USING THE MANAGERIAL ACCOUNTING VIDEO SERIES WITH THIS TEXT

COMPANY	TOPIC	CHAPTER
Multiple	What is Managerial Accounting?	Chapter 1
Pizza Hut	Managerial Accounting Today	Chapter 1
Making a Hollywood Movie	Job Order Costing	Chapter 2
Jones Soda Co.	Process Costing	Chapter 3
Precor	Activity-Based Costing	Chapter 4
Southwest Airlines	Cost-Volume-Profit	Chapter 5
Whole Foods Market	Cost-Volume-Profit Calculations	Chapter 6
Method	Incremental Analysis	Chapter 7
Zappos	Pricing	Chapter 8
Babycakes	Budgetary Planning	Chapter 9
Tribeca Grand	Budgetary Control and Responsibility Accounting	Chapter 10
Starbucks	Standard Costing	Chapter 11
Southwest Airlines	Balanced Scorecard	Chapter 11
Holland America Line	Capital Budgeting	Chapter 12

To see a sample video, go to:
www.wiley.com/college/managerialvideos

WILEY

weygandt
kimmel
kieso
team for success

MANAGERIAL
ACCOUNTING
TOOLS FOR BUSINESS DECISION MAKING
SIXTH EDITION

Jerry J. Weygandt PhD, CPA
University of Wisconsin—Madison
Madison, Wisconsin

Paul D. Kimmel PhD, CPA
University of Wisconsin—Milwaukee
Milwaukee, Wisconsin

Donald E. Kieso PhD, CPA
Northern Illinois University
DeKalb, Illinois

WILEY

John Wiley & Sons, Inc.

*Dedicated to
the **Wiley sales representatives**
who sell our books and service
our adopters in a professional
and ethical manner, and to
Enid, Merlynn, and Donna*

Vice President & Executive Publisher	George Hoffman
Associate Publisher	Christopher DeJohn
Senior Acquisitions Editor	Michael McDonald
Operations Manager	Yana Mermel
Senior Content Editor	Brian Kamins
Senior Content Editor	Ed Brislin
Development Editor	Terry Ann Tatro
Project Manager	Aaron Riccio
Content Manager	Dorothy Sinclair
Senior Production Editor	Valerie Vargas
Associate Director of Marketing	Amy Scholz
Marketing Manager	Karolina Zarychta Honsa
Lead Product Designer	Allison Morris
Product Designer	Greg Chaput
Interactive Product Designer	Daniela DiMaggio
Design Director	Harry Nolan
Senior Designer	Maureen Eide
Designer	Kristine Carney
Production Management Services	Ingrao Associates
Senior Illustration Editor	Anna Melhorn
Senior Photo Editor	Mary Ann Price
Senior Editorial Assistant	Jacqueline Kepping
Senior Marketing Assistant	Courtney Luzzi
Cover Design	Maureen Eide
Cover Photo	Robert Zaleski/Aurora Photos

This book was set in New Aster by Aptara®, Inc. and printed and bound by Courier Kendallville. The cover was printed by Courier Kendallville.

To order books or for customer service, please call 1-800-CALL WILEY (225-5945).

Jerry J. Weygandt, PhD, CPA; Paul D. Kimmel, PhD, CPA; and Donald E. Kieso, PhD, CPA
Managerial Accounting, Sixth Edition

ISBN-13 978-1-118-09689-5

Printed in the United States of America

10 9 8 7 6 5 4 3 2 1

From the Authors

Dear Student,

Why This Course? *Remember your biology course in high school? Did you have one of those "invisible man" models (or maybe something more high-tech than that) that gave you the opportunity to look "inside" the human body? This accounting course offers something similar: To understand a business, you have to understand the financial insides of a business organization. A managerial accounting course will help you understand the essential financial components of businesses. Whether you are looking at a large multinational company like Microsoft or Starbucks or a single-owner software consulting business or coffee shop, knowing the fundamentals of managerial accounting will help you understand what is happening. As an employee, a manager, an investor, a business owner, or a director of your own personal finances—any of which roles you will have at some point in your life—you will make better decisions for having taken this course.*

Why This Book? *Hundreds of thousands of students have used this textbook. Your instructor has chosen it for you because of its trusted reputation. The authors have worked hard to keep the book fresh, timely, and accurate.*

> "Whether you are looking at a large multinational company like Microsoft or Starbucks or a single-owner software consulting business or coffee shop, knowing the fundamentals of managerial accounting will help you understand what is happening."

This textbook contains features to help you learn best, whatever your learning style. To understand what your learning style is, spend about 10 minutes to take the learning style quiz at the book's companion website. Then, look at page xi for how you can apply an understanding of your learning style to this course. When you know more about your own learning style, browse through pages xii–xiii. These pages describe the main features you will find in this textbook and explain their purpose.

How To Succeed? *We've asked many students and many instructors whether there is a secret for success in this course. The nearly unanimous answer turns out to be not much of a secret: "Do the homework." This is one course where doing is learning, and the more time you spend on the homework assignments—using the various tools that this textbook provides—the more likely you are to learn the essential concepts, techniques, and methods of accounting. Besides the textbook itself, the textbook companion website offers various support resources.*

Good luck in this course. We hope you enjoy the experience and that you put to good use throughout a lifetime of success the knowledge you obtain in this course. We are sure you will not be disappointed.

Jerry J. Weygandt
Paul D. Kimmel
Donald E. Kieso

Your Team for Success in Accounting

Wiley Accounting is your partner in accounting education. We want to be the first publisher you think of when it comes to quality content, reliable technology, innovative resources, professional training, and unparalleled support for your accounting classroom.

Your Wiley Accounting Team for Success is comprised of three distinctive advantages that you won't find with any other publisher:

- Author Commitment
- Wiley Faculty Network
- WileyPLUS

kieso
weygandt
kimmel
warfield
team for success

Author Commitment:
A Proven Author Team of Inspired Teachers

The Team for Success authors bring years of industry and academic experience to the development of each textbook that relates accounting concepts to real-world experiences. This cohesive team brings continuity of writing style, pedagogy, and problem material to each course from Principles to Intermediate so you and your students can seamlessly progress from introductory through advanced courses in accounting.

The authors understand the mindset and time limitations of today's students. They demonstrate an intangible ability to effectively deliver complex information so it is clear and understandable while staying one step ahead of emerging global trends in business.

Wiley Faculty Network:
A Team of Educators Dedicated to Your Professional Development

The Wiley Faculty Network (WFN) is a global group of seasoned accounting professionals who share best practices in teaching with their peers. Our Virtual Guest Lecture Series provides the opportunity you need for professional development in an online environment that is relevant, convenient, and collaborative. The quality of these seminars and workshops meets the strictest standards, so we are proud to be able to offer valuable CPE credits to attendees.

With 24 faculty mentors in accounting, it's easy to find help with your most challenging curriculum questions—just ask our experts!

www.wileyplus.com

WileyPLUS:
An Experienced Team of Support Professionals

The *WileyPLUS* Account Managers understand the time constraints of busy instructors who want to provide the best resources available to their students with minimal headaches and planning time. They know how intimidating new software can be, so they are sure to make the transition easy and painless.

Account Managers act as your personal contact and expert resource for training, course set-up, and shortcuts throughout the *WileyPLUS* experience.

Your success as an educator directly correlates to student success, and that's our goal. The Wiley Accounting Team for Success truly strives for YOUR success! Partner with us today!

www.wileyteamforsuccess.com

Author Commitment
Collaboration. Innovation. Experience.

After decades of success as authors of textbooks like this one, Jerry Weygandt, Paul Kimmel, and Don Kieso understand that teaching accounting goes beyond simply presenting data. The authors are truly effective because they know that teaching is about telling compelling stories in ways that make each concept come to life.

Teacher / Author / Professional

Through their textbooks, supplements, online learning tools, and classrooms, these authors have developed a comprehensive pedagogy that engages students in learning and faculty with teaching.

These authors collaborate throughout the entire process. The end result is a true collaboration where each author brings his individual experience and talent to the development of every paragraph, page, and chapter, thus creating a truly well-rounded, thorough view on any given accounting topic.

Many Ways in One Direction

Our **Team for Success** has developed a teaching system that addresses every learning style. Each year brings new insights, feedback, ideas, and improvements on how to deliver the material to every student with a passion for the subject in a format that gives them the best chance to succeed.

The key to the team's approach is in understanding that, just as there are many different ways to learn, there are also many different ways to teach.

In Their Own Words

Visit the Wiley **Team for Success** website to hear from the authors first-hand as they discuss their teaching styles, collaboration, and the future of accounting.

www.wileyteamforsuccess.com

Author Commitment

Jerry Weygandt

Jerry J. Weygandt, PhD, CPA, is Arthur Andersen Alumni Emeritus Professor of Accounting at the University of Wisconsin—Madison. He holds a Ph.D. in accounting from the University of Illinois. Articles by Professor Weygandt have appeared in the *Accounting Review*, *Journal of Accounting Research*, *Accounting Horizons*, *Journal of Accountancy*, and other academic and professional journals. These articles have examined such financial reporting issues as accounting for price-level adjustments, pensions, convertible securities, stock option contracts, and interim reports. Professor Weygandt is author of other accounting and financial reporting books and is a member of the American Accounting Association, the American Institute of Certified Public Accountants, and the Wisconsin Society of Certified Public Accountants. He has served on numerous committees of the American Accounting Association and as a member of the editorial board of the Accounting Review; he also has served as President and Secretary-Treasurer of the American Accounting Association. In addition, he has been actively involved with the American Institute of Certified Public Accountants and has been a member of the Accounting Standards Executive Committee (AcSEC) of that organization. He has served on the FASB task force that examined the reporting issues related to accounting for income taxes and served as a trustee of the Financial Accounting Foundation. Professor Weygandt has received the Chancellor's Award for Excellence in Teaching and the Beta Gamma Sigma Dean's Teaching Award. He is on the board of directors of M & I Bank of Southern Wisconsin. He is the recipient of the Wisconsin Institute of CPA's Outstanding Educator's Award and the Lifetime Achievement Award. In 2001 he received the American Accounting Association's Outstanding Educator Award.

Paul Kimmel

Paul D. Kimmel, PhD, CPA, received his bachelor's degree from the University of Minnesota and his doctorate in accounting from the University of Wisconsin. He is an Associate Professor at the University of Wisconsin—Milwaukee, and has public accounting experience with Deloitte & Touche (Minneapolis). He was the recipient of the UWM School of Business Advisory Council Teaching Award, the Reggie Taite Excellence in Teaching Award and a three-time winner of the Outstanding Teaching Assistant Award at the University of Wisconsin. He is also a recipient of the Elijah Watts Sells Award for Honorary Distinction for his results on the CPA exam. He is a member of the American Accounting Association and the Institute of Management Accountants and has published articles in *Accounting Review*, *Accounting Horizons*, *Advances in Management Accounting*, *Managerial Finance*, *Issues in Accounting Education*, *Journal of Accounting Education*, as well as other journals. His research interests include accounting for financial instruments and innovation in accounting education. He has published papers and given numerous talks on incorporating critical thinking into accounting education, and helped prepare a catalog of critical thinking resources for the Federated Schools of Accountancy.

Don Kieso

Donald E. Kieso, PhD, CPA, received his bachelor's degree from Aurora University and his doctorate in accounting from the University of Illinois. He has served as chairman of the Department of Accountancy and is currently the KPMG Emeritus Professor of Accountancy at Northern Illinois University. He has public accounting experience with Price Waterhouse & Co. (San Francisco and Chicago) and Arthur Andersen & Co. (Chicago) and research experience with the Research Division of the American Institute of Certified Public Accountants (New York). He has done post doctorate work as a Visiting Scholar at the University of California at Berkeley and is a recipient of NIU's Teaching Excellence Award and four Golden Apple Teaching Awards. Professor Kieso is the author of other accounting and business books and is a member of the American Accounting Association, the American Institute of Certified Public Accountants, and the Illinois CPA Society. He has served as a member of the Board of Directors of the Illinois CPA Society, then AACSB's Accounting Accreditation Committees, the State of Illinois Comptroller's Commission, as Secretary-Treasurer of the Federation of Schools of Accountancy, and as Secretary-Treasurer of the American Accounting Association. Professor Kieso is currently serving on the Board of Trustees and Executive Committee of Aurora University, as a member of the Board of Directors of Kishwaukee Community Hospital, and as Treasurer and Director of Valley West Community Hospital. From 1989 to 1993 he served as a charter member of the national Accounting Education Change Commission. He is the recipient of the Outstanding Accounting Educator Award from the Illinois CPA Society, the FSA's Joseph A. Silvoso Award of Merit, the NIU Foundation's Humanitarian Award for Service to Higher Education, a Distinguished Service Award from the Illinois CPA Society, and in 2003 an honorary doctorate from Aurora University.

for Students

WileyPLUS

WileyPLUS is an innovative, research-based, online environment for effective teaching and learning.

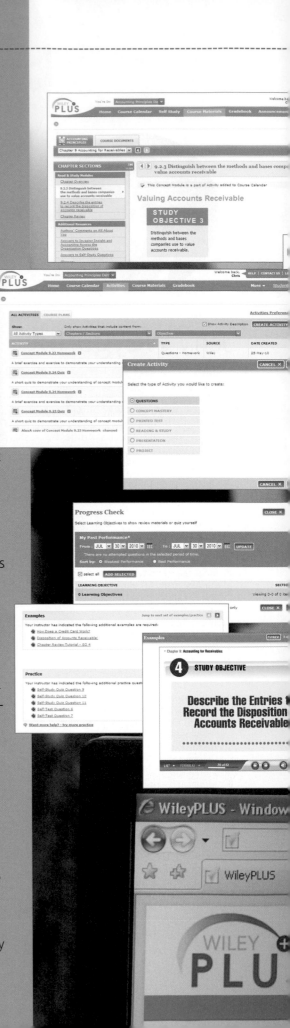

What do STUDENTS receive with *WileyPLUS*?

WileyPLUS increases confidence through an innovative **design** that allows greater **engagement**, which leads to improved learning **outcomes**.

Design

The *WileyPLUS* design integrates relevant resources, including the entire digital textbook, in an easy-to-navigate framework that helps students study more effectively and ensures student engagement. Innovative features, such as calendars and visual progress tracking, as well as a variety of self-evaluation tools, are all designed to improve time-management and increase student confidence.

Engagement

WileyPLUS organizes the textbook content into smaller, more manageable learning units with demonstrable study objectives and outcomes. Related media, examples, and sample practice items are integrated within each section to reinforce the study objectives. Throughout each study session, students can assess progress and gain immediate feedback on strengths and weaknesses in order to ensure they are spending their time most effectively.

Outcomes

Throughout each study session, *WileyPLUS* provides precise reporting of strengths and weaknesses, as well as individualized quizzes. As a result, students can be confident they are spending their time on the right things. With *WileyPLUS*, students always know the exact outcome of their efforts.

With increased confidence, motivation is sustained so students stay on task longer, leading to success.

www.wiley**plus**.com

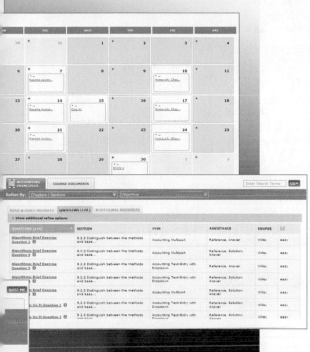

What do INSTRUCTORS receive with *WileyPLUS*?
Support and Insight into Student Progress

WileyPLUS provides reliable, customizable resources that reinforce course goals inside and outside of the classroom, as well as visibility into individual student progress. Pre-created materials and activities help instructors optimize their time.

For class preparation and classroom use:
- Interactive Tutorials
- Problem Walkthrough Videos
- Managerial Accounting Videos

For assignments and testing:
- Gradable Reading Assignment Questions (embedded with online text)
- Question Assignments: all end-of-chapter problems coded algorithmically with hints, links to text

For course planning: *WileyPLUS* comes with a pre-created **Course Plan** designed by a subject matter expert uniquely for this course. Simple drag-and-drop tools make it easy to assign the course plan as-is or modify it to reflect your course syllabus.

For progress monitoring: *WileyPLUS* provides instant access to reports on trends in class performance, student use of course materials, and progress toward learning objectives, helping inform decisions and drive classroom discussions.

Experience *WileyPLUS* for effective teaching and learning at **www.wileyplus.com**.

Powered by proven technology and built on a foundation of cognitive research, *WileyPLUS* has enriched the education of millions of students in numerous countries around the world.

The Wiley Faculty Network

The Place Where Faculty Connect ...

The Wiley Faculty Network is a global community of faculty connected by a passion for teaching and a drive to learn and share. Connect with the Wiley Faculty Network to collaborate with your colleagues, find a mentor, attend virtual and live events, and view a wealth of resources all designed to help you grow as an educator. Embrace the art of teaching—great things happen where faculty connect!

Attend

Discover innovative ideas and gain knowledge you can use.

- Training
- Virtual Guest Lectures
- Live Events

View

Explore your resources and development opportunities.

- Teaching Resources
- Archived Guest Lectures
- Recorded Presentations
- Professional Development Modules

Collaborate

Connect with colleagues— your greatest resource.

- Find a Mentor
- Interest Groups
- Blog

Find out more at
www.WHEREFACULTYCONNECT.com

Virtual Guest Lectures

Connect with recognized leaders across disciplines and collaborate with your peers on timely topics and discipline specific issues, many of which offer CPE credit.

Live and Virtual Events

These invitation-only, discipline-specific events are organized through a close partnership between the WFN, Wiley, and the academic community near the event location.

Technology Training

Discover a wealth of topic- and technology-specific training presented by subject matter experts, authors, and faculty where and when you need it.

Teaching Resources

Propel your teaching and student learning to the next level with quality peer-reviewed case studies, testimonials, classroom tools, and checklists.

Connect with Colleagues

Achieve goals and tackle challenges more easily by enlisting the help of your peers. Connecting with colleagues through the WFN can help you improve your teaching experience.

What TYPE of learner are you?

Understanding each of these basic learning styles enables the authors to engage students' minds and motivate them to do their best work, ultimately improving the experience for both students and faculty.

	Intake: To take in the information	To make a study package	Text features that may help you the most	Output: To do well on exams
VISUAL	• Pay close attention to charts, drawings, and handouts your instructors use. • Underline. • Use different colors. • Use symbols, flow charts, graphs, different arrangements on the page, white spaces.	Convert your lecture notes into "page pictures." Therefore: • Use the "Intake" strategies. • Reconstruct images in different ways. • Redraw pages from memory. • Replace words with symbols and initials. • Look at your pages.	The Navigator/Feature Story/Preview Infographics/Illustrations Accounting Equation Analyses Highlighted words Questions/Exercises/Problems Real-World Focus Decision-Making at Current Designs Managerial Analysis Problem	• Recall your "page pictures." • Draw diagrams where appropriate. • Practice turning your visuals back into words.
AURAL	• Attend lectures and tutorials. • Discuss topics with students and instructors. • Explain new ideas to other people. • Use a tape recorder. • Leave spaces in your lecture notes for later recall. • Describe overheads, pictures, and visuals to somebody who was not in class.	You may take poor notes because you prefer to listen. Therefore: • Expand your notes by talking with others and with information from your textbook. • Tape-record summarized notes and listen. • Read summarized notes out loud. • Explain your notes to another "aural" person.	Preview Insight Boxes DO IT!/Action Plan Summary of Learning Objectives Glossary Self-Test Questions Questions/Exercises/Problems Real-World Focus Decision-Making at Current Designs Managerial Analysis Problem Decision-Making Across the Organization Communication Activity Ethics Case	• Talk with the instructor. • Spend time in quiet places recalling the ideas. • Practice writing answers to old exam questions. • Say your answers out loud.
READING/ WRITING	• Use lists and headings. • Use dictionaries, glossaries, and definitions. • Read handouts, textbooks, and supplementary library readings. • Use lecture notes.	• Write out words again and again. • Reread notes silently. • Rewrite ideas and principles into other words. • Turn charts, diagrams, and other illustrations into statements.	The Navigator/Feature Story/Study Objectives/Preview DO IT!/Action Plan Summary of Learning Objectives Glossary/Self-Test Questions Questions/Exercises/Problems Writing Problems Real-World Focus Decision-Making at Current Designs Considering Your Costs and Benefits Managerial Analysis Problem Decision-Making Across the Organization Communication Activity	• Write exam answers. • Practice with multiple-choice questions. • Write paragraphs, beginnings, and endings. • Write your lists in outline form. • Arrange your words into hierarchies and points.
KINESTHETIC	• Use all your senses. • Go to labs, take field trips. • Listen to real-life examples. • Pay attention to applications. • Use hands-on approaches. • Use trial-and-error methods.	You may take poor notes because topics do not seem concrete or relevant. Therefore: • Put examples in your summaries. • Use case studies and applications to help with principles and abstract concepts. • Talk about your notes with another "kinesthetic" person. • Use pictures and photographs that illustrate an idea.	The Navigator/Feature Story/Preview Infographics/Illustrations DO IT!/Action Plan Summary of Learning Objectives Self-Test Questions Questions/Exercises/Problems Real-World Focus Decision-Making at Current Designs Managerial Analysis Problem Decision-Making Across the Organization Ethics Case Considering Your Costs and Benefits	• Write practice answers. • Role-play the exam situation.

Features of the Sixth Edition

The Sixth Edition expands our emphasis on student learning and improves upon a teaching and learning package that instructors and students have rated the highest in customer satisfaction.

What's New?

Integrated Company Coverage

Beginning in Chapter 1, we introduce Current Designs, a kayak-making company based in Winona, Minnesota. We then follow-up with a new decision-making problem in every chapter based on this real-world company. Each problem presents realistic managerial accounting situations that students must analyze to determine the best course of action. In addition, many of these end-of-chapter activities also have an accompanying video.

People, Planet, and Profit

Today's companies are evaluating not just their profitability but also their corporate social responsibility. In this edition, we have profiled some of these companies, such as Starbucks, to highlight their sustainable business practices. We also have added a new *Broadening Your Perspective* problem, "Considering People, Planet, and Profit," which requires students to assess and determine how best to balance a company's profitability with its corporate social responsibility.

New Feature Stories

Students will be more willing to commit time and energy to a topic when they believe it is relevant to their future careers. There is no better way to demonstrate relevance than to ground discussions in the real world. To that end, we have written new Feature Stories about such companies as Starbucks, Amazon.com, and Zappos.com.

Managerial Accounting Video Series

Through the use of real-world, cutting-edge companies, these videos engage students with a dynamic overview of managerial accounting topics and motivate them through the detailed tools, examples, and discussions presented in their textbook, *WileyPLUS* course, and classroom lectures.

Continued Focus on Decision-Making

In the Sixth Edition, we continue to demonstrate how invaluable management accounting information is to business decision-making. New to this edition is another new *Broadening Your Perspective* problem, "Considering Your Costs and Benefits," which presents a realistic situation in which students must weigh the pros and cons of two alternatives.

Enhanced Features of the Sixth Edition

This edition was also subject to an overall, comprehensive revision to ensure that it is technically accurate, relevant, and up-to-date. We have continued and enhanced many of the features of the Fifth Edition of *Managerial Accounting,* including the following:

Real-World Emphasis

One of the goals of the managerial accounting course is to orient students to the application of accounting principles and techniques in practice. Accordingly, we have continued our practice of using numerous examples from real companies throughout the textbook. The names of these real companies are highlighted in red.

Also, throughout the chapters, **Insight** and **Accounting Across the Organization** boxes show how people, often in non-accounting functions, in actual companies make decisions using accounting information. *Guideline Answers* to the critical thinking questions are provided at the end of each chapter. Finally, examples, exercises, and problems that focus on accounting situations faced by **service companies** are identified by the icon shown here.

Decision Toolkit

The **Decision Toolkits** highlight the important analytical tools integrated throughout the textbook, designed to assist students in evaluation and using the information at hand. A **Using the Decision Toolkit** exercise, just before the chapter summary, asks students to use the decision tools presented in the chapter and takes them through the problem-solving steps.

DO IT! Exercises

Brief **DO IT!** exercises ask students to apply their newly acquired knowledge. The **DO IT!** exercises include an *Action Plan,* which reviews the necessary steps to complete the exercise, as well as a *Solution* so students can have immediate feedback. A **Comprehensive DO IT!** problem at the end of each chapter allows students a final check of their understanding before they do their homework. **DO IT! Review** problems are part of the end-of-chapter homework material.

Marginal Notes

Helpful Hints in the margin further clarify concepts being discussed. **Ethics Notes** point out ethical points related to the nearby text discussion. **Alternative Terminology** lets students know about interchangeable words and phrases.

Comprehensive Homework Material

Each chapter concludes with revised Self-Test Questions, Questions, Brief Exercises, **DO IT!** Review, Exercises, and Problems. An icon, shown here, identifies Exercises and Problems that can be solved using **Excel templates** at the book's companion website. The **Waterways Continuing Problem** uses the business activities of a fictional company, to help students apply managerial accounting topics to a realistic entrepreneurial situation.

Broadening Your Perspective Section

We have revised and updated the **Broadening Your Perspective** section at the end of each chapter. Elements in this section include the following:

- Decision-Making at Current Designs
- Decision-Making Across the Organization
- Managerial Analysis
- Real-World Focus
- Communication Activity
- Ethics Case
- All About You
- Considering People, Planet, and Profit
- Considering Your Costs and Benefits

These assignments are designed to help develop students' decision-making and critical-thinking skills.

Content Changes by Chapter

Chapter 1 Managerial Accounting
- New Feature Story, on history and operations of Current Designs (kayak-making company).
- First section, Managerial Accounting Basics, rewritten to discuss managerial accounting activities within context of Current Designs' kayak-making business.
- New Management Insight, "Why Manufacturing Matters for U.S. Workers," about importance of U.S. factory jobs.
- Revised section, Managerial Accounting Today, now includes Focus on the Value Chain section (discussing value chain, JIT, TQM, TOC, ERP, ABC), Balanced Scorecard section, and new Corporate Social Responsibility section.
- Deleted chapter appendix (Accounting Cycle for a Manufacturing Company).

Chapter 2 Job Order Costing
- New Feature Story, on Lynn Tilton, founder and CEO of Patriarch Partners, the largest, woman-owned U.S. business.
- In the Accumulating Manufacturing Costs section, included the individual T-accounts in the margin, next to where discussed in the text. Also, provided additional explanations for Raw Materials Cost, Factory Labor Costs, and Manufacturing Overhead Costs, to increase student understanding.
- Added more detail (such as totals of T-accounts) within illustrations of job cost sheets, so students can better understand assignment of costs.

Chapter 3 Process Costing
- Changed example of company in Process Cost Flow section to roller blade/skateboard wheel manufacturer instead of can opener manufacturer, to increase student appeal.
- New People, Planet, and Profit Insight, about costs/benefits of remanufactured goods.

Chapter 4 Activity-Based Costing
- New Feature Story (and accompanying video) on why Precor (fitness equipment) switched from traditional costing to activity-based costing.
- Changed example company, in Example of ABC versus Traditional Costing section, to producing abdominal trainers instead of car-antitheft devices, to tie in with Precor.
- Rewrote definition/explanation of value-added and non–value-added activities, as well as of activity levels, to ensure student understanding of these concepts.
- Simplified the ABC costing example for the service company illustration, to avoid needless detail and potential student confusion.
- New Management Insight, summarizing a recent survey of ABC practices by companies worldwide.
- New Real-World Focus BYP problem, on use of ABC in the financial services industry.

Chapter 5 Cost-Volume-Profit
- New Feature Story, on how Jeff Bezos started and expanded Amazon.com's operations.
- New People, Planet, and Profit Insight, on hydroponic farming/vertical farming.
- Added material on use of scatter plots in High-Low Method section, as well as provided supplement on regression analysis on book's companion website.
- Added more detailed explanations and illustrations to Contribution Margin per Unit, Contribution Margin Ratio, and Break-Even Analysis sections, to ensure student understanding.
- New Real-World Focus BYP problem, on how Barnes and Noble's current structure left it ill-prepared for an e-book environment.

Chapter 6 Cost-Volume-Profit Analysis: Additional Issues
- New Feature Story, still about Intel, but now explaining why the computer chip giant experiences huge swings in its earnings.
- Provided more step-by-step explanations and illustrations in the Basic Computations section, so students will improve their understanding of why and how to compute break-even points, target net income, and margin of safety.
- New Service Company Insight, about why Warren Buffett acquired Burlington Northern Railroad.
- New Real-World Focus BYP problem, on Smart Balance's employment and cost structure.
- New Considering People, Planet, and Profit BYP problem, about whether companies should incorporate environmental costs into their decision-making process.

Chapter 7 Incremental Analysis
- New Service Company Insight, about the relevant revenues and costs of Amazon.com's Prime free shipping program.
- Expanded sunk cost discussion and illustrations, to improve student understanding.
- New material on how behavioral decision-making can affect whether or not to replace equipment.
- Expanded discussion of elimination of an unprofitable segment to include fixed cost analysis.
- New Considering Your Costs and Benefits BYP problem, about whether or not to drop out of college due to financial considerations.

Chapter 8 Pricing
- New Feature Story (and accompanying video) on origins and operating principles of Zappos.com.
- New Management Insight, about how competition affected online subscription prices.
- Rewrote Cost-Plus Pricing section, adding more explanations and illustrations to increase student understanding.
- New Considering Your Costs and Benefits BYP problem, about difference between "low-cost" and "low-price" suppliers as well as implications of full-cost accounting for corporate social responsibility.

Chapter 9 Budgetary Planning
- Added more detailed explanation to the Budgeting and Human Behavior section about participative budgeting.
- Added marginal T-accounts to Production Budget and Direct Materials Budget sections, to illustrate flow of costs.
- New Service Company Insight, on the implications of budgetary optimism as it pertains to governments.
- New Management Insight, on the potential costs and benefits of a company stockpiling raw materials.
- Added a second Comprehensive DO IT! problem on budgeted income statement and balance sheet.
- New Considering Your Costs and Benefits BYP problem about whether student loans should be considered as a source of income.

Chapter 10 Budgetary Control and Responsibility Accounting
- New Service Company Insight, about NBCUniversal's response to Fox wanting to reduce its licensing fee for the TV show "House."
- Added graph to the solution for the DO IT! on flexible budgets, to increase student understanding.

- Moved Management by Exception to within Performance Evaluation discussion, now included in Responsibility Accounting section, for better flow of chapter topics.
- New Considering Your Costs and Benefits BYP problem, addressing the decision of whether or not to purchase a home.

Chapter 11 Standard Costs and Balanced Scorecard
- New Feature Story (and accompanying video) on Starbucks' origins and vision.
- New case study example on producing caffeinated energy drink (replaces weed-killer manufacturer), to increase student appeal.
- New material and illustrations added, to enhance explanation of the components of variances as well as how to compute them.
- New People, Planet, and Profit Insight, highlighting Starbucks' 10th annual *Global Responsibility Report* and the company's commitment to corporate social responsibility.
- Reformatted the illustration of the objectives within the four perspectives of a balanced scorecard, to increase student understanding.
- New Real-World Focus BYP problem referencing the *Wall Street Journal* article, "In Risky Move, GM to Run Plants Around Clock."
- New Considering Your Costs and Benefits BYP problem, addressing the extent to which financial measures should influence medical care.

Chapter 12 Planning for Capital Investments
- New Feature Story, on how timing can affect capital investments by the cruise-line industry.
- New Management Insight, about whether Verizon's investment in its 4G wireless service will pay off and whether there is too much plant capacity for manufacturing big-screen TVs.
- New Considering Your Costs and Benefits BYP problem, about calculating the NPVs of solar panels.

Chapter 13 Statement of Cash Flows
- New Anatomy of a Fraud, about Parmalat's multiple frauds.
- New Appendix 13C, Statement of Cash Flows—T-Account Approach.

Chapter 14 Financial Statement Analysis
- New Anatomy of a Fraud, on using Benford's Law statistical law to detect fraud.
- New Investor Insight, "How to Manage the Current Ratio," about its limitations.

Teaching and Learning Supplementary Material

For Instructors

In addition to the support instructors receive from *WileyPLUS* and the Wiley Faculty Network, we offer the following useful supplements.

Book's Companion Website. On this website, *www.wiley.com/college/weygandt*, instructors will find the Solutions Manual, Test Bank, Instructor's Manual, Computerized Test Bank, and other resources.

Instructor's Resource CD. The Instructor's Resource CD (IRCD) contains all the instructor supplements. The IRCD gives instructors the flexibility to access and prepare instructional materials based on their individual needs.

Solutions Manual. The Solutions Manual contains detailed solutions to all questions, brief exercises, exercises, and problems in the textbook, as well as suggested answers to the questions and cases. The estimated time to complete exercises, problems, and cases is provided.

Solution Transparencies. The solution transparencies feature detailed solutions to brief exercises, exercises, problems, and *Broadening Your Perspective* activities. Transparencies can be easily ordered from the book's companion website.

Instructor's Manual. Included in each chapter are lecture outlines with teaching tips, chapter reviews, illustrations, and review quizzes.

Teaching Transparencies. The teaching transparencies are 4-color acetate images of the illustrations found in the Instructor's Manual. Transparencies can be easily ordered from the book's companion website.

Test Bank and Computerized Test Bank. The test bank and computerized test bank allow instructors to tailor examinations according to study objectives and learning outcomes, including AACSB, AICPA, and IMA professional standards. Achievement tests, comprehensive examinations, and a final exam are included.

PowerPoint™. The new PowerPoint™ presentations contain a combination of key concepts, images, and problems from the textbook.

WebCT and Desire2Learn. WebCT and Desire2Learn offer an integrated set of course management tools that enable instructors to easily design, develop, and manage Web-based and Web-enhanced courses.

For Students

Book's Companion Website. On this website, students will find:

- *Exercises: Set B* and *Challenge Exercises*
- *Problems: Set C*
- *Self-Tests and Additional Self-Tests*
- *Cases for Managerial Decision-Making*
- A complete *Glossary* of all the key terms used in the text

Student Study Guide. Each chapter of the Study Guide contains a chapter review, chapter outline, and a glossary of key terms. Demonstration problems, multiple-choice, true/false, matching, and other exercises are also included.

Working Papers. The working papers are printed templates that can help students correctly format their textbook accounting solutions. Working paper templates are available for all end-of-chapter brief exercises, exercises, problems, and cases.

Excel Working Papers. The *Excel Working Papers* are Excel templates that students can use to correctly format their textbook accounting solutions.

Excel Primer: Using Excel in Accounting. The online Excel primer and accompanying Excel templates allow students to complete select end-of-chapter exercises and problems identified by a spreadsheet icon in the margin of the textbook.

Managerial Accounting Video Series. Through the examples of real-world, cutting-edge companies, these videos engage students with a dynamic overview of managerial accounting topics and motivate them through the detailed tools, examples, and discussions presented in their textbook, *WileyPLUS* course, and classroom lectures.

Mobile Applications. Quizzing and reviewing content is available for download on iTunes.

Acknowledgments

Managerial Accounting has benefited greatly from the input of focus group participants, manuscript reviewers, those who have sent comments by letter or e-mail, ancillary authors, and proofers. We greatly appreciate the constructive suggestions and innovative ideas of reviewers and the creativity and accuracy of the ancillary authors and checkers.

Sixth Edition

Dawn Addington
Central New Mexico Community College

Bruce Bradford
Fairfield University

Leroy Bugger
Edison State College

Lisa Capozzoli
College of DuPage

Renee Castrigano
Cleveland State University

Gayle Chaky
Dutchess Community College

Toni Clegg
Delta College

Cheryl Copeland
California State University, Fresno

Larry DeGaetano
Montclair State University

Ron Dustin
Fresno City College

Barbara Eide
University of Wisconsin—La Crosse

Janet Farler
Pima Community College

Bambi Hora
University of Central Oklahoma

Don Kovacic
California State University, San Marcos

Richard Larkin

Jason Lee
SUNY Plattsburgh

Harold Little
Western Kentucky University

Lois Mahoney
Eastern Michigan University

Florence McGovern
Bergen Community College

Mary Michel
Manhattan College

Earl Mitchell
Santa Ana College

Michael Newman
University of Houston

Judy Peterson
Monmouth College

Robert Rambo
Roger Williams University

Luther Ross
Central Piedmont Community College

Susan Sadowski
Shippensburg University/UMUC

Richard Sarkisian
Camden County College

Karl Schindl
University of Wisconsin—Manitowoc

Debbie Seifert
Illinois State University

Valerie Simmons
University of Southern Mississippi

Mike Skaff
College of the Sequoias

Patrick Stegman
College of Lake County

Karen Tabak
Maryville University

Diane Tanner
University of North Florida

Joan Van Hise
Fairfield University

Sheila Viel
University of Wisconsin—Milwaukee

Prior Edition

Eric Blazer
Millersville University

Rita Kingery Cook
University of Delaware

Cheryl Copeland
California State University, Fresno

Robin D'Agati
Palm Beach Community College

Rafik Elias
University of California, Los Angeles

Annette Fisher
Glendale Community College

Michael Haselkorn
Bentley University

M.A. Maggie Houston
Wright State University

Mehmet Kocakulah
University of Southern Indiana

Wikil Kwak
University of Nebraska, Omaha

James Lukawitz
University of Memphis

Barbara Lamberton
University of Hartford

D. Jordan Lowe
Arizona State University

Sue Marcum
American University

Florence McGovern
Bergen Community College

Matthew Muller
Adirondack Community College

Joseph Nicassio
Westmoreland County Community College

Margaret O'Reilly-Allen
Rider University

Sandra Pelfrey
Oakland University

Karl Putnam
University of Texas—El Paso

Luther Ross
Central Piedmont Community College

Nancy Sill
Modesto Junior College

Howard Switkay
Community College of Philadelphia

Ron Vogel
College of Eastern Utah

WileyPLUS Developers and Reviewers

Carole Brandt-Fink
Laura McNally
Melanie Yon

Ancillary Authors, Contributors, Proofers, and Accuracy Checkers

Jack Borke
University of Wisconsin, Platteville

LuAnn Bean
Florida Institute of Technology

Jim Emig
Villanova University

Larry Falcetto
Emporia State University

Coby Harmon
University of California, Santa Barbara

Benjamin Huegel
St. Mary's University

Doug Kieso
Aurora University

Jill Misuraca
University of Tampa

Patricia Mounce
University of Central Arkansas

Barbara Muller
Arizona State University

John Plouffe
California State University—Los Angeles

Rex Schildhouse
San Diego Community College

Teresa Speck
St. Mary's University

Lynn Stallworth
Appalachian State University

Ellen Sweatt
Georgia Perimeter College

Diane Tanner
University of North Florida

Joan Van Hise
Fairfield University

Doris Warmflash
SUNY, Westchester Community College

Dick Wasson
Southwestern College

We thank Benjamin Huegel and Teresa Speck of St. Mary's University for their extensive efforts in the preparation of the homework materials related to Current Designs. We also appreciate the considerable support provided to us by the following people at Current Designs: Mike Cichanowski, Jim Brown, Diane Buswell, and Jake Greseth. We also benefited from the assistance and suggestions provided to us by Joan Van Hise in the preparation of materials related to sustainability.

We appreciate the exemplary support and commitment given to us by senior acquisitions editor Michael McDonald, marketing manager Karolina Zarychta Honsa, operations manager Yana Mermel, senior content editor Brian Kamins, senior content editor Ed Brislin, development editor Terry Ann Tatro, lead product designer Allie Morris, product designer Greg Chaput, vice president of higher education production and manufacturing Ann Berlin, designers Maureen Eide and Kristine Carney, illustration editor Anna Melhorn, photo editor Mary Ann Price, permissions editor Joan Naples, project editor Suzanne Ingrao of Ingrao Associates, indexer Steve Ingle, Denise Showers at Aptara, Cyndy Taylor, and project manager Angel Chavez at Integra. All of these professionals provided innumerable services that helped the textbook take shape.

Finally, our thanks to Amy Scholz, Susan Elbe, George Hoffman, Tim Stookesberry, Joe Heider, and Steve Smith for their support and leadership in Wiley's College Division. We will appreciate suggestions and comments from users—instructors and students alike. You can send your thoughts and ideas about the textbook to us via email at: *AccountingAuthors@yahoo.com*.

Jerry J. Weygandt   Paul D. Kimmel   Donald E. Kieso
Madison, Wisconsin Milwaukee, Wisconsin DeKalb, Illinois

Brief Contents

Cost Concepts for Decision-Makers

1 Managerial Accounting   2
2 Job Order Costing   48
3 Process Costing   94
4 Activity-Based Costing   144

Decision-Making Concepts

5 Cost-Volume-Profit   196
6 Cost-Volume-Profit Analysis: Additional Issues   236
7 Incremental Analysis   292
8 Pricing   332

Planning and Control Concepts

9 Budgetary Planning   382
10 Budgetary Control and Responsibility Accounting   434
11 Standard Costs and Balanced Scorecard   494
12 Planning for Capital Investments   546

Performance Evaluation Concepts

13 Statement of Cash Flows   586
14 Financial Statement Analysis   650

APPENDICES

A Time Value of Money   A-1
B Standards of Ethical Conduct for Management Accountants   B-1

Cases for Managerial Decision-Making   CA-1

(The full text of these cases is available online at *www.wiley.com/college/weygandt.*)

COMPANY INDEX   I-1
SUBJECT INDEX   I-3

Contents

Chapter 1

Managerial Accounting 2

Just Add Water . . . and Paddle 2
Managerial Accounting Basics 4
    Comparing Managerial and Financial Accounting 4
    Management Functions 4
    Organizational Structure 6
    Business Ethics 7
Managerial Cost Concepts 9
    Manufacturing Costs 9
    Product versus Period Costs 11
Manufacturing Costs in Financial Statements 12
    Income Statement 12
    Cost of Goods Manufactured 13
    Cost of Goods Manufactured Schedule 14
    Balance Sheet 15
    Cost Concepts—A Review 16
    Product Costing for Service Industries 18
Managerial Accounting Today 19
    Focus on the Value Chain 19
    Balanced Scorecard 20
    Corporate Social Responsibility 21

Chapter 2

Job Order Costing 48

She Succeeds Where Others Have Failed 48
Cost Accounting Systems 50
    Job Order Cost System 50
    Process Cost System 50
Job Order Cost Flow 51
    Accumulating Manufacturing Costs 52
    Assigning Manufacturing Costs to Work
      in Process 54
    Manufacturing Overhead Costs 58
    Assigning Costs to Finished Goods 62
    Assigning Costs to Cost of Goods Sold 63
    Summary of Job Order Cost Flows 64
    Job Order Costing for Service Companies 65
    Advantages and Disadvantages of Job Order
      Costing 67
Reporting Job Cost Data 68
    Under- or Overapplied Manufacturing Overhead 69

Chapter 3

Process Costing 94

Ben & Jerry's Tracks Its Mix-Ups 94
The Nature of Process Cost Systems 96
    Uses of Process Cost Systems 96
    Process Costing for Service Companies 97

    Similarities and Differences Between Job Order
      Cost and Process Cost Systems 97
    Process Cost Flow 99
    Assigning Manufacturing Costs—Journal
      Entries 99
Equivalent Units 102
    Weighted-Average Method 102
    Refinements on the Weighted-Average
      Method 103
Production Cost Report 105
    Compute the Physical Unit Flow (Step 1) 106
    Compute the Equivalent Units of Production
      (Step 2) 107
    Compute Unit Production Costs (Step 3) 107
    Prepare a Cost Reconciliation Schedule
      (Step 4) 108
    Preparing the Production Cost Report 109
    Costing Systems—Final Comments 111
APPENDIX 3A **FIFO Method   115**
    Equivalent Units Under FIFO 115
    Comprehensive Example 116
    FIFO and Weighted-Average 120

Chapter 4

Activity-Based Costing 144

Precor Is on Your Side 144
**Traditional Costing and Activity-Based
Costing 146**
    Traditional Costing Systems 146
    The Need for a New Approach 146
    Activity-Based Costing 147
Example of ABC versus Traditional Costing 149
    Identify and Classify Activities and Allocate
      Overhead to Cost Pools (Step 1) 150
    Identify Cost Drivers (Step 2) 150
    Compute Activity-Based Overhead Rates
      (Step 3) 150
    Assign Overhead Costs to Products
      (Step 4) 151
    Comparing Units Costs 152
Activity-Based Costing: A Closer Look 155
    Benefits of ABC 155
    Limitations of ABC 155
    When to Use ABC 156
    Value-Added versus Non–Value-Added
      Activities 157
    Classification of Activity Levels 159
**Activity-Based Costing in Service
Industries 161**
    Traditional Costing Example 162
    Activity-Based Costing Example 162

APPENDIX 4A: **Just-in-Time Processing 166**
    Objective of JIT Processing 167
    Elements of JIT Processing 168
    Benefits of JIT Processing 168

Chapter 5

Cost-Volume-Profit 196

Don't Worry—Just Get Big 196
Cost Behavior Analysis 198
    Variable Costs 198
    Fixed Costs 199
    Relevant Range 200
    Mixed Costs 201
    Importance of Identifying Variable and
        Fixed Costs 205
Cost-Volume-Profit Analysis 206
    Basic Components 206
    CVP Income Statement 206
    Break-Even Analysis 209
    Target Net Income 213
    Margin of Safety 215

Chapter 6

Cost-Volume-Profit Analysis: Additional Issues 236

Rapid Replay 236
Cost-Volume-Profit (CVP) Review 238
    Basic Concepts 238
    Basic Computations 239
    CVP and Changes in the Business Environment 241
Sales Mix 244
    Break-Even Sales in Units 244
    Break-Even Sales in Dollars 246
    Determining Sales Mix with Limited Resources 248
Cost Structure and Operating Leverage 251
    Effect on Contribution Margin Ratio 252
    Effect on Break-Even Point 252
    Effect on Margin of Safety Ratio 252
    Operating Leverage 252
APPENDIX 6A: **Absorption Costing versus
Variable Costing 256**
    Example: Comparing Absorption Costing with
        Variable Costing 256
    An Extended Example 258
    Decision-Making Concerns 262
    Potential Advantages of Variable Costing 264

Chapter 7

Incremental Analysis 292

Make It or Buy It? 292
Management's Decision-Making Process 294
    Incremental Analysis Approach 294
    How Incremental Analysis Works 295

Types of Incremental Analysis 296
    Accept an Order at a Special Price 296
    Make or Buy 298
    Sell or Process Further 301
    Repair, Retain, or Replace Equipment 304
    Eliminate an Unprofitable Segment or Product 305
Other Considerations in Decision-Making 308
    Qualitative Factors 308
    Relationship of Incremental Analysis and
        Activity-Based Costing 308

Chapter 8

Pricing 332

They've Got Your Size—and Color 332
Pricing Goods for External Sales 334
    Target Costing 335
    Cost-Plus Pricing 337
    Variable-Cost Pricing 339
Pricing Services 341
Transfer Pricing for Internal Sales 345
    Negotiated Transfer Prices 346
    Cost-Based Transfer Prices 349
    Market-Based Transfer Prices 350
    Effect of Outsourcing on Transfer Pricing 351
**Transfers Between Divisions in Different
Countries 351**
APPENDIX 8A: **Other Cost Approaches
to Pricing 355**
    Absorption-Cost Pricing 355
    Variable-Cost Pricing 357

Chapter 9

Budgetary Planning 382

Was This the Next Amazon.com? Not Quite 382
Budgeting Basics 384
    Budgeting and Accounting 384
    The Benefits of Budgeting 384
    Essentials of Effective Budgeting 384
    Length of the Budget Period 385
    The Budgeting Process 385
    Budgeting and Human Behavior 386
    Budgeting and Long-Range Planning 387
    The Master Budget 387
Preparing the Operating Budgets 389
    Sales Budget 389
    Production Budget 390
    Direct Materials Budget 392
    Direct Labor Budget 395
    Manufacturing Overhead Budget 395
    Selling and Administrative Expense Budget 396
    Budgeted Income Statement 396
Preparing the Financial Budgets 399
    Cash Budget 399
    Budgeted Balance Sheet 402

Budgeting in Nonmanufacturing Companies 404
   Merchandisers 404
   Service Companies 405
   Not-for-Profit Organizations 405

Chapter 10

Budgetary Control and Responsibility Accounting 434

Turning Trash Into Treasure 434
Budgetary Control 436
Static Budget Reports 437
   Examples 437
   Uses and Limitations 438
Flexible Budgets 438
   Why Flexible Budgets? 439
   Developing the Flexible Budget 440
   Flexible Budget—A Case Study 442
   Flexible Budget Reports 445
Responsibility Accounting 447
   Controllable versus Noncontrollable Revenues
     and Costs 449
   Principles of Performance Evaluation 449
   Responsibility Reporting System 451
Types of Responsibility Centers 454
   Responsibility Accounting for Cost Centers 455
   Responsibility Accounting for Profit Centers 455
   Responsibility Accounting for Investment
     Centers 458
APPENDIX 10A: **Residual Income—Another
Performance Measurement 465**
   Residual Income Compared to ROI 466
   Residual Income Weakness 466

Chapter 11

Standard Costs and Balanced Scorecard 494

80,000 Different Caffeinated Combinations 494
The Need for Standards 496
   Distinguishing Between Standards and
     Budgets 496
   Why Standard Costs? 496
Setting Standard Costs 496
   Ideal versus Normal Standards 497
   A Case Study 498
**Analyzing and Reporting Variances from
Standards 502**
   Direct Materials Variances 503
   Direct Labor Variances 506
   Manufacturing Overhead Variances 508
   Reporting Variances 511
   Statement Presentation of Variances 512
Balanced Scorecard 512

APPENDIX 11A: **Standard Cost Accounting
System 518**
   Journal Entries 518
   Ledger Accounts 520
APPENDIX 11B: **A Closer Look at Overhead
Variances 521**
   Overhead Controllable Variance 521
   Overhead Volume Variance 522

Chapter 12

Planning for Capital Investments 546

Floating Hotels 546
The Capital Budgeting Evaluation Process 548
   Cash Flow Information 548
   Illustrative Data 549
Cash Payback 550
Net Present Value Method 551
   Equal Annual Cash Flows 552
   Unequal Annual Cash Flows 553
   Choosing a Discount Rate 554
   Simplifying Assumptions 555
   Comprehensive Example 556
Additional Considerations 557
   Intangible Benefits 557
   Profitability Index for Mutually Exclusive
     Projects 559
   Risk Analysis 560
   Post-Audit of Investment Projects 561
Other Capital Budgeting Techniques 561
   Internal Rate of Return Method 562
   Comparing Discounted Cash Flow
     Methods 564
   Annual Rate of Return Method 564

Chapter 13

Statement of Cash Flows 586

"Got Cash?" 586
**Statement of Cash Flows: Usefulness
and Format 588**
   Usefulness of the Statement of Cash Flows 588
   Classification of Cash Flows 588
   Significant Noncash Activities 590
   Format of the Statement of Cash Flows 590
   Preparing the Statement of Cash Flows 592
   Indirect and Direct Methods 592
**Preparing the Statement of Cash Flows—Indirect
Method 593**
   Step 1: Operating Activities 594
   Summary of Conversion to Net Cash Provided by
     Operating Activities—Indirect Method 598
   Step 2: Investing and Financing Activities 600
   Step 3: Net Change in Cash 601

Using Cash Flows to Evaluate a
  Company 604
    Free Cash Flow 604
APPENDIX 13A: **Using a Worksheet to**
Prepare the Statement of Cash Flows—Indirect
Method 608
    Preparing the Worksheet 609
APPENDIX 13B **Statement of Cash Flows—Direct**
Method 615
    Step 1: Operating Activities 616
    Step 2: Investing and Financing
      Activities 620
    Step 3: Net Change in Cash 621
APPENDIX 13C: **Statement of Cash Flows—**
T-Account Approach 624

Chapter 14

Financial Statement Analysis 650

It Pays to Be Patient 650
Basics of Financial Statement
  Analysis 652
    Need for Comparative Analysis 652
    Tools of Analysis 652
Horizontal Analysis 653
    Balance Sheet 654
    Income Statement 655
    Retained Earnings Statement 655
Vertical Analysis 657
    Balance Sheet 657
    Income Statement 657
Ratio Analysis 659
    Liquidity Ratios 660
    Profitability Ratios 664
    Solvency Ratios 668
    Summary of Ratios 669
Earning Power and Irregular Items 671
    Discontinued Operations 672
    Extraordinary Items 673
    Changes in Accounting Principle 675
    Comprehensive Income 675
Quality of Earnings 676
    Alternative Accounting Methods 676
    Pro Forma Income 676
    Improper Recognition 677

Appendix A

Time Value of Money A-1

Nature of Interest A-1
    Simple Interest A-1
    Compound Interest A-2
Future Value Concepts A-2
    Future Value of a Single
      Amount A-2
    Future Value of an Annuity A-4
Present Value Concepts A-7
    Present Value Variables A-7
    Present Value of a Single Amount A-7
    Present Value of an Annuity A-9
    Time Periods and Discounting A-11
    Computing the Present Value of a Long-Term
      Note or Bond A-11
    Computing the Present Values in a Capital
      Budgeting Decision A-14
Using Financial Calculators A-16
    Present Value of a Single Sum A-16
    Present Value of an Annuity A-17
    Useful Applications of the Financial
      Calculator A-18

Appendix B

Standards of Ethical Conduct for Management Accountants B-1

IMA Statement of Ethical Professional
Practice B-1
    Principles B-1
    Standards B-1
    Resolution of Ethical Conflict B-2

Cases for Management Decision-Making CA-1

(The full text of these cases is available online at
***www.wiley.com/college/weygandt*).**

Photo Credits PC-1
Company Index I-1
Subject Index I-3

Chapter 1

Managerial Accounting

Feature Story

Just Add Water ... and Paddle

Mike Cichanowski grew up on the Mississippi River in Winona, Minnesota. At a young age, he learned to paddle a canoe so he could explore the river. Before long, Mike began crafting his own canoes from bent wood and fiberglass in his dad's garage. Then, when his canoe-making shop outgrew the garage, he moved it into an old warehouse. When that was going to be torn down, Mike came to a critical juncture in his life. He took out a bank loan and built his own small shop, giving birth to the company Wenonah Canoe.

Wenonah Canoe soon became known as a pioneer in developing techniques to get the most out of new materials such as plastics, composites, and carbon fibers—maximizing strength while minimizing weight.

In the 1990s, as kayaking became popular, Mike made another critical decision when he acquired Current Designs, a premier Canadian kayak manufacturer. This venture allowed Wenonah to branch out with new product lines while providing Current Designs with much-needed capacity expansion as well as manufacturing expertise. Mike moved Current Designs' headquarters to Minnesota and made a big (and potentially risky) investment in a new production facility. Today, the company's 90 employees produce and sell about

The Navigator is designed to prompt you to use the learning aids in the chapter and to help you set priorities as you study.

Learning Objectives give you a framework for learning the specific concepts covered in the chapter.

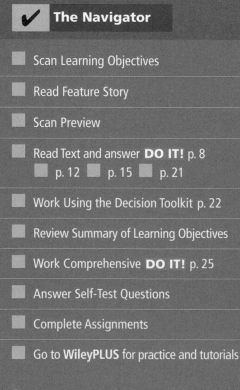

✔ The Navigator

☐ Scan Learning Objectives

☐ Read Feature Story

☐ Scan Preview

☐ Read Text and answer **DO IT!** p. 8
  ☐ p. 12 ☐ p. 15 ☐ p. 21

☐ Work Using the Decision Toolkit p. 22

☐ Review Summary of Learning Objectives

☐ Work Comprehensive **DO IT!** p. 25

☐ Answer Self-Test Questions

☐ Complete Assignments

☐ Go to **WileyPLUS** for practice and tutorials

Learning Objectives

After studying this chapter, you should be able to:

1 Explain the distinguishing features of managerial accounting.

2 Identify the three broad functions of management.

3 Define the three classes of manufacturing costs.

4 Distinguish between product and period costs.

5 Explain the difference between a merchandising and a manufacturing income statement.

6 Indicate how cost of goods manufactured is determined.

7 Explain the difference between a merchandising and a manufacturing balance sheet.

8 Identify trends in managerial accounting.

 **✔ The Navigator**

12,000 canoes and kayaks per year, across the country and around the world.

Mike will tell you that business success is "a three-legged stool." The first leg is the knowledge and commitment to make a great product. Wenonah's canoes and Current Designs' kayaks are widely regarded as among the very best. The second leg is the ability to sell your product. Mike's company started off making great canoes, but it took a little longer to figure out how to sell them. The third leg is not something that most of you would immediately associate with entrepreneurial success. It is what goes on behind the scenes—accounting. Good accounting

Source: www.wenonah.com.

information is absolutely critical to the countless decisions, big and small, that ensure the survival and growth of the company.

Bottom line: No matter how good your product is, and no matter how many units you sell, if you don't have a firm grip on your numbers, you are up a creek without a paddle.

Watch the **What Is Managerial Accounting?** *video in WileyPLUS for an introduction to managerial accounting and the topics presented in this course.*

The **Feature Story** *helps you picture how the chapter topic relates to the real world of business and accounting.*

✔ The Navigator

The **Preview** *describes the purpose of the chapter and outlines the major topics and subtopics you will find in it.*

Preview of **Chapter 1**

This chapter focuses on issues illustrated in the Feature Story about Current Designs and its parent company Wenonah Canoe. To succeed, the company needs to determine and control the costs of material, labor, and overhead, and understand the relationship between costs and profits. Managers often make decisions that determine their company's fate—and their own. Managers are evaluated on the results of their decisions. Managerial accounting provides tools for assisting management in making decisions and for evaluating the effectiveness of those decisions.

The content and organization of this chapter are as follows.

MANAGERIAL ACCOUNTING			
Managerial Accounting Basics	**Managerial Cost Concepts**	**Manufacturing Costs in Financial Statements**	**Managerial Accounting Today**
• Comparing managerial and financial accounting • Management functions • Organizational structure • Business ethics	• Manufacturing costs • Product vs. period costs	• Income statement • Cost of goods manufactured • Balance sheet • Cost concepts—A review • Product costing for service industries	• Focus on the value chain • Balanced scorecard • Corporate social responsibility

✔ The Navigator

Managerial Accounting Basics

Essential terms and concepts are printed in blue where they first appear and are defined in the end-of-chapter Glossary.

Managerial accounting provides economic and financial information for managers and other internal users. The skills that you will learn in this course will be vital to your future success in business. You don't believe us? Let's look at some examples of some of the crucial activities of employees at Current Designs, and where those activities are addressed in this textbook.

In order to know whether it is making a profit, Current Designs needs accurate information about the cost of each kayak (Chapters 2, 3, and 4). And to stay profitable, Current Designs must adjust the number of kayaks it produces in light of changes in economic conditions and consumer tastes. It then needs to understand how changes in the number of kayaks it produces impact its production costs and profitability (Chapters 5 and 6). Further, Current Designs' managers must often consider alternative courses of action. For example, should the company accept a special order from a customer, produce a particular kayak component internally or outsource it, or continue or discontinue a particular product line (Chapter 7)? Finally, one of the most important, and most difficult, decisions is what price to charge for the kayaks (Chapter 8).

In order to plan for the future, Current Designs prepares budgets (Chapter 9), and it then compares its budgeted numbers with its actual results to evaluate performance and identify areas that need to change (Chapters 10 and 11). Finally, it sometimes needs to make substantial investment decisions, such as the building of a new plant or the purchase of new equipment (Chapter 12).

Someday, you are going to face decisions just like these. You may end up in sales, marketing, management, production, or finance. You may work for a company that provides medical care, produces software, or serves up mouth-watering meals. No matter what your position is, and no matter what your product, the skills you acquire in this class will increase your chances of business success. Put another way, in business you can either guess, or you can make an informed decision. As the CEO of Microsoft once noted: "If you're supposed to be making money in business and supposed to be satisfying customers and building market share, there are numbers that characterize those things. And if somebody can't speak to me quantitatively about it, then I'm nervous." This course gives you the skills you need to quantify information so you can make informed business decisions.

Comparing Managerial and Financial Accounting

LEARNING OBJECTIVE 1

Explain the distinguishing features of managerial accounting.

There are both similarities and differences between managerial and financial accounting. First, each field of accounting deals with the economic events of a business. For example, *determining* the unit cost of manufacturing a product is part of managerial accounting. *Reporting* the total cost of goods manufactured and sold is part of financial accounting. In addition, both managerial and financial accounting require that a company's economic events be quantified and communicated to interested parties. Illustration 1-1 summarizes the principal differences between financial accounting and managerial accounting.

Management Functions

LEARNING OBJECTIVE 2

Identify the three broad functions of management.

Managers' activities and responsibilities can be classified into three broad functions:
1. Planning.
2. Directing.
3. Controlling.

Feature	Financial Accounting	Managerial Accounting
Primary Users of Reports	External users: stockholders, creditors, and regulators.	Internal users: officers and managers.
Types and Frequency of Reports	Financial statements. Quarterly and annually.	Internal reports. As frequently as needed.
Purpose of Reports	General-purpose.	Special-purpose for specific decisions.
Content of Reports	Pertains to business as a whole. Highly aggregated (condensed). Limited to double-entry accounting and cost data. Generally accepted accounting principles.	Pertains to subunits of the business. Very detailed. Extends beyond double-entry accounting to any relevant data. Standard is relevance to decisions.
Verification Process	Audited by CPA.	No independent audits.

Illustration 1-1
Differences between financial and managerial accounting

In performing these functions, managers make decisions that have a significant impact on the organization.

Planning requires managers to look ahead and to establish objectives. These objectives are often diverse: maximizing short-term profits and market share, maintaining a commitment to environmental protection, and contributing to social programs. For example, Hewlett-Packard, in an attempt to gain a stronger foothold in the computer industry, has greatly reduced its prices to compete with Dell. A key objective of management is to **add value** to the business under its control. Value is usually measured by the trading price of the company's stock and by the potential selling price of the company.

Directing involves coordinating a company's diverse activities and human resources to produce a smooth-running operation. This function relates to implementing planned objectives and providing necessary incentives to motivate employees. For example, manufacturers such as Campbell Soup Company, General Motors, and Dell must coordinate purchasing, manufacturing, warehousing, and selling. Service corporations such as American Airlines, Federal Express, and AT&T must coordinate scheduling, sales, service, and acquisitions of equipment and supplies. Directing also involves selecting executives, appointing managers and supervisors, and hiring and training employees.

The third management function, **controlling**, is the process of keeping the company's activities on track. In controlling operations, managers determine whether planned goals are being met. When there are deviations from targeted objectives, managers must decide what changes are needed to get back on track. Scandals at companies like Enron, Lucent, and Xerox attest to the fact that companies must have adequate controls to ensure that the company develops and distributes accurate information.

How do managers achieve control? A smart manager in a very small operation can make personal observations, ask good questions, and know how to evaluate the answers. But using this approach in a larger organization would result in chaos. Imagine the president of Current Designs attempting to determine whether the company is meeting its planned objectives, without some record of what has happened and what is expected to occur. Thus, large businesses typically use a formal system of evaluation. These systems include such features as budgets, responsibility centers, and performance evaluation reports—all of which are features of managerial accounting.

Decision-making is not a separate management function. Rather, it is the outcome of the exercise of good judgment in planning, directing, and controlling.

Insight boxes illustrate interesting situations in real companies and show how managers make decisions using accounting information. Guideline answers to the critical thinking questions appear on the last page of the chapter.

MANAGEMENT INSIGHT

Even the Best Have to Get Better

Louis Vuitton is a French manufacturer of high-end handbags, wallets, and suitcases. Its reputation for quality and style allows it to charge extremely high prices–for example, $700 for a tote bag. But often in the past, when demand was hot, supply was nonexistent–shelves were empty, and would-be buyers left empty-handed.

Luxury-goods manufacturers used to consider stockouts to be a good thing, but recently Louis Vuitton changed its attitude. The company adopted "lean" processes used by car manufacturers and electronics companies to speed up production of "hot" products. Work is done by flexible teams, with jobs organized based on how long a task takes. By reducing wasted time and eliminating bottlenecks, what used to take 20 to 30 workers eight days to do now takes 6 to 12 workers one day. Also, production employees who used to specialize on a single task on a single product are now multiskilled. This allows them to quickly switch products to meet demand.

To make sure that the factory is making the right products, within a week of a product launch, Louis Vuitton stores around the world feed sales information to the headquarters in France, and production is adjusted accordingly. Finally, the new production processes have also improved quality. Returns of some products are down by two-thirds, which makes quite a difference to the bottom line when the products are pricey.

Source: Christina Passariello, "Louis Vuitton Tries Modern Methods on Factory Lines," *Wall Street Journal* (October 9, 2006).

 What are some of the steps that this company has taken in order to ensure that production meets demand? (See page 47.)

Organizational Structure

Most companies prepare **organization charts** to show the interrelationships of activities and the delegation of authority and responsibility within the company. Illustration 1-2 shows a typical organization chart.

Stockholders own the corporation, but they manage it indirectly through a **board of directors** they elect. The board formulates the operating policies for the company or organization. The board also selects officers, such as a president and one or more vice presidents, to execute policy and to perform daily management functions.

The **chief executive officer (CEO)** has overall responsibility for managing the business. As the organization chart on page 7 shows, the CEO delegates responsibilities to other officers.

Responsibilities within the company are frequently classified as either line or staff positions. Employees with **line positions** are directly involved in the company's primary revenue-generating operating activities. Examples of line positions include the vice president of operations, vice president of marketing, plant managers, supervisors, and production personnel. Employees with **staff positions** are involved in activities that support the efforts of the line employees. In a company like General Electric or Facebook, employees in finance, legal, and human

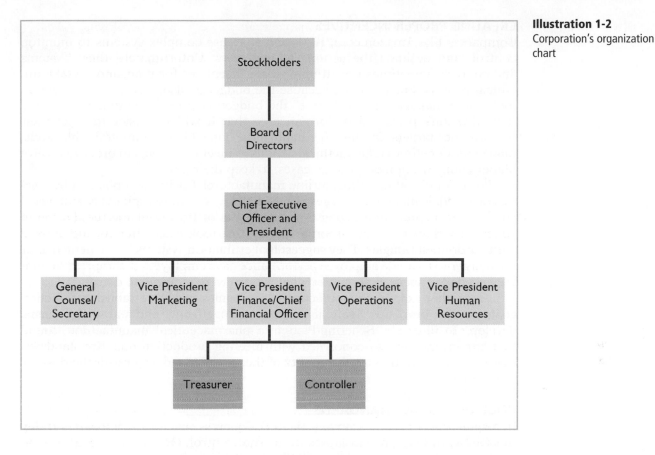

Illustration 1-2
Corporation's organization chart

resources have staff positions. While activities of staff employees are vital to the company, these employees are nonetheless there to serve the line employees who engage in the company's primary operations.

The **chief financial officer (CFO)** is responsible for all of the accounting and finance issues the company faces. The CFO is supported by the **controller** and the **treasurer**. The controller's responsibilities include (1) maintaining the accounting records, (2) maintaining an adequate system of internal control, and (3) preparing financial statements, tax returns, and internal reports. The treasurer has custody of the corporation's funds and is responsible for maintaining the company's cash position.

Also serving the CFO is the internal audit staff. The staff's responsibilities include reviewing the reliability and integrity of financial information provided by the controller and treasurer. Staff members also ensure that internal control systems are functioning properly to safeguard corporate assets. In addition, they investigate compliance with policies and regulations, and in many companies they determine whether resources are being used in the most economical and efficient fashion.

The vice president of operations oversees employees with line positions. For example, the company might have multiple plant managers, each of whom would report to the vice president of operations. Each plant would also have department managers, such as fabricating, painting, and shipping, each of whom would report to the plant manager.

Business Ethics

All employees within an organization are expected to act ethically in their business activities. Given the importance of ethical behavior to corporations and their owners (stockholders), an increasing number of organizations provide codes of business ethics for their employees.

CREATING PROPER INCENTIVES

Companies like Amazon.com, IBM, and Nike use complex systems to monitor, control, and evaluate the actions of managers. Unfortunately, these systems and controls sometimes unwittingly create incentives for managers to take unethical actions. For example, because the budget is also used as an evaluation tool, some managers try to "game" the budgeting process by underestimating their division's predicted performance so that it will be easier to meet their performance targets. On the other hand, if the budget is set at unattainable levels, managers sometimes take unethical actions to meet the targets in order to receive higher compensation or, in some cases, to keep their jobs.

For example, at one time, airline manufacturer Boeing was plagued by a series of scandals including charges of over-billing, corporate espionage, and illegal conflicts of interest. Some long-time employees of Boeing blame the decline in ethics on a change in the corporate culture that took place after Boeing merged with McDonnell Douglas. They suggest that evaluation systems implemented after the merger to evaluate employee performance gave employees the impression that they needed to succeed no matter what actions were required to do so.

As another example, manufacturing companies need to establish production goals for their processes. Again, if controls are not effective and realistic, problems develop. To illustrate, Schering-Plough, a pharmaceutical manufacturer, found that employees were so concerned with meeting production quantity standards that they failed to monitor the quality of the product, and as a result the dosages were often wrong.

CODE OF ETHICAL STANDARDS

In response to corporate scandals, the U.S. Congress enacted the **Sarbanes-Oxley Act (SOX)** to help prevent lapses in internal control. One result of SOX was to clarify top management's responsibility for the company's financial statements. CEOs and CFOs must now certify that financial statements give a fair presentation of the company's operating results and its financial condition. In addition, top managers must certify that the company maintains an adequate system of internal controls to safeguard the company's assets and ensure accurate financial reports.

Another result of SOX is that companies now pay more attention to the composition of the board of directors. In particular, the audit committee of the board of directors must be comprised entirely of independent members (that is, non-employees) and must contain at least one financial expert. Finally, the law substantially increases the penalties for misconduct.

DO IT! exercises ask you to put newly acquired knowledge to work. They outline the Action Plan necessary to complete the exercise, and they show a Solution.

To provide guidance for managerial accountants, the Institute of Management Accountants (IMA) has developed a code of ethical standards, entitled *IMA Statement of Ethical Professional Practice*. Management accountants should not commit acts in violation of these standards. Nor should they condone such acts by others within their organizations. We include the IMA code of ethical standards in Appendix B at the end of the textbook. Throughout the textbook, we will address various ethical issues managers face.

> DO IT!

Managerial Accounting Concepts

Indicate whether the following statements are true or false.

1. Managerial accountants have a single role within an organization, collecting and reporting costs to management.

2. Financial accounting reports are general-purpose and intended for external users.

3. Managerial accounting reports are special-purpose and issued as frequently as needed.

4. Managers' activities and responsibilities can be classified into three broad functions: cost accounting, budgeting, and internal control.

5. As a result of the Sarbanes-Oxley Act, managerial accounting reports must now comply with generally accepted accounting principles (GAAP).

6. Top managers must certify that a company maintains an adequate system of internal controls.

Action Plan

✔ Understand that managerial accounting is a field of accounting that provides economic and financial information for managers and other internal users.

✔ Understand that financial accounting provides information for external users.

✔ Analyze which users require which different types of information.

Solution

1. False. Managerial accountants determine product costs. In addition, managerial accountants are now held responsible for evaluating how well the company is employing its resources. As a result, when the company makes critical strategic decisions, managerial accountants serve as team members alongside personnel from production, marketing, and engineering.

2. True.

3. True.

4. False. Managers' activities are classified into three broad functions: planning, directing, and controlling. Planning requires managers to look ahead to establish objectives. Directing involves coordinating a company's diverse activities and human resources to produce a smooth-running operation. Controlling keeps the company's activities on track.

5. False. SOX clarifies top management's responsibility for the company's financial statements. In addition, top managers must certify that the company maintains an adequate system of internal control to safeguard the company's assets and ensure accurate financial reports.

6. True.

Related exercise material: **BE1-1, BE1-2, BE1-3, E1-1, and** **DO IT!** **1-1.**

✔ **The Navigator**

Managerial Cost Concepts

In order for managers at a company like Current Designs to plan, direct, and control operations effectively, they need good information. One very important type of information is related to costs. Managers should ask questions such as the following.

1. What costs are involved in making a product or providing a service?

2. If we decrease production volume, will costs decrease?

3. What impact will automation have on total costs?

4. How can we best control costs?

To answer these questions, managers need reliable and relevant cost information. We now explain and illustrate the various cost categories that companies use.

Manufacturing Costs

Manufacturing consists of activities and processes that convert raw materials into finished goods. Contrast this type of operation with merchandising, which sells merchandise in the form in which it is purchased. Manufacturing costs are classified as direct materials, direct labor, and manufacturing overhead.

LEARNING OBJECTIVE **3**

Define the three classes of manufacturing costs.

DIRECT MATERIALS

To obtain the materials that will be converted into the finished product, the manufacturer purchases raw materials. **Raw materials** are the basic materials and parts used in the manufacturing process.

Direct Materials

Raw materials that can be physically and directly associated with the finished product during the manufacturing process are **direct materials**. Examples include flour in the baking of bread, syrup in the bottling of soft drinks, and steel in the making of automobiles. A primary direct material of many Current Designs' kayaks is polyethylene powder. Some of its high-performance kayaks use Kevlar®.

Some raw materials cannot be easily associated with the finished product. These are called indirect materials. **Indirect materials** have one of two characteristics: (1) They do not physically become part of the finished product (such as lubricants used by Current Designs in its equipment and polishing compounds used for the finishing touches on kayaks). Or, (2) they are impractical to trace to the finished product because their physical association with the finished product is too small in terms of cost (such as cotter pins and lock washers). Companies account for indirect materials as part of **manufacturing overhead**.

DIRECT LABOR

The work of factory employees that can be physically and directly associated with converting raw materials into finished goods is **direct labor**. Bottlers at Coca-Cola, bakers at Sara Lee, and equipment operators at Current Designs are employees whose activities are usually classified as direct labor. **Indirect labor** refers to the work of employees that has no physical association with the finished product, or for which it is impractical to trace costs to the goods produced. Examples include wages of factory maintenance people, factory time-keepers, and factory supervisors. Like indirect materials, companies classify indirect labor as **manufacturing overhead**.

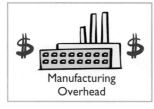
Direct Labor

MANUFACTURING OVERHEAD

Manufacturing overhead consists of costs that are indirectly associated with the manufacture of the finished product. Overhead costs also include manufacturing costs that cannot be classified as direct materials or direct labor. Manufacturing overhead includes indirect materials, indirect labor, depreciation on factory buildings and machines, and insurance, taxes, and maintenance on factory facilities.

One study of manufactured goods found the following magnitudes of the three different product costs as a percentage of the total product cost: direct materials 54%, direct labor 13%, and manufacturing overhead 33%. Note that the direct labor component is the smallest. This component of product cost is dropping substantially because of automation. Companies are working hard to increase productivity by decreasing labor. In some companies, direct labor has become as little as 5% of the total cost.

Allocating direct materials and direct labor costs to specific products is fairly straightforward. Good recordkeeping can tell a company how much plastic it used in making each type of gear, or how many hours of factory labor it took to assemble a part. But allocating overhead costs to specific products presents problems. How much of the purchasing agent's salary is attributable to the hundreds of different products made in the same plant? What about the grease that keeps the machines humming, or the computers that make sure paychecks come out on time? Boiled down to its simplest form, the question becomes: Which products cause the incurrence of which costs? In subsequent chapters, we show various methods of allocating overhead to products.

Alternative Terminology
Some companies use terms such as *factory overhead*, *indirect manufacturing costs*, and *burden* instead of manufacturing overhead.

Alternative Terminology notes present synonymous terms used in practice.

MANAGEMENT INSIGHT

Why Manufacturing Matters for U.S. Workers

Prior to 2010, U.S. manufacturing employment fell at an average rate of 0.1% per year for 60 years. At the same time, U.S. factory output increased by an average rate of 3.4%. As manufacturers relied more heavily on automation, the number of people they needed declined. However, factory jobs are important because the average wage of a factory worker is $22, twice the average wage of employees in the service sector. Fortunately, manufacturing jobs in the United States increased by 1.2% in 2010, and they are forecast to continue to increase through at least 2015. Why? Because companies like Whirlpool, Caterpillar, and Dow are building huge new plants in the United States to replace old, inefficient U.S. facilities. For many products that are ultimately sold in the United States, it makes more sense to produce them domestically and save on the shipping costs. In addition, these efficient new plants, combined with an experienced workforce, will make it possible to compete with manufacturers in other countries, thereby increasing export potential.

Source: Bob Tita, "Whirlpool to Invest in Tennessee Plant," *Wall Street Journal Online* (September 1, 2010); and James R. Hagerty, "U.S. Factories Buck Decline," *Wall Street Journal Online* (January 19, 2011).

? In what ways does the shift to automated factories change the amount and composition of product costs? (See page 47.)

Product Versus Period Costs

Each of the manufacturing cost components—direct materials, direct labor, and manufacturing overhead—are product costs. As the term suggests, **product costs** are costs that are a necessary and integral part of producing the finished product. Companies record product costs, when incurred, as inventory. These costs do not become expenses until the company sells the finished goods inventory. At that point, the company records the expense as cost of goods sold.

Period costs are costs that are matched with the revenue of a specific time period rather than included as part of the cost of a salable product. These are nonmanufacturing costs. Period costs include selling and administrative expenses. In order to determine net income, companies deduct these costs from revenues in the period in which they are incurred.

Illustration 1-3 summarizes these relationships and cost terms. Our main concern in this chapter is with product costs.

> **LEARNING OBJECTIVE   4**
>
> **Distinguish between product and period costs.**

Alternative Terminology
Product costs are also called *inventoriable costs.*

Illustration 1-3
Product versus period costs

All Costs

Product Costs
Manufacturing Costs

- Direct Materials
- Direct Labor
- Manufacturing Overhead
  - Indirect materials
  - Indirect labor
  - Other indirect costs

Period Costs
Nonmanufacturing Costs

- Selling Expenses
- Administrative Expenses

> DO IT!

Managerial Cost Concepts

Action Plan

✔ Classify as direct materials any raw materials that can be physically and directly associated with the finished product.

✔ Classify as direct labor the work of factory employees that can be physically and directly associated with the finished product.

✔ Classify as manufacturing overhead any costs that are indirectly associated with the finished product.

A bicycle company has these costs: tires, salaries of employees who put tires on the wheels, factory building depreciation, lubricants, spokes, salary of factory manager, handlebars, and salaries of factory maintenance employees. Classify each cost as direct materials, direct labor, or overhead.

Solution

Tires, spokes, and handlebars are direct materials. Salaries of employees who put tires on the wheels are direct labor. All of the other costs are manufacturing overhead.

Related exercise material: **BE1-4, BE1-5, BE1-6, BE1-7, E1-2, E1-3, E1-4, E1-5, E1-6, E1-7, and DO IT! 1-2.**

✔ **The Navigator**

Manufacturing Costs in Financial Statements

The financial statements of a manufacturer are very similar to those of a merchandiser. For example, you will find many of the same sections and same accounts in the financial statements of Procter & Gamble that you find in the financial statements of Dick's Sporting Goods. The principal differences between their financial statements occur in two places: the cost of goods sold section in the income statement and the current assets section in the balance sheet.

Income Statement

LEARNING OBJECTIVE   5

Explain the difference between a merchandising and a manufacturing income statement.

Under a periodic inventory system, the income statements of a merchandiser and a manufacturer differ in the cost of goods sold section. Merchandisers compute cost of goods sold by adding the beginning merchandise inventory to the **cost of goods purchased** and subtracting the ending merchandise inventory. Manufacturers compute cost of goods sold by adding the beginning finished goods inventory to the **cost of goods manufactured** and subtracting the ending finished goods inventory. Illustration 1-4 shows these different methods.

A number of accounts are involved in determining the cost of goods manufactured. To eliminate excessive detail, income statements typically show only the total cost of goods manufactured. A separate statement, called a Cost of Goods Manufactured Schedule, presents the details. (See the discussion on pages 13–14 and Illustration 1-7.)

Illustration 1-5 shows the different presentations of the cost of goods sold sections for merchandising and manufacturing companies. The other sections of an income statement are similar for merchandisers and manufacturers.

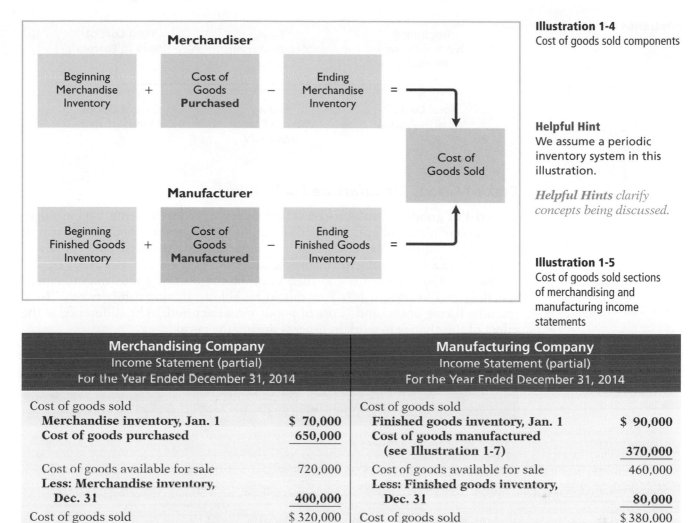

Illustration 1-4
Cost of goods sold components

Helpful Hint
We assume a periodic inventory system in this illustration.

Helpful Hints clarify concepts being discussed.

Illustration 1-5
Cost of goods sold sections of merchandising and manufacturing income statements

Merchandising Company Income Statement (partial) For the Year Ended December 31, 2014		Manufacturing Company Income Statement (partial) For the Year Ended December 31, 2014	
Cost of goods sold		Cost of goods sold	
Merchandise inventory, Jan. 1	$ 70,000	**Finished goods inventory, Jan. 1**	$ 90,000
Cost of goods purchased	650,000	**Cost of goods manufactured** (see Illustration 1-7)	370,000
Cost of goods available for sale	720,000	Cost of goods available for sale	460,000
Less: Merchandise inventory, Dec. 31	400,000	**Less: Finished goods inventory, Dec. 31**	80,000
Cost of goods sold	$ 320,000	Cost of goods sold	$ 380,000

Cost of Goods Manufactured

An example may help show how companies determine the cost of goods manufactured. Assume that on January 1, Current Designs has a number of kayaks in various stages of production. In total, these partially completed units are called **beginning work in process inventory**. The costs the company assigns to beginning work in process inventory are based on the **manufacturing costs incurred in the prior period**.

Current Designs first incurs manufacturing costs in the current year to complete the work that was in process on January 1. It then incurs manufacturing costs for production of new orders. The sum of the direct materials costs, direct labor costs, and manufacturing overhead incurred in the current year is the **total manufacturing costs** for the current period.

We now have two cost amounts: (1) the cost of the beginning work in process and (2) the total manufacturing costs for the current period. The sum of these costs is the **total cost of work in process** for the year.

At the end of the year, Current Designs may have some kayaks that are only partially completed. The costs of these units become the cost of the **ending work in process inventory**. To find the **cost of goods manufactured**, we subtract this cost from the total cost of work in process. Illustration 1-6 (page 14) shows the formula for determining the cost of goods manufactured.

LEARNING OBJECTIVE 6

Indicate how cost of goods manufactured is determined.

Illustration 1-6
Cost of goods manufactured
formula

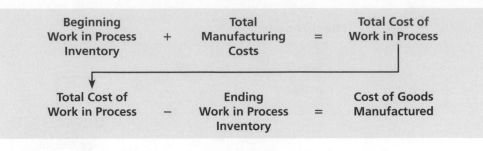

| Beginning Work in Process Inventory | + | Total Manufacturing Costs | = | Total Cost of Work in Process |
| Total Cost of Work in Process | − | Ending Work in Process Inventory | = | Cost of Goods Manufactured |

Cost of Goods Manufactured Schedule

The **cost of goods manufactured schedule** reports cost elements used in calculating cost of goods manufactured. Illustration 1-7 shows the schedule for Current Designs (using assumed data). The schedule presents detailed data for direct materials and for manufacturing overhead.

Review Illustration 1-6 and then examine the cost of goods manufactured schedule in Illustration 1-7. You should be able to distinguish between "Total manufacturing costs" and "Cost of goods manufactured." The difference is the effect of the change in work in process during the period.

Illustration 1-7
Cost of goods manufactured
schedule

*Often, numbers or categories in the financial statements are highlighted in **red type** to draw your attention to key information.*

*Each chapter presents useful information about how decision-makers analyze and solve business problems. **Decision Toolkits** summarize the key features of a decision tool and review why and how to use it.*

Current Designs Cost of Goods Manufactured Schedule For the Year Ended December 31, 2014			
Work in process, January 1			**$ 18,400**
Direct materials			
Raw materials inventory, January 1	$ 16,700		
Raw materials purchases	152,500		
Total raw materials available for use	169,200		
Less: Raw materials inventory, December 31	22,800		
Direct materials used		$146,400	
Direct labor		175,600	
Manufacturing overhead			
Indirect labor	14,300		
Factory repairs	12,600		
Factory utilities	10,100		
Factory depreciation	9,440		
Factory insurance	8,360		
Total manufacturing overhead		54,800	
Total manufacturing costs			**376,800**
Total cost of work in process			395,200
Less: Work in process, December 31			**25,200**
Cost of goods manufactured			**$370,000**

DECISION TOOLKIT

DECISION CHECKPOINTS	INFO NEEDED FOR DECISION	TOOL TO USE FOR DECISION	HOW TO EVALUATE RESULTS
Is the company maintaining control over the costs of production?	Cost of material, labor, and overhead	Cost of goods manufactured schedule	Compare the cost of goods manufactured to revenue expected from product sales.

> ## DO IT!

Cost of Goods Manufactured

The following information is available for Keystone Company.

	March 1	March 31
Raw materials inventory	$12,000	$10,000
Work in process inventory	2,500	4,000
Materials purchased in March	$ 90,000	
Direct labor in March	75,000	
Manufacturing overhead in March	220,000	

Prepare the cost of goods manufactured schedule for the month of March.

Solution

Action Plan

✔ Start with beginning work in process as the first item in the cost of goods manufactured schedule.

✔ Sum direct materials used, direct labor, and manufacturing overhead to determine total manufacturing costs.

✔ Sum beginning work in process and total manufacturing costs to determine total cost of work in process.

✔ Cost of goods manufactured is the total cost of work in process less ending work in process.

Keystone Company
Cost of Goods Manufactured Schedule
For the Month Ended March 31

Work in process, March 1		$ 2,500
Direct materials		
Raw materials, March 1	$ 12,000	
Raw material purchases	90,000	
Total raw materials available for use	102,000	
Less: Raw materials, March 31	10,000	
Direct materials used	$ 92,000	
Direct labor	75,000	
Manufacturing overhead	220,000	
Total manufacturing costs		387,000
Total cost of work in process		389,500
Less: Work in process, March 31		4,000
Cost of goods manufactured		$385,500

Related exercise material: **BE1-8, BE1-10, BE1-11, E1-8, E1-9, E1-10, E1-11, E1-12, E1-13, E1-14, E1-15, E1-16, E1-17, and DO IT! 1-3.**

✔ **The Navigator**

Balance Sheet

The balance sheet for a merchandising company shows just one category of inventory. In contrast, the balance sheet for a manufacturer may have three inventory accounts, as shown in Illustration 1-8.

LEARNING OBJECTIVE 7

Explain the difference between a merchandising and a manufacturing balance sheet.

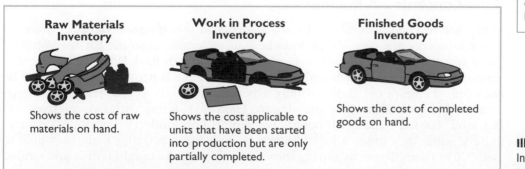

Raw Materials Inventory	**Work in Process Inventory**	**Finished Goods Inventory**
Shows the cost of raw materials on hand.	Shows the cost applicable to units that have been started into production but are only partially completed.	Shows the cost of completed goods on hand.

Illustration 1-8
Inventory accounts for a manufacturer

Finished Goods Inventory is to a manufacturer what Merchandise Inventory is to a merchandiser. Each of these classifications represents the goods that the company has available for sale.

The current assets sections presented in Illustration 1-9 contrast the presentations of inventories for merchandising and manufacturing companies. Manufacturing companies generally list their inventories in the order of their liquidity—the order in which they are expected to be realized in cash. Thus, finished goods inventory comes first. The remainder of the balance sheet is similar for the two types of companies.

Illustration 1-9
Current assets sections of merchandising and manufacturing balance sheets

Merchandising Company Balance Sheet December 31, 2014		Manufacturing Company Balance Sheet December 31, 2014		
Current assets		Current assets		
Cash	$100,000	Cash		$180,000
Receivables (net)	210,000	Receivables (net)		210,000
Merchandise inventory	**400,000**	**Inventories**		
Prepaid expenses	22,000	**Finished goods**	**$80,000**	
Total current assets	$732,000	**Work in process**	**25,200**	
		Raw materials	**22,800**	128,000
		Prepaid expenses		18,000
		Total current assets		$536,000

Each step in the accounting cycle for a merchandiser applies to a manufacturer. For example, prior to preparing financial statements, manufacturers make adjusting entries. The adjusting entries are essentially the same as those of a merchandiser. The closing entries are also similar for manufacturers and merchandisers.

DECISION TOOLKIT

DECISION CHECKPOINTS	INFO NEEDED FOR DECISION	TOOL TO USE FOR DECISION	HOW TO EVALUATE RESULTS
What is the composition of a manufacturing company's inventory?	Amount of raw materials, work in process, and finished goods inventories	Balance sheet	Determine whether there are sufficient finished goods, raw materials, and work in process inventories to meet forecasted demand.

Cost Concepts—A Review

You have learned a number of cost concepts in this chapter. Because many of these concepts are new, we provide here an extended example for review. Suppose you started your own snowboard factory, Terrain Park Boards. Think that's impossible? Burton Snowboards was started by Jake Burton Carpenter, when he was only 23 years old. Jake initially experimented with 100 different prototype designs before settling on a final design. Then Jake, along with two relatives and a friend, started making 50 boards per day in Londonderry, Vermont. Unfortunately, while they made a lot of boards in their first year, they were only able to sell 300 of them. To get by during those early years, Jake taught tennis and tended bar to pay the bills.

Here are some of the costs that your snowboard factory would incur.

1. The materials cost of each snowboard (wood cores, fiberglass, resins, metal screw holes, metal edges, and ink) is $30.

2. The labor costs (for example, to trim and shape each board using jig saws and band saws) are $40.

3. Depreciation on the factory building and equipment (for example, presses, grinding machines, and lacquer machines) used to make the snowboards is $25,000 per year.

4. Property taxes on the factory building (where the snowboards are made) are $6,000 per year.

5. Advertising costs (mostly online and catalogue) are $60,000 per year.

6. Sales commissions related to snowboard sales are $20 per snowboard.

7. Salaries for factory maintenance employees are $45,000 per year.

8. The salary of the plant manager is $70,000.

9. The cost of shipping is $8 per snowboard.

Illustration 1-10 shows how Terrain Park Boards would assign these manufacturing and selling costs to the various categories.

Terrain Park Boards

Illustration 1-10
Assignment of costs to cost categories

	Product Costs			
Cost Item	Direct Materials	Direct Labor	Manufacturing Overhead	Period Costs
1. Material cost ($30 per board)	X			
2. Labor costs ($40 per board)		X		
3. Depreciation on factory equipment ($25,000 per year)			X	
4. Property taxes on factory building ($6,000 per year)			X	
5. Advertising costs ($60,000 per year)				X
6. Sales commissions ($20 per board)				X
7. Maintenance salaries (factory facilities) ($45,000 per year)			X	
8. Salary of plant manager ($70,000 per year)			X	
9. Cost of shipping boards ($8 per board)				X

Remember that total manufacturing costs are the sum of the **product costs**—direct materials, direct labor, and manufacturing overhead. If Terrain Park Boards produces 10,000 snowboards the first year, the total manufacturing costs would be $846,000 as shown in Illustration 1-11 (page 18).

Illustration 1-11
Computation of total
manufacturing costs

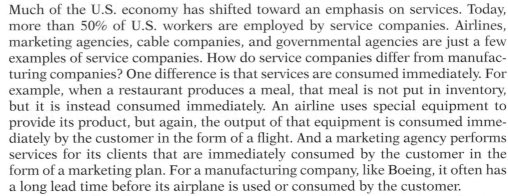

Cost Number and Item	Manufacturing Cost
1. Material cost ($30 × 10,000)	$300,000
2. Labor cost ($40 × 10,000)	400,000
3. Depreciation on factory equipment	25,000
4. Property taxes on factory building	6,000
7. Maintenance salaries (factory facilities)	45,000
8. Salary of plant manager	70,000
Total manufacturing costs	**$846,000**

Knowing the total manufacturing costs, Terrain Park Boards can compute the manufacturing cost per unit. Assuming 10,000 units, the cost to produce one snowboard is $84.60 ($846,000 ÷ 10,000 units).

In subsequent chapters, we will use extensively the cost concepts discussed in this chapter. So study Illustration 1-10 carefully. If you do not understand any of these classifications, go back and reread the appropriate section in this chapter.

Product Costing for Service Industries

Much of the U.S. economy has shifted toward an emphasis on services. Today, more than 50% of U.S. workers are employed by service companies. Airlines, marketing agencies, cable companies, and governmental agencies are just a few examples of service companies. How do service companies differ from manufacturing companies? One difference is that services are consumed immediately. For example, when a restaurant produces a meal, that meal is not put in inventory, but it is instead consumed immediately. An airline uses special equipment to provide its product, but again, the output of that equipment is consumed immediately by the customer in the form of a flight. And a marketing agency performs services for its clients that are immediately consumed by the customer in the form of a marketing plan. For a manufacturing company, like Boeing, it often has a long lead time before its airplane is used or consumed by the customer.

This chapter's examples used manufacturing companies because accounting for the manufacturing environment requires the use of the broadest range of accounts. That is, the accounts used by service companies represent a subset of those used by manufacturers because service companies are not producing inventory. Neither the restaurant, the airline, or the marketing agency discussed above produces an inventoriable product. However, just like a manufacturer, each needs to keep track of the costs of its services in order to know whether it is generating a profit. A successful restaurateur needs to know the cost of each offering on the menu, an airline needs to know the cost of flight service to each destination, and a marketing agency needs to know the cost to develop a marketing plan. Thus, the techniques shown in this chapter, to accumulate manufacturing costs to determine manufacturing inventory, are equally useful for determining the costs of providing services.

For example, let's consider the costs that Hewlett-Packard (HP) might incur on a consulting engagement. A significant portion of its costs would be salaries of consulting personnel. It might also incur travel costs, materials, software costs, and depreciation charges on equipment used by the employees to provide the consulting service. In the same way that it needs to keep track of the cost of manufacturing its computers and printers, HP needs to know what its costs are on each consulting job. It could prepare a cost of services provided schedule similar to the cost of goods manufactured schedule in Illustration 1-7 (page 14). The structure would be essentially the same as the cost of goods manufactured schedule, but section headings would be reflective of the costs of the particular service organization.

Ethics Note

Do telecommunications companies have an obligation to provide service to remote or low-user areas for a fee that may be less than the cost of the service?

Ethics Notes help sensitize you to some of the ethical issues in accounting.

Many of the examples we present in subsequent chapters will be based on service companies. To highlight the relevance of the techniques used in this course for service companies, we have placed a service company icon 👤 next to those items in the text and end-of-chapter materials that relate to nonmanufacturing companies.

SERVICE COMPANY INSIGHT 👤

Low Fares but Decent Profits

During 2008, when other airlines were cutting flight service due to the recession, Allegiant Airlines increased capacity by 21%. Sounds crazy, doesn't it? But it must know something, because while the other airlines were losing money, it was generating profits. Consider also that its average one-way fare is only $83. So how does it make money? As a low-budget airline, it focuses on controlling costs. It purchases used planes for $4 million each rather than new planes for $40 million. It flies out of small towns, so wages are low and competition is nonexistent. It only flies a route if its 150-passenger planes are nearly full (it averages about 90% of capacity). If a route isn't filling up, it quits flying it as often or cancels it altogether. It adjusts its prices weekly. The bottom line is that it knows its costs to the penny. Knowing what your costs are might not be glamorous, but it sure beats losing money.

Source: Susan Carey, "For Allegiant, Getaways Mean Profits," *Wall Street Journal Online* (February 18, 2009).

? What are some of the line items that would appear in the cost of services provided schedule of an airline? (See page 47.)

Managerial Accounting Today

The business environment never stands still. Regulations are always changing, global competition continues to intensify, and technology is a source of constant upheaval. In this rapidly changing world, managerial accounting must continue to innovate in order to provide managers with the information they need.

LEARNING OBJECTIVE 8

Identify trends in managerial accounting.

Focus on the Value Chain

The **value chain** refers to all business processes associated with providing a product or service. Illustration 1-12 depicts the value chain for a manufacturer. Many of the most significant business innovations in recent years have resulted either directly, or indirectly, from a focus on the value chain. For example, so-called **lean manufacturing**, originally pioneered by Japanese automobile manufacturer Toyota but now widely practiced, reviews all business processes in an effort to increase productivity and eliminate waste, all while continually trying to improve quality.

Illustration 1-12
A manufacturer's value chain

Research & development and product design	Acquisition of raw materials	Production	Sales and marketing	Delivery	Customer relations and subsequent services

Just-in-time (JIT) inventory methods, which have significantly lowered inventory levels and costs for many companies, are one innovation that resulted from the focus on the value chain. Under the JIT inventory method, goods are manufactured or purchased just in time for sale. For example, Dell can deliver a computer within 48 hours of a customer's custom order. However, JIT also necessitates increased emphasis on product quality. Because JIT companies do not have excess inventory on hand, they cannot afford to stop production because of defects or machine breakdowns. If they have to stop production, deliveries will be delayed and customers will be unhappy. For example, a recent design flaw in an Intel computer chip was estimated to cost the company $1 billion in repairs and reduced revenue. As a consequence, many companies now focus on **total quality management (TQM)** to reduce defects in finished products, with the goal of zero defects. The TQM philosophy has been employed by some of the most successful businesses to improve all aspects of the value chain.

Another innovation, the **theory of constraints**, involves identification of "bottlenecks"—constraints within the value chain that limit a company's profitability. Once a major constraint has been identified and eliminated, the company moves on to fix the next most significant constraint. General Motors found that by eliminating bottlenecks, it improved its use of overtime labor while meeting customer demand. An application of the theory of constraints is presented in Chapter 6.

Technology has played a big role in the focus on the value chain and the implementation of lean manufacturing. For example, **enterprise resource planning (ERP) systems**, such as those provided by SAP, provide a comprehensive, centralized, integrated source of information to manage all major business processes—from purchasing, to manufacturing, to sales, to human resources. ERP systems have, in some large companies, replaced as many as 200 individual software packages. In addition, the focus on improving efficiency in the value chain has also resulted in adoption of automated manufacturing processes. Many companies now use computer-integrated manufacturing. These systems often reduce the reliance on manual labor by using robotic equipment. This increases overhead costs as a percentage of total product costs.

As overhead costs increased because of factory automation, the accuracy of overhead cost allocation to specific products became more important. Managerial accounting devised an approach, called **activity-based costing (ABC)**, which allocates overhead based on each product's use of particular activities in making the product. In addition to providing more accurate product costing, ABC also can contribute to increased efficiency in the value chain. For example, suppose one of a company's overhead pools is allocated based on the number of setups that each product requires. If a particular product's cost is high because it is allocated a lot of overhead due to a high number of setups, management will be motivated to try to reduce the number of setups and thus reduce its overhead allocation. ABC is discussed further in Chapter 4.

Balanced Scorecard

As companies implement various business practice innovations, managers sometimes focus too enthusiastically on the latest innovation, to the detriment of other areas of the business. For example, by focusing on total quality management, companies sometimes lose sight of cost/benefit considerations. Similarly, in focusing on reducing inventory levels through just-in-time inventory methods, companies sometimes lose sales due to inventory shortages. The **balanced scorecard** corrects for this limited perspective: This approach uses both financial and nonfinancial measures to evaluate all aspects of a company's operations in an integrated fashion. The performance measures are linked in a cause-and-effect fashion to ensure that they all tie to the company's overall objectives. For example, to increase return on assets, the company could try to increase sales. To increase sales, the company could try to increase customer satisfaction. To increase customer satisfaction, the company could try to reduce product defects. Finally, to reduce product defects, the company could increase employee training. The balanced scorecard, which is discussed further in Chapter 11, is now used by many companies, including Hilton Hotels, Wal-Mart Stores, Inc., and HP.

Corporate Social Responsibility

The balanced scorecard attempts to take a broader, more inclusive view of corporate profitability measures. Many companies, however, have begun to evaluate not just corporate profitability but also **corporate social responsibility**. In addition to profitability, corporate social responsibility considers a company's efforts to employ sustainable business practices with regard to its employees and the environment. This is sometimes referred to as the **triple bottom line** because it evaluates a company's performance with regard to **people, planet, and profit**. Make no mistake, these companies are still striving to maximize profits—in a competitive world, they won't survive long if they don't. In fact, you might recognize a few of the names on the Forbes.com list of the 100 most sustainable companies in the world. Ever hear of General Electric, adidas, Toyota, Coca-Cola, or Starbucks? These companies have learned that with a long-term, sustainable approach, they can maximize profits while also acting in the best interest of their employees, their communities, and the environment. At various points within this textbook, we will discuss situations where real companies use the very skills that you are learning to evaluate decisions from a sustainable perspective.

> **DO IT!**

Trends in Managerial Accounting

Action Plan

✔ Develop a forward-looking view, in order to advise and provide information to various members of the organization.

✔ Understand current business trends and issues.

Match the descriptions that follow with the corresponding terms.

Descriptions:

1. _____ All activities associated with providing a product or service.

2. _____ A method of allocating overhead based on each product's use of activities in making the product.

3. _____ Systems implemented to reduce defects in finished products with the goal of achieving zero defects.

4. _____ A performance-measurement approach that uses both financial and nonfinancial measures, tied to company objectives, to evaluate a company's operations in an integrated fashion.

5. _____ Inventory system in which goods are manufactured or purchased just as they are needed for use.

Terms:

a. Activity-based costing

b. Balanced scorecard

c. Just-in-time (JIT) inventory

d. Total quality management (TQM)

e. Value chain

Solution

1. e   2. a   3. d   4. b   5. c

Related exercise material: **E1-18 and DO IT! 1-4.**

✔ **The Navigator**

USING THE **DECISION TOOLKIT**

Giant Bike Co. Ltd. produces many different models of bicycles. Assume that the market has responded enthusiastically to a new model, the Jaguar. As a result, the company has established a separate manufacturing facility to produce these bicycles. The company produces 1,000 bicycles per month. Giant's monthly manufacturing costs and other data are as follows.

1. Rent on manufacturing equipment (lease cost)	$2,000/month	
2. Insurance on manufacturing building	$750/month	
3. Raw materials (frames, tires, etc.)	$80/bicycle	
4. Utility costs for manufacturing facility	$1,000/month	
5. Supplies for administrative office	$800/month	
6. Wages for assembly line workers in manufacturing facility	$30/bicycle	
7. Depreciation on office equipment	$650/month	

8. Miscellaneous manufacturing materials (lubricants, solders, etc.) $1.20/bicycle
9. Property taxes on manufacturing building $2,400/year
10. Manufacturing supervisor's salary $3,000/month
11. Advertising for bicycles $30,000/year
12. Sales commissions $10/bicycle
13. Depreciation on manufacturing building $1,500/month

Instructions

(a) Prepare an answer sheet with the following column headings.

	Product Costs			
Cost Item	Direct Materials	Direct Labor	Manufacturing Overhead	Period Costs

Enter each cost item on your answer sheet, placing an "X" mark under the appropriate headings.

(b) Compute total manufacturing costs for the month.

Solution

(a)

	Product Costs			
Cost Item	Direct Materials	Direct Labor	Manufacturing Overhead	Period Costs
1. Rent on manufacturing equipment ($2,000/month)			X	
2. Insurance on manufacturing building ($750/month)			X	
3. Raw materials ($80/bicycle)	X			
4. Manufacturing utilities ($1,000/month)			X	
5. Office supplies ($800/month)				X
6. Wages for assembly workers ($30/bicycle)		X		
7. Depreciation on office equipment ($650/month)				X
8. Miscellaneous manufacturing materials ($1.20/bicycle)			X	

| | Product Costs | | | |
Cost Item	Direct Materials	Direct Labor	Manufacturing Overhead	Period Costs
9. Property taxes on manufacturing building ($2,400/year)			X	
10. Manufacturing supervisor's salary ($3,000/month)			X	
11. Advertising cost ($30,000/year)				X
12. Sales commissions ($10/bicycle)				X
13. Depreciation on manufacturing building ($1,500/month)			X	

(b)

Cost Item	Manufacturing Cost
Rent on manufacturing equipment	$ 2,000
Insurance on manufacturing building	750
Raw materials ($80 × 1,000)	80,000
Manufacturing utilities	1,000
Labor ($30 × 1,000)	30,000
Miscellaneous materials ($1.20 × 1,000)	1,200
Property taxes on manufacturing building ($2,400 ÷ 12)	200
Manufacturing supervisor's salary	3,000
Depreciation on manufacturing building	1,500
Total manufacturing costs	$119,650

✔ The Navigator

*The **Summary of Learning Objectives** reiterates the main points related to the Learning Objectives. It provides you with an opportunity to review what you have learned.*

SUMMARY OF LEARNING OBJECTIVES   ✔ The Navigator

1 Explain the distinguishing features of managerial accounting. The *primary users* of managerial accounting reports are internal users, who are officers, department heads, managers, and supervisors in the company. Managerial accounting issues internal reports as frequently as the need arises. The purpose of these reports is to provide special-purpose information for a particular user for a specific decision. The content of managerial accounting reports pertains to subunits of the business, may be very detailed, and may extend beyond the double-entry accounting system. The reporting standard is relevance to the decision being made. No independent audits are required in managerial accounting.

2 Identify the three broad functions of management. The three functions are planning, directing, and controlling. Planning requires management to look ahead and to establish objectives. Directing involves coordinating the diverse activities and human resources of a

company to produce a smooth-running operation. Controlling is the process of keeping the activities on track.

3 Define the three classes of manufacturing costs. Manufacturing costs are typically classified as either (1) direct materials, (2) direct labor, or (3) manufacturing overhead. Raw materials that can be physically and directly associated with the finished product during the manufacturing process are called direct materials. The work of factory employees that can be physically and directly associated with converting raw materials into finished goods is considered direct labor. Manufacturing overhead consists of costs that are indirectly associated with the manufacture of the finished product.

4 Distinguish between product and period costs. Product costs are costs that are a necessary and integral part of producing the finished product. Product costs are also called inventoriable costs. Under the expense recognition principle, these costs do not become expenses until the company sells the finished goods inventory. Period costs are costs that are identified with a specific time period rather than with a salable product. These costs relate to nonmanufacturing costs and therefore are not inventoriable costs.

5 Explain the difference between a merchandising and a manufacturing income statement. The difference between a merchandising and a manufacturing income statement is in the cost of goods sold section. A manufacturing cost of goods sold section shows beginning and ending finished goods inventories and the cost of goods manufactured.

6 Indicate how cost of goods manufactured is determined. Companies add the cost of the beginning work in process to the total manufacturing costs for the current year to arrive at the total cost of work in process for the year. They then subtract the ending work in process from the total cost of work in process to arrive at the cost of goods manufactured.

7 Explain the difference between a merchandising and a manufacturing balance sheet. The difference between a merchandising and a manufacturing balance sheet is in the current assets section. The current assets section of a manufacturing company's balance sheet presents three inventory accounts: finished goods inventory, work in process inventory, and raw materials inventory.

8 Identify trends in managerial accounting. Managerial accounting has experienced many changes in recent years. Improved practices include a focus on managing the value chain through techniques such as just-in-time inventory, total quality management, activity-based costing, and theory of constraints. The balanced scorecard is now used by many companies in order to attain a more comprehensive view of the company's operations. Finally, companies are now evaluating their performance with regard to their corporate social responsibility.

The **Decision Toolkit—A Summary** reviews the contexts and techniques useful for decision-making that were covered in the chapter.

DECISION TOOLKIT A SUMMARY

DECISION CHECKPOINTS	INFO NEEDED FOR DECISION	TOOL TO USE FOR DECISION	HOW TO EVALUATE RESULTS
Is the company maintaining control over the costs of production?	Cost of material, labor, and overhead	Cost of goods manufactured schedule	Compare the cost of goods manufactured to revenue expected from product sales.
What is the composition of a manufacturing company's inventory?	Amount of raw materials, work in process, and finished goods inventories	Balance sheet	Determine whether there are sufficient finished goods, raw materials, and work in process inventories to meet forecasted demand.

GLOSSARY

Activity-based costing (ABC) A method of allocating overhead based on each product's use of activities in making the product. (p. 20).

Balanced scorecard A performance-measurement approach that uses both financial and nonfinancial measures, tied to company objectives, to evaluate a company's operations in an integrated fashion. (p. 20).

Board of directors The group of officials elected by the stockholders of a corporation to formulate operating policies, select officers, and otherwise manage the company. (p. 6).

Chief executive officer (CEO) Corporate officer who has overall responsibility for managing the business and delegates responsibilities to other corporate officers. (p. 6).

Chief financial officer (CFO) Corporate officer who is responsible for all of the accounting and finance issues of the company. (p. 7).

Controller Financial officer responsible for a company's accounting records, system of internal control, and preparation of financial statements, tax returns, and internal reports. (p. 7).

Corporate social responsibility The efforts of a company to employ sustainable business practices with regard to its employees and the environment. (p. 21).

Cost of goods manufactured Total cost of work in process less the cost of the ending work in process inventory. (p. 13).

Direct labor The work of factory employees that can be physically and directly associated with converting raw materials into finished goods. (p. 10).

Direct materials Raw materials that can be physically and directly associated with manufacturing the finished product. (p. 10).

Enterprise resource planning (ERP) system Software that provides a comprehensive, centralized, integrated source of information used to manage all major business processes. (p. 20).

Indirect labor Work of factory employees that has no physical association with the finished product, or for which it is impractical to trace the costs to the goods produced. (p. 10).

Indirect materials Raw materials that do not physically become part of the finished product or for which it is impractical to trace to the finished product because their physical association with the finished product is too small. (p. 10).

Just-in-time (JIT) inventory Inventory system in which goods are manufactured or purchased just in time for sale. (p. 20).

Line positions Jobs that are directly involved in a company's primary revenue-generating operating activities. (p. 6).

Managerial accounting A field of accounting that provides economic and financial information for managers and other internal users. (p. 4).

Manufacturing overhead Manufacturing costs that are indirectly associated with the manufacture of the finished product. (p. 10).

Period costs Costs that are matched with the revenue of a specific time period and charged to expense as incurred. (p. 11).

Product costs Costs that are a necessary and integral part of producing the finished product. (p. 11).

Sarbanes-Oxley Act (SOX) Law passed by Congress intended to reduce unethical corporate behavior. (p. 8).

Staff positions Jobs that support the efforts of line employees. (p. 6).

Theory of constraints A specific approach used to identify and manage constraints in order to achieve the company's goals. (p. 20).

Total cost of work in process Cost of the beginning work in process plus total manufacturing costs for the current period. (p. 13).

Total manufacturing costs The sum of direct materials, direct labor, and manufacturing overhead incurred in the current period. (p. 13).

Total quality management (TQM) Systems implemented to reduce defects in finished products with the goal of achieving zero defects. (p. 20).

Treasurer Financial officer responsible for custody of a company's funds and for maintaining its cash position. (p. 7).

Triple bottom line The evaluation of a company's social responsibility performance with regard to people, planet, and profit. (p. 21).

Value chain All activities that a business processes with providing a product or service. (p. 19).

> ## Comprehensive **DO IT!**

*Comprehensive DO IT! exercises are a final review before you begin homework. An **Action Plan** that appears in the margin gives you tips about how to approach the problem, and the **Solution** provided demonstrates both the form and content of complete answers.*

Superior Company has the following cost and expense data for the year ending December 31, 2014.

Raw materials, 1/1/14	$ 30,000		Insurance, factory	$ 14,000
Raw materials, 12/31/14	20,000		Property taxes, factory building	6,000
Raw materials purchases	205,000		Sales revenue	1,500,000
Indirect materials	15,000		Delivery expenses	100,000
Work in process, 1/1/14	80,000		Sales commissions	150,000
Work in process, 12/31/14	50,000		Indirect labor	90,000
Finished goods, 1/1/14	110,000		Factory machinery rent	40,000
Finished goods, 12/31/14	120,000		Factory utilities	65,000
Direct labor	350,000		Depreciation, factory building	24,000
Factory manager's salary	35,000		Administrative expenses	300,000

Instructions

(a) Prepare a cost of goods manufactured schedule for Superior Company for 2014.

(b) Prepare an income statement for Superior Company for 2014.

(c) Assume that Superior Company's accounting records show the balances of the following current asset accounts: Cash $17,000, Accounts Receivable (net) $120,000, Prepaid Expenses $13,000, and Short-Term Investments $26,000. Prepare the current assets section of the balance sheet for Superior Company as of December 31, 2014.

Solution to Comprehensive `DO IT!`

Action Plan

✔ Start with beginning work in process as the first item in the cost of goods manufactured schedule.

✔ Sum direct materials used, direct labor, and total manufacturing overhead to determine total manufacturing costs.

✔ Sum beginning work in process and total manufacturing costs to determine total cost of work in process.

✔ Cost of goods manufactured is the total cost of work in process less ending work in process.

✔ In the cost of goods sold section of the income statement, show beginning and ending finished goods inventory and cost of goods manufactured.

✔ In the balance sheet, list manufacturing inventories in the order of their expected realization in cash, with finished goods first.

(a)

Superior Company
Cost of Goods Manufactured Schedule
For the Year Ended December 31, 2014

Work in process, 1/1			$ 80,000
Direct materials			
Raw materials inventory, 1/1	$ 30,000		
Raw materials purchases	205,000		
Total raw materials available for use	235,000		
Less: Raw materials inventory, 12/31	20,000		
Direct materials used		$215,000	
Direct labor		350,000	
Manufacturing overhead			
Indirect labor	90,000		
Factory utilities	65,000		
Factory machinery rent	40,000		
Factory manager's salary	35,000		
Depreciation, factory building	24,000		
Indirect materials	15,000		
Insurance, factory	14,000		
Property taxes, factory building	6,000		
Total manufacturing overhead		289,000	
Total manufacturing costs			854,000
Total cost of work in process			934,000
Less: Work in process, 12/31			50,000
Cost of goods manufactured			$ 884,000

(b)

Superior Company
Income Statement
For the Year Ended December 31, 2014

Sales revenue		$1,500,000
Cost of goods sold		
Finished goods inventory, January 1	$110,000	
Cost of goods manufactured	884,000	
Cost of goods available for sale	994,000	
Less: Finished goods inventory, December 31	120,000	
Cost of goods sold		874,000
Gross profit		626,000
Operating expenses		
Administrative expenses	300,000	
Sales commissions	150,000	
Delivery expenses	100,000	
Total operating expenses		550,000
Net income		$ 76,000

(c)

Superior Company
Balance Sheet (partial)
December 31, 2014

Current assets		
Cash		$ 17,000
Short-term investments		26,000
Accounts receivable (net)		120,000
Inventories		
Finished goods	$120,000	
Work in process	50,000	
Raw materials	20,000	190,000
Prepaid expenses		13,000
Total current assets		$366,000

✔ **The Navigator**

*This would be a good time to return to the **Preface** at the beginning of the textbook (or look at it for the first time if you skipped it before) to read about the various types of homework materials that appear at the ends of chapters. Knowing the purpose of different assignments will help you appreciate what each contributes to your accounting skills and competencies.*

WILEY PLUS Self-Test, Brief Exercises, Exercises, Problem Set A, and many more resources are available for practice in WileyPLUS.

SELF-TEST QUESTIONS

Answers are at the end of the chapter.

(LO 1) **1.** Managerial accounting:
  (a) is governed by generally accepted accounting principles.
  (b) places emphasis on special-purpose information.
  (c) pertains to the entity as a whole and is highly aggregated.
  (d) is limited to cost data.

(LO 2) **2.** The management of an organization performs several broad functions. They are:
  (a) planning, directing, and selling.
  (b) planning, directing, and controlling.
  (c) planning, manufacturing, and controlling.
  (d) directing, manufacturing, and controlling.

(LO 2) **3.** After passage of the Sarbanes-Oxley Act:
  (a) reports prepared by managerial accountants must by audited by CPAs.
  (b) CEOs and CFOs must certify that financial statements give a fair presentation of the company's operating results.
  (c) the audit committee, rather than top management, is responsible for the company's financial statements.
  (d) reports prepared by managerial accountants must comply with generally accepted accounting principles (GAAP).

4. Direct materials are a: (LO 3)

	Product Cost	Manufacturing Overhead	Period Cost
(a)	Yes	Yes	No
(b)	Yes	No	No
(c)	Yes	Yes	Yes
(d)	No	No	No

5. Which of the following costs would a computer man- (LO 3)
ufacturer include in manufacturing overhead?
  (a) The cost of the disk drives.
  (b) The wages earned by computer assemblers.
  (c) The cost of the memory chips.
  (d) Depreciation on testing equipment.

6. Which of the following is *not* an element of manufac- (LO 3)
turing overhead?
  (a) Sales manager's salary.
  (b) Plant manager's salary.
  (c) Factory repairman's wages.
  (d) Product inspector's salary.

7. Indirect labor is a: (LO 4)
  (a) nonmanufacturing cost.
  (b) raw material cost.
  (c) product cost.
  (d) period cost.

(LO 4) **8.** Which of the following costs are classified as a period cost?
(a) Wages paid to a factory custodian.
(b) Wages paid to a production department supervisor.
(c) Wages paid to a cost accounting department supervisor.
(d) Wages paid to an assembly worker.

(LO 5) **9.** For the year, Redder Company has cost of goods manufactured of $600,000, beginning finished goods inventory of $200,000, and ending finished goods inventory of $250,000. The cost of goods sold is:
(a) $450,000.
(b) $500,000.
(c) $550,000.
(d) $600,000.

(LO 5) **10.** Cost of goods available for sale is a step in the calculation of cost of goods sold of:
(a) a merchandising company but not a manufacturing company.
(b) a manufacturing company but not a merchandising company.
(c) a merchandising company and a manufacturing company.
(d) neither a manufacturing company nor a merchandising company.

(LO 6) **11.** A cost of goods manufactured schedule shows beginning and ending inventories for:
(a) raw materials and work in process only.
(b) work in process only.
(c) raw materials only.
(d) raw materials, work in process, and finished goods.

(LO 6) **12.** The formula to determine the cost of goods manufactured is:
(a) Beginning raw materials inventory + Total manufacturing costs − Ending work in process inventory.

(b) Beginning work in process inventory + Total manufacturing costs − Ending finished goods inventory.
(c) Beginning finished good inventory + Total manufacturing costs − Ending finished goods inventory.
(d) Beginning work in process inventory + Total manufacturing costs − Ending work in process inventory.

13. A manufacturer may report three inventories on its (LO 7) balance sheet: (1) raw materials, (2) work in process, and (3) finished goods. Indicate in what sequence these inventories generally appear on a balance sheet.
(a) (1), (2), (3)
(b) (2), (3), (1)
(c) (3), (1), (2)
(d) (3), (2), (1)

14. Which of the following managerial accounting tech- (LO 8) niques attempts to allocate manufacturing overhead in a more meaningful fashion?
(a) Just-in-time inventory.
(b) Total quality management.
(c) Balanced scorecard.
(d) Activity-based costing.

15. Corporate social responsibility refers to: (LO 8)
(a) the practice by management of reviewing all business processes in an effort to increase productivity and eliminate waste.
(b) an approach used to allocate overhead based on each product's use of activities.
(c) the attempt by management to identify and eliminate constraints within the value chain.
(d) efforts by companies to employ sustainable business practices with regard to employees and the environment.

Go to the book's companion website, **www.wiley.com/college/weygandt**, for additional Self-Test Questions.

✔ **The Navigator**

QUESTIONS

1. (a) "Managerial accounting is a field of accounting that provides economic information for all interested parties." Do you agree? Explain.
(b) Joe Delong believes that managerial accounting serves only manufacturing firms. Is Joe correct? Explain.

2. Distinguish between managerial and financial accounting as to (a) primary users of reports, (b) types and frequency of reports, and (c) purpose of reports.

3. How do the content of reports and the verification of reports differ between managerial and financial accounting?

4. In what ways can the budgeting process create incentives for unethical behavior?

5. Linda Olsen is studying for the next accounting midterm examination. Summarize for Linda what she should know about management functions.

6. "Decision-making is management's most important function." Do you agree? Why or why not?

7. Explain the primary difference between line positions and staff positions, and give examples of each.

8. What new rules were enacted under the Sarbanes-Oxley Act to address unethical accounting practices?

9. Tony Andres is studying for his next accounting examination. Explain to Tony what he should know about the differences between the income statements for a manufacturing and for a merchandising company.

10. Jerry Lang is unclear as to the difference between the balance sheets of a merchandising company and a manufacturing company. Explain the difference to Jerry.

11. How are manufacturing costs classified?

12. Mel Finney claims that the distinction between direct and indirect materials is based entirely on physical association with the product. Is Mel correct? Why?

13. Tina Burke is confused about the differences between a product cost and a period cost. Explain the differences to Tina.

14. Identify the differences in the cost of goods sold section of an income statement between a merchandising company and a manufacturing company.

15. The determination of the cost of goods manufactured involves the following factors: (A) beginning work in process inventory, (B) total manufacturing costs, and (C) ending work in process inventory. Identify the meaning of x in the following formulas:
    (a) A + B = x
    (b) A + B − C = x

16. Sealy Company has beginning raw materials inventory $12,000, ending raw materials inventory $15,000, and raw materials purchases $170,000. What is the cost of direct materials used?

17. Tate Inc. has beginning work in process $26,000, direct materials used $240,000, direct labor $220,000, total manufacturing overhead $180,000, and ending work in process $32,000. What are the total manufacturing costs?

18. Using the data in Question 17, what are (a) the total cost of work in process and (b) the cost of goods manufactured?

19. In what order should manufacturing inventories be listed in a balance sheet?

20. How does the output of manufacturing operations differ from that of service operations?

21. Discuss whether the product costing techniques discussed in this chapter apply equally well to manufacturers and service companies.

22. What is the value chain? Describe, in sequence, the main components of a manufacturer's value chain.

23. What is an enterprise resource planning (ERP) system? What are its primary benefits?

24. Why is product quality important for companies that implement a just-in-time inventory system?

25. Explain what is meant by "balanced" in the balanced scorecard approach.

26. What is activity-based costing, and what are its potential benefits?

BRIEF EXERCISES

BE1-1 Complete the following comparison table between managerial and financial accounting.

	Financial Accounting	Managerial Accounting
Primary users of reports		
Types of reports		
Frequency of reports		
Purpose of reports		
Content of reports		
Verification process		

Distinguish between managerial and financial accounting.

(LO 1), C

BE1-2 The Sarbanes-Oxley Act (SOX) has important implications for the financial community. Explain two implications of SOX.

Identify important regulatory changes.

(LO 2), C

BE1-3 Listed below are the three functions of the management of an organization.
1. Planning   2. Directing   3. Controlling

Identify which of the following statements best describes each of the above functions.
(a) _____ requires management to look ahead and to establish objectives. A key objective of management is to add value to the business.
(b) _____ involves coordinating the diverse activities and human resources of a company to produce a smooth-running operation. This function relates to the implementation of planned objectives.
(c) _____ is the process of keeping the activities on track. Management must determine whether goals are being met and what changes are necessary when there are deviations.

Identify the three management functions.

(LO 2), C

BE1-4 Determine whether each of the following costs should be classified as direct materials (DM), direct labor (DL), or manufacturing overhead (MO).
(a) _____ Frames and tires used in manufacturing bicycles.
(b) _____ Wages paid to production workers.
(c) _____ Insurance on factory equipment and machinery.
(d) _____ Depreciation on factory equipment.

Classify manufacturing costs.

(LO 3), C

Classify manufacturing costs.

(LO 3), C

BE1-5 Indicate whether each of the following costs of an automobile manufacturer would be classified as direct materials, direct labor, or manufacturing overhead.

(a) _____ Windshield.
(b) _____ Engine.
(c) _____ Wages of assembly line worker.
(d) _____ Depreciation of factory machinery.

(e) _____ Factory machinery lubricants.
(f) _____ Tires.
(g) _____ Steering wheel.
(h) _____ Salary of painting supervisor.

Identify product and period costs.

(LO 4), C

BE1-6 Identify whether each of the following costs should be classified as product costs or period costs.

(a) _____ Manufacturing overhead.
(b) _____ Selling expenses.
(c) _____ Administrative expenses.

(d) _____ Advertising expenses.
(e) _____ Direct labor.
(f) _____ Direct material.

Classify manufacturing costs.

(LO 3), C

BE1-7 Presented below are Dieker Company's monthly manufacturing cost data related to its personal computer products.

(a) Utilities for manufacturing equipment $116,000
(b) Raw material (CPU, chips, etc.) $ 85,000
(c) Depreciation on manufacturing building $880,000
(d) Wages for production workers $191,000

Enter each cost item in the following table, placing an "X" under the appropriate headings.

	Product Costs		
	Direct Materials	**Direct Labor**	**Factory Overhead**
(a)			
(b)			
(c)			
(d)			

Compute total manufacturing costs and total cost of work in process.

(LO 6), AP

BE1-8 Francum Company has the following data: direct labor $209,000, direct materials used $180,000, total manufacturing overhead $208,000, and beginning work in process $25,000. Compute (a) total manufacturing costs and (b) total cost of work in process.

Prepare current assets section.

(LO 7), AP

BE1-9 In alphabetical order below are current asset items for Ruiz Company's balance sheet at December 31, 2014. Prepare the current assets section (including a complete heading).

Accounts receivable	$200,000
Cash	62,000
Finished goods	91,000
Prepaid expenses	38,000
Raw materials	73,000
Work in process	87,000

Determine missing amounts in computing total manufacturing costs.

(LO 6), AP

BE1-10 Presented below are incomplete manufacturing cost data. Determine the missing amounts for three different situations.

	Direct Materials Used	**Direct Labor Used**	**Factory Overhead**	**Total Manufacturing Costs**
(1)	$40,000	$61,000	$ 50,000	?
(2)	?	$75,000	$140,000	$296,000
(3)	$55,000	?	$111,000	$310,000

Determine missing amounts in computing cost of goods manufactured.

(LO 6), AP

BE1-11 Use the same data from BE1–10 above and the data below. Determine the missing amounts.

	Total Manufacturing Costs	**Work in Process (1/1)**	**Work in Process (12/31)**	**Cost of Goods Manufactured**
(1)	?	$120,000	$82,000	?
(2)	$296,000	?	$98,000	$321,000
(3)	$310,000	$463,000	?	$715,000

> DO IT! REVIEW

DO IT! **1-1** Indicate whether the following statements are true or false.

1. Managerial accountants explain and report manufacturing and nonmanufacturing costs, determine cost behaviors, and perform cost-volume-profit analysis, but are not involved in the budget process.
2. Financial accounting reports pertain to subunits of the business and are very detailed.
3. Managerial accounting reports must follow GAAP and are audited by CPAs.
4. Managers' activities and responsibilities can be classified into three broad functions: planning, directing, and controlling.
5. As a result of the Sarbanes-Oxley Act (SOX), top managers must certify that the company maintains an adequate system of internal control.
6. Management accountants follow a code of ethics developed by the Institute of Management Accountants.

Identify managerial accounting concepts.

(LO 1, 2), C

DO IT! **1-2** A music company has these costs:

Advertising	Paper inserts for CD cases
Blank CDs	CD plastic cases
Depreciation of CD image burner	Salaries of sales representatives
	Salaries of factory maintenance employees
Salary of factory manager	Salaries of employees who burn music onto CDs
Factory supplies used	

Classify each cost as a period or a product cost. Within the product cost category, indicate if the cost is part of direct materials (DM), direct labor (DL), or manufacturing overhead (MO).

Identify managerial cost concepts.

(LO 3, 4), C

DO IT! **1-3** The following information is available for Fishel Company.

	April 1	April 30
Raw materials inventory	$10,000	$14,000
Work in process inventory	5,000	3,500

Materials purchased in April	$ 98,000
Direct labor in April	80,000
Manufacturing overhead in April	180,000

Prepare the cost of goods manufactured schedule for the month of April.

Prepare cost of goods manufactured schedule.

(LO 6), AP

DO IT! **1-4** Match the descriptions that follow with the corresponding terms.
Descriptions:

1. _____ Inventory system in which goods are manufactured or purchased just as they are needed for sale.
2. _____ A method of allocating overhead based on each product's use of activities in making the product.
3. _____ Systems that are especially important to firms adopting just-in-time inventory methods.
4. _____ One part of the value chain for a manufacturing company.
5. _____ The U.S. economy is trending toward this.
6. _____ A performance-measurement approach that uses both financial and nonfinancial measures, tied to company objectives, to evaluate a company's operations in an integrated fashion.

Identify trends in managerial accounting.

(LO 8), C

Terms:

(a) Activity-based costing
(b) Balanced scorecard
(c) Total quality management (TQM)
(d) Research and development, and product design
(e) Service industries
(f) Just-in-time (JIT) inventory

EXERCISES

Identify distinguishing features of managerial accounting.

(LO 1), C

E1-1 Richard Larkin has prepared the following list of statements about managerial accounting and financial accounting.

1. Financial accounting focuses on providing information to internal users.
2. Analyzing cost-volume-profit relationships is part of managerial accounting.
3. Preparation of budgets is part of financial accounting.
4. Managerial accounting applies only to merchandising and manufacturing companies.
5. Both managerial accounting and financial accounting deal with many of the same economic events.
6. Managerial accounting reports are prepared only quarterly and annually.
7. Financial accounting reports are general-purpose reports.
8. Managerial accounting reports pertain to subunits of the business.
9. Managerial accounting reports must comply with generally accepted accounting principles.
10. Although managerial accountants are expected to behave ethically, there is no code of ethical standards for managerial accountants.

Instructions
Identify each statement as true or false. If false, indicate how to correct the statement.

Classify costs into three classes of manufacturing costs.

(LO 3), C

E1-2 Presented below is a list of costs and expenses usually incurred by Barnum Corporation, a manufacturer of furniture, in its factory.

1. Salaries for assembly line inspectors.
2. Insurance on factory machines.
3. Property taxes on the factory building.
4. Factory repairs.
5. Upholstery used in manufacturing furniture.
6. Wages paid to assembly line workers.
7. Factory machinery depreciation.
8. Glue, nails, paint, and other small parts used in production.
9. Factory supervisors' salaries.
10. Wood used in manufacturing furniture.

Instructions
Classify the above items into the following categories: (a) direct materials, (b) direct labor, and (c) manufacturing overhead.

Identify types of cost and explain their accounting.

(LO 3, 4), C

E1-3 Ryan Corporation incurred the following costs while manufacturing its product.

Materials used in product	$100,000	Advertising expense	$45,000
Depreciation on plant	60,000	Property taxes on plant	14,000
Property taxes on store	7,500	Delivery expense	21,000
Labor costs of assembly-line workers	110,000	Sales commissions	35,000
Factory supplies used	13,000	Salaries paid to sales clerks	50,000

Instructions
(a) Identify each of the above costs as direct materials, direct labor, manufacturing overhead, or period costs.
(b) Explain the basic difference in accounting for product costs and period costs.

Determine the total amount of various types of costs.

(LO 3, 4), AP

E1-4 Knight Company reports the following costs and expenses in May.

Factory utilities	$ 15,500	Direct labor	$69,100
Depreciation on factory		Sales salaries	46,400
equipment	12,650	Property taxes on factory	
Depreciation on delivery trucks	3,800	building	2,500
Indirect factory labor	48,900	Repairs to office equipment	1,300
Indirect materials	80,800	Factory repairs	2,000
Direct materials used	137,600	Advertising	15,000
Factory manager's salary	8,000	Office supplies used	2,640

Instructions
From the information, determine the total amount of:
(a) Manufacturing overhead.
(b) Product costs.
(c) Period costs.

E1-5 Ikerd Company is a manufacturer of personal computers. Various costs and expenses associated with its operations are as follows.

1. Property taxes on the factory building.
2. Production superintendents' salaries.
3. Memory boards and chips used in assembling computers.
4. Depreciation on the factory equipment.
5. Salaries for assembly-line quality control inspectors.
6. Sales commissions paid to sell personal computers.
7. Electrical components used in assembling computers.
8. Wages of workers assembling personal computers.
9. Soldering materials used on factory assembly lines.
10. Salaries for the night security guards for the factory building.

The company intends to classify these costs and expenses into the following categories: (a) direct materials, (b) direct labor, (c) manufacturing overhead, and (d) period costs.

Classify various costs into different cost categories.

(LO 3, 4), C

Instructions
List the items (1) through (10). For each item, indicate the cost category to which it belongs.

E1-6 The administrators of Crawford County's Memorial Hospital are interested in identifying the various costs and expenses that are incurred in producing a patient's X-ray. A list of such costs and expenses is presented below.

1. Salaries for the X-ray machine technicians.
2. Wages for the hospital janitorial personnel.
3. Film costs for the X-ray machines.
4. Property taxes on the hospital building.
5. Salary of the X-ray technicians' supervisor.
6. Electricity costs for the X-ray department.
7. Maintenance and repairs on the X-ray machines.
8. X-ray department supplies.
9. Depreciation on the X-ray department equipment.
10. Depreciation on the hospital building.

The administrators want these costs and expenses classified as: (a) direct materials, (b) direct labor, or (c) service overhead.

Classify various costs into different cost categories.

(LO 3), C

Homework materials related to service companies are indicated by this icon.

Instructions
List the items (1) through (10). For each item, indicate the cost category to which the item belongs.

E1-7 Kwik Delivery Service reports the following costs and expenses in June 2014.

Indirect materials	$ 5,400	Drivers' salaries	$16,000
Depreciation on delivery equipment	11,200	Advertising	3,600
Dispatcher's salary	5,000	Delivery equipment repairs	300
Property taxes on office building	870	Office supplies	650
CEO's salary	12,000	Office utilities	990
Gas and oil for delivery trucks	2,200	Repairs on office equipment	180

Classify various costs into different cost categories.

(LO 4), AP

Instructions
Determine the total amount of (a) delivery service (product) costs and (b) period costs.

E1-8 Lopez Corporation incurred the following costs while manufacturing its product.

Materials used in product	$120,000	Advertising expense	$45,000
Depreciation on plant	60,000	Property taxes on plant	14,000
Property taxes on store	7,500	Delivery expense	21,000
Labor costs of assembly-line		Sales commissions	35,000
workers	110,000	Salaries paid to sales	
Factory supplies used	23,000	clerks	50,000

Compute cost of goods manufactured and sold.

(LO 5, 6), AP

Work in process inventory was $12,000 at January 1 and $15,500 at December 31. Finished goods inventory was $60,000 at January 1 and $45,600 at December 31.

Instructions
(a) Compute cost of goods manufactured.
(b) Compute cost of goods sold.

Determine missing amounts in cost of goods manufactured schedule.

(LO 6), AP

E1-9 An incomplete cost of goods manufactured schedule is presented below.

Molina Company
Cost of Goods Manufactured Schedule
For the Year Ended December 31, 2014

Work in process (1/1)			$210,000
Direct materials			
Raw materials inventory (1/1)	$?		
Add: Raw materials purchases	158,000		
Total raw materials available for use	?		
Less: Raw materials inventory (12/31)	22,500		
Direct materials used		$190,000	
Direct labor		?	
Manufacturing overhead			
Indirect labor	18,000		
Factory depreciation	36,000		
Factory utilities	68,000		
Total overhead		122,000	
Total manufacturing costs			?
Total cost of work in process			?
Less: Work in process (12/31)			81,000
Cost of goods manufactured			$530,000

Instructions
Complete the cost of goods manufactured schedule for Molina Company.

Determine the missing amount of different cost items.

(LO 6), AN

E1-10 Manufacturing cost data for Copa Company are presented below.

	Case A	Case B	Case C
Direct materials used	$ (a)	$68,400	$130,000
Direct labor	57,000	86,000	(g)
Manufacturing overhead	46,500	81,600	102,000
Total manufacturing costs	195,650	(d)	253,700
Work in process 1/1/14	(b)	16,500	(h)
Total cost of work in process	221,500	(e)	337,000
Work in process 12/31/14	(c)	11,000	70,000
Cost of goods manufactured	185,275	(f)	(i)

Instructions
Indicate the missing amount for each letter (a) through (i).

Determine the missing amount of different cost items, and prepare a condensed cost of goods manufactured schedule.

(LO 6), AN

E1-11 Incomplete manufacturing cost data for Colaw Company for 2014 are presented as follows for four different situations.

	Direct Materials Used	Direct Labor Used	Manufac-turing Overhead	Total Manufac-turing Costs	Work in Process 1/1	Work in Process 12/31	Cost of Goods Manufac-tured
(1)	$127,000	$140,000	$ 87,000	$ (a)	$33,000	$ (b)	$360,000
(2)	(c)	200,000	132,000	450,000	(d)	40,000	470,000
(3)	80,000	100,000	(e)	255,000	60,000	80,000	(f)
(4)	70,000	(g)	75,000	288,000	45,000	(h)	270,000

Instructions

(a) Indicate the missing amount for each letter.
(b) Prepare a condensed cost of goods manufactured schedule for situation (1) for the year ended December 31, 2014.

E1-12 Cepeda Corporation has the following cost records for June 2014.

Prepare a cost of goods manufactured schedule and a partial income statement.

(LO 5, 6), AP

Indirect factory labor	$ 4,500	Factory utilities	$ 400
Direct materials used	20,000	Depreciation, factory equipment	1,400
Work in process, 6/1/14	3,000	Direct labor	40,000
Work in process, 6/30/14	3,800	Maintenance, factory equipment	1,800
Finished goods, 6/1/14	5,000	Indirect materials	2,200
Finished goods, 6/30/14	7,500	Factory manager's salary	3,000

Instructions

(a) Prepare a cost of goods manufactured schedule for June 2014.
(b) Prepare an income statement through gross profit for June 2014 assuming sales revenue is $92,100.

E1-13 Joyce Tombert, the bookkeeper for Marks Consulting, a political consulting firm, has recently completed a managerial accounting course at her local college. One of the topics covered in the course was the cost of goods manufactured schedule. Joyce wondered if such a schedule could be prepared for her firm. She realized that, as a service-oriented company, it would have no work in process inventory to consider.

Classify various costs into different categories and prepare cost of services provided schedule.

(LO 4, 5, 6), AN

Listed below are the costs her firm incurred for the month ended August 31, 2014.

Supplies used on consulting contracts	$ 1,200
Supplies used in the administrative offices	1,500
Depreciation on equipment used for contract work	900
Depreciation used on administrative office equipment	1,050
Salaries of professionals working on contracts	15,600
Salaries of administrative office personnel	7,700
Janitorial services for professional offices	400
Janitorial services for administrative offices	500
Insurance on contract operations	800
Insurance on administrative operations	900
Utilities for contract operations	1,400
Utilities for administrative offices	1,300

Instructions

(a) Prepare a schedule of cost of contract services provided (similar to a cost of goods manufactured schedule) for the month.
(b) For those costs not included in (a), explain how they would be classified and reported in the financial statements.

E1-14 The following information is available for Aikman Company.

Prepare a cost of goods manufactured schedule and a partial income statement.

(LO 5, 6, 7), AP

	January 1, 2014	2014	December 31, 2014
Raw materials inventory	$21,000		$30,000
Work in process inventory	13,500		17,200
Finished goods inventory	27,000		21,000
Materials purchased		$150,000	
Direct labor		220,000	
Manufacturing overhead		180,000	
Sales revenue		910,000	

Instructions

(a) Compute cost of goods manufactured.
(b) Prepare an income statement through gross profit.
(c) Show the presentation of the ending inventories on the December 31, 2014, balance sheet.
(d) How would the income statement and balance sheet of a merchandising company be different from Aikman's financial statements?

Indicate in which schedule or financial statement(s) different cost items will appear.

(LO 5, 6, 7), C

E1-15 Chambers Company produces blankets. From its accounting records, it prepares the following schedule and financial statements on a yearly basis.
(a) Cost of goods manufactured schedule.
(b) Income statement.
(c) Balance sheet.

The following items are found in its ledger and accompanying data.

1. Direct labor
2. Raw materials inventory, 1/1
3. Work in process inventory, 12/31
4. Finished goods inventory, 1/1
5. Indirect labor
6. Depreciation on factory machinery
7. Work in process, 1/1
8. Finished goods inventory, 12/31
9. Factory maintenance salaries
10. Cost of goods manufactured
11. Depreciation on delivery equipment
12. Cost of goods available for sale
13. Direct materials used
14. Heat and electricity for factory
15. Repairs to roof of factory building
16. Cost of raw materials purchases

Instructions
List the items (1)–(16). For each item, indicate by using the appropriate letter or letters, the schedule and/or financial statement(s) in which the item will appear.

Prepare a cost of goods manufactured schedule, and present the ending inventories on the balance sheet.

(LO 6, 7), AP

E1-16 An analysis of the accounts of Roberts Company reveals the following manufacturing cost data for the month ended June 30, 2014.

Inventories	Beginning	Ending
Raw materials	$9,000	$13,100
Work in process	5,000	7,000
Finished goods	9,000	8,000

Costs incurred: raw materials purchases $54,000, direct labor $47,000, manufacturing overhead $19,900. The specific overhead costs were: indirect labor $5,500, factory insurance $4,000, machinery depreciation $4,000, machinery repairs $1,800, factory utilities $3,100, miscellaneous factory costs $1,500. Assume that all raw materials used were direct materials.

Instructions
(a) Prepare the cost of goods manufactured schedule for the month ended June 30, 2014.
(b) Show the presentation of the ending inventories on the June 30, 2014, balance sheet.

Determine the amount of cost to appear in various accounts, and indicate in which financial statements these accounts would appear.

(LO 5, 6, 7), AP

E1-17 Buhler Motor Company manufactures automobiles. During September 2014, the company purchased 5,000 head lamps at a cost of $10 per lamp. Buhler withdrew 4,650 lamps from the warehouse during the month. Fifty of these lamps were used to replace the head lamps in autos used by traveling sales staff. The remaining 4,600 lamps were put in autos manufactured during the month.

Of the autos put into production during September 2014, 90% were completed and transferred to the company's storage lot. Of the cars completed during the month, 70% were sold by September 30.

Instructions
(a) Determine the cost of head lamps that would appear in each of the following accounts at September 30, 2014: Raw Materials, Work in Process, Finished Goods, Cost of Goods Sold, and Selling Expenses.
(b) ▭▭▭▷ Write a short memo to the chief accountant, indicating whether and where each of the accounts in (a) would appear on the income statement or on the balance sheet at September 30, 2014.

E1-18 The following is a list of terms related to managerial accounting practices.

1. Activity-based costing.
2. Just-in-time inventory.
3. Balanced scorecard.
4. Value chain.

Identify various managerial accounting practices.

(LO 8), C

Instructions

Match each of the terms with the statement below that best describes the term.

(a) _____ A performance-measurement technique that attempts to consider and evaluate all aspects of performance using financial and nonfinancial measures in an integrated fashion.

(b) _____ The group of activities associated with providing a product or service.

(c) _____ An approach used to reduce the cost associated with handling and holding inventory by reducing the amount of inventory on hand.

(d) _____ A method used to allocate overhead to products based on each product's use of the activities that cause the incurrence of the overhead cost.

EXERCISES: SET B AND CHALLENGE EXERCISES

Visit the book's companion website, at **www.wiley.com/college/weygandt**, and choose the Student Companion site to access Exercise Set B and Challenge Exercises.

PROBLEMS: SET A

P1-1A Lott Company specializes in manufacturing a unique model of bicycle helmet. The model is well accepted by consumers, and the company has enough orders to keep the factory production at 10,000 helmets per month (80% of its full capacity). Lott's monthly manufacturing cost and other expense data are as follows.

Classify manufacturing costs into different categories and compute the unit cost.

(LO 3, 4), AP

Rent on factory equipment	$ 9,000
Insurance on factory building	1,500
Raw materials (plastics, polystyrene, etc.)	75,000
Utility costs for factory	900
Supplies for general office	300
Wages for assembly line workers	53,000
Depreciation on office equipment	800
Miscellaneous materials (glue, thread, etc.)	1,100
Factory manager's salary	5,700
Property taxes on factory building	400
Advertising for helmets	14,000
Sales commissions	10,000
Depreciation on factory building	1,500

Marginal check figures for parts of some problems, in most chapters, provide key numbers to confirm that you are on the right track in your computations.

Instructions

(a) Prepare an answer sheet with the following column headings.

	Product Costs			
Cost Item	**Direct Materials**	**Direct Labor**	**Manufacturing Overhead**	**Period Costs**

(a) DM $75,000
DL $53,000
MO $20,100
PC $25,100

Enter each cost item on your answer sheet, placing the dollar amount under the appropriate headings. Total the dollar amounts in each of the columns.

(b) Compute the cost to produce one helmet.

P1-2A Bell Company, a manufacturer of audio systems, started its production in October 2014. For the preceding 3 years, Bell had been a retailer of audio systems. After a thorough survey of audio system markets, Bell decided to turn its retail store into an audio equipment factory.

Classify manufacturing costs into different categories and compute the unit cost.

(LO 3, 4), AP

Raw materials cost for an audio system will total $74 per unit. Workers on the production lines are on average paid $12 per hour. An audio system usually takes 5 hours to complete. In addition, the rent on the equipment used to assemble audio systems amounts to $4,900 per month. Indirect materials cost $5 per system. A supervisor was hired to oversee production; her monthly salary is $3,000.

Factory janitorial costs are $1,300 monthly. Advertising costs for the audio system will be $9,500 per month. The factory building depreciation expense is $7,800 per year. Property taxes on the factory building will be $9,000 per year.

Instructions

(a) DM $111,000
    DL $ 90,000
    MO $ 18,100
    PC $ 9,500

(a) Prepare an answer sheet with the following column headings.

	Product Costs			
Cost Item	**Direct Materials**	**Direct Labor**	**Manufacturing Overhead**	**Period Costs**

Assuming that Bell manufactures, on average, 1,500 audio systems per month, enter each cost item on your answer sheet, placing the dollar amount per month under the appropriate headings. Total the dollar amounts in each of the columns.

(b) Compute the cost to produce one audio system.

Indicate the missing amount of different cost items, and prepare a condensed cost of goods manufactured schedule, an income statement, and a partial balance sheet.

(LO 5, 6, 7), AN

P1-3A Incomplete manufacturing costs, expenses, and selling data for two different cases are as follows.

	Case	
	1	**2**
Direct materials used	$ 9,600	$ (g)
Direct labor	5,000	8,000
Manufacturing overhead	8,000	4,000
Total manufacturing costs	(a)	16,000
Beginning work in process inventory	1,000	(h)
Ending work in process inventory	(b)	3,000
Sales revenue	24,500	(i)
Sales discounts	2,500	1,400
Cost of goods manufactured	17,000	22,000
Beginning finished goods inventory	(c)	3,300
Goods available for sale	20,000	(j)
Cost of goods sold	(d)	(k)
Ending finished goods inventory	3,400	2,500
Gross profit	(e)	7,000
Operating expenses	2,500	(l)
Net income	(f)	5,000

Instructions

(a) Indicate the missing amount for each letter.

(b) Ending WIP $ 6,600
(c) Current assets $30,000

(b) Prepare a condensed cost of goods manufactured schedule for Case 1.

(c) Prepare an income statement and the current assets section of the balance sheet for Case 1. Assume that in Case 1 the other items in the current assets section are as follows: Cash $4,000, Receivables (net) $15,000, Raw Materials $600, and Prepaid Expenses $400.

Prepare a cost of goods manufactured schedule, a partial income statement, and a partial balance sheet.

(LO 5, 6, 7), AP

P1-4A The following data were taken from the records of Clarkson Company for the fiscal year ended June 30, 2014.

Raw Materials		Factory Insurance	$ 4,600
Inventory 7/1/13	$ 48,000	Factory Machinery	
Raw Materials		Depreciation	16,000
Inventory 6/30/14	39,600	Factory Utilities	27,600
Finished Goods		Office Utilities Expense	8,650
Inventory 7/1/13	96,000	Sales Revenue	534,000
Finished Goods		Sales Discounts	4,200
Inventory 6/30/14	75,900	Plant Manager's Salary	58,000

Work in Process		Factory Property Taxes	$ 9,600
Inventory 7/1/13	$ 19,800	Factory Repairs	1,400
Work in Process		Raw Materials Purchases	96,400
Inventory 6/30/14	18,600	Cash	32,000
Direct Labor	139,250		
Indirect Labor	24,460		
Accounts Receivable	27,000		

Instructions

(a) Prepare a cost of goods manufactured schedule. (Assume all raw materials used were direct materials.)

(b) Prepare an income statement through gross profit.

(c) Prepare the current assets section of the balance sheet at June 30, 2014.

(a) CGM $386,910

(b) Gross profit $122,790
(c) Current assets $193,100

P1-5A Phillips Company is a manufacturer of computers. Its controller resigned in October 2014. An inexperienced assistant accountant has prepared the following income statement for the month of October 2014.

Prepare a cost of goods manufactured schedule and a correct income statement.

(LO 5, 6), AN

Phillips Company
Income Statement
For the Month Ended October 31, 2014

Sales revenue		$780,000
Less: Operating expenses		
Raw materials purchases	$264,000	
Direct labor cost	190,000	
Advertising expense	90,000	
Selling and administrative salaries	75,000	
Rent on factory facilities	60,000	
Depreciation on sales equipment	45,000	
Depreciation on factory equipment	31,000	
Indirect labor cost	28,000	
Utilities expense	12,000	
Insurance expense	8,000	803,000
Net loss		$ (23,000)

Prior to October 2014, the company had been profitable every month. The company's president is concerned about the accuracy of the income statement. As her friend, you have been asked to review the income statement and make necessary corrections. After examining other manufacturing cost data, you have acquired additional information as follows.

1. Inventory balances at the beginning and end of October were:

	October 1	October 31
Raw materials	$18,000	$29,000
Work in process	16,000	14,000
Finished goods	30,000	45,000

2. Only 75% of the utilities expense and 60% of the insurance expense apply to factory operations. The remaining amounts should be charged to selling and administrative activities.

Instructions

(a) Prepare a schedule of cost of goods manufactured for October 2014.

(b) Prepare a correct income statement for October 2014.

(a) CGM $577,800
(b) NI $ 1,000

Classify manufacturing costs into different categories and compute the unit cost.

P1-1B Agler Company specializes in manufacturing motorcycle helmets. The company has enough orders to keep the factory production at 1,000 motorcycle helmets per month. Agler's monthly manufacturing cost and other expense data are shown on the next page.

(LO 3, 4), AP

Maintenance costs on factory building	$ 1,500
Factory manager's salary	5,500
Advertising for helmets	8,000
Sales commissions	4,000
Depreciation on factory building	700
Rent on factory equipment	6,000
Insurance on factory building	3,000
Raw materials (plastic, polystyrene, etc.)	25,000
Utility costs for factory	800
Supplies for general office	200
Wages for assembly line workers	54,000
Depreciation on office equipment	500
Miscellaneous materials (glue, thread, etc.)	2,000

Instructions

(a) DM $25,000
DL $54,000
MO $19,500
PC $12,700

(a) Prepare an answer sheet with the following column headings.

	Product Costs			
Cost Item	Direct Materials	Direct Labor	Manufacturing Overhead	Period Costs

Enter each cost item on your answer sheet, placing the dollar amount under the appropriate headings. Total the dollar amounts in each of the columns.

(b) Compute the cost to produce one motorcycle helmet.

Classify manufacturing costs into different categories and compute the unit cost.

(LO 3, 4), AP

P1-2B Elliott Company, a manufacturer of tennis rackets, started production in November 2013. For the preceding 5 years, Elliott had been a retailer of sports equipment. After a thorough survey of tennis racket markets, Elliott decided to turn its retail store into a tennis racket factory.

Raw materials cost for a tennis racket will total $23 per racket. Workers on the production lines are paid on average $15 per hour. A racket usually takes 2 hours to complete. In addition, the rent on the equipment used to produce rackets amounts to $1,300 per month. Indirect materials cost $3 per racket. A supervisor was hired to oversee production; her monthly salary is $3,500.

Janitorial costs are $1,400 monthly. Advertising costs for the rackets will be $8,000 per month. The factory building depreciation expense is $8,400 per year. Property taxes on the factory building will be $9,600 per year.

Instructions

(a) DM $57,500
DL $75,000
MO $15,200
PC $ 8,000

(a) Prepare an answer sheet with the following column headings.

	Product Costs			
Cost Item	Direct Materials	Direct Labor	Manufacturing Overhead	Period Costs

Assuming that Elliott manufactures, on average, 2,500 tennis rackets per month, enter each cost item on your answer sheet, placing the dollar amount per month under the appropriate headings. Total the dollar amounts in each of the columns.

(b) Compute the cost to produce one racket.

Indicate the missing amount of different cost items, and prepare a condensed cost of goods manufactured schedule, an income statement, and a partial balance sheet.

(LO 5, 6, 7), AN

P1-3B Incomplete manufacturing costs, expenses, and selling data for two different cases are as follows.

	Case	
	A	B
Direct materials used	$ 6,300	$ (g)
Direct labor	3,000	4,000
Manufacturing overhead	6,000	5,000
Total manufacturing costs	(a)	16,000
Beginning work in process inventory	1,000	(h)
Ending work in process inventory	(b)	2,000
Sales revenue	22,500	(i)
Sales discounts	1,500	1,200
Cost of goods manufactured	15,800	20,000

	Case	
	A	B
Beginning finished goods inventory	$ (c)	$ 5,000
Goods available for sale	18,300	(j)
Cost of goods sold	(d)	(k)
Ending finished goods inventory	1,200	2,500
Gross profit	(e)	6,000
Operating expenses	2,700	(l)
Net income	(f)	2,200

Instructions
(a) Indicate the missing amount for each letter.
(b) Prepare a condensed cost of goods manufactured schedule for Case A.
(c) Prepare an income statement and the current assets section of the balance sheet for Case A. Assume that in Case A the other items in the current assets section are as follows: Cash $3,000, Receivables (net) $10,000, Raw Materials $700, and Prepaid Expenses $200.

(b) Beg. WIP $1,000
(c) Current assets $15,600

P1-4B The following data were taken from the records of Moxie Company for the year ended December 31, 2014.

Prepare a cost of goods manufactured schedule, a partial income statement, and a partial balance sheet.

(LO 5, 6, 7), AP

Raw Materials		Factory Insurance	$ 7,400	
Inventory 1/1/14	$ 47,000	Factory Machinery		
Raw Materials		Depreciation	7,700	
Inventory 12/31/14	44,200	Factory Utilities	12,900	
Finished Goods		Office Utilities Expense	8,600	
Inventory 1/1/14	85,000	Sales Revenue	465,000	
Finished Goods		Sales Discounts	2,500	
Inventory 12/31/14	57,800	Plant Manager's Salary	60,000	
Work in Process		Factory Property Taxes	6,100	
Inventory 1/1/14	9,500	Factory Repairs	800	
Work in Process		Raw Materials Purchases	62,500	
Inventory 12/31/14	8,000	Cash	18,000	
Direct Labor	145,100			
Indirect Labor	18,100			
Accounts Receivable	27,000			

Instructions
(a) Prepare a cost of goods manufactured schedule. (Assume all raw materials used were direct materials.)
(b) Prepare an income statement through gross profit.
(c) Prepare the current assets section of the balance sheet at December 31.

(a) CGM $324,900

(b) Gross profit $110,400
(c) Current assets $155,000

P1-5B Ortiz Company is a manufacturer of toys. Its controller resigned in August 2014. An inexperienced assistant accountant has prepared the following income statement for the month of August 2014.

Prepare a cost of goods manufactured schedule and a correct income statement.

(LO 5, 6), AN

Ortiz Company
Income Statement
For the Month Ended August 31, 2014

Sales revenue		$675,000
Less: Operating expenses		
Raw materials purchases	$220,000	
Direct labor cost	160,000	
Advertising expense	75,000	
Selling and administrative salaries	70,000	
Rent on factory facilities	60,000	
Depreciation on sales equipment	50,000	
Depreciation on factory equipment	35,000	
Indirect labor cost	20,000	
Utilities expense	10,000	
Insurance expense	5,000	705,000
Net loss		$ (30,000)

Prior to August 2014, the company had been profitable every month. The company's president is concerned about the accuracy of the income statement. As her friend, you have been asked to review the income statement and make necessary corrections. After examining other manufacturing cost data, you have acquired additional information as follows.

1. Inventory balances at the beginning and end of August were:

	August 1	**August 31**
Raw materials	$19,500	$35,000
Work in process	25,000	21,000
Finished goods	40,000	52,000

2. Only 60% of the utilities expense and 70% of the insurance expense apply to factory operations; the remaining amounts should be charged to selling and administrative activities.

Instructions

(a) CGM $493,000

(b) NL $ (6,500)

(a) Prepare a cost of goods manufactured schedule for August 2014.

(b) Prepare a correct income statement for August 2014.

PROBLEMS: SET C

Visit the book's companion website, at **www.wiley.com/college/weygandt**, and choose the Student Companion site to access Problem Set C.

WATERWAYS CONTINUING PROBLEM

*The **Waterways Problem** starts in this chapter and continues in every chapter. You will find the complete problem for each chapter at the book's companion website.*

(*Note:* The Waterways Problem begins in Chapter 1 and continues in the remaining chapters. You can also find this problem at the book's Student Companion site.)

WCP1 Waterways Corporation is a private corporation formed for the purpose of providing the products and the services needed to irrigate farms, parks, commercial projects, and private lawns. It has a centrally located factory in a U.S. city that manufactures the products it markets to retail outlets across the nation. It also maintains a division that provides installation and warranty servicing in six metropolitan areas.

The mission of Waterways is to manufacture quality parts that can be used for effective irrigation projects that also conserve water. By that effort, the company hopes to satisfy its customers, provide rapid and responsible service, and serve the community and the employees who represent them in each community.

The company has been growing rapidly, so management is considering new ideas to help the company continue its growth and maintain the high quality of its products.

Waterways was founded by Will Winkman, who is the company president and chief executive officer (CEO). Working with him from the company's inception is Will's brother, Ben, whose sprinkler designs and ideas about the installation of proper systems have been a major basis of the company's success. Ben is the vice president who oversees all aspects of design and production in the company.

The factory itself is managed by Todd Senter who hires his line managers to supervise the factory employees. The factory makes all of the parts for the irrigation systems. The purchasing department is managed by Hector Hines.

The installation and training division is overseen by vice president Henry Writer, who supervises the managers of the six local installation operations. Each of these local managers hires his or her own local service people. These service employees are trained by the home office under Henry Writer's direction because of the uniqueness of the company's products.

There is a small human resources department under the direction of Sally Fenton, a vice president who handles the employee paperwork, though hiring is actually performed by the separate departments. Sam Totter is the vice president who heads the sales and marketing area; he oversees 10 well-trained salespeople.

The accounting and finance division of the company is run by Abe Headman, who is the chief financial officer (CFO) and a company vice president. He is a member of the Institute of Management Accountants and holds a certificate in management accounting.

He has a small staff of certified public accountants, including a controller and a treasurer, and a staff of accounting input operators who maintain the financial records.

A partial list of Waterways' accounts and their balances for the month of November follows.

Accounts Receivable	$ 275,000
Advertising Expenses	54,000
Cash	260,000
Depreciation—Factory Equipment	16,800
Depreciation—Office Equipment	2,400
Direct Labor	42,000
Factory Supplies Used	16,800
Factory Utilities	10,200
Finished Goods Inventory, November 30	68,800
Finished Goods Inventory, October 31	72,550
Indirect Labor	48,000
Office Supplies Expense	1,600
Other Administrative Expenses	72,000
Prepaid Expenses	41,250
Raw Materials Inventory, November 30	52,700
Raw Materials Inventory, October 31	38,000
Raw Materials Purchases	184,500
Rent—Factory Equipment	47,000
Repairs—Factory Equipment	4,500
Salaries	325,000
Sales Revenue	1,350,000
Sales Commissions	40,500
Work in Process Inventory, October 31	52,700
Work in Process Inventory, November 30	42,000

Instructions

(a) Based on the information given, construct an organizational chart of Waterways Corporation.

(b) A list of accounts and their values are given above. From this information, prepare a cost of goods manufactured schedule, an income statement, and a partial balance sheet for Waterways Corporation for the month of November.

Broadening Your PERSPECTIVE

Management Decision-Making

Each chapter contains an exercise based on Current Designs, the company that was featured at the beginning of this chapter. We are excited to present managerial accounting situations that are based on the operations of a real company. However, to protect the proprietary nature of this information, the amounts in these exercises are realistic but not necessarily the actual data that would be found in Current Designs' accounting records. We sincerely appreciate the cooperation of the people at Current Designs, particularly Mike Cichanowski, Jim Brown, Diane Buswell, and Jake Greseth, who made these exercises possible.

Decision-Making at Current Designs

BYP1-1 Mike Cichanowski founded Wenonah Canoe and later purchased Current Designs, a company that designs and manufactures kayaks. The kayak-manufacturing facility is located just a few minutes from the canoe company's headquarters in Winona, Minnesota.

Current Designs makes kayaks using two different processes. (See *www.cdkayak.com/craftsmanship/index.php* for the details of each method.) The rotational molding process uses high

temperature to melt polyethylene powder in a closed rotating metal mold to produce a complete kayak hull and deck in a single piece. These kayaks are less labor-intensive and less expensive for the company to produce and sell.

Its other kayaks use the vacuum-bagged composite lamination process (which we will refer to as the composite process). Layers of fiberglass or Kevlar® are carefully placed by hand in a mold and are bonded with resin. Then, a high-pressure vacuum is used to eliminate any excess resin that would otherwise add weight and reduce strength of the finished kayak. These kayaks require a great deal of skilled labor as each boat is individually finished. The exquisite finish of the vacuum-bagged composite kayaks gave rise to Current Designs' tag line, "A work of art, made for life."

Current Designs has the following managers:

Mike Cichanowski, CEO
Diane Buswell, Controller
Deb Welch, Purchasing Manager
Bill Johnson, Sales Manager
Dave Thill, Kayak Plant Manager
Rick Thrune, Production Manager for Composite Kayaks

Instructions
(a) What are the primary information needs of each manager?
(b) Name one special-purpose management accounting report that could be designed for each manager. Include the name of the report, the information it would contain, and how frequently it should be issued.
(c) When Diane Buswell, controller for Current Designs, reviewed the accounting records for a recent period, she noted the following items. Classify each item as a product cost or a period cost. If an item is a product cost, note if it is a direct materials, direct labor, or manufacturing overhead item.

Payee	Purpose	Product Costs			Period Costs
		Direct Materials	Direct Labor	Manufacturing Overhead	
Winona Agency	Property insurance for the manufacturing plant				
Bill Johnson (sales manager)	Payroll check—payment to sales manager				
Xcel Energy	Electricity for manufacturing plant				
Winona Printing	Price lists for salespeople				
Jim Kaiser (sales representative)	Sales commissions				
Dave Thill (plant manager)	Payroll check—payment to plant manager				
Dana Schultz (kayak assembler)	Payroll check—payment to kayak assembler				
Composite One	Bagging film used when kayaks are assembled; it is discarded after use				
Fastenal	Shop supplies—brooms, paper towels, etc.				
Ravago	Polyethylene powder which is the main ingredient for the rotational molded kayaks				
Winona County	Property taxes on manufacturing plant				
North American Composites	Kevlar® fabric for composite kayaks				
Waste Management	Trash disposal for the company office building				
None	Journal entry to record depreciation of manufacturing equipment				

Decision-Making Across the Organization

BYP1-2 Wendall Company specializes in producing fashion outfits. On July 31, 2014, a tornado touched down at its factory and general office. The inventories in the warehouse and the factory were completely destroyed as was the general office nearby. Next morning, through a careful search of the disaster site, however, Bill Francis, the company's controller, and Elizabeth Walton, the cost accountant, were able to recover a small part of manufacturing cost data for the current month.

"What a horrible experience," sighed Bill "And the worst part is that we may not have enough records to use in filing an insurance claim."

"It was terrible," replied Elizabeth. "However, I managed to recover some of the manufacturing cost data that I was working on yesterday afternoon. The data indicate that our direct labor cost in July totaled $250,000 and that we had purchased $365,000 of raw materials. Also, I recall that the amount of raw materials used for July was $350,000. But I'm not sure this information will help. The rest of our records are blown away."

"Well, not exactly," said Bill. "I was working on the year-to-date income statement when the tornado warning was announced. My recollection is that our sales in July were $1,240,000 and our gross profit ratio has been 40% of sales. Also, I can remember that our cost of goods available for sale was $770,000 for July."

"Maybe we can work something out from this information!" exclaimed Elizabeth. "My experience tells me that our manufacturing overhead is usually 60% of direct labor."

"Hey, look what I just found," cried Elizabeth. "It's a copy of this June's balance sheet, and it shows that our inventories as of June 30 are Finished goods $38,000, Work in process $25,000, and Raw materials $19,000."

"Super," yelled Bill. "Let's go work something out."

In order to file an insurance claim, Wendall Company must determine the amount of its inventories as of July 31, 2014, the date of the tornado touchdown.

Instructions
With the class divided into groups, determine the amount of cost in the Raw Materials, Work in Process, and Finished Goods inventory accounts as of the date of the tornado touchdown.

Managerial Analysis

BYP1-3 Tenrack is a fairly large manufacturing company located in the southern United States. The company manufactures tennis rackets, tennis balls, tennis clothing, and tennis shoes, all bearing the company's distinctive logo, a large green question mark on a white flocked tennis ball. The company's sales have been increasing over the past 10 years.

The tennis racket division has recently implemented several advanced manufacturing techniques. Robot arms hold the tennis rackets in place while glue dries, and machine vision systems check for defects. The engineering and design team uses computerized drafting and testing of new products. The following managers work in the tennis racket division:

Jason Dennis, Sales Manager (supervises all sales representatives)
Peggy Groneman, Technical Specialist (supervises computer programmers)
Dave Marley, Cost Accounting Manager (supervises cost accountants)
Kevin Carson, Production Supervisor (supervises all manufacturing employees)
Sally Renner, Engineer (supervises all new-product design teams)

Instructions
(a) What are the primary information needs of each manager?
(b) Which, if any, financial accounting report(s) is each likely to use?
(c) Name one special-purpose management accounting report that could be designed for each manager. Include the name of the report, the information it would contain, and how frequently it should be issued.

Real-World Focus

BYP1-4 Anchor Glass Container Corporation, the third largest manufacturer of glass containers in the United States, supplies beverage and food producers and consumer products manufacturers nationwide. Parent company Consumers Packaging Inc. (*Toronto Stock Exchange:* CGC) is a leading international designer and manufacturer of glass containers.

The management discussion on page 46 appeared in a recent annual report of Anchor Glass.

Anchor Glass Container Corporation
Management Discussion

Cost of Products Sold   Cost of products sold as a percentage of net sales was 89.3% in the current year compared to 87.6% in the prior year. The increase in cost of products sold as a percentage of net sales principally reflected the impact of operational problems during the second quarter of the current year at a major furnace at one of the Company's plants, higher downtime, and costs and expenses associated with an increased number of scheduled capital improvement projects, increases in labor, and certain other manufacturing costs (with no corresponding selling price increases in the current year). Reduced fixed costs from the closing of the Streator, Illinois, plant in June of the current year and productivity and efficiency gains partially offset these cost increases.

Instructions
What factors affect the costs of products sold at Anchor Glass Container Corporation?

BYP1-5 The Institute of Management Accountants (IMA) is an organization dedicated to excellence in the practice of management accounting and financial management.

Address: **www.imanet.org**, or go to **www.wiley.com/college/weygandt**

Instructions
At the IMA's home page, locate the answers to the following questions.
(a) How many members does the IMA have, and what are their job titles?
(b) What are some of the benefits of joining the IMA as a student?
(c) Use the chapter locator function to locate the IMA chapter nearest you, and find the name of the chapter president.

Critical Thinking

Communication Activity

BYP1-6 Refer to P1–5A and add the following requirement.

Prepare a letter to the president of the company, Shelly Phillips, describing the changes you made. Explain clearly why net income is different after the changes. Keep the following points in mind as you compose your letter.

1. This is a letter to the president of a company, who is your friend. The style should be generally formal, but you may relax some requirements. For example, you may call the president by her first name.
2. Executives are very busy. Your letter should tell the president your main results first (for example, the amount of net income).
3. You should include brief explanations so that the president can understand the changes you made in the calculations.

Ethics Case

BYP1-7 Steve Morgan, controller for Newton Industries, was reviewing production cost reports for the year. One amount in these reports continued to bother him—advertising. During the year, the company had instituted an expensive advertising campaign to sell some of its slower-moving products. It was still too early to tell whether the advertising campaign was successful.

There had been much internal debate as how to report advertising cost. The vice president of finance argued that advertising costs should be reported as a cost of production, just like direct materials and direct labor. He therefore recommended that this cost be identified as manufacturing overhead and reported as part of inventory costs until sold. Others disagreed. Morgan believed that this cost should be reported as an expense of the current period, so as not to overstate net income. Others argued that it should be reported as prepaid advertising and reported as a current asset.

The president finally had to decide the issue. He argued that these costs should be reported as inventory. His arguments were practical ones. He noted that the company was experiencing financial difficulty and expensing this amount in the current period might jeopardize a planned bond offering. Also, by reporting the advertising costs as inventory rather than as prepaid advertising, less attention would be directed to it by the financial community.

Instructions
(a) Who are the stakeholders in this situation?
(b) What are the ethical issues involved in this situation?
(c) What would you do if you were Steve Morgan?

All About You

BYP1-8 The primary purpose of managerial accounting is to provide information useful for management decisions. Many of the managerial accounting techniques that you learn in this course will be useful for decisions you make in your everyday life.

Instructions
For each of the following managerial accounting techniques, read the definition provided and then provide an example of a personal situation that would benefit from use of this technique.
(a) Break-even point (page 207).
(b) Budget (page 384).
(c) Balanced scorecard (page 513).
(d) Capital budgeting (page 547).

Considering Your Costs and Benefits

BYP1-9 As noted in this chapter, because of global competition, companies have become increasingly focused on reducing costs. To reduce costs and remain competitive, many companies are turning to outsourcing. Outsourcing means hiring an outside supplier to provide elements of a product or service rather than producing them internally.

Suppose you are the managing partner in a CPA firm with 30 full-time staff. Larger firms in your community have begun to outsource basic tax-return preparation work to India. Should you outsource your basic tax-return work to India as well? You estimate that you would have to lay off six staff members if you outsource the work. The basic arguments for and against are as follows.

YES: The wages paid to Indian accountants are very low relative to U.S. wages. You will not be able to compete unless you outsource.
NO: Tax-return data is highly sensitive. Many customers will be upset to learn that their data is being emailed around the world.

Instructions
Write a response indicating your position regarding this situation. Provide support for your view.

Answers to Chapter Questions

Answers to Insight and Accounting Across the Organization Questions

p. 6 Even the Best Have to Get Better Q: What are some of the steps that this company has taken in order to ensure that production meets demand? **A:** The company has organized flexible teams, with jobs arranged by the amount of time a task takes. Employees now are multiskilled, so they can switch between tasks and products. Also, the stores now provide sales data more quickly to the manufacturing facility, so that production levels can be changed more quickly in response to demand.

p. 11 Why Manufacturing Matters for U.S. Workers Q: In what ways does the shift to automated factories change the amount and composition of product costs? **A:** As factories become more automated, they become more efficient, increasing output and decreasing cost per unit. The composition of those costs also switches: Factory labor costs decline, and factory overhead costs (e.g., depreciation and maintenance on equipment) increase.

p. 19 Low Fares but Decent Profits Q: What are some of the line items that would appear in the cost of services provided schedule of an airline? **A:** Some of the line items that would appear in the cost of services provided schedule of an airline would be fuel, flight crew salaries, maintenance wages, depreciation on equipment, airport gate fees, and food-service costs.

Answers to Self-Test Questions

1. b **2.** b **3.** b **4.** b **5.** d **6.** a **7.** c **8.** c **9.** c ($200,000 + $600,000 − $250,000) **10.** c
11. a **12.** d **13.** d **14.** d **15.** d

✔ **Remember to go back to The Navigator box on the chapter opening page and check off your completed work.**

She Succeeds Where Others Have Failed

The financial press is fond of highlighting the fact that, sporting stilettos and leather skirts, Lynn Tilton does not dress like your typical manufacturing executive. Much more important, however, is the fact that her business success is also far from typical. In fact, as the full or partial owner of 74 companies with revenues of more than $8 billion, Tilton is one of the wealthiest female entrepreneurs in the United States. Her company, Patriarch Partners, is sometimes referred to as the largest woman-owned business in America.

Her path to success is an inspiring tale of determination. Tilton started on Wall Street as a single mother, working 15-hour days as she put herself through business school. During years of employment at numerous financial institutions, she developed a knack for analyzing balance sheets and interpreting complex financial information. Eventually, Tilton started her own company, Patriarch Partners, and invested in the debt of a number of distressed companies. She quickly figured out that the only way she was going to make money on those investments was to take control of the companies and try to make them profitable. Thus, seemingly almost by accident, she became the CEO of dozens of failing manufacturing companies. Amazingly, she was able to make these companies profitable when others had given up on them.

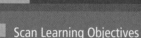

The Navigator

- Scan Learning Objectives
- Read Feature Story
- Read Preview
- Read Text and answer **DO IT!** p. 54
  - p. 62 ▪ p. 65 ▪ p. 70
- Work Using the Decision Toolkit p. 70
- Review Summary of Learning Objectives
- Work Comprehensive **DO IT!** p. 73
- Answer Self-Test Questions
- Complete Assignments
- Go to **WileyPLUS** for practice and tutorials

Learning Objectives

After studying this chapter, you should be able to:

1 Explain the characteristics and purposes of cost accounting.

2 Describe the flow of costs in a job order cost system.

3 Explain the nature and importance of a job cost sheet.

4 Indicate how the predetermined overhead rate is determined and used.

5 Prepare entries for jobs completed and sold.

6 Distinguish between under- and overapplied manufacturing overhead.

The Navigator

As a result of this initial success, Tilton made corporate turn-arounds the focus of her company. Once a business is acquired, she installs a new management team, improves productivity, and identifies new products for the company to produce. For example, she turned a failed paper mill into a producer of alternative fuels, and saved a helicopter company by identifying new customers. When others were fleeing the auto industry, she dove in and bought a number of auto-parts companies.

While she is a tough negotiator, Tilton also has the respect of her workers. Duane Ludgon, a union negotiator says, "Workers really take to Lynn. She's just human and honest with people. I don't say that about many CEOs." In fact, Tilton is a crusader for U.S. manufacturing. She says, "The key to America's future is manufacturing. We simply have to become a country that can make things again."

Not all of her investments are immediate successes. Her investment in a fire-truck manufacturer, American LaFrance, was slow to turn a profit. But everyone involved figured it was only a matter of time before her persistent approach made this fire-truck maker another business that she saved before it went up in smoke.

*Watch the **Making a Hollywood Movie** video in WileyPLUS to learn more about job order costing in the real world.*

Source: Robert Frank, "Tilton Flaunts Her Style at Patriarch," *Wall Street Journal Online* (January 8, 2011).

✔ **The Navigator**

Preview of **Chapter 2**

The Feature Story about Patriarch Partners describes the approach Lynn Tilton uses to turn around a failing company. Accurate costing is critical to this process. For example, in order to submit accurate bids on new jobs and to know whether it profited from past jobs, the company needs a good costing system. This chapter illustrates how these costs are assigned to specific jobs, such as the manufacture of individual fire trucks at one of Tilton's companies, American LaFrance. We begin the discussion in this chapter with an overview of the flow of costs in a job order cost accounting system. We then use a case study to explain and illustrate the documents, entries, and accounts in this type of cost accounting system.

The content and organization of Chapter 2 are as follows.

JOB ORDER COSTING

Cost Accounting Systems	Job Order Cost Flow	Reporting Job Cost Data
• Job order cost system • Process cost system	• Accumulating costs • Assigning costs to work in process • Assigning costs to finished goods • Assigning costs to cost of goods sold • Summary of job order cost flows • Job order costing for service companies • Advantages and disadvantages	• Cost of goods manufactured schedule • Income statement presentation • Under- or overapplied manufacturing overhead

✔ **The Navigator**

Cost Accounting Systems

Cost accounting involves measuring, recording, and reporting product costs. Companies determine both the total cost and the unit cost of each product. The accuracy of the product cost information is critical to the success of the company. Companies use this information to determine which products to produce, what price to charge, and the amounts to produce. Accurate product cost information is also vital for effective evaluation of employee performance.

A **cost accounting system** consists of accounts for the various manufacturing costs. These accounts are fully integrated into the general ledger of a company. An important feature of a cost accounting system is the use of **a perpetual inventory system**. Such a system **provides immediate, up-to-date information on the cost of a product**.

There are two basic types of cost accounting systems: (1) a job order cost system and (2) a process cost system. Although cost accounting systems differ widely from company to company, most involve one of these two traditional product costing systems.

Job Order Cost System

Under a **job order cost system**, the company assigns costs to each **job** or to each **batch** of goods. An example of a job is the manufacture of a mainframe computer by IBM, the production of a movie by Disney, or the making of a fire truck by American LaFrance. An example of a batch is the printing of 225 wedding invitations by a local print shop, or the printing of a weekly issue of *Fortune* magazine by a high-tech printer such as Quad Graphics.

An important feature of job order costing is that each job or batch has its own distinguishing characteristics. For example, each house is custom built, each consulting engagement by a CPA firm is unique, and each printing job is different. **The objective is to compute the cost per job**. At each point in manufacturing a product or providing a service, the company can identify the job and its associated costs. A job order cost system measures costs for each completed job, rather than for set time periods. Illustration 2-1 shows the recording of costs in a job order cost system.

Illustration 2-1
Job order cost system

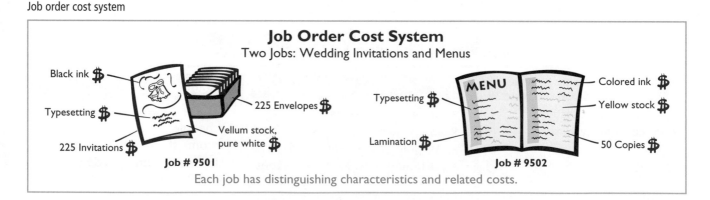

Job Order Cost System
Two Jobs: Wedding Invitations and Menus

Black ink $

Typesetting $

225 Invitations $

225 Envelopes $

Vellum stock, pure white $

Job # 9501

Typesetting $

Lamination $

MENU

Colored ink $

Yellow stock $

50 Copies $

Job # 9502

Each job has distinguishing characteristics and related costs.

Process Cost System

A company uses a **process cost system** when it manufactures a large volume of similar products. Production is continuous. Examples of a process cost system are the manufacture of cereal by Kellogg, the refining of petroleum by ExxonMobil, and the production of ice cream by Ben & Jerry's. Process costing accumulates product-related costs **for a period of time** (such as a week or a month) instead of assigning costs to specific products or job orders. In process costing, companies assign the costs to departments or processes for the specified period of time. Illustration 2-2 shows examples of the use of a process cost system. We will discuss the process cost system further in Chapter 3.

Illustration 2-2
Process cost system

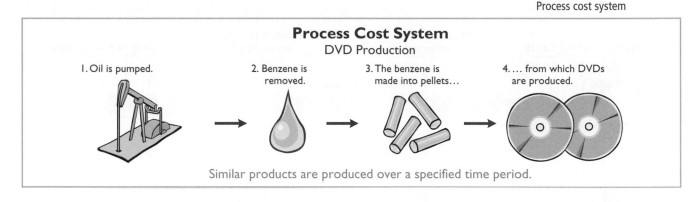

Process Cost System
DVD Production

I. Oil is pumped. 2. Benzene is removed. 3. The benzene is made into pellets... 4. ... from which DVDs are produced.

Similar products are produced over a specified time period.

Can a company use both types of cost systems? Yes. For example, General Motors uses process cost accounting for its standard model cars, such as Malibus and Corvettes, and job order cost accounting for a custom-made limousine for the President of the United States.

The objective of both cost accounting systems is to provide unit cost information for product pricing, cost control, inventory valuation, and financial statement presentation.

MANAGEMENT INSIGHT

Jobs Won, Money Lost

Many companies suffer from poor cost accounting. As a result, they sometimes make products they should not be selling at all, or they buy product components that they could more profitably make themselves. Also, inaccurate cost data leads companies to misallocate capital and frustrates efforts by plant managers to improve efficiency.

For example, consider the case of a diversified company in the business of rebuilding diesel locomotives. The managers thought they were making money, but a consulting firm found that the company had seriously underestimated costs. The company bailed out of the business, and not a moment too soon. Says the consultant who advised the company, "The more contracts it won, the more money it lost." Given that situation, a company cannot stay in business very long!

? What type of costs do you think the company had been underestimating? (See page 92.)

Job Order Cost Flow

The flow of costs (direct materials, direct labor, and manufacturing overhead) in job order cost accounting parallels the physical flow of the materials as they are converted into finished goods. As shown in Illustration 2-3 (page 52), companies first **accumulate** manufacturing costs in the form of raw materials, factory labor,

LEARNING OBJECTIVE   2

Describe the flow of costs in a job order cost system.

or manufacturing overhead. They then **assign** manufacturing costs to the Work in Process Inventory account. When a job is completed, the company transfers the cost of the job to Finished Goods Inventory. Later when the goods are sold, the company transfers their cost to Cost of Goods Sold.

Illustration 2-3
Flow of costs in job order costing

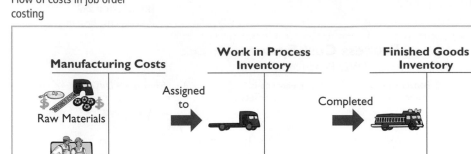

Illustration 2-3 provides a basic overview of the flow of costs in a manufacturing setting. A more detailed presentation of the flow of costs is summarized near the end of this chapter in Illustration 2-15. There are two major steps in the flow of costs: (1) *accumulating* the manufacturing costs incurred, and (2) *assigning* the accumulated costs to the work done. The following discussion shows that the company accumulates manufacturing costs incurred by debits to Raw Materials Inventory, Factory Labor, and Manufacturing Overhead. When the company incurs these costs, it does not attempt to associate the costs with specific jobs. The company makes additional entries to assign manufacturing costs incurred. In the remainder of this chapter, we will use a case study to explain how a job order cost system operates.

Accumulating Manufacturing Costs

To illustrate a job order cost system, we will use the January transactions of Wallace Company, which makes custom electronic sensors for corporate safety applications (such as fire and carbon monoxide) and security applications (such as theft and corporate espionage).

RAW MATERIALS COSTS

When Wallace receives the raw materials it has purchased, **it debits the cost of the materials to Raw Materials Inventory**. The company would debit this account for the invoice cost of the raw materials and freight costs chargeable to the purchaser. It would credit the account for purchase discounts taken and purchase returns and allowances. Wallace makes **no effort at this point to associate the cost of materials with specific jobs or orders**.

To illustrate, assume that Wallace purchases 2,000 lithium batteries (Stock No. AA2746) at $5 per unit ($10,000) and 800 electronic modules (Stock No. AA2850) at $40 per unit ($32,000) for a total cost of $42,000 ($10,000 + $32,000). The entry to record this purchase on January 4 is:

		(1)[1]			**Raw Materials Inventory**	
Jan. 4	Raw Materials Inventory		42,000		42,000	
	Accounts Payable			42,000		
	(Purchase of raw materials					
	on account)					

At this point, Raw Materials Inventory has a balance of $42,000, as shown in the T-account in the margin. As we will explain later in the chapter, the company subsequently assigns direct raw materials inventory to work in process and indirect raw materials inventory to manufacturing overhead.

FACTORY LABOR COSTS

Some of a company's employees are involved in the manufacturing process, while others are not. As discussed in Chapter 1, wages and salaries of nonmanufacturing employees are expensed as period costs (e.g., Salaries and Wages Expense). Costs related to manufacturing employees are accumulated in Factory Labor to ensure their treatment as product costs. Factory labor consists of three costs: (1) gross earnings of factory workers, (2) employer payroll taxes on these earnings, and (3) fringe benefits (such as sick pay, pensions, and vacation pay) incurred by the employer. **Companies debit labor costs to Factory Labor as they incur those costs**.

To illustrate, assume that Wallace incurs $32,000 of factory labor costs. Of that amount, $27,000 relates to wages payable and $5,000 relates to payroll taxes payable in February. The entry to record factory labor for the month is:

		(2)			**Factory Labor**	
Jan. 31	Factory Labor		32,000		32,000	
	Factory Wages Payable			27,000		
	Employer Payroll Taxes Payable			5,000		
	(To record factory labor costs)					

At this point, Factory Labor has a balance of $32,000, as shown in the T-account in the margin. The company subsequently assigns direct factory labor to work in process and indirect factory labor to manufacturing overhead.

MANUFACTURING OVERHEAD COSTS

A company has many types of overhead costs. If these overhead costs, such as property taxes, depreciation, insurance, and repairs, relate to overhead costs of a nonmanufacturing facility, such as an office building, then these costs are expensed as period costs (e.g., Property Tax Expense, Depreciation Expense, Insurance Expense, and Repairs Expense). If the costs relate to the manufacturing process, then they are accumulated in Manufacturing Overhead, to ensure their treatment as product costs.

Using assumed data, the summary entry for manufacturing overhead in Wallace Company is:

		(3)			**Manufacturing Overhead**	
Jan. 31	Manufacturing Overhead		13,800		13,800	
	Utilities Payable			4,800		
	Prepaid Insurance			2,000		
	Accounts Payable (for repairs)			2,600		
	Accumulated Depreciation			3,000		
	Property Taxes Payable			1,400		
	(To record overhead costs)					

---

[1]The numbers placed above the entries for Wallace Company are used for reference purposes in the summary provided in Illustration 2-15.

At this point, Manufacturing Overhead has a balance of $13,800, as shown in the T-account in the margin. The company subsequently assigns manufacturing overhead to work in process.

> **DO IT!**

Manufacturing Costs

Action Plan

✔ In accumulating manufacturing costs, debit at least one of three accounts: Raw Materials Inventory, Factory Labor, and Manufacturing Overhead.

✔ Manufacturing overhead costs may be recognized daily. Or manufacturing overhead may be recorded periodically through a summary entry.

During the current month, Ringling Company incurs the following manufacturing costs:

(a) Raw material purchases of $4,200 on account.

(b) Incurs factory labor of $18,000. Of that amount, $15,000 relates to wages payable and $3,000 relates to payroll taxes payable.

(c) Factory utilities of $2,200 are payable, prepaid factory insurance of $1,800 has expired, and depreciation on the factory building is $3,500.

Prepare journal entries for each type of manufacturing cost.

Solution

(a) Raw Materials Inventory	4,200	
Accounts Payable		4,200
(Purchases of raw materials on account)		
(b) Factory Labor	18,000	
Factory Wages Payable		15,000
Employer Payroll Taxes Payable		3,000
(To record factory labor costs)		
(c) Manufacturing Overhead	7,500	
Utilities Payable		2,200
Prepaid Insurance		1,800
Accumulated Depreciation		3,500
(To record overhead costs)		

Related exercise material: **BE2-1, BE2-2, E2-1, E2-7, E2-8, E2-11, and** **DO IT!** **2-1.**

✔ **The Navigator**

Assigning Manufacturing Costs to Work in Process

LEARNING OBJECTIVE **3**

Explain the nature and importance of a job cost sheet.

Assigning manufacturing costs to work in process results in the following entries.

1. **Debits** made to Work in Process Inventory.

2. **Credits** made to Raw Materials Inventory, Factory Labor, and Manufacturing Overhead.

An essential accounting record in assigning costs to jobs is a **job cost sheet**, as shown in Illustration 2-4. A **job cost sheet** is a form used to record the costs chargeable to a specific job and to determine the total and unit costs of the completed job.

Companies keep a separate job cost sheet for each job. The job cost sheets constitute the subsidiary ledger for the Work in Process Inventory account. A **subsidiary ledger** consists of individual records for each individual item—in this case, each job. The Work in Process account is referred to as a **control account** because it summarizes the detailed data regarding specific jobs contained in the job cost sheets. **Each entry to Work in Process Inventory must be accompanied by a corresponding posting to one or more job cost sheets**.

Illustration 2-4
Job cost sheet

Job Cost Sheet

Job No. _____   Quantity _____
Item _____   Date Requested _____
For _____   Date Completed _____

Date	Direct Materials	Direct Labor	Manufacturing Overhead

Cost of completed job
 Direct materials $ _____
 Direct labor   _____
 Manufacturing overhead   _____
Total cost $ _____
Unit cost (total dollars ÷ quantity) $ _____

Helpful Hint
In today's electronic environment, companies typically maintain job cost sheets as computer files.

RAW MATERIALS COSTS

Companies assign raw materials costs to jobs when their materials storeroom issues the materials in response to requests. Requests for issuing raw materials are made on a prenumbered **materials requisition slip**. The materials issued may be used directly on a job, or they may be considered indirect materials. As Illustration 2-5 shows, the requisition should indicate the quantity and type of materials withdrawn and the account to be charged. The company will charge direct materials to Work in Process Inventory, and indirect materials to Manufacturing Overhead.

Helpful Hint
Approvals are an important part of a materials requisition slip because they help to establish individual accountability over inventory.

Illustration 2-5
Materials requisition slip

Wallace Company
Materials Requisition Slip

Deliver to: _____ Assembly Department _____   Req. No.   R247
Charge to: _____ Work in Process—Job No. 101 _____   Date: 1/6/14

Quantity	Description	Stock No.	Cost per Unit	Total
200	Lithium batteries	AA2746	$5.00	$1,000

Requested by *Bruce Howart*   Received by *Herb Crowley*
Approved by *Kap Shin*   Costed by *Heather Remmers*

Helpful Hint
Note the specific job to be charged.

Ethics Note
The internal control principle of documentation includes prenumbering to enhance accountability.

The company may use any of the inventory costing methods (FIFO, LIFO, or average-cost) in costing the requisitions **to the individual job cost sheets**.

Periodically, the company journalizes the requisitions. For example, if Wallace uses $24,000 of direct materials and $6,000 of indirect materials in January, the entry is:

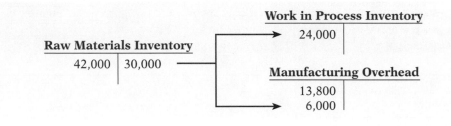

		(4)		
Jan. 31	Work in Process Inventory		24,000	
	Manufacturing Overhead		6,000	
	Raw Materials Inventory			30,000
	(To assign materials to jobs and			
	overhead)			

This entry reduces Raw Materials Inventory by $30,000, increases Work in Process Inventory by $24,000, and increases Manufacturing Overhead by $6,000, as shown below.

Work in Process Inventory

24,000	

Raw Materials Inventory

42,000	30,000

Manufacturing Overhead

13,800	
6,000	

Illustration 2-6 shows the posting of requisition slip R247 to Job No. 101 and other assumed postings to the job cost sheets for materials. The requisition slips provide

Illustration 2-6
Job cost sheets–direct materials

Helpful Hint
Companies post to control accounts monthly, and post to job cost sheets daily.

Helpful Hint
Prove the $24,000 direct materials charge to Work in Process Inventory by totaling the charges by jobs:

101	$12,000
102	7,000
103	5,000
	$24,000

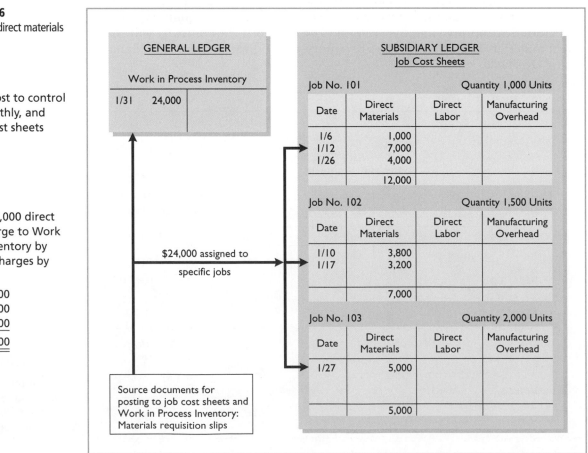

the basis for total direct materials costs of $12,000 for Job No. 101, $7,000 for Job No. 102, and $5,000 for Job No. 103. After the company has completed all postings, the sum of the direct materials columns of the job cost sheets (the subsidiary account amounts of $12,000, $7,000, and $5,000) should equal the direct materials debited to Work in Process Inventory (the control account amount of $24,000).

MANAGEMENT INSIGHT

The Cost of an iPhone? Just Tear One Apart

All companies need to know what it costs to make their own products—but a lot of companies would also like to know the cost of their competitors' products as well. That's where iSuppli steps in. For a price, iSuppli will tear apart sophisticated electronic devices to tell you what it would cost to replicate. In the case of smart-phones, which often have more than 1,000 tiny components, that is no small feat. As shown in the chart below, components of many smart-phones cost about $170. Assembly is only about another $6.50. The difference between what you pay and the "cost" is not all profit. Consider the additional nonproduction costs of research, design, marketing, patent fees, and selling costs.

Sum of the Parts
Cost of components[a], 2009

	Palm Pre	Apple iPhone[b]	Toshiba TG01	Motorola Droid
Integrated circuits	$ 83.96	$ 91.38	$ 68.39	$ 60.83
Display/ touchscreen	38.80	34.65	35.30	35.25
Mechanical[c]	19.63	17.80	21.88	20.23
Camera	7.50	9.35	12.80	14.25
Battery	4.25	5.07	4.71	4.25
Other	16.51	11.82	30.60	44.30
Total	$170.65	$170.07	$173.68	$179.11

[a] Latest data available
[b] 3GS 16GB
[c] Includes electromechanical
Source: iSuppli.

Source: "The Business of Dissecting Electronics: The Lowdown on Teardowns," *The Economist.com* (January 21, 2010).

? What type of costs are marketing and selling costs, and how are they treated for accounting purposes? (See page 92.)

FACTORY LABOR COSTS

Companies assign factory labor costs to jobs on the basis of time tickets prepared when the work is performed. The **time ticket** indicates the employee, the hours worked, the account and job to be charged, and the total labor cost. Many companies accumulate these data through the use of bar coding and scanning devices. When they start and end work, employees scan bar codes on their identification badges and bar codes associated with each job they work on. When direct labor is involved, the time ticket must indicate the job number, as shown in Illustration 2-7 (page 58). The employee's supervisor should approve all time tickets.

The time tickets are later sent to the payroll department, which applies the employee's hourly wage rate and computes the total labor cost. Finally, the company journalizes the time tickets. It debits the account Work in Process Inventory for

Illustration 2-7
Time ticket

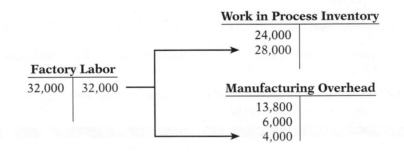

direct labor and debits Manufacturing Overhead for indirect labor. For example, if the $32,000 total factory labor cost consists of $28,000 of direct labor and $4,000 of indirect labor, the entry is:

(5)

Jan. 31	Work in Process Inventory		28,000	
	Manufacturing Overhead		4,000	
	Factory Labor			32,000
	(To assign labor to jobs and			
	overhead)			

As a result of this entry, Factory Labor is reduced by $32,000 so it has a zero balance, and labor costs are assigned to the appropriate manufacturing accounts. The entry increases Work in Process Inventory by $28,000 and increases Manufacturing Overhead by $4,000, as shown below.

Work in Process Inventory

24,000	
28,000	

Factory Labor

32,000	32,000

Manufacturing Overhead

13,800	
6,000	
4,000	

    Let's assume that the labor costs chargeable to Wallace's three jobs are $15,000, $9,000, and $4,000. Illustration 2-8 shows the Work in Process Inventory and job cost sheets after posting. As in the case of direct materials, the postings to the direct labor columns of the job cost sheets should equal the posting of direct labor to Work in Process Inventory.

LEARNING OBJECTIVE   4

Indicate how the predetermined overhead rate is determined and used.

Manufacturing Overhead Costs

Companies charge the actual costs of direct materials and direct labor to specific jobs. In contrast, manufacturing **overhead** relates to production operations **as a whole**. As a result, overhead costs cannot be assigned to specific jobs on the basis

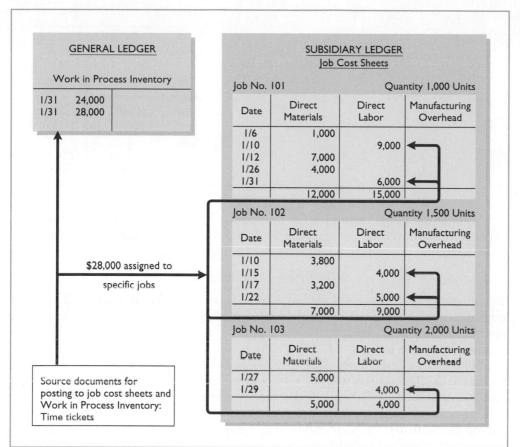

Illustration 2-8
Job cost sheets—direct labor

Helpful Hint
Prove the $28,000 direct labor charge to Work in Process Inventory by totaling the charges by jobs:

101	$15,000
102	9,000
103	4,000
	$28,000

of actual costs incurred. Instead, companies assign manufacturing overhead to work in process and to specific jobs **on an estimated basis through the use of a predetermined overhead rate**.

The **predetermined overhead rate** is based on the relationship between estimated annual overhead costs and expected annual operating activity, expressed in terms of a common **activity base**. The company may state the activity in terms of direct labor costs, direct labor hours, machine hours, or any other measure that will provide an equitable basis for applying overhead costs to jobs. Companies establish the predetermined overhead rate at the beginning of the year. Small companies often use a single, company-wide predetermined overhead rate. Large companies often use rates that vary from department to department. The formula for a predetermined overhead rate is as follows.

Estimated Annual Overhead Costs	÷	Expected Annual Operating Activity	=	Predetermined Overhead Rate

Illustration 2-9
Formula for predetermined overhead rate

Overhead relates to production operations as a whole. To know what "the whole" is, the logical thing is to wait until the end of the year's operations. At that time, the company knows all of its costs for the period. As a practical matter, though, managers cannot wait until the end of the year. To price products effectively as they are completed, managers need information about product costs of specific jobs completed during the year. Using a predetermined overhead rate enables a cost to be determined for the job immediately. Illustration 2-10 (page 60) indicates how manufacturing overhead is assigned to work in process.

Illustration 2-10
Using predetermined overhead rates

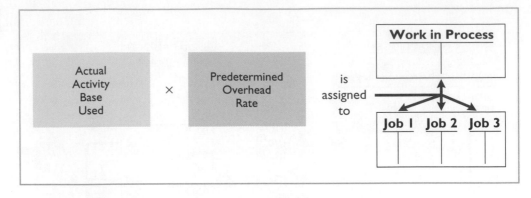

Wallace uses direct labor cost as the activity base. Assuming that the company expects annual overhead costs to be $280,000 and direct labor costs for the year to be $350,000, the overhead rate is 80%, computed as follows.

$$\$280,000 \div \$350,000 = 80\%$$

This means that for every dollar of direct labor, Wallace will assign 80 cents of manufacturing overhead to a job. The use of a predetermined overhead rate enables the company to determine the approximate total cost of each job **when it completes the job**.

Historically, companies used direct labor costs or direct labor hours as the activity base. The reason was the relatively high correlation between direct labor and manufacturing overhead. Today more companies are using **machine hours as the activity base, due to increased reliance on automation in manufacturing operations**. Or, as mentioned in Chapter 1 (and discussed more fully in Chapter 4), many companies now use activity-based costing to more accurately allocate overhead costs based on the activities that give rise to the costs.

A company may use more than one activity base. For example, if a job is manufactured in more than one factory department, each department may have its own overhead rate. In the Feature Story, American LaFrance might use two bases in assigning overhead to fire-truck jobs: direct materials dollars for indirect materials, and direct labor hours for such costs as insurance and supervisors' salaries.

Wallace Company applies manufacturing overhead to work in process when it assigns direct labor costs. It also applies manufacturing overhead to specific jobs at the same time. For January, Wallace applied overhead of $22,400 in response to its assignment of $28,000 of direct labor costs (direct labor cost of $28,000 × 80%). The following entry records this application.

(6)

Jan. 31	Work in Process Inventory	22,400	
	Manufacturing Overhead		22,400
	(To assign overhead to jobs)		

This entry reduces the balance in Manufacturing Overhead and increases Work in Process Inventory by $22,400, as shown below.

Manufacturing Overhead		Work in Process Inventory	
13,800	22,400	24,000	
6,000		28,000	
4,000		22,400	

The overhead that Wallace applies to each job will be 80% of the direct labor cost of the job for the month. Illustration 2-11 shows the Work in Process Inventory account and the job cost sheets after posting. Note that the debit of $22,400 to

Illustration 2-11
Job cost sheets–manufacturing overhead applied

Work in Process Inventory equals the sum of the overhead applied to jobs: Job 101 $12,000 + Job 102 $7,200 + Job 103 $3,200.

At the end of each month, the **balance in Work in Process Inventory should equal the sum of the costs shown on the job cost sheets of unfinished jobs**. Illustration 2-12 presents proof of the agreement of the control and subsidiary accounts in Wallace. (It assumes that all jobs are still in process.)

Work in Process Inventory				Job Cost Sheets	
Jan. 31	24,000			No. 101	$ 39,000
31	28,000			102	23,200
31	22,400			103	12,200
	74,400	←			**$74,400**

Illustration 2-12
Proof of job cost sheets to work in process inventory

DECISION TOOLKIT

DECISION CHECKPOINTS	INFO NEEDED FOR DECISION	TOOL TO USE FOR DECISION	HOW TO EVALUATE RESULTS
What is the cost of a job?	Cost of material, labor, and overhead assigned to a specific job	Job cost sheet	Compare costs to those of previous periods and to those of competitors to ensure that costs are in line. Compare costs to expected selling price or service fees charged to determine overall profitability.

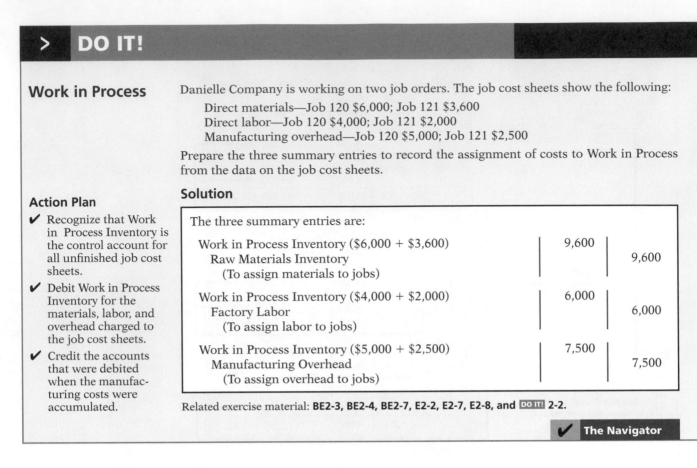

> **DO IT!**

Work in Process

Danielle Company is working on two job orders. The job cost sheets show the following:

     Direct materials—Job 120 $6,000; Job 121 $3,600
     Direct labor—Job 120 $4,000; Job 121 $2,000
     Manufacturing overhead—Job 120 $5,000; Job 121 $2,500

Prepare the three summary entries to record the assignment of costs to Work in Process from the data on the job cost sheets.

Action Plan

✔ Recognize that Work in Process Inventory is the control account for all unfinished job cost sheets.

✔ Debit Work in Process Inventory for the materials, labor, and overhead charged to the job cost sheets.

✔ Credit the accounts that were debited when the manufacturing costs were accumulated.

Solution

The three summary entries are:

Work in Process Inventory ($6,000 + $3,600)	9,600	
Raw Materials Inventory		9,600
(To assign materials to jobs)		
Work in Process Inventory ($4,000 + $2,000)	6,000	
Factory Labor		6,000
(To assign labor to jobs)		
Work in Process Inventory ($5,000 + $2,500)	7,500	
Manufacturing Overhead		7,500
(To assign overhead to jobs)		

Related exercise material: **BE2-3, BE2-4, BE2-7, E2-2, E2-7, E2-8, and DO IT! 2-2.**

✔ **The Navigator**

Assigning Costs to Finished Goods

LEARNING OBJECTIVE   **5**

Prepare entries for jobs completed and sold.

When a job is completed, Wallace summarizes the costs and completes the lower portion of the applicable job cost sheet. For example, if we assume that Wallace completes Job No. 101, a batch of electronic sensors, on January 31, the job cost sheet appears as shown in Illustration 2-13.

    When a job is finished, Wallace makes an entry to transfer its total cost to finished goods inventory. The entry is as follows.

(7)

Jan. 31	Finished Goods Inventory	39,000	
	Work in Process Inventory		39,000
	(To record completion of		
	Job No. 101)		

This entry increases Finished Goods Inventory and reduces Work in Process Inventory by $39,000, as shown in the T-accounts below.

Work in Process Inventory		Finished Goods Inventory	
24,000	39,000 ———→	39,000	
28,000			
22,400			

Finished Goods Inventory is a control account. It controls individual finished goods records in a finished goods subsidiary ledger. The company posts directly from completed job cost sheets to the receipts columns. Illustration 2-14 shows the finished goods inventory record for Job No. 101.

Illustration 2-13
Completed job cost sheet

Job Cost Sheet

Job No. ___101___ Quantity ___1,000___
Item ___Electronic Sensors___ Date Requested ___February 5___
For ___Tanner Company___ Date Completed ___January 31___

Date	Direct Materials	Direct Labor	Manufacturing Overhead
1/6	$ 1,000		
1/10		$ 9,000	$ 7,200
1/12	7,000		
1/26	4,000		
1/31		6,000	4,800
	$12,000	$15,000	$12,000

Cost of completed job
Direct materials $ 12,000
Direct labor   15,000
Manufacturing overhead   12,000
Total cost $ 39,000
Unit cost ($39,000 ÷ 1,000) $ 39.00

Assigning Costs to Cost of Goods Sold

Companies recognize cost of goods sold when each sale occurs. To illustrate the entries a company makes when it sells a completed job, assume that on January 31 Wallace sells on account Job 101. The job cost $39,000, and it sold for $50,000. The entries to record the sale and recognize cost of goods sold are:

(8)

Jan. 31	Accounts Receivable	50,000	
	Sales Revenue		50,000
	(To record sale of Job No. 101)		
31	Cost of Goods Sold	39,000	
	Finished Goods Inventory		39,000
	(To record cost of Job No. 101)		

As Illustration 2-14 shows, Wallace records, in the issues section of the finished goods record, the units sold, the cost per unit, and the total cost of goods sold for each job sold.

Illustration 2-14
Finished goods record

Finished Goods.xls

Home Insert Page Layout Formulas Data Review View

P18 fx

	A	B	C	D	E	F	G	H	I	J
1	**Item: Electronic Sensors**								**Job No: 101**	
2										
3			Receipts			Issues			Balance	
4	Date	Units	Cost	Total	Units	Cost	Total	Units	Cost	Total
5	1/31	1,000	$39	$39,000				1,000	$39	$39,000
6	1/31				1,000	$39	$39,000			– 0 –
7										

Summary of Job Order Cost Flows

Illustration 2-15 shows a completed flowchart for a job order cost accounting system. All postings are keyed to entries 1–8 in the example presented in the previous pages for Wallace Company.

The cost flows in the diagram can be categorized as one of four types:

- **Accumulation.** The company first accumulates costs by (1) purchasing raw materials, (2) incurring labor costs, and (3) incurring manufacturing overhead costs.

- **Assignment to jobs.** Once the company has incurred manufacturing costs, it must assign them to specific jobs. For example, as it uses raw materials on specific jobs (4), it assigns them to work in process, or treats them as manufacturing overhead if the raw materials cannot be associated with a specific job. Similarly, it either assigns factory labor (5) to work in process, or treats it as manufacturing overhead if the factory labor cannot be associated with a specific job. Finally it assigns manufacturing overhead (6) to work in process using a *predetermined overhead rate*. This deserves emphasis: **Do not assign overhead using actual overhead costs, but instead use a predetermined rate.**

- **Completed jobs.** As jobs are completed (7), the company transfers the cost of the completed job out of work in process inventory into finished goods inventory.

- **When goods are sold.** As specific items are sold (8), the company transfers their cost out of finished goods inventory into cost of goods sold.

Illustration 2-15
Flow of costs in a job order cost system

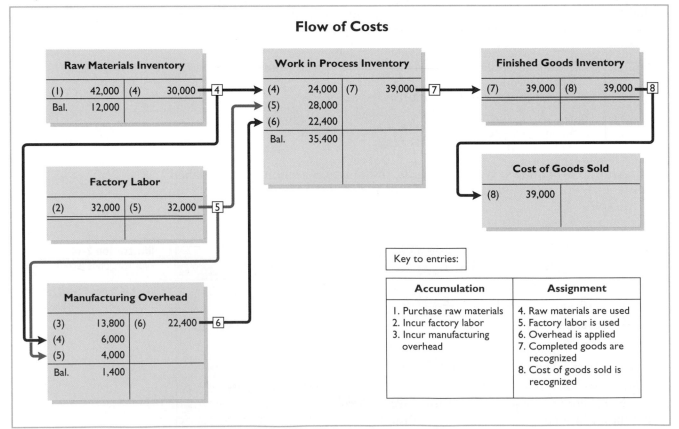

Illustration 2-16 summarizes the flow of documents in a job order cost system.

Illustration 2-16
Flow of documents in a job order cost system

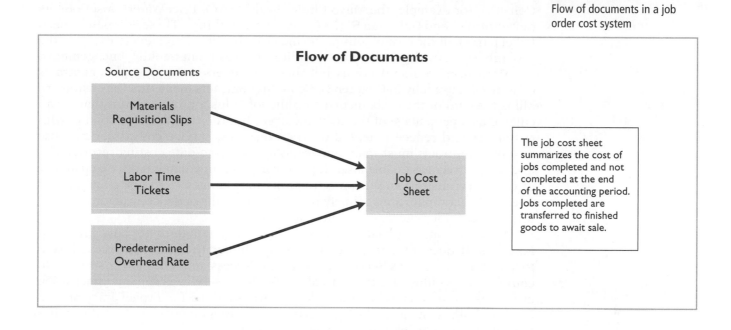

Flow of Documents

Source Documents

Materials Requisition Slips

Labor Time Tickets

Predetermined Overhead Rate

Job Cost Sheet

The job cost sheet summarizes the cost of jobs completed and not completed at the end of the accounting period. Jobs completed are transferred to finished goods to await sale.

> ## DO IT!

Completion and Sale of Jobs

During the current month, Onyx Corporation completed Job 109 and Job 112. Job 109 cost $19,000 and Job 112 cost $27,000. Job 112 was sold on account for $42,000. Journalize the entries for the completion of the two jobs and the sale of Job 112.

Solution

Action Plan

✔ Debit Finished Goods Inventory for the cost of completed jobs.

✔ Debit Cost of Goods Sold for the cost of jobs sold.

Finished Goods Inventory	46,000	
Work in Process Inventory		46,000
(To record completion of Job 109,		
costing $19,000 and Job 112,		
costing $27,000)		
Accounts Receivable	42,000	
Sales Revenue		42,000
(To record sale of Job 112)		
Cost of Goods Sold	27,000	
Finished Goods Inventory		27,000
(To record cost of goods sold for Job 112)		

Related exercise material: **BE2-8, E2-2, E2-3, E2-4, E2-6, E2-7, E2-10, and DO IT! 2-3.**

✔ **The Navigator**

Job Order Costing for Service Companies

Our extended job order costing example focuses on a manufacturer so that you see the flow of costs through the inventory accounts. It is important to understand, however, that job order costing is also commonly used by service companies. While service companies do not have inventory, the techniques of job order costing are still quite useful in many service-industry environments. Consider, for example, the Mayo Clinic (health care), PriceWaterhouseCoopers (accounting), and Goldman Sachs (investment banking). These companies need to keep track of the cost of jobs performed for specific customers to evaluate the profitability of medical treatments, audits, or investment banking engagements.

Many service organizations bill their customers using cost-plus contracts (discussed more fully in Chapter 8). Cost-plus contracts mean that the customer's bill is the sum of the costs incurred on the job, plus a profit amount that is calculated as a percentage of the costs incurred. In order to minimize conflict with customers and reduce potential contract disputes, service companies that use cost-plus contracts must maintain accurate and up-to-date costing records. Up-to-date cost records enable a service company to immediately notify a customer of cost overruns due to customer requests for changes to the original plan or unexpected complications. Timely recordkeeping allows the contractor and customer to consider alternatives before it is too late.

A service company that uses a job order cost system does not have inventory accounts. It does, however, use an account similar to Work in Process Inventory, referred to here as Service Contracts in Process, to record job costs prior to completion. To illustrate the journal entries for a service company under a job order cost system, consider the following transactions for Frugal Interiors, an interior design company. The entry to record the assignment of $9,000 of supplies to projects ($7,000 direct and $2,000 indirect) is:

Service Contracts in Process	7,000	
Operating Overhead	2,000	
Supplies		9,000
(To assign supplies to projects)		

The entry to record the assignment of service salaries and wages of $100,000 ($84,000 direct and $16,000 indirect) is:

Service Contracts in Process	84,000	
Operating Overhead	16,000	
Service Salaries and Wages		100,000
(To assign personnel costs to projects)		

Frugal Interiors applies operating overhead at a rate of 50% of direct labor costs. The entry to record the application of overhead ($84,000 × 50%) based on the direct labor costs is:

Service Contracts in Process	42,000	
Operating Overhead		42,000
(To assign operating overhead to projects)		

Finally, upon completion, the job cost sheet of a design project for Sampson Corporation shows a total cost of $34,000. The entry to record completion of this project is:

Cost of Completed Service Contracts	34,000	
Service Contracts in Process		34,000
(To record completion of Sampson project)		

Job cost sheets for a service company keep track of materials, labor, and overhead used on a particular job similar to a manufacturer. A number of exercises at the end of this chapter apply job order costing to service companies.

SERVICE COMPANY INSIGHT

Sales Are Nice, but Service Revenue Pays the Bills

Jet engines are one of the many products made by the industrial operations division of General Electric (GE). At prices as high as $30 million per engine, you can bet that GE does its best to keep track of costs. It might surprise you that GE doesn't make much profit on the sale of each engine. So why does it bother making them? Service revenue–during one recent year, about 75% of the division's revenues came from servicing its own products. One estimate is that the $13 billion in aircraft engines sold during a recent three-year period will generate about $90 billion in service revenue over the 30-year life of the engines. Because of the high product costs, both the engines themselves and the subsequent service are most likely accounted for using job order costing. Accurate service cost records are important because GE needs to generate high profit margins on its service jobs to make up for the low margins on the original sale. It also needs good cost records for its service jobs in order to control its costs. Otherwise, a competitor, such as Pratt and Whitney, might submit lower bids for service contracts and take lucrative service jobs away from GE.

Source: Paul Glader, "GE's Focus on Services Faces Test," *Wall Street Journal Online* (March 3, 2009).

? Explain why GE would use job order costing to keep track of the cost of repairing a malfunctioning engine for a major airline. (See page 92.)

Advantages and Disadvantages of Job Order Costing

An advantage of job order costing is it is more precise in assignment of costs to projects than process costing. For example, assume that a construction company, Juan Company, builds 10 custom homes a year at a total cost of $2,000,000. One way to determine the cost of the homes is to divide the total construction cost incurred during the year by the number of homes produced during the year. For Juan Company, an average cost of $200,000 ($2,000,000 ÷ 10) is computed. If the homes are nearly identical, then this approach is adequate for purposes of determining profit per home. But if the homes vary in terms of size, style, and material types, using the average cost of $200,000 to determine profit per home is inappropriate. Instead, Juan Company should use a job order cost system to determine the specific cost incurred to build each home and the amount of profit made on each. Thus, job order costing provides more useful information for determining the profitability of particular projects and for estimating costs when preparing bids on future jobs.

One disadvantage of job order costing is that it requires a significant amount of data entry. For Juan Company, it is much easier to simply keep track of total costs incurred during the year than it is to keep track of the costs incurred on each job (home built). Recording this information is time-consuming, and if the data is not entered accurately, then the product costs are not accurate. In recent years, technological advances, such as bar-coding devices for both labor costs and materials, have increased the accuracy and reduced the effort needed to record costs on specific jobs. These innovations expand the opportunities to apply job order costing in a wider variety of business settings, thus improving management's ability to control costs and make better informed decisions.

A common problem of all costing systems is how to allocate overhead to the finished product. Overhead often represents more than 50% of a product's cost, and this cost is often difficult to allocate meaningfully to the product. How, for example, is the salary of a project manager allocated to the various homes, which may differ in size, style, and materials used, that she oversees? The accuracy of the job order cost system is largely dependent on the accuracy of the overhead allocation process. Even if the company does a good job of keeping track of the specific amounts of materials and labor used on each job, if the overhead costs are not allocated to individual jobs in a meaningful way, the product costing information is not useful. This issue will be addressed in more detail in Chapter 4.

Reporting Job Cost Data

LEARNING OBJECTIVE 6

Distinguish between under- and overapplied manufacturing overhead.

At the end of a period, companies prepare financial statements that present aggregate data on all jobs manufactured and sold. The cost of goods manufactured schedule in job order costing is the same as in Chapter 1 with one exception: **The schedule shows manufacturing overhead applied, rather than actual overhead costs. The company adds this amount to direct materials and direct labor to determine total manufacturing costs.**

Companies prepare the cost of goods manufactured schedule directly from the Work in Process Inventory account. Illustration 2-17 shows a condensed schedule for Wallace Company for January.

Helpful Hint
Companies usually prepare monthly financial statements for management use only.

Wallace Company
Cost of Goods Manufactured Schedule
For the Month Ending January 31, 2014

Work in process, January 1		$ –0–
Direct materials used	$ 24,000	
Direct labor	28,000	
Manufacturing overhead applied	**22,400**	
Total manufacturing costs		74,400
Total cost of work in process		74,400
Less: Work in process, January 31		35,400
Cost of goods manufactured		$39,000

Illustration 2-17
Cost of goods manufactured schedule

Note that the cost of goods manufactured ($39,000) agrees with the amount transferred from Work in Process Inventory to Finished Goods Inventory in journal entry No. 7 in Illustration 2-15 (page 64).

The income statement and balance sheet are the same as those illustrated in Chapter 1. For example, Illustration 2-18 shows the partial income statement for Wallace for the month of January.

Illustration 2-18
Partial income statement

Wallace Company
Income Statement (partial)
For the Month Ending January 31, 2014

Sales revenue		$50,000
Cost of goods sold		
Finished goods inventory, January 1	$ –0–	
Cost of goods manufactured (see Illustration 2-17)	**39,000**	
Cost of goods available for sale	39,000	
Less: Finished goods inventory, January 31	–0–	
Cost of goods sold		39,000
Gross profit		$11,000

Under- or Overapplied Manufacturing Overhead

When Manufacturing Overhead has a **debit balance**, overhead is said to be un-derapplied. **Underapplied overhead** means that the overhead assigned to work in process is less than the overhead incurred. Conversely, when manufacturing overhead has a **credit balance**, overhead is overapplied. **Overapplied overhead** means that the overhead assigned to work in process is greater than the overhead incurred. Illustration 2-19 shows these concepts.

Illustration 2-19
Under- and overapplied overhead

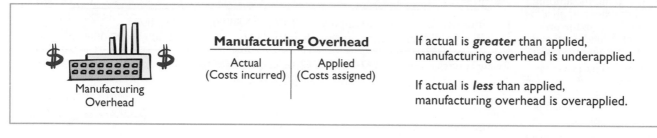

Manufacturing Overhead	
Actual (Costs incurred)	Applied (Costs assigned)

If actual is *greater* than applied, manufacturing overhead is underapplied.

If actual is *less* than applied, manufacturing overhead is overapplied.

YEAR-END BALANCE

At the end of the year, all manufacturing overhead transactions are complete. There is no further opportunity for offsetting events to occur. At this point, Wallace eliminates any balance in Manufacturing Overhead by an adjusting en-try. It considers under- or overapplied overhead to be an **adjustment to cost of goods sold**. Thus, Wallace **debits underapplied overhead to Cost of Goods Sold.** It **credits overapplied overhead to Cost of Goods Sold**.

To illustrate, assume that Wallace has a $2,500 credit balance in Manufac-turing Overhead at December 31. The adjusting entry for the overapplied over-head is:

Dec. 31	Manufacturing Overhead	2,500	
	Cost of Goods Sold		2,500
	(To transfer overapplied overhead to cost of goods sold)		

After Wallace posts this entry, Manufacturing Overhead has a zero balance. In preparing an income statement for the year, Wallace reports cost of goods sold **after adjusting it** for either under- or overapplied overhead.

Conceptually, some argue, under- or overapplied overhead at the end of the year should be allocated among ending work in process, finished goods, and cost of goods sold. The discussion of this possible allocation approach is left to more advanced courses.

DECISION TOOLKIT

DECISION CHECKPOINTS	INFO NEEDED FOR DECISION	TOOL TO USE FOR DECISION	HOW TO EVALUATE RESULTS
Has the company over- or underapplied overhead for the period?	Actual overhead costs and overhead applied	Manufacturing Overhead account	If the account balance is a credit, overhead applied exceeded actual overhead costs. If the account balance is a debit, overhead applied was less than actual overhead costs.

> **DO IT!**

Applied Manufacturing Overhead

Action Plan

✔ Calculate the amount of overhead applied by multiplying the pre-determined overhead rate by actual activity.

✔ If actual manufacturing overhead is greater than applied, manufacturing overhead is underapplied.

✔ If actual manufacturing overhead is less than applied, manufacturing overhead is overapplied.

For Karr Company, the predetermined overhead rate is 140% of direct labor cost. During the month, Karr incurred $90,000 of factory labor costs, of which $80,000 is direct labor and $10,000 is indirect labor. Actual overhead incurred was $119,000.

Compute the amount of manufacturing overhead applied during the month. Determine the amount of under- or overapplied manufacturing overhead.

Solution

Manufacturing overhead applied = (140% × $80,000) = $112,000
Underapplied manufacturing overhead = ($119,000 − $112,000) = $7,000

Related exercise material: **BE2-10, E2-5, E2-12, E2-13, and DO IT! 2-4.**

✔ **The Navigator**

USING THE DECISION TOOLKIT

Martinez Building Products Company is one of the largest manufacturers and marketers of unique, custom-made residential garage doors in the United States. It also is a major supplier of industrial and commercial doors, grills, and counter shutters for the new-construction, repair, and remodel markets. Martinez has developed plans for continued expansion of a network of service operations that sell, install, and service manufactured fireplaces, garage doors, and related products.

Martinez uses a job order cost system and applies overhead to production on the basis of direct labor cost. In computing a predetermined overhead rate for the year 2014, the company estimated manufacturing overhead to be $24 million and direct labor costs to be $20 million. In addition, it developed the following information.

Actual Costs Incurred During 2014

Direct materials used	$30,000,000
Direct labor cost incurred	21,000,000
Insurance, factory	500,000
Indirect labor	7,500,000
Factory maintenance	1,000,000
Rent on factory building	11,000,000
Depreciation on factory equipment	2,000,000

Instructions

Answer each of the following.

(a) Why is Martinez Building Products Company using a job order cost system?

(b) On what basis does Martinez allocate its manufacturing overhead? Compute the predetermined overhead rate for 2014.

(c) Compute the amount of the under- or overapplied overhead for 2014.

(d) Martinez had balances in the beginning and ending work in process and finished goods accounts as follows.

	1/1/14	12/31/14
Work in process	$ 5,000,000	$ 4,000,000
Finished goods	13,000,000	11,000,000

Determine the (1) cost of goods manufactured and (2) cost of goods sold for Martinez during 2014. Assume that any under- or overapplied overhead should be included in the cost of goods sold.

(e) During 2014, Job G408 was started and completed. Its cost sheet showed a total cost of $100,000, and the company prices its product at 50% above its cost. What is the price to the customer if the company follows this pricing strategy?

Solution

(a) The company is using a job order cost system because it custom-makes garage doors. Each job has its own distinguishing characteristics. For example, each garage door would be different, and therefore a different cost per garage door can be assigned.

(b) The company allocates its overhead on the basis of direct labor cost. The predetermined overhead rate is 120%, computed as follows.

$$\$24,000,000 \div 20,000,000 = 120\%$$

(c)

Actual manufacturing overhead		$22,000,000
Applied overhead cost ($21,000,000 × 120%)		25,200,000
Overapplied overhead		$ 3,200,000

(d) (1)

Work in process, 1/1/14		$ 5,000,000
Direct materials used	$30,000,000	
Direct labor	21,000,000	
Manufacturing overhead applied	25,200,000	
Total manufacturing costs		76,200,000
Total cost of work in process		81,200,000
Less: Work in process, 12/31/14		4,000,000
Cost of goods manufactured		$77,200,000

(2)

Finished goods inventory, 1/1/14	$13,000,000	
Cost of goods manufactured (see above)	77,200,000	
Cost of goods available for sale	90,200,000	
Finished goods inventory, 12/31/14	11,000,000	
Cost of goods sold (unadjusted)	79,200,000	
Less: Overapplied overhead	3,200,000	
Cost of goods sold	$76,000,000	

(e)

G408 cost	$ 100,000	
Markup percentage	× 50%	
Profit	$ 50,000	

Price to customer: $150,000 ($100,000 + $50,000)

✔ **The Navigator**

SUMMARY OF LEARNING OBJECTIVES

✔ **The Navigator**

1 Explain the characteristics and purposes of cost accounting. Cost accounting involves the procedures for measuring, recording, and reporting product costs. From the data accumulated, companies determine the total cost and the unit cost of each product. The two basic types of cost accounting systems are job order cost and process cost.

2 Describe the flow of costs in a job order cost system. In job order costing, companies first accumulate manufacturing costs in three accounts: Raw Materials Inventory, Factory Labor, and Manufacturing Overhead. They then assign the accumulated costs to Work in Process Inventory and eventually to Finished Goods Inventory and Cost of Goods Sold.

3 Explain the nature and importance of a job cost sheet. A job cost sheet is a form used to record the costs chargeable to a specific job and to determine the total and unit costs of the completed job. Job cost sheets constitute the subsidiary ledger for the Work in Process Inventory control account.

4 Indicate how the predetermined overhead rate is determined and used. The predetermined overhead rate is based on the relationship between estimated annual overhead costs and expected annual operating activity. This is expressed in terms of a common activity base, such as direct labor cost. Companies use this rate to assign overhead costs to work in process and to specific jobs.

5 Prepare entries for jobs completed and sold. When jobs are completed, companies debit the cost to Finished Goods Inventory and credit it to Work in Process Inven-

tory. When a job is sold, the entries are (a) debit Cash or Accounts Receivable and credit Sales Revenue for the selling price; and (b) debit Cost of Goods Sold and credit Finished Goods Inventory for the cost of the goods.

6 Distinguish between under- and overapplied manufacturing overhead. Underapplied manufacturing overhead indicates that the overhead assigned to work in process is less than the overhead incurred. Overapplied overhead indicates that the overhead assigned to work in process is greater than the overhead incurred.

DECISION TOOLKIT A SUMMARY

DECISION CHECKPOINTS	INFO NEEDED FOR DECISION	TOOL TO USE FOR DECISION	HOW TO EVALUATE RESULTS
What is the cost of a job?	Cost of material, labor, and overhead assigned to a specific job	Job cost sheet	Compare costs to those of previous periods and to those of competitors to ensure that costs are in line. Compare costs to expected selling price or service fees charged to determine overall profitability.
Has the company over- or underapplied overhead for the period?	Actual overhead costs and overhead applied	Manufacturing Overhead account	If the account balance is a credit, overhead applied exceeded actual overhead costs. If the account balance is a debit, overhead applied was less than actual overhead costs.

GLOSSARY

Cost accounting An area of accounting that involves measuring, recording, and reporting product costs. (p. 50).

Cost accounting system Manufacturing-cost accounts that are fully integrated into the general ledger of a company. (p. 50).

Job cost sheet A form used to record the costs chargeable to a specific job and to determine the total and unit costs of the completed job. (p. 54).

Job order cost system A cost accounting system in which costs are assigned to each job or batch. (p. 50).

Materials requisition slip A document authorizing the issuance of raw materials from the storeroom to production. (p. 55).

Overapplied overhead A situation in which overhead assigned to work in process is greater than the overhead incurred. (p. 69).

Predetermined overhead rate A rate based on the relationship between estimated annual overhead costs and expected annual operating activity, expressed in terms of a common activity base. (p. 59).

Process cost system A cost accounting system used when a company manufactures a large volume of similar products. (p. 50).

Time ticket A document that indicates the employee, the hours worked, the account and job to be charged, and the total labor cost. (p. 57).

Underapplied overhead A situation in which overhead assigned to work in process is less than the overhead incurred. (p. 69).

Cardella Company applies overhead on the basis of direct labor costs. The company estimates annual overhead costs will be $760,000, and annual direct labor costs will be $950,000. During February, Cardella works on two jobs: A16 and B17. Summary data concerning these jobs are as follows.

Manufacturing Costs Incurred

Purchased $54,000 of raw materials on account.
Factory labor $76,000, plus $4,000 employer payroll taxes.
Manufacturing overhead exclusive of indirect materials and indirect labor $59,800.

Assignment of Costs

Direct materials:	Job A16 $27,000, Job B17 $21,000
Indirect materials:	$3,000
Direct labor:	Job A16 $52,000, Job B17 $26,000
Indirect labor:	$2,000

The company completed Job A16 and sold it on account for $150,000. Job B17 was only partially completed.

Instructions

(a) Compute the predetermined overhead rate.

(b) Journalize the February transactions in the sequence followed in the chapter.

(c) What was the amount of under- or overapplied manufacturing overhead?

Solution to Comprehensive DO IT!

Action Plan

✔ Predetermined overhead rate = Estimated annual overhead cost ÷ Expected annual operating activity.

✔ In accumulating costs, debit three accounts: Raw Materials Inventory, Factory Labor, and Manufacturing Overhead.

✔ When Work in Process Inventory is debited, credit one of the three accounts listed above.

✔ Debit Finished Goods Inventory for the cost of completed jobs. Debit Cost of Goods Sold for the cost of jobs sold.

✔ Overhead is underapplied when Manufacturing Overhead has a debit balance.

(a)
Estimated annual overhead costs	÷	Expected annual operating activity	=	Predetermined overhead rate
$760,000	÷	$950,000	=	80%

(b)

1.

Feb. 28	Raw Materials Inventory	54,000	
	Accounts Payable		54,000
	(Purchase of raw materials on account)		

2.

28	Factory Labor	80,000	
	Factory Wages Payable		76,000
	Employer Payroll Taxes Payable		4,000
	(To record factory labor costs)		

3.

28	Manufacturing Overhead	59,800	
	Accounts Payable, Accumulated Depreciation, and Prepaid Insurance		59,800
	(To record overhead costs)		

4.

28	Work in Process Inventory	48,000	
	Manufacturing Overhead	3,000	
	Raw Materials Inventory		51,000
	(To assign raw materials to production)		

5.

28	Work in Process Inventory	78,000	
	Manufacturing Overhead	2,000	
	Factory Labor		80,000
	(To assign factory labor to production)		

6.

28	Work in Process Inventory	62,400	
	Manufacturing Overhead		62,400
	(To assign overhead to jobs—		
	80% × $78,000)		

7.

28	Finished Goods Inventory	120,600	
	Work in Process Inventory		120,600
	(To record completion of Job A16: direct		
	materials $27,000, direct labor $52,000,		
	and manufacturing overhead $41,600)		

8.

28	Accounts Receivable	150,000	
	Sales Revenue		150,000
	(To record sale of Job A16)		
28	Cost of Goods Sold	120,600	
	Finished Goods Inventory		120,600
	(To record cost of sale for Job A16)		

(c) Manufacturing Overhead has a debit balance of $2,400 as shown below.

Manufacturing Overhead			
(3)	59,800	(6)	62,400
(4)	3,000		
(5)	2,000		
Bal.	2,400		

Thus, manufacturing overhead is underapplied for the month.

✔ **The Navigator**

 Self-Test, Brief Exercises, Exercises, Problem Set A, and many more resources are available for practice in WileyPLUS.

SELF-TEST QUESTIONS

Answers are at the end of the chapter.

(LO 1) **1.** Cost accounting involves the measuring, recording, and reporting of:
(a) product costs.
(b) future costs.
(c) manufacturing processes.
(d) managerial accounting decisions.

(LO 1) **2.** A company is more likely to use a job order cost system if:
(a) it manufactures a large volume of similar products.
(b) its production is continuous.
(c) it manufactures products with unique characteristics.
(d) it uses a periodic inventory system.

(LO 2) **3.** In accumulating raw materials costs, companies debit the cost of raw materials purchased in a perpetual system to:

(a) Raw Materials Purchases.
(b) Raw Materials Inventory.
(c) Purchases.
(d) Work in Process.

4. When incurred, factory labor costs are debited to: (LO 2)
(a) Work in Process.
(b) Factory Wages Expense.
(c) Factory Labor.
(d) Factory Wages Payable.

5. The flow of costs in job order costing: (LO 2)
(a) begins with work in process inventory and ends with finished goods inventory.
(b) begins as soon as a sale occurs.
(c) parallels the physical flow of materials as they are converted into finished goods.
(d) is necessary to prepare the cost of goods manufactured schedule.

(LO 3) **6.** Raw materials are assigned to a job when:
  (a) the job is sold.
  (b) the materials are purchased.
  (c) the materials are received from the vendor.
  (d) the materials are issued by the materials storeroom.

(LO 3) **7.** The source documents for assigning costs to job cost sheets are:
  (a) invoices, time tickets, and the predetermined overhead rate.
  (b) materials requisition slips, time tickets, and the actual overhead costs.
  (c) materials requisition slips, payroll register, and the predetermined overhead rate.
  (d) materials requisition slips, time tickets, and the predetermined overhead rate.

(LO 3) **8.** In recording the issuance of raw materials in a job order cost system, it would be *incorrect* to:
  (a) debit Work in Process Inventory.
  (b) debit Finished Goods Inventory.
  (c) debit Manufacturing Overhead.
  (d) credit Raw Materials Inventory.

(LO 3) **9.** The entry when direct factory labor is assigned to jobs is a debit to:
  (a) Work in Process Inventory and a credit to Factory Labor.
  (b) Manufacturing Overhead and a credit to Factory Labor.
  (c) Factory Labor and a credit to Manufacturing Overhead.
  (d) Factory Labor and a credit to Work in Process Inventory.

(LO 4) **10.** The formula for computing the predetermined manufacturing overhead rate is estimated annual overhead costs divided by an expected annual operating activity, expressed as:
  (a) direct labor cost.   (c) machine hours.
  (b) direct labor hours.   (d) Any of the above.

(LO 4) **11.** In Crawford Company, the predetermined overhead rate is 80% of direct labor cost. During the month, Crawford incurs $210,000 of factory labor costs, of which $180,000 is direct labor and $30,000 is indirect labor. Actual overhead incurred was $200,000. The amount of overhead debited to Work in Process Inventory should be:
  (a) $200,000.   (c) $168,000.
  (b) $144,000.   (d) $160,000.

(LO 5) **12.** Mynex Company completes Job No. 26 at a cost of $4,500 and later sells it for $7,000 cash. A *correct* entry is:

  (a) debit Finished Goods Inventory $7,000 and credit Work in Process Inventory $7,000.
  (b) debit Cost of Goods Sold $7,000 and credit Finished Goods Inventory $7,000.
  (c) debit Finished Goods Inventory $4,500 and credit Work in Process Inventory $4,500.
  (d) debit Accounts Receivable $7,000 and credit Sales Revenue $7,000.

13. At the end of an accounting period, a company using (LO 5) a job order cost system calculates the cost of goods manufactured:
  (a) from the job cost sheet.
  (b) from the Work in Process Inventory account.
  (c) by adding direct materials used, direct labor incurred, and manufacturing overhead incurred.
  (d) from the Cost of Goods Sold account.

14. Which of the following statements is *true*?   (LO 5)
  (a) Job order costing requires less data entry than process costing.
  (b) Allocation of overhead is easier under job order costing than process costing.
  (c) Job order costing provides more precise costing for custom jobs than process costing.
  (d) The use of job order costing has declined because more companies have adopted automated accounting systems.

15. At end of the year, a company has a $1,200 debit bal- (LO 6) ance in Manufacturing Overhead. The company:
  (a) makes an adjusting entry by debiting Manufacturing Overhead Applied for $1,200 and crediting Manufacturing Overhead for $1,200.
  (b) makes an adjusting entry by debiting Manufacturing Overhead Expense for $1,200 and crediting Manufacturing Overhead for $1,200.
  (c) makes an adjusting entry by debiting Cost of Goods Sold for $1,200 and crediting Manufacturing Overhead for $1,200.
  (d) makes no adjusting entry because differences between actual overhead and the amount applied are a normal part of job order costing and will average out over the next year.

16. Manufacturing overhead is underapplied if: (LO 6)
  (a) actual overhead is less than applied.
  (b) actual overhead is greater than applied.
  (c) the predetermined rate equals the actual rate.
  (d) actual overhead equals applied overhead.

Go to the book's companion website, www.wiley.com/college/weygandt, for additional Self-Test Questions.

✔ **The Navigator**

QUESTIONS

1. (a) Mary Barett is not sure about the difference between cost accounting and a cost accounting system. Explain the difference to Mary.
  (b) What is an important feature of a cost accounting system?
2. (a) Distinguish between the two types of cost accounting systems.

  (b) Can a company use both types of cost accounting systems?
3. What type of industry is likely to use a job order cost system? Give some examples.
4. What type of industry is likely to use a process cost system? Give some examples.

5. Your roommate asks your help in understanding the major steps in the flow of costs in a job order cost system. Identify the steps for your roommate.

6. There are three inventory control accounts in a job order system. Identify the control accounts and their subsidiary ledgers.

7. What source documents are used in accumulating direct labor costs?

8. "Entries to Manufacturing Overhead normally are only made daily." Do you agree? Explain.

9. Stan Kaiser is confused about the source documents used in assigning materials and labor costs. Identify the documents and give the entry for each document.

10. What is the purpose of a job cost sheet?

11. Indicate the source documents that are used in charging costs to specific jobs.

12. Explain the purpose and use of a "materials requisition slip" as used in a job order cost system.

13. Sam Bowden believes actual manufacturing overhead should be charged to jobs. Do you agree? Why or why not?

14. What elements are involved in computing a predetermined overhead rate?

15. How can the agreement of Work in Process Inventory and job cost sheets be verified?

16. Jane Neff believes that the cost of goods manufactured schedule in job order cost accounting is the same as shown in Chapter 1. Is Jane correct? Explain.

17. Matt Litkee is confused about under- and overapplied manufacturing overhead. Define the terms for Matt, and indicate the balance in the manufacturing overhead account applicable to each term.

18. "At the end of the year, under- or overapplied overhead is closed to Income Summary." Is this correct? If not, indicate the customary treatment of this amount.

BRIEF EXERCISES

Prepare a flowchart of a job order cost accounting system, and identify transactions.

(LO 2), C

BE2-1 Knox Company begins operations on January 1. Because all work is done to customer specifications, the company decides to use a job order cost system. Prepare a flowchart of a typical job order system with arrows showing the flow of costs. Identify the eight transactions.

Prepare entries in accumulating manufacturing costs.

(LO 2), AP

BE2-2 During January, its first month of operations, Knox Company accumulated the following manufacturing costs: raw materials $4,000 on account, factory labor $6,000 of which $5,200 relates to factory wages payable and $800 relates to payroll taxes payable, and utilities payable $2,000. Prepare separate journal entries for each type of manufacturing cost.

Prepare entry for the assignment of raw materials costs.

(LO 3), AP

BE2-3 In January, Knox Company requisitions raw materials for production as follows: Job 1 $900, Job 2 $1,400, Job 3 $700, and general factory use $600. Prepare a summary journal entry to record raw materials used.

Prepare entry for the assignment of factory labor costs.

(LO 3), AP

BE2-4 Factory labor data for Knox Company is given in BE2-2. During January, time tickets show that the factory labor of $6,000 was used as follows: Job 1 $2,200, Job 2 $1,600, Job 3 $1,400, and general factory use $800. Prepare a summary journal entry to record factory labor used.

Prepare job cost sheets.

(LO 3), AP

BE2-5 Data pertaining to job cost sheets for Knox Company are given in BE2-3 and BE2-4. Prepare the job cost sheets for each of the three jobs. (*Note:* You may omit the column for Manufacturing Overhead.)

Compute predetermined overhead rates.

(LO 4), AP

BE2-6 Marquis Company estimates that annual manufacturing overhead costs will be $900,000. Estimated annual operating activity bases are direct labor cost $500,000, direct labor hours 50,000, and machine hours 100,000. Compute the predetermined overhead rate for each activity base.

Assign manufacturing overhead to production.

(LO 4), AP

BE2-7 During the first quarter, Roland Company incurs the following direct labor costs: January $40,000, February $30,000, and March $50,000. For each month, prepare the entry to assign overhead to production using a predetermined rate of 80% of direct labor cost.

Prepare entries for completion and sale of completed jobs.

(LO 5), AP

BE2-8 In March, Stinson Company completes Jobs 10 and 11. Job 10 cost $20,000 and Job 11 $30,000. On March 31, Job 10 is sold to the customer for $35,000 in cash. Journalize the entries for the completion of the two jobs and the sale of Job 10.

Prepare entries for service salaries and wages and operating overhead.

(LO 5), AP

BE2-9 Preprah Engineering Contractors incurred service salaries and wages of $32,000 ($24,000 direct and $8,000 indirect) on an engineering project. The company applies overhead at a rate of 25% of direct labor. Record the entries to assign service salaries and wages and to apply overhead.

Prepare adjusting entries for under- and overapplied overhead.

(LO 6), C

BE2-10 At December 31, balances in Manufacturing Overhead are Shimeca Company—debit $1,200, Garcia Company—credit $900. Prepare the adjusting entry for each company at December 31, assuming the adjustment is made to cost of goods sold.

> DO IT! REVIEW

DO IT! 2-1 During the current month, Tomlin Company incurs the following manufacturing costs.

(a) Purchased raw materials of $16,000 on account.
(b) Incurred factory labor of $40,000. Of that amount, $31,000 relates to wages payable and $9,000 relates to payroll taxes payable.
(c) Factory utilities of $3,100 are payable, prepaid factory property taxes of $2,400 have expired, and depreciation on the factory building is $9,500.

Prepare journal entries for each type of manufacturing cost. (Use a summary entry to record manufacturing overhead.)

Prepare journal entries for manufacturing costs.
(LO 2), AP

DO IT! 2-2 Milner Company is working on two job orders. The job cost sheets show the following.

	Job 201	**Job 202**
Direct materials	$7,200	$9,000
Direct labor	4,000	8,000
Manufacturing overhead	5,200	9,800

Prepare the three summary entries to record the assignment of costs to Work in Process from the data on the job cost sheets.

Assign costs to work in process.
(LO 3, 4), AP

DO IT! 2-3 During the current month, Reyes Corporation completed Job 310 and Job 312. Job 310 cost $60,000 and Job 312 cost $50,000. Job 312 was sold on account for $90,000. Journalize the entries for the completion of the two jobs and the sale of Job 312.

Prepare entries for completion and sale of jobs.
(LO 5), AP

DO IT! 2-4 For Eckstein Company, the predetermined overhead rate is 130% of direct labor cost. During the month, Eckstein incurred $100,000 of factory labor costs, of which $85,000 is direct labor and $15,000 is indirect labor. Actual overhead incurred was $115,000. Compute the amount of manufacturing overhead applied during the month. Determine the amount of under- or overapplied manufacturing overhead.

Apply manufacturing overhead and determine under- or overapplication.
(LO 6), AN

✔ **The Navigator**

EXERCISES

E2-1 The gross earnings of the factory workers for Vargas Company during the month of January are $66,000. The employer's payroll taxes for the factory payroll are $8,000. The fringe benefits to be paid by the employer on this payroll are $6,000. Of the total accumulated cost of factory labor, 85% is related to direct labor and 15% is attributable to indirect labor.

Prepare entries for factory labor.
(LO 2, 3), AP

Instructions
(a) Prepare the entry to record the factory labor costs for the month of January.
(b) Prepare the entry to assign factory labor to production.

E2-2 Stine Company uses a job order cost system. On May 1, the company has a balance in Work in Process Inventory of $3,500 and two jobs in process: Job No. 429 $2,000, and Job No. 430 $1,500. During May, a summary of source documents reveals the following.

Prepare journal entries for manufacturing costs.
(LO 2, 3, 4, 5), AP

Job Number	Materials Requisition Slips		Labor Time Tickets	
429	$2,500		$1,900	
430	3,500		3,000	
431	4,400	$10,400	7,600	$12,500
General use		800		1,200
		$11,200		$13,700

Stine Company applies manufacturing overhead to jobs at an overhead rate of 60% of direct labor cost. Job No. 429 is completed during the month.

Instructions

(a) Prepare summary journal entries to record (i) the requisition slips, (ii) the time tickets, (iii) the assignment of manufacturing overhead to jobs, and (iv) the completion of Job No. 429.

(b) Post the entries to Work in Process Inventory, and prove the agreement of the control account with the job cost sheets. (Use a T-account.)

Analyze a job cost sheet and prepare entries for manufacturing costs.

(LO 2, 3, 4, 5), AP

E2-3 A job order cost sheet for Lowry Company is shown below.

Job No. 92			For 2,000 Units
Date	Direct Materials	Direct Labor	Manufacturing Overhead
Beg. bal. Jan. 1	5,000	6,000	5,100
8	6,000		
12		8,000	6,400
25	2,000		
27		4,000	3,200
	13,000	18,000	14,700

Cost of completed job:	
Direct materials	$13,000
Direct labor	18,000
Manufacturing overhead	14,700
Total cost	$45,700
Unit cost ($45,700 ÷ 2,000)	$22.85

Instructions

(a) ▭▭▭▷ On the basis of the foregoing data, answer the following questions.

(1) What was the balance in Work in Process Inventory on January 1 if this was the only unfinished job?

(2) If manufacturing overhead is applied on the basis of direct labor cost, what overhead rate was used in each year?

(b) Prepare summary entries at January 31 to record the current year's transactions pertaining to Job No. 92.

Analyze costs of manufacturing and determine missing amounts.

(LO 2, 6), AN

E2-4 Manufacturing cost data for Orlando Company, which uses a job order cost system, are presented below.

	Case A	Case B	Case C
Direct materials used	$ (a)	$ 83,000	$ 63,150
Direct labor	50,000	140,000	(h)
Manufacturing overhead applied	42,500	(d)	(i)
Total manufacturing costs	145,650	(e)	213,000
Work in process 1/1/14	(b)	15,500	18,000
Total cost of work in process	201,500	(f)	(j)
Work in process 12/31/14	(c)	11,800	(k)
Cost of goods manufactured	192,300	(g)	222,000

Instructions

Indicate the missing amount for each letter. Assume that in all cases manufacturing overhead is applied on the basis of direct labor cost and the rate is the same.

Compute the manufacturing overhead rate and under- or overapplied overhead.

(LO 4, 6), AN

XLS

E2-5 Duggan Company applies manufacturing overhead to jobs on the basis of machine hours used. Overhead costs are expected to total $325,000 for the year, and machine usage is estimated at 125,000 hours.

For the year, $342,000 of overhead costs are incurred and 130,000 hours are used.

Instructions
(a) Compute the manufacturing overhead rate for the year.
(b) What is the amount of under- or overapplied overhead at December 31?
(c) Prepare the adjusting entry to assign the under- or overapplied overhead for the year to cost of goods sold.

E2-6 A job cost sheet of Sandoval Company is given below.

Analyze job cost sheet and prepare entry for completed job.

(LO 2, 3, 4, 5), AP

Job Cost Sheet			
JOB NO. 469		Quantity 2,500	
ITEM White Lion Cages		Date Requested 7/2	
FOR Todd Company		Date Completed 7/31	
Date	Direct Materials	Direct Labor	Manufacturing Overhead
7/10	700		
12	900		
15		440	550
22		380	475
24	1,600		
27	1,500		
31		540	675

Cost of completed job:	
Direct materials	_____
Direct labor	_____
Manufacturing overhead	_____
Total cost	_____
Unit cost	_____

Instructions
(a) ▭▭▭▶ Answer the following questions.
  (1)   What are the source documents for direct materials, direct labor, and manufacturing overhead costs assigned to this job?
  (2)   What is the predetermined manufacturing overhead rate?
  (3)   What are the total cost and the unit cost of the completed job? (Round unit cost to nearest cent.)
(b) Prepare the entry to record the completion of the job.

E2-7 Torre Corporation incurred the following transactions.

1. Purchased raw materials on account $46,300.
2. Raw materials of $36,000 were requisitioned to the factory. An analysis of the materials requisition slips indicated that $6,800 was classified as indirect materials.
3. Factory labor costs incurred were $55,900, of which $51,000 pertained to factory wages payable and $4,900 pertained to employer payroll taxes payable.
4. Time tickets indicated that $50,000 was direct labor and $5,900 was indirect labor.
5. Manufacturing overhead costs incurred on account were $80,500.
6. Depreciation on the company's office building was $8,100.
7. Manufacturing overhead was applied at the rate of 150% of direct labor cost.
8. Goods costing $88,000 were completed and transferred to finished goods.
9. Finished goods costing $75,000 to manufacture were sold on account for $103,000.

Prepare entries for manufacturing and nonmanufacturing costs.

(LO 2, 3, 4, 5), AP

Instructions
Journalize the transactions. (Omit explanations.)

E2-8 Enos Printing Corp. uses a job order cost system. The following data summarize the operations related to the first quarter's production.

Prepare entries for manufacturing and nonmanufacturing costs.

(LO 2, 3, 4, 5), AP

1. Materials purchased on account $192,000, and factory wages incurred $87,300.
2. Materials requisitioned and factory labor used by job:

Job Number	Materials	Factory Labor
A20	$ 35,240	$18,000
A21	42,920	22,000
A22	36,100	15,000
A23	39,270	25,000
General factory use	4,470	7,300
	$158,000	$87,300

3. Manufacturing overhead costs incurred on account $49,500.
4. Depreciation on factory equipment $14,550.
5. Depreciation on the company's office building was $14,300.
6. Manufacturing overhead rate is 90% of direct labor cost.
7. Jobs completed during the quarter: A20, A21, and A23.

Instructions
Prepare entries to record the operations summarized above. (Prepare a schedule showing the individual cost elements and total cost for each job in item 7.)

Prepare a cost of goods manufactured schedule and partial financial statements.

(LO 2, 5), AP

E2-9 At May 31, 2014, the accounts of Mantle Company show the following.

1. May 1 inventories—finished goods $12,600, work in process $14,700, and raw materials $8,200.
2. May 31 inventories—finished goods $9,500, work in process $17,900, and raw materials $7,100.
3. Debit postings to work in process were direct materials $62,400, direct labor $50,000, and manufacturing overhead applied $40,000.
4. Sales revenue totaled $210,000.

Instructions
(a) Prepare a condensed cost of goods manufactured schedule.
(b) Prepare an income statement for May through gross profit.
(c) Indicate the balance sheet presentation of the manufacturing inventories at May 31, 2014.

Compute work in process and finished goods from job cost sheets.

(LO 3, 5), AP

E2-10 Tierney Company begins operations on April 1. Information from job cost sheets shows the following.

Job Number	Manufacturing Costs Assigned			Month Completed
	April	May	June	
10	$5,200	$4,400		May
11	4,100	3,900	$2,000	June
12	1,200			April
13		4,700	4,500	June
14		5,900	3,600	Not complete

Job 12 was completed in April. Job 10 was completed in May. Jobs 11 and 13 were completed in June. Each job was sold for 25% above its cost in the month following completion.

Instructions
(a) What is the balance in Work in Process Inventory at the end of each month?
(b) What is the balance in Finished Goods Inventory at the end of each month?
(c) What is the gross profit for May, June, and July?

Prepare entries for costs of services provided.

(LO 2, 4, 5), AP

E2-11 Shown below are the job cost related accounts for the law firm of Jack, Bob, and Will and their manufacturing equivalents:

Law Firm Accounts	Manufacturing Firm Accounts
Supplies	Raw Materials
Salaries and Wages Payable	Factory Wages Payable
Operating Overhead	Manufacturing Overhead
Service Contracts in Process	Work in Process
Cost of Completed Service Contracts	Cost of Goods Sold

Cost data for the month of March follow.

1. Purchased supplies on account $1,500.
2. Issued supplies $1,200 (60% direct and 40% indirect).
3. Assigned labor costs based on time cards for the month which indicated labor costs of $60,000 (80% direct and 20% indirect).
4. Operating overhead costs incurred for cash totaled $40,000.
5. Operating overhead is applied at a rate of 90% of direct attorney cost.
6. Work completed totaled $75,000.

Instructions
(a) Journalize the transactions for March. (Omit explanations.)
(b) Determine the balance of the Service Contracts in Process account. (Use a T-account.)

E2-12 Don Lieberman and Associates, a CPA firm, uses job order costing to capture the costs of its audit jobs. There were no audit jobs in process at the beginning of November. Listed below are data concerning the three audit jobs conducted during November.

Determine cost of jobs and ending balance in work in process and overhead accounts.

(LO 3, 4, 6), AP

	Lynn	Brian	Mike
Direct materials	$600	$400	$200
Auditor labor costs	$5,400	$6,600	$3,375
Auditor hours	72	88	45

Overhead costs are applied to jobs on the basis of auditor hours, and the predetermined overhead rate is $50 per auditor hour. The Lynn job is the only incomplete job at the end of November. Actual overhead for the month was $11,000.

Instructions
(a) Determine the cost of each job.
(b) Indicate the balance of the Service Contracts in Process account at the end of November.
(c) Calculate the ending balance of the Operating Overhead account for November.

E2-13 Pure Decorating uses a job order cost system to collect the costs of its interior decorating business. Each client's consultation is treated as a separate job. Overhead is applied to each job based on the number of decorator hours incurred. Listed below are data for the current year.

Determine predetermined overhead rate, apply overhead and determine whether balance under- or overapplied

(LO 4, 6), AP

Estimated overhead	$920,000
Actual overhead	$942,800
Estimated decorator hours	40,000
Actual decorator hours	40,500

The company uses Operating Overhead in place of Manufacturing Overhead.

Instructions
(a) Compute the predetermined overhead rate.
(b) Prepare the entry to apply the overhead for the year.
(c) Determine whether the overhead was under- or overapplied and by how much.

EXERCISES: SET B AND CHALLENGE EXERCISES

Visit the book's companion website, at **www.wiley.com/college/weygandt**, and choose the Student Companion site to access Exercise Set B and Challenge Exercises.

PROBLEMS: SET A

P2-1A Degelman Company uses a job order cost system and applies overhead to production on the basis of direct labor costs. On January 1, 2014, Job No. 50 was the only job in process. The costs incurred prior to January 1 on this job were as follows: direct materials

Prepare entries in a job order cost system and job cost sheets.

(LO 2, 3, 4, 5, 6), AP

$20,000, direct labor $12,000, and manufacturing overhead $16,000. As of January 1, Job No. 49 had been completed at a cost of $90,000 and was part of finished goods inventory. There was a $15,000 balance in the Raw Materials Inventory account.

During the month of January, Degelman Company began production on Jobs 51 and 52, and completed Jobs 50 and 51. Jobs 49 and 50 were also sold on account during the month for $122,000 and $158,000, respectively. The following additional events occurred during the month.

1. Purchased additional raw materials of $90,000 on account.
2. Incurred factory labor costs of $70,000. Of this amount $16,000 related to employer payroll taxes.
3. Incurred manufacturing overhead costs as follows: indirect materials $17,000; indirect labor $20,000; depreciation expense on equipment $19,000; and various other manufacturing overhead costs on account $16,000.
4. Assigned direct materials and direct labor to jobs as follows.

Job No.	Direct Materials	Direct Labor
50	$10,000	$ 5,000
51	39,000	25,000
52	30,000	20,000

Instructions
(a) Calculate the predetermined overhead rate for 2014, assuming Degelman Company estimates total manufacturing overhead costs of $980,000, direct labor costs of $700,000, and direct labor hours of 20,000 for the year.
(b) Open job cost sheets for Jobs 50, 51, and 52. Enter the January 1 balances on the job cost sheet for Job No. 50.
(c) Prepare the journal entries to record the purchase of raw materials, the factory labor costs incurred, and the manufacturing overhead costs incurred during the month of January.
(d) Prepare the journal entries to record the assignment of direct materials, direct labor, and manufacturing overhead costs to production. In assigning manufacturing overhead costs, use the overhead rate calculated in (a). Post all costs to the job cost sheets as necessary.

(e) Job 50, $70,000
Job 51, $99,000

(e) Total the job cost sheets for any job(s) completed during the month. Prepare the journal entry (or entries) to record the completion of any job(s) during the month.
(f) Prepare the journal entry (or entries) to record the sale of any job(s) during the month.
(g) What is the balance in the Finished Goods Inventory account at the end of the month? What does this balance consist of?
(h) What is the amount of over- or underapplied overhead?

Prepare entries in a job order cost system and partial income statement.

(LO 2, 3, 4, 5, 6), AN

P2-2A For the year ended December 31, 2014, the job cost sheets of Cinta Company contained the following data.

Job Number	Explanation	Direct Materials	Direct Labor	Manufacturing Overhead	Total Costs
7640	Balance 1/1	$25,000	$24,000	$28,800	$ 77,800
	Current year's costs	30,000	36,000	43,200	109,200
7641	Balance 1/1	11,000	18,000	21,600	50,600
	Current year's costs	43,000	48,000	57,600	148,600
7642	Current year's costs	58,000	55,000	66,000	179,000

Other data:

1. Raw materials inventory totaled $15,000 on January 1. During the year, $140,000 of raw materials were purchased on account.
2. Finished goods on January 1 consisted of Job No. 7638 for $87,000 and Job No. 7639 for $92,000.
3. Job No. 7640 and Job No. 7641 were completed during the year.
4. Job Nos. 7638, 7639, and 7641 were sold on account for $530,000.

5. Manufacturing overhead incurred on account totaled $120,000.
6. Other manufacturing overhead consisted of indirect materials $14,000, indirect labor $18,000, and depreciation on factory machinery $8,000.

Instructions

(a) Prove the agreement of Work in Process Inventory with job cost sheets pertaining to unfinished work. (*Hint:* Use a single T-account for Work in Process Inventory.) Calculate each of the following, then post each to the T-account: (1) beginning balance, (2) direct materials, (3) direct labor, (4) manufacturing overhead, and (5) completed jobs.

(b) Prepare the adjusting entry for manufacturing overhead, assuming the balance is allocated entirely to Cost of Goods Sold.

(c) Determine the gross profit to be reported for 2014.

(a) $179,000; Job 7642: $179,000

(b) Amount = $6,800

(c) $158,600

P2-3A Stellar Inc. is a construction company specializing in custom patios. The patios are constructed of concrete, brick, fiberglass, and lumber, depending upon customer preference. On June 1, 2014, the general ledger for Stellar Inc. contains the following data.

Prepare entries in a job order cost system and cost of goods manufactured schedule.

(LO 2, 3, 4, 5), AP

Raw Materials Inventory	$4,200	Manufacturing Overhead Applied	$32,640
Work in Process Inventory	$5,540	Manufacturing Overhead Incurred	$31,650

Subsidiary data for Work in Process Inventory on June 1 are as follows.

Job Cost Sheets

	Customer Job		
Cost Element	**Gannon**	**Rosenthal**	**Linton**
Direct materials	$ 600	$ 800	$ 900
Direct labor	320	540	580
Manufacturing overhead	400	675	725
	$1,320	$2,015	$2,205

During June, raw materials purchased on account were $4,900, and all wages were paid. Additional overhead costs consisted of depreciation on equipment $700 and miscellaneous costs of $400 incurred on account.

A summary of materials requisition slips and time tickets for June shows the following.

Customer Job	**Materials Requisition Slips**	**Time Tickets**
Gannon	$ 800	$ 450
Koss	2,000	800
Rosenthal	500	360
Linton	1,300	1,200
Gannon	300	390
	4,900	3,200
General use	1,500	1,200
	$6,400	$4,400

Overhead was charged to jobs at the same rate of $1.25 per dollar of direct labor cost. The patios for customers Gannon, Rosenthal, and Linton were completed during June and sold for a total of $18,900. Each customer paid in full.

Instructions

(a) Journalize the June transactions: (i) for purchase of raw materials, factory labor costs incurred, and manufacturing overhead costs incurred; (ii) assignment of direct materials, labor, and overhead to production; and (iii) completion of jobs and sale of goods.

(b) Post the entries to Work in Process Inventory.

(c) Reconcile the balance in Work in Process Inventory with the costs of unfinished jobs.

(d) Prepare a cost of goods manufactured schedule for June.

(d) Cost of goods manufactured $13,840

Compute predetermined over-head rates, apply overhead, and calculate under- or overapplied overhead.

(LO 4, 6), AP

P2-4A Agassi Company uses a job order cost system in each of its three manufacturing departments. Manufacturing overhead is applied to jobs on the basis of direct labor cost in Department D, direct labor hours in Department E, and machine hours in Department K.

In establishing the predetermined overhead rates for 2014, the following estimates were made for the year.

	Department		
	D	**E**	**K**
Manufacturing overhead	$1,200,000	$1,500,000	$900,000
Direct labor costs	$1,500,000	$1,250,000	$450,000
Direct labor hours	100,000	125,000	40,000
Machine hours	400,000	500,000	120,000

During January, the job cost sheets showed the following costs and production data.

	Department		
	D	**E**	**K**
Direct materials used	$140,000	$126,000	$78,000
Direct labor costs	$120,000	$110,000	$37,500
Manufacturing overhead incurred	$ 99,000	$124,000	$79,000
Direct labor hours	8,000	11,000	3,500
Machine hours	34,000	45,000	10,400

(a) 80%, $12, $7.50
(b) $356,000, $368,000, $193,500
(c) $3,000, $(8,000), $1,000

Instructions
(a) Compute the predetermined overhead rate for each department.
(b) Compute the total manufacturing costs assigned to jobs in January in each department.
(c) Compute the under- or overapplied overhead for each department at January 31.

Analyze manufacturing accounts and determine missing amounts.

(LO 2, 3, 4, 5, 6), AN

P2-5A Rodman Corporation's fiscal year ends on November 30. The following accounts are found in its job order cost accounting system for the first month of the new fiscal year.

Raw Materials Inventory

Dec. 1	Beginning balance	(a)	Dec. 31	Requisitions	16,850
31	Purchases	19,225			
Dec. 31	Ending balance	7,975			

Work in Process Inventory

Dec. 1	Beginning balance	(b)	Dec. 31	Jobs completed	(f)
31	Direct materials	(c)			
31	Direct labor	8,800			
31	Overhead	(d)			
Dec. 31	Ending balance	(e)			

Finished Goods Inventory

Dec. 1	Beginning balance	(g)	Dec. 31	Cost of goods sold	(i)
31	Completed jobs	(h)			
Dec. 31	Ending balance	(j)			

Factory Labor

Dec. 31	Factory wages	12,025	Dec. 31	Wages assigned	(k)

Manufacturing Overhead

Dec. 31	Indirect materials	1,900	Dec. 31	Overhead applied	(m)
31	Indirect labor	(l)			
31	Other overhead	1,245			

Other data:
1. On December 1, two jobs were in process: Job No. 154 and Job No. 155. These jobs had combined direct materials costs of $9,750 and direct labor costs of $15,000. Overhead was applied at a rate that was 75% of direct labor cost.

2. During December, Job Nos. 156, 157, and 158 were started. On December 31, Job No. 158 was unfinished. This job had charges for direct materials $3,800 and direct labor $4,800, plus manufacturing overhead. All jobs, except for Job No. 158, were completed in December.
3. On December 1, Job No. 153 was in the finished goods warehouse. It had a total cost of $5,000. On December 31, Job No. 157 was the only job finished that was not sold. It had a cost of $4,000.
4. Manufacturing overhead was $230 overapplied in December.

Instructions

List the letters (a) through (m) and indicate the amount pertaining to each letter.

(c) $14,950
(f) $54,150
(i) $55,150

PROBLEMS: SET B

P2-1B Pedriani Company uses a job order cost system and applies overhead to production on the basis of direct labor hours. On January 1, 2014, Job No. 25 was the only job in process. The costs incurred prior to January 1 on this job were as follows: direct materials $10,000; direct labor $6,000; and manufacturing overhead $9,000. Job No. 23 had been completed at a cost of $42,000 and was part of finished goods inventory. There was a $5,000 balance in the Raw Materials Inventory account.

Prepare entries in a job order cost system and job cost sheets.

(LO 2, 3, 4, 5, 6), AP

During the month of January, the company began production on Jobs 26 and 27, and completed Jobs 25 and 26. Jobs 23 and 25 were sold on account during the month for $63,000 and $74,000, respectively. The following additional events occurred during the month.

1. Purchased additional raw materials of $45,000 on account.
2. Incurred factory labor costs of $33,500. Of this amount, $7,500 related to employer payroll taxes.
3. Incurred manufacturing overhead costs as follows: indirect materials $10,000; indirect labor $9,500; depreciation expense on equipment $12,000; and various other manufacturing overhead costs on account $11,000.
4. Assigned direct materials and direct labor to jobs as follows.

Job No.	Direct Materials	Direct Labor
25	$ 5,000	$ 3,000
26	17,000	12,000
27	13,000	9,000

5. The company uses direct labor hours as the activity base to assign overhead. Direct labor hours incurred on each job were as follows: Job No. 25, 200; Job No. 26, 800; and Job No. 27, 600.

Instructions

(a) Calculate the predetermined overhead rate for the year 2014, assuming Pedriani Company estimates total manufacturing overhead costs of $440,000, direct labor costs of $300,000, and direct labor hours of 20,000 for the year.
(b) Open job cost sheets for Jobs 25, 26, and 27. Enter the January 1 balances on the job cost sheet for Job No. 25.
(c) Prepare the journal entries to record the purchase of raw materials, the factory labor costs incurred, and the manufacturing overhead costs incurred during the month of January.
(d) Prepare the journal entries to record the assignment of direct materials, direct labor, and manufacturing overhead costs to production. In assigning manufacturing overhead costs, use the overhead rate calculated in (a). Post all costs to the job cost sheets as necessary.
(e) Total the job cost sheets for any job(s) completed during the month. Prepare the journal entry (or entries) to record the completion of any job(s) during the month.
(f) Prepare the journal entry (or entries) to record the sale of any job(s) during the month.
(g) What is the balance in the Work in Process Inventory account at the end of the month? What does this balance consist of?
(h) What is the amount of over- or underapplied overhead?

(e) Job 25, $37,400
    Job 26, $46,600

Prepare entries in a job order cost system and partial income statement.

(LO 2, 3, 4, 5, 6), AN

P2-2B For the year ended December 31, 2014, the job cost sheets of Dosey Company contained the following data.

Job Number	Explanation	Direct Materials	Direct Labor	Manufacturing Overhead	Total Costs
7650	Balance 1/1	$18,000	$20,000	$25,000	$ 63,000
	Current year's costs	32,000	36,000	45,000	113,000
7651	Balance 1/1	12,000	16,000	20,000	48,000
	Current year's costs	30,000	40,000	50,000	120,000
7652	Current year's costs	35,000	68,000	85,000	188,000

Other data:

1. Raw materials inventory totaled $20,000 on January 1. During the year, $100,000 of raw materials were purchased on account.
2. Finished goods on January 1 consisted of Job No. 7648 for $93,000 and Job No. 7649 for $62,000.
3. Job No. 7650 and Job No. 7651 were completed during the year.
4. Job Nos. 7648, 7649, and 7650 were sold on account for $490,000.
5. Manufacturing overhead incurred on account totaled $135,000.
6. Other manufacturing overhead consisted of indirect materials $12,000, indirect labor $16,000, and depreciation on factory machinery $19,500.

Instructions

(a) Prove the agreement of Work in Process Inventory with job cost sheets pertaining to unfinished work. (*Hint:* Use a single T-account for Work in Process Inventory.) Calculate each of the following, then post each to the T-account: (1) beginning balance, (2) direct materials, (3) direct labor, (4) manufacturing overhead, and (5) completed jobs.

(b) Prepare the adjusting entry for manufacturing overhead, assuming the balance is allocated entirely to cost of goods sold.

(c) Determine the gross profit to be reported for 2014.

(a) (1) $111,000
    (4) $180,000
    Unfinished job 7652,
    $188,000
(b) Amount = $2,500

(c) $156,500

Prepare entries in a job order cost system and cost of goods manufactured schedule.

(LO 2, 3, 4, 5), AP

P2-3B Robert Perez is a contractor specializing in custom-built jacuzzis. On May 1, 2014, his ledger contains the following data.

Raw Materials Inventory	$30,000
Work in Process Inventory	12,200
Manufacturing Overhead	2,500 (dr.)

The Manufacturing Overhead account has debit totals of $12,500 and credit totals of $10,000. Subsidiary data for Work in Process Inventory on May 1 include:

Job Cost Sheets

Job by Customer	Direct Materials	Direct Labor	Manufacturing Overhead
Stiner	$2,500	$2,000	$1,400
Alton	2,000	1,200	840
Herman	900	800	560
	$5,400	$4,000	$2,800

During May, the following costs were incurred: raw materials purchased on account $4,000, labor paid $7,000, and manufacturing overhead paid $1,400.

A summary of materials requisition slips and time tickets for the month of May reveals the following.

Job by Customer	Materials Requisition Slips	Time Tickets
Stiner	$ 500	$ 400
Alton	600	1,000
Herman	2,300	1,300
Smith	1,900	2,300
	5,300	5,000
General use	1,500	2,000
	$6,800	$7,000

Overhead was charged to jobs on the basis of $0.70 per dollar of direct labor cost. The jacuzzis for customers Stiner, Alton, and Herman were completed during May. The three jacuzzis were sold for a total of $36,000.

Instructions
(a) Prepare journal entries for the May transactions: (i) for purchase of raw materials, factory labor costs incurred, and manufacturing overhead costs incurred; (ii) assignment of raw materials, labor, and overhead to production; and (iii) completion of jobs and sale of goods.
(b) Post the entries to Work in Process Inventory.
(c) Reconcile the balance in Work in Process Inventory with the costs of unfinished jobs.
(d) Prepare a cost of goods manufactured schedule for May.

(d) Cost of goods manufactured $20,190

P2-4B Net Play Company uses a job order cost system in each of its three manufacturing departments. Manufacturing overhead is applied to jobs on the basis of direct labor cost in Department A, direct labor hours in Department B, and machine hours in Department C.

In establishing the predetermined overhead rates for 2014, the following estimates were made for the year.

Compute predetermined overhead rates, apply overhead, and calculate under- or overapplied overhead.

(LO 4, 6), AP

| | **Department** | | |
	A	B	C
Manufacturing overhead	$720,000	$640,000	$900,000
Direct labor cost	$600,000	$100,000	$600,000
Direct labor hours	50,000	40,000	40,000
Machine hours	100,000	120,000	150,000

During January, the job cost sheets showed the following costs and production data.

| | **Department** | | |
	A	B	C
Direct materials used	$92,000	$86,000	$64,000
Direct labor cost	$48,000	$35,000	$50,400
Manufacturing overhead incurred	$60,000	$60,000	$72,100
Direct labor hours	4,000	3,500	4,200
Machine hours	8,000	10,500	12,600

Instructions
(a) Compute the predetermined overhead rate for each department.
(b) Compute the total manufacturing costs assigned to jobs in January in each department.
(c) Compute the under- or overapplied overhead for each department at January 31.

(a) 120%, $16, $6
(b) $197,600, $177,000, $190,000
(c) $2,400 $4,000, $(3,500)

P2-5B Bell Company's fiscal year ends on June 30. The following accounts are found in its job order cost accounting system for the first month of the new fiscal year.

Analyze manufacturing accounts and determine missing amounts.

(LO 2, 3, 4, 5, 6), AN

Raw Materials Inventory

July 1	Beginning balance	19,000	July 31	Requisitions	(a)
31	Purchases	90,400			
July 31	Ending balance	(b)			

Work in Process Inventory

July 1	Beginning balance	(c)	July 31	Jobs completed	(f)
31	Direct materials	80,000			
31	Direct labor	(d)			
31	Overhead	(e)			
July 31	Ending balance	(g)			

Finished Goods Inventory

July 1	Beginning balance	(h)	July 31	Cost of goods sold	(j)
31	Completed jobs	(i)			
July 31	Ending balance	(k)			

Factory Labor

July 31	Factory wages	(l)	July 31	Wages assigned	(m)

Manufacturing Overhead

July 31	Indirect materials	8,900	July 31	Overhead applied	117,000
31	Indirect labor	16,000			
31	Other overhead	(n)			

Other data:

1. On July 1, two jobs were in process: Job No. 4085 and Job No. 4086, with costs of $19,000 and $8,200, respectively.
2. During July, Job Nos. 4087, 4088, and 4089 were started. On July 31, only Job No. 4089 was unfinished. This job had charges for direct materials $2,000 and direct labor $1,500, plus manufacturing overhead. Manufacturing overhead was applied at the rate of 130% of direct labor cost.
3. On July 1, Job No. 4084, costing $145,000, was in the finished goods warehouse. On July 31, Job No. 4088, costing $138,000, was in finished goods.
4. Overhead was $3,000 underapplied in July.

(d) $ 90,000
(f) $308,750
(l) $106,000

Instructions
List the letters (a) through (n) and indicate the amount pertaining to each letter. Show computations.

PROBLEMS: SET C

Visit the book's companion website, at **www.wiley.com/college/weygandt**, and choose the Student Companion site to access Problem Set C.

WATERWAYS CONTINUING PROBLEM

(*Note:* This is a continuation of the Waterways Problem from Chapter 1.)

WCP2 Waterways has two major public-park projects to provide with comprehensive irrigation in one of its service locations this month. Job J57 and Job K52 involve 15 acres of landscaped terrain which will require special-order sprinkler heads to meet the specifications of the project. This problem asks you to help Waterways use a job order cost system to account for production of these parts.

Go to the book's companion website, at **www.wiley.com/college/weygandt**, *to find the completion of this problem.*

Broadening Your PERSPECTIVE

Management Decision-Making

Decision-Making at Current Designs

BYP2-1 Huegel Hollow Resort has ordered 20 rotomolded kayaks from Current Designs. Each kayak will be formed in the rotomolded oven, cooled, and then the excess plastic trimmed away. Then, the hatches, seat, ropes, and bungees will be attached to the kayak.

Dave Thill, the kayak plant manager, knows that manufacturing each kayak requires 54 pounds of polyethylene powder and a finishing kit (rope, seat, hardware, etc.). The polyethylene powder used in these kayaks costs $1.50 per pound, and the finishing kits cost $170 each. Each kayak will use two kinds of labor: 2 hours of more-skilled type I labor from people who run the oven and trim the plastic, and 3 hours of less-skilled type II labor from people who attach the hatches and seat and other hardware. The type I employees are paid $15 per hour, and the type II employees are paid $12 per hour. For purposes of this problem, assume that overhead is allocated to all jobs at a rate of 150% of direct labor costs.

Instructions
Determine the total cost of the Huegel Hollow order and the cost of each individual kayak in the order. Identify costs as direct materials, direct labor, or manufacturing overhead.

Decision-Making Across the Organization

BYP2-2 Khan Products Company uses a job order cost system. For a number of months, there has been an ongoing rift between the sales department and the production department concerning a special-order product, TC-1. TC-1 is a seasonal product that is manufactured in batches of 1,000 units. TC-1 is sold at cost plus a markup of 40% of cost.

The sales department is unhappy because fluctuating unit production costs significantly affect selling prices. Sales personnel complain that this has caused excessive customer complaints and the loss of considerable orders for TC-1.

The production department maintains that each job order must be fully costed on the basis of the costs incurred during the period in which the goods are produced. Production personnel maintain that the only real solution to the problem is for the sales department to increase sales in the slack periods.

Andrea Parley, president of the company, asks you as the company accountant to collect quarterly data for the past year on TC-1. From the cost accounting system, you accumulate the following production quantity and cost data.

| | Quarter | | | |
Costs	1	2	3	4
Direct materials	$100,000	$220,000	$ 80,000	$200,000
Direct labor	60,000	132,000	48,000	120,000
Manufacturing overhead	105,000	153,000	97,000	125,000
Total	$265,000	$505,000	$225,000	$445,000
Production in batches	5	11	4	10
Unit cost (per batch)	$ 53,000	$ 45,909	$ 56,250	$ 44,500

Instructions
With the class divided into groups, answer the following questions.
(a) What manufacturing cost element is responsible for the fluctuating unit costs? Why?
(b) What is your recommended solution to the problem of fluctuating unit cost?
(c) Restate the quarterly data on the basis of your recommended solution.

Managerial Analysis

BYP2-3 In the course of routine checking of all journal entries prior to preparing year-end reports, Betty Eller discovered several strange entries. She recalled that the president's son Joe had come in to help out during an especially busy time and that he had recorded some journal entries. She was relieved that there were only a few of his entries, and even more relieved that he had included rather lengthy explanations. The entries Joe made were:

1.

Work in Process Inventory	25,000	
Cash		25,000

(This is for materials put into process. I don't find the record that we paid for these, so I'm crediting Cash because I know we'll have to pay for them sooner or later.)

2.

| Manufacturing Overhead | 12,000 | |
| Cash | | 12,000 |

(This is for bonuses paid to salespeople. I know they're part of overhead, and I can't find an account called "Non-Factory Overhead" or "Other Overhead" so I'm putting it in Manufacturing Overhead. I have the check stubs, so I know we paid these.)

3.

| Wages Expense | 120,000 | |
| Cash | | 120,000 |

(This is for the factory workers' wages. I have a note that payroll taxes are $18,000. I still think that's part of wages expense and that we'll have to pay it all in cash sooner or later, so I credited Cash for the wages and the taxes.)

4.

| Work in Process Inventory | 3,000 | |
| Raw Materials Inventory | | 3,000 |

(This is for the glue used in the factory. I know we used this to make the products, even though we didn't use very much on any one of the products. I got it out of inventory, so I credited an inventory account.)

Instructions
(a) How should Joe have recorded each of the four events?
(b) If the entry was not corrected, which financial statements (income statement or balance sheet) would be affected? What balances would be overstated or understated?

Real-World Focus

BYP 2-4 Founded in 1970, Parlex Corporation is a world leader in the design and manufacture of flexible interconnect products. Utilizing proprietary and patented technologies, Parlex produces custom flexible interconnects including flexible circuits, polymer thick film, laminated cables, and value-added assemblies for sophisticated electronics used in automotive, telecommunications, computer, diversified electronics, and aerospace applications. In addition to manufacturing sites in Methuen, Massachusetts; Salem, New Hampshire; Cranston, Rhode Island; San Jose, California; Shanghai, China; Isle of Wight, UK; and Empalme, Mexico, Parlex has logistic support centers and strategic alliances throughout North America, Asia, and Europe.

The following information was provided in the company's annual report.

| **Parlex Company** |
| Notes to the Financial Statements |

The Company's products are manufactured on a job order basis to customers' specifications. Customers submit requests for quotations on each job, and the Company prepares bids based on its own cost estimates. The Company attempts to reflect the impact of changing costs when establishing prices. However, during the past several years, the market conditions for flexible circuits and the resulting price sensitivity haven't always allowed this to transpire. Although still not satisfactory, the Company was able to reduce the cost of products sold as a percentage of sales to 85% this year versus 87% that was experienced in the two immediately preceding years. Management continues to focus on improving operational efficiency and further reducing costs.

Instructions
(a) Parlex management discusses the job order cost system employed by their company. What are several advantages of using the job order approach to costing?
(b) Contrast the products produced in a job order environment, like Parlex, to those produced when process cost systems are used.

BYP2-5 The Institute of Management Accountants sponsors a certification for management accountants, allowing them to obtain the title of Certified Management Accountant.

Address: **www.imanet.org**, or go to **www.wiley.com/college/weygandt**

Steps
1. Go to the site shown above.
2. Choose **CMA Certification**, and then, **Earning & Maintaining Your Credential**.

Instructions
(a) What is the experience qualification requirement?
(b) How many hours of continuing education are required, and what types of courses qualify?

Critical Thinking

Communication Activity

BYP2-6 You are the management accountant for Williams Company. Your company does custom carpentry work and uses a job order cost system. Williams sends detailed job cost sheets to its customers, along with an invoice. The job cost sheets show the date materials were used, the dollar cost of materials, and the hours and cost of labor. A predetermined overhead application rate is used, and the total overhead applied is also listed.

Nancy Kopay is a customer who recently had custom cabinets installed. Along with her check in payment for the work done, she included a letter. She thanked the company for including the detailed cost information but questioned why overhead was estimated. She stated that she would be interested in knowing exactly what costs were included in overhead, and she thought that other customers would, too.

Instructions
Prepare a letter to Ms. Kopay (address: 123 Cedar Lane, Altoona, KS 66651) and tell her why you did not send her information on exact costs of overhead included in her job. Respond to her suggestion that you provide this information.

Ethics Case

BYP2-7 LRF Printing provides printing services to many different corporate clients. Although LRF bids most jobs, some jobs, particularly new ones, are negotiated on a "cost-plus" basis. Cost-plus means that the buyer is willing to pay the actual cost plus a return (profit) on these costs to LRF.

Alice Reiley, controller for LRF, has recently returned from a meeting where LRF's president stated that he wanted her to find a way to charge more costs to any project that was on a cost-plus basis. The president noted that the company needed more profits to meet its stated goals this period. By charging more costs to the cost-plus projects and therefore fewer costs to the jobs that were bid, the company should be able to increase its profit for the current year.

Alice knew why the president wanted to take this action. Rumors were that he was looking for a new position and if the company reported strong profits, the president's opportunities would be enhanced. Alice also recognized that she could probably increase the cost of certain jobs by changing the basis used to allocate manufacturing overhead.

Instructions
(a) Who are the stakeholders in this situation?
(b) What are the ethical issues in this situation?
(c) What would you do if you were Alice Reiley?

All About You

BYP2-8 Many of you will work for a small business. Some of you will even own your own business. In order to operate a small business, you will need a good understanding of managerial accounting, as well as many other skills. Much information is available to assist people who are interested in starting a new business. A great place to start is the website provided by the Small Business Administration, which is an agency of the federal government whose purpose is to support small business.

Instructions

Go to **www.sba.gov** and in the Small Business Planner, Plan Your Business link, review the material under "Get Ready." Answer the following questions.

(a) What are some of the characteristics required of a small business owner?

(b) What are the top 10 reasons given for business failure?

Considering Your Costs and Benefits

BYP2-9 After graduating, you might decide to start a small business. As discussed in this chapter, owners of any business need to know how to calculate the cost of their products. In fact, many small businesses fail because they don't accurately calculate their product costs, so they don't know if they are making a profit or losing money—until it's too late.

Suppose that you decide to start a landscape business. You use an old pickup truck that you've fully paid for. You store the truck and other equipment in your parents' barn, and you store trees and shrubs on their land. Your parents will not charge you for the use of these facilities for the first two years, but beginning in the third year they will charge a reasonable rent. Your mother helps you by answering phone calls and providing customers with information. She doesn't charge you for this service, but she plans on doing it for only your first two years in business. In pricing your services, should you include charges for the truck, the barn, the land, and your mother's services when calculating your product cost? The basic arguments for and against are as follows.

YES: If you don't include charges for these costs, your costs are understated and your profitability is overstated.

NO: At this point, you are not actually incurring costs related to these activities; therefore, you shouldn't record charges.

Instructions

Write a response indicating your position regarding this situation. Provide support for your view.

Answers to Chapter Questions

Answers to Insight and Accounting Across the Organization Questions

p. 51 Jobs Won, Money Lost Q: What type of costs do you think the company had been underestimating? **A:** It is most likely that the company failed to estimate and track overhead. In a highly diversified company, overhead associated with the diesel locomotive jobs may have been "lost" in the total overhead pool for the entire company.

p. 57 The Cost of an iPhone? Just Tear One Apart Q: What type of costs are marketing and selling costs, and how are they treated for accounting purposes? **A:** Product costs include materials, labor, and overhead. Costs not related to production, such as marketing and selling costs, are period costs which are expensed in the period that they are incurred.

p. 67 Sales Are Nice, but Service Revenue Pays the Bills Q: Explain why GE would use job order costing to keep track of the cost of repairing a malfunctioning engine for a major airline. **A:** GE operates in a competitive environment. Other companies offer competing bids to win service contracts on GE's airplane engines. GE needs to know what it costs to repair engines, so that it can present competitive bids while still generating a reasonable profit.

Answers to Self-Test Questions

1. a **2.** c **3.** b **4.** c **5.** c **6.** d **7.** d **8.** b **9.** a **10.** d **11.** b ($180,000 \times 80\%$) **12.** c **13.** b **14.** c **15.** c **16.** b

Chapter 3

Process Costing

Ben & Jerry's Tracks Its Mix-Ups

Ben & Jerry's Homemade, Inc., based in Waterbury, Vermont, started its first ice cream shop in a former gas station in 1978.

Making ice cream is a process—a movement of product from a mixing department to a prepping department to a pint department. The mixing department is where the ice cream is created. In the prep area, the production process adds extras such as cherries and dark chocolate to make plain ice cream into "Cherry Garcia," Ben & Jerry's most popular flavor, or fudge-covered waffle cone pieces

and a swirl of caramel for "Stephen Colbert's Americone Dream." The pint department is where the ice cream is actually put into containers. As the product is processed from one department to the next, the appropriate materials, labor, and overhead are added to determine its cost.

"The incoming ingredients from the shipping and receiving departments are stored in certain locations, either in a freezer or dry warehouse," says Beecher Eurich, staff accountant. "As ingredients get added, so do the costs associated with them." How much ice cream is produced? Running plants around the clock, the company produces 18 million gallons a year.

✔ **The Navigator**

☐ Scan Learning Objectives

☐ Read Feature Story

☐ Read Preview

☐ Read Text and answer **DO IT!** p. 98
   ☐ p. 101 ☐ p. 105 ☐ p. 110

☐ Work Using the Decision Toolkit p. 112

☐ Review Summary of Learning Objectives

☐ Work Comprehensive **DO IT!** p. 122

☐ Answer Self-Test Questions

☐ Complete Assignments

☐ Go to **WileyPLUS** for practice and tutorials

Learning Objectives

After studying this chapter, you should be able to:

1 Understand who uses process cost systems.

2 Explain the similarities and differences between job order cost and process cost systems.

3 Explain the flow of costs in a process cost system.

4 Make the journal entries to assign manufacturing costs in a process cost system.

5 Compute equivalent units.

6 Explain the four steps necessary to prepare a production cost report.

7 Prepare a production cost report.

With the company's process cost system, Eurich can tell you how much a certain batch of ice cream costs to make—its materials, labor, and overhead in each of the production departments. She generates reports for the production department heads but makes sure not to overdo it. "You can get bogged down in numbers," says Eurich. "If you're generating a report that no one can use, then that's a waste of time."

It's more likely, though, that Ben & Jerry's production people want to know how efficient they are. Why? Many own stock in the company.

Watch the Jones Soda video in WileyPLUS to learn more about process costing in the real world.

✔ **The Navigator**

Preview of **Chapter 3**

The cost accounting system used by companies such as *Ben & Jerry's* is **process cost accounting**. In contrast to job order cost accounting, which focuses on the individual job, process cost accounting focuses on the *processes* involved in mass producing products that are identical or very similar in nature. The primary objective of this chapter is to explain and illustrate process costing.

The content and organization of this chapter are as follows.

PROCESS COSTING		
Nature of Process Cost Systems	**Equivalent Units**	**Production Cost Report**
• Uses • Service companies • Similarities and differences • Process cost flow • Assigning manufacturing costs	• Weighted-average method • Refinements	• Physical units • Equivalent units of production • Unit production costs • Cost reconciliation schedule • Production cost report • Costing systems—Final comments

✔ **The Navigator**

The Nature of Process Cost Systems

Uses of Process Cost Systems

Companies use **process cost systems** to apply costs to similar products that are mass-produced in a continuous fashion. Ben & Jerry's uses a process cost system: Production of the ice cream, once it begins, continues until the ice cream emerges, and the processing is the same for the entire run—with precisely the same amount of materials, labor, and overhead. Each finished pint of ice cream is indistinguishable from another.

A company such as USX uses process costing in the manufacturing of steel. Kellogg and General Mills use process costing for cereal production; Exxon-Mobil uses process costing for its oil refining. Sherwin Williams uses process costing for its paint products. At a bottling company like Coca-Cola, the manufacturing process begins with the blending of ingredients. Next, automated machinery moves the bottles into position and fills them. The production process then caps, packages, and forwards the bottles to the finished goods warehouse. Illustration 3-1 shows this process.

Illustration 3-1
Manufacturing processes

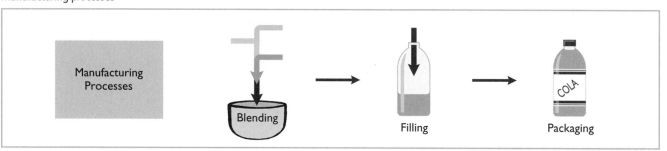

For Coca-Cola, as well as the other companies just mentioned, once production begins, it continues until the finished product emerges, and each unit of finished product is like every other unit.

In comparison, a job order cost system assigns costs to a *specific job*. Examples are the construction of a customized home, the making of a motion picture, or the manufacturing of a specialized machine. Illustration 3-2 provides examples of companies that primarily use either a process cost system or a job order cost system.

Illustration 3-2
Process cost and job order cost companies and products

Process Cost System		Job Order Cost System	
Company	**Product**	**Company**	**Product**
Coca-Cola, PepsiCo	Soft drinks	Young & Rubicam, J. Walter Thompson	Advertising
ExxonMobil, Royal Dutch Shell	Oil	Walt Disney, Warner Brothers	Motion pictures
Intel, Advanced Micro Devices	Computer chips	Center Ice Consultants, Ice Pro	Ice rinks
Dow Chemical, DuPont	Chemicals	Kaiser, Mayo Clinic	Patient health care

Process Costing for Service Companies

Frequently, when we think of service companies, we think of specific, nonroutine tasks, such as rebuilding an automobile engine, providing consulting services on a business acquisition, or working on a major lawsuit. However, many service companies specialize in performing repetitive, routine aspects of a particular business. For example, auto-care vendors such as Jiffy Lube focus on the routine aspects of car care. H&R Block focuses on the routine aspects of basic tax practice, and many large law firms focus on routine legal services, such as uncomplicated divorces. Service companies that provide specific, nonroutine services will probably benefit from using a job order cost system. Those that perform routine, repetitive services will probably be better off with a process cost system.

Similarities and Differences Between Job Order Cost and Process Cost Systems

In a job order cost system, companies assign costs to each job. In a process cost system, companies track costs through a series of connected manufacturing processes or departments, rather than by individual jobs. Thus, companies use process cost systems when they produce a large volume of uniform or relatively homogeneous products. Illustration 3-3 shows the basic flow of costs in these two systems.

The following analysis highlights the basic similarities and differences between these two systems.

> **LEARNING OBJECTIVE 2**
>
> Explain the similarities and differences between job order cost and process cost systems.

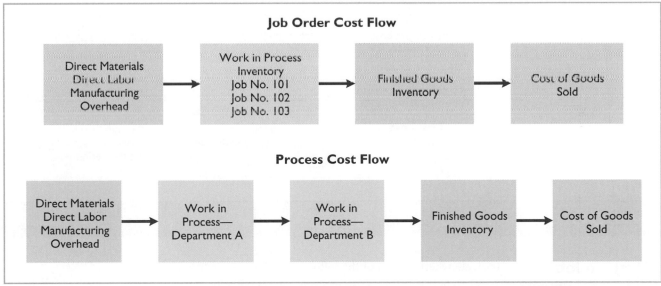

Illustration 3-3
Job order cost and process cost flow

SIMILARITIES

Job order cost and process cost systems are similar in three ways:

1. **The manufacturing cost elements.** Both costing systems track three manufacturing cost elements—direct materials, direct labor, and manufacturing overhead.

2. **The accumulation of the costs of materials, labor, and overhead.** Both costing systems debit raw materials to Raw Materials Inventory, factory labor to Factory Labor, and manufacturing overhead costs to Manufacturing Overhead.

3. **The flow of costs.** As noted above, both systems accumulate all manufacturing costs by debits to Raw Materials Inventory, Factory Labor, and Manufacturing

Overhead. Both systems then assign these costs to the same accounts—Work in Process, Finished Goods Inventory, and Cost of Goods Sold. **The methods of assigning costs, however, differ significantly.** These differences are explained and illustrated later in the chapter.

DIFFERENCES

The differences between a job order cost and a process cost system are as follows.

1. **The number of work in process accounts used.** A job order cost system uses only one work in process account. A process cost system uses multiple work in process accounts.

2. **Documents used to track costs.** A job order cost system charges costs to individual jobs and summarizes them in a job cost sheet. A process cost system summarizes costs in a production cost report for each department.

3. **The point at which costs are totaled.** A job order cost system totals costs when the job is completed. A process cost system totals costs at the end of a period of time.

4. **Unit cost computations.** In a job order cost system, the unit cost is the total cost per job divided by the units produced. In a process cost system, the unit cost is total manufacturing costs for the period divided by the units produced during the period.

Illustration 3-4 summarizes the major differences between a job order cost and a process cost system.

Illustration 3-4
Job order versus process cost systems

Feature	Job Order Cost System	Process Cost System
Work in process accounts	One work in process account	Multiple work in process accounts
Documents used	Job cost sheets	Production cost reports
Determination of total manufacturing costs	Each job	Each period
Unit-cost computations	Cost of each job ÷ Units produced for the job	Total manufacturing costs ÷ Equivalent units produced during the period

> ## DO IT!

Compare Job Order and Process Cost Systems

Action Plan

✔ Use job order costing in situations where unit costs are high, unit volume is low, and products are unique.

✔ Use process costing when there is a large volume of relatively homogeneous products.

Indicate whether each of the following statements is true or false.

1. A law firm is likely to use process costing for major lawsuits.

2. A manufacturer of paintballs is likely to use process costing.

3. Both job order and process costing determine product costs at the end of a period of time, rather than when a product is completed.

4. Process costing does not keep track of manufacturing overhead.

Solution

1. false.   2. true.   3. false.   4. false.

Related exercise material: **E3-1** and **DO IT! 3-1.**

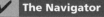 ✔ The Navigator

Process Cost Flow

Illustration 3-5 shows the flow of costs in the process cost system for Tyler Company. Tyler Company manufactures roller blade and skateboard wheels that it sells to manufacturers and retail outlets. Manufacturing consists of two processes: machining and assembly. The Machining Department shapes, hones, and drills the raw materials. The Assembly Department assembles and packages the parts.

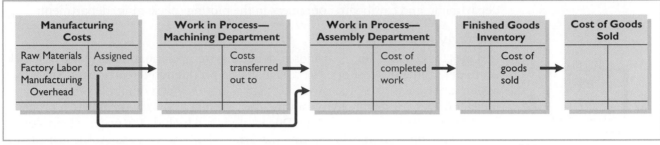

Illustration 3-5
Flow of costs in process cost system

As the flow of costs indicates, the company can add materials, labor, and manufacturing overhead in both the Machining and Assembly departments. When it finishes its work, the Machining Department transfers the partially completed units to the Assembly Department. The Assembly Department finishes the goods and then transfers them to the finished goods inventory. Upon sale, Tyler removes the goods from the finished goods inventory. Within each department, a similar set of activities is performed on each unit processed.

Assigning Manufacturing Costs—Journal Entries

As indicated, the accumulation of the costs of materials, labor, and manufacturing overhead is the same in a process cost system as in a job order cost system. That is, both systems follow these procedures:

- Companies debit all raw materials to Raw Materials Inventory at the time of purchase.
- They debit all factory labor to Factory Labor as the labor costs are incurred.
- They debit overhead costs to Manufacturing Overhead as these costs are incurred.

However, the assignment of the three manufacturing cost elements to Work in Process in a process cost system is different from a job order cost system. Here we'll look at how companies assign these manufacturing cost elements in a process cost system.

MATERIALS COSTS

All raw materials issued for production are a materials cost to the producing department. A process cost system may use materials requisition slips, but **it generally requires fewer requisitions than in a job order cost system, because the materials are used for processes rather than for specific jobs** and therefore typically are for larger quantities.

At the beginning of the first process, a company usually adds most of the materials needed for production. However, other materials may be added at various points. For example, in the manufacture of Hershey candy bars, the chocolate and other ingredients are added at the beginning of the first process, and the wrappers and cartons are added at the end of the packaging process. Tyler Company adds materials at the beginning of each process. Tyler makes the following entry to record the materials used.

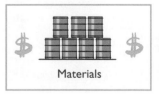

Materials

Work in Process—Machining	XXXX	
Work in Process—Assembly	XXXX	
Raw Materials Inventory		XXXX
(To record materials used)		

Ice cream maker Ben & Jerry's adds materials in three departments: milk and flavoring in the mixing department, extras such as cherries and dark chocolate in the prepping department, and cardboard containers in the pinting (packaging) department.

FACTORY LABOR COSTS

Factory Labor

In a process cost system, as in a job order cost system, companies may use time tickets to determine the cost of labor assignable to production departments. Since they assign labor costs to a process rather than a job, they can obtain, from the payroll register or departmental payroll summaries, the labor cost chargeable to a process.

Labor costs for the Machining Department will include the wages of employees who shape, hone, and drill the raw materials. The entry to assign these costs for Tyler Company is:

Work in Process—Machining	XXXX	
Work in Process—Assembly	XXXX	
Factory Labor		XXXX
(To assign factory labor to production)		

MANUFACTURING OVERHEAD COSTS

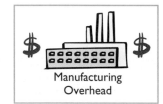

Manufacturing Overhead

The objective in assigning overhead in a process cost system is to allocate the overhead costs to the production departments on an objective and equitable basis. That basis is the activity that "drives" or causes the costs. A primary driver of overhead costs in continuous manufacturing operations is **machine time used**, not direct labor. Thus, companies **widely use machine hours** in allocating manufacturing overhead costs using predetermined overhead rates. Tyler's entry to allocate overhead to the two processes is:

Work in Process—Machining	XXXX	
Work in Process—Assembly	XXXX	
Manufacturing Overhead		XXXX
(To assign overhead to production)		

MANAGEMENT INSIGHT

Choosing a Cost Driver

In one of its automated cost centers, Caterpillar feeds work into the cost center, where robotic machines process it and transfer the finished job to the next cost center without human intervention. One person tends all of the machines and spends more time maintaining machines than operating them. In such cases, overhead rates based on direct labor hours may be misleading. Surprisingly, some companies continue to assign manufacturing overhead on the basis of direct labor despite the fact that there is no cause-and-effect relationship between labor and overhead.

 What is the result if a company uses the wrong "cost driver" to assign manufacturing overhead? (See page 143.)

TRANSFER TO NEXT DEPARTMENT

At the end of the month, Tyler needs an entry to record the cost of the goods transferred out of the Machining Department. In this case, the transfer is to the Assembly Department, and Tyler makes the following entry.

Work in Process—Assembly	XXXXX	
Work in Process—Machining		XXXXX
(To record transfer of units to the Assembly		
Department)		

TRANSFER TO FINISHED GOODS

When the Assembly Department completes the units, it transfers them to the finished goods warehouse. The entry for this transfer is as follows.

Finished Goods Inventory	XXXXX	
Work in Process—Assembly		XXXXX
(To record transfer of units to finished goods)		

TRANSFER TO COST OF GOODS SOLD

When Tyler sells the finished goods, it records the cost of goods sold as follows.

Cost of Goods Sold	XXXXX	
Finished Goods Inventory		XXXXX
(To record cost of units sold)		

> **DO IT!**

Manufacturing Costs in Process Costing

Ruth Company manufactures ZEBO through two processes: blending and bottling. In June, raw materials used were Blending $18,000 and Bottling $4,000. Factory labor costs were Blending $12,000 and Bottling $5,000. Manufacturing overhead costs were Blending $6,000 and Bottling $2,500. The company transfers units completed at a cost of $19,000 in the Blending Department to the Bottling Department. The Bottling Department transfers units completed at a cost of $11,000 to Finished Goods. Journalize the assignment of these costs to the two processes and the transfer of units as appropriate.

Solution

Action Plan

✔ In process cost accounting, keep separate work in process accounts for each process.

✔ When the costs are assigned to production, debit the separate work in process accounts.

✔ Transfer cost of completed units to the next process or to Finished Goods.

The entries are:

Work in Process—Blending	18,000	
Work in Process—Bottling	4,000	
Raw Materials Inventory		22,000
(To record materials used)		
Work in Process—Blending	12,000	
Work in Process—Bottling	5,000	
Factory Labor		17,000
(To assign factory labor to production)		
Work in Process—Blending	6,000	
Work in Process—Bottling	2,500	
Manufacturing Overhead		8,500
(To assign overhead to production)		

Work in Process—Bottling		19,000	
Work in Process—Blending			19,000
(To record transfer of units to the Bottling Department)			
Finished Goods Inventory		11,000	
Work in Process—Bottling			11,000
(To record transfer of units to finished goods)			

Related exercise material: **BE3-1, BE3-2, BE3-3, E3-2, E3-4, and DO IT! 3-2.**

✔ **The Navigator**

Equivalent Units

LEARNING OBJECTIVE 5

Compute equivalent units.

Suppose you have a work-study job in the office of your college's president, and she asks you to compute the cost of instruction per full-time equivalent student at your college. The college's vice president for finance provides the following information.

Illustration 3-6
Information for full-time student example

Costs:
  Total cost of instruction $9,000,000

Student population:
  Full-time students   900
  Part-time students   1,000

Part-time students take 60% of the classes of a full-time student during the year. To compute the number of full-time equivalent students per year, you would make the following computation.

Illustration 3-7
Full-time equivalent unit computation

Full-Time Students	+	Equivalent Units of Part-Time Students	=	Full-Time Equivalent Students
900	+	(60% × 1,000)	=	1,500

The cost of instruction per full-time equivalent student is therefore the total cost of instruction ($9,000,000) divided by the number of full-time equivalent students (1,500), which is $6,000 ($9,000,000 ÷ 1,500).

A process cost system uses the same idea, called equivalent units of production. **Equivalent units of production** measure the work done during the period, expressed in fully completed units. Companies use this measure to determine the cost per unit of completed product.

Weighted-Average Method

The formula to compute equivalent units of production is as follows.

Illustration 3-8
Equivalent units of production formula

Units Completed and Transferred Out	+	Equivalent Units of Ending Work in Process	=	Equivalent Units of Production

To better understand this concept of equivalent units, consider the following two separate examples.

Example 1. In a specific period, the entire output of Sullivan Company's Blending Department consists of ending work in process of 4,000 units which are 60% complete as to materials, labor, and overhead. The equivalent units of production for the Blending Department are therefore 2,400 units (4,000 × 60%).

Example 2. The output of Kori Company's Packaging Department during the period consists of 10,000 units completed and transferred out, and 5,000 units in ending work in process which are 70% completed. The equivalent units of production are therefore 13,500 [10,000 + (5,000 × 70%)].

This method of computing equivalent units is referred to as the **weighted-average method**. It considers the degree of completion (weighting) of the units completed and transferred out and the ending work in process.

Refinements on the Weighted-Average Method

Kellogg Company has produced Eggo® Waffles since 1970. Three departments produce these waffles: Mixing, Baking, and Freezing/Packaging. The Mixing Department combines dry ingredients, including flour, salt, and baking powder, with liquid ingredients, including eggs and vegetable oil, to make waffle batter. Illustration 3-9 provides information related to the Mixing Department at the end of June.

Mixing Department			
		Percentage Complete	
	Physical Units	**Materials**	**Conversion Costs**
Work in process, June 1	100,000	100%	70%
Started into production	800,000		
Total units	900,000		
Units transferred out	700,000		
Work in process, June 30	200,000	100%	60%
Total units	900,000		

Illustration 3-9
Information for Mixing Department

Illustration 3-9 indicates that the beginning work in process is 100% complete as to materials cost and 70% complete as to conversion costs. **Conversion costs are the sum of labor costs and overhead costs.** In other words, Kellogg adds both the dry and liquid ingredients (materials) at the beginning of the waffle-making process, and the conversion costs (labor and overhead) related to the mixing of these ingredients are incurred uniformly and are 70% complete. The ending work in process is 100% complete as to materials cost and 60% complete as to conversion costs.

We then use the Mixing Department information to determine equivalent units. **In computing equivalent units, the beginning work in process is not part of the equivalent-units-of-production formula.** The units transferred out to the Baking Department are fully complete as to both materials and conversion costs. The ending work in process is fully complete as to materials, but only 60% complete as to conversion costs. We therefore need to make **two equivalent unit computations**: one

Helpful Hint
When are separate unit cost computations needed for materials and conversion costs? Answer: Whenever the two types of costs do not occur in the process at the same time.

Ethics Note
An unethical manager might use incorrect completion percentages when determining equivalent units. This results in either raising or lowering costs. Since completion percentages are somewhat subjective, this form of income manipulation can be difficult to detect.

for materials, and the other for conversion costs. Illustration 3-10 shows these computations.

Illustration 3-10
Computation of equivalent units—Mixing Department

Mixing Department		
	Equivalent Units	
	Materials	Conversion Costs
Units transferred out	700,000	700,000
Work in process, June 30		
200,000 × 100%	200,000	
200,000 × 60%		120,000
Total equivalent units	900,000	820,000

We can refine the earlier formula used to compute equivalent units of production (Illustration 3-8, page 102) to show the computations for materials and for conversion costs, as follows.

Illustration 3-11
Refined equivalent units of production formula

Units Completed and Transferred Out— Materials	+	Equivalent Units of Ending Work in Process—Materials	=	Equivalent Units of Production— Materials
Units Completed and Transferred Out— Conversion Costs	+	Equivalent Units of Ending Work in Process—Conversion Costs	=	Equivalent Units of Production— Conversion Costs

PEOPLE, PLANET, AND PROFIT INSIGHT

Haven't I Seen That Before?

For a variety of reasons, many companies, including Caterpillar, General Electric, and Eastman Kodak, are making a big push to remanufacture goods that have been thrown away. Items getting a second chance include cell phones, computers, home appliances, car parts, vacuum cleaners, and medical equipment. Businesses have figured out that profit margins on remanufactured goods are significantly higher than on new goods. As commodity prices such as copper and steel increase, reusing parts makes more sense. Also, as more local governments initiate laws requiring that electronics and appliances be recycled rather than thrown away, the cost of remanufacturing declines because the gathering of used goods becomes far more efficient. Besides benefitting the manufacturer, remanufacturing provides goods at a much lower price to consumers, reduces waste going to landfills, saves energy, reuses scarce resources, and reduces emissions. For example, it was estimated that a remanufactured car starter results in about 50% less carbon dioxide emissions than making a new one.

Source: James R. Hagerty and Paul Glader, "From Trash Heap to Store Shelf," *Wall Street Journal Online* (January 24, 2011).

 In what ways might the relative composition (materials, labor, and overhead) of a remanufactured product's cost differ from that of a newly made product? (See page 143.)

> DO IT!

Equivalent Units

The fabricating department has the following production and cost data for the current month.

Beginning Work in Process	Units Transferred Out	Ending Work in Process
–0–	15,000	10,000

Materials are entered at the beginning of the process. The ending work in process units are 30% complete as to conversion costs. Compute the equivalent units of production for (a) materials and (b) conversion costs.

Action Plan

✔ To measure the work done during the period, expressed in fully completed units, compute equivalent units of production.

✔ Use the appropriate formula: Units completed and transferred out + Equivalent units of ending work in process = Equivalent units of production.

Solution

(a) Since materials are entered at the beginning of the process, the equivalent units of ending work in process are 10,000. Thus, 15,000 units + 10,000 units = 25,000 equivalent units of production for materials.

(b) Since ending work in process is only 30% complete as to conversion costs, the equivalent units of ending work in process are 3,000 (30% × 10,000 units). Thus, 15,000 units + 3,000 units = 18,000 equivalent units of production for conversion costs.

Related exercise material: **BE3-5, BE3-10, E3-5, E3-6, E3-8, E3-9, E3-10, E3-11, E3-13, E3-14, E3-15, and DO IT! 3-3.**

✔ **The Navigator**

Production Cost Report

As mentioned earlier, companies prepare a production cost report for each department. A **production cost report** is the key document that management uses to understand the activities in a department; it shows the production quantity and cost data related to that department. For example, in producing Eggo® Waffles, Kellogg Company uses three production cost reports: Mixing, Baking, and Freezing/Packaging. Illustration 3-12 shows the flow of costs to make an Eggo® Waffle and the related production cost reports for each department.

LEARNING OBJECTIVE   6

Explain the four steps necessary to prepare a production cost report.

Illustration 3-12
Flow of costs in making Eggo® Waffles

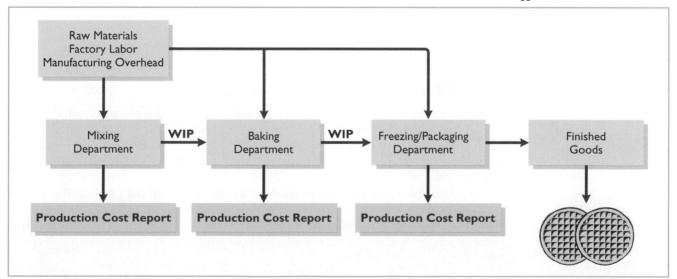

In order to complete a production cost report, the company must perform four steps, which, as a whole, make up the process cost system.

1. Compute the physical unit flow.
2. Compute the equivalent units of production.
3. Compute unit production costs.
4. Prepare a cost reconciliation schedule.

Illustration 3-13 shows assumed data for the Mixing Department at Kellogg Company for the month of June. We will use this information to complete a production cost report for the Mixing Department.

Illustration 3-13
Unit and cost data—Mixing Department

Mixing Department	
Units	
Work in process, June 1	100,000
Direct materials: 100% complete	
Conversion costs: 70% complete	
Units started into production during June	800,000
Units completed and transferred out to Baking Department	700,000
Work in process, June 30	200,000
Direct materials: 100% complete	
Conversion costs: 60% complete	
Costs	
Work in process, June 1	
Direct materials: 100% complete	$ 50,000
Conversion costs: 70% complete	35,000
Cost of work in process, June 1	$ 85,000
Costs incurred during production in June	
Direct materials	$400,000
Conversion costs	170,000
Costs incurred in June	$570,000

Compute the Physical Unit Flow (Step 1)

Physical units are the actual units to be accounted for during a period, irrespective of any work performed. To keep track of these units, add the units started (or transferred) into production during the period to the units in process at the beginning of the period. This amount is referred to as the **total units to be accounted for**.

The total units then are accounted for by the output of the period. The output consists of units transferred out during the period and any units in process at the end of the period. This amount is referred to as the **total units accounted for**. Illustration 3-14 shows the flow of physical units for Kellogg's Mixing Department for the month of June.

Mixing Department	
	Physical Units
Units to be accounted for	
Work in process, June 1	100,000
Started (transferred) into production	800,000
Total units	**900,000**
Units accounted for	
Completed and transferred out	700,000
Work in process, June 30	200,000
Total units	**900,000**

Illustration 3-14
Physical unit flow—Mixing
Department

The records indicate that the Mixing Department must account for 900,000 units. Of this sum, 700,000 units were transferred to the Baking Department and 200,000 units were still in process.

Compute the Equivalent Units of Production (Step 2)

Once the physical flow of the units is established, Kellogg must measure the Mixing Department's productivity in terms of equivalent units of production. The Mixing Department adds materials at the beginning of the process, and it incurs conversion costs uniformly during the process. Thus, we need two computations of equivalent units: one for materials and one for conversion costs. The equivalent unit computation is as follows.

Helpful Hint
Materials are not always added at the beginning of the process. For example, materials are sometimes added uniformly during the process.

	Equivalent Units	
	Materials	**Conversion Costs**
Units transferred out	700,000	700,000
Work in process, June 30		
200,000 × 100%	200,000	
200,000 × 60%		120,000
Total equivalent units	900,000	820,000

Illustration 3-15
Computation of equivalent units—Mixing Department

Helpful Hint
Remember that we ignore the beginning work in process in this computation.

Compute Unit Production Costs (Step 3)

Armed with the knowledge of the equivalent units of production, we can now compute the unit production costs. **Unit production costs** are costs expressed in terms of equivalent units of production. When equivalent units of production are different for materials and conversion costs, we compute three unit costs: (1) materials, (2) conversion, and (3) total manufacturing.

The computation of total materials cost related to Eggo® Waffles is as follows.

Work in process, June 1	
Direct materials cost	$ 50,000
Costs added to production during June	
Direct materials cost	400,000
Total materials cost	$450,000

Illustration 3-16
Total materials cost computation

The computation of unit materials cost is as follows.

Illustration 3-17
Unit materials cost
computation

Total Materials Cost	÷	Equivalent Units of Materials	=	Unit Materials Cost
$450,000	÷	900,000	=	$0.50

Illustration 3-18 shows the computation of total conversion costs.

Illustration 3-18
Total conversion costs
computation

Work in process, June 1	
Conversion costs	$ 35,000
Costs added to production during June	
Conversion costs	170,000
Total conversion costs	$205,000

The computation of unit conversion cost is as follows.

Illustration 3-19
Unit conversion cost
computation

Total Conversion Costs	÷	Equivalent Units of Conversion Costs	=	Unit Conversion Cost
$205,000	÷	820,000	=	$0.25

Total manufacturing cost per unit is therefore computed as shown in Illustration 3-20.

Illustration 3-20
Total manufacturing cost
per unit

Unit Materials Cost	+	Unit Conversion Cost	=	Total Manufacturing Cost per Unit
$0.50	+	$0.25	=	$0.75

Prepare a Cost Reconciliation Schedule (Step 4)

We are now ready to determine the cost of goods transferred out of the Mixing Department to the Baking Department and the costs in ending work in process. Kellogg charged total costs of $655,000 to the Mixing Department in June, calculated as follows.

Illustration 3-21
Costs charged to Mixing
Department

Costs to be accounted for	
Work in process, June 1	$ 85,000
Started into production	570,000
Total costs	**$655,000**

The company then prepares a cost reconciliation schedule to assign these costs to (a) units transferred out to the Baking Department and (b) ending work in process.

Illustration 3-22
Cost reconciliation schedule—Mixing Department

Mixing Department		
Cost Reconciliation Schedule		
Costs accounted for		
Transferred out (700,000 × $0.75)		$ 525,000
Work in process, June 30		
Materials (200,000 × $0.50)	$100,000	
Conversion costs (120,000 × $0.25)	30,000	130,000
Total costs		$655,000

Kellogg uses the total manufacturing cost per unit, $0.75, in costing the **units completed** and transferred to the Baking Department. In contrast, the unit cost of materials and the unit cost of conversion are needed in costing **units in process**. The **cost reconciliation schedule** shows that the **total costs accounted for** (Illustration 3-22) equal the **total costs to be accounted for** (Illustration 3-21).

Preparing the Production Cost Report

At this point, Kellogg is ready to prepare the production cost report for the Mixing Department. As indicated earlier, this report is an internal document for management that shows production quantity and cost data for a production department.

There are four steps in preparing a production cost report:

1. Compute the physical unit flow.
2. Compute the equivalent units of production.
3. Compute unit production costs.
4. Prepare a cost reconciliation schedule.

Illustration 3-23 (page 110) shows the production cost report for the Mixing Department. The report identifies the four steps.

Production cost reports provide a basis for evaluating the productivity of a department. In addition, managers can use the cost data to assess whether unit costs and total costs are reasonable. By comparing the quantity and cost data with predetermined goals, top management can also judge whether current performance is meeting planned objectives.

LEARNING OBJECTIVE   7

Prepare a production cost report.

DECISION TOOLKIT

DECISION CHECKPOINTS	INFO NEEDED FOR DECISION	TOOL TO USE FOR DECISION	HOW TO EVALUATE RESULTS
What is the cost of a product?	Cost of materials, labor, and overhead assigned to processes used to make the product	Production cost report	Compare costs to previous periods, to competitors, and to expected selling price to evaluate overall profitability.

Illustration 3-23
Production cost report

	A	B	C	D	E
			Mixing Department.xls		
			Home Insert Page Layout Formulas Data Review View		
		P18 ▾ *fx*			
1			**Mixing Department**		
2			**Production Cost Report**		
3			**For the Month Ended June 30, 2014**		
4			_Equivalent Units_		
5		Physical Units	Materials	Conversion Costs	
6	QUANTITIES	Step 1	Step 2		
7	Units to be accounted for				
8	Work in process, June 1	100,000			
9	Started into production	800,000			
10	Total units	900,000			
11	Units accounted for				
12	Transferred out	700,000	700,000	700,000	
13	Work in process, June 30	200,000	200,000	120,000	(200,000 × 60%)
14	Total units	900,000	900,000	820,000	
15	COSTS				
16	Unit costs Step 3		Materials	Conversion Costs	Total
17	Total cost (a)		$450,000	$205,000	$655,000
18	Equivalent units (b)		900,000	820,000	
19	Unit costs [(a) ÷ (b)]		$0.50	$0.25	$0.75
20	Costs to be accounted for				
21	Work in process, June 1				$85,000
22	Started into production				570,000
23	Total costs				$655,000
24	Cost Reconciliation Schedule Step 4				
25	Costs accounted for				
26	Transferred out (700,000 × $0.75)				$525,000
27	Work in process, June 30				
28	Materials (200,000 × $0.50)			$100,000	
29	Conversion costs (120,000 × $0.25)			30,000	130,000
30	Total costs				$655,000
31					

> **DO IT!**

Cost Reconciliation Schedule

In March, Rodayo Manufacturing had the following unit production costs: materials $6 and conversion costs $9. On March 1, it had zero work in process. During March, Rodayo transferred out 12,000 units. As of March 31, 800 units that were 25% complete as to conversion costs and 100% complete as to materials were in ending work in process. Assign the costs to the units transferred out and in process.

Action Plan

✔ Assign the total manufacturing cost of $15 per unit to the 12,000 units transferred out.

✔ Assign the materials cost and conversion costs based on equivalent units of production to units in ending work in process.

Solution

The assignment of costs is as follows.

Costs accounted for		
Transferred out (12,000 × $15)		$180,000
Work in process, March 31		
Materials (800 × $6)	$4,800	
Conversion costs (200[a] × $9)	1,800	6,600
Total costs		$186,600
[a]800 × 25%		

Related exercise material: **BE3-4, BE3-6, BE3-7, BE3-8, BE3-9, BE3-10, E3-5, E3-6, E3-8, E3-9, E3-10, E3-11, E3-14, E3-15, and** **DO IT!** **3-4.**

✔ **The Navigator**

Costing Systems—Final Comments

Companies often use a combination of a process cost and a job order cost system. Called **operations costing**, this hybrid system is similar to process costing in its assumption that standardized methods are used to manufacture the product. At the same time, the product may have some customized, individual features that require the use of a job order cost system.

Consider, for example, the automobile manufacturer Ford Motor Company. Each vehicle at a given plant goes through the same assembly line, but Ford uses different materials (such as seat coverings, paint, and tinted glass) for different vehicles. Similarly, Kellogg's Pop-Tarts® toaster pastries go through numerous standardized processes—mixing, filling, baking, frosting, and packaging. The pastry dough, though, comes in different flavors—plain, chocolate, and graham—and fillings include Smucker's® real fruit, chocolate fudge, vanilla creme, brown sugar cinnamon, and s'mores.

A cost-benefit trade-off occurs as a company decides which costing system to use. A job order cost system, for example, provides detailed information related to the cost of the product. Because each job has its own distinguishing characteristics, the system can provide an accurate cost per job. This information is useful in controlling costs and pricing products. However, the cost of implementing a job order cost system is often expensive because of the accounting costs involved.

On the other hand, for a company like Intel, which makes computer chips, is there a benefit in knowing whether the cost of the one-hundredth chip produced is different from the one-thousandth chip produced? Probably not. An average cost of the product will suffice for control and pricing purposes.

In summary, when deciding to use one of these systems, or a combination system, a company must weigh the costs of implementing the system against the benefits from the additional information provided.

DECISION TOOLKIT

DECISION CHECKPOINTS	INFO NEEDED FOR DECISION	TOOL TO USE FOR DECISION	HOW TO EVALUATE RESULTS
What costing method should be used?	Type of product or service produced	Cost of accounting system; benefits of additional information	The benefits of providing the additional information should exceed the costs of the accounting system needed to develop the information.

USING THE **DECISION TOOLKIT**

Essence Company manufactures a high-end after-shave lotion, called Eternity, in 10-ounce plastic bottles. Because the market for after-shave lotion is highly competitive, the company is very concerned about keeping its costs under control. Eternity is manufactured through three processes: mixing, filling, and corking. Materials are added at the beginning of the process, and labor and overhead are incurred uniformly throughout each process. The company uses a weighted-average method to cost its product. A partially completed production cost report for the month of May for the Mixing Department is shown below.

Essence Company
Mixing Department
Production Cost Report
For the Month Ended May 31, 2014

| | | Equivalent Units | |
| | Physical | | Conversion |
Quantities	Units	Materials	Costs
Units to be accounted for	Step 1	Step 2	
Work in process, May 1	1,000		
Started into production	2,000		
Total units	3,000		
Units accounted for			
Transferred out	2,200	?	?
Work in process, May 31	800	?	?
Total units	3,000	?	?

| | | | Conversion | |
Costs		Materials	Costs	Total
Unit costs Step 3				
Total cost	(a)	?	?	?
Equivalent units	(b)	?	?	
Unit costs [(a) ÷ (b)]		?	?	?
Costs to be accounted for				
Work in process, May 1				$ 56,300
Started into production				119,320
Total costs				$175,620

Cost Reconciliation Schedule Step 4

Costs accounted for		
Transferred out		?
Work in process, May 31		
Materials	?	
Conversion costs	?	?
Total costs		?

Additional information:
Work in process, May 1, 1000 units

Materials cost, 1,000 units (100% complete)	$49,100	
Conversion costs, 1,000 units (70% complete)	7,200	$ 56,300
Materials cost for May, 2,000 units		$100,000

Work in process, May 31, 800 units, 100% complete as to materials and 50% complete as to conversion costs.

Instructions

(a) Prepare a production cost report for the Mixing Department for the month of May.

(b) Prepare the journal entry to record the transfer of goods from the Mixing Department to the Filling Department.

(c) Explain why Essence Company is using a process cost system to account for its costs.

Solution

(a) A completed production cost report for the Mixing Department is shown below. Computations to support the amounts reported follow the report.

Action Plan

✔ Compute the physical unit flow—that is, the total units to be accounted for.

✔ Compute the equivalent units of production.

✔ Compute the unit production costs, expressed in terms of equivalent units of production.

✔ Prepare a cost reconciliation schedule, which shows that the total costs accounted for equal the total costs to be accounted for.

Essence Company
Mixing Department
Production Cost Report
For the Month Ended May 31, 2014

| | | Equivalent Units | |
Quantities	Physical Units	Materials	Conversion Costs
Units to be accounted for	Step 1	Step 2	
Work in process, May 1	1,000		
Started into production	2,000		
Total units	3,000		
Units accounted for			
Transferred out	2,200	2,200	2,200
Work in process, May 31	800	800	400 (800 × 50%)
Total units	3,000	3,000	2,600

Costs		Materials	Conversion Costs	Total
Unit costs Step 3				
Total cost*	(a)	$149,100	$26,520	$175,620
Equivalent units	(b)	3,000	2,600	
Unit costs [(a) ÷ (b)]		$49.70	$10.20	$59.90
Costs to be accounted for				
Work in process, May 1				$ 56,300
Started into production				119,320
Total costs				$175,620

*Additional computations to support production cost report data:
Materials cost—$49,100 + $100,000
Conversion costs—$7,200 + $19,320 ($119,320 − $100,000)

Cost Reconciliation Schedule Step 4

Costs accounted for		
Transferred out (2,200 × $59.90)		$131,780
Work in process, May 31		
Materials (800 × $49.70)	$39,760	
Conversion costs (400 × $10.20)	4,080	43,840
Total costs		$175,620

(b)
Work in Process—Filling	131,780	
Work in Process—Mixing		131,780

(c) Companies use process cost systems to apply costs to similar products that are mass-produced in a continuous fashion. Essence Company uses a process cost system because production of the after-shave lotion, once it begins, continues until the after-shave lotion emerges. The processing is the same for the entire run—with precisely the same amount of materials, labor, and overhead. Each bottle of Eternity after-shave lotion is indistinguishable from another.

✔ **The Navigator**

1 Understand who uses process cost systems. Companies that mass-produce similar products in a continuous fashion use process cost systems. Once production begins, it continues until the finished product emerges. Each unit of finished product is indistinguishable from every other unit.

2 Explain the similarities and differences between job order cost and process cost systems. Job order cost systems are similar to process cost systems in three ways: (1) Both systems track the same cost elements—direct materials, direct labor, and manufacturing overhead. (2) Both accumulate costs in the same accounts—Raw Materials Inventory, Factory Labor, and Manufacturing Overhead. (3) Both assign accumulated costs to the same accounts—Work in Process, Finished Goods Inventory, and Cost of Goods Sold. However, the method of assigning costs differs significantly.

There are four main differences between the two cost systems: (1) A process cost system uses separate accounts for each department or manufacturing process, rather than only one work in process account used in a job order cost system. (2) A process cost system summarizes costs in a production cost report for each department. A job order cost system charges costs to individual jobs and summarizes them in a job cost sheet. (3) Costs are totaled at the end of a time period in a process cost system, but at the completion of a job in a job order cost system. (4) A process cost system calculates unit cost as: Total manufacturing costs for the period ÷ Units produced during the period. A job order cost system calculates unit cost as: Total cost per job ÷ Units produced.

3 Explain the flow of costs in a process cost system. A process cost system assigns manufacturing costs for raw materials, labor, and overhead to work in process accounts for various departments or manufacturing processes. It transfers the costs of partially completed units from one department to another as those units move through the manufacturing process. The system transfers the costs of completed work to Finished

Goods Inventory. Finally, when inventory is sold, the system transfers the costs to Cost of Goods Sold.

4 Make the journal entries to assign manufacturing costs in a process cost system. Entries to assign the costs of raw materials, labor, and overhead consist of a credit to Raw Materials Inventory, Factory Labor, and Manufacturing Overhead, and a debit to Work in Process for each department. Entries to record the cost of goods transferred to another department are a credit to Work in Process for the department whose work is finished and a debit to the department to which the goods are transferred. The entry to record units completed and transferred to the warehouse is a credit to Work in Process for the department whose work is finished and a debit to Finished Goods Inventory. The entry to record the sale of goods is a credit to Finished Goods Inventory and a debit to Cost of Goods Sold.

5 Compute equivalent units. Equivalent units of production measure work done during a period, expressed in fully completed units. Companies use this measure to determine the cost per unit of completed product. Equivalent units are the sum of units completed and transferred out plus equivalent units of ending work in process.

6 Explain the four steps necessary to prepare a production cost report. The four steps to complete a production cost report are: (1) Compute the physical unit flow—that is, the total units to be accounted for. (2) Compute the equivalent units of production. (3) Compute the unit production costs, expressed in terms of equivalent units of production. (4) Prepare a cost reconciliation schedule, which shows that the total costs accounted for equal the total costs to be accounted for.

7 Prepare a production cost report. The production cost report contains both quantity and cost data for a production department. There are four sections in the report: (1) number of physical units, (2) equivalent units determination, (3) unit costs, and (4) cost reconciliation schedule.

DECISION TOOLKIT A SUMMARY

DECISION CHECKPOINTS	INFO NEEDED FOR DECISION	TOOL TO USE FOR DECISION	HOW TO EVALUATE RESULTS
What is the cost of a product?	Costs of materials, labor, and overhead assigned to processes used to make the product	Production cost report	Compare costs to previous periods, to competitors, and to expected selling price to evaluate overall profitability.
Which costing method should be used?	Type of product or service produced	Cost of accounting system; benefits of additional information	The benefits of providing the additional information should exceed the costs of the accounting system needed to develop the information.

APPENDIX 3A   FIFO METHOD

In this chapter, we demonstrated the weighted-average method of computing equivalent units. Some companies use a different method, referred to as the **first-in, first-out (FIFO) method**, to compute equivalent units. The purpose of this appendix is to illustrate how companies use the FIFO method to prepare a production cost report.

> **LEARNING OBJECTIVE   8**
>
> **Compute equivalent units using the FIFO method.**

Equivalent Units Under FIFO

Under the FIFO method, companies compute equivalent units on a first-in, first-out basis. Some companies favor the FIFO method because the FIFO cost assumption usually corresponds to the actual physical flow of the goods. Under the FIFO method, companies therefore assume that the beginning work in process is completed before new work is started.

Using the FIFO method, equivalent units are the sum of the work performed to:

1. Finish the units of beginning work in process inventory.
2. Complete the units started into production during the period (referred to as the **units started and completed**).
3. Start, but only partially complete, the units in ending work in process inventory.

Normally, in a process cost system, some units will always be in process at both the beginning and end of the period.

ILLUSTRATION

Illustration 3A-1 shows the physical flow of units for the Assembly Department of Shutters Inc. In addition, it indicates the degree of completion of the work in process accounts in regard to conversion costs.

Assembly Department	
	Physical Units
Units to be accounted for	
Work in process, June 1 (40% complete)	500
Started (transferred) into production	8,000
Total units	8,500
Units accounted for	
Completed and transferred out	8,100
Work in process, June 30 (75% complete)	400
Total units	8,500

Illustration 3A-1
Physical unit flow—Assembly Department

In Illustration 3A-1, the units completed and transferred out (8,100) plus the units in ending work in process (400) equal the total units to be accounted for (8,500). Using FIFO, we then compute equivalent units as follows.

1. The 500 units of beginning work in process were 40% complete. Thus, 300 equivalent units (60% × 500 units) were required to complete the beginning inventory.
2. The units started and completed during the current month are the units transferred out minus the units in beginning work in process. For the Assembly Department, units started and completed are 7,600 (8,100 − 500).
3. The 400 units of ending work in process were 75% complete. Thus, equivalent units were 300 (75% × 400).

Equivalent units for the Assembly Department are 8,200, computed as follows.

Illustration 3A-2
Computation of equivalent
units—FIFO method

		Assembly Department		
Production Data	**Physical Units**	**Work Added This Period**	**Equivalent Units**	
Work in process, June 1	500	60%	300	
Started and completed	7,600	100%	7,600	
Work in process, June 30	400	75%	300	
Total	8,500		8,200	

Comprehensive Example

To provide a complete illustration of the FIFO method, we will use the data for the Mixing Department at Kellogg Company for the month of June, as shown in Illustration 3A-3.

Illustration 3A-3
Unit and cost data—Mixing
Department

Mixing Department	
Units	
Work in process, June 1	100,000
Direct materials: 100% complete	
Conversion costs: 70% complete	
Units started into production during June	800,000
Units completed and transferred out to Baking Department	700,000
Work in process, June 30	200,000
Direct materials: 100% complete	
Conversion costs: 60% complete	
Costs	
Work in process, June 1	
Direct materials: 100% complete	$ 50,000
Conversion costs: 70% complete	35,000
Cost of work in process, June 1	$ 85,000
Costs incurred during production in June	
Direct materials	$400,000
Conversion costs	170,000
Costs incurred in June	$570,000

COMPUTE THE PHYSICAL UNIT FLOW (STEP 1)
Illustration 3A-4 (page 117) shows the physical flow of units for Kellogg for the month of June for the Mixing Department.

Under the FIFO method, companies often expand the physical units schedule, as shown in Illustration 3A-5 (page 117) to explain the transferred-out section. As a result, this section reports the beginning work in process and the units started and completed. These two items further explain the completed and transferred-out section.

Mixing Department	
	Physical Units
Units to be accounted for	
Work in process, June 1	100,000
Started (transferred) into production	800,000
Total units	900,000
Units accounted for	
Completed and transferred out	700,000
Work in process, June 30	200,000
Total units	900,000

Illustration 3A-4
Physical unit flow—Mixing Department

Mixing Department	
	Physical Units
Units to be accounted for	
Work in process, June 1	100,000
Started (transferred) into production	800,000
Total units	900,000
Units accounted for	
Completed and transferred out	
Work in process, June 1	100,000
Started and completed	600,000
	700,000
Work in process, June 30	200,000
Total units	900,000

Illustration 3A-5
Physical unit flow (FIFO)—Mixing Department

The records indicate that the Mixing Department must account for 900,000 units. Of this sum, 700,000 units were transferred to the Baking Department and 200,000 units were still in process.

COMPUTE EQUIVALENT UNITS OF PRODUCTION (STEP 2)

As with the method presented in the chapter, once they determine the physical flow of the units, companies need to determine equivalent units of production. The Mixing Department adds materials at the beginning of the process, and it incurs conversion costs uniformly during the process. Thus, Kellogg must make two computations of equivalent units: one for materials and one for conversion costs.

Helpful Hint
Materials are not always added at the beginning of the process. For example, companies sometimes add materials uniformly during the process.

EQUIVALENT UNITS FOR MATERIALS Since Kellogg adds materials at the beginning of the process, no additional materials costs are required to complete the beginning work in process. In addition, 100% of the materials costs has been incurred on the ending work in process. Thus, the computation of equivalent units for materials is as follows.

Illustration 3A-6
Computation of equivalent
units—materials

Mixing Department—Materials			
Production Data	**Physical Units**	**Materials Added This Period**	**Equivalent Units**
Work in process, June 1	100,000	–0–	–0–
Started and finished	600,000	100%	600,000
Work in process, June 30	200,000	100%	200,000
Total	900,000		800,000

EQUIVALENT UNITS FOR CONVERSION COSTS The 100,000 units of beginning work in process were 70% complete in terms of conversion costs. Thus, the Mixing Department required 30,000 equivalent units (30% $\times$ 100,000 units) of conversion costs to complete the beginning inventory. In addition, the 200,000 units of ending work in process were 60% complete in terms of conversion costs. Thus, the equivalent units for conversion costs is 750,000, computed as follows.

Illustration 3A-7
Computation of equivalent
units—conversion costs

Mixing Department—Conversion Costs			
Production Data	**Physical Units**	**Work Added This Period**	**Equivalent Units**
Work in process, June 1	100,000	30%	30,000
Started and finished	600,000	100%	600,000
Work in process, June 30	200,000	60%	120,000
Total	900,000		750,000

COMPUTE UNIT PRODUCTION COSTS (STEP 3)

Armed with the knowledge of the equivalent units of production, Kellogg can now compute the unit production costs. Unit production costs are costs expressed in terms of equivalent units of production. When equivalent units of production are different for materials and conversion costs, companies compute three unit costs: (1) materials, (2) conversion, and (3) total manufacturing.

Under the FIFO method, the unit costs of production are based entirely on the production costs incurred during the month. Thus, the costs in the beginning work in process are not relevant, because they were incurred on work done in the preceding month. As Illustration 3A-3 (page 116) indicated, the costs incurred during production in June were:

Illustration 3A-8
Costs incurred during
production in June

Direct materials	$400,000
Conversion costs	170,000
Total costs	$570,000

Illustration 3A-9 shows the computation of unit materials cost, unit conversion costs, and total unit cost related to Eggo® Waffles.

(1)	Total Materials Cost	÷	Equivalent Units of Materials	=	Unit Materials Cost
	$400,000	÷	800,000	=	$0.50
(2)	Total Conversion Costs	÷	Equivalent Units of Conversion Costs	=	Unit Conversion Cost
	$170,000	÷	750,000	=	$0.227 (rounded)*
(3)	Unit Materials Cost	+	Unit Conversion Cost	=	Total Manufacturing Cost per Unit
	$0.50	+	$0.227	=	$0.727

For homework problems, round unit costs to three decimal places.

Illustration 3A-9
Unit cost formulas and computations—Mixing Department

As shown, the unit costs are $0.50 for materials, $0.227 for conversion costs, and $0.727 for total manufacturing costs.

PREPARE A COST RECONCILIATION SCHEDULE (STEP 4)

Kellogg is now ready to determine the cost of goods transferred out of the Mixing Department to the Baking Department and the costs in ending work in process. The total costs charged to the Mixing Department in June are $655,000, calculated as follows.

Costs to be accounted for	
Work in process, June 1	$ 85,000
Started into production	570,000
Total costs	$655,000

Illustration 3A-10
Costs charged to Mixing Department

Kellogg next prepares a cost reconciliation to assign these costs to (1) units transferred out to the Baking Department and (2) ending work in process. Under the FIFO method, the first goods to be completed during the period are the units in beginning work in process. Thus, the cost of the beginning work in process is always assigned to the goods transferred to the next department (or finished goods, if processing is complete). Under the FIFO method, ending work in process also will be assigned only the production costs incurred in the current period. Illustration 3A-11 shows a cost reconciliation schedule for the Mixing Department.

Illustration 3A-11
Cost reconciliation report

Mixing Department Cost Reconciliation Schedule		
Costs accounted for		
Transferred out		
Work in process, June 1		$ 85,000
Costs to complete beginning work in process		
Conversion costs (30,000 × $0.227)		6,810
Total costs		91,810
Units started and completed (600,000 × $0.727)		435,950*
Total costs transferred out		527,760
Work in process, June 30		
Materials (200,000 × $0.50)	$100,000	
Conversion costs (120,000 × $0.227)	27,240	127,240
Total costs		$655,000

*Any rounding errors should be adjusted in the "Units started and completed" calculation.

As you can see, the total costs accounted for ($655,000 from Illustration 3A-11) equal the total costs to be accounted for ($655,000 from Illustration 3A-10).

PREPARING THE PRODUCTION COST REPORT

At this point, Kellogg is ready to prepare the production cost report for the Mixing Department. This report is an internal document for management that shows production quantity and cost data for a production department.

As discussed on page 109 there are four steps in preparing a production cost report:

1. Compute the physical unit flow.
2. Compute the equivalent units of production.
3. Compute unit production costs.
4. Prepare a cost reconciliation schedule.

Illustration 3A-12 shows the production cost report for the Mixing Department, with the four steps identified in the report.

As indicated in the chapter, production cost reports provide a basis for evaluating the productivity of a department. In addition, managers can use the cost data to assess whether unit costs and total costs are reasonable. By comparing the quantity and cost data with predetermined goals, top management can also judge whether current performance is meeting planned objectives.

FIFO and Weighted-Average

The weighted-average method of computing equivalent units has **one major advantage**: It is simple to understand and apply. In cases where prices do not fluctuate significantly from period to period, the weighted-average method will be very similar to the FIFO method. In addition, companies that have been using just-in-time procedures effectively for inventory control purposes will have minimal inventory balances, and therefore differences between the weighted- average and the FIFO methods will not be material.

Conceptually, the FIFO method is superior to the weighted-average method because it measures **current performance** using only costs incurred in the current period. Managers are, therefore, not held responsible for costs from prior periods over which they may not have had control. In addition, the FIFO method **provides current cost information**, which the company can use to establish **more accurate pricing strategies** for goods manufactured and sold in the current period.

Helpful Hint
What are the two self-checks in the report? Answer: (1) Total physical units accounted for must equal the total units to be accounted for. (2) Total costs accounted for must equal the total costs to be accounted for.

Mixing Department.xls

| | Home | Insert | Page Layout | Formulas | Data | Review | View |

P18

	A	B	C	D	E
1		**Mixing Department**			
2		**Production Cost Report**			
3		**For the Month Ended June 30, 2014**			
4			_Equivalent Units_		
5		Physical Units	Materials	Conversion Costs	
6	QUANTITIES	Step 1	Step 2		
7	Units to be accounted for				
8	Work in process (WIP), June 1	100,000			
9	Started into production	800,000			
10	Total units	900,000			
11	Units accounted for				
12	Completed and transferred out				
13	Work in process, June 1	100,000	0	30,000	
14	Started and completed	600,000	600,000	600,000	
15	Work in process, June 30	200,000	200,000	120,000	
16	Total units	900,000	800,000	750,000	
17	COSTS				
18	Unit costs Step 3		Materials	Conversion Costs	Total
19	Costs in June (excluding beginning WIP) (a)		$400,000	$170,000	$570,000
20	Equivalent units (b)		800,000	750,000	
21	Unit costs [(a) ÷ (b)]		$0.50	$0.227	$0.727
22	Costs to be accounted for				
23	Work in process, June 1				$85,000
24	Started into production				570,000
25	Total costs				$655,000
26	**Cost Reconciliation Schedule** Step 4				
27	Costs accounted for				
28	Transferred out				
29	Work in process, June 1				$85,000
30	Costs to complete beginning work in process				
31	Conversion costs (30,000 × $0.227)				6,810
32	Total costs				91,810
33	Units started and completed (600,000 × $0.727)*				435,950
34	Total costs transferred out				527,760
35	Work in process, June 30				
36	Materials (200,000 × $0.50)			$100,000	
37	Conversions costs (120,000 × $0.227)			27,240	127,240
38	Total costs				$655,000
39	*Any rounding errors should be adjusted in the "Units started and completed"				

Illustration 3A-12
Production cost
report—FIFO method

✔ The Navigator

SUMMARY OF LEARNING OBJECTIVE FOR APPENDIX 3A

8 Compute equivalent units using the FIFO method.
Equivalent units under the FIFO method are the sum of
the work performed to: (1) Finish the units of beginning
work in process inventory, if any; (2) complete the units

started into production during the period; and (3) start,
but only partially complete, the units in ending work in
process inventory.

GLOSSARY

Conversion costs The sum of labor costs and overhead costs. (p. 103).

Cost reconciliation schedule A schedule that shows that the total costs accounted for equal the total costs to be accounted for. (p. 109).

Equivalent units of production A measure of the work done during the period, expressed in fully completed units. (p. 102).

Operations costing A combination of a process cost and a job order cost system, in which products are manufactured primarily by standardized methods, with some customization. (p. 111).

Physical units Actual units to be accounted for during a period, irrespective of any work performed. (p. 106).

Process cost system An accounting system used to apply costs to similar products that are mass-produced in a continuous fashion. (p. 96).

Production cost report An internal report for management that shows both production quantity and cost data for a production department. (p. 105).

Total units (costs) accounted for The sum of the units (costs) transferred out during the period plus the units (costs) in process at the end of the period. (p. 106).

Total units (costs) to be accounted for The sum of the units (costs) started (or transferred) into production during the period plus the units (costs) in process at the beginning of the period. (p. 106).

Unit production costs Costs expressed in terms of equivalent units of production. (p. 107).

Weighted-average method Method of computing equivalent units of production which considers the degree of completion (weighting) of the units completed and transferred out and the ending work in process. (p. 103).

> Comprehensive **DO IT!**

Karlene Industries produces plastic ice cube trays in two processes: heating and stamping. All materials are added at the beginning of the Heating Department process. Karlene uses the weighted-average method to compute equivalent units.

On November 1, the Heating Department had in process 1,000 trays that were 70% complete. During November, it started into production 12,000 trays. On November 30, 2014, 2,000 trays that were 60% complete were in process.

The following cost information for the Heating Department was also available.

Work in process, November 1:		Costs incurred in November:	
Materials	$ 640	Material	$3,000
Conversion costs	360	Labor	2,300
Cost of work in process, Nov. 1	$1,000	Overhead	4,050

Instructions

(a) Prepare a production cost report for the Heating Department for the month of November 2014, using the weighted-average method.

(b) Journalize the transfer of costs to the Stamping Department.

Action Plan

✔ Compute the physical unit flow—that is, the total units to be accounted for.

✔ Compute the equivalent units of production.

✔ Compute the unit production costs, expressed in terms of equivalent units of production.

✔ Prepare a cost reconciliation schedule, which shows that the total costs accounted for equal the total costs to be accounted for.

Solution to Comprehensive DO IT!

(a)

Karlene Industries
Heating Department
Production Cost Report
For the Month Ended November 30, 2014

	Physical Units	Equivalent Units	
		Materials	Conversion Costs
Quantities	Step 1	Step 2	
Units to be accounted for			
Work in process, November 1	1,000		
Started into production	12,000		
Total units	13,000		
Units accounted for			
Transferred out	11,000	11,000	11,000
Work in process, November 30	2,000	2,000	1,200
Total units	13,000	13,000	12,200

Costs			Conversion	
Unit costs Step 3		Materials	Costs	Total
Total cost	(a)	$ 3,640*	$ 6,710**	$10,350
Equivalent units	(b)	13,000	12,200	
Unit costs [(a) ÷ (b)]		$0.28	$0.55	$0.83
Costs to be accounted for				
Work in process, November 1				$ 1,000
Started into production				9,350
Total costs				$10,350

*$640 + $3,000
**$360 + $2,300 + $4,050

Cost Reconciliation Schedule Step 4

Costs accounted for			
Transferred out (11,000 × $0.83)			$ 9,130
Work in process, November 30			
Materials (2,000 × $0.28)		$560	
Conversion costs (1,200 × $0.55)		660	1,220
Total costs			$10,350

(b)	Work in Process—Stamping	9,130	
	Work in Process—Heating		9,130
	(To record transfer of units to the Stamping Department)		

✔ **The Navigator**

Self-Test, Brief Exercises, Exercises, Problem Set A, and many more resources are available for practice in WileyPLUS.

Note: All asterisked Questions, Exercises, and Problems relate to material in the appendix to the chapter.

SELF-TEST QUESTIONS

Answers are at the end of the chapter.

(LO 1) **1.** Which of the following items is *not* characteristic of a process cost system?
- (a) Once production begins, it continues until the finished product emerges.
- (b) The products produced are heterogeneous in nature.
- (c) The focus is on continually producing homogeneous products.
- (d) When the finished product emerges, all units have precisely the same amount of materials, labor, and overhead.

(LO 2) **2.** Indicate which of the following statements is *not* correct.
- (a) Both a job order and a process cost system track the same three manufacturing cost elements—direct materials, direct labor, and manufacturing overhead.
- (b) A job order cost system uses only one work in process account, whereas a process cost system uses multiple work in process accounts.
- (c) Manufacturing costs are accumulated the same way in a job order and in a process cost system.
- (d) Manufacturing costs are assigned the same way in a job order and in a process cost system.

(LO 3) **3.** In a process cost system, the flow of costs is:
- (a) work in process, cost of goods sold, finished goods.
- (b) finished goods, work in process, cost of goods sold.
- (c) finished goods, cost of goods sold, work in process.
- (d) work in process, finished goods, cost of goods sold.

(LO 4) **4.** In making journal entries to assign raw materials costs, a company using process costing:
- (a) debits Finished Goods Inventory.
- (b) often debits two or more work in process accounts.
- (c) generally credits two or more work in process accounts.
- (d) credits Finished Goods Inventory.

(LO 4) **5.** In a process cost system, manufacturing overhead:
- (a) is assigned to finished goods at the end of each accounting period.
- (b) is assigned to a work in process account for each job as the job is completed.
- (c) is assigned to a work in process account for each production department on the basis of a predetermined overhead rate.
- (d) is assigned to a work in process account for each production department as overhead costs are incurred.

(LO 5) **6.** Conversion costs are the sum of:
- (a) fixed and variable overhead costs.
- (b) labor costs and overhead costs.
- (c) direct material costs and overhead costs.
- (d) direct labor and indirect labor costs.

7. The Mixing Department's output during the period (LO 5) consists of 20,000 units completed and transferred out, and 5,000 units in ending work in process 60% complete as to materials and conversion costs. Beginning inventory is 1,000 units, 40% complete as to materials and conversion costs. The equivalent units of production are:
- (a) 22,600.
- (c) 24,000.
- (b) 23,000.
- (d) 25,000.

8. In RYZ Company, there are zero units in beginning (LO 6) work in process, 7,000 units started into production, and 500 units in ending work in process 20% completed. The physical units to be accounted for are:
- (a) 7,000.
- (c) 7,500.
- (b) 7,360.
- (d) 7,340.

9. Mora Company has 2,000 units in beginning work in (LO 6) process, 20% complete as to conversion costs, 23,000 units transferred out to finished goods, and 3,000 units in ending work in process $33\frac{1}{3}$% complete as to conversion costs.

The beginning and ending inventory is fully complete as to materials costs. Equivalent units for materials and conversion costs are, respectively:
- (a) 22,000, 24,000.
- (c) 26,000, 24,000.
- (b) 24,000, 26,000.
- (d) 26,000, 26,000.

10. Fortner Company has no beginning work in process; (LO 6) 9,000 units are transferred out and 3,000 units in ending work in process are one-third finished as to conversion costs and fully complete as to materials cost. If total materials cost is $60,000, the unit materials cost is:
- (a) $5.00.
- (b) $5.45 rounded.
- (c) $6.00.
- (d) No correct answer is given.

11. Largo Company has unit costs of $10 for materials (LO 6) and $30 for conversion costs. If there are 2,500 units in ending work in process, 40% complete as to conversion costs, and fully complete as to materials cost, the total cost assignable to the ending work in process inventory is:
- (a) $45,000.
- (c) $75,000.
- (b) $55,000.
- (d) $100,000.

12. A production cost report: (LO 7)
- (a) is an external report.
- (b) shows both the production quantity and cost data related to a department.
- (c) shows equivalent units of production but not physical units.
- (d) contains six sections.

13. In a production cost report, units to be accounted for (LO 7) are calculated as:
- (a) Units started into production + Units in ending work in process.

(b) Units started into production − Units in beginning work in process.
(c) Units transferred out + Units in beginning work in process.
(d) Units started into production + Units in beginning work in process.

(LO 8)*14. Hollins Company uses the FIFO method to compute equivalent units. It has 2,000 units in beginning work in process, 20% complete as to conversion costs, 25,000 units started and completed, and 3,000 units in ending work in process, 30% complete as to conversion costs. All units are 100% complete as to materials. Equivalent units for materials and conversion costs are, respectively:
(a) 28,000 and 26,600.
(b) 28,000 and 27,500.
(c) 27,000 and 26,200.
(d) 27,000 and 29,600.

*15. KLM Company uses the FIFO method to compute (LO 8) equivalent units. It has no beginning work in process; 9,000 units are started and completed and 3,000 units in ending work in process are one-third completed. All material is added at the beginning of the process. If total materials cost is $60,000, the unit materials cost is:
(a) $5.00.
(b) $6.00.
(c) $6.67 (rounded).
(d) No correct answer given.

*16. Toney Company uses the FIFO method to compute (LO 3) equivalent units. It has unit costs of $10 for materials and $30 for conversion costs. If there are 2,500 units in ending work in process, 100% complete as to materials and 40% complete as to conversion costs, the total cost assignable to the ending work in process inventory is:
(a) $45,000.   (c) $75,000.
(b) $55,000.   (d) $100,000.

Go to the book's companion website, www.wiley.com/college/weygandt, for additional Self-Test Questions.

✔ **The Navigator**

QUESTIONS

1. Identify which costing system—job order or process cost—the following companies would primarily use: (a) Quaker Oats, (b) Jif Peanut Butter, (c) Gulf Craft (luxury yachts), and (d) Warner Bros. Motion Pictures.
2. Contrast the primary focus of job order cost accounting and of process cost accounting.
3. What are the similarities between a job order and a process cost system?
4. Your roommate is confused about the features of process cost accounting. Identify and explain the distinctive features for your roommate.
5. Sam Bowyer believes there are no significant differences in the flow of costs between job order cost accounting and process cost accounting. Is Bowyer correct? Explain.
6. (a) What source documents are used in assigning (1) materials and (2) labor to production in a process cost system?
   (b) What criterion and basis are commonly used in allocating overhead to processes?
7. At Ely Company, overhead is assigned to production departments at the rate of $5 per machine hour. In July, machine hours were 3,000 in the Machining Department and 2,400 in the Assembly Department. Prepare the entry to assign overhead to production.
8. Mark Haley is uncertain about the steps used to prepare a production cost report. State the procedures that are required in the sequence in which they are performed.
9. John Harbeck is confused about computing physical units. Explain to John how physical units to be accounted for and physical units accounted for are determined.
10. What is meant by the term "equivalent units of production"?

11. How are equivalent units of production computed?
12. Coats Company had zero units of beginning work in process. During the period, 9,000 units were completed, and there were 600 units of ending work in process. What were the units started into production?
13. Sanchez Co. has zero units of beginning work in process. During the period, 12,000 units were completed, and there were 500 units of ending work in process one-fifth complete as to conversion cost and 100% complete as to materials cost. What were the equivalent units of production for (a) materials and (b) conversion costs?
14. Hindi Co. started 3,000 units during the period. Its beginning inventory is 500 units one-fourth complete as to conversion costs and 100% complete as to materials costs. Its ending inventory is 300 units one-fifth complete as to conversion costs and 100% complete as to materials costs. How many units were transferred out this period?
15. Clauss Company transfers out 14,000 units and has 2,000 units of ending work in process that are 25% complete. Materials are entered at the beginning of the process and there is no beginning work in process. Assuming unit materials costs of $3 and unit conversion costs of $5, what are the costs to be assigned to units (a) transferred out and (b) in ending work in process?
16. (a) Ann Quinn believes the production cost report is an external report for stockholders. Is Ann correct? Explain.
   (b) Identify the sections in a production cost report.
17. What purposes are served by a production cost report?
18. At Trent Company, there are 800 units of ending work in process that are 100% complete as to materials and 40% complete as to conversion costs. If the unit cost of materials is $3 and the total costs assigned to the 800 units is $6,000, what is the per unit conversion cost?

19. What is the difference between operations costing and a process cost system?

20. How does a company decide whether to use a job order or a process cost system?

*21. Soria Co. started and completed 2,000 units for the period. Its beginning inventory is 800 units 25% complete and its ending inventory is 400 units 20% complete. Soria uses the FIFO method to compute equivalent units. How many units were transferred out this period?

*22. Reyes Company transfers out 12,000 units and has 2,000 units of ending work in process that are 25% complete. Materials are entered at the beginning of the process and there is no beginning work in process. Reyes uses the FIFO method to compute equivalent units. Assuming unit materials costs of $3 and unit conversion costs of $7, what are the costs to be assigned to units (a) transferred out and (b) in ending work in process?

BRIEF EXERCISES

Journalize entries for accumulating costs.

(LO 4), AP

BE3-1 Weber Company purchases $45,000 of raw materials on account, and it incurs $60,000 of factory labor costs. Journalize the two transactions on March 31 assuming the labor costs are not paid until April.

Journalize the assignment of materials and labor costs.

(LO 4), AP

BE3-2 Data for Weber Company are given in BE3-1. Supporting records show that (a) the Assembly Department used $24,000 of raw materials and $35,000 of the factory labor, and (b) the Finishing Department used the remainder. Journalize the assignment of the costs to the processing departments on March 31.

Journalize the assignment of overhead costs.

(LO 4), AP

BE3-3 Factory labor data for Weber Company are given in BE3-2. Manufacturing overhead is assigned to departments on the basis of 200% of labor costs. Journalize the assignment of overhead to the Assembly and Finishing Departments.

Compute equivalent units of production.

(LO 5), AP

BE3-4 Goode Company has the following production data for selected months.

Month	Beginning Work in Process	Units Transferred Out	Ending Work in Process	
			Units	% Complete as to Conversion Cost
January	–0–	35,000	10,000	40%
March	–0–	40,000	8,000	75
July	–0–	45,000	16,000	25

Compute equivalent units of production for materials and conversion costs, assuming materials are entered at the beginning of the process.

Compute unit costs of production.

(LO 6), AP

BE3-5 In Lopez Company, total material costs are $36,000, and total conversion costs are $54,000. Equivalent units of production are materials 10,000 and conversion costs 12,000. Compute the unit costs for materials, conversion costs, and total manufacturing costs.

Assign costs to units transferred out and in process.

(LO 6), AP

BE3-6 Trek Company has the following production data for April: units transferred out 40,000, and ending work in process 5,000 units that are 100% complete for materials and 40% complete for conversion costs. If unit materials cost is $4 and unit conversion cost is $7, determine the costs to be assigned to the units transferred out and the units in ending work in process.

Compute unit costs.

(LO 6), AP

BE3-7 Production costs chargeable to the Finishing Department in June in Cascio Company are materials $16,000, labor $29,500, overhead $18,000. Equivalent units of production are materials 20,000 and conversion costs 19,000. Compute the unit costs for materials and conversion costs.

Prepare cost reconciliation schedule.

(LO 6), AP

BE3-8 Data for Cascio Company are given in BE3-7. Production records indicate that 18,000 units were transferred out, and 2,000 units in ending work in process were 50% complete as to conversion cost and 100% complete as to materials. Prepare a cost reconciliation schedule.

Compute equivalent units of production.

(LO 5), AP

BE3-9 The Smelting Department of Mathews Company has the following production and cost data for November.

Production: Beginning work in process 2,000 units that are 100% complete as to materials and 20% complete as to conversion costs; units transferred out 8,000 units; and ending work in process 7,000 units that are 100% complete as to materials and 40% complete as to conversion costs.

Compute the equivalent units of production for (a) materials and (b) conversion costs for the month of November.

***BE3-10** Sanderson Company has the following production data for March: no beginning work in process, units started and completed 30,000, and ending work in process 5,000 units that are 100% complete for materials and 40% complete for conversion costs. Sanderson uses the FIFO method to compute equivalent units. If unit materials cost is $6 and unit conversion cost is $12, determine the costs to be assigned to the units transferred out and the units in ending work in process. The total costs to be assigned are $594,000.

Assign costs to units transferred out and in process.

(LO 8), AP

***BE3-11** Using the data in BE3-10, prepare the cost section of the production cost report for Sanderson Company.

Prepare a partial production cost report.

(LO 7, 8), AP

***BE3-12** Production costs chargeable to the Finishing Department in May at Kim Company are materials $8,000, labor $20,000, overhead $18,000, and transferred-in costs $67,000. Equivalent units of production are materials 20,000 and conversion costs 19,000. Kim uses the FIFO method to compute equivalent units. Compute the unit costs for materials and conversion costs. Transferred-in costs are considered materials costs.

Compute unit costs.

(LO 8), AP

> DO IT! REVIEW

DO IT! 3-1 Indicate whether each of the following statements is true or false.

1. Many hospitals use job order costing for small, routine medical procedures.
2. A manufacturer of computer flash drives would use a job order cost system.
3. A process cost system uses multiple work in process accounts.
4. A process cost system keeps track of costs on job cost sheets.

Compare job order and process cost systems.

(LO 1, 2), C

DO IT! 3-2 Kopa Company manufactures CH-21 through two processes: Mixing and Packaging. In July, the following costs were incurred.

Assign and journalize manufacturing costs.

(LO 4), AP

	Mixing	Packaging
Raw materials used	$10,000	$28,000
Factory labor costs	8,000	36,000
Manufacturing overhead costs	12,000	54,000

Units completed at a cost of $21,000 in the Mixing Department are transferred to the Packaging Department. Units completed at a cost of $106,000 in the Packaging Department are transferred to Finished Goods. Journalize the assignment of these costs to the two processes and the transfer of units as appropriate.

DO IT! 3-3 The assembly department has the following production data for the current month.

Compute equivalent units.

(LO 5), AP

Beginning Work in Process	Units Transferred Out	Ending Work in Process
–0–	20,000	12,000

Materials are entered at the beginning of the process. The ending work in process units are 70% complete as to conversion costs. Compute the equivalent units of production for (a) materials and (b) conversion costs.

DO IT! 3-4 In March, Kelly Company had the following unit production costs: materials $10 and conversion costs $8. On March 1, it had zero work in process. During March, Kelly transferred out 22,000 units. As of March 31, 4,000 units that were 40% complete as to conversion costs and 100% complete as to materials were in ending work in process.

Prepare cost reconciliation schedule.

(LO 6, 7), AP

(a) Compute the total units to be accounted for.
(b) Compute the equivalent units of production.
(c) Prepare a cost reconciliation schedule, including the costs of materials transferred out and the costs of materials in process.

EXERCISES

Understand process cost accounting.

(LO 1, 2), C

E3-1 Robert Mallory has prepared the following list of statements about process cost accounting.

1. Process cost systems are used to apply costs to similar products that are mass-produced in a continuous fashion.
2. A process cost system is used when each finished unit is indistinguishable from another.
3. Companies that produce soft drinks, motion pictures, and computer chips would all use process cost accounting.
4. In a process cost system, costs are tracked by individual jobs.
5. Job order costing and process costing track different manufacturing cost elements.
6. Both job order costing and process costing account for direct materials, direct labor, and manufacturing overhead.
7. Costs flow through the accounts in the same basic way for both job order costing and process costing.
8. In a process cost system, only one work in process account is used.
9. In a process cost system, costs are summarized in a job cost sheet.
10. In a process cost system, the unit cost is total manufacturing costs for the period divided by the equivalent units produced during the period.

Instructions
Identify each statement as true or false. If false, indicate how to correct the statement.

Journalize transactions.

(LO 4), AP

E3-2 Harrelson Company manufactures pizza sauce through two production departments: Cooking and Canning. In each process, materials and conversion costs are incurred evenly throughout the process. For the month of April, the work in process accounts show the following debits.

	Cooking	Canning
Beginning work in process	$ –0–	$ 4,000
Materials	21,000	9,000
Labor	8,500	7,000
Overhead	31,500	25,800
Costs transferred in		53,000

Instructions
Journalize the April transactions.

Answer questions on costs and production.

(LO 3, 5, 6), AP

E3-3 The ledger of Custer Company has the following work in process account.

Work in Process—Painting

5/1	Balance	3,590	5/31	Transferred out	?
5/31	Materials	5,160			
5/31	Labor	2,740			
5/31	Overhead	1,380			
5/31	Balance	?			

Production records show that there were 400 units in the beginning inventory, 30% complete, 1,400 units started, and 1,500 units transferred out. The beginning work in process had materials cost of $2,040 and conversion costs of $1,550. The units in ending inventory were 40% complete. Materials are entered at the beginning of the painting process.

Instructions
(a) How many units are in process at May 31?
(b) What is the unit materials cost for May?
(c) What is the unit conversion cost for May?
(d) What is the total cost of units transferred out in May?
(e) What is the cost of the May 31 inventory?

Journalize transactions for two processes.

(LO 4), AP

E3-4 Schrager Company has two production departments: Cutting and Assembly. July 1 inventories are Raw Materials $4,200, Work in Process—Cutting $2,900, Work in Process—

Assembly $10,600, and Finished Goods $31,000. During July, the following transactions occurred.

1. Purchased $62,500 of raw materials on account.
2. Incurred $60,000 of factory labor. (Credit Wages Payable.)
3. Incurred $70,000 of manufacturing overhead; $40,000 was paid and the remainder is unpaid.
4. Requisitioned materials for Cutting $15,700 and Assembly $8,900.
5. Used factory labor for Cutting $33,000 and Assembly $27,000.
6. Applied overhead at the rate of $18 per machine hour. Machine hours were Cutting 1,680 and Assembly 1,720.
7. Transferred goods costing $67,600 from the Cutting Department to the Assembly Department.
8. Transferred goods costing $134,900 from Assembly to Finished Goods.
9. Sold goods costing $150,000 for $200,000 on account.

Instructions
Journalize the transactions. (Omit explanations.)

E3-5 In Wayne Company, materials are entered at the beginning of each process. Work in process inventories, with the percentage of work done on conversion costs, and production data for its Sterilizing Department in selected months during 2014 are as follows.

Compute physical units and equivalent units of production.
(LO 5, 6), AP

| Month | Beginning Work in Process | | Units Transferred Out | Ending Work in Process | |
	Units	Conversion Cost%		Units	Conversion Cost%
January	–0–	—	9,000	2,000	60
March	–0–	—	12,000	3,000	30
May	–0–	—	16,000	7,000	80
July	–0–	—	10,000	1,500	40

Instructions
(a) Compute the physical units for January and May.
(b) Compute the equivalent units of production for (1) materials and (2) conversion costs for each month.

E3-6 The Cutting Department of Cassel Company has the following production and cost data for July.

Determine equivalent units, unit costs, and assignment of costs.
(LO 5, 6), AP

Production	Costs	
1. Transferred out 12,000 units.	Beginning work in process	$ –0–
2. Started 3,000 units that are 60% complete as to conversion costs and 100% complete as to materials at July 31.	Materials	45,000
	Labor	16,200
	Manufacturing overhead	18,300

Materials are entered at the beginning of the process. Conversion costs are incurred uniformly during the process.

Instructions
(a) Determine the equivalent units of production for (1) materials and (2) conversion costs.
(b) Compute unit costs and prepare a cost reconciliation schedule.

Prepare a production cost report.
(LO 5, 6, 7), AP

E3-7 The Sanding Department of Richards Furniture Company has the following production and manufacturing cost data for March 2014, the first month of operation.

Production: 9,000 units finished and transferred out; 3,000 units started that are 100% complete as to materials and 20% complete as to conversion costs.

Manufacturing costs: Materials $33,000; labor $24,000; overhead $36,000.

Instructions
Prepare a production cost report.

Determine equivalent units, unit costs, and assignment of costs.
(LO 5, 6), AP

E3-8 The Blending Department of Luongo Company has the following cost and production data for the month of April.

Costs:
Work in process, April 1

Direct materials: 100% complete	$100,000
Conversion costs: 20% complete	70,000
Cost of work in process, April 1	$170,000

Costs incurred during production in April

Direct materials	$ 800,000
Conversion costs	365,000
Costs incurred in April	$1,165,000

Units transferred out totaled 17,000. Ending work in process was 1,000 units that are 100% complete as to materials and 40% complete as to conversion costs.

Instructions
(a) Compute the equivalent units of production for (1) materials and (2) conversion costs for the month of April.
(b) Compute the unit costs for the month.
(c) Determine the costs to be assigned to the units transferred out and in ending work in process.

Determine equivalent units, unit costs, and assignment of costs.

(LO 5, 6), AP

E3-9 Kostrivas Company has gathered the following information.

Units in beginning work in process	–0–
Units started into production	40,000
Units in ending work in process	6,000
Percent complete in ending work in process:	
Conversion costs	40%
Materials	100%
Costs incurred:	
Direct materials	$72,000
Direct labor	$81,000
Overhead	$101,000

Instructions
(a) Compute equivalent units of production for materials and for conversion costs.
(b) Determine the unit costs of production.
(c) Show the assignment of costs to units transferred out and in process.

Determine equivalent units, unit costs, and assignment of costs.

(LO 5, 6), AP

E3-10 Overton Company has gathered the following information.

Units in beginning work in process	20,000
Units started into production	164,000
Units in ending work in process	24,000
Percent complete in ending work in process:	
Conversion costs	60%
Materials	100%
Costs incurred:	
Direct materials	$101,200
Direct labor	$164,800
Overhead	$184,000

Instructions
(a) Compute equivalent units of production for materials and for conversion costs.
(b) Determine the unit costs of production.
(c) Show the assignment of costs to units transferred out and in process.

Compute equivalent units, unit costs, and costs assigned.

(LO 5, 6), AP

E3-11 The Polishing Department of Harbin Company has the following production and manufacturing cost data for September. Materials are entered at the beginning of the process.

Production: Beginning inventory 1,600 units that are 100% complete as to materials and 30% complete as to conversion costs; units started during the period are 38,400; ending inventory of 5,000 units 10% complete as to conversion costs.

Manufacturing costs: Beginning inventory costs, comprised of $20,000 of materials and $43,180 of conversion costs; materials costs added in Polishing during the month, $177,200; labor and overhead applied in Polishing during the month, $125,680 and $257,140, respectively.

Instructions

(a) Compute the equivalent units of production for materials and conversion costs for the month of September.
(b) Compute the unit costs for materials and conversion costs for the month.
(c) Determine the costs to be assigned to the units transferred out and in process.

E3-12 David Skaros has recently been promoted to production manager, and so he has just started to receive various managerial reports. One of the reports he has received is the production cost report that you prepared. It showed that his department had 2,000 equivalent units in ending inventory. His department has had a history of not keeping enough inventory on hand to meet demand. He has come to you, very angry, and wants to know why you credited him with only 2,000 units when he knows he had at least twice that many on hand.

Explain the production cost report.

(LO 7), S

Instructions

▭▭▭▭▷ Explain to him why his production cost report showed only 2,000 equivalent units in ending inventory. Write an informal memo. Be kind and explain very clearly why he is mistaken.

E3-13 The Welding Department of Thorpe Company has the following production and manufacturing cost data for February 2014. All materials are added at the beginning of the process.

Prepare a production cost report.

(LO 5, 6, 7), AP

Manufacturing Costs			Production Data		
Beginning work in process			Beginning work in process	15,000 units	
Materials	$18,000			1/10 complete	
Conversion costs	14,175	$ 32,175	Units transferred out	49,000	
Materials		180,000	Units started	45,000	
Labor		52,380	Ending work in process	11,000 units	
Overhead		61,445		1/5 complete	

Instructions

Prepare a production cost report for the Welding Department for the month of February.

E3-14 Remington Shipping, Inc. is contemplating the use of process costing to track the costs of its operations. The operation consists of three segments (departments): receiving, shipping, and delivery. Containers are received at Remington's docks and sorted according to the ship they will be carried on. The containers are loaded onto a ship, which carries them to the appropriate port of destination. The containers are then off-loaded and delivered to the receiving company.

Compute physical units and equivalent units of production.

(LO 5, 6), AP

Remington Shipping wants to begin using process costing in the shipping department. Direct materials represent the fuel costs to run the ship, and "Containers in transit" represents work in process. Listed below is information about the shipping department's first month's activity.

Containers in transit, April 1	0
Containers loaded	1,200
Containers in transit, April 30	350, 40% of direct materials and 20% of conversion costs

Instructions

(a) Determine the physical flow of containers for the month.
(b) Calculate the equivalent units for direct materials and conversion costs.

E3-15 Royale Mortgage Company uses a process cost system to accumulate costs in its loan application department. When an application is completed, it is forwarded to the loan department for final processing. The following processing and cost data pertain to September.

Determine equivalent units, unit costs, and assignment of costs.

(LO 5, 6), AP

1. Applications in process on September 1, 100	Beginning WIP:	
	Direct materials	$ 1,000
2. Applications started in September, 900	Conversion costs	3,960
	September costs:	
3. Completed applications during September, 800	Direct materials	$ 4,500
	Direct labor	12,000
4. Applications still in process at September 30 were 100% complete as to materials (forms) and 60% complete as to conversion costs.	Overhead	9,340

Materials are the forms used in the application process, and these costs are incurred at the beginning of the process. Conversion costs are incurred uniformly during the process.

Instructions
(a) Determine the equivalent units of service (production) for materials and conversion costs.
(b) Compute the unit costs and prepare a cost reconciliation schedule.

Compute equivalent units, unit costs, and costs assigned.

(LO 6, 8), AP

*E3-16 Using the data in E3-15, assume Royale Mortgage Company uses the FIFO method. Also assume that the applications in process on September 1 were 100% complete as to materials (forms) and 40% complete as to conversion costs.

Instructions
(a) Determine the equivalent units of service (production) for materials and conversion costs.
(b) Compute the unit costs and prepare a cost reconciliation schedule.

Determine equivalent units, unit costs, and assignment of costs.

(LO 6, 8), AP

*E3-17 The Cutting Department of Keigi Company has the following production and cost data for August.

Production	Costs	
1. Started and completed 8,000 units.	Beginning work in process	$ –0–
2. Started 2,000 units that are 40% completed at August 31.	Materials	45,000
	Labor	14,700
	Manufacturing overhead	16,100

Materials are entered at the beginning of the process. Conversion costs are incurred uniformly during the process. Keigi Company uses the FIFO method to compute equivalent units.

Instructions
(a) Determine the equivalent units of production for (1) materials and (2) conversion costs.
(b) Compute unit costs and show the assignment of manufacturing costs to units transferred out and in work in process.

Compute equivalent units, unit costs, and costs assigned.

(LO 6, 8), AP

*E3-18 The Smelting Department of Polzin Company has the following production and cost data for September.

Production: Beginning work in process 2,000 units that are 100% complete as to materials and 20% complete as to conversion costs; units started and finished 9,000 units; and ending work in process 1,000 units that are 100% complete as to materials and 40% complete as to conversion costs.

Manufacturing costs: Work in process, September 1, $15,200; materials added $60,000; labor and overhead $132,000.

Polzin uses the FIFO method to compute equivalent units.

Instructions
(a) Compute the equivalent units of production for (1) materials and (2) conversion costs for the month of September.
(b) Compute the unit costs for the month.
(c) Determine the costs to be assigned to the units transferred out and in process.

*E3-19 The ledger of Hannon Company has the following work in process account.

Answer questions on costs and production.

(LO 6, 8), AP

Work in Process—Painting

3/1	Balance	3,680	3/31	Transferred out	?
3/31	Materials	6,600			
3/31	Labor	2,500			
3/31	Overhead	1,150			
3/31	Balance	?			

Production records show that there were 800 units in the beginning inventory, 30% complete, 1,200 units started, and 1,500 units transferred out. The units in ending inventory were 40% complete. Materials are entered at the beginning of the painting process. Hannon uses the FIFO method to compute equivalent units.

Instructions
Answer the following questions.
(a) How many units are in process at March 31?
(b) What is the unit materials cost for March?
(c) What is the unit conversion cost for March?
(d) What is the total cost of units started in February and completed in March?
(e) What is the total cost of units started and finished in March?
(f) What is the cost of the March 31 inventory?

*E3-20 The Welding Department of Majestic Company has the following production and manufacturing cost data for February 2014. All materials are added at the beginning of the process. Majestic uses the FIFO method to compute equivalent units.

Prepare a production cost report for a second process.

(LO 8), AP

Manufacturing Costs		Production Data	
Beginning work in process	$ 32,175	Beginning work in process	15,000 units,
Costs transferred in	135,000		10% complete
Materials	57,000	Units transferred out	54,000
Labor	35,100	Units transferred in	64,000
Overhead	68,400	Ending work in process	25,000,
			20% complete

Instructions
Prepare a production cost report for the Welding Department for the month of February. Transferred-in costs are considered materials costs.

EXERCISES: SET B AND CHALLENGE EXERCISES

Visit the book's companion website, at **www.wiley.com/college/weygandt**, and choose the Student Companion site to access Exercise Set B and Challenge Exercises.

PROBLEMS: SET A

P3-1A Conwell Company manufactures its product, Vitadrink, through two manufacturing processes: Mixing and Packaging. All materials are entered at the beginning of each process. On October 1, 2014, inventories consisted of Raw Materials $26,000, Work in Process—Mixing $0, Work in Process—Packaging $250,000, and Finished Goods $289,000. The beginning inventory for Packaging consisted of 10,000 units that were 50% complete as to conversion costs and fully complete as to materials. During October, 50,000 units were started into production in the Mixing Department and the following transactions were completed.

Journalize transactions.

(LO 3, 4), AP

1. Purchased $300,000 of raw materials on account.
2. Issued raw materials for production: Mixing $210,000 and Packaging $45,000.

3. Incurred labor costs of $258,900.
4. Used factory labor: Mixing $182,500 and Packaging $76,400.
5. Incurred $810,000 of manufacturing overhead on account.
6. Applied manufacturing overhead on the basis of $24 per machine hour. Machine hours were 28,000 in Mixing and 6,000 in Packaging.
7. Transferred 45,000 units from Mixing to Packaging at a cost of $979,000.
8. Transferred 53,000 units from Packaging to Finished Goods at a cost of $1,315,000.
9. Sold goods costing $1,604,000 for $2,500,000 on account.

Instructions
Journalize the October transactions.

Complete four steps necessary to prepare a production cost report.

(LO 5, 6, 7), AP

P3-2A Rosenthal Company manufactures bowling balls through two processes: Molding and Packaging. In the Molding Department, the urethane, rubber, plastics, and other materials are molded into bowling balls. In the Packaging Department, the balls are placed in cartons and sent to the finished goods warehouse. All materials are entered at the beginning of each process. Labor and manufacturing overhead are incurred uniformly throughout each process. Production and cost data for the Molding Department during June 2014 are presented below.

Production Data	June
Beginning work in process units	–0–
Units started into production	22,000
Ending work in process units	2,000
Percent complete—ending inventory	40%

Cost Data	
Materials	$198,000
Labor	53,600
Overhead	112,800
Total	$364,400

Instructions
(a) Prepare a schedule showing physical units of production.
(b) Determine the equivalent units of production for materials and conversion costs.
(c) Compute the unit costs of production.
(d) Determine the costs to be assigned to the units transferred out and in process for June.
(e) Prepare a production cost report for the Molding Department for the month of June.

(c) Materials $9.00
     CC $8.00
(d) Transferred
     out $340,000
     WIP $ 24,400

Complete four steps necessary to prepare a production cost report.

(LO 5, 6, 7), AP

P3-3A Seagren Industries Inc. manufactures in separate processes furniture for homes. In each process, materials are entered at the beginning, and conversion costs are incurred uniformly. Production and cost data for the first process in making two products in two different manufacturing plants are as follows.

	Cutting Department	
	Plant 1	Plant 2
Production Data—July	T12-Tables	C10-Chairs
Work in process units, July 1	–0–	–0–
Units started into production	19,000	16,000
Work in process units, July 31	3,000	500
Work in process percent complete	60	80

Cost Data—July		
Work in process, July 1	$ –0–	$ –0–
Materials	380,000	288,000
Labor	234,200	110,000
Overhead	104,000	96,700
Total	$718,200	$494,700

Instructions

(a) For each plant:
  (1) Compute the physical units of production.
  (2) Compute equivalent units of production for materials and for conversion costs.
  (3) Determine the unit costs of production.
  (4) Show the assignment of costs to units transferred out and in process.
(b) Prepare the production cost report for Plant 1 for July 2014.

P3-4A Rivera Company has several processing departments. Costs charged to the Assembly Department for November 2014 totaled $2,280,000 as follows.

Work in process, November 1		
Materials	$79,000	
Conversion costs	48,150	$ 127,150
Materials added		1,589,000
Labor		225,920
Overhead		337,930

Production records show that 35,000 units were in beginning work in process 30% complete as to conversion costs, 660,000 units were started into production, and 25,000 units were in ending work in process 40% complete as to conversion costs. Materials are entered at the beginning of each process.

Instructions

(a) Determine the equivalent units of production and the unit production costs for the Assembly Department.
(b) Determine the assignment of costs to goods transferred out and in process.
(c) Prepare a production cost report for the Assembly Department.

P3-5A Morse Company manufactures basketballs. Materials are added at the beginning of the production process and conversion costs are incurred uniformly. Production and cost data for the month of July 2014 are as follows.

Production Data—Basketballs	Units	Percent Complete
Work in process units, July 1	500	60%
Units started into production	1,250	
Work in process units, July 31	600	40%

Cost Data—Basketballs		
Work in process, July 1		
Materials	$750	
Conversion costs	600	$1,350
Direct materials		2,400
Direct labor		1,580
Manufacturing overhead		1,295

Instructions

(a) Calculate the following.
  (1) The equivalent units of production for materials and conversion costs.
  (2) The unit costs of production for materials and conversion costs.
  (3) The assignment of costs to units transferred out and in process at the end of the accounting period.
(b) Prepare a production cost report for the month of July for the basketballs.

P3-6A Hamilton Processing Company uses a weighted-average process cost system and manufactures a single product—a premium rug shampoo and cleaner. The manufacturing activity for the month of October has just been completed. A partially completed production cost report for the month of October for the Mixing and Cooking Department is shown on the next page.

Instructions

(a) Prepare a schedule that shows how the equivalent units were computed so that you can complete the "Quantities: Units accounted for" equivalent units section shown in the production cost report, and compute October unit costs.
(b) Complete the "Cost Reconciliation Schedule" part of the production cost report below.

(a) (3) T12:
  Materials $20
  CC $19
(4) T12:
  Transferred
    out $624,000
  WIP $ 94,200

Assign costs and prepare production cost report.

(LO 5, 6, 7), AP

(b) Transferred
  out $2,211,000
  WIP $ 69,000

Determine equivalent units and unit costs and assign costs.

(LO 5, 6, 7), AP

(a) (2) Materials $1.80
  (3) Transferred
    out $4,945
    WIP $1,680

Compute equivalent units and complete production cost report.

(LO 5, 7), AP

(a) Materials $1.60
(b) Transferred
  out $282,000
  WIP $ 63,000

Hamilton Processing Company
Mixing and Cooking Department
Production Cost Report
For the Month Ended October 31

		Equivalent Units	
Quantities	Physical Units	Materials	Conversion Costs
Units to be accounted for			
Work in process, October 1 (all materials, 70% conversion costs)	20,000		
Started into production	150,000		
Total units	170,000		
Units accounted for			
Transferred out	120,000	?	?
Work in process, October 31 (60% materials, 40% conversion costs)	50,000	?	?
Total units accounted for	170,000	?	?

Costs

Unit costs

	Materials	Conversion Costs	Total
Total cost	$240,000	$105,000	$345,000
Equivalent units	?	?	
Unit costs	$? +	$? =	$?
Costs to be accounted for			
Work in process, October 1			$ 30,000
Started into production			315,000
Total costs			$345,000

Cost Reconciliation Schedule

Costs accounted for			
Transferred out			$?
Work in process, October 31			
Materials		$?	
Conversion costs		?	?
Total costs			$?

Determine equivalent units and unit costs and assign costs for processes; prepare production cost report.

(LO 8), AP

*P3-7A Rondeli Company manufactures bicycles and tricycles. For both products, materials are added at the beginning of the production process, and conversion costs are incurred uniformly. Rondeli Company uses the FIFO method to compute equivalent units. Production and cost data for the month of March are as follows.

Production Data—Bicycles	Units	Percent Complete
Work in process units, March 1	200	80%
Units started into production	1,250	
Work in process units, March 31	300	40%

Cost Data—Bicycles	Units	Percent Complete
Work in process, March 1	$19,280	
Direct materials	50,000	
Direct labor	25,500	
Manufacturing overhead	30,000	

Production Data—Tricycles	Units	Percent Complete
Work in process units, March 1	100	75%
Units started into production	800	
Work in process units, March 31	60	25%

Cost Data—Tricycles	
Work in process, March 1	$ 6,125
Direct materials	30,400
Direct labor	15,100
Manufacturing overhead	20,000

Instructions

(a) Calculate the following for both the bicycles and the tricycles.
　(1) The equivalent units of production for materials and conversion costs.
　(2) The unit costs of production for materials and conversion costs.
　(3) The assignment of costs to units transferred out and in process at the end of the accounting period.
(b) Prepare a production cost report for the month of March for the bicycles only.

(a) Bicycles:
(1) Materials　　1,250
(2) Materials　　$40
(3) Transferred
　　out　　$106,780
　　WIP　　$ 18,000

PROBLEMS: SET B

P3-1B Wilbury Company manufactures a nutrient, Everlife, through two manufacturing processes: Blending and Packaging. All materials are entered at the beginning of each process. On August 1, 2014, inventories consisted of Raw Materials $5,000, Work in Process—Blending $0, Work in Process—Packaging $3,945, and Finished Goods $7,500. The beginning inventory for Packaging consisted of 500 units, two-fifths complete as to conversion costs and fully complete as to materials. During August, 9,000 units were started into production in Blending, and the following transactions were completed.

Journalize transactions.
(LO 3, 4), AP

1. Purchased $25,000 of raw materials on account.
2. Issued raw materials for production: Blending $18,930 and Packaging $9,140.
3. Incurred labor costs of $25,770.
4. Used factory labor: Blending $15,320 and Packaging $10,450.
5. Incurred $36,500 of manufacturing overhead on account.
6. Applied manufacturing overhead at the rate of $28 per machine hour. Machine hours were Blending 900 and Packaging 300.
7. Transferred 8,200 units from Blending to Packaging at a cost of $44,940.
8. Transferred 8,600 units from Packaging to Finished Goods at a cost of $67,490.
9. Sold goods costing $62,000 for $90,000 on account.

Instructions
Journalize the August transactions.

P3-2B Steiner Corporation manufactures water skis through two processes: Molding and Packaging. In the Molding Department, fiberglass is heated and shaped into the form of a ski. In the Packaging Department, the skis are placed in cartons and sent to the finished goods warehouse. Materials are entered at the beginning of both processes. Labor and manufacturing overhead are incurred uniformly throughout each process. Production and cost data for the Molding Department for January 2014 are presented below.

Complete four steps necessary to prepare a production cost report.
(LO 5, 6, 7), AP

Production Data	January
Beginning work in process units	–0–
Units started into production	50,000
Ending work in process units	2,500
Percent complete—ending inventory	40%

Cost Data	January
Materials	$510,000
Labor	92,500
Overhead	150,000
Total	$752,500

Instructions
(a) Compute the physical units of production.
(b) Determine the equivalent units of production for materials and conversion costs.

(c) Materials $10.20
    CC $5
(d) Transferred out $722,000
    WIP $ 30,500

(c) Compute the unit costs of production.
(d) Determine the costs to be assigned to the units transferred out and in process.
(e) Prepare a production cost report for the Molding Department for the month of January.

Complete four steps necessary to prepare a production cost report.

(LO 5, 6, 7), AP

P3-3B Borman Corporation manufactures in separate processes refrigerators and freezers for homes. In each process, materials are entered at the beginning and conversion costs are incurred uniformly. Production and cost data for the first process in making two products in two different manufacturing plants are as follows.

	Stamping Department	
	Plant A	**Plant B**
Production Data—June	**R12 Refrigerators**	**F24 Freezers**
Work in process units, June 1	–0–	–0–
Units started into production	20,000	20,000
Work in process units, June 30	4,000	2,500
Work in process percent complete	75	60

Cost Data—June		
Work in process, June 1	$ –0–	$ –0–
Materials	840,000	720,000
Labor	245,000	259,000
Overhead	420,000	292,000
Total	$1,505,000	$1,271,000

(a) (3) R12:
      Materials $42
      CC $35
    (4) R12:
      Transferred
        out $1,232,000
      WIP $ 273,000

Instructions
(a) For each plant:
   (1) Compute the physical units of production.
   (2) Compute equivalent units of production for materials and for conversion costs.
   (3) Determine the unit costs of production.
   (4) Show the assignment of costs to units transferred out and in process.
(b) Prepare the production cost report for Plant A for June 2014.

Assign costs and prepare production cost report.

(LO 5, 6, 7), AP

P3-4B Luxman Company has several processing departments. Costs charged to the Assembly Department for October 2014 totaled $1,298,400 as follows.

Work in process, October 1		
Materials	$29,000	
Conversion costs	16,500	$ 45,500
Materials added		1,006,000
Labor		138,900
Overhead		108,000

Production records show that 25,000 units were in beginning work in process 40% complete as to conversion cost, 435,000 units were started into production, and 35,000 units were in ending work in process 40% complete as to conversion costs. Materials are entered at the beginning of each process.

Instructions
(a) Determine the equivalent units of production and the unit production costs for the Assembly Department.

(b) Transferred out $1,211,250
    WIP $ 87,150

(b) Determine the assignment of costs to goods transferred out and in process.
(c) Prepare a production cost report for the Assembly Department.

P3-5B Swinn Company manufactures bicycles. Materials are added at the beginning of the production process, and conversion costs are incurred uniformly. Production and cost data for the month of May are as follows.

Determine equivalent units and unit costs and assign costs.

(LO 5, 6, 7), AP

Production Data—Bicycles	Units	Percent Complete
Work in process units, May 1	500	80%
Units started in production	2,000	
Work in process units, May 31	800	40%

Cost Data—Bicycles		
Work in process, May 1 Materials	$15,000	
Conversion costs	18,000	$33,000
Direct materials		50,000
Direct labor		19,020
Manufacturing overhead		33,680

Instructions

(a) Calculate the following.
  (1) The equivalent units of production for materials and conversion.
  (2) The unit costs of production for materials and conversion costs.
  (3) The assignment of costs to units transferred out and in process at the end of the accounting period.
(b) Prepare a production cost report for the month of May for the bicycles.

(2) Materials $26
　　CC　　　 $35
(3) Transferred
　　out　　　 $103,700
　　WIP　　 $ 32,000

P3-6B Venuchi Cleaner Company uses a weighted-average process cost system and manufactures a single product—an all-purpose liquid cleaner. The manufacturing activity for the month of March has just been completed. A partially completed production cost report for the month of March for the mixing and blending department is shown below.

Compute equivalent units and complete production cost report.

(LO 5, 7), AP

Venuchi Cleaner Company
Mixing and Blending Department
Production Cost Report
For the Month Ended March 31

Quantities	Physical Units	Equivalent Units Materials	Equivalent Units Conversion Costs
Units to be accounted for			
Work in process, March 1	10,000		
Started into production	76,000		
Total units	86,000		
Units accounted for			
Transferred out	66,000	?	?
Work in process, March 31			
(60% materials, 20% conversion costs)	20,000	?	?
Total units	86,000	?	?

Costs			
Unit costs	Materials	Conversion Costs	Total
Total cost	$156,000	$98,000	$254,000
Equivalent units	?	?	
Unit costs	$? +	$? =	$?
Costs to be accounted for			
Work in process, March 1			$ 8,700
Started into production			245,300
Total costs			$254,000

Cost Reconciliation Schedule	Materials	Conversion Costs	Total
Costs accounted for			
Transferred out			$?
Work in process, March 31			
Materials		?	
Conversion costs		$?	?
Total costs			$?

Instructions

(a) Materials $2.00
(b) Transferred out $224,400
    WIP $ 29,600

(a) Prepare a schedule that shows how the equivalent units were computed so that you can complete the "Quantities: Units accounted for" equivalent units section shown in the production cost report above, and compute March unit costs.

(b) Complete the "Cost Reconciliation Schedule" part of the production cost report above.

Determine equivalent units and unit costs and assign costs for processes; prepare production cost report.

(LO 8), AP

*P3-7B Holiday Company manufactures basketballs and soccer balls. For both products, materials are added at the beginning of the production process and conversion costs are incurred uniformly. Holiday uses the FIFO method to compute equivalent units. Production and cost data for the month of August are shown below.

Production Data—Basketballs	Units	Percent Complete	Production Data—Soccer Balls	Units	Percent Complete
Work in process units, August 1	500	60%	Work in process units, August 1	200	80%
Units started into production	2,000		Units started into production	2,000	
Work in process units, August 31	600	50%	Work in process units, August 31	150	70%

Cost Data—Basketballs		Cost Data—Soccer Balls	
Work in process, August 1	$1,125	Work in process, August 1	$ 450
Direct materials	1,600	Direct materials	2,800
Direct labor	1,280	Direct labor	1,000
Manufacturing overhead	1,000	Manufacturing overhead	1,394

Instructions

(a) Basketballs:
(1) Materials   2,000
(2) Materials $.80
(3) Transferred out $4,165
    WIP $840

(a) Calculate the following for both the basketballs and the soccer balls.
  (1) The equivalent units of production for materials and conversion costs.
  (2) The unit costs of production for materials and conversion costs.
  (3) The assignment of costs to units transferred out and in process at the end of the accounting period.

(b) Prepare a production cost report for the month of August for the basketballs only.

PROBLEMS: SET C

Visit the book's companion website, at **www.wiley.com/college/weygandt**, and choose the Student Companion site to access Problem Set C.

WATERWAYS CONTINUING PROBLEM

(*Note:* This is a continuation of the Waterways Problem from Chapters 1–2.)

WCP3 Because most of the parts for its irrigation systems are standard, Waterways handles the majority of its manufacturing as a process cost system. There are multiple process departments. Three of these departments are the Molding, Cutting, and Welding departments. All items eventually end up in the Packaging department which prepares items for sale in kits or individually. This problem asks you to help Waterways calculate equivalent units and prepare a production cost report.

Go to the book's companion website, at **www.wiley.com/college/weygandt**, *to see the completion of this problem.*

Management Decision-Making

Decision-Making at Current Designs

BYP3-1 Building a kayak using the composite method is a very labor-intensive process. In the fabrication department, the kayaks go through several steps as employees carefully place layers of Kevlar® in a mold and then use resin to fuse together the layers. The excess resin is removed with a vacuum process, and the upper shell and lower shell are removed from the molds and assembled. The seat, hatch, and other components are added in the finishing department.

At the beginning of April, Current Designs had 30 kayaks in process in the fabrication department. Rick Thrune, the production manager, estimated that about 80% of the material costs had been added to these boats, which were about 50% complete with respect to the conversion costs. The cost of this inventory had been calculated to be $8,400 in materials and $9,000 in conversion costs.

During April, 72 boats were started. At the end of the month, the 35 kayaks in the ending inventory had 20% of the materials and 40% of the conversion costs already added to them.

A review of the accounting records for April showed that materials with a cost of $17,500 had been requisitioned by this department and that the conversion costs for the month were $39,600.

Instructions
Complete a production cost report for April 2014 for the fabrication department using the weighted-average method.

Decision-Making Across the Organization

BYP3-2 Florida Beach Company manufactures suntan lotion, called Surtan, in 11-ounce plastic bottles. Surtan is sold in a competitive market. As a result, management is very cost-conscious. Surtan is manufactured through two processes: mixing and filling. Materials are entered at the beginning of each process, and labor and manufacturing overhead occur uniformly throughout each process. Unit costs are based on the cost per gallon of Surtan using the weighted-average costing approach.

On June 30, 2014, Mary Ritzman, the chief accountant for the past 20 years, opted to take early retirement. Her replacement, Joe Benili, had extensive accounting experience with motels in the area but only limited contact with manufacturing accounting. During July, Joe correctly accumulated the following production quantity and cost data for the Mixing Department.

Production quantities: Work in process, July 1, 8,000 gallons 75% complete; started into production 100,000 gallons; work in process, July 31, 5,000 gallons 20% complete. Materials are added at the beginning of the process.

Production costs: Beginning work in process $88,000, comprised of $21,000 of materials costs and $67,000 of conversion costs; incurred in July: materials $573,000, conversion costs $765,000.

Joe then prepared a production cost report on the basis of physical units started into production. His report showed a production cost of $14.26 per gallon of Surtan. The management of Florida Beach was surprised at the high unit cost. The president comes to you, as Mary's top assistant, to review Joe's report and prepare a correct report if necessary.

Instructions
With the class divided into groups, answer the following questions.
(a) Show how Joe arrived at the unit cost of $14.26 per gallon of Surtan.
(b) What error(s) did Joe make in preparing his production cost report?
(c) Prepare a correct production cost report for July.

Managerial Analysis

BYP3-3 Harris Furniture Company manufactures living room furniture through two departments: Framing and Upholstering. Materials are entered at the beginning of each process. For May, the following cost data are obtained from the two work in process accounts.

	Framing	Upholstering
Work in process, May 1	$ –0–	$?
Materials	450,000	?
Conversion costs	261,000	330,000
Costs transferred in	–0–	600,000
Costs transferred out	600,000	?
Work in process, May 31	111,000	?

Instructions

Answer the following questions.

(a) If 3,000 sofas were started into production on May 1 and 2,500 sofas were transferred to Upholstering, what was the unit cost of materials for May in the Framing Department?

(b) Using the data in (a) above, what was the per unit conversion cost of the sofas transferred to Upholstering?

(c) Continuing the assumptions in (a) above, what is the percentage of completion of the units in process at May 31 in the Framing Department?

Real-World Focus

BYP3-4 Paintball is now played around the world. The process of making paintballs is actually quite similar to the process used to make certain medical pills. In fact, paintballs were previously often made at the same factories that made pharmaceuticals.

Address: **http://video.google.com/videoplay?docid=6864066340713942400**, or go to **www.wiley. com/college/weygandt**

Instructions

View that video at the site listed above and then answer the following questions.

(a) Describe in sequence the primary steps used to manufacture paintballs.

(b) Explain the costs incurred by the company that would fall into each of the following categories: materials, labor, and overhead. Of these categories, which do you think would be the greatest cost in making paintballs?

(c) Discuss whether a paintball manufacturer would use job order costing or process costing.

Critical Thinking

Communication Activity

BYP3-5 Diane Barone was a good friend of yours in high school and is from your home town. While you chose to major in accounting when you both went away to college, she majored in marketing and management. You have recently been promoted to accounting manager for the Snack Foods Division of Melton Enterprises, and your friend was promoted to regional sales manager for the same division of Melton. Diane recently telephoned you. She explained that she was familiar with job cost sheets, which had been used by the Special Projects division where she had formerly worked. She was, however, very uncomfortable with the production cost reports prepared by your division. She emailed you a list of her particular questions:

1. Since Melton occasionally prepares snack foods for special orders in the Snack Foods Division, why don't we track costs of the orders separately?
2. What is an equivalent unit?
3. Why am I getting four production cost reports? Isn't there one Work in Process account?

Instructions

Prepare a memo to Diane. Answer her questions, and include any additional information you think would be helpful. You may write informally, but do use proper grammar and punctuation.

Ethics Case

BYP3-6 R. B. Dillman Company manufactures a high-tech component that passes through two production processing departments, Molding and Assembly. Department managers are partially compensated on the basis of units of products completed and transferred out relative to units of

product put into production. This was intended as encouragement to be efficient and to minimize waste.

Jan Wooten is the department head in the Molding Department, and Tony Ferneti is her quality control inspector. During the month of June, Jan had three new employees who were not yet technically skilled. As a result, many of the units produced in June had minor molding defects. In order to maintain the department's normal high rate of completion, Jan told Tony to pass through inspection and on to the Assembly Department all units that had defects nondetectable to the human eye. "Company and industry tolerances on this product are too high anyway," says Jan. "Less than 2% of the units we produce are subjected in the market to the stress tolerance we've designed into them. The odds of those 2% being any of this month's units are even less. Anyway, we're saving the company money."

Instructions

(a) Who are the potential stakeholders involved in this situation?

(b) What alternatives does Tony have in this situation? What might the company do to prevent this situation from occurring?

Considering People, Planet, and Profit

BYP3-7 In a recent year, an oil refinery in Texas City, Texas, on the Houston Ship Channel exploded. The explosion killed 14 people and sent a plume of smoke hundreds of feet into the air. The blast started as a fire in the section of the plant that increased the octane of the gasoline that was produced at the refinery. The Houston Ship Channel is the main waterway that allows commerce to flow from the Gulf of Mexico into Houston.

The Texas Commission on Environmental Quality expressed concern about the release of nitrogen oxides, benzene, and other known carcinogens as a result of the blast. Neighbors of the plant complained that the plant had been emitting carcinogens for years and that the regulators had ignored their complaints about emissions and unsafe working conditions.

Instructions

Answer the following questions.

(a) Outline the costs that the company now faces as a result of the accident.

(b) How could the company have reduced the costs associated with the accident?

Answers to Chapter Questions

Answers to Insight and Accounting Across the Organization Questions

p. 100 Choosing a Cost Driver Q: What is the result if a company uses the wrong "cost driver" to assign manufacturing overhead? **A:** Incorrect assignment of manufacturing overhead will result in some products receiving too much overhead and others receiving too little.

p. 104 Haven't I Seen That Before? Q: In what ways might the relative composition (materials, labor, and overhead) of a remanufactured product's cost differ from that of a newly made product? **A:** We would expect that the materials costs would be substantially reduced since the bulk of the physical product is being reused. The labor component might increase, and the level of automation might decrease, since remanufacturing a product requires identification and replacement of malfunctioning components. This process might not be as easily automated as the production of a new product.

Answers to Self-Test Questions

1. b   **2.** d   **3.** d   **4.** b   **5.** c   **6.** b   **7.** b $[20,000 + (5,000 \times 60\%)]$ **8.** a $(7,000 + 0)$ **9.** c $(23,000 + 3,000)$, $[23,000 + (3,000 \times 33\frac{1}{3}\%)]$ **10.** a $[\$60,000 \div (9,000 + 3,000)]$ **11.** b $[(\$10 \times 2,500) + (\$30 \times 2,500 \times 40\%)]$ **12.** b   **13.** d   ***14.** b $[25,000 + (3,000 \times 100\%)]$; $[(2,000 \times 80\%) + 25,000 + (3,000 \times 30\%)]$ ***15.** a $[\$60,000 \div (9,000 + 3,000)]$ ***16.** b $[(\$10 \times 2,500) + (\$30 \times 2,500 \times 40\%)]$

✔   **Remember to go back to The Navigator box on the chapter opening page and check off your completed work.**

Chapter 4

Activity-Based Costing

Precor Is on Your Side

Do you feel like the whole world is conspiring against your efforts to get in shape? Is it humanly possible to resist the constant barrage of advertisements and fast-food servers who pleasantly encourage us to "supersize" it? Lest we think that we have no allies in our battle against the bulge, consider Precor.

Ever since it made the first ergonomically sound rowing machine in 1980, Precor's sole mission has been to provide exercise equipment. It makes elliptical trainers, exercise bikes, rowing machines, treadmills, multi-station strength systems, and many other forms of equipment designed to erase the cumulative effects of a fast-food nation. Its equipment is widely used in Hilton hotels, Gold's Gym franchises, and even in Madonna's Hard Candy fitness center in Moscow.

Building high-quality fitness equipment requires sizable investments by Precor in buildings and machinery. For example, Precor recently moved its facilities from Valencia, California, to Greensboro, North Carolina. In order to reduce costs and minimize environmental impact, the company installed low-flow water fixtures, high-efficiency heating and cooling systems, and state-of-the-art lighting in its $26 million, 230,000-square-foot facility. As a result of these efforts, Precor's new facility received a Leadership in Energy and Efficient Design (LEED) CI Gold Certification.

✔ The Navigator

- ☐ Scan Learning Objectives
- ☐ Read Feature Story
- ☐ Read Preview
- ☐ Read Text and answer **DO IT!** p. 149
  ☐ p. 153 ☐ p. 158 ☐ p. 161
- ☐ Work Using the Decision Toolkit p. 164
- ☐ Review Summary of Learning Objectives
- ☐ Work Comprehensive **DO IT!** p. 169
- ☐ Answer Self-Test Questions
- ☐ Complete Assignments
- ☐ Go to **WileyPLUS** for practice and tutorials

Learning Objectives

After studying this chapter, you should be able to:

1 Recognize the difference between traditional costing and activity-based costing.

2 Identify the steps in the development of an activity-based costing system.

3 Know how companies identify the activity cost pools used in activity-based costing.

4 Know how companies identify and use cost drivers in activity-based costing.

5 Understand the benefits and limitations of activity-based costing.

6 Differentiate between value-added and non–value-added activities.

7 Understand the value of using activity levels in activity-based costing.

8 Apply activity-based costing to service industries.

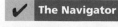

Because of its huge investments in property, plant, and equipment, overhead costs represent a large percentage of the cost of Precor's exercise equipment. The combination of high overhead costs and a wide variety of products means that it is important that Precor allocates its overhead accurately to its various products. Without accurate cost information, Precor would not know whether its elliptical trainers and recumbent bicycles are making money, whether its AMT 100i adaptive motion trainer is priced high enough to cover its costs, or if its 240i Stretchtrainer is losing money. To increase the accuracy of its costs, Precor uses a method of overhead allocation

that focuses on identifying the types of activities that cause the company to incur costs. It then assigns more overhead to those products that rely most heavily on cost-incurring activities. By doing this, the allocation of overhead is less arbitrary than traditional overhead allocation methods. In short, before it can help us burn off the pounds, Precor needs to understand what drives its overhead costs.

Watch the Precor video in WileyPLUS to learn more about activity-based costing in the real world.

Source: www.precor.com.

✔ **The Navigator**

Preview of **Chapter 4**

As indicated in the Feature Story about Precor, the traditional costing systems described in earlier chapters are not the best answer for every company. Because Precor suspected that the traditional system was masking significant differences in its real cost structure, it sought a new method of assigning costs. Similar searches by other companies for ways to improve operations and gather more accurate data for decision-making have resulted in the development of powerful new management tools, including **activity-based costing (ABC)**. The primary objective of this chapter is to explain and illustrate this concept.

The content and organization of this chapter are as follows.

ACTIVITY-BASED COSTING			
Traditional Costing and ABC	**Example of ABC versus Traditional Costing**	**ABC: A Closer Look**	**ABC in Service Industries**
• Traditional costing • Need for a new approach • Activity-based costing	• Identify activities and allocate to cost pools • Identify cost drivers • Compute overhead rates • Assign overhead costs to products • Compare unit costs	• Benefits • Limitations • When to use ABC • Value-added versus non–value-added activities • Classification of activity levels	• Traditional costing example • ABC example

✔ **The Navigator**

Traditional Costing and Activity-Based Costing

LEARNING OBJECTIVE   **1**

Recognize the difference between traditional costing and activity-based costing.

Traditional Costing Systems

It is probably impossible to determine the *exact* cost of a product or service. However, in order to achieve improved management decisions, companies strive to provide decision-makers with the most accurate cost estimates they can. The most accurate estimate of product cost occurs when the costs are traceable directly to the product produced or the service provided. Direct material and direct labor costs are the easiest to trace directly to the product through the use of material requisition forms and payroll time sheets. Overhead costs, on the other hand, are an indirect or common cost that generally cannot be easily or directly traced to individual products or services. Instead, companies use estimates to assign overhead costs to products and services.

Often the most difficult part of computing accurate unit costs is determining the proper amount of **overhead cost** to assign to each product, service, or job. In our coverage of job order costing in Chapter 2 and of process costing in Chapter 3, we used a single or plantwide overhead rate throughout the year for the entire factory operation. That rate was called the **predetermined overhead rate**. For job order costing, we assumed that **direct labor cost** was the relevant activity base for assigning all overhead costs to jobs. For process costing, we assumed that **machine hours** was the relevant activity base for assigning all overhead to the process or department.

The use of direct labor as the activity base made sense when overhead cost allocation systems were first developed. At that time, direct labor made up a large portion of total manufacturing cost. Therefore, it was widely accepted that there was a high correlation between direct labor and the incurrence of overhead cost. As a result, direct labor became the most popular basis for allocating overhead.

Even in today's increasingly automated environment, direct labor is sometimes the appropriate basis for assigning overhead cost to products. It is appropriate to use direct labor when (a) direct labor constitutes a significant part of total product cost, and (b) a high correlation exists between direct labor and changes in the amount of overhead costs. Illustration 4-1 displays a simplified (one-stage) traditional costing system relying on direct labor to assign overhead.

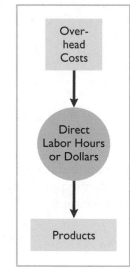

Illustration 4-1
Traditional one-stage costing system

The Need for a New Approach

In recent years, manufacturers and service providers have experienced tremendous change. Advances in computerized systems, technological innovation, global competition, and automation have changed the manufacturing environment drastically. As a result, the amount of direct labor used in many industries has greatly decreased, and total overhead costs resulting from depreciation on expensive equipment and machinery, utilities, repairs, and maintenance have significantly increased. When there is not a correlation between direct labor and overhead, it is inappropriate to use plantwide predetermined overhead rates based on direct labor. Companies that use overhead rates based on direct labor when this correlation does not exist experience significant product-cost distortions.

To avoid such distortions, many companies now use machine hours as the basis on which to allocate overhead in an automated manufacturing environment. But even machine hours may not suffice as the only plantwide basis for allocating all overhead. If the manufacturing process is complex, then only multiple allocation bases can result in more accurate product-cost computations. In such situations, managers need to consider an overhead cost allocation method that uses *multiple* bases. That method is **activity-based costing**.

Activity-Based Costing

Broadly, **activity-based costing (ABC)** is an approach for allocating overhead costs. More specifically, ABC allocates overhead to multiple activity cost pools, and it then assigns the activity cost pools to products and services by means of cost drivers. To understand this more clearly, we need to apply some new meanings to the rather common-sounding words that make up the definition: In activity-based costing, an **activity** is any event, action, transaction, or work sequence that incurs costs when producing a product or providing a service. An **activity cost pool** is the overhead cost attributed to a distinct type of activity (e.g., ordering materials or setting up machines). A **cost driver** is any factor or activity that has a direct cause-effect relationship with the resources consumed. The reasoning behind ABC cost allocation is simple: **Products consume activities, and activities consume resources**.

These definitions of terms will become clearer as we look more closely at how ABC works. ABC allocates overhead in a two-stage process. The first stage allocates overhead costs to activity cost pools. (Traditional costing systems, in contrast, allocate these costs to departments or to jobs.) Examples of overhead cost pools are ordering materials, setting up machines, assembling products, and inspecting products.

The second stage assigns the overhead allocated to the activity cost pools to products, using cost drivers. The cost drivers measure the number of individual activities undertaken or performed to produce products or provide services. Examples are number of purchase orders, number of setups, labor hours, and number of inspections. Illustration 4-2 shows examples of activities, and possible

Illustration 4-2
Activities and related cost drivers

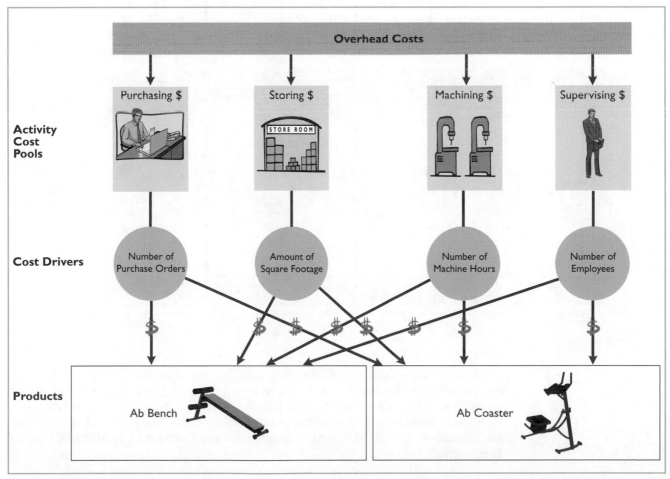

cost drivers to measure them, for a company that manufactures two types of abdominal exercise equipment—Ab Benches and Ab Coasters.

In the first step (as shown at the top of Illustration 4-2 on page 147), the company allocates overhead costs to activity cost pools. In this simplified example, the company has identified four activity cost pools: purchasing, storing, machining, and supervising. After the costs are allocated to the activity cost pools, the company uses cost drivers to determine the costs to assign to the individual products based on each product's use of each activity. For example, if Ab Benches require more activity by the purchasing department, as measured by the number of required purchase orders, then more of the overhead costs from the purchasing pool are allocated to the Ab Benches.

The more complex a product's manufacturing operation, the more activities and cost drivers it is likely to have. If there is little or no correlation between changes in the cost driver and consumption of the overhead cost, inaccurate product costs are inevitable.

Illustration 4-3 shows the design of a more complex activity-based costing system with seven activity cost pools for Lift Jack Company. Lift Jack Company manufactures two automotive jacks—an automobile scissors jack and a truck hydraulic jack.

Illustration 4-3
ABC system design—Lift Jack Company

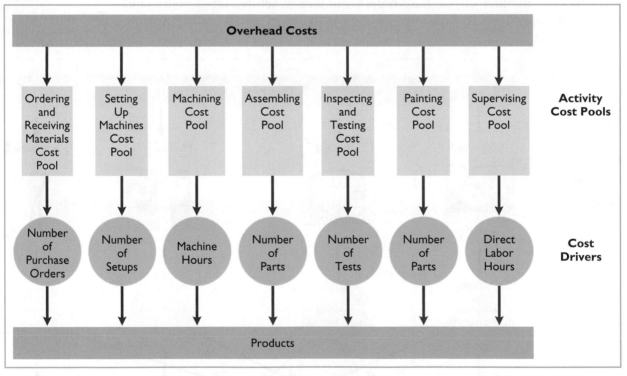

The Lift Jack Company illustration contains seven activity cost pools. In some companies, the number of activities can be substantial. For example, Clark-Hurth (a division of Clark Equipment Company), a manufacturer of axles and transmissions, identified over 170 activities. Compumotor (a division of Parker Hannifin) identified over 80 activities in just the procurement function of its Material Control Department.

> DO IT!

Costing Systems

Action Plan

✔ Understand that a traditional costing system allocates overhead on the basis of a single predetermined overhead rate.

✔ Understand that an ABC system allocates overhead to identified activity cost pools, and then assigns costs to products using related cost drivers that measure the resources consumed.

Indicate whether the following statements are true or false.

1. A traditional costing system allocates overhead by means of multiple overhead rates.
2. Activity-based costing allocates overhead costs in a two-stage process.
3. Direct material and direct labor costs are easier to trace to products than overhead.
4. As manufacturing processes have become more automated, more companies have chosen to allocate overhead on the basis of direct labor costs.
5. In activity-based costing, an activity is any event, action, transaction, or work sequence that incurs cost when producing a product.

Solution

1. false.   2. true.   3. true.   4. false.   5. true.

Related exercise material: **BE4-1, BE4-2, E4-1, and** **DO IT!** **4-1.**

✔ **The Navigator**

Example of ABC versus Traditional Costing

In this section, we present a simple case example that compares activity-based costing with traditional costing. It illustrates how ABC eliminates the distortion that can occur in traditional overhead cost allocation. As you study this example, you should understand that ABC does not *replace* an existing job order or process cost system. What ABC does is to segregate overhead into various cost pools in an effort to provide more accurate cost information. As a result, ABC supplements—rather than replaces—these cost systems.

LEARNING OBJECTIVE   2

Identify the steps in the development of an activity-based costing system.

Assume that Atlas Company produces two products—the Ab Bench and the Ab Coaster abdominal trainers. The Ab Bench is a high-volume item totaling 25,000 units annually. The Ab Coaster is a low-volume item totaling only 5,000 units per year. The direct materials cost per unit is $40 for the Ab Bench and $30 for the Ab Coaster. The direct labor cost is $12 per unit for each product. Each product requires one hour of direct labor for completion. Therefore, total annual direct labor hours are 30,000 (25,000 + 5,000). Expected annual manufacturing overhead costs are $900,000. Thus, the predetermined overhead rate under traditional costing, using direct labor hours, is $30 ($900,000 ÷ 30,000) per direct labor hour. Since both products require one direct labor hour per unit, both products are allocated overhead costs of **$30 per unit under traditional costing**.

Let's now calculate unit costs under ABC. Activity-based costing involves the following four steps.

1. **Identify and classify the activities** involved in the manufacture of specific products, and **allocate overhead to cost pools**.
2. **Identify the cost driver** that has a strong correlation to the costs accumulated in the cost pool.
3. **Compute the activity-based overhead rate** for each cost driver.
4. **Assign overhead costs to products**, using the overhead rates determined for each cost pool (cost per driver).

Identify and Classify Activities and Allocate Overhead to Cost Pools (Step 1)

Activity-based costing starts with an analysis of the activities performed to manufacture a product or provide a service. This analysis should identify all resource-consuming activities. It requires documenting every activity undertaken to accomplish a task. Atlas Company identified three activity cost pools: setting up machines, machining, and inspecting.

Next, the system assigns overhead costs directly to the appropriate activity cost pool. For example, all overhead costs directly associated with Atlas Company's machine setups (such as salaries, supplies, and depreciation) would be assigned to the machine setup cost pool. Illustration 4-4 shows the three cost pools, along with the estimated overhead allocated to each cost pool.

Illustration 4-4
Activity cost pools and estimated overhead

Activity Cost Pools	Estimated Overhead
Setting up machines	**$300,000**
Machining	**500,000**
Inspecting	**100,000**
Total	**$ 900,000**

Identify Cost Drivers (Step 2)

After costs are allocated to the activity cost pools, the company must identify the cost drivers for each cost pool. The cost driver must accurately measure the actual consumption of the activity by the various products. To achieve accurate costing, a **high degree of correlation** must exist between the cost driver and the actual consumption of the overhead costs in the cost pool.

Illustration 4-5 shows the cost drivers identified by Atlas and their total expected use per activity cost pool.

Illustration 4-5
Cost drivers and their expected use

Activity Cost Pools	Cost Drivers	Expected Use of Cost Drivers per Activity
Setting up machines	Number of setups	**1,500** setups
Machining	Machine hours	**50,000** machine hours
Inspecting	Number of inspections	**2,000** inspections

Availability and ease of obtaining data relating to the cost driver is an important factor that must be considered in its selection.

Compute Activity-Based Overhead Rates (Step 3)

Next, the company computes an **activity-based overhead rate** per cost driver by dividing the estimated overhead per activity by the number of cost drivers expected to be used per activity. Illustration 4-6 shows the formula for this computation.

Illustration 4-6
Formula for computing activity-based overhead rate

$$\frac{\text{Estimated Overhead per Activity}}{\text{Expected Use of Cost Drivers per Activity}} = \text{Activity-Based Overhead Rate}$$

Atlas Company computes its activity-based overhead rates by using the estimated overhead per activity cost pool, shown in Illustration 4-4, and the expected use of cost drivers per activity, shown in Illustration 4-5. These computations are presented in Illustration 4-7.

Activity Cost Pools	Estimated Overhead	÷	Expected Use of Cost Drivers per Activity	=	Activity-Based Overhead Rates
Setting up machines	$300,000		1,500 setups		$200 per setup
Machining	500,000		50,000 machine hours		$10 per machine hour
Inspecting	100,000		2,000 inspections		$50 per inspection
Total	$900,000				

Illustration 4-7
Computation of activity-based overhead rates

Assign Overhead Costs to Products (Step 4)

In assigning overhead costs, it is necessary to know the expected use of cost drivers **for each product**. Because of its low volume, the Ab Coaster requires more setups and inspections than the Ab Bench. Illustration 4-8 shows the expected use of cost drivers per product for each of Atlas's products.

Activity Cost Pools	Cost Drivers	Expected Use of Cost Drivers per Activity	Expected Use of Cost Drivers per Product	
			Ab Bench	Ab Coaster
Setting up machines	Number of setups	1,500 setups	500	1,000
Machining	Machine hours	50,000 machine hours	30,000	20,000
Inspecting	Number of inspections	2,000 inspections	500	1,500

Illustration 4-8
Expected use of cost drivers per product

To assign overhead costs to each product, Atlas multiplies the activity-based overhead rates per cost driver (Illustration 4-7) by the number of cost drivers expected to be used per product (Illustration 4-8). Illustration 4-9 shows the overhead cost assigned to each product.

Illustration 4-9
Assignment of activity cost pools to products

	Activity Cost Pools	Expected Use of Cost Drivers per Product	×	Activity-Based Overhead Rates	=	Cost Assigned	Expected Use of Cost Drivers per Product	×	Activity-Based Overhead Rates	=	Cost Assigned
		Ab Bench					Ab Coaster				
4	Setting up machines	500		$200		$100,000	1,000		$200		$200,000
5	Machining	30,000		$10		300,000	20,000		$10		200,000
6	Inspecting	500		$50		25,000	1,500		$50		75,000
7	Total costs assigned [(a)]					$425,000					$475,000
8	Units produced [(b)]					25,000					5,000
9	Overhead cost per unit [(a) ÷ (b)]					$17					$95

Atlas Company.xls

Under ABC, the overhead cost per unit is $17 for the Ab Bench and $95 for the Ab Coaster. When compared to the $30 per unit overhead charge under traditional costing, ABC shifts costs from the high-volume product (Ab Bench) to the low-volume product (Ab Coaster). This shift occurs because low-volume products often require more special handling, such as machine setups and inspections. This is true for Atlas Company. Thus, the low-volume product frequently is responsible for more overhead costs per unit than is a high-volume product.[1] Assigning overhead using ABC will usually increase the cost per unit for low-volume products as compared to a traditional overhead allocation. Therefore, traditional cost drivers such as direct labor hours are usually not appropriate for assigning overhead costs to low-volume products.

Comparing Unit Costs

Illustration 4-10 shows the unit cost for each product under traditional costing.

Illustration 4-10
Computation of unit costs—traditional costing

	Products	
Manufacturing Costs	**Ab Bench**	**Ab Coaster**
Direct materials	$40	$30
Direct labor	12	12
Overhead	30*	30*
Total unit cost	**$82**	**$72**

*Predetermined overhead rate × Direct labor hours = $30 × 1 hr. = $30

A comparison of unit manufacturing costs under traditional costing and ABC shows the following significant differences.

Illustration 4-11
Comparison of unit product costs

	Ab Bench		**Ab Coaster**	
	Traditional		**Traditional**	
Manufacturing Costs	**Costing**	**ABC**	**Costing**	**ABC**
Direct materials	$40	$40	$30	$ 30
Direct labor	12	12	12	12
Overhead	30	17*	30	95*
Total cost per unit	**$82**	**$69**	**$72**	**$137**
		Overstated		**Understated**
		$13		**$65**

*Overhead per Illustration 4-9

The comparison shows that unit costs under traditional costing are significantly distorted. The cost of producing the Ab Bench is overstated by $13 per unit ($82 − $69), and the cost of producing the Ab Coaster is understated by $65 per unit ($137 − $72). These differences are attributable entirely to how Atlas Company assigns manufacturing overhead. A likely consequence of the differences in assigning overhead is that Atlas has been overpricing the Ab Bench and possibly losing market share to competitors. It also has been sacrificing profitability by underpricing the Ab Coaster.

Activity-based costing was pioneered in the United States: John Deere Company coined the term about 25 years ago. Numerous well-known U.S. companies,

---

[1]Robin Cooper and Robert S. Kaplan, "How Cost Accounting Distorts Product Costs," *Management Accounting* 69, No. 10 (April 1988), pp. 20–27.

including IBM, AT&T, Hewlett-Packard, Procter & Gamble, Tektronix, Hughes Aircraft, Caterpillar, and American Express, have adopted ABC. Its use outside the United States, however, is limited. The cost of implementation may discourage some foreign companies.

In Japan, activity-based costing is less widely used. Companies prefer volume measures such as direct labor hours to assign overhead cost to products. Japanese managers are convinced that reducing direct labor is essential to continuous cost reduction. Using direct labor as the basis for overhead allocation forces Japanese companies to watch direct labor more closely.

SERVICE COMPANY INSIGHT

Traveling Light

Have you flown on an airplane since baggage fees have been implemented? Did the fee make you so mad that you swore that the next time you flew, you would pack fewer clothes so you could use a carry-on bag instead? That is exactly how the airlines hoped that you would react. Baggage handling is extremely labor-intensive. All that tagging, sorting, loading on carts, loading in planes, unloading, and sorting again add up to about $9 per bag. They also have equipment costs: sorters, carts, conveyors, tractors, and storage facilities. That's about another $4 of equipment-related overhead per bag. Finally, there is additional fuel cost of a 40-pound item—about $2 in fuel for a 3-hour flight. These costs add up to $15 ($9 + $4 + $2). Since airlines have implemented their baggage fees, fewer customers are checking bags. Not only does this save the airlines money, it also increases the amount of space available for hauling cargo. An airline can charge at least $80 for hauling a small parcel for same-day delivery service.

Source: Scott McCartney, "What It Costs an Airline to Fly Your Luggage," *Wall Street Journal Online* (November 25, 2008).

? Why do airlines charge even higher rates for heavier bags, bags that are odd shapes (e.g., ski bags), and bags with hazardous materials in them? (see page 193.)

> DO IT!

Apply ABC

Casey Company has five activity cost pools and two products. It expects to produce 200,000 units of its automobile scissors jack and 80,000 units of its truck hydraulic jack. Having identified its activity cost pools and the cost drivers for each cost pool, Casey Company accumulated the following data relative to those activity cost pools and cost drivers.

	Annual Overhead Data			Expected Use of Cost Drivers per Product	
Activity Cost Pools	**Cost Drivers**	**Estimated Overhead**	**Expected Use of Cost Drivers per Activity**	**Scissors Jacks**	**Hydraulic Jacks**
Ordering and receiving	Purchase orders	$ 200,000	2,500 orders	1,000	1,500
Machine setup	Setups	600,000	1,200 setups	500	700
Machining	Machine hours	2,000,000	800,000 hours	300,000	500,000
Assembling	Parts	1,800,000	3,000,000 parts	1,800,000	1,200,000
Inspecting and testing	Tests	700,000	35,000 tests	20,000	15,000
		$5,300,000			

Using the above data, do the following.

(a) Prepare a schedule showing the computations of the activity-based overhead rates per cost driver.

(b) Prepare a schedule assigning each activity's overhead cost to the two products.

(c) Compute the overhead cost per unit for each product.

(d) Comment on the comparative overhead cost per unit.

Solution

Action Plan

✔ Determine the activity-based overhead rate by dividing the estimated overhead per activity by the expected use of cost drivers per activity.

✔ Assign the overhead of each activity cost pool to the individual products by multiplying the expected use of cost driver per product times the activity-based overhead rate.

✔ Determine overhead cost per unit by dividing the overhead assigned to each product by the number of units of that product.

(a) Computations of activity-based overhead rates per cost driver:

Activity Cost Pools	Estimated Overhead	÷	Expected Use of Cost Drivers per Activity	=	Activity-Based Overhead Rates
Ordering and receiving	$ 200,000		2,500 purchase orders		$80 per order
Machine setup	600,000		1,200 setups		$500 per setup
Machining	2,000,000		800,000 machine hours		$2.50 per machine hour
Assembling	1,800,000		3,000,000 parts		$0.60 per part
Inspecting and testing	700,000		35,000 tests		$20 per test
	$5,300,000				

(b) Assignment of each activity's overhead cost to products using ABC:

	Scissors Jacks				Hydraulic Jacks			
Activity Cost Pools	Expected Use of Cost Drivers per Product ×	Activity-Based Overhead Rates =		Cost Assigned	Expected Use of Cost Drivers per Product ×	Activity-Based Overhead Rates =		Cost Assigned
Ordering and receiving	1,000	$80		$ 80,000	1,500	$80		$ 120,000
Machine setup	500	$500		250,000	700	$500		350,000
Machining	300,000	$2.50		750,000	500,000	$2.50		1,250,000
Assembling	1,800,000	$0.60		1,080,000	1,200,000	$0.60		720,000
Inspecting and testing	20,000	$20		400,000	15,000	$20		300,000
Total assigned costs				$2,560,000				$2,740,000

(c) Computation of overhead cost per unit:

	Scissors Jack	Hydraulic Jack
Total costs assigned	$2,560,000	$2,740,000
Total units produced	200,000	80,000
Overhead cost per unit	$12.80	$34.25

(d) These data show that the total overhead assigned to 80,000 hydraulic jacks exceeds the overhead assigned to 200,000 scissors jacks. The overhead cost per hydraulic jack is $34.25, but it is only $12.80 per scissors jack.

Related exercise material: **BE4-5, BE4-6, BE4-7, E4-1, E4-2, E4-3, E4-4, E4-5, E4-6, E4-11, and DO IT! 4-2.**

✔ The Navigator

Activity-Based Costing: A Closer Look

As the use of activity-based costing has grown, both its practical benefits and its limitations have become apparent.

Benefits of ABC

The primary benefit of ABC is **more accurate product costing**. Here's why:

1. **ABC leads to more cost pools** being used to assign overhead costs to products. Instead of one plantwide pool (or even departmental pools) and a single cost driver, companies use numerous activity cost pools with more relevant cost drivers. Costs are assigned more directly on the basis of the cost drivers used to produce each product.

2. **ABC leads to enhanced control over overhead costs.** Under ABC, companies can trace many overhead costs directly to activities—allowing some indirect costs to be identified as direct costs. Thus, managers have become more aware of their responsibility to control the activities that generate those costs.

3. **ABC leads to better management decisions.** More accurate product costing should contribute to setting selling prices that can help achieve desired product profitability levels. In addition, more accurate cost data could be helpful in deciding whether to make or buy a product part or component, and sometimes even whether to eliminate a product.

Activity-based costing does not change the amount of overhead costs. What it does do is allocate those overhead costs in a more accurate manner. Furthermore, if the scorekeeping is more realistic and more accurate, managers should be able to better understand cost behavior and overall profitability.

Limitations of ABC

Although ABC systems often provide better product cost data than traditional volume-based systems, there are limitations:

1. **ABC can be expensive to use.** The increased cost of identifying multiple activities and applying numerous cost drivers discourages many companies from using ABC. Activity-based costing systems are more complex than traditional costing systems—sometimes significantly more complex. So companies must ask, is the cost of implementation greater than the benefit of greater accuracy? Sometimes it may be. For some companies, there may be no need to consider ABC at all because their existing system is sufficient. If the costs of ABC outweigh the benefits, then the company should not implement ABC.

2. **Some arbitrary allocations continue.** Even though more overhead costs can be assigned directly to products through ABC's multiple activity cost pools, certain overhead costs remain to be allocated by means of some arbitrary volume-based cost driver such as labor or machine hours.

SERVICE COMPANY INSIGHT

Using ABC to Aid in Employee Evaluation

Although most publicized ABC applications are in manufacturing companies or large service firms, very small service businesses can apply it also. Mahany Welding Supply, a small family-run welding service business in Rochester, New York, used ABC to determine the cost of servicing customers and to identify feasible cost-reduction opportunities.

Application of ABC at Mahany Welding's operations provided information about the five employees who were involved in different activities of revenue generation—i.e., delivery of supplies (rural versus city), welding services, repairs, telephone sales, field or door-to-door sales, repeat business sales, and cold-call sales. Managers applied activity cost pools to the five revenue-producing employees using relevant cost drivers. ABC revealed annual net income (loss) by employee as follows.

Employee #1	$65,431		Employee #4	$(10,957)
Employee #2	$35,154		Employee #5	$(46,180)
Employee #3	$13,731			

This comparative information was an eye-opener to the owner of Mahany Welding—who was Employee #5!

Source: Michael Krupnicki and Thomas Tyson, "Using ABC to Determine the Cost of Servicing Customers," *Management Accounting* (December 31, 1997), pp. 40–46.

 What positive implications does application of ABC have for the employees of this company? (See page 194.)

When to Use ABC

How does a company know when to use ABC? The presence of one or more of the following factors would point to its possible use:

1. Product lines differ greatly in volume and manufacturing complexity.
2. Product lines are numerous and diverse, and they require differing degrees of support services.
3. Overhead costs constitute a significant portion of total costs.
4. The manufacturing process or the number of products has changed significantly—for example, from labor-intensive to capital-intensive due to automation.
5. Production or marketing managers are ignoring data provided by the existing system and are instead using "bootleg" costing data or other alternative data when pricing or making other product decisions.

The redesign and installation of a product costing system is a significant decision that requires considerable cost and a major effort to accomplish. Therefore, financial managers need to be very cautious and deliberate when initiating changes in costing systems. A key factor in implementing a successful ABC system is the support of top management.

DECISION TOOLKIT

DECISION CHECKPOINTS	INFO NEEDED FOR DECISION	TOOL TO USE FOR DECISION	HOW TO EVALUATE RESULTS
When should we use ABC?	Knowledge of the products or product lines, the manufacturing process, and overhead costs	A detailed and accurate cost accounting system; cooperation between accountants and operating managers	Compare the results under both costing systems. If managers are better able to understand and control their operations using ABC, and the costs are not prohibitive, use of ABC would be beneficial.

Value-Added versus Non–Value-Added Activities

Some companies that have experienced the benefits of activity-based costing have applied it to a broader range of management activities. **Activity-based management (ABM)** extends the use of ABC from product costing to a comprehensive management tool that focuses on reducing costs and improving processes and decision-making. A refinement of activity-based costing used in ABM is the classification of activities as either value-added or non–value-added.

Value-added activities are those activities of **a company's operations** that increase the perceived worth of a product or service to customers. Examples for the manufacture of Precor exercise equipment include engineering design, machining, assembly, and painting. Examples of value-added activities in a service company include performing surgery at a hospital, providing legal research at a law firm, or delivering packages by a freight company.

Non–value-added activities are those activities that, if eliminated, would not hinder the company's operations or reduce the perceived worth of its product or service. These activities simply **add cost to, or increase the time spent on, a product or service without increasing its perceived value**. One example is inventory storage. If a company eliminated the need to store inventory (for example, through just-in-time inventory processes), it would not hinder its operations or reduce the worth of its product, but it would decrease its product costs. Other examples include moving materials, work in process, or finished goods from one location to another in the plant during the production process; waiting for manufacturing equipment to become available; inspecting goods; and fixing defective goods under warranty.

Companies often use **activity flowcharts** to help identify the ABC activities. Illustration 4-12 (page 158) shows an activity flowchart. The top part of this flowchart identifies activities as value-added or non–value-added. The value-added activities are highlighted in red. Two rows in the lower part of the flowchart show the number of days spent on each activity. The first row shows the number of days spent on each activity under the current manufacturing process. The second row shows the number of days expected to be spent on each activity under management's proposed reengineered manufacturing process.

The proposed changes would reduce time spent on non–value-added activities by 17 days. This 17-day improvement would be due entirely to moving inventory more quickly through the non–value-added processes—that is, by reducing inventory time in moving, storage, and waiting. The appendix at the end of this

LEARNING OBJECTIVE   6

Differentiate between value-added and non–value-added activities.

	Heartland Company											
	Activity Flowchart											

					Activities							
NVA	**NVA**	**NVA**	**NVA**	**VA**		**NVA**	**NVA**	**VA**	**NVA**	**NVA**	**NVA**	**VA**
Receive and Inspect Materials	Move and Store Materials	Move Materials to Production and Wait	Set Up Machines	Machining:		Inspect	Move and Wait	Assembly	Inspect and Test	Move to Storage	Store Finished Goods	Package and Ship
				Drill	Lathe							

Current Days 1 · 12 · 2.5 · 1.5 · 2 · 1 · 0.2 · 6 · 2 · 0.3 · 0.5 · 14 · 1

← ———————————— *Total Current Average Time = 44 days* ———————————— →

Proposed Days 1 · 4 · 1.5 · 1.5 · 2 · 1 · 0.2 · 2 · 2 · 0.3 · 0.5 · 10 · 1

← ———————————— *Total Proposed Average Time = 27 days* ———————————— →

Proposed reduction in non–value-added time = 17 days

VA = Value-added   NVA = Non–value-added

Illustration 4-12
Flowchart showing value-added and non–value-added activities

chapter discusses a just-in-time inventory system, which some companies use to eliminate non–value-added activities related to inventory.

Not all activities labeled non–value-added are totally wasteful, nor can they be totally eliminated. For example, although inspection time is a non–value-added activity from a customer's perspective, few companies would eliminate their quality control functions. Similarly, moving and waiting time is non–value-added, but it would be impossible to completely eliminate. Nevertheless, when managers recognize the non–value-added characteristic of these activities, they are motivated to minimize them as much as possible. Attention to such matters is part of the growing practice of activity-based management, which helps managers concentrate on **continuous improvement** of operations and activities.

> **DO IT!**

Value-Added Activities

Action Plan

✔ Recognize that value-added activities increase the worth of a product or service to customers.

✔ Understand that non–value-added activities simply add cost to or increase the time spent on a product or service without increasing its market value.

Classify each of the following activities within a water-ski manufacturer as value-added (VA) or non–value-added (NVA).

1. Inspecting completed skis.
2. Storing raw materials.
3. Machine setups.
4. Installing bindings on skis.
5. Packaging skis for shipment.
6. Reworking defective skis.

Solution

1. NVA.   2. NVA.   3. NVA.   4. VA.   5. VA.   6. NVA.

Related exercise material: **BE4-8, BE4-9, E4-13, E4-14, E4-15, E4-16, and DO IT! 4-3.**

✔ **The Navigator**

MANAGEMENT INSIGHT

What Does NASCAR Have to Do with Breakfast Cereal?

Often the best way to improve a process is to learn from observing a different process. Production-line technicians from giant food producer General Mills were flown to North Carolina to observe firsthand how race-car pit crews operate. In a NASCAR race, the value-added activity is driving toward the finish line; any time spent in the pit is non–value-added. Every split second saved in the pit increases the chances of winning. From what the General Mills' technicians learned at the car race, as well as other efforts, they were able to reduce setup time from 5 hours to just 20 minutes.

? What are the benefits of reducing setup time? (See page 194.)

DECISION TOOLKIT

DECISION CHECKPOINTS	INFO NEEDED FOR DECISION	TOOL TO USE FOR DECISION	HOW TO EVALUATE RESULTS
How can activity-based management help managers?	Activities classified as value added and non–value-added	Activity flowchart	The flowchart should motivate managers to minimize non–value-added activities. Managers should better understand the relationship between activities and the resources they consume.

Classification of Activity Levels

As mentioned earlier, traditional costing systems are volume-driven—driven by unit-based cost drivers such as direct labor or machine hours. Some activity costs are strictly variable and are caused by the production or acquisition of a single unit of product or the performance of a single unit of service. However, the recognition that other activity costs are not driven by unit-based cost drivers has led to the development of a classification of ABC activities consisting of four levels, as follows.

LEARNING OBJECTIVE   7

Understand the value of using activity levels in activity-based costing.

1. **Unit-level activities** are performed for each unit of production. For example, the assembly of cell phones is a unit-level activity because the amount of assembly the company performs increases with each additional cell phone assembled.

2. **Batch-level activities** are performed every time a company produces another batch of a product. For example, suppose that to start processing a new batch of ice cream, an ice cream producer needs to set up its machines. The amount of time spent setting up machines increases with the number of batches produced, not with the number of units produced.

3. **Product-level activities** are performed every time a company produces a new type of product. For example, before a pharmaceutical company can produce and sell a new type of medicine, it must undergo very substantial product tests to ensure the product is effective and safe. The amount of time spent on testing activities increases with the number of products the company produces.

4. **Facility-level activities** are required to support or sustain an entire production process. Consider, for example, a hospital. The hospital building must be insured and heated, and the property taxes must be paid, no matter how many patients the hospital treats. These costs do not vary as a function of the number of units, batches, or products.

Companies may achieve greater accuracy in overhead cost allocation by recognizing these four different levels of activities and, from them, developing specific activity cost pools and their related cost drivers. Illustration 4-13 graphically displays this four-level activity hierarchy, along with the types of activities and examples of cost drivers for those activities at each level.

Illustration 4-13
Hierarchy of activity levels

Four Levels	Types of Activities	Examples of Cost Drivers
Unit-Level Activities		
	Machine-related Drilling, cutting, milling, trimming, pressing	Machine hours
	Labor-related Assembling, painting, sanding, sewing	Direct labor hours or cost
Batch-Level Activities		
	Equipment setups	Number of setups or setup time
	Purchase ordering	Number of purchase orders
	Inspection	Number of inspections or inspection time
	Material handling	Number of material moves
Product-Level Activities		
	Product design	Number of product designs
	Engineering changes	Number of changes
Facility-Level Activities		
There. This baby should keep the building cool.	Plant management salaries	Number of employees managed
CUTTING EDGE APPAREL COMPANY	Plant depreciation	Square footage
	Property taxes	Square footage
	Utilities	Square footage

This classification provides managers a structured way of thinking about the relationships between activities and the resources they consume. In contrast, traditional volume-based costing recognizes only unit-level costs. **Failure to recognize this classification of activities is one of the reasons that volume-based cost allocation causes distortions in product costing.**

As indicated earlier, allocating all overhead costs by unit-based cost drivers can send false signals to managers: Dividing batch-, product-, or facility-level costs by the number of units produced gives the mistaken impression that these costs vary with the number of units. **The resources consumed by batch-, product-, and facility-level supporting activities do not vary at the unit level**, nor can managers control them at the unit level. The number of activities performed at the batch level goes up as the *number of batches* rises—not as the number of units within the batches changes. Similarly, the number of product-level activities performed depends on the *number of different products*—not on how many units or batches are produced. Furthermore, facility-sustaining activity costs are not dependent upon the number of products, batches, or units produced. Companies can control batch-, product-, and facility-level costs only by modifying batch-, product-, and facility-level activities.

> DO IT!

Classify Activity Levels

Action Plan

✔ You should use: **unit-level** activities for each unit of product; **batch-level** activities for each batch of product; **product-level** activities for an entire product line; and **facility-level** activities for across the entire range of products.

Morgan Toy Company manufactures six primary product lines of toys in its Morganville plant. As a result of an activity analysis, the accounting department has identified eight activity cost pools. Each of the toy products is produced in large batches, with the whole plant devoted to one product at a time. Classify each of the following activities as either unit-level, batch-level, product-level, or facility-level: (a) engineering design, (b) machine setup, (c) toy design, (d) interviews of prospective employees, (e) inspections after each setup, (f) polishing parts, (g) assembling parts, (h) health and safety.

Solution

(a) product-level. (b) batch-level. (c) product-level. (d) facility-level. (e) batch-level. (f) unit-level. (g) unit-level. (h) facility-level.

Related exercise material: **BE4-10, BE4-11, BE4-12, E4-17, E4-18, and** DO IT! **4-4.**

✔ **The Navigator**

Activity-Based Costing in Service Industries

Although initially developed and implemented by manufacturers, activity-based costing has been widely adopted in service industries as well. ABC is used by airlines, railroads, hotels, hospitals, banks, insurance companies, telephone companies, and financial services firms. The overall objective of ABC in service firms is no different than it is in a manufacturing company. That objective is to identify the key activities that generate costs and to keep track of how many of those activities are performed for each service provided (by job, service, contract, or customer).

LEARNING OBJECTIVE **8**

Apply activity-based costing to service industries.

The general approach to identifying activities, activity cost pools, and cost drivers is the same for service companies and for manufacturers. Also, the labeling of activities as value-added and non–value-added, and the attempt to reduce or eliminate non–value-added activities as much as possible, is just as valid in service industries as in manufacturing operations. What sometimes makes implementation of activity-based costing difficult in service industries is that, compared to manufacturers, **a larger proportion of overhead costs are company-wide costs** that cannot be directly traced to specific services provided by the company.

To illustrate the application of activity-based costing to a service company, contrasted to traditional costing, we use a public accounting firm. This illustration is equally applicable to a law firm, consulting firm, architect, or any service firm that performs numerous services for a client as part of a job.

Traditional Costing Example

Assume that the public accounting firm of Check and Doublecheck prepares the condensed annual budget shown in Illustration 4-14. The firm engages in a number of services, including audit, tax, and computer consulting.

Illustration 4-14
Condensed annual budget of a service firm under traditional costing

Check and Doublecheck, CPAs		
Annual Budget		
Revenue		$4,000,000
Direct labor	$1,200,000	
Overhead (expected)	600,000	
Total costs		1,800,000
Operating income		$2,200,000

$$\frac{\text{Estimated overhead}}{\text{Direct labor cost}} = \text{Predetermined overhead rate}$$

$$\frac{\$600,000}{\$1,200,000} = 50\%$$

Direct labor is the professional service performed. Under traditional costing, direct labor is the basis for overhead application to each job. As shown in Illustration 4-14, the predetermined overhead rate of 50% is calculated by dividing the total estimated overhead costs by the total direct labor cost. To determine the operating income earned on any job, Check and Doublecheck applies overhead at the rate of 50% of actual direct professional labor costs incurred. For example, assume that Check and Doublecheck records $140,000 of actual direct professional labor cost during its audit of Plano Molding Company, which was billed an audit fee of $260,000. Under traditional costing, using 50% as the rate for applying overhead to the job, Check and Doublecheck would compute applied overhead and operating income related to the Plano Molding Company audit, as shown in Illustration 4-15.

Illustration 4-15
Overhead applied under traditional costing system

Check and Doublecheck, CPAs		
Plano Molding Company Audit		
Revenue		$260,000
Less: Direct professional labor	$140,000	
Applied overhead (50% × $140,000)	70,000	210,000
Operating income		$ 50,000

This example, under traditional costing, uses only one direct cost item and one overhead application rate.

Activity-Based Costing Example

Under *activity-based costing*, Check and Doublecheck distributes its estimated annual overhead costs of $600,000 to three activity cost pools. The firm computes activity-based overhead rates per cost driver by dividing each activity overhead cost pool by the expected number of cost drivers used per activity. Illustration 4-16 shows an annual overhead budget using an ABC system.

Check and Doublecheck, CPAs
Annual Overhead Budget

Activity Cost Pools	Cost Drivers	Estimated Overhead	÷	Expected Use of Cost Drivers per Activity	=	Activity-Based Overhead Rates
Administration	Number of partner-hours	$335,000		3,350		$100 per partner-hour
Customer development	Revenue billed	160,000		$4,000,000		$0.04 per $1 of revenue
Recruiting and training	Direct professional hours	105,000		30,000		$3.50 per hour
		$600,000				

Illustration 4-16
Condensed annual budget of a service firm under activity-based costing

The assignment of the individual overhead activity rates to the actual number of activities used in the performance of the Plano Molding Company audit results in total overhead assigned of $57,200, as shown in Illustration 4-17.

Illustration 4-17
Assigning overhead in a service company

	Check and Doublecheck CPA.xls				
	Home Insert Page Layout Formulas Data Review View				
	P18 fx				
	A	B	C	D	E
1	Check and Doublecheck, CPAs				
2	Plano Molding Company Audit				
3				Activity-	
4			Actual Use of	Based Overhead	Cost
5	Activity Cost Pools	Cost Drivers	Drivers	Rates	Assigned
6	Administration	Number of partner-hours	335	$100.00	$33,500
7	Customer development	Revenue billed	$260,000	$0.04	10,400
8	Recruiting and training	Direct professional hours	3,800	$3.50	13,300
9					$57,200
10					

Under activity-based costing, Check and Doublecheck assigns overhead costs of $57,200 to the Plano Molding Company audit, as compared to $70,000 under traditional costing. Illustration 4-18 compares total costs and operating margins under the two costing systems.

Check and Doublecheck, CPAS
Plano Molding Company Audit

	Traditional Costing		ABC	
Revenue		$260,000		$260,000
Expenses				
Direct professional labor	$140,000		$140,000	
Applied overhead	70,000		57,200	
Total expenses		210,000		197,200
Operating income		$ 50,000		$ 62,800
Profit margin		19.2%		24.2%

Illustration 4-18
Comparison of traditional costing with ABC in a service company

The comparison shows that the assignment of overhead costs under traditional costing is distorted. The total cost assigned to performing the audit of Plano Molding Company is greater under traditional costing by $12,800, and the profit margin is significantly lower. Traditional costing understates the profitability of the audit.

MANAGEMENT INSIGHT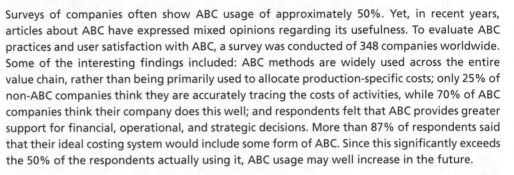

ABC Evaluated

Surveys of companies often show ABC usage of approximately 50%. Yet, in recent years, articles about ABC have expressed mixed opinions regarding its usefulness. To evaluate ABC practices and user satisfaction with ABC, a survey was conducted of 348 companies worldwide. Some of the interesting findings included: ABC methods are widely used across the entire value chain, rather than being primarily used to allocate production-specific costs; only 25% of non-ABC companies think they are accurately tracing the costs of activities, while 70% of ABC companies think their company does this well; and respondents felt that ABC provides greater support for financial, operational, and strategic decisions. More than 87% of respondents said that their ideal costing system would include some form of ABC. Since this significantly exceeds the 50% of the respondents actually using it, ABC usage may well increase in the future.

Source: William Stratton, Denis Desroches, Raef Lawson, and Toby Hatch, "Activity-Based Costing: Is It Still Relevant?" *Management Accounting Quarterly* (Spring, 2009), pp. 31–39.

 What might explain why so many companies say that ideally they would use ABC, but they haven't adopted it yet? (See page 194.)

USING THE **DECISION TOOLKIT**

As mentioned in the Feature Story, Precor manufactures a line of high-end exercise equipment of commercial quality. Assume that the chief accountant has proposed changing from a traditional costing system to an activity-based costing system. The financial vice president is not convinced, so she requests that the next large order for equipment be costed under both systems for purposes of comparison and analysis. An order from Slim-Way Salons, Inc., for 150 low-impact treadmills is received and is identified as the order to be subjected to dual costing. The following cost data relate to the Slim-Way order.

Data relevant to both costing systems

Direct materials	$55,500
Direct labor hours	820
Direct labor rate per hour	$ 18.00

Data relevant to the traditional costing system

Predetermined overhead rate is 300% of direct labor cost.

Data relevant to the activity-based costing system

Activity Cost Pools	Cost Drivers	Activity-Based Overhead Rate	Expected Use of Cost Drivers for Treadmill Order
Engineering design	Engineering hours	$30 per hour	330
Machine setup	Setups	$200 per setup	22
Machining	Machine hours	$25 per hour	732
Assembly	Number of subassemblies	$8 per subassembly	1,500
Packaging and shipping	Packaging/shipping hours	$15 per hour	152
Building occupancy	Machine hours	$6 per hour	732

Instructions

Compute the total cost of the Slim-Way Salons, Inc. order under (a) the traditional costing system and (b) the activity-based costing system. (c) As a result of this comparison, which costing system is Precor likely to adopt? Why?

Solution

(a) Traditional costing system:

Direct materials	$ 55,500
Direct labor (820 × $18)	14,760
Overhead assigned ($14,760 × 300%)	44,280
Total costs assigned to Slim-Way order	$114,540
Number of low-impact treadmills	150
Cost per unit	$ 763.60

(b) Activity-based costing system:

Direct materials		$ 55,500
Direct labor (820 × $18)		14,760
Overhead activities costs:		
Engineering design (330 hours @ $30)	$ 9,900	
Machine setup (22 setups @ $200)	4,400	
Machining (732 machine hours @ $25)	18,300	
Assembly (1,500 subassemblies @ $8)	12,000	
Packaging and shipping (152 hours @ $15)	2,280	
Building occupancy (732 hours @ $6)	4,392	51,272
Total costs assigned to Slim-Way order		$121,532
Number of low-impact treadmills		150
Cost per unit		$ 810.21

(c) Precor will likely adopt ABC because of the difference in the cost per unit (which ABC found to be higher). More importantly, ABC provides greater insight into the sources and causes of the cost per unit. Managers are given greater insight into which activities to control in order to reduce costs. ABC will provide better product costing and greater profitability for the company.

✔ The Navigator

SUMMARY OF LEARNING OBJECTIVES

✔ The Navigator

1 **Recognize the difference between traditional costing and activity-based costing.** A traditional costing system allocates overhead to products on the basis of predetermined plantwide or departmentwide rates such as direct labor or machine hours. An ABC system allocates overhead to identified activity cost pools, and then assigns costs to products using related cost drivers that measure the activities (resources) consumed.

2 **Identify the steps in the development of an activity-based costing system.** The development of an activity-based costing system involves four steps: (1) Identify and classify the major activities involved in the manufacture of specific products, and allocate manufacturing overhead costs to the appropriate cost pools. (2) Identify the cost driver that has a strong correlation to the costs accumulated in the cost pool. (3) Compute the overhead rate per cost driver. (4) Assign manufacturing overhead costs for each cost pool to products or services using the overhead rates.

3 **Know how companies identify the activity cost pools used in activity-based costing.** To identify activity cost pools, a company must perform an analysis of each operation or process, documenting and timing every task, action, or transaction.

4 **Know how companies identify and use cost drivers in activity-based costing.** Cost drivers identified for assigning activity cost pools must (a) accurately measure the actual consumption of the activity by the various products and (b) have related data easily available.

5 **Understand the benefits and limitations of activity-based costing.** Features of ABC that make it a more

accurate product costing system include: (1) the increased number of cost pools used to assign overhead, (2) the enhanced control over overhead costs, and (3) the better management decisions it makes possible. The limitations of ABC are: (1) the higher analysis and measurement costs that accompany multiple activity centers and cost drivers, and (2) the necessity still to allocate some costs arbitrarily.

6 Differentiate between value-added and non–value-added activities. Value-added activities are essential to operations of the business and often increase the worth of a product or service. Non–value-added are non-essential activities that simply add cost to or increase the time spent on a product or service without increasing its market value. Awareness of these classifications encourages managers to reduce or eliminate the time spent on non–value-added activities.

7 Understand the value of using activity levels in activity-based costing. Activities may be classified as unit-level, batch-level, product-level, and facility-level. Companies control overhead costs at unit-, batch-, product-, and facility-levels by modifying unit-, batch-, product-, and facility-level activities, respectively. Failure to recognize this classification of levels can result in distorted product costing.

8 Apply activity-based costing to service industries. The overall objective of using ABC in service industries is no different than for manufacturing industries—that is, improved costing of services provided (by job, service, contract, or customer). The general approach to costing is the same: analyze operations, identify activities, accumulate overhead costs by activity cost pools, and identify and use cost drivers to assign the cost pools to the services.

DECISION TOOLKIT A SUMMARY

DECISION CHECKPOINTS	INFO NEEDED FOR DECISION	TOOL TO USE FOR DECISION	HOW TO EVALUATE RESULTS
When should we use ABC?	Knowledge of the products or product lines, the manufacturing process, and overhead costs	A detailed and accurate cost accounting system; cooperation between accountants and operating managers	Compare the results under both costing systems. If managers are better able to understand and control their operations using ABC, and the costs are not prohibitive, the use of ABC would be beneficial.
How can activity-based management help managers?	Activities classified as value-added and non–value-added	Activity flowchart	The flowchart should motivate managers to minimize non–value-added activities. Managers should better understand the relationship between activities and the resources they consume.

APPENDIX 4A   JUST-IN-TIME PROCESSING

LEARNING OBJECTIVE   9

Explain just-in-time (JIT) processing.

Traditionally, continuous process manufacturing has been based on a **just-in-case** philosophy: Inventories of raw materials are maintained *just in case* some items are of poor quality or a key supplier is shut down by a strike. Similarly, subassembly parts are manufactured and stored *just in case* they are needed later in the manufacturing process. Finished goods are completed and stored *just in case* unexpected and rush customer orders are received. This philosophy often results in a "**push approach**," in which raw materials and subassembly parts are pushed through each process. Traditional processing often results in the buildup of extensive manufacturing inventories.

Primarily in response to foreign competition, many U.S. firms have switched to **just-in-time (JIT) processing**. JIT manufacturing is dedicated to having the right amount of materials, parts, or products just as they are needed. JIT first hit the United States in the early 1980s when automobile companies adopted it to compete with foreign automakers. Many companies, including Dell, Caterpillar, and Harley-Davidson, now successfully use JIT. Under JIT processing, companies receive raw materials **just in time** for use in production, they complete subassembly parts **just in time** for use in finished goods, and they complete finished goods **just in time** to be sold. Illustration 4A-1 shows the sequence of activities in just-in-time processing.

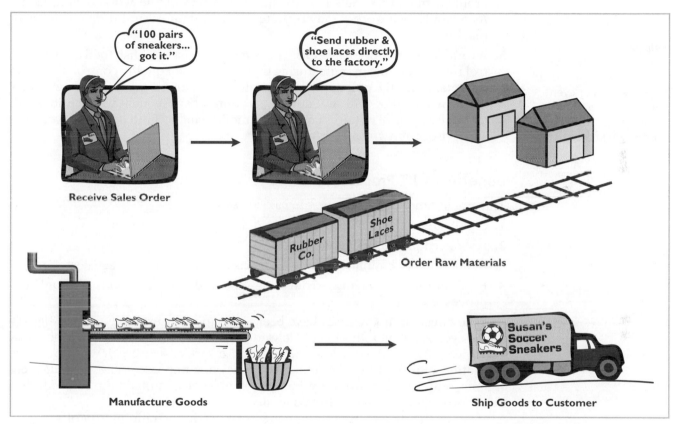

Illustration 4A-1
Just-in-time processing

Objective of JIT Processing

A primary objective of JIT is to eliminate all manufacturing inventories. Inventories have an adverse effect on net income because they tie up funds and storage space that could be put to more productive uses. JIT strives to eliminate inventories by using a "**pull approach**" in manufacturing. This approach begins with the customer placing an order with the company, which starts the process of pulling the product through the manufacturing process. A computer at the final workstation sends a signal to the preceding workstation. This signal indicates the exact materials (parts and subassemblies) needed to complete the production of a specified product for a specified time period, such as an eight-hour shift. The next-preceding process, in turn, sends its signal to other processes back up the line. The goal is a smooth continuous flow in the manufacturing process, with no buildup of inventories at any point.

Elements of JIT Processing

There are three important elements in JIT processing:

1. **Dependable suppliers.** Suppliers must be willing to deliver on short notice exact quantities of raw materials according to precise quality specifications (even including multiple deliveries within the same day). Suppliers must also be willing to deliver the raw materials at specified workstations rather than at a central receiving department. This type of purchasing requires constant and direct communication. Such communication is facilitated by an online computer linkage between the company and its suppliers.

2. **A multiskilled work force.** Under JIT, machines are often strategically grouped into work cells or workstations. Much of the work is automated. As a result, one worker may operate and maintain several different types of machines.

3. **A total quality control system.** The company must establish total quality control throughout the manufacturing operations. Total quality control means **no defects**. Since the pull approach signals only required quantities, any defects at any workstation will shut down operations at subsequent workstations. Total quality control requires continuous monitoring by both line employees and supervisors at each workstation.

Benefits of JIT Processing

The major benefits of implementing JIT processing are:

1. Significant reduction or elimination of manufacturing inventories.

2. Enhanced product quality.

3. Reduction or elimination of rework costs and inventory storage costs.

4. Production cost savings from the improved flow of goods through the processes.

The effects in many cases have been dramatic. For example, after using JIT for two years, a major division of Hewlett-Packard found that work in process inventories (in dollars) were down 82%, scrap/rework costs were down 30%, space utilization improved by 40%, and labor efficiency improved 50%. As indicated, JIT not only reduces inventory but also enables a manufacturer to produce a better product faster and with less waste.

One of the major accounting benefits of JIT is the elimination of separate raw materials and work in process inventory accounts. These accounts are replaced by **one account**, Raw and In-Process Inventory. All materials and conversion costs are charged to this account. The reduction (or elimination) of in-process inventories results in a simpler computation of equivalent units of production.

SUMMARY OF LEARNING OBJECTIVE FOR APPENDIX 4A ✔ The Navigator

9 Explain just-in-time (JIT) processing. JIT is a processing system dedicated to having on hand the right materials and products just at the time they are needed, thereby reducing the amount of inventory and the time inventory is held. One of the principal accounting effects is that one account, Raw and In-Process Inventory, replaces both the raw materials and work-in-process inventory accounts.

GLOSSARY

Activity Any event, action, transaction, or work sequence that incurs cost when producing a product or providing a service. (p. 147).

Activity-based costing (ABC) An overhead cost-allocation system that allocates overhead to multiple activity cost pools and assigns the activity cost pools to products or services by means of cost drivers that represent the activities used. (p. 147).

Activity-based management (ABM) Extends ABC from product costing to a comprehensive management tool that focuses on reducing costs and improving processes and decision-making. (p. 157).

Activity cost pool The overhead cost attributed to a distinct type of activity or related activities. (p. 147).

Batch-level activities Activities performed for each batch of products rather than for each unit. (p. 159).

Cost driver Any factor or activity that has a direct cause–effect relationship with the resources consumed. In ABC, cost drivers are used to assign activity cost pools to products or services. (p. 147).

Facility-level activities Activities required to support or sustain an entire production process. (p. 160).

Just-in-time (JIT) processing A processing system dedicated to having the right amount of materials, parts, or products arrive as they are needed, thereby reducing the amount of inventory. (p. 167).

Non–value-added activity An activity that, if eliminated, would not hinder the company's operations or reduce the perceived worth of its product or service. (p. 157).

Product-level activities Activities performed in support of an entire product line, but not always performed every time a new unit or batch of products is produced. (p. 159).

Unit-level activities Activities performed for each unit of production. (p. 159).

Value-added activity An activity that increases the perceived worth of a product or service to a customer. (p. 157).

> Comprehensive DO IT!

Spreadwell Paint Company manufactures two high-quality base paints: an *oil-based* paint and a *latex* paint. Both are housepaints and are manufactured in neutral white color only. Spreadwell sells the white base paints to franchised retail paint and decorating stores where pigments are added to tint (color) the paint as the customer desires. The oil-based paint is made with organic solvents (petroleum products) such as mineral spirits or turpentine. The latex paint is made with water; synthetic resin particles are suspended in the water, and dry and harden when exposed to the air.

Spreadwell uses the same processing equipment to produce both paints in different production runs. Between batches, the vats and other processing equipment must be washed and cleaned.

After analyzing the company's entire operations, Spreadwell's accountants and production managers have identified activity cost pools and accumulated annual budgeted overhead costs by pool as follows.

Activity Cost Pools	Estimated Overhead
Purchasing	$ 240,000
Processing (weighing and mixing, grinding, thinning and drying, straining)	1,400,000
Packaging (quarts, gallons, and 5-gallons)	580,000
Testing	240,000
Storage and inventory control	180,000
Washing and cleaning equipment	560,000
Total annual budgeted overhead	$3,200,000

Following further analysis, activity cost drivers were identified and their expected use by product and activity were scheduled as follows.

Activity Cost Pools	Cost Drivers	Expected Cost Drivers per Activity	Expected Use of Drivers per Product	
			Oil-Based	Latex
Purchasing	Purchase orders	1,500 orders	800	700
Processing	Gallons processed	1,000,000 gallons	400,000	600,000
Packaging	Containers filled	400,000 containers	180,000	220,000
Testing	Number of tests	4,000 tests	2,100	1,900
Storing	Avg. gals. on hand	18,000 gallons	10,400	7,600
Washing	Number of batches	800 batches	350	450

Spreadwell has budgeted 400,000 gallons of oil-based paint and 600,000 gallons of latex paint for processing during the year.

Instructions

(a) Prepare a schedule showing the computations of the activity-based overhead rates.

(b) Prepare a schedule assigning each activity's overhead cost pool to each product.

(c) Compute the overhead cost per unit for each product.

Solution to Comprehensive DO IT!

Action Plan

✔ Identify the major activities that pertain to the manufacture of specific products and allocate manufacturing overhead costs to activity cost pools.

✔ Identify the cost drivers that accurately measure each activity's contribution to the finished product.

✔ Compute the activity-based overhead rates.

✔ Assign manufacturing overhead costs for each activity cost pool to products, using the activity-based overhead rates.

(a) Computations of activity-based overhead rates:

Activity Cost Pools	Estimated Overhead	÷	Expected Use of Cost Drivers	=	Activity-Based Overhead Rates
Purchasing	$ 240,000		1,500 orders		$160 per order
Processing	1,400,000		1,000,000 gallons		$1.40 per gallon
Packaging	580,000		400,000 containers		$1.45 per container
Testing	240,000		4,000 tests		$60 per test
Storing	180,000		18,000 gallons		$10 per gallon
Washing	560,000		800 batches		$700 per batch
	$3,200,000				

(b) Assignment of activity cost pools to products:

Activity Cost Pools	Oil-Based Paint			Latex Paint		
	Expected Use of Drivers	Overhead Rates	Cost Assigned	Expected Use of Drivers	Overhead Rates	Cost Assigned
Purchasing	800	$160	$ 128,000	700	$160	$ 112,000
Processing	400,000	$1.40	560,000	600,000	$1.40	840,000
Packaging	180,000	$1.45	261,000	220,000	$1.45	319,000
Testing	2,100	$60	126,000	1,900	$60	114,000
Storing	10,400	$10	104,000	7,600	$10	76,000
Washing	350	$700	245,000	450	$700	315,000
Total overhead assigned			$1,424,000			$1,776,000

(c) Computation of overhead cost assigned per unit:

	Oil-Based Paint	Latex Paint
Total overhead cost assigned	$1,424,000	$1,776,000
Total gallons produced	400,000	600,000
Overhead cost per gallon	$3.56	$2.96

✔ The Navigator

Self-Test, Brief Exercises, Exercises, Problem Set A, and many more resources are available for practice in WileyPLUS.

Note: All asterisked Questions, Exercises, and Problems relate to material in the appendix to the chapter.

SELF-TEST QUESTIONS

Answers are at the end of the chapter.

(LO 1) **1.** Activity-based costing (ABC):
  (a) can be used only in a process cost system.
  (b) focuses on units of production.
  (c) focuses on activities performed to produce a product.
  (d) uses only a single basis of allocation.

(LO 1) **2.** Activity-based costing:
  (a) is the initial phase of converting to a just-in-time operating environment.
  (b) can be used only in a job order costing system.
  (c) is a two-stage overhead cost allocation system that identifies activity cost pools and cost drivers.
  (d) uses direct labor as its primary cost driver.

(LO 1, 4) **3.** Any activity that causes resources to be consumed is called a:
  (a) just-in-time activity.
  (b) facility-level activity.
  (c) cost driver.
  (d) non–value-added activity.

(LO 2) **4.** The first step in the development of an activity-based costing system is:
  (a) identify and classify activities and allocate overhead to cost pools.
  (b) assign overhead costs to products.
  (c) identify cost drivers.
  (d) compute overhead rates.

(LO 4) **5.** Which of the following would be the *best* cost driver for the assembling cost pool?
  (a) Number of product lines.
  (b) Number of parts.
  (c) Number of orders.
  (d) Amount of square footage.

(LO 4) **6.** The overhead rate for Machine Setups is $100 per setup. Products A and B have 80 and 60 setups, respectively. The overhead assigned to each product is:
  (a) Product A $8,000, Product B $8,000.
  (b) Product A $8,000, Product B $6,000.
  (c) Product A $6,000, Product B $6,000.
  (d) Product A $6,000, Product B $8,000.

(LO 4) **7.** Donna Crawford Co. has identified an activity cost pool to which it has allocated estimated overhead of $1,920,000. It has determined the expected use of cost drivers for that activity to be 160,000 inspections. Widgets require 40,000 inspections, Gadgets 30,000 inspections, and Targets 90,000 inspections. The overhead assigned to each product is:
  (a) Widgets $40,000, Gadgets $30,000, Targets $90,000.
  (b) Widgets $640,000, Gadgets $640,000, Targets $640,000.
  (c) Widgets $360,000, Gadgets $480,000, Targets $1,080,000.
  (d) Widgets $480,000, Gadgets $360,000, Targets $1,080,000.

(LO 5) **8.** A frequently cited limitation of activity-based costing is:
  (a) ABC results in more cost pools being used to assign overhead costs to products.
  (b) certain overhead costs remain to be allocated by means of some arbitrary volume-based cost driver such as labor or machine hours.
  (c) ABC leads to poorer management decisions.
  (d) ABC results in less control over overhead costs.

(LO 5) **9.** A company should consider using ABC if:
  (a) overhead costs constitute a small portion of total product costs.
  (b) it has only a few product lines that require similar degrees of support services.
  (c) direct labor constitutes a significant part of the total product cost and a high correlation exists between direct labor and changes in overhead costs.
  (d) its product lines differ greatly in volume and manufacturing complexity.

(LO 6) **10.** An activity that adds costs to the product but does not increase its perceived market value is a:
  (a) value-added activity.
  (b) cost driver.
  (c) cost/benefit activity.
  (d) non–value-added activity.

(LO 6) **11.** The following activity is value-added:
  (a) Storage of raw materials.
  (b) Moving parts from machine to machine.
  (c) Shaping a piece of metal on a lathe.
  (d) All of the above.

(LO 7) **12.** A relevant facility-level cost driver for heating costs is:
  (a) machine hours.   (c) floor space.
  (b) direct material.   (d) direct labor cost.

(LO 9) *****13.** Under just-in-time processing:
  (a) raw materials are received just in time for use in production.
  (b) subassembly parts are completed just in time for use in assembling finished goods.
  (c) finished goods are completed just in time to be sold.
  (d) All of the above.

(LO 9) *****14.** The primary objective of just-in-time processing is to:
  (a) accumulate overhead in activity cost pools.
  (b) eliminate or reduce all manufacturing inventories.
  (c) identify relevant activity cost drivers.
  (d) identify value-added activities.

Go to the book's companion website, www.wiley.com/college/weygandt, for additional Self-Test Questions.

✔ **The Navigator**

QUESTIONS

1. Under what conditions is direct labor a valid basis for allocating overhead?
2. What has happened in recent industrial history to reduce the usefulness of direct labor as the primary basis for allocating overhead to products?
3. In an automated manufacturing environment, what basis of overhead allocation is frequently more relevant than direct labor hours?
4. What is generally true about overhead allocation to high-volume products versus low-volume products under a traditional costing system?
5. What are the principal differences between activity-based costing (ABC) and traditional product costing?
6. What is the formula for computing activity-based overhead rates?
7. What steps are involved in developing an activity-based costing system?
8. Explain the preparation and use of a value-added/non–value-added activity flowchart in an ABC system.
9. What is an activity cost pool?
10. What is a cost driver?

11. What makes a cost driver accurate and appropriate?
12. What is the formula for assigning activity cost pools to products?
13. What are the benefits of activity-based costing?
14. What are the limitations of activity-based costing?
15. Under what conditions is ABC generally the superior overhead costing system?
16. What refinement has been made to enhance the efficiency and effectiveness of ABC for use in managing costs?
17. Of what benefit is classifying activities as value-added and non–value-added?
18. In what ways is the application of ABC to service industries the same as its application to manufacturing companies?
19. What is the relevance of the classification of levels of activity to ABC?
*20. (a) Describe the philosophy and approach of just-in-time processing.
    (b) Identify the major elements of JIT processing.

BRIEF EXERCISES

Identify differences between costing systems.

(LO 1), AP

BE4-1 Warner Inc. sells a high-speed retrieval system for mining information. It provides the following information for the year.

	Budgeted	Actual
Overhead cost	$1,000,000	$950,000
Machine hours	50,000	45,000
Direct labor hours	100,000	92,000

Overhead is applied on the basis of direct labor hours. (a) Compute the predetermined overhead rate. (b) Determine the amount of overhead applied for the year. (c) Explain how an activity-based costing system might differ in terms of computing a predetermined overhead rate.

Identify differences between costing systems.

(LO 1), AP

BE4-2 Finney Inc. has conducted an analysis of overhead costs related to one of its product lines using a traditional costing system (volume-based) and an activity-based costing system. Here are its results.

	Traditional Costing	ABC
Sales revenue	$600,000	$600,000
Overhead costs:		
Product RX3	$ 34,000	$ 50,000
Product Y12	36,000	20,000
	$ 70,000	$ 70,000

Explain how a difference in the overhead costs between the two systems may have occurred.

Identify cost drivers.

(LO 4), AP

BE4-3 Storrer Co. identifies the following activities that pertain to manufacturing overhead: materials handling, machine setups, factory machine maintenance, factory supervision, and quality control. For each activity, identify an appropriate cost driver.

BE4-4 Mason Company manufactures four products in a single production facility. The company uses activity-based costing. The following activities have been identified through the company's activity analysis: (a) inventory control, (b) machine setups, (c) employee training, (d) quality inspections, (e) material ordering, (f) drilling operations, and (g) building maintenance.

Identify cost drivers.
(LO 4), AP

For each activity, name a cost driver that might be used to assign overhead costs to products.

BE4-5 Mordica Company identifies three activities in its manufacturing process: machine setups, machining, and inspections. Estimated annual overhead cost for each activity is $150,000, $325,000, and $87,500, respectively. The cost driver for each activity and the expected annual usage are: number of setups 2,500, machine hours 25,000, and number of inspections 1,750. Compute the overhead rate for each activity.

Compute activity-based overhead rates.
(LO 4), AP

BE4-6 Weisman, Inc. uses activity-based costing as the basis for information to set prices for its six lines of seasonal coats. Compute the activity-based overhead rates using the following budgeted data for each of the activity cost pools.

Compute activity-based overhead rates.
(LO 4), AP

Activity Cost Pools	Estimated Overhead	Expected Use of Cost Drivers per Activity
Designing	$ 450,000	10,000 designer hours
Sizing and cutting	4,000,000	160,000 machine hours
Stitching and trimming	1,440,000	80,000 labor hours
Wrapping and packing	336,000	32,000 finished units

BE4-7 Hollins, Inc., a manufacturer of computer chips, employs activity based costing. The budgeted data for each of the activity cost pools is provided below for the year 2014.

Compute activity-based overhead rates.
(LO 4), AP

Activity Cost Pools	Estimated Overhead	Expected Use of Cost Drivers per Activity
Ordering and receiving	$ 90,000	12,000 orders
Etching	480,000	60,000 machine hours
Soldering	1,760,000	440,000 labor hours

For 2014, the company had 11,000 orders and used 50,000 machine hours, and labor hours totaled 500,000. What is the total overhead applied?

BE4-8 Rich Novelty Company identified the following activities in its production and support operations. Classify each of these activities as either value-added or non–value-added.
(a) Machine setup.   (d) Moving work in process.
(b) Design engineering.   (e) Inspecting and testing.
(c) Storing inventory.   (f) Painting and packing.

Classify activities as value- or non–value-added.
(LO 6), AN

BE4-9 Mendle and Kiner is an architectural firm that is contemplating the installation of activity-based costing. The following activities are performed daily by staff architects. Classify these activities as value-added or non–value-added: (a) designing and drafting, 2.5 hours; (b) staff meetings, 1 hour; (c) on-site supervision, 2 hours; (d) lunch, 1 hour; (e) consultation with client on specifications, 1.5 hours; (f) entertaining a prospective client for dinner, 2 hours.

Classify service company activities as value- or non–value-added.
(LO 6, 8), AN

BE4-10 Kwik Pix is a large digital processing center that serves 130 outlets in grocery stores, service stations, camera and photo shops, and drug stores in 16 nearby towns. Kwik Pix operates 24 hours a day, 6 days a week. Classify each of the following activity costs of Kwik Pix as either unit-level, batch-level, product-level, or facility-level.
(a) Color printing materials.
(b) Photocopy paper.
(c) Depreciation of machinery.
(d) Setups for enlargements.
(e) Supervisor's salary.
(f) Ordering materials.
(g) Pickup and delivery.

Classify activities according to level.
(LO 7, 8), AN

(h) Commission to dealers.
(i) Insurance on building.
(j) Loading developing machines.

Classify activities according to level.

(LO 7), AP

BE4-11 Trammell, Inc. operates 20 injection molding machines in the production of tool boxes of four different sizes, named the Apprentice, the Handyman, the Journeyman, and the Professional. Classify each of the following costs as unit-level, batch-level, product-level, or facility-level.
(a) First-shift supervisor's salary.
(b) Powdered raw plastic.
(c) Dies for casting plastic components.
(d) Depreciation on injection molding machines.
(e) Changing dies on machines.
(f) Moving components to assembly department.
(g) Engineering design.
(h) Employee health and medical insurance coverage.

Compute rates and activity levels.

(LO 4, 7), AP

BE4-12 Spin Cycle Company uses three activity pools to apply overhead to its products. Each activity has a cost driver used to allocate the overhead costs to the product. The activities and related overhead costs are as follows: product design $40,000; machining $300,000; and material handling $100,000. The cost drivers and expected use are as follows.

Activities	Cost Drivers	Expected Use of Cost Drivers per Activity
Product design	Number of product changes	10
Machining	Machine hours	150,000
Material handling	Number of setups	100

(a) Compute the predetermined overhead rate for each activity. (b) Classify each of these activities as unit-level, batch-level, product-level, or facility-level.

> DO IT! REVIEW

Identify characteristics of traditional and ABC costing systems.

(LO 1, 2), K

DO IT! 4-1 Indicate whether the following statements are true or false.
(a) The reasoning behind ABC cost allocation is that products consume activities and activities consume resources.
(b) Activity-based costing is an approach for allocating direct labor to products.
(c) In today's increasingly automated environment, direct labor is never an appropriate basis for allocating costs to products.
(d) A cost driver is any factor or activity that has a direct cause-effect relationship with resources consumed.
(e) Activity-based costing segregates overhead into various cost pools in an effort to provide more accurate cost information.

Compute activity-based overhead rates and assign overhead using ABC.

(LO 4), AP

DO IT! 4-2 Flynn Industries has three activity cost pools and two products. It expects to produce 3,000 units of Product BC113 and 1,500 of Product AD908. Having identified its activity cost pools and the cost drivers for each pool, Flynn accumulated the following data relative to those activity cost pools and cost drivers.

	Annual Overhead Data			Expected Use of Cost Drivers per Product	
Activity Cost Pool	**Cost Drivers**	**Estimated Overhead**	**Expected Use of Cost Drivers per Activity**	**Product BC113**	**Product AD908**
Machine setup	Setups	$ 16,000	40	25	15
Machining	Machine hours	110,000	5,000	1,000	4,000
Packing	Orders	30,000	500	150	350

Using the above data, do the following:

(a) Prepare a schedule showing the computations of the activity-based overhead rates per cost driver.
(b) Prepare a schedule assigning each activity's overhead cost to the two products.
(c) Compute the overhead cost per unit for each product. (Round to nearest cent.)
(d) Comment on the comparative overhead cost per product.

DO IT! 4-3 Classify each of the following activities within a tax-preparation business as value-added (VA) or non–value-added (NVA).

Classify activities as value- or non–value-added.

(a) Advertising.
(b) Completing tax returns.
(c) Billing clients.
(d) Answering client questions.
(e) Accompanying clients to audit proceedings.

(LO 6, 8), AP

DO IT! 4-4 Adamson Company manufactures four lines of garden tools. As a result of an activity analysis, the accounting department has identified eight activity cost pools. Each of the product lines is produced in large batches, with the whole plant devoted to one product at a time. Classify each of the following activities or costs as either unit-level, batch level, product-level, or facility-level.

Classify activities according to level.

(LO 7), C

(a) Machining parts.
(b) Product design.
(c) Plant maintenance.
(d) Machine setup.

(e) Assembling parts.
(f) Purchasing raw materials.
(g) Property taxes.
(h) Painting.

✔ **The Navigator**

EXERCISES

E4-1 Wilkins Inc. has two types of handbags: standard and custom. The controller has decided to use a plantwide overhead rate based on direct labor costs. The president has heard of activity-based costing and wants to see how the results would differ if this system were used. Two activity cost pools were developed: machining and machine setup. Presented below is information related to the company's operations.

Assign overhead using traditional costing and ABC.

(LO 1, 4), AP

XLS

	Standard	Custom
Direct labor costs	$50,000	$100,000
Machine hours	1,000	1,000
Setup hours	100	400

Total estimated overhead costs are $270,000. Overhead cost allocated to the machining activity cost pool is $170,000, and $100,000 is allocated to the machine setup activity cost pool.

Instructions

(a) Compute the overhead rate using the traditional (plantwide) approach.
(b) Compute the overhead rates using the activity-based costing approach.
(c) Determine the difference in allocation between the two approaches.

E4-2 Ayala Inc. has conducted the following analysis related to its product lines, using a traditional costing system (volume-based) and an activity-based costing system. Both the traditional and the activity-based costing systems include direct materials and direct labor costs.

Explain difference between traditional and activity-based costing.

(LO 1), AP

Products	Sales Revenue	Total Costs	
		Traditional	ABC
Product 540X	$180,000	$55,000	$50,000
Product 137Y	160,000	50,000	35,000
Product 249S	70,000	15,000	35,000

Instructions
(a) For each product line, compute operating income using the traditional costing system.
(b) For each product line, compute operating income using the activity-based costing system.
(c) Using the following formula, compute the percentage difference in operating income for each of the product lines of Ayala: [Operating Income (ABC) − Operating Income (traditional cost)] ÷ Operating Income (traditional cost). (Round the percentage to two decimals.)
(d) Provide a rationale as to why the costs for Product 540X are approximately the same using either the traditional or activity-based costing system.

Assign overhead using traditional costing and ABC.

(LO 1, 4), AN

E4-3 American Fabrics has budgeted overhead costs of $990,000. It has allocated overhead on a plantwide basis to its two products (wool and cotton) using direct labor hours which are estimated to be 450,000 for the current year. The company has decided to experiment with activity-based costing and has created two activity cost pools and related activity cost drivers. These two cost pools are: cutting (cost driver is machine hours) and design (cost driver is number of setups). Overhead allocated to the cutting cost pool is $360,000 and $630,000 is allocated to the design cost pool. Additional information related to these pools is as follows.

	Wool	Cotton	Total
Machine hours	100,000	100,000	200,000
Number of setups	1,000	500	1,500

Instructions
(a) Determine the amount of overhead allocated to the wool product line and the cotton product line using activity-based costing.
(b) What amount of overhead would be allocated to the wool and cotton product lines using the traditional approach, assuming direct labor hours were incurred evenly between the wool and cotton? How does this compare with the amount allocated using ABC in part (a)?

Assign overhead using traditional costing and ABC.

(LO 1, 4), AN

E4-4 Altex Inc. manufactures two products: car wheels and truck wheels. To determine the amount of overhead to assign to each product line, the controller, Robert Hermann, has developed the following information.

	Car	Truck
Estimated wheels produced	40,000	10,000
Direct labor hours per wheel	1	3

Total estimated overhead costs for the two product lines are $770,000.

Instructions
(a) Compute the overhead cost assigned to the car wheels and truck wheels, assuming that direct labor hours is used to allocate overhead costs.
(b) Hermann is not satisfied with the traditional method of allocating overhead because he believes that most of the overhead costs relate to the truck wheel product line because of its complexity. He therefore develops the following three activity cost pools and related cost drivers to better understand these costs.

Activity Cost Pools	Expected Use of Cost Drivers	Estimated Overhead Costs
Setting up machines	1,000 setups	$220,000
Assembling	70,000 labor hours	280,000
Inspection	1,200 inspections	270,000

Compute the activity-based overhead rates for these three cost pools.
(c) Compute the cost that is assigned to the car wheels and truck wheels product lines using an activity-based costing system, given the following information.

Expected Use of Cost Drivers per Product		
	Car	Truck
Number of setups	200	800
Direct labor hours	40,000	30,000
Number of inspections	100	1,100

(d) What do you believe Hermann should do?

E4-5 Shady Lady sells window coverings (shades, blinds, and awnings) to both commercial and residential customers. The following information relates to its budgeted operations for the current year.

Assign overhead using traditional costing and ABC.
(LO 1, 4), AP

	Commercial		Residential	
Revenues		$300,000		$480,000
Direct material costs	$ 30,000		$ 50,000	
Direct labor costs	100,000		300,000	
Overhead costs	85,000	215,000	150,000	500,000
Operating income (loss)		$ 85,000		($ 20,000)

The controller, Peggy Kingman, is concerned about the residential product line. She cannot understand why this line is not more profitable given that the installations of window coverings are less complex for residential customers. In addition, the residential client base resides in close proximity to the company office, so travel costs are not as expensive on a per client visit for residential customers. As a result, she has decided to take a closer look at the overhead costs assigned to the two product lines to determine whether a more accurate product costing model can be developed. Here are the three activity cost pools and related information she developed:

Activity Cost Pools	Estimated Overhead	Cost Drivers
Scheduling and travel	$105,000	Hours of travel
Setup time	70,000	Number of setups
Supervision	60,000	Direct labor cost

Expected Use of Cost Drivers per Product		
	Commercial	Residential
Scheduling and travel	1,000	500
Setup time	450	250

Instructions

(a) Compute the activity-based overhead rates for each of the three cost pools, and determine the overhead cost assigned to each product line.

(b) Compute the operating income for each product line, using the activity-based overhead rates.

(c) What do you believe Peggy Kingman should do?

E4-6 Perdon Corporation manufactures safes—large mobile safes, and large walk-in stationary bank safes. As part of its annual budgeting process, Perdon is analyzing the profitability of its two products. Part of this analysis involves estimating the amount of overhead to be allocated to each product line. The information shown below relates to overhead.

Assign overhead using traditional costing and ABC.
(LO 1, 4), AN

	Mobile Safes	Walk-In Safes
Units planned for production	200	50
Material moves per product line	300	200
Purchase orders per product line	450	350
Direct labor hours per product line	800	1,700

Instructions

(a) The total estimated manufacturing overhead was $260,000. Under traditional costing (which assigns overhead on the basis of direct labor hours), what amount of manufacturing overhead costs are assigned to:
  (1) One mobile safe?
  (2) One walk-in safe?

(b) The total estimated manufacturing overhead of $260,000 was comprised of $160,000 for material handling costs and $100,000 for purchasing activity costs. Under activity-based costing (ABC):
  (1) What amount of material handling costs are assigned to:
    (a) One mobile safe?
    (b) One walk-in safe?
  (2) What amount of purchasing activity costs are assigned to:
    (a) One mobile safe?
    (b) One walk-in safe?

(c) Compare the amount of overhead allocated to one mobile safe and to one walk-in safe under the traditional costing approach versus under ABC.

Identify activity cost pools.

(LO 3), AP

E4-7 Quik Prints Company is a small printing and copying firm with three high-speed off-set printing presses, five copiers (two color and three black-and-white), one collator, one cutting and folding machine, and one fax machine. To improve its pricing practices, owner-manager Terry Morton is installing activity-based accounting. Additionally, Terry employs five employees: two printers/designers, one receptionist/bookkeeper, one salesperson/copy-machine operator, and one janitor/delivery clerk. Terry can operate any of the machines and, in addition to managing the entire operation, he performs the training, designing, selling, and marketing functions.

Instructions

As Quik Prints' independent accountant who prepares tax forms and quarterly financial statements, you have been asked to identify the activities that would be used to accumulate overhead costs for assignment to jobs and customers. Using your knowledge of a small printing and copying firm (and some imagination), identify at least 12 activity cost pools as the start of an activity-based costing system for Quik Prints Company.

Identify activity cost pools and cost drivers.

(LO 3, 4), AN

E4-8 Santana Corporation manufactures snowmobiles in its Blue Mountain, Wisconsin, plant. The following costs are budgeted for the first quarter's operations.

Machine setup, indirect materials	$ 4,000
Inspections	16,000
Tests	4,000
Insurance, plant	110,000
Engineering design	140,000
Depreciation, machinery	520,000
Machine setup, indirect labor	20,000
Property taxes	29,000
Oil, heating	19,000
Electricity, plant lighting	21,000
Engineering prototypes	60,000
Depreciation, plant	210,000
Electricity, machinery	36,000
Machine maintenance wages	19,000

Instructions

Classify the above costs of Santana Corporation into activity cost pools using the following: engineering, machinery, machine setup, quality control, factory utilities, maintenance. Next, identify a cost driver that may be used to assign each cost pool to each line of snowmobiles.

Identify activity cost drivers.

(LO 4), AN

E4-9 Danny Baden's Verde Vineyards in Oakville, California, produces three varieties of wine: Merlot, Viognier, and Pinot Noir. His winemaster, Russel Hansen, has identified the following activities as cost pools for accumulating overhead and assigning it to products.

1. Culling and replanting. Dead or overcrowded vines are culled, and new vines are planted or relocated. (Separate vineyards by variety.)
2. Tying. The posts and wires are reset, and vines are tied to the wires for the dormant season.
3. Trimming. At the end of the harvest, the vines are cut and trimmed back in preparation for the next season.
4. Spraying. The vines are sprayed with chemicals for protection against insects and fungi.
5. Harvesting. The grapes are hand-picked, placed in carts, and transported to the crushers.
6. Stemming and crushing. Cartfuls of bunches of grapes of each variety are separately loaded into machines which remove stems and gently crush the grapes.
7. Pressing and filtering. The crushed grapes are transferred to presses which mechanically remove the juices and filter out bulk and impurities.
8. Fermentation. The grape juice, by variety, is fermented in either stainless-steel tanks or oak barrels.
9. Aging. The wines are aged in either stainless-steel tanks or oak barrels for one to three years depending on variety.
10. Bottling and corking. Bottles are machine-filled and corked.

11. Labeling and boxing. Each bottle is labeled, as is each nine-bottle case, with the name of the vintner, vintage, and variety.
12. Storing. Packaged and boxed bottles are stored awaiting shipment.
13. Shipping. The wine is shipped to distributors and private retailers.
14. Heating and air-conditioning of plant and offices.
15. Maintenance of buildings and equipment. Printing, repairs, replacements, and general maintenance are performed in the off-season.

Instructions

For each of Verde's 15 activity cost pools, identify a probable cost driver that might be used to assign overhead costs to its three wine varieties.

E4-10 Wilmington, Inc. manufactures five models of kitchen appliances at its Mesa plant. The company is installing activity-based costing and has identified the following activities performed at its Mesa plant.

Identify activity cost drivers.

(LO 4), AN

1. Designing new models.
2. Purchasing raw materials and parts.
3. Storing and managing inventory.
4. Receiving and inspecting raw materials and parts.
5. Interviewing and hiring new personnel.
6. Machine forming sheet steel into appliance parts.
7. Manually assembling parts into appliances.
8. Training all employees of the company.
9. Insuring all tangible fixed assets.
10. Supervising production.
11. Maintaining and repairing machinery and equipment.
12. Painting and packaging finished appliances.

Having analyzed its Mesa plant operations for purposes of installing activity-based costing, Wilmington, Inc. identified its activity cost centers. It now needs to identify relevant activity cost drivers in order to assign overhead costs to its products.

Instructions

Using the activities listed above, identify for each activity one or more cost drivers that might be used to assign overhead to Wilmington's five products.

E4-11 Major Instrument, Inc. manufactures two products: missile range instruments and space pressure gauges. During April, 50 range instruments and 300 pressure gauges were produced, and overhead costs of $94,500 were estimated. An analysis of estimated overhead costs reveals the following activities.

Compute overhead rates and assign overhead using ABC.

(LO 4, 5), AP

| XLS |

Activities	Cost Drivers	Total Cost
1. Materials handling	Number of requisitions	$40,000
2. Machine setups	Number of setups	27,500
3. Quality inspections	Number of inspections	27,000
		$94,500

The cost driver volume for each product was as follows.

Cost Drivers	Instruments	Gauges	Total
Number of requisitions	400	600	1,000
Number of setups	200	300	500
Number of inspections	200	400	600

Instructions

(a) Determine the overhead rate for each activity.
(b) Assign the manufacturing overhead costs for April to the two products using activity-based costing.
(c) ▯▮▭▷ Write a memorandum to the president of Major Instrument explaining the benefits of activity-based costing.

E4-12 Kragan Clothing Company manufactures its own designed and labeled sports attire and sells its products through catalog sales and retail outlets. While Kragan has for years used activity-based costing in its manufacturing activities, it has always used traditional

Assign overhead using traditional costing and ABC.

(LO 1, 4, 6), AP

costing in assigning its selling costs to its product lines. Selling costs have traditionally been assigned to Kragan's product lines at a rate of 70% of direct material costs. Its direct material costs for the month of March for Kragan's "high-intensity" line of attire are $400,000. The company has decided to extend activity-based costing to its selling costs. Data relating to the "high-intensity" line of products for the month of March are as follows.

Activity Cost Pools	Cost Drivers	Overhead Rate	Number of Cost Drivers Used per Activity
Sales commissions	Dollar sales	$0.05 per dollar sales	$900,000
Advertising—TV/Radio	Minutes	$300 per minute	250
Advertising—Newspaper	Column inches	$10 per column inch	2,000
Catalogs	Catalogs mailed	$2.50 per catalog	60,000
Cost of catalog sales	Catalog orders	$1 per catalog order	9,000
Credit and collection	Dollar sales	$0.03 per dollar sales	$900,000

Instructions
(a) Compute the selling costs to be assigned to the "high-intensity" line of attire for the month of March (1) using the traditional product costing system (direct material cost is the cost driver), and (2) using activity-based costing.
(b) By what amount does the traditional product costing system undercost or overcost the "high-intensity" product line?

Assign overhead using traditional costing and ABC; classify activities as value- or non–value-added.

(LO 1, 4, 6), AP

E4-13 Healthy Products, Inc., uses a traditional product costing system to assign overhead costs uniformly to all products. To meet Food and Drug Administration requirements and to assure its customers of safe, sanitary, and nutritious food, Healthy engages in a high level of quality control. Healthy assigns its quality-control overhead costs to all products at a rate of 17% of direct labor costs. Its direct labor cost for the month of June for its low-calorie dessert line is $65,000. In response to repeated requests from its financial vice president, Healthy's management agrees to adopt activity-based costing. Data relating to the low-calorie dessert line for the month of June are as follows.

Activity Cost Pools	Cost Drivers	Overhead Rate	Number of Cost Drivers Used per Activity
Inspections of material received	Number of pounds	$0.80 per pound	6,000 pounds
In-process inspections	Number of servings	$0.33 per serving	10,000 servings
FDA certification	Customer orders	$12.00 per order	420 orders

Instructions
(a) Compute the quality-control overhead cost to be assigned to the low-calorie dessert product line for the month of June (1) using the traditional product costing system (direct labor cost is the cost driver), and (2) using activity-based costing.
(b) By what amount does the traditional product costing system undercost or overcost the low-calorie dessert line?
(c) Classify each of the activities as value-added or non–value-added.

Classify service company activities as value-added or non–value-added.

(LO 6), AN

E4-14 Lasso and Markowitz is a law firm that is initiating an activity-based costing system. Sam Lasso, the senior partner and strong supporter of ABC, has prepared the following list of activities performed by a typical attorney in a day at the firm.

Activities	Hours
Writing contracts and letters	1.5
Attending staff meetings	0.5
Taking depositions	1.0
Doing research	1.0
Traveling to/from court	1.0
Contemplating legal strategy	1.0
Eating lunch	1.0
Litigating a case in court	2.5
Entertaining a prospective client	1.5

Instructions
Classify each of the activities listed by Sam Lasso as value-added or non–value-added, and defend your classification. How much was value-added time and how much was non–value-added?

E4-15 Having itemized its costs for the first quarter of next year's budget, Santana Corporation desires to install an activity-based costing system. First, it identified the activity cost pools in which to accumulate factory overhead. Second, it identified the relevant cost drivers. (This was done in E4-8.)

Classify activities by level.
(LO 7), AN

Instructions
Using the activity cost pools identified in E4-8, classify each of those cost pools as either unit-level, batch-level, product-level, or facility-level.

E4-16 William Mendel & Sons, Inc. is a small manufacturing company in La Jolla that uses activity-based costing. Mendel & Sons accumulates overhead in the following activity cost pools.

Classify activities by level.
(LO 7), AN

1. Hiring personnel.
2. Managing parts inventory.
3. Purchasing.
4. Testing prototypes.
5. Designing products.
6. Setting up equipment.
7. Training employees.
8. Inspecting machined parts.
9. Machining.
10. Assembling.

Instructions
For each activity cost pool, indicate whether the activity cost pool would be unit-level, batch-level, product-level, or facility-level.

EXERCISES: SET B AND CHALLENGE EXERCISES

Visit the book's companion website, at **www.wiley.com/college/weygandt**, and choose the Student Companion site to access Exercise Set B and Challenge Exercises.

PROBLEMS: SET A

P4-1A FireOut, Inc. manufactures steel cylinders and nozzles for two models of fire extinguishers: (1) a home fire extinguisher and (2) a commercial fire extinguisher. The *home model* is a high-volume (54,000 units), half-gallon cylinder that holds 2 1/2 pounds of multi-purpose dry chemical at 480 PSI. The *commercial model* is a low-volume (10,200 units), two-gallon cylinder that holds 10 pounds of multi-purpose dry chemical at 390 PSI. Both products require 1.5 hours of direct labor for completion. Therefore, total annual direct labor hours are 96,300 or [1.5 hrs. × (54,000 + 10,200)]. Expected annual manufacturing overhead is $1,557,480. Thus, the predetermined overhead rate is $16.17 or ($1,557,480 ÷ 96,300) per direct labor hour. The direct materials cost per unit is $18.50 for the home model and $26.50 for the commercial model. The direct labor cost is $19 per unit for both the home and the commercial models.

The company's managers identified six activity cost pools and related cost drivers and accumulated overhead by cost pool as follows.

Assign overhead using traditional costing and ABC; compute unit costs; classify activities as value- or non–value-added.

(LO 1, 4, 6), AP

Activity Cost Pools	Cost Drivers	Estimated Overhead	Expected Use of Cost Drivers	Expected Use of Drivers by Product	
				Home	**Commercial**
Receiving	Pounds	$ 70,350	335,000	215,000	120,000
Forming	Machine hours	150,500	35,000	27,000	8,000
Assembling	Number of parts	412,300	217,000	165,000	52,000
Testing	Number of tests	51,000	25,500	15,500	10,000
Painting	Gallons	52,580	5,258	3,680	1,578
Packing and shipping	Pounds	820,750	335,000	215,000	120,000
		$1,557,480			

Instructions

(a) Unit cost—H.M. $61.76

(a) Under traditional product costing, compute the total unit cost of each product. Prepare a simple comparative schedule of the individual costs by product (similar to Illustration 4-10 on page 152).

(b) Under ABC, prepare a schedule showing the computations of the activity-based overhead rates (per cost driver).

(c) Cost assigned—H.M. $1,069,300

(c) Prepare a schedule assigning each activity's overhead cost pool to each product based on the use of cost drivers. (Include a computation of overhead cost per unit, rounding to the nearest cent.)

(d) Cost/unit—H.M. $57.30

(d) Compute the total cost per unit for each product under ABC.

(e) Classify each of the activities as a value-added activity or a non–value-added activity.

(f) Comment on (1) the comparative overhead cost per unit for the two products under ABC, and (2) the comparative total costs per unit under traditional costing and ABC.

Assign overhead to products using ABC and evaluate decision.

(LO 4), AP

P4-2A Schultz Electronics manufactures two large-screen television models: the Royale which sells for $1,600, and a new model, the Majestic, which sells for $1,300. The production cost computed per unit under traditional costing for each model in 2014 was as follows.

Traditional Costing	Royale	Majestic
Direct materials	$ 700	$420
Direct labor ($20 per hour)	120	100
Manufacturing overhead ($38 per DLH)	228	190
Total per unit cost	$1,048	$710

In 2014, Schultz manufactured 25,000 units of the Royale and 10,000 units of the Majestic. The overhead rate of $38 per direct labor hour was determined by dividing total expected manufacturing overhead of $7,600,000 by the total direct labor hours (200,000) for the two models.

Under traditional costing, the gross profit on the models was Royale $552 or ($1,600 − $1,048), and Majestic $590 or ($1,300 − $710). Because of this difference, management is considering phasing out the Royale model and increasing the production of the Majestic model.

Before finalizing its decision, management asks Schultz's controller to prepare an analysis using activity-based costing (ABC). The controller accumulates the following information about overhead for the year ended December 31, 2014.

Activities	Cost Drivers	Estimated Overhead	Expected Use of Cost Drivers	Activity-Based Overhead Rate
Purchasing	Number of orders	$1,200,000	40,000	$30/order
Machine setups	Number of setups	900,000	18,000	$50/setup
Machining	Machine hours	4,800,000	120,000	$40/hour
Quality control	Number of inspections	700,000	28,000	$25/inspection

The cost drivers used for each product were:

Cost Drivers	Royale	Majestic	Total
Purchase orders	17,000	23,000	40,000
Machine setups	5,000	13,000	18,000
Machine hours	75,000	45,000	120,000
Inspections	11,000	17,000	28,000

Instructions

(a) Assign the total 2014 manufacturing overhead costs to the two products using activity-based costing (ABC) and determine the overhead cost per unit.

(a) Royale $4,035,000

(b) What was the cost per unit and gross profit of each model using ABC costing?

(b) Cost/unit—Royale $981.40

(c) ▭▭▭▷ Are management's future plans for the two models sound? Explain.

P4-3A Thakin Stairs Co. designs and builds factory-made premium wooden stairways for homes. The manufactured stairway components (spindles, risers, hangers, hand rails) permit installation of stairways of varying lengths and widths. All are of white oak wood. Budgeted manufacturing overhead costs for the year 2014 are as follows.

Assign overhead costs using traditional costing and ABC; compare results.

(LO 1, 4), AN

Overhead Cost Pools	Amount
Purchasing	$ 69,000
Handling materials	82,000
Production (cutting, milling, finishing)	210,000
Setting up machines	95,000
Inspecting	90,000
Inventory control (raw materials and finished goods)	126,000
Utilities	180,000
Total budgeted overhead costs	$852,000

For the last 4 years, Thakin Stairs Co. has been charging overhead to products on the basis of machine hours. For the year 2014, 100,000 machine hours are budgeted.

Jeremy Nolan, owner-manager of Thakin Stairs Co., recently directed his accountant, Bill Seagren, to implement the activity-based costing system that he has repeatedly proposed. At Jeremy Nolan's request, Bill and the production foreman identify the following cost drivers and their usage for the previously budgeted overhead cost pools.

Activity Cost Pools	Cost Drivers	Expected Use of Cost Drivers
Purchasing	Number of orders	600
Handling materials	Number of moves	8,000
Production (cutting, milling, finishing)	Direct labor hours	100,000
Setting up machines	Number of setups	1,250
Inspecting	Number of inspections	6,000
Inventory control (raw materials and finished goods)	Number of components	168,000
Utilities	Square feet occupied	90,000

Steve Hannon, sales manager, has received an order for 250 stairways from Community Builders, Inc., a large housing development contractor. At Steve's request, Bill prepares cost estimates for producing components for 250 stairways so Steve can submit a contract price per stairway to Community Builders. He accumulates the following data for the production of 250 stairways.

Direct materials	$103,600
Direct labor	$112,000
Machine hours	14,500
Direct labor hours	5,000
Number of purchase orders	60
Number of material moves	800
Number of machine setups	100
Number of inspections	450
Number of components	16,000
Number of square feet occupied	8,000

Instructions

(a) Compute the predetermined overhead rate using traditional costing with machine hours as the basis.

(b) Cost/stairway $1,356.56

(b) What is the manufacturing cost per stairway under traditional costing? (Round to the nearest cent.)

(c) Cost/stairway $1,134.20

(c) What is the manufacturing cost per stairway under the proposed activity-based costing? (Round to the nearest cent. Prepare all of the necessary schedules.)

(d) ▭▭▭▭▷ Which of the two costing systems is preferable in pricing decisions and why?

Assign overhead costs using traditional costing and ABC; compare results.

(LO 1, 4), AN

P4-4A Benton Corporation produces two grades of wine from grapes that it buys from California growers. It produces and sells roughly 3,000,000 liters per year of a low-cost, high-volume product called CoolDay. It sells this in 600,000 5-liter jugs. Benton also produces and sells roughly 300,000 liters per year of a low-volume, high-cost product called LiteMist. LiteMist is sold in 1-liter bottles. Based on recent data, the CoolDay product has not been as profitable as LiteMist. Management is considering dropping the inexpensive CoolDay line so it can focus more attention on the LiteMist product. The LiteMist product already demands considerably more attention than the CoolDay line.

Jack Eller, president and founder of Benton, is skeptical about this idea. He points out that for many decades the company produced only the CoolDay line and that it was always quite profitable. It wasn't until the company started producing the more complicated LiteMist wine that the profitability of CoolDay declined. Prior to the introduction of LiteMist, the company had simple equipment, simple growing and production procedures, and virtually no need for quality control. Because LiteMist is bottled in 1-liter bottles, it requires considerably more time and effort, both to bottle and to label and box than does CoolDay. The company must bottle and handle 5 times as many bottles of LiteMist to sell the same quantity as CoolDay. CoolDay requires 1 month of aging; LiteMist requires 1 year. CoolDay requires cleaning and inspection of equipment every 10,000 liters; LiteMist requires such maintenance every 600 liters.

Jack has asked the accounting department to prepare an analysis of the cost per liter using the traditional costing approach and using activity-based costing. The following information was collected.

	CoolDay	LiteMist
Direct materials per liter	$0.40	$1.20
Direct labor cost per liter	$0.50	$0.90
Direct labor hours per liter	0.05	0.09
Total direct labor hours	150,000	27,000

Activity Cost Pools	Cost Drivers	Estimated Overhead	Expected Use of Cost Drivers	Expected Use of Cost Drivers Per Product	
				CoolDay	LiteMist
Grape processing	Cart of grapes	$ 145,860	6,600	6,000	600
Aging	Total months	396,000	6,600,000	3,000,000	3,600,000
Bottling and corking	Number of bottles	270,000	900,000	600,000	300,000
Labeling and boxing	Number of bottles	189,000	900,000	600,000	300,000
Maintain and inspect equipment	Number of inspections	240,800	800	350	450
		$1,241,660			

Instructions

Answer each of the following questions. (Round all calculations to three decimal places.)

(a) Cost/liter—C.D. $1.251

(a) Under traditional product costing using direct labor hours, compute the total manufacturing cost per **liter** of both products.

(b) Under ABC, prepare a schedule showing the computation of the activity-based overhead rates (per cost driver).

(c) Prepare a schedule assigning each activity's overhead cost pool to each product, based
on the use of cost drivers. Include a computation of overhead cost per liter.

(c) Cost/liter—C.D. $.241

(d) Compute the total manufacturing cost per liter for both products under ABC.

(e) ▱▱▱▱➡ Write a memo to Jack Eller discussing the implications of your analysis for
the company's plans. In this memo, provide a brief description of ABC as well as an
explanation of how the traditional approach can result in distortions.

P4-5A Polk and Stoneman is a public accounting firm that offers two primary services,
auditing and tax-return preparation. A controversy has developed between the partners
of the two service lines as to who is contributing the greater amount to the bottom line.
The area of contention is the assignment of overhead. The tax partners argue for assigning overhead on the basis of 40% of direct labor dollars, while the audit partners argue
for implementing activity-based costing. The partners agree to use next year's budgeted
data for purposes of analysis and comparison. The following overhead data are collected
to develop the comparison.

*Assign overhead costs to
services using traditional
costing and ABC; compute
overhead rates and unit costs;
compare results.*

(LO 1, 4, 6, 8), AN

Activity Cost Pools	Cost Drivers	Estimated Overhead	Expected Use of Cost Drivers	Expected Use of Cost Drivers Per Service	
				Audit	Tax
Employee training	Direct labor dollars	$216,000	$1,800,000	$1,050,000	$750,000
Typing and secretarial	Number of reports/ forms	76,200	2,500	800	1,700
Computing	Number of minutes	204,000	60,000	25,000	35,000
Facility rental	Number of employees	142,500	40	22	18
Travel	Per expense reports	81,300	Direct	56,000	25,300
		$720,000			

Instructions

(a) Using traditional product costing as proposed by the tax partners, compute the total
overhead cost assigned to both services (audit and tax) of Polk and Stoneman.

(b) (1) Using activity-based costing, prepare a schedule showing the computations of the
activity-based overhead rates (per cost driver).

*(b) (2) Cost assigned—Tax
$350,241*

(2) Prepare a schedule assigning each activity's overhead cost pool to each service
based on the use of the cost drivers.

(c) ▱▱▱▱➡ Comment on the comparative overhead cost for the two services under both
traditional costing and ABC.

(c) Difference—Audit $50,241

PROBLEMS: SET B

P4-1B VideoPlus, Inc. manufactures two types of DVD players, a deluxe model and a
standard model. The deluxe model is a multi-format progressive-scan DVD player with
networking capability, Dolby digital, and DTS decoder. The standard model's primary feature is progressive-scan. Annual production is 50,000 units for the deluxe and 20,000 units
for the standard.

*Assign overhead using
traditional costing and ABC;
compute unit costs; classify
activities as value- or non–
value-added.*

Both products require 2 hours of direct labor for completion. Therefore, total annual
direct labor hours are 140,000 [2 hrs. × (20,000 + 50,000)]. Expected annual manufacturing overhead is $1,050,000. Thus, the predetermined overhead rate is $7.50 ($1,050,000 ÷
140,000) per direct labor hour. The direct materials cost per unit is $42 for the deluxe
model and $11 for the standard model. The direct labor cost is $18 per unit for both the
deluxe and the standard models.

(LO 1, 4, 6), AP

The company's managers identified six activity cost pools and related cost drivers and
accumulated overhead by cost pool as follows.

Activity Cost Pool	Cost Driver	Estimated Overhead	Expected Use of Cost Drivers	Expected Use of Drivers by Product	
				Standard	Deluxe
Purchasing	Orders	$ 126,000	400	100	300
Receiving	Pounds	30,000	20,000	4,000	16,000
Assembling	Number of parts	444,000	74,000	20,000	54,000
Testing	Number of tests	115,000	23,000	10,000	13,000
Finishing	Units	140,000	70,000	20,000	50,000
Packing and shipping	Pounds	195,000	80,000	18,000	62,000
		$1,050,000			

Instructions

(a) Unit cost—Standard $44

(a) Under traditional product costing, compute the total unit cost of both products. Prepare a simple comparative schedule of the individual costs by product (similar to Illustration 4-10 on page 152).

(b) Under ABC, prepare a schedule showing the computations of the activity-based overhead rates (per cost driver).

(c) Cost assigned—Standard $291,375

(c) Prepare a schedule assigning each activity's overhead cost pool to each product based on the use of cost drivers. (Include a computation of overhead cost per unit, rounding to the nearest cent.)

(d) Cost/unit—Standard $43.57

(d) Compute the total cost per unit for each product under ABC.

(e) Classify each of the activities as a value-added activity or a non–value-added activity.

(f) Comment on (1) the comparative overhead cost per unit for the two products under ABC, and (2) the comparative total costs per unit under traditional costing and ABC.

Assign overhead to products using ABC and evaluate decision.

(LO 4), AP

P4-2B Kinnard Electronics manufactures two home theater systems: the Elite which sells for $1,400, and a new model, the Preferred, which sells for $1,100. The production cost computed per unit under traditional costing for each model in 2014 was as follows.

Traditional Costing	Elite	Preferred
Direct materials	$600	$320
Direct labor ($20 per hour)	100	80
Manufacturing overhead ($35 per DLH)	175	140
Total per unit cost	$875	$540

In 2014, Kinnard manufactured 20,000 units of the Elite and 10,000 units of the Preferred. The overhead rate of $35 per direct labor hour was determined by dividing total expected manufacturing overhead of $4,900,000 by the total direct labor hours (140,000) for the two models.

Under traditional costing, the gross profit on the models was Elite $525 ($1,400 − $875), and Preferred $560 ($1,100 − $540). Because of this difference, management is considering phasing out the Elite model and increasing the production of the Preferred model.

Before finalizing its decision, management asks Kinnard's controller to prepare an analysis using activity-based costing (ABC). The controller accumulates the following information about overhead for the year ended December 31, 2014.

Activity	Cost Driver	Estimated Overhead	Expected Use of Cost Drivers	Activity-Based Overhead Rate
Purchasing	Number of orders	$ 775,000	25,000	$31
Machine setups	Number of setups	580,000	20,000	29
Machining	Machine hours	3,100,000	100,000	31
Quality control	Number of inspections	445,000	5,000	89

The cost drivers used for each product were:

Cost Driver	Elite	Preferred	Total
Purchase orders	11,250	13,750	25,000
Machine setups	11,000	9,000	20,000
Machine hours	40,000	60,000	100,000
Inspections	2,750	2,250	5,000

Instructions

(a) Assign the total 2014 manufacturing overhead costs to the two products using activity-based costing (ABC) and determine the overhead cost per unit.

(b) What was the cost per unit and gross profit of each model using ABC costing?

(c) ▮▮▮▭▶ Are management's future plans for the two models sound? Explain.

(a) Elite $2,152,500

(b) Cost/unit—Elite $807.63

P4-3B Luxury Furniture designs and builds factory-made, premium, wood armoires for homes. All are of white oak. Its budgeted manufacturing overhead costs for the year 2014 are as follows.

Assign overhead costs using traditional costing and ABC; compare results.

(LO 1, 4), AN

Overhead Cost Pools	Amount
Purchasing	$ 45,000
Handling materials	50,000
Production (cutting, milling, finishing)	130,000
Setting up machines	85,000
Inspecting	60,000
Inventory control (raw materials and finished goods)	80,000
Utilities	100,000
Total budgeted overhead costs	$550,000

For the last 4 years, Luxury Furniture has been charging overhead to products on the basis of materials cost. For the year 2014, materials cost of $500,000 were budgeted.

Jim Brigham, owner-manager of Luxury Furniture, recently directed his accountant, Bob Borke, to implement the activity-based costing system that he has repeatedly proposed. At Jim Brigham's request, Bob and the production foreman identify the following cost drivers and their usage for the previously budgeted overhead cost pools.

Overhead Cost Pools	Activity Cost Drivers	Expected Use of Cost Drivers
Purchasing	Number of orders	500
Handling materials	Number of moves	5,000
Production (cutting, milling, finishing)	Direct labor hours	65,000
Setting up machines	Number of setups	1,000
Inspecting	Number of inspections	4,000
Inventory control (raw materials and finished goods)	Number of components	40,000
Utilities	Square feet occupied	50,000

Debbie Steiner, sales manager, has received an order for 12 luxury armoires from Thom's Interior Design. At Debbie's request, Bob prepares cost estimates for producing 12 armoires so Debbie can submit a contract price per armoire to Thom's. He accumulates the following data for the production of 12 armoires.

Direct materials	$5,200
Direct labor	$3,500
Direct labor hours	200
Number of purchase orders	3
Number of material moves	32
Number of machine setups	4
Number of inspections	20
Number of components	640
Number of square feet occupied	320

Instructions

(a) Compute the predetermined overhead rate using traditional costing with materials cost as the basis.

(b) Cost/armoire $1,201.67
(c) Cost/armoire $1,020.83

(b) What is the manufacturing cost per armoire under traditional costing?

(c) What is the manufacturing cost per armoire under the proposed activity-based costing? (Prepare all of the necessary schedules.)

(d) ▯▭▭▭▭▷ Which of the two costing systems is preferable in pricing decisions and why?

Assign overhead costs using traditional costing and ABC; compare results.

(LO 1, 4), AN

P4-4B Merando Corporation produces two grades of wine from grapes that it buys from California growers. It produces and sells roughly 600,000 gallon jugs per year of a low-cost, high-volume product called Valley Fresh. Merando also produces and sells roughly 200,000 gallons per year of a low-volume, high-cost product called Merando Valley. Merando Valley is sold in 1-liter bottles. Based on recent data, the Valley Fresh product has not been as profitable as Merando Valley. Management is considering dropping the inexpensive Valley Fresh line so it can focus more attention on the Merando Valley product. The Merando Valley product already demands considerably more attention than the Valley Fresh line.

Frankie Merando, president and founder of Merando, is skeptical about this idea. He points out that for many decades the company produced only the Valley Fresh line, and that it was always quite profitable. It wasn't until the company started producing the more complicated Merando Valley wine that the profitability of Valley Fresh declined. Prior to the introduction of Merando Valley, the company had simple equipment, simple growing and production procedures, and virtually no need for quality control. Because Merando Valley is bottled in 1-liter bottles, it requires considerably more time and effort, both to bottle and to label and box, than does Valley Fresh. The company must bottle and handle 4 times as many bottles of Merando Valley to sell the same quantity as Valley Fresh, since there are approximately 4 liters in a gallon. Valley Fresh requires 1 month of aging; Merando Valley requires 1 year. Valley Fresh requires cleaning and inspection of equipment every 2,500 gallons; Merando Valley requires such maintenance every 250 gallons.

Frankie has asked the accounting department to prepare an analysis of the cost per gallon using the traditional costing approach and using activity-based costing. The following information was collected.

	Valley Fresh	**Merando Valley**
Direct materials per gallon	$1.35	$3.60
Direct labor cost per gallon	$0.75	$1.50
Direct labor hours per gallon	0.05	0.10
Total direct labor hours	30,000	20,000

Activity Cost Pool	Cost Driver	Estimated Overhead	Expected Use of Cost Drivers	Expected Use of Cost Drivers per Product	
				Valley Fresh	**Merando Valley**
Grape processing	Cart of grapes	$ 146,000	8,000	6,000	2,000
Aging	Total months	420,000	3,000,000	600,000	2,400,000
Bottling and corking	Number of bottles	210,000	1,400,000	600,000	800,000
Labeling and boxing	Number of bottles	140,000	1,400,000	600,000	800,000
Maintain and inspect equipment	Number of inspections	234,000	1,040	240	800
		$1,150,000			

Instructions

Answer each of the following questions. (Round all calculations to three decimal places.)

(a) Cost/gallon—V.F. $3.25

(a) Under traditional product costing using direct labor hours, compute the total manufacturing cost per **gallon** of both products.

(b) Under ABC, prepare a schedule showing the computation of the activity-based overhead rates (per cost driver).

(c) Prepare a schedule assigning each activity's overhead cost pool to each product, based
on the use of cost drivers. Include a computation of overhead cost per gallon.

(d) Compute the total manufacturing cost per gallon for both products under ABC.

(e) ▰▰▰▰▷ Write a memo to Frankie Merando discussing the implications of your analysis for the company's plans. In this memo, provide a brief description of ABC as well
as an explanation of how the traditional approach can result in distortions.

(c) Cost/gallon—V.F. $0.663

P4-5B Smith and Jones is a law firm that serves both individuals and corporations. A
controversy has developed between the partners of the two service lines as to who is contributing the greater amount to the bottom line. The area of contention is the assignment
of overhead. The individual partners argue for assigning overhead on the basis of 30% of
direct labor dollars, while the corporate partners argue for implementing activity-based
costing. The partners agree to use next year's budgeted data for purposes of analysis and
comparison. The following overhead data are collected to develop the comparison.

*Assign overhead costs to
services using traditional
costing and ABC; compute
overhead rates and unit costs;
compare results.*

(LO 1, 4, 6, 8), AN

Activity Cost Pool	Cost Driver	Estimated Overhead	Expected Use of Cost Drivers	Expected Use of Cost Drivers per Service	
				Corporate	Individual
Employee training	Direct labor dollars	$120,000	$1,600,000	$900,000	$700,000
Typing and secretarial	Number of reports/ forms	60,000	2,000	500	1,500
Computing	Number of minutes	130,000	40,000	17,000	23,000
Facility rental	Number of employees	100,000	25	14	11
Travel	Per expense reports	70,000	Direct	48,000	22,000
		$480,000			

Instructions

(a) Using traditional product costing, compute the total overhead cost assigned to both
services (individual and corporate) of Smith and Jones.

(b) (1) Using activity-based costing, prepare a schedule showing the computations of the
activity-based overhead rates (per cost driver).

(2) Prepare a schedule assigning each activity's overhead cost pool to each service
based on the use of the cost drivers.

(c) ▰▰▰▰▷ Comment on the comparative overhead for the two service lines under both
traditional costing and ABC.

*(b) (2) Cost assigned—
Individual $238,250*

*(c) Difference—Corporate
$28,250*

PROBLEMS: SET C

Visit the book's companion website, at **www.wiley.com/college/weygandt**, and choose
the Student Companion site to access Problem Set C.

WATERWAYS CONTINUING PROBLEM

(Note: This is a continuation of the Waterways Problem from Chapters 1–3.)

WCP4 Waterways looked into ABC as a method of costing because of the variety of items it
produces and the many different activities in which it is involved. This problem asks you to
help Waterways use an activity-based costing system to account for its production activities.

Go to the book's companion website, at **www.wiley.com/college/weygandt**, *to find the
completion of this problem.*

Broadening Your **PERSPECTIVE**

Management Decision-Making

Decision-Making at Current Designs

BYP4-1 As you learned in the previous chapters, Current Designs has two main product lines—composite kayaks, which are handmade and very labor-intensive, and rotomolded kayaks, which require less labor but employ more expensive equipment. Current Designs' controller, Diane Buswell, is now evaluating several different methods of assigning overhead to these products. It is important to ensure that costs are appropriately assigned to the company's products. At the same time, the system that is used must not be so complex that its costs are greater than its benefits.

Diane has decided to use the following activities and costs to evaluate the methods of assigning overhead.

Activity	Cost
Designing new models	$121,100
Creating and testing prototypes	152,000
Creating molds for kayaks	188,500
Operating oven for the rotomolded kayaks	40,000
Operating the vacuum line for the composite kayaks	28,000
Supervising production employees	180,000
Curing time (the time that is needed for the chemical processes to finish before the next step in the production process; many of these costs are related to the space required in the building)	190,400
Total	$900,000

As Diane examines the data, she decides that the cost of operating the oven for the rotomolded kayaks and the cost of operating the vacuum line for the composite kayaks can be directly assigned to each of these product lines and do not need to be allocated with the other costs.

Instructions

For purposes of this analysis, assume that Current Designs uses $234,000 in direct labor costs to produce 1,000 composite kayaks and $286,000 in direct labor costs to produce 4,000 rotomolded kayaks each year.

(a) One method of allocating overhead would allocate the common costs to each product line by using an allocation basis such as the number of employees in working on each type of kayak or the amount of factory space used for the production of each type of kayak. Diane knows that about 50% of the area of the plant and 50% of the employees work on the composite kayaks, and the remaining space and other employees work on the rotomolded kayaks. Using this information, and remembering that the cost of operating the oven and vacuum line have been directly assigned, determine the total amount to be assigned to the composite kayak line and the rotomolded kayak line, and the amount to be assigned to each of the units in each line.

(b) Another method of allocating overhead is to use direct labor dollars as an allocation basis. Remembering that the costs of the oven and the vacuum line have been assigned directly to the product lines, allocate the remaining costs using direct labor dollars as the allocation basis. Then, determine the amount of overhead that should be assigned to each unit of each product line using this method.

(c) Activity-based costing requires a cost driver for each cost pool. Use the following information to assign the costs to the product lines using the activity-based costing approach.

Activity	Cost Driver	Driver Amount for Composite Kayaks	Driver Amount for Rotomolded Kayaks
Designing new models	Number of models	3	1
Creating and testing prototypes	Number of prototypes	6	2
Creating molds for kayaks	Number of molds	12	1
Supervising production employees	Number of employees	12	12
Curing time	Number of days of curing time	15,000	2,000

What amount of overhead should be assigned to each composite kayak using this method? What amount of overhead should be assigned to each rotomolded kayak using this method?

(d) Which of the three methods do you think Current Designs should use? Why?

Decision-Making Across the Organization

BYP4-2 East Valley Hospital is a primary medical care facility and trauma center that serves 11 small, rural midwestern communities within a 40-mile radius. The hospital offers all the medical/surgical services of a typical small hospital. It has a staff of 18 full-time doctors and 20 part-time visiting specialists. East Valley has a payroll of 150 employees consisting of technicians, nurses, therapists, managers, directors, administrators, dieticians, secretaries, data processors, and janitors.

Instructions

With the class divided into groups, discuss and answer the following.

(a) Using your (limited, moderate, or in-depth) knowledge of a hospital's operations, identify as many **activities** as you can that would serve as the basis for implementing an activity-based costing system.

(b) For each of the activities listed in (a), identify a **cost driver** that would serve as a valid measure of the resources consumed by the activity.

Managerial Analysis

BYP4-3 Ideal Manufacturing Company of Sycamore, Illinois, has supported a research and development (R&D) department that has for many years been the sole contributor to the company's new farm machinery products. The R&D activity is an overhead cost center that provides services only to in-house manufacturing departments (four different product lines), all of which produce agricultural/farm/ranch-related machinery products.

The department has never sold its services outside, but because of its long history of success, larger manufacturers of agricultural products have approached Ideal to hire its R&D department for special projects. Because the costs of operating the R&D department have been spiraling uncontrollably, Ideal's management is considering entertaining these outside approaches to absorb the increasing costs. But, (1) management doesn't have any cost basis for charging R&D services to outsiders, and (2) it needs to gain control of its R&D costs. Management decides to implement an activity-based costing system in order to determine the charges for both outsiders and the in-house users of the department's services.

R&D activities fall into four pools with the following annual costs.

Market analysis	$1,050,000
Product design	2,350,000
Product development	3,600,000
Prototype testing	1,400,000

Activity analysis determines that the appropriate cost drivers and their usage for the four activities are:

Activities	Cost Drivers	Total Estimated Drivers
Market analysis	Hours of analysis	15,000 hours
Product design	Number of designs	2,500 designs
Product development	Number of products	90 products
Prototype testing	Number of tests	500 tests

Instructions

(a) Compute the activity-based overhead rate for each activity cost pool.

(b) How much cost would be charged to an in-house manufacturing department that consumed 1,800 hours of market analysis time, was provided 280 designs relating to 10 products, and requested 92 engineering tests?

(c) How much cost would serve as the basis for pricing an R&D bid with an outside company on a contract that would consume 800 hours of analysis time, require 178 designs relating to 3 products, and result in 70 engineering tests?

(d) What is the benefit to Ideal Manufacturing of applying activity-based costing to its R&D activity for both in-house and outside charging purposes?

Real-World Focus

BYP4-4 An article in *Cost Management*, by Kocakulah, Bartlett, and Albin entitled "ABC for Calculating Mortgage Loan Servicing Expenses" (July/August 2009, p. 36), discusses a use of ABC in the financial services industry.

Instructions

Read the article and answer the following questions.

(a) What are some of the benefits of ABC that relate to the financial services industry?

(b) What are three things that the company's original costing method did not take into account?

(c) What were some of the cost drivers used by the company in the ABC approach?

BYP4-5 Activity-based costing methods are constantly being improved upon, and many websites discuss suggestions for improvement. The article in this activity outlines an alternative perspective on activity-based costing.

Address: **http://hbswk.hbs.edu/item/4587.html,** or go to **www.wiley.com/college/weygandt**

Instructions

Read the article provided at the site and answer the following questions.

(a) What concerns do the authors say are raised by "real-world use" of ABC? According to the authors, what benefits have companies enjoyed from the use of ABC?

(b) What method do the authors suggest for estimating practical capacity? How important is it to be precise in this estimate?

(c) Describe the steps that are taken after practical capacity has been estimated.

(d) What is one of the primary benefits obtained by management in the report entitled "ABC, the Time-Driven Way"? What is an example of how this worked for a real company?

Critical Thinking

Ethics Case

BYP4-6 Curtis Rich, the cost accountant for Hi-Power Mower Company, recently installed activity-based costing at Hi-Power's St. Louis lawn tractor (riding mower) plant where three models—the 8-horsepower Bladerunner, the 12-horsepower Quickcut, and the 18-horsepower Supercut—are manufactured. Curtis's new product costs for these three models show that the company's traditional costing system had been significantly undercosting the 18-horsepower Supercut. This was due primarily to the lower sales volume of the Supercut compared to the Bladerunner and the Quickcut.

Before completing his analysis and reporting these results to management, Curtis is approached by his friend Ed Gray, who is the production manager for the 18-horsepower Supercut model. Ed has heard from one of Curtis's staff about the new product costs and is upset and worried for his job because the new costs show the Supercut to be losing, rather than making, money.

At first, Ed condemns the new cost system, whereupon Curtis explains the practice of activity-based costing and why it is more accurate than the company's present system. Even more worried now, Ed begs Curtis, "Massage the figures just enough to save the line from being discontinued. You don't want me to lose my job, do you? Anyway, nobody will know."

Curtis holds firm but agrees to recompute all his calculations for accuracy before submitting his costs to management.

Instructions
(a) Who are the stakeholders in this situation?
(b) What, if any, are the ethical considerations in this situation?
(c) What are Curtis's ethical obligations to the company? To his friend?

All About You

BYP4-7 There are many resources available on the Web to assist people in time management. Some of these resources are designed specifically for college students.

Instructions
Go to **http://www.dartmouth.edu/~acskills/videos/video_tm.html** (or do an Internet search of Dartmouth's time-management video). Watch the video and then answer the following questions.
(a) What are the main tools of time management for students, and what is each used for?
(b) At what time of day are students most inclined to waste time? What time of day is the best for studying complex topics?
(c) How can employing time-management practices be a "liberating" experience?
(d) Why is goal-setting important? What are the characteristics of good goals, and what steps should you take to help you develop your goals?

Considering Your Costs and Benefits

BYP4-8 As discussed in the chapter, the principles underlying activity-based costing have evolved into the broader approach known as *activity-based management*. One of the common practices of activity-based management is to identify all business activities, classify each activity as either a value-added or a non–value-added activity, and then try to reduce or eliminate the time spent on non–value-added activities. Consider the implications of applying this same approach to your everyday life, at work and at school. How do you spend your time each day? How much of your day is spent on activities that help you accomplish your objectives, and how much of your day is spent on activities that do not add value?

Many "self-help" books and websites offer suggestions on how to improve your time management. Should you minimize the "non–value-added" hours in your life by adopting the methods suggested by these sources? The basic arguments for and against are as follows.

> **YES:** There are a limited number of hours in a day. You should try to maximize your chances of achieving your goals by eliminating the time that you waste.
>
> **NO:** Life is about more than working yourself to death. Being an efficiency expert doesn't guarantee that you will be happy. Schedules and daily planners are too constraining.

Instructions
Write a response indicating your position regarding this situation. Provide support for your view.

Answers to Chapter Questions

Answers to Insight and Accounting Across the Organization Questions

p. 153 Traveling Light Q: Why do airlines charge even higher rates for heavier bags, bags that are odd shapes (e.g., ski bags), and bags with hazardous materials in them? **A:** Each of these factors increases the costs to the airlines. Heavier baggage is more difficult to handle, thus increasing labor costs. It also uses up more fuel. Bags that are odd shapes complicate handling both for humans and machines. In addition, odd shapes take up more space in the cargo area. Finally, hazardous materials require special handling and storage procedures. All of these factors should be considered by an airline when it decides how much to charge for special baggage.

p. 156 Using ABC to Aid in Employee Evaluation Q: What positive implications does application of ABC have for the employees of this company? **A:** ABC will make these employees more aware of which activities cost the company more money. They will be motivated to reduce their use of these activities in order to improve their individual performance.

p. 159 What Does NASCAR Have to Do with Breakfast Cereal? Q: What are the benefits of reducing setup time? **A:** Setup time is a non–value-added activity. Customers are not willing to pay extra for more setup time. By reducing the time spent on setups, the company can reduce non–value-added costs. Also, by reducing setup time, the company can switch from producing one product to producing a different product more quickly. This enables it to respond to customers' demands more quickly, thus avoiding stockouts.

p. 164 ABC Evaluated Q: What might explain why so many companies say that ideally they would use ABC, but they haven't adopted it yet? **A:** As noted in the chapter, implementation of an ABC system can be very expensive. It may be difficult to justify an expenditure for a system that allocates overhead costs more accurately. The benefits of more accurate costing may not be as obvious as some of the other things a company might spend its money on, such as a machine that produces goods more efficiently.

Answers to Self-Test Questions

1. c **2.** c **3.** c **4.** a **5.** b **6.** b ($100 × 80), ($100 × 60) **7.** d [($1,920,000/160,000) × 40,000], [($1,920,000/160,000) × 30,000)], [($1,920,000/160,000) × 90,000)] **8.** b **9.** d **10.** d **11.** c **12.** c *13. d *14. b

Don't Worry— Just Get Big

It wasn't that Jeff Bezos didn't have a good job. He was a vice president at a Wall Street firm. But, he quit his job, moved to Seattle, and started an online retailer, which he named Amazon.com. Like any good entrepreneur, Jeff strove to keep his initial investment small. Operations were run out of his garage. And, to avoid the need for a warehouse, he took orders for books and had them shipped from other distributors' warehouses. One board member recalls how excited the board was whenever an order came in from a customer in a state that Amazon had never serviced before.

By its fourth month, Amazon was selling 100 books a day. In its first full year, it had $15.7 million in sales. The next year, sales increased eightfold. Two years later, sales were $1.6 billion.

Although its sales growth was impressive, Amazon's ability to lose money was equally amazing. One analyst nicknamed it *Amazon.bomb*, while another, predicting its demise, called it *Amazon.toast*. Why was it losing money? The company used every available dollar to reinvest in itself. It built massive warehouses and bought increasingly sophisticated (and expensive) computer systems to improve its distribution system. This desire to grow as fast as possible was

✔ The Navigator

- [ ] Scan Learning Objectives
- [ ] Read Feature Story
- [ ] Scan Preview
- [ ] Read Text and answer **DO IT!** p. 202
  - [ ] p. 205　[ ] p. 213　[ ] p. 216
- [ ] Work Using the Decision Toolkit p. 216
- [ ] Review Summary of Learning Objectives
- [ ] Work Comprehensive **DO IT!** p. 218
- [ ] Answer Self-Test Questions
- [ ] Complete Assignments
- [ ] Go to **WileyPLUS** for practice and tutorials

Learning Objectives

After studying this chapter, you should be able to:

1 Distinguish between variable and fixed costs.

2 Explain the significance of the relevant range.

3 Explain the concept of mixed costs.

4 List the five components of cost-volume-profit analysis.

5 Indicate what contribution margin is and how it can be expressed.

6 Identify the three ways to determine the break-even point.

7 Give the formulas for determining sales required to earn target net income.

8 Define margin of safety, and give the formulas for computing it.

✔ The Navigator

captured in a T-shirt slogan at its company picnic, which read "Eat another hot dog, get big fast." This buying binge was increasing the company's fixed costs at a rate that exceeded its sales growth. Skeptics were predicting that Amazon would soon run out of cash. It didn't.

In the fourth quarter of 2010 (only 15 years after its world headquarters were located in a garage), Amazon reported quarterly revenues of $12.95 billion and quarterly income of $416 million. But, even as it announced record profits, its share price fell by 9%. Why? Because although the company was predicting that its sales revenue in the next quarter would increase by at least 28%, it predicted that its operating profit would fall by at least 2% and perhaps by as much as 34%.

The company made no apologies. It explained that it was in the process of expanding from 39 distribution centers to 52. As Amazon's finance chief noted, "You're not as productive on those assets for some time. I'm very pleased with the investments we're making and we've shown over our history that we've been able to make great returns on the capital we invest in." In other words, eat another hot dog.

Watch the Southwest Airlines video in WileyPLUS to learn more about cost-volume-profit analysis in the real world.

Source: Christine Frey and John Cook, "How Amazon.com Survived, Thrived and Turned a Profit," *Seattle Post* (January 28, 2008); and Stu Woo, "Sticker Shock Over Amazon Growth," *Wall Street Journal Online* (January 28, 2011).

✔ **The Navigator**

Preview of **Chapter 5**

As the Feature Story indicates, to manage any size business you must understand how costs respond to changes in sales volume and the effect of costs and revenues on profits. A prerequisite to understanding cost-volume-profit (CVP) relationships is knowledge of how costs behave. In this chapter, we first explain the considerations involved in cost behavior analysis. Then, we discuss and illustrate CVP analysis.

The content and organization of Chapter 5 are as follows.

COST-VOLUME-PROFIT

Cost Behavior Analysis	Cost-Volume-Profit Analysis
• Variable costs • Fixed costs • Relevant range • Mixed costs • Identifying variable and fixed costs	• Basic components • CVP income statement • Break-even analysis • Target net income • Margin of safety

✔ **The Navigator**

Cost Behavior Analysis

Cost behavior analysis is the study of how specific costs respond to changes in the level of business activity. As you might expect, some costs change, and others remain the same. For example, for an airline company such as Southwest or United, the longer the flight, the higher the fuel costs. On the other hand, Massachusetts General Hospital's costs to staff the emergency room on any given night are relatively constant regardless of the number of patients treated. A knowledge of cost behavior helps management plan operations and decide between alternative courses of action. Cost behavior analysis applies to all types of entities.

The starting point in cost behavior analysis is measuring the key business activities. Activity levels may be expressed in terms of sales dollars (in a retail company), miles driven (in a trucking company), room occupancy (in a hotel), or dance classes taught (by a dance studio). Many companies use more than one measurement base. A manufacturer, for example, may use direct labor hours or units of output for manufacturing costs, and sales revenue or units sold for selling expenses.

For an activity level to be useful in cost behavior analysis, changes in the level or volume of activity should be correlated with changes in costs. The activity level selected is referred to as the activity (or volume) index. The **activity index** identifies the activity that causes changes in the behavior of costs. With an appropriate activity index, companies can classify the behavior of costs in response to changes in activity levels into three categories: variable, fixed, or mixed.

Variable Costs

Variable costs are costs that vary **in total** directly and proportionately with changes in the activity level. If the level increases 10%, total variable costs will increase 10%. If the level of activity decreases by 25%, variable costs will decrease 25%. Examples of variable costs include direct materials and direct labor for a manufacturer; cost of goods sold, sales commissions, and freight-out for a merchandiser; and gasoline in airline and trucking companies. A variable cost may also be defined as a cost that **remains the same *per unit* at every level of activity**.

To illustrate the behavior of a variable cost, assume that Damon Company manufactures tablet computers that contain a $10 camera. The activity index is the number of tablet computers produced. As Damon manufactures each tablet, the total cost of cameras used increases by $10. As part (a) of Illustration 5-1

Illustration 5-1
Behavior of total and unit variable costs

Helpful Hint
True or false: Variable costs per unit change directly and proportionately with changes in activity.
Answer: False. Per unit costs remain constant at all levels of activity.

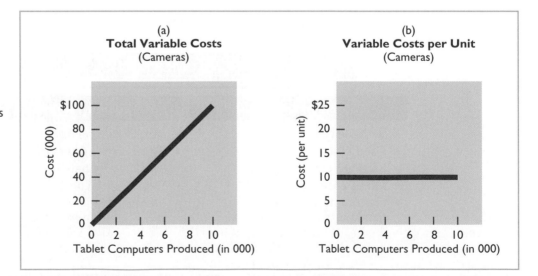

shows, total cost of the cameras will be $20,000 if Damon produces 2,000 tablets, and $100,000 when it produces 10,000 tablets. We also can see that a variable cost remains the same per unit as the level of activity changes. As part (b) of Illustration 5-1 shows, the unit cost of $10 for the cameras is the same whether Damon produces 2,000 or 10,000 tablets.

Companies that rely heavily on labor to manufacture a product, such as Nike or Reebok, or to provide a service, such as Hilton or Marriott, are likely to have many variable costs. In contrast, companies that use a high proportion of machinery and equipment in producing revenue, such as AT&T or Duke Energy Co., may have few variable costs.

Fixed Costs

Fixed costs are costs that **remain the same in total** regardless of changes in the activity level. Examples include property taxes, insurance, rent, supervisory salaries, and depreciation on buildings and equipment. Because total fixed costs remain constant as activity changes, it follows that **fixed costs *per unit* vary inversely with activity: As volume increases, unit cost declines, and vice versa**.

To illustrate the behavior of fixed costs, assume that Damon Company leases its productive facilities at a cost of $10,000 per month. Total fixed costs of the facilities will remain constant at every level of activity, as part (a) of Illustration 5-2 shows. But, **on a per unit basis, the cost of rent will decline as activity increases**, as part (b) of Illustration 5-2 shows. At 2,000 units, the unit cost per tablet computer is $5 ($10,000 ÷ 2,000). When Damon produces 10,000 tablets, the unit cost of the rent is only $1 per tablet ($10,000 ÷ 10,000).

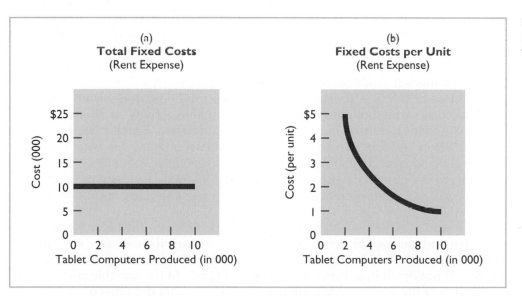

Illustration 5-2
Behavior of total and unit fixed costs

The trend for many manufacturers is to have more fixed costs and fewer variable costs. This trend is the result of increased use of automation and less use of employee labor. As a result, depreciation and lease charges (fixed costs) increase, whereas direct labor costs (variable costs) decrease.

PEOPLE, PLANET, AND PROFIT INSIGHT

Gardens in the Sky

Because of population increases, the United Nations' Food and Agriculture Organization estimates that food production will need to increase by 70% by 2050. Also, by 2050, roughly 70% of people will live in cities, which means more food needs to be hauled further to get it to the consumer. To address the lack of farmable land and reduce the cost of transporting produce, some have suggested building "vertical farming" skyscrapers in cities. This sounds great, but do the numbers work? Some variable costs would be reduced. For example, the use of pesticides, herbicides, fuel costs for shipping, and water would all drop. Soil erosion would be a non-issue since plants would be grown hydroponically (in a solution of water and minerals), and land requirements would be reduced because of vertical structures. But, other costs would be higher. First, there is the cost of the building. Also, any multistory building would require artificial lighting for plants on lower floors.

Until these cost challenges can be overcome, it appears that these skyscrapers will not break even. On the other hand, rooftop greenhouses on existing city structures already appear financially viable. For example, a 15,000 square-foot rooftop greenhouse in Brooklyn already produces roughly 30 tons of vegetables per year for local residents.

Source: "Vertical Farming: Does It Really Stack Up?" *The Economist* (December 9, 2010).

? What are some of the variable and fixed costs that are impacted by hydroponic farming? (See page 234.)

Relevant Range

LEARNING OBJECTIVE **2**

Explain the significance of the relevant range.

In Illustration 5-1 part (a) (page 198), a straight line is drawn throughout the entire range of the activity index for total variable costs. In essence, the assumption is that the costs are **linear**. If a relationship is linear (that is, straight-line), then changes in the activity index will result in a direct, proportional change in the variable cost. For example, if the activity level doubles, the cost doubles.

It is now necessary to ask: Is the straight-line relationship realistic? Does the linear assumption produce useful data for CVP analysis?

In most business situations, a straight-line relationship **does not exist** for variable costs throughout the entire range of possible activity. At abnormally low levels of activity, it may be impossible to be cost-efficient. Small-scale operations may not allow the company to obtain quantity discounts for raw materials or to use specialized labor. In contrast, at abnormally high levels of activity, labor costs may increase sharply because of overtime pay. Also, at high activity levels, materials costs may jump significantly because of excess spoilage caused by worker fatigue.

As a result, in the real world, the relationship between the behavior of a variable cost and changes in the activity level is often **curvilinear**, as shown in part (a) of Illustration 5-3. In the curved sections of the line, a change in the activity index will not result in a direct, proportional change in the variable cost. That is, a doubling of the activity index will not result in an exact doubling of the variable cost. The variable cost may more than double, or it may be less than double.

Total fixed costs also do not have a straight-line relationship over the entire range of activity. Some fixed costs will not change. But it is possible for management to change other fixed costs. For example, in some instances, salaried employees (fixed) are replaced with freelance workers (variable). Illustration 5-3, part (b), shows an example of the behavior of total fixed costs through all potential levels of activity.

Helpful Hint
Fixed costs that may be changeable include research, such as new product development, and management training programs.

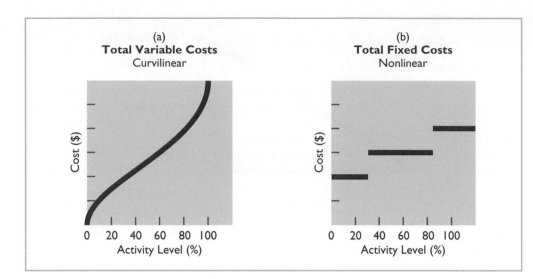

Illustration 5-3
Nonlinear behavior of variable and fixed costs

For most companies, operating at almost zero or at 100% capacity is the exception rather than the rule. Instead, companies often operate over a somewhat narrower range, such as 40–80% of capacity. The range over which a company expects to operate during a year is called the **relevant range** of the activity index. Within the relevant range, as both diagrams in Illustration 5-4 show, a straight-line relationship generally exists for both variable and fixed costs.

Alternative Terminology
The relevant range is also called the *normal* or *practical range*.

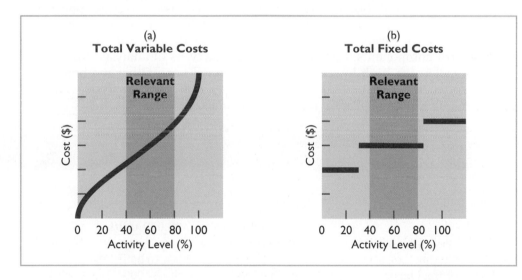

Illustration 5-4
Linear behavior within relevant range

As you can see, although the linear (straight-line) relationship may not be completely realistic, **the linear assumption produces useful data for CVP analysis as long as the level of activity remains within the relevant range**.

Mixed Costs

Mixed costs are costs that contain both a variable element and a fixed element. **Mixed costs, therefore, change in total but not proportionately with changes in the activity level.**

The rental of a U-Haul truck is a good example of a mixed cost. Assume that local rental terms for a 17-foot truck, including insurance, are $50 per day plus 50 cents per mile. When determining the cost of a one-day rental, the per day charge is a fixed cost (with respect to miles driven), whereas the mileage charge is a variable cost. The graphic presentation of the rental cost for a one-day rental is as follows.

LEARNING OBJECTIVE   3

Explain the concept of mixed costs.

Illustration 5-5
Behavior of a mixed cost

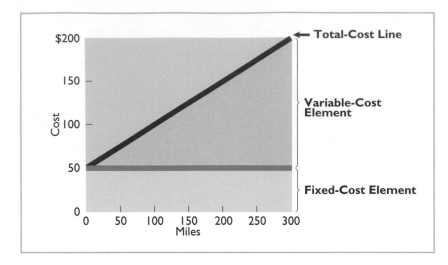

In this case, the fixed-cost element is the cost of having the service available. The variable-cost element is the cost of actually using the service. Another example of a mixed cost is utility costs (electric, telephone, and so on), where there is a flat service fee plus a usage charge.

For purposes of CVP analysis, **mixed costs must be classified into their fixed and variable elements**. How does management make the classification? One possibility is to determine the variable and fixed components each time a mixed cost is incurred. But because of time and cost constraints, this approach is rarely followed. Instead, the usual approach is to collect data on the behavior of the mixed costs at various levels of activity. Analysts then identify the fixed- and variable-cost components. Companies use various types of analysis. One type of analysis, called the **high-low method**, is discussed next. Other methods, such as the scatter diagram method and least squares regression analysis, are more appropriately explained in cost accounting courses.

> ## DO IT!

Types of Costs

Action Plan

✔ Recall that a variable cost varies in total directly and proportionately with each change in activity level.

✔ Recall that a fixed cost remains the same in total with each change in activity level.

✔ Recall that a mixed cost changes in total but not proportionately with each change in activity level.

Helena Company reports the following total costs at two levels of production.

	10,000 Units	**20,000 Units**
Direct materials	$20,000	$40,000
Maintenance	8,000	10,000
Direct labor	17,000	34,000
Indirect materials	1,000	2,000
Depreciation	4,000	4,000
Utilities	3,000	5,000
Rent	6,000	6,000

Classify each cost as variable, fixed, or mixed.

Solution

Direct materials, direct labor, and indirect materials are variable costs.
Depreciation and rent are fixed costs.
Maintenance and utilities are mixed costs.

Related exercise material: **BE5-1, BE5-2, E5-1, E5-2, E5-4, and** DO IT! **5-1.**

✔ **The Navigator**

HIGH-LOW METHOD

The **high-low method** uses the total costs incurred at the high and low levels of activity to classify mixed costs into fixed and variable components. The difference in costs between the high and low levels represents variable costs, since only the variable-cost element can change as activity levels change.

The steps in computing fixed and variable costs under this method are as follows.

1. Determine variable cost per unit from the following formula.

Change in Total Costs	÷	High minus Low Activity Level	=	Variable Cost per Unit

To illustrate, assume that Metro Transit Company has the following maintenance costs and mileage data for its fleet of buses over a 6-month period.

Month	Miles Driven	Total Cost	Month	Miles Driven	Total Cost
January	20,000	$30,000	April	50,000	$63,000
February	40,000	48,000	May	30,000	42,000
March	35,000	49,000	June	43,000	61,000

The high and low levels of activity are 50,000 miles in April and 20,000 miles in January. The maintenance costs at these two levels are $63,000 and $30,000, respectively. The difference in maintenance costs is $33,000 ($63,000 − $30,000), and the difference in miles is 30,000 (50,000 − 20,000). Therefore, for Metro Transit, variable cost per unit is $1.10, computed as follows.

$$\$33,000 \div 30,000 = \$1.10$$

2. Determine the fixed costs by subtracting the total variable costs at either the high or the low activity level from the total cost at that activity level.

For Metro Transit, the computations are shown in Illustration 5-8.

	A	B	C	D
	METRO TRANSIT.xls			
	Home Insert Page Layout Formulas Data Review View			
	P18 fx			
1			Metro Transit	
2				Activity Level
3			High	Low
4	Total cost		$63,000	$30,000
5	Less:	Variable costs		
6		50,000 × $1.10	55,000	
7		20,000 × $1.10		22,000
8	Total fixed costs		$ 8,000	$ 8,000
9				
10				

Maintenance costs are therefore $8,000 per month of fixed costs plus $1.10 per mile of variable costs. This is represented by the following formula:

$$\text{Maintenance costs} = \$8,000 + (\$1.10 \times \text{Miles driven})$$

For example, at 45,000 miles, estimated maintenance costs would be $8,000 fixed and $49,500 variable ($1.10 × 45,000) for a total of $57,500.

The graph in Illustration 5-9 plots the 6-month data for Metro Transit Company. The red line drawn in the graph connects the high and low data points, and therefore represents the equation that we just solved using the high-low method. The red, "high-low" line intersects the y-axis at $8,000 (the fixed-cost level), and it rises by $1.10 per unit (the variable cost per unit). Note that a completely different line would result if we chose any two of the other data points. That is, by choosing any two other data points, we would end up with a different estimate of fixed costs and a different variable cost per unit. Thus, from this scatter plot, we can see that while the high-low method is simple, the result is rather arbitrary. A better approach, which uses information from all the data points to estimate fixed and variable costs, is called *regression analysis*. A discussion of regression analysis is provided in a supplement on the book's companion website.

Illustration 5-9
Scatter plot for Metro Transit Company

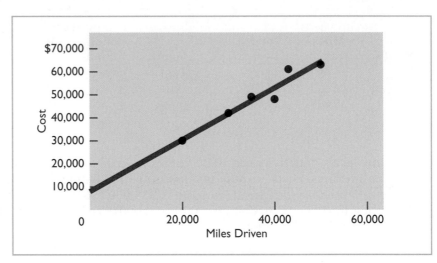

MANAGEMENT INSIGHT

Skilled Labor Is Truly Essential

The recession that started in 2008 had devastating implications for employment. But one surprise was that for some manufacturers, the number of jobs lost was actually lower than in previous recessions. One of the main explanations for this was that between 2000 and 2008, many factories adopted lean manufacturing practices. This meant that production relied less on large numbers of low-skilled workers, and more on machines and a few highly skilled workers. As a result of this approach, a single employee was supporting far more dollars in sales. Thus, it would require a larger decline in sales before an employee would need to be laid-off in order to continue to break even. Also, because the employees are highly skilled, employers are reluctant to lose them. Instead of lay-offs, many manufacturers have resorted to cutting employees hours.

Source: Timothy Aeppel and Justin Lahart, "Lean Factories Find It Hard to Cut Jobs Even in a Slump," *Wall Street Journal Online* (March 9, 2009).

 Would you characterize labor costs as being a fixed cost, a variable cost, or something else in this situation? (See page 234.)

Importance of Identifying Variable and Fixed Costs

Why is it important to segregate costs into variable and fixed elements? The answer may become apparent if we look at the following four business decisions.

1. If American Airlines is to make a profit when it reduces all domestic fares by 30%, what reduction in costs or increase in passengers will be required?
Answer: To make a profit when it cuts domestic fares by 30%, American Airlines will have to increase the number of passengers or cut its variable costs for those flights. Its fixed costs will not change.

2. If Ford Motor Company meets workers' demands for higher wages, what increase in sales revenue will be needed to maintain current profit levels?
Answer: Higher wages at Ford Motor Company will increase the variable costs of manufacturing automobiles. To maintain present profit levels, Ford will have to cut other variable costs or increase the price of its automobiles.

3. If United States Steel Corp.'s program to modernize plant facilities through significant equipment purchases reduces the work force by 50%, what will be the effect on the cost of producing one ton of steel?
Answer: The modernizing of plant facilities at United States Steel Corp. changes the proportion of fixed and variable costs of producing one ton of steel. Fixed costs increase because of higher depreciation charges, whereas variable costs decrease due to the reduction in the number of steelworkers.

4. What happens if Kellogg's increases its advertising expenses but cannot increase prices because of competitive pressure?
Answer: Sales volume must be increased to cover the increase in fixed advertising costs.

> **DO IT!**

High-Low Method

Byrnes Company accumulates the following data concerning a mixed cost, using units produced as the activity level.

	Units Produced	Total Cost
March	9,800	$14,740
April	8,500	13,250
May	7,000	11,100
June	7,600	12,000
July	8,100	12,460

Action Plan

✔ Determine the highest and lowest levels of activity.

✔ Compute variable cost per unit as: Change in total costs ÷ (High − low activity level) = Variable cost per unit.

✔ Compute fixed cost as: Total cost − (Variable cost per unit × Units produced) = Fixed cost.

(a) Compute the variable- and fixed-cost elements using the high-low method.
(b) Estimate the total cost if the company produces 6,000 units.

Solution

(a) Variable cost: ($14,740 − $11,100) ÷ (9,800 − 7,000) = $1.30 per unit
   Fixed cost: $14,740 − $12,740 ($1.30 × 9,800 units) = $2,000
          or $11,100 − $9,100 ($1.30 × 7,000) = $2,000
(b) Total cost to produce 6,000 units: $2,000 + $7,800 ($1.30 × 6,000) = $9,800

Related exercise material: **BE5-3, BE5-4, BE5-5, E5-3, E5-5, E5-6, and DO IT! 5-2.**

✔ **The Navigator**

Cost-Volume-Profit Analysis

Cost-volume-profit (CVP) analysis is the study of the effects of changes in costs and volume on a company's profits. CVP analysis is important in profit planning. It also is a critical factor in such management decisions as setting selling prices, determining product mix, and maximizing use of production facilities.

LEARNING OBJECTIVE 4

List the five components of cost-volume-profit analysis.

Basic Components

CVP analysis considers the interrelationships among the components shown in Illustration 5-10.

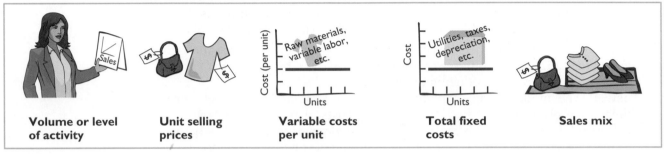

| Volume or level of activity | Unit selling prices | Variable costs per unit | Total fixed costs | Sales mix |

Illustration 5-10
Components of CVP analysis

The following assumptions underlie each CVP analysis.

1. The behavior of both costs and revenues is linear throughout the relevant range of the activity index.
2. Costs can be classified accurately as either variable or fixed.
3. Changes in activity are the only factors that affect costs.
4. All units produced are sold.
5. When more than one type of product is sold, the sales mix will remain constant. That is, the percentage that each product represents of total sales will stay the same. Sales mix complicates CVP analysis because different products will have different cost relationships. In this chapter, we assume a single product. (In Chapter 6, we relax this assumption.)

When these assumptions are not valid, the CVP analysis may be inaccurate.

CVP Income Statement

LEARNING OBJECTIVE 5

Indicate what contribution margin is and how it can be expressed.

Because CVP is so important for decision-making, management often wants this information reported in a **cost-volume-profit (CVP) income statement** format for internal use. The CVP income statement classifies costs as variable or fixed and computes a contribution margin. **Contribution margin (CM)** is the amount of revenue remaining after deducting variable costs. It is often stated both as a total amount and on a per unit basis.

We will use Vargo Video Company to illustrate a CVP income statement. Vargo Video produces a high-definition digital camcorder with 15× optical zoom and a wide-screen, high-resolution LCD monitor. Relevant data for the camcorders sold by this company in June 2014 are as follows.

Illustration 5-11
Assumed selling and cost data for Vargo Video

Unit selling price of camcorder	$500
Unit variable costs	$300
Total monthly fixed costs	$200,000
Units sold	1,600

The CVP income statement for Vargo Video therefore would be reported as follows.

Vargo Video Company
CVP Income Statement
For the Month Ended June 30, 2014

	Total
Sales (1,600 camcorders)	$ 800,000
Variable costs	480,000
Contribution margin	320,000
Fixed costs	200,000
Net income	**$120,000**

Illustration 5-12
CVP income statement, with
net income

A traditional income statement and a CVP income statement both report the same net income of $120,000. However a traditional income statement does not classify costs as variable or fixed, and therefore it does not report a contribution margin. In addition, sometimes per unit amounts and percentage of sales amounts are shown on a CVP income statement to facilitate CVP analysis. *Homework assignments specify which columns to present.*

In the applications of CVP analysis that follow, we assume that the term "cost" includes all costs and expenses related to production and sale of the product. That is, cost includes manufacturing costs plus selling and administrative expenses.

CONTRIBUTION MARGIN PER UNIT

Illustration 5-14 shows Vargo Video's CVP income statement at the point where net income equals zero. It shows a contribution margin of $200,000, and a contribution margin per unit of $200 ($500 − $300). The formula for **contribution margin per unit** and the computation for Vargo Video are:

Unit Selling Price	−	Unit Variable Costs	=	Contribution Margin per Unit
$500	−	$300	=	**$200**

Illustration 5-13
Formula for contribution
margin per unit

Contribution margin per unit indicates that for every camcorder sold, the selling price exceeds the variable costs by $200. Vargo generates $200 per unit sold to cover fixed costs and contribute to net income. Because Vargo Video has fixed costs of $200,000, it must sell 1,000 camcorders ($200,000 ÷ $200) to cover its fixed costs. At the point where total contribution margin exactly equals fixed costs, Vargo will report net income of zero. At this point, referred to as the **break-even point**, total costs (variable plus fixed) exactly equal total revenue.

Vargo Video Company
CVP Income Statement
For the Month Ended June 30, 2014

	Total	Per Unit
Sales (1,000 camcorders)	$ 500,000	$ 500
Variable costs	300,000	300
Contribution margin	200,000	**$200**
Fixed costs	200,000	
Net income	$ –0–	

Illustration 5-14
CVP income statement, with
zero net income

It follows that for every camcorder sold above the break-even point of 1,000 units, **net income increases by the amount of the contribution margin per unit, $200**. For example, assume that Vargo sold one more camcorder, for a total of 1,001 camcorders sold. In this case, Vargo reports net income of $200, as shown in Illustration 5-15.

Illustration 5-15
CVP income statement, with net income and per unit data

Vargo Video Company
CVP Income Statement
For the Month Ended June 30, 2014

	Total	Per Unit
Sales (1,001 camcorders)	$500,500	$500
Variable costs	300,300	300
Contribution margin	**200,200**	**$200**
Fixed costs	200,000	
Net income	**$ 200**	

CONTRIBUTION MARGIN RATIO

Some managers prefer to use a contribution margin ratio in CVP analysis. The contribution margin ratio is the contribution margin expressed as a percentage of sales, as shown in Illustration 5-16.

Illustration 5-16
CVP income statement, with net income and percent of sales data

Vargo Video Company
CVP Income Statement
For the Month Ended June 30, 2014

	Total	Percent of Sales
Sales (1,001 camcorders)	$500,500	100%
Variable costs	300,300	60
Contribution margin	**200,200**	**40%**
Fixed costs	200,000	
Net income	**$ 200**	

Alternatively, the **contribution margin ratio** is the contribution margin per unit divided by the unit selling price. For Vargo Video, the ratio is as follows.

Illustration 5-17
Formula for contribution margin ratio

Contribution Margin per Unit	÷	Unit Selling Price	=	Contribution Margin Ratio
$200	÷	$500	=	40%

The contribution margin ratio of 40% means that Vargo generates 40 cents of contribution margin with each dollar of sales. That is, $0.40 of each sales dollar (40% × $1) is available to apply to fixed costs and to contribute to net income.

This expression of contribution margin is very helpful in determining the effect of changes in sales on net income. For example, if Vargo's sales increase $100,000, net income will increase $40,000 (40% × $100,000). Thus, by using the contribution margin ratio, managers can quickly determine increases in net income from any change in sales.

We can also see this effect through a CVP income statement. Assume that Vargo Video's current sales are $500,000 and it wants to know the effect of a $100,000 (200-unit) increase in sales. Vargo prepares a comparative CVP income statement analysis as follows.

Illustration 5-18
Comparative CVP income statements

Vargo Video Company
CVP Income Statements
For the Month Ended June 30, 2014

	No Change			With Change		
	Total	Per Unit	Percent of Sales	Total	Per Unit	Percent of Sales
Sales	$500,000	$500	100%	$600,000	$500	100%
Variable costs	300,000	300	60	360,000	300	60
Contribution margin	**200,000**	**$200**	**40%**	**240,000**	**$200**	**40%**
Fixed costs	200,000			200,000		
Net income	**$ –0–**			**$ 40,000**		

The $40,000 increase in net income can be calculated on either a contribution margin per unit basis (200 units × $200 per unit) or using the contribution margin ratio times the increase in sales dollars (40% × $100,000). Note that the contribution margin per unit and contribution margin as a percentage of sales remain unchanged by the increase in sales.

Study these CVP income statements carefully. The concepts presented in these statements are used extensively in this and later chapters.

DECISION TOOLKIT

DECISION CHECKPOINTS	INFO NEEDED FOR DECISION	TOOL TO USE FOR DECISION	HOW TO EVALUATE RESULTS
What was the contribution toward fixed costs and income from each unit sold?	Selling price per unit and variable cost per unit	Contribution margin per unit = Unit selling price − Unit variable cost	Every unit sold will increase income by the contribution margin.
What was the increase in income as a result of an increase in sales?	Contribution margin per unit and unit selling price	Contribution margin ratio = Contribution margin per unit ÷ Unit selling price	Every dollar of sales will increase income by the contribution margin ratio.

Break-Even Analysis

A key relationship in CVP analysis is the level of activity at which total revenues equal total costs (both fixed and variable)—the **break-even point**. At this volume of sales, the company will realize no income but will suffer no loss. The process of finding the break-even point is called **break-even analysis**. Knowledge of the break-even point is useful to management when it decides whether to introduce new product lines, change sales prices on established products, or enter new market areas.

The break-even point can be:

1. Computed from a mathematical equation.

2. Computed by using contribution margin.

3. Derived from a cost-volume-profit (CVP) graph.

The break-even point can be expressed either in **sales units** or **sales dollars**.

LEARNING OBJECTIVE 6

Identify the three ways to determine the break-even point.

MATHEMATICAL EQUATION

The first line of Illustration 5-19 shows a common equation used for CVP analysis. When net income is set to zero, this equation can be used to calculate the break-even point.

Illustration 5-19
Basic CVP equation

Required Sales	−	Variable Costs	−	Fixed Costs	=	Net Income
$500Q	−	$300Q	−	$200,000	=	$0

As shown in Illustration 5-14 (page 207), net income equals zero when the contribution margin (sales minus variable costs) is equal to fixed costs.

To reflect this, Illustration 5-20 rewrites the equation with contribution margin (sales minus variable costs) on the left side, and fixed costs and net income on the right. We can compute the break-even point **in units** by **using unit selling prices** and **unit variable costs**. The computation for Vargo Video is:

Illustration 5-20
Computation of break-even point in units

Required Sales	−	Variable Costs	−	Fixed Costs	=	Net Income
$500Q	−	$300Q	−	$200,000	=	$0
$500Q	−	$300Q	=	$200,000	+	$0

$$\$200Q = \$200,000$$

$$Q = \frac{\$200,000}{\$200} = \frac{\text{Fixed Costs}}{\text{Contribution Margin per Unit}}$$

$$Q = 1,000 \text{ units}$$

where

$$Q = \text{sales volume in units}$$
$$\$500 = \text{selling price}$$
$$\$300 = \text{variable costs per unit}$$
$$\$200,000 = \text{total fixed costs}$$

Thus, Vargo Video must sell 1,000 units to break even.

To find the amount of **sales dollars** required to break even, we multiply the units sold at the break-even point times the selling price per unit, as shown below.

$$1,000 \times \$500 = \$500,000 \text{ (break-even sales dollars)}$$

CONTRIBUTION MARGIN TECHNIQUE

Many managers employ the contribution margin to compute the break-even point.

CONTRIBUTION MARGIN IN UNITS The final step in Illustration 5-20 divides fixed costs by the contribution margin per unit (highlighted in red). Thus, rather than walk through all of the steps of the equation approach, we can simply employ this formula shown in Illustration 5-21.

Illustration 5-21
Formula for break-even point in units using contribution margin per unit

Fixed Costs	÷	Contribution Margin per Unit	=	Break-Even Point in Units
$200,000	÷	$200	=	1,000 units

Why does this formula work? The contribution margin per unit is the net amount by which each sale exceeds the variable costs per unit. Every sale generates this much money to pay off fixed costs. Consequently, if we divide fixed costs by the contribution margin per unit, we know how many units we need to sell to break even.

CONTRIBUTION MARGIN RATIO As we will see in the next chapter, when a company has numerous products, it is not practical to determine the contribution margin per unit for each product. In this case, using the contribution margin ratio is very useful for determining the break-even point in total dollars (rather than units). Recall that the contribution margin ratio is the amount of contribution margin that is generated from each dollar of sales. Therefore, to determine the sales dollars needed to cover fixed costs, we divide fixed costs by the contribution margin ratio, as shown in Illustration 5-22.

Fixed Costs	÷	Contribution Margin Ratio	=	Break-Even Point in Dollars
$200,000	÷	40%	=	$500,000

Illustration 5-22
Formula for break-even point in dollars using contribution margin ratio

To apply this formula to Vargo, consider that its 40% contribution margin ratio means that for every dollar sold, it generates 40 cents of contribution margin. The question is, how many dollars of sales does Vargo need in order to generate total contribution margin of $200,000 to pay off fixed costs? We divide the fixed costs of $200,000 by the 40 cents of contribution margin generated by each dollar of sales to arrive at $500,000 ($200,000 ÷ 40%). To prove this result, if we generate 40 cents of contribution margin for each dollar of sales, then the total contribution margin generated by $500,000 in sales is $200,000 ($500,000 × 40%).

SERVICE COMPANY INSIGHT

Charter Flights Offer a Good Deal

The Internet is wringing inefficiencies out of nearly every industry. While commercial aircraft spend roughly 4,000 hours a year in the air, chartered aircraft are flown only 500 hours annually. That means that they are sitting on the ground—not making any money—about 90% of the time. One company, FlightServe, saw a business opportunity in that fact. For about the same cost as a first-class ticket, FlightServe decided to match up executives with charter flights in small "private jets." The executive would get a more comfortable ride and could avoid the hassle of big airports. FlightServe noted that the average charter jet has eight seats. When all eight seats were full, the company would have an 80% profit margin. It would break even at an average of 3.3 full seats per flight.

Source: "Jet Set Go," *The Economist* (March 18, 2000), p. 68.

? How did FlightServe determine that it would break even with 3.3 seats full per flight? (See page 234.)

GRAPHIC PRESENTATION

An effective way to find the break-even point is to prepare a break-even graph. Because this graph also shows costs, volume, and profits, it is referred to as a **cost-volume-profit (CVP) graph**.

As the CVP graph in Illustration 5-23 (page 212) shows, sales volume is recorded along the horizontal axis. This axis should extend to the maximum level of expected sales. Both total revenues (sales) and total costs (fixed plus variable) are recorded on the vertical axis.

Illustration 5-23
CVP graph

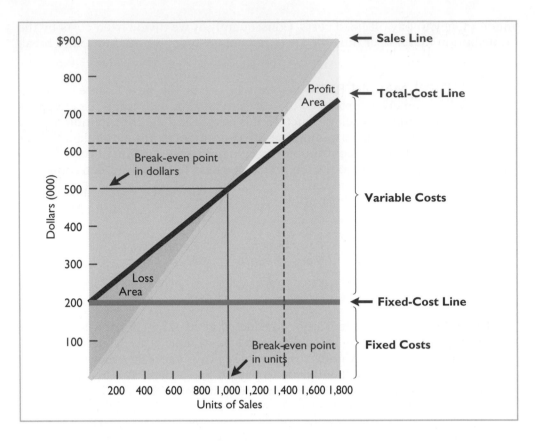

The construction of the graph, using the data for Vargo Video, is as follows.

1. Plot the sales line, starting at the zero activity level. For every camcorder sold, total revenue increases by $500. For example, at 200 units, sales are $100,000. At the upper level of activity (1,800 units), sales are $900,000. The revenue line is assumed to be linear through the full range of activity.

2. Plot the total fixed costs using a horizontal line. For the camcorders, this line is plotted at $200,000. The fixed costs are the same at every level of activity.

3. Plot the total-cost line. This starts at the fixed-cost line at zero activity. It increases by the variable costs at each level of activity. For each camcorder, variable costs are $300. Thus, at 200 units, total variable costs are $60,000, and the total cost is $260,000. At 1,800 units, total variable costs are $540,000, and total cost is $740,000. On the graph, the amount of the variable costs can be derived from the difference between the total-cost and fixed-cost lines at each level of activity.

4. Determine the break-even point from the intersection of the total-cost line and the sales line. The break-even point in dollars is found by drawing a horizontal line from the break-even point to the vertical axis. The break-even point in units is found by drawing a vertical line from the break-even point to the horizontal axis. For the camcorders, the break-even point is $500,000 of sales, or 1,000 units. At this sales level, Vargo Video will cover costs but make no profit.

The CVP graph also shows both the net income and net loss areas. Thus, the amount of income or loss at each level of sales can be derived from the sales and total-cost lines.

A CVP graph is useful because the effects of a change in any element in the CVP analysis can be quickly seen. For example, a 10% increase in selling price will change the location of the sales line. Likewise, the effects on total costs of wage increases can be quickly observed.

DECISION TOOLKIT

DECISION CHECKPOINTS	INFO NEEDED FOR DECISION	TOOL TO USE FOR DECISION	HOW TO EVALUATE RESULTS
At what amount of sales does a company cover its costs?	Unit selling price, unit variable cost, and total fixed costs	Break-even point analysis *In units:* $$\text{Break-even point} = \frac{\text{Fixed costs}}{\text{Unit contribution margin}}$$ *In dollars:* $$\text{Break-even point} = \frac{\text{Fixed costs}}{\text{Contribution margin ratio}}$$	Below the break-even point, the company is unprofitable.

> DO IT!

Break-Even Analysis

Lombardi Company has a unit selling price of $400, variable costs per unit of $240, and fixed costs of $180,000. Compute the break-even point in units using (a) a mathematical equation and (b) contribution margin per unit.

Action Plan

✔ Apply the formula: Sales = Variable costs + Fixed costs + Net income.

✔ Apply the formula: Fixed costs ÷ Contribution margin per unit = Break-even point in units.

Solution

(a) The equation is $400Q − $240Q − $180,000 = $0; ($400Q − $240Q) = $180,000. The break-even point in units is 1,125. (b) The contribution margin per unit is $160 ($400 − $240). The formula therefore is $180,000 ÷ $160, and the break-even point in units is 1,125.

Related exercise material: **BE5-6, BE5-7, BE5-8, BE5-9, E5-8, E5-9, E5-10, E5-11, E5-12, E5-13, and DO IT! 5-3.**

✔ **The Navigator**

Target Net Income

Rather than simply "breaking even," management usually sets an income objective often called **target net income**. It indicates the sales necessary to achieve a specified level of income. Companies determine the sales necessary to achieve target net income by using one of the three approaches discussed earlier.

LEARNING OBJECTIVE 7

Give the formulas for determining sales required to earn target net income.

MATHEMATICAL EQUATION

We know that at the break-even point no profit or loss results for the company. By adding an amount for target net income to the same basic equation, we obtain the following formula for determining required sales.

Required Sales	−	Variable Costs	−	Fixed Costs	=	Target Net Income

Illustration 5-24
Formula for required sales to meet target net income

Recall that once the break-even point has been reached so that fixed costs are covered, each additional unit sold increases net income by the amount of the contribution margin per unit. We can rewrite the equation with contribution margin (sales minus variable costs) on the left-hand side, and fixed costs and net income on the right. Assuming that target net income is $120,000 for Vargo Video, the computation of required sales in units is as follows.

Illustration 5-25
Computation of required sales

	Required Sales	−	Variable Costs	−	Fixed Costs	=	Target Net Income
	$500Q	−	$300Q	−	$200,000	=	$120,000
	$500Q	−	$300Q			=	$200,000 + $120,000

$$\$200Q = \$200,000 + \$120,000$$

$$Q = \frac{\$200,000 + \$120,000}{\$200} = \frac{\text{Fixed Costs} + \text{Net Target Income}}{\text{Contribution Margin per Unit}}$$

$$Q = 1,600$$

where
$$\begin{align}
Q &= \text{sales volume} \\
\$500 &= \text{selling price} \\
\$300 &= \text{variable costs per unit} \\
\$200,000 &= \text{total fixed costs} \\
\$120,000 &= \text{target net income}
\end{align}$$

Vargo must sell 1,600 units to achieve target net income of $120,000. The sales dollars required to achieve the target net income is found by multiplying the units sold by the unit selling price [(1,600 × $500) = $800,000].

CONTRIBUTION MARGIN TECHNIQUE

As in the case of break-even sales, we can compute in either units or dollars the sales required to meet target net income. The formula to compute required sales in units for Vargo Video using the contribution margin per unit can be seen in the final step of the equation approach in Illustration 5-25 (shown in red). We simply divide the sum of fixed costs and target net income by the contribution margin per unit. Illustration 5-26 shows this for Vargo.

Illustration 5-26
Formula for required sales in units using contribution margin per unit

(Fixed Costs + Target Net Income)	÷	Contribution Margin per Unit	=	Required Sales in Units
($200,000 + $120,000)	÷	$200	=	1,600 units

To achieve its desired target net income of $120,000, Vargo must sell 1,600 camcorders.

The formula to compute the required sales in dollars for Vargo Video using the contribution margin ratio is shown below.

Illustration 5-27
Formula for required sales in dollars using contribution margin ratio

(Fixed Costs + Target Net Income)	÷	Contribution Margin Ratio	=	Required Sales in Dollars
($200,000 + $120,000)	÷	40%	=	$800,000

To achieve its desired target net income of $120,000, Vargo must generate sales of $800,000.

GRAPHIC PRESENTATION

We also can use the CVP graph in Illustration 5-23 (on page 212) to find the sales required to meet target net income. In the profit area of the graph, the distance between the sales line and the total-cost line at any point equals net income. We can find required sales by analyzing the differences between the two lines until the desired net income is found.

For example, suppose Vargo Video sells 1,400 camcorders. Illustration 5-23 shows that a vertical line drawn at 1,400 units intersects the sales line at $700,000 and the total cost line at $620,000. The difference between the two amounts represents the net income (profit) of $80,000.

Margin of Safety

Margin of safety is the difference between actual or expected sales and sales at the break-even point. It measures the "cushion" that a particular level of sales provides. It tells us how far sales could fall before the company begins operating at a loss. The margin of safety is expressed in dollars or as a ratio.

The formula for stating the **margin of safety in dollars** is actual (or expected) sales minus break-even sales. Assuming that actual (expected) sales for Vargo Video are $750,000, the computation is:

LEARNING OBJECTIVE 6
Define margin of safety, and give the formulas for computing it.

Actual (Expected) Sales	−	Break-Even Sales	=	Margin of Safety in Dollars
$750,000	−	$500,000	=	$250,000

Illustration 5-28
Formula for margin of safety in dollars

Vargo's margin of safety is $250,000. Its sales could fall $250,000 before it operates at a loss.

The **margin of safety ratio** is the margin of safety in dollars divided by actual (or expected) sales. The formula and computation for determining the margin of safety ratio are:

Margin of Safety in Dollars	÷	Actual (Expected) Sales	=	Margin of Safety Ratio
$250,000	÷	$750,000	=	33%

Illustration 5-29
Formula for margin of safety ratio

This means that the company's sales could fall by 33% before it would be operating at a loss.

The higher the dollars or the percentage, the greater the margin of safety. Management continuously evaluates the adequacy of the margin of safety in terms of such factors as the vulnerability of the product to competitive pressures and to downturns in the economy.

SERVICE COMPANY INSIGHT

How a Rolling Stones' Tour Makes Money

Computation of break-even and margin of safety is important for service companies. Consider how the promoter for the Rolling Stones' tour used the break-even point and margin of safety. For example, one outdoor show should bring 70,000 individuals for a gross of $2.45 million. The promoter guarantees $1.2 million to the Rolling Stones. In addition, 20% of gross goes to the stadium in which the performance is staged. Add another $400,000 for other expenses such as ticket takers, parking attendants, advertising, and so on. The promoter also shares in sales of T-shirts and memorabilia for which the promoter will net over $7 million during the tour. From a successful Rolling Stones' tour, the promoter could make $35 million!

? What amount of sales dollars are required for the promoter to break even? (See page 234.)

> **DO IT!**

Break-Even, Margin of Safety, Target Net Income

Zootsuit Inc. makes travel bags that sell for $56 each. For the coming year, management expects fixed costs to total $320,000 and variable costs to be $42 per unit. Compute the following: (a) break-even point in dollars using the contribution margin (CM) ratio; (b) the margin of safety and margin of safety ratio assuming actual sales are $1,382,400; and (c) the sales dollars required to earn net income of $410,000.

Action Plan

✔ Apply the formula for the break-even point in dollars.

✔ Apply the formulas for the margin of safety in dollars and the margin of safety ratio.

✔ Apply the formula for the required sales in dollars.

Solution

(a) Contribution margin ratio = [($56 − $42) ÷ $56] = 25%
    Break-even sales in dollars = $320,000 ÷ 25% = $1,280,000

(b) Margin of safety = $1,382,400 − $1,280,000 = $102,400
    Margin of safety ratio = $102,400 ÷ $1,382,400 = 7.4%

(c) Required sales in dollars = ($320,000 + $410,000) ÷ 25% = $2,920,000

Related exercise material: **BE5-10, BE5-11, BE5-12, E5-14, E5-15, E5-16, and DO IT! 5-4.**

✔ **The Navigator**

USING THE **DECISION TOOLKIT**

B.T. Hernandez Company, maker of high-quality flashlights, has experienced steady growth over the last 6 years. However, increased competition has led Mr. Hernandez, the president, to believe that an aggressive campaign is needed next year to maintain the company's present growth. The company's accountant has presented Mr. Hernandez with the following data for the current year, 2013, for use in preparing next year's advertising campaign.

Cost Schedules

Variable costs	
Direct labor per flashlight	$ 8.00
Direct materials	4.00
Variable overhead	3.00
Variable cost per flashlight	$15.00
Fixed costs	
Manufacturing	$ 25,000
Selling	40,000
Administrative	70,000
Total fixed costs	$135,000
Selling price per flashlight	$25.00
Sales, 2013 (20,000 flashlights)	$500,000

Mr. Hernandez has set the sales target for the year 2014 at a level of $550,000 (22,000 flashlights).

Instructions

(Ignore any income tax considerations.)

(a) What is the operating income for 2013?

(b) What is the contribution margin per unit for 2013?

(c) What is the break-even point in units for 2013?

(d) Mr. Hernandez believes that to attain the sales target in the year 2014, the company must incur an additional selling expense of $10,000 for advertising in 2014, with all other costs remaining constant. What will be the break-even point in sales dollars for 2014 if the company spends the additional $10,000?

(e) If the company spends the additional $10,000 for advertising in 2014, what is the sales level in dollars required to equal 2013 operating income?

Solution

(a) Sales $500,000
    Less:
        Variable costs (20,000 flashlights × $15)   300,000
        Fixed costs   135,000
    Operating income $ 65,000

(b) Selling price per flashlight $25
    Variable cost per flashlight   15
    Contribution margin per unit $10

(c) Fixed costs ÷ Contribution margin per unit = Break-even point in units $135,000 ÷ $10 = 13,500 units

(d) Fixed costs ÷ Contribution margin ratio = Break-even point in dollars $145,000* ÷ 40%** = $362,500

    *Fixed costs (from 2013) $135,000
     Additional advertising expense   10,000
    Fixed costs (2014) $145,000

    **Contribution margin ratio = Contribution margin per unit ÷ Unit selling price 40% = $10 ÷ $25

(e) Required sales = (Fixed costs + Target net income) ÷ Contribution margin ratio
        $525,000 = ($145,000 + $65,000) ÷ 40%

✔ **The Navigator**

SUMMARY OF LEARNING OBJECTIVES

✔ **The Navigator**

1 **Distinguish between variable and fixed costs.** Variable costs are costs that vary in total directly and proportionately with changes in the activity index. Fixed costs are costs that remain the same in total regardless of changes in the activity index.

2 **Explain the significance of the relevant range.** The relevant range is the range of activity in which a company expects to operate during a year. It is important in CVP analysis because the behavior of costs is assumed to be linear throughout the relevant range.

3 **Explain the concept of mixed costs.** Mixed costs increase in total but not proportionately with changes in the activity level. For purposes of CVP analysis, mixed costs must be classified into their fixed and variable elements. One method that management may use to classify these costs is the high-low method.

4 **List the five components of cost-volume-profit analysis.** The five components of CVP analysis are (a) volume or level of activity, (b) unit selling prices, (c) variable costs per unit, (d) total fixed costs, and (e) sales mix.

5 **Indicate what contribution margin is and how it can be expressed.** Contribution margin is the amount of revenue remaining after deducting variable costs. It is identified in a CVP income statement, which classifies costs as variable or fixed. It can be expressed as a total amount, as a per unit amount, or as a ratio.

6 **Identify the three ways to determine the break-even point.** The break-even point can be (a) computed from a mathematical equation, (b) computed by using a contribution margin technique, and (c) derived from a CVP graph.

7 **Give the formulas for determining sales required to earn target net income.** The general formula for required sales is: Required sales − Variable costs − Fixed costs = Target net income. Two other formulas are Required sales in units = (Fixed costs + Target net income) ÷ Contribution margin per unit, and Required sales in dollars = (Fixed costs + Target net income) ÷ Contribution margin ratio.

8 **Define margin of safety, and give the formulas for computing it.** Margin of safety is the difference between actual or expected sales and sales at the break-even point. The formulas for margin of safety are Actual (expected) sales − Break-even sales = Margin of safety in dollars; Margin of safety in dollars ÷ Actual (expected) sales = Margin of safety ratio.

DECISION TOOLKIT A SUMMARY

DECISION CHECKPOINTS	INFO NEEDED FOR DECISION	TOOL TO USE FOR DECISION	HOW TO EVALUATE RESULTS
What was the contribution toward fixed costs and income from each unit sold?	Selling price per unit and variable cost per unit	$$\begin{array}{c}\text{Contribution}\\\text{margin}\\\text{per unit}\end{array} = \begin{array}{c}\text{Unit}\\\text{selling}\\\text{price}\end{array} - \begin{array}{c}\text{Unit}\\\text{variable}\\\text{cost}\end{array}$$	Every unit sold will increase income by the contribution margin.
What was the increase in income as a result of an increase in sales?	Contribution margin per unit and unit selling price	$$\begin{array}{c}\text{Contribution}\\\text{margin}\\\text{ratio}\end{array} = \begin{array}{c}\text{Contribution}\\\text{margin}\\\text{per unit}\end{array} \div \begin{array}{c}\text{Unit}\\\text{selling}\\\text{price}\end{array}$$	Every dollar of sales will increase income by the contribution margin ratio
At what amount of sales does a company cover its costs?	Unit selling price, unit variable cost, and total fixed costs	Break-even point analysis *In units:* $$\frac{\text{Break-even}}{\text{point}} = \frac{\text{Fixed costs}}{\text{Unit contribution margin}}$$ *In dollars:* $$\frac{\text{Break-even}}{\text{point}} = \frac{\text{Fixed costs}}{\text{Contribution margin ratio}}$$	Below the break-even point, the company is unprofitable.

GLOSSARY

Activity index The activity that causes changes in the behavior of costs. (p. 198).

Break-even point The level of activity at which total revenues equal total costs. (p. 207).

Contribution margin (CM) The amount of revenue remaining after deducting variable costs. (p. 206).

Contribution margin per unit The amount of revenue remaining per unit after deducting variable costs; calculated as unit selling price minus unit variable cost. (p. 207).

Contribution margin ratio The percentage of each dollar of sales that is available to apply to fixed costs and contribute to net income; calculated as contribution margin per unit divided by unit selling price. (p. 208).

Cost behavior analysis The study of how specific costs respond to changes in the level of business activity. (p. 198).

Cost-volume-profit (CVP) analysis The study of the effects of changes in costs and volume on a company's profits. (p. 206).

Cost-volume-profit (CVP) graph A graph showing the relationship between costs, volume, and profits. (p. 211).

Cost-volume-profit (CVP) income statement A statement for internal use that classifies costs as fixed or variable and reports contribution margin in the body of the statement. (p. 206).

Fixed costs Costs that remain the same in total regardless of changes in the activity level. (p. 199).

High-low method A mathematical method that uses the total costs incurred at the high and low levels of activity to classify mixed costs into fixed and variable components. (p. 203).

Margin of safety The difference between actual or expected sales and sales at the break-even point. (p. 215).

Mixed costs Costs that contain both a variable- and a fixed-cost element and change in total but not proportionately with changes in the activity level. (p. 201).

Relevant range The range of the activity index over which the company expects to operate during the year. (p. 201).

Target net income The income objective set by management. (p. 213).

Variable costs Costs that vary in total directly and proportionately with changes in the activity level. (p. 198).

> Comprehensive DO IT!

Mabo Company makes calculators that sell for $20 each. For the coming year, management expects fixed costs to total $220,000 and variable costs to be $9 per unit.

Instructions
(a) Compute break-even point in units using the mathematical equation.
(b) Compute break-even point in dollars using the contribution margin (CM) ratio.

(c) Compute the margin of safety percentage assuming actual sales are $500,000.

(d) Compute the sales required in dollars to earn net income of $165,000.

Solution to Comprehensive DO IT!

Action Plan

✔ Know the formulas.

✔ Recognize that variable costs change with sales volume; fixed costs do not.

✔ Avoid computational errors.

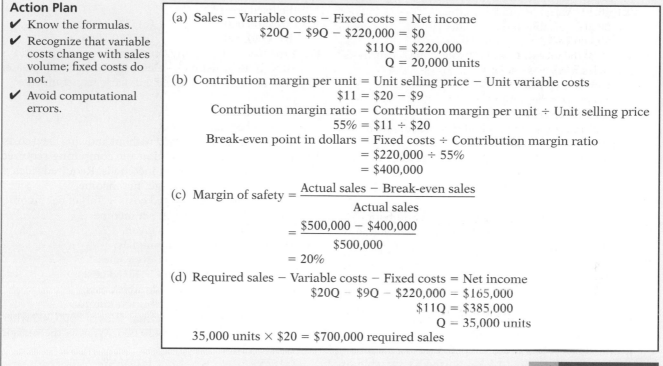

(a) Sales − Variable costs − Fixed costs = Net income
$$\$20Q - \$9Q - \$220,000 = \$0$$
$$\$11Q = \$220,000$$
$$Q = 20,000 \text{ units}$$

(b) Contribution margin per unit = Unit selling price − Unit variable costs
$$\$11 = \$20 - \$9$$
Contribution margin ratio = Contribution margin per unit ÷ Unit selling price
$$55\% = \$11 \div \$20$$
Break-even point in dollars = Fixed costs ÷ Contribution margin ratio
$$= \$220,000 \div 55\%$$
$$= \$400,000$$

(c) Margin of safety $= \dfrac{\text{Actual sales} - \text{Break-even sales}}{\text{Actual sales}}$
$$= \dfrac{\$500,000 - \$400,000}{\$500,000}$$
$$= 20\%$$

(d) Required sales − Variable costs − Fixed costs = Net income
$$\$20Q - \$9Q - \$220,000 = \$165,000$$
$$\$11Q = \$385,000$$
$$Q = 35,000 \text{ units}$$
$$35,000 \text{ units} \times \$20 = \$700,000 \text{ required sales}$$

✔ **The Navigator**

Self-Test, Brief Exercises, Exercises, Problem Set A, and many more resources are available for practice in WileyPLUS.

SELF-TEST QUESTIONS

Answers are at the end of the chapter.

(LO 1) **1.** Variable costs are costs that:
(a) vary in total directly and proportionately with changes in the activity level.
(b) remain the same per unit at every activity level.
(c) Neither of the above.
(d) Both (a) and (b) above.

(LO 2) **2.** The relevant range is:
(a) the range of activity in which variable costs will be curvilinear.
(b) the range of activity in which fixed costs will be curvilinear.
(c) the range over which the company expects to operate during a year.
(d) usually from zero to 100% of operating capacity.

3. Mixed costs consist of a: (LO 3)
(a) variable-cost element and a fixed-cost element.
(b) fixed-cost element and a controllable-cost element.
(c) relevant-cost element and a controllable-cost element.
(d) variable-cost element and a relevant-cost element.

4. Your phone service provider offers a plan that is clas- (LO 3)
sified as a mixed cost. The cost per month for 1,000 minutes is $50. If you use 2,000 minutes this month, your cost will be:
(a) $50.   (c) more than $100.
(b) $100.   (d) between $50 and $100.

5. Kendra Corporation's total utility costs during the (LO 3)
past year were $1,200 during its highest month and $600 during its lowest month. These costs

corresponded with 10,000 units of production during the high month and 2,000 units during the low month. What are the fixed and variable components of its utility costs using the high-low method?
(a) $0.075 variable and $450 fixed.
(b) $0.120 variable and $0 fixed.
(c) $0.300 variable and $0 fixed.
(d) $0.060 variable and $600 fixed.

(LO 4) 6. Which of the following is *not* involved in CVP analysis?
(a) Sales mix.
(b) Unit selling prices.
(c) Fixed costs per unit.
(d) Volume or level of activity.

(LO 5) 7. When comparing a traditional income statement to a CVP income statement:
(a) net income will always be greater on the traditional statement.
(b) net income will always be less on the traditional statement.
(c) net income will always be identical on both.
(d) net income will be greater or less depending on the sales volume.

(LO 5) 8. Contribution margin:
(a) is revenue remaining after deducting variable costs.
(b) may be expressed as contribution margin per unit.
(c) is selling price less cost of goods sold.
(d) Both (a) and (b) above.

(LO 5) 9. Cournot Company sells 100,000 wrenches for $12 a unit. Fixed costs are $300,000, and net income is $200,000. What should be reported as variable expenses in the CVP income statement?

(a) $700,000.   (c) $500,000.
(b) $900,000.   (d) $1,000,000.

10. Gossen Company is planning to sell 200,000 pliers for **(LO 6)** $4 per unit. The contribution margin ratio is 25%. If Gossen will break even at this level of sales, what are the fixed costs?
(a) $100,000.   (c) $200,000.
(b) $160,000.   (d) $300,000.

11. Brownstone Company's contribution margin ratio is **(LO 6)** 30%. If Brownstone's sales revenue is $100 greater than its break-even sales in dollars, its net income:
(a) will be $100.
(b) will be $70.
(c) will be $30.
(d) cannot be determined without knowing fixed costs.

12. The mathematical equation for computing required **(LO 7)** sales to obtain target net income is: Required sales =
(a) Variable costs + Target net income.
(b) Variable costs + Fixed costs + Target net income.
(c) Fixed costs + Target net income.
(d) No correct answer is given.

13. Margin of safety is computed as: **(LO 8)**
(a) Actual sales − Break-even sales.
(b) Contribution margin − Fixed costs.
(c) Break-even sales − Variable costs.
(d) Actual sales − Contribution margin.

14. Marshall Company had actual sales of $600,000 when **(LO 8)** break-even sales were $420,000. What is the margin of safety ratio?
(a) 25%.   (c) 33⅓%.
(b) 30%.   (d) 45%.

Go to the book's companion website, www.wiley.com/college/weygandt, for additional Self-Test Questions.

✔ **The Navigator**

QUESTIONS

1. (a) What is cost behavior analysis?
   (b) Why is cost behavior analysis important to management?
2. (a) Scott Winter asks your help in understanding the term "activity index." Explain the meaning and importance of this term for Scott.
   (b) State the two ways that variable costs may be defined.
3. Contrast the effects of changes in the activity level on total fixed costs and on unit fixed costs.
4. J. P. Alexander claims that the relevant range concept is important only for variable costs.
   (a) Explain the relevant range concept.
   (b) Do you agree with J. P.'s claim? Explain.
5. "The relevant range is indispensable in cost behavior analysis." Is this true? Why or why not?
6. Adam Antal is confused. He does not understand why rent on his apartment is a fixed cost and rent on a Hertz rental truck is a mixed cost. Explain the difference to Adam.

7. How should mixed costs be classified in CVP analysis? What approach is used to effect the appropriate classification?
8. At the high and low levels of activity during the month, direct labor hours are 90,000 and 40,000, respectively. The related costs are $165,000 and $100,000. What are the fixed and variable costs at any level of activity?
9. "Cost-volume-profit (CVP) analysis is based entirely on unit costs." Do you agree? Explain.
10. Faye Dunn defines contribution margin as the amount of profit available to cover operating expenses. Is there any truth in this definition? Discuss.
11. Marshall Company's GWhiz calculator sells for $40. Variable costs per unit are estimated to be $26. What are the contribution margin per unit and the contribution margin ratio?
12. "Break-even analysis is of limited use to management because a company cannot survive by just breaking even." Do you agree? Explain.

13. Total fixed costs are $26,000 for Daz Inc. It has a contribution margin per unit of $15, and a contribution margin ratio of 25%. Compute the break-even sales in dollars.

14. Peggy Turnbull asks your help in constructing a CVP graph. Explain to Peggy (a) how the break-even point is plotted, and (b) how the level of activity and dollar sales at the break-even point are determined.

15. Define the term "margin of safety." If Revere Company expects to sell 1,250 units of its product at $12 per unit, and break-even sales for the product are $13,200, what is the margin of safety ratio?

16. Huang Company's break-even sales are $500,000. Assuming fixed costs are $180,000, what sales volume is needed to achieve a target net income of $90,000?

17. The traditional income statement for Pace Company shows sales $900,000, cost of goods sold $600,000, and operating expenses $200,000. Assuming all costs and expenses are 70% variable and 30% fixed, prepare a CVP income statement through contribution margin.

BRIEF EXERCISES

BE5-1 Monthly production costs in Pesavento Company for two levels of production are as follows.

Cost	2,000 Units	4,000 Units
Indirect labor	$10,000	$20,000
Supervisory salaries	5,000	5,000
Maintenance	4,000	7,000

Indicate which costs are variable, fixed, and mixed, and give the reason for each answer.

Classify costs as variable, fixed, or mixed.

(LO 1, 3), C

BE5-2 For Lodes Company, the relevant range of production is 40–80% of capacity. At 40% of capacity, a variable cost is $4,000 and a fixed cost is $6,000. Diagram the behavior of each cost within the relevant range assuming the behavior is linear.

Diagram the behavior of costs within the relevant range.

(LO 2), AN

BE5-3 For Hunt Company, a mixed cost is $15,000 plus $18 per direct labor hour. Diagram the behavior of the cost using increments of 500 hours up to 2,500 hours on the horizontal axis and increments of $15,000 up to $60,000 on the vertical axis.

Diagram the behavior of a mixed cost.

(LO 3), AN

BE5-4 Bruno Company accumulates the following data concerning a mixed cost, using miles as the activity level.

Determine variable- and fixed-cost elements using the high-low method.

(LO 3), AP

	Miles Driven	Total Cost		Miles Driven	Total Cost
January	8,000	$14,150	March	8,500	$15,000
February	7,500	13,500	April	8,200	14,490

Compute the variable- and fixed-cost elements using the high-low method.

BE5-5 Stiever Corp. has collected the following data concerning its maintenance costs for the past 6 months.

Determine variable- and fixed-cost elements using the high-low method.

(LO 3), AP

	Units Produced	Total Cost
July	18,000	$32,000
August	32,000	48,000
September	36,000	55,000
October	22,000	38,000
November	40,000	66,100
December	38,000	62,000

Compute the variable- and fixed-cost elements using the high-low method.

BE5-6 Determine the missing amounts.

Determine missing amounts for contribution margin.

(LO 5), AN

	Unit Selling Price	Unit Variable Costs	Contribution Margin per Unit	Contribution Margin Ratio
1.	$640	$352	(a)	(b)
2.	$300	(c)	$93	(d)
3.	(e)	(f)	$325	25%

BE5-7 Radial Inc. had sales of $2,400,000 for the first quarter of 2014. In making the sales, the company incurred the costs and expenses shown on page 222.

Prepare CVP income statement.

(LO 5), AP

	Variable	Fixed
Cost of goods sold	$920,000	$440,000
Selling expenses	70,000	45,000
Administrative expenses	86,000	98,000

Prepare a CVP income statement for the quarter ended March 31, 2014.

Compute the break-even point.
(LO 6), AP

BE5-8 Rice Company has a unit selling price of $520, variable costs per unit of $286, and fixed costs of $163,800. Compute the break-even point in units using (a) the mathematical equation and (b) contribution margin per unit.

Compute the break-even point.
(LO 6), AP

BE5-9 Acorn Corp. had total variable costs of $180,000, total fixed costs of $170,000, and total revenues of $300,000. Compute the required sales in dollars to break even.

Compute sales for target net income.
(LO 7), AP

BE5-10 For Flynn Company, variable costs are 70% of sales, and fixed costs are $195,000. Management's net income goal is $75,000. Compute the required sales in dollars needed to achieve management's target net income of $75,000. (Use the contribution margin approach.)

Compute the margin of safety and the margin of safety ratio.
(LO 8), AP

BE5-11 For Stevens Company, actual sales are $1,000,000 and break-even sales are $840,000. Compute (a) the margin of safety in dollars and (b) the margin of safety ratio.

Compute the required sales in units for target net income.
(LO 7), AP

BE5-12 Deines Corporation has fixed costs of $480,000. It has a unit selling price of $6, unit variable costs of $4.40, and a target net income of $1,500,000. Compute the required sales in units to achieve its target net income.

> DO IT! REVIEW

Classify types of costs.
(LO 1, 3), C

DO IT! **5-1** Helena Company reports the following total costs at two levels of production.

	5,000 Units	**10,000 Units**
Indirect labor	$ 3,000	$ 6,000
Property taxes	7,000	7,000
Direct labor	28,000	56,000
Direct materials	22,000	44,000
Depreciation	4,000	4,000
Utilities	5,000	7,000
Maintenance	9,000	11,000

Classify each cost as variable, fixed, or mixed.

Compute costs using high-low method and estimate total cost.
(LO 3), AP

DO IT! **5-2** Westerville Company accumulates the following data concerning a mixed cost, using units produced as the activity level.

	Units Produced	**Total Cost**
March	10,000	$18,000
April	9,000	16,650
May	10,500	18,580
June	8,800	16,200
July	9,500	17,100

(a) Compute the variable- and fixed-cost elements using the high-low method.
(b) Estimate the total cost if the company produces 9,200 units.

Compute break-even point in units.
(LO 6), AP

DO IT! **5-3** Larissa Company has a unit selling price of $250, variable costs per unit of $170, and fixed costs of $140,000. Compute the break-even point in units using (a) the mathematical equation and (b) contribution margin per unit.

Compute break-even point, margin of safety ratio, and sales for target net income.
(LO 6, 7, 8), AP

DO IT! **5-4** Presto Company makes radios that sell for $30 each. For the coming year, management expects fixed costs to total $220,000 and variable costs to be $18 per unit.

(a) Compute the break-even point in dollars using the contribution margin (CM) ratio.
(b) Compute the margin of safety ratio assuming actual sales are $800,000.
(c) Compute the sales dollars required to earn net income of $140,000.

✔ **The Navigator**

EXERCISES

E5-1 Turgro Company manufactures a single product. Annual production costs incurred in the manufacturing process are shown below for two levels of production.

Define and classify variable, fixed, and mixed costs.

(LO 1, 3), C

	Costs Incurred			
Production in Units	**5,000**		**10,000**	
Production Costs	**Total Cost**	**Cost/ Unit**	**Total Cost**	**Cost/ Unit**
Direct materials	$8,000	$1.60	$16,000	$1.60
Direct labor	9,500	1.90	19,000	1.90
Utilities	2,000	0.40	3,500	0.35
Rent	4,000	0.80	4,000	0.40
Maintenance	800	0.16	1,100	0.11
Supervisory salaries	1,000	0.20	1,000	0.10

Instructions

(a) Define the terms variable costs, fixed costs, and mixed costs.

(b) Classify each cost above as either variable, fixed, or mixed.

E5-2 Shingle Enterprises is considering manufacturing a new product. It projects the cost of direct materials and rent for a range of output as shown below.

Diagram cost behavior, determine relevant range, and classify costs.

(LO 1, 2), C

Output in Units	Rent Expense	Direct Materials
1,000	$ 5,000	$ 4,000
2,000	5,000	7,200
3,000	8,000	9,000
4,000	8,000	12,000
5,000	8,000	15,000
6,000	8,000	18,000
7,000	8,000	21,000
8,000	8,000	24,000
9,000	10,000	29,300
10,000	10,000	35,000
11,000	10,000	44,000

Instructions

(a) Diagram the behavior of each cost for output ranging from 1,000 to 11,000 units.

(b) Determine the relevant range of activity for this product.

(c) Calculate the variable costs per unit within the relevant range.

(d) Indicate the fixed cost within the relevant range.

E5-3 The controller of Furgee Industries has collected the following monthly expense data for use in analyzing the cost behavior of maintenance costs.

Determine fixed and variable costs using the high-low method and prepare graph.

(LO 1, 3), AN

Month	Total Maintenance Costs	Total Machine Hours
January	$2,500	300
February	3,000	350
March	3,600	500
April	4,500	690
May	3,200	400
June	4,900	700

Instructions

(a) Determine the fixed- and variable-cost components using the high-low method.

(b) Prepare a graph showing the behavior of maintenance costs, and identify the fixed- and variable-cost elements. Use 100-hour increments and $1,000 cost increments.

E5-4 Family Furniture Corporation incurred the following costs.

Classify variable, fixed, and mixed costs.

(LO 1, 3), C

1. Wood used in the production of furniture.

2. Fuel used in delivery trucks.

3. Straight-line depreciation on factory building.
4. Screws used in the production of furniture.
5. Sales staff salaries.
6. Sales commissions.
7. Property taxes.
8. Insurance on buildings.
9. Hourly wages of furniture craftsmen.
10. Salaries of factory supervisors.
11. Utilities expense.
12. Telephone bill.

Instructions
Identify the costs above as variable, fixed, or mixed.

Determine fixed and variable costs using the high-low method and prepare graph.

(LO 1, 3), AP

E5-5 The controller of Dousmann Industries has collected the following monthly expense data for use in analyzing the cost behavior of maintenance costs.

Month	Total Maintenance Costs	Total Machine Hours
January	$2,750	3,500
February	3,000	4,000
March	3,600	6,000
April	4,500	7,900
May	3,200	5,000
June	5,000	8,000

Instructions
(a) Determine the fixed- and variable-cost components using the high-low method.
(b) Prepare a graph showing the behavior of maintenance costs, and identify the fixed- and variable-cost elements. Use 2,000-hour increments and $1,000 cost increments.

Determine fixed, variable, and mixed costs.

(LO 1, 3), AP

E5-6 PCB Corporation manufactures a single product. Monthly production costs incurred in the manufacturing process are shown below for the production of 3,000 units. The utilities and maintenance costs are mixed costs. The fixed portions of these costs are $300 and $200, respectively.

Production in Units	3,000
Production Costs	
Direct materials	$ 7,500
Direct labor	18,000
Utilities	2,100
Property taxes	1,000
Indirect labor	4,500
Supervisory salaries	1,900
Maintenance	1,100
Depreciation	2,400

Instructions
(a) Identify the above costs as variable, fixed, or mixed.
(b) Calculate the expected costs when production is 5,000 units.

Explain assumptions underlying CVP analysis.

(LO 4), K

E5-7 Jim Taylor wants Taylor Company to use CVP analysis to study the effects of changes in costs and volume on the company. Taylor has heard that certain assumptions must be valid in order for CVP analysis to be useful.

Instructions
▭▭▭▷ Prepare a memo to Jim Taylor concerning the assumptions that underlie CVP analysis.

Compute break-even point in units and dollars.

(LO 5, 6), AP

E5-8 All That Blooms provides environmentally friendly lawn services for homeowners. Its operating costs are as follows.

Depreciation	$1,400 per month
Advertising	$200 per month
Insurance	$2,000 per month

Weed and feed materials	$12 per lawn
Direct labor	$10 per lawn
Fuel	$2 per lawn

All That Blooms charges $60 per treatment for the average single-family lawn.

Instructions
Determine the company's break-even point in (a) number of lawns serviced per month and (b) dollars.

E5-9 The Green Acres Inn is trying to determine its break-even point. The inn has 50 rooms that it rents at $60 a night. Operating costs are as follows.

Compute break-even point.
(LO 5, 6), AP

Salaries	$6,200 per month
Utilities	$1,100 per month
Depreciation	$1,000 per month
Maintenance	$100 per month
Maid service	$11 per room
Other costs	$28 per room

Instructions
Determine the inn's break-even point in (a) number of rented rooms per month and (b) dollars.

E5-10 In the month of March, Style Salon services 560 clients at an average price of $120. During the month, fixed costs were $21,024 and variable costs were 60% of sales.

Compute contribution margin and break-even point.
(LO 5, 6), AP

Instructions
(a) Determine the contribution margin in dollars, per unit, and as a ratio.
(b) Using the contribution margin technique, compute the break-even point in dollars and in units.

E5-11 Kare Kars provides shuttle service between four hotels near a medical center and an international airport. Kare Kars uses two 10-passenger vans to offer 12 round trips per day. A recent month's activity in the form of a cost-volume-profit income statement is shown below.

Compute break-even point.
(LO 5, 6), AP

Fare revenues (1,440 fares)		$36,000
Variable costs		
Fuel	$ 5,040	
Tolls and parking	3,100	
Maintenance	860	9,000
Contribution margin		27,000
Fixed costs		
Salaries	12,700	
Depreciation	1,300	
Insurance	1,000	15,000
Net income		$12,000

Instructions
(a) Calculate the break-even point in (1) dollars and (2) number of fares.
(b) Without calculations, determine the contribution margin at the break-even point.

E5-12 In 2013, Manhoff Company had a break-even point of $350,000 based on a selling price of $5 per unit and fixed costs of $112,000. In 2014, the selling price and the variable costs per unit did not change, but the break-even point increased to $420,000.

Compute variable costs per unit, contribution margin ratio, and increase in fixed costs.
(LO 5, 6), AP

Instructions
(a) Compute the variable costs per unit and the contribution margin ratio for 2013.
(b) Compute the increase in fixed costs for 2014.

E5-13 Cannes Company has the following information available for September 2014.

Prepare CVP income statements.
(LO 5, 6), AP

Unit selling price of video game consoles	$ 400
Unit variable costs	$ 275
Total fixed costs	$52,000
Units sold	600

Instructions

(a) Compute the contribution margin per unit.

(b) Prepare a CVP income statement that shows both total and per unit amounts.

(c) Compute Cannes' break-even point in units.

(d) Prepare a CVP income statement for the break-even point that shows both total and per unit amounts.

Compute various components to derive target net income under different assumptions.

(LO 6, 7), AP

E5-14 Naylor Company had $210,000 of net income in 2013 when the selling price per unit was $150, the variable costs per unit were $90, and the fixed costs were $570,000. Management expects per unit data and total fixed costs to remain the same in 2014. The president of Naylor Company is under pressure from stockholders to increase net income by $52,000 in 2014.

Instructions

(a) Compute the number of units sold in 2013.

(b) Compute the number of units that would have to be sold in 2014 to reach the stockholders' desired profit level.

(c) Assume that Naylor Company sells the same number of units in 2014 as it did in 2013. What would the selling price have to be in order to reach the stockholders' desired profit level?

Compute net income under different alternatives.

(LO 7), AP

E5-15 Cottonwood Company reports the following operating results for the month of August: sales $400,000 (units 5,000); variable costs $210,000; and fixed costs $90,000. Management is considering the following independent courses of action to increase net income.

1. Increase selling price by 10% with no change in total variable costs or units sold.

2. Reduce variable costs to 45% of sales.

Instructions

Compute the net income to be earned under each alternative. Which course of action will produce the highest net income?

Prepare a CVP graph and compute break-even point and margin of safety.

(LO 6, 8), AP

E5-16 Glacial Company estimates that variable costs will be 62.5% of sales, and fixed costs will total $600,000. The selling price of the product is $4.

Instructions

(a) Prepare a CVP graph, assuming maximum sales of $3,200,000. (*Note:* Use $400,000 increments for sales and costs and 100,000 increments for units.)

(b) Compute the break-even point in (1) units and (2) dollars.

(c) Compute the margin of safety in (1) dollars and (2) as a ratio, assuming actual sales are $2 million.

Determine contribution margin ratio, break-even point in dollars, and margin of safety.

(LO 5, 6, 7, 8), AP

E5-17 Oak Bucket Co., a manufacturer of wood buckets, had the following data for 2013:

Sales	2,600 units
Sales price	$40 per unit
Variable costs	$16 per unit
Fixed costs	$19,500

Instructions

(a) What is the contribution margin ratio?

(b) What is the break-even point in dollars?

(c) What is the margin of safety in dollars and as a ratio?

(d) If the company wishes to increase its total dollar contribution margin by 30% in 2014, by how much will it need to increase its sales if all other factors remain constant?

(CGA adapted)

EXERCISES: SET B AND CHALLENGE EXERCISES

Visit the book's companion website, at **www.wiley.com/college/weygandt**, and choose the Student Companion site to access Exercise Set B and Challenge Exercises.

PROBLEMS: SET A

P5-1A Telly Savalas owns the Bonita Barber Shop. He employs four barbers and pays each a base rate of $1,000 per month. One of the barbers serves as the manager and receives an extra $500 per month. In addition to the base rate, each barber also receives a commission of $4.50 per haircut.

Other costs are as follows.

Advertising	$200 per month
Rent	$1,100 per month
Barber supplies	$0.30 per haircut
Utilities	$175 per month plus $0.20 per haircut
Magazines	$25 per month

Telly currently charges $10 per haircut.

Determine variable and fixed costs, compute break-even point, prepare a CVP graph, and determine net income.

(LO 1, 3, 5, 6), AN

Instructions
(a) Determine the variable costs per haircut and the total monthly fixed costs.
(b) Compute the break-even point in units and dollars.
(c) Prepare a CVP graph, assuming a maximum of 1,800 haircuts in a month. Use increments of 300 haircuts on the horizontal axis and $3,000 on the vertical axis.
(d) Determine net income, assuming 1,700 haircuts are given in a month.

(a) VC $5

P5-2A Jorge Company bottles and distributes B-Lite, a diet soft drink. The beverage is sold for 50 cents per 16-ounce bottle to retailers, who charge customers 75 cents per bottle. For the year 2014, management estimates the following revenues and costs.

Prepare a CVP income statement, compute break-even point, contribution margin ratio, margin of safety ratio, and sales for target net income.

(LO 5, 6, 7, 8), AN

Sales	$1,800,000	Selling expenses—variable	$70,000
Direct materials	430,000	Selling expenses—fixed	65,000
Direct labor	360,000	Administrative expenses—	
Manufacturing overhead—		variable	20,000
variable	380,000	Administrative expenses—	
Manufacturing overhead—		fixed	60,000
fixed	280,000		

Instructions
(a) Prepare a CVP income statement for 2014 based on management's estimates. (Show column for total amounts only.)
(b) Compute the break-even point in (1) units and (2) dollars.
(c) Compute the contribution margin ratio and the margin of safety ratio. (Round to nearest full percent.)
(d) Determine the sales dollars required to earn net income of $180,000.

(b) (1) 2,700,000 units
(c) CM ratio 30%

P5-3A Dousmann Corp.'s sales slumped badly in 2014. For the first time in its history, it operated at a loss. The company's income statement showed the following results from selling 500,000 units of product: sales $2,500,000; total costs and expenses $2,600,000; and net loss $100,000. Costs and expenses consisted of the amounts shown below.

Compute break-even point under alternative courses of action.

(LO 5, 6), E

	Total	Variable	Fixed
Cost of goods sold	$2,140,000	$1,540,000	$600,000
Selling expenses	250,000	92,000	158,000
Administrative expenses	210,000	68,000	142,000
	$2,600,000	$1,700,000	$900,000

Management is considering the following independent alternatives for 2015.

1. Increase unit selling price 20% with no change in costs, expenses, and sales volume.
2. Change the compensation of salespersons from fixed annual salaries totaling $150,000 to total salaries of $60,000 plus a 5% commission on sales.

Instructions
(a) Compute the break-even point in dollars for 2014.
(b) Compute the break-even point in dollars under each of the alternative courses of action. (Round all ratios to nearest full percent.) Which course of action do you recommend?

(b) Alternative 1 $2,093,023

Compute break-even point and margin of safety ratio, and prepare a CVP income statement before and after changes in business environment.

(LO 5, 6, 8), E

P5-4A Mary Willis is the advertising manager for Bargain Shoe Store. She is currently working on a major promotional campaign. Her ideas include the installation of a new lighting system and increased display space that will add $24,000 in fixed costs to the $270,000 currently spent. In addition, Mary is proposing that a 5% price decrease ($40 to $38) will produce a 20% increase in sales volume (20,000 to 24,000). Variable costs will remain at $24 per pair of shoes. Management is impressed with Mary's ideas but concerned about the effects that these changes will have on the break-even point and the margin of safety.

Instructions

(a) Compute the current break-even point in units, and compare it to the break-even point in units if Mary's ideas are used.

(b) Current margin of safety ratio 16%

(b) Compute the margin of safety ratio for current operations and after Mary's changes are introduced. (Round to nearest full percent.)

(c) Prepare a CVP income statement for current operations and after Mary's changes are introduced. (Show column for total amounts only.) Would you make the changes suggested?

Compute contribution margin, fixed costs, break-even point, sales for target net income, and margin of safety ratio.

(LO 5, 6, 7, 8), AN

P5-5A Mozena Corporation has collected the following information after its first year of sales. Sales were $1,500,000 on 100,000 units; selling expenses $250,000 (40% variable and 60% fixed); direct materials $511,000; direct labor $290,000; administrative expenses $270,000 (20% variable and 80% fixed); manufacturing overhead $350,000 (70% variable and 30% fixed). Top management has asked you to do a CVP analysis so that it can make plans for the coming year. It has projected that unit sales will increase by 10% next year.

Instructions

(a) Compute (1) the contribution margin for the current year and the projected year, and (2) the fixed costs for the current year. (Assume that fixed costs will remain the same in the projected year.)

(b) 157,000 units

(b) Compute the break-even point in units and sales dollars for the current year.

(c) The company has a target net income of $200,000. What is the required sales in dollars for the company to meet its target?

(d) If the company meets its target net income number, by what percentage could its sales fall before it is operating at a loss? That is, what is its margin of safety ratio?

Determine contribution margin ratio, break-even point, and margin of safety.

(LO 1, 5, 7, 8), E

P5-6A Kaiser Industries carries no inventories. Its product is manufactured only when a customer's order is received. It is then shipped immediately after it is made. For its fiscal year ended October 31, 2014, Kaiser's break-even point was $1.3 million. On sales of $1.2 million, its income statement showed a gross profit of $180,000, direct materials cost of $400,000, and direct labor costs of $500,000. The contribution margin was $180,000, and variable manufacturing overhead was $50,000.

Instructions

(a) Calculate the following:
   (1) Variable selling and administrative expenses.
   (2) Fixed manufacturing overhead.
   (3) Fixed selling and administrative expenses.

(a) (2) $70,000

(b) Ignoring your answer to part (a), assume that fixed manufacturing overhead was $100,000 and the fixed selling and administrative expenses were $80,000. The marketing vice president feels that if the company increased its advertising, sales could be increased by 25%. What is the maximum increased advertising cost the company can incur and still report the same income as before the advertising expenditure?

(CGA adapted)

PROBLEMS: SET B

Determine variable and fixed costs, compute break-even point, prepare a CVP graph, and determine net income.

(LO 1, 3, 5, 6), AN

P5-1B The Sasoon Barber Shop employs four barbers. One barber, who also serves as the manager, is paid a salary of $3,000 per month. The other barbers are paid $1,500 per month. In addition, each barber is paid a commission of $3 per haircut. Other monthly costs are store rent $700 plus 60 cents per haircut, depreciation on equipment $400, barber supplies 40 cents per haircut, utilities $300, and advertising $100. The price of a haircut is $10.

Instructions

(a) Determine the variable costs per haircut and the total monthly fixed costs.
(b) Compute the break-even point in units and dollars.
(c) Prepare a CVP graph, assuming a maximum of 1,800 haircuts in a month. Use increments of 300 haircuts on the horizontal axis and $3,000 increments on the vertical axis.
(d) Determine the net income, assuming 1,800 haircuts are given in a month.

P5-2B All Frute Company bottles and distributes Frute Ade, a fruit drink. The beverage is sold for 50 cents per 16-ounce bottle to retailers, who charge customers 70 cents per bottle. For the year 2014, management estimates the following revenues and costs.

Sales	$2,500,000	Selling expenses—variable	$ 80,000
Direct materials	360,000	Selling expenses—fixed	250,000
Direct labor	450,000	Administrative expenses—	
Manufacturing overhead—		variable	40,000
variable	270,000	Administrative expenses—	
Manufacturing overhead—		fixed	150,000
fixed	380,000		

Instructions

(a) Prepare a CVP income statement for 2014 based on management's estimates. (Show column for total amounts only.)
(b) Compute the break-even point in (1) units and (2) dollars.
(c) Compute the contribution margin ratio and the margin of safety ratio.
(d) Determine the sales dollars required to earn net income of $624,000.

P5-3B Olgivie Company had a bad year in 2013. For the first time in its history, it operated at a loss. The company's income statement showed the following results from selling 60,000 units of product: sales $1,800,000; total costs and expenses $2,010,000; and net loss $210,000. Costs and expenses consisted of the amounts shown below.

	Total	Variable	Fixed
Cost of goods sold	$1,350,000	$ 930,000	$420,000
Selling expenses	480,000	125,000	355,000
Administrative expenses	180,000	115,000	65,000
	$2,010,000	$1,170,000	$840,000

Management is considering the following independent alternatives for 2014.

1. Increase unit selling price 25% with no change in costs, expenses, and sales volume.
2. Change the compensation of salespersons from fixed annual salaries totaling $200,000 to total salaries of $20,000 plus a 5% commission on net sales.
3. Purchase new high-tech factory machinery that will change the proportion between variable and fixed cost of goods sold to 50:50.

Instructions

(a) Compute the break-even point in dollars for 2013.
(b) Compute the break-even point in dollars under each of the alternative courses of action. (Round all ratios to nearest full percent.) Which course of action do you recommend?

P5-4B Alma Ortiz is the advertising manager for CostLess Shoe Store. She is currently working on a major promotional campaign. Her ideas include the installation of a new lighting system and increased display space that will add $18,000 in fixed costs to the $216,000 currently spent. In addition, Alma is proposing that a 10% price decrease (from $30 to $27) will produce an increase in sales volume from 20,000 to 24,000 units. Variable costs will remain at $12 per pair of shoes. Management is impressed with Alma's ideas but concerned about the effects that these changes will have on the break-even point and the margin of safety.

Instructions

(a) Compute the current break-even point in units, and compare it to the break-even point in units if Alma's ideas are used.
(b) Compute the margin of safety ratio for current operations and after Alma's changes are introduced. (Round to nearest full percent.)
(c) Prepare a CVP income statement for current operations and after Alma's changes are introduced. (Show column for total amounts only.) Would you make the changes suggested?

(a) VC $4

Prepare a CVP income statement, compute break-even point, contribution margin ratio, margin of safety ratio, and sales for target net income.

(LO 5, 6, 7, 8), AN

(b) (1) 3,000,000 units
(c) CM ratio 52%

Compute break-even point under alternative courses of action.

(LO 5, 6), E

(b) Alternative 1, $1,750,000

Compute break-even point and margin of safety ratio, and prepare a CVP income statement before and after changes in business environment.

(LO 5, 6, 8), E

(b) Current margin of safety ratio 40%

Compute break-even point and margin of safety ratio, and prepare a CVP income statement before and after changes in business environment.

(LO 5, 6, 7, 8), AN

P5-5B Isaac Corporation has collected the following information after its first year of sales. Sales were $1,800,000 on 100,000 units; selling expenses $400,000 (30% variable and 70% fixed); direct materials $456,000; direct labor $250,000; administrative expenses $484,000 (50% variable and 50% fixed); manufacturing overhead $480,000 (40% variable and 60% fixed). Top management has asked you to do a CVP analysis so that it can make plans for the coming year. It has projected that unit sales will increase by 20% next year.

Instructions

(a) Compute (1) the contribution margin for the current year and the projected year, and (2) the fixed costs for the current year. (Assume that fixed costs will remain the same in the projected year.)

(b) 150,000 units

(b) Compute the break-even point in units and sales dollars.

(c) The company has a target net income of $213,000. What is the required sales in dollars for the company to meet its target?

(d) If the company meets its target net income number, by what percentage could its sales fall before it is operating at a loss? That is, what is its margin of safety ratio?

(e) The company is considering a purchase of equipment that would reduce its direct labor costs by $100,000 and would change its manufacturing overhead costs to 10% variable and 90% fixed (assume total manufacturing overhead cost is $480,000, as above). It is also considering switching to a pure commission basis for its sales staff. This would change selling expenses to 80% variable and 20% fixed (assume total selling expense is $400,000, as above). Compute (1) the contribution margin and (2) the contribution margin ratio, and recompute (3) the break-even point in sales dollars. Comment on the effect each of management's proposed changes has on the break-even point.

Determine contribution margin ratio, break-even point, and margin of safety.

(LO 1, 5, 7, 8), E

P5-6B Mega Electronix carries no inventories. Its product is manufactured only when a customer's order is received. It is then shipped immediately after it is made. For its fiscal year ended October 31, 2014, Mega's break-even point was $2.4 million. On sales of $2 million, its income statement showed a gross profit of $400,000, direct materials cost of $600,000, and direct labor costs of $700,000. The contribution margin was $150,000, and variable manufacturing overhead was $200,000.

Instructions

(a) Calculate the following:
   1. Variable selling and administrative expenses.
   2. Fixed manufacturing overhead.
   3. Fixed selling and administrative expenses.

(a) 2. $100,000

(b) Ignoring your answer to part (a), assume that fixed manufacturing overhead was $100,000 and the fixed selling and administrative expenses were $80,000. The marketing vice president feels that if the company increased its advertising, sales could be increased by 15%. What is the maximum increased advertising cost the company can incur and still report the same income as before the advertising expenditure?

(CGA adapted)

PROBLEMS: SET C

Visit the book's companion website, at **www.wiley.com/college/weygandt**, and choose the Student Companion site to access Problem Set C.

WATERWAYS CONTINUING PROBLEM

(*Note:* This is a continuation of the Waterways Problem from Chapters 1–4.)

WCP5 The Vice President for Sales and Marketing at Waterways Corporation is planning for production needs to meet sales demand in the coming year. He is also trying to determine how the company's profits might be increased in the coming year. This problem asks you to use cost-volume-profit concepts to help Waterways understand contribution margins of some of its products and to decide whether to mass-produce certain products.

Go to the book's companion website, **www.wiley.com/college/weygandt**, *to find the remainder of this problem.*

Broadening Your **PERSPECTIVE**

Management Decision-Making

Decision-Making at Current Designs

BYP5-1 Bill Johnson, sales manager, and Diane Buswell, controller, at Current Designs are beginning to analyze the cost considerations for one of the composite models of the kayak division. They have provided the following production and operational costs necessary to produce one composite kayak.

Kevlar®	$250 per kayak
Resin and supplies	$100 per kayak
Finishing kit (seat, rudder, ropes, etc.)	$170 per kayak
Labor	$420 per kayak
Selling and administrative expenses—variable	$400 per kayak
Selling and administrative expenses—fixed	$119,700 per year
Manufacturing overhead—fixed	$240,000 per year

Bill and Diane have asked you to provide a cost-volume-profit analysis, to help them finalize the budget projections for the upcoming year. Bill has informed you that the selling price of the composite kayak will be $2,000.

Instructions
(a) Calculate variable costs per unit.
(b) Determine the contribution margin per unit.
(c) Using the contribution margin per unit, determine the break-even point in units for this product line.
(d) Assume that Current Designs plans to earn $270,600 on this product line. Using the contribution margin per unit, calculate the number of units that need to be sold to achieve this goal.
(e) Based on the most recent sales forecast, Current Designs plans to sell 1,000 units of this model. Using your results from part (c), calculate the margin of safety and the margin of safety ratio.

Decision-Making Across the Organization

BYP5-2 Creative Ideas Company has decided to introduce a new product. The new product can be manufactured by either a capital-intensive method or a labor-intensive method. The manufacturing method will not affect the quality of the product. The estimated manufacturing costs by the two methods are as follows.

	Capital-Intensive	Labor-Intensive
Direct materials	$5 per unit	$5.50 per unit
Direct labor	$6 per unit	$8.00 per unit
Variable overhead	$3 per unit	$4.50 per unit
Fixed manufacturing costs	$2,524,000	$1,550,000

Creative Ideas' market research department has recommended an introductory unit sales price of $32. The incremental selling expenses are estimated to be $502,000 annually plus $2 for each unit sold, regardless of manufacturing method.

Instructions
With the class divided into groups, answer the following.
(a) Calculate the estimated break-even point in annual unit sales of the new product if Creative Ideas Company uses the:
   (1) Capital-intensive manufacturing method.
   (2) Labor-intensive manufacturing method.
(b) Determine the annual unit sales volume at which Creative Ideas Company would be indifferent between the two manufacturing methods.
(c) Explain the circumstance under which Creative Ideas should employ each of the two manufacturing methods.

(CMA adapted)

Managerial Analysis

BYP5-3 The condensed income statement for the Peri and Paul partnership for 2014 is as follows.

Peri and Paul Company
Income Statement
For the Year Ended December 31, 2014

Sales (240,000 units)		$1,200,000
Cost of goods sold		800,000
Gross profit		400,000
Operating expenses		
Selling	$280,000	
Administrative	150,000	430,000
Net loss		($30,000)

A cost behavior analysis indicates that 75% of the cost of goods sold are variable, 42% of the selling expenses are variable, and 40% of the administrative expenses are variable.

Instructions

(Round to nearest unit, dollar, and percentage, where necessary. Use the CVP income statement format in computing profits.)

(a) Compute the break-even point in total sales dollars and in units for 2014.

(b) Peri has proposed a plan to get the partnership "out of the red" and improve its profitability. She feels that the quality of the product could be substantially improved by spending $0.25 more per unit on better raw materials. The selling price per unit could be increased to only $5.25 because of competitive pressures. Peri estimates that sales volume will increase by 25%. What effect would Peri's plan have on the profits and the break-even point in dollars of the partnership? (Round the contribution margin ratio to two decimal places.)

(c) Paul was a marketing major in college. He believes that sales volume can be increased only by intensive advertising and promotional campaigns. He therefore proposed the following plan as an alternative to Peri's: (1) Increase variable selling expenses to $0.59 per unit, (2) lower the selling price per unit by $0.25, and (3) increase fixed selling expenses by $40,000. Paul quoted an old marketing research report that said that sales volume would increase by 60% if these changes were made. What effect would Paul's plan have on the profits and the break-even point in dollars of the partnership?

(d) Which plan should be accepted? Explain your answer.

Real-World Focus

BYP5-4 The Coca-Cola Company hardly needs an introduction. A line taken from the cover of a recent annual report says it all: If you measured time in servings of Coca-Cola, "a billion Coca-Cola's ago was yesterday morning." On average, every U.S. citizen drinks 363 8-ounce servings of Coca-Cola products each year. Coca-Cola's primary line of business is the making and selling of syrup to bottlers. These bottlers then sell the finished bottles and cans of Coca-Cola to the consumer.

In the annual report of Coca-Cola, the information shown below was provided.

The Coca-Cola Company
Management Discussion

Our gross margin declined to 61 percent this year from 62 percent in the prior year, primarily due to costs for materials such as sweeteners and packaging.

The increases [in selling expenses] in the last two years were primarily due to higher marketing expenditures in support of our Company's volume growth.

We measure our sales volume in two ways: (1) gallon shipments of concentrates and syrups and (2) unit cases of finished product (bottles and cans of Coke sold by bottlers).

Instructions

Answer the following questions.

(a) Are sweeteners and packaging a variable cost or a fixed cost? What is the impact on the contribution margin of an increase in the per unit cost of sweeteners or packaging? What are the implications for profitability?

(b) In your opinion, are marketing expenditures a fixed cost, variable cost, or mixed cost to The Coca-Cola Company? Give justification for your answer.

(c) Which of the two measures cited for measuring volume represents the activity index as defined in this chapter? Why might Coca-Cola use two different measures?

BYP5-5 The May 21, 2010, edition of the *Wall Street Journal* includes an article by Jeffrey Trachtenberg entitled "E-Books Rewrite Bookselling."

Instructions

Read the article and answer the following questions.

(a) What aspect of Barnes and Noble's current structure puts it at risk if electronic books become a significant portion of book sales?

(b) What was Barnes and Noble's primary competitive advantage in a "paper book" world? How has this advantage been eliminated by e-books?

(c) What event do the authors say might eventually be viewed as the big turning point for e-books?

(d) What amount does Barnes and Noble earn on a $25 hardcover book? How much would it likely earn on an e-book version of the same title? What implications does this have for Barnes and Noble versus its competitors?

(e) What two mistakes does the author suggest that Barnes and Noble made that left it ill-prepared for an e book environment?

Critical Thinking

Communication Activity

BYP5-6 Your roommate asks for your help on the following questions about CVP analysis formulas.

(a) How can the mathematical equation for break-even sales show both sales units and sales dollars?

(b) How do the formulas differ for contribution margin per unit and contribution margin ratio?

(c) How can contribution margin be used to determine break-even sales in units and in dollars?

Instructions

Write a memo to your roommate stating the relevant formulas and answering each question.

Ethics Case

BYP5-7 Scott Bestor is an accountant for Westfield Company. Early this year, Scott made a highly favorable projection of sales and profits over the next 3 years for Westfield's hot-selling computer PLEX. As a result of the projections Scott presented to senior management, the company decided to expand production in this area. This decision led to dislocations of some plant personnel who were reassigned to one of the company's newer plants in another state. However, no one was fired, and in fact the company expanded its work force slightly.

  Unfortunately, Scott rechecked his computations on the projections a few months later and found that he had made an error that would have reduced his projections substantially. Luckily, sales of PLEX have exceeded projections so far, and management is satisfied with its decision. Scott, however, is not sure what to do. Should he confess his honest mistake and jeopardize his possible promotion? He suspects that no one will catch the error because sales of PLEX have exceeded his projections, and it appears that profits will materialize close to his projections.

Instructions

(a) Who are the stakeholders in this situation?

(b) Identify the ethical issues involved in this situation.

(c) What are the possible alternative actions for Scott? What would you do in Scott's position?

All About You

BYP5-8 Cost-volume-profit analysis can also be used in making personal financial decisions. For example, the purchase of a new car is one of your biggest personal expenditures. It is important that you carefully analyze your options.

Suppose that you are considering the purchase of a hybrid vehicle. Let's assume the following facts: The hybrid will initially cost an additional $4,500 above the cost of a traditional vehicle. The hybrid will get 40 miles per gallon of gas, and the traditional car will get 30 miles per gallon. Also, assume that the cost of gas is $3.60 per gallon.

Instructions
Using the facts above, answer the following questions.
(a) What is the variable gasoline cost of going one mile in the hybrid car? What is the variable cost of going one mile in the traditional car?
(b) Using the information in part (a), if "miles" is your unit of measure, what is the "contribution margin" of the hybrid vehicle relative to the traditional vehicle? That is, express the variable cost savings on a per-mile basis.
(c) How many miles would you have to drive in order to break even on your investment in the hybrid car?
(d) What other factors might you want to consider?

Answers to Chapter Questions

Answers to Insight and Accounting Across the Organization Questions

p. 200 Gardens in the Sky Q: What are some of the variable and fixed costs that are impacted by hydroponic farming? **A:** Compared to traditional methods, hydroponic farming would reduce the use of pesticides, herbicides, fuel, and water. Soil erosion would be eliminated, and land requirements would drop. But, fixed costs related to constructing greenhouses, suitable vertical planters, as well as investments in artificial lighting could be high.

p. 204 Skilled Labor Is Truly Essential Q: Would you characterize labor costs as being a fixed cost, a variable cost, or something else in this situation? **A:** Because these labor costs are essentially unchanged for most levels of production, they are primarily fixed. However, it could be described as being a "step function." If production gets too far outside the normal range, workers' hours will change. If production goes too low, hours are cut, and if it goes too high, overtime hours are needed.

p. 211 Charter Flights Offer a Good Deal Q: How did FlightServe determine that it would break even with 3.3 seats full per flight? **A:** FlightServe determined its break-even point with the following formula: Fixed costs ÷ Contribution margin per seat occupied = Break-even point in seats.

p. 215 How a Rolling Stones' Tour Makes Money Q: What amount of sales dollars are required for the promoter to break even?
A: Fixed costs = $1,200,000 + $400,000 = $1,600,000
Contribution margin ratio = 80%
Break-even sales = $1,600,000 ÷ .80 = $2,000,000

Answers to Self-Test Questions

1. d **2.** c **3.** a **4.** d **5.** a [($1,200 − $600) ÷ (10,000 − 2,000)] **6.** c **7.** c **8.** d
9. a [(100,000 × $12) − $300,000 − $200,000] **10.** c (200,000 × $4 × 25%) **11.** c ($100 × 30%)
12. b **13.** a **14.** b [($600,000 − $420,000) ÷ $600,000]

✔ Remember to go back to The Navigator box on the chapter opening page and check off your completed work.

Chapter 6

Cost-Volume-Profit Analysis: Additional Issues

Feature Story

Rapid Replay

Intel doesn't do things half-way. If you own a PC, then there is a roughly 85% chance that the microprocessor chip that runs your machine was made by Intel. In fact, for as long as most people can remember, Intel has had at least an 85% share of the market for PC computer chips. That doesn't mean, however, that life is easy for Intel. Its earnings swings, like every-thing else about the company, are major league. Consider these two *Wall Street Journal* headlines: "Intel's Net Plunges as Demand Dries Up" and then, only slightly more than a year later, "Intel Earnings Set High Bar."

If Intel is so dominant in the computer chip market, why does it experience such huge swings in its earnings? First, to produce computer chips, Intel must continually make huge investments in sophisticated equipment. Now, consider what you learned in the previous chapter. The higher a company's fixed costs, the more units it must sell to break even. In this chapter, you will learn that if a company has high fixed costs as a percentage of total costs, then its earnings will be very susceptible to economic swings.

Another way of saying this is that when the economy gets the sniffles,

✔ The Navigator

- [ ] Scan Learning Objectives
- [ ] Read Feature Story
- [ ] Scan Preview
- [ ] Read Text and answer **DO IT!** p. 239
  - [ ] p. 243 [ ] p. 248 [ ] p. 250
  - [ ] p. 265
- [ ] Work Using the Decision Toolkit p. 254
- [ ] Review Summary of Learning Objectives
- [ ] Work Comprehensive **DO IT!** p. 266
- [ ] Answer Self-Test Questions
- [ ] Complete Assignments
- [ ] Go to **WileyPLUS** for practice and tutorials

Learning Objectives

After studying this chapter, you should be able to:

1. Describe the essential features of a cost-volume-profit income statement.
2. Apply basic CVP concepts.
3. Explain the term sales mix and its effects on break-even sales.
4. Determine sales mix when a company has limited resources.
5. Understand how operating leverage affects profitability.

✔ The Navigator

Intel gets the flu. A drop in Intel's sales results in a disproportionately large drop in its profits. For example, during a recent
quarter when Intel's sales fell
23%, its profits fell 90%. On the
other hand, the minute the
economy turns upward, Intel's
profits do a sharp about-face.
After the recent downturn,
Intel's sales jumped 44%. While
this was a nice bump in sales,
consider what happened to its
net income. Its net income
increased by almost 10 times as
much—nearly 400%.

Is there anything that Intel can do to tame this roller coaster
ride? It can try to change its cost structure by reducing its

reliance on fixed costs. But to do this, it would have to rely
more heavily on outside suppliers rather than producing its
own chips. Intel is probably
reluctant to make this change
because it would lose some of
its control over product
quality.

*Watch the Whole Foods
video in WileyPLUS to learn
more about the use of
cost-volume-profit analysis
in a changing business
environment.*

Source: Don Clark and Ben Worthen, "Intel's Net Plunges as Demand Dries Up,"
Wall Street Journal Online (January 16, 2009); and Don Clark, "Intel Earnings
Set High Bar," *Wall Street Journal Online* (April 13, 2010).

✔ **The Navigator**

Preview of **Chapter 6**

As the Feature Story about Intel suggests, the relationship between a company's fixed and variable costs
can have a huge impact on its profitability. In particular, the trend toward cost structures dominated by
fixed costs has significantly increased the volatility of many companies' net income. The purpose of this
chapter is to demonstrate additional uses of cost-volume-profit analysis in making sound business decisions.

The content and organization of this chapter are as follows.

COST-VOLUME-PROFIT ANALYSIS: ADDITIONAL ISSUES		
Cost-Volume-Profit (CVP) Review	**Sales Mix**	**Cost Structure and Operating Leverage**
• Basic concepts • Basic computations • CVP and changes in the business environment	• Break-even sales in units • Break-even sales in dollars • Sales mix with limited resources	• Effect on contribution margin ratio • Effect on break-even point • Effect on margin of safety ratio • Operating leverage

✔ **The Navigator**

Cost-Volume-Profit (CVP) Review

As indicated in Chapter 5, cost-volume-profit (CVP) analysis is the study of the effects of changes in costs and volume on a company's profit. CVP analysis is important to profit planning. It is also a critical factor in determining product mix, maximizing use of production facilities, and setting selling prices.

Basic Concepts

LEARNING OBJECTIVE   1

Describe the essential features of a cost-volume-profit income statement.

Because CVP is so important for decision-making, management often wants this information reported in a CVP income statement format for internal use. The CVP income statement classifies costs as *variable* or *fixed* and computes a contribution margin. **Contribution margin** is the amount of revenue remaining after deducting variable costs. It is often stated both as a total amount and on a per unit basis.

Illustration 6-1 presents the CVP income statement for Vargo Video (which was shown in Illustration 5-12, on page 207). Note that Vargo's sales included 1,600 camcorders at $500 per unit.

Illustration 6-1
Basic CVP income statement

Vargo Video Company
CVP Income Statement
For the Month Ended June 30, 2014

	Total	Per Unit
Sales (1,600 camcorders)	$ 800,000	$ 500
Variable costs	480,000	300
Contribution margin	**320,000**	**$200**
Fixed costs	200,000	
Net income	**$120,000**	

Companies often prepare detailed CVP income statements. The CVP income statement in Illustration 6-2 uses the same base information as that presented in Illustration 6-1 but provides more detailed information (using assumed data) about the composition of expenses.

Illustration 6-2
Detailed CVP income statement

Vargo Video Company
CVP Income Statement
For the Month Ended June 30, 2014

		Total	Per Unit
Sales		$ 800,000	$ 500
Variable expenses			
Cost of goods sold	$400,000		
Selling expenses	60,000		
Administrative expenses	20,000		
Total variable expenses		480,000	300
Contribution margin		**320,000**	**$200**
Fixed expenses			
Cost of goods sold	120,000		
Selling expenses	40,000		
Administrative expenses	40,000		
Total fixed expenses		200,000	
Net income		**$120,000**	

Helpful Hint
The appendix to this chapter provides additional discussion of income statements used for decision-making.

In the applications of CVP analysis that follow, we assume that the term "cost" includes all costs and expenses related to production and sale of the product. That is, **cost includes manufacturing costs plus selling and administrative expenses.**

> ## DO IT!

CVP Income Statement

Garner Inc. sold 20,000 units and recorded sales of $800,000 for the first quarter of 2014. In making the sales, the company incurred the following costs and expenses.

	Variable	Fixed
Cost of goods sold	$250,000	$110,000
Selling expenses	100,000	25,000
Administrative expenses	82,000	73,000

(a) Prepare a CVP income statement for the quarter ended March 31, 2014.

(b) Compute the contribution margin per unit.

(c) Compute the contribution margin ratio.

Solution

Action Plan

✔ Use the CVP income statement format.

✔ Use the formula for contribution margin per unit.

✔ Use the formula for the contribution margin ratio.

(a)

Garner Inc.
Income Statement
For the Quarter Ended March 31, 2014

Sales (20,000 units)		$800,000
Variable expenses		
Cost of goods sold	$250,000	
Selling expenses	100,000	
Administrative expenses	82,000	
Total variable expenses		432,000
Contribution margin		368,000
Fixed expenses		
Cost of goods sold	110,000	
Selling expenses	25,000	
Administrative expenses	73,000	
Total fixed expenses		208,000
Net income		$160,000

(b) Contribution margin per unit:
   $368,000 ÷ 20,000 units = $18.40 per unit.

(c) Contribution margin ratio:
   $368,000 ÷ $800,000 = 46% (or $18.40 ÷ $40 = 46%).

Related exercise material: **BE6-1, BE6-2, and** DO IT! **6-1.**

✔ **The Navigator**

Basic Computations

Before we introduce additional issues of CVP analysis, let's review some of the basic concepts that you learned in Chapter 5, specifically break-even analysis, target net income, and margin of safety.

LEARNING OBJECTIVE **2**

Apply basic CVP concepts.

BREAK-EVEN ANALYSIS

Vargo Video's CVP income statement (Illustration 6-2) shows that total contribution margin (sales minus variable expenses) is $320,000, and the company's contribution margin per unit is $200. Recall that contribution margin can also be expressed in the form of the **contribution margin ratio** (contribution margin divided by sales), which in the case of Vargo is 40% ($200 ÷ $500).

Illustration 6-3 demonstrates how to compute Vargo's break-even point in units (using contribution margin per unit).

Illustration 6-3
Break-even point in units

Fixed Costs	÷	Contribution Margin per Unit	=	Break-Even Point in Units
$200,000	÷	$200	=	1,000 units

Illustration 6-4 shows the computation for the break-even point in dollars (using contribution margin ratio).

Illustration 6-4
Break-even point in dollars

Fixed Costs	÷	Contribution Margin Ratio	=	Break-Even Point in Dollars
$200,000	÷	.40	=	$500,000

When a company is in its early stages of operation, its primary goal is to break even. Failure to break even will lead eventually to financial failure.

TARGET NET INCOME

Once a company achieves break-even, it then sets a sales goal that will generate a target net income. For example, assume that Vargo's management has a target net income of $250,000. Illustration 6-5 shows the required sales in units to achieve its target net income.

Illustration 6-5
Target net income in units

(Fixed Costs + Target Net Income)	÷	Contribution Margin per Unit	=	Required Sales in Units
($200,000 + $250,000)	÷	$200	=	2,250 units

Illustration 6-6 uses the contribution margin ratio to compute the required sales in dollars.

Illustration 6-6
Target net income in dollars

(Fixed Costs + Target Net Income)	÷	Contribution Margin Ratio	=	Required Sales in Dollars
($200,000 + $250,000)	÷	.40	=	$1,125,000

In order to achieve net income of $250,000, Vargo has to sell 2,250 camcorders, for a total price of $1,125,000.

MARGIN OF SAFETY

Another measure managers use to assess profitability is the margin of safety. The **margin of safety** tells us **how far sales can drop** before the company will be operating at a loss. Managers like to have a sense of how much cushion they have between their current situation and operating at a loss. This can be expressed in dollars or as a ratio. In Illustration 6-2, for example, Vargo reported sales of $800,000. At that sales level, its margin of safety in dollars and as a ratio are as follows.

Illustration 6-7
Margin of safety in dollars

Actual (Expected) Sales	−	Break-Even Sales	=	Margin of Safety in Dollars
$800,000	−	$500,000	=	$300,000

As shown in Illustration 6-8, Vargo's sales could drop by $300,000, or 37.5%, before the company would operate at a loss.

Illustration 6-8
Margin of safety ratio

Margin of Safety in Dollars	÷	Actual (Expected) Sales	=	Margin of Safety Ratio
$300,000	÷	$800,000	=	37.5%

CVP and Changes in the Business Environment

To better understand how CVP analysis works, let's look at three independent situations that might occur at Vargo Video. Each case uses the original camcorder sales and cost data, which were:

Illustration 6-9
Original camcorder sales
and cost data

Unit selling price	$500
Unit variable cost	$300
Total fixed costs	$200,000
Break-even sales	$500,000 or 1,000 units

CASE I

A competitor is offering a 10% discount on the selling price of its camcorders. Management must decide whether to offer a similar discount.

Question: What effect will a 10% discount on selling price have on the break-even point for camcorders?

Answer: A 10% discount on selling price reduces the selling price per unit to $450 [$500 − ($500 × 10%)]. Variable costs per unit remain unchanged at $300. Thus, the contribution margin per unit is $150. Assuming no change in fixed costs, break-even sales are 1,333 units, computed as follows.

Illustration 6-10
Computation of break-even
sales in units

Fixed Costs	÷	Contribution Margin per Unit	=	Break-Even Sales
$200,000	÷	$150	=	1,333 units (rounded)

For Vargo Video, this change requires monthly sales to increase by 333 units, or 33⅓%, in order to break even. In reaching a conclusion about offering a 10% discount to customers, management must determine how likely it is to achieve the increased sales. Also, management should estimate the possible loss of sales if the competitor's discount price is not matched.

CASE II

To meet the threat of foreign competition, management invests in new robotic equipment that will lower the amount of direct labor required to make camcorders. The company estimates that total fixed costs will increase 30% and that variable cost per unit will decrease 30%.

Question: What effect will the new equipment have on the sales volume required to break even?

Answer: Total fixed costs become $260,000 [$200,000 + (30% × $200,000)]. The variable cost per unit becomes $210 [$300 − (30% × $300)]. The new break-even point is approximately 897 units, computed as shown on the next page.

Illustration 6-11
Computation of break-even sales in units

Fixed Costs	÷	Contribution Margin per Unit	=	Break-Even Sales
$260,000	÷	($500 − $210)	=	897 units (rounded)

These changes appear to be advantageous for Vargo Video. The break-even point is reduced by approximately 10%, or 100 units.

CASE III

Vargo's principal supplier of raw materials has just announced a price increase. The higher cost is expected to increase the variable cost of camcorders by $25 per unit. Management decides to hold the line on the selling price of the camcorders. It plans a cost-cutting program that will save $17,500 in fixed costs per month. Vargo is currently realizing monthly net income of $80,000 on sales of 1,400 camcorders.

Question: What increase in units sold will be needed to maintain the same level of net income?

Answer: The variable cost per unit increases to $325 ($300 + $25). Fixed costs are reduced to $182,500 ($200,000 − $17,500). Because of the change in variable cost, the contribution margin per unit becomes $175 ($500 − $325). The required number of units sold to achieve the target net income is computed as follows.

Illustration 6-12
Computation of required sales

$\left(\begin{array}{c}\text{Fixed Costs + Target} \\ \text{Net Income}\end{array}\right)$	÷	Contribution Margin per Unit	=	Required Sales in Units
($182,500 + $80,000)	÷	$175	=	1,500

To achieve the required sales, Vargo Video will have to sell 1,500 camcorders, an increase of 100 units. If this does not seem to be a reasonable expectation, management will either have to make further cost reductions or accept less net income if the selling price remains unchanged.

We hope that the concepts reviewed in this section are now familiar to you. We are now ready to examine additional ways that companies use CVP analysis to assess profitability and to help in making effective business decisions.

MANAGEMENT INSIGHT

Don't Just Look—Buy Something

When analyzing an Internet business, analysts closely watch the so-called "conversion rate." This rate is calculated by dividing the number of people who actually take action at an Internet site (buy something) by the total number of people who visit the site. Average conversion rates are from 3% to 5%. A rate below 2% is poor, while a rate above 10% is great.

Conversion rates have an obvious effect on the break-even point. Suppose you spend $10,000 on your site, and you attract 5,000 visitors. If you get a 2% conversion rate (100 purchases), your site costs $100 per purchase ($10,000 ÷ 100). A 4% conversion rate gets you down to a cost of $50 per transaction, and an 8% conversion rate gets you down to $25. Studies show that conversion rates increase if the site has an easy-to-use interface, fast-performing screens, a convenient ordering process, and advertising that is both clever and clear.

Source: J. William Gurley, "The One Internet Metric That Really Counts" *Fortune* (March 6, 2000), p. 392.

? Besides increasing their conversion rates, what steps can online merchants use to lower their break-even points? (See page 290.)

DECISION TOOLKIT 🧰

DECISION CHECKPOINTS	INFO NEEDED FOR DECISION	TOOL TO USE FOR DECISION	HOW TO EVALUATE RESULTS
How can a company use CVP analysis to improve profitability?	Data on what effect a price change, a fixed-cost change, or a trade-off between fixed and variable costs would have on volume and costs	Measurement of income at new volume levels	If profitability increases under proposed change, adopt change.

> ## DO IT!

CVP Analysis

Krisanne Company reports the following operating results for the month of June.

Krisanne Company
CVP Income Statement
For the Month Ended June 30, 2014

	Total	Per Unit
Sales (5,000 units)	$300,000	$60
Variable costs	180,000	36
Contribution margin	120,000	$24
Fixed expenses	100,000	
Net income	$ 20,000	

To increase net income, management is considering reducing the selling price by 10%, with no changes to unit variable costs or fixed costs. Management is confident that this change will increase unit sales by 25%.

Using the contribution margin technique, compute the break-even point in units and dollars and margin of safety in dollars (a) assuming no changes to sales price or costs, and (b) assuming changes to sales price and volume as described above. (c) Comment on your findings.

Solution

Action Plan

✔ Apply the formula for the break-even point in units.

✔ Apply the formula for the break-even point in dollars.

✔ Apply the formula for the margin of safety in dollars.

(a) Assuming no changes to sales price or costs:
   Break-even point in units = 4,167 units (rounded) ($100,000 ÷ $24).
   Break-even point in sales dollars = $250,000 ($100,000 ÷ .40[a]).
   Margin of safety in dollars = $50,000 ($300,000 − $250,000).
   [a]$24 ÷ $60.

(b) Assuming changes to sales price and volume:
   Break-even point in units = 5,556 units (rounded) ($100,000 ÷ $18[b]).
   Break-even point in sales dollars = $300,000 ($100,000 ÷ ($18 ÷ $54)).
   Margin of safety in dollars = $37,500 ($337,500[c] − $300,000).
   [b]$60 − (.10 × $60) − 36 = $18.
   [c]5,000 + (.25 × 5,000) = 6,250 units, 6,250 units × $54 = $337,500.

(c) The increase in the break-even point and the decrease in the margin of safety indicate that management should not implement the proposed change. The increase in sales volume will result in contribution margin of $112,500 (6,250 × $18), which is $7,500 less than the current amount.

Related exercise material: **BE6-3, BE6-4, BE6-5, BE6-6, E6-1, E6-2, E6-3, E6-4, E6-5, and DO IT! 6-2.**

✔ **The Navigator**

Sales Mix

LEARNING OBJECTIVE 3

Explain the term sales mix and its effects on break-even sales.

To this point, our discussion of CVP analysis has assumed that a company sells only one product. However, most companies sell multiple products. When a company sells many products, it is important that management understand its sales mix.

Sales mix is the relative percentage in which a company sells its multiple products. For example, if 80% of Hewlett Packard's unit sales are printers and the other 20% are PCs, its sales mix is 80% printers to 20% PCs.

Sales mix is important to managers because different products often have substantially different contribution margins. For example, Ford's SUVs and F150 pickup trucks have higher contribution margins compared to its economy cars. Similarly, first-class tickets sold by United Airlines provide substantially higher contribution margins than coach-class tickets. Intel's sales of computer chips for netbook computers have increased, but the contribution margin on these chips is lower than for notebook and desktop PCs.

Break-Even Sales in Units

Companies can compute break-even sales for a mix of two or more products by determining the **weighted-average unit contribution margin of all the products**. To illustrate, assume that Vargo Video sells not only camcorders but high-definition TVs as well. Vargo sells its two products in the following amounts: 1,500 camcorders and 500 TVs. The sales mix, expressed as a percentage of the 2,000 total units sold, is as follows.

Illustration 6-13
Sales mix as a function of units sold

Camcorders	TVs
1,500 units ÷ 2,000 units = 75%	500 units ÷ 2,000 units = 25%

That is, 75% of the 2,000 units sold are camcorders, and 25% of the 2,000 units sold are TVs.

Illustration 6-14 shows additional information related to Vargo Video. The unit contribution margin for camcorders is $200, and for TVs it is $500. Vargo's fixed costs total $275,000.

Illustration 6-14
Per unit data—sales mix

Unit Data	Camcorders	TVs
Selling price	$500	$1,000
Variable costs	300	500
Contribution margin	$200	$500
Sales mix—units	**75%**	**25%**
Fixed costs = $275,000		

To compute break-even for Vargo, we must determine the weighted-average unit contribution margin for the two products. We use the ***weighted-average*** contribution margin because Vargo sells three times as many camcorders as TVs. As a result, in determining an average unit contribution margin, three times as much weight should be placed on the contribution margin of the camcorders as on the TVs. Therefore, the camcorders must be counted three times for every TV sold. The weighted-average contribution margin for a sales mix of 75% camcorders and 25% TVs is $275, which is computed as follows.

	Camcorders				TVs			
$\left(\begin{array}{c}\text{Unit}\\\text{Contribution}\\\text{Margin}\end{array}\right.$	$\times$	$\left.\begin{array}{c}\text{Sales Mix}\\\text{Percentage}\end{array}\right)$	$+$	$\left(\begin{array}{c}\text{Unit}\\\text{Contribution}\\\text{Margin}\end{array}\right.$	$\times$	$\left.\begin{array}{c}\text{Sales Mix}\\\text{Percentage}\end{array}\right)$	$=$	$\begin{array}{c}\text{Weighted-Average}\\\text{Unit Contribution}\\\text{Margin}\end{array}$
($200	$\times$	.75)	$+$	($500	$\times$	.25)	$=$	$275

Illustration 6-15
Weighted-average unit contribution margin

Similar to our calculation in the single-product setting, we can compute the break-even point in units by dividing the fixed costs by the weighted-average unit contribution margin. Then, we use the weighted-average unit contribution margin of $275 to compute the break-even point in unit sales. The computation of break-even sales in units for Vargo Video, assuming $275,000 of fixed costs, is as follows.

Illustration 6-16
Break-even point in units

Fixed Costs	$\div$	Weighted-Average Unit Contribution Margin	$=$	Break-Even Point in Units
$275,000	$\div$	$275	$=$	1,000 units

Illustration 6-16 shows the break-even point for Vargo Video is 1,000 units—camcorders and TVs combined. Management needs to know how many of these 1,000 units are camcorders and how many are TVs. Applying the sales mix percentages that we computed previously of 75% for camcorders and 25% for TVs, these 1,000 units would be comprised of 750 camcorders (.75 × 1,000 units) and 250 TVs (.25 × 1,000). This can be verified by the computations in Illustration 6-17, which shows that the total contribution margin is $275,000 when 1,000 units are sold, which equals the fixed costs of $275,000.

Illustration 6-17
Break-even proof—sales units

Product	Unit Sales	$\times$	Unit Contribution Margin	$=$	Total Contribution Margin
Camcorders	750	$\times$	$200	$=$	$ 150,000
TVs	250	$\times$	500	$=$	125,000
	1,000				**$275,000**

Management should continually review the company's sales mix. At any level of units sold, **net income will be greater if higher contribution margin units are sold, rather than lower contribution margin units**. For Vargo Video, the TVs produce the higher contribution margin. Consequently, if Vargo sells 300 TVs and 700 camcorders, net income would be higher than in the current sales mix even though total units sold are the same.

An analysis of these relationships shows that a shift from low-margin sales to high-margin sales may increase net income even though there is a decline in total units sold. Likewise, a shift from high- to low-margin sales may result in a decrease in net income even though there is an increase in total units sold.

DECISION TOOLKIT

DECISION CHECKPOINTS	INFO NEEDED FOR DECISION	TOOL TO USE FOR DECISION	HOW TO EVALUATE RESULTS
How many units of product A and product B do we need to sell to break even?	Fixed costs, weighted-average unit contribution margin, sales mix	$\text{Break-even point in units} = \dfrac{\text{Fixed costs}}{\text{Weighted-average unit contribution margin}}$	To determine number of units of product A and B, allocate total units based on sales mix.

Break-Even Sales in Dollars

The calculation of the break-even point presented for Vargo Video in the previous section works well if a company has only a *small number* of products. In contrast, consider 3M, the maker of Post-it Notes, which has more than 30,000 products. In order to calculate the break-even point for 3M using a weighted-average unit contribution margin, we would need to calculate 30,000 different unit contribution margins. That is not realistic.

Therefore, for a company with many products, we calculate the break-even point in terms of sales dollars (rather than units sold), using sales information for divisions or product lines (rather than individual products). This requires that we compute sales mix as a percentage of total dollars sales (rather than units sold) and we compute the contribution margin ratio (rather than contribution margin per unit).

To illustrate, suppose that Kale Garden Supply Company has two divisions—Indoor Plants and Outdoor Plants. Each division has hundreds of different types of plants and plant-care products. Illustration 6-18 provides information necessary for determining the sales mix percentages for the two divisions of Kale Garden Supply.

Illustration 6-18
Cost-volume-profit data for Kale Garden Supply

	Indoor Plant Division	Outdoor Plant Division	Total
Sales	$ 200,000	$ 800,000	$1,000,000
Variable costs	120,000	560,000	680,000
Contribution margin	$ 80,000	$ 240,000	$ 320,000
Sales mix percentage (Division sales ÷ Total sales)	$\frac{\$200{,}000}{\$1{,}000{,}000} = .20$	$\frac{\$800{,}000}{\$1{,}000{,}000} = .80$	

Illustration 6-19
Contribution margin ratio for each division

As shown in Illustration 6-19, the contribution margin ratio for the combined company is 32%, which is computed by dividing the total contribution margin by total sales.

	Indoor Plant Division	Outdoor Plant Division	Total
Contribution margin ratio (Contribution margin ÷ Sales)	$\frac{\$80{,}000}{\$200{,}000} = .40$	$\frac{\$240{,}000}{\$800{,}000} = .30$	$\frac{\$320{,}000}{\$1{,}000{,}000} = .32$

It is useful to note that the contribution margin ratio of 32% is a weighted average of the individual contribution margin ratios of the two divisions (40% and 30%). To illustrate, in Illustration 6-20 we multiply each division's contribution margin ratio by its sales mix percentage, based on dollar sales, and then sum these amounts. As shown later, the calculation in Illustration 6-20 is useful because it enables us to determine how the break-even point changes when the sales mix changes.

Illustration 6-20
Calculation of weighted-average contribution margin

Indoor Plant Division		Outdoor Plant Division		Weighted-Average Contribution Margin Ratio
(Contribution Margin Ratio	× Sales Mix Percentage)	+ (Contribution Margin Ratio	× Sales Mix Percentage)	= Weighted-Average Contribution Margin Ratio
(.40	× .20)	+ (.30	× .80)	= .32

Kale Garden Supply's break-even point in dollars is then computed by dividing its fixed costs of $300,000 by the weighted-average contribution margin ratio of 32%, as shown in Illustration 6-21.

Fixed Costs	÷	Weighted-Average Contribution Margin Ratio	=	Break-Even Point in Dollars
$300,000	÷	.32	=	$937,500

Illustration 6-21
Calculation of break-even point in dollars

The break-even point is based on the sales mix of 20% to 80%. We can determine the amount of sales contributed by each division by multiplying the sales mix percentage of each division by the total sales figure. Of the company's total break-even sales of $937,500, a total of $187,500 (.20 × $937,500) will come from the Indoor Plant Division, and $750,000 (.80 × $937,500) will come from the Outdoor Plant Division.

What would be the impact on the break-even point if a higher percentage of Kale Garden Supply's sales were to come from the Indoor Plant Division? Because the Indoor Plant Division enjoys a higher contribution margin ratio, this change in the sales mix would result in a higher weighted-average contribution margin ratio, and consequently a lower break-even point in dollars. For example, if the sales mix changes to 50% for the Indoor Plant Division and 50% for the Outdoor Plant Division, the weighted-average contribution margin ratio would be 35% [(.40 × .50) + (.30 × .50)]. The new, lower, break-even point is $857,143 ($300,000 ÷ .35). The opposite would occur if a higher percentage of sales were expected from the Outdoor Plant Division. As you can see, the information provided using CVP analysis can help managers better understand the impact of sales mix on profitability.

SERVICE COMPANY INSIGHT

Healthy for You, and Great for the Bottom Line

Zoom Kitchen, a chain of four restaurants in the Chicago area, is known for serving sizable portions of meat and potatoes. But the company's management is quite pleased with the fact that during the past four years, salad sales have increased from 18% of its sales mix to 40%. Why are they pleased? Because the contribution margin on salads is much higher than on meat. The restaurant made a conscious effort to encourage people to buy more salads by offering an interesting assortment of salad ingredients including jicama, beets, marinated mushrooms, grilled tuna, and carved turkey. Management has to be very sensitive to contribution margin—it costs about $600,000 to open up a new Zoom Kitchen restaurant.

Source: Amy Zuber, "Salad Sales 'Zoom' at Meat-and-Potatoes Specialist," *Nation's Restaurant News* (November 12, 2001), p. 26.

? Why do you suppose restaurants are so eager to sell beverages and desserts? (See page 290.)

DECISION TOOLKIT

DECISION CHECKPOINTS	INFO NEEDED FOR DECISION	TOOL TO USE FOR DECISION	HOW TO EVALUATE RESULTS
How many dollars of sales are required from each division in order to break even?	Fixed costs, weighted-average contribution margin ratio, sales mix	$$\text{Break-even point in dollars} = \frac{\text{Fixed costs}}{\text{Weighted-average contribution margin ratio}}$$	To determine the sales dollars required from each division, allocate the total break-even sales using the sales mix.

> **DO IT!**

Sales Mix Break-Even

Manzeck Bicycles International produces and sells three different types of mountain bikes. Information regarding the three models is shown below.

	Pro	Intermediate	Standard	Total
Units sold	5,000	10,000	25,000	40,000
Selling price	$800	$500	$350	
Variable costs	$500	$300	$250	

The company's total fixed costs to produce the bicycles are $7,500,000.

(a) Determine the sales mix as a function of units sold for the three products.

(b) Determine the weighted-average unit contribution margin.

(c) Determine the total number of units that the company must produce to break even.

(d) Determine the number of units of each model that the company must produce to break even.

Action Plan

✔ The sales mix is the relative percentage of each product sold in units.

✔ The weighted-average unit contribution margin is the sum of the per unit contribution margins multiplied by the respective sales mix percentage.

✔ Determine the break-even point in units by dividing the fixed costs by the weighted-average unit contribution margin.

✔ Determine the number of units of each model to produce by multiplying the total break-even units by the respective sales mix percentage for each product.

Solution

(a) The sales mix percentages as a function of units sold are:

Pro	Intermediate	Standard
5,000/40,000 = 12.5%	10,000/40,000 = 25%	25,000/40,000 = 62.5%

(b) The weighted-average unit contribution margin is:

$$[.125 \times (\$800 - \$500)] + [.25 \times (\$500 - \$300)] + [.625 \times (\$350 - \$250)] = \$150$$

(c) The break-even point in units is:

$$\$7,500,000 \div \$150 = 50,000 \text{ units}$$

(d) The break-even units to produce for each product are:

Pro:	50,000 units × 12.5% =	6,250 units
Intermediate:	50,000 units × 25% =	12,500 units
Standard:	50,000 units × 62.5% =	31,250 units
		50,000 units

Related exercise material: **BE6-7, BE6-8, BE6-9, BE6-10, E6-6, E6-7, E6-8, E6-9, E6-10, and** **DO IT!** **6-3.**

✔ **The Navigator**

Determining Sales Mix with Limited Resources

LEARNING OBJECTIVE **4**

Determine sales mix when a company has limited resources.

In the previous discussion, we assumed a certain sales mix and then determined the break-even point given that sales mix. We now discuss how limited resources influence the sales-mix decision.

Everyone's resources are limited. The limited resource may be floor space in a retail department store, or raw materials, direct labor hours, or machine capacity in a manufacturing company. When a company has limited resources, management must decide which products to make and sell in order to maximize net income.

To illustrate, recall that Vargo manufactures camcorders and TVs. The limiting resource is machine capacity, which is 3,600 hours per month. Relevant data consist of the following.

Illustration 6-22
Contribution margin and machine hours

	Camcorders	TVs
Contribution margin per unit	$200	$500
Machine hours required per unit	.2	.625

The TVs may appear to be more profitable since they have a higher contribution margin per unit ($500) than the camcorders ($200). However, the camcorders take fewer machine hours to produce than the TVs. Therefore, it is necessary to find the **contribution margin per unit of limited resource**—in this case, contribution margin per machine hour. This is obtained by dividing the contribution margin per unit of each product by the number of units of the limited resource required for each product, as shown in Illustration 6-23.

Helpful Hint
CM alone is not enough to make this decision. The key factor is CM per unit of limited resource.

	Camcorders	TVs
Contribution margin per unit (a)	$200	$500
Machine hours required (b)	0.2	0.625
Contribution margin per unit of limited resource [(a) ÷ (b)]	**$1,000**	**$800**

Illustration 6-23
Contribution margin per unit of limited resource

The computation shows that the camcorders have a higher contribution margin per unit of limited resource. This would suggest that, given sufficient demand for camcorders, Vargo should shift the sales mix to produce more camcorders or increase machine capacity.

As indicated in Illustration 6-23, the constraint for the production of the TVs is the larger number of machine hours needed to produce them. In addressing this problem, we have taken the limited number of machine hours as a given and have attempted to maximize the contribution margin given the constraint. One question that Vargo should ask, however, is whether this constraint can be reduced or eliminated. If Vargo is able to increase machine capacity from 3,600 hours to 4,200 hours, the additional 600 hours could be used to produce either the camcorders or TVs. The total contribution margin under each alternative is found by multiplying the machine hours by the contribution margin per unit of limited resource, as shown below

	Camcorders	TVs
Machine hours (a)	600	600
Contribution margin per unit of limited resource (b)	$ 1,000	$ 800
Contribution margin [(a) × (b)]	**$600,000**	**$480,000**

Illustration 6-24
Incremental analysis—computation of total contribution margin

From this analysis, we can see that to maximize net income, all of the increased capacity should be used to make and sell the camcorders.

Vargo's manufacturing constraint might be due to a bottleneck in production or to poorly trained machine operators. In addition to finding ways to solve those problems, the company should consider other possible solutions, such as outsourcing part of the production, acquiring additional new equipment (discussed in Chapter 12), or striving to eliminate any non–value-added activities (see Chapter 4). As discussed in Chapter 1, this approach to evaluating constraints is referred to as the theory of constraints. The **theory of constraints** is a specific approach used to identify and manage constraints in order to achieve the company's goals. According to this theory, a company must continually identify its constraints and find ways to reduce or eliminate them, where appropriate.

MANAGEMENT INSIGHT

Something Smells

When fragrance sales went flat, retailers turned up the heat on fragrance manufacturers. They reduced the amount of floor space devoted to fragrances, leaving fragrance manufacturers fighting each other for the smaller space. The retailer doesn't just choose the fragrance with the highest contribution margin. Instead, it chooses the fragrance with the highest contribution margin per square foot for a given period of time. In this game, a product with a lower contribution margin, but a higher turnover, could well be the winner.

? What is the limited resource for a retailer, and what implications does this have for sales mix? (See page 290.)

DECISION TOOLKIT

DECISION CHECKPOINTS	INFO NEEDED FOR DECISION	TOOL TO USE FOR DECISION	HOW TO EVALUATE RESULTS
How many units of product A and B should we produce in light of a limited resource?	Contribution margin per unit, limited resource required per unit	$\dfrac{\text{Contribution margin per unit of limited resource}}{} = \dfrac{\text{Contribution margin per unit}}{\text{Limited resource per unit}}$	Any additional capacity of limited resource should be applied toward the product with higher contribution margin per unit of limited resource.

> DO IT!

Sales Mix with Limited Resources

Carolina Corporation manufactures and sells three different types of high-quality sealed ball bearings. The bearings vary in terms of their quality specifications—primarily with respect to their smoothness and roundness. They are referred to as Fine, Extra-Fine, and Super-Fine bearings. Machine time is limited. More machine time is required to manufacture the Extra-Fine and Super-Fine bearings. Additional information is provided below.

	Product		
	Fine	**Extra-Fine**	**Super-Fine**
Selling price	$6.00	$10.00	$16.00
Variable costs and expenses	4.00	6.50	11.00
Contribution margin	$2.00	$ 3.50	$ 5.00
Machine hours required	0.02	0.04	0.08

(a) Ignoring the machine time constraint, what strategy would appear optimal?

(b) What is the contribution margin per unit of limited resource for each type of bearing?

(c) If additional machine time could be obtained, how should the additional capacity be used?

Solution

Action Plan

✔ Calculate the contribution margin per unit of limited resource for each product.

(a) The Super-Fine bearings have the highest contribution margin per unit. Thus, ignoring any manufacturing constraints, it would appear that the company should shift toward production of more Super-Fine units.

Action Plan (cont'd.)	(b) The contribution margin per unit of limited resource (machine hours) is calculated as:

Action Plan (cont'd.)

✔ Apply the formula for the contribution margin per unit of limited resource.

✔ To maximize net income, shift sales mix to the product with the highest contribution margin per unit of limited resource.

(b) The contribution margin per unit of limited resource (machine hours) is calculated as:

	Fine	**Extra-Fine**	**Super-Fine**
$\dfrac{\text{Contribution margin per unit}}{\text{Limited resource consumed per unit}}$	$\dfrac{\$2}{.02} = \$100$	$\dfrac{\$3.5}{.04} = \$87.50$	$\dfrac{\$5}{.08} = \$62.50$

(c) The Fine bearings have the highest contribution margin per unit of limited resource even though they have the lowest contribution margin per unit. Given the resource constraint, any additional capacity should be used to make Fine bearings.

Related exercise material: **BE6-11, E6-11, E6-12, E6-13, and** DO IT! **6-4.**

✔ **The Navigator**

Cost Structure and Operating Leverage

Cost structure refers to the relative proportion of fixed versus variable costs that a company incurs. Cost structure can have a significant effect on profitability. For example, computer equipment manufacturer Cisco Systems has substantially reduced its fixed costs by choosing to outsource much of its production. By minimizing its fixed costs, Cisco is now less susceptible to economic swings. However, as the following discussion shows, its reduced reliance on fixed costs has also reduced its ability to experience the incredible profitability that it used to have during economic booms.

> **LEARNING OBJECTIVE   5**
>
> **Understand how operating leverage affects profitability.**

The choice of cost structure should be carefully considered. There are many ways that companies can influence their cost structure. For example, by acquiring sophisticated robotic equipment, many companies have reduced their use of manual labor. Similarly, some brokerage firms, such as E*Trade, have reduced their reliance on human brokers and have instead invested heavily in computers and online technology. In so doing, they have increased their reliance on fixed costs (through depreciation on the robotic equipment or computer equipment) and reduced their reliance on variable costs (the variable employee labor cost). Alternatively, some companies have reduced their fixed costs and increased their variable costs by outsourcing their production. Nike, for example, does very little manufacturing but instead outsources the manufacture of nearly all of its shoes. It has consequently converted many of its fixed costs into variable costs and therefore changed its cost structure.

Consider the following example of Vargo Video and one of its competitors, New Wave Company. Both make camcorders. Vargo Video uses a traditional, labor-intensive manufacturing process. New Wave Company has invested in a completely automated system. The factory employees are involved only in setting up, adjusting, and maintaining the machinery. Illustration 6-25 shows CVP income statements for each company.

	Vargo Video	**New Wave Company**
Sales	$800,000	$800,000
Variable costs	480,000	160,000
Contribution margin	320,000	640,000
Fixed costs	200,000	520,000
Net income	$120,000	$120,000

Illustration 6-25
CVP income statements for two companies

Both companies have the same sales and the same net income. However, because of the differences in their cost structures, they differ greatly in the risks and rewards related to increasing or decreasing sales. Let's evaluate the impact of cost structure on the profitability of the two companies.

Effect on Contribution Margin Ratio

First let's look at the contribution margin ratio. Illustration 6-26 shows the computation of the contribution margin ratio for each company.

Illustration 6-26
Contribution margin ratio for two companies

	Contribution Margin	÷	Sales	=	Contribution Margin Ratio
Vargo Video	$320,000	÷	$800,000	=	.40
New Wave	$640,000	÷	$800,000	=	.80

Because of its lower variable costs, New Wave has a contribution margin ratio of 80% versus only 40% for Vargo. That means that with every dollar of sales, New Wave generates 80 cents of contribution margin (and thus an 80-cent increase in net income), versus only 40 cents for Vargo. However, it also means that for every dollar that sales decline, New Wave loses 80 cents in net income, whereas Vargo will lose only 40 cents. New Wave's cost structure, which relies more heavily on fixed costs, makes it more sensitive to changes in sales revenue.

Effect on Break-Even Point

The difference in cost structure also affects the break-even point. The break-even point for each company is calculated in Illustration 6-27.

Illustration 6-27
Computation of break-even point for two companies

	Fixed Costs	÷	Contribution Margin Ratio	=	Break-Even Point in Dollars
Vargo Video	$200,000	÷	.40	=	$500,000
New Wave	$520,000	÷	.80	=	$650,000

New Wave needs to generate $150,000 ($650,000 − $500,000) more in sales than Vargo before it breaks even. This makes New Wave riskier than Vargo because a company cannot survive for very long unless it at least breaks even.

Effect on Margin of Safety Ratio

We can also evaluate the relative impact that changes in sales would have on the two companies by computing the margin of safety ratio. Illustration 6-28 shows the computation of the **margin of safety ratio** for the two companies.

Illustration 6-28
Computation of margin of safety ratio for two companies

	(Actual Sales	−	Break-Even Sales)	÷	Actual Sales	=	Margin of Safety Ratio
Vargo Video	($800,000	−	$500,000)	÷	$800,000	=	.38
New Wave	($800,000	−	$650,000)	÷	$800,000	=	.19

The difference in the margin of safety ratio also reflects the difference in risk between the two companies. Vargo could sustain a 38% decline in sales before it would be operating at a loss. New Wave could sustain only a 19% decline in sales before it would be "in the red."

Operating Leverage

Operating leverage refers to the extent to which a company's net income reacts to a given change in sales. Companies that have higher fixed costs relative to variable costs have higher operating leverage. When a company's sales revenue is increasing, high operating leverage is a good thing because it means that profits will increase rapidly. But when sales are declining, too much operating leverage can have devastating consequences.

DEGREE OF OPERATING LEVERAGE

How can we compare operating leverage between two companies? The **degree of operating leverage** provides a measure of a company's earnings volatility and can be used to compare companies. Degree of operating leverage is computed by dividing contribution margin by net income. This formula is presented in Illustration 6-29 and applied to our two manufacturers of camcorders.

	Contribution Margin	÷	Net Income	=	Degree of Operating Leverage
Vargo Video	$320,000	÷	$120,000	=	2.67
New Wave	$640,000	÷	$120,000	=	5.33

Illustration 6-29
Computation of degree of operating leverage

New Wave's earnings would go up (or down) by about two times (5.33 ÷ 2.67 = 1.99) as much as Vargo's with an equal increase (or decrease) in sales. For example, suppose both companies experience a 10% decrease in sales. Vargo's net income will decrease by 26.7% (2.67 × 10%), while New Wave's will decrease by 53.3% (5.33 × 10%). Thus, New Wave's higher operating leverage exposes it to greater earnings volatility risk.

You should be careful not to conclude from this analysis that a cost structure that relies on higher fixed costs, and consequently has higher operating leverage, is necessarily bad. Some have suggested that Internet radio company Pandora has limited potential for growth in its profitability because it has very little operating leverage. When its revenues grow, its variable costs (fees it pays for the right to use music) grow proportionally. When used carefully, operating leverage can add considerably to a company's profitability. For example, computer equipment manufacturer Komag enjoyed a 66% increase in net income when its sales increased by only 8%. As one commentator noted, "Komag's fourth quarter illustrates the company's significant operating leverage; a small increase in sales leads to a big profit rise." However, as our illustration demonstrates, increased reliance on fixed costs increases a company's risk.

DECISION TOOLKIT

DECISION CHECKPOINTS	INFO NEEDED FOR DECISION	TOOL TO USE FOR DECISION	HOW TO EVALUATE RESULTS
How sensitive is the company's net income to changes in sales?	Contribution margin and net income	$$\text{Degree of operating leverage} = \frac{\text{Contribution margin}}{\text{Net income}}$$	Reports the change in net income that will occur with a given change in sales. A high degree of operating leverage means that the company's net income is very sensitive to changes in sales.

USING THE DECISION TOOLKIT

Rexfield Corp. is contemplating a huge investment in automated mass-spectrometers for its medical laboratory testing services. Its current process relies heavily on the expertise of a high number of lab technicians. The new equipment would employ a computer expert system that integrates much of the decision process and knowledge base that is used by a skilled lab technician.

Rex Field, the company's CEO, has requested that an analysis of projected results using the old technology versus the new technology be done for the coming year. The accounting department has prepared the following CVP income statements for use in your analysis.

	Old	New
Sales	$2,000,000	$2,000,000
Variable costs	1,400,000	600,000
Contribution margin	600,000	1,400,000
Fixed costs	400,000	1,200,000
Net income	$ 200,000	$ 200,000

Instructions

Use the information provided above to do the following.

(a) Compute the degree of operating leverage for the company under each scenario, and discuss your results.

(b) Compute the break-even point in dollars and margin of safety ratio for the company under each scenario, and discuss your results.

Solution

(a)

	Contribution Margin	÷	Net Income	=	Degree of Operating Leverage
Old	$600,000	÷	$200,000	=	3
New	$1,400,000	÷	$200,000	=	7

The degree of operating leverage measures the company's sensitivity to changes in sales. By switching to a cost structure dominated by fixed costs, the company would significantly increase its operating leverage. As a result, with a percentage change in sales, its percentage change in net income would be 2.33 times as much (7 ÷ 3) under the new structure as it would under the old.

(b) To compute the break-even point in sales dollars, we need first to compute the contribution margin ratio under each scenario. Under the old structure, the contribution margin ratio would be .30 ($600,000 ÷ $2,000,000), and under the new it would be .70 ($1,400,000 ÷ $2,000,000).

	Fixed Costs	÷	Contribution Margin Ratio	=	Break-Even Point in Dollars
Old	$400,000	÷	.30	=	$1,333,333
New	$1,200,000	÷	.70	=	$1,714,286

Because the company's fixed costs would be substantially higher under the new cost structure, its break-even point would increase significantly, from $1,333,333 to $1,714,286. A higher break-even point is riskier because it means that the company must generate higher sales to be profitable.

The margin of safety ratio tells how far sales can fall before the company is operating at a loss.

	$\left(\begin{array}{c}\text{Actual} \\ \text{Sales}\end{array}\right.$	$-$	$\left.\begin{array}{c}\text{Break-Even} \\ \text{Sales}\end{array}\right)$	$\div$	Actual Sales	$=$	Margin of Safety Ratio
Old	($2,000,000	$-$	$1,333,333)	$\div$	$2,000,000	$=$	.33
New	($2,000,000	$-$	$1,714,286)	$\div$	$2,000,000	$=$	.14

Under the old structure, sales could fall by 33% before the company would be operating at a loss. Under the new structure, sales could fall by only 14%.

✔ **The Navigator**

SUMMARY OF LEARNING OBJECTIVES

✔ **The Navigator**

1 Describe the essential features of a cost-volume-profit income statement. The CVP income statement classifies costs and expenses as variable or fixed and reports contribution margin in the body of the statement.

2 Apply basic CVP concepts. Contribution margin is the amount of revenue remaining after deducting variable costs. It can be expressed as a per unit amount or as a ratio. The break-even point in units is fixed costs divided by contribution margin per unit. The break-even point in dollars is fixed costs divided by the contribution margin ratio. These formulas can also be used to determine units or sales dollars needed to achieve target net income, simply by adding target net income to fixed costs before dividing by the contribution margin. Margin of safety indicates how much sales can decline before the company is operating at a loss. It can be expressed in dollar terms or as a percentage.

3 Explain the term sales mix and its effects on break-even sales. Sales mix is the relative proportion in which each product is sold when a company sells more than one product. For a company with a small number of products, break-even sales in units is determined by using the weighted-average unit contribution margin of all the products. If the company sells many different products, then calculating the break-even point using unit information is not practical. Instead, in a company with many products, break-even sales in dollars is calculated using the weighted-average contribution margin ratio.

4 Determine sales mix when a company has limited resources. When a company has limited resources, it is necessary to find the contribution margin per unit of limited resource. This amount is then multiplied by the units of limited resource to determine which product maximizes net income.

5 Understand how operating leverage affects profitability. Operating leverage refers to the degree to which a company's net income reacts to a change in sales. Operating leverage is determined by a company's relative use of fixed versus variable costs. Companies with high fixed costs relative to variable costs have high operating leverage. A company with high operating leverage will experience a sharp increase (decrease) in net income with a given increase (decrease) in sales. The degree of operating leverage can be measured by dividing contribution margin by net income.

DECISION TOOLKIT A SUMMARY

DECISION CHECKPOINTS	INFO NEEDED FOR DECISION	TOOL TO USE FOR DECISION	HOW TO EVALUATE RESULTS
How can a company use CVP analysis to improve profitability?	Data on what effect a price change, a fixed-cost change, or a trade-off between fixed and variable costs would have on volume and costs	Measurement of income at new volume levels	If profitability increases under proposed change, adopt change.
How many units of product A and product B do we need to sell to break even?	Fixed costs, weighted-average unit contribution margin, sales mix	$$\text{Break-even point in units} = \frac{\text{Fixed costs}}{\text{Weighted-average unit contribution margin}}$$	To determine number of units of product A and B, allocate total units based on sales mix.
How many dollars of sales are required from each division in order to break even?	Fixed costs, weighted-average contribution margin ratio, sales mix	$$\text{Break-even point in dollars} = \frac{\text{Fixed costs}}{\text{Weighted-average contribution margin ratio}}$$	To determine the sales dollars required from each division, allocate the total break-even sales using the sales mix.

DECISION CHECKPOINTS	INFO NEEDED FOR DECISION	TOOL TO USE FOR DECISION	HOW TO EVALUATE RESULTS
How many units of product A and B should we produce in light of a limited resource?	Contribution margin per unit, limited resource required per unit	$$\text{Contribution margin per unit of limited resource} = \frac{\text{Contribution margin per unit}}{\text{Limited resource per unit}}$$	Any additional capacity of limited resource should be applied toward the product with higher contribution margin per unit of limited resource.
How sensitive is the company's net income to changes in sales?	Contribution margin and net income	$$\text{Degree of operating leverage} = \frac{\text{Contribution margin}}{\text{Net income}}$$	Reports the change in net income that will occur with a given change in sales. A high degree of operating leverage means that the company's net income is very sensitive to changes in sales.

APPENDIX **6A**　ABSORPTION COSTING VERSUS VARIABLE COSTING

LEARNING OBJECTIVE　**6**

Explain the difference between absorption costing and variable costing.

In the earlier chapters, we classified both variable and fixed manufacturing costs as product costs. In job order costing, for example, a job is assigned the costs of direct materials, direct labor, and **both** variable and fixed manufacturing overhead. This costing approach is referred to as **full** or **absorption costing**. It is so named because all manufacturing costs are charged to, or absorbed by, the product. Absorption costing is the approach used for external reporting under generally accepted accounting principles.

An alternative approach is to use **variable costing**. Under variable costing, only direct materials, direct labor, and variable manufacturing overhead costs are considered product costs. Companies recognize fixed manufacturing overhead costs as period costs (expenses) when incurred. The difference between absorption costing and variable costing is shown graphically as follows.

Illustration 6A-1
Difference between absorption costing and variable costing

Absorption Costing		Variable Costing
	Fixed	
Product Cost ◄——— Manufacturing ———► Period Cost		
	Overhead	

Under both absorption and variable costing, selling and administrative expenses are period costs.

Companies may not use variable costing for external financial reports because generally accepted accounting principles require that fixed manufacturing overhead be accounted for as a product cost.

Example Comparing Absorption Costing with Variable Costing

To illustrate absorption and variable costing, assume that Premium Products Corporation manufactures a polyurethane sealant, called Fix-It, for car windshields. Relevant data for Fix-It in January 2014, the first month of production, are as shown on the next page.

Selling price	$20 per unit.
Units	Produced 30,000; sold 20,000; beginning inventory zero.
Variable unit costs	Manufacturing $9 (direct materials $5, direct labor $3, and variable overhead $1).
	Selling and administrative expenses $2.
Fixed costs	Manufacturing overhead $120,000.
	Selling and administrative expenses $15,000.

Illustration 6A-2
Sealant sales and cost data for Premium Products Corporation

The per unit manufacturing cost under each costing approach is computed in Illustration 6A-3.

Type of Cost	Absorption Costing	Variable Costing
Direct materials	$ 5	$5
Direct labor	3	3
Variable manufacturing overhead	1	1
Fixed manufacturing overhead		
($120,000 ÷ 30,000 units produced)	4	0
Manufacturing cost per unit	**$13**	**$9**

Illustration 6A-3
Computation of per unit manufacturing cost

The manufacturing cost per unit is $4 higher ($13 − $9) for absorption costing. This occurs because fixed manufacturing overhead costs are a product cost under absorption costing. Under variable costing, they are, instead, a period cost, and so they are expensed. Based on these data, each unit sold and each unit remaining in inventory is costed under absorption costing at $13 and under variable costing at $9.

ABSORPTION COSTING EXAMPLE

Illustration 6A-4 shows the income statement for Premium Products using absorption costing. It shows that cost of goods manufactured is $390,000, computed by multiplying the 30,000 units produced times the manufacturing cost per unit of $13 (see Illustration 6A-3). Cost of goods sold is $260,000, after subtracting ending inventory of $130,000. Under absorption costing, $40,000 of the fixed overhead (10,000 units × $4) is deferred to a future period as part of the cost of ending inventory.

Illustration 6A-4
Absorption costing income statement

Premium Products Corporation		
Income Statement		
For the Month Ended January 31, 2014		
Absorption Costing		
Sales (20,000 units × $20)		$400,000
Cost of goods sold		
Inventory, January 1	$ −0−	
Cost of goods manufactured (30,000 units × $13)	390,000	
Cost of goods available for sale	390,000	
Inventory, January 31 (10,000 units × $13)	**130,000**	
Cost of goods sold (20,000 units × $13)		260,000
Gross profit		140,000
Variable selling and administrative expenses		
(20,000 × $2)	40,000	
Fixed selling and administrative expenses	15,000	55,000
Net income		**$ 85,000**

Helpful Hint
The income statement format in Illustration 6A-4 is the same as that used under generally accepted accounting principles.

VARIABLE COSTING EXAMPLE

As Illustration 6A-5 shows, companies use the cost-volume-profit format in preparing a variable costing income statement. The variable manufacturing cost of $270,000 is computed by multiplying the 30,000 units produced times variable manufacturing cost of $9 per unit (see Illustration 6A-3). As in absorption costing, both variable and fixed selling and administrative expenses are treated as period costs.

Illustration 6A-5
Variable costing income statement

Helpful Hint
Note the difference in the computation of the ending inventory: $9 per unit here, $13 per unit in Illustration 6A-4.

Premium Products Corporation Income Statement For the Month Ended January 31, 2014 Variable Costing			
Sales (20,000 units × $20)			$400,000
Variable cost of goods sold			
Inventory, January 1	$ –0–		
Variable cost of goods manufactured			
(30,000 units × $9)	270,000		
Variable cost of goods available for sale	270,000		
Inventory, January 31 (10,000 units × $9)	**90,000**		
Variable cost of goods sold	180,000		
Variable selling and administrative expenses			
(20,000 units × $2)	40,000	220,000	
Contribution margin		180,000	
Fixed manufacturing overhead	120,000		
Fixed selling and administrative expenses	15,000	135,000	
Net income		**$ 45,000**	

There is one primary difference between variable and absorption costing: Under variable costing, companies charge the fixed manufacturing overhead as an expense in the current period. Fixed manufacturing overhead costs of the current period, therefore, are not deferred to future periods through the ending inventory. As a result, absorption costing will show a **higher net income number** than variable costing **whenever units produced exceed units sold.** This difference can be seen in the income statements in Illustrations 6A-4 and 6A-5. There is a $40,000 difference in the ending inventories ($130,000 under absorption costing versus $90,000 under variable costing). Under absorption costing, $40,000 of the fixed overhead costs (10,000 units × $4) has been deferred to a future period as part of inventory. In contrast, under variable costing, all fixed manufacturing costs are expensed in the current period.

As shown, when units produced exceed units sold, income under absorption costing is *higher.* When units produced are less than units sold, income under absorption costing is *lower.* When units produced and sold are the same, net income will be *equal* under the two costing approaches. In this case, there is no increase in ending inventory. So fixed overhead costs of the current period are not deferred to future periods through the ending inventory.

LEARNING OBJECTIVE   7

Discuss net income effects under absorption costing versus variable costing.

An Extended Example

To further illustrate the concepts underlying absorption and variable costing, we will look at an extended example using Overbay Inc., a manufacturer of small airplane drones. We assume that production volume stays the same each year over the 3-year period, but the number of units sold varies each year.

2013 RESULTS

As indicated in Illustration 6A-6 below, the variable manufacturing cost per drone is $240,000, and the fixed manufacturing overhead cost per drone is $60,000 (assuming 10 drones). Total manufacturing cost per drone under absorption costing is therefore $300,000 ($240,000 + $60,000). Overbay also has variable selling and administrative expenses of $5,000 per drone. The fixed selling and administrative expenses are $80,000.

	2013	2014	2015
Volume information			
Drones in beginning inventory	0	0	2
Drones produced	10	10	10
Drones sold	10	8	12
Drones in ending inventory	0	2	0

Financial information	
Selling price per drone	$400,000
Variable manufacturing cost per drone	$240,000
Fixed manufacturing overhead for the year	$600,000
Fixed manufacturing overhead per drone	$ 60,000 ($600,000 ÷ 10)
Variable selling and administrative expenses	
per drone	$ 5,000
Fixed selling and administrative expenses	$ 80,000

Illustration 6A-6
Information for Overbay Inc.

An absorption costing income statement for 2013 for Overbay Inc. is shown in Illustration 6A-7.

Overbay Inc.
Income Statement
For the Year Ended December 31, 2013
Absorption Costing

Sales (10 drones × $400,000)		$4,000,000
Cost of goods sold (10 drones × $300,000)		3,000,000
Gross profit		1,000,000
Variable selling and administrative expenses		
(10 drones × $5,000)	$50,000	
Fixed selling and administrative expenses	80,000	130,000
Net income		$ 870,000

Illustration 6A-7
Absorption costing income statement—2013

Overbay reports net income of $870,000 under absorption costing.

Under a variable costing system, the income statement follows a cost-volume-profit (CVP) format. In this case, the manufacturing cost is comprised solely of the variable manufacturing costs of $240,000 per drone. The fixed manufacturing overhead costs of $600,000 for the year are expensed in 2013. As in absorption costing, the fixed and variable selling and administrative expenses are period costs expensed in 2013. A variable costing income statement for Overbay Inc. for 2013 is shown in Illustration 6A-8 (page 260).

As shown in Illustration 6A-8, the variable costing net income of $870,000 is the same as the absorption costing net income computed in Illustration 6A-7. **When the numbers of units produced and sold are the same, net income is equal under the two costing approaches.** Because no increase in ending inventory occurs, no fixed manufacturing overhead costs incurred in 2013 are deferred to future periods using absorption costing.

Illustration 6A-8
Variable costing income statement—2013

Overbay Inc. Income Statement For the Year Ended December 31, 2013 Variable Costing		
Sales (10 drones × $400,000)		$4,000,000
Variable cost of goods sold (10 drones × $240,000)	$2,400,000	
Variable selling and administrative expenses (10 drones × $5,000)	50,000	2,450,000
Contribution margin		1,550,000
Fixed manufacturing overhead	600,000	
Fixed selling and administrative expenses	80,000	680,000
Net income		$ 870,000

2014 RESULTS

In 2014, Overbay produced 10 drones but sold only eight drones. As a result, there are two drones in ending inventory. The absorption costing income statement for 2014 is shown in Illustration 6A-9.

Illustration 6A-9
Absorption costing income statement—2014

Overbay Inc. Income Statement For the Year Ended December 31, 2014 Absorption Costing		
Sales (8 drones × $400,000)		$3,200,000
Cost of goods sold (8 drones × $300,000)		2,400,000
Gross profit		800,000
Variable selling and administrative expenses (8 drones × $5,000)	$40,000	
Fixed selling and administrative expenses	80,000	120,000
Net income		$ 680,000

Under absorption costing, the ending inventory of two drones is $600,000 ($300,000 × 2). Each unit of ending inventory includes $60,000 of fixed manufacturing overhead. Therefore, fixed manufacturing overhead costs of $120,000 ($60,000 × 2 drones) are deferred until a future period.

The variable costing income statement for 2014 is shown in Illustration 6A-10.

Illustration 6A-10
Variable costing income statement—2014

Overbay Inc. Income Statement For the Year Ended December 31, 2014 Variable Costing		
Sales (8 drones × $400,000)		$3,200,000
Variable cost of goods sold (8 drones × $240,000)	$1,920,000	
Variable selling and administrative expenses (8 drones × $5,000)	40,000	1,960,000
Contribution margin		1,240,000
Fixed manufacturing overhead	600,000	
Fixed selling and administrative expenses	80,000	680,000
Net income		$ 560,000

As shown, when units produced (10) exceeds units sold (8), net income under absorption costing ($680,000) is higher than net income under variable costing ($560,000). The reason: The cost of the ending inventory is higher under absorption costing than under variable costing. In 2014, under absorption costing, fixed manufacturing overhead of $120,000 is deferred and carried to future periods as part of inventory. Under variable costing, the $120,000 is expensed in the current period and, therefore the difference in the two net income numbers is $120,000 ($680,000 − $560,000).

2015 RESULTS

In 2015, Overbay produced 10 drones and sold 12 (10 drones from the current year's production and 2 drones from the beginning inventory). As a result, there are no drones in ending inventory. The absorption costing income statement for 2015 is shown in Illustration 6A-11.

Overbay Inc. Income Statement For the Year Ended December 31, 2015 Absorption Costing		
Sales (12 drones × $400,000)		$4,800,000
Cost of goods sold (12 drones × $300,000)		3,600,000
Gross profit		1,200,000
Variable selling and administrative expenses		
(12 drones × $5,000)	$60,000	
Fixed selling and administrative expenses	80,000	140,000
Net income		$1,060,000

Illustration 6A-11
Absorption costing income statement—2015

Fixed manufacturing costs of $720,000 ($60,000 × 12 drones) are expensed as part of cost of goods sold in 2015. This $720,000 includes $120,000 of fixed manufacturing costs incurred during 2014 and included in beginning inventory, plus $600,000 of fixed manufacturing costs incurred during 2015. Given this result for the absorption costing statement, what would you now expect the result to be under variable costing? Let's take a look.

The variable costing income statement for 2015 is shown in Illustration 6A-12.

Overbay Inc. Income Statement For the Year Ended December 31, 2015 Variable Costing		
Sales (12 drones × $400,000)		$4,800,000
Variable cost of goods sold		
(12 drones × $240,000)	$2,880,000	
Variable selling and administrative expenses		
(12 drones × $5,000)	60,000	2,940,000
Contribution margin		1,860,000
Fixed manufacturing overhead	600,000	
Fixed selling and administrative expenses	80,000	680,000
Net income		$1,180,000

Illustration 6A-12
Variable costing income statement—2015

When Drones produced (10) are less than Drones sold (12), net income under absorption costing ($1,060,000) is less than net income under variable costing

($1,180,000). This difference of $120,000 ($1,180,000 − $1,060,000) results because $120,000 of fixed manufacturing overhead costs in beginning inventory are charged to 2015 under absorption costing. Under variable costing, there is no fixed manufacturing overhead cost in beginning inventory.

Illustration 6A-13 summarizes the results of the three years.

Illustration 6A-13
Comparison of net income under two costing approaches

	Net Income under Two Costing Approaches		
	2013 Production = Sales	2014 Production > Sales	2015 Production < Sales
Absorption costing	$870,000	$ 680,000	$1,060,000
Variable costing	870,000	560,000	1,180,000
Difference	$ -0-	$120,000	$(120,000)

This relationship between production and sales and its effect on net income under the two costing approaches is shown graphically in Illustration 6A-14.

Illustration 6A-14
Summary of income effects under absorption costing and variable costing

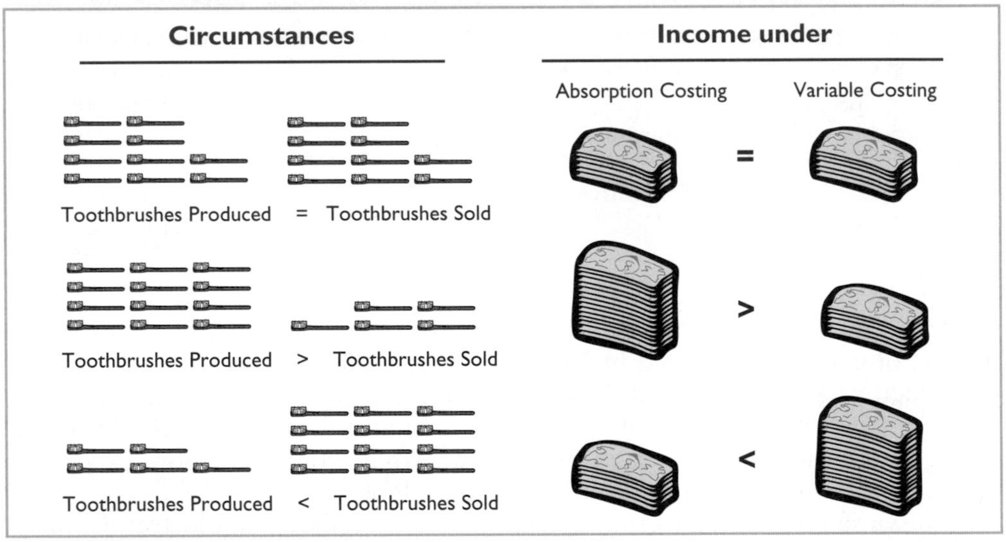

Decision-Making Concerns

LEARNING OBJECTIVE 8

Discuss the merits of absorption versus variable costing for management decision-making.

Generally accepted accounting principles require that absorption costing be used for the costing of inventory for external reporting purposes. Net income measured under GAAP (absorption costing) is often used internally to evaluate performance, justify cost reductions, or evaluate new projects. Some companies, however, have recognized that net income calculated using GAAP does not highlight differences between variable and fixed costs and may lead to poor business decisions. Consequently, these companies use variable costing for internal reporting purposes. The following discussion and example highlight a significant problem related to the use of absorption costing for decision-making purposes.

When production exceeds sales, absorption costing reports a higher net income than variable costing. The reason is that some fixed manufacturing costs are not expensed in the current period but are deferred to future periods as part of inventory. As a result, management may be tempted to overproduce in a given period in order to increase net income. Although net income will increase, this decision to overproduce may not be in the company's best interest.

Suppose, for example, a division manager's compensation is based upon the division's net income. In such a case, the manager may decide to meet the net income targets by increasing production. While this overproduction may increase the manager's compensation, the buildup of inventories in the long run will lead to additional costs to the company. Variable costing avoids this situation because net income under variable costing is unaffected by changes in production levels, as the following illustration shows.

Warren Lund, a division manager of Walker Enterprises, is under pressure to boost the performance of the Lighting Division in 2014. Unfortunately, recent profits have not met expectations. The expected sales for this year are 20,000 units. As he plans for the year, Warren has to decide whether to produce 20,000 or 30,000 units. The following facts are available for the division.

Beginning inventory	0	
Expected sales in units	20,000	
Selling price per unit	$15	
Variable manufacturing cost per unit	$6	
Fixed manufacturing overhead cost (total)	$60,000	
Fixed manufacturing overhead costs per unit		
Based on 20,000 units	$3 per unit ($60,000 ÷ 20,000 units)	
Based on 30,000 units	$2 per unit ($60,000 ÷ 30,000 units)	
Total manufacturing cost per unit		
Based on 20,000 units	$9 per unit ($6 variable + $3 fixed)	
Based on 30,000 units	$8 per unit ($6 variable + $2 fixed)	
Variable selling and administrative expenses		
per unit	$1	
Fixed selling and administrative expenses	$15,000	

Illustration 6A-15
Facts for Lighting Division—2014

Illustration 6A-16 presents the division's results based upon the two possible levels of output under absorption costing.

Illustration 6A-16
Absorption costing income statement—2014

Lighting Division Income Statement For the Year Ended December 31, 2014 Absorption Costing		
	20,000 Produced	**30,000 Produced**
Sales (20,000 units × $15)	$300,000	$ 300,000
Cost of goods sold	180,000*	160,000**
Gross profit	120,000	140,000
Variable selling and administrative expenses		
(20,000 units × $1)	20,000	20,000
Fixed selling and administrative expenses	15,000	15,000
Net income	**$ 85,000**	**$105,000**

*20,000 units × $9
**20,000 units × $8

If the Lighting Division produces 20,000 units, its net income under absorption costing is $85,000. If it produces 30,000 units, its net income is $105,000. By producing 30,000 units, the division has inventory of 10,000 units. This excess inventory causes net income to increase $20,000 because $20,000 of fixed costs

(10,000 units × $2) are not charged to the current year, but are deferred to future periods.

What do you think Warren Lund might do in this situation? Given his concern about the profit numbers of the Lighting Division, he may be tempted to increase production. Although this increased production will increase 2014 net income, it may be costly to the company in the long run.

Now let's evaluate the same situation under variable costing. A variable costing income statement is shown for production at both 20,000 and 30,000 units, using the information from Illustration 6A-15.

Illustration 6A-17
Variable costing income statement—2014

	20,000 Produced	**30,000 Produced**
Lighting Division Income Statement For the Year Ended December 31, 2014 Variable Costing		
Sales (20,000 units × $15)	$300,000	$300,000
Variable cost of goods sold (20,000 units × $6)	120,000	120,000
Variable selling and administrative expenses (20,000 units × $1)	20,000	20,000
Contribution margin	160,000	160,000
Fixed manufacturing overhead	60,000	60,000
Fixed selling and administrative expenses	15,000	15,000
Net income	$ 85,000	$ 85,000

From this example, we see that under variable costing, net income is not affected by the number of units produced. Net income is $85,000 whether the division produces 20,000 or 30,000 units. Why? Because fixed manufacturing overhead is treated as a period expense. Unlike absorption costing, no fixed manufacturing overhead is deferred through inventory buildup. Therefore, under variable costing, production does not increase income; sales do. As a result, if the company uses variable costing, managers like Warren Lund cannot affect profitability by increasing production.

Potential Advantages of Variable Costing

Variable costing has a number of potential advantages relative to absorption costing:

1. Net income computed under variable costing is unaffected by changes in production levels. As a result, it is much easier to understand the impact of fixed and variable costs on the computation of net income when variable costing is used.

2. The use of variable costing is consistent with the cost-volume-profit material presented in Chapters 5 and 6.

3. Net income computed under variable costing is closely tied to changes in sales levels (not production levels), and therefore provides a more realistic assessment of the company's success or failure during a period.

4. The presentation of fixed and variable cost components on the face of the variable costing income statement makes it easier to identify these costs and understand their effect on the business. Under absorption costing, the allocation of fixed costs to inventory makes it difficult to evaluate the impact of fixed costs on the company's results.

Companies that use just-in-time processing techniques to minimize their inventories will not have significant differences between absorption and variable costing net income.

> DO IT!

Variable Costing

Franklin Company produces and sells tennis balls. The following costs are available for the year ended December 31, 2014. The company has no beginning inventory. In 2014, 8,000,000 units were produced, but only 7,500,000 units were sold. The unit selling price was $0.50 per ball. Costs and expenses were:

Variable costs per unit	
Direct materials	$0.10
Direct labor	0.05
Variable manufacturing overhead	0.08
Variable selling and administrative expenses	0.02
Annual fixed costs and expenses	
Manufacturing overhead	$500,000
Selling and administrative expenses	100,000

(a) Compute the manufacturing cost of one unit of product using variable costing.

(b) Prepare a 2014 income statement for Franklin Company using variable costing.

Solution

Action Plan

✔ Recall that under variable costing, only variable manufacturing costs are treated as manufacturing (product) costs.

✔ Subtract all fixed costs, both manufacturing overhead and selling and administrative expenses, as period costs.

(a) The cost of one unit of product under variable costing would be:

Direct materials	$0.10
Direct labor	0.05
Variable manufacturing overhead	0.08
	$0.23

(b) The variable costing income statement would be as follows.

Franklin Company
Income Statement
For the Year Ended December 31, 2014
Variable Costing

Sales (7,500,000 × $0.50)		$3,750,000
Variable cost of goods sold (7,500,000 × $0.23)	$1,725,000	
Variable selling and administrative expenses (7,500,000 × .02)	150,000	1,875,000
Contribution margin		1,875,000
Fixed manufacturing overhead	500,000	
Fixed selling and administrative expenses	100,000	600,000
Net income		$1,275,000

Related exercise material: **BE6-16, BE6-17, BE6-18, BE6-19, E6-17, E6-18, and E6-19.**

✔ The Navigator

SUMMARY OF LEARNING OBJECTIVES FOR APPENDIX 6A ✔ The Navigator

6 Explain the difference between absorption costing and variable costing. Under absorption costing, fixed manufacturing costs are product costs. Under variable costing, fixed manufacturing costs are period costs.

7 Discuss net income effects under absorption costing versus variable costing. If production volume exceeds sales volume, net income under absorption costing will exceed net income under variable costing by the amount of fixed manufacturing costs included in ending inventory that results from units produced but not sold during the period. If production volume is less than sales volume, net income under absorption costing will be

less than under variable costing by the amount of fixed manufacturing costs included in the units sold during the period that were not produced during the period.

8 Discuss the merits of absorption versus variable costing for management decision-making. The use of variable costing is consistent with cost–volume–profit analysis. Net income under variable costing is unaffected by changes in production levels. Instead, it is closely tied to changes in sales. The presentation of fixed costs in the variable costing approach makes it easier to identify fixed costs and to evaluate their impact on the company's profitability.

GLOSSARY

Absorption costing A costing approach in which all manufacturing costs are charged to the product. (p. 256).

Cost structure The relative proportion of fixed versus variable costs that a company incurs. (p. 251).

Degree of operating leverage A measure of the extent to which a company's net income reacts to a change in sales. It is calculated by dividing contribution margin by net income. (p. 253).

Operating leverage The extent to which a company's net income reacts to a change in sales. Operating leverage

is determined by a company's relative use of fixed versus variable costs. (p. 252).

Sales mix The relative percentage in which a company sells its multiple products. (p. 244).

Theory of constraints A specific approach used to identify and manage constraints in order to achieve the company's goals. (p. 249).

Variable costing A costing approach in which only variable manufacturing costs are product costs, and fixed manufacturing costs are period costs (expenses). (p. 256).

> Comprehensive **DO IT!**

Francis Corporation manufactures and sells three different types of water-sport wakeboards. The boards vary in terms of their quality specifications—primarily with respect to their smoothness and finish. They are referred to as Smooth, Extra-Smooth, and Super-Smooth boards. Machine time is limited. More machine time is required to manufacture the Extra-Smooth and Super-Smooth boards. Additional information is provided below.

	Product		
	Smooth	**Extra-Smooth**	**Super-Smooth**
Selling price	$60	$100	$160
Variable costs and expenses	50	75	130
Contribution margin	$10	$ 25	$ 30
Machine hours required	0.25	0.40	0.60

Total fixed costs: $234,000

Instructions

Answer each of the following questions.

(a) Ignoring the machine time constraint, what strategy would appear optimal?

(b) What is the contribution margin per unit of limited resource for each type of board?

(c) If additional machine time could be obtained, how should the additional capacity be used?

Solution to Comprehensive DO IT!

Action Plan

✔ To determine how best to use a limited resource, calculate the contribution margin per unit of limited resource for each product type.

(a) The Super-Smooth boards have the highest contribution margin per unit. Thus, ignoring any manufacturing constraints, it would appear that the company should shift toward production of more Super-Smooth units.

(b) The contribution margin per unit of limited resource is calculated as:

	Smooth	Extra-Smooth	Super-Smooth
$\dfrac{\text{Contribution margin per unit}}{\text{Limited resource consumed per unit}}$	$\dfrac{\$10}{.25} = \$40$	$\dfrac{\$25}{.40} = \$62.50$	$\dfrac{\$30}{.60} = \$50$

(c) The Extra-Smooth boards have the highest contribution margin per unit of limited resource. Given the resource constraint, any additional capacity should be used to make Extra-Smooth boards.

✔ **The Navigator**

Self-Test, Brief Exercises, Exercises, Problem Set A, and many more resources are available for practice in WileyPLUS.

Note: All asterisked Questions, Exercises, and Problems relate to material contained in the appendix to the chapter.

SELF-TEST QUESTIONS

Answers are at the end of the chapter.

(LO 1) 1. Which one of the following is the format of a CVP income statement?
    (a) Sales − Variable costs = Fixed costs + Net income.
    (b) Sales − Fixed costs − Variable costs − Operating expenses = Net income.
    (c) Sales − Cost of goods sold − Operating expenses = Net income.
    (d) Sales − Variable costs − Fixed costs = Net income.

(LO 1, 2) 2. Croc Catchers calculates its contribution margin to be less than zero. Which statement is *true*?
    (a) Its fixed costs are less than the variable costs per unit.
    (b) Its profits are greater than its total costs.
    (c) The company should sell more units.
    (d) Its selling price is less than its variable costs.

(LO 2) 3. Which one of the following describes the break-even point?
    (a) It is the point where total sales equals total variable plus total fixed costs.
    (b) It is the point where the contribution margin equals zero.
    (c) It is the point where total variable costs equal total fixed costs.
    (d) It is the point where total sales equals total fixed costs.

(LO 1) 4. The following information is available for Chap Company.

Sales	$350,000
Cost of goods sold	$120,000
Total fixed expenses	$60,000
Total variable expenses	$100,000

Which amount would you find on Chap's CVP income statement?
    (a) Contribution margin of $250,000.
    (b) Contribution margin of $190,000.
    (c) Gross profit of $230,000.
    (d) Gross profit of $190,000.

(LO 2) 5. Gabriel Corporation has fixed costs of $180,000 and variable costs of $8.50 per unit. It has a target income of $268,000. How many units must it sell at $12 per unit to achieve its target net income?
    (a) 51,429 units.   (c) 76,571 units.
    (b) 128,000 units.   (d) 21,176 units.

(LO 2) 6. Mackey Corporation has fixed costs of $150,000 and variable costs of $9 per unit. If sales price per unit is $12, what is break-even sales in dollars?
    (a) $200,000.   (c) $480,000.
    (b) $450,000.   (d) $600,000.

(LO 3) 7. Sales mix is:
    (a) important to sales managers but not to accountants.

(b) easier to analyze on absorption costing income statements.

(c) a measure of the relative percentage of a company's variable costs to its fixed costs.

(d) a measure of the relative percentage in which a company's products are sold.

(LO 3) **8.** Net income will be:

(a) greater if more higher-contribution margin units are sold than lower-contribution margin units.

(b) greater if more lower-contribution margin units are sold than higher-contribution margin units.

(c) equal as long as total sales remain equal, regardless of which products are sold.

(d) unaffected by changes in the mix of products sold.

(LO 4) **9.** If the contribution margin per unit is $15 and it takes 3.0 machine hours to produce the unit, the contribution margin per unit of limited resource is:

(a) $25.   (c) $4.

(b) $5.   (d) None of the above.

(LO 4) **10.** MEM manufactures two products. Product X has a contribution margin of $26 and requires 4 hours of machine time. Product Y has a contribution margin of $14 and requires 2 hours of machine time. Assuming that machine time is limited to 3,000 hours, how should it allocate the machine time to maximize its income?

(a) Use 1,500 hours to produce X and 1,500 hours to produce Y.

(b) Use 2,250 hours to produce X and 750 hours to produce Y.

(c) Use 3,000 hours to produce only X.

(d) Use 3,000 hours to produce only Y.

(LO 4) **11.** When a company has a limited resource, it should apply additional capacity of that resource to providing more units of the product or service that has:

(a) the highest contribution margin.

(b) the highest selling price.

(c) the highest gross profit.

(d) the highest contribution margin per unit of that limited resource.

12. The degree of operating leverage: (LO 5)

(a) can be computed by dividing total contribution margin by net income.

(b) provides a measure of the company's earnings volatility.

(c) affects a company's break-even point.

(d) All of the above.

13. A high degree of operating leverage: (LO 5)

(a) indicates that a company has a larger percentage of variable costs relative to its fixed costs.

(b) is computed by dividing fixed costs by contribution margin.

(c) exposes a company to greater earnings volatility risk.

(d) exposes a company to less earnings volatility risk.

14. Stevens Company has a degree of operating leverage (LO 5) of 3.5 at a sales level of $1,200,000 and net income of $200,000. If Stevens' sales fall by 10%, Stevens can be expected to experience a:

(a) decrease in net income of $70,000.

(b) decrease in contribution margin of $7,000.

(c) decrease in operating leverage of 35%.

(d) decrease in net income of $175,000.

***15.** Fixed manufacturing overhead costs are recognized as: (LO 6)

(a) period costs under absorption costing.

(b) product costs under absorption costs.

(c) product costs under variable costing.

(d) part of ending inventory costs under both absorption and variable costing.

***16.** Net income computed under absorption costing (LO 6) will be:

(a) higher than net income under variable costing in all cases.

(b) equal to net income under variable costing in all cases.

(c) higher than net income under variable costing when units produced are greater than units sold.

(d) higher than net income under variable costing when units produced are less than units sold.

Go to the book's companion website, www.wiley.com/college/weygandt, for additional Self-Test Questions.

✔ **The Navigator**

QUESTIONS

1. What is meant by CVP analysis?

2. Provide three examples of management decisions that benefit from CVP analysis.

3. Distinguish between a traditional income statement and a CVP income statement.

4. Describe the features of a CVP income statement that make it more useful for management decision-making than the traditional income statement that is prepared for external users.

5. The traditional income statement for Wheat Company shows sales $900,000, cost of goods sold $500,000, and operating expenses $200,000. Assuming all costs and

expenses are 75% variable and 25% fixed, prepare a CVP income statement through contribution margin.

6. If management chooses to reduce its selling price to match that of a competitor, how will the break-even point be affected?

7. What is meant by the term sales mix? How does sales mix affect the calculation of the break-even point?

8. Performance Company sells two types of performance tires. The lower-priced model is guaranteed for only 50,000 miles; the higher-priced model is guaranteed for 150,000 miles. The unit contribution margin on the higher-priced tire is twice as high as that of the lower-priced tire. If the sales mix shifts so that the company begins to sell more units of the lower-priced tire, explain how the company's break-even point in units will change.

9. What approach should be used to calculate the break-even point of a company that has many products?

10. How is the contribution margin per unit of limited resource computed?

11. What is the theory of constraints? Provide some examples of possible constraints for a manufacturer.

12. What is meant by "cost structure?" Explain how a company's cost structure affects its break-even point.

13. What is operating leverage? How does a company increase its operating leverage?

14. How does the replacement of manual labor with automated equipment affect a company's cost structure? What implications does this have for its operating leverage and break-even point?

15. What is a measure of operating leverage, and how is it calculated?

16. Pine Company has a degree of operating leverage of 8. Fir Company has a degree of operating leverage of 4. Interpret these measures.

*17. Distinguish between absorption costing and variable costing.

*18. (a) What is the major rationale for the use of variable costing?
   (b) Discuss why variable costing may not be used for financial reporting purposes.

*19. Doc Rowan Corporation sells one product, its waterproof hiking boot. It began operations in the current year and had an ending inventory of 8,500 units. The company sold 20,000 units throughout the year. Fixed manufacturing overhead is $5 per unit, and total manufacturing cost per unit is $20 (including fixed manufacturing overhead costs). What is the difference in net income between absorption and variable costing?

*20. If production equals sales, what, if any, is the difference between net income under absorption costing versus under variable costing?

*21. If production is greater than sales, how does absorption costing net income differ from variable costing net income?

*22. In the long run, will net income be higher or lower under variable costing compared to absorption costing?

BRIEF EXERCISES

BE6-1 Determine the missing amounts.

	Unit Selling Price	Unit Variable Costs	Contribution Margin per Unit	Contribution Margin Ratio
1.	$250	$180	(a)	(b)
2.	$500	(c)	$300	(d)
3.	(e)	(f)	$330	30%

Determine missing amounts for contribution margin.
(LO 1, 2), AN

BE6-2 Hamby Inc. has sales of $2,000,000 for the first quarter of 2014. In making the sales, the company incurred the following costs and expenses.

	Variable	Fixed
Cost of goods sold	$760,000	$600,000
Selling expenses	95,000	60,000
Administrative expenses	79,000	66,000

Prepare a CVP income statement for the quarter ended March 31, 2014.

Prepare CVP income statement.
(LO 1, 2), AP

BE6-3 Wesland Corp. had total variable costs of $175,000, total fixed costs of $120,000, and total revenues of $250,000. Compute the required sales in dollars to break even.

Compute the break-even point.
(LO 1, 2), AP

BE6-4 Dilts Company has a unit selling price of $400, variable costs per unit of $250, and fixed costs of $210,000. Compute the break-even point in units using (a) the mathematical equation and (b) contribution margin per unit.

Compute the break-even point.
(LO 1, 2), AP

BE6-5 For Ortega Company, variable costs are 60% of sales, and fixed costs are $210,000. Management's net income goal is $60,000. Compute the required sales needed to achieve management's target net income of $60,000. (Use the mathematical equation approach.)

Compute sales for target net income.
(LO 1, 2), AP

BE6-6 For Kosko Company actual sales are $1,200,000 and break-even sales are $960,000. Compute (a) the margin of safety in dollars and (b) the margin of safety ratio.

Compute the margin of safety and the margin of safety ratio.
(LO 1, 2), AP

BE6-7 Markowis Corporation sells three different models of mosquito "zapper." Model A12 sells for $50 and has variable costs of $40. Model B22 sells for $100 and has variable costs of $70. Model C124 sells for $400 and has variable costs of $300. The sales mix of the three models is: A12, 60%; B22, 15%; and C124, 25%. What is the weighted-average unit contribution margin?

Compute weighted-average unit contribution margin based on sales mix.
(LO 3), AP

Compute break-even point in units for company with multiple products.

(LO 3), AP

Compute break-even point in dollars for company with multiple product lines.

(LO 3), AP

BE6-8 Information for Markowis Corporation is given in BE6-7. If the company has fixed costs of $213,000, how many units of each model must the company sell in order to break even?

BE6-9 Peine Candle Supply makes candles. The sales mix (as a percentage of total dollar sales) of its three product lines is birthday candles 30%, standard tapered candles 50%, and large scented candles 20%. The contribution margin ratio of each candle type is shown below.

Candle Type	Contribution Margin Ratio
Birthday	20%
Standard tapered	20%
Large scented	45%

(a) What is the weighted-average contribution margin ratio?
(b) If the company's fixed costs are $440,000 per year, what is the dollar amount of each type of candle that must be sold to break even?

Determine weighted-average contribution margin.

(LO 3), AP

BE6-10 Faune Furniture Co. consists of two divisions, Bedroom Division and Dining Room Division. The results of operations for the most recent quarter are:

	Bedroom Division	Dining Room Division	Total
Sales	$500,000	$750,000	$1,250,000
Variable costs	225,000	450,000	675,000
Contribution margin	$275,000	$300,000	$ 575,000

(a) Determine the company's sales mix.
(b) Determine the company's weighted-average contribution margin ratio.

Show allocation of limited resources.

(LO 4), AP

BE6-11 In Briggs Company, data concerning two products are contribution margin per unit—Product A $12, Product B $15; machine hours required for one unit—Product A 2, Product B 3. Compute the contribution margin per unit of limited resource for each product.

Compute degree of operating leverage.

(LO 5), AP

BE6-12 Sam's Shingle Corporation is considering the purchase of a new automated shingle-cutting machine. The new machine will reduce variable labor costs but will increase depreciation expense. Contribution margin is expected to increase from $200,000 to $240,000. Net income is expected to be the same at $40,000. Compute the degree of operating leverage before and after the purchase of the new equipment. Interpret your results.

Compute break-even point with change in operating leverage.

(LO 5), AP

BE6-13 Presented below are variable costing income statements for Logan Company and Morgan Company. They are in the same industry, with the same net incomes, but different cost structures.

	Logan Co.	Morgan Co.
Sales	$200,000	$200,000
Variable costs	80,000	50,000
Contribution margin	120,000	150,000
Fixed costs	60,000	90,000
Net income	$ 60,000	$ 60,000

Compute the break-even point in dollars for each company and comment on your findings.

Determine contribution margin from degree of operating leverage.

(LO 5), AP

BE6-14 The degree of operating leverage for Montana Corp. and APK Co. are 1.6 and 5.4, respectively. Both have net incomes of $50,000. Determine their respective contribution margins.

Show allocation of limited resources.

(LO 4), AP

BE6-15 Ger Corporation manufactures two products with the following characteristics.

	Contribution Margin per Unit	Machine Hours Required for Production
Product 1	$42	.15 hours
Product 2	$35	.10 hours

If Ger's machine hours are limited to 2,000 per month, determine which product it should produce.

*BE6-16 The Rock Company produces basketballs. It incurred the following costs during the year.

Direct materials	$14,400
Direct labor	$25,600
Fixed manufacturing overhead	$12,000
Variable manufacturing overhead	$32,400
Selling costs	$21,000

What are the total product costs for the company under variable costing?

Compute product costs under variable costing.

(LO 6), AP

*BE6-17 Information concerning The Rock Company is provided in BE6-16. What are the total product costs for the company under absorption costing?

Compute product costs under absorption costing.

(LO 6), AP

*BE6-18 Burns Company incurred the following costs during the year: direct materials $20 per unit; direct labor $14 per unit; variable manufacturing overhead $15 per unit; variable selling and administrative costs $8 per unit; fixed manufacturing overhead $128,000; and fixed selling and administrative costs $10,000. Burns produced 8,000 units and sold 6,000 units. Determine the manufacturing cost per unit under (a) absorption costing and (b) variable costing.

Determine manufacturing cost per unit under absorption and variable costing.

(LO 6), AP

*BE6-19 ▭▭▭▭▷ Howser Company's fixed overhead costs are $4 per unit, and its variable overhead costs are $8 per unit. In the first month of operations, 50,000 units are produced, and 48,000 units are sold. Write a short memo to the chief financial officer explaining which costing approach will produce the higher income and what the difference will be.

Compute net income under absorption and variable costing.

(LO 7), AP

> ## DO IT! REVIEW

DO IT! 6-1 Amanda Inc. sold 10,000 units and recorded sales of $400,000 for the first month of 2014. In making the sales, the company incurred the following costs and expenses.

	Variable	Fixed
Cost of goods sold	$184,000	$70,000
Selling expenses	40,000	30,000
Administrative expenses	16,000	50,000

(a) Prepare a CVP income statement for the month ended January 31, 2014.
(b) Compute the contribution margin per unit.
(c) Compute the contribution margin ratio.

Prepare CVP income statement and compute contribution margin.

(LO 1), AP

DO IT! 6-2 Queensland Company reports the following operating results for the month of April.

Queensland Company
CVP Income Statement
For the Month Ended April 30, 2014

	Total	Per Unit
Sales (9,000 units)	$450,000	$50
Variable costs	270,000	30
Contribution margin	180,000	$20
Fixed expenses	150,000	
Net income	$ 30,000	

Management is considering the following course of action to increase net income: Reduce the selling price by 4%, with no changes to unit variable costs or fixed costs. Management is confident that this change will increase unit sales by 20%.

Compute the break-even point and margin of safety under different alternatives.

(LO 2), AP

Using the contribution margin technique, compute the break-even point in units and dollars and margin of safety in dollars:

(a) Assuming no changes to selling price or costs, and
(b) Assuming changes to sales price and volume as described above.

Comment on your findings.

Compute sales mix, weighted-average contribution margin, and break-even point.

(LO 3), AP

DO IT! 6-3 Snow Cap Springs produces and sells water filtration systems for homeowners. Information regarding its three models is shown below.

	Basic	Basic Plus	Premium	Total
Units sold	750	450	300	1,500
Selling price	$250	$400	$800	
Variable costs	$195	$288	$416	

The company's total fixed costs to produce the filtration systems are $165,480.

(a) Determine the sales mix as a function of units sold for the three products.
(b) Determine the weighted-average unit contribution margin.
(c) Determine the total number of units that the company must produce to break even.
(d) Determine the number of units of each model that the company must produce to break even.

Determine sales mix with limited resources.

(LO 4), AP

DO IT! 6-4 Eye Spy Corporation manufactures and sells three different types of binoculars. They are referred to as Good, Better, and Best binoculars. Grinding and polishing time is limited. More time is required to grind and polish the lenses used in the Better and Best binoculars. Additional information is provided below.

	Product		
	Good	Better	Best
Selling price	$90.00	$330.00	$900.00
Variable costs and expenses	50.00	180.00	480.00
Contribution margin	$40.00	$150.00	$420.00
Grinding and polishing time required	0.5 hrs	1.5 hrs	6 hrs

(a) Ignoring the time constraint, what strategy would appear to be optimal?
(b) What is the contribution margin per unit of limited resource for each type of binocular?
(c) If additional grinding and polishing time could be obtained, how should the additional capacity be used?

✔ **The Navigator**

EXERCISES

Compute break-even point and margin of safety.

(LO 2), AP

E6-1 The Bonita Inn is trying to determine its break-even point. The inn has 75 rooms that are rented at $60 a night. Operating costs are as follows.

Salaries	$8,800 per month
Utilities	2,400 per month
Depreciation	1,500 per month
Maintenance	800 per month
Maid service	8 per room
Other costs	37 per room

Instructions
(a) Determine the inn's break-even point in (1) number of rented rooms per month and (2) dollars.
(b) If the inn plans on renting an average of 50 rooms per day (assuming a 30-day month), what is (1) the monthly margin of safety in dollars and (2) the margin of safety ratio?

E6-2 In the month of June, Jose Hebert's Beauty Salon gave 4,000 haircuts, shampoos, and permanents at an average price of $30. During the month, fixed costs were $16,800 and variable costs were 75% of sales.

Compute contribution margin, break-even point, and margin of safety.

(LO 2), AP

Instructions

(a) Determine the contribution margin in dollars, per unit and as a ratio.

(b) Using the contribution margin technique, compute the break-even point in dollars and in units.

(c) Compute the margin of safety in dollars and as a ratio.

E6-3 Norton Company reports the following operating results for the month of August: sales $310,000 (units 5,000); variable costs $210,000; and fixed costs $75,000. Management is considering the following independent courses of action to increase net income.

Compute net income under different alternatives.

(LO 2), AP

1. Increase selling price by 10% with no change in total variable costs or sales volume.
2. Reduce variable costs to 58% of sales.
3. Reduce fixed costs by $20,000.

Instructions

Compute the net income to be earned under each alternative. Which course of action will produce the highest net income?

E6-4 Comfi Airways, Inc., a small two-plane passenger airline, has asked for your assistance in some basic analysis of its operations. Both planes seat 10 passengers each, and they fly commuters from Comfi's base airport to the major city in the state, Metropolis. Each month, 40 round-trip flights are made. Shown below is a recent month's activity in the form of a cost-volume-profit income statement.

Compute break-even point and prepare CVP income statement.

(LO 2), AP

Fare revenues (400 fares)		$48,000
Variable costs		
Fuel	$14,000	
Snacks and drinks	800	
Landing fees	2,000	
Supplies and forms	1,200	18,000
Contribution margin		30,000
Fixed costs		
Depreciation	3,000	
Salaries	15,000	
Advertising	500	
Airport hangar fees	1,750	20,250
Net income		$ 9,750

Instructions

(a) Calculate the break-even point in (1) dollars and (2) number of fares.

(b) Without calculations, determine the contribution margin at the break-even point.

(c) If fares were decreased by 10%, an additional 100 fares could be generated. However, total variable costs would increase by 20%. Should the fare decrease be adopted?

E6-5 Hall Company had sales in 2014 of $1,560,000 on 60,000 units. Variable costs totaled $720,000, and fixed costs totaled $500,000.

A new raw material is available that will decrease the variable costs per unit by 25% (or $3.00). However, to process the new raw material, fixed operating costs will increase by $150,000. Management feels that one-half of the decline in the variable costs per unit should be passed on to customers in the form of a sales price reduction. The marketing department expects that this sales price reduction will result in a 5% increase in the number of units sold.

Prepare a CVP income statement before and after changes in business environment.

(LO 2), AP

Instructions

Prepare a projected CVP income statement for 2014 (a) assuming the changes have not been made, and (b) assuming that changes are made as described.

Compute break-even point in units for a company with more than one product.

(LO 3), AP

E6-6 Yard Tools manufactures lawnmowers, weed-trimmers, and chainsaws. Its sales mix and contribution margin per unit are as follows.

	Sales Mix	Contribution Margin per Unit
Lawnmowers	20%	$30
Weed-trimmers	50%	$20
Chainsaws	30%	$40

Yard Tools has fixed costs of $4,200,000.

Instructions
Compute the number of units of each product that Yard Tools must sell in order to break even under this product mix.

Compute service line break-even point and target net income in dollars for a company with more than one service.

(LO 3), AN

E6-7 Qwik Repairs has over 200 auto-maintenance service outlets nationwide. It provides primarily two lines of service: oil changes and brake repair. Oil change–related services represent 70% of its sales and provide a contribution margin ratio of 20%. Brake repair represents 30% of its sales and provides a 60% contribution margin ratio. The company's fixed costs are $16,000,000 (that is, $80,000 per service outlet).

Instructions
(a) Calculate the dollar amount of each type of service that the company must provide in order to break even.
(b) The company has a desired net income of $60,000 per service outlet. What is the dollar amount of each type of service that must be provided by each service outlet to meet its target net income per outlet?

Compute break-even point in dollars for a company with more than one service.

(LO 3), AN

E6-8 Express Delivery is a rapidly growing delivery service. Last year, 80% of its revenue came from the delivery of mailing "pouches" and small, standardized delivery boxes (which provides a 20% contribution margin). The other 20% of its revenue came from delivering non-standardized boxes (which provides a 70% contribution margin). With the rapid growth of Internet retail sales, Express believes that there are great opportunities for growth in the delivery of non-standardized boxes. The company has fixed costs of $12,000,000.

Instructions
(a) What is the company's break-even point in total sales dollars? At the break-even point, how much of the company's sales are provided by each type of service?
(b) The company's management would like to hold its fixed costs constant but shift its sales mix so that 60% of its revenue comes from the delivery of non-standardized boxes and the remainder from pouches and small boxes. If this were to occur, what would be the company's break-even sales, and what amount of sales would be provided by each service type?

Compute break-even point in units for a company with multiple products.

(LO 3), AP

E6-9 Palmer Golf Accessories sells golf shoes, gloves, and a laser-guided range-finder that measures distance. Shown below are unit cost and sales data.

	Pairs of Shoes	Pairs of Gloves	Range-Finder
Unit sales price	$100	$30	$260
Unit variable costs	60	10	200
Unit contribution margin	$ 40	$20	$ 60
Sales mix	30%	60%	10%

Fixed costs are $630,000.

Instructions
(a) Compute the break-even point in units for the company.
(b) Determine the number of units to be sold at the break-even point for each product line.
(c) Verify that the mix of sales units determined in (b) will generate a zero net income.

E6-10 Personal Electronix sells iPads and iPods. The business is divided into two divisions along product lines. CVP income statements for a recent quarter's activity are presented below.

Determine break-even point in dollars for two divisions.

(LO 3), AP

	iPad Division	iPod Division	Total
Sales	$600,000	$400,000	$1,000,000
Variable costs	420,000	260,000	680,000
Contribution margin	$180,000	$140,000	320,000
Fixed costs			120,000
Net income			$ 200,000

Instructions

(a) Determine sales mix percentage and contribution margin ratio for each division.
(b) Calculate the company's weighted-average contribution margin ratio.
(c) Calculate the company's break-even point in dollars.
(d) Determine the sales level in dollars for each division at the break-even point.

E6-11 Spencer Company manufactures and sells three products. Relevant per unit data concerning each product are given below.

Compute contribution margin and determine the product to be manufactured.

(LO 4), AN

	Product		
	A	**B**	**C**
Selling price	$8	$12	$15
Variable costs and expenses	$3	$10	$12
Machine hours to produce	2	1	2

Instructions

(a) Compute the contribution margin per unit of the limited resource (machine hours) for each product.
(b) Assuming 1,500 additional machine hours are available, which product should be manufactured?
(c) Prepare an analysis showing the total contribution margin if the additional hours are (1) divided equally among the products, and (2) allocated entirely to the product identified in (b) above.

E6-12 Dalton Inc. produces and sells three products. Unit data concerning each product is shown below.

Compute contribution margin and determine the products to be manufactured.

(LO 4), AN

	Product		
	D	**E**	**F**
Selling price	$200	$300	$250
Direct labor costs	30	80	35
Other variable costs	95	80	145

The company has 2,000 hours of labor available to build inventory in anticipation of the company's peak season. Management is trying to decide which product should be produced. The direct labor hourly rate is $10.

Instructions

(a) Determine the number of direct labor hours per unit.
(b) Determine the contribution margin per direct labor hour.
(c) Determine which product should be produced and the total contribution margin for that product.

E6-13 Billings Company manufactures and sells two products. Relevant per unit data concerning each product follow.

Compute contribution margin and determine the products to be manufactured.

(LO 4), AN

	Product	
	Basic	**Deluxe**
Selling price	$40	$52
Variable costs	$20	$22
Machine hours	.5	.8

Instructions
(a) Compute the contribution margin per machine hour for each product.
(b) If 1,000 additional machine hours are available, which product should Billings manufacture?
(c) Prepare an analysis showing the total contribution margin if the additional hours are:
   (1) Divided equally between the products.
   (2) Allocated entirely to the product identified in part (b).

Compute degree of operating leverage and evaluate impact of alternative cost structures on net income.

(LO 5), AN

E6-14 The CVP income statements shown below are available for Armstrong Company and Contador Company.

	Armstrong Co.	Contador Co.
Sales	$500,000	$500,000
Variable costs	240,000	50,000
Contribution margin	260,000	450,000
Fixed costs	160,000	350,000
Net income	$100,000	$100,000

Instructions
(a) Compute the degree of operating leverage for each company and interpret your results.
(b) Assuming that sales revenue increases by 10%, prepare a variable costing income statement for each company.
(c) Discuss how the cost structure of these two companies affects their operating leverage and profitability.

Compute degree of operating leverage and evaluate impact of alternative cost structures on net income and margin of safety.

(LO 5), AN

E6-15 Arquitectos Interiores of Juarez, Mexico, is contemplating a major change in its cost structure. Currently, all of its drafting work is performed by skilled draftsmen. Alfonso Jiminez, Arquitectos' owner, is considering replacing the draftsmen with a computerized drafting system. However, before making the change, Alfonso would like to know the consequences of the change, since the volume of business varies significantly from year to year. Shown below are CVP income statements for each alternative.

	Manual System	Computerized System
Sales	$1,500,000	$1,500,000
Variable costs	1,200,000	600,000
Contribution margin	300,000	900,000
Fixed costs	50,000	650,000
Net income	$ 250,000	$ 250,000

Instructions
(a) Determine the degree of operating leverage for each alternative.
(b) Which alternative would produce the higher net income if sales increased by $150,000?
(c) Using the margin of safety ratio, determine which alternative could sustain the greater decline in sales before operating at a loss.

Compute degree of operating leverage and impact on net income of alternative cost structures.

(LO 5), AN

E6-16 An investment banker is analyzing two companies that specialize in the production and sale of candied yams. Traditional Yams uses a labor-intensive approach, and Auto-Yams uses a mechanized system. CVP income statements for the two companies are shown below.

	Traditional Yams	Auto-Yams
Sales	$400,000	$400,000
Variable costs	320,000	160,000
Contribution margin	80,000	240,000
Fixed costs	30,000	190,000
Net income	$ 50,000	$ 50,000

The investment banker is interested in acquiring one of these companies. However, she is concerned about the impact that each company's cost structure might have on its profitability.

Instructions

(a) Calculate each company's degree of operating leverage. Determine which company's cost structure makes it more sensitive to changes in sales volume.

(b) Determine the effect on each company's net income if sales decrease by 15% and if sales increase by 10%. Do not prepare income statements.

(c) Which company should the investment banker acquire? Discuss.

*E6-17 Felde Company builds custom fishing lures for sporting goods stores. In its first year of operations, 2014, the company incurred the following costs.

Compute product cost and prepare an income statement under variable and absorption costing.

(LO 6), AP

Variable Costs per Unit	
Direct materials	$7.50
Direct labor	$2.45
Variable manufacturing overhead	$5.80
Variable selling and administrative expenses	$3.90

Fixed Costs per Year	
Fixed manufacturing overhead	$225,000
Fixed selling and administrative expenses	$240,100

Felde Company sells the fishing lures for $25. During 2014, the company sold 80,000 lures and produced 90,000 lures.

Instructions

(a) Assuming the company uses variable costing, calculate Felde's manufacturing cost per unit for 2014.

(b) Prepare a variable costing income statement for 2014.

(c) Assuming the company uses absorption costing, calculate Felde's manufacturing cost per unit for 2014.

(d) Prepare an absorption costing income statement for 2014.

*E6-18 Langdon Company produced 9,000 units during the past year, but only 8,200 of the units were sold. The following additional information is also available.

Determine ending inventory under variable costing and determine whether absorption or variable costing would result in higher net income.

(LO 6, 7), AN

Direct materials used	$79,000
Direct labor incurred	$30,000
Variable manufacturing overhead	$21,500
Fixed manufacturing overhead	$45,000
Fixed selling and administrative expenses	$70,000
Variable selling and administrative expenses	$10,000

There was no work in process inventory at the beginning of the year, nor did Langdon have any beginning finished goods inventory.

Instructions

(a) What would be Langdon Company's finished goods inventory cost on December 31 under variable costing?

(b) Which costing method, absorption or variable costing, would show a higher net income for the year? By what amount?

*E6-19 Creative Crates Co. produces wooden crates used for shipping products by ocean liner. In 2014, Creative incurred the following costs.

Compute manufacturing cost under absorption and variable costing and explain difference.

(LO 6), AN

Wood used in crate production	$54,000
Nails (considered insignificant and a variable expense)	$ 350
Direct labor	$38,000
Utilities for the plant:	
$1,500 each month,	
plus $0.40 for each kilowatt-hour used each month	
Rent expense for the plant for the year	$21,400

Assume Creative used an average 500 kilowatt-hours each month over the past year.

Instructions

(a) What is Creative's total manufacturing cost if it uses a variable costing approach?

(b) What is Creative's total manufacturing cost if it uses an absorption costing approach?

(c) What accounts for the difference in manufacturing costs between these two costing approaches?

EXERCISES: SET B AND CHALLENGE EXERCISES

Visit the book's companion website, at **www.wiley.com/college/weygandt**, and choose the Student Companion site to access Exercise Set B and Challenge Exercises.

PROBLEMS: SET A

Compute break-even point under alternative courses of action.

(LO 1, 2), AN

P6-1A Fredonia Inc. had a bad year in 2013. For the first time in its history, it operated at a loss. The company's income statement showed the following results from selling 80,000 units of product: net sales $2,000,000; total costs and expenses $1,740,000; and net loss $135,000. Costs and expenses consisted of the following.

	Total	Variable	Fixed
Cost of goods sold	$1,468,000	$ 950,000	$ 518,000
Selling expenses	517,000	92,000	425,000
Administrative expenses	150,000	58,000	92,000
	$2,135,000	$1,100,000	$1,035,000

Management is considering the following independent alternatives for 2014.

1. Increase unit selling price 25% with no change in costs and expenses.
2. Change the compensation of salespersons from fixed annual salaries totaling $200,000 to total salaries of $40,000 plus a 5% commission on net sales.
3. Purchase new high-tech factory machinery that will change the proportion between variable and fixed cost of goods sold to 50:50.

Instructions
(a) Compute the break-even point in dollars for 2014.

(b) (2) $2,187,500

(b) Compute the break-even point in dollars under each of the alternative courses of action. (Round to the nearest dollar.) Which course of action do you recommend?

Compute break-even point and margin of safety ratio, and prepare a CVP income statement before and after changes in business environment.

(LO 1, 2), AN

P6-2A Lorge Corporation has collected the following information after its first year of sales. Sales were $1,500,000 on 100,000 units; selling expenses $250,000 (40% variable and 60% fixed); direct materials $511,000; direct labor $290,000; administrative expenses $270,000 (20% variable and 80% fixed); manufacturing overhead $350,000 (70% variable and 30% fixed). Top management has asked you to do a CVP analysis so that it can make plans for the coming year. It has projected that unit sales will increase by 10% next year.

Instructions
(a) Compute (1) the contribution margin for the current year and the projected year, and (2) the fixed costs for the current year. (Assume that fixed costs will remain the same in the projected year.)

(b) 157,000 units

(b) Compute the break-even point in units and sales dollars for the first year.
(c) The company has a target net income of $200,000. What is the required sales in dollars for the company to meet its target?
(d) If the company meets its target net income number, by what percentage could its sales fall before it is operating at a loss? That is, what is its margin of safety ratio?

(e) (3) $1,735,714

(e) The company is considering a purchase of equipment that would reduce its direct labor costs by $104,000 and would change its manufacturing overhead costs to 30% variable and 70% fixed (assume total manufacturing overhead cost is $350,000, as above). It is also considering switching to a pure commission basis for its sales staff. This would change selling expenses to 90% variable and 10% fixed (assume total selling expense is $250,000, as above). Compute (1) the contribution margin and (2) the contribution margin ratio, and recompute (3) the break-even point in sales dollars. Comment on the effect each of management's proposed changes has on the break-even point.

P6-3A Tanek Industries manufactures and sells three different models of wet-dry shop vacuum cleaners. Although the shop vacs vary in terms of quality and features, all are good sellers. Tanek is currently operating at full capacity with limited machine time. Sales and production information relevant to each model follows.

Determine sales mix with limited resources.

(LO 4), AN

	Product		
	Economy	Standard	Deluxe
Selling price	$30	$50	$100
Variable costs and expenses	$14	$15	$46
Machine hours required	.5	.8	1.6

Instructions
(a) Ignoring the machine time constraint, which single product should Tanek Industries produce?
(b) What is the contribution margin per unit of limited resource for each product?
(c) If additional machine time could be obtained, how should the additional time be used?

(b) Economy $32

P6-4A The Hillside Inn is a restaurant in Flagstaff, Arizona. It specializes in southwestern style meals in a moderate price range. Phil Weld, the manager of Hillside, has determined that during the last 2 years the sales mix and contribution margin ratio of its offerings are as follows.

Determine break-even sales under alternative sales strategies and evaluate results.

(LO 3), AN

	Percent of Total Sales	Contribution Margin Ratio
Appetizers	15%	50%
Main entrees	50%	25%
Desserts	10%	50%
Beverages	25%	80%

Phil is considering a variety of options to try to improve the profitability of the restaurant. His goal is to generate a target net income of $117,000. The company has fixed costs of $1,053,000 per year.

Instructions
(a) Calculate the total restaurant sales and the sales of each product line that would be necessary to achieve the desired target net income.
(b) Phil believes the restaurant could greatly improve its profitability by reducing the complexity and selling price of its entrees to increase the number of clients that it serves. It would then more heavily market its appetizers and beverages. He is proposing to reduce the contribution margin ratio on the main entrees to 10% by dropping the average selling price. He envisions an expansion of the restaurant that would increase fixed costs by $585,000. At the same time, he is proposing to change the sales mix to the following.

(a) Total sales $2,600,000

(b) Total sales $3,375,000

	Percent of Total Sales	Contribution Margin Ratio
Appetizers	25%	50%
Main entrees	25%	10%
Desserts	10%	50%
Beverages	40%	80%

Compute the total restaurant sales, and the sales of each product line that would be necessary to achieve the desired target net income.
(c) Suppose that Phil reduces the selling price on entrees and increases fixed costs as proposed in part (b), but customers are not swayed by the marketing efforts and the sales mix remains what it was in part (a). Compute the total restaurant sales and the sales of each product line that would be necessary to achieve the desired target net income. Comment on the potential risks and benefits of this strategy.

Compute degree of operating leverage and evaluate impact of operating leverage on financial results.

(LO 5), AN

P6-5A The following CVP income statements are available for Viejo Company and Nuevo Company.

	Viejo Company	**Nuevo Company**
Sales	$500,000	$500,000
Variable costs	280,000	180,000
Contribution margin	220,000	320,000
Fixed costs	180,000	280,000
Net income	$ 40,000	$ 40,000

Instructions

(a) BE, Viejo $409,091
    BE, Nuevo $437,500

(b) DOL, Viejo 5.5
    DOL, Nuevo 8.0

(a) Compute the break-even point in dollars and the margin of safety ratio for each company.
(b) Compute the degree of operating leverage for each company and interpret your results.
(c) Assuming that sales revenue increases by 20%, prepare a CVP income statement for each company.
(d) Assuming that sales revenue decreases by 20%, prepare a CVP income statement for each company.
(e) ▭▭▭▷ Discuss how the cost structure of these two companies affects their operating leverage and profitability.

Determine contribution margin, break-even point, target sales, and degree of operating leverage.

(LO 2, 5), AN

P6-6A Bonita Beauty Corporation manufactures cosmetic products that are sold through a network of sales agents. The agents are paid a commission of 18% of sales. The income statement for the year ending December 31, 2014, is as follows.

Bonita Beauty Corporation
Income Statement
For the Year Ended December 31, 2014

Sales		$75,000,000
Cost of goods sold		
Variable	$31,500,000	
Fixed	8,610,000	40,110,000
Gross margin		34,890,000
Selling and marketing expenses		
Commissions	13,500,000	
Fixed costs	10,260,000	23,760,000
Operating income		$11,130,000

The company is considering hiring its own sales staff to replace the network of agents. It will pay its salespeople a commission of 8% and incur additional fixed costs of $7.5 million.

Instructions

(a) $47,175

(c) (2) 3.37

(a) Under the current policy of using a network of sales agents, calculate the Bonita Beauty Corporation's break-even point in sales dollars for the year 2014.
(b) Calculate the company's break-even point in sales dollars for the year 2014 if it hires its own sales force to replace the network of agents.
(c) Calculate the degree of operating leverage at sales of $75 million if (1) Bonita Beauty uses sales agents, and (2) Bonita Beauty employs its own sales staff. Describe the advantages and disadvantages of each alternative.
(d) Calculate the estimated sales volume in sales dollars that would generate an identical net income for the year ending December 31, 2014, regardless of whether Bonita Beauty Corporation employs its own sales staff and pays them an 8% commission or continues to use the independent network of agents.

(CMA-Canada adapted)

Prepare income statements under absorption costing and variable costing for a company with beginning inventory, and reconcile differences.

(LO 6, 7), AN

*P6-7A Gardner Company produces plastic that is used for injection-molding applications such as gears for small motors. In 2013, the first year of operations, Gardner produced 4,000 tons of plastic and sold 2,500 tons. In 2014, the production and sales results were exactly reversed. In each year, the selling price per ton was $2,000, variable manufacturing costs were 15% of the sales price of units produced, variable selling expenses were 10%

of the selling price of units sold, fixed manufacturing costs were $2,000,000, and fixed administrative expenses were $500,000.

Instructions

(a) Prepare income statements for each year using variable costing. (Use the format from Illustration 6A-5.)

(b) Prepare income statements for each year using absorption costing. (Use the format from Illustration 6A-4.)

(c) Reconcile the differences each year in net income under the two costing approaches.

(d) ▭▭▭▭▭▷ Comment on the effects of production and sales on net income under the two costing approaches.

(a) 2014 $3,500,000

(b) 2014 $2,750,000

*P6-8A Dilithium Batteries is a division of Enterprise Corporation. The division manufactures and sells a long-life battery used in a wide variety of applications. During the coming year, it expects to sell 60,000 units for $30 per unit. Nyota Uthura is the division manager. She is considering producing either 60,000 or 90,000 units during the period. Other information is presented in the schedule.

Prepare absorption and variable costing income statements and reconcile differences between absorption and variable costing income statements when sales level and production level change. Discuss relative usefulness of absorption costing versus variable costing.

(LO 6, 7, 8), AN

Division Information for 2014

Beginning inventory	0
Expected sales in units	60,000
Selling price per unit	$30
Variable manufacturing costs per unit	$12
Fixed manufacturing overhead costs (total)	$540,000
Fixed manufacturing overhead costs per unit:	
Based on 60,000 units	$9 per unit ($540,000 ÷ 60,000)
Based on 90,000 units	$6 per unit ($540,000 ÷ 90,000)
Manufacturing costs per unit:	
Based on 60,000 units	$21 per unit ($12 variable + $9 fixed)
Based on 90,000 units	$18 per unit ($12 variable + $6 fixed)
Variable selling and administrative expenses	$2
Fixed selling and administrative expenses (total)	$50,000

Instructions

(a) Prepare an absorption costing income statement, with one column showing the results if 60,000 units are produced and one column showing the results if 90,000 units are produced.

(b) Prepare a variable costing income statement, with one column showing the results if 60,000 units are produced and one column showing the results if 90,000 units are produced.

(c) Reconcile the difference in net incomes under the two approaches and explain what accounts for this difference.

(d) ▭▭▭▭▭▷ Discuss the relative usefulness of the variable costing income statements versus the absorption costing income statements for decision making and for evaluating the manager's performance.

(a) 90,000 units: NI $550,000

(b) 90,000 units: NI $370,000

PROBLEMS: SET B

P6-1B McCure Corporation had a bad year in 2013, operating at a loss for the first time in its history. The company's income statement showed the following results from selling 200,000 units of product: net sales $2,400,000; total costs and expenses $2,472,000; and net loss $72,000. Costs and expenses consisted of the following.

Compute break-even point under alternative courses of action.

(LO 1, 2), AN

	Total	Variable	Fixed
Cost of goods sold	$1,486,000	$1,070,000	$416,000
Selling expenses	681,000	356,000	325,000
Administrative expenses	305,000	110,000	195,000
	$2,472,000	$1,536,000	$936,000

Management is considering the following independent alternatives for 2014.

1. Increase unit selling price 25% with no change in costs and expenses.
2. Change the compensation of salespersons from fixed annual salaries totaling $170,000 to total salaries of $50,000 plus a 6% commission on net sales.
3. Purchase new high-tech factory machinery that will change the proportion between variable and fixed cost of goods sold to 40:60.

Instructions
(a) Compute the break-even point in dollars for 2014.

(b) (2) $2,720,000

(b) Compute the break-even point in dollars under each of the alternative courses of action. Which course of action do you recommend? Round to the nearest dollar.

Compute break-even point and margin of safety ratio, and prepare a CVP income statement before and after changes in business environment.

(LO 1, 2), AN

P6-2B Huber Corporation has collected the following information after its first year of sales. Sales were $1,000,000 on 40,000 units; selling expenses $200,000 (30% variable and 70% fixed); direct materials $327,000; direct labor $190,000; administrative expenses $250,000 (30% variable and 70% fixed); manufacturing overhead $240,000 (20% variable and 80% fixed). Top management has asked you to do a CVP analysis so that it can make plans for the coming year. It has projected that unit sales will increase by 20% next year.

Instructions
(a) Compute (1) the contribution margin for the current year and the projected year, and (2) the fixed costs for the current year. (Assume that fixed costs will remain the same in the projected year.)

(b) 67,600 units

(b) Compute the break-even point in units and sales dollars for the current year.
(c) The company has a target net income of $120,000. What is the required sales in dollars for the company to meet its target?
(d) If the company meets its target net income number, by what percentage could its sales fall before it is operating at a loss? That is, what is its margin of safety ratio?

(e) (3) $1,372,611

(e) The company is considering a purchase of equipment that would reduce its direct labor costs by $90,000 and would change its manufacturing overhead costs to 10% variable and 90% fixed (assume total manufacturing overhead cost is $240,000, as above). It is also considering switching to a pure commission basis for its sales staff. This would change selling expenses to 80% variable and 20% fixed (assume total selling expense is $200,000, as above). Compute (1) the contribution margin and (2) the contribution margin ratio, and (3) recompute the break-even point in sales dollars. Comment on the effect each of management's proposed changes has on the break-even point.

Determine sales mix with limited resources.

(LO 4), AN

P6-3B Keppel Corporation manufactures and sells three different models of exterior doors. Although the doors vary in terms of quality and features, all are good sellers. Keppel is currently operating at full capacity with limited machine time.

Sales and production information relevant to each model is shown below.

	Product		
	Economy	**Standard**	**Deluxe**
Selling price	$270	$450	$650
Variable costs and expenses	$144	$260	$430
Machine hours required	.6	.8	1.1

Instructions
(a) Ignoring the machine time constraint, which single product should Keppel produce?

(b) Economy $210

(b) What is the contribution margin per unit of limited resource for each product?
(c) If additional machine time could be obtained, how should the additional time be used?

Determine break-even sales under alternative sales strategies and evaluate results.

(LO 3), AN

P6-4B The Eatery is a restaurant in DeKalb, Illinois. It specializes in deluxe sandwiches in a moderate price range. Michael Raye, the manager of The Eatery, has determined that during the last 2 years the sales mix and contribution margin ratio of its offerings are as follows.

	Percent of Total Sales	Contribution Margin Ratio
Appetizers	15%	60%
Main entrees	60%	25%
Desserts	10%	40%
Beverages	15%	80%

Michael is considering a variety of options to try to improve the profitability of the restaurant. His goal is to generate a target net income of $176,000. The company has fixed costs of $352,000 per year.

Instructions

(a) Calculate the total restaurant sales and the sales of each product line that would be necessary to achieve the desired target net income.

(b) Michael believes the restaurant could greatly improve its profitability by reducing the complexity and selling price of its entrees to increase the number of clients that it serves. It would then more heavily market its appetizers and beverages. He is proposing to reduce the contribution margin ratio on the main entrees to 10% by dropping the average selling price and increasing the contribution margin ratio on desserts to 50% by reducing costs. He envisions an expansion of the restaurant that would increase fixed costs by 50%. At the same time, he is proposing to change the sales mix to the following.

	Percent of Total Sales	Contribution Margin Ratio
Appetizers	25%	60%
Main entrees	40%	10%
Desserts	10%	50%
Beverages	25%	80%

Compute the total restaurant sales, and the sales of each product line that would be necessary to achieve the desired target net income.

(c) Suppose that Michael reduces the selling price on entrees and increases fixed costs as proposed in part (b), but customers are not swayed by the marketing efforts and the sales mix remains what it was in part (a). Compute the total restaurant sales and the sales of each product line that would be necessary to achieve the desired target net income. Comment on the potential risks and benefits of this strategy.

P6-5B The following variable costing income statements are available for Lyte Company and Darke Company.

	Lyte Company	Darke Company
Sales	$1,000,000	$1,000,000
Variable costs	600,000	200,000
Contribution margin	400,000	800,000
Fixed costs	200,000	600,000
Net income	$ 200,000	$ 200,000

Instructions

(a) Compute the break-even point in dollars and the margin of safety ratio for each company.

(b) Compute the degree of operating leverage for each company and interpret your results.

(c) Assuming that sales revenue increases by 30%, prepare a variable costing income statement for each company.

(d) Assuming that sales revenue decreases by 30%, prepare a variable costing income statement for each company.

(e) ▱▱▱▱▷ Discuss how the cost structure of these two companies affects their operating leverage and profitability.

P6-6B Peaches and Cream Corporation manufactures cosmetic products that are sold through a network of sales agents. The agents are paid a commission of 16.25% of sales. The income statement for the year ending December 31, 2014, is shown on the next page.

(Margin notes:)

(a) Total sales, $1,320,000

(b) Total sales, $1,600,000

(c) Total sales, $2,200,000

Compute degree of operating leverage and evaluate impact of operating leverage on financial results.

(LO 5), AN

(a) BE Lyte $500,000
   BE Darke $750,000

(b) DOL, Lyte 2.0
   DOL, Darke 4.0

Determine contribution margin, break-even point, target sales, and degree of operating leverage.

(LO 2, 5), AN

Peaches and Cream Corporation
Income Statement
For the Year Ended December 31, 2014

Sales		$120,000,000
Cost of goods sold		
Variable	$58,500,000	
Fixed	11,000,000	69,500,000
Gross margin		50,500,000
Selling and marketing expenses		
Commissions	19,500,000	
Fixed costs	10,000,000	29,500,000
Operating income		$ 21,000,000

The company is considering hiring its own sales staff to replace the network of agents. It will pay its salespeople a commission of 10% and incur additional fixed costs of $12.0 million.

Instructions

(a) $60,000

(a) Under the current policy of using a network of sales agents, calculate the Peaches and Cream Corporation's break-even point in sales dollars for the year 2014.

(b) Calculate the company's break-even point in sales dollars for the year 2014 if it hires its own sales force to replace the network of agents.

(c) (2) 3.0

(c) Calculate the degree of operating leverage at sales of $120 million if (1) Peaches and Cream uses sales agents, and (2) Peaches and Cream employs its own sales staff. Describe the advantages and disadvantages of each alternative.

(d) Calculate the estimated sales volume in sales dollars that would generate an identical net income for the year ending December 31, 2014, regardless of whether Peaches and Cream Corporation employs its own sales staff and pays them a 10% commission as well as incurring additional fixed costs of $12.0 million, or continues to use the independent network of agents.

(CMA Canada-adapted)

Prepare income statements under absorption costing and variable costing for a company with beginning inventory, and reconcile differences.

(LO 6, 7), AN

(a) 2013 Net income $100,000

(b) 2013 Net income $180,000

*P6-7B FAB produces fabrics that are used for clothing and other applications. In 2013, the first year of operations, FAB produced 500,000 yards of fabric and sold 400,000 yards. In 2014, the production and sales results were exactly reversed. In each year, selling price per yard was $2.50, variable manufacturing costs were 30% of the sales price of units produced, variable selling expenses were 10% of the selling price of units sold, fixed manufacturing costs were $400,000, and fixed administrative expenses were $100,000.

Instructions

(a) Prepare income statements for each year using variable costing. (Use the format from Illustration 6A-10.)

(b) Prepare income statements for each year using absorption costing. (Use the format from Illustration 6A-11.)

(c) Reconcile the differences each year in income from operations under the two costing approaches.

(d) ▭▭▭▷ Comment on the effects of production and sales on net income under the two costing approaches.

Prepare absorption and variable costing income statements and reconcile differences between absorption and variable costing income statements when sales level and production level change. Discuss relative usefulness of absorption costing versus variable costing.

(LO 6, 7, 8), AN

P6-8B Electricoil is a division of Meier Products Corporation. The division manufactures and sells an electric coil used in a wide variety of applications. During the coming year, it expects to sell 200,000 units for $9 per unit. Mark Barnes is the division manager. He is considering producing either 200,000 or 250,000 units during the period. Other information is presented in the schedule.

Division Information for 2014

Beginning inventory	0
Expected sales in units	200,000
Selling price per unit	$9
Variable manufacturing costs per unit	$3
Fixed manufacturing overhead costs (total)	$500,000

Fixed manufacturing overhead costs per unit:
    Based on 200,000 units $2.50 per unit ($50,000 ÷ 200,000)
    Based on 250,000 units $2.00 per unit ($500,000 ÷ 250,000)

Manufacturing costs per unit:
    Based on 200,000 units $5.50 per unit ($3 variable + $2.50 fixed)
    Based on 250,000 units $5.00 per unit ($3 variable + $2.00 fixed)
    Variable selling and administrative expense $0.40
    Fixed selling and administrative expense (total) $15,000

Instructions

(a) Prepare an absorption costing income statement, with one column showing the results if 200,000 units are produced and one column showing the results if 250,000 units are produced.

(b) Prepare a variable costing income statement, with one column showing the results if 200,000 units are produced and one column showing the results if 250,000 units are produced.

(c) Reconcile the difference in net incomes under the two approaches and explain what accounts for this difference.

(d) ◼▤▶ Discuss the relative usefulness of the variable costing income statements versus the absorption costing income statements for decision making and for evaluating the manager's performance.

(a) 250,000 produced
    NI, $705,000

(b) 250,000 produced
    NI, $605,000

PROBLEMS: SET C

Visit the book's companion website, at **www.wiley.com/college/weygandt**, and choose the Student Companion site to access Problem Set C.

WATERWAYS CONTINUING PROBLEM

(*Note:* This is a continuation of the Waterways Problem from Chapters 1–5.)

WCP6 This problem asks you to perform break-even analysis based on Waterways' sales mix and to make sales mix decisions related to Waterways' use of its productive facilities. An optional extension of the problem (related to the chapter appendix) also asks you to prepare a variable costing income statement and an absorption costing income statement.

Go to the book's companion website, **www.wiley.com/college/weygandt**, to find the remainder of this problem.

Broadening Your PERSPECTIVE

Management Decision-Making

Decision-Making at Current Designs

BYP6-1 Current Designs manufactures two different types of kayaks, rotomolded kayaks and composite kayaks. The following information is available for each product line.

	Rotomolded	Composite
Sales price/unit	$950	$2,000
Variable costs/unit	$570	$1,340

The company's fixed costs are $820,000. An analysis of the sales mix identifies that rotomolded kayaks make up 80% of the total units sold.

Instructions
(a) Determine the weighted-average unit contribution margin for Current Designs.
(b) Determine the break-even point in units for Current Designs and identify how many units of each type of kayak will be sold at the break-even point. (Round to the nearest whole number.)
(c) Assume that the sales mix changes, and rotomolded kayaks now make up 70% of total units sold. Calculate the total number of units that would need to be sold to earn a net income of $2,000,000 and identify how many units of each type of kayak will be sold at this level of income. (Round to the nearest whole number.)
(d) Assume that Current Designs will have sales of $3,000,000 with two-thirds of the sales dollars in rotomolded kayaks and one-third of the sales dollars in composite kayaks. Assuming $660,000 of fixed costs are allocated to the rotomolded kayaks and $160,000 to the composite kayaks, prepare a CVP income statement for each product line.
(e) Using the information in part (d), calculate the degree of operating leverage for each product line and interpret your findings. (Round to two decimal places.)

Decision-Making Across The Organization

BYP6-2 E-Z Seats manufactures swivel seats for customized vans. It currently manufactures 10,000 seats per year, which it sells for $500 per seat. It incurs variable costs of $200 per seat and fixed costs of $2,000,000. It is considering automating the upholstery process, which is now largely manual. It estimates that if it does so, its fixed costs will be $3,000,000, and its variable costs will decline to $100 per seat.

Instructions
With the class divided into groups, answer the following questions.
(a) Prepare a CVP income statement based on current activity.
(b) Compute contribution margin ratio, break-even point in dollars, margin of safety ratio, and degree of operating leverage based on current activity.
(c) Prepare a CVP income statement assuming that the company invests in the automated upholstery system.
(d) Compute contribution margin ratio, break-even point in dollars, margin of safety ratio, and degree of operating leverage assuming the new upholstery system is implemented.
(e) Discuss the implications of adopting the new system.

Managerial Analysis

BYP6-3 For nearly 20 years, Specialized Coatings has provided painting and galvanizing services for manufacturers in its region. Manufacturers of various metal products have relied on the quality and quick turnaround time provided by Specialized Coatings and its 20 skilled employees. During the last year, as a result of a sharp upturn in the economy, the company's sales have increased by 30% relative to the previous year. The company has not been able to increase its capacity fast enough, so Specialized Coatings has had to turn work away because it cannot keep up with customer requests.

Top management is considering the purchase of a sophisticated robotic painting booth. The booth would represent a considerable move in the direction of automation versus manual labor. If Specialized Coatings purchases the booth, it would most likely lay off 15 of its skilled painters. To analyze the decision, the company compiled production information from the most recent year and then prepared a parallel compilation assuming that the company would purchase the new equipment and lay off the workers. Those data are shown below. As you can see, the company projects that during the last year it would have been far more profitable if it had used the automated approach.

	Current Approach	Automated Approach
Sales	$2,000,000	$2,000,000
Variable costs	1,500,000	1,000,000
Contribution margin	500,000	1,000,000
Fixed costs	380,000	800,000
Net income	$ 120,000	$ 200,000

Instructions
(a) Compute and interpret the contribution margin ratio under each approach.
(b) Compute the break-even point in sales dollars under each approach. Discuss the implications of your findings.

(c) Using the current level of sales, compute the margin of safety ratio under each approach and interpret your findings.
(d) Determine the degree of operating leverage for each approach at current sales levels. How much would the company's net income decline under each approach with a 10% decline in sales?
(e) At what level of sales would the company's net income be the same under either approach?
(f) Discuss the issues that the company must consider in making this decision.

Real-World Focus

BYP6-4 In a recent report, the Del Monte Foods Company reported three separate operating segments: consumer products (which includes a variety of canned foods including tuna, fruit, and vegetables); pet products (which includes pet food and snacks and veterinary products); and soup and infant-feeding products (which includes soup, broth, and infant feeding and pureed products).

In its annual report, Del Monte uses absorption costing. As a result, information regarding the relative composition of its fixed and variable costs is not available. We have assumed that $860.3 million of its total operating expenses of $1,920.3 million are fixed and have allocated the remaining variable costs across the three divisions. Sales data, along with assumed expense data, are provided below.

	(in millions)	
	Sales	Variable Costs
Consumer products	$1,031.8	$ 610
Pet products	837.3	350
Soup and infant-feeding products	302.0	100
	$2,171.1	$1,060

Instructions
(a) Compute each segment's contribution margin ratio and the sales mix.
(b) Using the information computed in part (a), compute the company's break-even point in dollars, and then determine the amount of sales that would be generated by each division at the break-even point.

BYP6-5 The external financial statements published by publicly traded companies are based on absorption cost accounting. As a consequence, it is very difficult to gain an understanding of the relative composition of the companies' fixed and variable costs. It is possible, however, to learn about a company's sales mix and the relative profitability of its various divisions. This exercise looks at the financial statements of FedEx Corporation.

Address: **www.fedex.com/us/investorrelations**, or go to **www.wiley.com/college/weygandt**

Steps
1. Go to the site above.
2. Under "Financial Documents," choose "Annual Reports."
3. Choose "2008 Annual Report."

Instructions
(a) Read page 25 of the report under the heading "Description of Business." What are the three primary product lines of the company? What does the company identify as the key factors affecting operating results?
(b) Page 36 of the report lists the operating expenses of FedEx Ground. Assuming that rentals, depreciation, and "other" are all fixed costs, prepare a variable costing income statement for 2008, and compute the division's contribution margin ratio and the break-even point in dollars.
(c) Page 73, Note 13 ("Business segment information") provides additional information regarding the relative profitability of the three business segments.
   (i) Calculate the sales mix for 2006 and 2008. (*Note:* Exclude "other" when you calculate total revenue.)

(ii) The company does not provide the contribution margin for each division, but it does provide "operating margin" (operating income divided by revenues) on pages 34, 36, and 37. List these for each division for 2006 and 2008.

(iii) Assuming that the "operating margin" (operating income divided by revenues) moves in parallel with each division's contribution margin, how has the shift in sales mix affected the company's profitability from 2006 to 2008?

BYP6-6 The June 8, 2009, edition of the *Wall Street Journal* has an article by JoAnn Lublin entitled "Smart Balance Keeps Tight Focus on Creativity."

Instructions
Read the article and answer the following questions.
(a) Describe Smart Balance's approach to employment and cost structure.
(b) What function does it keep "in-house"?
(c) Based on the discussion in this chapter, what are the advantages to Smart Balance's approach?
(d) Based on the discussion in this chapter, what are the disadvantages to Smart Balance's approach?

Critical Thinking

Communication Activity

BYP6-7 Easton Corporation makes two different boat anchors—a traditional fishing anchor and a high-end yacht anchor—using the same production machinery. The contribution margin of the yacht anchor is three times as high as that of the other product. The company is currently operating at full capacity and has been doing so for nearly two years. Bjorn Borg, the company's CEO, wants to cut back on production of the fishing anchor so that the company can make more yacht anchors. He says that this is a "no-brainer" because the contribution margin of the yacht anchor is so much higher.

Instructions
Write a short memo to Bjorn Borg describing the analysis that the company should do before it makes this decision and any other considerations that would affect the decision.

Ethics Case

*BYP6-8 Brett Stern was hired during January 2014 to manage the home products division of Hi-Tech Products. As part of his employment contract, he was told that he would get $5,000 of additional bonus for every 1% increase that the division's profits exceeded those of the previous year.

Soon after coming on board, Brett met with his plant managers and explained that he wanted the plants to be run at full capacity. Previously, the plant had employed just-in-time inventory practices and had consequently produced units only as they were needed. Brett stated that under previous management the company had missed out on too many sales opportunities because it didn't have enough inventory on hand. Because previous management had employed just-in-time inventory practices, when Brett came on board there was virtually no beginning inventory. The selling price and variable costs per unit remained the same from 2013 to 2014. Additional information is provided below.

	2013	2014
Net income	$ 300,000	$ 525,000
Units produced	25,000	30,000
Units sold	25,000	25,000
Fixed manufacturing overhead costs	$1,350,000	$1,350,000
Fixed manufacturing overhead costs per unit	$ 54	$ 45

Instructions

(a) Calculate Brett's bonus based upon the net income shown above.
(b) Recompute the 2013 and 2014 results using variable costing.
(c) Recompute Brett's 2014 bonus under variable costing.
(d) Were Brett's actions unethical? Do you think any actions need to be taken by the company?

All About You

BYP6-9 Many of you will some day own your own business. One rapidly growing opportunity is no-frills workout centers. Such centers attract customers who want to take advantage of state-of-the-art fitness equipment but do not need the other amenities of full-service health clubs. One way to own your own fitness business is to buy a franchise. Snap Fitness is a Minnesota-based business that offers franchise opportunities. For a very low monthly fee ($26, without an annual contract), customers can access a Snap Fitness center 24 hours a day.

The Snap Fitness website (*www.snapfitness.com*) indicates that start-up costs range from $60,000 to $184,000. This initial investment covers the following pre-opening costs: franchise fee, grand opening marketing, leasehold improvements, utility/rent deposits, and training.

Instructions

(a) Suppose that Snap Fitness estimates that each location incurs $4,000 per month in fixed operating expenses plus $1,460 to lease equipment. A recent newspaper article describing no-frills fitness centers indicated that a Snap Fitness site might require only 300 members to break even. Using the information provided above and your knowledge of CVP analysis, estimate the amount of variable costs. (When performing your analysis, assume that the only fixed costs are the estimated monthly operating expenses and the equipment lease.)
(b) Using the information from part (a), what would monthly sales in members and dollars have to be to achieve a target net income of $3,640 for the month?
(c) Provide five examples of variable costs for a fitness center.
(d) Go to a fitness-business website, such as Curves, Snap Fitness, or Anytime Fitness, and find information about purchasing a franchise. Summarize the franchise information needed to decide whether entering into a franchise agreement would be a good idea.

Considering People, Planet, and Profit

BYP6-10 Many politicians, scientists, economists, and businesspeople have become concerned about the potential implications of global warming. The largest source of the emissions thought to contribute to global warming is from coal-fired power plants. The cost of alternative energy has declined, but it is still higher than coal. In 1980, wind-power electricity cost 80 cents per kilowatt hour. Using today's highly efficient turbines with rotor diameters of up to 125 meters, the cost can be as low as 4 cents (about the same as coal), or as much as 20 cents in places with less wind.

Some people have recently suggested that conventional cost comparisons are not adequate because they do not take environmental costs into account. For example, while coal is a very cheap energy source, it is also a significant contributor of greenhouse gases. Should environmental costs be incorporated into decision formulas when planners evaluate new power plants? The basic arguments for and against are as follows.

YES: As long as environmental costs are ignored, renewable energy will appear to be too expensive relative to coal.

NO: If one country decides to incorporate environmental costs into its decision-making process but other countries do not, the country that does so will be at a competitive disadvantage because its products will cost more to produce.

Instructions

Write a response indicating your position regarding this situation. Provide support for your view.

Answers to Chapter Questions

Answers to Insight and Accounting Across the Organization Questions

p. 242 Don't Just Look—Buy Something Q: Besides increasing their conversion rates, what steps can online merchants use to lower their break-even points? **A:** In theory, one of the principal advantages of online retailers is that they can minimize their investment in "bricks and mortar" and thus minimize their fixed costs. Some online merchants never even handle the merchandise they sell. Instead, they simply provide a centralized location for customers to view merchandise and to place orders. The online retailer then forwards the order to the supplier, and the supplier ships it directly to the customer.

However, some online merchants who originally planned on employing this model have since found it necessary to build their own warehouses and distribution centers to ensure timely and dependable product delivery. This increases their fixed costs and consequently increases their break-even point.

p. 247 Healthy for You, and Great for the Bottom Line Q: Why do you suppose restaurants are so eager to sell beverages and desserts? **A:** There is a reason why servers at restaurants keep your beverage glass full, and why they wave the dessert tray in your face at the end of the meal. Both of these items traditionally have very high contribution margins and require very minimal investments in fixed costs. As a consequence, they are a great mechanism by which a company can hit its break-even point.

p. 250 Something Smells Q: What is the limited resource for a retailer, and what implications does this have for sales mix? **A:** For retailers, the limited resource is not just shelf space, but shelf space per day. At first, you might think that a product that is small and has a high contribution margin would be the product of choice. But, you also have to factor in the amount of time that a product sits on the shelf.

For example, suppose Product A and B are the same size. Product A has twice the contribution margin as product B, but A sits on the shelf five times as long as product B. In this case, once time spent on the shelf is taken into account, B's superior turnover more than makes up for its lower contribution margin.

p. 253 There Is Something About a Train Q: Why did Warren Buffett think that this was a good time to invest in railroad stocks? **A:** Railroads have extremely high fixed costs. Mr. Buffett bought Burlington Northern Railroad at the bottom of a recession. He is counting on the railroad's high operating leverage to provide large profits once the economy rebounds.

Answers to Self-Test Questions

1. d **2.** d **3.** a **4.** a ($350,000 − $100,000) **5.** b [($180,000 + $268,000) ÷ ($12 − $8.50)]
6. d [$150,000 ÷ ($3 ÷ $12)] **7.** d **8.** a **9.** b ($15 ÷ 3.0) **10.** d [($26 ÷ 4) < ($14 ÷ 2)] **11.** d
12. d **13.** c **14.** a ($200,000 × 3.5 × 10%) ***15.** b ***16.** c

✔   **Remember to go back to The Navigator box on the chapter opening page and check off your completed work.**

Chapter 7

Incremental Analysis

Make It or Buy It?

When is a manufacturer not a manufacturer? When it outsources. An extension of the classic "make or buy" decision, outsourcing involves hiring other companies to make all or part of a product or to perform services. Who is outsourcing? Nike, General Motors, Sara Lee, and Hewlett-Packard, to name a few. Even a recent trade journal article for small cabinet-makers outlined the pros and cons of building cabinet doors and drawers internally, or outsourcing them to other shops.

Gibson Greetings, Inc., one of the country's largest sellers of greeting cards, has experienced both the pros and cons of outsourcing. In April one year, it announced it would outsource the manufacturing of all of its cards and gift wrap. Gibson's stock price shot up quickly because investors believed the strategy could save the company $10 million a year, primarily by reducing manufacturing costs. But later in the same year, Gibson got a taste of the negative side of outsourcing: When one of its suppliers was unable to meet its production schedule, about $20 million of Christmas cards went to stores a month later than scheduled.

Outsourcing is often a point of dispute in labor negotiations. Although many of the jobs lost to outsourcing go overseas, that is not always the case. In fact, a recent trend is to hire out work to vendors located close to the company. This reduces shipping costs and can improve coordination of efforts.

✔ The Navigator

- [ ] Scan Learning Objectives
- [ ] Read Feature Story
- [ ] Read Preview
- [ ] Read Text and answer **DO IT!** p. 297
  - [ ] p. 299 [ ] p. 304 [ ] p. 307
- [ ] Work Using the Decision Toolkit p. 309
- [ ] Review Summary of Learning Objectives
- [ ] Work Comprehensive **DO IT!** p. 310
- [ ] Answer Self-Test Questions
- [ ] Complete Assignments
- [ ] Go to **WileyPLUS** for practice and tutorials

Learning Objectives

After studying this chapter, you should be able to:

1 Identify the steps in management's decision-making process.

2 Describe the concept of incremental analysis.

3 Identify the relevant costs in accepting an order at a special price.

4 Identify the relevant costs in a make-or-buy decision.

5 Identify the relevant costs in determining whether to sell or process materials further.

6 Identify the relevant costs to be considered in repairing, retaining, or replacing equipment.

7 Identify the relevant costs in deciding whether to eliminate an unprofitable segment or product.

✔ The Navigator

One company that has benefited from local outsourcing is Solectron Corporation in Silicon Valley. It makes things like cell phones, printers, and computers for high-tech companies in the region. To the surprise of many, it has kept thousands of people employed in California rather than watching those jobs go overseas. What is its secret? It produces high-quality products efficiently. Solectron has to be efficient because it

operates on a very thin profit margin—that is, it makes a tiny amount of money on each part—but it makes millions and millions of parts. It has proved the logic of outsourcing as a management decision, both for the companies for which it makes parts and for its owners and employees.

Watch the Method video in WileyPLUS to learn more about incremental analysis in the real world.

✔ The Navigator

Preview of **Chapter 7**

An important purpose of management accounting is to provide managers with relevant information for decision-making. Companies of all sorts must make product decisions. Philip Morris decided to cut prices to raise market share. Oral-B Laboratories opted to produce a new, higher-priced ($5) toothbrush. General Motors discontinued making the Buick Riviera and announced the closure of its Oldsmobile Division. Quaker Oats decided to sell off a line of beverages, at a price more than $1 billion less than it paid for that product line only a few years before. Ski manufacturers like Dynastar had to decide whether to use their limited resources to make snowboards instead of downhill skis.

This chapter explains management's decision-making process and a decision-making approach called incremental analysis. The use of incremental analysis is demonstrated in a variety of situations.

The content and organization of this chapter are as follows.

INCREMENTAL ANALYSIS		
Management's Decision-Making Process	**Types of Incremental Analysis**	**Other Considerations**
• Incremental analysis • How incremental analysis works	• Accept an order at a special price • Make or buy • Sell or process further • Repair, retain, or replace equipment • Eliminate an unprofitable segment or product	• Qualitative factors • Incremental analysis and ABC

✔ The Navigator

Management's Decision-Making Process

Making decisions is an important management function. Management's decision-making process does not always follow a set pattern because decisions vary significantly in their scope, urgency, and importance. It is possible, though, to identify some steps that are frequently involved in the process. These steps are shown in Illustration 7-1 below.

Accounting's contribution to the decision-making process occurs primarily in Steps 2 and 4—evaluating possible courses of action, and reviewing results. In Step 2, for each possible course of action, relevant revenue and cost data are provided. These show the expected overall effect on net income. In Step 4, internal reports are prepared that review the actual impact of the decision.

Illustration 7-1
Management's decision-making process

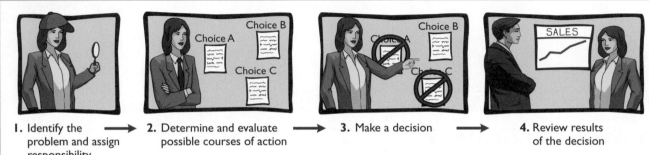

1. Identify the problem and assign responsibility ⟶ 2. Determine and evaluate possible courses of action ⟶ 3. Make a decision ⟶ 4. Review results of the decision

In making business decisions, management ordinarily considers both financial and nonfinancial information. **Financial** information is related to revenues and costs and their effect on the company's overall profitability. **Nonfinancial** information relates to such factors as the effect of the decision on employee turnover, the environment, or the overall image of the company in the community. (These are considerations that we touched on in our Chapter 1 discussion of corporate social responsibility.) Although nonfinancial information can be as important as financial information, we will focus primarily on financial information that is relevant to the decision.

Incremental Analysis Approach

Decisions involve a choice among alternative courses of action. Suppose you face the personal financial decision of whether to purchase or lease a car. The financial data relate to the cost of leasing versus the cost of purchasing. For example, leasing would involve periodic lease payments; purchasing would require "up-front" payment of the purchase price. In other words, the financial data relevant to the decision are the data that would vary in the future among the possible alternatives. The process used to identify the financial data that change under alternative courses of action is called **incremental analysis**. In some cases, you will find that when you use incremental analysis, both costs **and** revenues will vary. In other cases, only costs **or** revenues will vary.

Just as your decision to buy or lease a car will affect your future financial situation, similar decisions, on a larger scale, will affect a company's future. Incremental analysis identifies the probable effects of those decisions on future earnings. Such analysis inevitably involves estimates and uncertainty. Gathering data for incremental analyses may involve market analysts, engineers, and accountants. In quantifying the data, the accountant is expected to produce the most reliable information available at the time the decision must be made.

Alternative Terminology
Incremental analysis is also called *differential analysis* because the analysis focuses on differences.

How Incremental Analysis Works

The basic approach in incremental analysis is illustrated in the following example.

Illustration 7-2
Basic approach in incremental analysis

	Incremental Analysis.xls		
Home Insert Page Layout Formulas Data Review View			
P18 *fx*			
A	**B**	**C**	**D**
1	**Alternative A**	**Alternative B**	**Net Income Increase (Decrease)**
2 Revenues	$125,000	$110,000	$ (15,000)
3 Costs	100,000	80,000	20,000
4 Net income	$ 25,000	$ 30,000	$ 5,000
5			

This example compares alternative B with alternative A. The net income column shows the differences between the alternatives. In this case, incremental revenue will be $15,000 less under alternative B than under alternative A. But a $20,000 incremental cost saving will be realized.[1] Thus, alternative B will produce $5,000 more net income than alternative A.

In the following pages, you will encounter three important cost concepts used in incremental analysis, as defined and discussed in Illustration 7-3.

Illustration 7-3
Key cost concepts in incremental analysis

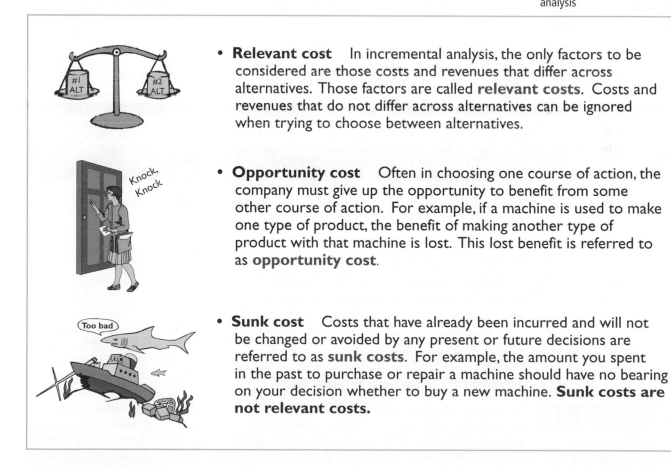

- **Relevant cost**   In incremental analysis, the only factors to be considered are those costs and revenues that differ across alternatives. Those factors are called **relevant costs**. Costs and revenues that do not differ across alternatives can be ignored when trying to choose between alternatives.

- **Opportunity cost**   Often in choosing one course of action, the company must give up the opportunity to benefit from some other course of action. For example, if a machine is used to make one type of product, the benefit of making another type of product with that machine is lost. This lost benefit is referred to as **opportunity cost**.

- **Sunk cost**   Costs that have already been incurred and will not be changed or avoided by any present or future decisions are referred to as **sunk costs**. For example, the amount you spent in the past to purchase or repair a machine should have no bearing on your decision whether to buy a new machine. **Sunk costs are not relevant costs.**

---

[1]Although income taxes are sometimes important in incremental analysis, they are ignored in the chapter for simplicity's sake.

Incremental analysis sometimes involves changes that at first glance might seem contrary to your intuition. For example, sometimes variable costs **do not change** under the alternative courses of action. Also, sometimes fixed costs **do change**. For example, direct labor, normally a variable cost, is not an incremental cost in deciding between two new factory machines if each asset requires the same amount of direct labor. In contrast, rent expense, normally a fixed cost, is an incremental cost in a decision whether to continue occupancy of a building or to purchase or lease a new building.

It is also important to understand that **the approaches to incremental analysis discussed in this chapter do not take into consideration the time value of money**. That is, amounts to be paid or received in future years are not discounted for the cost of interest. Time value of money is addressed in Chapter 12 and Appendix A.

SERVICE COMPANY INSIGHT

That Letter from AmEx Might Not Be a Bill

No doubt every one of you has received an invitation from a credit card company to open a new account—some of you have probably received three in one day. But how many of you have received an offer of $300 to close out your credit card account? American Express decided to offer some of its customers $300 if they would give back their credit card. You could receive the $300 even if you hadn't paid off your balance yet, as long as you agreed to give up your credit card.

Source: Aparajita Saha-Bubna and Lauren Pollock, "AmEx Offers Some Holders $300 to Pay and Leave," *Wall Street Journal Online* (February 23, 2009).

? What are the relevant costs that American Express would need to know in order to determine to whom to make this offer? (See page 331.)

Types of Incremental Analysis

A number of different types of decisions involve incremental analysis. The more common types of decisions are whether to:

1. Accept an order at a special price.
2. Make or buy component parts or finished products.
3. Sell products or process them further.
4. Repair, retain, or replace equipment.
5. Eliminate an unprofitable business segment or product.

We will consider each of these types of decisions in the following pages.

Accept an Order at a Special Price

LEARNING OBJECTIVE 3

Identify the relevant costs in accepting an order at a special price.

Sometimes a company may have an opportunity to obtain additional business if it is willing to make a major price concession to a specific customer. To illustrate, assume that Sunbelt Company produces 100,000 Smoothie blenders per month, which is 80% of plant capacity. Variable manufacturing costs are $8 per unit. Fixed manufacturing costs are $400,000, or $4 per unit. The Smoothie blenders are normally sold directly to retailers at $20 each. Sunbelt has an offer from Kensington Co. (a foreign wholesaler) to purchase an additional 2,000 blenders at

$11 per unit. Acceptance of the offer would not affect normal sales of the product, and the additional units can be manufactured without increasing plant capacity. What should management do?

If management makes its decision on the basis of the total cost per unit of $12 ($8 variable + $4 fixed), the order would be rejected because costs per unit ($12) would exceed revenues per unit ($11) by $1 per unit. However, since the units can be produced within existing plant capacity, the special order **will not increase fixed costs**. Let's identify the relevant data for the decision. First, the variable manufacturing costs will increase $16,000 ($8 × 2,000). Second, the expected revenue will increase $22,000 ($11 × 2,000). Thus, as shown in Illustration 7-4, Sunbelt will increase its net income by $6,000 by accepting this special order.

Helpful Hint

This is a good example of different costs for different purposes. In the long run all costs are relevant, but for this decision only costs that change are relevant.

		Incremental Analysis - Accepting an order at a special price.xls		
	Home Insert Page Layout Formulas Data Review View			
	P18 *fx*			
	A	B	C	D
1		Reject Order	Accept Order	Net Income Increase (Decrease)
2	Revenues	$0	$22,000	$ 22,000
3	Costs	0	16,000	(16,000)
4	Net income	$0	$ 6,000	$ 6,000
5				

Illustration 7-4
Incremental analysis—accepting an order at a special price

Two points should be emphasized: First, we assume that sales of the product in other markets **would not be affected by this special order**. If other sales were affected, then Sunbelt would have to consider the lost sales in making the decision. Second, if Sunbelt is operating **at full capacity**, it is likely that the special order would be rejected. Under such circumstances, the company would have to expand plant capacity. In that case, the special order would have to absorb these additional fixed manufacturing costs, as well as the variable manufacturing costs.

> **DO IT!**

Special Orders

Action Plan

✔ Identify all revenues that will change as a result of accepting the order.

✔ Identify all costs that will change as a result of accepting the order, and net this amount against the change in revenues.

Cobb Company incurs costs of $28 per unit ($18 variable and $10 fixed) to make a product that normally sells for $42. A foreign wholesaler offers to buy 5,000 units at $25 each. Cobb will incur additional shipping costs of $1 per unit. Compute the increase or decrease in net income Cobb will realize by accepting the special order, assuming Cobb has excess operating capacity. Should Cobb Company accept the special order?

Solution

	Reject	Accept	Net Income Increase (Decrease)
Revenue	$–0–	$125,000*	$125,000
Costs	–0–	95,000**	(95,000)
Net income	$–0–	$ 30,000	$ 30,000

*5,000 × $25
**(5,000 × $18) + (5,000 × $1)

The analysis indicates net income will increase by $30,000; therefore, Cobb Company should accept the special order.

Related exercise material: **BE7-3, E7-2, E7-3, E7-4, and DO IT! 7-1.**

✔ **The Navigator**

Make or Buy

When a manufacturer assembles component parts in producing a finished product, management must decide whether to make or buy the components. The decision to buy parts or services is often referred to as outsourcing. For example, as discussed in the Feature Story, a company such as General Motors Corporation may either make or buy the batteries, tires, and radios used in its cars. Similarly, Hewlett-Packard Corporation may make or buy the electronic circuitry, cases, and printer heads for its printers. Boeing recently sold some of its commercial aircraft factories in an effort to cut production costs and focus instead on engineering and final assembly rather than manufacturing. The decision to make or buy components should be made on the basis of incremental analysis.

Baron Company makes motorcycles and scooters. It incurs the following annual costs in producing 25,000 ignition switches for scooters.

Illustration 7-5
Annual product cost data

Direct materials	$ 50,000
Direct labor	75,000
Variable manufacturing overhead	40,000
Fixed manufacturing overhead	60,000
Total manufacturing costs	$225,000
Total cost per unit ($225,000 ÷ 25,000)	**$9.00**

Instead of making its own switches, Baron Company might purchase the ignition switches from Ignition, Inc. at a price of $8 per unit. What should management do?

At first glance, it appears that management should purchase the ignition switches for $8 rather than make them at a cost of $9. However, a review of operations indicates that if the ignition switches are purchased from Ignition, Inc., *all* of Baron's variable costs but only $10,000 of its fixed manufacturing costs will be eliminated (avoided). Thus, $50,000 of the fixed manufacturing costs will remain if the ignition switches are purchased. The relevant costs for incremental analysis, therefore, are as shown below.

Illustration 7-6
Incremental analysis—make or buy

Incremental Analysis - Make or buy.xls

Home | Insert | Page Layout | Formulas | Data | Review | View

P18   fx

	A	B	C	D
1		**Make**	**Buy**	**Net Income Increase (Decrease)**
2	Direct materials	$ 50,000	$ 0	$ 50,000
3	Direct labor	75,000	0	75,000
4	Variable manufacturing costs	40,000	0	40,000
5	Fixed manufacturing costs	60,000	50,000	10,000
6	Purchase price (25,000 × $8)	0	200,000	(200,000)
7	Total annual cost	$225,000	$250,000	$ (25,000)
8				

This analysis indicates that Baron Company would incur $25,000 of additional costs by buying the ignition switches rather than making them. Therefore, Baron should continue to make the ignition switches even though the total manufacturing cost is $1 higher per unit than the purchase price. The primary cause of this result is that, even if the company purchases the ignition switches, it will still have fixed costs of $50,000 to absorb.

OPPORTUNITY COST

The foregoing make-or-buy analysis is complete only if it is assumed that the productive capacity used to make the ignition switches cannot be converted to another purpose. If there is an opportunity to use this productive capacity in some other manner, then this opportunity cost must be considered. As indicated earlier, **opportunity cost** is the potential benefit that may be obtained by following an alternative course of action.

To illustrate, assume that through buying the switches, Baron Company can use the released productive capacity to generate additional income of $38,000 from producing a different product. This lost income is an additional cost of continuing to make the switches in the make-or-buy decision. This opportunity cost is therefore added to the "Make" column for comparison. As shown in Illustration 7-7, it is now advantageous to buy the ignition switches. The company's income would increase by $13,000.

> ### Ethics Note
> In the make-or-buy decision, it is important for management to take into account the social impact of its choice. For instance, buying may be the most economically feasible solution, but such action could result in the closure of a manufacturing plant that employs many good workers.

Illustration 7-7
Incremental analysis—make or buy, with opportunity cost

Incremental Analysis - Make or buy with opportunity cost.xls

Home   Insert   Page Layout   Formulas   Data   Review   View

P18

	A	B	C	D
1		Make	Buy	Net Income Increase (Decrease)
2	Total annual cost	$225,000	$250,000	$(25,000)
3	Opportunity cost	38,000	0	38,000
4	Total cost	$263,000	$250,000	$ 13,000
5				

The qualitative factors in this decision include the possible loss of jobs for employees who produce the ignition switches. In addition, management must assess how well the supplier will be able to satisfy the company's quality control standards at the quoted price per unit.

> DO IT!

Make or Buy

Juanita Company must decide whether to make or buy some of its components for the appliances it produces. The costs of producing 166,000 electrical cords for its appliances are as follows.

Direct materials	$90,000	Variable overhead	$32,000
Direct labor	$20,000	Fixed overhead	$24,000

Instead of making the electrical cords at an average cost per unit of $1.00 ($166,000 ÷ 166,000), the company has an opportunity to buy the cords at $0.90 per unit. If the company purchases the cords, all variable costs and one-fourth of the fixed costs will be eliminated.

(a) Prepare an incremental analysis showing whether the company should make or buy the electrical cords. (b) Will your answer be different if the released productive capacity will generate additional income of $5,000?

Action Plan

✔ Look for the costs that change.

✔ Ignore the costs that do not change.

✔ Use the format in the chapter for your answer.

✔ Recognize that opportunity cost can make a difference.

Solution

(a)

	Make	**Buy**	**Net Income Increase (Decrease)**
Direct materials	$ 90,000	$ –0–	$ 90,000
Direct labor	20,000	–0–	20,000
Variable manufacturing costs	32,000	–0–	32,000
Fixed manufacturing costs	24,000	18,000*	6,000
Purchase price	–0–	149,400**	(149,400)
Total cost	$166,000	$167,400	$ (1,400)

*.75 × $24,000
**$166,000 × .90

This analysis indicates that Juanita Company will incur $1,400 of additional costs if it buys the electrical cords rather than making them.

(b)

	Make	**Buy**	**Net Income Increase (Decrease)**
Total cost	$166,000	$167,400	$(1,400)
Opportunity cost	5,000	–0–	5,000
Total cost	$171,000	$167,400	$ 3,600

Yes, the answer is different: The analysis shows that net income will be increased by $3,600 if Juanita Company purchases the electrical cords rather than making them.

Related exercise material: **BE7-4, E7-5, E7-6, E7-7, E7-8, and DO IT! 7-2.**

✔ **The Navigator**

SERVICE COMPANY INSIGHT

Giving Away the Store?

In an earlier chapter, we discussed Amazon.com's incredible growth. However, some analysts have questioned whether some of the methods that Amazon uses to increase its sales make good business sense. For example, a few years ago, Amazon initiated a "Prime" free-shipping subscription program. For a $79 fee per year, Amazon's customers get free shipping on as many goods as they want to buy. At the time, CEO Jeff Bezos promised that the program would be costly in the short-term but benefit the company in the long-term. Six years later, it was true that Amazon's sales had grown considerably. It was also estimated that its Prime customers buy two to three times as much as non-Prime customers. But, its shipping costs rose from 2.8% of sales to 4% of sales, which is remarkably similar to the drop in its gross margin from 24% to 22.3%. Perhaps even less easy to justify is a proposal by Mr. Bezos to start providing a free Internet movie-streaming service to Amazon's Prime customers. Perhaps some incremental analysis is in order?

Source: Martin Peers, "Amazon's Prime Numbers," *Wall Street Journal Online* (February 3, 2011).

? What are the relevant revenues and costs that Amazon should consider relative to the decision whether to offer the Prime free-shipping subscription? (See page 331.)

Sell or Process Further

Many manufacturers have the option of selling products at a given point in the production cycle or continuing to process with the expectation of selling them at a later point at a higher price. For example, a bicycle manufacturer such as Trek could sell its bicycles to retailers either unassembled or assembled. A furniture manufacturer such as Ethan Allen could sell its dining room sets to furniture stores either unfinished or finished. The sell-or-process-further decision should be made on the basis of incremental analysis. The basic decision rule is: **Process further as long as the incremental revenue from such processing exceeds the incremental processing costs.**

> **LEARNING OBJECTIVE   5**
>
> **Identify the relevant costs in determining whether to sell or process materials further.**

SINGLE-PRODUCT CASE

Assume, for example, that Woodmasters Inc. makes tables. It sells unfinished tables for $50. The cost to manufacture an unfinished table is $35, computed as follows.

Direct materials	$15
Direct labor	10
Variable manufacturing overhead	6
Fixed manufacturing overhead	4
Manufacturing cost per unit	**$35**

Illustration 7-8
Per unit cost of unfinished table

Woodmasters currently has unused productive capacity that is expected to continue indefinitely. Some of this capacity could be used to finish the tables and sell them at $60 per unit. For a finished table, direct materials will increase $2 and direct labor costs will increase $4. Variable manufacturing overhead costs will increase by $2.40 (60% of direct labor). No increase is anticipated in fixed manufacturing overhead.

Should the company sell the unfinished tables, or should it process them further? The incremental analysis on a per unit basis is as follows.

> **Helpful Hint**
> Current net income is known. Net income from processing further is an estimate. In making its decision, management could add a "risk" factor for the estimate.

	Incremental Analysis - Sell or process further.xls			
	Home Insert Page Layout Formulas Data Review View			
	P18 *fx*			

	A	B	C	D
1		Sell Unfinished	Process Further	Net Income Increase (Decrease)
2	Sales price per unit	$50.00	$60.00	$10.00
3	Cost per unit			
4	Direct materials	15.00	17.00	(2.00)
5	Direct labor	10.00	14.00	(4.00)
6	Variable manufacturing overhead	6.00	8.40	(2.40)
7	Fixed manufacturing overhead	4.00	4.00	0.00
8	Total	35.00	43.40	(8.40)
9	Net income per unit	$ 15.00	$ 16.60	$ 1.60
10				

Illustration 7-9
Incremental analysis—sell or process further

It would be advantageous for Woodmasters to process the tables further. The incremental revenue of $10.00 from the additional processing is $1.60 higher than the incremental processing costs of $8.40.

MULTIPLE-PRODUCT CASE

Sell-or-process-further decisions are particularly applicable to production processes that produce multiple products simultaneously. In many industries, a number of end-products are produced from a single raw material and a common production process. These multiple end-products are commonly referred to as **joint products**. For example, in the meat-packing industry, Armour processes a cow or pig to produce meat, internal organs, hides, bones, and fat. In the petroleum industry, ExxonMobil refines crude oil to produce gasoline, lubricating oil, kerosene, paraffin, and ethylene.

Illustration 7-10 presents a joint product situation for Marais Creamery involving a decision **to sell or process further** cream and skim milk. Cream and skim milk are joint products that result from the processing of raw milk.

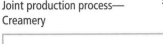

Illustration 7-10
Joint production process—
Creamery

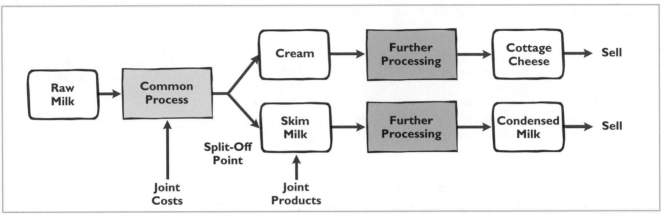

Marais incurs many costs prior to the manufacture of the cream and skim milk. All costs incurred prior to the point at which the two products are separately identifiable (the *split-off point*) are called **joint costs**. For purposes of determining the cost of each product, joint product costs must be allocated to the individual products. This is frequently done based on the relative sales value of the joint products. While this allocation is important for determination of product cost, **it is irrelevant for any sell-or-process-further decisions**. The reason is that these **joint product costs are sunk costs.** That is, they have already been incurred, and they cannot be changed or avoided by any subsequent decision.

Illustration 7-11 provides the daily cost and revenue data for Marais Creamery related to cream and cottage cheese.

Illustration 7-11
Cost and revenue data per day
for cream

Costs (per day)	
Joint cost allocated to cream	$ 9,000
Cost to process cream into cottage cheese	10,000

Revenues from Products (per day)	
Cream	$19,000
Cottage cheese	27,000

From this information, we can determine whether the company should simply sell the cream or process it further into cottage cheese. Illustration 7-12 shows the necessary analysis. Note that the joint cost that is allocated to the cream is not included in this decision. It is not relevant to the decision because it is a sunk cost. It has been incurred in the past and will remain the same no matter whether the cream is subsequently processed into cottage cheese or not.

	Sell	Process Further	Net Income Increase (Decrease)
Incremental Analysis - Sell or process further - Cottage cheese.xls			
P18 fx			
A	**B**	**C**	**D**
1	Sell	Process Further	Net Income Increase (Decrease)
2 Sales per day	$19,000	$27,000	$ 8,000
3 Cost per day to process cream into cottage cheese	0	10,000	(10,000)
4	$19,000	$ 17,000	$ (2,000)
5			

Illustration 7-12
Analysis of whether to sell cream or process into cottage cheese

From this analysis, we can see that Marais should not process the cream further because it will sustain an incremental loss of $2,000.

Illustration 7-13 provides the daily cost and revenue data for the company related to skim milk and condensed milk.

Illustration 7-13
Cost and revenue data per day for skim milk

Costs (per day)	
Joint cost allocated to skim milk	$ 5,000
Cost to process skim milk into condensed milk	8,000
Revenues from Products (per day)	
Skim milk	$11,000
Condensed milk	26,000

Illustration 7-14 shows that Marais Company should process the skim milk into condensed milk, as it will increase net income by $7,000.

	Sell	Process Further	Net Income Increase (Decrease)
Incremental Analysis - Sell or process further - Skim milk or process condensed milk.xls			
P18 fx			
A	**B**	**C**	**D**
1	Sell	Process Further	Net Income Increase (Decrease)
2 Sales per day	$11,000	$26,000	$15,000
3 Cost per day to process skim milk into condensed milk	0	8,000	(8,000)
4	$11,000	$ 18,000	$ 7,000
5			

Illustration 7-14
Analysis of whether to sell skim milk or process into condensed milk

Again, note that the $5,000 of joint cost allocated to the skim milk is irrelevant in deciding whether to sell or process further. Why? The joint cost remains the same, whether or not further processing is performed.

It is important to understand that these decisions need to be reevaluated as market conditions change. For example, if the price of skim milk increases relative to the price of condensed milk, it may become more profitable to sell the skim milk rather than process it into condensed milk. Consider also oil refineries. As market conditions change, they must constantly re-assess which products to produce from the oil they receive at their plants.

> **DO IT!**

Sell or Process Further

Easy Does It manufactures unpainted furniture for the do-it-yourself (DIY) market. It currently sells a child's rocking chair for $25. Production costs are $12 variable and $8 fixed. Easy Does It is considering painting the rocking chair and selling it for $35. Variable costs to paint each chair are expected to be $9, and fixed costs are expected to be $2.

Prepare an analysis showing whether Easy Does It should sell unpainted or painted chairs.

Action Plan

✔ Identify the revenues that will change as a result of painting the rocking chair.

✔ Identify all costs that will change as a result of painting the rocking chair, and net the amount against the revenues.

Solution

	Sell	Process Further	Net Income Increase (Decrease)
Revenues	$25	$35	$10
Variable costs	12	21	(9)
Fixed costs	8	10	(2)
Net income	$ 5	$ 4	$ (1)

The analysis indicates that the rocking chair should be sold unpainted because net income per chair will be $1 greater.

Related exercise material: **BE7-5, BE7-6, E7-9, E7-10, E7-11, E7-12, and** **DO IT!** **7-3.**

✔ **The Navigator**

Repair, Retain, or Replace Equipment

LEARNING OBJECTIVE **6**

Identify the relevant costs to be considered in repairing, retaining, or replacing equipment.

Management often has to decide whether to continue using an asset, repair, or replace it. For example, Delta Airlines must decide whether to replace old jets with new, more fuel-efficient ones. To illustrate, assume that Jeffcoat Company has a factory machine that originally cost $110,000. It has a balance in Accumulated Depreciation of $70,000, so its book value is $40,000. It has a remaining useful life of four years. The company is considering replacing this machine with a new machine. A new machine is available that costs $120,000. It is expected to have zero salvage value at the end of its four-year useful life. If the new machine is acquired, variable manufacturing costs are expected to decrease from $160,000 to $125,000 annually, and the old unit could be sold for $5,000. The incremental analysis for the **four-year period** is as follows.

Illustration 7-15
Incremental analysis—retain or replace equipment

	A	B	C	D	E	F
1		Retain Equipment		Replace Equipment		Net Income Increase (Decrease)
2	Variable manufacturing costs	$640,000	a	$500,000	b	$140,000
3	New machine cost			120,000		(120,000)
4	Sale of old machine			(5,000)		5,000
5	Total	$640,000		$ 615,000		$ 25,000
6						
7	a(4 years × $160,000)					
8	b(4 years × $125,000)					
9						

Incremental Analysis - Retain or replace equipment.xls

In this case, it would be to the company's advantage to replace the equipment. The lower variable manufacturing costs due to replacement more than offset the cost of the new equipment. Note that the $5,000 received from the sale of the old machine is relevant to the decision because it will only be received if the company chooses to replace its equipment. In general, any trade-in allowance or cash disposal value of existing assets is relevant to the decision to retain or replace equipment.

One other point should be mentioned regarding Jeffcoat's decision: **The book value of the old machine does not affect the decision.** Book value is a **sunk cost**, which is a cost that cannot be changed by any present or future decision. **Sunk costs are not relevant in incremental analysis.** In this example, if the asset is retained, book value will be depreciated over its remaining useful life. Or, if the new unit is acquired, book value will be recognized as a loss of the current period. Thus, the effect of book value on current and future earnings is the same regardless of the replacement decision.

Sometimes, decisions regarding whether to replace equipment are clouded by behavioral decision-making errors. For example, suppose a manager spent $90,000 repairing a machine two months ago. Now, suppose that the machine breaks down again today. The manager might be inclined to think that, because the company recently spent a large amount of money to repair the machine, the machine should now be repaired rather than replaced. However, the amount spent in the past to repair the machine is irrelevant to the current decision. It is a sunk cost.

Similarly, suppose a manager spent $5,000,000 to purchase a new machine. Six months later, a new machine comes on the market that is significantly more efficient than the one recently purchased. The manager might be inclined to think that he or she should not buy the new machine because of the recent purchase. In fact, the manager might fear that buying a different machine so quickly might call into question the merit of the previous decision. Again, the fact that the company recently bought a new machine is not relevant. Instead, the manager should use incremental analysis to determine whether the savings generated by the efficiencies of the new machine would justify its purchase.

Eliminate an Unprofitable Segment or Product

Management sometimes must decide whether to eliminate an unprofitable business segment or product. For example, in recent years, many airlines quit servicing certain cities or cut back on the number of flights. Goodyear quit producing several brands in the low-end tire market. Again, the key is to **focus on the relevant costs— the data that change under the alternative courses of action**. To illustrate, assume that Venus Company manufactures tennis racquets in three models: Pro, Master, and Champ. Pro and Master are profitable lines. Champ (highlighted in red in the table below) operates at a loss. Condensed income statement data are as follows.

LEARNING OBJECTIVE   7

Identify the relevant costs in deciding whether to eliminate an unprofitable segment or product.

	Pro	Master	Champ	Total
Sales	$800,000	$300,000	**$100,000**	$1,200,000
Variable costs	520,000	210,000	**90,000**	820,000
Contribution margin	280,000	90,000	**10,000**	380,000
Fixed costs	80,000	50,000	**30,000**	160,000
Net income	$200,000	$ 40,000	**$ (20,000)**	$ 220,000

Illustration 7-16
Segment income data

Helpful Hint
A decision to discontinue a segment based solely on the bottom line—net loss—is inappropriate.

You might think that total net income will increase by $20,000 to $240,000 if the unprofitable Champ line of racquets is eliminated. However, **net income may actually decrease if the Champ line is discontinued**. The reason is that the fixed costs allocated to the Champ racquets will have to be absorbed by the other products. To illustrate, assume that the $30,000 of fixed costs applicable to the unprofitable segment are allocated ⅔ to the Pro model and ⅓ to the Master model if the Champ model is eliminated. Fixed costs will increase to $100,000 ($80,000 + $20,000) in the Pro line and to $60,000 ($50,000 + $10,000) in the Master line. The revised income statement is:

Illustration 7-17
Income data after eliminating unprofitable product line

	Pro	Master	Total
Sales	$800,000	$300,000	$1,100,000
Variable costs	520,000	210,000	730,000
Contribution margin	280,000	90,000	370,000
Fixed costs	**100,000**	**60,000**	160,000
Net income	$180,000	$ 30,000	$ 210,000

Illustration 7-18
Incremental analysis—eliminating unprofitable segment with no reduction in fixed costs

Total net income has decreased $10,000 ($220,000 − $210,000). This result is also obtained in the following incremental analysis of the Champ racquets.

	A	B	C	D
		Continue	Eliminate	Net Income Increase (Decrease)
2	Sales	$100,000	$ 0	$(100,000)
3	Variable costs	90,000	0	90,000
4	Contribution margin	10,000	0	(10,000)
5	Fixed costs	30,000	30,000	0
6	Net income	$(20,000)	$(30,000)	$ (10,000)

The loss in net income is attributable to the Champ line's contribution margin ($10,000) that will not be realized if the segment is discontinued.

Assume the same facts as above, except now assume that $22,000 of the fixed costs attributed to the Champ line can be eliminated if the line is discontinued. Illustration 7-19 presents the incremental analysis based on this revised assumption.

Illustration 7-19
Incremental analysis—eliminating unprofitable segment with reduction in fixed costs

	A	B	C	D
1		Continue	Eliminate	Net Income Increase (Decrease)
2	Sales	$100,000	$ 0	$(100,000)
3	Variable costs	90,000	0	90,000
4	Contribution margin	10,000	0	(10,000)
5	Fixed costs	30,000	8,000	22,000
6	Net income	$(20,000)	$(8,000)	$ 12,000

In this case, because the company is able to eliminate some of its fixed costs by eliminating the division, it can increase its net income by $12,000. **This occurs because the $22,000 savings that results from the eliminated fixed costs exceeds the $10,000 in lost contribution margin by $12,000 ($22,000 − $10,000).**

In deciding on the future status of an unprofitable segment, management should consider the effect of elimination on related product lines. It may be possible for continuing product lines to obtain some or all of the sales lost by the discontinued product line. In some businesses, services or products may be linked—for example, free checking accounts at a bank, or coffee at a donut shop. In addition, management should consider the effect of eliminating the product line on employees who may have to be discharged or retrained.

> DO IT!

Unprofitable Segments

Lambert, Inc. manufactures several types of accessories. For the year, the knit hats and scarves line had sales of $400,000, variable expenses of $310,000, and fixed expenses of $120,000. Therefore, the knit hats and scarves line had a net loss of $30,000. If Lambert eliminates the knit hats and scarves line, $20,000 of fixed costs will remain. Prepare an analysis showing whether the company should eliminate the knit hats and scarves line.

Action Plan

✔ Identify the revenues that will change as a result of eliminating a product line.

✔ Identify all costs that will change as a result of eliminating a product line, and net the amount against the revenues.

Solution

	Continue	Eliminate	Net Income Increase (Decrease)
Sales	$400,000	$ 0	$(400,000)
Variable costs	310,000	0	310,000
Contribution margin	90,000	0	(90,000)
Fixed costs	120,000	20,000	100,000
Net income	$(30,000)	$(20,000)	$ 10,000

The analysis indicates that Lambert should eliminate the knit hats and scarves line because net income will increase $10,000.

Related exercise material: **BE7-8, E7-15, E7-16, E7-17, and** DO IT! **7-4.**

✔ The Navigator

MANAGEMENT INSIGHT

Time to Move to a New Neighborhood?

If you have ever moved, then you know how complicated and costly it can be. Now consider what it would be like for a manufacturing company with 260 employees and a 170,000-square-foot facility to move from southern California to Idaho. That is what Buck Knives did in order to save its company from financial ruin. Electricity rates in Idaho were half those in California, workers' compensation was one-third the cost, and factory wages were 20% lower. Combined, this would reduce manufacturing costs by $600,000 per year. Moving the factory would cost about $8.5 million, plus $4 million to move key employees. Offsetting these costs was the estimated $11 million selling price of the California property. Based on these estimates, the move would pay for itself in three years.

Ultimately, the company received only $7.5 million for its California property, only 58 of 75 key employees were willing to move, construction was delayed by a year which caused the new plant to increase in price by $1.5 million, and wages surged in Idaho due to low unemployment. Despite all of these complications, though, the company considers the move a great success.

Source: Chris Lydgate, "The Buck Stopped," *Inc. Magazine* (May 2006), pp. 87–95.

? What were some of the factors that complicated the company's decision to move? How should the company have incorporated such factors into its incremental analysis? (See page 331.)

DECISION TOOLKIT

DECISION CHECKPOINTS	INFO NEEDED FOR DECISION	TOOL TO USE FOR DECISION	HOW TO EVALUATE RESULTS
Which alternative should the company choose?	All relevant costs including opportunity cost	Compare relevant cost of each alternative	Choose the alternative that maximizes net income.

Other Considerations in Decision-Making

Qualitative Factors

In this chapter, we have focused primarily on the quantitative factors that affect a decision—those attributes that can be easily expressed in terms of numbers or dollars. However, many of the decisions involving incremental analysis have important qualitative features. Though not easily measured, they should not be ignored.

Consider, for example, the potential effects of the make-or-buy decision or of the decision to eliminate a line of business on existing employees and the community in which the plant is located. The cost savings that may be obtained from outsourcing or from eliminating a plant should be weighed against these qualitative attributes. One example would be the cost of lost morale that might result. Al "Chainsaw" Dunlap was a so-called "turnaround" artist who went into many companies, identified inefficiencies (using incremental analysis techniques), and tried to correct these problems to improve corporate profitability. Along the way, he laid off thousands of employees at numerous companies. As head of Sunbeam, it was Al Dunlap who lost his job because his Draconian approach failed to improve Sunbeam's profitability. It was widely reported that Sunbeam's employees openly rejoiced for days after his departure. Clearly, qualitative factors can matter.

Relationship of Incremental Analysis and Activity-Based Costing

In Chapter 4, we noted that many companies have shifted to activity-based costing to allocate overhead costs to products. The primary reason for using activity-based costing is that it results in a more accurate allocation of overhead. The concepts presented in this chapter are completely consistent with the use of activity-based costing. In fact, activity-based costing will result in better identification of relevant costs and, therefore, better incremental analysis.

MANAGEMENT INSIGHT

What Is the Real Cost of Packaging Options?

The existence of excess plant capacity is frequently the incentive for management to add new products. Adding one new product may not add much incremental cost. But continuing to add products will at some point create new constraints, perhaps requiring additional investments in people, equipment, and facilities.

The effects of product and product line proliferation are generally understood. But the effect on incremental overhead costs of changes *in servicing customers* is less understood. For example, if a company newly offers its customers the option of product delivery by case or by pallet, the new service may appear to be simple and low in cost. But, if the manufacturing process must be realigned to package in two different forms; if two sets of inventory records must be maintained; and if warehousing, handling, and shipping require two different arrangements or sets of equipment, the additional costs of this new option could be as high as a whole new product. If the customer service option were adopted for all products, the product line could effectively be doubled—but so might many overhead costs.

Source: Elizabeth Haas Edersheim and Joan Wilson, "Complexity at Consumer Goods Companies: Naming and Taming the Beast," *Journal of Cost Management* (Fall 1992), pp. 26–36.

? If your marketing director suggests that, in addition to selling your cereal in a standard-size box, you should sell a jumbo size and an individual size, what issues must you consider? (See page 331.)

USING THE **DECISION TOOLKIT**

Suppose Hewlett-Packard Company (HP) must decide whether to make or buy some of its components from Solectron Corp. The cost of producing 50,000 electrical connectors for its printers is $110,000, broken down as follows.

Direct materials	$60,000	Variable manufacturing overhead	$12,000
Direct labor	$30,000	Fixed manufacturing overhead	$ 8,000

Instead of making the electrical connectors at an average cost per unit of $2.20 ($110,000 ÷ 50,000), HP has an opportunity to buy the connectors at $2.15 per unit. If the connectors are purchased, all variable costs and one-half of the fixed costs will be eliminated.

Instructions

(a) Prepare an incremental analysis showing whether HP should make or buy the electrical connectors.

(b) Will your answer be different if the released productive capacity resulting from the purchase of the connectors will generate additional income of $25,000?

Solution

(a)

	Make	Buy	Net Income Increase (Decrease)
Direct materials	$ 60,000	$ –0–	$ 60,000
Direct labor	30,000	–0–	30,000
Variable manufacturing costs	12,000	–0–	12,000
Fixed manufacturing costs	8,000	4,000*	4,000
Purchase price	–0–	107,500**	(107,500)
Total cost	$110,000	$111,500	$ (1,500)

*$8,000 × .50; **$2.15 × 50,000

This analysis indicates that HP will incur $1,500 of additional costs if it buys the electrical connectors. HP therefore would choose to make the connectors.

(b)

	Make	Buy	Net Income Increase (Decrease)
Total cost	$110,000	$111,500	$ (1,500)
Opportunity cost	25,000	–0–	25,000
Total cost	$135,000	$111,500	$23,500

Yes, the answer is different. The analysis shows that if additional capacity is released, net income will be increased by $23,500 if the electrical connectors are purchased. In this case, HP would choose to purchase the connectors.

✔ **The Navigator**

SUMMARY OF LEARNING OBJECTIVES

✔ **The Navigator**

1 Identify the steps in management's decision-making process. Management's decision-making process consists of (a) identifying the problem and assigning responsibility for the decision, (b) determining and evaluating possible courses of action, (c) making the decision, and (d) reviewing the results of the decision.

2 Describe the concept of incremental analysis. Incremental analysis identifies financial data that change under alternative courses of action. These data are relevant to the decision because they will vary in the future among the possible alternatives.

3 Identify the relevant costs in accepting an order at a special price. The relevant costs are those that change if the order is accepted. The relevant information in accepting an order at a special price is the difference between the variable manufacturing costs to produce the special order and expected revenues. Any changes in fixed costs, opportunity cost, or other incremental costs or savings (such as additional shipping) should be considered.

4 Identify the relevant costs in a make-or-buy decision. In a make or buy decision, the relevant costs are (a) the variable manufacturing costs that will be saved as well as changes to fixed manufacturing costs, (b) the purchase price, and (c) opportunity cost.

5 Identify the relevant costs in determining whether to sell or process materials further. The decision rule for whether to sell or process materials further is: Process further as long as the incremental revenue from processing exceeds the incremental processing costs.

6 Identify the relevant costs to be considered in repairing, retaining, or replacing equipment. The relevant costs to be considered in determining whether equipment

should be repaired, retained, or replaced are the effects on variable costs and the cost of the new equipment. Also, any disposal value of the existing asset must be considered.

7 Identify the relevant costs in deciding whether to eliminate an unprofitable segment or product. In deciding whether to eliminate an unprofitable segment or product, the relevant costs are the variable costs that drive the contribution margin, if any, produced by the segment or product. Disposition of the segment's or the product's fixed expenses and opportunity cost must also be considered.

DECISION TOOLKIT A SUMMARY

DECISION CHECKPOINTS	INFO NEEDED FOR DECISION	TOOL TO USE FOR DECISION	HOW TO EVALUATE RESULTS
Which alternative should the company choose?	All relevant costs including opportunity cost	Compare the relevant cost of each alternative	Choose the alternative that maximizes net income.

GLOSSARY

Incremental analysis The process of identifying the financial data that change under alternative courses of action. (p. 294).

Joint costs For joint products, all costs incurred prior to the point at which the two products are separately identifiable (known as the *split-off point*). (p. 302).

Joint products Multiple end-products produced from a single raw material and a common production process. (p. 302).

Opportunity cost The potential benefit that is lost when one course of action is chosen rather than an alternative course of action. (p. 295).

Relevant costs Those costs and revenues that differ across alternatives. (p. 295).

Sunk cost A cost that cannot be changed or avoided by any present or future decision. (p. 295).

> ## Comprehensive **DO IT!**

Walston Company produces kitchen cabinets for homebuilders across the western United States. The cost of producing 5,000 cabinets is as follows.

Materials	$ 500,000
Labor	250,000
Variable overhead	100,000
Fixed overhead	400,000
Total	$1,250,000

Walston also incurs selling expenses of $20 per cabinet. Wellington Corp. has offered Walston $165 per cabinet for a special order of 1,000 cabinets. The cabinets would be sold to homebuilders in the eastern United States and thus would not conflict with Walston's current sales. Selling expenses per cabinet would be only $5 per cabinet. Walston has available capacity to do the work.

Instructions
(a) Prepare an incremental analysis for the special order.
(b) Should Walston accept the special order? Why or why not?

Solution to Comprehensive DO IT!

Action Plan

✔ Determine the relevant cost per unit of the special order.

✔ Identify the relevant costs and revenues for the units to be produced.

✔ Compare the results related to accepting the special order versus rejecting the special order.

(a) Relevant costs per unit would be:

Materials	$500,000/5,000 =	$100
Labor	250,000/5,000 =	50
Variable overhead	100,000/5,000 =	20
Selling expenses		5
Total relevant cost per unit		$175

	Reject Order	Accept Order	Net Income Increase (Decrease)
Revenues	$0	$165,000	$165,000
Costs	0	175,000	(175,000)
Net income	$0	$ (10,000)	$ (10,000)

(b) Walston should reject the offer. The incremental benefit of $165 per cabinet is less than the incremental cost of $175. By accepting the order, Walston's net income would actually decline by $10,000.

✔ **The Navigator**

Self-Test, Brief Exercises, Exercises, Problem Set A, and many more resources are available for practice in WileyPLUS.

SELF-TEST QUESTIONS

Answers are at the end of the chapter.

(LO 1) **1.** Three of the steps in management's decision-making process are (1) review results of decision, (2) determine and evaluate possible courses of action, and (3) make the decision. The steps are prepared in the following order:
   (a) (1), (2), (3).   (c) (2), (1), (3).
   (b) (3), (2), (1).   (d) (2), (3), (1).

(LO 2) **2.** Incremental analysis is the process of identifying the financial data that:
   (a) do not change under alternative courses of action.
   (b) change under alternative courses of action.
   (c) are mixed under alternative courses of action.
   (d) No correct answer is given.

(LO1, 2) **3.** In making business decisions, management ordinarily considers:
   (a) quantitative factors but not qualitative factors.
   (b) financial information only.
   (c) both financial and nonfinancial information.
   (d) relevant costs, opportunity cost, and sunk costs.

(LO 2) **4.** A company is considering the following alternatives:

	Alternative A	Alternative B
Revenues	$50,000	$50,000
Variable costs	24,000	24,000
Fixed costs	12,000	15,000

Which of the following are relevant in choosing between these alternatives?

   (a) Revenues, variable costs, and fixed costs.
   (b) Variable costs and fixed costs.
   (c) Variable costs only.
   (d) Fixed costs only.

5. It costs a company $14 of variable costs and $6 of (LO 3) fixed costs to produce product Z200 that sells for $30. A foreign buyer offers to purchase 3,000 units at $18 each. If the special offer is accepted and produced with unused capacity, net income will:
   (a) decrease $6,000.   (c) increase $12,000.
   (b) increase $6,000.   (d) increase $9,000.

6. It costs a company $14 of variable costs and $6 of (LO 3) fixed costs to produce product Z200. Product Z200 sells for $30. A buyer offers to purchase 3,000 units at $18 each. The seller will incur special shipping costs of $5 per unit. If the special offer is accepted and produced with unused capacity, net income will:
   (a) increase $3,000.   (c) decrease $12,000.
   (b) increase $12,000.   (d) decrease $3,000.

7. Jobart Company is currently operating at full capacity. (LO 3) It is considering buying a part from an outside supplier rather than making it in-house. If Jobart purchases the part, it can use the released productive capacity to generate additional income of $30,000 from producing a different product. When conducting incremental analysis in this make-or-buy decision, the company should:
   (a) ignore the $30,000.
   (b) add $30,000 to other costs in the "Make" column.

(c) add $30,000 to other costs in the "Buy" column.

(d) subtract $30,000 from the other costs in the "Make" column.

(LO 4) **8.** In a make-or-buy decision, relevant costs are:

(a) manufacturing costs that will be saved.

(b) the purchase price of the units.

(c) the opportunity cost.

(d) All of the above.

(LO 4) **9.** Derek is performing incremental analysis in a make-or-buy decision for Item X. If Derek buys Item X, he can use its released productive capacity to produce Item Z. Derek will sell Item Z for $12,000 and incur production costs of $8,000. Derek's incremental analysis should include an opportunity cost of:

(a) $12,000.   (c) $4,000.

(b) $8,000.   (d) $0.

(LO 5) **10.** The decision rule in a sell-or-process-further decision is: process further as long as the incremental revenue from processing exceeds:

(a) incremental processing costs.

(b) variable processing costs.

(c) fixed processing costs.

(d) No correct answer is given.

(LO 5) **11.** Walton, Inc. makes an unassembled product that it currently sells for $55. Production costs are $20. Walton is considering assembling the product and selling it for $68. The cost to assemble the product is estimated at $12. What decision should Walton make?

(a) Sell before assembly; net income per unit will be $12 greater.

(b) Sell before assembly; net income per unit will be $1 greater.

(c) Process further; net income per unit will be $13 greater.

(d) Process further; net income per unit will be $1 greater.

(LO 6) **12.** In a decision to retain or replace equipment, the book value of the old equipment is a (an):

(a) opportunity cost.   (c) incremental cost.

(b) sunk cost.   (d) marginal cost.

(LO 7) **13.** If an unprofitable segment is eliminated:

(a) net income will always increase.

(b) variable expenses of the eliminated segment will have to be absorbed by other segments.

(c) fixed expenses allocated to the eliminated segment will have to be absorbed by other segments.

(d) net income will always decrease.

(LO 7) **14.** A segment of Hazard Inc. has the following data.

Sales	$200,000
Variable expenses	140,000
Fixed expenses	100,000

If this segment is eliminated, what will be the effect on the remaining company? Assume that 50% of the fixed expenses will be eliminated and the rest will be allocated to the segments of the remaining company.

(a) $120,000 increase.   (c) $50,000 increase.

(b) $10,000 decrease.   (d) $10,000 increase.

Go to the book's companion website, www.wiley.com/college/weygandt, for additional Self-Test Questions.

✔ **The Navigator**

QUESTIONS

1. What steps are frequently involved in management's decision-making process?

2. Your roommate, Anna Polis, contends that accounting contributes to most of the steps in management's decision-making process. Is your roommate correct? Explain.

3. "Incremental analysis involves the accumulation of information concerning a single course of action." Do you agree? Why?

4. Sydney Greene asks for your help concerning the relevance of variable and fixed costs in incremental analysis. Help Sydney with her problem.

5. What data are relevant in deciding whether to accept an order at a special price?

6. Emil Corporation has an opportunity to buy parts at $9 each that currently cost $12 to make. What manufacturing costs are relevant to this make-or-buy decision?

7. Define the term "opportunity cost." How may this cost be relevant in a make-or-buy decision?

8. What is the decision rule in deciding whether to sell a product or process it further?

9. What are joint products? What accounting issue results from the production process that creates joint products?

10. How are allocated joint costs treated when making a sell-or-process-further decision?

11. Your roommate, Gale Dunham, is confused about sunk costs. Explain to your roommate the meaning of sunk costs and their relevance to a decision to retain or replace equipment.

12. Huang Inc. has one product line that is unprofitable. What circumstances may cause overall company net income to be lower if the unprofitable product line is eliminated?

BRIEF EXERCISES

BE7-1 The steps in management's decision-making process are listed in random order below. Indicate the order in which the steps should be executed.

_____ Make a decision

_____ Identify the problem and assign responsibility

_____ Review results of the decision

_____ Determine and evaluate possible courses of action

Identify the steps in management's decision-making process.
(LO 1), AP

BE7-2 Bogart Company is considering two alternatives. Alternative A will have revenues of $160,000 and costs of $100,000. Alternative B will have revenues of $180,000 and costs of $125,000. Compare Alternative A to Alternative B showing incremental revenues, costs, and net income.

Determine incremental changes.
(LO 2), AP

BE7-3 At Jaymes Company, it costs $30 per unit ($20 variable and $10 fixed) to make a product at full capacity that normally sells for $45. A foreign wholesaler offers to buy 3,000 units at $25 each. Jaymes will incur special shipping costs of $2 per unit. Assuming that Jaymes has excess operating capacity, indicate the net income (loss) Jaymes would realize by accepting the special order.

Determine whether to accept a special order.
(LO 3), AP

BE7-4 Manson Industries incurs unit costs of $8 ($5 variable and $3 fixed) in making a subassembly part for its finished product. A supplier offers to make 10,000 of the assembly part at $6 per unit. If the offer is accepted, Manson will save all variable costs but no fixed costs. Prepare an analysis showing the total cost saving, if any, Manson will realize by buying the part.

Determine whether to make or buy a part.
(LO 4), AP

BE7-5 Chudrick Inc. makes unfinished bookcases that it sells for $62. Production costs are $36 variable and $10 fixed. Because it has unused capacity, Chudrick is considering finishing the bookcases and selling them for $70. Variable finishing costs are expected to be $7 per unit with no increase in fixed costs. Prepare an analysis on a per unit basis showing whether Chudrick should sell unfinished or finished bookcases.

Determine whether to sell or process further.
(LO 5), AP

BE7-6 Each day, Adama Corporation processes 1 ton of a secret raw material into two resulting products, AB1 and XY1. When it processes 1 ton of the raw material, the company incurs joint processing costs of $60,000. It allocates $25,000 of these costs to AB1 and $35,000 of these costs to XY1. The resulting AB1 can be sold for $100,000. Alternatively, it can be processed further to make AB2 at an additional processing cost of $45,000, and sold for $150,000. Each day's batch of XY1 can be sold for $95,000. Alternatively, it can be processed further to create XY2, at an additional processing cost of $50,000, and sold for $130,000. Discuss what products Adama Corporation should make.

Determine whether to sell or process further, joint products.
(LO 5), AP

BE7-7 Kobe Company has a factory machine with a book value of $90,000 and a remaining useful life of 5 years. It can be sold for $30,000. A new machine is available at a cost of $300,000. This machine will have a 5-year useful life with no salvage value. The new machine will lower annual variable manufacturing costs from $600,000 to $500,000. Prepare an analysis showing whether the old machine should be retained or replaced.

Determine whether to retain or replace equipment.
(LO 6), AP

BE7-8 Lisah, Inc., manufactures golf clubs in three models. For the year, the Big Bart line has a net loss of $10,000 from sales $200,000, variable costs $180,000, and fixed costs $30,000. If the Big Bart line is eliminated, $20,000 of fixed costs will remain. Prepare an analysis showing whether the Big Bart line should be eliminated.

Determine whether to eliminate an unprofitable segment.
(LO 7), AP

> DO IT! REVIEW

DO IT! 7-1 Maize Company incurs a cost of $35 per unit, of which $20 is variable, to make a product that normally sells for $58. A foreign wholesaler offers to buy 6,000 units at $30 each. Maize will incur additional costs of $3 per unit to imprint a logo and to pay for shipping. Compute the increase or decrease in net income Maize will realize by accepting the special order, assuming Maize has sufficient excess operating capacity. Should Maize Company accept the special order?

Evaluate special order.
(LO 3), AN

Evaluate make-or-buy opportunity.

(LO 4), AN

DO IT! **7-2** Rubble Company must decide whether to make or buy some of its components. The costs of producing 60,000 switches for its generators are as follows.

Direct materials	$30,000	Variable overhead	$45,000
Direct labor	$42,000	Fixed overhead	$60,000

Instead of making the switches at an average cost of $2.95 ($177,000 ÷ 60,000), the company has an opportunity to buy the switches at $2.70 per unit. If the company purchases the switches, all the variable costs and one-fourth of the fixed costs will be eliminated.

(a) Prepare an incremental analysis showing whether the company should make or buy the switches. (b) Would your answer be different if the released productive capacity will generate additional income of $34,000?

Sell or process further.

(LO 5), AP

DO IT! **7-3** Mesa Verde manufactures unpainted furniture for the do-it-yourself (DIY) market. It currently sells a table for $75. Production costs are $40 variable and $10 fixed. Mesa Verde is considering staining and sealing the table to sell it for $100. Variable costs to finish each table are expected to be $17, and fixed costs are expected to be $3.

Prepare an analysis showing whether Mesa Verde should sell unpainted or finished tables.

Analyze whether to eliminate unprofitable segment.

(LO 7), AP

DO IT! **7-4** Gator Corporation manufactures several types of accessories. For the year, the gloves and mittens line had sales of $500,000, variable expenses of $370,000, and fixed expenses of $150,000. Therefore, the gloves and mittens line had a net loss of $20,000. If Gator eliminates the line, $38,000 of fixed costs will remain.

Prepare an analysis showing whether the company should eliminate the gloves and mittens line.

✔ **The Navigator**

EXERCISES

Analyze statements about decision-making and incremental analysis.

(LO 1, 2), C

E7-1 Ortega has prepared the following list of statements about decision-making and incremental analysis.

1. The first step in management's decision-making process is, "Determine and evaluate possible courses of action."
2. The final step in management's decision-making process is to actually make the decision.
3. Accounting's contribution to management's decision-making process occurs primarily in evaluating possible courses of action and in reviewing the results.
4. In making business decisions, management ordinarily considers only financial information because it is objectively determined.
5. Decisions involve a choice among alternative courses of action.
6. The process used to identify the financial data that change under alternative courses of action is called incremental analysis.
7. Costs that are the same under all alternative courses of action sometimes affect the decision.
8. When using incremental analysis, some costs will always change under alternative courses of action, but revenues will not.
9. Variable costs will change under alternative courses of action, but fixed costs will not.

Instructions
Identify each statement as true or false. If false, indicate how to correct the statement.

Use incremental analysis for special-order decision.

(LO 3), AN

E7-2 Gruden Company produces golf discs which it normally sells to retailers for $7 each. The cost of manufacturing 20,000 golf discs is:

Materials	$ 10,000
Labor	30,000
Variable overhead	20,000
Fixed overhead	40,000
Total	$100,000

Gruden also incurs 5% sales commission ($0.35) on each disc sold.

McGee Corporation offers Gruden $4.80 per disc for 5,000 discs. McGee would sell the discs under its own brand name in foreign markets not yet served by Gruden. If Gruden accepts the offer, its fixed overhead will increase from $40,000 to $46,000 due to the purchase of a new imprinting machine. No sales commission will result from the special order.

Instructions
(a) Prepare an incremental analysis for the special order.
(b) Should Gruden accept the special order? Why or why not?
(c) What assumptions underlie the decision made in part (b)?

E7-3 Leno Company manufactures toasters. For the first 8 months of 2014, the company reported the following operating results while operating at 75% of plant capacity:

Use incremental analysis for special order.

(LO 3), AN

Sales (350,000 units)	$4,375,000
Cost of goods sold	2,600,000
Gross profit	1,775,000
Operating expenses	840,000
Net income	$ 935,000

Cost of goods sold was 70% variable and 30% fixed; operating expenses were 75% variable and 25% fixed.

In September, Leno Company receives a special order for 15,000 toasters at $7.60 each from Centro Company of Ciudad Juarez. Acceptance of the order would result in an additional $3,000 of shipping costs but no increase in fixed operating expenses.

Instructions
(a) Prepare an incremental analysis for the special order.
(b) ▭▭▭▷ Should Leno Company accept the special order? Why or why not?

E7-4 Klean Fiber Company is the creator of Y-Go, a technology that weaves silver into its fabrics to kill bacteria and odor on clothing while managing heat. Y-Go has become very popular as an undergarment for sports activities. Operating at capacity, the company can produce 1,000,000 undergarments of Y-Go a year. The per unit and the total costs for an individual garment when the company operates at full capacity are as follows.

Use incremental analysis for special order.

(LO 3), AN

	Per Undergarment	Total
Direct materials	$2.00	$2,000,000
Direct labor	0.75	750,000
Variable manufacturing overhead	1.00	1,000,000
Fixed manufacturing overhead	1.50	1,500,000
Variable selling expenses	0.25	250,000
Totals	$5.50	$5,500,000

The U.S. Army has approached Klean Fiber and expressed an interest in purchasing 250,000 Y-Go undergarments for soldiers in extremely warm climates. The Army would pay the unit cost for direct materials, direct labor, and variable manufacturing overhead costs. In addition, the Army has agreed to pay an additional $1 per undergarment to cover all other costs and provide a profit. Presently, Klean Fiber is operating at 70% capacity and does not have any other potential buyers for Y-Go. If Klean Fiber accepts the Army's offer, it will not incur any variable selling expenses related to this order.

Instructions
Using incremental analysis, determine whether Klean Fiber should accept the Army's offer.

E7-5 Schopp Inc. has been manufacturing its own shades for its table lamps. The company is currently operating at 100% of capacity, and variable manufacturing overhead is charged to production at the rate of 70% of direct labor cost. The direct materials and direct labor cost per unit to make the lamp shades are $4 and $5, respectively. Normal production is 30,000 table lamps per year.

A supplier offers to make the lamp shades at a price of $12.75 per unit. If Schopp Inc. accepts the supplier's offer, all variable manufacturing costs will be eliminated, but the $45,000 of fixed manufacturing overhead currently being charged to the lamp shades will have to be absorbed by other products.

Use incremental analysis for make-or-buy decision.

(LO 4), AN

Instructions

(a) Prepare the incremental analysis for the decision to make or buy the lamp shades.
(b) ▭▭▶ Should Schopp Inc. buy the lamp shades?
(c) ▭▭▶ Would your answer be different in (b) if the productive capacity released by not making the lamp shades could be used to produce income of $25,000?

Use incremental analysis for make-or-buy decision.

(LO 4), E

E7-6 Jobs, Inc. has recently started the manufacture of Tri-Robo, a three-wheeled robot that can scan a home for fires and gas leaks and then transmit this information to a mobile phone. The cost structure to manufacture 20,000 Tri-Robos is as follows.

	Cost
Direct materials ($50 per robot)	$1,000,000
Direct labor ($40 per robot)	800,000
Variable overhead ($6 per robot)	120,000
Allocated fixed overhead ($30 per robot)	600,000
Total	$2,520,000

Jobs is approached by Tienh Inc., which offers to make Tri-Robo for $115 per unit or $2,300,000.

Instructions

(a) Using incremental analysis, determine whether Jobs should accept this offer under each of the following independent assumptions.
   (1) Assume that $405,000 of the fixed overhead cost can be reduced (avoided).
   (2) Assume that none of the fixed overhead can be reduced (avoided). However, if the robots are purchased from Tienh Inc., Jobs can use the released productive resources to generate additional income of $405,000.
(b) Describe the qualitative factors that might affect the decision to purchase the robots from an outside supplier.

Prepare incremental analysis for make-or-buy decision.

(LO 4), E

E7-7 Gibbs Company purchases sails and produces sailboats. It currently produces 1,200 sailboats per year, operating at normal capacity, which is about 80% of full capacity. Gibbs purchases sails at $250 each, but the company is considering using the excess capacity to manufacture the sails instead. The manufacturing cost per sail would be $100 for direct materials, $80 for direct labor, and $100 for overhead. The $100 overhead is based on $78,000 of annual fixed overhead that is allocated using normal capacity.

The president of Gibbs has come to you for advice. "It would cost me $280 to make the sails," she says, "but only $250 to buy them. Should I continue buying them, or have I missed something?"

Instructions

(a) Prepare a per unit analysis of the differential costs. Briefly explain whether Gibbs should make or buy the sails.
(b) If Gibbs suddenly finds an opportunity to rent out the unused capacity of its factory for $77,000 per year, would your answer to part (a) change? Briefly explain.
(c) Identify three qualitative factors that should be considered by Gibbs in this make-or-buy decision.

(CGA adapted)

Prepare incremental analysis concerning make-or-buy decision.

(LO 4), E

E7-8 Innova uses 1,000 units of the component IMC2 every month to manufacture one of its products. The unit costs incurred to manufacture the component are as follows.

Direct materials	$ 65.00
Direct labor	45.00
Overhead	126.50
Total	$236.50

Overhead costs include variable material handling costs of $6.50, which are applied to products on the basis of direct material costs. The remainder of the overhead costs are applied on the basis of direct labor dollars and consist of 60% variable costs and 40% fixed costs.

A vendor has offered to supply the IMC2 component at a price of $200 per unit.

Instructions

(a) Should Innova purchase the component from the outside vendor if Innova's capacity remains idle?

(b) Should Innova purchase the component from the outside vendor if it can use its facilities to manufacture another product? What information will Innova need to make an accurate decision? Show your calculations.

(c) What are the qualitative factors that Innova will have to consider when making this decision?

(CGA adapted)

E7-9 Rachel Rey recently opened her own basketweaving studio. She sells finished baskets in addition to the raw materials needed by customers to weave baskets of their own. Rachel has put together a variety of raw material kits, each including materials at various stages of completion. Unfortunately, owing to space limitations, Rachel is unable to carry all varieties of kits originally assembled and must choose between two basic packages.

Use incremental analysis for further processing of materials decision.

(LO 5), AN

The basic introductory kit includes undyed, uncut reeds (with dye included) for weaving one basket. This basic package costs Rachel $14 and sells for $30. The second kit, called Stage 2, includes cut reeds that have already been dyed. With this kit the customer need only soak the reeds and weave the basket. Rachel is able to produce the second kit by using the basic materials included in the first kit and adding one hour of her own time, which she values at $18 per hour. Because she is more efficient at cutting and dying reeds than her average customer, Rachel is able to make two kits of the dyed reeds, in one hour, from one kit of undyed reeds. The Stage 2 kit sells for $35.

Instructions

Determine whether Rachel's basketweaving shop should carry the basic introductory kit with undyed and uncut reeds or the Stage 2 kit with reeds already dyed and cut. Prepare an incremental analysis to support your answer.

E7-10 Stahl Inc. produces three separate products from a common process costing $100,000. Each of the products can be sold at the split-off point or can be processed further and then sold for a higher price. Shown below are cost and selling price data for a recent period.

Determine whether to sell or process further, joint products.

(LO 5), AN

	Sales Value at Split-Off Point	Cost to Process Further	Sales Value after Further Processing
Product 10	$60,000	$100,000	$190,000
Product 12	15,000	30,000	35,000
Product 14	55,000	150,000	215,000

Instructions

(a) Determine total net income if all products are sold at the split-off point.

(b) Determine total net income if all products are sold after further processing.

(c) Using incremental analysis, determine which products should be sold at the split-off point and which should be processed further.

(d) Determine total net income using the results from (c) and explain why the net income is different from that determined in (b).

E7-11 Chen Minerals processes materials extracted from mines. The most common raw material that it processes results in three joint products: Larco, Marco, and Narco. Each of these products can be sold as is, or each can be processed further and sold for a higher price. The company incurs joint costs of $180,000 to process one batch of the raw material that produces the three joint products. The following cost and sales information is available for one batch of each product.

Determine whether to sell or process further, joint products.

(LO 5), AN

	Sales Value at Split-Off Point	Allocated Joint Costs	Cost to Process Further	Sales Value of Processed Product
Larco	$200,000	$40,000	$110,000	$300,000
Marco	300,000	60,000	85,000	400,000
Narco	405,000	80,000	250,000	800,000

Instructions

Determine whether each of the three joint products should be sold as is, or processed further.

Prepare incremental analysis for whether to sell or process materials further.

(LO 5), E

E7-12 A company manufactures three products using the same production process. The costs incurred up to the split-off point are $200,000. These costs are allocated to the products on the basis of their sales value at the split-off point. The number of units produced, the selling prices per unit of the three products at the split-off point and after further processing, and the additional processing costs are as follows.

Product	Number of Units Produced	Selling Price at Split-Off	Selling Price after Processing	Additional Processing Costs
D	4,000	$10.00	$15.00	$14,000
E	6,000	11.60	16.20	20,000
F	2,000	19.40	22.60	9,000

Instructions
(a) Which information is relevant to the decision on whether or not to process the products further? Explain why this information is relevant.
(b) Which product(s) should be processed further and which should be sold at the split-off point?
(c) Would your decision be different if the company was using the quantity of output to allocate joint costs? Explain.

(CGA adapted)

Use incremental analysis for retaining or replacing equipment decision.

(LO 6), E

E7-13 On January 2, 2013, Benson Hospital purchased a $100,000 special radiology scanner from Picard Inc. The scanner had a useful life of 4 years and was estimated to have no disposal value at the end of its useful life. The straight-line method of depreciation is used on this scanner. Annual operating costs with this scanner are $105,000.

Approximately one year later, the hospital is approached by Dyno Technology salesperson, Meg Ryan, who indicated that purchasing the scanner in 2013 from Picard Inc. was a mistake. She points out that Dyno has a scanner that will save Benson Hospital $30,000 a year in operating expenses over its 3-year useful life. She notes that the new scanner will cost $110,000 and has the same capabilities as the scanner purchased last year. The hospital agrees that both scanners are of equal quality. The new scanner will have no disposal value. Ryan agrees to buy the old scanner from Benson Hospital for $40,000.

Instructions
(a) If Benson Hospital sells its old scanner on January 2, 2014, compute the gain or loss on the sale.
(b) Using incremental analysis, determine if Benson Hospital should purchase the new scanner on January 2, 2014.
(c) Explain why Benson Hospital might be reluctant to purchase the new scanner, regardless of the results indicated by the incremental analysis in (b).

Use incremental analysis for retaining or replacing equipment decision.

(LO 6), AN

E7-14 Johnson Enterprises uses a computer to handle its sales invoices. Lately, business has been so good that it takes an extra 3 hours per night, plus every third Saturday, to keep up with the volume of sales invoices. Management is considering updating its computer with a faster model that would eliminate all of the overtime processing.

	Current Machine	New Machine
Original purchase cost	$15,000	$25,000
Accumulated depreciation	$ 6,000	—
Estimated annual operating costs	$25,000	$20,000
Useful life	5 years	5 years

If sold now, the current machine would have a salvage value of $6,000. If operated for the remainder of its useful life, the current machine would have zero salvage value. The new machine is expected to have zero salvage value after 5 years.

Instructions
Should the current machine be replaced?

Use incremental analysis concerning elimination of division.

(LO 7), AN

XLS

E7-15 Judy Jean, a recent graduate of Rolling's accounting program, evaluated the operating performance of Artie Company's six divisions. Judy made the following presentation to Artie's board of directors and suggested the Huron Division be eliminated. "If the Huron Division is eliminated," she said, "our total profits would increase by $26,000."

	The Other Five Divisions	Huron Division	Total
Sales	$1,664,200	$100,000	$1,764,200
Cost of goods sold	978,520	76,000	1,054,520
Gross profit	685,680	24,000	709,680
Operating expenses	527,940	50,000	577,940
Net income	$ 157,740	$ (26,000)	$ 131,740

In the Huron Division, cost of goods sold is $61,000 variable and $15,000 fixed, and operating expenses are $26,000 variable and $24,000 fixed. None of the Huron Division's fixed costs will be eliminated if the division is discontinued.

Instructions

☐▐▭▭▭▷ Is Judy right about eliminating the Huron Division? Prepare a schedule to support your answer.

E7-16 Cawley Company makes three models of tasers. Information on the three products is given below.

Use incremental analysis for elimination of a product line.

(LO 7), AN

	Tingler	Shocker	Stunner
Sales	$300,000	$500,000	$200,000
Variable expenses	150,000	200,000	145,000
Contribution margin	150,000	300,000	55,000
Fixed expenses	120,000	230,000	95,000
Net income	$ 30,000	$ 70,000	$ (40,000)

Fixed expenses consist of $300,000 of common costs allocated to the three products based on relative sales, and additional fixed expenses of $30,000 (Tingler), $80,000 (Shocker), and $35,000 (Stunner). The common costs will be incurred regardless of how many models are produced. The other fixed expenses would be eliminated if a model is phased out.

James Watt, an executive with the company, feels the Stunner line should be discontinued to increase the company's net income.

Instructions

(a) Compute current net income for Cawley Company.
(b) Compute net income by product line and in total for Cawley Company if the company discontinues the Stunner product line. (*Hint:* Allocate the $300,000 common costs to the two remaining product lines based on their relative sales.)
(c) Should Cawley eliminate the Stunner product line? Why or why not?

E7-17 Twyla Company operates a small factory in which it manufactures two products: C and D. Production and sales results for last year were as follows.

Prepare incremental analysis concerning keeping or dropping a product to maximize operating income.

(LO 2, 7), AN

	C	D
Units sold	9,000	20,000
Selling price per unit	$95	$75
Variable cost per unit	50	40
Fixed cost per unit	22	22

For purposes of simplicity, the firm averages total fixed costs over the total number of units of C and D produced and sold.

The research department has developed a new product (E) as a replacement for product D. Market studies show that Twyla Company could sell 10,000 units of E next year at a price of $115; the variable cost per unit of E is $40. The introduction of product E will lead to a 10% increase in demand for product C and discontinuation of product D. If the company does not introduce the new product, it expects next year's results to be the same as last year's.

Instructions

Should Twyla Company introduce product E next year? Explain why or why not. Show calculations to support your decision.

(CMA-Canada adapted)

*Identify relevant costs for
different decisions.*

(LO 3, 4, 5, 6, 7), C

E7-18 The costs listed below relate to a variety of different decision situations.

Cost	Decision
1. Unavoidable fixed overhead	Eliminate an unprofitable segment
2. Direct labor	Make or buy
3. Original cost of old equipment	Equipment replacement
4. Joint production costs	Sell or process further
5. Opportunity cost	Accepting a special order
6. Segment manager's salary	Eliminate an unprofitable segment (manager will be terminated)
7. Cost of new equipment	Equipment replacement
8. Incremental production costs	Sell or process further
9. Direct materials	Equipment replacement (the amount of materials required does not change)
10. Rent expense	Purchase or lease a building

Instructions

For each cost listed above, indicate if it is relevant or not to the related decision. For those costs determined to be irrelevant, briefly explain why.

EXERCISES: SET B AND CHALLENGE EXERCISES

Visit the book's companion website, at **www.wiley.com/college/weygandt**, and choose the Student Companion site to access Exercise Set B and Challenge Exercises.

PROBLEMS: SET A

*Use incremental analysis
for special order and identify
nonfinancial factors in the
decision.*

(LO 3), E

P7-1A ShurShot Sports Inc. manufactures basketballs for the National Basketball Association (NBA). For the first 6 months of 2014, the company reported the following operating results while operating at 80% of plant capacity and producing 120,000 units.

	Amount
Sales	$4,800,000
Cost of goods sold	3,600,000
Selling and administrative expenses	405,000
Net income	$ 795,000

Fixed costs for the period were cost of goods sold $960,000, and selling and administrative expenses $225,000.

In July, normally a slack manufacturing month, ShurShot Sports receives a special order for 10,000 basketballs at $27 each from the Greek Basketball Association (GBA). Acceptance of the order would increase variable selling and administrative expenses $0.50 per unit because of shipping costs but would not increase fixed costs and expenses.

Instructions

(a) NI increase $30,000

(a) Prepare an incremental analysis for the special order.
(b) Should ShurShot Sports Inc. accept the special order? Explain your answer.
(c) What is the minimum selling price on the special order to produce net income of $4.00 per ball?
(d) ▭▭▭➤ What nonfinancial factors should management consider in making its decision?

*Use incremental analysis
related to make or buy,
consider opportunity cost,
and identify nonfinancial
factors.*

(LO 4), E

P7-2A The management of Shatner Manufacturing Company is trying to decide whether to continue manufacturing a part or to buy it from an outside supplier. The part, called CISCO, is a component of the company's finished product.

The following information was collected from the accounting records and production data for the year ending December 31, 2014.

1. 8,000 units of CISCO were produced in the Machining Department.
2. Variable manufacturing costs applicable to the production of each CISCO unit were: direct materials $4.80, direct labor $4.30, indirect labor $0.43, utilities $0.40.
3. Fixed manufacturing costs applicable to the production of CISCO were:

Cost Item	Direct	Allocated
Depreciation	$2,100	$ 900
Property taxes	500	200
Insurance	900	600
	$3,500	$1,700

All variable manufacturing and direct fixed costs will be eliminated if CISCO is purchased. Allocated costs will have to be absorbed by other production departments.
4. The lowest quotation for 8,000 CISCO units from a supplier is $80,000.
5. If CISCO units are purchased, freight and inspection costs would be $0.35 per unit, and receiving costs totaling $1,300 per year would be incurred by the Machining Department.

Instructions

(a) Prepare an incremental analysis for CISCO. Your analysis should have columns for (1) Make CISCO, (2) Buy CISCO, and (3) Net Income Increase/(Decrease).

(a) NI (decrease) $(1,160)

(b) Based on your analysis, what decision should management make?

(c) Would the decision be different if Shatner Company has the opportunity to produce $3,000 of net income with the facilities currently being used to manufacture CISCO? Show computations.

(c) NI increase $1,840

(d) ▱▱▱▱▶ What nonfinancial factors should management consider in making its decision?

P7-3A Sutton Industrial Products Inc. (SIPI) is a diversified industrial cleaner processing company. The company's Verde plant produces two products: a table cleaner and a floor cleaner from a common set of chemical inputs (CDG). Each week 900,000 ounces of chemical input are processed at a cost of $210,000 into 600,000 ounces of floor cleaner and 300,000 ounces of table cleaner. The floor cleaner has no market value until it is converted into a polish with the trade name FloorShine. The additional processing costs for this conversion amount to $240,000.

Determine if product should be sold or processed further.

(LO 5), AN

FloorShine sells at $20 per 30-ounce bottle. The table cleaner can be sold for $18 per 25-ounce bottle. However, the table cleaner can be converted into two other products by adding 300,000 ounces of another compound (TCP) to the 300,000 ounces of table cleaner. This joint process will yield 300,000 ounces each of table stain remover (TSR) and table polish (TP). The additional processing costs for this process amount to $100,000. Both table products can be sold for $14 per 25-ounce bottle.

The company decided not to process the table cleaner into TSR and TP based on the following analysis.

		Process Further		
	Table Cleaner	Table Stain Remover (TSR)	Table Polish (TP)	Total
Production in ounces	300,000	300,000	300,000	
Revenue	$216,000	$168,000	$168,000	$336,000
Costs:				
CDG costs	70,000*	52,500	52,500	105,000**
TCP costs	0	50,000	50,000	100,000
Total costs	70,000	102,500	102,500	205,000
Weekly gross profit	$146,000	$ 65,500	$ 65,500	$131,000

*If table cleaner is not processed further, it is allocated 1/3 of the $210,000 of CDG cost, which is equal to 1/3 of the total physical output.

**If table cleaner is processed further, total physical output is 1,200,000 ounces. TSR and TP combined account for 50% of the total physical output and are each allocated 25% of the CDG cost.

Instructions

(a) Determine if management made the correct decision to not process the table cleaner further by doing the following.
  (1) Calculate the company's total weekly gross profit assuming the table cleaner is not processed further.

(2) Gross profit $186,000

  (2) Calculate the company's total weekly gross profit assuming the table cleaner is processed further.
  (3) Compare the resulting net incomes and comment on management's decision.
(b) Using incremental analysis, determine if the table cleaner should be processed further.

(CMA adapted)

Compute gain or loss, and determine if equipment should be replaced.

(LO 6), S

P7-4A Last year (2013), Richter Condos installed a mechanized elevator for its tenants. The owner of the company, Ron Richter, recently returned from an industry equipment exhibition where he watched a computerized elevator demonstrated. He was impressed with the elevator's speed, comfort of ride, and cost efficiency. Upon returning from the exhibition, he asked his purchasing agent to collect price and operating cost data on the new elevator. In addition, he asked the company's accountant to provide him with cost data on the company's elevator. This information is presented below.

	Old Elevator	New Elevator
Purchase price	$120,000	$160,000
Estimated salvage value	0	0
Estimated useful life	5 years	4 years
Depreciation method	Straight-line	Straight-line
Annual operating costs other than depreciation:		
Variable	$ 35,000	$ 10,000
Fixed	23,000	8,500

Annual revenues are $240,000, and selling and administrative expenses are $29,000, regardless of which elevator is used. If the old elevator is replaced now, at the beginning of 2014, Richter Condos will be able to sell it for $25,000.

Instructions

(a) Determine any gain or loss if the old elevator is replaced.
(b) Prepare a 4-year summarized income statement for each of the following assumptions:
  (1) The old elevator is retained.
  (2) The old elevator is replaced.

(b) (2) NI $539,000
(c) NI increase $23,000

(c) Using incremental analysis, determine if the old elevator should be replaced.
(d) ▭▭▭▭▷ Write a memo to Ron Richter explaining why any gain or loss should be ignored in the decision to replace the old elevator.

Prepare incremental analysis concerning elimination of divisions.

(LO 7), AN

P7-5A Gutierrez Company has four operating divisions. During the first quarter of 2014, the company reported aggregate income from operations of $213,000 and the following divisional results.

	Division			
	I	**II**	**III**	**IV**
Sales	$250,000	$200,000	$500,000	$450,000
Cost of goods sold	200,000	192,000	300,000	250,000
Selling and administrative expenses	75,000	60,000	60,000	50,000
Income (loss) from operations	$ (25,000)	$ (52,000)	$140,000	$150,000

Analysis reveals the following percentages of variable costs in each division.

	I	**II**	**III**	**IV**
Cost of goods sold	75%	90%	80%	75%
Selling and administrative expenses	40	70	50	60

Discontinuance of any division would save 50% of the fixed costs and expenses for that division.

Top management is very concerned about the unprofitable divisions (I and II). Consensus is that one or both of the divisions should be discontinued.

Instructions

(a) Compute the contribution margin for Divisions I and II.

(b) Prepare an incremental analysis concerning the possible discontinuance of (1) Division I and (2) Division II. What course of action do you recommend for each division?

(c) Prepare a columnar condensed income statement for Gutierrez Company, assuming Division II is eliminated. (Use the CVP format.) Division II's unavoidable fixed costs are allocated equally to the continuing divisions.

(d) Reconcile the total income from operations ($213,000) with the total income from operations without Division II.

(a) I $70,000

(c) Income III $133,800

PROBLEMS: SET B

P7-1B Morello Inc. manufactures basketballs for the National Basketball Association (NBA). For the first 6 months of 2014, the company reported the following operating results while operating at 90% of plant capacity and producing 90,000 units.

Use incremental analysis for special order and identify nonfinancial factors in decision.

(LO 3), E

	Amount	Per Unit
Sales	$4,500,000	$50
Cost of goods sold	3,060,000	34
Selling and administrative expenses	360,000	4
Net income	$1,080,000	$12

Fixed costs for the period were cost of goods sold $900,000, and selling and administrative expenses $180,000.

In July, normally a slack manufacturing month, Morello receives a special order for 10,000 basketballs at $30 each from the Chinese Basketball Association (CBA). Acceptance of the order would increase variable selling and administrative expenses $0.50 per unit because of shipping costs but would not increase fixed costs and expenses.

Instructions

(a) Prepare an incremental analysis for the special order.

(b) Should Morello Inc. accept the special order?

(c) What is the minimum selling price on the special order to produce net income of $5.50 per ball?

(d) ▭▭▭▷ What nonfinancial factors should management consider in making its decision?

(a) NI increase $35,000

P7-2B The management of Gill Corporation is trying to decide whether to continue manufacturing a part or to buy it from an outside supplier. The part, called FIZBE, is a component of the company's finished product.

The following information was collected from the accounting records and production data for the year ending December 31, 2014.

Use incremental analysis related to make or buy; consider opportunity cost and identify nonfinancial factors.

(LO 4), E

1. 5,000 units of FIZBE were produced in the Machining Department.

2. Variable manufacturing costs applicable to the production of each FIZBE unit were: direct materials $4.75, direct labor $4.60, indirect labor $0.45, utilities $0.35.

3. Fixed manufacturing costs applicable to the production of FIZBE were:

Cost Item	Direct	Allocated
Depreciation	$1,100	$ 900
Property taxes	500	200
Insurance	900	600
	$2,500	$1,700

All variable manufacturing and direct fixed costs will be eliminated if FIZBE is purchased. Allocated costs will have to be absorbed by other production departments.

4. The lowest quotation for 5,000 FIZBE units from a supplier is $56,000.

5. If FIZBE units are purchased, freight and inspection costs would be $0.30 per unit, and receiving costs totaling $500 per year would be incurred by the Machining Department.

(a) NI (decrease) ($4,750)

(c) NI increase $1,250

Instructions
(a) Prepare an incremental analysis for FIZBE. Your analysis should have columns for (1) Make FIZBE, (2) Buy FIZBE, and (3) Net Income Increase/Decrease.
(b) Based on your analysis, what decision should management make?
(c) Would the decision be different if Gill Corporation has the opportunity to produce $6,000 of net income with the facilities currently being used to manufacture FIZBE? Show computations.
(d) ▱▱▱▱▱▷ What nonfinancial factors should management consider in making its decision?

Determine if product should be sold or processed further.

(LO 5), AN

P7-3B Ohio Household Products Co. (OHPC) is a diversified household-cleaner processing company. The company's Mishawaka plant produces two products: an appliance cleaner and a general-purpose cleaner from a common set of chemical inputs (NPR). Each week 1,000,000 ounces of chemical input are processed at a cost of $200,000 into 750,000 ounces of appliance cleaner and 250,000 ounces of general-purpose cleaner. The appliance cleaner has no market value until it is converted into a polish with the trade name Shine Brite. The additional processing costs for this conversion amount to $300,000. Shine Brite sells at $15 per 25-ounce bottle. The general-purpose cleaner can be sold for $20 per 20-ounce bottle. However, the general-purpose cleaner can be converted into two other products by adding 250,000 ounces of another compound (PST) to the 250,000 ounces of general-purpose cleaner. This joint process will yield 250,000 ounces each of premium cleaner (PC) and premium stain remover (PSR). The additional processing costs for this process amount to $140,000. Both premium products can be sold for $16 per 20-ounce bottle.

The company decided not to process the general-purpose cleaner into PC and PSR based on the following analysis.

| | General-Purpose Cleaner | Process Further | | |
		Premium Cleaner (PC)	Premium Stain Remover (PSR)	Total
Production in ounces	250,000	250,000	250,000	
Revenue	$250,000	$200,000	$200,000	$400,000
Costs:				
NPR costs	50,000*	40,000	40,000	80,000**
PST costs	0	70,000	70,000	140,000
Total costs	50,000	110,000	110,000	220,000
Weekly gross profit	$200,000	$ 90,000	$ 90,000	$180,000

*If general-purpose cleaner is not processed further, it is allocated 1/4 of the $200,000 of NPR cost, which is equal to 1/4 of the total physical output.
**If general-purpose cleaner is processed further, total physical output is 1,250,000 ounces. PC and PSR combined account for 40% of the total output and are each allocated 20% of the NPR cost.

Instructions
(a) Determine if management made the correct decision to not process the general-purpose cleaner further by doing the following.
   (1) Calculate the company's total weekly gross profit assuming the general-purpose cleaner is not processed further.
   (2) Calculate the company's total weekly gross profit assuming the general-purpose cleaner is processed further.
   (3) Compare the resulting net incomes and comment on management's decision.
(b) Using incremental analysis, determine if the general-purpose cleaner should be processed further.

(a) (2) Gross profit $210,000

(CMA adapted)

Compute gain or loss, and determine if equipment should be replaced.

(LO 6), S

P7-4B Last year (2013), Simmons Company installed new factory equipment. The owner of the company, Gene Simmons, recently returned from an industry equipment exhibition where he watched computerized equipment demonstrated. He was impressed with the equipment's speed and cost efficiency. Upon returning from the exhibition, he asked his purchasing agent to collect price and operating cost data on the new equipment. In addition, he asked the company's accountant to provide him with cost data on the company's equipment. This information is presented below.

	Old Equipment	New Equipment
Purchase price	$210,000	$250,000
Estimated salvage value	0	0
Estimated useful life	5 years	4 years
Depreciation method	Straight-line	Straight-line
Annual operating costs other than depreciation:		
Variable	$50,000	$12,000
Fixed	30,000	5,000

Annual revenues are $360,000, and selling and administrative expenses are $45,000, regardless of which equipment is used. If the old equipment is replaced now, at the beginning of 2014, Simmons Company will be able to sell it for $58,000.

Instructions
(a) Determine any gain or loss if the old equipment is replaced.
(b) Prepare a 4-year summarized income statement for each of the following assumptions:
(1) The old equipment is retained.
(2) The old equipment is replaced.
(c) Using incremental analysis, determine if the old equipment should be replaced.
(d) ▭▭▭▷ Write a memo to Gene Simmons explaining why any gain or loss should be ignored in the decision to replace the old equipment.

(b) (2) NI $832,000
(c) NI increase $60,000

P7-5B Panda Corporation has four operating divisions. During the first quarter of 2014, the company reported aggregate income from operations of $129,000 and the divisional results shown below.

Prepare incremental analysis concerning elimination of divisions.

(LO 7), AN

	Division			
	I	**II**	**III**	**IV**
Sales	$510,000	$400,000	$310,000	$170,000
Cost of goods sold	300,000	250,000	270,000	156,000
Selling and administrative expenses	60,000	80,000	75,000	70,000
Income (loss) from operations	$150,000	$ 70,000	$ (35,000)	$ (56,000)

Analysis reveals the following percentages of variable costs in each division.

	I	**II**	**III**	**IV**
Cost of goods sold	70%	80%	70%	90%
Selling and administrative expenses	40	50	60	70

Discontinuance of any division would save 50% of the fixed costs and expenses for that division.

Top management is very concerned about the unprofitable divisions (III and IV). Consensus is that one or both of the divisions should be discontinued.

Instructions
(a) Compute the contribution margin for Divisions III and IV.
(b) Prepare an incremental analysis concerning the possible discontinuance of (1) Division III and (2) Division IV. What course of action do you recommend for each division?
(c) Prepare a columnar condensed income statement for Panda Corporation, assuming Division IV is eliminated. (Use the CVP format.) Division IV's unavoidable fixed costs are allocated equally to the continuing divisions.
(d) Reconcile the total income from operations ($129,000) with the total income from operations without Division IV.

(a) III $76,000

(c) II $63,900

PROBLEMS: SET C

Visit the book's companion website, at **www.wiley.com/college/weygandt**, and choose the Student Companion site to access Problem Set C.

WATERWAYS CONTINUING PROBLEM

(This is a continuation of the Waterways Problem from Chapters 1–6.)

WCP7 Waterways Corporation is considering various business opportunities. It wants to make the best use of its production facilities to maximize income. This problem asks you to help Waterways do incremental analysis on these various opportunities.

*Go to the book's companion website, **www.wiley.com/college/weygandt**, to find the remainder of this problem.*

Broadening Your PERSPECTIVE

Management Decision-Making

Decision-Making at Current Designs

BYP7-1 Current Designs faces a number of important decisions that require incremental analysis. Consider each of the following situations independently.

Situation 1

Recently, Mike Cichanowski, owner and CEO of Current Designs, received a phone call from the president of a brewing company. He was calling to inquire about the possibility of Current Designs producing "floating coolers" for a promotion his company was planning. These coolers resemble a kayak but are about one-third the size. They are used to float food and beverages while paddling down the river on a weekend leisure trip. The company would be interested in purchasing 100 coolers for the upcoming summer. It is willing to pay $250 per cooler. The brewing company would pick up the coolers upon completion of the order.

Mike met with Diane Buswell, controller, to identify how much it would cost Current Designs to produce the coolers. After careful analysis, the following costs were identified.

Direct materials	$80/unit	Variable overhead	$20/unit
Direct labor	$60/unit	Fixed overhead	$1,000

Current Designs would be able to modify an existing mold to produce the coolers. The cost of these modifications would be approximately $2,000.

Instructions

(a) Prepare an incremental analysis to determine whether Current Designs should accept this special order to produce the coolers.

(b) Discuss additional factors that Mike and Diane should consider if Current Designs is currently operating at full capacity.

Situation 2

Current Designs is always working to identify ways to increase efficiency while becoming more environmentally conscious. During a recent brainstorming session, one employee suggested to Diane Buswell, controller, that the company should consider replacing the current rotomold oven as a way to realize savings from reduced energy consumption. The oven operates on natural gas, using 17,000 therms of natural gas for an entire year. A new, energy-efficient rotomold oven would operate on 15,000 therms of natural gas for an entire year. After seeking out price quotes from a few suppliers, Diane determined that it would cost approximately $250,000 to purchase a new, energy-efficient rotomold oven. She determines that the expected useful life of the new oven would be 10 years, and it would have no salvage value at the end of its useful life. Current Designs would be able to sell the current oven for $10,000.

Instructions
(a) Prepare an incremental analysis to determine if Current Designs should purchase the new roto-mold oven, assuming that the average price for natural gas over the next 10 years will be $0.65 per therm.
(b) Diane is concerned that natural gas prices might increase at a faster rate over the next 10 years. If the company projects that the average natural gas price of the next 10 years could be as high as $0.85 per therm, discuss how that might change your conclusion in (a).

Situation 3

One of Current Designs' competitive advantages is found in the ingenuity of its owner and CEO, Mike Cichanowski. His involvement in the design of kayak molds and production techniques has led to Current Designs being recognized as an industry leader in the design and production of kay-aks. This ingenuity was evident in an improved design of one of the most important components of a kayak, the seat. The "Revolution Seating System" is a one-of-a-kind, rotating axis seat that gives unmatched, full-contact, under-leg support. It is quickly adjustable with a lever-lock system that allows for a customizable seat position that maximizes comfort for the rider.

Having just designed the "Revolution Seating System," Current Designs must now decide whether to produce the seats internally or buy them from an outside supplier. The costs for Current Designs to produce the seats are as follows.

| Direct materials | $20/unit | Direct labor | $15/unit |
| Variable overhead | $12/unit | Fixed overhead | $20,000 |

Current Designs will need to produce 3,000 seats this year; 25% of the fixed overhead will be avoided if the seats are purchased from an outside vendor. After soliciting prices from outside suppliers, the company determined that it will cost $50 to purchase a seat from an outside vendor.

Instructions
(a) Prepare an incremental analysis showing whether Current Designs should make or buy the "Revolution Seating System."
(b) Would your answer in (a) change if the productive capacity released by not making the seats could be used to produce income of $20,000?

Decision-Making Across the Organization

BYP7-2 Aurora Company is considering the purchase of a new machine. The invoice price of the machine is $140,000, freight charges are estimated to be $4,000, and installation costs are expected to be $6,000. Salvage value of the new equipment is expected to be zero after a useful life of 5 years. Existing equipment could be retained and used for an additional 5 years if the new machine is not pur-chased. At that time, the salvage value of the equipment would be zero. If the new machine is purchased now, the existing machine would have to be scrapped. Aurora's accountant, Lisah Huang, has accumu-lated the following data regarding annual sales and expenses with and without the new machine.

1. Without the new machine, Aurora can sell 12,000 units of product annually at a per unit selling price of $100. If the new machine is purchased, the number of units produced and sold would increase by 10%, and the selling price would remain the same.
2. The new machine is faster than the old machine, and it is more efficient in its usage of materials. With the old machine the gross profit rate will be 25% of sales, whereas the rate will be 30% of sales with the new machine.
3. Annual selling expenses are $180,000 with the current equipment. Because the new equipment would produce a greater number of units to be sold, annual selling expenses are expected to increase by 10% if it is purchased.
4. Annual administrative expenses are expected to be $100,000 with the old machine, and $113,000 with the new machine.
5. The current book value of the existing machine is $36,000. Aurora uses straight-line depreciation.

Instructions
With the class divided into groups, prepare an incremental analysis for the 5 years showing whether Aurora should keep the existing machine or buy the new machine. (Ignore income tax effects.)

Managerial Analysis

BYP7-3 MiniTek manufactures private-label small electronic products, such as alarm clocks, calculators, kitchen timers, stopwatches, and automatic pencil sharpeners. Some of the products are sold as sets, and others are sold individually. Products are studied as to their sales potential, and then cost estimates are made. The Engineering Department develops production plans, and then production begins. The company has generally had very successful product introductions. Only two products introduced by the company have been discontinued.

One of the products currently sold is a multi-alarm clock. The clock has four alarms that can be programmed to sound at various times and for varying lengths of time. The company has experienced a great deal of difficulty in making the circuit boards for the clocks. The production process has never operated smoothly. The product is unprofitable at the present time, primarily because of warranty repairs and product recalls. Two models of the clocks were recalled, for example, because they sometimes caused an electric shock when the alarms were being shut off. The Engineering Department is attempting to revise the manufacturing process, but the revision will take another 6 months at least.

The clocks were very popular when they were introduced, and since they are private-label, the company has not suffered much from the recalls. Presently, the company has a very large order for several items from Kmart Stores. The order includes 5,000 of the multi-alarm clocks. When the company suggested that Kmart purchase the clocks from another manufacturer, Kmart threatened to rescind the entire order unless the clocks were included.

The company has therefore investigated the possibility of having another company make the clocks for them. The clocks were bid for the Kmart order based on an estimated $6.90 cost to manufacture:

Circuit board, 1 each @ $2.00	$2.00
Plastic case, 1 each @ $0.80	0.80
Alarms, 4 @ $0.15 each	0.60
Labor, 15 minutes @ $12/hour	3.00
Overhead, $2.00 per labor hour	0.50

MiniTek could purchase clocks to fill the Kmart order for $10 from Trans-Tech Asia, a Korean manufacturer with a very good quality record. Trans-Tech has offered to reduce the price to $7.50 after MiniTek has been a customer for 6 months, placing an order of at least 1,000 units per month. If MiniTek becomes a "preferred customer" by purchasing 15,000 units per year, the price would be reduced still further to $4.50.

Omega Products, a local manufacturer, has also offered to make clocks for MiniTek. They have offered to sell 5,000 clocks for $5 each. However, Omega Products has been in business for only 6 months. They have experienced significant turnover in their labor force, and the local press has reported that the owners may face tax evasion charges soon. The owner of Omega Products is an electronic engineer, however, and the quality of the clocks is likely to be good.

If MiniTek decides to purchase the clocks from either Trans-Tech or Omega, all the costs to manufacture could be avoided, except a total of $5,000 in overhead costs for machine depreciation. The machinery is fairly new, and has no alternate use.

Instructions

(a) What is the difference in profit under each of the alternatives if the clocks are to be sold for $14.50 each to Kmart?
(b) What are the most important nonfinancial factors that MiniTek should consider when making this decision?
(c) What do you think MiniTek should do in regard to the Kmart order? What should it do in regard to continuing to manufacture the multi-alarm clocks? Be prepared to defend your answer.

Real-World Focus

BYP7-4 Founded in 1983, Beverly Hills Fan Company is located in Woodland Hills, California. With 23 employees and sales of less than $10 million, the company is relatively small. Management feels that there is potential for growth in the upscale market for ceiling fans and lighting. They are particularly optimistic about growth in Mexican and Canadian markets.

Presented below is information from the president's letter in the company's annual report.

| **Beverly Hills Fan Company** |
| President's Letter |

An aggressive product development program was initiated during the past year resulting in new ceiling fan models planned for introduction this year. Award winning industrial designer Ron Rezek created several new fan models for the Beverly Hills Fan and L.A. Fan lines, including a new Showroom Collection, designed specifically for the architectural and designer markets. Each of these models has received critical acclaim, and order commitments for this year have been outstanding. Additionally, our Custom Color and special order fans continued to enjoy increasing popularity and sales gains as more and more customers desire fans that match their specific interior decors. Currently, Beverly Hills Fan Company offers a product line of over 100 models of contemporary, traditional, and transitional ceiling fans.

Instructions

(a) What points did the company management need to consider before deciding to offer the special-order fans to customers?

(b) How would incremental analysis be employed to assist in this decision?

BYP7-5 Outsourcing by both manufacturers and service companies is becoming increasingly common. There are now many firms that specialize in outsourcing consulting.

Address: **www.alsbridge.com**, or go to **www.wiley.com/college/weygandt**

Instructions

Go to the Web page of Alsbridge, Inc. at the address shown above, and answer the following questions.

(a) What are some of the types of outsourcing for which the company provides assistance?

(b) What is insourcing?

(c) What are some of the potential benefits of insourcing?

Critical Thinking

Communication Activity

BYP7-6 Hank Jewell is a production manager at a metal fabricating plant. Last night, he read an article about a new piece of equipment that would dramatically reduce his division's costs. Hank was very excited about the prospect, and the first thing he did this morning was to bring the article to his supervisor, Preston Thiese, the plant manager. The following conversation occurred:

Hank: Preston, I thought you would like to see this article on the new PDD1130; they've made some fantastic changes that could save us millions of dollars.

Preston: I appreciate your interest, Hank, but I actually have been aware of the new machine for two months. The problem is that we just bought a new machine last year. We spent $2 million on that machine, and it was supposed to last us 12 years. If we replace it now, we would have to write its book value off of the books for a huge loss. If I go to top management now and say that I want a new machine, they will fire me. I think we should use our existing machine for a couple of years, and then when it becomes obvious that we have to have a new machine, I will make the proposal.

Instructions

Hank just completed a course in managerial accounting, and he believes that Preston is making a big mistake. Write a memo from Hank to Preston explaining Preston's decision-making error.

Ethics Case

BYP7-7 Blake Romney became Chief Executive Officer of Peters Inc. two years ago. At the time, the company was reporting lagging profits, and Blake was brought in to "stir things up." The company has three divisions, electronics, fiber optics, and plumbing supplies. Blake has no interest in plumbing supplies, and one of the first things he did was to put pressure on his accountants to reallocate some of the company's fixed costs away from the other two divisions to the plumbing division. This had the effect of causing the plumbing division to report losses during the last two years; in the past it had always reported low, but acceptable, net income. Blake felt that this reallocation would shine a favorable light on him in front of the board of directors because it meant that the electronics and fiber optics divisions would look like they were improving. Given that these are "businesses of the future," he believed that the stock market would react favorably to these increases, while not penalizing the poor results of the plumbing division. Without this shift in the allocation of fixed costs, the profits of the electronics and fiber optics divisions would not have improved. But now the board of directors has suggested that the plumbing division be closed because it is reporting losses. This would mean that nearly 500 employees, many of whom have worked for Peters their whole lives, would lose their jobs.

Instructions
(a) If a division is reporting losses, does that necessarily mean that it should be closed?
(b) Was the reallocation of fixed costs across divisions unethical?
(c) What should Blake do?

All About You

BYP7-8 Managerial accounting techniques can be used in a wide variety of settings. As we have frequently pointed out, you can use them in many personal situations. They also can be useful in trying to find solutions for societal issues that appear to be hard to solve.

Instructions
Read the Fortune article, "The Toughest Customers: How Hardheaded Business Metrics Can Help the Hard-core Homeless," by Cait Murphy, available at *http://money.cnn.com/magazines/fortune/fortune_archive/2006/04/03/8373067/index.htm*. Answer the following questions.
(a) How does the article define "chronic" homelessness?
(b) In what ways does homelessness cost a city money? What are the estimated costs of a chronic homeless person to various cities?
(c) What are the steps suggested to address the problem?
(d) What is the estimated cost of implementing this program in New York? What results have been seen?
(e) In terms of incremental analysis, frame the relevant costs in this situation.

Considering Your Costs and Benefits

BYP7-9 School costs money. Is this an expenditure that you should have avoided? A year of tuition at a public four-year college costs about $8,655, and a year of tuition at a public two-year college costs about $1,359. If you did not go to college, you might avoid mountains of school-related debt. In fact, each year, about 600,000 students decide to drop out of school. Many of them never return. Suppose that you are working two jobs and going to college, and that you are not making ends meet. Your grades are suffering due to your lack of available study time. You feel depressed. Should you drop out of school?

> **YES:** You can always go back to school. If your grades are bad and you are depressed, what good is school doing you anyway?
> **NO:** Once you drop out, it is very hard to get enough momentum to go back. Dropping out will dramatically reduce your long-term opportunities. It is better to stay in school, even if you take only one class per semester. While you cannot go back and redo your initial decision, you can look at some facts to evaluate the wisdom of your decision.

Instructions
Write a response indicating your position regarding this situation. Provide support for your view.

Answers to Chapter Questions

Answers to Insight and Accounting Across the Organization Questions

p. 296 That Letter from AmEx Might Not Be a Bill Q: What are the relevant costs that American Express would need to know in order to determine to whom to make this offer? **A:** Clearly, American Express would make this offer to those customers that are most likely to default on their bills. The most important relevant cost would be the "expected loss" that an at-risk customer posed. If a customer has a high probability of defaulting and if the expected loss exceeds the $300 cost, then American Express can probably save money by paying that customer to quit using its card so that the customer doesn't ring up an even bigger bill.

p. 300 Giving Away the Store? Q: What are the relevant revenues and costs that Amazon should consider relative to the decision whether to offer the Prime free-shipping subscription? **A:** The relevant revenues to consider would be the estimated change in revenue that would result from offering free shipping and the $79 annual fee for a Prime subscription. The relevant costs would be the estimated additional shipping costs that the company would incur.

p. 307 Time to Move to a New Neighborhood? Q: What were some of the factors that complicated the company's decision to move? How should the company have incorporated such factors into its incremental analysis? **A:** The company received only $7.5 million for its California property, only 58 of 75 key employees were willing to move, construction was delayed by a year which caused the new plant to increase in price by $1.5 million, and wages surged in Idaho due to low unemployment. In performing incremental analysis of the decision to move, a company should perform sensitivity analysis. This would include evaluating the impact on the decision if all costs were, for example, 10% higher than expected or if cost savings were 10% lower than expected.

p. 308 What Is the Real Cost of Packaging Options? Q: If your marketing director suggests that, in addition to selling your cereal in a standard-size box, you should sell a jumbo size and an individual size, what issues must you consider? **A:** In evaluating this decision, you should identify the incremental revenues as well as incremental costs. The marketing manager is most likely focusing on the fact that by offering alternative packaging options, the company can market the product to a broader range of customers. However, alternative packaging options will also result in additional costs. It will increase the number of setups, require different types of storage and handling, and increase the need for additional storage space for the packages and the packaged products.

Answers to Self-Test Questions

1. d 2. b 3. c 4. d 5. c $(3,000 \times \$4)$ 6. d $[\$18 - (\$14 + \$5)] \times 3,000$ 7. b 8. d
9. c $(\$12,000 - \$8,000)$ 10. a 11. d $[(\$68 - \$55) - \$12]$ 12. b 13. c 14. b $(.5 \times \$100,000) - (\$200,000 - \$140,000)$

✔ Remember to go back to The Navigator box on the chapter opening page and check off your completed work.

Feature Story

They've Got Your Size—and Color

Nick Swinmum was shopping for a pair of shoes. He found a store with the right style, but not the right color. The next store had the right color, but not the right size. After visiting numerous stores, he went home, figuring he would buy them on the Web. After all, it was 1999, so you could buy everything on the Web, right? Well, apparently not shoes. After an exhaustive search, Nick still came up shoeless.

Nick lived in San Francisco, where, in 1999, everybody with even half an idea started an Internet company and became a millionaire. Or so it seemed. So Nick started Zappos.com. The company is dedicated to providing the best selection in shoes in terms of brands, styles, colors, size, and most importantly service.

To make sure that Zappos.com had a fighting chance of evolving from a half-baked idea to a thriving business, Nick brought in Tony Hsieh. At the age of 24, Tony had developed and recently sold a business to Microsoft for $265 million. Tony originally contributed to Zappos as an investor and advisor, but soon he took over as CEO. Tony then brought in Alfred Lin to manage the company's finances. Tony and Alfred had met when Tony was running a pizza business. (Alfred was Tony's best pizza customer, but his competencies apparently extended

✔ **The Navigator**

- Scan Learning Objectives
- Read Feature Story
- Read Preview
- Read Text and answer **DO IT!** p. 336
  - p. 340 p. 344 p. 349
- Work Using the Decision Toolkit p. 353
- Review Summary of Learning Objectives
- Work Comprehensive **DO IT!** p. 360
- Answer Self-Test Questions
- Complete Assignments
- Go to **WileyPLUS** for practice and tutorials

Learning Objectives

After studying this chapter, you should be able to:

1 Compute a target cost when the market determines a product price.

2 Compute a target selling price using cost-plus pricing.

3 Use time-and-material pricing to determine the cost of services provided.

4 Determine a transfer price using the negotiated, cost-based, and market-based approaches.

5 Explain issues involved in transferring goods between divisions in different countries.

✔ **The Navigator**

beyond pizza consumption.) Together, Tony and Alfred have run Zappos based on 10 basic principles:

1. Deliver WOW through service.
2. Embrace and drive change.
3. Create fun and a little weirdness.
4. Be adventurous, creative, and open-minded.
5. Pursue growth and learning.
6. Build open and honest relationships with communication.
7. Build a positive team and family spirit.
8. Do more with less.
9. Be passionate and determined.
10. Be humble.

Are you looking for a pair of size 6 Giuseppe Zanotti heels for $1,295 or a pair of Keen size 17 sandals for $95? Zappos is

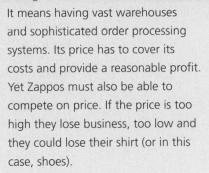

committed to having what you want and getting it to you as fast as possible. Providing this kind of service is not cheap. It means having vast warehouses and sophisticated order processing systems. Its price has to cover its costs and provide a reasonable profit. Yet Zappos must also be able to compete on price. If the price is too high they lose business, too low and they could lose their shirt (or in this case, shoes).

Watch the Zappos.com video in WileyPLUS to learn more about how the company sets prices.

Source: www.zappos.com.

✔ **The Navigator**

Preview of **Chapter 8**

As the Feature Story about Zappos.com indicates, few management decisions are more important than setting prices. Intel, for example, must sell computer chips at a price that is high enough to cover its costs and ensure a reasonable profit. But if the price is too high, the chips will not sell. In this chapter, we examine two types of pricing situations. The first part of the chapter addresses pricing for goods sold or services provided to external parties. The second part of the chapter addresses pricing decisions managers face when they sell goods to other divisions within the company.

The content and organization of this chapter are as follows.

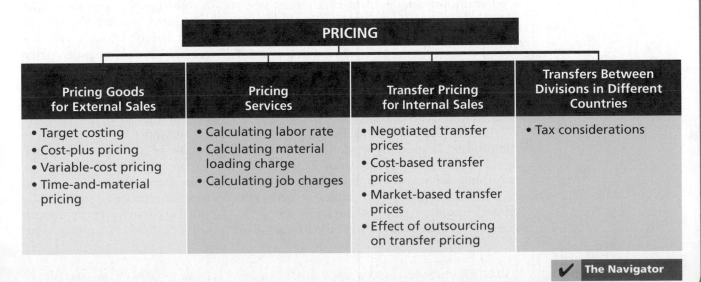

PRICING			
Pricing Goods for External Sales	**Pricing Services**	**Transfer Pricing for Internal Sales**	**Transfers Between Divisions in Different Countries**
• Target costing • Cost-plus pricing • Variable-cost pricing • Time-and-material pricing	• Calculating labor rate • Calculating material loading charge • Calculating job charges	• Negotiated transfer prices • Cost-based transfer prices • Market-based transfer prices • Effect of outsourcing on transfer pricing	• Tax considerations

✔ **The Navigator**

Pricing Goods for External Sales

Establishing the price for any good or service is affected by many factors. Take the pharmaceutical industry as an example. Its approach to profitability has been to spend heavily on research and development in an effort to find and patent a few new drugs, price them high, and market them aggressively. However, the AIDS crisis in Africa placed the drug industry under considerable pressure to lower prices on drugs used to treat the disease. For example, Merck Co. lowered the price of its AIDS drug Crixivan to $600 per patient in these countries. This compares with the $6,016 it typically charged in the United States.[1] As a consequence, individuals in the United States questioned whether prices in the U.S. market were too high. The drug companies countered that to cover their substantial financial risks to develop these products, they need to set the prices high. Illustration 8-1 indicates the many factors that can affect pricing decisions.

Illustration 8-1
Pricing factors

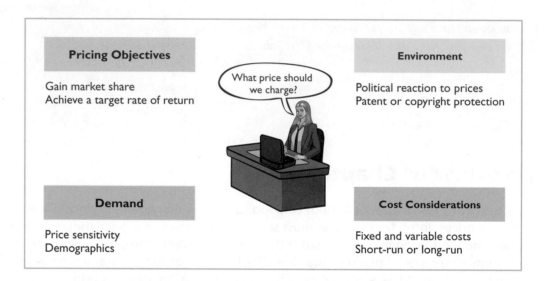

In the long run, a company must price its product to cover its costs and earn a reasonable profit. But to price its product appropriately, it must have a good understanding of market forces at work. In most cases, a company does not set the prices. Instead, the price is set by the competitive market (the laws of supply and demand). For example, a company such as ChevronTexaco or Exxon-Mobil cannot set the price of gasoline by itself. These companies are called **price takers** because the price of gasoline is set by market forces (the supply of oil and the demand by customers). This is the case for any product that is not easily differentiated from competing products, such as farm products (corn or wheat) or minerals (coal or sand).

In other situations, the company sets the prices. This would be the case where the product is specially made for a customer, as in a one-of-a-kind product such as a designer dress by Zoran or Armani. This also occurs when there are few or no other producers capable of manufacturing a similar item. An example would be a company that has a patent or copyright on a unique process, such as the case of computer chips by Intel. However, it is also the case when a company can effectively differentiate its product or service from others. Even in a competitive

---

[1]"AIDS Gaffes in Africa Come Back to Haunt Drug Industry at Home," *Wall Street Journal* (April 23, 2001), p. 1.

market like coffee, Starbucks has been able to differentiate its product and charge a premium for a cup of java.

MANAGEMENT INSIGHT

The Only Game in Town?

Pricing plays a critical role in corporate strategy. For example, almost 50% of tablet computer users say that they use them to read newspapers and magazines. And since Apple's iPad tablet computer at one time represented 75% of the tablets being sold, Apple felt like it had the newspaper and magazine publishers right where it wanted them. So it decided to charge the publishers a fee of 30% of subscription revenue for subscriptions sold at Apple's App Store. Publishers were outraged, but it didn't take long for somebody to come to their rescue. Within 1 day of Apple's announcement, Google announced that it would only charge a fee of about 10% of subscription revenue for users of its Android system. That might at least partially explain why *Sports Illustrated* provided an app to run on Android tablets before it provided one for iPads, even though at that time Android tablets only had a small share of the market.

Source: Martin Peers, "Apple Risks App-lash on iPad," *Wall Street Journal Online* (February 17, 2011).

? Do the substantially different prices that Apple and Google charge for a similar service reflect different costs incurred by each company, or is the price difference due to something else? (See page 381.)

Target Costing

Automobile manufacturers like Ford or Toyota face a competitive market. The price of an automobile is affected greatly by the laws of supply and demand, so no company in this industry can affect the price to a significant degree. Therefore, to earn a profit, companies in the auto industry must focus on controlling costs. This requires setting a **target cost** that provides a desired profit. Illustration 8-2 shows the relationship and importance of a target cost to the price and desired profit.

LEARNING OBJECTIVE 1

Compute a target cost when the market determines a product price.

Market Price	−	Desired Profit	=	Target Cost

Illustration 8-2
Target cost as related to price and profit

If General Motors can produce its automobiles for the target cost (or less), it will meet its profit goal. If it cannot achieve its target cost, it will fail to produce the desired profit, which will disappoint its stockholders.

In a competitive market, a company chooses the segment of the market it wants to compete in—that is, its market niche. For example, it may choose between selling luxury goods or economy goods in order to focus its efforts on one segment or the other. Once the company has identified the segment of the market that it wants to compete in, it conducts market research. This determines the features its product should have, and what the market price is for a product with those features. Once the company has determined this price, it can determine its target cost by setting a desired profit. The difference between the market price and the desired profit is the target cost of the product (shown in Illustration 8-2). After the company determines the target cost, it assembles a team of employees with expertise in a variety of areas (production and operations, marketing, and finance). The team's task is to design and develop a product that can meet quality specifications while not exceeding the target cost. The target cost includes all product and period costs necessary to make and market the product or service.

MANAGEMENT INSIGHT

Wal-Mart Says the Price Is Too High

"And the price should be $19 per pair of jeans instead of $23," said the retailer Wal-Mart Stores Inc. to jean maker Levi Strauss. What happened to Levi Strauss is what happens to many manufacturers who deal with Wal-Mart. Wal-Mart often sets the price, and the manufacturer has to figure out how to make a profit, given that price. In Levi Strauss's case, it revamped its distribution and production to serve Wal-Mart and improve its overall record of timely deliveries. Producing a season of new jeans styles, from conception to store shelves, used to take Levi 12 to 15 months. Today, it takes just 10 months for Levi Strauss signature jeans; for regular Levi's, the time is down to 7 1/2 months. As the chief executive of Levi Strauss noted, "We had to change people and practice. It's been somewhat of a D-Day invasion approach."

Source: "In Bow to Retailers' New Clout, Levi Strauss Makes Alterations," *Wall Street Journal* (June 17, 2004), p A1.

? What are some issues that Levi Strauss should consider in deciding whether it should agree to meet Wal-Mart's target price? (See page 381.)

DECISION TOOLKIT

DECISION CHECKPOINTS	INFO NEEDED FOR DECISION	TOOL TO USE FOR DECISION	HOW TO EVALUATE RESULTS
How does management use target costs to make decisions about manufacturing products or providing services?	Target selling price, desired profit, target cost	Target selling price less desired profit equals target cost	If actual cost exceeds target cost, the company will not earn desired profit. If desired profit is not achieved, company must evaluate whether to manufacture the product or provide the service.

> DO IT!

Target Costing

Fine Line Phones is considering introducing a fashion cover for its phones. Market research indicates that 200,000 units can be sold if the price is no more than $20. If Fine Line decides to produce the covers, it will need to invest $1,000,000 in new production equipment. Fine Line requires a minimum rate of return of 25% on all investments.

Determine the target cost per unit for the cover.

Solution

Action Plan

✔ Recall that Market price − Desired profit = Target cost.

✔ The minimum rate of return is a company's desired profit.

The desired profit for this new product line is $250,000 ($1,000,000 × 25%).

Each cover must result in $1.25 of profit ($250,000/200,000 units).

Market price	−	Desired profit	=	Target cost per unit
$20	−	$1.25	=	$18.75 per unit

Related exercise material: **BE8-1, E8-1, E8-2, and DO IT! 8-1.**

✔ **The Navigator**

Cost-Plus Pricing

As discussed, in a competitive product environment, the price of a product is set by the market. In order to achieve its desired profit, the company focuses on achieving a target cost. In a less competitive environment, companies have a greater ability to set the product price. Commonly, when a company sets a product price, it does so as a function of, or relative to, the cost of the product or service. This is referred to as **cost-plus pricing**. Under cost-plus pricing, a company first determines a cost base and then adds a **markup** to the cost base to determine the **target selling price**.

LEARNING OBJECTIVE   **2**

Compute a target selling price using cost-plus pricing.

If the cost base includes all of the costs required to produce and sell the product, then the markup represents the desired profit. This can be seen in Illustration 8-3, where the markup represents the difference between the selling price and cost—the profit on the product.

> **Selling Price − Cost = Markup (Profit)**

Illustration 8-3
Relation of markup to cost and selling price

The size of the markup (profit) depends on the return the company hopes to generate on the amount it has invested. In determining the optimal markup, the company must consider competitive and market conditions, political and legal issues, and other relevant factors. Once the company has determined its cost base and its desired markup, it can add the two together to determine the target selling price. The basic cost-plus pricing formula is expressed as follows.

> **Cost + Markup = Target Selling Price**

Illustration 8-4
Cost-plus pricing formula

To illustrate, assume that Thinkmore Products, Inc. is in the process of setting a selling price on its new video camera pen. It is a functioning pen that will record up to 2 hours of audio and video. The per unit variable cost estimates for the video camera pen are as follows.

	Per Unit
Direct materials	$23
Direct labor	17
Variable manufacturing overhead	12
Variable selling and administrative expenses	8
Variable cost per unit	**$60**

Illustration 8-5
Variable cost per unit

To produce and sell its product, Thinkmore incurs fixed manufacturing overhead of $280,000 and fixed selling and administrative expenses of $240,000. To arrive at the cost per unit, we divide total fixed costs by the number of units the company expects to produce. Illustration 8-6 shows the computation of fixed cost per unit for Thinkmore, assuming the production of 10,000 units.

	Total Costs	÷	Budgeted Volume	=	Cost per Unit
Fixed manufacturing overhead	$280,000	÷	10,000	=	$28
Fixed selling and administrative expenses	240,000	÷	10,000	=	24
Fixed cost per unit					**$52**

Illustration 8-6
Fixed cost per unit, 10,000 units

Management is ultimately evaluated based on its ability to generate a high return on the company's investment. This is frequently expressed as a return on investment (ROI) percentage, calculated as income divided by the average amount invested in a product or service. A higher percentage reflects a greater success in generating profits from the investment in a product or service. Chapter 10 provides a more in-depth discussion of the use of ROI to evaluate the performance of investment center managers.

To achieve a desired return on investment percentage, a product's markup should be determined by calculating the desired return on investment (ROI) per unit. This is calculated by multiplying the desired ROI percentage times the amount invested to produce the product, and then dividing this by the number of units produced. Illustration 8-7 shows the computation used to determine a markup amount based on a desired ROI per unit for Thinkmore, assuming that the company desires a 20% ROI and that it has invested $1,000,000.

Illustration 8-7
Calculation of markup based on desired ROI per unit

$$\frac{\text{Desired ROI Percentage} \times \text{Amount Invested}}{\text{Units Produced}} = \text{Markup}$$

$$\frac{20\% \times \$1,000,000}{10,000 \text{ units}} = \$20$$

Thinkmore expects to receive income of $200,000 (20% × $1,000,000) on its $1,000,000 investment. On a per unit basis, the markup based on the desired ROI per unit is $20 ($200,000 ÷ 10,000 units). Given the per unit costs shown above, Illustration 8-8 computes the sales price to be $132.

Illustration 8-8
Computation of selling price, 10,000 units

	Per Unit
Variable cost	$ 60
Fixed cost	52
Total cost	112
Markup (desired ROI)	20
Selling price per unit	**$132**

In most cases, companies like Thinkmore use a percentage markup on cost to determine the selling price. The formula to compute the markup percentage to achieve a desired ROI of $20 per unit is as follows.

Illustration 8-9
Computation of markup percentage

Markup (Desired ROI per Unit)	÷	Total Unit Cost	=	Markup Percentage
$20	÷	$112	=	17.86%

Using a 17.86% markup on cost, Thinkmore Products would compute the target selling price as follows.

Illustration 8-10
Computation of selling price—markup approach

$$\text{Total Unit Cost} + \left(\text{Total Unit Cost} \times \text{Markup Percentage} \right) = \text{Target Selling Price per Unit}$$

$$\$112 + (\$112 \times 17.86\%) = \$132$$

Thinkmore should set the price for its video camera pen at $132 per unit.

LIMITATIONS OF COST-PLUS PRICING

The cost-plus pricing approach has a major advantage: It is simple to compute. However, the cost model does not give consideration to the demand side. That is, will customers pay the price Thinkmore computed for its video camera pen? In addition, sales volume plays a large role in determining per unit costs. The lower the sales volume, for example, the higher the price Thinkmore must charge to meet its desired ROI. To illustrate, if the budgeted sales volume was 8,000 instead of 10,000, Thinkmore's variable cost per unit would remain the same. However, the fixed cost per unit would change as follows.

	Total Costs	÷	Budgeted Volume	=	Cost per Unit
Fixed manufacturing overhead	$280,000	÷	8,000	=	$35
Fixed selling and administrative expenses	240,000	÷	8,000	=	30
Fixed cost per unit					$65

Illustration 8-11
Fixed cost per unit, 8,000 units

As indicated in Illustration 8-6, the fixed cost per unit for 10,000 units was $52. However, at a lower sales volume of 8,000 units, the fixed cost per unit increases to $65. Thinkmore's desired 20% ROI now results in a $25 ROI per unit $[(20\% \times \$1,000,000) \div 8,000]$. Thinkmore computes the selling price at 8,000 units as follows.

	Per Unit
Variable cost	$ 60
Fixed cost	65
Total cost	125
Desired ROI	25
Selling price per unit	$150

Illustration 8-12
Computation of selling price, 8,000 units

As shown, the lower the budgeted volume, the higher the per unit price. The reason: Fixed costs and ROI are spread over fewer units, and therefore the fixed cost and ROI per unit increase. In this case, at 8,000 units, Thinkmore would have to mark up its total unit costs 20% to earn a desired ROI of $25 per unit, as shown below.

$$20\% = \frac{\$25 \text{ (desired ROI)}}{\$125 \text{ (total unit cost)}}$$

The target selling price would then be $150, as indicated earlier:

$$\$125 + (\$125 \times 20\%) = \$150$$

The opposite effect will occur if budgeted volume is higher (say, at 12,000 units) because fixed costs and ROI can be spread over more units. As a result, the cost-plus model of pricing will achieve its desired ROI only when Thinkmore sells the quantity it budgeted. If actual volume is much less than budgeted volume, Thinkmore may sustain losses unless it can raise its prices.

Variable-Cost Pricing

In determining the target price for Thinkmore's video camera pen, we calculated the cost base by including all costs incurred. This approach is referred to as **full-cost pricing**. Instead of using full costs to set prices, some companies simply add a markup to their variable costs (thus excluding fixed manufacturing and fixed selling and administrative costs). Using **variable-cost pricing** as the basis for setting prices avoids the problem of using uncertain cost information (as shown in Illustration 8-11) related to fixed-cost-per-unit computations. Variable-cost pricing also is helpful in pricing special orders or when excess capacity exists.

The major disadvantage of variable-cost pricing is that managers may set the price too low and consequently fail to cover their fixed costs. In the long run, failure to cover fixed costs will lead to losses. As a result, companies that use variable-cost pricing must adjust their markups to make sure that the price set will provide a fair return. The use of variable costs as the basis for setting prices is discussed in the appendix to this chapter.

MANAGEMENT INSIGHT

At Least It Was Simple

For nearly 90 years, Parker Hannifin used the same simple approach to price its industrial parts. It calculated the production cost, then added on a percentage of the cost (about 35%) to arrive at the price. It didn't matter if a product was a premium product or a standard product. And if Parker reduced its production costs, it then also cut the price for the product. The problem with this approach was that it made it difficult for the company to ever substantially increase its profit margins. So the company's CEO decided to break with tradition and implement strategic pricing schemes similar to those used by retailers. It determined that for about a third of its products, it had a competitive advantage that would allow it to charge a higher markup. For example, there might be limited competition for the product, or its product might be of higher quality, or it might have the ability to produce a product faster. The company determined that the price increases raised net income by $200 million—not bad considering that net income was $130 million before the price increases.

Source: Timothy Aeppel, "Changing the Formula: Seeking Perfect Prices, CEO Tears Up the Rules," *Wall Street Journal Online* (March 27, 2007).

? **What kind of help might the sales staff need in implementing this new approach?** (See page 381.)

DECISION TOOLKIT

DECISION CHECKPOINTS	INFO NEEDED FOR DECISION	TOOL TO USE FOR DECISION	HOW TO EVALUATE RESULTS
What factors should be considered in determining selling price in a less competitive environment?	Total cost per unit and desired profit (cost-plus pricing)	Total cost per unit plus desired profit equals target selling price	Does company make its desired profit? If not, does the profit shortfall result from less volume?

> DO IT!

Target Selling Price

Air Corporation produces air purifiers. The following per unit cost information is available: direct materials $16, direct labor $18, variable manufacturing overhead $11, variable selling and administrative expenses $6. Fixed selling and administrative expenses are $50,000, and fixed manufacturing overhead is $150,000. Using a 45% markup percentage on total per unit cost and assuming 10,000 units, compute the target selling price.

Action Plan

✔ Calculate the total cost per unit.

✔ Multiply the total cost per unit by the markup percentage, then add this amount to the total cost per unit to determine the target selling price.

Solution

Direct materials	$16
Direct labor	18
Variable manufacturing overhead	11
Variable selling and administrative expenses	6
Fixed selling and administrative expenses	5*
Fixed manufacturing overhead	15**
Total unit cost	$71

$$\text{Total unit cost} + \left(\text{Total unit cost} \times \text{Markup percentage} \right) = \text{Target selling price}$$

$$\$71 \quad + \quad (\$71 \quad \times \quad 45\%) \quad = \quad \$102.95$$

*$50,000 ÷ 10,000; **$150,000 ÷ 10,000

Related exercise material: **BE8-2, BE8-3, BE8-4, BE8-5, E8-3, E8-4, E8-5, E8-6, E8-7, and** **DO IT!** **8-2.**

✔ **The Navigator**

Pricing Services

Another variation on cost-plus pricing is **time-and-material pricing**. Under this approach, the company sets two pricing rates—one for the **labor** used on a job and another for the **material**. The labor rate includes direct labor time and other employee costs. The material charge is based on the cost of direct parts and materials used and a **material loading charge** for related overhead costs. Time-and-material pricing is widely used in service industries, especially professional firms such as public accounting, law, engineering, and consulting firms, as well as construction companies, repair shops, and printers.

To illustrate a time-and-material pricing situation, assume the following data for Lake Holiday Marina, a boat and motor repair shop.

LEARNING OBJECTIVE 3

Use time-and-material pricing to determine the cost of services provided.

Lake Holiday Marina Budgeted Costs for the Year 2014		
	Time Charges	**Material Loading Charges***
Mechanics' wages and benefits	$103,500	—
Parts manager's salary and benefits	—	$11,500
Office employee's salary and benefits	20,700	2,300
Other overhead (supplies, depreciation, property taxes, advertising, utilities)	26,800	14,400
Total budgeted costs	$151,000	$28,200

*The material loading charges exclude the invoice cost of the materials.

Illustration 8-13
Total annual budgeted time and material costs

Using time-and-material pricing involves three steps: (1) calculate the per hour labor charge, (2) calculate the charge for obtaining and holding materials, and (3) calculate the charges for a particular job.

STEP 1: CALCULATE THE LABOR RATE. The first step for time-and-material pricing is to determine a charge for labor time. The charge for labor time is expressed as a rate per hour of labor. This rate includes (1) the direct labor cost of the employee, including hourly rate or salary and fringe benefits; (2) selling, administrative, and similar overhead costs; and (3) an allowance for a desired profit or ROI per hour of employee time. In some industries, such as repair shops for autos and boats, the same hourly labor rate is charged regardless of which employee performs the work. In other industries, the rate that is charged is adjusted according to classification or level of the employee. A public accounting firm, for example, would charge different rates for the services of an assistant, senior, manager, or partner; a law firm would charge different rates for the work of a paralegal, associate, or partner.

Illustration 8-14 shows computation of the hourly charges for Lake Holiday Marina during 2014. The marina budgets 5,000 annual labor hours in 2014, and it desires a profit margin of $8 per hour of labor.

Illustration 8-14
Computation of hourly time-charge rate

	A	B	C	D	E	F
	Per Hour	**Total Cost**	÷	**Total Hours**	=	**Per Hour Charge**
1						
2	Hourly labor rate for repairs					
3	Mechanics' wages and benefits	$103,500	÷	5,000	=	$20.70
4	Overhead costs					
5	Office employee's salary and benefits	20,700	÷	5,000	=	4.14
6	Other overhead	26,800	÷	5,000	=	5.36
7	Total hourly cost	$151,000	÷	5,000	=	30.20
8	Profit margin					8.00
9	Rate charged per hour of labor					$38.20
10						

The marina multiplies this rate of $38.20 by the number of hours of labor used on any particular job to determine the labor charge for that job.

STEP 2: CALCULATE THE MATERIAL LOADING CHARGE. The charge for materials typically includes the invoice price of any materials used on the job plus a material loading charge. The **material loading charge** covers the costs of purchasing, receiving, handling, and storing materials, plus any desired profit margin on the materials themselves. The material loading charge is expressed as a **percentage** of the total estimated costs of parts and materials for the year. To determine this percentage, the company does the following: (1) It estimates its total annual costs for purchasing, receiving, handling, and storing materials. (2) It divides this amount by the total estimated cost of parts and materials. (3) It adds a desired profit margin on the materials themselves.

Illustration 8-15 shows computation of the material loading charge used by Lake Holiday Marina during 2014. The marina estimates that the total invoice cost of parts and materials used in 2014 will be $120,000. The marina desires a 20% profit margin on the invoice cost of parts and materials.

The marina's material loading charge on any particular job is 43.50% multiplied by the cost of materials used on the job. For example, if the marina used $100 of parts, the additional material loading charge would be $43.50.

STEP 3: CALCULATE CHARGES FOR A PARTICULAR JOB. The charges for any particular job are the sum of (1) the labor charge, (2) the charge for the materials,

	A	B	C	D	E	F
1		**Material Loading Charges**	÷	**Total Invoice Cost, Parts and Materials**	=	**Material Loading Percentage**
2	Overhead costs					
3	Parts manager's salary and benefits	$11,500				
4	Office employee's salary	2,300				
5		13,800	÷	$120,000	=	11.50%
6						
7	Other overhead	14,400	÷	120,000	=	12.00%
8		$28,200	÷	120,000	=	23.50%
9	Profit margin					20.00%
10	Material loading percentage					43.50%
11						

Illustration 8-15
Computation of material loading charge

and (3) the material loading charge. For example, suppose that Lake Holiday Marina prepares a price quotation to estimate the cost to refurbish a used 28-foot pontoon boat. Lake Holiday Marina estimates the job will require 50 hours of labor and $3,600 in parts and materials. Illustration 8-16 shows the marina's price quotation.

Illustration 8-16
Price quotation for time and material

Lake Holiday Marina
Time-and-Material Price Quotation

Job: Marianne Perino, repair of 28-foot pontoon boat

Labor charges: 50 hours @ $38.20		$1,910
Material charges		
Cost of parts and materials	$3,600	
Material loading charge (43.5% × $3,600)	1,566	5,166
Total price of labor and material		$7,076

Included in the $7,076 price quotation for the boat repair are charges for labor costs, overhead costs, materials costs, materials handling and storage costs, and a profit margin on both labor and parts. Lake Holiday Marina used labor hours as a basis for computing the time rate. Other companies, such as machine shops, plastic molding shops, and printers, might use machine hours.

DECISION TOOLKIT

DECISION CHECKPOINTS	INFO NEEDED FOR DECISION	TOOL TO USE FOR DECISION	HOW TO EVALUATE RESULTS
How do we set prices when it is difficult to estimate total cost per unit?	Two pricing rates needed: one for labor use and another for materials	Compute labor rate charge and material rate charge. In each of these calculations, add a profit margin.	Is the company profitable under this pricing approach? Are employees earning reasonable wages?

> DO IT!

Time-and-Material Pricing

Presented below are data for Harmon Electrical Repair Shop for next year.

Repair-technicians' wages	$130,000
Fringe benefits	30,000
Overhead	20,000

The desired profit margin per labor hour is $10. The material loading charge is 40% of invoice cost. Harmon estimates that 8,000 labor hours will be worked next year. If Harmon repairs a TV that takes 4 hours to repair and uses parts costing $50, compute the bill for this job.

Solution

Action Plan

✔ Calculate the labor charge.

✔ Calculate the material loading charge.

✔ Compute the bill for specific repair.

	Total Cost	÷	Total Hours	=	Per Hour Charge
Repair-technicians' wages	$130,000	÷	8,000	=	$16.25
Fringe benefits	30,000	÷	8,000	=	3.75
Overhead	20,000	÷	8,000	=	2.50
	$180,000	÷	8,000	=	22.50
Profit margin					10.00
Rate charged per hour of labor					$32.50

Job: Repair TV		
Labor charges: 4 hours @ $32.50		$130
Material charges		
Cost of parts and materials	$50	
Material loading charge (40% × $50)	20	70
Total price of labor and material		$200

Related exercise material: **BE8-6, E8-8, E8-9, E8-10, and** DO IT! **8-3.**

✔ **The Navigator**

SERVICE COMPANY INSIGHT

It Ain't Like It Used to Be

For many decades, professionals in most service industries have used some form of hourly based price, regardless of the outcome. But the most recent recession appears to have brought an end to that practice. Many customers are now demanding that the bill be tied to actual performance, rather than to the amount of hours worked. For example, one communications company that used to charge about $15,000 or more per month as its "retainer fee" now instead charges based on achieving particular outcomes. Now, it might charge $10,000 if it obtains a desirable public speaking engagement for a company executive. Similarly, a digital marketing agency reduced its hourly fee from $135 to $80, but it gets a bonus if it achieves specified increases in the sales volume on a customer's website.

Source: Simona Covel, "Firms Try Alternative to Hourly Fees," *Wall Street Journal Online* (April 2, 2009).

?   **What implications does this have for a service company's need for managerial accounting?** (See page 381.)

Transfer Pricing for Internal Sales

In today's global economy, growth is often vital to survival. Some companies grow "vertically," meaning the company expands in the direction of either its suppliers or its customers. For example, a manufacturer of bicycles like Trek may acquire a bicycle component manufacturer or a chain of bicycle shops. A movie production company like Walt Disney or Time Warner may acquire a movie theater chain or a cable television company.

Divisions within vertically integrated companies normally transfer goods or services to other divisions within the same company, as well as make sales to customers outside the company. When goods are transferred between divisions of the same company, the price used to record the transaction is the **transfer price**. Illustration 8-17 shows transfers between divisions for Aerobic Bicycle Company. As shown, the Component Division sells goods to the Company's Assembly Division, as well as to outside parties. Units sold to the Assembly Division are recorded at the transfer price.

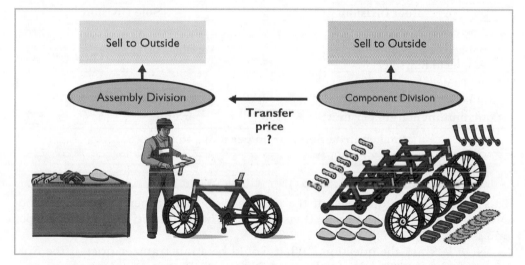

Illustration 8-17
Transfer pricing example

The primary objective of transfer pricing is the same as that of pricing a product to an outside party. The objective is to maximize the return to the company. An additional objective of transfer pricing is to measure divisional performance accurately. Setting a transfer price is complicated because of competing interests among divisions within the company. For example, in the case of the bicycle company shown in Illustration 8-17, setting the transfer price high will benefit the Component Division (the selling division), but will hurt the Assembly Division (the purchasing division).

There are three possible approaches for determining a transfer price:

1. Negotiated transfer prices.

2. Cost-based transfer prices.

3. Market-based transfer prices.

Conceptually, a negotiated transfer price should work best, but due to practical considerations, companies often use the other two methods.

Negotiated Transfer Prices

LEARNING OBJECTIVE   **4**

Determine a transfer price using the negotiated, cost-based, and market-based approaches.

A **negotiated transfer price** is determined through agreement of division managers. To illustrate negotiated transfer pricing, we examine Alberta Company. Until recently, Alberta focused exclusively on making rubber soles for work boots and hiking boots. It sold these rubber soles to boot manufacturers. However, last year the company decided to take advantage of its strong reputation by expanding into the business of making hiking boots. As a consequence of this expansion, the company is now structured as two independent divisions, the Boot Division and the Sole Division. The company compensates the manager of each division based on achievement of profitability targets for that division.

The Boot Division manufactures leather uppers for hiking boots and attaches these uppers to rubber soles. During its first year, the Boot Division purchased its rubber soles from an *outside supplier* so as not to disrupt the operations of the Sole Division. However, top management now wants the Sole Division to provide at least some of the soles used by the Boot Division. Illustration 8-18 shows the computation of the contribution margin per unit for each division when the Boot Division purchases soles from an outside supplier.

Illustration 8-18
Computation of contribution margin for two divisions, when Boot Division purchases soles from an outside supplier

Boot Division		**Sole Division**	
Selling price of boots	$90	Selling price of sole	$18
Variable cost of boot (not including sole)	35	Variable cost per sole	11
Cost of sole purchased from outside supplier	17	**Contribution margin per unit**	**$ 7**
Contribution margin per unit	**$38**		

Total contribution margin per unit $45 ($38 + $7)

This information indicates that the contribution margin per unit for the Boot Division is $38 and for the Sole Division is $7. The total contribution margin per unit is $45 ($38 + $7).

Now let's ask the question, "What would be a fair transfer price if the Sole Division sold 10,000 soles to the Boot Division?" The answer depends on how busy the Sole Division is—that is, whether it has excess capacity.

NO EXCESS CAPACITY

As indicated in Illustration 8-18, the Sole Division charges outside customers $18 and derives a contribution margin of $7 per sole. The Sole Division has **no excess capacity** and produces and sells 80,000 units (soles) to outside customers. Therefore, the Sole Division must receive from the Boot Division a payment that will at least cover its variable cost per sole **plus** its lost contribution margin per sole. (This lost contribution margin is often referred to as **opportunity cost**.) If the Sole Division cannot recover that amount—called the **minimum transfer price**—it should not sell its soles to the Boot Division. The minimum transfer price that would be acceptable to the Sole Division is $18, as shown below.

Illustration 8-19
Minimum transfer price—no excess capacity

Variable Cost	+	Opportunity Cost	=	Minimum Transfer Price
$11	+	$7	=	$18

From the perspective of the Boot Division (the buyer), the most it will pay is what the sole would cost from an outside supplier. In this case, therefore, the Boot Division would pay no more than $17. As shown in Illustration 8-20, an acceptable transfer price is not available in this situation.

Illustration 8-20
Transfer price negotiations—no deal

EXCESS CAPACITY

What happens if the Sole Division **has excess capacity**? For example, assume the Sole Division can produce 80,000 soles but can sell only 70,000 soles in the open market. As a result, it has available capacity of 10,000 units. Because it has excess capacity, the Sole Division could provide 10,000 units to the Boot Division without losing its $7 contribution margin on these units. Therefore, the minimum price it would now accept is $11, as shown below.

Variable Cost	+	Opportunity Cost	=	Minimum Transfer Price
$11	+	$0	=	$11

Illustration 8-21
Minimum transfer price formula—excess capacity

In this case, the Boot Division and the Sole Division should negotiate a transfer price within the range of $11 to $17, as shown in Illustration 8-22.

Illustration 8-22
Transfer pricing negotiations—deal

Given excess capacity, Alberta Company will increase its overall net income if the Boot Division purchases the 10,000 soles internally. This is true as long as the Sole Division's variable cost is less than the outside price of $17. The Sole

Division will receive a positive contribution margin from any transfer price above its variable cost of $11. The Boot Division will benefit from any price below $17. At any transfer price above $17 the Boot Division will go to an outside supplier, a solution that would be undesirable to both divisions, as well as to the company as a whole.

VARIABLE COSTS

In the minimum transfer price formula, **variable cost is defined as the variable cost of units sold** *internally*. In some instances, the variable cost of units sold internally will differ from the variable cost of units sold externally. For example, companies often can avoid some variable selling expenses when units are sold internally. In this case, the variable cost of units sold internally will be lower than that of units sold externally.

Alternatively, the variable cost of units sold internally could be higher than normal if the internal division requests a special order that requires more expensive materials or additional labor. For example, assume that the Boot Division designs a new high-margin, heavy-duty boot. The sole for this boot will use denser rubber with an intricate lug design. Alberta Company is not aware of any supplier that currently makes such a sole, nor does it feel that any other supplier can meet its quality expectations. As a consequence, there is no available market price to use as the transfer price.

We can, however, employ the formula for the minimum transfer price to assist in arriving at a reasonable solution. After evaluating the special sole, the Sole Division determines that its variable cost would be $19 per sole. The Sole Division is at full capacity. The Sole Division's opportunity cost at full capacity is the $7 ($18 − $11) per sole that it earns producing the standard sole and selling it to an outside customer. Therefore, the minimum transfer price that the Sole Division would be willing to accept for the special-order sole would be:

Illustration 8-23
Minimum transfer price
formula—special order

Variable Cost	+	Opportunity Cost	=	Minimum Transfer Price
$19	+	$7	=	$26

The transfer price of $26 provides the Sole Division with enough revenue to cover its increased variable cost and its opportunity cost (contribution margin on its standard sole).

SUMMARY OF NEGOTIATED TRANSFER PRICING

Under negotiated transfer pricing, the selling division establishes a minimum transfer price, and the purchasing division establishes a maximum transfer price. This system provides a sound basis for establishing a transfer price because both divisions are better off if the proper decision rules are used. However, companies often do not use negotiated transfer pricing because:

- Market price information is sometimes not easily obtainable.
- A lack of trust between the two negotiating divisions may lead to a breakdown in the negotiations.
- Negotiations often lead to different pricing strategies from division to division, which is cumbersome and sometimes costly to implement.

Many companies, therefore, often use simple systems based on cost or market information to develop transfer prices.

> **DO IT!**

Transfer Pricing

Action Plan

✔ Determine whether the company is at full capacity or not.

✔ Determine variable cost and opportunity cost.

✔ Apply minimum transfer price formula.

The clock division of Control Central Corporation manufactures clocks and then sells them to customers for $10 per unit. Its variable cost is $4 per unit, and its fixed cost per unit is $2.50. Management would like the clock division to transfer 8,000 of these clocks to another division within the company at a price of $5. The clock division could avoid $0.50 per clock of variable packaging costs by selling internally.

(a) Determine the minimum transfer price, assuming the clock division is not operating at full capacity. (b) Determine the minimum transfer price, assuming the clock division is operating at full capacity.

Solution

(a) If the clock division is not operating at full capacity, the opportunity cost for the clocks is $0. Since internal sales will eliminate $0.50 of packaging costs, the variable cost per clock is $3.50 ($4 − $0.50).

Minimum transfer price	=	Variable cost	+	Opportunity cost
$3.50	=	$3.50	+	$0

(b) If the clock division is already operating at full capacity, the opportunity cost for the clocks is $6 ($10 − $4). Since internal sales will eliminate $0.50 of packaging costs, the variable cost per clock is $3.50 ($4 − $0.50).

Minimum transfer price	=	Variable cost	+	Opportunity cost
$9.50	=	$3.50	+	$6

Related exercise material: **BE8-7, BE8-8, BE8-9, E8-11, E8-12, E8-13, E8-14, E8-15, and DO IT! 8-4.**

✔ **The Navigator**

Cost-Based Transfer Prices

An alternative to negotiated transfer pricing is cost-based pricing. A **cost-based transfer price** is based on the costs incurred by the division producing the goods or services. A cost-based transfer price can be based on variable costs alone, or on variable costs plus fixed costs. Also, in some cases the selling division may add a markup.

The cost-based approach sometimes results in improper transfer prices. Improper transfer prices can reduce company profits and provide unfair evaluations of division performance. To illustrate, assume that Alberta Company requires the division to use a transfer price based on the variable cost of the sole. With no excess capacity, the contribution margins per unit for the two divisions are:

Illustration 8-24
Cost-based transfer price—10,000 units

Boot Division		Sole Division	
Selling price of boots	$90	Selling price of sole	$11
Variable cost of boot (not including sole)	35	Variable cost per sole	11
Cost of sole purchased from sole division	11		
Contribution margin per unit	**$44**	**Contribution margin per unit**	**$ 0**

Total contribution margin per unit $44 ($44 + $0)

This cost-based transfer system is a bad deal for the Sole Division as it reports no profit on the transfer of 10,000 soles to the Boot Division. If the Sole Division could sell these soles to an outside customer, it would make $70,000 [10,000 × ($18 − $11)]. The Boot Division, on the other hand, is delighted: its contribution margin per unit increases from $38 to $44, or $6 per boot. Thus, this transfer price results in an unfair evaluation of these two divisions.

Further examination of this example reveals that this transfer price reduces the company's overall profits. The Sole Division lost a contribution margin per unit of $7 (Illustration 8-18, page 346), and the Boot Division experiences only a $6 increase in its contribution margin per unit. Overall, Alberta Company loses $10,000 [10,000 boots × ($7 − $6)]. Illustration 8-25 illustrates this deficiency.

Illustration 8-25
Cost-based transfer price results—no excess capacity

The overall results change if the Sole Division **has excess capacity**. In this case, the Sole Division continues to report a zero profit on these 10,000 units but does not lose the $7 per unit of contribution margin (because it had excess capacity). The Boot Division gains $6. So overall, the company is better off by $60,000 (10,000 × $6). However, with a cost-based system, the Sole Division continues to report a zero profit on these 10,000 units.

We can see that a cost-based system does not reflect the division's true profitability. What's more, **it does not provide adequate incentive for the Sole Division to control costs**. The division's costs are simply passed on to the next division.

Notwithstanding these disadvantages, the cost system is simple to understand and easy to use because the information is already available in the accounting system. In addition, market information is sometimes not available, so the only alternative is some type of cost-based system. As a result, it is the most common method used by companies to establish transfer prices.

Market-Based Transfer Prices

The **market-based transfer price** is based on existing market prices of competing goods or services. A market-based system is often considered the best approach because it is objective and generally provides the proper economic incentives. For example, if the Sole Division can charge the market price, it is indifferent as to whether soles are sold to outside customers or internally to the Boot Division—it does not lose any contribution margin. Similarly, the Boot Division pays a price for the soles that is at or reasonably close to market.

When the Sole Division has no excess capacity, the market-based system works reasonably well. The Sole Division receives market price, and the Boot Division pays market price.

If the Sole Division has excess capacity, however, the market-based system can lead to actions that are not in the best interest of the company. The minimum transfer price that the Sole Division should receive is its variable cost plus opportunity cost. If the Sole Division has excess capacity, its opportunity cost is zero. However, under the market-based system, the Sole Division transfers the goods at the market price of $18, for a contribution margin per unit of $7 ($18 − $11). The Boot Division manager has to accept the $18 sole price. This price may not accurately reflect a fair cost of the sole, given that the Sole Division had excess capacity. As a result, the Boot Division may overprice its boots in the market if it uses the market price of the sole plus a markup in setting the price of the boot. This action can lead to losses for Alberta overall.

As indicated earlier, in many cases, there simply is not a well-defined market for the good or service being transferred. When this is the case, a reasonable market value cannot be developed, so companies often resort to a cost-based system.

Effect of Outsourcing on Transfer Pricing

An increasing number of companies rely on **outsourcing**. Outsourcing involves contracting with an external party to provide a good or service, rather than performing the work internally. Some companies have taken outsourcing to the extreme by outsourcing all of their production. Many of these so-called **virtual companies** have well-established brand names though they do not manufacture any of their own products. Companies use incremental analysis (Chapter 7) to determine whether outsourcing is profitable. When companies outsource, fewer components are transferred internally between divisions. This reduces the need for transfer prices.

Transfers Between Divisions in Different Countries

As more companies "globalize" their operations, an increasing number of intercompany transfers are between divisions that are located in different countries. One estimate suggests that 60% of trade between countries is simply transfers between company divisions. Differences in tax rates across countries can complicate the determination of the appropriate transfer price.

Companies must pay income tax in the country where they generate the income. In order to maximize income and minimize income tax, many companies prefer to report more income in countries with low tax rates, and less income in countries with high tax rates. They accomplish this by adjusting the transfer prices they use on internal transfers between divisions located in different countries. They allocate more contribution margin to the division in the low-tax-rate country, and allocate less to the division in the high-tax-rate country.

To illustrate, suppose that Alberta's Boot Division is located in a country with a corporate tax rate of 10%, and the Sole Division is located in a country with a tax rate of 30%. Illustration 8-26 (page 352) compares the after-tax contribution margin to the company using a transfer price of $18 versus a transfer price of $11.

Note that the *before-tax* total contribution margin to Alberta Company is $44 regardless of whether the transfer price is $18 or $11. However, the *after-tax* total contribution margin to Alberta Company is $38.20 using the $18 transfer price, and $39.60 using the $11 transfer price. The reason: When Alberta uses the $11 transfer price, more of the contribution margin is attributed to the division that is in the country with the lower tax rate, so it pays $1.40 less per shoe in taxes [($3.70 + $2.10) − $4.40].

As this analysis shows, Alberta Company would be better off using the $11 transfer price. However, this presents some concerns. First, the Sole Division

Illustration 8-26
After-tax contribution margin per unit under alternative transfer prices

At $18 Transfer Price

Boot Division		Sole Division	
Selling price of boots	$90.00	Selling price of sole	$18.00
Variable cost of boot (not including sole)	35.00	Variable cost per sole	11.00
Cost of sole purchased internally	18.00		
Before-tax contribution margin	37.00	Before-tax contribution margin	7.00
Tax at 10%	3.70	Tax at 30%	2.10
After-tax contribution margin	$33.30	After-tax contribution margin	$ 4.90

Before-tax total contribution margin per unit to company = $37 + $7 = **$44**
After-tax total contribution margin per unit to company = $33.30 + $4.90 = **$38.20**

At $11 Transfer Price

Boot Division		Sole Division	
Selling price of boots	$90.00	Selling price of sole	$11.00
Variable cost of boot (not including sole)	35.00	Variable cost per sole	11.00
Cost of sole purchased internally	11.00		
Before-tax contribution margin	44.00	Before-tax contribution margin	0.00
Tax at 10%	4.40	Tax at 30%	0.00
After-tax contribution margin	$39.60	After-tax contribution margin	$ 0.00

Before-tax total contribution margin per unit to company = $44 + $0 = **$44**
After-tax total contribution margin per unit to company = $39.60 + $0 = **$39.60**

manager won't be happy with an $11 transfer price. This price may lead to unfair evaluations of the Sole Division's manager. Second, the company must ask whether it is legal and ethical to use an $11 transfer price when the market price clearly is higher than that.

Additional consideration of international transfer pricing is presented in advanced accounting texts.

ETHICS INSIGHT

Transferring Profits and Reducing Taxes

International transfer pricing issues create a huge headache for the Internal Revenue Service. Some estimates suggest that the United States loses over $25 billion in underpaid taxes due to transfer price abuses. Occasionally, violators are caught. Toyota, for example, reportedly paid a $1 billion settlement. But enforcement is complicated and time-consuming, and many foreign firms are reluctant to give access to their records.

U.S. companies have also been accused of transfer pricing abuse. It has been noted that at one time, U.S. giant Westinghouse booked over 25% of its profit in the tiny island of Puerto Rico. At the time, the corporate tax rate there was zero. The rules require that the transfer price be based on the current market price that a nonrelated party would pay for the goods. But often this current market price is difficult to determine.

? What are the implications for other taxpayers if companies reduce their taxes by using improper transfer prices to shift profits to lower-tax countries? (See page 381.)

DECISION TOOLKIT

DECISION CHECKPOINTS	INFO NEEDED FOR DECISION	TOOL TO USE FOR DECISION	HOW TO EVALUATE RESULTS
What price should be charged for transfer of goods between divisions of a company?	Variable cost, opportunity cost, market prices	Variable cost plus opportunity cost provides minimum transfer price for seller	If income of division provides fair evaluation of managers, then transfer price is useful. Also, income of the company overall should not be reduced due to the transfer pricing approach.

USING THE DECISION TOOLKIT

Cedarburg Lumber specializes in building "high-end" playhouses for kids. It builds the components in its factory and then ships the parts to the customer's home. It has contracted with carpenters across the country to do the final assembly. Each year, the company introduces a new model. This year's model looks like a miniature castle, complete with spires and drawbridge. The accounting department provided the following cost estimates for this new product for a budgeted volume of 1,000 units.

	Per Unit	Total
Direct materials	$ 840	
Direct labor	$1,600	
Variable manufacturing overhead	$ 400	
Fixed manufacturing overhead		$540,000
Variable selling and administrative expenses	$ 510	
Fixed selling and administrative expenses		$320,000

Cedarburg Lumber uses cost-plus pricing to set its selling price. Management also directs that the target price be set to provide a 25% return on investment (ROI) on invested assets of $4,200,000.

Instructions

(a) Compute the markup percentage and target selling price on this new playhouse.

(b) Assuming that the volume is 1,500 units instead of 1,000 units, compute the markup percentage and target selling price that will allow Cedarburg Lumber to earn its desired ROI of 25%.

Solution

(a)

Variable cost per unit

	Per Unit
Direct materials	$ 840
Direct labor	1,600
Variable manufacturing overhead	400
Variable selling and administrative expenses	510
Variable cost per unit	$3,350

Fixed cost per unit

	Total Costs	÷	Budgeted Volume	=	Cost per Unit
Fixed manufacturing overhead	$540,000	÷	1,000	=	$540
Fixed selling and administrative expenses	320,000	÷	1,000	=	320
Fixed cost per unit	$860,000				$860

Computation of selling price (1,000 units)

Variable cost per unit	$3,350
Fixed cost per unit	860
Total unit cost	4,210
Desired ROI per unit*	1,050
Selling price	$5,260

*($4,200,000 × .25) ÷ 1,000

The markup percentage is:

$$\frac{\text{Desired ROI per unit}}{\text{Total unit cost}} = \frac{\$1,050}{\$4,210} = 24.9\%$$

(b) If the company produces 1,500 units, its selling price and markup percentage would be:

Computation of selling price (1,500 units)

Variable cost per unit	$3,350
Fixed cost per unit ($860,000 ÷ 1,500)	573**
Total unit cost	3,923
Desired ROI per unit*	700
Selling price	$4,623

*($4,200,000 × .25) ÷ 1,500
**Rounded

The markup percentage would be:

$$\frac{\text{Desired ROI per unit}}{\text{Total unit cost}} = \frac{\$700}{\$3,923} = 17.8\%$$

✔ **The Navigator**

SUMMARY OF LEARNING OBJECTIVES

✔ **The Navigator**

1 **Compute a target cost when the market determines a product price.** To compute a target cost, the company determines its target selling price. Once the target selling price is set, it determines its target cost by setting a desired profit. The difference between the target price and desired profit is the target cost of the product.

2 **Compute a target selling price using cost-plus pricing.** Cost-plus pricing involves establishing a cost base and adding to this cost base a markup to determine a target selling price. The cost-plus pricing formula is expressed as follows: Target selling price = Cost + (Markup percentage × Cost).

3 **Use time-and-material pricing to determine the cost of services provided.** Under time-and-material pricing, two pricing rates are set—one for the labor used on a job and another for the material. The labor rate includes direct labor time and other employee costs. The material charge is based on the cost of direct parts and materials used and a material loading charge for related overhead costs.

4 **Determine a transfer price using the negotiated, cost-based, and market-based approaches.** The negotiated price is determined through agreement of division managers. Under a cost-based approach, the transfer price may be based on variable cost alone or on variable costs plus fixed costs. Companies may add a markup to these numbers. The cost-based approach often leads to poor performance evaluations and purchasing decisions. The advantage of the cost-based system is its simplicity. A market-based transfer price is based on existing competing market prices and services. A market-based system is often considered the best approach because it is objective and generally provides the proper economic incentives.

5 **Explain issues involved in transferring goods between divisions in different countries.** Companies must pay income tax in the country where they generate the income. In order to maximize income and minimize income tax, many companies prefer to report more income in countries with low tax rates, and less income in countries with high tax rates. This is accomplished by adjusting the transfer prices they use on internal transfers between divisions located in different countries.

DECISION TOOLKIT A SUMMARY

DECISION CHECKPOINTS	INFO NEEDED FOR DECISION	TOOL TO USE FOR DECISION	HOW TO EVALUATE RESULTS
How does management use target costs to make decisions about manufacturing products or providing services?	Target selling price, desired profit, target cost	Target selling price less desired profit equals target cost	If actual cost exceeds target cost, the company will not earn desired profit. If desired profit is not achieved, company must evaluate whether to manufacture the product or provide the service.
What factors should be considered in determining selling price in a less competitive environment?	Total cost per unit and desired profit (cost-plus pricing)	Total cost per unit plus desired profit equals target selling price	Does company make its desired profit? If not, does the profit shortfall result from less volume?
How do we set prices when it is difficult to estimate total cost per unit?	Two pricing rates needed: one for labor use and another for materials	Compute labor rate charge and materials rate charge. In each of these calculations, add a profit margin.	Is the company profitable under this pricing approach? Are employees earning reasonable wages?
What price should be charged for transfer of goods between divisions of a company?	Variable cost, opportunity cost, market prices	Variable cost plus opportunity cost provides minimum transfer price for seller	If income of division provides fair evaluation of managers, then transfer price is useful. Also, income of the company overall should not be reduced due to the transfer pricing approach.

APPENDIX 8A OTHER COST APPROACHES TO PRICING

In determining the target price for Thinkmore's video camera pen in the chapter, we calculated the cost base **by including all costs incurred**. This approach is referred to as **full-cost pricing**. Using total cost as the basis of the markup makes sense conceptually because, in the long run, the price must cover all costs and provide a reasonable profit. However, total cost is difficult to determine in practice. This is because period costs (selling and administrative expenses) are difficult to trace to a specific product. Activity-based costing can be used to overcome this difficulty to some extent.

In practice, companies sometimes use two other cost approaches: (1) absorption cost pricing or (2) variable-cost pricing. Absorption-cost pricing is more popular than variable-cost pricing.[2] We illustrate both approaches because both have merit.

> **LEARNING OBJECTIVE   6**
>
> Determine prices using absorption-cost pricing and variable-cost pricing.

Absorption-Cost Pricing

Absorption-cost pricing is consistent with generally accepted accounting principles (GAAP). The reason: It includes both variable and fixed manufacturing costs as product costs. **It excludes from this cost base both variable and fixed**

---

[2]For a discussion of cost-plus pricing, see Eunsup Skim and Ephraim F. Sudit, "How Manufacturers Price Products," *Management Accounting* (February 1995), pp. 37–39; and V. Govindarajan and R.N. Anthony, "How Firms Use Cost Data in Pricing Decisions," *Management Accounting* (65, no. 1), pp. 30–36.

selling and administrative costs. Thus, companies must somehow provide for selling and administrative costs plus the target ROI, and they do this through the markup.

The **first step** in absorption-cost pricing is to compute the unit **manufacturing cost**. For Thinkmore Products, Inc., this amounts to $80 per unit at a volume of 10,000 units, as shown in Illustration 8A-1.

Illustration 8A-1
Computation of unit manufacturing cost

	Per Unit
Direct materials	$23
Direct labor	17
Variable manufacturing overhead	12
Fixed manufacturing overhead ($280,000 ÷ 10,000)	28
Total unit manufacturing cost (absorption cost)	$80

In addition, Thinkmore provides the following information regarding selling and administrative expenses per unit and desired ROI per unit.

Illustration 8A-2
Other information

Variable selling and administrative expenses	$ 8
Fixed selling and administrative expenses ($240,000 ÷ 10,000)	$24
Desired ROI per unit	$20

The **second step** in absorption-cost pricing is to compute the markup percentage using the formula in Illustration 8A-3. Note that when companies use manufacturing cost per unit as the cost base to compute the markup percentage, the **percentage must cover the desired ROI and also the selling and administrative expenses**.

Illustration 8A-3
Markup percentage—absorption-cost pricing

Desired ROI per Unit	+	Selling and Administrative Expenses per Unit	=	Markup Percentage	×	Manufacturing Cost per Unit
$20	+	$32	=	**MP**	×	$80

Solving we find:

$$\text{MP} = (\$20 + \$32) \div \$80 = 65\%$$

The **third** and final **step** is to set the target selling price. Using a markup percentage of 65% and absorption-cost pricing, Thinkmore computes the target selling price as shown in Illustration 8A-4.

Illustration 8A-4
Computation of target price—absorption-cost pricing

Manufacturing Cost per Unit	+	(Markup Percentage	×	Manufacturing Cost per Unit)	=	Target Selling Price
$80	+	(65%	×	$80)	=	$132

Using a target price of $132 will produce the desired 20% return on investment for Thinkmore Products on its video camera pen at a volume level of 10,000 units, as shown in Illustration 8A-5.

Thinkmore Products, Inc.
Budgeted Absorption-Cost Income Statement

Revenue (10,000 camera pens × $132)	$1,320,000
Cost of goods sold (10,000 camera pens × $80)	800,000
Gross profit	520,000
Selling and administrative expenses	
[10,000 camera pens × ($8 + $24)]	320,000
Net income	**$ 200,000**

Budgeted ROI

$$\frac{\text{Net income}}{\text{Invested assets}} = \frac{\$200,000}{\$1,000,000} = \underline{\underline{\mathbf{20\%}}}$$

Markup Percentage

$$\frac{\text{Net income} + \text{Selling and administrative expenses}}{\text{Cost of goods sold}} = \frac{\$200,000 + \$320,000}{\$800,000} = \underline{\underline{\mathbf{65\%}}}$$

Because of the fixed-cost element, if Thinkmore sells more than 10,000 units, the ROI will be greater than 20%. If it sells fewer than 10,000 units, the ROI will be less than 20%. The markup percentage is also verified by adding $200,000 (the net income) and $320,000 (selling and administrative expenses) and then dividing by $800,000 (the cost of goods sold or the cost base).

Most companies that use cost-plus pricing use either absorption cost or full cost as the basis. The reasons for this tendency are as follows.

1. Absorption-cost information is most readily provided by a company's cost accounting system. Because absorption-cost data already exist in general ledger accounts, it is cost-effective to use the data for pricing.

2. Basing the cost-plus formula on only variable costs could encourage managers to set too low a price to boost sales. There is the fear that if managers use only variable costs, they will substitute variable costs for full costs, which can lead to suicidal price cutting.

3. Absorption-cost or full-cost pricing provides the most defensible base for justifying prices to all interested parties—managers, customers, and government.

Variable-Cost Pricing

Under **variable-cost pricing**, the cost base consists of all of the **variable costs** associated with a product, including variable selling and administrative costs. **Because fixed costs are not included in the base, the markup must provide for all fixed costs (manufacturing, and selling and administrative) and the target ROI.** Variable-cost pricing is more useful for making short-run decisions because it considers variable-cost and fixed-cost behavior patterns separately.

The **first step** in variable-cost pricing is to compute the unit variable cost. For Thinkmore Products, Inc., this amounts to $60 per unit, as shown in Illustration 8A-6 (page 358).

Illustration 8A-6
Computation of unit variable cost

	Per Unit
Direct materials	$23
Direct labor	17
Variable manufacturing overhead	12
Variable selling and administrative expense	8
Total unit variable cost	$60

The **second step** in variable-cost pricing is to compute the markup percentage. Illustration 8A-7 shows the formula for the markup percentage. For Thinkmore, fixed costs include fixed manufacturing overhead of $28 per unit ($280,000 ÷ 10,000) and fixed selling and administrative expenses of $24 per unit ($240,000 ÷ 10,000).

Illustration 8A-7
Computation of markup percentage—variable-cost pricing

Desired ROI per Unit	+	Fixed Cost per Unit	=	Markup Percentage	×	Variable Cost per Unit
$20	+	($28 + $24)	=	MP	×	$60

Solving, we find:

$$MP = \frac{\$20 + (\$28 + \$24)}{\$60} = 120\%$$

The **third step** is to set the target selling price. Using a markup percentage of 120% and the contribution approach, Thinkmore computes the selling price as shown in Illustration 8A-8.

Illustration 8A-8
Computation of target price—variable-cost pricing

Variable Cost per Unit	+	(Markup Percentage	×	Variable Cost per Unit)	=	Target Selling Price
$60	+	(120%	×	$60)	=	$132

Using a target price of $132 will produce the desired 20% return on investment for Thinkmore Products on its video camera pen at a volume level of 10,000 units, as shown in Illustration 8A-9.

Illustration 8A-9
Proof of 20% ROI—contribution approach

Thinkmore Products, Inc.
Budgeted Variable-Cost Income Statement

Revenue (10,000 camera pens × $132)		$1,320,000
Variable costs (10,000 camera pens × $60)		600,000
Contribution margin		720,000
Fixed manufacturing overhead (10,000 camera pens × $28)	$280,000	
Fixed selling and administrative expenses (10,000 camera pens × $24)	240,000	520,000
Net income		$ 200,000

Budgeted ROI

$$\frac{\text{Net income}}{\text{Invested assets}} = \frac{\$200,000}{\$1,000,000} = 20\%$$

Markup Percentage

$$\frac{\text{Net income + Fixed costs}}{\text{Variable costs}} = \frac{\$200,000 + \$520,000}{\$600,000} = 120\%$$

Under any of the three pricing approaches we have looked at (full-cost, absorption-cost, and variable-cost), the desired ROI will be attained only if the budgeted sales volume for the period is attained. None of these approaches guarantees a profit or a desired ROI. Achieving a desired ROI is the result of many factors, some of which are beyond the company's control, such as market conditions, political and legal issues, customers' tastes, and competitive actions.

Because absorption-cost pricing includes allocated fixed costs, it does not make clear how the company's costs will change as volume changes. To avoid blurring the effects of cost behavior on net income, some managers therefore prefer variable-cost pricing. The specific reasons for using variable-cost pricing, even though the basic accounting data are less accessible, are as follows.

1. Variable-cost pricing, being based on variable cost, is more consistent with cost-volume-profit analysis used by managers to measure the profit implications of changes in price and volume.

2. Variable-cost pricing provides the type of data managers need for pricing special orders. It shows the incremental cost of accepting one more order.

3. Variable-cost pricing avoids arbitrary allocation of common fixed costs (such as executive salaries) to individual product lines.

SUMMARY OF LEARNING OBJECTIVE FOR APPENDIX 8A ✔ The Navigator

6 **Determine prices using absorption-cost pricing and variable-cost pricing.** Absorption-cost pricing uses total manufacturing cost as the cost base and provides for selling and administrative costs plus the target ROI through the markup. The target selling price is computed as: Manufacturing cost per unit + (Markup percentage × Manufacturing cost per unit).

Variable-cost pricing uses all of the variable costs, including selling and administrative costs, as the cost base and provides for fixed costs and target ROI through the markup. The target selling price is computed as: Variable cost per unit + (Markup percentage × Variable cost per unit).

GLOSSARY

Absorption-cost pricing An approach to pricing that defines the cost base as the manufacturing cost; it excludes both variable and fixed selling and administrative costs. (p. 355).

Cost-based transfer price A transfer price that uses as its foundation the costs incurred by the division producing the goods. (p. 349).

Cost-plus pricing A process whereby a product's selling price is determined by adding a markup to a cost base. (p. 337).

Full-cost pricing An approach to pricing that defines the cost base as all costs incurred. (p. 339).

Market-based transfer price A transfer price that is based on existing market prices of competing products. (p. 350).

Markup The amount added to a product's cost base to determine the product's selling price. (p. 337).

Material loading charge A charge added to cover the cost of purchasing, receiving, handling, and storing materials, plus any desired profit margin on the materials themselves. (p. 342).

Negotiated transfer price A transfer price that is determined by the agreement of the division managers. (p. 346).

Outsourcing Contracting with an external party to provide a good or service, rather than performing the work internally. (p. 351).

Target cost The cost that will provide the desired profit on a product when the seller does not have control over the product's price. (p. 335).

Target selling price The selling price that will provide the desired profit on a product when the seller has the ability to determine the product's price. (p. 337).

Time-and-material pricing An approach to cost-plus pricing in which the company uses two pricing rates, one for the labor used on a job and another for the material. (p. 341).

Transfer price The price used to record the transfer of goods between two divisions of a company. (p. 345).

Variable-cost pricing An approach to pricing that defines the cost base as all variable costs; it excludes both fixed manufacturing and fixed selling and administrative costs. (pp. 340, 357).

> **Comprehensive DO IT!**

Revco Electronics is a division of International Motors, an automobile manufacturer. Revco produces car radio/CD players. Revco sells its products to International Motors, as well as to other car manufacturers and electronics distributors. The following information is available regarding Revco's car radio/CD player.

Selling price of car radio/CD player to external customers	$49
Variable cost per unit	$28
Capacity	200,000 units

Instructions

Determine whether the goods should be transferred internally or purchased externally and what the appropriate transfer price should be under each of the following **independent** situations.

(a) Revco Electronics is operating at full capacity. There is a saving of $4 per unit for variable cost if the car radio is made for internal sale. International Motors can purchase a comparable car radio from an outside supplier for $47.

(b) Revco Electronics has sufficient existing capacity to meet the needs of International Motors. International Motors can purchase a comparable car radio from an outside supplier for $47.

(c) International Motors wants to purchase a special-order car radio/CD player with additional features. It needs 15,000 units. Revco Electronics has determined that the additional variable cost would be $12 per unit. Revco Electronics has no spare capacity. It will have to forgo sales of 15,000 units to external parties in order to provide this special order.

Solution to Comprehensive DO IT!

Action Plan

✔ Determine whether company is at full capacity or not.

✔ Find the minimum transfer price, using formulas.

✔ Compare maximum price the buyer would pay to the minimum price for the seller.

✔ Determine if a deal can be made.

(a) Revco Electronics' opportunity cost (its lost contribution margin) would be $21 ($49 − $28). Using the formula for minimum transfer price, we determine:

$$\text{Minimum transfer price} = \text{Variable cost} + \text{Opportunity cost}$$
$$\$45 = (\$28 - \$4) + \$21$$

Since this minimum transfer price is less than the $47 it would cost if International Motors purchases from an external party, internal transfer should take place. Revco Electronics and International Motors should negotiate a transfer price between $45 and $47.

(b) Since Revco Electronics has available capacity, its opportunity cost (its lost contribution margin) would be $0. Using the formula for minimum transfer price, we determine the following.

$$\text{Minimum transfer price} = \text{Variable cost} + \text{Opportunity cost}$$
$$\$28 = \$28 + \$0$$

Since International Motors can purchase the unit for $47 from an external party, the most it would be willing to pay would be $47. It is in the best interest of the company as a whole, as well as the two divisions, for a transfer to take place. The two divisions must reach a negotiated transfer price between $28 and $47 that recognizes the costs and benefits to each party and is acceptable to both.

(c) Revco Electronics' opportunity cost (its lost contribution margin per unit) would be $21 ($49 − $28). Its variable cost would be $40 ($28 + $12). Using the formula for minimum transfer price, we determine the following.

$$\text{Minimum transfer price} = \text{Variable cost} + \text{Opportunity cost}$$
$$\$61 = \$40 + \$21$$

Note that in this case Revco Electronics has no available capacity. Its management may decide that it does not want to provide this special order because to do so will require that it cut off the supply of the standard unit to some of its existing customers. This may anger those customers and result in the loss of customers.

 **The Navigator**

Self-Test, Brief Exercises, Exercises, Problem Set A, and many more resources are available for practice in WileyPLUS.

Note: All asterisked Questions, Exercises, and Problems relate to material in the appendix to the chapter.

SELF-TEST QUESTIONS

Answers are at the end of the chapter.

(LO 1) 1. Target cost related to price and profit means that:
   (a) cost and desired profit must be determined before selling price.
   (b) cost and selling price must be determined before desired profit.
   (c) price and desired profit must be determined before costs.
   (d) costs can be achieved only if the company is at full capacity.

(LO 1) 2. Classic Toys has examined the market for toy train locomotives. It believes there is a market niche in which it can sell locomotives at $80 each. It estimates that it could sell 10,000 of these locomotives annually. Variable costs to make a locomotive are expected to be $25. Classic anticipates a profit of $15 per locomotive. The target cost for the locomotive is:
   (a) $80.   (c) $40.
   (b) $65.   (d) $25.

(LO 1, 2) 3. In a competitive, common-product environment, a seller would most likely use:
   (a) time-and-material pricing.
   (b) variable costing.
   (c) target costing.
   (d) cost-plus pricing.

(LO 2) 4. Cost-plus pricing means that:
   (a) Selling price = Variable cost + (Markup percentage + Variable cost).
   (b) Selling price = Cost + (Markup percentage × Cost).
   (c) Selling price = Manufacturing cost + (Markup percentage + Manufacturing cost).
   (d) Selling price = Fixed cost + (Markup percentage × Fixed cost).

(LO 2) 5. Adler Company is considering developing a new product. The company has gathered the following information on this product.

Expected total unit cost	$25
Estimated investment for new product	$500,000
Desired ROI	10%
Expected number of units to be produced and sold	1,000

Given this information, the desired markup percentage and selling price are:
   (a) markup percentage 10%; selling price $55.
   (b) markup percentage 200%; selling price $75.
   (c) markup percentage 10%; selling price $50.
   (d) markup percentage 100%; selling price $55.

(LO 2) 6. Mystique Co. provides the following information for the new product it recently introduced.

Total unit cost	$30
Desired ROI per unit	$10
Target selling price	$40

What would be Mystique Co.'s percentage markup on cost?
   (a) 125%.   (c) 33⅓%.
   (b) 75%.   (d) 25%.

(LO 3) 7. Crescent Electrical Repair has decided to price its work on a time-and-material basis. It estimates the following costs for the year related to labor.

Technician wages and benefits	$100,000
Office employee's salary and benefits	$ 40,000
Other overhead	$ 80,000

Crescent desires a profit margin of $10 per labor hour and budgets 5,000 hours of repair time for the year. The office employee's salary, benefits, and other overhead costs should be divided evenly between time charges and material loading charges. Crescent labor charge per hour would be:
   (a) $42.   (c) $32.
   (b) $34.   (d) $30.

(LO 3) 8. Time-and-material pricing would most likely be used by a:
   (a) garden-fertilizer producer.
   (b) lawn-mower manufacturer.
   (c) tree farm.
   (d) lawn-care provider.

(LO 4) 9. The Plastics Division of Weston Company manufactures plastic molds and then sells them to customers for $70 per unit. Its variable cost is $30 per unit, and its fixed cost per unit is $10. Management would like the Plastics Division to transfer 10,000 of these molds to another division within the company at a price of $40. The Plastics Division is operating at full capacity. What is the minimum transfer price that the Plastics Division should accept?
   (a) $10.   (c) $40.
   (b) $30.   (d) $70.

(LO 4) 10. Assume the same information as Question 9, except that the Plastics Division has available capacity of 10,000 units for plastic moldings. What is the minimum transfer price that the Plastics Division should accept?
   (a) $10.   (c) $40.
   (b) $30.   (d) $70.

(LO 4) **11.** The most common method used to establish transfer prices is the:
  (a) negotiated transfer pricing approach.
  (b) opportunity costing transfer pricing approach.
  (c) cost-based transfer pricing approach.
  (d) market-based transfer pricing approach.

(LO 4) **12.** When a company uses time-and-material pricing, the material loading charge is expressed as a percentage of:
  (a) the total estimated labor costs for the year.
  (b) the total estimated costs of parts and materials for the year.
  (c) the total estimated overhead costs for the year.
  (d) the total estimated costs of parts, materials, and labor for the year.

(LO 5) **13.** Global Industries transfers parts between divisions in two countries, Eastland and Westland. Eastland's tax rate is 8%, and Westland's tax rate is 16%. To minimize tax payments and maximize net income, Global should establish transfer prices that:
  (a) allocate contribution margin equally between Eastland and Westland.
  (b) allocate more contribution margin to Eastland.
  (c) allocate more contribution margin to Westland.
  (d) allocate half as much contribution margin to Eastland as it does to Westland.

*14. AST Electrical provides the following cost information (LO 6) related to its production of electronic circuit boards.

	Per Unit
Variable manufacturing cost	$40
Fixed manufacturing cost	$30
Variable selling and administrative expenses	$ 8
Fixed selling and administrative expenses	$12
Desired ROI per unit	$15

What is its markup percentage assuming that AST Electrical uses absorption-cost pricing?
  (a) 16.67%.   (c) 54.28%.
  (b) 50%.   (d) 118.75%.

*15. Assume the same information as question 14 and (LO 6) determine AST Electrical's markup percentage using variable-cost pricing.
  (a) 16.67%.   (c) 54.28%.
  (b) 50%.   (d) 118.75%.

Go to the book's companion website, www.wiley.com/college/weygandt, for additional Self-Test Questions.

✔ **The Navigator**

QUESTIONS

1. What are the two types of pricing environments for sales to external parties?

2. In what situation does a company place the greatest focus on its target cost? How is the target cost determined?

3. What is the basic formula to determine the target selling price in cost-plus pricing?

4. Benz Corporation produces a filter that has a per unit cost of $18. The company would like a 30% markup. Using cost-plus pricing, determine the per unit selling price.

5. What is the basic formula for the markup percentage?

6. What are some of the factors that affect a company's desired ROI?

7. Stanley Corporation manufactures an electronic switch for dishwashers. The cost base per unit, excluding selling and administrative expenses, is $60. The per unit cost of selling and administrative expenses is $15. The company's desired ROI per unit is $6. Calculate its markup percentage on total unit cost.

8. Sheen Co. manufactures a standard cabinet for a DVD player. The variable cost per unit is $16. The fixed cost per unit is $9. The desired ROI per unit is $6. Compute the markup percentage on total unit cost and the target selling price for the cabinet.

9. In what circumstances is time-and-material pricing most often used?

10. What is the material loading charge? How is it expressed?

11. What is a transfer price? Why is determining a fair transfer price important to division managers?

12. When setting a transfer price, what objective(s) should the company have in mind?

13. What are the three approaches for determining transfer prices?

14. Describe the cost-based approach to transfer pricing. What is the strength of this approach? What are the weaknesses of this approach?

15. What is the general formula for determining the minimum transfer price that the selling division should be willing to accept?

16. When determining the minimum transfer price, what is meant by the "opportunity cost"?

17. In what circumstances will a negotiated transfer price be used instead of a market-based price?

18. Explain how companies use transfer pricing between divisions located in different countries to reduce tax payments, and discuss the propriety of this approach.

*19. What costs are excluded from the cost base when absorption-cost pricing is used to determine the markup percentage?

*20. Marie Corporation manufactures a fiber optic connector. The variable cost per unit is $16. The fixed cost per unit is $9. The company's desired ROI per unit is $3. Compute the markup percentage using variable-cost pricing.

BRIEF EXERCISES

BE8-1 Voorhees Company manufactures computer hard drives. The market for hard drives is very competitive. The current market price for a computer hard drive is $45. Voorhees would like a profit of $15 per drive. How can Voorhees Company accomplish this objective?

Compute target cost.

(LO 1), AP

BE8-2 Mussatto Corporation produces snowboards. The following per unit cost information is available: direct materials $12; direct labor $8; variable manufacturing overhead $6; fixed manufacturing overhead $14; variable selling and administrative expenses $4; and fixed selling and administrative expenses $12. Using a 30% markup percentage on total per unit cost, compute the target selling price.

Use cost-plus pricing to determine selling price.

(LO 2), AP

BE8-3 Hannon Corporation produces high-performance rotors. It expects to produce 50,000 rotors in the coming year. It has invested $10,000,000 to produce rotors. The company has a required return on investment of 16%. What is its ROI per unit?

Compute ROI per unit.

(LO 2), AP

BE8-4 Morales Corporation produces microwave units. The following per unit cost information is available: direct materials $36; direct labor $24; variable manufacturing overhead $18; fixed manufacturing overhead $40; variable selling and administrative expenses $14; and fixed selling and administrative expenses $28. Its desired ROI per unit is $30. Compute its markup percentage using a total-cost approach.

Compute markup percentage.

(LO 2), AP

BE8-5 During the current year, Mast Corporation expects to produce 10,000 units and has budgeted the following: net income $300,000; variable costs $1,100,000; and fixed costs $100,000. It has invested assets of $1,500,000. The company's budgeted ROI was 24%. What was its budgeted markup percentage using a full-cost approach?

Compute ROI and markup percentage.

(LO 2), AP

BE8-6 Rooney Small Engine Repair charges $42 per hour of labor. It has a material loading percentage of 40%. On a recent job replacing the engine of a riding lawnmower, Rooney worked 10.5 hours and used parts with a cost of $700. Calculate Rooney's total bill.

Use time-and-material pricing to determine bill.

(LO 3), AP

BE8-7 The Heating Division of KLM International produces a heating element that it sells to its customers for $45 per unit. Its variable cost per unit is $20, and its fixed cost per unit is $10. Top management of KLM International would like the Heating Division to transfer 15,000 heating units to another division within the company at a price of $29. The Heating Division is operating at full capacity. What is the minimum transfer price that the Heating Division should accept?

Determine minimum transfer price.

(LO 4), AP

BE8-8 Use the data from BE8-7, but assume that the Heating Division has sufficient excess capacity to provide the 15,000 heating units to the other division. What is the minimum transfer price that the Heating Division should accept?

Determine minimum transfer price with excess capacity.

(LO 4), AP

BE8-9 Use the data from BE8-7, but assume that the units being requested are special high-performance units and that the division's variable cost would be $24 per unit (rather than $20). What is the minimum transfer price that the Heating Division should accept?

Determine minimum transfer price for special order.

(LO 4), AP

*BE8-10 Using the data in BE8-4, compute the markup percentage using absorption-cost pricing.

Compute markup percentage using absorption-cost pricing.

(LO 6), AP

*BE8-11 Using the data in BE8-4, compute the markup percentage using variable-cost pricing.

Compute markup percentage using variable-cost pricing.

(LO 6), AP

> DO IT! REVIEW

DO IT! 8-1 Krystal Water is considering introducing a water filtration device for its 20-ounce water bottles. Market research indicates that 1,000,000 units can be sold if the price is no more than $3. If Krystal Water decides to produce the filters, it will need to

Determine target cost.

(LO 1), AP

invest $2,000,000 in new production equipment. Krystal Water requires a minimum rate of return of 18% on all investments.

Determine the target cost per unit for the filter.

Use cost-plus pricing to determine various amounts.

(LO 2), AP

DO IT! **8-2** Gundy Corporation produces area rugs. The following per unit cost information is available: direct materials $18, direct labor $9, variable manufacturing overhead $5, fixed manufacturing overhead $6, variable selling and administrative expenses $3, and fixed selling and administrative expenses $7.

Using a 30% markup on total per unit cost, compute the target selling price.

Use time-and-material pricing to determine bill.

(LO 3), AP

DO IT! **8-3** Presented below are data for Kwik Appliance Repair Shop.

Repair-technicians' wages	$120,000
Fringe benefits	40,000
Overhead	50,000

The desired profit margin per hour is $20. The material loading charge is 60% of invoice cost. Kwik estimates that 5,000 labor hours will be worked next year. If Kwik repairs a dishwasher that takes 1.5 hours to repair and uses parts of $80, compute the bill for the job.

Determine transfer prices.

(LO 4), AP

DO IT! **8-4** The fastener division of Southern Fasteners manufactures zippers and then sells them to customers for $8 per unit. Its variable cost is $3 per unit, and its fixed cost per unit is $1.50. Management would like the fastener division to transfer 12,000 of these zippers to another division within the company at a price of $3. The fastener division could avoid $0.20 per zipper of variable packaging costs by selling internally.

Determine the minimum transfer price (a) assuming the fastener division is not operating at full capacity, and (b) assuming the fastener division is operating at full capacity.

✔ **The Navigator**

EXERCISES

Compute target cost.

(LO 1), AP

XLS

E8-1 Jarlsberg Cheese Company has developed a new cheese slicer called Slim Slicer. The company plans to sell this slicer through its catalog, which it issues monthly. Given market research, Jarlsberg believes that it can charge $20 for the Slim Slicer. Prototypes of the Slim Slicer, however, are costing $22. By using cheaper materials and gaining efficiencies in mass production, Jarlsberg believes it can reduce Slim Slicer's cost substantially. Jarlsberg wishes to earn a return of 30% of the selling price.

Instructions
(a) Compute the target cost for the Slim Slicer.
(b) When is target costing particularly helpful in deciding whether to produce a given product?

Compute target cost.

(LO 1), AP

E8-2 Eckert Company is involved in producing and selling high-end golf equipment. The company has recently been involved in developing various types of laser guns to measure yardages on the golf course. One small laser gun, called LittleLaser, appears to have a very large potential market. Because of competition, Eckert does not believe that it can charge more than $90 for LittleLaser. At this price, Eckert believes it can sell 100,000 of these laser guns. Eckert will require an investment of $8,000,000 to manufacture, and the company wants an ROI of 20%.

Instructions
Determine the target cost for one LittleLaser.

Compute target cost and cost-plus pricing.

(LO 1, 2), AP

E8-3 Hannon Company makes swimsuits and sells these suits directly to retailers. Although Hannon has a variety of suits, it does not make the All-Body suit used by highly skilled swimmers. The market research department believes that a strong market exists for this type of suit. The department indicates that the All-Body suit would sell for approximately $100. Given its experience, Hannon believes the All-Body suit would have the following manufacturing costs.

Direct materials	$ 25
Direct labor	30
Manufacturing overhead	45
Total costs	$100

Instructions

(a) Assume that Hannon uses cost-plus pricing, setting the selling price 20% above its costs. (1) What would be the price charged for the All-Body swimsuit? (2) Under what circumstances might Hannon consider manufacturing the All-Body swimsuit given this approach?

(b) Assume that Hannon uses target costing. What is the price that Hannon would charge the retailer for the All-Body swimsuit?

(c) What is the highest acceptable manufacturing cost Hannon would be willing to incur to produce the All-Body swimsuit, if it desired a profit of $20 per unit? (Assume target costing.)

E8-4 Kaspar Corporation makes a commercial-grade cooking griddle. The following information is available for Kaspar Corporation's anticipated annual volume of 30,000 units.

Use cost-plus pricing to determine selling price.

(LO 2), AP

	Per Unit	Total
Direct materials	$17	
Direct labor	$ 8	
Variable manufacturing overhead	$11	
Fixed manufacturing overhead		$300,000
Variable selling and administrative expenses	$ 4	
Fixed selling and administrative expenses		$150,000

The company uses a 40% markup percentage on total cost.

Instructions

(a) Compute the total cost per unit.

(b) Compute the target selling price.

E8-5 Paige Corporation makes a mechanical stuffed alligator that sings the Martian national anthem. The following information is available for Paige Corporation's anticipated annual volume of 500,000 units.

Use cost-plus pricing to determine various amounts.

(LO 2), AP

	Per Unit	Total
Direct materials	$ 7	
Direct labor	$ 9	
Variable manufacturing overhead	$15	
Fixed manufacturing overhead		$3,000,000
Variable selling and administrative expenses	$14	
Fixed selling and administrative expenses		$1,500,000

The company has a desired ROI of 25%. It has invested assets of $26,000,000.

Instructions

(a) Compute the total cost per unit.

(b) Compute the desired ROI per unit.

(c) Compute the markup percentage using total cost per unit.

(d) Compute the target selling price.

E8-6 Alma's Recording Studio rents studio time to musicians in 2-hour blocks. Each session includes the use of the studio facilities, a digital recording of the performance, and a professional music producer/mixer. Anticipated annual volume is 1,000 sessions. The company has invested $2,352,000 in the studio and expects a return on investment (ROI) of 20%. Budgeted costs for the coming year are as follows.

Use cost-plus pricing to determine various amounts.

(LO 2), AP

	Per Session	Total
Direct materials (tapes, CDs, etc)	$ 20	
Direct labor	$400	
Variable overhead	$ 50	
Fixed overhead		$950,000
Variable selling and administrative expenses	$ 40	
Fixed selling and administrative expenses		$500,000

Instructions
(a) Determine the total cost per session.
(b) Determine the desired ROI per session.
(c) Calculate the markup percentage on the total cost per session.
(d) Calculate the target price per session.

Use cost-plus pricing to determine various amounts.

(LO 2), AP

E8-7 Pargo Corporation produces industrial robots for high-precision manufacturing. The following information is given for Pargo Corporation.

	Per Unit	Total
Direct materials	$380	
Direct labor	$290	
Variable manufacturing overhead	$ 72	
Fixed manufacturing overhead		$1,800,000
Variable selling and administrative expenses	$ 55	
Fixed selling and administrative expenses		$ 324,000

The company has a desired ROI of 20%. It has invested assets of $51,000,000. It anticipates production of 3,000 units per year.

Instructions
(a) Compute the cost per unit of the fixed manufacturing overhead and the fixed selling and administrative expenses.
(b) Compute the desired ROI per unit. (Round to the nearest dollar.)
(c) Compute the target selling price.

Use time-and-material pricing to determine bill.

(LO 3), AP

E8-8 Second Chance Welding rebuilds spot welders for manufacturers. The following budgeted cost data for 2014 is available for Second Chance.

	Time Charges	Material Loading Charges
Technicians' wages and benefits	$228,000	—
Parts manager's salary and benefits	—	$42,500
Office employee's salary and benefits	38,000	9,000
Other overhead	15,200	24,000
Total budgeted costs	$281,200	$75,500

The company desires a $30 profit margin per hour of labor and a 20% profit margin on parts. It has budgeted for 7,600 hours of repair time in the coming year, and estimates that the total invoice cost of parts and materials in 2014 will be $400,000.

Instructions
(a) Compute the rate charged per hour of labor.
(b) Compute the material loading percentage. (Round to three decimal places.)
(c) Pace Corporation has requested an estimate to rebuild its spot welder. Second Chance estimates that it would require 40 hours of labor and $2,000 of parts. Compute the total estimated bill.

Use time-and-material pricing to determine bill.

(LO 3), AP

E8-9 Ignatenko's Custom Electronics (ICE) sells and installs complete security, computer, audio, and video systems for homes. On newly constructed homes it provides bids using time-and-material pricing. The following budgeted cost data are available.

	Time Charges	Material Loading Charges
Technicians' wages and benefits	$150,000	—
Parts manager's salary and benefits	—	$34,000
Office employee's salary and benefits	28,000	15,000
Other overhead	15,000	42,000
Total budgeted costs	$193,000	$91,000

The company has budgeted for 6,250 hours of technician time during the coming year. It desires a $38 profit margin per hour of labor and a 100% profit on parts. It estimates the total invoice cost of parts and materials in 2014 will be $700,000.

Instructions
(a) Compute the rate charged per hour of labor. (Round to two decimal places.)
(b) Compute the material loading percentage. (Round to two decimal places.)
(c) ICE has just received a request for a bid from Buil Builders on a $1,200,000 new home. The company estimates that it would require 80 hours of labor and $40,000 of parts. Compute the total estimated bill.

E8-10 Wasson's Classic Cars restores classic automobiles to showroom status. Budgeted data for the current year are:

Use time-and-material pricing to determine bill.

(LO 3), AP

	Time Charges	Material Loading Charges
Restorers' wages and fringe benefits	$270,000	
Purchasing agent's salary and fringe benefits		$ 67,500
Administrative salaries and fringe benefits	54,000	21,960
Other overhead costs	24,000	77,490
Total budgeted costs	$348,000	$166,950

The company anticipated that the restorers would work a total of 12,000 hours this year. Expected parts and materials were $1,260,000.

In late January, the company experienced a fire in its facilities that destroyed most of the accounting records. The accountant remembers that the hourly labor rate was $70.00 and that the material loading charge was 83.25%.

Instructions
(a) Determine the profit margin per hour on labor.
(b) Determine the profit margin on materials.
(c) Determine the total price of labor and materials on a job that was completed after the fire that required 150 hours of labor and $60,000 in parts and materials.

E8-11 Wellstone Company's Small Motor Division manufactures a number of small motors used in household and office appliances. The Household Division of Wellstone then assembles and packages such items as blenders and juicers. Both divisions are free to buy and sell any of their components internally or externally. The following costs relate to small motor LN233 on a per unit basis.

Determine minimum transfer price.

(LO 4), AP

Fixed cost per unit	$ 5
Variable cost per unit	$ 9
Selling price per unit	$30

Instructions
(a) Assuming that the Small Motor Division has excess capacity, compute the minimum acceptable price for the transfer of small motor LN233 to the Household Division.
(b) Assuming that the Small Motor Division does not have excess capacity, compute the minimum acceptable price for the transfer of the small motor to the Household Division.
(c) ▭▭▭▭▷ Explain why the level of capacity in the Small Motor Division has an effect on the transfer price.

*Determine effect on income
from transfer price.*

(LO 4), AN

E8-12 The Cycle Division of Ayala Company has the following per unit data related to its most recent cycle called Roadbuster.

Selling price		$2,200
Variable cost of goods sold		
Body frame	$300	
Other variable costs	900	1,200
Contribution margin		$1,000

Presently, the Cycle Division buys its body frames from an outside supplier. However Ayala has another division, FrameBody, that makes body frames for other cycle companies. The Cycle Division believes that FrameBody's product is suitable for its new Roadbuster cycle. Presently, FrameBody sells its frames for $350 per frame. The variable cost for FrameBody is $270. The Cycle Division is willing to pay $280 to purchase the frames from FrameBody.

Instructions

(a) Assume that FrameBody has excess capacity and is able to meet all of the Cycle Division's needs. If the Cycle Division buys 1,000 frames from FrameBody, determine the following: (1) effect on the income of the Cycle Division; (2) effect on the income of FrameBody; and (3) effect on the income of Ayala.

(b) Assume that FrameBody does not have excess capacity and therefore would lose sales if the frames were sold to the Cycle Division. If the Cycle Division buys 1,000 frames from FrameBody, determine the following: (1) effect on the income of the Cycle Division; (2) effect on the income of FrameBody; and (3) effect on the income of Ayala.

Determine minimum transfer price.

(LO 4), AP

E8-13 Venetian Corporation manufactures car stereos. It is a division of Berna Motors, which manufactures vehicles. Venetian sells car stereos to Berna, as well as to other vehicle manufacturers and retail stores. The following information is available for Venetian's standard unit: variable cost per unit $35; fixed cost per unit $23; and selling price to outside customer $86. Berna currently purchases a standard unit from an outside supplier for $80. Because of quality concerns and to ensure a reliable supply, the top management of Berna has ordered Venetian to provide 200,000 units per year at a transfer price of $35 per unit. Venetian is already operating at full capacity. Venetian can avoid $4 per unit of variable selling costs by selling the unit internally.

Instructions

Answer each of the following questions.

(a) What is the minimum transfer price that Venetian should accept?

(b) What is the potential loss to the corporation as a whole resulting from this forced transfer?

(c) How should the company resolve this situation?

Compute minimum transfer price.

(LO 4), AP

E8-14 The Bathtub Division of Kirk Plumbing Corporation has recently approached the Faucet Division with a proposal. The Bathtub Division would like to make a special "ivory" tub with gold-plated fixtures for the company's 50-year anniversary. It would make only 5,000 of these units. It would like the Faucet Division to make the fixtures and provide them to the Bathtub Division at a transfer price of $160. If sold externally, the estimated variable cost per unit would be $140. However, by selling internally, the Faucet Division would save $6 per unit on variable selling expenses. The Faucet Division is currently operating at full capacity. Its standard unit sells for $50 per unit and has variable costs of $29.

Instructions

Compute the minimum transfer price that the Faucet Division should be willing to accept, and discuss whether it should accept this offer.

Determine minimum transfer price.

(LO 4), AP

E8-15 The Appraisal Department of Bonita Bank performs appraisals of business properties for loans being considered by the bank and appraisals for home buyers that are financing their purchase through some other financial institution. The department charges $162 per home appraisal, and its variable costs are $130 per appraisal.

Recently, Bonita Bank has opened its own Home-Loan Department and wants the Appraisal Department to perform 1,200 appraisals on all Bonita Bank–financed home loans. Bank management feels that the cost of these appraisals to the Home-Loan Department should be $150. The variable cost per appraisal to the Home-Loan Department would be $6 less than those performed for outside customers due to savings in administrative costs.

Instructions

(a) Determine the minimum transfer price, assuming the Appraisal Department has excess capacity.

(b) Determine the minimum transfer price, assuming the Appraisal Department has no excess capacity.

(c) Assuming the Appraisal Department has no excess capacity, should management force the department to charge the Home-Loan Department only $150? Discuss.

E8-16 Crede Inc. has two divisions. Division A makes and sells student desks. Division B manufactures and sells reading lamps.

Determine minimum transfer price under different situations.

(LO 4), AP

Each desk has a reading lamp as one of its components. Division A can purchase reading lamps at a cost of $10 from an outside vendor. Division A needs 10,000 lamps for the coming year.

Division B has the capacity to manufacture 50,000 lamps annually. Sales to outside customers are estimated at 40,000 lamps for the next year. Reading lamps are sold at $12 each. Variable costs are $7 per lamp and include $1 of variable sales costs that are not incurred if lamps are sold internally to Division A. The total amount of fixed costs for Division B is $80,000.

Instructions

Consider the following independent situations.

(a) What should be the minimum transfer price accepted by Division B for the 10,000 lamps and the maximum transfer price paid by Division A? Justify your answer.

(b) Suppose Division B could use the excess capacity to produce and sell externally 15,000 units of a new product at a price of $7 per unit. The variable cost for this new product is $5 per unit. What should be the minimum transfer price accepted by Division B for the 10,000 lamps and the maximum transfer price paid by Division A? Justify your answer.

(c) If Division A needs 15,000 lamps instead of 10,000 during the next year, what should be the minimum transfer price accepted by Division B and the maximum transfer price paid by Division A? Justify your answer.

(CGA adapted)

E8-17 The Pacific Company is a multidivisional company. Its managers have full responsibility for profits and complete autonomy to accept or reject transfers from other divisions. Division A produces a subassembly part for which there is a competitive market. Division B currently uses this subassembly for a final product that is sold outside at $2,400. Division A charges Division B market price for the part, which is $1,500 per unit. Variable costs are $1,050 and $1,200 for Divisions A and B, respectively.

Determine minimum transfer price under different situations.

(LO 4), AP

The manager of Division B feels that Division A should transfer the part at a lower price than market because at market, Division B is unable to make a profit.

Instructions

(a) Calculate Division B's contribution margin if transfers are made at the market price, and calculate the company's total contribution margin.

(b) Assume that Division A can sell all its production in the open market. Should Division A transfer the goods to Division B? If so, at what price?

(c) Assume that Division A can sell in the open market only 500 units at $1,500 per unit out of the 1,000 units that it can produce every month. Assume also that a 20% reduction in price is necessary to sell all 1,000 units each month. Should transfers be made? If so, how many units should the division transfer and at what price? To support your decision, submit a schedule that compares the contribution margins under three different alternatives.

(CMA-Canada adapted)

*E8-18 Information for Paige Corporation is given in E8-5.

Compute total cost per unit, ROI, and markup percentages using absorption-cost pricing and variable-cost pricing.

(LO 6), AP

Instructions

Using the information given in E8-5, answer the following.

(a) Compute the total cost per unit.

(b) Compute the desired ROI per unit.

(c) Using absorption-cost pricing, compute the markup percentage.

(d) Using variable-cost pricing, compute the markup percentage.

Compute markup percentage using absorption-cost pricing and variable-cost pricing.

(LO 6), AP

*E8-19 Rensing Corporation produces outdoor portable fireplace units. The following per unit cost information is available: direct materials $20; direct labor $25; variable manufacturing overhead $14; fixed manufacturing overhead $21; variable selling and administrative expenses $9; and fixed selling and administrative expenses $11. The company's ROI per unit is $20.

Instructions

Compute Rensing Corporation's markup percentage using (a) absorption-cost pricing and (b) variable-cost pricing.

Compute various amounts using absorption-cost pricing and variable-cost pricing.

(LO 6), AP

*E8-20 Information for Pargo Corporation is given in E8-7.

Instructions

Using the information given in E8-7, answer the following.

(a) Compute the cost per unit of the fixed manufacturing overhead and the fixed selling and administrative expenses.
(b) Compute the desired ROI per unit. (Round to the nearest dollar.)
(c) Compute the markup percentage and target selling price using absorption-cost pricing. (Round the markup percentage to three decimal places.)
(d) Compute the markup percentage and target selling price using variable-cost pricing. (Round the markup percentage to three decimal places.)

EXERCISES: SET B AND CHALLENGE EXERCISES

Visit the book's companion website, at **www.wiley.com/college/weygandt**, and choose the Student Companion site to access Exercise Set B and Challenge Exercises.

PROBLEMS: SET A

Use cost-plus pricing to determine various amounts.

(LO 2), AP

XLS

P8-1A Dewitt Corporation needs to set a target price for its newly designed product M14–M16. The following data relate to this new product.

	Per Unit	Total
Direct materials	$20	
Direct labor	$40	
Variable manufacturing overhead	$10	
Fixed manufacturing overhead		$1,440,000
Variable selling and administrative expenses	$ 5	
Fixed selling and administrative expenses		$ 960,000

These costs are based on a budgeted volume of 80,000 units produced and sold each year. Dewitt uses cost-plus pricing methods to set its target selling price. The markup percentage on total unit cost is 30%.

Instructions

(a) Variable cost per unit $75

(a) Compute the total variable cost per unit, total fixed cost per unit, and total cost per unit for M14–M16.
(b) Compute the desired ROI per unit for M14–M16.
(c) Compute the target selling price for M14–M16.
(d) Compute variable cost per unit, fixed cost per unit, and total cost per unit assuming that 60,000 M14–M16s are sold during the year.

Use cost-plus pricing to determine various amounts.

(LO 2), AP

P8-2A Lovell Computer Parts Inc. is in the process of setting a selling price on a new component it has just designed and developed. The following cost estimates for this new component have been provided by the accounting department for a budgeted volume of 50,000 units.

	Per Unit	Total
Direct materials	$50	
Direct labor	$26	
Variable manufacturing overhead	$20	
Fixed manufacturing overhead		$600,000
Variable selling and administrative expenses	$19	
Fixed selling and administrative expenses		$400,000

Lovell Computer Parts management requests that the total cost per unit be used in cost-plus pricing its products. On this particular product, management also directs that the target price be set to provide a 25% return on investment (ROI) on invested assets of $1,000,000.

Instructions
(Round all calculations to two decimal places.)

(a) Compute the markup percentage and target selling price that will allow Lovell Computer Parts to earn its desired ROI of 25% on this new component.
(b) Assuming that the volume is 40,000 units, compute the markup percentage and target selling price that will allow Lovell Computer Parts to earn its desired ROI of 25% on this new component.

(b) Target selling price $146.25

P8-3A Jose's Electronic Repair Shop has budgeted the following time and material for 2014.

Use time-and-material pricing to determine bill.

(LO 3), AP

Jose's Electronic Repair Shop
Budgeted Costs for the Year 2014

	Time Charges	Material Loading Charges
Shop employees' wages and benefits	$108,000	—
Parts manager's salary and benefits	—	$25,400
Office employee's salary and benefits	23,500	13,600
Overhead (supplies, depreciation, advertising, utilities)	26,000	16,000
Total budgeted costs	$157,500	$55,000

Jose's budgets 5,000 hours of repair time in 2014 and will bill a profit of $5 per labor hour along with a 30% profit markup on the invoice cost of parts. The estimated invoice cost for parts to be used is $100,000.

On January 5, 2014, Jose's is asked to submit a price estimate to fix a 72-inch flat-screen TV. Jose's estimates that this job will consume 5 hours of labor and $200 in parts.

Instructions
(a) Compute the labor rate for Jose's Electronic Repair Shop for the year 2014.
(b) Compute the material loading charge percentage for Jose's Electronic Repair Shop for the year 2014.
(c) Prepare a time-and-material price quotation for fixing the flat-screen TV.

(c) $1,655

P8-4A Word Wizard is a publishing company with a number of different book lines. Each line has contracts with a number of different authors. The company also owns a printing operation called Quick Press. The book lines and the printing operation each operate as a separate profit center. The printing operation earns revenue by printing books by authors under contract with the book lines owned by Word Wizard, as well as authors under contract with other companies. The printing operation bills out at $0.01 per page, and a typical book requires 500 pages of print. A manager from Business Books, one of the Word Wizard's book lines, has approached the manager of the printing operation offering to pay $0.007 per page for 1,500 copies of a 500-page book. The book line pays outside printers $0.009 per page. The printing operation's variable cost per page is $0.004.

Determine minimum transfer price with no excess capacity and with excess capacity.

(LO 4), AP

Instructions
Determine whether the printing should be done internally or externally, and the appropriate transfer price, under each of the following situations.

(a) Assume that the printing operation is booked solid for the next 2 years, and it would have to cancel an obligation with an outside customer in order to meet the needs of the internal division.

(b) Assume that the printing operation has available capacity.

(c) ◼▭▭▭▷ The top management of Word Wizard believes that the printing operation should always do the printing for the company's authors. On a number of occasions, it has forced the printing operation to cancel jobs with outside customers in order to meet the needs of its own lines. Discuss the pros and cons of this approach.

(d) Loss to company ($750)

(d) Calculate the change in contribution margin to each division, and to the company as a whole, if top management forces the printing operation to accept the $0.007 per page transfer price when it has no available capacity.

Determine minimum transfer price with no excess capacity.

(LO 4), AP

P8-5A Watts Company makes various electronic products. The company is divided into a number of autonomous divisions that can either sell to internal units or sell externally. All divisions are located in buildings on the same piece of property. The Board Division has offered the Chip Division $20 per unit to supply it with chips for 30,000 boards. It has been purchasing these chips for $22 per unit from outside suppliers. The Chip Division receives $22.50 per unit for sales made to outside customers on this type of chip. The variable cost of chips sold externally by the Chip Division is $14.50. It estimates that it will save $4.50 per chip of selling expenses on units sold internally to the Board Division. The Chip Division has no excess capacity.

Instructions

(a) Calculate the minimum transfer price that the Chip Division should accept. Discuss whether it is in the Chip Division's best interest to accept the offer.

(b) Total loss to company $120,000

(b) Suppose that the Chip Division decides to reject the offer. What are the financial implications for each division, and for the company as a whole, of this decision?

Determine minimum transfer price under different situations.

(LO 4), AP

P8-6A Comm Devices (CD) is a division of Worldwide Communications, Inc. CD produces pagers and other personal communication devices. These devices are sold to other Worldwide divisions, as well as to other communication companies. CD was recently approached by the manager of the Personal Communications Division regarding a request to make a special pager designed to receive signals from anywhere in the world. The Personal Communications Division has requested that CD produce 12,000 units of this special pager. The following facts are available regarding the Comm Devices Division.

Selling price of standard pager	$95
Variable cost of standard pager	$50
Additional variable cost of special pager	$30

Instructions

For each of the following independent situations, calculate the minimum transfer price, and discuss whether the internal transfer should take place or whether the Personal Communications Division should purchase the pager externally.

(a) The Personal Communications Division has offered to pay the CD Division $105 per pager. The CD Division has no available capacity. The CD Division would have to forgo sales of 10,000 pagers to existing customers in order to meet the request of the Personal Communications Division.

(b) Minimum price $140

(b) The Personal Communications Division has offered to pay the CD Division $150 per pager. The CD Division has no available capacity. The CD Division would have to forego sales of 16,000 pagers to existing customers in order to meet the request of the Personal Communications Division.

(c) The Personal Communications Division has offered to pay the CD Division $100 per pager. The CD Division has available capacity.

Compute the target price using absorption-cost pricing and variable-cost pricing.

(LO 6), AP

*P8-7A Gonzalez Corporation needs to set a target price for its newly designed product EverReady. The following data relate to this new product.

	Per Unit	Total
Direct materials	$20	
Direct labor	$40	
Variable manufacturing overhead	$10	
Fixed manufacturing overhead		$1,200,000
Variable selling and administrative expenses	$ 5	
Fixed selling and administrative expenses		$1,120,000

The costs shown above are based on a budgeted volume of 80,000 units produced and sold each year. Gonzalez uses cost-plus pricing methods to set its target selling price. Because some managers prefer absorption-cost pricing and others prefer variable-cost pricing, the accounting department provides information under both approaches using a markup of 50% on absorption cost and a markup of 70% on variable cost.

Instructions

(a) Compute the target price for one unit of EverReady using absorption-cost pricing.

(b) Compute the target price for one unit of EverReady using variable-cost pricing.

(a) Markup $42.50

(b) Markup $52.50

*P8-8A Anderson Windows Inc. is in the process of setting a target price on its newly designed tinted window. Cost data relating to the window at a budgeted volume of 4,000 units are as follows.

Compute various amounts using absorption-cost pricing and variable-cost pricing.

(LO 6), AP

	Per Unit	Total
Direct materials	$100	
Direct labor	$ 70	
Variable manufacturing overhead	$ 20	
Fixed manufacturing overhead		$120,000
Variable selling and administrative expenses	$ 10	
Fixed selling and administrative expenses		$102,000

Anderson Windows uses cost-plus pricing methods that are designed to provide the company with a 25% ROI on its tinted window line. A total of $1,016,000 in assets is committed to production of the new tinted window.

Instructions

(a) Compute the markup percentage under absorption-cost pricing that will allow Anderson Windows to realize its desired ROI.

(a) 45%

(b) Compute the target price of the window under absorption-cost pricing, and show proof that the desired ROI is realized.

(c) Compute the markup percentage under variable-cost pricing that will allow Anderson Windows to realize its desired ROI. (Round to three decimal places.)

(d) Compute the target price of the window under variable-cost pricing, and show proof that the desired ROI is realized.

(e) ▮▮▮✏▷ Since both absorption-cost pricing and variable-cost pricing produce the same target price and provide the same desired ROI, why do both methods exist? Isn't one method clearly superior to the other?

PROBLEMS: SET B

P8-1B Harrington Corporation needs to set a target price for its newly designed product R2–D2. The following data relate to this new product.

Use cost-plus pricing to determine various amounts.

(LO 2), AP

	Per Unit	Total
Direct materials	$ 8	
Direct labor	$14	
Variable manufacturing overhead	$ 7	
Fixed manufacturing overhead		$2,000,000
Variable selling and administrative expenses	$ 6	
Fixed selling and administrative expenses		$1,200,000

These costs are based on a budgeted volume of 100,000 units produced and sold each year. Harrington uses cost-plus pricing methods to set its target selling price. The markup on total unit cost is 30%.

Instructions

(a) Compute the total variable cost per unit, total fixed cost per unit, and total cost per unit for R2–D2.

(a) Variable cost per unit $35

(b) Compute the desired ROI per unit for R2–D2.

(c) Compute the target selling price for R2–D2.

(d) Compute variable cost per unit, fixed cost per unit, and total cost per unit assuming that 80,000 R2–D2s are sold during the year.

Use cost-plus pricing to determine various amounts.

(LO 2), AP

P8-2B Robo Parts Inc. is in the process of setting a selling price on a new robotics component it has just designed and developed. The following cost estimates for this new component have been provided by the accounting department for a budgeted volume of 100,000 units.

	Per Unit	Total
Direct materials	$30	
Direct labor	$20	
Variable manufacturing overhead	$17	
Fixed manufacturing overhead		$2,500,000
Variable selling and administrative expenses	$ 8	
Fixed selling and administrative expenses		$ 500,000

Robo's management requests that the total cost per unit be used in cost-plus pricing its products. On this particular product, management also directs that the target price be set to provide a 30% return on investment (ROI) on invested assets of $3,000,000.

Instructions

(Round all calculations to two decimal places.)

(a) Compute the markup percentage and target selling price that will allow Robo to earn its desired ROI of 30% on this new component.

(b) Target selling price $123.75

(b) Assuming that the volume is 80,000 units, compute the markup percentage and target selling price that will allow Robo to earn its desired ROI of 30% on this new component.

Use time-and-material pricing to determine bill.

(LO 3), AP

P8-3B Armstrong Bike Repair Shop has budgeted the following time and material for 2014.

Armstrong Bike Repair Shop
Budgeted Costs for the Year 2014

	Time Charges	Material Loading Charges
Shop employees' wages and benefits	$36,000	—
Parts supervisor's salary and benefits	—	$20,000
Office employee's salary and benefits	15,000	10,000
Overhead (supplies, depreciation, advertising, utilities)	19,000	15,000
Total budgeted costs	$70,000	$45,000

Armstrong budgets 2,500 hours of repair time in 2014 and will bill a profit of $5 per labor hour along with a 15% profit markup on the invoice cost of parts. The estimated invoice cost for parts to be used is $75,000.

On January 5, 2014, Armstrong is asked to submit a price estimate to fix a Superior Mountain bike. Armstrong estimates that this job will consume 4 hours of labor and $200 in parts.

Instructions

(a) Compute the labor rate for Armstrong Bike Repair Shop for the year 2014.

(b) Compute the material loading charge percentage for Armstrong Bike Repair Shop for the year 2014.

(c) $482.00

(c) Prepare a time-and-material price quotation for fixing the Superior Mountain bike.

Determine minimum transfer price with no excess capacity and with excess capacity.

(LO 4), AP

P8-4B Deitz is a publishing company with a number of different magazines and other publications. The company also owns a printing operation called Saira Press. The publications and the printing operation each operate as a separate profit center. The printing operation earns revenue by printing magazines and other publications owned by Deitz, as well as publications of other companies. The printing operation bills out at $0.025 per page. A manager from *Winner!*, one of Deitz's magazines, has approached the manager of the printing operation offering to pay $0.016 per page for 20,000 copies of a 64-page magazine. The magazine pays outside printers $0.018 per page. The printing operation's variable cost per page is $0.014.

Instructions

Determine whether the printing should be done internally or externally, and the appropriate transfer price, under each of the following situations.

(a) Assume that the printing operation is booked solid for the next two years, and it would have to cancel an obligation with an outside customer in order to meet the needs of the internal division.

(b) Assume that the printing operation has available capacity.

(c) ▭▭▭▭▷ The top management of Deitz believes that the printing operation should always do the printing for the company's magazines. On a number of occasions, it has forced the printing operation to cancel jobs with outside customers in order to meet the needs of its own publications. Discuss the pros and cons of this approach.

(d) Calculate the change in contribution margin to each division, and to the company as a whole, if top management forces the printing operation to accept the $0.016 per page transfer price when it has no available capacity.

(d) Loss to company $8,960

P8-5B Dolby Ukes makes various types of ukeleles. The company is divided into a number of autonomous divisions that can either sell to internal units or sell externally. All divisions are located in buildings on the same piece of property. The Alto Division has offered the Peg Division $0.26 per peg to supply it with 200,000 pegs. It has been purchasing these pegs for $0.28 per unit from outside suppliers. The Peg Division receives $0.30 per unit for sales made to outside customers on this type of peg. The variable cost of pegs sold externally by the Peg Division is $0.18. It estimates that it will save $0.04 per peg of selling expenses on units sold internally to the Alto Division. The Peg Division has no excess capacity.

Determine minimum transfer price with no excess capacity.

(LO 4), AP

Instructions

(a) Calculate the minimum transfer price that the Peg Division should accept. Discuss whether it is in the Peg Division's best interest to accept the offer.

(b) Suppose that the Peg Division decides to reject the offer. What are the financial implications for each division, and for the company as a whole, of this decision?

(b) Total loss to company $4,000

P8-6B Innovative Systems (IS) is a division of Global Electronics, Inc. IS produces video-game systems. These systems are sold to retailers. IS recently approached the manager of the Laptop Computer Division regarding a request to buy a special circuit board for a new advanced video game system. IS has requested that the laptop computer division produce 200,000 units of this special circuit board. The following facts are available regarding the Laptop (LT) Division.

Determine minimum transfer price under different situations.

(LO 4), AP

Selling price of standard circuit board	$54
Variable cost of standard circuit board	30
Additional variable cost of special circuit board	20

Instructions

For each of the following independent situations, calculate the minimum transfer price, and discuss whether the internal transfer should take place or whether IS should purchase the circuit board externally.

(a) IS has offered to pay the LT Division $62 per circuit board. The LT Division has no available capacity. The LT Division would have to forgo sales of 200,000 circuit boards to existing customers in order to meet the request of IS.

(b) IS has offered to pay the LT Division $90 per circuit board. The LT Division has no available capacity. The LT Division would have to forgo sales of 250,000 circuit boards to existing customers in order to meet the request of IS.

(b) Minimum price $80

(c) IS has offered to pay the LT Division $62 per circuit board. The LT Division has available capacity.

*P8-7B Zelmer Corporation needs to set a target price for its newly designed product QB-14. The following data relate to this new product.

Compute the target price using absorption-cost and variable-cost pricing.

(LO 6), AP

	Per Unit	Total
Direct materials	$50	
Direct labor	$30	
Variable manufacturing overhead	$13	
Fixed manufacturing overhead		$8,000,000
Variable selling and administrative expenses	$ 7	
Fixed selling and administrative expenses		$2,000,000

The costs above are based on a budgeted volume of 250,000 units produced and sold each year. Zelmer uses cost-plus pricing methods to set its target selling price. Because some managers prefer absorption-cost pricing and others prefer variable-cost pricing, the accounting department provides information under both approaches using a markup of 60% on unit manufacturing cost and a markup of 100% on variable cost.

Instructions

(a) Markup $75

(b) Markup $100

(a) Compute the target price for one unit of QB-14 using absorption-cost pricing.

(b) Compute the target price for one unit of QB-14 using variable-cost pricing.

Compute various amounts using absorption-cost pricing and variable-cost pricing.

(LO 6), AP

*P8-8B Georgia Gould Bikes Inc. is in the process of setting a target price on its newly designed mountain bike. Cost data relating to the bike at a budgeted volume of 20,000 units are as follows.

	Per Unit	Total
Direct materials	$200	
Direct labor	$100	
Variable manufacturing overhead	$ 30	
Fixed manufacturing overhead		$1,400,000
Variable selling and administrative expenses	$ 20	
Fixed selling and administrative expenses		$ 200,000

Georgia Gould Bikes uses cost-plus pricing methods that are designed to provide the company with a 25% ROI on its mountain bike line. A total of $20,000,000 in assets is committed to production of the new mountain bike.

Instructions

(a) 70%

(a) Compute the markup percentage under absorption-cost pricing that will allow Georgia Gould Bikes to realize its desired ROI.

(b) Compute the target price of the bike under absorption-cost pricing, and show proof that the desired ROI is realized.

(c) Compute the markup percentage under variable-cost pricing that will allow Georgia Gould Bikes to realize its desired ROI. (Round to three decimal places.)

(d) Compute the target price of the bike under variable-cost pricing, and show proof that the desired ROI is realized. (Round to nearest dollar.)

(e) Since both the absorption-cost pricing and variable-cost pricing produce the same target price and provide the same desired ROI, why do both methods exist? Isn't one method clearly superior to the other?

PROBLEMS: SET C

Visit the book's companion website, at **www.wiley.com/college/weygandt**, and choose the Student Companion site to access Problem Set C.

WATERWAYS CONTINUING PROBLEM

(This is a continuation of the Waterways Problem from Chapters 1–7.)

WCP8 Waterways Corporation competes in a market economy in which its products must be sold at market prices. Its emphasis is therefore on manufacturing its products at a cost that allows the company to earn its desired profit. This problem asks you to consider various pricing situations for Waterways' projects.

Go to the book's companion website, **www.wiley.com/college/weygandt**, *to find the remainder of this problem.*

Broadening Your PERSPECTIVE

Management Decision-Making

Decision-Making at Current Designs

BYP8-1 As a service to its customers, Current Designs repairs damaged kayaks. This is especially valuable to customers that have made a significant investment in the composite kayaks. To price the repair jobs, Current Designs uses time-and-material pricing with a desired profit margin of $20 per labor hour and a 50% materials loading charge.

Recently, Bill Johnson, Vice President of Sales and Marketing, received a phone call from a dealer in Brainerd, Minnesota. The dealer has a customer who recently damaged his composite kayak and would like an estimate of the cost to repair it. After the dealer emailed pictures of the damage, Bill reviewed the pictures with the repair technician and determined that the total materials charges for the repair would be $100. Bill estimates that the job will take 3 labor hours to complete. Following is the budgeted cost data for Current Designs:

Repair technician wages	$30,000
Fringe benefits	$10,000
Overhead	$10,000

Current Designs has allocated 2,000 hours of repair time for the upcoming year. The customer has agreed to transport the kayak to the Winona production facility for the repairs.

Instructions
Determine the price that Current Designs would charge to complete the repairs for the customer.

Decision-Making Across the Organization

BYP8-2 Lanier Manufacturing has multiple divisions that make a wide variety of products. Recently, the Bearing Division and the Wheel Division got into an argument over a transfer price. The Wheel Division needed bearings for garden tractor wheels. It normally buys its bearings from an outside supplier for $25 per set. The company's top management recently initiated a campaign to persuade the different divisions to buy their materials from within the company whenever possible. As a result, Hank Sherril, the purchasing manager for the Wheel Division, received a letter from the vice president of Purchasing, ordering him to contact the Bearing Division to discuss buying bearings from this division.

To comply with this request, Hank from the Wheel Division called Mary Plimpton of the Bearing Division, and asked the price for 15,000 bearings. Mary responded that the bearings normally sell for $36 per set. However, Mary noted that the Bearing Division would save $3 on marketing costs by selling internally, and would pass this cost savings on to the Wheel Division. She further commented that they were at full capacity, and therefore would not be able to provide any bearings presently. In the future, if they had available capacity, they would be happy to provide bearings.

Hank responded indignantly, "Thanks but no thanks." He said, "We can get all the bearings we need from Falk Manufacturing for $24 per set." Mary snorted back, "Falk makes junk. It costs us $22 per set just to make our bearings. Our bearings can withstand heat of 2,000 degrees centigrade, and are good to within .00001 centimeters. If you guys are happy buying junk, then go ahead and buy from Falk."

Two weeks later, Hank's boss from the central office stopped in to find out whether he had placed an order with the Bearing Division. Hank responded that he would sooner buy his bearings from his worst enemy than from the Bearing Division.

Instructions
With the class divided into groups, prepare answers to the following questions.

(a) Why might the company's top management want the divisions to start doing more business with one another?

(b) Under what conditions should a buying division be forced to buy from an internal supplier? Under what conditions should a selling division be forced to sell to an internal division rather than to an outside customer?

(c) The vice president of Purchasing thinks that this problem should be resolved by forcing the Bearing Division to sell to the Wheel Division at its cost of $22. Is this a good solution for the Wheel Division? Is this a good solution for the Bearing Division? Is this a good solution for the company?

(d) Provide at least two other possible solutions to this problem. Discuss the merits and drawbacks of each.

Managerial Analysis

BYP8-3 Construction on the Bonita Full-Service Car Wash is nearing completion. The owner is Dave Kear, a retired accounting professor. The car wash is strategically located on a busy street that separates an affluent suburban community from a middle-class community. It has two state-of-the-art stalls. Each stall can provide anything from a basic two-stage wash and rinse to a five-stage luxurious bath. It is all "touchless," that is, there are no brushes to potentially damage the car. Outside each stall, there is also a 400 horse-power vacuum. Dave likes to joke that these vacuums are so strong that they will pull the carpet right out of your car if you aren't careful.

Dave has some important decisions to make before he can open the car wash. First, he knows that there is one drive-through car wash only a 10-minute drive away. It is attached to a gas station; it charges $5 for a basic wash, and $4 if you also buy at least 8 gallons of gas. It is a "brush"-type wash with rotating brush heads. There is also a self-serve "stand outside your car and spray until you are soaked" car wash a 15-minute drive away from Dave's location. He went over and tried this out. He went through $3 in quarters to get the equivalent of a basic wash. He knows that both of these locations always have long lines, which is one reason why he decided to build a new car wash.

Dave is planning to offer three levels of wash service—Basic, Deluxe, and Premium. The Basic is all automated; it requires no direct intervention by employees. The Deluxe is all automated except that at the end an employee will wipe down the car and will put a window treatment on the windshield that reduces glare and allows rainwater to run off more quickly. The Premium level is a "pampered" service. This will include all the services of the Deluxe, plus a special wax after the machine wax, and an employee will vacuum the car, wipe down the entire interior, and wash the inside of the windows. To provide the Premium service, Dave will have to hire a couple of "car wash specialists" to do the additional pampering.

Dave has pulled together the following estimates, based on data he received from the local Chamber of Commerce and information from a trade association.

	Per Unit	Total
Direct materials per Basic wash	$0.30	
Direct materials per Deluxe wash	$0.80	
Direct materials per Premium wash	$1.10	
Direct labor per Basic wash	na	
Direct labor per Deluxe wash	$0.40	
Direct labor per Premium wash	$2.40	
Variable overhead per Basic wash	$0.10	
Variable overhead per Deluxe and Premium washes	$0.20	
Fixed overhead		$117,000
Variable selling and administrative expenses all washes	$0.10	
Fixed selling and administrative expenses		$130,500

The total estimated number of washes of any type is 45,000. Dave has invested assets of $393,750. He would like a return on investment (ROI) of 20%.

Instructions

Answer each of the following questions.

(a) Identify the issues that Dave must consider in deciding on the price of each level of service of his car wash. Also discuss what issues he should consider in deciding on what levels of service to provide.

(b) Dave estimates that of the total 45,000 washes, 20,000 will be Basic, 20,000 will be Deluxe, and 5,000 will be Premium. Calculate the selling price, using cost-plus pricing, that Dave should use for each type of wash to achieve his desired ROI of 20%.

(c) During the first year, instead of selling 45,000 washes, Dave sold 43,000 washes. He was quite accurate in his estimate of first-year sales, but he was way off on the types of washes that he sold. He sold 3,000 Basic, 31,000 Deluxe, and 9,000 Premium. His actual total fixed expenses were as he expected, and his variable cost per unit was as estimated. Calculate Dave's actual net income and his actual ROI. (Round to two decimal places.)

(d) Dave is using a traditional approach to allocate overhead. As a consequence, he is allocating overhead equally to all three types of washes, even though the Basic wash is considerably less complicated and uses very little of the technical capabilities of the machinery. What should Dave do to determine more accurate costs per unit? How will this affect his pricing and, consequently, his sales?

Real-World Focus

BYP8-4 Merck & Co., Inc. is a global, research-driven pharmaceutical company that discovers, develops, manufactures, and markets a broad range of human and animal health products. The following are excerpts from the financial review section of the company's annual report.

Merck & Co., Inc.
Financial Review Section (partial)

In the United States, the Company has been working with private and governmental employers to slow the increase of health care costs.

Outside of the United States, in difficult environments encumbered by government cost containment actions, the Company has worked with payers to help them allocate scarce resources to optimize health care outcomes, limiting potentially detrimental effects of government actions on sales growth.

Several products face expiration of product patents in the near term.

The Company, along with other pharmaceutical manufacturers, received a notice from the Federal Trade Commission (FTC) that it was conducting an investigation into pricing practices.

Instructions
Answer each of the following questions.

(a) In light of the above excerpts from Merck's annual report, discuss some unique pricing issues faced by companies that operate in the pharmaceutical industry.

(b) What are some reasons why the same company often sells identical drugs for dramatically different prices in different countries? How can the same drug used for both humans and animals cost significantly different prices?

(c) Suppose that Merck has just developed a revolutionary new drug. Discuss the steps it would go through in setting a price. Include a discussion of the information it would need to gather, and the issues it would need to consider.

BYP8-5 Shopping "robots" have become very popular on the Web. These are sites that will find the price of a specified product that is listed by retailers on the Web ("e-tailers"). This allows the customer to search for the lowest possible price.

Address: **www.dealtime.com** or go to **www.wiley.com/college/weygandt**

Steps
1. Go to the Web page of DealTime.
2. Under the heading "**Electronics**," click on **DVD players**.
3. Choose one of the models.

Instructions
(a) Write down the name of the retailer and the price of the two lowest-priced units and the two highest-priced units.

(b) As a consumer, what concerns might you have in clicking on the "buy" button?

(c) Why might a consumer want to purchase a unit from a retailer that isn't offering the lowest price?

(d) What implications does the existence of these sites have for retailers?

Critical Thinking

Communication Activity

BYP8-6 Jane Fleming recently graduated from college with a degree in landscape architecture. Her father runs a tree, shrub, and perennial-flower nursery, and her brother has a business delivering topsoil, mulch, and compost. Jane has decided that she would like to start a landscape business. She believes that she can generate a nice profit for herself, while providing an opportunity for both her brother's and father's businesses to grow.

One potential problem that Jane is concerned about is that her father and brother tend to charge the highest prices of any local suppliers for their products. She is hoping that she can demonstrate that it would be in her interest, as well as theirs, for them to sell to her at a discounted price.

Instructions

Write a memo to Jane explaining what information she must gather, and what issues she must consider in working out an arrangement with her father and brother. In your memo, discuss how this situation differs from a "standard" transfer pricing problem, but also how it has many of the characteristics of a transfer pricing problem.

Ethics Case

BYP8-7 Jumbo Airlines operates out of three main "hub" airports in the United States. Recently, Econo Airlines began operating a flight from Reno, Nevada, into Jumbo's Metropolis hub for $190. Jumbo Airlines offers a price of $425 for the same route. The management of Jumbo is not happy about Econo invading its turf. In fact, Jumbo has driven off nearly every other competing airline from its hub, so that today 90% of flights into and out of Metropolis are Jumbo Airline flights. Econo is able to offer a lower fare because its pilots are paid less, it uses older planes, and it has lower overhead costs. Econo has been in business for only 6 months, and it services only two other cities. It expects the Metropolis route to be its most profitable.

Jumbo estimates that it would have to charge $210 just to break even on this flight. It estimates that Econo can break even at a price of $160. Within one day of Econo's entry into the market, Jumbo dropped its price to $140, whereupon Econo matched its price. They both maintained this fare for a period of 9 months, until Econo went out of business. As soon as Econo went out of business, Jumbo raised its fare back to $425.

Instructions
Answer each of the following questions.

(a) Who are the stakeholders in this case?
(b) What are some of the reasons why Econo's break-even point is lower than that of Jumbo?
(c) What are the likely reasons why Jumbo was able to offer this price for this period of time, while Econo couldn't?
(d) What are some of the possible courses of action available to Econo in this situation?
(e) Do you think that this kind of pricing activity is ethical? What are the implications for the stakeholders in this situation?

Considering Your Costs and Benefits

BYP8-8 The January 2011 issue of *Strategic Finance* includes an article by J. Lockhart, A. Taylor, K. Thomas, B. Levetsovitis, and J. Wise entitled "When a Higher Price Pays Off."

Instructions
Read the article and answer the following questions.

(a) Explain what is meant by a "low-cost" supplier versus a "low-priced" supplier.
(b) Clarus Technologies' products are typically priced significantly higher than its competitors' products. How is it able to overcome the initial "sticker shock"?
(c) List the five categories of costs that the authors used to compare the Tornado to competing products. Give examples of specific types of costs in each category.
(d) The article discusses full-cost accounting as developed by the Environmental Protection Agency (EPA). What are the characteristics of this approach, and what implications does the approach used in this article have for corporate social responsibility?

Answers to Chapter Questions

Answers to Insight and Accounting Across the Organization Questions

p. 335 The Only Game in Town? Q: Do the substantially different prices that Apple and Google charge for a similar service reflect different costs incurred by each company, or is the price difference due to something else? **A:** While it is possible that the companies incur different costs to provide this service, that would not explain this huge price difference. Instead, Apple apparently felt that its commanding lead in terms of the percentage of tablet computer users enabled it to charge a substantial premium for subscription services. On the other hand, Google's decision most likely reflects a strategic decision to try to grow its market share by providing a substantially lower price.

p. 336 Wal-Mart Says the Price Is Too High Q: What are some issues that Levi Strauss should consider in deciding whether it should agree to meet Wal-Mart's target price? **A:** Levi may be tempted to reduce the quality of its product, or it may be forced to move more of its operations to low-wage suppliers. A big concern is that other retailers may complain that Levi is selling its jeans to Wal-Mart at a price that is lower than they receive. Also, customers may no longer be willing to pay for Levi's other models of higher-priced jeans that it sells in other stores because they can get the low-price jeans (those with the lower gross margin) at Wal-Mart. All of these are issues that a manufacturer must consider in deciding whether to be a supplier to Wal-Mart.

p. 340 At Least It Was Simple Q: What kind of help might the sales staff need in implementing this new approach? **A:** Many customers might object to the price increases, and some might even threaten to buy a competing product. The company needed to provide the sales staff with justifications for the product. For example, salespeople needed evidence to demonstrate that the superior quality of the product justified the higher price.

p. 344 It Ain't Like It Used to Be Q: What implications does this have for a service company's need for managerial accounting? **A:** When service companies billed by the hour, they were better able to ensure their profitability because labor hours is their primary cost. But when billing schemes become performance-based, the company cannot be assured that the bill will cover its hourly costs. As a consequence, companies will need to be far more accurate in their estimates of the likelihood of achieving desired outcomes, or their costs may well exceed their revenues.

p. 352 Transferring Profits and Reducing Taxes Q: What are the implications for other taxpayers if companies reduce their taxes by using improper transfer prices to shift profits to lower-tax countries? **A:** If companies reduce their taxes by using improper transfer prices, then more of the tax burden will fall on law-abiding companies or on individual taxpayers. As countries such as Ireland, for example, have drawn increased foreign investment by non-Irish companies, many other European countries have complained that Ireland is using unfair tax incentives. Many countries are beginning to scrutinize the transfer pricing practices of multinational companies more closely in order to reduce cheating and increase tax revenues.

Answers to Self-Test Questions

1. c   **2.** b ($80 − $15)   **3.** c   **4.** b   **5.** b [(.10 × $500,000) ÷ 1,000]/$25; $25 + $50   **6.** c ($10 ÷ $30)   **7.** a $10 + [$100,000 + .5(40,000) + .5(80,000)] ÷ 5,000   **8.** d   **9.** d ($70 − $30) + $30   **10.** b   **11.** c   **12.** b   **13.** b   ***14.** b [$15 + ($8 + 12)] ÷ ($40 + $30)   ***15.** d [$15 + ($30 + $12)] ÷ ($40 + $8)

✔ Remember to go back to The Navigator box on the chapter opening page and check off your completed work.

Chapter 9

Budgetary Planning

Was This the Next Amazon.com? Not Quite

So you came up with a great idea for a product. You started a company, and you are selling stuff so fast that you can barely keep up. No problem, right? However, without proper planning and budgeting, your success could be short-lived. In some cases, failure is actually brought on by rapid, uncontrolled growth.

One such example was online discount bookseller, www.Positively-You.com. One of the website's co-founders, Lyle Bowline, had never run a business. However, his experience as an assistant director of an entrepreneurial center had provided him with knowledge about the do's and don'ts of small business. To minimize costs, he started the company small and simple. He invested $5,000 in computer equipment and ran the business out of his basement. In the early months, even though sales were only about $2,000 a month, the company actually made a profit because it kept its costs low (a feat few other dot-coms could boast of).

Things changed dramatically when the company received national publicity in the financial press. Suddenly, the company's sales increased to $50,000 a month—fully 25 times the previous level. The "simple" little business suddenly needed a business plan, a strategic plan, and a budget. It needed to rent office space and to hire employees.

✔ The Navigator

- ☐ Scan Learning Objectives

- ☐ Read Feature Story

- ☐ Scan Preview

- ☐ Read Text and answer **DO IT!** p. 388
  - ☐ p. 391 ☐ p. 393 ☐ p. 398 ☐ p. 404

- ☐ Work Using the Decision Toolkit p. 406

- ☐ Review Summary of Learning Objectives

- ☐ Work Comprehensive **DO IT!** **1** p. 409
  - ☐ **2** p. 411

- ☐ Answer Self-Test Questions

- ☐ Complete Assignments

- ☐ Go to **WileyPLUS** for practice and tutorials

Learning Objectives

After studying this chapter, you should be able to:

1 Indicate the benefits of budgeting.

2 State the essentials of effective budgeting.

3 Identify the budgets that comprise the master budget.

4 Describe the sources for preparing the budgeted income statement.

5 Explain the principal sections of a cash budget.

6 Indicate the applicability of budgeting in nonmanufacturing companies.

✔ The Navigator

Initially, members of a local book club donated time to help meet the sudden demand. Some put in so much time that eventually the company hired them. Quickly, the number of paid employees ballooned. The sudden growth necessitated detailed planning and budgeting. The need for a proper budget was accentuated by the fact that the company's gross profit was only 16 cents on each dollar of goods sold. This meant that after paying for its inventory, the company had only 16 cents of every dollar to cover its remaining operating costs.

Unfortunately, the company never got things under control. Within a few months, sales had plummeted to $12,000 per month. At this level of sales, the company could not meet the mountain of monthly expenses that it had accumulated in trying to grow. Ironically, the company's sudden success, and the turmoil it created, appears to have been what eventually caused the company to fail.

Watch the Babycakes video in WileyPLUS to learn more about budgetary planning in the real world.

✔ **The Navigator**

Preview of **Chapter 9**

As the Feature Story about Positively-You.com indicates, budgeting is critical to financial well-being. As a student, you budget your study time and your money. Families budget income and expenses. Governmental agencies budget revenues and expenditures. Businesses use budgets in planning and controlling their operations.

Our primary focus in this chapter is budgeting—specifically, how budgeting is used as a *planning tool* by management. Through budgeting, it should be possible for management to maintain enough cash to pay creditors, to have sufficient raw materials to meet production requirements, and to have adequate finished goods to meet expected sales.

The content and organization of Chapter 9 are as follows.

BUDGETARY PLANNING			
Budgeting Basics	**Preparing the Operating Budgets**	**Preparing the Financial Budgets**	**Budgeting in Non-manufacturing Companies**
• Budgeting and accounting • Benefits • Essentials of effective budgeting • Length of budget period • Budgeting process • Budgeting and human behavior • Budgeting and long-range planning • The master budget	• Sales • Production • Direct materials • Direct labor • Manufacturing overhead • Selling and administrative expense • Budgeted income statement	• Cash • Budgeted balance sheet	• Merchandisers • Service • Not-for-profit

✔ **The Navigator**

Budgeting Basics

One of management's major responsibilities is planning. As explained in Chapter 1, **planning** is the process of establishing company-wide objectives. A successful organization makes both long-term and short-term plans. These plans establish the objectives of the company and the proposed way of accomplishing them.

A **budget** is a formal written statement of management's plans for a specified future time period, expressed in financial terms. It represents the primary method of communicating agreed-upon objectives throughout the organization. Once adopted, a budget becomes an important basis for evaluating performance. It promotes efficiency and serves as a deterrent to waste and inefficiency. We consider the role of budgeting as a **control device** in Chapter 10.

Budgeting and Accounting

Accounting information makes major contributions to the budgeting process. From the accounting records, companies can obtain historical data on revenues, costs, and expenses. These data are helpful in formulating future budget goals.

Normally, accountants have the responsibility for presenting management's budgeting goals in financial terms. In this role, they translate management's plans and communicate the budget to employees throughout the company. They prepare periodic budget reports that provide the basis for measuring performance and comparing actual results with planned objectives. The budget itself, and the administration of the budget, however, are entirely management responsibilities.

The Benefits of Budgeting

LEARNING OBJECTIVE 1

Indicate the benefits of budgeting.

The primary benefits of budgeting are:

1. It requires all levels of management to **plan ahead** and to formalize goals on a recurring basis.
2. It provides **definite objectives** for evaluating performance at each level of responsibility.
3. It creates an **early warning system** for potential problems so that management can make changes before things get out of hand.
4. It facilitates the **coordination of activities** within the business. It does this by correlating the goals of each segment with overall company objectives. Thus, the company can integrate production and sales promotion with expected sales.
5. It results in greater **management awareness** of the entity's overall operations and the impact on operations of external factors, such as economic trends.
6. It **motivates personnel** throughout the organization to meet planned objectives.

A budget is an aid to management; it is not a *substitute* for management. A budget cannot operate or enforce itself. Companies can realize the benefits of budgeting only when managers carefully administer budgets.

Essentials of Effective Budgeting

LEARNING OBJECTIVE 2

State the essentials of effective budgeting.

Effective budgeting depends on a **sound organizational structure**. In such a structure, authority and responsibility for all phases of operations are clearly defined. Budgets based on **research and analysis** are more likely to result in realistic goals that will contribute to the growth and profitability of a company. And, the effectiveness of a budget program is directly related to its **acceptance by all levels of management**.

Once adopted, the budget is an important tool for evaluating performance. Managers should systematically and periodically review variations between actual and expected results to determine their cause(s). However, individuals should not be held responsible for variations that are beyond their control.

Length of the Budget Period

The budget period is not necessarily one year in length. **A budget may be prepared for any period of time.** Various factors influence the length of the budget period. These factors include the type of budget, the nature of the organization, the need for periodic appraisal, and prevailing business conditions.

The budget period should be long enough to provide an attainable goal under normal business conditions. Ideally, the time period should minimize the impact of seasonal or cyclical fluctuations. On the other hand, the budget period should not be so long that reliable estimates are impossible.

The **most common budget period is one year**. The annual budget, in turn, is often supplemented by monthly and quarterly budgets. Many companies use **continuous 12-month budgets**. These budgets drop the month just ended and add a future month. One advantage of continuous budgeting is that it keeps management planning a full year ahead.

ACCOUNTING ACROSS THE ORGANIZATION

Businesses Often Feel Too Busy to Plan for the Future

A study by Willard & Shullman Group Ltd. found that fewer than 14% of businesses with less than 500 employees do an annual budget or have a written business plan. For many small businesses, the basic assumption is that, "As long as I sell as much as I can, and keep my employees paid, I'm doing OK." A few small business owners even say that they see no need for budgeting and planning. Most small business owners, though, say that they understand that budgeting and planning are critical for survival and growth. But given the long hours that they already work addressing day-to-day challenges, they also say that they are "just too busy to plan for the future."

? Describe a situation in which a business "sells as much as it can" but cannot "keep its employees paid." (See page 431.)

The Budgeting Process

The development of the budget for the coming year generally starts several months before the end of the current year. The budgeting process usually begins with the collection of data from each organizational unit of the company. Past performance is often the starting point from which future budget goals are formulated.

The budget is developed within the framework of a **sales forecast**. This forecast shows potential sales for the industry and the company's expected share of such sales. Sales forecasting involves a consideration of various factors: (1) general economic conditions, (2) industry trends, (3) market research studies, (4) anticipated advertising and promotion, (5) previous market share, (6) changes in prices, and (7) technological developments. The input of sales personnel and top management is essential to the sales forecast.

In small companies like Positively-You.com, the budgeting process is often informal. In larger companies, a **budget committee** has responsibility for coordinating the preparation of the budget. The committee ordinarily includes the president, treasurer, chief accountant (controller), and management personnel from each of the major areas of the company, such as sales, production, and research. The budget committee serves as a review board where managers can defend their budget goals and requests. Differences are reviewed, modified if necessary, and reconciled. The budget is then put in its final form by the budget committee, approved, and distributed.

Budgeting and Human Behavior

A budget can have a significant impact on human behavior. If done well, it can inspire managers to higher levels of performance. However, if done poorly, budgets can discourage additional effort and pull down the morale of managers. Why do these diverse effects occur? The answer is found in how the budget is developed and administered.

In developing the budget, each level of management should be invited to participate. This "bottom-to-top" approach is referred to as **participative budgeting**. One advantage of participative budgeting is that lower-level managers have more detailed knowledge of their specific area and thus are able to provide more accurate budgetary estimates. Also, when lower-level managers participate in the budgeting process, they are more likely to perceive the resulting budget as fair. The overall goal is to reach agreement on a budget that the managers consider fair and achievable, but which also meets the corporate goals set by top management. When this goal is met, the budget will provide positive motivation for the managers. In contrast, if managers view the budget as unfair and unrealistic, they may feel discouraged and uncommitted to budget goals. The risk of having unrealistic budgets is generally greater when the budget is developed from top management down to lower management than vice versa. Illustration 9-1 graphically displays the flow of budget data from bottom to top under participative budgeting.

Illustration 9-1
Flow of budget data under participative budgeting

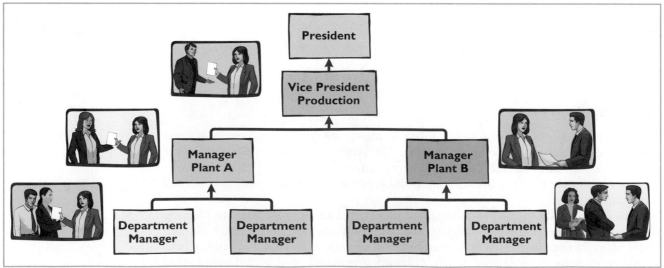

For example, at one time, in an effort to revive its plummeting stock, Time Warner's top management determined and publicly announced bold new financial goals for the coming year. Unfortunately, these goals were not reached. The next year, the company got a new CEO who said the company would now actually set reasonable goals that it could meet. The new budgets were developed with each operating unit setting what it felt were optimistic but attainable goals. In the words of one manager, using this approach created a sense of teamwork.

Participative budgeting does, however, have potential disadvantages. First, the "give and take" of participative budgeting is time-consuming (and thus more costly). Under a "top-down" approach, the budget is simply developed by top management and then dictated to lower-level managers. A second disadvantage is that participative budgeting can foster budgetary "gaming" through budgetary slack. **Budgetary slack** occurs when managers intentionally underestimate budgeted revenues or overestimate budgeted expenses in order to make it easier to achieve budgetary goals. To minimize budgetary slack, higher-level managers must carefully review and thoroughly question the budget projections provided to them by employees whom they supervise.

For the budget to be effective, top management must completely support the budget. The budget is an important basis for evaluating performance. It also can be used as a positive aid in achieving projected goals. The effect of an evaluation is positive when top management tempers criticism with advice and assistance. In contrast, a manager is likely to respond negatively if top management uses the budget exclusively to assess blame. A budget should not be used as a pressure device to force improved performance. In sum, a budget can be a manager's friend or a foe.

> ### Ethics Note
> Unrealistic budgets can lead to unethical employee behavior such as cutting corners on the job or distorting internal financial reports.

Budgeting and Long-Range Planning

Budgeting and long-range planning are not the same. One important difference is the **time period involved**. The maximum length of a budget is usually one year, and budgets are often prepared for shorter periods of time, such as a month or a quarter. In contrast, long-range planning usually encompasses a period of at least five years.

A second significant difference is in **emphasis**. Budgeting focuses on achieving specific short-term goals, such as meeting annual profit objectives. **Long-range planning**, on the other hand, identifies long-term goals, selects strategies to achieve those goals, and develops policies and plans to implement the strategies. In long-range planning, management also considers anticipated trends in the economic and political environment and how the company should cope with them.

The final difference between budgeting and long-range planning relates to the **amount of detail presented**. Budgets, as you will see in this chapter, can be very detailed. Long-range plans contain considerably less detail. The data in long-range plans are intended more for a review of progress toward long-term goals than as a basis of control for achieving specific results. The primary objective of long-range planning is to develop the best strategy to maximize the company's performance over an extended future period.

> **Helpful Hint**
> In comparing a budget with a long-range plan:
> (1) Which has more detail?
> (2) Which is done for a longer period of time?
> (3) Which is more concerned with short-term goals?
> Answers: (1) Budget.
> (2) Long-range plan.
> (3) Budget.

The Master Budget

The term "budget" is actually a shorthand term to describe a variety of budget documents. All of these documents are combined into a master budget. The **master budget** is a set of interrelated budgets that constitutes a plan of action for a specified time period.

The master budget contains two classes of budgets. **Operating budgets** are the individual budgets that result in the preparation of the budgeted income statement.

> **LEARNING OBJECTIVE 3**
>
> **Identify the budgets that comprise the master budget.**

These budgets establish goals for the company's sales and production personnel. In contrast, **financial budgets** focus primarily on the cash resources needed to fund expected operations and planned capital expenditures. Financial budgets include the capital expenditure budget, the cash budget, and the budgeted balance sheet.

Illustration 9-2 pictures the individual budgets included in a master budget, and the sequence in which they are prepared. The company first develops the operating budgets, beginning with the sales budget. Then, it prepares the financial budgets. We will explain and illustrate each budget shown in Illustration 9-2 except the capital expenditure budget. That budget is discussed under the topic of capital budgeting in Chapter 12.

Illustration 9-2
Components of the master budget

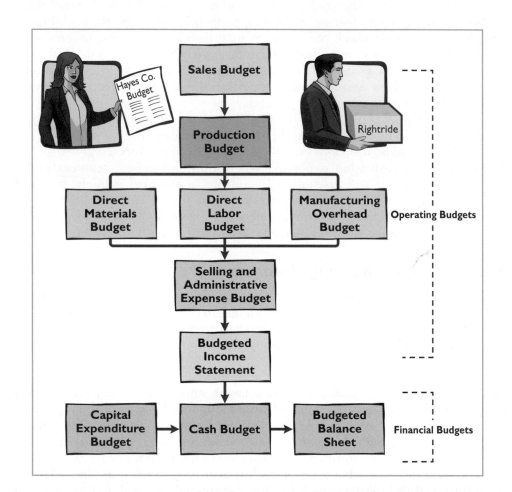

Budget Terminology

Use this list of terms to complete the sentences that follow.

Long-range planning	Participative budgeting
Sales forecast	Operating budgets
Master budget	Financial budgets

1. A _____ shows potential sales for the industry and a company's expected share of such sales.

2. _____ are used as the basis for the preparation of the budgeted income statement.

3. The _____ is a set of interrelated budgets that constitutes a plan of action for a specified time period.

Action Plan

✔ Understand the budgeting process, including the importance of the sales forecast.

✔ Understand the difference between an operating budget and a financial budget.

✔ Differentiate budgeting from long-range planning.

✔ Realize that the master budget is a set of inter-related budgets.

4. _____ identifies long-term goals, selects strategies to achieve these goals, and develops policies and plans to implement the strategies.

5. Lower-level managers are more likely to perceive results as fair and achievable under a _____ approach.

6. _____ focus primarily on the cash resources needed to fund expected operations and planned capital expenditures.

Solution

1. Sales forecast.	4. Long-range planning.
2. Operating budgets.	5. Participative budgeting.
3. Master budget.	6. Financial budgets.

Related exercise material: **BE9-1, E9-1, and** **DO IT!** **9-1.**

✔ **The Navigator**

Preparing the Operating Budgets

We use a case study of Hayes Company in preparing the operating budgets. Hayes manufactures and sells a single product, an ergonomically designed bike seat with multiple customizable adjustments, called the Rightride. The budgets are prepared by quarters for the year ending December 31, 2014. Hayes Company begins its annual budgeting process on September 1, 2013, and it completes the budget for 2014 by December 1, 2013.

Sales Budget

As shown in the master budget in Illustration 9-2, **the sales budget is prepared first**. Each of the other budgets depends on the sales budget. The **sales budget** is derived from the sales forecast. It represents management's best estimate of sales revenue for the budget period. An inaccurate sales budget may adversely affect net income. For example, an overly optimistic sales budget may result in excessive inventories that may have to be sold at reduced prices. In contrast, an unduly pessimistic sales budget may result in loss of sales revenue due to inventory shortages.

For example, at one time Amazon.com significantly underestimated demand for its e-book reader, the Kindle. As a consequence, it did not produce enough Kindles and was completely sold out well before the holiday shopping season. Not only did this represent a huge lost opportunity for Amazon.com, but it exposed it to potential competitors, who were eager to provide customers with alternatives to the Kindle.

Forecasting sales is challenging. For example, consider the forecasting challenges faced by major sports arenas, whose revenues depend on the success of the home team. Madison Square Garden's revenues from April to June were $193 million during a year when the Knicks made the NBA playoffs. But revenues were only $133.2 million a couple of years later when the team did not make the playoffs. Or, consider the challenges faced by Hollywood movie producers in predicting the complicated revenue stream produced by a new movie. Movie theater ticket sales represent only 20% of total revenue. The bulk of revenue comes from global sales, DVDs, video-on-demand, merchandising products, and videogames, all of which are difficult to forecast.

The sales budget is prepared by multiplying the expected unit sales volume for each product by its anticipated unit selling price. Hayes Company expects sales volume to be 3,000 units in the first quarter, with 500-unit increases in each succeeding quarter. Illustration 9-3 (page 390) shows the sales budget for the year, by quarter, based on a sales price of $60 per unit.

Helpful Hint

For a retail or manufacturing company, what is the starting point in preparing the master budget, and why? Answer: The sales budget is the starting point for the master budget. It sets the level of activity for other functions such as production and purchasing.

Illustration 9-3
Sales budget

Hayes Company Sales Budget.xls
Home   Insert   Page Layout   Formulas   Data   Review   View
P18   *fx*

	A	B	C	D	E	F
1			Hayes Company			
2			Sales Budget			
3			For the Year Ending December 31, 2014			
4				Quarter		
5		1	2	3	4	Year
6	Expected unit sales	3,000	3,500	4,000	4,500	15,000
7	Unit selling price	× $60	× $60	× $60	× $60	× $60
8	Total sales	$180,000	$210,000	$240,000	$270,000	$900,000

Some companies classify the anticipated sales revenue as cash or credit sales and by geographical regions, territories, or salespersons.

SERVICE COMPANY INSIGHT

The Implications of Budgetary Optimism

Companies aren't the only ones that have to estimate revenues. Governments at all levels (e.g., local, state or federal) prepare annual budgets. Most are required to submit balanced budgets, that is, estimated revenues are supposed to cover anticipated expenditures. Unfortunately, estimating government revenues can be as difficult as, or even more difficult than, estimating company revenues. The accuracy of government estimates is most critical during economic downturns. If governments fail to anticipate lower revenues during the planning stage, they then often have to make much larger, more disruptive cuts than would have been originally necessary.

For example, during 2009, the median state government overestimated revenues by 10.2%, with four state governments missing by more than 25%. What makes estimation so difficult for these governments? Most states rely on income taxes, which fluctuate widely with economic gyrations. Some states rely on sales taxes, which are problematic because the laws regarding sales taxes haven't adjusted for the shift from manufacturing to service companies and from brick-and-mortar stores to online sales.

Source: Conor Dougherty, "States Fumble Revenue Forecasts," *Wall Street Journal Online* (March 2, 2011).

? Why is it important that government budgets accurately estimate future revenues during economic downturns? (See page 432.)

Production Budget

The **production budget** shows the number of units of a product to produce to meet anticipated sales demand. Production requirements are determined from the following formula.[1]

Illustration 9-4
Production requirements formula

Budgeted Sales Units	+	Desired Ending Finished Goods Units	−	Beginning Finished Goods Units	=	Required Production Units

A realistic estimate of ending inventory is essential in scheduling production requirements. Excessive inventories in one quarter may lead to cutbacks in

---

[1]This formula ignores any work in process inventories, which are assumed to be nonexistent in Hayes Company.

production and employee layoffs in a subsequent quarter. On the other hand, inadequate inventories may result either in added costs for overtime work or in lost sales. Hayes Company believes it can meet future sales requirements by maintaining an ending inventory equal to 20% of the next quarter's budgeted sales volume. For example, the ending finished goods inventory for the first quarter is 700 units (20% × anticipated second-quarter sales of 3,500 units). Illustration 9-5 shows the production budget.

Units of Finished Goods Inventory

Beg. Inv.	
Required Prod. Units	Sales
End. Inv.	

Hayes Company Production Budget.xls

Home   Insert   Page Layout   Formulas   Data   Review   View

P18   fx

	A	B	C	D	E	F	G	H	I	J
1				**Hayes Company**						
2				**Production Budget**						
3				**For the Year Ending December 31, 2014**						
4					Quarter					
5			1	2		3		4		Year
6	Expected unit sales (Illustration 9-3)		3,000	3,500		4,000		4,500		
7	Add: Desired ending finished goods units^a		700	800		900		1,000 ^b		
8	Total required units		3,700	4,300		4,900		5,500		
9	Less: Beginning finished goods units		600 ^c	700		800		900		
10	**Required production units**		3,100	3,600		4,100		4,600		15,400
11										
12	^a20% of next quarter's sales									
13	^bExpected 2015 first-quarter sales, 5,000 units × 20%									
14	^c20% of estimated first-quarter 2014 sales units									

Units of Finished Goods Inventory

600	
3,100	3,000
700	

Illustration 9-5
Production budget

The production budget, in turn, provides the basis for the budgeted costs for each manufacturing cost element, as explained in the following pages.

> **DO IT!**

Production Budget

Becker Company estimates that 2014 unit sales will be 12,000 in quarter 1, 16,000 in quarter 2, and 20,000 in quarter 3, at a unit selling price of $30. Management desires to have ending finished goods inventory equal to 15% of the next quarter's expected unit sales. Prepare a production budget by quarter for the first six months of 2014.

Solution

Action Plan

✔ Begin with budgeted sales in units.

✔ Add desired ending finished goods inventory.

✔ Subtract beginning finished goods inventory.

		Quarter	Six Months
	1	**2**	
Expected unit sales	12,000	16,000	
Add: Desired ending finished goods	2,400	3,000	
Total required units	14,400	19,000	
Less: Beginning finished goods inventory	1,800	2,400	
Required production units	12,600	16,600	29,200

Becker Company
Production Budget
For the Six Months Ending June 30, 2014

Related exercise material: **BE9-3, E9-4, E9-6, and** **DO IT!** **9-2.**

✔ **The Navigator**

Direct Materials Budget

The **direct materials budget** shows both the quantity and cost of direct materials to be purchased. The quantities of direct materials are derived from the following formula.

Illustration 9-6
Formula for direct materials quantities

Direct Materials Units Required for Production	+	Desired Ending Direct Materials Units	−	Beginning Direct Materials Units	=	Required Direct Materials Units to Be Purchased

Units of Direct Materials

Beg. Inv.	
Direct Materials to Prod.	Direct Materials Required for Prod.
End. Inv.	

After the company determines the number of units to purchase, it can compute the budgeted cost of direct materials to be purchased. It does so by multiplying the required units of direct materials by the anticipated cost per unit.

   The desired ending inventory is again a key component in the budgeting process. For example, inadequate inventories could result in temporary shutdowns of production. Because of its close proximity to suppliers, Hayes Company maintains an ending inventory of raw materials equal to 10% of the next quarter's production requirements. The manufacture of each Rightride requires 2 pounds of raw materials, and the expected cost per pound is $4. Illustration 9-7 shows the direct materials budget. Assume that the desired ending direct materials amount is 1,020 pounds for the fourth quarter of 2014.

Illustration 9-7
Direct materials budget

Units of Direct Materials
(1ˢᵗ Qtr.)

620	
6,300	6,200
720	

Hayes Company Direct Materials Budget.xls

Home   Insert   Page Layout   Formulas   Data   Review   View

P18   fx

Hayes Company
Direct Materials Budget
For the Year Ending December 31, 2014

	Quarter				
	1	2	3	4	Year
Units to be produced (Illustration 9-5)	3,100	3,600	4,100	4,600	
Direct materials per unit	× 2	× 2	× 2	× 2	
Total pounds needed for production	6,200	7,200	8,200	9,200	
Add: Desired ending direct materials (pounds)[a]	720	820	920	1,020	
Total materials required	6,920	8,020	9,120	10,220	
Less: Beginning direct materials (pounds)	620 [b]	720	820	920	
Direct materials purchases	6,300	7,300	8,300	9,300	
Cost per pound	× $4	× $4	× $4	× $4	
Total cost of direct materials purchases	**$25,200**	**$29,200**	**$33,200**	**$37,200**	**$124,800**

[a]10% of next quarter's production requirements
[b]10% of estimated first-quarter pounds needed for production

MANAGEMENT INSIGHT

Betting That Prices Won't Fall

Sometimes things happen that cause managers to reevaluate their normal purchasing patterns. Consider, for example, the predicament that businesses faced when the price of many raw materials recently skyrocketed. Rubber, cotton, oil, corn, wheat, steel, copper, and spices—prices for seemingly everything were going straight up. Anticipating that prices might continue to go up, many managers decided to stockpile much larger quantities of raw materials to avoid paying even higher prices in the future. For example, after cotton prices rose 92%, one manager of a printed T-shirt manufacturer decided to stockpile a huge supply of plain T-shirts in anticipation of additional price increases. While he normally has about 30 boxes of T-shirts in inventory, he purchased 2,500 boxes.

Source: Liam Pleven and Matt Wirz, "Companies Stock Up as Commodities Prices Rise," *Wall Street Journal Online* (February 3, 2011).

? What are the potential downsides of stockpiling a huge amount of raw materials? (See page 432.)

> DO IT!

Master Budget

Action Plan

✔ Know the form and content of the sales budget.

✔ Prepare the sales budget first, as the basis for the other budgets.

✔ Determine the units that must be produced to meet anticipated sales.

✔ Know how to compute the beginning and ending finished goods units.

✔ Determine the materials required to meet production needs.

✔ Know how to compute the beginning and ending direct materials units.

Soriano Company is preparing its master budget for 2014. Relevant data pertaining to its sales, production, and direct materials budgets are as follows.

Sales. Sales for the year are expected to total 1,200,000 units. Quarterly sales, as a percentage of total sales, are 20%, 25%, 30%, and 25%, respectively. The sales price is expected to be $50 per unit for the first three quarters and $55 per unit beginning in the fourth quarter. Sales in the first quarter of 2015 are expected to be 10% higher than the budgeted sales for the first quarter of 2014.

Production. Management desires to maintain the ending finished goods inventories at 25% of the next quarter's budgeted sales volume.

Direct materials. Each unit requires 3 pounds of raw materials at a cost of $5 per pound. Management desires to maintain raw materials inventories at 5% of the next quarter's production requirements. Assume the production requirements for the first quarter of 2015 are 810,000 pounds.

Prepare the sales, production, and direct materials budgets by quarters for 2014.

Solution

🖫 ⤾ ⤿ ⤸ ￬		Soriano Company Sales Budget.xls				
Home	Insert	Page Layout Formulas Data Review View				
P18		*fx*				
	A	B	C	D	E	F
1		**Soriano Company**				
2		Sales Budget				
3		For the Year Ending December 31, 2014				
4				Quarter		
5		1	2	3	4	Year
6	Expected unit sales	240,000	300,000	360,000	300,000	1,200,000
7	Unit selling price	× $50	× $50	× $50	× $55	—
8	Total sales	$12,000,000	$15,000,000	$18,000,000	$16,500,000	$61,500,000

Soriano Company Production Budget.xls

Home   Insert   Page Layout   Formulas   Data   Review   View

P18   fx

Soriano Company
Production Budget
For the Year Ending December 31, 2014

	Quarter				
	1	2	3	4	Year
Expected unit sales	240,000	300,000	360,000	300,000	
Add: Desired ending finished goods units[a]	75,000	90,000	75,000	66,000 [b]	
Total required units	315,000	390,000	435,000	366,000	
Less: Beginning finished goods units	60,000 [c]	75,000	90,000	75,000	
Required production units	**255,000**	**315,000**	**345,000**	**291,000**	**1,206,000**

[a]25% of next quarter's unit sales

[b]Estimated first-quarter 2015 sales units: 240,000 + (240,000 × 10%) = 264,000: 264,000 × 25%

[c]25% of estimated first-quarter 2014 sales units (240,000 × 25%)

Soriano Company Direct Materials Budget.xls

Home   Insert   Page Layout   Formulas   Data   Review   View

P18   fx

Soriano Company
Direct Materials Budget
For the Year Ending December 31, 2014

	Quarter				
	1	2	3	4	Year
Units to be produced	255,000	315,000	345,000	291,000	
Direct materials per unit	× 3	× 3	× 3	× 3	
Total pounds needed for production	765,000	945,000	1,035,000	873,000	
Add: Desired ending direct materials (pounds)	47,250	51,750	43,650	40,500 [a]	
Total materials required	812,250	996,750	1,078,650	913,500	
Less: Beginning direct materials (pounds)	38,250 [b]	47,250	51,750	43,650	
Direct materials purchases	774,000	949,500	1,026,900	869,850	
Cost per pound	× $5	× $5	× $5	× $5	
Total cost of direct materials purchases	**$3,870,000**	**$4,747,500**	**$5,134,500**	**$4,349,250**	**$18,101,250**

[a]Estimated first-quarter 2015 production requirements: 810,000 × 5% = 40,500

[b]5% of estimated first-quarter pounds needed for production

Related exercise material: **BE9-2, BE9-3, BE9-4, E9-2, E9-3, E9-4, E9-5, E9-6, and** DO IT! **9-3.**

✔ **The Navigator**

Direct Labor Budget

Like the direct materials budget, the **direct labor budget** contains the quantity (hours) and cost of direct labor necessary to meet production requirements. The total direct labor cost is derived from the following formula.

Units to Be Produced	×	Direct Labor Time per Unit	×	Direct Labor Cost per Hour	=	Total Direct Labor Cost

Illustration 9-8
Formula for direct labor cost

Direct labor hours are determined from the production budget. At Hayes Company, two hours of direct labor are required to produce each unit of finished goods. The anticipated hourly wage rate is $10. Illustration 9-9 shows these data.

Illustration 9-9
Direct labor budget

Hayes Company Direct Labor Budget.xls

	Home Insert Page Layout Formulas Data Review View

P18	fx

	A	B	C	D	E	F	G	H	I	J
1			**Hayes Company**							
2			**Direct Labor Budget**							
3			**For the Year Ending December 31, 2014**							
4					Quarter					
5			1		2		3		4	Year
6	Units to be produced (Illustration 9-5)		3,100		3,600		4,100		4,600	
7	Direct labor time (hours) per unit		× 2		× 2		× 2		× 2	
8	Total required direct labor hours		6,200		7,200		8,200		9,200	
9	Direct labor cost per hour		× $10		× $10		× $10		× $10	
10	**Total direct labor cost**		**$62,000**		**$72,000**		**$82,000**		**$92,000**	**$308,000**
11										

The direct labor budget is critical in maintaining a labor force that can meet the expected levels of production.

Manufacturing Overhead Budget

The **manufacturing overhead budget** shows the expected manufacturing overhead costs for the budget period. As Illustration 9-10 (page 396) shows, **this budget distinguishes between variable and fixed overhead costs**. Hayes Company expects variable costs to fluctuate with production volume on the basis of the following rates per direct labor hour: indirect materials $1.00, indirect labor $1.40, utilities $0.40, and maintenance $0.20. Thus, for the 6,200 direct labor hours to produce 3,100 units, budgeted indirect materials are $6,200 (6,200 × $1), and budgeted indirect labor is $8,680 (6,200 × $1.40). Hayes also recognizes that some maintenance is fixed. The amounts reported for fixed costs are assumed for our example. The accuracy of budgeted overhead cost estimates can be greatly improved by employing activity-based costing.

Helpful Hint
An important assumption in Illustration 9-9 is that the company can add to and subtract from its work force as needed so that the $10 per hour labor cost applies to a wide range of possible production activity.

Illustration 9-10
Manufacturing overhead
budget

	Hayes Company Manufacturing Overhead Budget.xls					
	Home Insert Page Layout Formulas Data Review View					
	P18					
	A	B	C	D	E	F
1	**Hayes Company**					
2	**Manufacturing Overhead Budget**					
3	**For the Year Ending December 31, 2014**					
4		Quarter				
5		1	2	3	4	Year
6	Variable costs					
7	Indirect materials ($1.00/hour)	$ 6,200	$ 7,200	$ 8,200	$ 9,200	$ 30,800
8	Indirect labor ($1.40/hour)	8,680	10,080	11,480	12,880	43,120
9	Utilities ($0.40/hour)	2,480	2,880	3,280	3,680	12,320
10	Maintenance ($0.20/hour)	1,240	1,440	1,640	1,840	6,160
11	Total variable costs	18,600	21,600	24,600	27,600	92,400
12	Fixed costs					
13	Supervisory salaries	20,000	20,000	20,000	20,000	80,000
14	Depreciation	3,800	3,800	3,800	3,800	15,200
15	Property taxes and insurance	9,000	9,000	9,000	9,000	36,000
16	Maintenance	5,700	5,700	5,700	5,700	22,800
17	Total fixed costs	38,500	38,500	38,500	38,500	154,000
18	**Total manufacturing overhead**	**$57,100**	**$60,100**	**$63,100**	**$66,100**	**$246,400**
19	Direct labor hours (Illustration 9-9)	6,200	7,200	8,200	9,200	30,800
20	Manufacturing overhead rate per direct labor hour ($246,400 ÷ 30,800)					$8
21						

At Hayes Company, overhead is applied to production on the basis of direct labor hours. Thus, as Illustration 9-10 shows, the budgeted annual rate is $8 per hour ($246,400 ÷ 30,800).

Selling and Administrative Expense Budget

Hayes Company combines its operating expenses into one budget, the **selling and administrative expense budget**. This budget projects anticipated selling and administrative expenses for the budget period. This budget (Illustration 9-11) also classifies expenses as either variable or fixed. In this case, the variable expense rates per unit of sales are sales commissions $3 and freight-out $1. Variable expenses per quarter are based on the unit sales from the sales budget (Illustration 9-3, page 390). For example, Hayes expects sales in the first quarter to be 3,000 units. Thus, Sales Commissions Expense is $9,000 (3,000 × $3), and Freight-Out is $3,000 (3,000 × $1). Fixed expenses are based on assumed data.

LEARNING OBJECTIVE   4

Describe the sources for preparing the budgeted income statement.

Budgeted Income Statement

The **budgeted income statement** is the important end-product of the operating budgets. This budget indicates the expected profitability of operations for the budget period. The budgeted income statement provides the basis for evaluating company performance. Budgeted income statements often act as a call to action.

◢	A	B	C	D	E	F

Hayes Company Manufacturing Selling and Administrative Expense Budget.xls

Home   Insert   Page Layout   Formulas   Data   Review   View

P18   fx

	A	B	C	D	E	F
1		**Hayes Company**				
2		**Selling and Administrative Expense Budget**				
3		**For the Year Ending December 31, 2014**				
4				Quarter		
5		1	2	3	4	Year
6	Budgeted sales in units (Illustration 9-3)	3,000	3,500	4,000	4,500	15,000
7	Variable expenses					
8	Sales commissions ($3 per unit)	$ 9,000	$10,500	$12,000	$13,500	$ 45,000
9	Freight-out ($1 per unit)	3,000	3,500	4,000	4,500	15,000
10	Total variable expenses	12,000	14,000	16,000	18,000	60,000
11	Fixed expenses					
12	Advertising	5,000	5,000	5,000	5,000	20,000
13	Sales salaries	15,000	15,000	15,000	15,000	60,000
14	Office salaries	7,500	7,500	7,500	7,500	30,000
15	Depreciation	1,000	1,000	1,000	1,000	4,000
16	Property taxes and insurance	1,500	1,500	1,500	1,500	6,000
17	Total fixed expenses	30,000	30,000	30,000	30,000	120,000
18	Total selling and administrative expenses	$42,000	$44,000	$46,000	$48,000	$180,000
19						

Illustration 9-11
Selling and administrative expense budget

For example, a board member at XM Satellite Radio Holdings felt that budgeted costs were too high relative to budgeted revenues. When management refused to cut its marketing and programming costs, the board member resigned. He felt that without the cuts, the company risked financial crisis.

As you would expect, the budgeted income statement is prepared from the various operating budgets. For example, to find the cost of goods sold, Hayes Company must first determine the total unit cost of producing one Rightride, as follows.

Cost of One Rightride

Cost Element	Illustration	Quantity	Unit Cost	Total
Direct materials	9-7	2 pounds	$ 4.00	$ 8.00
Direct labor	9-9	2 hours	$10.00	20.00
Manufacturing overhead	9-10	2 hours	$ 8.00	16.00
Total unit cost				**$44.00**

Illustration 9-12
Computation of total unit cost

Hayes Company then determines cost of goods sold by multiplying the units sold by the unit cost. Its budgeted cost of goods sold is $660,000 (15,000 × $44). All data for the income statement come from the individual operating budgets except the following: (1) interest expense is expected to be $100, and (2) income taxes are estimated to be $12,000. Illustration 9-13 (page 398) shows the budgeted income statement.

Illustration 9-13
Budgeted income statement

Hayes Company	
Budgeted Income Statement	
For the Year Ending December 31, 2014	
Sales (Illustration 9-3)	$900,000
Cost of goods sold (15,000 × $44)	660,000
Gross profit	240,000
Selling and administrative expenses (Illustration 9-11)	180,000
Income from operations	60,000
Interest expense	100
Income before income taxes	59,900
Income tax expense	12,000
Net income	$ 47,900

DECISION TOOLKIT

DECISION CHECKPOINTS	INFO NEEDED FOR DECISION	TOOL TO USE FOR DECISION	HOW TO EVALUATE RESULTS
Has the company met its targets for sales, production expenses, selling and administrative expenses, and net income?	Sales forecasts, inventory levels, projected materials, labor, overhead, and selling and administrative requirements	Master budget—a set of interrelated budgets including sales, production, materials, labor, overhead, and selling and administrative budgets	Results are favorable if revenues exceed budgeted amounts, or if expenses are less than budgeted amounts.

> DO IT!

Budgeted Income Statement

Soriano Company is preparing its budgeted income statement for 2014. Relevant data pertaining to its sales, production, and direct materials budgets can be found in the DO IT! exercise on page 393.

In addition, Soriano budgets 0.5 hours of direct labor per unit, labor costs at $15 per hour, and manufacturing overhead at $25 per direct labor hour. Its budgeted selling and administrative expenses for 2014 are $12,000,000.

(a) Calculate the budgeted total unit cost. (b) Prepare the budgeted income statement for 2014.

Solution

Action Plan

✔ Recall that total unit cost consists of direct materials, direct labor, and manufacturing overhead.

(a)

Cost Element	Quantity	Unit Cost	Total
Direct materials	3.0 pounds	$ 5	$ 15.00
Direct labor	0.5 hours	$15	7.50
Manufacturing overhead	0.5 hours	$25	12.50
Total unit cost			**$35.00**

Action Plan (cont'd.)

✔ Recall that direct materials costs are included in the direct materials budget.

✔ Know the form and content of the income statement.

✔ Use the total unit sales information from the sales budget to compute annual sales and cost of goods sold.

(b)

Soriano Company
Budgeted Income Statement
For the Year Ending December 31, 2014

Sales (1,200,000 units from sales budget, page 393)	$61,500,000
Cost of goods sold (1,200,000 × $35.00/unit)	42,000,000
Gross profit	19,500,000
Selling and administrative expenses	12,000,000
Net income	$ 7,500,000

Related exercise material: **BE9-8, E9-11, E9-13, and** DO IT! **9-4.**

✔ **The Navigator**

Preparing the Financial Budgets

As shown in Illustration 9-2 (page 388), the financial budgets consist of the capital expenditure budget, the cash budget, and the budgeted balance sheet. We will discuss the capital expenditure budget in Chapter 12. The other budgets are explained in the following sections.

Cash Budget

The **cash budget** shows anticipated cash flows. Because cash is so vital, this budget is often considered to be the most important financial budget.

The cash budget contains three sections (cash receipts, cash disbursements, and financing) and the beginning and ending cash balances, as shown in Illustration 9-14.

LEARNING OBJECTIVE 5

Explain the principal sections of a cash budget.

Any Company
Cash Budget

Beginning cash balance	$X,XXX
Add: Cash receipts (itemized)	X,XXX
Total available cash	X,XXX
Less: Cash disbursements (itemized)	X,XXX
Excess (deficiency) of available cash over cash disbursements	X,XXX
Financing	X,XXX
Ending cash balance	$X,XXX

Illustration 9-14
Basic form of a cash budget

Helpful Hint
Why is the cash budget prepared after the other budgets are prepared? Answer: Because the information generated by the other budgets dictates the expected inflows and outflows of cash.

The **cash receipts section** includes expected receipts from the company's principal source(s) of revenue. These are usually cash sales and collections from customers on credit sales. This section also shows anticipated receipts of interest and dividends, and proceeds from planned sales of investments, plant assets, and the company's capital stock.

The **cash disbursements section** shows expected cash payments. Such payments include direct materials, direct labor, manufacturing overhead, and selling and administrative expenses. This section also includes projected payments for income taxes, dividends, investments, and plant assets.

The **financing section** shows expected borrowings and the repayment of the borrowed funds plus interest. Companies need this section when there is a cash deficiency or when the cash balance is below management's minimum required balance.

Data in the cash budget are prepared in sequence. The ending cash balance of one period becomes the beginning cash balance for the next period. Companies obtain data for preparing the cash budget from other budgets and from information provided by management. In practice, cash budgets are often prepared for the year on a monthly basis.

To minimize detail, we will assume that Hayes Company prepares an annual cash budget by quarters. Its cash budget is based on the following assumptions.

1. The January 1, 2014, cash balance is expected to be $38,000. Hayes wishes to maintain a balance of at least $15,000.

2. Sales (Illustration 9-3, page 390): 60% are collected in the quarter sold and 40% are collected in the following quarter. Accounts receivable of $60,000 at December 31, 2013, are expected to be collected in full in the first quarter of 2014.

3. Short-term investments are expected to be sold for $2,000 cash in the first quarter.

4. Direct materials (Illustration 9-7, page 392): 50% are paid in the quarter purchased and 50% are paid in the following quarter. Accounts payable of $10,600 at December 31, 2013, are expected to be paid in full in the first quarter of 2014.

5. Direct labor (Illustration 9-9, page 395): 100% is paid in the quarter incurred.

6. Manufacturing overhead (Illustration 9-10, page 396) and selling and administrative expenses (Illustration 9-11, page 397): All items except depreciation are paid in the quarter incurred.

7. Management plans to purchase a truck in the second quarter for $10,000 cash.

8. Hayes makes equal quarterly payments of its estimated annual income taxes.

9. Loans are repaid in the earliest quarter in which there is sufficient cash (that is, when the cash on hand exceeds the $15,000 minimum required balance).

In preparing the cash budget, it is useful to prepare schedules for collections from customers (assumption No. 2) and cash payments for direct materials (assumption No. 4). These schedules are shown in Illustrations 9-15 and 9-16.

Illustration 9-15
Collections from customers

		Collections by Quarter			
	Sales[a]	1	2	3	4
Accounts receivable, 12/31/13		$ 60,000			
First quarter	$180,000	108,000[b]	$ 72,000[c]		
Second quarter	210,000		126,000	$ 84,000	
Third quarter	240,000			144,000	$ 96,000
Fourth quarter	270,000				162,000
Total collections		$168,000	$198,000	$228,000	$258,000

Hayes Company
Schedule of Expected Collections from Customers

[a]Per Illustration 9-3; [b]$180,000 × .60; [c]$180,000 × .40

Illustration 9-16
Payments for direct materials

Hayes Company
Schedule of Expected Payments for Direct Materials

		Payments by Quarter			
	Purchases[a]	1	2	3	4
Accounts payable, 12/31/13		$10,600			
First quarter	$25,200	12,600[b]	$12,600[c]		
Second quarter	29,200		14,600	$14,600	
Third quarter	33,200			16,600	$16,600
Fourth quarter	37,200				18,600
Total payments		$23,200	$27,200	$31,200	$35,200

[a]Per Illustration 9-7; [b]$25,200 × .50; [c]$25,200 × .50

Illustration 9-17 shows the cash budget for Hayes Company. The budget indicates that Hayes will need $3,000 of financing in the second quarter to maintain a minimum cash balance of $15,000. Since there is an excess of available cash over disbursements of $22,500 at the end of the third quarter, the borrowing, plus $100 interest, is repaid in this quarter.

Illustration 9-17
Cash budget

Hayes Company Cash Budget.xls

Home   Insert   Page Layout   Formulas   Data   Review   View

P18

	A	B	C	D	E	F	G	H	I	J
1			Hayes Company							
2			Cash Budget							
3			For the Year Ending December 31, 2014							
4							Quarter			
5		Assumption	1		2		3		4	
6	Beginning cash balance	1	$ 38,000		$ 25,500		$ 15,000		$ 19,400	
7	**Add: Receipts**									
8	Collections from customers	2	168,000		198,000		228,000		258,000	
9	Sale of securities	3	2,000		0		0		0	
10	Total receipts		170,000		198,000		228,000		258,000	
11	Total available cash		208,000		223,500		243,000		277,400	
12	**Less: Disbursements**									
13	Direct materials	4	23,200		27,200		31,200		35,200	
14	Direct labor	5	62,000		72,000		82,000		92,000	
15	Manufacturing overhead	6	53,300	[a]	56,300		59,300		62,300	
16	Selling and administrative expenses	6	41,000	[b]	43,000		45,000		47,000	
17	Purchase of truck	7	0		10,000		0		0	
18	Income tax expense	8	3,000		3,000		3,000		3,000	
19	Total disbursements		182,500		211,500		220,500		239,500	
20	Excess (deficiency) of available cash over cash disbursements		25,500		12,000		22,500		37,900	
21	**Financing**									
22	Add: Borrowings		0		**3,000**		0		0	
23	Less: Repayments including interest	9	0		0		**3,100**		0	
24	Ending cash balance		$ 25,500		$ 15,000		$ 19,400		$ 37,900	
25										
26	[a]$57,100 − $3,800 depreciation									
27	[b]$42,000 − $1,000 depreciation									

A cash budget contributes to more effective cash management. It shows managers when additional financing is necessary well before the actual need arises. And, it indicates when excess cash is available for investments or other purposes.

DECISION TOOLKIT

DECISION CHECKPOINTS	INFO NEEDED FOR DECISION	TOOL TO USE FOR DECISION	HOW TO EVALUATE RESULTS
Is the company going to need to borrow funds in the coming quarter?	Beginning cash balance, cash receipts, cash disbursements, and desired cash balance	Cash budget	The company will need to borrow money if the cash budget indicates a projected cash deficiency of available cash over cash disbursements for the quarter.

Budgeted Balance Sheet

The **budgeted balance sheet** is a projection of financial position at the end of the budget period. This budget is developed from the budgeted balance sheet for the preceding year and the budgets for the current year. Pertinent data from the budgeted balance sheet at December 31, 2013, are as follows.

Buildings and equipment	$182,000	Common stock	$225,000
Accumulated depreciation	$ 28,800	Retained earnings	$ 46,480

Illustration 9-18 shows Hayes Company's budgeted balance sheet at December 31, 2014.

Illustration 9-18
Budgeted balance sheet

Hayes Company
Budgeted Balance Sheet
December 31, 2014

Assets

Cash		$ 37,900
Accounts receivable		108,000
Finished goods inventory		44,000
Raw materials inventory		4,080
Buildings and equipment	$192,000	
Less: Accumulated depreciation	48,000	144,000
Total assets		$337,980

Liabilities and Stockholders' Equity

Accounts payable		$ 18,600
Common stock		225,000
Retained earnings		94,380
Total liabilities and stockholders' equity		$337,980

The computations and sources of the amounts are explained below.

Cash: Ending cash balance $37,900, shown in the cash budget (Illustration 9-17, page 401).

Accounts receivable: 40% of fourth-quarter sales $270,000, shown in the schedule of expected collections from customers (Illustration 9-15, page 400).

Finished goods inventory: Desired ending inventory 1,000 units, shown in the production budget (Illustration 9-5, page 391) times the total unit cost $44 (shown in Illustration 9-12, page 397).

Raw materials inventory: Desired ending inventory 1,020 pounds, times the cost per pound $4, shown in the direct materials budget (Illustration 9-7, page 392).

Buildings and equipment: December 31, 2013, balance $182,000, plus purchase of truck for $10,000 (Illustration 9-17, page 401).

Accumulated depreciation: December 31, 2013, balance $28,800, plus $15,200 depreciation shown in manufacturing overhead budget (Illustration 9-10, page 396) and $4,000 depreciation shown in selling and administrative expense budget (Illustration 9-11, page 397).

Accounts payable: 50% of fourth-quarter purchases $37,200, shown in schedule of expected payments for direct materials (Illustration 9-16, page 401).

Common stock: Unchanged from the beginning of the year.

Retained earnings: December 31, 2013, balance $46,480, plus net income $47,900, shown in budgeted income statement (Illustration 9-13, page 398).

After budget data are entered into the computer, Hayes prepares the various budgets (sales, cash, etc.), as well as the budgeted financial statements. Using spreadsheets, management can also perform "what if" (sensitivity) analyses based on different hypothetical assumptions. For example, suppose that sales managers project that sales will be 10% higher in the coming quarter. What impact does this change have on the rest of the budgeting process and the financing needs of the business? The impact of the various assumptions on the budget is quickly determined by the spreadsheet. Armed with these analyses, managers make more informed decisions about the impact of various projects. They also anticipate future problems and business opportunities. As seen in this chapter, budgeting is an excellent use of electronic spreadsheets.

> ## DO IT!

Cash Budget

Martian Company management wants to maintain a minimum monthly cash balance of $15,000. At the beginning of March, the cash balance is $16,500, expected cash receipts for March are $210,000, and cash disbursements are expected to be $220,000. How much cash, if any, must be borrowed to maintain the desired minimum monthly balance?

Solution

Action Plan

✔ Write down the basic form of the cash budget, starting with the beginning cash balance, adding cash receipts for the period, deducting cash disbursements, and identifying the needed financing to achieve the desired minimum ending cash balance.

✔ Insert the data given into the outlined form of the cash budget.

Martian Company
Cash Budget
For the Month Ending March 31, 2014

Beginning cash balance	$ 16,500
Add: Cash receipts for March	210,000
Total available cash	226,500
Less: Cash disbursements for March	220,000
Excess of available cash over cash disbursements	6,500
Financing	8,500
Ending cash balance	$ 15,000

To maintain the desired minimum cash balance of $15,000, Martian Company must borrow $8,500 of cash.

Related exercise material: **BE9-9, E9-13, E9-14, E9-15, E9-16, and DO IT! 9-5.**

✔ **The Navigator**

Budgeting in Nonmanufacturing Companies

Budgeting is not limited to manufacturers. Budgets are also used by merchandisers, service companies, and not-for-profit organizations.

Merchandisers

As in manufacturing operations, the sales budget for a merchandiser is both the starting point and the key factor in the development of the master budget. The major differences between the master budgets of a merchandiser and a manufacturer are these:

1. A merchandiser **uses a merchandise purchases budget instead of a production budget**.

2. A merchandiser **does not use the manufacturing budgets (direct materials, direct labor, and manufacturing overhead)**.

The **merchandise purchases budget** shows the estimated cost of goods to be purchased to meet expected sales. The formula for determining budgeted merchandise purchases is:

Illustration 9-19
Merchandise purchases formula

Budgeted Cost of Goods Sold	+	Desired Ending Merchandise Inventory	−	Beginning Merchandise Inventory	=	Required Merchandise Purchases

To illustrate, assume that the budget committee of Lima Company is preparing the merchandise purchases budget for July 2014. It estimates that budgeted sales will be $300,000 in July and $320,000 in August. Cost of goods sold is expected to be 70% of sales—that is, $210,000 in July (.70 × $300,000) and $224,000 in August (.70 × $320,000). The company's desired ending inventory is 30% of the following month's cost of goods sold. Required merchandise purchases for July are $214,200, computed as follows.

Lima Company
Merchandise Purchases Budget
For the Month Ending July 31, 2014

Budgeted cost of goods sold ($300,000 × 70%)	$ 210,000
Add: Desired ending merchandise inventory ($224,000 × 30%)	67,200
Total	277,200
Less: Beginning merchandise inventory ($210,000 × 30%)	63,000
Required merchandise purchases for July	**$214,200**

When a merchandiser is departmentalized, it prepares separate budgets for each department. For example, a grocery store prepares sales budgets and purchases budgets for each of its major departments, such as meats, dairy, and produce. The store then combines these budgets into a master budget for the store. When a retailer has branch stores, it prepares separate master budgets for each store. Then, it incorporates these budgets into master budgets for the company as a whole.

Departmentalized budgets

Service Companies

In a service company, such as a public accounting firm, a law office, or a medical practice, the critical factor in budgeting is **coordinating professional staff needs with anticipated services**. If a firm is overstaffed, several problems may result: Labor costs are disproportionately high. Profits are lower because of the additional salaries. Staff turnover sometimes increases because of lack of challenging work. In contrast, if a service company is understaffed, it may lose revenue because existing and prospective client needs for service cannot be met. Also, professional staff may seek other jobs because of excessive work loads.

Service companies can obtain budget data for service revenue from **expected output** or **expected input**. When output is used, it is necessary to determine the expected billings of clients for services provided. In a public accounting firm, for example, output is the sum of its billings in auditing, tax, and consulting services. When input data are used, each professional staff member projects his or her billable time. The firm then applies billing rates to billable time to produce expected service revenue.

Not-For-Profit Organizations

Budgeting is just as important for not-for-profit organizations as for profit-oriented businesses. The budget process, however, is different. In most cases, not-for-profit entities budget **on the basis of cash flows (expenditures and receipts), rather than on a revenue and expense basis**. Further, the starting point in the process is usually expenditures, not receipts. For the not-for-profit entity, management's task generally is to find the receipts needed to support the planned expenditures. The activity index is also likely to be significantly different. For example, in a not-for-profit entity, such as a university, budgeted faculty positions may be based on full-time equivalent students or credit hours expected to be taught in a department.

For some governmental units, voters approve the budget. In other cases, such as state governments and the federal government, legislative approval is required.

After the budget is adopted, it must be followed. Overspending is often illegal. In governmental budgets, authorizations tend to be on a line-by-line basis. That is, the budget for a municipality may have a specified authorization for police and fire protection, garbage collection, street paving, and so on. The line-item authorization of governmental budgets significantly limits the amount of discretion management can exercise. The city manager often cannot use savings from one line item, such as street paving, to cover increased spending in another line item, such as snow removal.

SERVICE COMPANY INSIGHT

Budget Shortfalls as Far as the Eye Can See

All organizations need to stick to budgets. The Museum of Contemporary Art in Los Angeles learned this the hard way. Over a 10-year period, its endowment shrunk from $50 million to $6 million as its newly hired director strove to build the museum's reputation through spending. The director consistently ran budget deficits, which eventually threatened the museum's survival.

The most recent recession has created budgeting challenges for nearly all governmental agencies. Tax revenues dropped rapidly as earnings declined and unemployment skyrocketed. At the same time, sources of debt financing dried up. To meet a projected shortfall of nearly $50 billion, California proposed to cut the school year by five days, give state workers two unpaid days off per month, and raise the state's sales tax percentage. Even Princeton University, with the largest endowment per student of any U.S. university ($2 million per student), experienced a 25% drop in the value of its endowment when the financial markets plunged. Because the endowment supports 45% of the university's $1.25 billion budget, when the endowment fell the university had to make cuts. Many raises were capped at $2,000, administrative budgets were cut by 5%, and major construction projects were put on hold.

Source: Edward Wyatt and Jori Finkel, "Soaring in Art, Museum Trips Over Finances," *Wall Street Journal Online* (December 4, 2008); and Stu Woo, "California's Plans to Close Gap Become More Drastic," *Wall Street Journal Online* (January 8, 2009); and John Hechinger, "Princeton Cuts Budget as Endowment Slides," *Wall Street Journal Online* (January 9, 2009).

? Why would a university's budgeted scholarships probably fall when the stock market suffers a serious drop? (See page 432.)

USING THE DECISION TOOLKIT

The University of Wisconsin and its subunits must prepare budgets. One unique subunit of the University of Wisconsin is Babcock Ice Cream, a functioning producer of dairy products (and famous, at least on campus, for its delicious ice cream).

Assume that Babcock Ice Cream prepares monthly cash budgets. Relevant data from assumed operating budgets for 2014 are:

	January	February
Sales	$460,000	$412,000
Direct materials purchases	185,000	210,000
Direct labor	70,000	85,000
Manufacturing overhead	50,000	65,000
Selling and administrative expenses	85,000	95,000

Babcock sells its ice cream in shops on campus, as well as to local stores. Collections are expected to be 75% in the month of sale, and 25% in the month following sale. Babcock pays 60% of direct materials purchases in cash in the month of purchase, and the balance due in the month following the purchase. All other items above are paid in the month incurred. (Depreciation has been excluded from manufacturing overhead and selling and administrative expenses.)

Other data:

(1) Sales: December 2013, $320,000
(2) Purchases of direct materials: December 2013, $175,000
(3) Other receipts: January—Donation received, $2,000
               February—Sale of used equipment, $4,000
(4) Other disbursements: February—Purchased equipment, $10,000
(5) Repaid debt: January, $30,000

The company's cash balance on January 1, 2014, is expected to be $50,000. The company wants to maintain a minimum cash balance of $45,000.

Instructions

(a) Prepare schedules for (1) expected collections from customers and (2) expected payments for direct materials purchases for January and February.
(b) Prepare a cash budget for January and February in columnar form.

Solution

(a) (1)

Expected Collections from Customers

	Sales	January	February
December	$320,000	$ 80,000	$ 0
January	460,000	345,000	115,000
February	412,000	0	309,000
Totals		$425,000	$424,000

(2)

Expected Payments for Direct Materials

	Purchases	January	February
December	$175,000	$ 70,000	$ 0
January	185,000	111,000	74,000
February	210,000	0	126,000
Totals		$181,000	$200,000

(b)

Babcock Ice Cream
Cash Budget
For the Two Months Ending February 28, 2014

	January	February
Beginning cash balance	$ 50,000	$ 61,000
Add: Receipts		
Collections from customers	425,000	424,000
Donations received	2,000	0
Sale of used equipment	0	4,000
Total receipts	427,000	428,000
Total available cash	477,000	489,000
Less: Disbursements		
Direct materials	181,000	200,000
Direct labor	70,000	85,000
Manufacturing overhead	50,000	65,000
Selling and administrative expenses	85,000	95,000
Purchase of equipment	0	10,000
Total disbursements	386,000	455,000
Excess (deficiency) of available cash over cash disbursements	91,000	34,000
Financing		
Add: Borrowings	0	11,000
Less: Repayments	30,000	0
Ending cash balance	$ 61,000	$ 45,000

✔ **The Navigator**

SUMMARY OF LEARNING OBJECTIVES

1 **Indicate the benefits of budgeting.** The primary advantages of budgeting are that it (a) requires management to plan ahead, (b) provides definite objectives for evaluating performance, (c) creates an early warning system for potential problems, (d) facilitates coordination of activities, (e) results in greater management awareness, and (f) motivates personnel to meet planned objectives.

2 **State the essentials of effective budgeting.** The essentials of effective budgeting are (a) sound organizational structure, (b) research and analysis, and (c) acceptance by all levels of management.

3 **Identify the budgets that comprise the master budget.** The master budget consists of the following budgets: (a) sales, (b) production, (c) direct materials, (d) direct labor, (e) manufacturing overhead, (f) selling and administrative expense, (g) budgeted income statement, (h) capital expenditure budget, (i) cash budget, and (j) budgeted balance sheet.

4 **Describe the sources for preparing the budgeted income statement.** The budgeted income statement is prepared from (a) the sales budget; (b) the budgets for direct materials, direct labor, and manufacturing overhead; and (c) the selling and administrative expense budget.

5 **Explain the principal sections of a cash budget.** The cash budget has three sections (receipts, disbursements, and financing) and the beginning and ending cash balances.

6 **Indicate the applicability of budgeting in nonmanufacturing companies.** Budgeting may be used by merchandisers for development of a merchandise purchases budget. In service companies, budgeting is a critical factor in coordinating staff needs with anticipated services. In not-for-profit organizations, the starting point in budgeting is usually expenditures, not receipts.

DECISION TOOLKIT A SUMMARY

DECISION CHECKPOINTS	INFO NEEDED FOR DECISION	TOOL TO USE FOR DECISION	HOW TO EVALUATE RESULTS
Has the company met its targets for sales, production expenses, selling and administrative expenses, and net income?	Sales forecasts, inventory levels, projected materials, labor, overhead, and selling and administrative requirements	Master budget—a set of interrelated budgets including sales, production, materials, labor, overhead, and selling and administrative budgets	Results are favorable if revenues exceed budgeted amounts, or if expenses are less than budgeted amounts.
Is the company going to need to borrow funds in the coming quarter?	Beginning cash balance, cash receipts, cash disbursements, and desired cash balance	Cash budget	The company will need to borrow money if the cash budget indicates a projected cash deficiency of available cash over cash disbursements for the quarter.

GLOSSARY

Budget A formal written statement of management's plans for a specified future time period, expressed in financial terms. (p. 384).

Budget committee A group responsible for coordinating the preparation of the budget. (p. 386).

Budgetary slack The amount by which a manager intentionally underestimates budgeted revenues or overestimates budgeted expenses in order to make it easier to achieve budgetary goals. (p. 387).

Budgeted balance sheet A projection of financial position at the end of the budget period. (p. 402).

Budgeted income statement An estimate of the expected profitability of operations for the budget period. (p. 396).

Cash budget A projection of anticipated cash flows. (p. 399).

Direct labor budget A projection of the quantity and cost of direct labor necessary to meet production requirements. (p. 395).

Direct materials budget An estimate of the quantity and cost of direct materials to be purchased. (p. 392).

Financial budgets Individual budgets that focus primarily on the cash resources needed to fund expected operations and planned capital expenditures. (p. 388).

Long-range planning A formalized process of identifying long-term goals, selecting strategies to achieve those goals, and developing policies and plans to implement the strategies. (p. 387).

Manufacturing overhead budget An estimate of expected manufacturing overhead costs for the budget period. (p. 395).

Master budget A set of interrelated budgets that constitutes a plan of action for a specific time period. (p. 387).

Merchandise purchases budget The estimated cost of goods to be purchased by a merchandiser to meet expected sales. (p. 404).

Operating budgets Individual budgets that result in a budgeted income statement. (p. 387).

Participative budgeting A budgetary approach that starts with input from lower-level managers and works upward so that managers at all levels participate. (p. 386).

Production budget A projection of the units that must be produced to meet anticipated sales. (p. 390).

Sales budget An estimate of expected sales revenue for the budget period. (p. 389).

Sales forecast The projection of potential sales for the industry and the company's expected share of such sales. (p. 385).

Selling and administrative expense budget A projection of anticipated selling and administrative expenses for the budget period. (p. 396).

> ## Comprehensive DO IT! 1

Barrett Company has completed all operating budgets other than the income statement for 2014. Selected data from these budgets follow.

Sales: $300,000
Purchases of raw materials: $145,000
Ending inventory of raw materials: $15,000
Direct labor: $40,000
Manufacturing overhead: $73,000, including $3,000 of depreciation expense
Selling and administrative expenses: $36,000 including depreciation expense of $1,000
Interest expense: $1,000
Principal payment on note: $2,000
Dividends declared: $2,000
Income tax rate: 30%

Other information:

Assume that the number of units produced equals the number sold.
Year-end accounts receivable: 4% of 2014 sales.
Year-end accounts payable: 50% of ending inventory of raw materials.
Interest, direct labor, manufacturing overhead, and selling and administrative expenses other than depreciation are paid as incurred.
Dividends declared and income taxes for 2014 will not be paid until 2015.

Barrett Company
Balance Sheet
December 31, 2013

Assets

Cash		$20,000
Raw materials inventory		10,000
Equipment	$40,000	
Less: Accumulated depreciation	4,000	36,000
Total assets		$66,000

Liabilities and Stockholders' Equity

Accounts payable	$ 5,000	
Notes payable	22,000	
Total liabilities		$27,000
Common stock	25,000	
Retained earnings	14,000	39,000
Total liabilities and stockholders' equity		$66,000

Instructions

(a) Calculate budgeted cost of goods sold.

(b) Prepare a budgeted income statement for the year ending December 31, 2014.

(c) Prepare a budgeted balance sheet as of December 31, 2014.

Solution to Comprehensive DO IT! 1

Action Plan

✔ Recall that beginning raw materials inventory plus purchases less ending raw materials inventory equals direct materials used.

✔ Prepare the budgeted income statement before the budgeted balance sheet.

✔ Use the standard form of a cash budget to determine cash on the budgeted balance sheet.

✔ Add budgeted depreciation expense to accumulated depreciation at the beginning of the year to determine accumulated depreciation on the budgeted balance sheet.

✔ Add budgeted net income to retained earnings from the beginning of the year and subtract dividends declared to determine retained earnings on the budgeted balance sheet.

✔ Verify that total assets equal total liabilities and stockholders' equity on the budgeted balance sheet.

(a) Beginning raw materials + Purchases − Ending raw materials = Cost of direct materials used ($10,000 + $145,000 − $15,000 = $140,000)

Direct materials used + Direct labor + Manufacturing overhead = Cost of goods sold ($140,000 + $40,000 + $73,000 = $253,000)

(b)

Barrett Company
Budgeted Income Statement
For the Year Ending December 31, 2014

Sales		$300,000
Cost of goods sold		253,000
Gross profit		47,000
Selling and administrative expenses	$36,000	
Interest expense	1,000	37,000
Income before income tax expense		10,000
Income tax expense (30%)		3,000
Net income		$ 7,000

(c)

Barrett Company
Budgeted Balance Sheet
December 31, 2014

Assets

Cash[(1)]		$17,500
Accounts receivable (4% × $300,000)		12,000
Raw materials inventory		15,000
Equipment	$40,000	
Less: Accumulated depreciation	8,000	32,000
Total assets		$76,500

[(1)]Beginning cash balance		$ 20,000
Add: Collections from customers		
(96% × $300,000 sales)		288,000
Total available cash		308,000
Less: Disbursements		
Direct materials ($5,000 + $145,000 − $7,500)	$142,500	
Direct labor	40,000	
Manufacturing overhead	70,000	
Selling and administrative expenses	35,000	
Total disbursements		287,500
Excess of available cash over cash disbursements		20,500
Financing		
Less: Repayment of principal and interest		3,000
Ending cash balance		$ 17,500

Liabilities and Stockholders' Equity

Accounts payable (50% × $15,000)	$ 7,500	
Income taxes payable	3,000	
Dividends payable	2,000	
Note payable	20,000	
Total liabilities		$32,500
Common stock	25,000	
Retained earnings[2]	19,000	44,000
Total liabilities and stockholders' equity		$76,500

[2]Beginning retained earnings + Net income − Dividends declared = Ending retained earnings ($14,000 + $7,000 − $2,000 = $19,000)

✔ **The Navigator**

> ## Comprehensive DO IT! 2

Action Plan

✔ Know the form and content of the sales budget.

✔ Prepare the sales budget first as the basis for the other budgets.

✔ Determine the units that must be produced to meet anticipated sales.

✔ Know how to compute the beginning and ending finished goods units.

Asheville Company is preparing its master budget for 2014. Relevant data pertaining to its sales and production budgets are as follows.

Sales. Sales for the year are expected to total 2,100,000 units. Quarterly sales, as a percentage of total sales, are 15%, 25%, 35%, and 25%, respectively. The sales price is expected to be $70 per unit for the first three quarters and $75 per unit beginning in the fourth quarter. Sales in the first quarter of 2015 are expected to be 10% higher than the budgeted sales volume for the first quarter of 2014.

Production. Management desires to maintain ending finished goods inventories at 20% of the next quarter's budgeted sales volume.

Instructions

Prepare the sales budget and production budget by quarters for 2014.

Solution to Comprehensive DO IT! 2

Asheville Company
Sales Budget
For the Year Ending December 31, 2014

	Quarter				
	1	**2**	**3**	**4**	**Year**
Expected unit sales	315,000	525,000	735,000	525,000	2,100,000
Unit selling price	× $70	× $70	× $70	× $75	—
Total sales	$22,050,000	$36,750,000	$51,450,000	$39,375,000	$149,625,000

Asheville Company
Production Budget
For the Year Ending December 31, 2014

	Quarter				
	1	**2**	**3**	**4**	**Year**
Expected unit sales	315,000	525,000	735,000	525,000	
Add: Desired ending finished goods units	105,000	147,000	105,000	69,300[a]	
Total required units	420,000	672,000	840,000	594,300	
Less: Beginning finished goods units	63,000[b]	105,000	147,000	105,000	
Required production units	357,000	567,000	693,000	489,300	2,106,300

[a]Estimated first-quarter 2015 sales volume 315,000 + (315,000 × 10%) = 346,500; 346,500 × 20%
[b]20% of estimated first-quarter 2014 sales units (315,000 × 20%)

✔ **The Navigator**

SELF-TEST QUESTIONS

Answers are at the end of the chapter.

(LO 1) **1.** Which of the following is *not* a benefit of budgeting?
  (a) Management can plan ahead.
  (b) An early warning system is provided for potential problems.
  (c) It enables disciplinary action to be taken at every level of responsibility.
  (d) The coordination of activities is facilitated.

(LO 1) **2.** A budget:
  (a) is the responsibility of management accountants.
  (b) is the primary method of communicating agreed-upon objectives throughout an organization.
  (c) ignores past performance because it represents management's plans for a future time period.
  (d) may promote efficiency but has no role in evaluating performance.

(LO 2) **3.** The essentials of effective budgeting do *not* include:
  (a) top-down budgeting.
  (b) management acceptance.
  (c) research and analysis.
  (d) sound organizational structure.

(LO 2) **4.** Compared to budgeting, long-range planning generally has the:
  (a) same amount of detail.
  (b) longer time period.
  (c) same emphasis.
  (d) same time period.

(LO 3) **5.** A sales budget is:
  (a) derived from the production budget.
  (b) management's best estimate of sales revenue for the year.
  (c) not the starting point for the master budget.
  (d) prepared only for credit sales.

(LO 3) **6.** The formula for the production budget is budgeted sales in units plus:
  (a) desired ending merchandise inventory less beginning merchandise inventory.
  (b) beginning finished goods units less desired ending finished goods units.
  (c) desired ending direct materials units less beginning direct materials units.
  (d) desired ending finished goods units less beginning finished goods units.

(LO 3) **7.** Direct materials inventories are kept in pounds in Byrd Company, and the total pounds of direct materials needed for production is 9,500. If the beginning inventory is 1,000 pounds and the desired ending inventory is 2,200 pounds, the total pounds to be purchased is:
  (a) 9,400.   (c) 9,700.
  (b) 9,500.   (d) 10,700.

(LO 3) **8.** The formula for computing the direct labor budget is to multiply the direct labor cost per hour by the:
  (a) total required direct labor hours.
  (b) physical units to be produced.
  (c) equivalent units to be produced.
  (d) No correct answer is given.

(LO 4) **9.** Each of the following budgets is used in preparing the budgeted income statement *except* the:
  (a) sales budget.
  (b) selling and administrative budget.
  (c) capital expenditure budget.
  (d) direct labor budget.

(LO 4) **10.** The budgeted income statement is:
  (a) the end-product of the operating budgets.
  (b) the end-product of the financial budgets.
  (c) the starting point of the master budget.
  (d) dependent on cash receipts and cash disbursements.

(LO 5) **11.** The budgeted balance sheet is:
  (a) developed from the budgeted balance sheet for the preceding year and the budgets for the current year.
  (b) the last operating budget prepared.
  (c) used to prepare the cash budget.
  (d) All of the above.

(LO 5) **12.** The format of a cash budget is:
  (a) Beginning cash balance + Cash receipts + Cash from financing − Cash disbursements = Ending cash balance.
  (b) Beginning cash balance + Cash receipts − Cash disbursements +/− Financing = Ending cash balance.
  (c) Beginning cash balance + Net income − Cash dividends = Ending cash balance.
  (d) Beginning cash balance + Cash revenues − Cash expenses = Ending cash balance.

(LO 5) **13.** Expected direct materials purchases in Read Company are $70,000 in the first quarter and $90,000 in the second quarter. Forty percent of the purchases are paid in cash as incurred, and the balance is paid in the following quarter. The budgeted cash payments for purchases in the second quarter are:
  (a) $96,000.   (c) $78,000.
  (b) $90,000.   (d) $72,000.

(LO 6) **14.** The budget for a merchandiser differs from a budget for a manufacturer because:
  (a) a merchandise purchases budget replaces the production budget.
  (b) the manufacturing budgets are not applicable.
  (c) None of the above.
  (d) Both (a) and (b) above.

(LO 6) 15. In most cases, not-for-profit entities:
(a) prepare budgets using the same steps as those used by profit-oriented businesses.
(b) know budgeted cash receipts at the beginning of a time period, so they budget only for expenditures.
(c) begin the budgeting process by budgeting expenditures rather than receipts.
(d) can ignore budgets because they are not expected to generate net income.

Go to the book's companion website, www.wiley.com/college/weygandt, for additional Self-Test Questions.

✔ The Navigator

QUESTIONS

1. (a) What is a budget?
   (b) How does a budget contribute to good management?
2. Kate Cey and Joe Coulter are discussing the benefits of budgeting. They ask you to identify the primary advantages of budgeting. Comply with their request.
3. Jane Gilligan asks your help in understanding the essentials of effective budgeting. Identify the essentials for Jane.
4. (a) "Accounting plays a relatively unimportant role in budgeting." Do you agree? Explain.
   (b) What responsibilities does management have in budgeting?
5. What criteria are helpful in determining the length of the budget period? What is the most common budget period?
6. Lori Wilkins maintains that the only difference between budgeting and long-range planning is time. Do you agree? Why or why not?
7. What is participative budgeting? What are its potential benefits? What are its potential disadvantages?
8. What is budgetary slack? What incentive do managers have to create budgetary slack?
9. Distinguish between a master budget and a sales forecast.
10. What budget is the starting point in preparing the master budget? What may result if this budget is inaccurate?
11. "The production budget shows both unit production data and unit cost data." Is this true? Explain.
12. Alou Company has 20,000 beginning finished goods units. Budgeted sales units are 160,000. If management desires 15,000 ending finished goods units, what are the required units of production?
13. In preparing the direct materials budget for Quan Company, management concludes that required purchases are 64,000 units. If 52,000 direct materials units are required in production and there are 9,000 units of beginning direct materials, what is the desired units of ending direct materials?

14. The production budget of Justus Company calls for 80,000 units to be produced. If it takes 45 minutes to make one unit and the direct labor rate is $16 per hour, what is the total budgeted direct labor cost?
15. Ortiz Company's manufacturing overhead budget shows total variable costs of $198,000 and total fixed costs of $162,000. Total production in units is expected to be 150,000. It takes 20 minutes to make one unit, and the direct labor rate is $15 per hour. Express the manufacturing overhead rate as (a) a percentage of direct labor cost, and (b) an amount per direct labor hour.
16. Everly Company's variable selling and administrative expenses are 12% of net sales. Fixed expenses are $50,000 per quarter. The sales budget shows expected sales of $200,000 and $240,000 in the first and second quarters, respectively. What are the total budgeted selling and administrative expenses for each quarter?
17. For Goody Company, the budgeted cost for one unit of product is direct materials $10, direct labor $20, and manufacturing overhead 80% of direct labor cost. If 25,000 units are expected to be sold at $65 each, what is the budgeted gross profit?
18. Indicate the supporting schedules used in preparing a budgeted income statement through gross profit for a manufacturer.
19. Identify the three sections of a cash budget. What balances are also shown in this budget?
20. Noterman Company has credit sales of $600,000 in January. Past experience suggests that 40% is collected in the month of sale, 50% in the month following the sale, and 10% in the second month following the sale. Compute the cash collections from January sales in January, February, and March.
21. What is the formula for determining required merchandise purchases for a merchandiser?
22. How may expected revenues in a service company be computed?

BRIEF EXERCISES

BE9-1 Chicksaw Company uses the following budgets: Balance Sheet, Capital Expenditure, Cash, Direct Labor, Direct Materials, Income Statement, Manufacturing Overhead, Production, Sales, and Selling and Administrative. Prepare a diagram of the interrelationships

Prepare a diagram of a master budget.

(LO 3), AN

of the budgets in the master budget. Indicate whether each budget is an operating or a financial budget.

Prepare a sales budget.
(LO 3), AP

BE9-2 Palermo Company estimates that unit sales will be 10,000 in quarter 1; 12,000 in quarter 2; 15,000 in quarter 3; and 18,000 in quarter 4. Using a sales price of $70 per unit, prepare the sales budget by quarters for the year ending December 31, 2014.

Prepare a production budget for 2 quarters.
(LO 3), AP

BE9-3 Sales budget data for Palermo Company are given in BE9-2. Management desires to have an ending finished goods inventory equal to 25% of the next quarter's expected unit sales. Prepare a production budget by quarters for the first 6 months of 2014.

Prepare a direct materials budget for 1 month.
(LO 3), AP

BE9-4 Perine Company has 2,000 pounds of raw materials in its December 31, 2013, ending inventory. Required production for January and February of 2014 are 4,000 and 5,000 units, respectively. Two pounds of raw materials are needed for each unit, and the estimated cost per pound is $6. Management desires an ending inventory equal to 25% of next month's materials requirements. Prepare the direct materials budget for January.

Prepare a direct labor budget for 2 quarters.
(LO 3), AP

BE9-5 For Mize Company, units to be produced are 5,000 in quarter 1 and 6,000 in quarter 2. It takes 1.6 hours to make a finished unit, and the expected hourly wage rate is $15 per hour. Prepare a direct labor budget by quarters for the 6 months ending June 30, 2014.

Prepare a manufacturing overhead budget.
(LO 3), AP

BE9-6 For Roche Inc., variable manufacturing overhead costs are expected to be $20,000 in the first quarter of 2014, with $5,000 increments in each of the remaining three quarters. Fixed overhead costs are estimated to be $40,000 in each quarter. Prepare the manufacturing overhead budget by quarters and in total for the year.

Prepare a selling and administrative expense budget.
(LO 3), AP

BE9-7 Noble Company classifies its selling and administrative expense budget into variable and fixed components. Variable expenses are expected to be $22,000 in the first quarter, and $4,000 increments are expected in the remaining quarters of 2014. Fixed expenses are expected to be $40,000 in each quarter. Prepare the selling and administrative expense budget by quarters and in total for 2014.

Prepare a budgeted income statement for the year.
(LO 4), AP

BE9-8 North Company has completed all of its operating budgets. The sales budget for the year shows 50,000 units and total sales of $2,250,000. The total unit cost of making one unit of sales is $25. Selling and administrative expenses are expected to be $300,000. Income taxes are estimated to be $210,000. Prepare a budgeted income statement for the year ending December 31, 2014.

Prepare data for a cash budget.
(LO 5), AP

BE9-9 Bruno Industries expects credit sales for January, February, and March to be $200,000, $260,000, and $300,000, respectively. It is expected that 75% of the sales will be collected in the month of sale, and 25% will be collected in the following month. Compute cash collections from customers for each month.

Determine required merchandise purchases for 1 month.
(LO 6), AP

BE9-10 Moore Wholesalers is preparing its merchandise purchases budget. Budgeted sales are $400,000 for April and $480,000 for May. Cost of goods sold is expected to be 65% of sales. The company's desired ending inventory is 20% of the following month's cost of goods sold. Compute the required purchases for April.

> DO IT! REVIEW

Identify budget terminology.
(LO 2, 3), K

DO IT! 9-1 Use this list of terms to complete the sentences that follow.

Long-range plans	Participative budgeting
Sales forecast	Operating budgets
Master budget	Financial budgets

1. _____ establish goals for the company's sales and production personnel.
2. The _____ is a set of interrelated budgets that constitutes a plan of action for a specified time period.
3. _____ reduces the risk of having unrealistic budgets.
4. _____ include the cash budget and the budgeted balance sheet.
5. The budget is formed within the framework of a _____.
6. _____ contain considerably less detail than budgets.

DO IT! **9-2** Zeller Company estimates that 2014 unit sales will be 20,000 in quarter 1, 24,000 in quarter 2, and 29,000 in quarter 3, at a unit selling price of $20. Management desires to have ending finished goods inventory equal to 10% of the next quarter's expected unit sales. Prepare a production budget by quarter for the first 6 months of 2014.

Production budget.

(LO 3), AP

DO IT! **9-3** Ash Creek Company is preparing its master budget for 2014. Relevant data pertaining to its sales, production, and direct materials budgets are as follows.

Prepare sales, production, and direct materials budgets.

(LO 3), AP

Sales. Sales for the year are expected to total 1,000,000 units. Quarterly sales are 20%, 20%, 30%, and 30%, respectively. The sales price is expected to be $40 per unit for the first three quarters and $45 per unit beginning in the fourth quarter. Sales in the first quarter of 2015 are expected to be 20% higher than the budgeted sales for the first quarter of 2014.

Production. Management desires to maintain the ending finished goods inventories at 25% of the next quarter's budgeted sales volume.

Direct materials. Each unit requires 2 pounds of raw materials at a cost of $12 per pound. Management desires to maintain raw materials inventories at 10% of the next quarter's production requirements. Assume the production requirements for first quarter of 2015 are 450,000 pounds.

Prepare the sales, production, and direct materials budgets by quarters for 2014.

DO IT! **9-4** Ash Creek Company is preparing its budgeted income statement for 2014. Relevant data pertaining to its sales, production, and direct materials budgets can be found in **DO IT!** 9-3.

In addition, Ash Creek budgets 0.3 hours of direct labor per unit, labor costs at $15 per hour, and manufacturing overhead at $20 per direct labor hour. Its budgeted selling and administrative expenses for 2014 are $6,000,000.

(a) Calculate the budgeted total unit cost.
(b) Prepare the budgeted income statement for 2014.

Calculate budgeted total unit cost and prepare budgeted income statement.

(LO 4), AP

DO IT! **9-5** Batista Company management wants to maintain a minimum monthly cash balance of $20,000. At the beginning of April, the cash balance is $25,000, expected cash receipts for April are $245,000, and cash disbursements are expected to be $255,000. How much cash, if any, must be borrowed to maintain the desired minimum monthly balance?

Determine amount of financing needed.

(LO 5), AP

✔ **The Navigator**

EXERCISES

E9-1 ✏️ Adler Company has always done some planning for the future, but the company has never prepared a formal budget. Now that the company is growing larger, it is considering preparing a budget.

Explain the concept of budgeting.

(LO 1, 2, 3), C

Instructions
Write a memo to Jim Dixon, the president of Adler Company, in which you define budgeting, identify the budgets that comprise the master budget, identify the primary benefits of budgeting, and discuss the essentials of effective budgeting.

E9-2 Edington Electronics Inc. produces and sells two models of pocket calculators, XQ-103 and XQ-104. The calculators sell for $15 and $25, respectively. Because of the intense competition Edington faces, management budgets sales semiannually. Its projections for the first 2 quarters of 2014 are as follows.

Prepare a sales budget for 2 quarters.

(LO 3), AP

	Unit Sales	
Product	**Quarter 1**	**Quarter 2**
XQ-103	20,000	22,000
XQ-104	12,000	15,000

No changes in selling prices are anticipated.

Instructions

Prepare a sales budget for the 2 quarters ending June 30, 2014. List the products and show for each quarter and for the 6 months, units, selling price, and total sales by product and in total.

Prepare a sales budget for 4 quarters.

(LO 3, 6), AP

E9-3 Garza and Neely, CPAs, are preparing their service revenue (sales) budget for the coming year (2014). The practice is divided into three departments: auditing, tax, and consulting. Billable hours for each department, by quarter, are provided below.

Department	Quarter 1	Quarter 2	Quarter 3	Quarter 4
Auditing	2,300	1,600	2,000	2,400
Tax	3,000	2,200	2,000	2,500
Consulting	1,500	1,500	1,500	1,500

Average hourly billing rates are auditing $80, tax $90, and consulting $100.

Instructions

Prepare the service revenue (sales) budget for 2014 by listing the departments and showing for each quarter and the year in total, billable hours, billable rate, and total revenue.

Prepare quarterly production budgets.

(LO 3), AP

E9-4 Turney Company produces and sells automobile batteries, the heavy-duty HD-240. The 2014 sales forecast is as follows.

Quarter	HD-240
1	5,000
2	7,000
3	8,000
4	10,000

The January 1, 2014, inventory of HD-240 is 2,000 units. Management desires an ending inventory each quarter equal to 40% of the next quarter's sales. Sales in the first quarter of 2015 are expected to be 25% higher than sales in the same quarter in 2014.

Instructions

Prepare quarterly production budgets for each quarter and in total for 2014.

Prepare a direct materials purchases budget.

(LO 3), AP

E9-5 Dallas Industries has adopted the following production budget for the first 4 months of 2014.

Month	Units	Month	Units
January	10,000	March	5,000
February	8,000	April	4,000

Each unit requires 2 pounds of raw materials costing $2 per pound. On December 31, 2013, the ending raw materials inventory was 4,000 pounds. Management wants to have a raw materials inventory at the end of the month equal to 20% of next month's production requirements.

Instructions

Prepare a direct materials purchases budget by month for the first quarter.

Prepare production and direct materials budgets by quarters for 6 months.

(LO 3), AP

E9-6 On January 1, 2014, the Hardin Company budget committee has reached agreement on the following data for the 6 months ending June 30, 2014.

Sales units: First quarter 5,000; second quarter 6,000; third quarter 7,000.

Ending raw materials inventory: 40% of the next quarter's production requirements.

Ending finished goods inventory: 25% of the next quarter's expected sales units.

Third-quarter production: 7,200 units.

The ending raw materials and finished goods inventories at December 31, 2013, follow the same percentage relationships to production and sales that occur in 2014. Three pounds of raw materials are required to make each unit of finished goods. Raw materials purchased are expected to cost $4 per pound.

Instructions

(a) Prepare a production budget by quarters for the 6-month period ended June 30, 2014.
(b) Prepare a direct materials budget by quarters for the 6-month period ended June 30, 2014.

E9-7 Chandler Ltd. estimates sales for the second quarter of 2014 will be as follows.

Month	Units
April	2,550
May	2,475
June	2,390

Prepare raw materials purchase budget in dollars.

(LO 3), AP

The target ending inventory of finished products is as follows.

March 31	2,000
April 30	2,230
May 31	2,200
June 30	2,310

Two units of material are required for each unit of finished product. Production for July is estimated at 2,700 units to start building inventory for the fall sales period. Chandler's policy is to have an inventory of raw materials at the end of each month equal to 50% of the following month's production requirements.

Raw materials are expected to cost $4 per unit throughout the period.

Instructions

Calculate the May raw materials purchases in dollars.

(CGA adapted)

E9-8 Rodriguez, Inc., is preparing its direct labor budget for 2014 from the following production budget based on a calendar year.

Prepare a direct labor budget.

(LO 3), AP

Quarter	Units	Quarter	Units
1	20,000	3	35,000
2	25,000	4	30,000

Each unit requires 1.5 hours of direct labor.

Instructions

Prepare a direct labor budget for 2014. Wage rates are expected to be $16 for the first 2 quarters and $18 for quarters 3 and 4.

E9-9 Donnegal Company makes and sells artistic frames for pictures. The controller is responsible for preparing the master budget and has accumulated the following information for 2014.

Prepare production and direct labor budgets.

(LO 3), AP

	January	February	March	April	May
Estimated unit sales	12,000	14,000	10,000	11,000	11,000
Sales price per unit	$50.00	$47.50	$47.50	$47.50	$47.50
Direct labor hours per unit	2.0	2.0	1.5	1.5	1.5
Wage per direct labor hour	$8.00	$8.00	$8.00	$9.00	$9.00

Donnegal has a labor contract that calls for a wage increase to $9.00 per hour on April 1. New labor-saving machinery has been installed and will be fully operational by March 1.

Donnegal expects to begin the year with 17,600 frames on hand and has a policy of carrying an end-of-month inventory of 100% of the following month's sales, plus 40% of the second following month's sales.

Instructions

Prepare a production budget and a direct labor budget for Donnegal Company by month and for the first quarter of the year. The direct labor budget should include direct labor hours.

(CMA-Canada adapted)

E9-10 Atlanta Company is preparing its manufacturing overhead budget for 2014. Relevant data consist of the following.

Prepare a manufacturing overhead budget for the year.

(LO 3), AP

Units to be produced (by quarters): 10,000, 12,000, 14,000, 16,000.

Direct labor: time is 1.5 hours per unit.

Variable overhead costs per direct labor hour: indirect materials $0.80; indirect labor $1.20; and maintenance $0.50.

Fixed overhead costs per quarter: supervisory salaries $35,000; depreciation $15,000; and maintenance $12,000.

Prepare a selling and administrative expense budget for 2 quarters.

(LO 3), AP

Instructions
Prepare the manufacturing overhead budget for the year, showing quarterly data.

E9-11 Duncan Company combines its operating expenses for budget purposes in a selling and administrative expense budget. For the first 6 months of 2014, the following data are available.

1. Sales: 20,000 units quarter 1; 22,000 units quarter 2.
2. Variable costs per dollar of sales: sales commissions 5%, delivery expense 2%, and advertising 4%.
3. Fixed costs per quarter: sales salaries $10,000, office salaries $8,000, depreciation $4,200, insurance $1,500, utilities $800, and repairs expense $500.
4. Unit selling price: $20.

Instructions
Prepare a selling and administrative expense budget by quarters for the first 6 months of 2014.

Prepare a production and a direct materials budget.

(LO 3), AP

E9-12 Fuqua Company's sales budget projects unit sales of part 198Z of 10,000 units in January, 12,000 units in February, and 13,000 units in March. Each unit of part 198Z requires 4 pounds of materials, which cost $2 per pound. Fuqua Company desires its ending raw materials inventory to equal 40% of the next month's production requirements, and its ending finished goods inventory to equal 20% of the next month's expected unit sales. These goals were met at December 31, 2013.

Instructions
(a) Prepare a production budget for January and February 2014.
(b) Prepare a direct materials budget for January 2014.

Prepare a budgeted income statement for the year.

(LO 4), AP

E9-13 Dalby Company has accumulated the following budget data for the year 2014.

1. Sales: 30,000 units, unit selling price $85.
2. Cost of one unit of finished goods: direct materials 2 pounds at $5 per pound, direct labor 3 hours at $15 per hour, and manufacturing overhead $5 per direct labor hour.
3. Inventories (raw materials only): beginning, 10,000 pounds; ending, 15,000 pounds.
4. Selling and administrative expenses: $200,000.
5. Income taxes: 30% of income before income taxes.

Instructions
(a) Prepare a schedule showing the computation of cost of goods sold for 2014.
(b) Prepare a budgeted income statement for 2014.

Prepare a cash budget for 2 months.

(LO 5), AP

E9-14 Danner Company expects to have a cash balance of $45,000 on January 1, 2014. Relevant monthly budget data for the first 2 months of 2014 are as follows.

Collections from customers: January $85,000, February $150,000.

Payments for direct materials: January $50,000, February $75,000.

Direct labor: January $30,000, February $45,000. Wages are paid in the month they are incurred.

Manufacturing overhead: January $21,000, February $25,000. These costs include depreciation of $1,500 per month. All other overhead costs are paid as incurred.

Selling and administrative expenses: January $15,000, February $20,000. These costs are exclusive of depreciation. They are paid as incurred.

Sales of marketable securities in January are expected to realize $12,000 in cash. Danner Company has a line of credit at a local bank that enables it to borrow up to $25,000. The company wants to maintain a minimum monthly cash balance of $20,000.

Instructions
Prepare a cash budget for January and February.

Prepare a cash budget.

(LO 5), AP

E9-15 Aaron Corporation is projecting a cash balance of $30,000 in its December 31, 2013, balance sheet. Aaron's schedule of expected collections from customers for the first quarter of 2014 shows total collections of $180,000. The schedule of expected payments for direct materials for the first quarter of 2014 shows total payments of $41,000. Other information gathered for the first quarter of 2014 is sale of equipment $3,000; direct labor $70,000, manufacturing overhead $35,000, selling and administrative expenses $45,000; and purchase of securities $14,000. Aaron wants to maintain a balance of at least $25,000 cash at the end of each quarter.

Instructions
Prepare a cash budget for the first quarter.

E9-16 The controller of Trenshaw Company wants to improve the company's control system by preparing a month-by-month cash budget. The following information is for the month ending July 31, 2014.

Prepare cash budget for a month.

(LO 5), AN

June 30, 2014, cash balance	$45,000
Dividends to be declared on July 15*	12,000
Cash expenditures to be paid in July for operating expenses	40,800
Amortization expense in July	4,500
Cash collections to be received in July	90,000
Merchandise purchases to be paid in cash in July	56,200
Equipment to be purchased for cash in July	20,000

*Dividends are payable 30 days after declaration to shareholders of record on the declaration date.

Trenshaw Company wants to keep a minimum cash balance of $25,000.

Instructions
(a) Prepare a cash budget for the month ended July 31, 2014, and indicate how much money, if any, Trenshaw Company will need to borrow to meet its minimum cash requirement.
(b) Explain how cash budgeting can reduce the cost of short-term borrowing.

(CGA adapted)

E9-17 LRF Company's budgeted sales and direct materials purchases are as follows.

Prepare schedules of expected collections and payments.

(LO 5), AP

	Budgeted Sales	Budgeted D.M. Purchases
January	$200,000	$30,000
February	220,000	36,000
March	270,000	40,000

LRF's sales are 30% cash and 70% credit. Credit sales are collected 10% in the month of sale, 50% in the month following sale, and 36% in the second month following sale; 4% are uncollectible. LRF's purchases are 50% cash and 50% on account. Purchases on account are paid 40% in the month of purchase, and 60% in the month following purchase.

Instructions
(a) Prepare a schedule of expected collections from customers for March.
(b) Prepare a schedule of expected payments for direct materials for March.

E9-18 Green Landscaping Inc. is preparing its budget for the first quarter of 2014. The next step in the budgeting process is to prepare a cash receipts schedule and a cash payments schedule. To that end the following information has been collected.

Prepare schedules for cash receipts and cash payments, and determine ending balances for balance sheet.

(LO 5, 6), AP

Clients usually pay 60% of their fee in the month that service is provided, 30% the month after, and 10% the second month after receiving service.

Actual service revenue for 2013 and expected service revenues for 2014 are November 2013, $80,000; December 2013, $90,000; January 2014, $100,000; February 2014, $120,000; March 2014, $140,000.

Purchases of landscaping supplies (direct materials) are paid 60% in the month of purchase and 40% the following month. Actual purchases for 2013 and expected purchases for 2014 are December 2013, $14,000; January 2014, $12,000; February 2014, $15,000; March 2014, $18,000.

Instructions
(a) Prepare the following schedules for each month in the first quarter of 2014 and for the quarter in total:
(1) Expected collections from clients.
(2) Expected payments for landscaping supplies.

(b) Determine the following balances at March 31, 2014:
   (1) Accounts receivable.
   (2) Accounts payable.

Prepare a cash budget for 2 quarters.

(LO 5, 6), AP

E9-19 Lager Dental Clinic is a medium-sized dental service specializing in family dental care. The clinic is currently preparing the master budget for the first 2 quarters of 2014. All that remains in this process is the cash budget. The following information has been collected from other portions of the master budget and elsewhere.

Beginning cash balance	$ 30,000
Required minimum cash balance	25,000
Payment of income taxes (2nd quarter)	4,000
Professional salaries:	
1st quarter	140,000
2nd quarter	140,000
Interest from investments (2nd quarter)	7,000
Overhead costs:	
1st quarter	75,000
2nd quarter	100,000
Selling and administrative costs, including	
$2,000 depreciation:	
1st quarter	50,000
2nd quarter	70,000
Purchase of equipment (2nd quarter)	50,000
Sale of equipment (1st quarter)	12,000
Collections from clients:	
1st quarter	230,000
2nd quarter	380,000
Interest payments (2nd quarter)	400

Instructions
Prepare a cash budget for each of the first two quarters of 2014.

Prepare a purchases budget and budgeted income statement for a merchandiser.

(LO 6), AP

E9-20 In May 2014, the budget committee of Grand Stores assembles the following data in preparation of budgeted merchandise purchases for the month of June.

1. Expected sales: June $500,000, July $600,000.
2. Cost of goods sold is expected to be 75% of sales.
3. Desired ending merchandise inventory is 30% of the following (next) month's cost of goods sold.
4. The beginning inventory at June 1 will be the desired amount.

Instructions
(a) Compute the budgeted merchandise purchases for June.
(b) Prepare the budgeted income statement for June through gross profit.

EXERCISES: SET B AND CHALLENGE EXERCISES

Visit the book's companion website, at **www.wiley.com/college/weygandt**, and choose the Student Companion site to access Exercise Set B and Challenge Exercises.

PROBLEMS: SET A

Prepare budgeted income statement and supporting budgets.

(LO 3, 4), AP

P9-1A Glendo Farm Supply Company manufactures and sells a pesticide called Snare. The following data are available for preparing budgets for Snare for the first 2 quarters of 2014.

1. Sales: quarter 1, 30,000 bags; quarter 2, 42,000 bags. Selling price is $60 per bag.
2. Direct materials: each bag of Snare requires 4 pounds of Gumm at a cost of $3.80 per pound and 6 pounds of Tarr at $1.50 per pound.
3. Desired inventory levels:

Type of Inventory	January 1	April 1	July 1
Snare (bags)	8,000	15,000	18,000
Gumm (pounds)	9,000	10,000	13,000
Tarr (pounds)	14,000	20,000	25,000

4. Direct labor: direct labor time is 15 minutes per bag at an hourly rate of $16 per hour.
5. Selling and administrative expenses are expected to be 15% of sales plus $175,000 per quarter.
6. Income taxes are expected to be 30% of income from operations.

Your assistant has prepared two budgets: (1) The manufacturing overhead budget shows expected costs to be 150% of direct labor cost. (2) The direct materials budget for Tarr shows the cost of Tarr purchases to be $297,000 in quarter 1 and $439,500 in quarter 2.

Instructions
Prepare the budgeted income statement for the first 6 months and all required operating budgets by quarters. (*Note:* Use variable and fixed in the selling and administrative expense budget.) Do not prepare the manufacturing overhead budget or the direct materials budget for Tarr.

Net income $601,720
Cost per bag $34.20

P9-2A Deleon Inc. is preparing its annual budgets for the year ending December 31, 2014. Accounting assistants furnish the data shown below.

Prepare sales, production, direct materials, direct labor, and income statement budgets.

(LO 3, 4), AP

	Product JB 50	Product JB 60
Sales budget:		
Anticipated volume in units	400,000	200,000
Unit selling price	$20	$25
Production budget:		
Desired ending finished goods units	30,000	15,000
Beginning finished goods units	25,000	10,000
Direct materials budget:		
Direct materials per unit (pounds)	2	3
Desired ending direct materials pounds	30,000	10,000
Beginning direct materials pounds	40,000	15,000
Cost per pound	$3	$4
Direct labor budget:		
Direct labor time per unit	0.4	0.6
Direct labor rate per hour	$12	$12
Budgeted income statement:		
Total unit cost	$13	$20

An accounting assistant has prepared the detailed manufacturing overhead budget and the selling and administrative expense budget. The latter shows selling expenses of $560,000 for product JB 50 and $360,000 for product JB 60, and administrative expenses of $540,000 for product JB 50 and $340,000 for product JB 60. Income taxes are expected to be 30%.

Instructions
Prepare the following budgets for the year. Show data for each product. Quarterly budgets should not be prepared.

(a) Sales
(b) Production
(c) Direct materials
(d) Direct labor
(e) Income statement (*Note:* Income taxes are not allocated to the products.)

(a) Total sales $13,000,000
(b) Required production units:
JB 50, 405,000
JB 60, 205,000
(c) Total cost of direct materials purchases $4,840,000
(d) Total direct labor cost $3,420,000
(e) Net income $1,400,000

P9-3A Marsh Industries had sales in 2013 of $6,400,000 and gross profit of $1,100,000. Management is considering two alternative budget plans to increase its gross profit in 2014.

Plan A would increase the selling price per unit from $8.00 to $8.40. Sales volume would decrease by 10% from its 2013 level. Plan B would decrease the selling price per unit by $0.50. The marketing department expects that the sales volume would increase by 100,000 units.

At the end of 2013, Marsh has 38,000 units of inventory on hand. If Plan A is accepted, the 2014 ending inventory should be equal to 5% of the 2014 sales. If Plan B is accepted,

Prepare sales and production budgets and compute cost per unit under two plans.

(LO 3, 4), E

the ending inventory should be equal to 60,000 units. Each unit produced will cost $1.80 in direct labor, $1.30 in direct materials, and $1.20 in variable overhead. The fixed overhead for 2014 should be $1,895,000.

Instructions

(c) Unit cost: Plan A $6.94
    Plan B $6.36
(d) Gross profit:
    Plan A $1,051,200
    Plan B $1,026,000

(a) Prepare a sales budget for 2014 under each plan.
(b) Prepare a production budget for 2014 under each plan.
(c) Compute the production cost per unit under each plan. Why is the cost per unit different for each of the two plans? (Round to two decimals.)
(d) Which plan should be accepted? (*Hint:* Compute the gross profit under each plan.)

Prepare cash budget for 2 months.

(LO 5), AP

P9-4A Colter Company prepares monthly cash budgets. Relevant data from operating budgets for 2014 are:

	January	February
Sales	$360,000	$400,000
Direct materials purchases	120,000	125,000
Direct labor	90,000	100,000
Manufacturing overhead	70,000	75,000
Selling and administrative expenses	79,000	85,000

All sales are on account. Collections are expected to be 50% in the month of sale, 30% in the first month following the sale, and 20% in the second month following the sale. Sixty percent (60%) of direct materials purchases are paid in cash in the month of purchase, and the balance due is paid in the month following the purchase. All other items above are paid in the month incurred except for selling and administrative expenses that include $1,000 of depreciation per month.

Other data:

1. Credit sales: November 2013, $250,000; December 2013, $320,000.
2. Purchases of direct materials: December 2013, $100,000.
3. Other receipts: January—collection of December 31, 2013, notes receivable $15,000; February—proceeds from sale of securities $6,000.
4. Other disbursements: February—payment of $6,000 cash dividend.

The company's cash balance on January 1, 2014, is expected to be $60,000. The company wants to maintain a minimum cash balance of $50,000.

(a) January: collections
    $326,000 payments
    $112,000
(b) Ending cash balance:
    January $51,000
    February $50,000

Instructions

(a) Prepare schedules for (1) expected collections from customers and (2) expected payments for direct materials purchases for January and February.
(b) Prepare a cash budget for January and February in columnar form.

Prepare purchases and income statement budgets for a merchandiser.

(LO 6), AP

P9-5A The budget committee of Litwin Company collects the following data for its San Miguel Store in preparing budgeted income statements for May and June 2014.

1. Sales for May are expected to be $800,000. Sales in June and July are expected to be 5% higher than the preceding month.
2. Cost of goods sold is expected to be 75% of sales.
3. Company policy is to maintain ending merchandise inventory at 15% of the following month's cost of goods sold.
4. Operating expenses are estimated to be:

Sales salaries	$30,000 per month
Advertising	6% of monthly sales
Delivery expense	3% of monthly sales
Sales commissions	5% of monthly sales
Rent expense	$5,000 per month
Depreciation	$800 per month
Utilities	$600 per month
Insurance	$500 per month

5. Income taxes are estimated to be 30% of income from operations.

Instructions

(a) Prepare the merchandise purchases budget for each month in columnar form.
(b) Prepare budgeted income statements for each month in columnar form. Show in the statements the details of cost of goods sold.

P9-6A Krause Industries' balance sheet at December 31, 2013, is presented below.

(a) Purchases:
   May $604,500
   June $634,725
(b) Net income:
   May $35,770
   June $38,850

Prepare budgeted income statement and balance sheet.

(LO 4, 5), AP

Krause Industries
Balance Sheet
December 31, 2013

Assets

Current assets		
Cash		$ 7,500
Accounts receivable		82,500
Finished goods inventory (1,000 units)		15,000
Total current assets		105,000
Property, plant, and equipment		
Equipment	$40,000	
Less: Accumulated depreciation	10,000	30,000
Total assets		$135,000

Liabilities and Stockholders' Equity

Liabilities		
Notes payable		$ 25,000
Accounts payable		45,000
Total liabilities		70,000
Stockholders' equity		
Common stock	$40,000	
Retained earnings	25,000	
Total stockholders' equity		65,000
Total liabilities and stockholders' equity		$135,000

Additional information accumulated for the budgeting process is as follows.
Budgeted data for the year 2014 include the following.

	4th Qtr. of 2014	Year 2014 Total
Sales budget (8,000 units at $32)	$76,800	$256,000
Direct materials used	17,000	62,500
Direct labor	12,500	50,900
Manufacturing overhead applied	10,000	48,600
Selling and administrative expenses	18,000	75,000

To meet sales requirements and to have 3,000 units of finished goods on hand at December 31, 2014, the production budget shows 9,000 required units of output. The total unit cost of production is expected to be $18. Krause Industries uses the first-in, first-out (FIFO) inventory costing method. Selling and administrative expenses include $4,000 for depreciation on equipment. Interest expense is expected to be $3,500 for the year. Income taxes are expected to be 40% of income before income taxes.

All sales and purchases are on account. It is expected that 60% of quarterly sales are collected in cash within the quarter and the remainder is collected in the following quarter. Direct materials purchased from suppliers are paid 50% in the quarter incurred and the remainder in the following quarter. Purchases in the fourth quarter were the same as the materials used. In 2014, the company expects to purchase additional equipment costing $9,000. It expects to pay $8,000 on notes payable plus all interest due and payable to December 31 (included in interest expense $3,500, above). Accounts payable at December 31, 2014, include amounts due suppliers (see above) plus other accounts payable of $6,500. In 2014, the company expects to declare and pay an $8,000 cash dividend. Unpaid income taxes at December 31 will be $5,000. The company's cash budget shows an expected cash balance of $6,980 at December 31, 2014.

Instructions

Net income $32,700
Total assets $126,700

Prepare a budgeted income statement for 2014 and a budgeted balance sheet at December 31, 2014. In preparing the income statement, you will need to compute cost of goods manufactured (direct materials + direct labor + manufacturing overhead) and finished goods inventory (December 31, 2014).

PROBLEMS: SET B

Prepare budgeted income statement and supporting budgets.

(LO 3, 4), AP

P9-1B Mercer Farm Supply Company manufactures and sells a fertilizer called Basic II. The following data are available for preparing budgets for Basic II for the first 2 quarters of 2014.

1. Sales: quarter 1, 40,000 bags; quarter 2, 50,000 bags. Selling price is $63 per bag.
2. Direct materials: each bag of Basic II requires 5 pounds of Crup at a cost of $3.80 per pound and 10 pounds of Dert at $1.50 per pound.
3. Desired inventory levels:

Type of Inventory	January 1	April 1	July 1
Basic II (bags)	10,000	15,000	20,000
Crup (pounds)	9,000	12,000	15,000
Dert (pounds)	15,000	20,000	25,000

4. Direct labor: direct labor time is 15 minutes per bag at an hourly rate of $12 per hour.
5. Selling and administrative expenses are expected to be 10% of sales plus $150,000 per quarter.
6. Income taxes are expected to be 30% of income from operations.

Your assistant has prepared two budgets: (1) The manufacturing overhead budget shows expected costs to be 100% of direct labor cost. (2) The direct materials budget for Dert which shows the cost of Dert to be $682,500 in quarter 1 and $832,500 in quarter 2.

Instructions

Net income $842,100
Cost per bag $40.00

Prepare the budgeted income statement for the first 6 months of 2014 and all required supporting budgets by quarters. (*Note:* Use variable and fixed in the selling and administrative expense budget.) Do not prepare the manufacturing overhead budget or the direct materials budget for Dert.

Prepare sales, production, direct materials, direct labor, and income statement budgets.

(LO 3, 4), AP

P9-2B Urbina Inc. is preparing its annual budgets for the year ending December 31, 2014. Accounting assistants furnish the following data.

	Product LN 35	Product LN 40
Sales budget:		
Anticipated volume in units	400,000	240,000
Unit selling price	$25	$35
Production budget:		
Desired ending finished goods units	20,000	25,000
Beginning finished goods units	30,000	15,000
Direct materials budget:		
Direct materials per unit (pounds)	2	3
Desired ending direct materials pounds	50,000	10,000
Beginning direct materials pounds	40,000	20,000
Cost per pound	$2	$3
Direct labor budget:		
Direct labor time per unit	0.5	0.75
Direct labor rate per hour	$12	$12
Budgeted income statement:		
Total unit cost	$12	$22

An accounting assistant has prepared the detailed manufacturing overhead budget and the selling and administrative expense budget. The latter shows selling expenses of $750,000 for product LN 35 and $580,000 for product LN 40, and administrative expenses of $420,000 for product LN 35 and $380,000 for product LN 40. Income taxes are expected to be 30%.

Instructions
Prepare the following budgets for the year. Show data for each product. You do not need to prepare quarterly budgets.

(a) Sales
(b) Production
(c) Direct materials
(d) Direct labor
(e) Income statement (*Note:* Income taxes are not allocated to the products.)

(a) Total sales $18,400,000
(b) Required production units: LN 35, 390,000
(c) Total cost of direct materials purchases $3,800,000
(d) Total direct labor cost $4,590,000
(e) Net income $4,333,000

P9-3B Ogleby Industries has sales in 2013 of $5,600,000 (800,000 units) and gross profit of $1,344,000. Management is considering two alternative budget plans to increase its gross profit in 2014.

Prepare sales and production budgets and compute cost per unit under two plans.

(LO 3, 4), E

Plan A would increase the selling price per unit from $7.00 to $7.60. Sales volume would decrease by 5% from its 2013 level. Plan B would decrease the selling price per unit by 5%. The marketing department expects that the sales volume would increase by 150,000 units.

At the end of 2013, Ogleby has 70,000 units on hand. If Plan A is accepted, the 2014 ending inventory should be equal to 90,000 units. If Plan B is accepted, the ending inventory should be equal to 100,000 units. Each unit produced will cost $2.00 in direct materials, $1.50 in direct labor, and $0.50 in variable overhead. The fixed overhead for 2014 should be $980,000.

Instructions
(a) Prepare a sales budget for 2014 under (1) Plan A and (2) Plan B.
(b) Prepare a production budget for 2014 under (1) Plan A and (2) Plan B.
(c) Compute the cost per unit under (1) Plan A and (2) Plan B. Explain why the cost per unit is different for each of the two plans. (Round to two decimals.)
(d) Which plan should be accepted? (*Hint:* Compute the gross profit under each plan.)

(c) Unit cost:
    Plan A $5.26
    Plan B $5.00
(d) Gross profit:
    Plan A $1,778,400
    Plan B $1,567,500

P9-4B Derby Company prepares monthly cash budgets. Relevant data from operating budgets for 2014 are:

Prepare cash budget for 2 months.

(LO 5), AP

	January	February
Sales	$350,000	$400,000
Direct materials purchases	110,000	120,000
Direct labor	85,000	115,000
Manufacturing overhead	60,000	75,000
Selling and administrative expenses	75,000	80,000

All sales are on account. Collections are expected to be 60% in the month of sale, 25% in the first month following the sale, and 15% in the second month following the sale. Thirty percent (30%) of direct materials purchases are paid in cash in the month of purchase, and the balance due is paid in the month following the purchase. All other items above are paid in the month incurred. Depreciation has been excluded from manufacturing overhead and selling and administrative expenses.

Other data:
1. Credit sales: November 2013, $200,000; December 2013, $290,000.
2. Purchases of direct materials: December 2013, $90,000.
3. Other receipts: January—collection of December 31, 2013, interest receivable $3,000; February—proceeds from sale of securities $5,000.
4. Other disbursements: February—payment of $20,000 for land.

The company's cash balance on January 1, 2014, is expected to be $50,000. The company wants to maintain a minimum cash balance of $40,000.

Instructions
(a) Prepare schedules for (1) expected collections from customers and (2) expected payments for direct materials purchases.
(b) Prepare a cash budget for January and February in columnar form.

(a) January:
    collections $312,500
    payments $96,000
(b) Ending cash balance:
    January $49,500
    February $40,000

Prepare purchases and income statement budgets for a merchandiser.

(LO 6), AP

P9-5B The budget committee of Widner Company collects the following data for its West-wood Store in preparing budgeted income statements for July and August 2014.

1. Expected sales: July $400,000, August $450,000, September $500,000.
2. Cost of goods sold is expected to be 65% of sales.
3. Company policy is to maintain ending merchandise inventory at 15% of the following month's cost of goods sold.
4. Operating expenses are estimated to be:

Sales salaries	$50,000 per month
Advertising	5% of monthly sales
Delivery expense	2% of monthly sales
Sales commissions	4% of monthly sales
Rent expense	$3,000 per month
Depreciation	$700 per month
Utilities	$500 per month
Insurance	$300 per month

5. Income taxes are estimated to be 30% of income from operations.

(a) Purchases: July $264,875
        August $297,375

(b) Net income: July $29,050
        August $37,450

Instructions
(a) Prepare the merchandise purchases budget for each month in columnar form.
(b) Prepare budgeted income statements for each month in columnar form. Show the details of cost of goods sold in the statements.

PROBLEMS: SET C

Visit the book's companion website, at **www.wiley.com/college/weygandt**, and choose the Student Companion site to access Problem Set C.

WATERWAYS CONTINUING PROBLEM

(This is a continuation of the Waterways Problem from Chapters 1–8.)

WCP9 Waterways Corporation is preparing its budget for the coming year, 2014. The first step is to plan for the first quarter of that coming year. The company has gathered information from its managers in preparation of the budgeting process. This problem asks you to prepare the various budgets that comprise the master budget for 2014.

Go to the book's companion website, at **www.wiley.com/college/weygandt**, *to see the completion of this problem.*

Broadening Your **PERSPECTIVE**

Management Decision-Making

Decision-Making at Current Designs

BYP9-1 Diane Buswell is preparing the 2013 budget for one of Current Designs' rotomolded kayaks. Extensive meetings with members of the sales department and executive team have resulted in the following unit sales projections for 2013.

Quarter 1	1,000 kayaks
Quarter 2	1,500 kayaks
Quarter 3	750 kayaks
Quarter 4	750 kayaks

Current Designs' policy is to have finished goods ending inventory in a quarter equal to 20% of the next quarter's anticipated sales. Preliminary sales projections for 2014 are 1,100 units for the first quarter and 1,500 units for the second quarter. Ending inventory of finished goods at December 31, 2012, will be 200 rotomolded kayaks.

Production of each kayak requires 54 pounds of polyethylene powder and a finishing kit (rope, seat, hardware, etc). Company policy is that the ending inventory of polyethylene powder should be 25% of the amount needed for production in the next quarter. Assume that the ending inventory of polyethylene powder on December 31, 2012, is 19,400 pounds. The finishing kits can be assembled as they are needed. As a result, Current Designs does not maintain a significant inventory of the finishing kits.

The polyethylene powder used in these kayaks costs $1.50 per pound, and the finishing kits cost $170 each. Production of a single kayak requires 2 hours of time by more experienced, type I employees and 3 hours of finishing time by type II employees. The type I employees are paid $15 per hour, and the type II employees are paid $12 per hour.

Selling and administrative expenses for this line are expected to be $45 per unit sold plus $7,500 per quarter. Manufacturing overhead is assigned at 150% of labor costs.

Instructions

Prepare the production budget, direct materials budget, direct labor budget, manufacturing overhead budget, and selling and administrative budget for this product line by quarter and in total for 2013.

Decision-Making Across the Organization

BYP9-2 Palmer Corporation operates on a calendar-year basis. It begins the annual budgeting process in late August when the president establishes targets for the total dollar sales and net income before taxes for the next year.

The sales target is given first to the marketing department. The marketing manager formulates a sales budget by product line in both units and dollars. From this budget, sales quotas by product line in units and dollars are established for each of the corporation's sales districts. The marketing manager also estimates the cost of the marketing activities required to support the target sales volume and prepares a tentative marketing expense budget.

The executive vice president uses the sales and profit targets, the sales budget by product line, and the tentative marketing expense budget to determine the dollar amounts that can be devoted to manufacturing and corporate office expense. The executive vice president prepares the budget for corporate expenses. She then forwards to the production department the product-line sales budget in units and the total dollar amount that can be devoted to manufacturing.

The production manager meets with the factory managers to develop a manufacturing plan that will produce the required units when needed within the cost constraints set by the executive vice president. The budgeting process usually comes to a halt at this point because the production department does not consider the financial resources allocated to be adequate.

When this standstill occurs, the vice president of finance, the executive vice president, the marketing manager, and the production manager meet together to determine the final budgets for each of the areas. This normally results in a modest increase in the total amount available for manufacturing costs and cuts in the marketing expense and corporate office expense budgets. The total sales and net income figures proposed by the president are seldom changed. Although the participants are seldom pleased with the compromise, these budgets are final. Each executive then develops a new detailed budget for the operations in his or her area.

None of the areas has achieved its budget in recent years. Sales often run below the target. When budgeted sales are not achieved, each area is expected to cut costs so that the president's profit target can be met. However, the profit target is seldom met because costs are not cut enough. In fact, costs often run above the original budget in all functional areas (marketing, production, and corporate office).

The president is disturbed that Palmer has not been able to meet the sales and profit targets. He hired a consultant with considerable experience with companies in Palmer's industry. The consultant reviewed the budgets for the past 4 years. He concluded that the product line sales budgets were reasonable and that the cost and expense budgets were adequate for the budgeted sales and production levels.

Instructions

With the class divided into groups, answer the following.

(a) Discuss how the budgeting process employed by Palmer Corporation contributes to the failure to achieve the president's sales and profit targets.
(b) Suggest how Palmer Corporation's budgeting process could be revised to correct the problems.
(c) Should the functional areas be expected to cut their costs when sales volume falls below budget? Explain your answer.

(CMA adapted)

Managerial Analysis

BYP9-3 Elliot & Hesse Inc. manufactures ergonomic devices for computer users. Some of its more popular products include glare screens (for computer monitors), keyboard stands with wrist rests, and carousels that allow easy access to discs. Over the past 5 years, it experienced rapid growth, with sales of all products increasing 20% to 50% each year.

Last year, some of the primary manufacturers of computers began introducing new products with some of the ergonomic designs, such as glare screens and wrist rests, already built in. As a result, sales of Elliot & Hesse's accessory devices have declined somewhat. The company believes that the disc carousels will probably continue to show growth, but that the other products will probably continue to decline. When the next year's budget was prepared, increases were built into research and development so that replacement products could be developed or the company could expand into some other product line. Some product lines being considered are general-purpose ergonomic devices including back supports, foot rests, and sloped writing pads.

The most recent results have shown that sales decreased more than was expected for the glare screens. As a result, the company may have a shortage of funds. Top management has therefore asked that all expenses be reduced 10% to compensate for these reduced sales. Summary budget information is as follows.

Direct materials	$240,000
Direct labor	110,000
Insurance	50,000
Depreciation	90,000
Machine repairs	30,000
Sales salaries	50,000
Office salaries	80,000
Factory salaries (indirect labor)	50,000
Total	$700,000

Instructions

Using the information above, answer the following questions.

(a) What are the implications of reducing each of the costs? For example, if the company reduces direct materials costs, it may have to do so by purchasing lower-quality materials. This may affect sales in the long run.
(b) Based on your analysis in (a), what do you think is the best way to obtain the $70,000 in cost savings requested? Be specific. Are there any costs that cannot or should not be reduced? Why?

Real-World Focus

BYP9-4 Network Computing Devices, Inc. was founded in 1988 in Mountain View, California. The company develops software products such as X-terminals, Z-mail, PC X-ware, and related hardware products. The following is a discussion by management in its annual report.

Network Computing Devices, Inc.
Management Discussion

The Company's operating results have varied significantly, particularly on a quarterly basis, as a result of a number of factors, including general economic conditions affecting industry demand for computer products, the timing and market acceptance of new product introductions by the Company and its competitors, the timing of significant orders from large customers, periodic changes in product pricing and discounting due to competitive factors, and the availability of key components, such as video monitors and electronic subassemblies, some of which require substantial order lead times. The Company's operating results may fluctuate in the future as a result of these and other factors, including the Company's success in developing and introducing new products, its product and customer mix, and the level of competition which it experiences. The Company operates with a small backlog. Sales and operating results, therefore, generally depend on the volume and timing of orders received, which are difficult to forecast. The Company has experienced slowness in orders from some customers during the first quarter of each calendar year due to budgeting cycles common in the computer industry. In addition, sales in Europe typically are adversely affected in the third calendar quarter as many European customers reduce their business activities during the month of August.

Due to the Company's rapid growth rate and the effect of new product introductions on quarterly revenues, these seasonal trends have not materially impacted the Company's results of operations to date. However, as the Company's product lines mature and its rate of revenue growth declines, these seasonal factors may become more evident. Additionally, the Company's international sales are denominated in U.S. dollars, and an increase or decrease in the value of the U.S. dollar relative to foreign currencies could make the Company's products less or more competitive in those markets.

Instructions
(a) Identify the factors that affect the budgeting process at Network Computing Devices, Inc.
(b) Explain the additional budgeting concerns created by the international operations of the company.

BYP9-5 Information regarding many approaches to budgeting can be found on the Web. The following activity investigates the merits of "zero-based" budgeting, as discussed by Michael LaFaive, Director of Financial Policy of the Mackinac Center for Public Policy.

Address: **www.mackinac.org/article.aspx?ID=5928**, or go to **www.wiley.com/college/weygandt**

Instructions
Read the article at the website and answer the following questions.

(a) How does zero-based budgeting differ from standard budgeting procedures?
(b) What are some potential advantages of zero-based budgeting?
(c) What are some potential disadvantages of zero-based budgeting?
(d) How often do departments in Oklahoma undergo zero-based budgeting?

Critical Thinking

Communication Activity

BYP9-6 In order to better serve their rural patients, Drs. Joe and Rick Parcells (brothers) began giving safety seminars. Especially popular were their "emergency-preparedness" talks given to farmers. Many people asked whether the "kit" of materials the doctors recommended for common farm emergencies was commercially available.

After checking with several suppliers, the doctors realized that no other company offered the supplies they recommended in their seminars, packaged in the way they described. Their wives, Megan and Sue, agreed to make a test package by ordering supplies from various medical supply companies and assembling them into a "kit" that could be sold at the seminars. When these kits proved a runaway success, the sisters-in-law decided to market them. At the advice of their accountant, they organized this venture as a separate company, called Life Protection Products (LPP), with Megan Parcells as CEO and Sue Parcells as Secretary-Treasurer.

LPP soon started receiving requests for the kits from all over the country, as word spread about their availability. Even without advertising, LPP was able to sell its full inventory every month. However, the company was becoming financially strained. Megan and Sue had about $100,000 in savings, and they invested about half that amount initially. They believed that this venture would allow them to make money. However, at the present time, only about $30,000 of the cash remains, and the company is constantly short of cash.

Megan has come to you for advice. She does not understand why the company is having cash flow problems. She and Sue have not even been withdrawing salaries. However, they have rented a local building and have hired two more full-time workers to help them cope with the increasing demand. They do not think they could handle the demand without this additional help.

Megan is also worried that the cash problems mean that the company may not be able to support itself. She has prepared the cash budget shown below. All seminar customers pay for their products in full at the time of purchase. In addition, several large companies have ordered the kits for use by employees who work in remote sites. They have requested credit terms and have been allowed to pay in the month following the sale. These large purchasers amount to about 25% of the sales at the present time. LPP purchases the materials for the kits about 2 months ahead of time. Megan and Sue are considering slowing the growth of the company by simply purchasing less materials, which will mean selling fewer kits.

The workers are paid weekly. Megan and Sue need about $15,000 cash on hand at the beginning of the month to pay for purchases of raw materials. Right now they have been using cash from their savings, but as noted, only $30,000 is left.

Instructions

Write a response to Megan Parcells. Explain why LPP is short of cash. Will this company be able to support itself? Explain your answer. Make any recommendations you deem appropriate.

Life Protection Products
Cash Budget
For the Quarter Ending June 30, 2014

	April	May	June
Cash balance, beginning	$15,000	$15,000	$15,000
Cash received			
From prior month sales	5,000	7,500	12,500
From current sales	15,000	22,500	37,500
Total cash on hand	35,000	45,000	65,000
Cash payments			
To employees	3,000	3,000	3,000
For products	25,000	35,000	45,000
Miscellaneous expenses	5,000	6,000	7,000
Postage	1,000	1,000	1,000
Total cash payments	34,000	45,000	56,000
Cash balance	$ 1,000	$ 0	$ 9,000
Borrow from savings	$14,000	$15,000	$ 1,000
Borrow from bank?	$ 0	$ 0	$ 5,000

Ethics Case

BYP9-7 You are an accountant in the budgetary, projections, and special projects department of Fernetti Conductor, Inc., a large manufacturing company. The president, Richard Brown, asks you on very short notice to prepare some sales and income projections covering the next 2 years of the company's much heralded new product lines. He wants these projections for a series of speeches he is making while on a 2-week trip to eight East Coast brokerage firms. The president hopes to bolster Fernetti's stock sales and price.

You work 23 hours in 2 days to compile the projections, hand-deliver them to the president, and are swiftly but graciously thanked as he departs. A week later, you find time to go over some of your computations and discover a miscalculation that makes the projections grossly overstated. You quickly inquire about the president's itinerary and learn that he has made half of his speeches and has half yet to make. You are in a quandary as to what to do.

Instructions
(a) What are the consequences of telling the president of your gross miscalculations?
(b) What are the consequences of not telling the president of your gross miscalculations?
(c) What are the ethical considerations to you and the president in this situation?

All About You

BYP9-8 In order to get your personal finances under control, you need to prepare a personal budget. Assume that you have compiled the following information regarding your expected cash flows for a typical month.

Rent payment	$ 500	Miscellaneous costs	$210
Interest income	50	Savings	50
Income tax withheld	300	Eating out	150
Electricity bill	85	Telephone and Internet costs	125
Groceries	100	Student loan payments	375
Wages earned	2,500	Entertainment costs	250
Insurance	100	Transportation costs	150

Instructions
Using the information above, prepare a personal budget. In preparing this budget, use the format found at *http://financialplan.about.com/cs/budgeting/l/blbudget.htm*. Just skip any unused line items.

Considering Your Costs and Benefits

BYP9-9 You might hear people say that they "need to learn to live within a budget." The funny thing is that most people who say this haven't actually prepared a personal budget, nor do they intend to. Instead, what they are referring to is a vaguely defined, poorly specified collection of rough ideas of how much they should spend on various aspects of their lives. However, you can't live within or even outside of something that doesn't exist. With that in mind, let's take a look at one aspect of personal-budget templates.

Many personal-budget worksheet templates that are provided for college students treat student loans as an income source. See, for example, the template provided at *http://financialplan. about.com/cs/budgeting/l/blmocolbud.htm*. Based on your knowledge of accounting, is this correct?

YES: Student loans provide a source of cash, which can be used to pay costs. As the saying goes, "It all spends the same." Therefore, student loans are income.
NO: Student loans must eventually be repaid; therefore, they are not income. As the name suggests, they are loans.

Instructions
Write a response indicating your position regarding this situation. Provide support for your view.

Answers to Chapter Questions

Answers to Insight and Accounting Across the Organization Questions

p. 385 Businesses Often Feel Too Busy to Plan for the Future Q: Describe a situation in which a business "sells as much as it can" but cannot "keep its employees paid." **A:** If sales are made to customers on credit and collection is slow, the company may find that it does not have enough cash to pay employees or suppliers. Without these resources, the company will fail to survive.

p. 390 The Implications of Budgetary Optimism Q: Why is it important that government budgets accurately estimate future revenues during economic downturns? **A:** Accuracy of government revenue estimates is especially important during economic downturns because most governments must balance their budgets. If anticipated revenues in one period do not match expectations, then the shortfall must be made up in the next period. This can result in much steeper, more disruptive cuts than might have been necessary had the government anticipated the revenue decline more accurately and consequently started cutting expenditures sooner.

p. 393 Betting That Prices Won't Fall Q: What are the potential downsides of stockpiling a huge amount of raw materials? **A:** If prices continue to go up, these managers will avoid paying higher prices until their inventory runs out. However, it is a risky strategy. First of all, prices fluctuate. If a price goes up by 90% in a year, it can also go down by 90%. If this happens, the managers will be stuck with overpriced raw materials. Second, if the economy slows down, it might take a lot longer to sell their inventory than they had planned. There are many costs associated with holding large quantities of inventory. The additional storage, insurance, and handling costs can be very expensive, and obsolescence can occur.

p. 402 Without a Budget, Can the Games Begin? Q: Why does it matter whether the Olympic Games exceed their budget? **A:** If the Olympic Games exceed their budget, taxpayers of the sponsoring community and country will end up footing the bill. Depending on the size of the losses, and the resources of the community, this could produce a substantial burden. As a result, other communities might be reluctant to host the Olympics in the future.

p. 406 Budget Shortfalls as Far as the Eye Can See Q: Why would a university's budgeted scholarships probably fall when the stock market suffers a serious drop? **A:** Scholarships typically cannot be paid out of the "principal" portion of donations made to scholarship endowment funds. Instead, scholarships are usually funded through earnings generated by endowment investments. Any excess earnings above current-year scholarship needs can be used for scholarships in subsequent years. But a serious drop in the value of endowment investments can wipe out previous earnings, in some cases completely eliminating funds available for scholarships.

Answers to Self-Test Questions

1. c **2.** b **3.** a **4.** b **5.** b **6.** d **7.** d (9,500 + 2,200 − 1,000) **8.** a **9.** c **10.** a **11.** a **12.** b **13.** c [($70,000 × 60%) + ($90,000 × 40%)] **14.** d **15.** c

Chapter 10

Budgetary Control and Responsibility Accounting

Turning Trash Into Treasure

Vancouver teenager Brian Scudamore needed to raise money to pay his way through college. With $700 and a strong desire to do it on his own, he established a junk removal company. Fifteen years later, 1-800-GOT-JUNK? had 113 franchise partners across Canada and the United States, and projected revenues of more than $60 million.

"It was a high-school business project that was out of control," says Cameron Herold, vice president of operations.

While the exponential growth of 1-800-GOT-JUNK? may seem unwieldy (at one point it had five consecutive years of 100-percent compounded growth), it has in fact involved sound financial planning, budgeting, and cash management. The company only spends money it has; it has no outside investors or debt.

Managing this growth involves forecasting everything by creating a "painted picture" of what the company will look like in three years. The company knows its staffing plans, training requirements, and overhead and office space needs well in advance. "That filters back to our budgeting process," Mr. Herold says. "We'll sit down and say, 'If this is where we're going, what are all the components of that?' . . . Then we

✔ The Navigator

☐ Scan Learning Objectives

☐ Read Feature Story

☐ Scan Preview

☐ Read Text and answer **DO IT!** p. 444
  ☐ p. 446 ☐ p. 457 ☐ p. 461

☐ Work Using the Decision Toolkit p. 462

☐ Review Summary of Learning Objectives

☐ Work Comprehensive **DO IT!** p. 467

☐ Answer Self-Test Questions

☐ Complete Assignments

☐ Go to **WileyPLUS** for practice and tutorials

Learning Objectives

After studying this chapter, you should be able to:

1 Describe the concept of budgetary control.

2 Evaluate the usefulness of static budget reports.

3 Explain the development of flexible budgets and the usefulness of flexible budget reports.

4 Describe the concept of responsibility accounting.

5 Indicate the features of responsibility reports for cost centers.

6 Identify the content of responsibility reports for profit centers.

7 Explain the basis and formula used in evaluating performance in investment centers.

✔ The Navigator

bring it back to zero and say, 'What's it going to cost us? Where does it fit into the budget?'"

Key to the company's growth management was the introduction of franchising. "We chose franchising because our franchise partners would actually finance our growth," Mr. Herold says. In addition to the initial franchise fee, franchisees pay the head office 8 percent of their sales, plus another 7 percent to run the centralized call center.

While the company has used franchising to manage growth, a frugal approach to

day-to-day costs has also been integral to its budgeting success. "We're always looking for ways to cut costs," Mr. Herold says. This includes establishing strategic relationships with the local coffee shop, doing regular cost analyses of office equipment and changing suppliers when needed, and buying office furniture in bulk from liquidators at 10 cents on the dollar. "All those little things start to really add up," he says.

Watch the Tribeca Grand video in WileyPLUS to learn more about budgeting in the real world.

✔ **The Navigator**

Preview of **Chapter 10**

In contrast to Chapter 9, we now consider how budgets are used by management to control operations. In the Feature Story on 1-800-GOT-JUNK?, we saw that management uses the budget to adapt to the business environment. This chapter focuses on two aspects of management control: (1) budgetary control and (2) responsibility accounting.

The content and organization of Chapter 10 are as follows.

BUDGETARY CONTROL AND RESPONSIBILITY ACCOUNTING				
Budgetary Control	**Static Budget Reports**	**Flexible Budgets**	**Responsibility Accounting**	**Types of Responsibility Centers**
• Budget reports • Control activities • Reporting systems	• Examples • Uses and limitations	• Why flexible budgets? • Development • Case study • Reports	• Controllable vs. noncontrollable • Performance evaluation • Reporting system	• Cost centers • Profit centers • Investment centers

✔ **The Navigator**

Budgetary Control

LEARNING OBJECTIVE **1**

Describe the concept of budgetary control.

One of management's functions is to control company operations. Control consists of the steps taken by management to see that planned objectives are met. We now ask: How do budgets contribute to control of operations?

The use of budgets in controlling operations is known as **budgetary control**. Such control takes place by means of **budget reports** that compare actual results with planned objectives. The use of budget reports is based on the belief that planned objectives lose much of their potential value without some monitoring of progress along the way. Just as your professors give midterm exams to evaluate your progress, top management requires periodic reports on the progress of department managers toward their planned objectives.

Budget reports provide management with feedback on operations. The feedback for a crucial objective, such as having enough cash on hand to pay bills, may be made daily. For other objectives, such as meeting budgeted annual sales and operating expenses, monthly budget reports may suffice. Budget reports are prepared as frequently as needed. From these reports, management analyzes any differences between actual and planned results and determines their causes. Management then takes corrective action, or it decides to modify future plans. Budgetary control involves the activities shown in Illustration 10-1.

Illustration 10-1
Budgetary control activities

Budgetary control works best when a company has a formalized reporting system. The system does the following:

1. Identifies the name of the budget report, such as the sales budget or the manufacturing overhead budget.
2. States the frequency of the report, such as weekly or monthly.
3. Specifies the purpose of the report.
4. Indicates the primary recipient(s) of the report.

Illustration 10-2 provides a partial budgetary control system for a manufacturing company. Note the frequency of the reports and their emphasis on control. For example, there is a daily report on scrap and a weekly report on labor.

Name of Report	Frequency	Purpose	Primary Recipient(s)
Sales	Weekly	Determine whether sales goals are met	Top management and sales manager
Labor	Weekly	Control direct and indirect labor costs	Vice president of production and production department managers
Scrap	Daily	Determine efficient use of materials	Production manager
Departmental overhead costs	Monthly	Control overhead costs	Department manager
Selling expenses	Monthly	Control selling expenses	Sales manager
Income statement	Monthly and quarterly	Determine whether income goals are met	Top management

Illustration 10-2
Budgetary control reporting system

Static Budget Reports

You learned in Chapter 9 that the master budget formalizes management's planned objectives for the coming year. When used in budgetary control, each budget included in the master budget is considered to be static. A **static budget** is a projection of budget data **at one level of activity**. These budgets do not consider data for different levels of activity. As a result, companies always compare actual results with budget data at the activity level that was used in developing the master budget.

LEARNING OBJECTIVE 2

Evaluate the usefulness of static budget reports.

Examples

To illustrate the role of a static budget in budgetary control, we will use selected data prepared for Hayes Company in Chapter 9. Budget and actual sales data for the Rightride product in the first and second quarters of 2014 are as follows.

Sales	First Quarter	Second Quarter	Total
Budgeted	$180,000	$210,000	$390,000
Actual	179,000	199,500	378,500
Difference	$ 1,000	$ 10,500	$ 11,500

Illustration 10-3
Budget and actual sales data

The sales budget report for Hayes Company's first quarter is shown below. The right-most column reports the difference between the budgeted and actual amounts.

Illustration 10-4
Sales budget report—first quarter

Hayes Company
Sales Budget Report
For the Quarter Ended March 31, 2014

Product Line	Budget	Actual	Difference Favorable F Unfavorable U
Rightride[a]	$180,000	$179,000	**$1,000 U**

[a]In practice, each product line would be included in the report.

The report shows that sales are $1,000 under budget—an unfavorable result. This difference is less than 1% of budgeted sales ($1,000 ÷ $180,000 = .0056).

Alternative Terminology
The difference between budget and actual is sometimes called a *budget variance*.

Top management's reaction to unfavorable differences is often influenced by the materiality (significance) of the difference. Since the difference of $1,000 is immaterial in this case, we assume that Hayes Company management takes no specific corrective action.

Illustration 10-5 shows the budget report for the second quarter. It contains one new feature: cumulative year-to-date information. This report indicates that sales for the second quarter are $10,500 below budget. This is 5% of budgeted sales ($10,500 ÷ $210,000). Top management may now conclude that the difference between budgeted and actual sales requires investigation.

	Hayes Company					
	Sales Budget Report					
	For the Quarter Ended June 30, 2014					

	Second Quarter				**Year-to-Date**		
			Difference				**Difference**
			Favorable F				**Favorable F**
Product Line	**Budget**	**Actual**	**Unfavorable U**	**Budget**	**Actual**	**Unfavorable U**
Rightride	$210,000	$199,500	**$10,500 U**	$390,000	$378,500	**$11,500 U**

Illustration 10-5
Sales budget report—second quarter

Management's analysis should start by asking the sales manager the cause(s) of the shortfall. Managers should consider the need for corrective action. For example, management may decide to spur sales by offering sales incentives to customers or by increasing the advertising of Rightrides. Or, if management concludes that a downturn in the economy is responsible for the lower sales, it may modify planned sales and profit goals for the remainder of the year.

Uses and Limitations

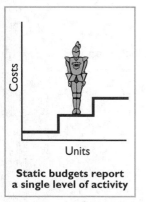

Static budgets report a single level of activity

From these examples, you can see that a master sales budget is useful in evaluating the performance of a sales manager. It is now necessary to ask: Is the master budget appropriate for evaluating a manager's performance in controlling costs? Recall that in a static budget, data are not modified or adjusted, regardless of changes in activity. It follows, then, that a static budget is appropriate in evaluating a manager's effectiveness in controlling costs when:

1. The actual level of activity closely approximates the master budget activity level, and/or
2. The behavior of the costs in response to changes in activity is fixed.

A static budget report is, therefore, appropriate for **fixed manufacturing costs** and for **fixed selling and administrative expenses**. But, as you will see shortly, static budget reports may not be a proper basis for evaluating a manager's performance in controlling variable costs.

Flexible Budgets

LEARNING OBJECTIVE   3

Explain the development of flexible budgets and the usefulness of flexible budget reports.

In contrast to a static budget, which is based on one level of activity, a **flexible budget** projects budget data for various levels of activity. In essence, **the flexible budget is a series of static budgets at different levels of activity**. The flexible budget recognizes that the budgetary process is more useful if it is adaptable to changed operating conditions.

Flexible budgets can be prepared for each of the types of budgets included in the master budget. For example, Marriott Hotels can budget revenues and net income on the basis of 60%, 80%, and 100% of room occupancy. Similarly, American Van Lines can budget its operating expenses on the basis of various levels of truck-miles driven. Duke Energy can budget revenue and net income on the basis of estimated billions of kwh (kilowatt hours) of residential, commercial, and industrial electricity generated. In the following pages, we will illustrate a flexible budget for manufacturing overhead.

Why Flexible Budgets?

Assume that you are the manager in charge of manufacturing overhead in the Assembly Department of Barton Robotics. In preparing the manufacturing overhead budget for 2014, you prepare the following static budget based on a production volume of 10,000 units of robotic controls.

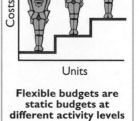

Flexible budgets are static budgets at different activity levels

Barton Robotics	
Manufacturing Overhead Budget (Static)	
Assembly Department	
For the Year Ended December 31, 2014	
Budgeted production in units (robotic controls)	10,000
Budgeted costs	
Indirect materials	$ 250,000
Indirect labor	260,000
Utilities	190,000
Depreciation	280,000
Property taxes	70,000
Supervision	50,000
	$1,100,000

Helpful Hint
The master budget described in Chapter 9 is based on a static budget.

Illustration 10-6
Static overhead budget

Fortunately for the company, the demand for robotic controls has increased, and Barton produces and sells 12,000 units during the year, rather than 10,000. You are elated: Increased sales means increased profitability, which should mean a bonus or a raise for you and the employees in your department. Unfortunately, a comparison of Assembly Department actual and budgeted costs has put you on the spot. The budget report is shown below.

Illustration 10-7
Overhead static budget report

	Barton Robotics.xls				
Home Insert Page Layout Formulas Data Review View					
P18	fx				
	A	B	C	D	E
1		Barton Robotics			
2		Manufacturing Overhead Static Budget Report			
3		For the Year Ended December 31, 2014			
4				Difference	
5		Budget	Actual	Favorable - F Unfavorable - U	
6	Production in units	10,000	12,000		
7					
8	Costs				
9	Indirect materials	$ 250,000	$ 295,000	$ 45,000	U
10	Indirect labor	260,000	312,000	52,000	U
11	Utilities	190,000	225,000	35,000	U
12	Depreciation	280,000	280,000	0	
13	Property taxes	70,000	70,000	0	
14	Supervision	50,000	50,000	0	
15		$1,100,000	$1,232,000	$132,000	U
16					

This comparison uses budget data based on the original activity level (10,000 robotic controls). It indicates that the Assembly Department is significantly **over budget** for three of the six overhead costs. There is a total unfavorable difference of $132,000, which is 12% over budget ($132,000 ÷ $1,100,000). Your supervisor is very unhappy! Instead of sharing in the company's success, you may find yourself looking for another job. What went wrong?

When you calm down and carefully examine the manufacturing overhead budget, you identify the problem: The budget data are not relevant! At the time the budget was developed, the company anticipated that only 10,000 units would be produced, **not** 12,000. Comparing actual with budgeted variable costs is meaningless. As production increases, the budget allowances for variable costs should increase proportionately. The variable costs in this example are indirect materials, indirect labor, and utilities.

Analyzing the budget data for these costs at 10,000 units, you arrive at the following per unit results.

Illustration 10-8
Variable costs per unit

Item	Total Cost	Per Unit
Indirect materials	$250,000	$25
Indirect labor	260,000	26
Utilities	190,000	19
	$700,000	$70

Illustration 10-9 calculates the budgeted variable costs at 12,000 units.

Illustration 10-9
Budgeted variable costs, 12,000 units

Item	Computation	Total
Indirect materials	$25 × 12,000	$300,000
Indirect labor	26 × 12,000	312,000
Utilities	19 × 12,000	228,000
		$840,000

Because fixed costs do not change in total as activity changes, the budgeted amounts for these costs remain the same. Illustration 10-10 shows the budget report based on the flexible budget for **12,000 units** of production. (Compare this with Illustration 10-7.)

This report indicates that the Assembly Department's costs are *under budget*—a favorable difference. Instead of worrying about being fired, you may be in line for a bonus or a raise after all! As this analysis shows, the only appropriate comparison is between actual costs at 12,000 units of production and budgeted costs at 12,000 units. Flexible budget reports provide this comparison.

Developing the Flexible Budget

The flexible budget uses the master budget as its basis. To develop the flexible budget, management uses the following steps.

1. Identify the activity index and the relevant range of activity.
2. Identify the variable costs, and determine the budgeted variable cost per unit of activity for each cost.
3. Identify the fixed costs, and determine the budgeted amount for each cost.
4. Prepare the budget for selected increments of activity within the relevant range.

Illustration 10-10
Overhead flexible budget report

	A	B	C	D	E
1			Barton Robotics		
2			Manufacturing Overhead Flexible Budget Report		
3			For the Year Ended December 31, 2014		
4				Difference	
5		Budget	Actual	Favorable - F Unfavorable - U	
6	Production in units	12,000	12,000		
7					
8	Variable costs				
9	Indirect materials ($25)	$ 300,000	$ 295,000	$5,000	F
10	Indirect labor ($26)	312,000	312,000	0	
11	Utilities ($19)	228,000	225,000	3,000	F
12	Total variable costs	840,000	832,000	8,000	F
13					
14	Fixed costs				
15	Depreciation	280,000	280,000	0	
16	Property taxes	70,000	70,000	0	
17	Supervision	50,000	50,000	0	
18	Total fixed costs	400,000	400,000	0	
19	Total costs	$1,240,000	$1,232,000	$8,000	F
20					

The activity index chosen should significantly influence the costs being budgeted. For manufacturing overhead costs, for example, the activity index is usually the same as the index used in developing the predetermined overhead rate—that is, direct labor hours or machine hours. For selling and administrative expenses, the activity index usually is sales or net sales.

The choice of the increment of activity is largely a matter of judgment. For example, if the relevant range is 8,000 to 12,000 direct labor hours, increments of 1,000 hours may be selected. The flexible budget is then prepared for each increment within the relevant range.

SERVICE COMPANY INSIGHT

Just What the Doctor Ordered?

Nobody is immune from the effects of declining revenues—not even movie stars. When the number of viewers of the television show "House," a medical drama, declined by almost 20%, Fox Broadcasting said it wanted to cut the license fee that it paid to NBCUniversal by 20%. What would NBCUniversal do in response? It might cut the size of the show's cast, which would reduce the payroll costs associated with the show. Or, it could reduce the number of episodes that take advantage of the full cast. Alternatively, it might threaten to quit providing the show to Fox altogether and instead present the show on its own NBC-affiliated channels.

Source: Sam Schechner, "Media Business Shorts: NBCU, Fox Taking Scalpel to 'House'," *Wall Street Journal Online* (April 17, 2011).

? Explain how the use of flexible budgets might help to identify the best solution to this problem. (See page 492.)

DECISION TOOLKIT

DECISION CHECKPOINTS	INFO NEEDED FOR DECISION	TOOL TO USE FOR DECISION	HOW TO EVALUATE RESULTS
Are the increased costs resulting from increased production reasonable?	Variable costs projected at different levels of production	Flexible budget	After taking into account different production levels, results are favorable if expenses are less than budgeted amounts.

Flexible Budget—a Case Study

To illustrate the flexible budget, we use Fox Company. Fox's management uses a **flexible budget for monthly comparisons** of actual and budgeted manufacturing overhead costs of the Finishing Department. The master budget for the year ending December 31, 2014, shows expected **annual** operating capacity of 120,000 direct labor hours and the following overhead costs.

Illustration 10-11
Master budget data

Variable Costs		Fixed Costs	
Indirect materials	$180,000	Depreciation	$180,000
Indirect labor	240,000	Supervision	120,000
Utilities	60,000	Property taxes	60,000
Total	$480,000	Total	$360,000

The four steps for developing the flexible budget are applied as follows.

STEP 1. Identify the activity index and the relevant range of activity. The activity index is direct labor hours. The relevant range is 8,000–12,000 direct labor hours per **month**.

STEP 2. Identify the variable costs, and determine the budgeted variable cost per unit of activity for each cost. There are three variable costs. The variable cost per unit is found by dividing each total budgeted cost by the direct labor hours used in preparing the annual master budget (120,000 hours). For Fox Company, the computations are:

Illustration 10-12
Computation of variable cost per direct labor hour

Variable Costs	Computation	Variable Cost per Direct Labor Hour
Indirect materials	$180,000 ÷ 120,000	$1.50
Indirect labor	$240,000 ÷ 120,000	2.00
Utilities	$ 60,000 ÷ 120,000	0.50
Total		$4.00

STEP 3. Identify the fixed costs, and determine the budgeted amount for each cost. There are three fixed costs. Since Fox desires **monthly budget data**, it divides each annual budgeted cost by 12 to find the monthly amounts. For Fox

Company, the monthly budgeted fixed costs are depreciation $15,000, supervision $10,000, and property taxes $5,000.

STEP 4. Prepare the budget for selected increments of activity within the relevant range. Management prepares the budget in increments of 1,000 direct labor hours.

Illustration 10-13 shows Fox's flexible budget.

Illustration 10-13
Monthly overhead flexible budget

	A	B	C	D	E	F
1				Fox Company		
2			Monthly Manufacturing Overhead Flexible Budget			
3			Finishing Department			
4			For Months During the Year 2014			
5	Activity level					
6	Direct labor hours	8,000	9,000	10,000	11,000	12,000
7	Variable costs					
8	Indirect materials ($1.50)[a]	$12,000[b]	$13,500	$15,000	$16,500	$18,000
9	Indirect labor ($2.00)[a]	16,000[c]	18,000	20,000	22,000	24,000
10	Utilities ($0.50)[a]	4,000[d]	4,500	5,000	5,500	6,000
11	Total variable costs	32,000	36,000	40,000	44,000	48,000
12	Fixed costs					
13	Depreciation	15,000	15,000	15,000	15,000	15,000
14	Supervision	10,000	10,000	10,000	10,000	10,000
15	Property taxes	5,000	5,000	5,000	5,000	5,000
16	Total fixed costs	30,000	30,000	30,000	30,000	30,000
17	Total costs	$62,000	$66,000	$70,000	$74,000	$78,000
18						
19	[a]Cost per direct labor hour; [b]8,000 x $1.50; [c]8,000 x $2.00; [d]8,000 x $0.50					

Fox uses the formula below to determine total budgeted costs at any level of activity.

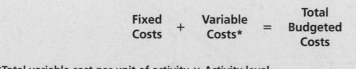

$$\text{Fixed Costs} + \text{Variable Costs*} = \text{Total Budgeted Costs}$$

*Total variable cost per unit of activity × Activity level.

Illustration 10-14
Formula for total budgeted costs

For Fox, fixed costs are $30,000, and total variable cost per direct labor hour is $4 ($1.50 + $2.00 + $0.50). At 9,000 direct labor hours, total budgeted costs are $66,000 [$30,000 + ($4 × 9,000)]. At 8,622 direct labor hours, total budgeted costs are $64,488 [$30,000 + ($4 × 8,622)].

Total budgeted costs can also be shown graphically, as in Illustration 10-15 (page 444). In the graph, the horizontal axis represents the activity index, and

Helpful Hint
Using the data given for Fox, what amount of total costs would be budgeted for 10,600 direct labor hours? Answer: $30,000 fixed + $42,400 variable (i.e., 10,600 × $4) = $72,400 total.

Illustration 10-15
Graphic flexible budget data highlighting 10,000 and 12,000 activity levels

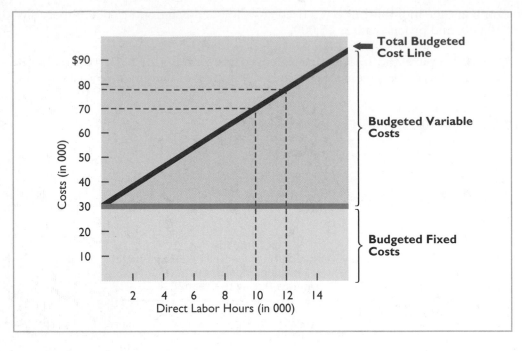

costs are indicated on the vertical axis. The graph highlights two activity levels (10,000 and 12,000). As shown, total budgeted costs at these activity levels are $70,000 [$30,000 + ($4 × 10,000)] and $78,000 [$30,000 + ($4 × 12,000)], respectively.

> **DO IT!**

Flexible Budgets

In Strassel Company's flexible budget graph, the fixed cost line and the total budgeted cost line intersect the vertical axis at $36,000. The total budgeted cost line is $186,000 at an activity level of 50,000 direct labor hours. Compute total budgeted costs at 30,000 direct labor hours.

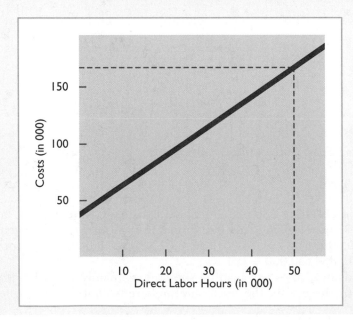

Action Plan

✔ Apply the formula: Fixed costs + Variable costs (Total variable cost per unit × Activity level) = Total budgeted costs.

Solution

Using the graph, fixed costs are $36,000, and variable costs are $3 per direct labor hour [($186,000 − $36,000) ÷ 50,000]. Thus, at 30,000 direct labor hours, total budgeted costs are $126,000 [$36,000 + ($3 × 30,000)].

Related exercise material: **BE10-4, E10-3, E10-5, and DO IT! 10-1.**

Flexible Budget Reports

Flexible budget reports are another type of internal report. The flexible budget report consists of two sections: (1) production data for a selected activity index, such as direct labor hours, and (2) cost data for variable and fixed costs. The report provides a basis for evaluating a manager's performance in two areas: production control and cost control. Flexible budget reports are widely used in production and service departments.

Illustration 10-16 shows a budget report for the Finishing Department of Fox Company for the month of January. In this month, 9,000 hours are worked. The budget data are therefore based on the flexible budget for 9,000 hours in Illustration 10-13 (page 443). The actual cost data are assumed.

Illustration 10-16
Overhead flexible budget report

	Fox Company.xls			
Home	Insert	Page Layout	Formulas	Data Review View
P18	fx			
	A	B	C	D	E

	A	B	C	D	E
1		**Fox Company**			
2		**Manufacturing Overhead Flexible Budget Report**			
3		**Finishing Department**			
4		**For the Month Ended January 31, 2014**			
5				Difference	
6		Budget at	Actual costs at	Favorable - F	
7	Direct labor hours (DLH)	9,000 DLH	9,000 DLH	Unfavorable - U	
8					
9	Variable costs				
10	Indirect materials ($1.50)ᵃ	$13,500	$14,000	$ 500	U
11	Indirect labor ($2.00)ᵃ	18,000	17,000	1,000	F
12	Utilities ($0.50)ᵃ	4,500	4,600	100	U
13	Total variable costs	36,000	35,600	400	F
14					
15	Fixed costs				
16	Depreciation	15,000	15,000	0	
17	Supervision	10,000	10,000	0	
18	Property taxes	5,000	5,000	0	
19	Total fixed costs	30,000	30,000	0	
20	Total costs	$66,000	$65,600	$ 400	F
21					
22	ᵃCost per direct labor hour				

How appropriate is this report in evaluating the Finishing Department manager's performance in controlling overhead costs? The report clearly provides a reliable basis. Both actual and budget costs are based on the activity level worked during January. Since variable costs generally are incurred directly by the department, the difference between the budget allowance for those hours and the actual costs is the responsibility of the department manager.

In subsequent months, Fox Company will prepare other flexible budget reports. For each month, the budget data are based on the actual activity level attained. In February that level may be 11,000 direct labor hours, in July 10,000, and so on.

Note that this flexible budget is based on a single cost driver. A more accurate budget often can be developed using the activity-based costing concepts explained in Chapter 4.

SERVICE COMPANY INSIGHT

Budgets and the Exotic Newcastle Disease

Exotic Newcastle Disease, one of the most infectious bird diseases in the world, kills so swiftly that many victims die before any symptoms appear. When it broke out in Southern California, it could have spelled disaster for the San Diego Zoo. "We have one of the most valuable collections of birds in the world, if not *the* most valuable," says Paula Brock, CFO of the Zoological Society of San Diego, which operates the zoo.

Bird exhibits were closed to the public for several months (the disease, which is harmless to humans, can be carried on clothes and shoes). The tires of arriving delivery trucks were sanitized, as were the shoes of anyone visiting the zoo's nonpublic areas. Zookeeper uniforms had to be changed and cleaned daily. And ultimately, the zoo, with $150 million in revenues, spent almost half a million dollars on quarantine measures.

It worked: No birds got sick. Better yet, the damage to the rest of the zoo's budget was minimized by another protective measure: the monthly budget reforecast. "When we get a hit like this, we still have to find a way to make our bottom line," says Brock. Thanks to a new planning process Brock had introduced a year earlier, the zoo's scientists were able to raise the financial alarm as they redirected resources to ward off the disease. "Because we had timely awareness," she says, "we were able to make adjustments to weather the storm."

Budget reforecasting is nothing new. (The San Diego Zoo's annual static budget was behind the times before Brock took over as CFO.) But the reaction of the zoo's staff shows the benefits of Brock's immediate efforts to link strategy to the process. It's a move long touted by consultants as a key way to improve people's involvement in budgeting.

"To keep your company on a path, it has to have some kind of map," says Brock. "The budgeting-and-planning process is that map. I cannot imagine an organization feeling in control if it didn't have that sort of discipline."

Source: Tim Reason, "Budgeting in the Real World," *CFO Magazine* (July 12, 2005), *www.cfodirect.com/ cfopublic.nsf/vContentPrint/649A82C8FF8AB06B85257037004* (accessed July 2005).

? What is the major benefit of tying a budget to the overall goals of the company? (See page 492.)

> DO IT!

Flexible Budget Reports

Lawler Company expects to produce 40,000 units of product CV93 during the current year. Budgeted variable manufacturing costs per unit are direct materials $6, direct labor $15, and overhead $24. Annual budgeted fixed manufacturing overhead costs are $120,000 for depreciation and $60,000 for supervision.

In the current month, Lawler produced 5,000 units and incurred the following costs: direct materials $33,900, direct labor $74,200, variable overhead $120,500, depreciation $10,000, and supervision $5,000.

Prepare a flexible budget report. (*Note:* You do not have to prepare the heading.) Were costs controlled?

Solution

Action Plan

✔ Use budget for actual units produced.

✔ Classify each cost as variable or fixed.

✔ Determine monthly fixed costs by dividing annual amounts by 12.

✔ Determine the difference as favorable or unfavorable.

✔ Determine the difference in total variable costs, total fixed costs, and total costs.

Lawler Company.xls

Home   Insert   Page Layout   Formulas   Data   Review   View

P18   *fx*

	A	B	C	D	
1				Difference	
2		Budget at	Actual costs at	Favorable - F	
3	Units produced	5,000 units	5,000 units	Unfavorable - U	
4					
5	Variable costs				
6	Direct materials ($6)	$ 30,000	$ 33,900	$3,900	U
7	Direct labor ($15)	75,000	74,200	800	F
8	Overhead ($24)	120,000	120,500	500	U
9	Total variable costs	225,000	228,600	3,600	U
10					
11	Fixed costs				
12	Depreciation	10,000	10,000	0	
13	Supervision	5,000	5,000	0	
14	Total fixed costs	15,000	15,000	0	
15	Total costs	$240,000	$243,600	$3,600	U
16					
17					

The responsibility report indicates that actual direct labor was only about 1% different from the budget, and overhead was less than half a percent different. Both appear to have been well-controlled.

This was not the case for direct materials. Its 13% unfavorable difference should probably be investigated.

Actual fixed costs had no difference from budget and were well-controlled.

Related exercise material: **BE10-5, E10-4, E10-6, E10-7, E10-8, E10-10, and DO IT! 10-2.**

✔ **The Navigator**

Responsibility Accounting

Like budgeting, responsibility accounting is an important part of management accounting. **Responsibility accounting** involves accumulating and reporting costs (and revenues, where relevant) on the basis of the manager who has the authority to make the day-to-day decisions about the items. Under responsibility accounting, a manager's performance is evaluated on matters directly under that manager's control. Responsibility accounting can be used at every level of management in which the following conditions exist.

LEARNING OBJECTIVE   4

Describe the concept of responsibility accounting.

1. Costs and revenues can be directly associated with the specific level of management responsibility.

2. The costs and revenues can be controlled by employees at the level of responsibility with which they are associated.

3. Budget data can be developed for evaluating the manager's effectiveness in controlling the costs and revenues.

Illustration 10-17 depicts levels of responsibility for controlling costs.

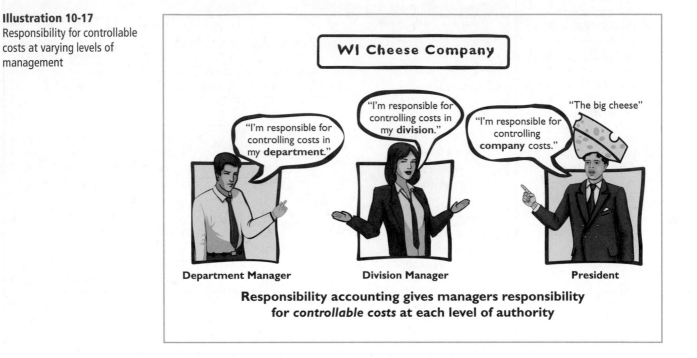

Under responsibility accounting, any individual who controls a specified set of activities can be a responsibility center. Thus, responsibility accounting may extend from the lowest level of control to the top strata of management. Once responsibility is established, the company first measures and reports the effectiveness of the individual's performance for the specified activity. It then reports that measure upward throughout the organization.

Responsibility accounting is especially valuable in a decentralized company. **Decentralization** means that the control of operations is delegated to many managers throughout the organization. The term **segment** is sometimes used to identify an area of responsibility in decentralized operations. Under responsibility accounting, companies prepare segment reports periodically, such as monthly, quarterly, and annually, to evaluate managers' performance.

Responsibility accounting is an essential part of any effective system of budgetary control. The reporting of costs and revenues under responsibility accounting differs from budgeting in two respects:

1. A distinction is made between controllable and noncontrollable items.

2. Performance reports either emphasize or include only items controllable by the individual manager.

Responsibility accounting applies to both profit and not-for-profit entities. For-profit entities seek to maximize net income. Not-for-profit entities wish to provide services as efficiently as possible.

MANAGEMENT INSIGHT

Competition versus Collaboration

Many compensation and promotion programs encourage competition among employees for pay raises. To get ahead you have to perform better than your fellow employees. While this may encourage hard work, it does not foster collaboration, and it can lead to distrust and disloyalty. Such results have led some companies to believe that cooperation and collaboration are essential in order to succeed in today's environment. For example, division managers might increase collaboration (and reduce costs) by sharing design and marketing resources or by jointly negotiating with suppliers. In addition, companies can reduce the need to hire and lay off employees by sharing employees across divisions as human resource needs increase and decrease.

As a consequence, many companies now explicitly include measures of collaboration in their performance measures. For example, Procter & Gamble measures collaboration in employees' annual performance reviews. At Cisco Systems the assessment of an employee's teamwork can affect the annual bonus by as much as 20%.

Source: Carol Hymowitz, "Rewarding Competitors Over Collaboration No Longer Makes Sense," *Wall Street Journal* (February 13, 2006).

? How might managers of separate divisions be able to reduce division costs through collaboration? (See page 492.)

Controllable versus Noncontrollable Revenues and Costs

All costs and revenues are controllable at some level of responsibility within a company. This truth underscores the adage by the CEO of any organization that "the buck stops here." Under responsibility accounting, the critical issue is **whether the cost or revenue is controllable at the level of responsibility with which it is associated**. A cost over which a manager has control is called a **controllable cost**. From this definition, it follows that:

1. All costs are controllable by top management because of the broad range of its authority.
2. Fewer costs are controllable as one moves down to each lower level of managerial responsibility because of the manager's decreasing authority.

In general, **costs incurred directly by a level of responsibility are controllable at that level**. In contrast, costs incurred indirectly and allocated to a responsibility level are **noncontrollable costs** at that level.

> **Helpful Hint**
> Are there more or fewer controllable costs as you move to higher levels of management?
> Answer: More.

> **Helpful Hint**
> The longer the time span, the more likely that the cost becomes controllable.

Principles of Performance Evaluation

Performance evaluation is at the center of responsibility accounting. It is a management function that compares actual results with budget goals. It involves both behavioral and reporting principles.

MANAGEMENT BY EXCEPTION

Management by exception means that top management's review of a budget report is focused either entirely or primarily on differences between actual results and planned objectives. This approach enables top management to focus on problem areas. For example, many companies now use online reporting systems for employees to file their travel and entertainment expense reports. In addition to cutting reporting time in half, the online system enables managers to quickly analyze variances from travel budgets. This cuts down on expense account "padding" such as spending too much on meals or falsifying documents for costs that were never actually incurred.

Management by exception does not mean that top management will investigate every difference. For this approach to be effective, there must be guidelines for identifying an exception. The usual criteria are materiality and controllability.

MATERIALITY Without quantitative guidelines, management would have to investigate every budget difference regardless of the amount. Materiality is usually expressed as a percentage difference from budget. For example, management may set the percentage difference at 5% for important items and 10% for other items. Managers will investigate all differences either over or under budget by the specified percentage. Costs over budget warrant investigation to determine why they were not controlled. Likewise, costs under budget merit investigation to determine whether costs critical to profitability are being curtailed. For example, if maintenance costs are budgeted at $80,000 but only $40,000 is spent, major unexpected breakdowns in productive facilities may occur in the future.

Alternatively, a company may specify a single percentage difference from budget for all items and supplement this guideline with a minimum dollar limit. For example, the exception criteria may be stated at 5% of budget or more than $10,000.

CONTROLLABILITY OF THE ITEM Exception guidelines are more restrictive for controllable items than for items the manager cannot control. In fact, there may be no guidelines for noncontrollable items. For example, a large unfavorable difference between actual and budgeted property tax expense may not be flagged for investigation because the only possible causes are an unexpected increase in the tax rate or in the assessed value of the property. An investigation into the difference would be useless: The manager cannot control either cause.

BEHAVIORAL PRINCIPLES

The human factor is critical in evaluating performance. Behavioral principles include the following.

1. **Managers of responsibility centers should have direct input into the process of establishing budget goals of their area of responsibility.** Without such input, managers may view the goals as unrealistic or arbitrarily set by top management. Such views adversely affect the managers' motivation to meet the targeted objectives.

2. **The evaluation of performance should be based entirely on matters that are controllable by the manager being evaluated.** Criticism of a manager on matters outside his or her control reduces the effectiveness of the evaluation process. It leads to negative reactions by a manager and to doubts about the fairness of the company's evaluation policies.

3. **Top management should support the evaluation process.** As explained earlier, the evaluation process begins at the lowest level of responsibility and extends upward to the highest level of management. Managers quickly lose faith in the process when top management ignores, overrules, or bypasses established procedures for evaluating a manager's performance.

4. **The evaluation process must allow managers to respond to their evaluations.** Evaluation is not a one-way street. Managers should have the opportunity to defend their performance. Evaluation without feedback is both impersonal and ineffective.

5. The evaluation should identify both good and poor performance. Praise for good performance is a powerful motivating factor for a manager. This is especially true when a manager's compensation includes rewards for meeting budget goals.

REPORTING PRINCIPLES

Performance evaluation under responsibility accounting should be based on certain reporting principles. These principles pertain primarily to the internal reports that provide the basis for evaluating performance. Performance reports should:

1. Contain only data that are controllable by the manager of the responsibility center.

2. Provide accurate and reliable budget data to measure performance.

3. Highlight significant differences between actual results and budget goals.

4. Be tailor-made for the intended evaluation.

5. Be prepared at reasonable time intervals.

In recent years, companies have come under increasing pressure from influential shareholder groups to do a better job of linking executive pay to corporate performance. For example, software maker Siebel Systems unveiled a new incentive plan after lengthy discussions with the California Public Employees' Retirement System. One unique feature of the plan is that managers' targets will be publicly disclosed at the beginning of each year for investors to evaluate.

MANAGEMENT INSIGHT

Flexible Manufacturing Requires Flexible Accounting

Flexible budgeting is useful because it enables managers to evaluate performance in light of changing conditions. But the ability to react quickly to changing conditions is even more important. Among automobile manufacturing facilities in the U.S., nobody's plants are more flexible than Honda. The manufacturing facilities of some auto companies can make slight alterations to the features of a vehicle in response to changes in demand for particular features. But for most plants, to switch from production of one type of vehicle to a completely different type of vehicle, when demand for types of vehicles shifts, typically takes months and costs hundreds of millions of dollars. But at the Honda plant, the switch takes minutes. For example, it takes about five minutes to install different hand-like parts on the robots so they can switch from making Civic compacts to the longer, taller CR-V crossover. This ability to adjust quickly to changing demand gave Honda a huge advantage when gas prices surged and demand for more fuel-efficient cars increased quickly.

Source: Kate Linebaugh, "Honda's Flexible Plants Provide Edge," *Wall Street Journal Online* (September 23, 2008).

 What implications do these improvements in production capabilities have for management accounting information and performance evaluation within the organization? (See page 493.)

Responsibility Reporting System

A **responsibility reporting system** involves the preparation of a report for each level of responsibility in the company's organization chart. To illustrate such a system, we use the partial organization chart and production departments of Francis Chair Company in Illustration 10-18 (page 452).

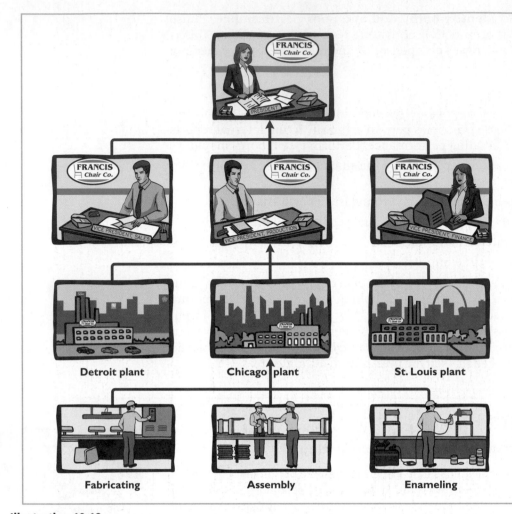

Report A
President sees summary data of vice presidents.

Report B
Vice president sees summary of controllable costs in his/her functional area.

Report C
Plant manager sees summary of controllable costs for each department in the plant.

Report D
Department manager sees controllable costs of his/her department.

Illustration 10-18
Partial organization chart

The responsibility reporting system begins with the lowest level of responsibility for controlling costs and moves upward to each higher level. Illustration 10-19 details the connections between levels.

A brief description of the four reports for Francis Chair Company is as follows.

1. **Report D** is typical of reports that go to department managers. Similar reports are prepared for the managers of the Fabricating, Assembly, and Enameling Departments.

2. **Report C** is an example of reports that are sent to plant managers. It shows the costs of the Chicago plant that are controllable at the second level of responsibility. In addition, Report C shows summary data for each department that is controlled by the plant manager. Similar reports are prepared for the Detroit and St. Louis plant managers.

3. **Report B** illustrates the reports at the third level of responsibility. It shows the controllable costs of the vice president of production and summary data on the three assembly plants for which this officer is responsible. Similar reports are prepared for the vice presidents of sales and finance.

4. **Report A** is typical of reports that go to the top level of responsibility—the president. It shows the controllable costs and expenses of this office and summary data on the vice presidents that are accountable to the president.

Illustration 10-19
Responsibility reporting system

Report A
President sees summary data of vice presidents.

Report A.xls

	A	B	C	D	E
1		**Report A**			
2					
3	To President			Month: January	
4	Controllable Costs:	Budget	Actual	Fav/Unfav	
5	President	$ 150,000	$ 151,500	$ 1,500	U
6	Vice Presidents:				
7	Sales	185,000	187,000	2,000	U
8	**Production**	**1,179,000**	**1,186,300**	**7,300**	U
9	Finance	100,000	101,000	1,000	U
10	Total	$1,614,000	$1,625,800	$11,800	U
11					

Report B
Vice president sees summary of controllable costs in his/her functional area.

Report B.xls

	A	B	C	D	E
1		**Report B**			
2					
3	To Vice President Production			Month: January	
4	Controllable Costs:	Budget	Actual	Fav/Unfav	
5	VP Production	$ 125,000	$ 126,000	$ 1,000	U
6	Assembly Plants:				
7	Detroit	420,000	418,000	2,000	F
8	**Chicago**	**304,000**	**309,300**	**5,300**	U
9	St. Louis	330,000	333,000	3,000	U
10	Total	$1,179,000	$1,186,300	$ 7,300	U
11					

Report C
Plant manager sees summary of controllable costs for each department in the plant.

Report C.xls

	A	B	C	D	E
1		**Report C**			
2					
3	To Plant Manager-Chicago			Month: January	
4	Controllable Costs:	Budget	Actual	Fav/Unfav	
5	Chicago Plant	$110,000	$113,000	$3,000	U
6	Departments:				
7	**Fabricating**	**84,000**	**85,300**	**1,300**	U
8	Enameling	62,000	64,000	2,000	U
9	Assembly	48,000	47,000	1,000	F
10	Total	$304,000	$309,300	$5,300	U
11					

Report D
Department manager sees controllable costs of his/her department.

Report D.xls

	A	B	C	D	E
1		**Report D**			
2					
3	To Fabricating Dept. Manager			Month: January	
4	Controllable Costs:	Budget	Actual	Fav/Unfav	
5	Direct Materials	$20,000	$20,500	$ 500	U
6	Direct Labor	40,000	41,000	1,000	U
7	Overhead	24,000	23,800	200	F
8	Total	$84,000	$85,300	$1,300	U
9					

A responsibility reporting system permits management by exception at each level of responsibility. And, each higher level of responsibility can obtain the detailed report for each lower level of responsibility. For example, the vice president of production in the Francis Chair Company may request the Chicago plant manager's report because this plant is $5,300 over budget.

This type of reporting system also permits comparative evaluations. In Illustration 10-19, the Chicago plant manager can easily rank the department managers' effectiveness in controlling manufacturing costs. Comparative rankings provide further incentive for a manager to control costs.

Types of Responsibility Centers

There are three basic types of responsibility centers: cost centers, profit centers, and investment centers. These classifications indicate the degree of responsibility the manager has for the performance of the center.

A **cost center** incurs costs (and expenses) but does not directly generate revenues. Managers of cost centers have the authority to incur costs. They are evaluated on their ability to control costs. **Cost centers are usually either production departments or service departments.** Production departments participate directly in making the product. Service departments provide only support services. In a Ford Motor Company automobile plant, the welding, painting, and assembling departments are production departments. Ford's maintenance, cafeteria, and human resources departments are service departments. All of them are cost centers.

A **profit center** incurs costs (and expenses) and also generates revenues. Managers of profit centers are judged on the profitability of their centers. Examples of profit centers include the individual departments of a retail store, such as clothing, furniture, and automotive products, and branch offices of banks.

Like a profit center, an **investment center** incurs costs (and expenses) and generates revenues. In addition, an investment center has control over decisions regarding the assets available for use. Investment center managers are evaluated on both the profitability of the center and the rate of return earned on the funds invested. Investment centers are often associated with subsidiary companies. Utility Duke Energy has operating divisions such as electric utility, energy trading, and natural gas. Investment center managers control or significantly influence investment decisions related to such matters as plant expansion and entry into new market areas. Illustration 10-20 depicts the three types of responsibility centers.

Helpful Hint
(1) Is the jewelry department of Macy's department store a profit center or a cost center?
(2) Is the props department of a movie studio a profit center or a cost center?
Answers: (1) Profit center.
(2) Cost center.

Illustration 10-20
Types of responsibility centers

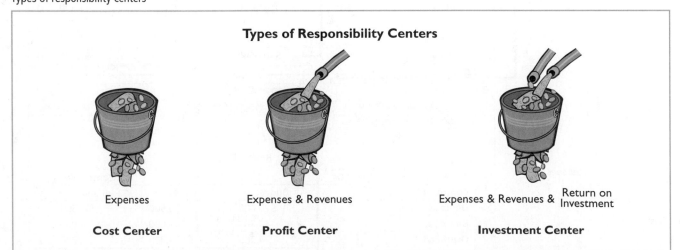

Types of Responsibility Centers

Expenses

Cost Center

Expenses & Revenues

Profit Center

Expenses & Revenues & Return on Investment

Investment Center

Responsibility Accounting for Cost Centers

The evaluation of a manager's performance for cost centers is based on his or her ability to meet budgeted goals for controllable costs. **Responsibility reports for cost centers compare actual controllable costs with flexible budget data.**

Illustration 10-21 shows a responsibility report. The report is adapted from the flexible budget report for Fox Company in Illustration 10-16 (page 445). It assumes that the Finishing Department manager is able to control all manufacturing overhead costs except depreciation, property taxes, and his own monthly salary of $6,000. The remaining $4,000 ($10,000 − $6,000) of supervision costs are assumed to apply to other supervisory personnel within the Finishing Department, whose salaries are controllable by the manager.

LEARNING OBJECTIVE **5**

Indicate the features of responsibility reports for cost centers.

	Fox Company.xls			
Home Insert Page Layout Formulas Data Review View				
P18 fx				
	A	B	C	D	E

	A	B	C	D	E
1					
2		Fox Company			
3		Finishing Department			
3		Responsibility Report			
4		For the Month Ended January 31, 2014			
5				Difference	
6				Favorable - F	
6	Controllable Costs	Budget	Actual	Unfavorable - U	
7	Indirect materials	$13,500	$14,000	$ 500	U
8	Indirect labor	18,000	17,000	$1,000	F
9	Utilities	4,500	4,600	100	U
10	**Supervision**	4,000	4,000	0	
11		$40,000	$39,600	$ 400	F
12					

Illustration 10-21
Responsibility report for a cost center

The report in Illustration 10-21 includes **only controllable costs**, and no distinction is made between variable and fixed costs. The responsibility report continues the concept of management by exception. In this case, top management may request an explanation of the $1,000 favorable difference in indirect labor and/or the $500 unfavorable difference in indirect materials.

Responsibility Accounting for Profit Centers

To evaluate the performance of a profit center manager, upper management needs detailed information about both controllable revenues and controllable costs. The operating revenues earned by a profit center, such as sales, are controllable by the manager. All variable costs (and expenses) incurred by the center are also controllable by the manager because they vary with sales. However, to determine the controllability of fixed costs, it is necessary to distinguish between direct and indirect fixed costs.

LEARNING OBJECTIVE **6**

Identify the content of responsibility reports for profit centers.

DIRECT AND INDIRECT FIXED COSTS

A profit center may have both direct and indirect fixed costs. **Direct fixed costs** relate specifically to one center and are incurred for the sole benefit of that center. Examples of such costs include the salaries established by the profit center manager for supervisory personnel and the cost of a timekeeping department for the center's employees. Since these fixed costs can be traced directly to a center, they are also called **traceable costs**. **Most direct fixed costs are controllable by the profit center manager.**

In contrast, **indirect fixed costs** pertain to a company's overall operating activities and are incurred for the benefit of more than one profit center. Management allocates indirect fixed costs to profit centers on some type of equitable basis. For example, property taxes on a building occupied by more than one center may be allocated on the basis of square feet of floor space used by each center. Or, the costs of a company's human resources department may be allocated to profit centers on the basis of the number of employees in each center. Because these fixed costs apply to more than one center, they are also called **common costs**. **Most indirect fixed costs are not controllable by the profit center manager.**

Helpful Hint
Recognize that we are emphasizing *financial* measures of performance. These days companies are also making an effort to stress *nonfinancial* performance measures such as product quality, labor productivity, market growth, materials' yield, manufacturing flexibility, and technological capability.

RESPONSIBILITY REPORT

The responsibility report for a profit center shows budgeted and actual **controllable revenues and costs**. The report is prepared using the cost-volume-profit income statement explained in Chapter 5. In the report:

1. Controllable fixed costs are deducted from contribution margin.

2. The excess of contribution margin over controllable fixed costs is identified as **controllable margin**.

3. Noncontrollable fixed costs are not reported.

Illustration 10-22 shows the responsibility report for the manager of the Marine Division, a profit center of Mantle Company. For the year, the Marine Division also had $60,000 of indirect fixed costs that were not controllable by the profit center manager.

Illustration 10-22
Responsibility report for profit center

	A	B	C	D	E
			Mantle Company		
			Marine Division		
			Responsibility Report		
			For the Year Ended December 31, 2014		
5				Difference	
6		Budget	Actual	Favorable - F Unfavorable - U	
7	Sales	$1,200,000	$1,150,000	$50,000	U
8	Variable costs				
9	Cost of goods sold	500,000	490,000	10,000	F
10	Selling and administrative	160,000	156,000	4,000	F
11	Total	660,000	646,000	14,000	F
12	Contribution margin	540,000	504,000	36,000	U
13	**Controllable fixed costs**				
14	Cost of goods sold	100,000	100,000	0	
15	Selling and administrative	80,000	80,000	0	
16	Total	180,000	180,000	0	
17	**Controllable margin**	$ 360,000	$ 324,000	$36,000	U
18					

Controllable margin is considered to be the best measure of the manager's performance **in controlling revenues and costs**. The report in Illustration 10-22 shows that the manager's performance was below budgeted expectations by 10% ($36,000 ÷ $360,000). Top management would likely investigate the causes of this unfavorable result. Note that the report does not show the Marine Division's noncontrollable fixed costs of $60,000. These costs would be included in a report on the profitability of the profit center.

Management also may choose to see **monthly** responsibility reports for profit centers. In addition, responsibility reports may include cumulative year-to-date results.

DECISION TOOLKIT

DECISION CHECKPOINTS	INFO NEEDED FOR DECISION	TOOL TO USE FOR DECISION	HOW TO EVALUATE RESULTS
Have the individual managers been held accountable for the costs and revenues under their control?	Review costs and revenues, where the individual manager has authority to make day-to-day decisions about the items	Responsibility reports focused on cost centers, profit centers, and investment centers as appropriate	Compare budget to actual costs and revenues for controllable items.

> DO IT!

Profit Center Responsibility Report

Midwest Division operates as a profit center. It reports the following for the year:

	Budget	Actual
Sales	$1,500,000	$1,700,000
Variable costs	700,000	800,000
Controllable fixed costs	400,000	400,000
Noncontrollable fixed costs	200,000	200,000

Prepare a responsibility report for the Midwest Division for December 31, 2014.

Solution

Action Plan

✔ Deduct variable costs from sales to show contribution margin.

✔ Deduct controllable fixed costs from the contribution margin to show controllable margin.

✔ Do not report noncontrollable fixed costs.

Midwest Division
Responsibility Report
For the Year Ended December 31, 2014

	Budget	Actual	Difference Favorable F Unfavorable U
Sales	$1,500,000	$1,700,000	$200,000 F
Variable costs	700,000	800,000	100,000 U
Contribution margin	800,000	900,000	100,000 F
Controllable fixed costs	400,000	400,000	–0–
Controllable margin	$ 400,000	$ 500,000	$100,000 F

Related exercise material: **BE10-7, E10-15, and DO IT! 10-3.**

✔ The Navigator

Responsibility Accounting for Investment Centers

LEARNING OBJECTIVE 7

Explain the basis and formula used in evaluating performance in investment centers.

As explained earlier, an investment center manager can control or significantly influence the investment funds available for use. Thus, the primary basis for evaluating the performance of a manager of an investment center is **return on investment (ROI)**. The return on investment is considered to be a useful performance measurement because it shows the **effectiveness of the manager in utilizing the assets at his or her disposal**.

RETURN ON INVESTMENT (ROI)

The formula for computing ROI for an investment center, together with assumed illustrative data, is shown in Illustration 10-23.

Illustration 10-23
ROI formula

Controllable Margin	÷	Average Operating Assets	=	Return on Investment (ROI)
$1,000,000	÷	$5,000,000	=	20%

Both factors in the formula are controllable by the investment center manager. Operating assets consist of current assets and plant assets used in operations by the center and controlled by the manager. Nonoperating assets such as idle plant assets and land held for future use are excluded. Average operating assets are usually based on the cost or book value of the assets at the beginning and end of the year.

RESPONSIBILITY REPORT

The scope of the investment center manager's responsibility significantly affects the content of the performance report. Since an investment center is an independent entity for operating purposes, **all fixed costs are controllable by its manager**. For example, the manager is responsible for depreciation on investment center assets. Therefore, more fixed costs are identified as controllable in the performance report for an investment center manager than in a performance report for a profit center manager. The report also shows budgeted and actual ROI below controllable margin.

To illustrate this responsibility report, we will now assume that the Marine Division of Mantle Company is an investment center. It has budgeted and actual average operating assets of $2,000,000. The manager can control $60,000 of fixed costs that were not controllable when the division was a profit center. Illustration 10-24 shows the division's responsibility report.

The report shows that the manager's performance based on ROI was below budget expectations by 1.8% (15.0% versus 13.2%). Top management would likely want an explanation of the reasons for this unfavorable result.

JUDGMENTAL FACTORS IN ROI

The return on investment approach includes two judgmental factors:

1. **Valuation of operating assets.** Operating assets may be valued at acquisition cost, book value, appraised value, or fair value. The first two bases are readily available from the accounting records.

2. **Margin (income) measure.** This measure may be controllable margin, income from operations, or net income.

Illustration 10-24
Responsibility report for
investment center

	Mantle Company.xls			
Home Insert Page Layout Formulas Data Review View				
P18	fx			

	A	B	C	D	E
1		**Mantle Company**			
2		**Marine Division**			
3		**Responsibility Report**			
4		**For the Year Ended December 31, 2014**			
5				Difference	
6		Budget	Actual	Favorable - F Unfavorable - U	
7	Sales	$ 1,200,000	$ 1,150,000	$ 50,000	U
8	Variable costs				
9	Cost of goods sold	500,000	490,000	10,000	F
10	Selling and administrative	160,000	156,000	4,000	F
11	Total	660,000	646,000	14,000	F
12	Contribution margin	540,000	504,000	36,000	U
13	**Controllable fixed costs**				
14	Cost of goods sold	100,000	100,000	0	
15	Selling and administrative	80,000	80,000	0	
16	**Other fixed costs**	**60,000**	60,000	0	
17	Total	$ 240,000	$ 240,000	0	
18	Controllable margin	$ 300,000	$ 264,000	$ 36,000	U
19	**Return on investment**	15.0%	13.2%	1.8%	U
20		(a)	(b)	(c)	
21					
22		(a) $ 300,000 $2,000,000	(b) $ 264,000 $2,000,000	(c) $ 36,000 $2,000,000	
23					

Each of the alternative values for operating assets can provide a reliable basis for evaluating a manager's performance as long as it is consistently applied between reporting periods. However, the use of income measures other than controllable margin will not result in a valid basis for evaluating the performance of an investment center manager.

IMPROVING ROI
The manager of an investment center can improve ROI by increasing controllable margin, and/or reducing average operating assets. To illustrate, we will use the following assumed data for the Laser Division of Berra Company.

Sales	$2,000,000
Variable costs	1,100,000
Contribution margin (45%)	900,000
Controllable fixed costs	300,000
Controllable margin (a)	$ 600,000
Average operating assets (b)	$5,000,000
Return on investment (a) ÷ (b)	**12%**

Illustration 10-25
Assumed data for Laser
Division

INCREASING CONTROLLABLE MARGIN Controllable margin can be increased by increasing sales or by reducing variable and controllable fixed costs as follows.

1. **Increase sales 10%.** Sales will increase $200,000 ($2,000,000 × .10). Assuming no change in the contribution margin percentage of 45%, contribution margin will increase $90,000 ($200,000 × .45). Controllable margin will increase by the same amount because controllable fixed costs will not change. Thus, controllable margin becomes $690,000 ($600,000 + $90,000). The new ROI is 13.8%, computed as follows.

Illustration 10-26
ROI computation—increase in sales

$$\text{ROI} = \frac{\text{Controllable margin}}{\text{Average operating assets}} = \frac{\$690,000}{\$5,000,000} = \textbf{13.8\%}$$

An increase in sales benefits both the investment center and the company if it results in new business. It would not benefit the company if the increase was achieved at the expense of other investment centers.

2. **Decrease variable and fixed costs 10%.** Total costs decrease $140,000 [($1,100,000 + $300,000) × .10]. This reduction results in a corresponding increase in controllable margin. Thus, controllable margin becomes $740,000 ($600,000 + $140,000). The new ROI is 14.8%, computed as follows.

Illustration 10-27
ROI computation—decrease in costs

$$\text{ROI} = \frac{\text{Controllable margin}}{\text{Average operating assets}} = \frac{\$740,000}{\$5,000,000} = \textbf{14.8\%}$$

This course of action is clearly beneficial when the reduction in costs is the result of eliminating waste and inefficiency. But, a reduction in costs that results from cutting expenditures on vital activities, such as required maintenance and inspections, is not likely to be acceptable to top management.

REDUCING AVERAGE OPERATING ASSETS Assume that average operating assets are reduced 10% or $500,000 ($5,000,000 × .10). Average operating assets become $4,500,000 ($5,000,000 − $500,000). Since controllable margin remains unchanged at $600,000, the new ROI is 13.3%, computed as follows.

Illustration 10-28
ROI computation—decrease in operating assets

$$\text{ROI} = \frac{\text{Controllable margin}}{\text{Average operating assets}} = \frac{\$600,000}{\$4,500,000} = \textbf{13.3\%}$$

Reductions in operating assets may or may not be prudent. It is beneficial to eliminate overinvestment in inventories and to dispose of excessive plant assets. However, it is unwise to reduce inventories below expected needs or to dispose of essential plant assets.

ACCOUNTING ACROSS THE ORGANIZATION

Does Hollywood Look at ROI?

If Hollywood were run like a real business, where things like return on investment mattered, there would be one unchallenged, sacred principle that studio chieftains would never violate: Make lots of G-rated movies.

No matter how you slice the movie business—by star vehicles, by budget levels, or by sequels or franchises—by far the best return on investment comes from the not-so-glamorous world of G-rated films. The problem is, these movies represent only 3% of the total films made in a typical year.

Take 2003: According to Motion Picture Association of America statistics, of the 940 movies released that year, only 29 were G-rated. Yet the highest-grossing movie of the year, *Finding Nemo*, was G-rated. . . . On the flip side are the R-rated films, which dominate the total releases and yet yield the worst return on investment. A whopping 646 R-rated films were released in 2003—69% of the total output—but only four of the top-20 grossing movies of the year were R-rated films.

This trend—G-rated movies are good for business but underproduced; R-rated movies are bad for business, and yet overdone—is something that has been driving economists batty for the past several years.

Source: David Grainger, "The Dysfunctional Family-Film Business," *Fortune* (January 10, 2005), pp. 20–21.

? What might be the reason that movie studios do not produce G-rated movies as much as R-rated ones? (See page 493.)

DECISION TOOLKIT

DECISION CHECKPOINTS	INFO NEEDED FOR DECISION	TOOL TO USE FOR DECISION	HOW TO EVALUATE RESULTS
Has the investment center performed up to expectations?	Controllable margin (contribution margin minus controllable fixed costs), and average investment center operating assets	Return on Investment	Compare actual ROI to expected ROI.

> DO IT!

Performance Evaluation

The service division of Metro Industries reported the following results for 2014.

Sales	$400,000
Variable costs	320,000
Controllable fixed costs	40,800
Average operating assets	280,000

Management is considering the following independent courses of action in 2015 in order to maximize the return on investment for this division.

1. Reduce average operating assets by $80,000, with no change in controllable margin.
2. Increase sales $80,000, with no change in the contribution margin percentage.

(a) Compute the controllable margin and the return on investment for 2014.

(b) Compute the controllable margin and the expected return on investment for each proposed alternative.

Solution

Action Plan

✔ Recall key formulas: Sales − Variable costs = Contribution margin.

✔ Contribution margin ÷ Sales = Contribution margin percentage.

✔ Contribution margin − Controllable fixed costs = Controllable margin.

✔ Return on investment = Controllable margin ÷ Average operating assets.

(a) Return on investment for 2014

Sales	$400,000
Variable costs	320,000
Contribution margin	80,000
Controllable fixed costs	40,800
Controllable margin	$ 39,200

$$\text{Return on investment} \qquad \frac{\$39,200}{\$280,000} = 14\%$$

(b) Expected return on investment for alternative 1:

$$\frac{\$39,200}{\$280,000 - \$80,000} = 19.6\%$$

Expected return on investment for alternative 2:

Sales ($400,000 + $80,000)	$480,000
Variable costs ($320,000/$400,000 × $480,000)	384,000
Contribution margin	96,000
Controllable fixed costs	40,800
Controllable margin	$ 55,200

$$\text{Return on investment} \qquad \frac{\$55,200}{\$280,000} = 19.7\%$$

Related exercise material: **BE10-8, BE10-9, BE10-10, E10-16, E10-17, and** DO IT! **10-4.**

✔ **The Navigator**

USING THE **DECISION TOOLKIT**

The manufacturing overhead budget for Reebles Company contains the following items.

Variable costs	
Indirect materials	$25,000
Indirect labor	12,000
Maintenance expenses	10,000
Manufacturing supplies	6,000
Total variable	$53,000
Fixed costs	
Supervision	$17,000
Inspection costs	1,000
Insurance expenses	2,000
Depreciation	15,000
Total fixed	$35,000

The budget was based on an estimated 2,000 units being produced. During November, 1,500 units were produced, and the following costs incurred.

Variable costs

Indirect materials	$25,200
Indirect labor	13,500
Maintenance expenses	8,200
Manufacturing supplies	5,100
Total variable	$52,000

Fixed costs

Supervision	$19,300
Inspection costs	1,200
Insurance expenses	2,200
Depreciation	14,700
Total fixed	$37,400

Instructions

(a) Determine which items would be controllable by Ed Lopat, the production manager. (Assume "supervision" excludes Lopat's own salary.)

(b) How much should have been spent during the month for the manufacture of the 1,500 units?

(c) Prepare a flexible manufacturing overhead budget report for Mr. Lopat.

(d) Prepare a responsibility report. Include only the costs that would have been controllable by Mr. Lopat. In an attached memo, describe clearly for Mr. Lopat the areas in which his performance needs to be improved.

Solution

(a) Ed Lopat should be able to control all the variable costs and the fixed costs of supervision and inspection. Insurance and depreciation ordinarily are not the responsibility of the department manager.

(b) The total variable cost per unit is $26.50 ($53,000 ÷ 2,000). The total budgeted cost during the month to manufacture 1,500 units is variable costs $39,750 (1,500 × $26.50) plus fixed costs ($35,000), for a total of $74,750 ($39,750 + $35,000).

(c)

Reebles Company
Production Department
Manufacturing Overhead Budget Report (Flexible)
For the Month Ended November 30, 2014

	Budget at 1,500 Units	Actual at 1,500 Units	Difference Favorable F Unfavorable U
Variable costs			
Indirect materials ($12.50)	$18,750	$25,200	$ 6,450 U
Indirect labor ($6)	9,000	13,500	4,500 U
Maintenance ($5)	7,500	8,200	700 U
Manufacturing supplies ($3)	4,500	5,100	600 U
Total variable	39,750	52,000	12,250 U
Fixed costs			
Supervision	17,000	19,300	2,300 U
Inspection	1,000	1,200	200 U
Insurance	2,000	2,200	200 U
Depreciation	15,000	14,700	300 F
Total fixed	35,000	37,400	2,400 U
Total costs	$74,750	$89,400	$14,650 U

(d) Because a production department is a cost center, the responsibility report should include only the costs that are controllable by the production manager. In this type of report, no distinction is made between variable and fixed costs. Budget data in the report should be based on the units actually produced.

Reebles Company
Production Department
Manufacturing Overhead Responsibility Report
For the Month Ended November 30, 2014

Controllable Costs	Budget	Actual	Difference Favorable F Unfavorable U
Indirect materials	$18,750	$25,200	$ 6,450 U
Indirect labor	9,000	13,500	4,500 U
Maintenance	7,500	8,200	700 U
Manufacturing supplies	4,500	5,100	600 U
Supervision	17,000	19,300	2,300 U
Inspection	1,000	1,200	200 U
Total	$57,750	$72,500	$14,750 U

To: Mr. Ed Lopat, Production Manager

From: _____, Vice President of Production

Subject: Performance Evaluation for the Month of November

Your performance in controlling costs that are your responsibility was very disappointing in the month of November. As indicated in the accompanying responsibility report, total costs were $14,750 over budget. On a percentage basis, costs were 26% over budget. As you can see, actual costs were over budget for every cost item. In three instances, costs were significantly over budget (indirect materials 34%, indirect labor 50%, and supervision 14%).

Ed, it is imperative that you get costs under control in your department as soon as possible.

I think we need to talk about ways to implement more effective cost control measures. I would like to meet with you in my office at 9 a.m. on Wednesday to discuss possible alternatives.

✔ **The Navigator**

SUMMARY OF LEARNING OBJECTIVES

✔ **The Navigator**

1 Describe the concept of budgetary control. Budgetary control consists of (a) preparing periodic budget reports that compare actual results with planned objectives, (b) analyzing the differences to determine their causes, (c) taking appropriate corrective action, and (d) modifying future plans, if necessary.

2 Evaluate the usefulness of static budget reports. Static budget reports are useful in evaluating the progress toward planned sales and profit goals. They are also appropriate in assessing a manager's effectiveness in controlling costs when (a) actual activity closely approximates the master budget activity level, and/or (b) the behavior of the costs in response to changes in activity is fixed.

3 Explain the development of flexible budgets and the usefulness of flexible budget reports. To develop the flexible budget it is necessary to: (a) Identify the activity index and the relevant range of activity. (b) Identify the variable costs, and determine the budgeted variable cost per unit of activity for each cost. (c) Identify the fixed costs, and determine the budgeted amount for each cost. (d) Prepare the budget for selected increments of activity within the relevant range. Flexible budget reports permit an evaluation of a manager's performance in controlling production and costs.

4 Describe the concept of responsibility accounting. Responsibility accounting involves accumulating and reporting revenues and costs on the basis of the individual manager who has the authority to make the day-to-day decisions about the items. The evaluation of a manager's performance is based on the matters directly under the manager's control. In responsibility accounting, it is necessary to distinguish between controllable and non-controllable fixed costs and to identify three types of responsibility centers: cost, profit, and investment.

5 Indicate the features of responsibility reports for cost centers. Responsibility reports for cost centers compare actual costs with flexible budget data. The reports show only controllable costs, and no distinction is made between variable and fixed costs.

6 Identify the content of responsibility reports for profit centers. Responsibility reports show contribution margin, controllable fixed costs, and controllable margin for each profit center.

7 Explain the basis and formula used in evaluating performance in investment centers. The primary basis for evaluating performance in investment centers is return on investment (ROI). The formula for computing ROI for investment centers is: Controllable margin ÷ Average operating assets.

DECISION TOOLKIT A SUMMARY 🧰

DECISION CHECKPOINTS	INFO NEEDED FOR DECISION	TOOL TO USE FOR DECISION	HOW TO EVALUATE RESULTS
Are the increased costs resulting from increased production reasonable?	Variable costs projected at different levels of production	Flexible budget	After taking into account different production levels, results are favorable if expenses are less than budgeted amounts.
Have the individual managers been held accountable for the costs and revenues under their control?	Relevant costs and revenues, where the individual manager has authority to make day-to-day decisions about the items	Responsibility reports focused on cost centers, profit centers, and investment centers as appropriate	Compare budget to actual costs and revenues for controllable items.
Has the investment center performed up to expectations?	Controllable margin (contribution margin minus controllable fixed costs), and average investment center operating assets	Return on investment	Compare actual ROI to expected ROI.

APPENDIX 10A RESIDUAL INCOME—ANOTHER PERFORMANCE MEASUREMENT

Although most companies use ROI in evaluating their investment performance, ROI has a significant disadvantage. To illustrate, let's look at the Electronics Division of Pujols Company. It has an ROI of 20% computed as follows.

LEARNING OBJECTIVE   8

Explain the difference between ROI and residual income.

Controllable Margin	÷	Average Operating Assets	=	Return on Investment (ROI)
$1,000,000	÷	$5,000,000	=	20%

Illustration 10A-1
ROI formula

The Electronics Division is considering producing a new product, a GPS device (hereafter referred to as Tracker), for its boats. To produce Tracker, operating assets will have to increase $2,000,000. Tracker is expected to generate an additional $260,000 of controllable margin. Illustration 10A-2 shows how Tracker will effect ROI.

Illustration 10A-2
ROI comparison

	Without Tracker	Tracker	With Tracker
Controllable margin (a)	$1,000,000	$ 260,000	$1,260,000
Average operating assets (b)	$5,000,000	$2,000,000	$7,000,000
Return on investment [(a) ÷ (b)]	**20%**	**13%**	**18%**

The investment in Tracker reduces ROI from 20% to 18%.

Let's suppose that you are the manager of the Electronics Division and must make the decision to produce or not produce Tracker. If you were evaluated using ROI, you probably would not produce Tracker because your ROI would drop from 20% to 18%. The problem with this ROI analysis is that it ignores an important variable, the minimum rate of return on a company's operating assets.

The **minimum rate of return** is the rate at which the Electronics Division can cover its costs and earn a profit. Assuming that the Electronics Division has a minimum rate of return of 10%, it should invest in Tracker because its ROI of 13% is greater than 10%.

Residual Income Compared to ROI

To evaluate performance using the minimum rate of return, companies use the residual income approach. **Residual income** is the income that remains after subtracting from the controllable margin the minimum rate of return on a company's average operating assets. The residual income for Tracker would be computed as follows.

Illustration 10A-3
Residual income formula

Controllable Margin	−	Minimum Rate of Return × Average Operating Assets	=	Residual Income
$260,000	−	10% × $2,000,000	=	$60,000

As shown, the residual income related to the Tracker investment is $60,000. Illustration 10A-4 indicates how residual income changes as the additional investment is made.

Illustration 10A-4
Residual income comparison

	Without Tracker	Tracker	With Tracker
Controllable margin (a)	$1,000,000	$260,000	$1,260,000
Average operating assets × 10% (b)	500,000	200,000	700,000
Residual income [(a) − (b)]	$ 500,000	$ 60,000	$ 560,000

This example illustrates how performance evaluation based on ROI can be misleading and can even cause managers to reject projects that would actually increase income for the company. As a result, many companies such as Coca-Cola, Briggs and Stratton, Eli Lilly, and Siemens AG use residual income (or a variant often referred to as economic value added) to evaluate investment alternatives and measure company performance.

Residual Income Weakness

It might appear from the above discussion that the goal of any company should be to maximize the total amount of residual income in each division. This goal, however, ignores the fact that one division might use substantially fewer assets to attain the same level of residual income as another division. For example, we know that to produce Tracker, the Electronics Division of Pujols Company used $2,000,000 of average operating assets to generate $260,000 of controllable margin. Now let's say a different division produced a product called SeaDog, which used $4,000,000 to generate $460,000 of controllable margin, as shown in Illustration 10A-5.

Illustration 10A-5
Comparison of two products

	Tracker	SeaDog
Controllable margin (a)	$260,000	$460,000
Average operating assets × 10% (b)	200,000	400,000
Residual income [(a) − (b)]	$ 60,000	$ 60,000

If the performance of these two investments were evaluated using residual income, they would be considered equal: Both products have the same total residual income. This ignores, however, the fact that SeaDog required **twice** as many operating assets to achieve the same level of residual income.

SUMMARY OF LEARNING OBJECTIVE FOR APPENDIX 10A   ✔ The Navigator

8 Explain the difference between ROI and residual income. ROI is controllable margin divided by average operating assets. Residual income is the income that remains after subtracting the minimum rate of return on a company's average operating assets. ROI sometimes provides misleading results because profitable investments are often rejected when the investment reduces ROI but increases overall profitability.

GLOSSARY

Budgetary control The use of budgets to control operations. (p. 436).

Controllable cost A cost over which a manager has control. (p. 449).

Controllable margin Contribution margin less controllable fixed costs. (p. 456).

Cost center A responsibility center that incurs costs but does not directly generate revenues. (p. 454).

Decentralization Control of operations is delegated to many managers throughout the organization. (p. 448).

Direct fixed costs Costs that relate specifically to a responsibility center and are incurred for the sole benefit of the center. (p. 455).

Flexible budget A projection of budget data for various levels of activity. (p. 438).

Indirect fixed costs Costs that are incurred for the benefit of more than one profit center. (p. 456).

Investment center A responsibility center that incurs costs, generates revenues, and has control over decisions regarding the assets available for use. (p. 454).

Management by exception The review of budget reports by top management focused entirely or primarily on differences between actual results and planned objectives. (p. 449).

Noncontrollable costs Costs incurred indirectly and allocated to a responsibility center that are not controllable at that level. (p. 449).

Profit center A responsibility center that incurs costs and also generates revenues. (p. 454).

Residual income The income that remains after subtracting from the controllable margin the minimum rate of return on a company's average operating assets. (p. 466).

Responsibility accounting A part of management accounting that involves accumulating and reporting revenues and costs on the basis of the manager who has the authority to make the day-to-day decisions about the items. (p. 447).

Responsibility reporting system The preparation of reports for each level of responsibility in the company's organization chart. (p. 451).

Return on investment (ROI) A measure of management's effectiveness in utilizing assets at its disposal in an investment center. (p. 458).

Segment An area of responsibility in decentralized operations. (p. 448).

Static budget A projection of budget data at one level of activity. (p. 437).

> Comprehensive DO IT!

Glenda Company uses a flexible budget for manufacturing overhead based on direct labor hours. For 2014, the master overhead budget for the Packaging Department based on 300,000 direct labor hours was as follows.

Variable Costs		Fixed Costs	
Indirect labor	$360,000	Supervision	$ 60,000
Supplies and lubricants	150,000	Depreciation	24,000
Maintenance	210,000	Property taxes	18,000
Utilities	120,000	Insurance	12,000
	$840,000		$114,000

During July, 24,000 direct labor hours were worked. The company incurred the following variable costs in July: indirect labor $30,200, supplies and lubricants $11,600, maintenance $17,500, and utilities $9,200. Actual fixed overhead costs were the same as monthly budgeted fixed costs.

Instructions

Prepare a flexible budget report for the Packaging Department for July.

Solution to Comprehensive DO IT!

Action Plan

✔ Classify each cost as variable or fixed.
✔ Compute the budgeted cost per direct labor hour for all variable costs.
✔ Use budget data for actual direct labor hours worked.
✔ Determine the difference between budgeted and actual costs.
✔ Identify the difference as favorable or unfavorable.
✔ Determine the difference in total variable costs, total fixed costs, and total costs.

Glenda Company
Manufacturing Overhead Budget Report (Flexible)
Packaging Department
For the Month Ended July 31, 2014

Direct labor hours (DLH)	Budget 24,000 DLH	Actual Costs 24,000 DLH	Difference Favorable F Unfavorable U
Variable costs			
Indirect labor ($1.20ᵃ)	$28,800	$30,200	$1,400 U
Supplies and lubricants ($0.50ᵃ)	12,000	11,600	400 F
Maintenance ($0.70ᵃ)	16,800	17,500	700 U
Utilities ($0.40ᵃ)	9,600	9,200	400 F
Total variable	67,200	68,500	1,300 U
Fixed costs			
Supervision	$ 5,000ᵇ	$ 5,000	–0–
Depreciation	2,000ᵇ	2,000	–0–
Property taxes	1,500ᵇ	1,500	–0–
Insurance	1,000ᵇ	1,000	–0–
Total fixed	9,500	9,500	–0–
Total costs	$76,700	$78,000	$1,300 U

ᵃ($360,000 ÷ 300,000; $150,000 ÷ 300,000; $210,000 ÷ 300,000; $120,000 ÷ 300,000).
ᵇAnnual cost divided by 12.

✔ **The Navigator**

Self-Test, Brief Exercises, Exercises, Problem Set A, and many more resources are available for practice in WileyPLUS.

Note: All asterisked Questions, Exercises, and Problems relate to material in the appendix to the chapter.

SELF-TEST QUESTIONS

(LO 1) 1. Budgetary control involves all but one of the following:
(a) modifying future plans.
(b) analyzing differences.
(c) using static budgets.
(d) determining differences between actual and planned results.

2. Budget reports are prepared: (LO 1)
(a) daily.   (c) monthly.
(b) weekly.   (d) All of the above.

3. A production manager in a manufacturing company (LO 1) would most likely receive a:
(a) sales report.
(b) income statement.

(c) scrap report.

(d) shipping department overhead report.

(LO 2) **4.** A static budget is:

(a) a projection of budget data at several levels of activity within the relevant range of activity.

(b) a projection of budget data at a single level of activity.

(c) compared to a flexible budget in a budget report.

(d) never appropriate in evaluating a manager's effectiveness in controlling costs.

(LO 2) **5.** A static budget is useful in controlling costs when cost behavior is:

(a) mixed.   (c) variable.

(b) fixed.   (d) linear.

(LO 3) **6.** At zero direct labor hours in a flexible budget graph, the total budgeted cost line intersects the vertical axis at $30,000. At 10,000 direct labor hours, a horizontal line drawn from the total budgeted cost line intersects the vertical axis at $90,000. Fixed and variable costs may be expressed as:

(a) $30,000 fixed plus $6 per direct labor hour variable.

(b) $30,000 fixed plus $9 per direct labor hour variable.

(c) $60,000 fixed plus $3 per direct labor hour variable.

(d) $60,000 fixed plus $6 per direct labor hour variable.

(LO 3) **7.** At 9,000 direct labor hours, the flexible budget for indirect materials is $27,000. If $28,000 of indirect materials costs are incurred at 9,200 direct labor hours, the flexible budget report should show the following difference for indirect materials:

(a) $1,000 unfavorable.   (c) $400 favorable.

(b) $1,000 favorable.   (d) $400 unfavorable.

(LO 4) **8.** Under responsibility accounting, the evaluation of a manager's performance is based on matters that the manager:

(a) directly controls.

(b) directly and indirectly controls.

(c) indirectly controls.

(d) has shared responsibility for with another manager.

(LO 4) **9.** Responsibility centers include:

(a) cost centers.   (c) investment centers.

(b) profit centers.   (d) All of the above.

(LO 5) **10.** Responsibility reports for cost centers:

(a) distinguish between fixed and variable costs.

(b) use static budget data.

(c) include both controllable and noncontrollable costs.

(d) include only controllable costs.

(LO 5) **11.** The accounting department of a manufacturing company is an example of:

(a) a cost center.   (c) an investment center.

(b) a profit center.   (d) a contribution center.

(LO 6) **12.** To evaluate the performance of a profit center manager, upper management needs detailed information about:

(a) controllable costs.

(b) controllable revenues.

(c) controllable costs and revenues.

(d) controllable costs and revenues and average operating assets.

(LO 6) **13.** In a responsibility report for a profit center, controllable fixed costs are deducted from contribution margin to show:

(a) profit center margin.

(b) controllable margin.

(c) net income.

(d) income from operations.

(LO 7) **14.** In the formula for return on investment (ROI), the factors for controllable margin and operating assets are, respectively:

(a) controllable margin percentage and total operating assets.

(b) controllable margin dollars and average operating assets.

(c) controllable margin dollars and total assets.

(d) controllable margin percentage and average operating assets.

(LO 7) **15.** A manager of an investment center can improve ROI by:

(a) increasing average operating assets.

(b) reducing sales.

(c) increasing variable costs.

(d) reducing variable and/or controllable fixed costs.

Go to the book's companion website, www.wiley.com/college/weygandt, for additional Self-Test Questions.

✔ **The Navigator**

QUESTIONS

1. (a) What is budgetary control?

(b) Fred Barone is describing budgetary control. What steps should be included in Fred's description?

2. The following purposes are part of a budgetary reporting system: (a) Determine efficient use of materials. (b) Control overhead costs. (c) Determine whether income objectives are being met. For each purpose, indicate the name of the report, the frequency of the report, and the primary recipient(s) of the report.

3. How may a budget report for the second quarter differ from a budget report for the first quarter?

4. Ken Bay questions the usefulness of a master sales budget in evaluating sales performance. Is there justification for Ken's concern? Explain.

5. Under what circumstances may a static budget be an appropriate basis for evaluating a manager's effectiveness in controlling costs?

6. "A flexible budget is really a series of static budgets." Is this true? Why?

7. The static manufacturing overhead budget based on 40,000 direct labor hours shows budgeted indirect labor costs of $54,000. During March, the department incurs $64,000 of indirect labor while working 45,000 direct labor hours. Is this a favorable or unfavorable performance? Why?

8. A static overhead budget based on 40,000 direct labor hours shows Factory Insurance $6,500 as a fixed cost. At the 50,000 direct labor hours worked in March, factory insurance costs were $6,300. Is this a favorable or unfavorable performance? Why?

9. Megan Pedigo is confused about how a flexible budget is prepared. Identify the steps for Megan.

10. Cali Company has prepared a graph of flexible budget data. At zero direct labor hours, the total budgeted cost line intersects the vertical axis at $20,000. At 10,000 direct labor hours, the line drawn from the total budgeted cost line intersects the vertical axis at $85,000. How may the fixed and variable costs be expressed?

11. The flexible budget formula is fixed costs $50,000 plus variable costs of $4 per direct labor hour. What is the total budgeted cost at (a) 9,000 hours and (b) 12,345 hours?

12. What is management by exception? What criteria may be used in identifying exceptions?

13. What is responsibility accounting? Explain the purpose of responsibility accounting.

14. Eve Rooney is studying for an accounting examination. Describe for Eve what conditions are necessary for responsibility accounting to be used effectively.

15. Distinguish between controllable and noncontrollable costs.

16. How do responsibility reports differ from budget reports?

17. What is the relationship, if any, between a responsibility reporting system and a company's organization chart?

18. Distinguish among the three types of responsibility centers.

19. (a) What costs are included in a performance report for a cost center? (b) In the report, are variable and fixed costs identified?

20. How do direct fixed costs differ from indirect fixed costs? Are both types of fixed costs controllable?

21. Jane Nott is confused about controllable margin reported in an income statement for a profit center. How is this margin computed, and what is its primary purpose?

22. What is the primary basis for evaluating the performance of the manager of an investment center? Indicate the formula for this basis.

23. Explain the ways that ROI can be improved.

24. Indicate two behavioral principles that pertain to (a) the manager being evaluated and (b) top management.

*25. What is a major disadvantage of using ROI to evaluate investment and company performance?

*26. What is residual income, and what is one of its major weaknesses?

BRIEF EXERCISES

Prepare static budget report.
(LO 2), AP

BE10-1 For the quarter ended March 31, 2014, Maris Company accumulates the following sales data for its product, Garden-Tools: $310,000 budget; $305,000 actual. Prepare a static budget report for the quarter.

Prepare static budget report for 2 quarters.
(LO 2), AP

BE10-2 Data for Maris Company are given in BE10-1. In the second quarter, budgeted sales were $380,000, and actual sales were $384,000. Prepare a static budget report for the second quarter and for the year to date.

Show usefulness of flexible budgets in evaluating performance.
(LO 3), E

BE10-3 In Paige Company, direct labor is $20 per hour. The company expects to operate at 10,000 direct labor hours each month. In January 2014, direct labor totaling $204,000 is incurred in working 10,400 hours. Prepare (a) a static budget report and (b) a flexible budget report. Evaluate the usefulness of each report.

Prepare a flexible budget for variable costs.
(LO 3), AP

BE10-4 Gundy Company expects to produce 1,200,000 units of Product XX in 2014. Monthly production is expected to range from 80,000 to 120,000 units. Budgeted variable manufacturing costs per unit are direct materials $5, direct labor $6, and overhead $8. Budgeted fixed manufacturing costs per unit for depreciation are $2 and for supervision are $1. Prepare a flexible manufacturing budget for the relevant range value using 20,000 unit increments.

Prepare flexible budget report.
(LO 3), AN

BE10-5 Data for Gundy Company are given in BE10-4. In March 2014, the company incurs the following costs in producing 100,000 units: direct materials $525,000, direct labor $596,000, and variable overhead $805,000. Actual fixed costs were equal to budgeted fixed costs. Prepare a flexible budget report for March. Were costs controlled?

Prepare a responsibility report for a cost center.
(LO 5), AP

BE10-6 In the Assembly Department of Hannon Company, budgeted and actual manufacturing overhead costs for the month of April 2014 were as follows.

	Budget	Actual
Indirect materials	$16,000	$14,300
Indirect labor	20,000	20,600
Utilities	10,000	10,850
Supervision	5,000	5,000

All costs are controllable by the department manager. Prepare a responsibility report for April for the cost center.

BE10-7 Elbert Company accumulates the following summary data for the year ending December 31, 2014, for its Water Division, which it operates as a profit center: sales— $2,000,000 budget, $2,080,000 actual; variable costs—$1,000,000 budget, $1,060,000 actual; and controllable fixed costs—$300,000 budget, $305,000 actual. Prepare a responsibility report for the Water Division.

Prepare a responsibility report for a profit center.

(LO 6), AP

BE10-8 For the year ending December 31, 2014, Cobb Company accumulates the following data for the Plastics Division which it operates as an investment center: contribution margin—$700,000 budget, $710,000 actual; controllable fixed costs—$300,000 budget, $302,000 actual. Average operating assets for the year were $2,000,000. Prepare a responsibility report for the Plastics Division beginning with contribution margin.

Prepare a responsibility report for an investment center.

(LO 7), AP

BE10-9 For its three investment centers, Kaspar Company accumulates the following data:

	I	II	III
Sales	$2,000,000	$4,000,000	$ 4,000,000
Controllable margin	1,300,000	2,000,000	3,600,000
Average operating assets	5,000,000	8,000,000	12,000,000

Compute the return on investment (ROI) for each center.

Compute return on investment using the ROI formula.

(LO 7), AP

BE10-10 Data for the investment centers for Kaspar Company are given in BE10-9. The centers expect the following changes in the next year: (I) increase sales 15%; (II) decrease costs $400,000; (III) decrease average operating assets $500,000. Compute the expected return on investment (ROI) for each center. Assume center I has a contribution margin percentage of 70%.

Compute return on investment under changed conditions.

(LO 7), AP

***BE10-11** Voorhees, Inc. reports the following financial information.

Average operating assets	$3,000,000
Controllable margin	$ 660,000
Minimum rate of return	10%

Compute the return on investment and the residual income.

Compute ROI and residual income.

(LO 8), AP

***BE10-12** Presented below is information related to the Southern Division of Lumber, Inc.

Contribution margin	$1,200,000
Controllable margin	$ 800,000
Average operating assets	$4,000,000
Minimum rate of return	15%

Compute the Southern Division's return on investment and residual income.

Compute ROI and residual income.

(LO 8), AP

> ## DO IT! REVIEW

DO IT! 10-1 In Pargo Company's flexible budget graph, the fixed cost line and the total budgeted cost line intersect the vertical axis at $90,000. The total budgeted cost line is $330,000 at an activity level of 50,000 direct labor hours. Compute total budgeted costs at 65,000 direct labor hours.

Compute total budgeted costs in flexible budget.

(LO 3), AP

Prepare and evaluate a flexible budget report.

(LO 3), AP

DO IT! 10-2 Mussatto Company expects to produce 50,000 units of product IOA during the current year. Budgeted variable manufacturing costs per unit are direct materials $7, direct labor $13, and overhead $18. Annual budgeted fixed manufacturing overhead costs are $96,000 for depreciation and $45,600 for supervision.

In the current month, Mussatto produced 6,000 units and incurred the following costs: direct materials $38,850, direct labor $76,440, variable overhead $116,640, depreciation $8,000, and supervision $4,000.

Prepare a flexible budget report. (*Note:* You do not need to prepare the heading.) Were costs controlled?

Prepare a responsibility report.

(LO 6), AP

DO IT! 10-3 The Wellstone Division operates as a profit center. It reports the following for the year.

	Budget	Actual
Sales	$2,000,000	$1,860,000
Variable costs	800,000	760,000
Controllable fixed costs	550,000	550,000
Noncontrollable fixed costs	250,000	250,000

Prepare a responsibility report for the Wellstone Division at December 31, 2014.

Compute ROI and expected return on investments.

(LO 7), AP

DO IT! 10-4 The service division of Raney Industries reported the following results for 2013.

Sales	$500,000
Variable costs	300,000
Controllable fixed costs	75,000
Average operating assets	625,000

Management is considering the following independent courses of action in 2014 in order to maximize the return on investment for this division.

1. Reduce average operating assets by $125,000, with no change in controllable margin.
2. Increase sales $100,000, with no change in the contribution margin percentage.

(a) Compute the controllable margin and the return on investment for 2013. (b) Compute the controllable margin and the expected return on investment for each proposed alternative.

✔ **The Navigator**

EXERCISES

Understand the concept of budgetary control.

(LO 1, 2, 3), K

E10-1 Mike Trusler has prepared the following list of statements about budgetary control.

1. Budget reports compare actual results with planned objectives.
2. All budget reports are prepared on a weekly basis.
3. Management uses budget reports to analyze differences between actual and planned results and determine their causes.
4. As a result of analyzing budget reports, management may either take corrective action or modify future plans.
5. Budgetary control works best when a company has an informal reporting system.
6. The primary recipients of the sales report are the sales manager and the vice president of production.
7. The primary recipient of the scrap report is the production manager.
8. A static budget is a projection of budget data at one level of activity.
9. Top management's reaction to unfavorable differences is not influenced by the materiality of the difference.
10. A static budget is not appropriate in evaluating a manager's effectiveness in controlling costs unless the actual activity level approximates the static budget activity level or the behavior of the costs is fixed.

Instructions

Identify each statement as true or false. If false, indicate how to correct the statement.

E10-2 Crede Company budgeted selling expenses of $30,000 in January, $35,000 in February, and $40,000 in March. Actual selling expenses were $31,200 in January, $34,525 in February, and $46,000 in March.

Prepare and evaluate static budget report.

(LO 2), AN

Instructions

(a) Prepare a selling expense report that compares budgeted and actual amounts by month and for the year to date.

(b) What is the purpose of the report prepared in (a), and who would be the primary recipient?

(c) What would be the likely result of management's analysis of the report?

E10-3 Thome Company uses a flexible budget for manufacturing overhead based on direct labor hours. Variable manufacturing overhead costs per direct labor hour are as follows.

Prepare flexible manufacturing overhead budget.

(LO 3), AP

Indirect labor	$1.00
Indirect materials	0.60
Utilities	0.40

Fixed overhead costs per month are supervision $4,000, depreciation $1,200, and property taxes $800. The company believes it will normally operate in a range of 7,000–10,000 direct labor hours per month.

Instructions

Prepare a monthly manufacturing overhead flexible budget for 2014 for the expected range of activity, using increments of 1,000 direct labor hours.

E10-4 Using the information in E10-3, assume that in July 2014, Thome Company incurs the following manufacturing overhead costs.

Prepare flexible budget reports for manufacturing overhead costs, and comment on findings.

(LO 3), AN

Variable Costs		**Fixed Costs**	
Indirect labor	$8,800	Supervision	$4,000
Indirect materials	5,300	Depreciation	1,200
Utilities	3,200	Property taxes	800

Instructions

(a) Prepare a flexible budget performance report, assuming that the company worked 9,000 direct labor hours during the month.

(b) Prepare a flexible budget performance report, assuming that the company worked 8,500 direct labor hours during the month.

(c) [pencil icon] Comment on your findings.

E10-5 DeWitt Company uses flexible budgets to control its selling expenses. Monthly sales are expected to range from $170,000 to $200,000. Variable costs and their percentage relationship to sales are sales commissions 6%, advertising 4%, traveling 3%, and delivery 2%. Fixed selling expenses will consist of sales salaries $35,000, depreciation on delivery equipment $7,000, and insurance on delivery equipment $1,000.

Prepare flexible selling expense budget.

(LO 3), AP

Instructions

Prepare a monthly flexible budget for each $10,000 increment of sales within the relevant range for the year ending December 31, 2014.

E10-6 The actual selling expenses incurred in March 2014 by DeWitt Company are as follows.

Prepare flexible budget reports for selling expenses.

(LO 3), AN

Variable Expenses		**Fixed Expenses**	
Sales commissions	$11,000	Sales salaries	$35,000
Advertising	6,900	Depreciation	7,000
Travel	5,100	Insurance	1,000
Delivery	3,450		

Instructions

(a) Prepare a flexible budget performance report for March using the budget data in E10-5, assuming that March sales were $170,000.

(b) Prepare a flexible budget performance report, assuming that March sales were $180,000.

(c) [pencil icon] Comment on the importance of using flexible budgets in evaluating the performance of the sales manager.

Prepare flexible budget report for cost center.

(LO 3), AP

E10-7 Kitchen Help Inc. (KHI) is a manufacturer of toaster ovens. To improve control over operations, the president of KHI wants to begin using a flexible budgeting system, rather than use only the current master budget. The following data are available for KHI's expected costs at production levels of 90,000, 100,000, and 110,000 units.

Variable costs	
Manufacturing	$6 per unit
Administrative	$4 per unit
Selling	$2 per unit
Fixed costs	
Manufacturing	$160,000
Administrative	$ 80,000

Instructions
(a) Prepare a flexible budget for each of the possible production levels: 90,000, 100,000, and 110,000 units.
(b) If KHI sells the toaster ovens for $16 each, how many units will it have to sell to make a profit of $200,000 before taxes?

(CGA adapted)

Prepare flexible budget report; compare flexible and static budgets.

(LO 2, 3), E

E10-8 Rensing Groomers is in the dog-grooming business. Its operating costs are described by the following formulas:

Grooming supplies (variable)	$y = \$0 + \$5x$
Direct labor (variable)	$y = \$0 + \$14x$
Overhead (mixed)	$y = \$10,000 + \$1x$

Milo, the owner, has determined that direct labor is the cost driver for all three categories of costs.

Instructions
(a) Prepare a flexible budget for activity levels of 550, 600, and 700 direct labor hours.
(b) ▭▭▭▭▶ Explain why the flexible budget is more informative than the static budget.
(c) Calculate the total cost per direct labor hour at each of the activity levels specified in part (a).
(d) The groomers at Rensing normally work a total of 650 direct labor hours during each month. Each grooming job normally takes a groomer 1.3 hours. Milo wants to earn a profit equal to 40% of the costs incurred. Determine what he should charge each pet owner for grooming.

(CGA adapted)

Prepare flexible budget and responsibility report for manufacturing overhead.

(LO 3, 5), AP

E10-9 Lowell Company's manufacturing overhead budget for the first quarter of 2014 contained the following data.

Variable Costs		Fixed Costs	
Indirect materials	$12,000	Supervisory salaries	$36,000
Indirect labor	10,000	Depreciation	7,000
Utilities	8,000	Property taxes and insurance	8,000
Maintenance	6,000	Maintenance	5,000

Actual variable costs were indirect materials $13,900, indirect labor $9,500, utilities $8,700, and maintenance $5,000. Actual fixed costs equaled budgeted costs except for property taxes and insurance, which were $8,400. The actual activity level equaled the budgeted level.

All costs are considered controllable by the production department manager except for depreciation, and property taxes and insurance.

Instructions
(a) Prepare a manufacturing overhead flexible budget report for the first quarter.
(b) Prepare a responsibility report for the first quarter.

Prepare flexible budget report, and answer question.

(LO 2, 3), E

E10-10 As sales manager, Joe Batista was given the following static budget report for selling expenses in the Clothing Department of Soria Company for the month of October.

Soria Company
Clothing Department
Budget Report
For the Month Ended October 31, 2014

	Budget	Actual	Difference Favorable F Unfavorable U
Sales in units	8,000	10,000	2,000 F
Variable expenses			
Sales commissions	$ 2,400	$ 2,600	$ 200 U
Advertising expense	720	850	130 U
Travel expense	3,600	4,100	500 U
Free samples given out	1,600	1,400	200 F
Total variable	8,320	8,950	630 U
Fixed expenses			
Rent	1,500	1,500	–0–
Sales salaries	1,200	1,200	–0–
Office salaries	800	800	–0–
Depreciation—autos (sales staff)	500	500	–0–
Total fixed	4,000	4,000	–0–
Total expenses	$12,320	$12,950	$ 630 U

As a result of this budget report, Joe was called into the president's office and congratulated on his fine sales performance. He was reprimanded, however, for allowing his costs to get out of control. Joe knew something was wrong with the performance report that he had been given. However, he was not sure what to do, and comes to you for advice.

Instructions
(a) Prepare a budget report based on flexible budget data to help Joe.
(b) Should Joe have been reprimanded? Explain.

E10-11 Kirkland Plumbing Company is a newly formed company specializing in plumbing services for home and business. The owner, Lenny Kirkland, had divided the company into two segments: Home Plumbing Services and Business Plumbing Services. Each segment is run by its own supervisor, while basic selling and administrative services are shared by both segments.

Prepare and discuss a responsibility report.
(LO 3, 5), AP

Lenny has asked you to help him create a performance reporting system that will allow him to measure each segment's performance in terms of its profitability. To that end, the following information has been collected on the Home Plumbing Services segment for the first quarter of 2014.

	Budget	Actual
Service revenue	$25,000	$26,000
Allocated portion of:		
Building depreciation	11,000	11,000
Advertising	5,000	4,200
Billing	3,500	3,000
Property taxes	1,200	1,000
Material and supplies	1,600	1,200
Supervisory salaries	9,000	9,500
Insurance	4,000	3,600
Wages	3,000	3,250
Gas and oil	2,800	3,400
Equipment depreciation	1,500	1,300

Instructions
(a) Prepare a responsibility report for the first quarter of 2014 for the Home Plumbing Services segment.
(b) ▭▭▭▷ Write a memo to Lenny Kirkland discussing the principles that should be used when preparing performance reports.

State total budgeted cost formulas, and prepare flexible budget graph.

(LO 3), AP

E10-12 Venetian Company has two production departments, Fabricating and Assembling. At a department managers' meeting, the controller uses flexible budget graphs to explain total budgeted costs. Separate graphs based on direct labor hours are used for each department. The graphs show the following.

1. At zero direct labor hours, the total budgeted cost line and the fixed cost line intersect the vertical axis at $50,000 in the Fabricating Department and $40,000 in the Assembling Department.
2. At normal capacity of 50,000 direct labor hours, the line drawn from the total budgeted cost line intersects the vertical axis at $150,000 in the Fabricating Department, and $120,000 in the Assembling Department.

Instructions
(a) State the total budgeted cost formula for each department.
(b) Compute the total budgeted cost for each department, assuming actual direct labor hours worked were 53,000 and 47,000, in the Fabricating and Assembling Departments, respectively.
(c) Prepare the flexible budget graph for the Fabricating Department, assuming the maximum direct labor hours in the relevant range is 100,000. Use increments of 10,000 direct labor hours on the horizontal axis and increments of $50,000 on the vertical axis.

Prepare reports in a responsibility reporting system.

(LO 4, 5), AP

E10-13 Fultz Company's organization chart includes the president; the vice president of production; three assembly plants—Dallas, Atlanta, and Tucson; and two departments within each plant—Machining and Finishing. Budget and actual manufacturing cost data for July 2014 are as follows.

Finishing Department—Dallas: direct materials $41,500 actual, $44,000 budget; direct labor $83,400 actual, $82,000 budget; manufacturing overhead $51,000 actual, $49,200 budget.

Machining Department—Dallas: total manufacturing costs $220,000 actual, $219,000 budget.

Atlanta Plant: total manufacturing costs $424,000 actual, $421,000 budget.

Tucson Plant: total manufacturing costs $494,200 actual, $496,500 budget.

The Dallas plant manager's office costs were $95,000 actual and $92,000 budget. The vice president of production's office costs were $132,000 actual and $130,000 budget. Office costs are not allocated to departments and plants.

Instructions
Using the format on page 453, prepare the reports in a responsibility system for:
(a) The Finishing Department—Dallas.
(b) The plant manager—Dallas.
(c) The vice president of production.

Prepare a responsibility report for a cost center.

(LO 5), AN

E10-14 The Mixing Department manager of Malone Company is able to control all overhead costs except rent, property taxes, and salaries. Budgeted monthly overhead costs for the Mixing Department, in alphabetical order, are:

Indirect labor	$12,000	Property taxes	$ 1,000
Indirect materials	7,700	Rent	1,800
Lubricants	1,675	Salaries	10,000
Maintenance	3,500	Utilities	5,000

Actual costs incurred for January 2014 are indirect labor $12,250; indirect materials $10,200; lubricants $1,650; maintenance $3,500; property taxes $1,100; rent $1,800; salaries $10,000; and utilities $6,400.

Instructions
(a) Prepare a responsibility report for January 2014.
(b) What would be the likely result of management's analysis of the report?

Compute missing amounts in responsibility reports for three profit centers, and prepare a report.

(LO 6), AN

E10-15 Deitz Inc. has three divisions which are operated as profit centers. Actual operating data for the divisions listed alphabetically are as follows.

Operating Data	Women's Shoes	Men's Shoes	Children's Shoes
Contribution margin	$250,000	(3)	$180,000
Controllable fixed costs	100,000	(4)	(5)
Controllable margin	(1)	$ 90,000	95,000
Sales	600,000	450,000	(6)
Variable costs	(2)	320,000	250,000

Instructions

(a) Compute the missing amounts. Show computations.

(b) Prepare a responsibility report for the Women's Shoes Division assuming (1) the data are for the month ended June 30, 2014, and (2) all data equal budget except variable costs which are $10,000 over budget.

E10-16 The Sports Equipment Division of Harrington Company is operated as a profit center. Sales for the division were budgeted for 2014 at $900,000. The only variable costs budgeted for the division were cost of goods sold ($440,000) and selling and administrative ($60,000). Fixed costs were budgeted at $100,000 for cost of goods sold, $90,000 for selling and administrative, and $70,000 for noncontrollable fixed costs. Actual results for these items were:

Prepare a responsibility report for a profit center, and compute ROI.

(LO 6, 7), AP

Sales	$880,000
Cost of goods sold	
Variable	408,000
Fixed	105,000
Selling and administrative	
Variable	61,000
Fixed	66,000
Noncontrollable fixed	90,000

Instructions

(a) Prepare a responsibility report for the Sports Equipment Division for 2014.

(b) Assume the division is an investment center, and average operating assets were $1,000,000. The noncontrollable fixed costs are controllable at the investment center level. Compute ROI.

E10-17 The West Division of Nieto Company reported the following data for the current year.

Compute ROI for current year and for possible future changes.

(LO 7), AP

Sales	$3,000,000
Variable costs	1,980,000
Controllable fixed costs	600,000
Average operating assets	5,000,000

Top management is unhappy with the investment center's return on investment (ROI). It asks the manager of the West Division to submit plans to improve ROI in the next year. The manager believes it is feasible to consider the following independent courses of action.

1. Increase sales by $320,000 with no change in the contribution margin percentage.
2. Reduce variable costs by $150,000.
3. Reduce average operating assets by 4%.

Instructions

(a) Compute the return on investment (ROI) for the current year.

(b) Using the ROI formula, compute the ROI under each of the proposed courses of action. (Round to one decimal.)

E10-18 The Dinkle and Frizell Dental Clinic provides both preventive and orthodontic dental services. The two owners, Reese Dinkle and Anita Frizell, operate the clinic as two separate investment centers: Preventive Services and Orthodontic Services. Each of them is in charge of one of the centers: Reese for Preventive Services and Anita for Orthodontic Services. Each month, they prepare an income statement for the two centers to evaluate performance and make decisions about how to improve the operational efficiency and profitability of the clinic.

Prepare a responsibility report for an investment center.

(LO 7), AP

Recently, they have been concerned about the profitability of the Preventive Services operations. For several months, it has been reporting a loss. The responsibility report for the month of May 2014 is shown on page 478.

	Actual	Difference from Budget
Service revenue	$ 40,000	$1,000 F
Variable costs		
Filling materials	5,000	100 U
Novocain	3,900	100 U
Supplies	1,900	350 F
Dental assistant wages	2,500	–0–
Utilities	500	110 U
Total variable costs	13,800	40 F
Fixed costs		
Allocated portion of receptionist's salary	3,000	200 U
Dentist salary	9,800	400 U
Equipment depreciation	6,000	–0–
Allocated portion of building depreciation	15,000	1,000 U
Total fixed costs	33,800	1,600 U
Operating income (loss)	$ (7,600)	$ 560 U

In addition, the owners know that the investment in operating assets at the beginning of the month was $82,400, and it was $77,600 at the end of the month. They have asked for your assistance in evaluating their current performance reporting system.

Instructions

(a) Prepare a responsibility report for an investment center as illustrated in the chapter.

(b) ▱▱▱▱➤ Write a memo to the owners discussing the deficiencies of their current reporting system.

Prepare missing amounts in responsibility reports for three investment centers.

(LO 7), AN

E10-19 The Pletcher Transportation Company uses a responsibility reporting system to measure the performance of its three investment centers: Planes, Taxis, and Limos. Segment performance is measured using a system of responsibility reports and return on investment calculations. The allocation of resources within the company and the segment managers' bonuses are based in part on the results shown in these reports.

Recently, the company was the victim of a computer virus that deleted portions of the company's accounting records. This was discovered when the current period's responsibility reports were being prepared. The printout of the actual operating results appeared as follows.

	Planes	Taxis	Limos
Service revenue	$?	$500,000	$?
Variable costs	5,500,000	?	300,000
Contribution margin	?	250,000	480,000
Controllable fixed costs	1,500,000	?	?
Controllable margin	?	80,000	240,000
Average operating assets	25,000,000	?	1,500,000
Return on investment	13%	10%	?

Instructions

Determine the missing pieces of information above.

Compare ROI and residual income.

(LO 8), AN

*E10-20 Presented below is selected information for three regional divisions of Medina Company.

	Divisions		
	North	**West**	**South**
Contribution margin	$ 300,000	$ 500,000	$ 400,000
Controllable margin	$ 140,000	$ 360,000	$ 210,000
Average operating assets	$1,000,000	$2,000,000	$1,500,000
Minimum rate of return	13%	16%	10%

Instructions

(a) Compute the return on investment for each division.

(b) Compute the residual income for each division.

(c) Assume that each division has an investment opportunity that would provide a rate of return of 16%.

(1) If ROI is used to measure performance, which division or divisions will probably make the additional investment?

(2) If residual income is used to measure performance, which division or divisions will probably make the additional investment?

*E10-21 Presented below is selected financial information for two divisions of Yono Brewing.

Fill in information related to ROI and residual income.

(LO 8), AN

	Lager	Lite Lager
Contribution margin	$500,000	$ 300,000
Controllable margin	200,000	(c)
Average operating assets	(a)	$1,200,000
Minimum rate of return	(b)	13%
Return on investment	20%	(d)
Residual income	$100,000	$ 204,000

Instructions

Supply the missing information for the lettered items.

EXERCISES: SET B AND CHALLENGE EXERCISES

Visit the book's companion website, at **www.wiley.com/college/weygandt**, and choose the Student Companion site to access Exercise Set B and Challenge Exercises.

PROBLEMS: SET A

P10-1A Cook Company estimates that 300,000 direct labor hours will be worked during the coming year, 2014, in the Packaging Department. On this basis, the budgeted manufacturing overhead cost data, shown below, are computed for the year.

Prepare flexible budget and budget report for manufacturing overhead.

(LO 3), AN

Fixed Overhead Costs		Variable Overhead Costs	
Supervision	$ 96,000	Indirect labor	$126,000
Depreciation	72,000	Indirect materials	90,000
Insurance	30,000	Repairs	54,000
Rent	24,000	Utilities	72,000
Property taxes	18,000	Lubricants	18,000
	$240,000		$360,000

It is estimated that direct labor hours worked each month will range from 27,000 to 36,000 hours.

During October, 27,000 direct labor hours were worked and the following overhead costs were incurred.

Fixed overhead costs: supervision $8,000, depreciation $6,000, insurance $2,460, rent $2,000, and property taxes $1,500.

Variable overhead costs: indirect labor $12,432, indirect materials $7,680, repairs $4,800, utilities $6,840, and lubricants $1,920.

Instructions

(a) Prepare a monthly manufacturing overhead flexible budget for each increment of 3,000 direct labor hours over the relevant range for the year ending December 31, 2014.

(b) Prepare a flexible budget report for October.

(c) ▣▤▤▤▷ Comment on management's efficiency in controlling manufacturing overhead costs in October.

(a) Total costs: DLH 27,000, $52,400; DLH 36,000, $63,200

(b) Total $1,232 U

Prepare flexible budget, budget report, and graph for manufacturing overhead.

(LO 3), E

P10-2A Zelmer Company manufactures tablecloths. Sales have grown rapidly over the past 2 years. As a result, the president has installed a budgetary control system for 2014. The following data were used in developing the master manufacturing overhead budget for the Ironing Department, which is based on an activity index of direct labor hours.

Variable Costs	Rate per Direct Labor Hour	Annual Fixed Costs	
Indirect labor	$0.40	Supervision	$48,000
Indirect materials	0.50	Depreciation	18,000
Factory utilities	0.30	Insurance	12,000
Factory repairs	0.20	Rent	30,000

The master overhead budget was prepared on the expectation that 480,000 direct labor hours will be worked during the year. In June, 41,000 direct labor hours were worked. At that level of activity, actual costs were as shown below.

Variable—per direct labor hour: indirect labor $0.44, indirect materials $0.48, factory utilities $0.32, and factory repairs $0.25.

Fixed: same as budgeted.

Instructions

(a) Total costs: 35,000 DLH, $58,000; 50,000 DLH, $79,000

(b) Budget $66,400 Actual $70,090

(a) Prepare a monthly manufacturing overhead flexible budget for the year ending December 31, 2014, assuming production levels range from 35,000 to 50,000 direct labor hours. Use increments of 5,000 direct labor hours.
(b) Prepare a budget report for June comparing actual results with budget data based on the flexible budget.
(c) Were costs effectively controlled? Explain.
(d) State the formula for computing the total budgeted costs for the Ironing Department.
(e) Prepare the flexible budget graph, showing total budgeted costs at 35,000 and 45,000 direct labor hours. Use increments of 5,000 direct labor hours on the horizontal axis and increments of $10,000 on the vertical axis.

State total budgeted cost formula, and prepare flexible budget reports for 2 time periods.

(LO 2, 3), AN

P10-3A Hill Company uses budgets in controlling costs. The August 2014 budget report for the company's Assembling Department is as follows.

Hill Company
Budget Report
Assembling Department
For the Month Ended August 31, 2014

Manufacturing Costs	Budget	Actual	Difference Favorable F Unfavorable U
Variable costs			
Direct materials	$ 48,000	$ 47,000	$1,000 F
Direct labor	54,000	51,200	2,800 F
Indirect materials	24,000	24,200	200 U
Indirect labor	18,000	17,500	500 F
Utilities	15,000	14,900	100 F
Maintenance	6,000	6,200	200 U
Total variable	165,000	161,000	4,000 F
Fixed costs			
Rent	12,000	12,000	–0–
Supervision	17,000	17,000	–0–
Depreciation	6,000	6,000	–0–
Total fixed	35,000	35,000	–0–
Total costs	$200,000	$196,000	$4,000 F

The monthly budget amounts in the report were based on an expected production of 60,000 units per month or 720,000 units per year. The Assembling Department manager is pleased with the report and expects a raise, or at least praise for a job well done. The company president, however, is unhappy with the results for August because only 58,000 units were produced.

Instructions
(a) State the total monthly budgeted cost formula.
(b) Prepare a budget report for August using flexible budget data. Why does this report provide a better basis for evaluating performance than the report based on static budget data?

(b) Budget $194,500

(c) In September, 64,000 units were produced. Prepare the budget report using flexible budget data, assuming (1) each variable cost was 10% higher than its actual cost in August, and (2) fixed costs were the same in September as in August.

(c) Budget $211,000
Actual $212,100

P10-4A Clarke Inc. operates the Patio Furniture Division as a profit center. Operating data for this division for the year ended December 31, 2014, are as shown below.

Prepare responsibility report for a profit center.

(LO 6), AN

	Budget	Difference from Budget
Sales	$2,500,000	$50,000 F
Cost of goods sold		
Variable	1,300,000	41,000 F
Controllable fixed	200,000	3,000 U
Selling and administrative		
Variable	220,000	6,000 U
Controllable fixed	50,000	2,000 U
Noncontrollable fixed costs	70,000	4,000 U

In addition, Clarke incurs $180,000 of indirect fixed costs that were budgeted at $175,000. Twenty percent (20%) of these costs are allocated to the Patio Furniture Division.

Instructions
(a) Prepare a responsibility report for the Patio Furniture Division for the year.
(b) ▭▭▭▭▷ Comment on the manager's performance in controlling revenues and costs.
(c) Identify any costs excluded from the responsibility report and explain why they were excluded.

(a) Contribution margin
$85,000 F
Controllable margin
$80,000 F

P10-5A Suppan Company manufactures a variety of tools and industrial equipment. The company operates through three divisions. Each division is an investment center. Operating data for the Home Division for the year ended December 31, 2014, and relevant budget data are as follows.

Prepare responsibility report for an investment center, and compute ROI.

(LO 7), E

	Actual	Comparison with Budget
Sales	$1,400,000	$100,000 favorable
Variable cost of goods sold	675,000	55,000 unfavorable
Variable selling and administrative expenses	125,000	25,000 unfavorable
Controllable fixed cost of goods sold	170,000	On target
Controllable fixed selling and administrative expenses	80,000	On target

Average operating assets for the year for the Home Division were $2,000,000 which was also the budgeted amount.

Instructions
(a) Prepare a responsibility report (in thousands of dollars) for the Home Division.
(b) Evaluate the manager's performance. Which items will likely be investigated by top management?

(a) Controllable margin:
Budget $330;
Actual $350

(c) Compute the expected ROI in 2014 for the Home Division, assuming the following independent changes to actual data.
   (1) Variable cost of goods sold is decreased by 5%.
   (2) Average operating assets are decreased by 10%.
   (3) Sales are increased by $200,000, and this increase is expected to increase contribution margin by $85,000.

P10-6A Durham Company uses a responsibility reporting system. It has divisions in Denver, Seattle, and San Diego. Each division has three production departments: Cutting, Shaping, and Finishing. The responsibility for each department rests with a manager who reports to the division production manager. Each division manager reports to the vice

Prepare reports for cost centers under responsibility accounting, and comment on performance of managers.

(LO 4), AN

president of production. There are also vice presidents for marketing and finance. All vice presidents report to the president.

In January 2014, controllable actual and budget manufacturing overhead cost data for the departments and divisions were as shown below.

Manufacturing Overhead	Actual	Budget
Individual costs—Cutting Department—Seattle		
Indirect labor	$ 73,000	$ 70,000
Indirect materials	47,900	46,000
Maintenance	20,500	18,000
Utilities	20,100	17,000
Supervision	22,000	20,000
	$183,500	$171,000
Total costs		
Shaping Department—Seattle	$158,000	$148,000
Finishing Department—Seattle	210,000	205,000
Denver division	678,000	673,000
San Diego division	722,000	715,000

Additional overhead costs were incurred as follows: Seattle division production manager—actual costs $52,500, budget $51,000; vice president of production—actual costs $65,000, budget $64,000; president—actual costs $76,400, budget $74,200. These expenses are not allocated.

The vice presidents who report to the president, other than the vice president of production, had the following expenses.

Vice President	Actual	Budget
Marketing	$133,600	$130,000
Finance	109,000	104,000

Instructions

(a) Using the format on page 453, prepare the following responsibility reports.
   (1) Manufacturing overhead—Cutting Department manager—Seattle division.
   (2) Manufacturing overhead—Seattle division manager.
   (3) Manufacturing overhead—vice president of production.
   (4) Manufacturing overhead and expenses—president.
(b) Comment on the comparative performances of:
   (1) Department managers in the Seattle division.
   (2) Division managers.
   (3) Vice presidents.

(a) (1) $12,500 U
   (2) $29,000 U
   (3) $42,000 U
   (4) $52,800 U

Compare ROI and residual income.

(LO 8), AN

*P10-7A Delby Industries has manufactured prefabricated houses for over 20 years. The houses are constructed in sections to be assembled on customers' lots. Delby expanded into the precut housing market when it acquired Jensen Company, one of its suppliers. In this market, various types of lumber are precut into the appropriate lengths, banded into packages, and shipped to customers' lots for assembly. Delby designated the Jensen Division as an investment center.

Delby uses return on investment (ROI) as a performance measure with investment defined as average operating assets. Management bonuses are based in part on ROI. All investments are expected to earn a minimum rate of return of 18%. Jensen's ROI has ranged from 20.1% to 23.5% since it was acquired. Jensen had an investment opportunity in 2014 that had an estimated ROI of 19%. Jensen management decided against the investment because it believed the investment would decrease the division's overall ROI.

Selected financial information for Jensen are presented below. The division's average operating assets were $12,300,000 for the year 2014.

Jensen Division
Selected Financial Information
For the Year Ended December 31, 2014

Sales	$26,000,000
Contribution margin	9,100,000
Controllable margin	2,583,000

Instructions

(a) Calculate the following performance measures for 2014 for the Jensen Division.
   (1) Return on investment (ROI).
   (2) Residual income.
(b) ▭▭▭▭▷ Would the management of Jensen Division have been more likely to accept the investment opportunity it had in 2014 if residual income were used as a performance measure instead of ROI? Explain your answer.

(CMA adapted)

PROBLEMS: SET B

P10-1B Speier Company estimates that 240,000 direct labor hours will be worked during 2014 in the Assembly Department. On this basis, the following budgeted manufacturing overhead data are computed.

Prepare flexible budget and budget report for manufacturing overhead.

(LO 3), AN

Variable Overhead Costs		Fixed Overhead Costs	
Indirect labor	$ 72,000	Supervision	$ 75,600
Indirect materials	48,000	Depreciation	30,000
Repairs	36,000	Insurance	12,000
Utilities	24,000	Rent	9,600
Lubricants	12,000	Property taxes	6,000
	$192,000		$133,200

It is estimated that direct labor hours worked each month will range from 18,000 to 24,000 hours.

During January, 20,000 direct labor hours were worked and the following overhead costs were incurred.

Variable Overhead Costs		Fixed Overhead Costs	
Indirect labor	$ 6,200	Supervision	$ 6,300
Indirect materials	3,600	Depreciation	2,500
Repairs	2,300	Insurance	1,000
Utilities	1,700	Rent	850
Lubricants	1,050	Property taxes	500
	$14,850		$11,150

Instructions

(a) Prepare a monthly flexible manufacturing overhead budget for each increment of 2,000 direct labor hours over the relevant range for the year ending December 31, 2014.
(b) Prepare a manufacturing overhead budget report for January.
(c) ▭▭▭▭▷ Comment on management's efficiency in controlling manufacturing overhead costs in January.

(a) Total costs: 18,000 DLH, $25,500; 24,000 DLH, $30,300
(b) Budget $27,100 Actual $26,000

P10-2B Gonzalez Company produces one product, Olpe. Because of wide fluctuations in demand for Olpe, the Assembly Department experiences significant variations in monthly production levels.

The annual master manufacturing overhead budget is based on 300,000 direct labor hours. In July, 27,500 labor hours were worked. The master manufacturing overhead budget for the year and the actual overhead costs incurred in July are as follows.

Prepare flexible budget, budget report, and graph for manufacturing overhead.

(LO 3), E

Overhead Costs	Master Budget (annual)	Actual in July
Variable		
Indirect labor	$300,000	$26,000
Indirect materials	150,000	11,350
Utilities	90,000	8,050
Maintenance	60,000	5,400
Fixed		
Supervision	144,000	12,000
Depreciation	96,000	8,000
Insurance and taxes	60,000	5,000
Total	$900,000	$75,800

(a) Total costs: 22,500 DLH,
$70,000; 30,000 DLH,
$85,000

(b) Budget $80,000
Actual $75,800

Instructions

(a) Prepare a monthly flexible overhead budget for the year ending December 31, 2014, assuming monthly production levels range from 22,500 to 30,000 direct labor hours. Use increments of 2,500 direct labor hours.

(b) Prepare a budget report for the month of July 2014, comparing actual results with budget data based on the flexible budget.

(c) ▬▬▬▶ Were costs effectively controlled? Explain.

(d) State the formula for computing the total monthly budgeted costs in the Gonzalez Company.

(e) Prepare the flexible budget graph showing total budgeted costs at 25,000 and 27,500 direct labor hours. Use increments of 5,000 on the horizontal axis and increments of $10,000 on the vertical axis.

State total budgeted cost formula, and prepare flexible budget reports for 2 time periods.

(LO 2, 3), AN

P10-3B Hardesty Company uses budgets in controlling costs. The May 2014 budget report for the company's Packaging Department is as follows.

Hardesty Company
Budget Report
Packaging Department
For the Month Ended May 31, 2014

Manufacturing Costs	Budget	Actual	Difference Favorable F Unfavorable U
Variable costs			
Direct materials	$ 40,000	$ 41,000	$1,000 U
Direct labor	45,000	47,300	2,300 U
Indirect materials	15,000	15,200	200 U
Indirect labor	12,500	13,000	500 U
Utilities	10,000	9,600	400 F
Maintenance	7,500	8,000	500 U
Total variable	130,000	134,100	4,100 U
Fixed costs			
Rent	10,000	10,000	–0–
Supervision	7,000	7,000	–0–
Depreciation	4,000	4,000	–0–
Total fixed	21,000	21,000	–0–
Total costs	$151,000	$155,100	$4,100 U

The monthly budget amounts in the report were based on an expected production of 50,000 units per month or 600,000 units per year.

The company president was displeased with the department manager's performance. The department manager, who thought he had done a good job, could not understand the unfavorable results. In May, 55,000 units were produced.

Instructions

(b) Budget $164,000

(c) Budget $125,000
Actual $128,280

(a) State the total budgeted cost formula.

(b) Prepare a budget report for May using flexible budget data. Why does this report provide a better basis for evaluating performance than the report based on static budget data?

(c) In June, 40,000 units were produced. Prepare the budget report using flexible budget data, assuming (1) each variable cost was 20% less in June than its actual cost in May, and (2) fixed costs were the same in the month of June as in May.

Prepare responsibility report for a profit center.

(LO 6), AN

P10-4B Guzman Inc. operates the Home Appliance Division as a profit center. Operating data for this division for the year ended December 31, 2014, are shown on the next page.

	Budget	Difference from Budget
Sales	$2,400,000	$90,000 U
Cost of goods sold		
Variable	1,200,000	58,000 U
Controllable fixed	200,000	8,000 F
Selling and administrative		
Variable	240,000	8,000 F
Controllable fixed	60,000	3,000 U
Noncontrollable fixed costs	50,000	2,000 U

In addition, Guzman incurs $150,000 of indirect fixed costs that were budgeted at $155,000. Twenty percent (20%) of these costs are allocated to the Home Appliance Division. None of these costs are controllable by the division manager.

Instructions
(a) Prepare a responsibility report for the Home Appliance Division (a profit center) for the year.
(b) ▭▭▭▷ Comment on the manager's performance in controlling revenues and costs.
(c) Identify any costs excluded from the responsibility report and explain why they were excluded.

(a) Contribution margin
$140,000 U
Controllable margin
$135,000 U

P10-5B Strauss Company manufactures a variety of garden and lawn equipment. The company operates through three divisions. Each division is an investment center. Operating data for the Lawnmower Division for the year ended December 31, 2014, and relevant budget data are as follows.

Prepare responsibility report for an investment center, and compute ROI.

(LO 7), E

	Actual	Comparison with Budget
Sales	$2,900,000	$150,000 unfavorable
Variable cost of goods sold	1,400,000	100,000 unfavorable
Variable selling and administrative expenses	300,000	40,000 favorable
Controllable fixed cost of goods sold	270,000	On target
Controllable fixed selling and administrative expenses	140,000	On target

Average operating assets for the year for the Lawnmower Division were $5,000,000, which was also the budgeted amount.

Instructions
(a) Prepare a responsibility report (in thousands of dollars) for the Lawnmower Division.
(b) Evaluate the manager's performance. Which items will likely be investigated by top management?
(c) Compute the expected ROI in 2014 for the Lawnmower Division, assuming the following independent changes.
   (1) Variable cost of goods sold is decreased by 20%.
   (2) Average operating assets are decreased by 24%.
   (3) Sales are increased by $700,000, and this increase is expected to increase contribution margin by $260,000.

(a) Controllable margin:
Budget $1,000
Actual $790

P10-6B Gore Company uses a responsibility reporting system. It has divisions in San Francisco, Phoenix, and Tulsa. Each division has three production departments: Cutting, Shaping, and Finishing. The responsibility for each department rests with a manager who reports to the division production manager. Each division manager reports to the vice president of production. There are also vice presidents for marketing and finance. All vice presidents report to the president.

In January 2014, controllable actual and budget manufacturing overhead cost data for the departments and divisions were as shown on the next page.

Prepare reports for cost centers under responsibility accounting, and comment on performance of managers.

(LO 4), AN

Manufacturing Overhead	Actual	Budget
Individual costs—Cutting Department—Phoenix		
Indirect labor	$ 95,000	$ 90,000
Indirect materials	62,700	61,000
Maintenance	27,400	25,000
Utilities	25,200	20,000
Supervision	31,000	28,000
	$241,300	$224,000
Total costs		
Shaping Department—Phoenix	$190,000	$177,000
Finishing Department—Phoenix	250,000	245,000
San Francisco division	724,000	715,000
Tulsa division	760,000	750,000

Additional overhead costs were incurred as follows: Phoenix division production manager—actual costs $73,100, budget $70,000; vice president of production—actual costs $72,000, budget $70,000; president—actual costs $94,200, budget $91,300. These expenses are not allocated.

The vice presidents, who report to the president (other than the vice president of production), had the following expenses.

Vice President	Actual	Budget
Marketing	$167,200	$160,000
Finance	125,000	120,000

Instructions

(a) Using the format on page 453, prepare the following responsibility reports.
  (1) Manufacturing overhead—Cutting Department manager—Phoenix division.
  (2) Manufacturing overhead—Phoenix division manager.
  (3) Manufacturing overhead—vice president of production.
  (4) Manufacturing overhead and expenses—president.
(b) Comment on the comparative performances of:
  (1) Department managers in the Phoenix division.
  (2) Division managers.
  (3) Vice presidents.

(a) (1) $17,300 U
(2) $38,400 U
(3) $59,400 U
(4) $74,500 U

Compare ROI and residual income.

(LO 8), AN

*P10-7B Walton Industries has manufactured prefabricated garages for over 20 years. The garages are constructed in sections to be assembled on customers' lots. Walton expanded into the precut housing market when it acquired Washington Enterprises, one of its suppliers. In this market, various types of lumber are precut into the appropriate lengths, banded into packages, and shipped to customers' lots for assembly. Walton designated the Washington Division as an investment center.

Walton uses return on investment (ROI) as a performance measure, with investment defined as average operating assets. Management bonuses are based in part on ROI. All investments are expected to earn a minimum rate of return of 15%. Washington's ROI has ranged from 19.9% to 23.3% since it was acquired. Washington had an investment opportunity in 2014 that had an estimated ROI of 18%. Washington's management decided against the investment because it believed the investment would decrease the division's overall ROI.

Selected financial information for Washington is presented below. The division's average operating assets were $7,500,000 for the year 2014.

Washington Division
Selected Financial Information
For the Year Ended December 31, 2014

Sales	$16,000,000
Contribution margin	5,600,000
Controllable margin	1,500,000

Instructions

(a) Calculate the following performance measures for 2014 for the Washington Division.
   (1) Return on investment (ROI).
   (2) Residual income.
(b) ▣▰▰▰▶ Would the management of Washington have been more likely to accept the investment opportunity it had in 2014 if residual income were used as a performance measure instead of ROI? Explain your answer.

PROBLEMS: SET C

Visit the book's companion website, at **www.wiley.com/college/weygandt**, and choose the Student Companion site to access Problem Set C.

WATERWAYS CONTINUING PROBLEM

(*Note:* This is a continuation of the Waterways Problem from Chapters 1–9.)

WCP10 Waterways Corporation is continuing its budget preparations. This problem gives you static budget information as well as actual overhead costs, and asks you to calculate amounts related to budgetary control and responsibility accounting.

Go to the book's companion website, at **www.wiley.com/college/weygandt**, *to find the completion of this problem.*

Broadening Your PERSPECTIVE

Management Decision-Making

Decision-Making at Current Designs

BYP10-1 The Current Designs staff has prepared the annual manufacturing budget for the roto-molded line based on an estimated annual production of 4,000 kayaks during 2013. Each kayak will require 54 pounds of polyethylene powder and a finishing kit (rope, seat, hardware, etc.). The polyethylene powder used in these kayaks costs $1.50 per pound, and the finishing kits cost $170 each. Each kayak will use two kinds of labor—2 hours of type I labor from people who run the oven and trim the plastic, and 3 hours of work from type II workers who attach the hatches and seat and other hardware. The type I employees are paid $15 per hour, and the type II are paid $12 per hour.
   Manufacturing overhead is budgeted at $396,000 for 2013, broken down as follows.

Variable costs	
Indirect materials	$ 40,000
Manufacturing supplies	53,800
Maintenance and utilities	88,000
	181,800
Fixed costs	
Supervision	90,000
Insurance	14,400
Depreciation	109,800
	214,200
Total	$396,000

During the first quarter, ended March 31, 2013, 1,050 units were actually produced with the following costs.

Polyethylene powder	$ 87,000
Finishing kits	178,840
Type I labor	31,500
Type II labor	39,060
Indirect materials	10,500
Manufacturing supplies	14,150
Maintenance and utilities	26,000
Supervision	20,000
Insurance	3,600
Depreciation	27,450
Total	$438,100

Instructions
(a) Prepare the annual manufacturing budget for 2013, assuming that 4,000 kayaks will be produced.
(b) Prepare the flexible budget for manufacturing for the quarter ended March 31, 2013. Assume activity levels of 900, 1,000, and 1,050 units.
(c) Assuming the rotomolded line is treated as a profit center, prepare a flexible budget report for manufacturing for the quarter ended March 31, 2013, when 1,050 units were produced.

Decision-Making Across the Organization

BYP10-2 Green Pastures is a 400-acre farm on the outskirts of the Kentucky Bluegrass, specializing in the boarding of broodmares and their foals. A recent economic downturn in the thoroughbred industry has led to a decline in breeding activities, and it has made the boarding business extremely competitive. To meet the competition, Green Pastures planned in 2014 to entertain clients, advertise more extensively, and absorb expenses formerly paid by clients such as veterinary and blacksmith fees.

The budget report for 2014 is presented below. As shown, the static income statement budget for the year is based on an expected 21,900 boarding days at $25 per mare. The variable expenses per mare per day were budgeted: feed $5, veterinary fees $3, blacksmith fees $0.25, and supplies $0.55. All other budgeted expenses were either semifixed or fixed.

During the year, management decided not to replace a worker who quit in March, but it did issue a new advertising brochure and did more entertaining of clients.[1]

Green Pastures
Static Budget Income Statement
For the Year Ended December 31, 2014

	Actual	Master Budget	Difference
Number of mares	52	60	8 U
Number of boarding days	19,000	21,900	2,900 U
Sales	$380,000	$547,500	$167,500 U
Less: Variable expenses			
Feed	104,390	109,500	5,110 F
Veterinary fees	58,838	65,700	6,862 F
Blacksmith fees	4,984	5,475	491 F
Supplies	10,178	12,045	1,867 F
Total variable expenses	178,390	192,720	14,330 F
Contribution margin	201,610	354,780	153,170 U

---

[1]Data for this case are based on Hans Sprohge and John Talbott, "New Applications for Variance Analysis," *Journal of Accountancy* (AICPA, New York), April 1989, pp. 137–141.

	Actual	Master Budget	Difference
Less: Fixed expenses			
Depreciation	40,000	40,000	–0–
Insurance	11,000	11,000	–0–
Utilities	12,000	14,000	2,000 F
Repairs and maintenance	10,000	11,000	1,000 F
Labor	88,000	95,000	7,000 F
Advertisement	12,000	8,000	4,000 U
Entertainment	7,000	5,000	2,000 U
Total fixed expenses	180,000	184,000	4,000 F
Net income	$ 21,610	$170,780	$149,170 U

Instructions

With the class divided into groups, answer the following.

(a) Based on the static budget report:
   (1) What was the primary cause(s) of the loss in net income?
   (2) Did management do a good, average, or poor job of controlling expenses?
   (3) Were management's decisions to stay competitive sound?
(b) Prepare a flexible budget report for the year.
(c) Based on the flexible budget report, answer the three questions in part (a) above.
(d) What course of action do you recommend for the management of Green Pastures?

Managerial Analysis

BYP10-3 Lanier Company manufactures expensive watch cases sold as souvenirs. Three of its sales departments are Retail Sales, Wholesale Sales, and Outlet Sales. The Retail Sales Department is a profit center. The Wholesale Sales Department is a cost center. Its managers merely take orders from customers who purchase through the company's wholesale catalog. The Outlet Sales Department is an investment center because each manager is given full responsibility for an outlet store location. The manager can hire and discharge employees, purchase, maintain, and sell equipment, and in general is fairly independent of company control.

Mary Gammel is a manager in the Retail Sales Department. Stephen Flott manages the Wholesale Sales Department. Jose Gomez manages the Golden Gate Club outlet store in San Francisco. The following are the budget responsibility reports for each of the three departments.

	Budget		
	Retail Sales	Wholesale Sales	Outlet Sales
Sales	$ 750,000	$ 400,000	$200,000
Variable costs			
Cost of goods sold	150,000	100,000	25,000
Advertising	100,000	30,000	5,000
Sales salaries	75,000	15,000	3,000
Printing	10,000	20,000	5,000
Travel	20,000	30,000	2,000
Fixed costs			
Rent	50,000	30,000	10,000
Insurance	5,000	2,000	1,000
Depreciation	75,000	100,000	40,000
Investment in assets	1,000,000	1,200,000	800,000

	Actual Results		
	Retail Sales	**Wholesale Sales**	**Outlet Sales**
Sales	$ 750,000	$ 400,000	$200,000
Variable costs			
Cost of goods sold	192,000	122,000	26,500
Advertising	100,000	30,000	5,000
Sales salaries	75,000	15,000	3,000
Printing	10,000	20,000	5,000
Travel	14,000	21,000	1,500
Fixed costs			
Rent	40,000	50,000	12,300
Insurance	5,000	2,000	1,000
Depreciation	80,000	90,000	56,000
Investment in assets	1,000,000	1,200,000	800,000

Instructions
(a) Determine which of the items should be included in the responsibility report for each of the three managers.
(b) Compare the budgeted measures with the actual results. Decide which results should be called to the attention of each manager.

Real-World Focus

BYP10-4 Computer Associates International, Inc., the world's leading business software company, delivers the end-to-end infrastructure to enable e-business through innovative technology, services, and education. Computer Associates has 19,000 employees worldwide and recently had revenue of over $6 billion.

Presented below is information from the company's annual report.

Computer Associates International, Inc.
Management Discussion

The Company has experienced a pattern of business whereby revenue for its third and fourth fiscal quarters reflects an increase over first- and second-quarter revenue. The Company attributes this increase to clients' increased spending at the end of their calendar year budgetary periods and the culmination of its annual sales plan. Since the Company's costs do not increase proportionately with the third- and fourth-quarters' increase in revenue, the higher revenue in these quarters results in greater profit margins and income. Fourth-quarter profitability is traditionally affected by significant new hirings, training, and education expenditures for the succeeding year.

Instructions
(a) Why don't the company's costs increase proportionately as the revenues increase in the third and fourth quarters?
(b) What type of budgeting seems appropriate for the Computer Associates situation?

BYP10-5 There are many useful resources regarding budgeting available on websites. The following activity investigates the results of a comprehensive budgeting study.

Address: **http://www.accountingweb.com/whitepapers/centage_ioma.pdf**, or go to **www.wiley.com/college/weygandt**

Instructions
Go to the address above and then answer the following questions.

(a) What are cited as the two most common "pain points" of budgeting?
(b) What percentage of companies that participated in the survey said that they prepare annual budgets? Of those that prepare budgets, what percentage say that they start the budgeting process by first generating sales projections?
(c) What is the most common amount of time for the annual budgeting process?

(d) When evaluating variances from budgeted amounts, what was the most commonly defined range of acceptable tolerance levels?

(e) The study defines three types of consequences for varying from budgeted amounts. How does it describe "severe" consequences?

Critical Thinking

Communication Activity

BYP10-6 The manufacturing overhead budget for Fleming Company contains the following items.

Variable costs		Fixed costs	
Indirect materials	$22,000	Supervision	$17,000
Indirect labor	12,000	Inspection costs	1,000
Maintenance expense	10,000	Insurance expense	2,000
Manufacturing supplies	6,000	Depreciation	15,000
Total variable	$50,000	Total fixed	$35,000

The budget was based on an estimated 2,000 units being produced. During the past month, 1,500 units were produced, and the following costs incurred.

Variable costs		Fixed costs	
Indirect materials	$22,500	Supervision	$18,400
Indirect labor	13,500	Inspection costs	1,200
Maintenance expense	8,200	Insurance expense	2,200
Manufacturing supplies	5,000	Depreciation	14,700
Total variable	$49,200	Total fixed	$36,500

Instructions
(a) Determine which items would be controllable by Fred Bedner, the production manager.
(b) How much should have been spent during the month for the manufacture of the 1,500 units?
(c) Prepare a flexible manufacturing overhead budget report for Mr. Bedner.
(d) Prepare a responsibility report. Include only the costs that would have been controllable by Mr. Bedner. Assume that the supervision cost above includes Mr. Bedner's salary of $10,000, both at budget and actual. In an attached memo, describe clearly for Mr. Bedner the areas in which his performance needs to be improved.

Ethics Case

BYP10-7 American Products Corporation participates in a highly competitive industry. In order to meet this competition and achieve profit goals, the company has chosen the decentralized form of organization. Each manager of a decentralized investment center is measured on the basis of profit contribution, market penetration, and return on investment. Failure to meet the objectives established by corporate management for these measures has not been acceptable and usually has resulted in demotion or dismissal of an investment center manager.

An anonymous survey of managers in the company revealed that the managers feel the pressure to compromise their personal ethical standards to achieve the corporate objectives. For example, at certain plant locations there was pressure to reduce quality control to a level which could not assure that all unsafe products would be rejected. Also, sales personnel were encouraged to use questionable sales tactics to obtain orders, including gifts and other incentives to purchasing agents.

The chief executive officer is disturbed by the survey findings. In his opinion, such behavior cannot be condoned by the company. He concludes that the company should do something about this problem.

Instructions
(a) Who are the stakeholders (the affected parties) in this situation?
(b) Identify the ethical implications, conflicts, or dilemmas in the above described situation.
(c) What might the company do to reduce the pressures on managers and decrease the ethical conflicts?

(CMA adapted)

All About You

BYP10-8 It is one thing to prepare a personal budget; it is another thing to stick to it. Financial planners have suggested various mechanisms to provide support for enforcing personal budgets. One approach is called "envelope budgeting."

Instructions
Read the article provided at **http://en.wikipedia.org/wiki/Envelope_budgeting**, and answer the following questions.

(a) Summarize the process of envelope budgeting.
(b) Evaluate whether you think you would benefit from envelope budgeting. What do you think are its strengths and weaknesses relative to your situation?

Considering Your Costs and Benefits

BYP10-9 Preparing a personal budget is a great first step toward control over your personal finances. It is especially useful to prepare a budget when you face a big decision. For most people, the biggest decision they will ever make is whether to purchase a house. The percentage of people in the United States who own a home is high compared to many other countries. This is partially the result of U.S. government programs and incentives that encourage home ownership. For example, the interest on a home mortgage is tax-deductible.

Before purchasing a house, you should first consider whether buying it is the best choice for you. Suppose you just graduated from college and are moving to a new community. Should you immediately buy a new home?

> **YES:** If I purchase a home, I am making my housing cost more like a "fixed cost," thus minimizing increases in my future housing costs. Also, I benefit from the appreciation in my home's value. Although recent turbulence in the economy has caused home prices in many communities to decline, I know that over the long term, home prices have increased across the country.
>
> **NO:** I just moved to a new town, so I don't know the housing market. I am new to my job, so I don't know whether I will like it or my new community. Also, if my job does go well, it is likely that my income will increase in the next few years, so I will able to afford a better house if I wait. Therefore, the flexibility provided by renting is very valuable to me at this point in my life.

Instructions
Write a response indicating your position regarding this situation. Provide support for your view.

Answers to Chapter Questions

Answers to Insight and Accounting Across the Organization Questions

p. 441 Just What the Doctor Ordered? Q: Explain how the use of flexible budgets might help to identify the best solution to this problem. **A:** A fixed budget assumes a particular level of activity. In the case of television shows, the number of viewers can impact revenues and costs. NBCUniversal could prepare alternative budgets at varying levels of activities and assume various cost structures depending on the number of cast members and other factors. Experimenting with different scenarios could help the network identify an approach that maintains an acceptable level of income as revenues decline.

p. 446 Budgets and the Exotic Newcastle Disease Q: What is the major benefit of tying a budget to the overall goals of the company? **A:** People working on a budgeting process that is clearly guided and focused by strategic goals spend less time arguing about irrelevant details and more time focusing on the items that matter.

p. 449 Competition versus Collaboration Q: How might managers of separate divisions be able to reduce division costs through collaboration? **A:** Division managers might reduce costs by sharing design and marketing resources or by jointly negotiating with suppliers. In addition, they can reduce the need to hire and lay off employees by sharing staff across divisions as human resource needs change.

p. 451 Flexible Manufacturing Requires Flexible Accounting Q: What implications do these improvements in production capabilities have for management accounting information and performance evaluation within the organization? **A:** In order to maximize the potential of flexible manufacturing facilities, managers need to be supplied with information on a more frequent basis. In turn, the tools used to evaluate performance need to take into account what information management had at its disposal, and what decisions were made in response to this information.

p. 461 Does Hollywood Look at ROI? Q: What might be the reason that movie studios do not produce G-rated movies as much as R-rated ones? **A:** Perhaps Hollywood believes that big-name stars or large budgets, both of which are typical of R-rated movies, sell movies. However, one study recently concluded, "We can't find evidence that stars help movies, and we can't find evidence that bigger budgets increase return on investment." Some film companies are going out of their way to achieve at least a PG rating.

Answers to Self-Test Questions

1. c **2.** d **3.** c **4.** b **5.** b **6.** a ($90,000 − $30,000) ÷ 10,000 **7.** d $28,000 − [9,200 × ($2,700 ÷ 9,000)] **8.** a **9.** d **10.** d **11.** a **12.** c **13.** b **14.** b **15.** d

✔ Remember to go back to The Navigator box on the chapter opening page and check off your completed work.

Chapter 11

Standard Costs and Balanced Scorecard

80,000 Different Caffeinated Combinations

When Howard Schultz purchased a small Seattle coffee-roasting business in 1987, he set out to create a new kind of company. He thought the company should sell coffee by the cup in its store, in addition to the bags of roasted beans it already sold. He also felt that the store shouldn't just sell coffee but also a pleasant atmosphere and experience. Schultz saw the store as a place where you could order a beverage, custom-made to your unique tastes, in an environment that would give you the sense that you had escaped, if only momentarily, from the chaos we call life. Finally, Schultz believed that the company would prosper if employees shared in its success.

In a little more than 20 years, Howard Schultz's company, Starbucks, grew from that one store to over 17,000 locations in 54 countries. That is an incredible rate of growth, and it didn't happen by accident. While Starbucks does everything it can to maximize the customer's experience, behind the scenes it needs to control costs. Consider the almost infinite options of beverage combinations and variations at Starbucks. The company must determine the most efficient way to make each beverage, it must communicate these methods in the form of standards to its employees, and it must then evaluate whether those standards are being met.

✔ The Navigator

- Scan Learning Objectives

- Read Feature Story

- Scan Preview

- Read Text and answer **DO IT!** p. 501
    - p. 506   p. 510   p. 515

- Work Using the Decision Toolkit p. 516

- Review Summary of Learning Objectives

- Work Comprehensive **DO IT!** p. 524

- Answer Self-Test Questions

- Complete Assignments

- Go to **WileyPLUS** for practice and tutorials

Learning Objectives

After studying this chapter, you should be able to:

1 Distinguish between a standard and a budget.

2 Identify the advantages of standard costs.

3 Describe how companies set standards.

4 State the formulas for determining direct materials and direct labor variances.

5 State the formula for determining the total manufacturing overhead variance.

6 Discuss the reporting of variances.

7 Prepare an income statement for management under a standard costing system.

8 Describe the balanced scorecard approach to performance evaluation.

Schultz's book, *Onward: How Starbucks Fought for Its Life Without Losing Its Soul*, describes a painful period in which Starbucks had to close 600 stores and lay off thousands of employees. However, when a prominent shareholder suggested that the company eliminate its employee health-care plan, as so many other companies had done, Schultz refused. The health-care plan represented one of the company's most tangible commitments to employee

well-being as well as to corporate social responsibility. Schultz feels strongly that providing health care to the company's employees is an essential part of the standard cost of a cup of Starbucks' coffee.

Watch the Starbucks video in WileyPLUS to learn more about how the company sets standards. Watch the Southwest Airlines video in WileyPLUS to learn more about the use of the balanced scorecard in the real world.

✔ **The Navigator**

Preview of **Chapter 11**

Standards are a fact of life. You met the admission standards for the school you are attending. The vehicle that you drive had to meet certain governmental emissions standards. The hamburgers and salads that you eat in a restaurant have to meet certain health and nutritional standards before they can be sold. As described in our Feature Story, Starbucks has standards for the costs of its materials, labor, and overhead. The reason for standards in these cases is very simple: They help to ensure that overall product quality is high while keeping costs under control.

In this chapter, we continue the study of controlling costs. You will learn how to evaluate performance using standard costs and a balanced scorecard.

The content and organization of Chapter 11 are as follows.

STANDARD COSTS AND BALANCED SCORECARD

The Need for Standards	Setting Standard Costs	Analyzing and Reporting Variances from Standards	Balanced Scorecard
• Standards vs. budgets • Why standard costs?	• Ideal vs. normal • Case study	• Direct materials variances • Direct labor variances • Manufacturing overhead variances • Reporting variances • Statement presentation	• Financial perspective • Customer perspective • Internal process perspective • Learning and growth perspective

✔ **The Navigator**

The Need for Standards

Standards are common in business. Those imposed by government agencies are often called **regulations**. They include the Fair Labor Standards Act, the Equal Employment Opportunity Act, and a multitude of environmental standards. Standards established internally by a company may extend to personnel matters, such as employee absenteeism and ethical codes of conduct, quality control standards for products, and standard costs for goods and services. In managerial accounting, **standard costs** are predetermined unit costs, which companies use as measures of performance.

We will focus on manufacturing operations in this chapter. But you should also recognize that standard costs also apply to many types of service businesses as well. For example, a fast-food restaurant such as McDonald's knows the price it should pay for pickles, beef, buns, and other ingredients. It also knows how much time it should take an employee to flip hamburgers. If the company pays too much for pickles or if employees take too much time to prepare Big Macs, McDonald's notices the deviations and takes corrective action. Not-for-profit entities, such as universities, charitable organizations, and governmental agencies, also may use standard costs as measures of performance.

Distinguishing Between Standards and Budgets

LEARNING OBJECTIVE 1

Distinguish between a standard and a budget.

Both **standards** and **budgets** are predetermined costs, and both contribute to management planning and control. There is a difference, however, in the way the terms are expressed. A standard is a **unit** amount. A budget is a **total** amount. Thus, it is customary to state that the **standard cost** of direct labor for a unit of product is, say, $10. If the company produces 5,000 units of the product, the $50,000 of direct labor is the **budgeted** labor cost. A standard is the budgeted **cost per unit** of product. A standard is therefore concerned with each individual cost component that makes up the entire budget.

There are important accounting differences between budgets and standards. Except in the application of manufacturing overhead to jobs and processes, budget data are not journalized in cost accounting systems. In contrast, as we illustrate in the appendix to this chapter, standard costs may be incorporated into cost accounting systems. Also, a company may report its inventories at standard cost in its financial statements, but it would not report inventories at budgeted costs.

Why Standard Costs?

LEARNING OBJECTIVE 2

Identify the advantages of standard costs.

Standard costs offer a number of advantages to an organization, as shown in Illustration 11-1.

The organization will realize these advantages only when standard costs are carefully established and prudently used. Using standards solely as a way to place blame can have a negative effect on managers and employees. To minimize this effect, many companies offer wage incentives to those who meet the standards.

Setting Standard Costs

LEARNING OBJECTIVE 3

Describe how companies set standards.

The setting of standard costs to produce a unit of product is a difficult task. It requires input from all persons who have responsibility for costs and quantities. To determine the standard cost of direct materials, management consults purchasing agents, product managers, quality control engineers, and production supervisors. In setting the standard cost for direct labor, managers obtain pay

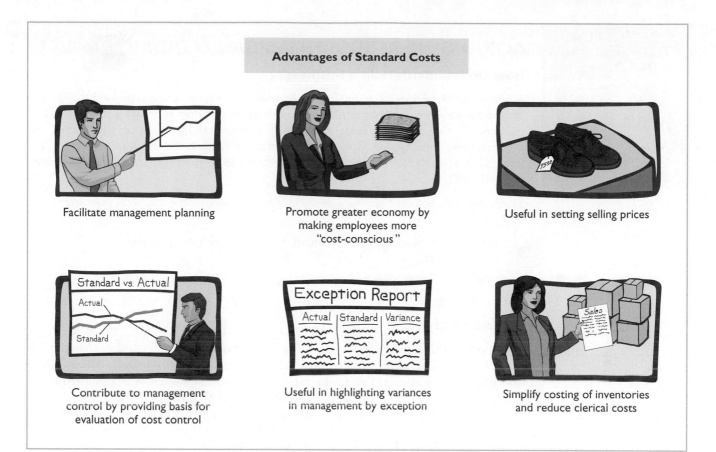

Advantages of Standard Costs

Facilitate management planning

Promote greater economy by making employees more "cost-conscious"

Useful in setting selling prices

Contribute to management control by providing basis for evaluation of cost control

Useful in highlighting variances in management by exception

Simplify costing of inventories and reduce clerical costs

Illustration 11-1
Advantages of standard costs

rate data from the payroll department. Industrial engineers generally determine the labor time requirements. The managerial accountant provides important input for the standard-setting process by accumulating historical cost data and by knowing how costs respond to changes in activity levels.

To be effective in controlling costs, standard costs need to be current at all times. Thus, standards are under continuous review. They should change whenever managers determine that the existing standard is not a good measure of performance. Circumstances that warrant revision of a standard include changed wage rates resulting from a new union contract, a change in product specifications, or the implementation of a new manufacturing method.

Ideal versus Normal Standards

Companies set standards at one of two levels: ideal or normal. **Ideal standards** represent optimum levels of performance under perfect operating conditions. **Normal standards** represent efficient levels of performance that are attainable under expected operating conditions.

Some managers believe ideal standards will stimulate workers to ever-increasing improvement. However, most managers believe that ideal standards lower the morale of the entire workforce because they are difficult, if not impossible, to meet. Very few companies use ideal standards.

Most companies that use standards set them at a normal level. Properly set, normal standards should be **rigorous but attainable**. Normal standards allow for rest periods, machine breakdowns, and other "normal" contingencies in the production process. In the remainder of this chapter, we will assume that standard costs are set at a normal level.

Ethics Note

When standards are set too high, employees sometimes feel pressure to consider unethical practices to meet these standards.

ACCOUNTING ACROSS THE ORGANIZATION

How Do Standards Help a Business?

A number of organizations, including corporations, consultants, and governmental agencies, share information regarding performance standards in an effort to create a standard set of measures for thousands of business processes. The group, referred to as the Open Standards Benchmarking Collaborative, includes IBM, Procter and Gamble, the U.S. Navy, and the World Bank. Companies that are interested in participating can go to the group's website and enter their information.

Source: William M. Bulkeley, "Business, Agencies to Standardize Their Benchmarks," *Wall Street Journal* (May 19, 2004).

? How will the creation of such standards help a business or organization?
(See page 544.)

A Case Study

To establish the standard cost of producing a product, it is necessary to establish standards for each manufacturing cost element—direct materials, direct labor, and manufacturing overhead. The standard for each element is derived from the standard price to be paid and the standard quantity to be used.

To illustrate, we use an extended example. Xonic Beverage Company uses standard costs to measure performance at the production facility of its caffeinated energy drink, Xonic Tonic. Xonic produces one-gallon containers of concentrated syrup that it sells to coffee and smoothie shops, and other retail outlets. The syrup is mixed with ice water or ice "slush" before serving. The potency of the beverage varies depending on the amount of concentrated syrup used.

DIRECT MATERIALS

The **direct materials price standard** is the cost per unit of direct materials that should be incurred. This standard is based on the purchasing department's best estimate of the **cost of raw materials**. This cost is frequently based on current purchase prices. The price standard also includes an amount for related costs such as receiving, storing, and handling. The materials price standard per pound of material for Xonic Tonic is:

Illustration 11-2
Setting direct materials price standard

Item	Price
Purchase price, net of discounts	$ 2.70
Freight	0.20
Receiving and handling	0.10
Standard direct materials price per pound	**$3.00**

The **direct materials quantity standard** is the quantity of direct materials that should be used per unit of finished goods. This standard is expressed as a physical measure, such as pounds, barrels, or board feet. In setting the standard, management considers both the quality and quantity of materials required to manufacture the product. The standard includes allowances for unavoidable waste and normal spoilage. The standard quantity per unit for Xonic Tonic is as follows.

Item	Quantity (Pounds)
Required materials	3.5
Allowance for waste	0.4
Allowance for spoilage	0.1
Standard direct materials quantity per unit	**4.0**

Illustration 11-3
Setting direct materials quantity standard

The standard direct materials cost per unit is the standard direct materials price times the standard direct materials quantity. For Xonic, the standard direct materials cost per gallon of Xonic Tonic is $12.00 ($3 × 4 pounds).

DIRECT LABOR

The **direct labor price standard** is the rate per hour that should be incurred for direct labor. This standard is based on current wage rates, adjusted for anticipated changes such as cost of living adjustments (COLAs). The price standard also generally includes employer payroll taxes and fringe benefits, such as paid holidays and vacations. For Xonic, the direct labor price standard is as follows.

Alternative Terminology
The direct labor price standard is also called the *direct labor rate standard*.

Item	Price
Hourly wage rate	$ 12.50
COLA	0.25
Payroll taxes	0.75
Fringe benefits	1.50
Standard direct labor rate per hour	**$15.00**

Illustration 11-4
Setting direct labor price standard

The **direct labor quantity standard** is the time that should be required to make one unit of the product. This standard is especially critical in labor-intensive companies. Allowances should be made in this standard for rest periods, cleanup, machine setup, and machine downtime. For Xonic, the direct labor quantity standard is as follows.

Alternative Terminology
The direct labor quantity standard is also called the *direct labor efficiency standard*.

Item	Quantity (Hours)
Actual production time	1.5
Rest periods and cleanup	0.2
Setup and downtime	0.3
Standard direct labor hours per unit	**2.0**

Illustration 11-5
Setting direct labor quantity standard

The standard direct labor cost per unit is the standard direct labor rate times the standard direct labor hours. For Xonic, the standard direct labor cost per gallon is $30 ($15 × 2 hours).

MANUFACTURING OVERHEAD

For manufacturing overhead, companies use a **standard predetermined overhead rate** in setting the standard. This overhead rate is determined by dividing budgeted overhead costs by an expected standard activity index. For example, the index may be standard direct labor hours or standard machine hours.

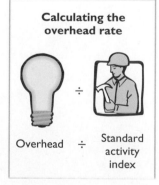

Calculating the overhead rate

Overhead ÷ Standard activity index

As discussed in Chapter 4, many companies employ activity-based costing (ABC) to allocate overhead costs. Because ABC uses multiple activity indices to allocate overhead costs, it results in a better correlation between activities and costs incurred than do other methods. As a result, the use of ABC can significantly improve the usefulness of standard costing for management decision-making.

Xonic uses standard direct labor hours as the activity index. The company expects to produce 13,200 gallons of Xonic Tonic during the year at normal capacity. **Normal capacity** is the average activity output that a company should experience over the long run. Since it takes two direct labor hours for each gallon, total standard direct labor hours are 26,400 (13,200 gallons × 2 hours).

At normal capacity of 26,400 direct labor hours, overhead costs are expected to be $132,000. Of that amount, $79,200 are variable and $52,800 are fixed. Illustration 11-6 shows computation of the standard predetermined overhead rates for Xonic.

Illustration 11-6
Computing predetermined overhead rates

Budgeted Overhead Costs	Amount	÷	Standard Direct Labor Hours	=	Overhead Rate per Direct Labor Hour
Variable	$ 79,200		26,400		$3.00
Fixed	52,800		26,400		2.00
Total	$132,000		26,400		**$5.00**

The standard manufacturing overhead rate per unit is the predetermined overhead rate times the activity index quantity standard. For Xonic, which uses direct labor hours as its activity index, the standard manufacturing overhead rate per gallon of Xonic Tonic is $10 ($5 × 2 hours).

TOTAL STANDARD COST PER UNIT

After a company has established the standard quantity and price per unit of product, it can determine the total standard cost. The total standard cost per unit is the sum of the standard costs of direct materials, direct labor, and manufacturing overhead. The total standard cost per gallon of Xonic Tonic is $52, as shown on the following standard cost card.

Illustration 11-7
Standard cost per gallon of Xonic Tonic

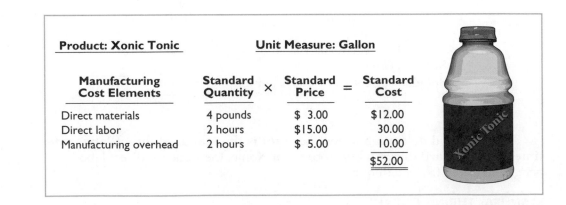

Product: Xonic Tonic		Unit Measure: Gallon		
Manufacturing Cost Elements	Standard Quantity ×	Standard Price =	Standard Cost	
Direct materials	4 pounds	$ 3.00	$12.00	
Direct labor	2 hours	$15.00	30.00	
Manufacturing overhead	2 hours	$ 5.00	10.00	
			$52.00	

The company prepares a standard cost card for each product. This card provides the basis for determining variances from standards.

MANAGEMENT INSIGHT

How Can We Make Susan's Chili Profitable?

Susan's Chili Factory manufactures and sells chili. The cost of manufacturing Susan's chili consists of the costs of raw materials, labor to convert the basic ingredients to chili, and overhead. Managers need to develop three standards for materials: (1) What should be the formula (mix) of ingredients for one gallon of chili? (2) What should be the normal wastage (or shrinkage) for the individual ingredients? (3) What should be the standard cost for the individual ingredients that go into the chili?

Susan's Chili Factory also illustrates how managers can use standard costs in controlling costs. Suppose that summer droughts have reduced crop yields. As a result, prices have doubled for beans, onions, and peppers. In this case, actual costs will be significantly higher than standard costs, which will cause management to evaluate the situation. Similarly, assume that poor maintenance caused the onion-dicing blades to become dull. As a result, usage of onions to make a gallon of chili tripled. Because this deviation is quickly highlighted through standard costs, managers can take corrective action promptly.

Source: Adapted from David R. Beran, "Cost Reduction Through Control Reporting," *Management Accounting* (April 1982), pp. 29–33.

? How might management use this raw materials cost information? (See page 545.)

> DO IT!

Standard Costs

Action Plan

✔ Know that standard costs are predetermined unit costs.

✔ To establish the standard cost of producing a product, establish the standard for each manufacturing cost element—direct materials, direct labor, and manufacturing overhead.

✔ Compute the standard cost for each element from the standard price to be paid and the standard quantity to be used.

Ridette Inc. accumulated the following standard cost data concerning product Cty31.

Direct materials per unit: 1.5 pounds at $4 per pound
Direct labor per unit: 0.25 hours at $13 per hour.
Manufacturing overhead: predetermined rate is 120% of direct labor cost.

Compute the standard cost of one unit of product Cty31.

Solution

Manufacturing Cost Element	Standard Quantity	×	Standard Price	=	Standard Cost
Direct materials	1.5 pounds		$4.00		$ 6.00
Direct labor	0.25 hours		$13.00		3.25
Manufacturing overhead	120% of direct labor cost		$3.25		3.90
Total					$13.15

Related exercise material: **BE11-2, BE11-3, E11-1, E11-2, E11-3, and DO IT! 11-1.**

✔ **The Navigator**

Analyzing and Reporting Variances from Standards

Alternative Terminology
In business, the term *variance* is also used to indicate differences between total budgeted and total actual costs.

One of the major management uses of standard costs is to identify variances from standards. **Variances** are the differences between total actual costs and total standard costs.

To illustrate, assume that in producing 1,000 gallons of Xonic Tonic in the month of June, Xonic incurred the following costs.

Illustration 11-8
Actual production costs

Direct materials	$13,020
Direct labor	31,080
Variable overhead	6,500
Fixed overhead	4,400
Total actual costs	$55,000

Companies determine total standard costs by multiplying the units produced by the standard cost per unit. The total standard cost of Xonic Tonic is $52,000 (1,000 gallons × $52). Thus, the total variance is $3,000, as shown below.

Illustration 11-9
Computation of total variance

Actual costs	$55,000
Less: Standard costs	52,000
Total variance	**$ 3,000**

Note that the variance is expressed in total dollars, and not on a per unit basis.

When actual costs exceed standard costs, the variance is **unfavorable**. The $3,000 variance in June for Xonic Tonic is unfavorable. An unfavorable variance has a negative connotation. It suggests that the company paid too much for one or more of the manufacturing cost elements or that it used the elements inefficiently.

If actual costs are less than standard costs, the variance is **favorable**. A favorable variance has a positive connotation. It suggests efficiencies in incurring manufacturing costs and in using direct materials, direct labor, and manufacturing overhead.

However, be careful: A favorable variance could be obtained by using inferior materials. In printing wedding invitations, for example, a favorable variance could result from using an inferior grade of paper. Or, a favorable variance might be achieved in installing tires on an automobile assembly line by tightening only half of the lug bolts. A variance is not favorable if the company has sacrificed quality control standards.

To interpret a variance, you must analyze its components. A variance can result from differences related to the cost of materials, labor, or overhead. Illustration 11-10 shows that the total variance is the sum of the materials, labor, and overhead variances.

Illustration 11-10
Components of total variance

Materials Variance   +   Labor Variance   +   Overhead Variance   =   Total Variance

In the following discussion, you will see that the materials variance and the labor variance are the sum of variances resulting from price differences and quantity differences. Illustration 11-11 shows a format for computing the price and quantity variances.

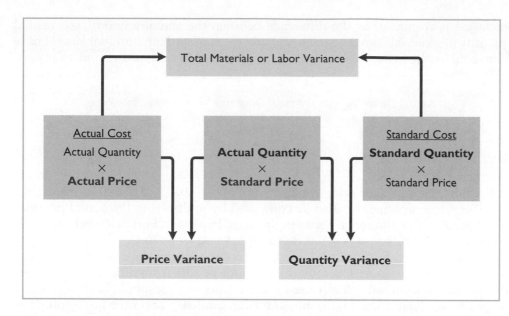

Illustration 11-11
Breakdown of materials or labor variance into price and quantity variances

Note that the left side of the matrix is actual cost (actual quantity times actual price). The right hand is standard cost (standard quantity times standard price). The only additional element you need in order to compute the price and quantity variances is the middle element, the actual quantity at the standard price.

Direct Materials Variances

Part of Xonic's total variance of $3,000 is due to a materials variance. In completing the order for 1,000 gallons of Xonic Tonic, the company used 4,200 pounds of direct materials. The direct materials were purchased at a price of $3.10 per unit. From Illustration 11-3, we know that Xonic's standards require it to use 4 pounds of materials per gallon produced, so it should have only used 4,000 (4 × 1,000) pounds of direct materials to produce 1,000 gallons. Illustration 11-2 shows that the standard cost of each pound of direct materials is $3 instead of the $3.10 actually paid. Illustration 11-12 shows that the **total materials variance** is computed as the difference between the amount paid (actual quantity times actual price) and the amount that should have been paid based on standards (standard quantity times standard price of materials).

LEARNING OBJECTIVE 4

State the formulas for determining direct materials and direct labor variances.

Actual Quantity × Actual Price (AQ) × (AP)		Standard Quantity × Standard Price (SQ) × (SP)		Total Materials Variance (TMV)
(4,200 × $3.10)	−	(4,000 × $3.00)	=	$1,020 U

Illustration 11-12
Formula for total materials variance

Thus, for Xonic, the total materials variance is $1,020 ($13,020 − $12,000) unfavorable.

The total materials variance could be caused by differences in the price paid for the materials or by differences in the amount of materials used. Illustration 11-13 shows that the total materials variance is the sum of the materials price variance and the materials quantity variance.

Materials Price Variance + Materials Quantity Variance = Total Materials Variance

Illustration 11-13
Components of total materials variance

The materials price variance results from a difference between the actual price and the standard price. Illustration 11-14 (page 504) shows that the **materials price**

variance is computed as the difference between the actual amount paid (actual quantity of materials times actual price) and the standard amount that should have been paid for the materials used (actual quantity of materials times standard price).[1]

Illustration 11-14
Formula for materials price variance

Actual Quantity × Actual Price (AQ) × (AP)	−	Actual Quantity × Standard Price (AQ) × (SP)	=	Materials Price Variance (MPV)
(4,200 × $3.10)	−	(4,200 × $3.00)	=	$420 U

Helpful Hint
The alternative formula is:
$$\boxed{AQ} \times \boxed{AP - SP} = \boxed{MPV}$$

For Xonic, the materials price variance is $420 ($13,020 − $12,600) unfavorable.

The price variance can also be computed by multiplying the actual quantity purchased by the difference between the actual and standard price per unit. The computation in this case is 4,200 × ($3.10 − $3.00) = $420 U.

As seen in Illustration 11-13, the other component of the materials variance is the quantity variance. The quantity variance results from differences between the amount of material actually used and the amount that should have been used. As shown in Illustration 11-15, the **materials quantity variance** is computed as the difference between the standard cost of the actual quantity (actual quantity times standard price) and the standard cost of the amount that should have been used (standard quantity times standard price for materials).

Illustration 11-15
Formula for materials quantity variance

Actual Quantity × Standard Price (AQ) × (SP)	−	Standard Quantity × Standard Price (SQ) × (SP)	=	Materials Quantity Variance (MQV)
(4,200 × $3.00)	−	(4,000 × $3.00)	=	$600 U

Thus, for Xonic, the materials quantity variance is $600 ($12,600 − $12,000) unfavorable.

Helpful Hint
The alternative formula is:
$$\boxed{SP} \times \boxed{AQ - SQ} = \boxed{MQV}$$

The quantity variance can also be computed by applying the standard price to the difference between actual and standard quantities used. The computation in this example is $3.00 × (4,200 − 4,000) = $600 U.

The total materials variance of $1,020 U, therefore, consists of the following.

Illustration 11-16
Summary of materials variances

Materials price variance	$ 420 U
Materials quantity variance	600 U
Total materials variance	**$1,020 U**

Companies sometimes use a matrix to analyze a variance. **When the matrix is used, a company computes the amounts using the formulas for each cost element first and then computes the variances.** Illustration 11-17 shows the completed matrix for the direct materials variance for Xonic. The matrix provides a convenient structure for determining each variance.

CAUSES OF MATERIALS VARIANCES

What are the causes of a variance? The causes may relate to both internal and external factors. The investigation of a **materials price variance usually begins in the purchasing department**. Many factors affect the price paid for raw

"What caused materials price variances?"
Purchasing Dept.

---

[1]Assume that all materials purchased during the period are used in production and that no units remain in inventory at the end of the period.

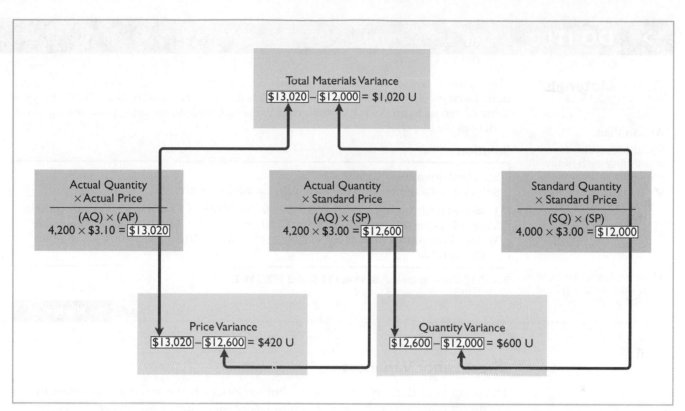

Illustration 11-17
Matrix for direct materials variances

materials. These include availability of quantity and cash discounts, the quality of the materials requested, and the delivery method used. To the extent that these factors are considered in setting the price standard, the purchasing department is responsible for any variances.

However, a variance may be beyond the control of the purchasing department. Sometimes, for example, prices may rise faster than expected. Moreover, actions by groups over which the company has no control, such as the OPEC nations' oil price increases, may cause an unfavorable variance. For example, during a recent year, Kraft Foods and Kellogg Company both experienced unfavorable materials price variances when the cost of dairy and wheat products jumped unexpectedly. There are also times when a production department may be responsible for the price variance. This may occur when a rush order forces the company to pay a higher price for the materials.

The starting point for determining the cause(s) of a significant **materials quantity variance is in the production department**. If the variances are due to inexperienced workers, faulty machinery, or carelessness, the production department is responsible. However, if the materials obtained by the purchasing department were of inferior quality, then the purchasing department is responsible.

DECISION TOOLKIT

DECISION CHECKPOINTS	INFO NEEDED FOR DECISION	TOOL TO USE FOR DECISION	HOW TO EVALUATE RESULTS
Has management accomplished its price and quantity objectives regarding materials?	Actual cost and standard cost of materials	Materials price and materials quantity variances	Positive (favorable) variances suggest that price and quantity objectives have been met.

> **DO IT!**

Direct Materials Variances

Action Plan

Use the formulas for computing each of the materials variances:

✔ Total materials variance = (AQ × AP) − (SQ × SP)

✔ Materials price variance = (AQ × AP) − (AQ × SP)

✔ Materials quantity variance = (AQ × SP) − (SQ × SP)

The standard cost of Wonder Walkers includes two units of direct materials at $8.00 per unit. During July, the company buys 22,000 units of direct materials at $7.50 and uses those materials to produce 10,000 Wonder Walkers. Compute the total, price, and quantity variances for materials.

Solution

Standard quantity = 10,000 × 2.
Substituting amounts into the formulas, the variances are:

Total materials variance = (22,000 × $7.50) − (20,000 × $8.00) = $5,000 unfavorable
Materials price variance = (22,000 × $7.50) − (22,000 × $8.00) = $11,000 favorable
Materials quantity variance = (22,000 × $8.00) − (20,000 × $8.00) = $16,000 unfavorable

Related exercise material: **BE11-4, E11-5, and** **DO IT!** **11-2.**

✔ **The Navigator**

Direct Labor Variances

The process of determining direct labor variances is the same as for determining the direct materials variances. In completing the Xonic Tonic order, the company incurred 2,100 direct labor hours at an average hourly rate of $14.80. The standard hours allowed for the units produced were 2,000 hours (1,000 gallons × 2 hours). The standard labor rate was $15 per hour.

The total labor variance is the difference between the amount actually paid for labor versus the amount that should have been paid. Illustration 11-18 shows that the **total labor variance** is computed as the difference between the amount actually paid for labor (actual hours times actual rate) and the amount that should have been paid (standard hours times standard rate for labor).

Illustration 11-18
Formula for total labor variance

Actual Hours × Actual Rate (AH) × (AR)	−	Standard Hours × Standard Rate (SH) × (SR)	=	Total Labor Variance (TLV)
(2,100 × $14.80)	−	(2,000 × $15.00)	=	$1,080 U

The total labor variance is $1,080 ($31,080 − $30,000) unfavorable.

The total labor variance is caused by differences in the labor rate or difference in labor hours. Illustration 11-19 shows that the total labor variance is the sum of the labor price variance and the labor quantity variance.

Illustration 11-19
Components of total labor variance

Labor Price Variance	+	Labor Quantity Variance	=	Total Labor Variance

The labor price variance results from the difference between the rate paid to workers versus the rate that was supposed to be paid. Illustration 11-20 shows that the **labor price variance** is computed as the difference between the actual amount paid (actual hours times actual rate) and the amount that should have been paid for the number of hours worked (actual hours times standard rate for labor).

Actual Hours × Actual Rate (AH) × (AR)	−	Actual Hours × Standard Rate (AH) × (SR)	=	Labor Price Variance (LPV)
(2,100 × $14.80)	−	(2,100 × $15.00)	=	$420 F

Illustration 11-20
Formula for labor price variance

For Xonic, the labor price variance is $420 ($31,080 − $31,500) favorable.

The labor price variance can also be computed by multiplying actual hours worked by the difference between the actual pay rate and the standard pay rate. The computation in this example is 2,100 × ($15.00 − $14.80) = $420 F.

The other component of the total labor variance is the labor quantity variance. The labor quantity variance results from the difference between the actual number of labor hours and the number of hours that should have been worked for the quantity produced. Illustration 11-21 shows that the **labor quantity variance** is computed as the difference between the amount that should have been paid for the hours worked (actual hours times standard rate) and the amount that should have been paid for the amount of hours that should have been worked (standard hours times standard rate for labor).

Helpful Hint
The alternative formula is:
$$\boxed{AH} \times \boxed{AR - SR} = \boxed{LPV}$$

Actual Hours × Standard Rate (AH) × (SR)	−	Standard Hours × Standard Rate (SH) × (SR)	=	Labor Quantity Variance (LQV)
(2,100 × $15.00)	−	(2,000 × $15.00)	=	$1,500 U

Illustration 11-21
Formula for labor quantity variance

Thus, for Xonic, the labor quantity variance is $1,500 ($31,500 − $30,000) unfavorable.

The same result can be obtained by multiplying the standard rate by the difference between actual hours worked and standard hours allowed. In this case, the computation is $15.00 × (2,100 − 2,000) = $1,500 U.

The total direct labor variance of $1,080 U, therefore, consists of:

Helpful Hint
The alternative formula is:
$$\boxed{SR} \times \boxed{AH - SH} = \boxed{LQV}$$

Labor price variance	$ 420 F
Labor quantity variance	1,500 U
Total direct labor variance	**$1,080 U**

Illustration 11-22
Summary of labor variances

These results can also be obtained from the matrix in Illustration 11-23 (page 508).

CAUSES OF LABOR VARIANCES

Labor price variances usually result from two factors: (1) paying workers **different wages than expected**, and (2) **misallocation of workers**. In companies where pay rates are determined by union contracts, labor price variances should be infrequent. When workers are not unionized, there is a much higher likelihood of such variances. The responsibility for these variances rests with the manager who authorized the wage change.

"What caused labor price variances?"

Personnel decisions

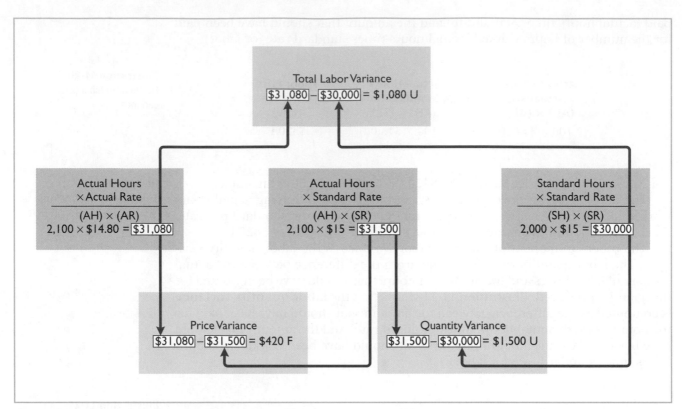

Illustration 11-23
Matrix for direct labor variances

"What caused labor quantity variances?"

Production Dept.

Misallocation of the workforce refers to using skilled workers in place of unskilled workers and vice versa. The use of an inexperienced worker instead of an experienced one will result in a favorable price variance because of the lower pay rate of the unskilled worker. An unfavorable price variance would result if a skilled worker were substituted for an inexperienced one. The production department generally is responsible for labor price variances resulting from misallocation of the workforce.

Labor quantity variances relate to the **efficiency of workers**. The cause of a quantity variance generally can be traced to the production department. The causes of an unfavorable variance may be poor training, worker fatigue, faulty machinery, or carelessness. These causes are the responsibility of the **production department**. However, if the excess time is due to inferior materials, the responsibility falls outside the production department.

DECISION TOOLKIT 🧰

DECISION CHECKPOINTS	INFO NEEDED FOR DECISION	TOOL TO USE FOR DECISION	HOW TO EVALUATE RESULTS
Has management accomplished its price and quantity objectives regarding labor?	Actual cost and standard cost of labor	Labor price and labor quantity variances	Positive (favorable) variances suggest that price and quantity objectives have been met.

LEARNING OBJECTIVE   5

State the formula for determining the total manufacturing overhead variance.

Manufacturing Overhead Variances

The **total overhead variance** is the difference between the actual overhead costs and overhead costs applied based on standard hours allowed for the amount of goods produced. As indicated in Illustration 11-8 (page 502), Xonic incurred overhead costs of $10,900 to produce 1,000 gallons of Xonic Tonic in June. The computation of the actual overhead is comprised of a variable and a fixed component. Illustration 11-24 shows this computation.

Illustration 11-24
Actual overhead costs

Variable overhead	$ 6,500
Fixed overhead	4,400
Total actual overhead	**$10,900**

To find the total overhead variance in a standard costing system, we determine the overhead costs applied based on standard hours allowed. **Standard hours allowed** are the hours that *should* have been worked for the units produced. Overhead costs for Xonic Tonic are applied based on direct labor hours. Because it takes two hours of direct labor to produce one gallon of Xonic Tonic, for the 1,000-gallon Xonic Tonic order, the standard hours allowed are 2,000 hours (1,000 gallons × 2 hours). We then apply the predetermined overhead rate to the 2,000 standard hours allowed.

Recall from Illustration 11-6 (page 500) that the amount of budgeted overhead costs at normal capacity of $132,000 was divided by normal capacity of 26,400 direct labor hours, to arrive at a predetermined overhead rate of $5 ($132,000 ÷ 26,400). The predetermined rate of $5 is then multiplied by the 2,000 standard hours allowed, to determine the overhead costs applied.

Illustration 11-25 shows the formula for the total overhead variance and the calculation for Xonic for the month of June.

Illustration 11-25
Formula for total overhead variance

Actual Overhead	−	Overhead Applied*	=	Total Overhead Variance
$10,900	−	$10,000	−	$900 U
($6,500 + $4,400)		($5 × 2,000 hours)		

*Based on standard hours allowed.

Thus, for Xonic, the total overhead variance is $900 unfavorable.

The overhead variance is generally analyzed through a price and a quantity variance. (These computations are discussed in more detail in advanced courses.) The name usually given to the price variance is the **overhead controllable variance**; the quantity variance is referred to as the **overhead volume variance**. Appendix 11B discusses how the total overhead variance can be broken down into these two variances.

CAUSES OF MANUFACTURING OVERHEAD VARIANCES

One reason for an overhead variance relates to over- or underspending on overhead items. For example, overhead may include indirect labor for which a company paid wages higher than the standard labor price allowed. Or, the price of electricity to run the company's machines increased, and the company did not anticipate this additional cost. Companies should investigate any spending variances, to determine whether they will continue in the future. Generally, the responsibility for these variances rests with the production department.

The overhead variance can also result from the inefficient use of overhead. For example, because of poor maintenance, a number of the manufacturing machines are experiencing breakdowns on a consistent basis, leading to reduced production. Or, the flow of materials through the production process is impeded because of a lack of skilled labor to perform the necessary production tasks, due

"What caused manufacturing overhead variances?"
Production Dept. or Sales Dept.

to a lack of planning. In both of these cases, the production department is responsible for the cause of these variances. On the other hand, overhead can also be underutilized because of a lack of sales orders. When the cause is a lack of sales orders, the responsibility rests outside the production department. For example, at one point Chrysler experienced a very significant unfavorable overhead variance because plant capacity was maintained at excessively high levels, due to overly optimistic sales forecasts.

DECISION TOOLKIT

DECISION CHECKPOINTS	INFO NEEDED FOR DECISION	TOOL TO USE FOR DECISION	HOW TO EVALUATE RESULTS
Has management accomplished its objectives regarding manufacturing overhead?	Actual cost and standard cost of manufacturing overhead	Total manufacturing overhead variance	Positive (favorable) variances suggest that manufacturing overhead objectives have been met.

PEOPLE, PLANET, AND PROFIT INSIGHT

What's Brewing at Starbucks?

It is one thing for a company to say it is committed to corporate social responsibility. It is another thing for the company to actually spell out measurable goals. Recently, Starbucks published its 10th annual *Global Responsibility Report* in which it describes its goals, achievements, and even its shortcomings related to corporate social responsibility. For example, the company achieved its goal of getting more than 50% of its electricity from renewable sources. It then set its sights higher by setting a goal of 100% within five years. The company also has numerous goals related to purchasing coffee from sources that are certified as responsibly grown and ethically traded; providing funds for loans to coffee farmers; and partnerships with Conservation International to provide training to farmers on ecologically friendly growing. Further, the company reduced water consumption by more than 20% in a two-year period. Finally, it made a significant investment in programs to increase recycling of paper and plastic at its stores.

The report also candidly explains that the company did not meet its goal to cut energy consumption by 25%. It also fell far short of its goal of getting customers to reuse their cups. In those instances where it didn't achieve its goals, Starbucks set new goals and described steps it would take to achieve them. You can view the company's *Global Responsibility Report* at *www.starbucks.com/2010report*.

Source: "Starbucks Launches 10th Global Responsibility Report," *Business Wire* (April 18, 2011).

? What implications does Starbucks' commitment to corporate social responsibility have for the standard cost of a cup of coffee? (See page 545.)

> DO IT!

Labor and Manufacturing Overhead Variances

The standard cost of Product YY includes 3 hours of direct labor at $12.00 per hour. The predetermined overhead rate is $20.00 per direct labor hour. During July, the company incurred 3,500 hours of direct labor at an average rate of $12.40 per hour and $71,300 of manufacturing overhead costs. It produced 1,200 units.

(a) Compute the total, price, and quantity variances for labor. (b) Compute the total overhead variance.

Action Plan

✔ Use the formulas for computing each of the variances:
Total labor variance = (AH × AR) − (SH × SR)
Labor price variance = (AH × AR) − (AH × SR)
Labor quantity variance = (AH × SR) − (SH × SR)
Total overhead variance = Actual overhead − Overhead applied*

*Based on standard hours allowed.

Solution

Substituting amounts into the formulas, the variances are:

Total labor variance = (3,500 × $12.40) − (3,600 × $12.00) = $200 unfavorable

Labor price variance = (3,500 × $12.40) − (3,500 × $12.00) = $1,400 unfavorable

Labor quantity variance = (3,500 × $12.00) − (3,600 × $12.00) = $1,200 favorable

Total overhead variance = $71,300 − $72,000* = $700 favorable

*3,600 hours × $20.00

Related exercise material: **BE11-5, BE11-6, E11-4, E11-6, E11-7, E11-8, E11-11, and DO IT! 11-3.**

✔ **The Navigator**

Reporting Variances

All variances should be reported to appropriate levels of management as soon as possible. The sooner managers are informed, the sooner they can evaluate problems and take corrective action.

The form, content, and frequency of variance reports vary considerably among companies. One approach is to prepare a weekly report for each department that has primary responsibility for cost control. Under this approach, materials price variances are reported to the purchasing department, and all other variances are reported to the production department that did the work. The following report for Xonic, with the materials for the Xonic Tonic order listed first, illustrates this approach.

LEARNING OBJECTIVE   6

Discuss the reporting of variances.

			Xonic		
		Variance Report—Purchasing Department			
		For Week Ended June 8, 2014			
Type of Materials	**Quantity Purchased**	**Actual Price**	**Standard Price**	**Price Variance**	**Explanation**
X100	4,200 lbs.	$3.10	$3.00	$ 420 U	Rush order
X142	1,200 units	2.75	2.80	60 F	Quantity discount
A85	600 doz.	5.20	5.10	60 U	Regular supplier on strike
Total price variance				**$420 U**	

Illustration 11-26
Materials price variance report

The explanation column is completed after consultation with the purchasing department manager.

Variance reports facilitate the principle of "management by exception" explained in Chapter 10. For example, the vice president of purchasing can use the report shown above to evaluate the effectiveness of the purchasing department manager. Or, the vice president of production can use production department variance reports to determine how well each production manager is controlling costs. In using variance reports, top management normally looks for **significant variances**. These may be judged on the basis of some quantitative measure, such as more than 10% of the standard or more than $1,000.

Statement Presentation of Variances

In income statements **prepared for management** under a standard cost accounting system, **cost of goods sold is stated at standard cost and the variances are disclosed separately**. Unfavorable variances increase cost of goods sold, while favorable variances decrease cost of goods sold. Illustration 11-27 shows the presentation of variances in an income statement. This income statement is based on the production and sale of 1,000 units of Xonic Tonic at $70 per unit. It also assumes selling and administrative costs of $3,000. Observe that each variance is shown, as well as the total net variance. In this example, variations from standard costs reduced net income by $3,000.

Illustration 11-27
Variances in income statement for management

Xonic Income Statement For the Month Ended June 30, 2014		
Sales revenue		$70,000
Cost of goods sold (at standard)		52,000
Gross profit (at standard)		18,000
Variances		
Materials price	$ 420 U	
Materials quantity	600 U	
Labor price	420 F	
Labor quantity	1,500 U	
Overhead	900 U	
Total variance unfavorable		3,000
Gross profit (actual)		15,000
Selling and administrative expenses		3,000
Net income		$12,000

Standard costs may be used in financial statements prepared for stockholders and other external users. The costing of inventories at standard costs is in accordance with generally accepted accounting principles when there are no significant differences between actual costs and standard costs. Hewlett-Packard and Jostens, Inc., for example, report their inventories at standard costs. However, if there are significant differences between actual and standard costs, the financial statements must report inventories and cost of goods sold at actual costs.

It is also possible to show the variances in an income statement prepared in the variable costing (CVP) format. To do so, it is necessary to analyze the overhead variances into variable and fixed components. This type of analysis is explained in cost accounting textbooks.

Balanced Scorecard

Financial measures (measurement of dollars), such as variance analysis and return on investment (ROI), are useful tools for evaluating performance. However, many companies now supplement these financial measures with nonfinancial measures to better assess performance and anticipate future results. For example, airlines like Delta, American, and United use capacity utilization as an important measure to understand and predict future performance. Newspaper publishers such as the *New York Times* and the *Chicago Tribune* use circulation figures as another measure by which to assess performance. Penske Automotive

Group, the owner of 300 dealerships, rewards executives for meeting employee retention targets. Illustration 11-28 lists some key nonfinancial measures used in various industries.

Industry	Measure
Automobiles	Capacity utilization of plants. Average age of key assets. Impact of strikes. Brand-loyalty statistics.
Computer Systems	Market profile of customer end-products. Number of new products. Employee stock ownership percentages. Number of scientists and technicians used in R&D.
Chemicals	Customer satisfaction data. Factors affecting customer product selection. Number of patents and trademarks held. Customer brand awareness.
Regional Banks	Number of ATMs by state. Number of products used by average customer. Percentage of customer service calls handled by interactive voice response units. Personnel cost per employee. Credit card retention rates.

Source: Financial Accounting Standards Board, *Business Reporting: Insights into Enhancing Voluntary Disclosures* (Norwalk, Conn.: FASB, 2001).

Illustration 11-28
Nonfinancial measures used in various industries

Most companies recognize that both financial and nonfinancial measures can provide useful insights into what is happening in the company. As a result, many companies now use a broad-based measurement approach, called the **balanced scorecard**, to evaluate performance. The **balanced scorecard** incorporates financial and nonfinancial measures in an integrated system that links performance measurement with a company's strategic goals. Nearly 50% of the largest companies in the United States, including Unilever, Chase, and Wal-Mart Stores Inc., are using the balanced scorecard approach.

The balanced scorecard evaluates company performance from a series of "perspectives." The four most commonly employed perspectives are as follows.

1. The **financial perspective** is the most traditional view of the company. It employs financial measures of performance used by most firms.

2. The **customer perspective** evaluates the company from the viewpoint of those people who buy its products or services. This view compares the company to competitors in terms of price, quality, product innovation, customer service, and other dimensions.

3. The **internal process perspective** evaluates the internal operating processes critical to success. All critical aspects of the value chain—including product development, production, delivery, and after-sale service—are evaluated to ensure that the company is operating effectively and efficiently.

4. The **learning and growth perspective** evaluates how well the company develops and retains its employees. This would include evaluation of such things as employee skills, employee satisfaction, training programs, and information dissemination.

Within each perspective, the balanced scorecard identifies objectives that contribute to attainment of strategic goals. Illustration 11-29 shows examples of objectives within each perspective.

Perspective		Objective
Financial		Return on assets
		Net income
		Credit rating
		Share price
		Profit per employee
Customer		Percentage of customers who would recommend product
		Customer retention
		Response time per customer request
		Brand recognition
		Customer service expense per customer
Internal Process		Percentage of defect-free products
		Stockouts
		Labor utilization rates
		Waste reduction
		Planning accuracy
Learning and Growth		Percentage of employees leaving in less than one year
		Number of cross-trained employees
		Ethics violations
		Training hours
		Reportable accidents

Illustration 11-29
Examples of objectives within the four perspectives of balanced scorecard

The objectives are linked across perspectives in order to tie performance measurement to company goals. The financial-perspective objectives are normally set first, and then objectives are set in the other perspectives in order to accomplish the financial goals.

For example, within the financial perspective, a common goal is to increase profit per dollars invested as measured by ROI. In order to increase ROI, a customer-perspective objective might be to increase customer satisfaction as measured by the percentage of customers who would recommend the product to a friend. In order to increase customer satisfaction, an internal-process-perspective objective might be to increase product quality as measured by the percentage of defect-free units. Finally, in order to increase the percentage of defect-free units, the learning-and-growth-perspective objective might be to reduce factory employee turnover as measured by the percentage of employees leaving in under one year.

Illustration 11-30 illustrates this linkage across perspectives.

Illustration 11-30
Linked process across balanced scorecard perspectives

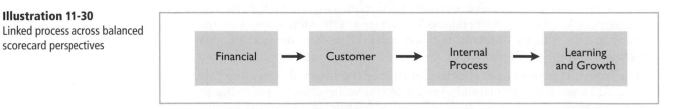

Through this linked process, the company can better understand how to achieve its goals and what measures to use to evaluate performance.

In summary, the balanced scorecard does the following:

1. Employs both **financial and nonfinancial measures**. (For example, ROI is a financial measure; employee turnover is a nonfinancial measure.)

2. Creates linkages so that high-level corporate goals can be communicated all the way down to the shop floor.

3. Provides measurable objectives for nonfinancial measures such as product quality, rather than vague statements such as "We would like to improve quality."

4. Integrates all of the company's goals into a single performance measurement system, so that **an inappropriate amount of weight will not be placed on any single goal**.

SERVICE COMPANY INSIGHT

It May Be Time to Fly United Again

Many of the benefits of a balanced scorecard approach are evident in the improved operations at United Airlines. At the time it filed for bankruptcy, United had a reputation for some of the worst service in the airline business. But when Glenn Tilton took over as United's chief executive officer, he recognized that things had to change.

He implemented an incentive program that allows all of United's 63,000 employees to earn a bonus of 2.5% or more of their wages if the company "exceeds its goals for on-time flight departures and for customer intent to fly United again." After instituting this program, the company's on-time departures were among the best, its customer complaints were reduced considerably, and the number of customers who said that they would fly United again was at its highest level ever.

Source: Susan Carey, "Friendlier Skies: In Bankruptcy, United Airlines Forges a Path to Better Service," *Wall Street Journal* (June 15, 2004).

? Which of the perspectives of a balanced scorecard were the focus of United's CEO? (See page 545.)

> DO IT!

Balanced Scorecard

Action Plan

✔ The financial perspective employs traditional financial measures of performance.

✔ The customer perspective evaluates company performance as seen by the people who buy its products or services.

✔ The internal process perspective evaluates the internal operating processes critical to success.

✔ The learning and growth perspective evaluates how well the company develops and retains its employees.

Indicate which of the four perspectives in the balanced scorecard is most likely associated with the objectives that follow.

1. Percentage of repeat customers.

2. Number of suggestions for improvement from employees.

3. Contribution margin.

4. Brand recognition.

5. Number of cross-trained employees.

6. Amount of setup time.

Solution

1. Customer perspective.

2. Learning and growth perspective.

3. Financial perspective.

4. Customer perspective.

5. Learning and growth perspective.

6. Internal process perspective.

Related exercise material: **BE11-7, E11-17, and** **DO IT!** **11-4.**

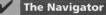 **The Navigator**

USING THE **DECISION TOOLKIT** 🧰

Assume that during the past month, Sanford produced 10,000 cartons of Liquid ACCENT® highlighters. Liquid ACCENT® offers a translucent barrel and cap with a visible ink supply for see-through color. The special fluorescent ink is fade- and water-resistant. Each carton contains 100 boxes of markers, and each box contains five markers. The markers come in boxes of one of five fluorescent colors—orange, blue, yellow, green, and pink—and in a five-color set.

Assume the following additional facts: The standard cost for one carton of 500 markers is as follows.

		Standard		
Manufacturing Cost Elements	**Quantity**	**×**	**Price**	**= Cost**
Direct materials				
Tips (boxes of 500)	500	×	$ 0.03	= $ 15.00
Translucent barrels and caps (boxes of 500)	500	×	$ 0.09	= 45.00
Fluorescent ink (100 oz. containers)	100 oz.	×	$ 0.32	= 32.00
Total direct materials				92.00
Direct labor	0.25 hours	×	$ 9.00	= 2.25
Overhead	0.25 hours	×	$48.00	= 12.00
				$106.25

During the month, the following transactions occurred in manufacturing the 10,000 cartons of highlighters.

1. Purchased 10,000 boxes of tips for $148,000 ($14.80 per 500 tips); purchased 10,200 boxes of translucent barrels and caps for $453,900 ($44.50 per 500 barrels and caps); and purchased 9,900 containers of fluorescent ink for $328,185 ($33.15 per 100 ounces).

2. All materials purchased during the period were used to make markers during the period.

3. 2,300 direct labor hours were worked at a total labor cost of $20,240 (an average hourly rate of $8.80).

4. Variable manufacturing overhead incurred was $34,600, and fixed overhead incurred was $84,000.

The manufacturing overhead rate of $48.00 is based on a normal capacity of 2,600 direct labor hours. The total budget at this capacity is $83,980 fixed and $40,820 variable.

Instructions

Determine whether Sanford met its price and quantity objectives relative to materials, labor, and overhead.

Solution

To determine whether Sanford met its price and quantity objectives, compute the total variance and the variances for direct materials and direct labor, and calculate the total variance for manufacturing overhead.

Total Variance

Actual cost incurred:		
Direct materials		
Tips	$148,000	
Translucent barrels and caps	453,900	
Fluorescent ink	328,185	
Total direct materials		$ 930,085
Direct labor		20,240
Overhead		118,600
Total actual costs		1,068,925
Less: Standard cost (10,000 × $106.25)		1,062,500
Total variance		$ 6,425 U

Direct Materials Variances

Total	=	$930,085	−	$920,000 (10,000 × $92)	= $10,085 U
Price (Tips)	=	$148,000 (10,000 × $14.80)	−	$150,000 (10,000 × $15.00)	= $ 2,000 F
Price (Barrels and caps)	=	$453,900 (10,200 × $44.50)	−	$459,000 (10,200 × $45.00)	= $ 5,100 F
Price (Ink)	=	$328,185 (9,900 × $33.15)	−	$316,800 (9,900 × $32.00)	= $11,385 U
Quantity (Tips)	=	$150,000 (10,000 × $15.00)	−	$150,000 (10,000 × $15.00)	= $ 0
Quantity (Barrels and caps)	=	$459,000 (10,200 × $45.00)	−	$450,000 (10,000 × $45.00)	= $ 9,000 U
Quantity (Ink)	=	$316,800 (9,900 × $32.00)	−	$320,000 (10,000 × $32.00)	= $ 3,200 F

Direct Labor Variances

Total	=	$20,240 (2,300 × $8.80)	−	$22,500 (2,500* × $9.00)	=	$ 2,260 F
Price	=	$20,240 (2,300 × $8.80)	−	$20,700 (2,300 × $9.00)	=	$ 460 F
Quantity	=	$20,700 (2,300 × $9.00)	−	$22,500 (2,500* × $9.00)	=	$ 1,800 F

*10,000 × .25

Overhead Variance

Total	=	$118,600 ($84,000 + $34,600)	−	$120,000 (2,500 × $48)	=	$ 1,400 F

Sanford's total variance was an unfavorable $6,425. The unfavorable materials variance outweighed the favorable labor and overhead variances. The primary determinants were an unfavorable price variance for ink and an unfavorable quantity variance for barrels and caps.

✔ **The Navigator**

SUMMARY OF LEARNING OBJECTIVES

✔ **The Navigator**

1 Distinguish between a standard and a budget. Both standards and budgets are predetermined costs. The primary difference is that a standard is a unit amount, whereas a budget is a total amount. A standard may be regarded as the budgeted cost per unit of product.

2 Identify the advantages of standard costs. Standard costs offer a number of advantages. They (a) facilitate management planning, (b) promote greater economy, (c) are useful in setting selling prices, (d) contribute to management control, (e) permit "management by exception," and (f) simplify the costing of inventories and reduce clerical costs.

3 Describe how companies set standards. The direct materials price standard should be based on the delivered cost of raw materials plus an allowance for receiving and handling. The direct materials quantity standard should establish the required quantity plus an allowance for waste and spoilage.

The direct labor price standard should be based on current wage rates and anticipated adjustments such as COLAs. It also generally includes payroll taxes and fringe benefits. Direct labor quantity standards should be based on required production time plus an allowance for rest periods, cleanup, machine setup, and machine downtime.

For manufacturing overhead, a standard pre determined overhead rate is used. It is based on an expected standard activity index such as standard direct labor hours or standard machine hours.

4 State the formulas for determining direct materials and direct labor variances. The formulas for the direct materials variances are:

$$\begin{pmatrix} \text{Actual quantity} \\ \times \text{ Actual price} \end{pmatrix} - \begin{pmatrix} \text{Standard quantity} \\ \times \text{ Standard price} \end{pmatrix} = \begin{matrix} \text{Total} \\ \text{materials} \\ \text{variance} \end{matrix}$$

$$\begin{pmatrix} \text{Actual quantity} \\ \times \text{ Actual price} \end{pmatrix} - \begin{pmatrix} \text{Actual quantity} \\ \times \text{ Standard price} \end{pmatrix} = \begin{matrix} \text{Materials} \\ \text{price} \\ \text{variance} \end{matrix}$$

$$\begin{pmatrix} \text{Actual quantity} \\ \times \text{ Standard price} \end{pmatrix} - \begin{pmatrix} \text{Standard quantity} \\ \times \text{ Standard price} \end{pmatrix} = \begin{matrix} \text{Materials} \\ \text{quantity} \\ \text{variance} \end{matrix}$$

The formulas for the direct labor variances are:

$$\begin{pmatrix} \text{Actual hours} \\ \times \text{ Actual rate} \end{pmatrix} - \begin{pmatrix} \text{Standard hours} \\ \times \text{ Standard rate} \end{pmatrix} = \begin{matrix} \text{Total} \\ \text{labor} \\ \text{variance} \end{matrix}$$

$$\begin{pmatrix} \text{Actual hours} \\ \times \text{ Actual rate} \end{pmatrix} - \begin{pmatrix} \text{Actual hours} \\ \times \text{ Standard rate} \end{pmatrix} = \begin{matrix} \text{Labor} \\ \text{price} \\ \text{variance} \end{matrix}$$

$$\begin{pmatrix} \text{Actual hours} \\ \times \text{ Standard rate} \end{pmatrix} - \begin{pmatrix} \text{Standard hours} \\ \times \text{ Standard rate} \end{pmatrix} = \begin{matrix} \text{Labor} \\ \text{quantity} \\ \text{variance} \end{matrix}$$

5 State the formula for determining the total manufacturing overhead variance. The formula for the total manufacturing overhead variance is:

$$\begin{pmatrix} \text{Actual} \\ \text{overhead} \end{pmatrix} - \begin{pmatrix} \text{Overhead} \\ \text{applied at} \\ \text{standard hours} \\ \text{allowed} \end{pmatrix} = \begin{matrix} \text{Total overhead} \\ \text{variance} \end{matrix}$$

6 Discuss the reporting of variances. Variances are reported to management in variance reports. The reports facilitate management by exception by highlighting significant differences.

7 Prepare an income statement for management under a standard costing system. Under a standard costing system, an income statement prepared for management will report cost of goods sold at standard cost and then disclose each variance separately.

8 Describe the balanced scorecard approach to performance evaluation. The balanced scorecard incorporates financial and nonfinancial measures in an integrated system that links performance measurement and a company's strategic goals. It employs four perspectives: financial, customer, internal process, and learning and growth. Objectives are set within each of these perspectives that link to objectives within the other perspectives.

DECISION TOOLKIT A SUMMARY

DECISION CHECKPOINTS	INFO NEEDED FOR DECISION	TOOL TO USE FOR DECISION	HOW TO EVALUATE RESULTS
Has management accomplished its price and quantity objectives regarding materials?	Actual cost and standard cost of materials	Materials price and materials quantity variances	Positive (favorable) variances suggest that price and quantity objectives have been met.
Has management accomplished its price and quantity objectives regarding labor?	Actual cost and standard cost of labor	Labor price and labor quantity variances	Positive (favorable) variances suggest that price and quantity objectives have been met.
Has management accomplished its objectives regarding manufacturing overhead?	Actual cost and standard cost of manufacturing overhead	Total manufacturing overhead variance	Positive (favorable) variances suggest that manufacturing overhead objectives have been met.

APPENDIX 11A STANDARD COST ACCOUNTING SYSTEM

A **standard cost accounting system** is a double-entry system of accounting. In this system, companies use standard costs in making entries, and they formally recognize variances in the accounts. Companies may use a standard cost system with either job order or process costing.

In this appendix, we will explain and illustrate a **standard cost, job order cost accounting system**. The system is based on two important assumptions:

1. Variances from standards are recognized at the earliest opportunity.
2. The Work in Process account is maintained exclusively on the basis of standard costs.

In practice, there are many variations among standard cost systems. The system described here should prepare you for systems you see in the "real world."

Journal Entries

We will use the transactions of Xonic to illustrate the journal entries. Note as you study the entries that the major difference between the entries here and those for the job order cost accounting system in Chapter 2 is the **variance accounts**.

1. Purchase raw materials on account for $13,020 when the standard cost is $12,600.

Raw Materials Inventory	12,600	
Materials Price Variance	420	
Accounts Payable		13,020
(To record purchase of materials)		

Xonic debits the inventory account for actual quantities at standard cost. This enables the perpetual materials records to show actual quantities. Xonic debits the price variance, which is unfavorable, to Materials Price Variance.

2. Incur direct labor costs of $31,080 when the standard labor cost is $31,500.

Factory Labor	31,500	
Labor Price Variance		420
Factory Wages Payable		31,080
(To record direct labor costs)		

Like the raw materials inventory account, Xonic debits Factory Labor for actual hours worked at the standard hourly rate of pay. In this case, the labor variance is favorable. Thus, Xonic credits Labor Price Variance.

3. Incur actual manufacturing overhead costs of $10,900.

Manufacturing Overhead	10,900	
Accounts Payable/Cash/Acc. Depreciation		10,900
(To record overhead incurred)		

The controllable overhead variance (see Appendix 11B) is not recorded at this time. It depends on standard hours applied to work in process. This amount is not known at the time overhead is incurred.

4. Issue raw materials for production at a cost of $12,600 when the standard cost is $12,000.

Work in Process Inventory	12,000	
Materials Quantity Variance	600	
Raw Materials Inventory		12,600
(To record issuance of raw materials)		

Xonic debits Work in Process Inventory for standard materials quantities used at standard prices. It debits the variance account because the variance is unfavorable. The company credits Raw Materials Inventory for actual quantities at standard prices.

5. Assign factory labor to production at a cost of $31,500 when standard cost is $30,000.

Work in Process Inventory	30,000	
Labor Quantity Variance	1,500	
Factory Labor		31,500
(To assign factory labor to jobs)		

Xonic debits Work in Process Inventory for standard labor hours at standard rates. It debits the unfavorable variance to Labor Quantity Variance. The credit to Factory Labor produces a zero balance in this account.

6. Apply manufacturing overhead to production $10,000.

Work in Process Inventory	10,000	
Manufacturing Overhead		10,000
(To assign overhead to jobs)		

Xonic debits Work in Process Inventory for standard hours allowed multiplied by the standard overhead rate.

7. Transfer completed work to finished goods $52,000.

Finished Goods Inventory	52,000	
Work in Process Inventory		52,000
(To record transfer of completed work to finished goods)		

In this example, both inventory accounts are at standard cost.

8. Sell the 1,000 gallons of Xonic Tonic for $70,000.

Accounts Receivable	70,000	
Cost of Goods Sold	52,000	
Sales		70,000
Finished Goods Inventory		52,000
(To record sale of finished goods and the		
cost of goods sold)		

The company debits Cost of Goods Sold at standard cost. Gross profit, in turn, is the difference between sales and the standard cost of goods sold.

9. Recognize unfavorable total overhead variance:

Overhead Variance	900	
Manufacturing Overhead		900
(To recognize overhead variances)		

Prior to this entry, a debit balance of $900 existed in Manufacturing Overhead. This entry therefore produces a zero balance in the Manufacturing Overhead account. The information needed for this entry is often not available until the end of the accounting period.

Ledger Accounts

Illustration 11A-1 shows the cost accounts for Xonic after posting the entries. Note that five variance accounts are included in the ledger. The remaining accounts are the same as those illustrated for a job order cost system in Chapter 2, in which only actual costs were used.

Illustration 11A-1
Cost accounts with variances

Helpful Hint
All debit balances in variance accounts indicate unfavorable variances; all credit balances indicate favorable variances.

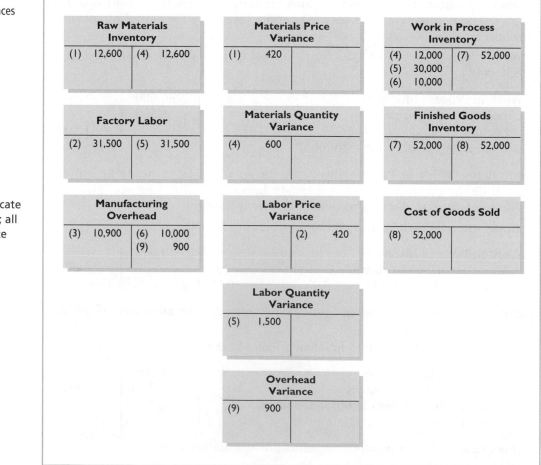

9 Identify the features of a standard cost accounting system. In a standard cost accounting system, companies journalize and post standard costs, and they maintain separate variance accounts in the ledger.

APPENDIX 11B   A CLOSER LOOK AT OVERHEAD VARIANCES

As indicated in the chapter, the total overhead variance is generally analyzed through a price variance and a quantity variance. The name usually given to the price variance is the **overhead controllable variance**; the quantity variance is referred to as the **overhead volume variance**.

> **LEARNING OBJECTIVE   10**
>
> Compute overhead controllable and volume variance.

Overhead Controllable Variance

The **overhead controllable variance** shows whether overhead costs are effectively controlled. To compute this variance, the company compares actual overhead costs incurred with budgeted costs for the **standard hours allowed**. The budgeted costs are determined from a flexible manufacturing overhead budget. The concepts related to a flexible budget were discussed in Chapter 10.

For Xonic, the budget formula for manufacturing overhead is variable manufacturing overhead cost of $3 per hour of labor plus fixed manufacturing overhead costs of $4,400 ($52,800 ÷ 12, per Illustration 11-6 on page 500). Illustration 11B-1 shows the monthly flexible budget for Xonic.

Illustration 11B-1
Flexible budget using standard direct labor hours

	A	B	C	D	E
1		**Xonic**			
2		**Flexible Manufacturing Overhead Monthly Budget**			
3	Activity Index				
4	Standard direct labor hours	1,800	**2,000**	2,200	2,400
5	Costs				
6	Variable costs				
7	Indirect materials	$1,800	**$ 2,000**	$ 2,200	$ 2,400
8	Indirect labor	2,700	**3,000**	3,300	3,600
9	Utilities	900	**1,000**	1,100	1,200
10	Total variable costs	5,400	**6,000**	6,600	7,200
11					
12	Fixed costs				
13	Supervision	3,000	**3,000**	3,000	3,000
14	Depreciation	1,400	**1,400**	1,400	1,400
15	Total fixed costs	4,400	**4,400**	4,400	4,400
16	Total costs	$9,800	**$10,400**	$11,000	$11,600
17					

As shown, the budgeted costs for 2,000 standard hours are $10,400 ($6,000 variable and $4,400 fixed).

Illustration 11B-2 (page 522) shows the formula for the overhead controllable variance and the calculation for Xonic at 1,000 units of output (2,000 standard labor hours).

Illustration 11B-2
Formula for overhead controllable variance

Actual Overhead	−	Overhead Budgeted*	=	Overhead Controllable Variance
$10,900	−	$10,400	=	$500 U
($6,500 + $4,400)		($6,000 + $4,400)		

*Based on standard hours allowed.

The overhead controllable variance for Xonic is $500 unfavorable.

Most controllable variances are associated with variable costs, which are controllable costs. Fixed costs are often known at the time the budget is prepared and are therefore not as likely to deviate from the budgeted amount. In Xonic's case, all of the overhead controllable variance is due to the difference between the actual variable overhead costs ($6,500) and the budgeted variable costs ($6,000).

Management can compare actual and budgeted overhead for each manufacturing overhead cost that contributes to the controllable variance. In addition, management can develop cost and quantity variances for each overhead cost, such as indirect materials and indirect labor.

Overhead Volume Variance

The **overhead volume variance** is the difference between normal capacity hours and standard hours allowed times the fixed overhead rate. The overhead volume variance relates to whether fixed costs were under- or overapplied during the year. For example, the overhead volume variance answers the question of whether Xonic effectively used its fixed costs. If Xonic produces less Xonic Tonic than normal capacity would allow, an unfavorable variance results. Conversely, if Xonic produces more Xonic Tonic than what is considered normal capacity, a favorable variance results.

The formula for computing the overhead volume variance is as follows.

Illustration 11B-3
Formula for overhead volume variance

Fixed Overhead Rate	×	(Normal Capacity Hours	−	Standard Hours Allowed)	=	Overhead Volume Variance

To illustrate the fixed overhead rate computation, recall that Xonic budgeted fixed overhead cost for the year of $52,800 (Illustration 11-6 on page 500). At normal capacity, 26,400 standard direct labor hours are required. The fixed overhead rate is therefore $2 per hour ($52,800 ÷ 26,400 hours).

Xonic produced 1,000 units of Xonic Tonic in June. The standard hours allowed for the 1,000 gallons produced in June is 2,000 (1,000 gallons × 2 hours). For Xonic, normal capacity for June is 1,100, so standard direct labor hours for June at normal capacity is 2,200 (26,400 annual hours ÷ 12 months). The computation of the overhead volume variance in this case is as follows.

Illustration 11B-4
Computation of overhead volume variance for Xonic

Fixed Overhead Rate	×	(Normal Capacity Hours	−	Standard Hours Allowed)	=	Overhead Volume Variance
$2	×	(2,200	−	2,000)	=	$400 U

In Xonic's case, a $400 unfavorable volume variance results. The volume variance is unfavorable because Xonic produced only 1,000 gallons rather than the normal capacity of 1,100 gallons in the month of June. As a result, it underapplied fixed overhead for that period.

In computing the overhead variances, it is important to remember the following.

1. Standard hours allowed are used in each of the variances.
2. Budgeted costs for the controllable variance are derived from the flexible budget.
3. The controllable variance generally pertains to variable costs.
4. The volume variance pertains solely to fixed costs.

SUMMARY OF LEARNING OBJECTIVE FOR APPENDIX 11B ✔ The Navigator

10 Compute overhead controllable and volume variance. The total overhead variance is generally analyzed through a price variance and a quantity variance. The name usually given to the price variance is the overhead controllable variance. The quantity variance is referred to as the overhead volume variance.

GLOSSARY

Balanced scorecard An approach that incorporates financial and nonfinancial measures in an integrated system that links performance measurement and a company's strategic goals. (p. 513).

Customer perspective A viewpoint employed in the balanced scorecard to evaluate the company from the perspective of those people who buy and use its products or services. (p. 513).

Direct labor price standard The rate per hour that should be incurred for direct labor. (p. 499).

Direct labor quantity standard The time that should be required to make one unit of product. (p. 499).

Direct materials price standard The cost per unit of direct materials that should be incurred. (p. 498).

Direct materials quantity standard The quantity of direct materials that should be used per unit of finished goods. (p. 498).

Financial perspective A viewpoint employed in the balanced scorecard to evaluate a company's performance using financial measures. (p. 513).

Ideal standards Standards based on the optimum level of performance under perfect operating conditions. (p. 497).

Internal process perspective A viewpoint employed in the balanced scorecard to evaluate the effectiveness and efficiency of a company's value chain, including product development, production, delivery, and after-sale service. (p. 513).

Labor price variance The difference between the actual hours times the actual rate and the actual hours times the standard rate for labor. (p. 506).

Labor quantity variance The difference between actual hours times the standard rate and standard hours times the standard rate for labor. (p. 507).

Learning and growth perspective A viewpoint employed in the balanced scorecard to evaluate how well a company develops and retains its employees. (p. 513).

Materials price variance The difference between the actual quantity times the actual price and the actual quantity times the standard price for materials. (p. 503).

Materials quantity variance The difference between the actual quantity times the standard price and the standard quantity times the standard price for materials. (p. 504).

Normal capacity The average activity output that a company should experience over the long run. (p. 500).

Normal standards Standards based on an efficient level of performance that are attainable under expected operating conditions. (p. 497).

Overhead controllable variance The difference between actual overhead incurred and overhead budgeted for the standard hours allowed. (p. 521).

Overhead volume variance The difference between normal capacity hours and standard hours allowed times the fixed overhead rate. (p. 522).

Standard cost accounting system A double-entry system of accounting in which standard costs are used in making entries, and variances are recognized in the accounts. (p. 518).

Standard costs Predetermined unit costs which companies use as measures of performance. (p. 496).

Standard hours allowed The hours that should have been worked for the units produced. (p. 509).

Standard predetermined overhead rate An overhead rate determined by dividing budgeted overhead costs by an expected standard activity index. (p. 499).

Total labor variance The difference between actual hours times the actual rate and standard hours times the standard rate for labor. (p. 506).

Total materials variance The difference between the actual quantity times the actual price and the standard quantity times the standard price of materials. (p. 503).

Total overhead variance The difference between actual overhead costs and overhead costs applied to work done, based on standard hours allowed. (p. 508).

Variance The difference between total actual costs and total standard costs. (p. 502).

> **Comprehensive DO IT!**

Manlow Company makes a cologne called Allure. The standard cost for one bottle of Allure is as follows.

	Standard				
Manufacturing Cost Elements	**Quantity**	**×**	**Price**	**=**	**Cost**
Direct materials	6 oz.	×	$ 0.90	=	$ 5.40
Direct labor	0.5 hrs.	×	$12.00	=	6.00
Manufacturing overhead	0.5 hrs.	×	$ 4.80	=	2.40
					$13.80

During the month, the following transactions occurred in manufacturing 10,000 bottles of Allure.

1. 58,000 ounces of materials were purchased at $1.00 per ounce.
2. All the materials purchased were used to produce the 10,000 bottles of Allure.
3. 4,900 direct labor hours were worked at a total labor cost of $56,350.
4. Variable manufacturing overhead incurred was $15,000 and fixed overhead incurred was $10,400.

The manufacturing overhead rate of $4.80 is based on a normal capacity of 5,200 direct labor hours. The total budget at this capacity is $10,400 fixed and $14,560 variable.

Instructions
(a) Compute the total variance and the variances for direct materials and direct labor elements.
(b) Compute the total variance for manufacturing overhead.

Solution to Comprehensive DO IT!

Action Plan
✔ Check to make sure the total variance and the sum of the individual variances are equal.
✔ Find the price variance first, then the quantity variance.
✔ Base budgeted overhead costs on flexible budget data.
✔ Base overhead applied on standard hours allowed.
✔ Ignore actual hours worked in computing overhead variances.

(a)
Total Variance

Actual costs incurred	
Direct materials	$ 58,000
Direct labor	56,350
Manufacturing overhead	25,400
	139,750
Standard cost (10,000 × $13.80)	138,000
Total variance	$ 1,750 U

Direct Materials Variances

Total   = $58,000 (58,000 × $1.00) − $54,000 (60,000 × $0.90) = $4,000 U
Price   = $58,000 (58,000 × $1.00) − $52,200 (58,000 × $0.90) = $5,800 U
Quantity = $52,200 (58,000 × $0.90) − $54,000 (60,000 × $0.90) = $1,800 F

Direct Labor Variances

Total   = $56,350 (4,900 × $11.50) − $60,000 (5,000 × $12.00) = $3,650 F
Price   = $56,350 (4,900 × $11.50) − $58,800 (4,900 × $12.00) = $2,450 F
Quantity = $58,800 (4,900 × $12.00) − $60,000 (5,000 × $12.00) = $1,200 F

(b)
Overhead Variance

Total   = $25,400 ($15,000 + $10,400) − $24,000 (5,000 × $4.80) = $1,400 U

✔ **The Navigator**

Self-Test, Brief Exercises, Exercises, Problem Set A, and many more resources are available for practice in WileyPLUS.

Note: All asterisked Questions, Exercises, and Problems relate to material in the appendix to the chapter.

SELF-TEST QUESTIONS

Answers are at the end of the chapter.

(LO 1) **1.** Standards differ from budgets in that:
(a) budgets but not standards may be used in valuing inventories.
(b) budgets but not standards may be journalized and posted.
(c) budgets are a total amount and standards are a unit amount.
(d) only budgets contribute to management planning and control.

(LO 1) **2.** Standard costs:
(a) are imposed by governmental agencies.
(b) are predetermined unit costs which companies use as measures of performance.
(c) can be used by manufacturing companies but not by service or not-for-profit companies.
(d) All of the above.

(LO 2) **3.** The advantages of standard costs include all of the following *except*:
(a) management by exception may be used.
(b) management planning is facilitated.
(c) they may simplify the costing of inventories.
(d) management must use a static budget.

(LO 3) **4.** Normal standards:
(a) allow for rest periods, machine breakdowns, and setup time.
(b) represent levels of performance under perfect operating conditions.
(c) are rarely used because managers believe they lower workforce morale.
(d) are more likely than ideal standards to result in unethical practices.

(LO 3) **5.** The setting of standards is:
(a) a managerial accounting decision.
(b) a management decision.
(c) a worker decision.
(d) preferably set at the ideal level of performance.

(LO 4) **6.** Each of the following formulas is correct *except*:
(a) Labor price variance = (Actual hours × Actual rate) − (Actual hours × Standard rate).
(b) Total overhead variance = Actual overhead − Overhead applied.
(c) Materials price variance = (Actual quantity × Actual price) − (Standard quantity × Standard price).
(d) Labor quantity variance = (Actual hours × Standard rate) − (Standard hours × Standard rate).

(LO 4) **7.** In producing product AA, 6,300 pounds of direct materials were used at a cost of $1.10 per pound. The standard was 6,000 pounds at $1.00 per pound. The direct materials quantity variance is:
(a) $330 unfavorable.   (c) $600 unfavorable.
(b) $300 unfavorable.   (d) $630 unfavorable.

(LO 4) **8.** In producing product ZZ, 14,800 direct labor hours were used at a rate of $8.20 per hour. The standard was 15,000 hours at $8.00 per hour. Based on these data, the direct labor:
(a) quantity variance is $1,600 favorable.
(b) quantity variance is $1,600 unfavorable.
(c) price variance is $2,960 favorable.
(d) price variance is $2,960 unfavorable.

(LO 5) **9.** Which of the following is *correct* about the total overhead variance?
(a) Budgeted overhead and budgeted overhead applied are the same.
(b) Total actual overhead is composed of variable overhead, fixed overhead, and period costs.
(c) Standard hours actually worked are used in computing the variance.
(d) Standard hours allowed for the work done is the measure used in computing the variance.

(LO 5) **10.** The formula for computing the total overhead variance is:
(a) actual overhead less overhead applied.
(b) overhead budgeted less overhead applied.
(c) actual overhead less overhead budgeted.
(d) No correct answer is given.

(LO 6) **11.** Which of the following is *incorrect* about variance reports?
(a) They facilitate "management by exception."
(b) They should only be sent to the top level of management.
(c) They should be prepared as soon as possible.
(d) They may vary in form, content, and frequency among companies.

(LO 6) **12.** In using variance reports to evaluate cost control, management normally looks into:
(a) all variances.
(b) favorable variances only.
(c) unfavorable variances only.
(d) both favorable and unfavorable variances that exceed a predetermined quantitative measure such as a percentage or dollar amount.

(LO 7) **13.** Generally accepted accounting principles allow a company to:
  (a) report inventory at standard cost but cost of goods sold must be reported at actual cost.
  (b) report cost of goods sold at standard cost but inventory must be reported at actual cost.
  (c) report inventory and cost of goods sold at standard cost as long as there are no significant differences between actual and standard cost.
  (d) report inventory and cost of goods sold only at actual costs; standard costing is never permitted.

(LO 8) **14.** Which of the following would *not* be an objective used in the customer perspective of the balanced scorecard approach?
  (a) Percentage of customers who would recommend product to a friend.
  (b) Customer retention.
  (c) Brand recognition.
  (d) Earnings per share.

*15. Which of the following is *incorrect* about a standard (LO 9) cost accounting system?
  (a) It is applicable to job order costing.
  (b) It is applicable to process costing.
  (c) It reports only favorable variances.
  (d) It keeps separate accounts for each variance.

*16. The formula to compute the overhead volume vari- (LO 10) ance is:
  (a) Fixed overhead rate × (Standard hours − Actual hours).
  (b) Fixed overhead rate × (Normal capacity hours − Actual hours).
  (c) Fixed overhead rate × (Normal capacity hours − Standard hours allowed).
  (d) (Variable overhead rate + Fixed overhead rate) × (Normal capacity hours − Standard hours allowed).

Go to the book's companion website, www.wiley.com/college/weygandt, for additional Self-Test Questions.

✔ **The Navigator**

QUESTIONS

1. (a) "Standard costs are the expected total cost of completing a job." Is this correct? Explain.
  (b) "A standard imposed by a governmental agency is known as a regulation." Do you agree? Explain.

2. (a) Explain the similarities and differences between standards and budgets.
  (b) Contrast the accounting for standards and budgets.

3. Standard costs facilitate management planning. What are the other advantages of standard costs?

4. Contrast the roles of the management accountant and management in setting standard costs.

5. Distinguish between an ideal standard and a normal standard.

6. What factors should be considered in setting (a) the direct materials price standard and (b) the direct materials quantity standard?

7. "The objective in setting the direct labor quantity standard is to determine the aggregate time required to make one unit of product." Do you agree? What allowances should be made in setting this standard?

8. How is the predetermined overhead rate determined when standard costs are used?

9. What is the difference between a favorable cost variance and an unfavorable cost variance?

10. In each of the following formulas, supply the words that should be inserted for each number in parentheses.
  (a) (Actual quantity × (1)) − (Standard quantity × (2)) = Total materials variance
  (b) ((3) × Actual price) − (Actual quantity × (4)) = Materials price variance
  (c) (Actual quantity × (5)) − ((6) × Standard price) = Materials quantity variance

11. In the direct labor variance matrix, there are three factors: (1) Actual hours × Actual rate, (2) Actual hours × Standard rate, and (3) Standard hours × Standard rate. Using the numbers, indicate the formulas for each of the direct labor variances.

12. Mikan Company's standard predetermined overhead rate is $9 per direct labor hour. For the month of June, 26,000 actual hours were worked, and 27,000 standard hours were allowed. How much overhead was applied?

13. How often should variances be reported to management? What principle may be used with variance reports?

14. What circumstances may cause the purchasing department to be responsible for both an unfavorable materials price variance and an unfavorable materials quantity variance?

15. What are the four perspectives used in the balanced scorecard? Discuss the nature of each, and how the perspectives are linked.

16. Kerry James says that the balanced scorecard was created to replace financial measures as the primary mechanism for performance evaluation. He says that it uses only nonfinancial measures. Is this true?

17. What are some examples of nonfinancial measures used by companies to evaluate performance?

18. (a) How are variances reported in income statements prepared for management? (b) May standard costs be used in preparing financial statements for stockholders? Explain.

*19. (a) Explain the basic features of a standard cost accounting system. (b) What type of balance will exist in the variance account when (1) the materials price variance is unfavorable and (2) the labor quantity variance is favorable?

*20. If the $9 per hour overhead rate in Question 12 includes $5 variable, and actual overhead costs were $248,000, what is the overhead controllable variance for June? The normal capacity hours were 28,000. Is the variance favorable or unfavorable?

*21. What is the purpose of computing the overhead volume variance? What is the basic formula for this variance?

*22. Alma Ortiz does not understand why the overhead volume variance indicates that fixed overhead costs are under- or overapplied. Clarify this matter for Alma.

*23. John Hsu is attempting to outline the important points about overhead variances on a class examination. List four points that John should include in his outline.

BRIEF EXERCISES

BE11-1 Perez Company uses both standards and budgets. For the year, estimated production of Product X is 500,000 units. Total estimated cost for materials and labor are $1,300,000 and $1,700,000. Compute the estimates for (a) a standard cost and (b) a budgeted cost.

Distinguish between a standard and a budget.
(LO 1), AP

BE11-2 Tang Company accumulates the following data concerning raw materials in making one gallon of finished product: (1) Price—net purchase price $2.30, freight-in $0.20, and receiving and handling $0.10. (2) Quantity—required materials 3.6 pounds, allowance for waste and spoilage 0.4 pounds. Compute the following.
(a) Standard direct materials price per gallon.
(b) Standard direct materials quantity per gallon.
(c) Total standard materials cost per gallon.

Set direct materials standard.
(LO 3), AP

BE11-3 Labor data for making one gallon of finished product in Tang Company are as follows: (1) Price—hourly wage rate $13.00, payroll taxes $0.80, and fringe benefits $1.20. (2) Quantity—actual production time 1.1 hours, rest periods and cleanup 0.25 hours, and setup and downtime 0.15 hours. Compute the following.
(a) Standard direct labor rate per hour.
(b) Standard direct labor hours per gallon.
(c) Standard labor cost per gallon.

Set direct labor standard.
(LO 3), AP

BE11-4 Simba Company's standard materials cost per unit of output is $10 (2 pounds × $5). During July, the company purchases and uses 3,200 pounds of materials costing $16,192 in making 1,500 units of finished product. Compute the total, price, and quantity materials variances.

Compute direct materials variances.
(LO 4), AP

BE11-5 Hartley Company's standard labor cost per unit of output is $22 (2 hours × $11 per hour). During August, the company incurs 2,100 hours of direct labor at an hourly cost of $10.80 per hour in making 1,000 units of finished product. Compute the total, price, and quantity labor variances.

Compute direct labor variances.
(LO 4), AP

BE11-6 In October, Roby Company reports 21,000 actual direct labor hours, and it incurs $118,000 of manufacturing overhead costs. Standard hours allowed for the work done is 20,400 hours. The predetermined overhead rate is $6 per direct labor hour. Compute the total overhead variance.

Compute total overhead variance.
(LO 5), AP

BE11-7 The four perspectives in the balanced scorecard are (1) financial, (2) customer, (3) internal process, and (4) learning and growth. Match each of the following objectives with the perspective it is most likely associated with: (a) Plant capacity utilization. (b) Employee work days missed due to injury. (c) Return on assets. (d) Brand recognition.

Match balanced scorecard perspectives.
(LO 8), AP

*BE11-8 Journalize the following transactions for Combs Company.
(a) Purchased 6,000 units of raw materials on account for $11,500. The standard cost was $12,000.
(b) Issued 5,600 units of raw materials for production. The standard units were 5,800.

Journalize materials variances.
(LO 9), AP

*BE11-9 Journalize the following transactions for Dewey, Inc.
(a) Incurred direct labor costs of $24,000 for 3,000 hours. The standard labor cost was $25,500.
(b) Assigned 3,000 direct labor hours costing $24,000 to production. Standard hours were 3,150.

Journalize labor variances.
(LO 9), AP

Compute the overhead controllable variance.

(LO 10), AP

*BE11-10 Some overhead data for Roby Company are given in BE11-6. In addition, the flexible manufacturing overhead budget shows that budgeted costs are $4 variable per direct labor hour and $50,000 fixed. Compute the overhead controllable variance.

Compute overhead volume variance.

(LO 10), AP

*BE11-11 Using the data in BE11-6 and BE11-10, compute the overhead volume variance. Normal capacity was 25,000 direct labor hours.

> DO IT! REVIEW

Compute standard cost.

(LO 3), AP

DO IT! 11-1 Jacque Company accumulated the following standard cost data concerning product I-Tal.

Direct materials per unit: 2 pounds at $5 per pound
Direct labor per unit: 0.2 hours at $15 per hour
Manufacturing overhead: Predetermined rate is 125% of direct labor cost

Compute the standard cost of one unit of product I-Tal.

Compute materials variance.

(LO 4), AP

DO IT! 11-2 The standard cost of product 777 includes 2 units of direct materials at $6.00 per unit. During August, the company bought 29,000 units of materials at $6.30 and used those materials to produce 16,000 units. Compute the total, price, and quantity variances for materials.

Compute labor and manufacturing overhead variances.

(LO 4, 5), AP

DO IT! 11-3 The standard cost of product 5252 includes 1.9 hours of direct labor at $14.00 per hour. The predetermined overhead rate is $22.00 per direct labor hour. During July, the company incurred 4,100 hours of direct labor at an average rate of $14.30 per hour and $81,300 of manufacturing overhead costs. It produced 2,000 units.

(a) Compute the total, price, and quantity variances for labor. (b) Compute the total overhead variance.

Match balance scorecard perspectives and their objectives.

(LO 8), C

DO IT! 11-4 Indicate which of the four perspectives in the balanced scorecard is most likely associated with the objectives that follow.

1. Ethics violations.
2. Credit rating.
3. Customer retention.
4. Stockouts.
5. Reportable accidents.
6. Brand recognition.

✔ **The Navigator**

EXERCISES

Compute budget and standard.

(LO 1, 2, 3), AP

E11-1 Shannon Company is planning to produce 2,000 units of product in 2014. Each unit requires 3 pounds of materials at $5 per pound and a half-hour of labor at $15 per hour. The overhead rate is 70% of direct labor.

Instructions
(a) Compute the budgeted amounts for 2014 for direct materials to be used, direct labor, and applied overhead.
(b) Compute the standard cost of one unit of product.
(c) What are the potential advantages to a corporation of using standard costs?

Compute standard materials costs.

(LO 3), AP

E11-2 Hank Itzek manufactures and sells homemade wine, and he wants to develop a standard cost per gallon. The following are required for production of a 50-gallon batch.

3,000 ounces of grape concentrate at $0.06 per ounce
54 pounds of granulated sugar at $0.30 per pound

60 lemons at $0.60 each
50 yeast tablets at $0.25 each
50 nutrient tablets at $0.20 each
2,600 ounces of water at $0.005 per ounce

Hank estimates that 4% of the grape concentrate is wasted, 10% of the sugar is lost, and 25% of the lemons cannot be used.

Instructions
Compute the standard cost of the ingredients for one gallon of wine. (Carry computations to two decimal places.)

E11-3 Kimm Company has gathered the following information about its product.

Direct materials. Each unit of product contains 4.5 pounds of materials. The average waste and spoilage per unit produced under normal conditions is 0.5 pounds. Materials cost $5 per pound, but Kimm always takes the 2% cash discount all of its suppliers offer. Freight costs average $0.25 per pound.

Direct labor. Each unit requires 2 hours of labor. Setup, cleanup, and downtime average 0.3 hours per unit. The average hourly pay rate of Kimm's employees is $12. Payroll taxes and fringe benefits are an additional $3 per hour.

Manufacturing overhead. Overhead is applied at a rate of $7 per direct labor hour.

Compute standard cost per unit.

(LO 3), AP

Instructions
Compute Kimm's total standard cost per unit.

E11-4 Monte Services, Inc. is trying to establish the standard labor cost of a typical oil change. The following data have been collected from time and motion studies conducted over the past month.

Compute labor cost and labor quantity variance.

(LO 3, 4), AP

Actual time spent on the oil change	1.0 hour
Hourly wage rate	$12
Payroll taxes	10% of wage rate
Setup and downtime	20% of actual labor time
Cleanup and rest periods	30% of actual labor time
Fringe benefits	25% of wage rate

Instructions
(a) Determine the standard direct labor hours per oil change.
(b) Determine the standard direct labor hourly rate.
(c) Determine the standard direct labor cost per oil change.
(d) If an oil change took 1.6 hours at the standard hourly rate, what was the direct labor quantity variance?

E11-5 The standard cost of Product B manufactured by MIT Company includes three units of direct materials at $5.00 per unit. During June, 29,000 units of direct materials are purchased at a cost of $4.70 per unit, and 29,000 units of direct materials are used to produce 9,500 units of Product B.

Compute materials price and quantity variances.

(LO 4), AP

Instructions
(a) Compute the total materials variance and the price and quantity variances.
(b) Repeat (a), assuming the purchase price is $5.15 and the quantity purchased and used is 28,000 units.

E11-6 Lewis Company's standard labor cost of producing one unit of Product DD is 4 hours at the rate of $12.00 per hour. During August, 40,600 hours of labor are incurred at a cost of $12.15 per hour to produce 10,000 units of Product DD.

Compute labor price and quantity variances.

(LO 4), AP

Instructions
(a) Compute the total labor variance.
(b) Compute the labor price and quantity variances.
(c) Repeat (b), assuming the standard is 4.1 hours of direct labor at $12.25 per hour.

E11-7 Nona Inc., which produces a single product, has prepared the following standard cost sheet for one unit of the product.

Compute materials and labor variances.

(LO 4), AP

Direct materials (8 pounds at $2.50 per pound)	$20
Direct labor (3 hours at $12.00 per hour)	$36

During the month of April, the company manufactures 235 units and incurs the following actual costs.

Direct materials purchased and used (1,900 pounds)	$5,035
Direct labor (700 hours)	$8,260

Instructions
Compute the total, price, and quantity variances for materials and labor.

Compute the materials and labor variances and list reasons for unfavorable variances.

(LO 4), AN

E11-8 The following direct materials and direct labor data pertain to the operations of Laurel Company for the month of August.

Costs		Quantities	
Actual labor rate	$13 per hour	Actual hours incurred and used	4,150 hours
Actual materials price	$128 per ton	Actual quantity of materials purchased and used	1,220 tons
Standard labor rate	$12.50 per hour	Standard hours used	4,300 hours
Standard materials price	$130 per ton	Standard quantity of materials used	1,200 tons

Instructions
(a) Compute the total, price, and quantity variances for materials and labor.
(b) ▮▮▮▭▭▷ Provide two possible explanations for each of the unfavorable variances calculated above, and suggest where responsibility for the unfavorable result might be placed.

Determine amounts from variance report.

(LO 4), AN

E11-9 You have been given the following information about the production of Horatio Co., and are asked to provide the plant manager with information for a meeting with the vice president of operations.

	Standard Cost Card
Direct materials (5 pounds at $4 per pound)	$20.00
Direct labor (0.8 hours at $10)	8.00
Variable overhead (0.8 hours at $3 per hour)	2.40
Fixed overhead (0.8 hours at $7 per hour)	5.60
	$36.00

The following is a variance report for the most recent period of operations.

			Variances	
Costs	Total Standard Cost		Price	Quantity
Direct materials	$405,000		$5,175 F	$9,000 U
Direct labor	180,000		3,840 U	6,000 U

Instructions
(a) How many units were produced during the period?
(b) How many pounds of raw materials were purchased and used during the period?
(c) What was the actual cost per pound of raw materials?
(d) How many actual direct labor hours were worked during the period?
(e) What was the actual rate paid per direct labor hour?

(CGA adapted)

Prepare a variance report for direct labor.

(LO 4, 6), AP

E11-10 During March 2014, Toby Tool & Die Company worked on four jobs. A review of direct labor costs reveals the following summary data.

Job Number	Actual		Standard		Total Variance
	Hours	Costs	Hours	Costs	
A257	221	$4,420	225	$4,500	$ 80 F
A258	450	9,450	430	8,600	850 U
A259	300	6,180	300	6,000	180 U
A260	116	2,088	110	2,200	112 F
Total variance					$838 U

Analysis reveals that Job A257 was a repeat job. Job A258 was a rush order that required overtime work at premium rates of pay. Job A259 required a more experienced replacement worker on one shift. Work on Job A260 was done for one day by a new trainee when a regular worker was absent.

Instructions
Prepare a report for the plant supervisor on direct labor cost variances for March. The report should have columns for (1) Job No., (2) Actual Hours, (3) Standard Hours, (4) Quantity Variance, (5) Actual Rate, (6) Standard Rate, (7) Price Variance, and (8) Explanation.

E11-11 Manufacturing overhead data for the production of Product H by Smart Company are as follows.

Compute overhead variance.
(LO 5), AN

Overhead incurred for 52,000 actual direct labor hours worked	$263,000
Overhead rate (variable $3; fixed $2) at normal capacity of 54,000	
direct labor hours	$5
Standard hours allowed for work done	51,000

Instructions
Compute the total overhead variance.

E11-12 Byrd Company produces one product, a putter called GO-Putter. Byrd uses a standard cost system and determines that it should take one hour of direct labor to produce one GO-Putter. The normal production capacity for this putter is 100,000 units per year. The total budgeted overhead at normal capacity is $850,000 comprised of $250,000 of variable costs and $600,000 of fixed costs. Byrd applies overhead on the basis of direct labor hours.

Compute overhead variances.
(LO 5), AP

During the current year, Byrd produced 95,000 putters, worked 94,000 direct labor hours, and incurred variable overhead costs of $256,000 and fixed overhead costs of $600,000.

Instructions
(a) Compute the predetermined variable overhead rate and the predetermined fixed overhead rate.
(b) Compute the applied overhead for Byrd for the year.
(c) Compute the total overhead variance.

E11-13 Wales Company purchased (at a cost of $10,800) and used 2,400 pounds of materials during May. Wales's standard cost of materials per unit produced is based on 2 pounds per unit at a cost $5 per pound. Production in May was 1,070 units.

Compute variances for materials.
(LO 4), AP

Instructions
(a) Compute the total, price, and quantity variances for materials.
(b) Assume Wales also had an unfavorable labor quantity variance. What is a possible scenario that would provide one cause for the variances computed in (a) and the unfavorable labor quantity variance?

E11-14 Picard Landscaping plants grass seed as the basic landscaping for business campuses. During a recent month, the company worked on three projects (Remington, Chang, and Wyco). The company is interested in controlling the materials costs, namely the grass seed, for these plantings projects.

Prepare a variance report.
(LO 4, 6), AP

In order to provide management with useful cost control information, the company uses standard costs and prepares monthly variance reports. Analysis reveals that the purchasing agent mistakenly purchased poor-quality seed for the Remington project. The Chang project, however, received higher-than-standard-quality seed that was on sale. The Wyco project received standard-quality seed. However, the price had increased and a new employee was used to spread the seed.

Shown below are quantity and cost data for each project.

Project	Actual Quantity	Costs	Standard Quantity	Costs	Total Variance
Remington	500 lbs.	$1,200	460 lbs.	$1,150	$ 50 U
Chang	400	920	410	1,025	105 F
Wyco	550	1,430	480	1,200	230 U
Total variance					$175 U

Instructions

(a) Prepare a variance report for the purchasing department with the following columns: (1) Project, (2) Actual Pounds Purchased, (3) Actual Price, (4) Standard Price, (5) Price Variance, and (6) Explanation.

(b) Prepare a variance report for the production department with the following columns: (1) Project, (2) Actual Pounds, (3) Standard Pounds, (4) Standard Price, (5) Quantity Variance, and (6) Explanation.

Complete variance report.

(LO 6), AP

E11-15 Burte Corporation prepared the following variance report.

Burte Corporation
Variance Report—Purchasing Department
For the Week Ended January 9, 2014

Type of Materials	Quantity Purchased	Actual Price	Standard Price	Price Variance	Explanation
Rogue11	? lbs.	$5.20	$5.00	$5,000 ?	Price increase
Storm17	7,000 oz.	?	3.30	1,050 U	Rush order
Beast29	22,000 units	0.40	?	440 F	Bought larger quantity

Instructions

Fill in the appropriate amounts or letters for the question marks in the report.

Prepare income statement for management.

(LO 7), AP

E11-16 Fisk Company uses a standard cost accounting system. During January, the company reported the following manufacturing variances.

Materials price variance	$1,200 U	Labor quantity variance	$750 U
Materials quantity variance	800 F	Overhead variance	800 U
Labor price variance	550 U		

In addition, 8,000 units of product were sold at $8 per unit. Each unit sold had a standard cost of $5. Selling and administrative expenses were $8,000 for the month.

Instructions

Prepare an income statement for management for the month ended January 31, 2014.

Identify performance evaluation terminology.

(LO 3, 8), C

E11-17 The following is a list of terms related to performance evaluation.
1. Balanced scorecard
2. Variance
3. Learning and growth perspective
4. Nonfinancial measures
5. Customer perspective
6. Internal process perspective
7. Ideal standards
8. Normal standards

Instructions

Match each of the following descriptions with one of the terms above.

(a) The difference between total actual costs and total standard costs.
(b) An efficient level of performance that is attainable under expected operating conditions.
(c) An approach that incorporates financial and nonfinancial measures in an integrated system that links performance measurement and a company's strategic goals.
(d) A viewpoint employed in the balanced scorecard to evaluate how well a company develops and retains its employees.
(e) An evaluation tool that is not based on dollars.
(f) A viewpoint employed in the balanced scorecard to evaluate the company from the perspective of those people who buy its products or services.
(g) An optimum level of performance under perfect operating conditions.
(h) A viewpoint employed in the balanced scorecard to evaluate the efficiency and effectiveness of the company's value chain.

Journalize entries in a standard cost accounting system.

(LO 9), AP

*E11-18 Vista Company installed a standard cost system on January 1. Selected transactions for the month of January are as follows.
1. Purchased 18,000 units of raw materials on account at a cost of $4.50 per unit. Standard cost was $4.40 per unit.

2. Issued 18,000 units of raw materials for jobs that required 17,500 standard units of raw materials.
3. Incurred 15,300 actual hours of direct labor at an actual rate of $5.00 per hour. The standard rate is $5.50 per hour. (Credit Factory Wages Payable.)
4. Performed 15,300 hours of direct labor on jobs when standard hours were 15,400.
5. Applied overhead to jobs at the rate of 100% of direct labor cost for standard hours allowed.

Instructions
Journalize the January transactions.

*E11-19 Stiller Company uses a standard cost accounting system. Some of the ledger accounts have been destroyed in a fire. The controller asks your help in reconstructing some missing entries and balances.

Answer questions concerning missing entries and balances.
(LO 4, 5, 9), AN

Instructions
Answer the following questions.

(a) Materials Price Variance shows a $2,000 unfavorable balance. Accounts Payable shows $128,000 of raw materials purchases. What was the amount debited to Raw Materials Inventory for raw materials purchased?
(b) Materials Quantity Variance shows a $3,000 favorable balance. Raw Materials Inventory shows a zero balance. What was the amount debited to Work in Process Inventory for direct materials used?
(c) Labor Price Variance shows a $1,500 favorable balance. Factory Labor shows a debit of $140,000 for wages incurred. What was the amount credited to Factory Wages Payable?
(d) Factory Labor shows a credit of $140,000 for direct labor used. Labor Quantity Variance shows a $900 favorable balance. What was the amount debited to Work in Process for direct labor used?
(e) Overhead applied to Work in Process totaled $165,000. If the total overhead variance was $1,200 favorable, what was the amount of overhead costs debited to Manufacturing Overhead?

*E11-20 Data for Nona Inc. are given in E11-7.

Journalize entries for materials and labor variances.
(LO 9), AP

Instructions
Journalize the entries to record the materials and labor variances.

*E11-21 The information shown below was taken from the annual manufacturing overhead cost budget of Samantha Company.

Compute manufacturing overhead variances and interpret findings.
(LO 10), AN

Variable manufacturing overhead costs	$34,650
Fixed manufacturing overhead costs	$19,800
Normal production level in labor hours	16,500
Normal production level in units	4,125
Standard labor hours per unit	4

During the year, 4,000 units were produced, 16,100 hours were worked, and the actual manufacturing overhead was $55,000. Actual fixed manufacturing overhead costs equaled budgeted fixed manufacturing overhead costs. Overhead is applied on the basis of direct labor hours.

Instructions
(a) Compute the total, fixed, and variable predetermined manufacturing overhead rates.
(b) Compute the total, controllable, and volume overhead variances.
(c) ▅▅▅▅▷ Briefly interpret the overhead controllable and volume variances computed in (b).

*E11-22 The loan department of Calgary Bank uses standard costs to determine the overhead cost of processing loan applications. During the current month, a fire occurred, and the accounting records for the department were mostly destroyed. The data shown on page 534 were salvaged from the ashes.

Compute overhead variances.
(LO 10), AN

Standard variable overhead rate per hour	$9
Standard hours per application	2
Standard hours allowed	2,000
Standard fixed overhead rate per hour	$6
Actual fixed overhead cost	$12,600
Variable overhead budget based on standard hours allowed	$18,000
Fixed overhead budget	$12,600
Overhead controllable variance	$ 1,200 U

Instructions

(a) Determine the following.
 (1) Total actual overhead cost.
 (2) Actual variable overhead cost.
 (3) Variable overhead costs applied.
 (4) Fixed overhead costs applied.
 (5) Overhead volume variance.
(b) Determine how many loans were processed.

Compute variances.

(LO 10), AP

*E11-23 Alona Company's overhead rate was based on estimates of $200,000 for overhead costs and 20,000 direct labor hours. Alona's standards allow 2 hours of direct labor per unit produced. Production in May was 900 units, and actual overhead incurred in May was $19,000. The overhead budgeted for 1,800 standard direct labor hours is $17,600 ($5,000 fixed and $12,600 variable).

Instructions

(a) Compute the total, controllable, and volume variances for overhead.
(b) What are possible causes of the variances computed in part (a)?

EXERCISES: SET B AND CHALLENGE EXERCISES

Visit the book's companion website, at **www.wiley.com/college/weygandt**, and choose the Student Companion site to access Exercise Set B and Challenge Exercises.

PROBLEMS: SET A

Compute variances.

(LO 4, 5), AP

P11-1A Costello Corporation manufactures a single product. The standard cost per unit of product is shown below.

Direct materials—1 pound plastic at $7.00 per pound	$ 7.00
Direct labor—1.6 hours at $12.00 per hour	19.20
Variable manufacturing overhead	12.00
Fixed manufacturing overhead	4.00
Total standard cost per unit	$42.20

The predetermined manufacturing overhead rate is $10 per direct labor hour ($16.00 ÷ 1.6). It was computed from a master manufacturing overhead budget based on normal production of 8,000 direct labor hours (5,000 units) for the month. The master budget showed total variable costs of $60,000 ($7.50 per hour) and total fixed overhead costs of $20,000 ($2.50 per hour). Actual costs for October in producing 4,900 units were as follows.

Direct materials (5,100 pounds)	$ 36,720
Direct labor (7,500 hours)	93,750
Variable overhead	59,700
Fixed overhead	21,000
Total manufacturing costs	$211,170

The purchasing department buys the quantities of raw materials that are expected to be used in production each month. Raw materials inventories, therefore, can be ignored.

Instructions
(a) Compute all of the materials and labor variances.
(b) Compute the total overhead variance.

(a) MPV $1,020 U

P11-2A Ayala Corporation accumulates the following data relative to jobs started and finished during the month of June 2014.

Compute variances, and prepare income statement.

(LO 4, 5, 7), AP

Costs and Production Data	Actual	Standard
Raw materials unit cost	$2.25	$2.10
Raw materials units used	10,600	10,000
Direct labor payroll	$120,960	$120,000
Direct labor hours worked	14,400	15,000
Manufacturing overhead incurred	$189,500	
Manufacturing overhead applied		$189,000
Machine hours expected to be used at normal capacity		42,500
Budgeted fixed overhead for June		$55,250
Variable overhead rate per machine hour		$3.00
Fixed overhead rate per machine hour		$1.30

Overhead is applied on the basis of standard machine hours. Three hours of machine time are required for each direct labor hour. The jobs were sold for $400,000. Selling and administrative expenses were $40,000. Assume that the amount of raw materials purchased equaled the amount used.

Instructions
(a) Compute all of the variances for (1) direct materials and (2) direct labor.
(b) Compute the total overhead variance.
(c) Prepare an income statement for management. (Ignore income taxes.)

(a) LQV $4,800 F

P11-3A Hopkins Clothiers is a small company that manufactures tall-men's suits. The company has used a standard cost accounting system. In May 2014, 11,200 suits were produced. The following standard and actual cost data applied to the month of May when normal capacity was 14,000 direct labor hours. All materials purchased were used.

Compute and identify significant variances.

(LO 4, 5, 6), AN

Cost Element	Standard (per unit)	Actual
Direct materials	8 yards at $4.40 per yard	$375,575 for 90,500 yards ($4.15 per yard)
Direct labor	1.2 hours at $13.40 per hour	$200,220 for 14,200 hours ($14.10 per hour)
Overhead	1.2 hours at $6.10 per hour (fixed $3.50; variable $2.60)	$49,000 fixed overhead $37,000 variable overhead

Overhead is applied on the basis of direct labor hours. At normal capacity, budgeted fixed overhead costs were $49,000, and budgeted variable overhead was $36,400.

Instructions
(a) Compute the total, price, and quantity variances for (1) materials and (2) labor.
(b) Compute the total overhead variance.
(c) ▥▥▥▷ Which of the materials and labor variances should be investigated if management considers a variance of more than 4% from standard to be significant?

(a) MPV $22,625 F

P11-4A Kansas Company uses a standard cost accounting system. In 2014, the company produced 28,000 units. Each unit took several pounds of direct materials and 1.6 standard hours of direct labor at a standard hourly rate of $12.00. Normal capacity was 50,000 direct labor hours. During the year, 117,000 pounds of raw materials were purchased at $0.92 per pound. All materials purchased were used during the year.

Answer questions about variances.

(LO 4, 5), AN

Instructions
(a) If the materials price variance was $3,510 favorable, what was the standard materials price per pound?
(b) If the materials quantity variance was $4,750 unfavorable, what was the standard materials quantity per unit?

(b) 4.0 pounds

(c) What were the standard hours allowed for the units produced?
(d) If the labor quantity variance was $7,200 unfavorable, what were the actual direct labor hours worked?
(e) If the labor price variance was $9,080 favorable, what was the actual rate per hour?

(f) $7.20 per DLH

(f) If total budgeted manufacturing overhead was $360,000 at normal capacity, what was the predetermined overhead rate?
(g) What was the standard cost per unit of product?
(h) How much overhead was applied to production during the year?
(i) Using one or more answers above, what were the total costs assigned to work in process?

Compute variances, prepare an income statement, and explain unfavorable variances.

(LO 4, 5, 7), AP

P11-5A Pace Labs, Inc. provides mad cow disease testing for both state and federal governmental agricultural agencies. Because the company's customers are governmental agencies, prices are strictly regulated. Therefore, Pace Labs must constantly monitor and control its testing costs. Shown below are the standard costs for a typical test.

Direct materials (2 test tubes @ $1.46 per tube)	$ 2.92
Direct labor (1 hour @ $24 per hour)	24.00
Variable overhead (1 hour @ $6 per hour)	6.00
Fixed overhead (1 hour @ $10 per hour)	10.00
Total standard cost per test	$42.92

The lab does not maintain an inventory of test tubes. Therefore, the tubes purchased each month are used that month. Actual activity for the month of November 2014, when 1,500 tests were conducted, resulted in the following.

Direct materials (3,050 test tubes)	$ 4,209
Direct labor (1,600 hours)	36,800
Variable overhead	7,400
Fixed overhead	15,000

Monthly budgeted fixed overhead is $14,000. Revenues for the month were $75,000, and selling and administrative expenses were $5,000.

Instructions

(a) LQV $2,400 U

(a) Compute the price and quantity variances for direct materials and direct labor.
(b) Compute the total overhead variance.
(c) Prepare an income statement for management.
(d) Provide possible explanations for each unfavorable variance.

Journalize and post standard cost entries, and prepare income statement.

(LO 4, 5, 7, 9), AP

*P11-6A Jorgensen Corporation uses standard costs with its job order cost accounting system. In January, an order (Job No. 12) for 1,900 units of Product B was received. The standard cost of one unit of Product B is as follows.

Direct materials	3 pounds at $1.00 per pound	$ 3.00
Direct labor	1 hour at $8.00 per hour	8.00
Overhead	2 hours (variable $4.00 per machine hour; fixed $2.25 per machine hour)	12.50
Standard cost per unit		$23.50

Normal capacity for the month was 4,200 machine hours. During January, the following transactions applicable to Job No. 12 occurred.

1. Purchased 6,200 pounds of raw materials on account at $1.05 per pound.
2. Requisitioned 6,200 pounds of raw materials for Job No. 12.
3. Incurred 2,000 hours of direct labor at a rate of $7.80 per hour.
4. Worked 2,000 hours of direct labor on Job No. 12.
5. Incurred manufacturing overhead on account $25,000.
6. Applied overhead to Job No. 12 on basis of standard machine hours allowed.
7. Completed Job No. 12.
8. Billed customer for Job No. 12 at a selling price of $65,000.

Instructions

(a) Journalize the transactions.
(b) Post to the job order cost accounts.

(c) Prepare the entry to recognize the total overhead variance.
(d) Prepare the January 2014 income statement for management. Assume selling and administrative expenses were $2,000.

(d) NI $15,890

*P11-7A Using the information in P11-1A, compute the overhead controllable variance and the overhead volume variance.

Compute overhead controllable and volume variances.

(LO 10), AP

*P11-8A Using the information in P11-2A, compute the overhead controllable variance and the overhead volume variance.

Compute overhead controllable and volume variances.

(LO 10), AP

*P11-9A Using the information in P11-3A, compute the overhead controllable variance and the overhead volume variance.

Compute overhead controllable and volume variances.

(LO 10), AP

*P11-10A Using the information in P11-5A, compute the overhead controllable variance and the overhead volume variance.

Compute overhead controllable and volume variances.

(LO 10), AP

PROBLEMS: SET B

P11-1B Buil Corporation manufactures a single product. The standard cost per unit of product is as follows.

Compute variances.

(LO 4, 5), AP

Direct materials—2 pounds of plastic at $6 per pound	$12
Direct labor—2 hours at $13 per hour	26
Variable manufacturing overhead	7
Fixed manufacturing overhead	5
Total standard cost per unit	$50

The master manufacturing overhead budget for the month based on normal productive capacity of 20,000 direct labor hours (10,000 units) shows total variable costs of $70,000 ($3.50 per labor hour) and total fixed costs of $50,000 ($2.50 per labor hour). Normal productive capacity is 20,000 direct labor hours. Overhead is applied on the basis of direct labor hours. Actual costs for November in producing 9,700 units were as follows.

Direct materials (20,000 pounds)	$119,000
Direct labor (19,600 hours)	256,760
Variable overhead	68,800
Fixed overhead	50,000
Total manufacturing costs	$494,560

The purchasing department normally buys the quantities of raw materials that are expected to be used in production each month. Raw materials inventories, therefore, can be ignored.

Instructions
(a) Compute all of the materials and labor variances.
(b) Compute the total overhead variance.

(a) MPV $1,000 F

P11-2B Huang Company uses a standard cost accounting system to account for the manufacture of exhaust fans. In July 2014, it accumulates the following data relative to 1,800 units started and finished.

Compute variances, and prepare income statement.

(LO 4, 5, 7), AP

Cost and Production Data	Actual	Standard
Raw materials		
Units purchased	21,000	
Units used	21,000	22,000
Unit cost	$3.70	$3.50
Direct labor		
Hours worked	3,450	3,600
Hourly rate	$11.50	$12.00
Manufacturing overhead		
Incurred	$94,800	
Applied		$100,800

Manufacturing overhead was applied on the basis of direct labor hours. Normal capacity for the month was 3,400 direct labor hours. At normal capacity, budgeted overhead costs were $16 per labor hour variable and $12 per labor hour fixed. Total budgeted fixed overhead costs were $40,800.

Jobs finished during the month were sold for $270,000. Selling and administrative expenses were $20,000.

Instructions

(a) LQV $1,800 F

(a) Compute all of the variances for (1) direct materials and (2) direct labor.
(b) Compute the total overhead variance.
(c) Prepare an income statement for management. (Ignore income taxes.)

Compute and identify significant variances.

(LO 4, 5, 6), AN

P11-3B Zimmerman Clothiers manufactures women's business suits. The company uses a standard cost accounting system. In March 2014, 15,700 suits were made. The following standard and actual cost data applied to the month of March when normal capacity was 20,000 direct labor hours. All materials purchased were used in production.

Cost Element	Standard (per unit)	Actual
Direct materials	5 yards at $6.75 per yard	$547,200 for 76,000 yards ($7.20 per yard)
Direct labor	1.0 hours at $11.45 per hour	$165,760 for 14,800 hours ($11.20 per hour)
Overhead	1.0 hours at $9.40 per hour (fixed $6.25; variable $3.15)	$120,000 fixed overhead $49,000 variable overhead

Overhead is applied on the basis of direct labor hours. At normal capacity, budgeted fixed overhead costs were $125,000, and budgeted variable overhead costs were $63,000.

Instructions

(a) MPV $34,200 U

(a) Compute the total, price, and quantity variances for (1) materials and (2) labor.
(b) Compute the total overhead variance.
(c) ▭▭▭▭▷ Which of the materials and labor variances should be investigated if management considers a variance of more than 5% from standard to be significant?

Answer questions about variances.

(LO 4, 5), AN

P11-4B Beta Company uses a standard cost accounting system. In 2014, 45,000 units were produced. Each unit took several pounds of direct materials and 2 standard hours of direct labor at a standard hourly rate of $12.00. Normal capacity was 86,000 direct labor hours. During the year, 200,000 pounds of raw materials were purchased at $1.00 per pound. All materials purchased were used during the year.

Instructions

(a) If the materials price variance was $10,000 unfavorable, what was the standard materials price per pound?

(b) 5.0 pounds

(b) If the materials quantity variance was $23,750 favorable, what was the standard materials quantity per unit?
(c) What were the standard hours allowed for the units produced?
(d) If the labor quantity variance was $10,080 unfavorable, what were the actual direct labor hours worked?
(e) If the labor price variance was $18,168 favorable, what was the actual rate per hour?

(f) $8.30 per DLH

(f) If total budgeted manufacturing overhead was $713,800 at normal capacity, what was the predetermined overhead rate per direct labor hour?
(g) What was the standard cost per unit of product?
(h) How much overhead was applied to production during the year?
(i) Using selected answers above, what were the total costs assigned to work in process?

Compute variances, prepare an income statement, and explain unfavorable variances.

(LO 4, 5, 7), AP

P11-5B Bonita Labs performs steroid testing services to high schools, colleges, and universities. Because the company deals solely with educational institutions, the price of each test is strictly regulated. Therefore, the costs incurred must be carefully monitored and controlled. Shown below are the standard costs for a typical test.

Direct materials (1 petri dish @ $1.80 per dish)	$ 1.80
Direct labor (0.5 hours @ $20.50 per hour)	10.25
Variable overhead (0.5 hours @ $8 per hour)	4.00
Fixed overhead (0.5 hours @ $5 per hour)	2.50
Total standard cost per test	$18.55

The lab does not maintain an inventory of petri dishes. Therefore, the dishes purchased each month are used that month. Actual activity for the month of May 2014, when 2,500 tests were conducted, resulted in the following.

Direct materials (2,530 dishes)	$ 5,060
Direct labor (1,240 hours)	26,040
Variable overhead	10,100
Fixed overhead	5,700

Monthly budgeted fixed overhead is $6,000. Revenues for the month were $55,000, and selling and administrative expenses were $2,000.

Instructions
(a) Compute the price and quantity variances for direct materials and direct labor.
(b) Compute the total overhead variance.
(c) Prepare an income statement for management.
(d) Provide possible explanations for each unfavorable variance.

(a) LQV $205 F

*P11-6B Frio Company uses standard costs with its job order cost accounting system. In January, an order (Job No. 84) was received for 5,500 units of Product D. The standard cost of 1 unit of Product D is as follows.

Journalize and post standard cost entries, and prepare income statement.

(LO 4, 5, 7, 9), AP

Direct materials—1.5 pounds at $4.00 per pound	$ 6.00
Direct labor—1 hour at $9.00 per hour	9.00
Overhead—1 hour (variable $7.40; fixed $8.00)	15.40
Standard cost per unit	$30.40

Overhead is applied on the basis of direct labor hours. Normal capacity for the month of January was 6,000 direct labor hours. During January, the following transactions applicable to Job No. 84 occurred.

1. Purchased 8,100 pounds of raw materials on account at $3.70 per pound.
2. Requisitioned 8,100 pounds of raw materials for production.
3. Incurred 5,200 hours of direct labor at $9.20 per hour.
4. Worked 5,200 hours of direct labor on Job No. 84.
5. Incurred $87,500 of manufacturing overhead on account.
6. Applied overhead to Job No. 84 on the basis of direct labor hours.
7. Transferred Job No. 84 to finished goods.
8. Billed customer for Job No. 84 at a selling price of $270,000.

Instructions
(a) Journalize the transactions.
(b) Post to the job order cost accounts.
(c) Prepare the entry to recognize the total overhead variance.
(d) Prepare the January 2014 income statement for management. Assume selling and administrative expenses were $60,000.

(d) NI $44,690

*P11-7B Using the information in P11-1B, compute the overhead controllable variance and the overhead volume variance.

Compute overhead controllable and volume variances.

(LO 10), AP

*P11-8B Using the information in P11-2B, compute the overhead controllable variance and the overhead volume variance.

Compute overhead controllable and volume variances.

(LO 10), AP

*P11-9B Using the information in P11-3B, compute the overhead controllable variance and the overhead volume variance.

Compute overhead controllable and volume variances.

(LO 10), AP

*P11-10B Using the information in P11-5B, compute the overhead controllable variance and the overhead volume variance.

Compute overhead controllable and volume variances.

(LO 10), AP

PROBLEMS: SET C

Visit the book's companion website, at **www.wiley.com/college/weygandt**, and choose the Student Companion site to access Problem Set C.

WATERWAYS CONTINUING PROBLEM

(This is a continuation of the Waterways Problem from Chapters 1–10.)

WCP11 Waterways Corporation uses very stringent standard costs in evaluating its manufacturing efficiency. These standards are not "ideal" at this point, but management is working toward that as a goal. This problem asks you to calculate and evaluate the company's variances.

Go to the book's companion website, at **www.wiley.com/college/weygandt**, *to find the completion of this problem.*

Broadening Your **PERSPECTIVE**

Management Decision-Making

Decision-Making at Current Designs

BYP11-1 The executive team at Current Designs has gathered to evaluate the company's operations for the last month. One of the topics on the agenda is the special order from Huegel Hollow, which was presented in BYP2-1. Recall that Current Designs had a special order to produce a batch of 20 kayaks for a client, and you were asked to determine the cost of the order and the cost per kayak.

Mike Cichanowski asked the others if the special order caused any particular problems in the production process. Dave Thill, the production manager, made the following comments: "Since we wanted to complete this order quickly and make a good first impression on this new customer, we had some of our most experienced type I workers run the rotomold oven and do the trimming. They were very efficient and were able to complete that part of the manufacturing process even more quickly than the regular crew. However, the finishing on these kayaks required a different technique than what we usually use, so our type II workers took a little longer than usual for that part of the process."

Deb Welch, who is in charge of the purchasing function, said, "We had to pay a little more for the polyethylene powder for this order because the customer wanted a color that we don't usually stock. We also ordered a little extra since we wanted to make sure that we had enough to allow us to calibrate the equipment. The calibration was a little tricky, and we used all of the powder that we had purchased. Since the number of kayaks in the order was fairly small, we were able to use some rope and other parts that were left over from last year's production in the finishing kits. We've seen a price increase for these components in the last year, so using the parts that we already had in inventory cut our costs for the finishing kits."

Instructions

(a) Based on the comments above, predict whether each of the following variances will be favorable or unfavorable. If you don't have enough information to make a prediction, use "NEI" to indicate "Not Enough Information."

(1) Quantity variance for polyethylene powder.   (5) Quantity variance for type I workers.
(2) Price variance for polyethylene powder.   (6) Price variance for type I workers.
(3) Quantity variance for finishing kits.   (7) Quantity variance for type II workers.
(4) Price variance for finishing kits.   (8) Price variance for type II workers.

(b) Diane Buswell examined some of the accounting records and reported that Current Designs purchased 1,200 pounds of pellets for this order at a total cost of $2,040. Twenty (20) finishing kits were assembled at a total cost of $3,240. The payroll records showed that the type I employees worked 38 hours on this project at a total cost of $570. The type II finishing employees worked 65 hours at a total cost of $796.25. A total of 20 kayaks were produced for this order.

The standards that had been developed for this model of kayak were used in BYP2-1 and are reproduced here. For each kayak:

54 pounds of polyethylene powder at $1.50 per pound

1 finishing kit (rope, seat, hardware, etc.) at $170

2 hours of type I labor from people who run the oven and trim the plastic at a standard wage rate of $15 per hour

3 hours of type II labor from people who attach the hatches and seat and other hardware at a standard wage rate of $12 per hour.

Calculate the eight variances that are listed in part (a) of this problem.

Decision-Making Across the Organization

BYP11-2 Milton Professionals, a management consulting firm, specializes in strategic planning for financial institutions. James Hahn and Sara Norton, partners in the firm, are assembling a new strategic planning model for use by clients. The model is designed for use on most personal computers and replaces a rather lengthy manual model currently marketed by the firm. To market the new model, James and Sara will need to provide clients with an estimate of the number of labor hours and computer time needed to operate the model. The model is currently being test-marketed at five small financial institutions. These financial institutions are listed below, along with the number of combined computer/labor hours used by each institution to run the model one time.

Financial Institutions	Computer/Labor Hours Required
Midland National	25
First State	45
Financial Federal	40
Pacific America	30
Lakeview National	30
Total	170
Average	34

Any company that purchases the new model will need to purchase user manuals for the system. User manuals will be sold to clients in cases of 20, at a cost of $320 per case. One manual must be used each time the model is run because each manual includes a nonreusable computer-accessed password for operating the system. Also required are specialized computer forms that are sold only by Milton. The specialized forms are sold in packages of 250, at a cost of $60 per package. One application of the model requires the use of 50 forms. This amount includes two forms that are generally wasted in each application due to printer alignment errors. The overall cost of the strategic planning model to clients is $12,000. Most clients will use the model four times annually.

Milton must provide its clients with estimates of ongoing costs incurred in operating the new planning model, and would like to do so in the form of standard costs.

Instructions
With the class divided into groups, answer the following.
(a) What factors should be considered in setting a standard for computer/labor hours?
(b) What alternatives for setting a standard for computer/labor hours might be used?
(c) What standard for computer/labor hours would you select? Justify your answer.
(d) Determine the standard materials cost associated with the user manuals and computer forms for each application of the strategic planning model.

Managerial Analysis

*BYP11-3 Ana Carillo and Associates is a medium-sized company located near a large metropolitan area in the Midwest. The company manufactures cabinets of mahogany, oak, and other fine woods for use in expensive homes, restaurants, and hotels. Although some of the work is custom, many of the cabinets are a standard size.

One such non-custom model is called Luxury Base Frame. Normal production is 1,000 units. Each unit has a direct labor hour standard of 5 hours. Overhead is applied to production based on standard direct labor hours. During the most recent month, only 900 units were produced; 4,500 direct labor hours were allowed for standard production, but only 4,000 hours were used. Standard and actual overhead costs were as follows.

	Standard (1,000 units)	Actual (900 units)
Indirect materials	$ 12,000	$ 12,300
Indirect labor	43,000	51,000
(Fixed) Manufacturing supervisors salaries	22,500	22,000
(Fixed) Manufacturing office employees salaries	13,000	12,500
(Fixed) Engineering costs	27,000	25,000
Computer costs	10,000	10,000
Electricity	2,500	2,500
(Fixed) Manufacturing building depreciation	8,000	8,000
(Fixed) Machinery depreciation	3,000	3,000
(Fixed) Trucks and forklift depreciation	1,500	1,500
Small tools	700	1,400
(Fixed) Insurance	500	500
(Fixed) Property taxes	300	300
Total	$144,000	$150,000

Instructions
(a) Determine the overhead application rate.
(b) Determine how much overhead was applied to production.
(c) Calculate the total overhead variance, controllable variance, and volume variance.
(d) Decide which overhead variances should be investigated.
(e) Discuss causes of the overhead variances. What can management do to improve its performance next month?

Real-World Focus

BYP11-4 Glassmaster Company is organized as two divisions and one subsidiary. One division focuses on the manufacture of filaments such as fishing line and sewing thread; the other division manufactures antennas and specialty fiberglass products. Its subsidiary manufactures flexible steel wire controls and molded control panels.

The annual report of Glassmaster provides the following information.

Glassmaster Company
Management Discussion

Gross profit margins for the year improved to 20.9% of sales compared to last year's 18.5%. All operations reported improved margins due in large part to improved operating efficiencies as a result of cost reduction measures implemented during the second and third quarters of the fiscal year and increased manufacturing throughout due to higher unit volume sales. Contributing to the improved margins was a favorable materials price variance due to competitive pricing by suppliers as a result of soft demand for petrochemical-based products. This favorable variance is temporary and will begin to reverse itself as stronger worldwide demand for commodity products improves in tandem with the economy. Partially offsetting these positive effects on profit margins were competitive pressures on sales prices of certain product lines. The company responded with pricing strategies designed to maintain and/or increase market share.

Instructions
(a) Is it apparent from the information whether Glassmaster utilizes standard costs?
(b) Do you think the price variance experienced should lead to changes in standard costs for the next fiscal year?

BYP11-5 The Balanced Scorecard Institute *(www.balancedscorecard.org)* is a great resource for information about implementing the balanced scorecard. One item of interest provided at its website is an example of a balanced scorecard for a regional airline.

Address: **http://www.balancedscorecard.org/portals/0/pdf/regional_airline.pdf**, or go to **www. wiley.com/college/weygandt**

Instructions
Go to the address above and answer the following questions.
(a) What are the objectives identified for the airline for each perspective?
(b) What measures are used for the objectives in the customer perspective?
(c) What initiatives are planned to achieve the objective in the learning perspective?

BYP11-6 The December 22, 2009, edition of the *Wall Street Journal* has an article by Kevin Kelliker entitled "In Risky Move, GM to Run Plants Around Clock."

Instructions
Read the article and answer the following questions.
(a) According to the article, what is the normal industry standard for plants to be considered operating at full capacity?
(b) What ideal standard is the company hoping to achieve?
(c) What reasons are given in the article for why most companies do not operate a third shift? How does GM propose to overcome these issues?
(d) What are some potential drawbacks of the midnight shift? What implications does this have for variances from standards?
(e) What potential sales/marketing disadvantage does the third shift create?

Critical Thinking

Communication Activity

BYP11-7 The setting of standards is critical to the effective use of standards in evaluating performance.

Instructions
Explain the following in a memo to your instructor.
(a) The comparative advantages and disadvantages of ideal versus normal standards.
(b) The factors that should be included in setting the price and quantity standards for direct materials, direct labor, and manufacturing overhead.

Ethics Case

BYP11-8 At Symond Company, production workers in the Painting Department are paid on the basis of productivity. The labor time standard for a unit of production is established through periodic time studies conducted by Douglas Management Consultants. In a time study, the actual time required to complete a specific task by a worker is observed. Allowances are then made for preparation time, rest periods, and cleanup time. Bill Carson is one of several veterans in the Painting Department.

Bill is informed by Douglas that he will be used in the time study for the painting of a new product. The findings will be the basis for establishing the labor time standard for the next 6 months. During the test, Bill deliberately slows his normal work pace in an effort to obtain a labor time standard that will be easy to meet. Because it is a new product, the Douglas representative who conducted the test is unaware that Bill did not give the test his best effort.

Instructions

(a) Who was benefited and who was harmed by Bill's actions?

(b) Was Bill ethical in the way he performed the time study test?

(c) What measure(s) might the company take to obtain valid data for setting the labor time standard?

All About You

BYP11-9 From the time you first entered school many years ago, instructors have been measuring and evaluating you by imposing standards. In addition, many of you will pursue professions that administer professional examinations to attain recognized certification. Recently, a federal commission presented proposals suggesting all public colleges and universities should require standardized tests to measure their students' learning.

Instructions

Read the article at **www.signonsandiego.com/uniontrib/20060811/news_1n11colleges.html**, and answer the following questions.

(a) What areas of concern did the panel's recommendations address?

(b) What are possible advantages of standard testing?

(c) What are possible disadvantages of standard testing?

(d) Would you be in favor of standardized tests?

Considering Your Costs and Benefits

BYP11-10 Do you think that standard costs are used only in making products like wheel bearings and hamburgers? Think again. Standards influence virtually every aspect of our lives. For example, the next time you call to schedule an appointment with your doctor, ask the receptionist how many minutes the appointment is scheduled for. Doctors are under increasing pressure to see more patients each day, which means the time spent with each patient is shorter. As insurance companies and employers push for reduced medical costs, every facet of medicine has been standardized and analyzed. Doctors, nurses, and other medical staff are evaluated in every part of their operations to ensure maximum efficiency. While keeping medical treatment affordable seems like a worthy goal, what are the potential implications for the quality of health care? Does a focus on the bottom line result in a reduction in the quality of health care?

A simmering debate has centered on a very basic question: To what extent should accountants, through financial measures, influence the type of medical care that you receive? Suppose that your local medical facility is in danger of closing because it has been losing money. Should the facility put in place incentives that provide bonuses to doctors if they meet certain standard-cost targets for the cost of treating specific ailments?

YES: If the facility is in danger of closing, then someone should take steps to change the medical practices to reduce costs. A closed medical facility is of no use to me, my family, or the community.

NO: I don't want an accountant deciding the right medical treatment for me. My family and I deserve the best medical care.

Instructions

Write a response indicating your position regarding this situation. Provide support for your view.

Answers to Chapter Questions

Answers to Insight and Accounting Across the Organization Questions

p. 498 How Do Standards Help a Business? Q: How will the creation of such standards help a business or organization? **A:** A business or organization may use the data to compare its performance relative to others with regard to common practices such as processing a purchase order or filling a sales order. Armed with this information, an organization can determine which areas to focus on with improvement campaigns.

p. 501 How Can We Make Susan's Chili Profitable? Q: How might management use this raw materials cost information? **A:** Management might decide to increase the price of its chili. Or, it might revise its recipes to use cheaper ingredients. Or, it might eliminate some products until ingredients are available at costs closer to standard. Regarding the waste due to dull blades, management should reconsider its maintenance policy, to balance the cost of maintenance versus the cost of wasted product.

p. 510 What's Brewing at Starbucks? Q: What implications does Starbucks' commitment to corporate social responsibility have for the standard cost of a cup of coffee? **A:** Starbucks' *Global Responsibility Report* explicitly describes its goals related to corporate social responsibility. By including measurable objectives, it signals that it is committed to meeting these goals. As a consequence of setting measurable objectives, when the company determines the standard costs of its products, it needs to factor in the costs of these programs. For example, if renewable energy costs more per kilowatt, then the company must include this added cost in its determination of its products' costs.

p. 515 It May Be Time to Fly United Again Q: Which of the perspectives of a balanced scorecard were the focus of United's CEO? **A:** Improving on-time flight departures is an objective within the internal process perspective. Customer intent to fly United again is an objective within the customer perspective.

Answers to Self-Test Questions

1. c **2.** b **3.** d **4.** a **5.** b **6.** c **7.** b $[(6,300 \times \$1.00) - (6,000 \times \$1.00)]$ **8.** a $[(14,800 \times \$8.00) - (15,000 \times \$8.00)]$ **9.** d **10.** a **11.** b **12.** d **13.** c **14.** d *15. c *16. c

✔ Remember to go back to The Navigator box on the chapter opening page and check off your completed work.

Chapter 12

Planning for Capital Investments

Feature Story

Floating Hotels

Do you own a boat? Maybe it's a nice boat, but how many swimming pools, movie theaters, shopping malls, or restaurants does it have on board? If you are in the cruise-line business, like Holland America Line, you need all of these amenities and more just to stay afloat. Holland America Line is considered by many to be the leader of the premium luxury-liner segment.

Carnival Corporation, which owns Holland America Line and other cruise lines, is one of the largest vacation companies in the world. During one recent three-year period, Carnival spent more than $3 billion per year on capital expenditures. Those are big numbers, but keep in mind that Carnival estimates that at any given time there are 270,000 people (200,000 customers and 70,000 crew) on one of its 100 ships somewhere in the world.

The cruise industry is a tricky business. When times are good, customers are looking for ways to splurge. But when times get tough, people are more inclined to take a trip in a minivan than a luxury yacht. So timing your investment properly is important. For example, during one stretch of solid global economic growth, many cruise lines decided to add capacity. The industry built 14 new ships at a total price of $4.7 billion. (That's an average price of about $330 million.) But, it takes

✔ The Navigator

- Scan Learning Objectives
- Read Feature Story
- Read Preview
- Read Text and answer **DO IT!** p. 551
  - p. 555 ■ p. 563 ■ p. 565
- Work Using the Decision Toolkit p. 566
- Review Summary of Learning Objectives
- Work Comprehensive **DO IT!** p. 569
- Answer Self-Test Questions
- Complete Assignments
- Go to **WileyPLUS** for practice and tutorials

Learning Objectives

After studying this chapter, you should be able to:

1 Discuss capital budgeting evaluation, and explain inputs used in capital budgeting.

2 Describe the cash payback technique.

3 Explain the net present value method.

4 Identify the challenges presented by intangible benefits in capital budgeting.

5 Describe the profitability index.

6 Indicate the benefits of performing a post-audit.

7 Explain the internal rate of return method.

8 Describe the annual rate of return method.

✔ The Navigator

up to three years to build one of these giant vessels Unfortunately, by the time these ships were completed, the economy was in a nose-dive.

To maintain passenger numbers, cruise prices had to be cut by up to 40%. While the lower prices attracted lots of customers, that wasn't enough to offset

an overall decline in revenue of 10% in the middle of the recession. The industry had added capacity at just the wrong time.

Watch the Holland America Line video in WileyPLUS to learn more about capital budgeting in the real world.

✔ The Navigator

Preview of **Chapter 12**

Companies like Holland America Line must constantly determine how to invest their resources. Other examples: Dell announced plans to spend $1 billion on data centers for cloud computing. Exxon announced that two wells off the Brazilian coast, which it had spent hundreds of millions to drill, would produce no oil. Renault and Nissan spent over $5 billion during a nearly 20-year period to develop electric cars, such as the Leaf.

The process of making such capital expenditure decisions is referred to as **capital budgeting**. Capital budgeting involves choosing among various capital projects to find the one(s) that will maximize a company's return on its financial investment. The purpose of this chapter is to discuss the various techniques used to make effective capital budgeting decisions.

The content and organization of this chapter are as follows.

PLANNING FOR CAPITAL INVESTMENTS

Capital Budgeting Evaluation Process	Cash Payback	Net Present Value Method	Additional Considerations	Other Capital Budgeting Techniques
• Cash flow information • Illustrative data	• Calculation • Evaluation	• Equal cash flows • Unequal cash flows • Choosing a discount rate • Simplifying assumptions • Comprehensive example	• Intangible benefits • Profitability index • Risk analysis • Post-audit of projects	• Internal rate of return method • Comparing discounted cash flow methods • Annual rate of return method

✔ The Navigator

547

The Capital Budgeting Evaluation Process

LEARNING OBJECTIVE	1

Discuss capital budgeting evaluation, and explain inputs used in capital budgeting.

Many companies follow a carefully prescribed process in capital budgeting. At least once a year, top management requests proposals for projects from each department. A capital budgeting committee screens the proposals and submits its findings to the officers of the company. The officers, in turn, select the projects they believe to be most worthy of funding. They submit this list of projects to the board of directors. Ultimately, the directors approve the capital expenditure budget for the year. Illustration 12-1 shows this process.

The involvement of top management and the board of directors in the process demonstrates the importance of capital budgeting decisions. These decisions often have a significant impact on a company's future profitability. In fact, poor capital budgeting decisions can cost a lot of money. Such decisions have even led to the bankruptcy of some companies.

1. Project proposals are requested from departments, plants, and authorized personnel.

2. Proposals are screened by a capital budget committee.

3. Officers determine which projects are worthy of funding.

4. Board of directors approves capital budget.

Illustration 12-1
Corporate capital budget authorization process

Cash Flow Information

In this chapter, we will look at several methods that help companies make effective capital budgeting decisions. Most of these methods employ **cash flow numbers**, rather than accrual accounting revenues and expenses. Remember from your financial accounting course that accrual accounting records *revenues* and *expenses*, rather than cash inflows and cash outflows. In fact, revenues and expenses measured during a period often differ significantly from their cash flow counterparts. Accrual accounting has advantages over cash accounting in many contexts. **For purposes of capital budgeting, though, estimated cash inflows and outflows are the preferred inputs.** Why? Because ultimately the value of all financial investments is determined by the value of cash flows received and paid.

Sometimes cash flow information is not available. In this case, companies can make adjustments to accrual accounting numbers to estimate cash flow. Often, they estimate net annual cash flow by adding back depreciation expense to net income. Depreciation expense is added back because it is an expense that does not require an outflow of cash. By adding back to net income the depreciation expense that was deducted in determining net income, companies approximate net annual cash flow. Suppose, for example, that Reno Company's net income of $13,000 includes a charge for depreciation expense of $26,000. Its estimated net annual cash flow would be $39,000 ($13,000 + $26,000).

Illustration 12-2 lists some typical cash outflows and inflows related to equipment purchase and replacement.

Cash Outflows

Initial investment
Repairs and maintenance
Increased operating costs
Overhaul of equipment

Cash Inflows

Sale of old equipment
Increased cash received from customers
Reduced cash outflows related to operating costs
Salvage value of equipment

Illustration 12-2
Typical cash flows relating to
capital budgeting decisions

These cash flows are the inputs that are considered relevant in capital budgeting decisions.

The capital budgeting decision, under any technique, depends in part on a variety of considerations:

- **The availability of funds:** Does the company have unlimited funds, or will it have to ration capital investments?

- **Relationships among proposed projects:** Are proposed projects independent of each other, or does the acceptance or rejection of one depend on the acceptance or rejection of another?

- **The company's basic decision-making approach:** Does the company want to produce an accept-reject decision or a ranking of desirability among possible projects?

- **The risk associated with a particular project:** How certain are the projected returns? The certainty of estimates varies with such issues as market considerations or the length of time before returns are expected.

Illustrative Data

For our initial discussion of quantitative capital budgeting techniques, we will use a continuing example, which will enable us to compare the results of the various techniques. Assume that Stewart Shipping Company is considering an investment of $130,000 in new equipment. The new equipment is expected to last 10 years. It will have a zero salvage value at the end of its useful life. The annual cash inflows are $200,000, and the annual cash outflows are $176,000. Illustration 12-3 summarizes these data.

Initial investment	$130,000
Estimated useful life	10 years
Estimated salvage value	–0–
Estimated annual cash flows	
Cash inflows from customers	$200,000
Cash outflows for operating costs	176,000
Net annual cash flow	$ 24,000

Illustration 12-3
Investment information for
Stewart Shipping example

In the following two sections, we will examine two popular techniques for evaluating capital investments: cash payback and the net present value method.

Cash Payback

LEARNING OBJECTIVE   **2**

Describe the cash payback technique.

The **cash payback technique** identifies the time period required to recover the cost of the capital investment from the net annual cash flow produced by the investment. Illustration 12-4 presents the formula for computing the cash payback period assuming equal annual cash flows.

Illustration 12-4
Cash payback formula

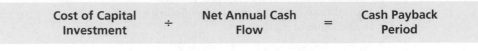

| Cost of Capital Investment | ÷ | Net Annual Cash Flow | = | Cash Payback Period |

Helpful Hint
Net annual cash flow can also be approximated by "Net cash provided by operating activities" from the statement of cash flows.

The cash payback period in the Stewart Shipping example is 5.42 years, computed as follows.

$$\$130{,}000 \div \$24{,}000 = 5.42 \text{ years}$$

The evaluation of the payback period is often related to the expected useful life of the asset. For example, assume that at Stewart Shipping a project is unacceptable if the payback period is longer than 60% of the asset's expected useful life. The 5.42-year payback period in this case is a bit over 50% of the project's expected useful life. Thus, the project is acceptable.

It follows that when the payback technique is used to decide among acceptable alternative projects, **the shorter the payback period, the more attractive the investment**. This is true for two reasons: First, the earlier the investment is recovered, the sooner the company can use the cash funds for other purposes. Second, the risk of loss from obsolescence and changed economic conditions is less in a shorter payback period.

The preceding computation of the cash payback period assumes **equal** net annual cash flows in each year of the investment's life. In many cases, this assumption is not valid. In the case of **uneven** net annual cash flows, the company determines the cash payback period when the cumulative net cash flows from the investment equal the cost of the investment.

To illustrate, assume that Chen Company proposes an investment in a new website that is estimated to cost $300,000. Illustration 12-5 shows the proposed investment cost, net annual cash flows, cumulative net cash flows, and the cash payback period.

Illustration 12-5
Computation of cash payback period—unequal cash flows

Year	Investment	Net Annual Cash Flow	Cumulative Net Cash Flow
0	$300,000		
1		$ 60,000	$ 60,000
2		90,000	150,000
3		90,000	240,000
4		120,000	360,000
5		100,000	460,000

Cash payback period = 3.5 years

As Illustration 12-5 shows, at the end of year 3, cumulative net cash flow of $240,000 is less than the investment cost of $300,000, but at the end of year 4 the cumulative cash inflow of $360,000 exceeds the investment cost. The cash flow needed in year 4 to equal the investment cost is $60,000 ($300,000 − $240,000). Assuming the cash inflow occurred evenly during year 4, we then divide this amount by the net annual cash flow in year 4 ($120,000) to determine the point during the year when the cash payback occurs. Thus, we get 0.50 ($60,000/$120,000), or half of the year, and the cash payback period is 3.5 years.

The cash payback technique may be useful as an initial screening tool. It may be the most critical factor in the capital budgeting decision for a company that desires a fast turnaround of its investment because of a weak cash position. It also is relatively easy to compute and understand.

However, cash payback should not ordinarily be the only basis for the capital budgeting decision because it **ignores the expected profitability of the project**. To illustrate, assume that Projects A and B have the same payback period, but Project A's useful life is double the useful life of Project B. Project A's earning power, therefore, is twice as long as Project B's. A further—and major—disadvantage of this technique is that it **ignores the time value of money**.

> **DO IT!**

Cash Payback Period

Action Plan

✔ Annual cash inflows − Annual cash outflows = Net annual cash flow.

✔ Cash payback period = Cost of capital investment/Net annual cash flow.

Watertown Paper Corporation is considering adding another machine for the manufacture of corrugated cardboard. The machine would cost $900,000. It would have an estimated life of 6 years and no salvage value. The company estimates that annual cash inflows would increase by $400,000 and that annual cash outflows would increase by $190,000. Compute the cash payback period.

Solution

Estimated annual cash inflows	$400,000
Estimated annual cash outflows	190,000
Net annual cash flow	$210,000

Cash payback period = $900,000/$210,000 − 4.3 years.

Related exercise material: **BE12-1** and **DO IT! 12-1**.

✔ **The Navigator**

Net Present Value Method

Recognition of the time value of money can make a significant difference in the long-term impact of the capital budgeting decision. For example, cash flows that occur early in the life of an investment will be worth more than those that occur later—because of the time value of money. Therefore, it is useful to recognize the timing of cash flows when evaluating projects.

LEARNING OBJECTIVE 3

Explain the net present value method.

Capital budgeting techniques that take into account both the time value of money and the estimated net cash flow from an investment are called **discounted cash flow techniques**. They are generally recognized as the most informative and best conceptual approaches to making capital budgeting decisions. The expected net cash flow used in discounting cash flows consists of the annual net cash flows plus the estimated liquidation proceeds (salvage value) when the asset is sold for salvage at the end of its useful life.

The primary discounted cash flow technique is the **net present value method**. A second method, discussed later in the chapter, is the **internal rate of return**. At this point, before you read on, **we recommend that you examine Appendix A** at the end of the book to review time value of money concepts, upon which these methods are based.

The **net present value (NPV) method** involves discounting net cash flows to their present value and then comparing that present value with the capital outlay required by the investment. The difference between these two amounts is referred to as **net present value (NPV)**. Company management determines what interest rate to use in discounting the future net cash flows. This rate, often referred to as the **discount rate** or **required rate of return**, is discussed in a later section.

The NPV decision rule is this: **A proposal is acceptable when net present value is zero or positive**. At either of those values, the rate of return on the investment equals or exceeds the required rate of return. When net present value is negative, the project is unacceptable. Illustration 12-6 shows the net present value decision criteria.

Illustration 12-6
Net present value decision criteria

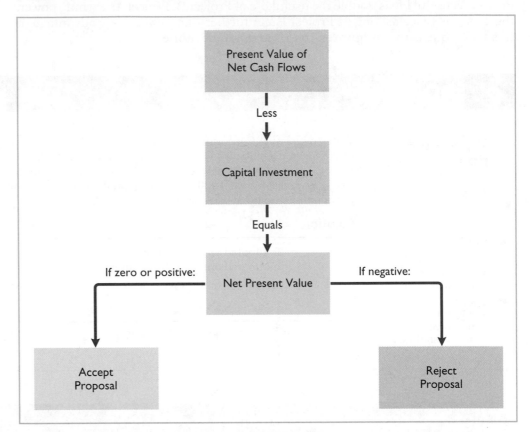

When making a selection among acceptable proposals, **the higher the positive net present value, the more attractive the investment**. The application of this method to two cases is described in the next two sections. In each case, we will assume that the investment has no salvage value at the end of its useful life.

Helpful Hint
The ABC Co. expects equal cash flows over an asset's 5-year useful life. What discount factor should it use in determining present values if management wants (1) a 12% return or (2) a 15% return? Answer: Using Table 4, the factors are (1) 3.60478 and (2) 3.35216.

Equal Annual Cash Flows

In our Stewart Shipping Company example, the company's net annual cash flows are $24,000. If we assume this amount **is uniform over the asset's useful life**, we can compute the present value of the net annual cash flows by using the present value of an annuity of 1 for 10 payments (from Table 4, Appendix A). Assuming a discount rate of 12%, the present value of net cash flows are as shown in Illustration 12-7 (rounded to the nearest dollar).

Illustration 12-7
Computation of present value of equal net annual cash flows

	Present Value at 12%
Discount factor for 10 periods	5.65022
Present value of net cash flows:	
$24,000 × 5.65022	**$135,605**

The analysis of the proposal by the net present value method is as follows.

	12%
Present value of net cash flows	$135,605
Capital investment	130,000
Net present value	**$ 5,605**

The proposed capital expenditure is acceptable at a required rate of return of 12% because the net present value is positive.

Unequal Annual Cash Flows

When net annual cash flows are unequal, we cannot use annuity tables to calculate their present value. Instead, we use tables showing the **present value of a single future amount for each annual cash flow**.

To illustrate, assume that Stewart Shipping Company expects the same total net cash flows of $240,000 over the life of the investment. But because of a declining market demand for the new product over the life of the equipment, the net annual cash flows are higher in the early years and lower in the later years. The present value of the net annual cash flows is calculated as follows, using Table 3 in Appendix A.

Year	Assumed Net Annual Cash Flows	Discount Factor 12%	Present Value 12%
	(1)	(2)	(1) × (2)
1	$ 34,000	.89286	$ 30,357
2	30,000	.79719	23,916
3	27,000	.71178	19,218
4	25,000	.63552	15,888
5	24,000	.56743	13,618
6	22,000	.50663	11,146
7	21,000	.45235	9,499
8	20,000	.40388	8,078
9	19,000	.36061	6,852
10	18,000	.32197	5,795
	$240,000		**$144,367**

Therefore, the analysis of the proposal by the net present value method is as follows.

	12%
Present value of net cash flows	$144,367
Capital investment	130,000
Net present value	**$ 14,367**

In this example, the present value of the net cash flows is greater than the $130,000 capital investment. Thus, the project is acceptable at a 12% required rate of return. The difference between the present values using the 12% rate under equal cash flows ($135,605) and unequal cash flows ($144,367) is due to the pattern of the flows. Since more money is received sooner under this particular uneven cash flow scenario, its present value is greater.

MANAGEMENT INSIGHT

Can You Hear Me—Better?

What's better than 3G wireless service? 4G. But the question for wireless service providers is whether customers will be willing to pay extra for that improvement. Verizon has already spent billions on the upgrade, but customer usage might be slow in coming. First, there aren't that many 4G-compatible devices, and coverage will be spotty. Also, most applications don't really need higher speeds. Verizon is hoping that its investment in 4G works out better than its $23 billion investment in its FIOS fiber-wired network for TV and ultrahigh-speed Internet. One analyst estimates that the present value of each FIOS customer is $800 less than the cost of the connection.

Source: Martin Peers, "Investors: Beware Verizon's Generation GAP," *Wall Street Journal Online* (January 26, 2010).

 Based on the potentially slow initial adoption of 4G by customers, how might the conclusions of a cash payback analysis of Verizon's 4G investment differ from a present value analysis? (See page 584.)

Choosing a Discount Rate

Now that you understand how companies apply the net present value method, it is logical to ask a related question: How is a discount rate (required rate of return) determined in real capital budgeting decisions? In most instances, a company uses a required rate of return equal to its **cost of capital**—that is, the rate that it must pay to obtain funds from creditors and stockholders.

Helpful Hint
Cost of capital is the rate that management expects to pay on all borrowed and equity funds. It does not relate to the cost of funding a *specific* project.

The cost of capital is a weighted average of the rates paid on borrowed funds as well as on funds provided by investors in the company's common stock and preferred stock. If management believes a project is riskier than the company's usual line of business, the discount rate should be increased. That is, the discount rate has two elements, a cost of capital element and a risk element. Often, companies assume the risk element is equal to zero.

Using an incorrect discount rate can lead to incorrect capital budgeting decisions. Consider again the Stewart Shipping example in Illustration 12-8, where we used a discount rate of 12%. Suppose that this rate does not take into account the fact that this project is riskier than most of the company's investments. A more appropriate discount rate, given the risk, might be 15%. Illustration 12-11 compares the net present values at the two rates. At the higher, more appropriate discount rate of 15%, the net present value is negative, and the company should reject the project (discount factors from Appendix A, Table 4).

Illustration 12-11
Comparison of net present values at different discount rates

	Present Values at Different Discount Rates	
	12%	**15%**
Discount factor for 10 payments	5.65022	5.01877
Present value of net cash flows:		
$24,000 × 5.65022	$135,605	
$24,000 × 5.01877		$120,450
Capital investment	130,000	130,000
Positive (negative) net present value	**$ 5,605**	**$ (9,550)**

The discount rate is often referred to by alternative names, including the **required rate of return**, the **hurdle rate**, and the **cutoff rate**. Determination of the cost of capital varies somewhat depending on whether the entity is a for-profit or not-for-profit business. Calculation of the cost of capital is discussed more fully in advanced accounting and finance courses.

Simplifying Assumptions

In our examples of the net present value method, we have made a number of simplifying assumptions:

- **All cash flows come at the end of each year.** In reality, cash flows will come at uneven intervals throughout the year. However, it is far simpler to assume that all cash flows come at the end (or in some cases the beginning) of the year. In fact, this assumption is frequently made in practice.

- **All cash flows are immediately reinvested in another project that has a similar return.** In most capital budgeting situations, companies receive cash flows during each year of a project's life. In order to determine the return on the investment, some assumption must be made about how the cash flows are reinvested in the year that they are received. It is customary to assume that cash flows received are reinvested in some other project of similar return until the end of the project's life.

- **All cash flows can be predicted with certainty.** The outcomes of business investments are full of uncertainty, as the Holland America Line Feature Story shows. There is no way of knowing how popular a new product will be, how long a new machine will last, or what competitors' reactions might be to changes in a product. But, in order to make investment decisions, analysts must estimate future outcomes. In this chapter, we have assumed that future amounts are known with certainty.[1] In reality, little is known with certainty. More advanced capital budgeting techniques deal with uncertainty by considering the probability that various outcomes will occur.

> DO IT!

Net Present Value

Watertown Paper Corporation is considering adding another machine for the manufacture of corrugated cardboard. The machine would cost $900,000. It would have an estimated life of 6 years and no salvage value. The company estimates that annual cash inflows would increase by $400,000 and that annual cash outflows would increase by $190,000. Management has a required rate of return of 9%. Calculate the net present value on this project and discuss whether it should be accepted.

Action Plan

✔ Estimated annual cash inflows − Estimated annual cash outflows = Net annual cash flow.

✔ Use the NPV technique to calculate the difference between net cash flows and the initial investment.

✔ Accept the project if the net present value is positive.

Solution

Estimated annual cash inflows	$400,000
Estimated annual cash outflows	190,000
Net annual cash flow	$210,000

	Cash Flow	9% Discount Factor	Present Value
Present value of net annual cash flows	$210,000	4.48592[a]	$942,043
Capital investment			900,000
Net present value			$ 42,043

[a]Table 4, Appendix A, 9%, 6 years

Since the net present value is greater than zero, Watertown should accept the project.

Related exercise material: **BE12-2, BE12-3, E12-1, E12-2, E12-3, and DO IT! 12-2.**

✔ **The Navigator**

---

[1]One exception is a brief discussion of sensitivity analysis later in the chapter.

Comprehensive Example

Best Taste Foods is considering investing in new equipment to produce fat-free snack foods. Management believes that although demand for fat-free foods has leveled off, fat-free foods are here to stay. The following estimated costs, cost of capital, and cash flows were determined in consultation with the marketing, production, and finance departments.

Illustration 12-12

Investment information for Best Taste Foods example

Initial investment	$1,000,000
Cost of equipment overhaul in 5 years	$200,000
Salvage value of equipment in 10 years	$20,000
Cost of capital (discount rate)	15%
Estimated annual cash flows	
Cash inflows received from sales	$500,000
Cash outflows for cost of goods sold	$200,000
Maintenance costs	$30,000
Other direct operating costs	$40,000

Remember that we are using cash flows in our analysis, not accrual revenues and expenses. Thus, for example, the direct operating costs would not include depreciation expense, since depreciation expense does not use cash. Illustration 12-13 presents the computation of the net annual cash flows of this project.

Illustration 12-13

Computation of net annual cash flow

Cash inflows received from sales	$ 500,000
Cash outflows for cost of goods sold	(200,000)
Maintenance costs	(30,000)
Other direct operating costs	(40,000)
Net annual cash flow	**$230,000**

Illustration 12-14 shows computation of the net present value for this proposed investment (discount factors from Appendix A, Table 4).

Illustration 12-14

Computation of net present value for Best Taste Foods investment

Event	Time Period	Cash Flow	×	15% Discount Factor	=	Present Value
Equipment purchase	0	$1,000,000		1.00000		$(1,000,000)
Equipment overhaul	5	200,000		.49718		(99,436)
Net annual cash flow	1–10	230,000		5.01877		1,154,317
Salvage value	10	20,000		.24719		4,944
Net present value						**$ 59,825**

Because the net present value of the project is positive, Best Taste should accept the project.

DECISION TOOLKIT

DECISION CHECKPOINTS	INFO NEEDED FOR DECISION	TOOL TO USE FOR DECISION	HOW TO EVALUATE RESULTS
Should the company invest in a proposed project?	Cash flow estimates, discount rate	Net present value $=$ Present value of net cash flows less capital investment	The investment is financially acceptable if net present value is positive.

Additional Considerations

Now that you understand how the net present value method works, we can add some "additional wrinkles." Specifically, these are the impact of intangible benefits, a way to compare mutually exclusive projects, refinements that take risk into account, and the need to conduct post-audits of investment projects.

Intangible Benefits

The NPV evaluation techniques employed thus far rely on tangible costs and benefits that can be relatively easily quantified. Some investment projects, especially high-tech projects, fail to make it through initial capital budget screens because only the project's tangible benefits are considered. *Intangible benefits* might include increased quality, improved safety, or enhanced employee loyalty. By ignoring intangible benefits, capital budgeting techniques might incorrectly eliminate projects that could be financially beneficial to the company.

To avoid rejecting projects that actually should be accepted, analysts suggest two possible approaches:

1. Calculate net present value ignoring intangible benefits. Then, if the NPV is negative, ask whether the project offers any intangible benefits that are worth at least the amount of the negative NPV.

2. Project rough, conservative estimates of the value of the intangible benefits, and incorporate these values into the NPV calculation.

EXAMPLE

Assume that Berg Company is considering the purchase of a new mechanical robot to be used for soldering electrical connections. Illustration 12-15 shows the estimates related to this proposed purchase (discount factors from Appendix A, Table 4).

Initial investment	$200,000
Annual cash inflows	$ 50,000
Annual cash outflows	20,000
Net annual cash flow	**$ 30,000**
Estimated life of equipment	10 years
Discount rate	12%

Illustration 12-15
Investment information for Berg Company example

	Cash Flows	×	12% Discount Factor	=	Present Value
Present value of net annual cash flows	$30,000	×	5.65022	=	$169,507
Initial investment					200,000
Net present value					**$(30,493)**

Based on the negative net present value of $30,493, the proposed project is not acceptable. This calculation, however, ignores important information. First, the company's engineers believe that purchasing this machine will dramatically improve the quality of electrical connections in the company's products. As a result, future warranty costs will be reduced. Also, the company believes that this higher quality will translate into higher future sales. Finally, the new machine will be much safer than the previous one.

Berg can incorporate this new information into the capital budgeting decision in the two ways discussed earlier. First, management might simply ask whether the reduced warranty costs, increased sales, and improved safety benefits have an estimated total present value to the company of at least $30,493. If yes, then the project is acceptable.

Alternatively, analysts can estimate the annual cash flows of these benefits. In our initial calculation, we assumed each of these benefits to have a value of zero. It seems likely that their actual values are much higher than zero. Given the difficulty of estimating these benefits, however, conservative values should be assigned to them. If, after using conservative estimates, the net present value is positive, Berg should accept the project.

To illustrate, assume that Berg estimates that improved sales will increase cash inflows by $10,000 annually as a result of an increase in perceived quality. Berg also estimates that annual cost outflows would be reduced by $5,000 as a result of lower warranty claims, reduced injury claims, and missed work. Consideration of the intangible benefits results in the following revised NPV calculation (discount factors from Appendix A, Table 4).

Illustration 12-16
Revised investment information for Berg Company example, including intangible benefits

Initial investment	$200,000	
Annual cash inflows (revised)	$ 60,000 ($50,000 + $10,000)	
Annual cash outflows (revised)	15,000 ($20,000 − $5,000)	
Net annual cash flow	**$ 45,000**	
Estimated life of equipment	10 years	
Discount rate	12%	

	Cash Flows	×	12% Discount Factor	=	Present Value
Present value of net annual cash flows	$45,000	×	5.65022	=	$254,260
Initial investment					200,000
Net present value					**$ 54,260**

Using these conservative estimates of the value of the additional benefits, Berg should accept the project.

ETHICS INSIGHT

It Need Not Cost an Arm and a Leg

Most manufacturers say that employee safety matters above everything else. But how many back up this statement with investments that improve employee safety? Recently, a woodworking hobbyist, who also happens to be a patent attorney with a Ph.D. in physics, invented a mechanism that automatically shuts down a power saw when the saw blade comes in contact with human flesh. The blade stops so quickly that only minor injuries result.

Power saws injure 40,000 Americans each year, and 4,000 of those injuries are bad enough to require amputation. Therefore, one might think that power-saw companies would be lined up to incorporate this mechanism into their saws. But, in the words of one power-tool company, "Safety doesn't sell." Since existing saw manufacturers were unwilling to incorporate the device into their saws, eventually the inventor started his own company to build the devices and sell them directly to businesses that use power saws.

Source: Melba Newsome, "An Edgy New Idea," *Time: Inside Business* (May 2006), p. A16.

? In addition to the obvious humanitarian benefit of reducing serious injuries, how else might the manufacturer of this product convince potential customers of its worth? (See page 584.)

Profitability Index for Mutually Exclusive Projects

In theory, companies should accept all projects with positive NPVs. However, companies rarely are able to adopt all positive-NPV proposals. First, proposals often are **mutually exclusive**. This means that if the company adopts one proposal, it would be impossible also to adopt the other proposal. For example, a company may be considering the purchase of a new packaging machine and is looking at various brands and models. It needs only one packaging machine. Once the company has determined which brand and model to purchase, the others will not be purchased—even though they also may have positive net present values.

LEARNING OBJECTIVE   5

Describe the profitability index.

Even in instances where projects are not mutually exclusive, managers often must choose between various positive-NPV projects because of **limited resources**. For example, the company might have ideas for two new lines of business, each of which has a projected positive NPV. However, both of these proposals require skilled personnel, and the company determines that it will not be able to find enough skilled personnel to staff both projects. Management will have to choose the project it thinks is a better option.

When choosing between alternative proposals, it is tempting simply to choose the project with the higher NPV. Consider the following example of two mutually exclusive projects. Each is assumed to have a 10-year life and a 12% discount rate (discount factors from Appendix A, Tables 3 and 4). Illustration 12-17 shows the estimates for each project and the computation of the present value of the net annual cash flows.

	Project A	Project B
Initial investment	$40,000	$ 90,000
Net annual cash inflow	10,000	19,000
Salvage value	5,000	10,000
Present value of net annual cash flows		
($10,000 × 5.65022) + ($5,000 × .32197)	58,112	
($19,000 × 5.65022) + ($10,000 × .32197)		110,574

Illustration 12-17
Investment information for mutually exclusive projects

Illustration 12-18 computes the net present values of Project A and Project B by subtracting the initial investment from the present value of the net annual cash flows.

	Project A	Project B
Present value of net annual cash flows	$ 58,112	$110,574
Initial investment	40,000	90,000
Net present value	**$18,112**	**$ 20,574**

Illustration 12-18
Net present value computation

Project B has the higher NPV, and so it would seem that the company should adopt B. Note, however, that Project B also requires more than twice the original investment of Project A. In choosing between the two projects, the company should also include in its calculations the amount of the original investment.

One relatively simple method of comparing alternative projects is the **profitability index**. This method takes into account both the size of the original investment and the discounted cash flows. The profitability index is calculated by dividing the present value of net cash flows that occur after the initial investment by the amount of the initial investment.

Present Value of Net Cash Flows	÷	**Initial Investment**	=	**Profitability Index**

Illustration 12-19
Formula for profitability index

The profitability index allows comparison of the relative desirability of projects that require differing initial investments. Note that any project with a positive

NPV will have a profitability index above 1. The profitability index for each of the mutually exclusive projects is calculated below.

Illustration 12-20
Calculation of profitability index

$$\text{Profitability Index} = \frac{\text{Present Value of Net Cash Flows}}{\text{Initial Investment}}$$

Project A	Project B
$\dfrac{\$58,112}{\$40,000} = 1.45$	$\dfrac{\$110,574}{\$90,000} = 1.23$

In this case, the profitability index of Project A exceeds that of Project B. Thus, Project A is more desirable. Again, if these were not mutually exclusive projects and if resources were not limited, then the company should invest in both projects since both have positive NPVs. Additional considerations related to preference decisions are discussed in more advanced courses.

DECISION TOOLKIT

DECISION CHECKPOINTS	INFO NEEDED FOR DECISION	TOOL TO USE FOR DECISION	HOW TO EVALUATE RESULTS
Which investment proposal should a company accept?	Estimated cash flows and discount rate for each proposal	$\text{Profitability index} = \dfrac{\text{Present value of net cash flows}}{\text{Initial investment}}$	The investment proposal with the highest profitability index should be accepted.

Risk Analysis

A simplifying assumption made by many financial analysts is that projected results are known with certainty. In reality, projected results are only estimates based upon the forecaster's belief as to the most probable outcome. One approach for dealing with such uncertainty is **sensitivity analysis**. Sensitivity analysis uses a number of outcome estimates to get a sense of the variability among potential returns. An example of sensitivity analysis was presented in Illustration 12-11 (page 554), where we illustrated the impact on NPV of different discount rate assumptions. A higher-risk project would be evaluated using a higher discount rate.

Similarly, to take into account that more distant cash flows are often more uncertain, a higher discount rate can be used to discount more distant cash flows. Other techniques to address uncertainty are discussed in advanced courses.

MANAGEMENT INSIGHT

Wide-Screen Capacity

Building a new factory to produce 50- and even 60-inch TV screens can cost $4 billion. But for more than 10 years, manufacturers of these screens have continued to build new plants. By building so many plants, they have expanded productive capacity at a rate that has exceeded the demand for big-screen TVs. In fact, during one recent year, the supply of big-screen TVs was estimated to exceed demand by 12%, rising to 16% in the future. One state-of-the-art plant built by Sharp was estimated to be operating at only 50% of capacity. Experts say that the price of big-screen TVs will have to fall much further than they already have before demand may eventually catch up with productive capacity.

Source: James Simms, "Sharp's Payoff Delayed," *Wall Street Journal Online* (September 14, 2010).

? What implications does the excess capacity have for the cash payback and net present value calculations of these investments? (See page 584.)

Post-Audit of Investment Projects

Any well-run organization should perform an evaluation, called a **post-audit**, of its investment projects after their completion. A post-audit is a thorough evaluation of how well a project's actual performance matches the original projections. An example of a post-audit is seen in a situation that occurred at Campbell Soup. The company made the original decision to invest in the Intelligent Quisine line based on management's best estimates of future cash flows. During the development phase of the project, Campbell hired an outside consulting firm to evaluate the project's potential for success. Because actual results during the initial years were far below the estimated results and because the future also did not look promising, the project was terminated.

LEARNING OBJECTIVE 6

Indicate the benefits of performing a post-audit.

Performing a post-audit is important for a variety of reasons. First, if managers know that the company will compare their estimates to actual results, they will be more likely to submit reasonable and accurate data when they make investment proposals. This clearly is better for the company than for managers to submit overly optimistic estimates in an effort to get pet projects approved. Second, as seen with Campbell Soup, a post-audit provides a formal mechanism by which the company can determine whether existing projects should be supported or terminated. Third, post-audits improve future investment proposals because, by evaluating past successes and failures, managers improve their estimation techniques.

A post-audit involves the same evaluation techniques used in making the original capital budgeting decision—for example, use of the NPV method. The difference is that, in the post-audit, analysts insert actual figures, where known, and they revise estimates of future amounts based on new information. The managers responsible for the estimates used in the original proposal must explain the reasons for any significant differences between their estimates and actual results.

Post-audits are not foolproof. In the case of Campbell Soup, some observers suggested that the company was too quick to abandon the project. Industry analysts suggested that with more time and more advertising expenditures, the company might have enjoyed success.

MANAGEMENT INSIGHT

Seeing the Big Picture

Inaccurate trend forecasting and market positioning are more detrimental to capital investment decisions than using the wrong discount rate. Ampex patented the VCR but failed to see its market potential. Westinghouse made the same mistake with the flat-screen video display. More often, companies adopt projects or businesses only to discontinue them in response to market changes. Texas Instruments announced it would stop manufacturing computer chips, after it had made substantial capital investments that enabled it to become one of the world's leading suppliers. The company dropped out of some 12 business lines in only a few years.

Source: World Research Advisory Inc. (London, August 1998), p. 4.

? How important is the choice of discount rate in making capital budgeting decisions? (See page 584.)

Other Capital Budgeting Techniques

Some companies use capital budgeting techniques other than, or in addition to, the cash payback and net present value methods. In this section, we will briefly discuss these other approaches.

Internal Rate of Return Method

The **internal rate of return method** differs from the net present value method in that it finds the **interest yield of the potential investment**. The **internal rate of return (IRR)** is the interest rate that will cause the present value of the proposed capital expenditure to equal the present value of the expected net annual cash flows (that is, NPV equal to zero). Because it recognizes the time value of money, the internal rate of return method is (like the NPV method) a discounted cash flow technique.

How do we determine the internal rate of return? One way is to use a financial calculator (see Appendix A, Section Three) or computerized spreadsheet to solve for this rate. Or, we can use a trial-and-error procedure.

To illustrate, assume that Stewart Shipping Company is considering the purchase of a new front-end loader at a cost of $244,371. Net annual cash flows from this loader are estimated to be $100,000 a year for three years. To determine the internal rate of return on this front-end loader, the company finds the discount rate that results in a net present value of zero. As Illustration 12-21 shows, at a rate of return of 10%, Stewart Shipping has a positive net present value of $4,315. At a rate of return of 12%, it has a negative net present value of $4,188. At an 11% rate, the net present value is zero. Therefore, 11% is the internal rate of return for this investment (discount factors from Appendix A, Table 3).

Illustration 12-21
Estimation of internal rate of return

Year	Net Annual Cash Flows	Discount Factor 10%	Present Value 10%	Discount Factor 11%	Present Value 11%	Discount Factor 12%	Present Value 12%
1	$100,000	.90909	$ 90,909	.90090	$ 90,090	.89286	$ 89,286
2	$100,000	.82645	82,645	.81162	81,162	.79719	79,719
3	$100,000	.75132	75,132	.73119	73,119	.71178	71,178
			248,686		244,371		240,183
Less: Initial investment			244,371		244,371		244,371
Net present value			$ 4,315		$ –0–		$ (4,188)

An easier approach to solving for the internal rate of return can be used if the net annual cash flows are **equal**, as in the Stewart Shipping example. In this special case, we can find the internal rate of return using the following formula.

Illustration 12-22
Formula for internal rate of return—even cash flows

$$\text{Capital Investment} \div \text{Net Annual Cash Flows} = \text{Internal Rate of Return Factor}$$

Applying this formula to the Stewart Shipping example, we find:

$$\$244,371 \div \$100,000 = 2.44371$$

We then look up the factor 2.44371 in Table 4 of Appendix A in the three-payment row and find it under 11%. Row 3 is reproduced below for your convenience.

Table 4 Present Value of an Annuity of 1										
(n) Payments	**4%**	**5%**	**6%**	**7%**	**8%**	**9%**	**10%**	**11%**	**12%**	**15%**
3	2.77509	2.72325	2.67301	2.62432	2.57710	2.53130	2.48685	**2.44371**	2.40183	2.28323

Recognize that if the cash flows are **uneven**, then a trial-and-error approach or a financial calculator or computerized spreadsheet must be used.

Once managers know the internal rate of return, they compare it to the company's required rate of return (the discount rate). The IRR decision rule is as follows: **Accept the project when the internal rate of return is equal to or greater than the required rate of return. Reject the project when the internal rate of return is less than the required rate of return.** Illustration 12-23 shows these relationships. The internal rate of return method is widely used in practice, largely because most managers find the internal rate of return easy to interpret.

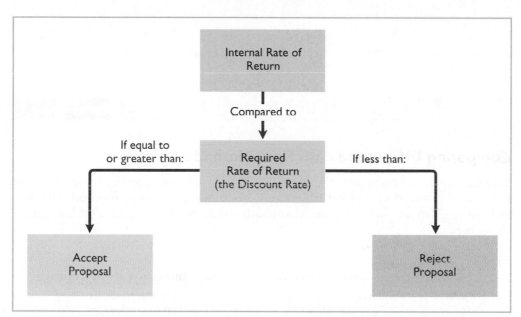

Illustration 12-23
Internal rate of return decision criteria

DECISION TOOLKIT

DECISION CHECKPOINTS	INFO NEEDED FOR DECISION	TOOL TO USE FOR DECISION	HOW TO EVALUATE RESULTS
Should the company invest in a proposed project?	Estimated cash flows and the required rate of return (hurdle rate)	Internal rate of return = Interest rate that results in a net present value of zero	If the internal rate of return exceeds the required rate of return for the project, then the project is financially acceptable.

> ## DO IT!

Internal Rate of Return

Watertown Paper Corporation is considering adding another machine for the manufacture of corrugated cardboard. The machine would cost $900,000. It would have an estimated life of 6 years and no salvage value. The company estimates that annual cash inflows would increase by $400,000 and that annual cash outflows would increase by $190,000. Management has a required rate of return of 9%. Calculate the internal rate of return on this project and discuss whether it should be accepted.

Action Plan

✔ Estimated annual cash inflows − Estimated annual cash outflows = Net annual cash flow.

✔ Capital investment/Net annual cash flows = Internal rate of return factor.

✔ Look up the factor in the present value of an annuity table to find the internal rate of return.

✔ Accept the project if the internal rate of return is equal to or greater than the required rate of return.

Solution

Estimated annual cash inflows	$400,000
Estimated annual cash outflows	190,000
Net annual cash flow	$210,000

$900,000/210,000 = 4.285714$. Using Table 4 of Appendix A and the factors that correspond with the six-payment row, 4.285714 is between the factors for 10% and 11%. Since the project has an internal rate that is greater than 10% and the required rate of return is only 9%, the project should be accepted.

Related exercise material: **BE12-7, BE12-8, E12-5, E12-6, E12-7,** and **DO IT! 12-3.**

✔ **The Navigator**

Comparing Discounted Cash Flow Methods

Illustration 12-24 compares the two discounted cash flow methods—net present value and internal rate of return. When properly used, either method will provide management with relevant quantitative data for making capital budgeting decisions.

Illustration 12-24
Comparison of discounted cash flow methods

	Net Present Value	Internal Rate of Return
1. Objective	Compute net present value (a dollar amount).	Compute internal rate of return (a percentage).
2. Decision Rule	If net present value is zero or positive, accept the proposal. If net present value is negative, reject the proposal.	If internal rate of return is equal to or greater than the required rate of return, accept the proposal. If internal rate of return is less than the required rate of return, reject the proposal.

Annual Rate of Return Method

LEARNING OBJECTIVE   8

Describe the annual rate of return method.

The final capital budgeting technique we will look at is the **annual rate of return method**. It is based directly on accrual accounting data rather than on cash flows. It indicates **the profitability of a capital expenditure** by dividing expected annual net income by the average investment. Illustration 12-25 shows the formula for computing annual rate of return.

Illustration 12-25
Annual rate of return formula

$$\frac{\text{Expected Annual}}{\text{Net Income}} \div \frac{\text{Average}}{\text{Investment}} = \frac{\text{Annual Rate}}{\text{of Return}}$$

Assume that Reno Company is considering an investment of $130,000 in new equipment. The new equipment is expected to last five years and have zero salvage value at the end of its useful life. Reno uses the straight-line method of depreciation for accounting purposes. The expected annual revenues and costs of the new product that will be produced from the investment are:

Sales			$200,000
Less: Costs and expenses			
Manufacturing costs (exclusive of depreciation)		$132,000	
Depreciation expense ($130,000 ÷ 5)		26,000	
Selling and administrative expenses		22,000	180,000
Income before income taxes			20,000
Income tax expense			7,000
Net income			$ 13,000

Illustration 12-26
Estimated annual net income from Reno Company's capital expenditure

Reno's expected annual net income is $13,000. Average investment is derived from the formula shown below.

$$\frac{\text{Original Investment} + \text{Value at End of Useful Life}}{2} = \text{Average Investment}$$

Illustration 12-27
Formula for computing average investment

The value at the end of useful life is equal to the asset's salvage value, if any. For Reno, average investment is $65,000 [($130,000 + $0) ÷ 2]. The expected annual rate of return for Reno's investment in new equipment is therefore 20%, computed as follows.

$$\$13,000 ÷ \$65,000 = 20\%$$

Management then compares the annual rate of return with its **required rate of return** for investments of similar risk. The required rate of return is generally based on the company's cost of capital. The decision rule is: **A project is acceptable if its rate of return is greater than management's required rate of return. It is unacceptable when the reverse is true.** When companies use the rate of return technique in deciding among several acceptable projects, **the higher the rate of return for a given risk, the more attractive the investment**.

The principal advantages of this method are the simplicity of its calculation and management's familiarity with the accounting terms used in the computation. A major limitation of the annual rate of return method is that it does not consider the time value of money. For example, no consideration is given as to whether cash inflows will occur early or late in the life of the investment. As explained in Appendix A, recognition of the time value of money can make a significant difference between the future value and the discounted present value of an investment. A second disadvantage is that this method relies on accrual accounting numbers rather than expected cash flows.

Helpful Hint
A capital budgeting decision based on only one technique may be misleading. It is often wise to analyze an investment from a number of different perspectives.

> **DO IT!**

Annual Rate of Return

Watertown Paper Corporation is considering adding another machine for the manufacture of corrugated cardboard. The machine would cost $900,000. It would have an estimated life of 6 years and no salvage value. The company estimates that annual revenues would increase by $400,000 and that annual expenses excluding depreciation would increase by $190,000. It uses the straight-line method to compute depreciation expense. Management has a required rate of return of 9%. Compute the annual rate of return.

Action Plan

✔ Expected annual net income = Annual revenues − Annual expenses (including depreciation expense).

✔ Annual rate of return = Expected annual net income/Average investment.

✔ Average investment = (Original investment + Value at end of useful life)/2.

Solution

Revenues		$400,000
Less:		
Expenses (excluding depreciation)	$190,000	
Depreciation ($900,000/6 years)	150,000	340,000
Annual net income		$ 60,000

Average investment = ($900,000 + 0)/2 = $450,000.
Annual rate of return = $60,000/$450,000 = 13.3%.

Since the annual rate of return (13.33%) is greater than Watertown's required rate of return (9%), the proposed project is acceptable.

Related exercise material: **BE12-9, E12-8, E12-9, E12-10, E12-11, and DO IT! 12-4.**

✔ **The Navigator**

USING THE DECISION TOOLKIT

Campbell Soup is considering expanding its international presence. It sells 38% of the soup consumed in the United States but only 2% of soup worldwide. Thus, the company believes that it has great potential for international sales. Recently, 20% of Campbell's sales were in foreign markets (and nearly all of that was in Europe). Its goal is to have 30% of its sales be in foreign markets. In order to accomplish this goal, the company will have to invest heavily.

In recent years, Campbell has spent between $300 and $400 million on capital expenditures. Suppose that Campbell is interested in expanding its South American presence by building a new production facility. After considering tax, marketing, labor, transportation, and political issues, Campbell has determined that the most desirable location is either in Buenos Aires or Rio de Janeiro. The following estimates have been provided. (All amounts are stated in U.S. dollars.)

	Buenos Aires	Rio de Janeiro
Initial investment	$2,500,000	$1,400,000
Estimated useful life	20 years	20 years
Annual revenues (accrual)	$500,000	$380,000
Annual expenses (accrual)	$200,000	$180,000
Annual cash inflows	$550,000	$430,000
Annual cash outflows	$222,250	$206,350
Estimated salvage value	$500,000	$0
Discount rate	9%	9%

Instructions

Evaluate each of these mutually exclusive proposals employing (a) cash payback, (b) net present value, (c) the profitability index, (d) the internal rate of return, and (e) annual rate of return. Discuss the implications of your findings.

Solution

	Buenos Aires	Rio de Janeiro
(a) Cash payback	$\dfrac{\$2,500,000}{\$327,750^{*}} = 7.63$ years	$\dfrac{\$1,400,000}{\$223,650^{**}} = 6.26$ years

*$550,000 − $222,250; **$430,000 − $206,350

(b) Net present value
Present value of net cash flows

$327,750 × 9.12855 =	$2,991,882	$223,650 × 9.12855 = $2,041,600	
$500,000 × 0.17843 =	89,215		
	3,081,097		
Less: Initial investment	2,500,000	1,400,000	
Net present value	$ 581,097	$ 641,600	

(c) Profitability index

$$\frac{\$3,081,097}{\$2,500,000} = 1.23 \qquad \frac{\$2,041,600}{\$1,400,000} = 1.46$$

(d) Internal rate of return: The internal rate of return can be approximated by experimenting with different discount rates to see which one comes the closest to resulting in a net present value of zero. Doing this, we find that Buenos Aires has an internal rate of return of approximately 12%, while the internal rate of return of the Rio de Janeiro location is approximately 15% as shown below. Rio, therefore, is preferable.

Buenos Aires

Internal rate of return

Cash Flows	×	12% Discount Factor	=	Present Value
$327,750	×	7.46944	=	$2,448,109
$500,000	×	0.10367	=	51,835
				$2,499,944
Less: Capital investment				2,500,000
Net present value				$ (56)

Rio de Janeiro

Cash Flows	×	15% Discount Factor	=	Present Value
$223,650	×	6.25933	=	$1,399,899
				1,400,000
				$ (101)

(e) Annual rate of return

Average investment
$$\frac{(\$2,500,000 + \$500,000)}{2} = \$1,500,000 \qquad \frac{(\$1,400,000 + \$0)}{2} = \$700,000$$

Annual rate of return $\dfrac{\$300,000^*}{\$1,500,000} = .20 = 20\%$ $\qquad \dfrac{\$200,000^{**}}{\$700,000} = .286 = 28.6\%$

*$500,000 − $200,000; **$380,000 − $180,000

Implications: Although the annual rate of return is higher for Rio de Janeiro, this method has the disadvantage of ignoring time value of money, as well as using accrual numbers rather than cash flows. The cash payback of Rio de Janeiro is also shorter, but this method also ignores the time value of money. Thus, while these two methods can be used for a quick assessment, neither should be relied upon as the sole evaluation tool.

From the net present value calculation, it would appear that the two projects are nearly identical in their acceptability. However, the profitability index indicates that the Rio de Janeiro investment is far more desirable because it generates its cash flows with a much smaller initial investment. A similar result is found by using the internal rate of return. Overall, assuming that the company will invest in only one project, it would appear that the Rio de Janeiro project should be chosen.

✔ **The Navigator**

SUMMARY OF LEARNING OBJECTIVES

✔ **The Navigator**

1 Discuss capital budgeting evaluation, and explain inputs used in capital budgeting. Management gathers project proposals from each department; a capital budget committee screens the proposals and recommends worthy projects. Company officers decide which projects to fund, and the board of directors approves the capital budget. In capital budgeting, estimated cash inflows and outflows, rather than accrual-accounting numbers, are the preferred inputs.

2 Describe the cash payback technique. The cash payback technique identifies the time period required to recover the cost of the investment. The formula when net annual cash flows are equal is: Cost of capital investment ÷ Estimated net annual cash flow = Cash payback period. The shorter the payback period, the more attractive the investment.

3 Explain the net present value method. The net present value method compares the present value of future cash inflows with the capital investment to determine net present value. The NPV decision rule is: Accept the project if net present value is zero or positive. Reject the project if net present value is negative.

4 Identify the challenges presented by intangible benefits in capital budgeting. Intangible benefits are difficult to quantify and thus are often ignored in capital budgeting decisions. This can result in incorrectly rejecting some projects. One method for considering intangible benefits is to calculate the NPV, ignoring intangible benefits. If the resulting NPV is below zero, evaluate whether the benefits are worth at least the amount of the negative net present value. Alternatively, intangible benefits can be incorporated into the NPV calculation, using conservative estimates of their value.

5 Describe the profitability index. The profitability index is a tool for comparing the relative merits of alternative capital investment opportunities. It is computed as: Present value of net cash flows ÷ Initial investment. The higher the index, the more desirable the project.

6 Indicate the benefits of performing a post-audit. A post-audit is an evaluation of a capital investment's actual performance. Post-audits create an incentive for managers to make accurate estimates. Post-audits also are useful for determining whether a company should continue, expand, or terminate a project. Finally, post-audits provide feedback that is useful for improving estimation techniques.

7 Explain the internal rate of return method. The objective of the internal rate of return method is to find the interest yield of the potential investment, which is expressed as a percentage rate. The IRR decision rule is: Accept the project when the internal rate of return is equal to or greater than the required rate of return. Reject the project when the internal rate of return is less than the required rate of return.

8 Describe the annual rate of return method. The annual rate of return uses accrual accounting data to indicate the profitability of a capital investment. It is calculated as: Expected annual net income ÷ Amount of the average investment. The higher the rate of return, the more attractive the investment.

DECISION TOOLKIT A SUMMARY

DECISION CHECKPOINTS	INFO NEEDED FOR DECISION	TOOL TO USE FOR DECISION	HOW TO EVALUATE RESULTS
Should the company invest in a proposed project?	Cash flow estimates, discount rate	Net present value $=$ Present value of net cash flows less capital investment	The investment is financially acceptable if net present value is positive.
Which investment proposal should a company accept?	Estimated cash flows and discount rate for each proposal	Profitability index $=$ $\dfrac{\text{Present value of net cash flows}}{\text{Initial investment}}$	The investment proposal with the highest profitability index should be accepted.
Should the company invest in a proposed project?	Estimated cash flows and the required rate of return (hurdle rate)	Internal rate of return $=$ Interest rate that results in a net present value of zero	If the internal rate of return exceeds the required rate of return for the project, then the project is financially acceptable.

GLOSSARY

Annual rate of return method The determination of the profitability of a capital expenditure, computed by dividing expected annual net income by the average investment. (p. 564).

Capital budgeting The process of making capital expenditure decisions in business. (p. 547).

Cash payback technique A capital budgeting technique that identifies the time period required to recover the cost of a capital investment from the net annual cash flow produced by the investment. (p. 550).

Cost of capital The average rate of return that the firm must pay to obtain funds from creditors and stockholders. (p. 554).

Discounted cash flow technique A capital budgeting technique that considers both the estimated net cash flows from the investment and the time value of money. (p. 551).

Discount rate The interest rate used in discounting the future net cash flows to determine present value. (p. 552).

Internal rate of return (IRR) The interest rate that will cause the present value of the proposed capital expenditure to equal the present value of the expected net annual cash flows. (p. 562).

Internal rate of return (IRR) method A method used in capital budgeting that results in finding the interest yield of the potential investment. (p. 562).

Net present value (NPV) The difference that results when the original capital outlay is subtracted from the discounted net cash flows. (p. 552).

Net present value (NPV) method A method used in capital budgeting in which net cash flows are discounted to their present value and then compared to the capital outlay required by the investment. (p. 551).

Post-audit A thorough evaluation of how well a project's actual performance matches the original projections. (p. 561).

Profitability index A method of comparing alternative projects that takes into account both the size of the investment and its discounted future net cash flows. It is computed by dividing the present value of net future cash flows by the initial investment. (p. 559).

Required rate of return The rate of return management expects on investments; also called the *discount rate or cost of capital*. (p. 565).

> Comprehensive **DO IT!**

Cornfield Company is considering a long-term capital investment project in laser equipment. This will require an investment of $280,000, and it will have a useful life of 5 years. Annual net income is expected to be $16,000 a year. Depreciation is computed by the straight-line method with no salvage value. The company's cost of capital is 10%. (*Hint:* Assume cash flows can be computed by adding back depreciation expense.)

Instructions
(Round all computations to two decimal places.)
(a) Compute the cash payback period for the project. (Round to two decimals.)
(b) Compute the net present value for the project. (Round to nearest dollar.)
(c) Compute the annual rate of return for the project.
(d) Should the project be accepted? Why?

Solution to Comprehensive DO IT!

Action Plan

✔ Calculate the time it will take to pay back the investment: cost of the investment divided by net annual cash flows.

✔ When calculating NPV, remember that net annual cash flow equals annual net income plus annual depreciation expense.

✔ Be careful to use the correct discount factor in using the net present value method.

✔ Calculate the annual rate of return: expected annual net income divided by average investment.

(a) $280,000 ÷ $72,000 ($16,000 + $56,000) = 3.89 years

(b)

	Present Value at 10%
Discount factor for 5 payments	3.79079
Present value of net cash flows: $72,000 × 3.79079	$272,937
Capital investment	280,000
Negative net present value	$ (7,063)

(c) $16,000 ÷ $140,000 ($280,000 ÷ 2) = 11.4%
(d) The annual rate of return of 11.4% is good. However, the cash payback period is 78% of the project's useful life, and net present value is negative. The recommendation is to reject the project.

✔ **The Navigator**

Self-Test, Brief Exercises, Exercises, Problem Set A, and many more resources are available for practice in WileyPLUS.

SELF-TEST QUESTIONS

Answers are at the end of the chapter.

(LO 1) **1.** Which of the following is *not* an example of a capital budgeting decision?
   (a) Decision to build a new plant.
   (b) Decision to renovate an existing facility.
   (c) Decision to buy a piece of machinery.
   (d) All of these are capital budgeting decisions.

(LO 1) **2.** What is the order of involvement of the following parties in the capital budgeting authorization process?
   (a) Plant managers, officers, capital budget committee, board of directors.

   (b) Board of directors, plant managers, officers, capital budget committee.
   (c) Plant managers, capital budget committee, officers, board of directors.
   (d) Officers, plant managers, capital budget committee, board of directors.

3. What is a weakness of the cash payback approach?   (LO 2)
   (a) It uses accrual-based accounting numbers.
   (b) It ignores the time value of money.
   (c) It ignores the useful life of alternative projects.
   (d) Both (b) and (c) are true.

(LO 2) **4.** Siegel Industries is considering two capital budgeting projects. Project A requires an initial investment of $48,000. It is expected to produce net annual cash flows of $7,000. Project B requires an initial investment of $75,000 and is expected to produce net annual cash flows of $12,000. Using the cash payback technique to evaluate the two projects, Siegel should accept:
(a) Project A because it has a shorter cash payback period.
(b) Project B because it has a shorter cash payback period.
(c) Project A because it requires a smaller initial investment.
(d) Project B because it produces a larger net annual cash flow.

(LO 3) **5.** Which is a true statement regarding using a higher discount rate to calculate the net present value of a project?
(a) It will make it less likely that the project will be accepted.
(b) It will make it more likely that the project will be accepted.
(c) It is appropriate to use a higher rate if the project is perceived as being less risky than other projects being considered.
(d) It is appropriate to use a higher rate if the project will have a short useful life relative to other projects being considered.

(LO 3) **6.** A positive net present value means that the:
(a) project's rate of return is less than the cutoff rate.
(b) project's rate of return exceeds the required rate of return.
(c) project's rate of return equals the required rate of return.
(d) project is unacceptable.

(LO 3) **7.** Which of the following is *not* an alternative name for the discount rate?
(a) Hurdle rate.
(b) Required rate of return.
(c) Cutoff rate.
(d) All of these are alternative names for the discount rate.

(LO 4) **8.** If a project has intangible benefits whose value is hard to estimate, the best thing to do is:
(a) ignore these benefits, since any estimate of their value will most likely be wrong.
(b) include a conservative estimate of their value.
(c) ignore their value in your initial net present value calculation, but then estimate whether their potential value is worth at least the amount of the net present value deficiency.
(d) Either (b) or (c) is correct.

(LO 4) **9.** An example of an intangible benefit provided by a capital budgeting project is:
(a) the salvage value of the capital investment.
(b) a positive net present value.
(c) a decrease in customer complaints due to poor quality.
(d) an internal rate of return greater than zero.

10. The following information is available for a potential (LO 5) capital investment.

Initial investment	$80,000
Salvage value	10,000
Net annual cash flow	14,820
Net present value	18,112
Useful life	10 years

The potential investment's profitability index (rounded to two decimals) is:
(a) 5.40.   (c) 1.23.
(b) 1.19.   (d) 1.40.

11. A post-audit of an investment project should be (LO 6) performed:
(a) on all significant capital expenditure projects.
(b) on all projects that management feels might be financial failures.
(c) on randomly selected projects.
(d) only on projects that enjoy tremendous success.

12. A project should be accepted if its internal rate of (LO 7) return exceeds:
(a) zero.
(b) the rate of return on a government bond.
(c) the company's required rate of return.
(d) the rate the company pays on borrowed funds.

13. The following information is available for a potential (LO 7) capital investment.

Initial investment	$60,000
Net annual cash flow	15,400
Net present value	3,143
Useful life	5 years

The potential investment's internal rate of return is approximately:
(a) 5%.   (c) 4%.
(b) 10%.   (d) 9%.

14. Which of the following is *incorrect* about the annual (LO 8) rate of return technique?
(a) The calculation is simple.
(b) The accounting terms used are familiar to management.
(c) The timing of the cash inflows is not considered.
(d) The time value of money is considered.

15. The following information is available for a potential (LO 8) capital investment.

Initial investment	$120,000
Annual net income	15,000
Net annual cash flow	27,500
Salvage value	20,000
Useful life	8 years

The potential investment's annual rate of return is approximately:
(a) 21%.   (c) 30%.
(b) 15%.   (d) 39%.

Go to the book's companion website, www.wiley.com/college/weygandt, for additional Self-Test Questions.

✔ **The Navigator**

QUESTIONS

1. Describe the process a company may use in screening and approving the capital expenditure budget.
2. What are the advantages and disadvantages of the cash payback technique?
3. Tom Wells claims the formula for the cash payback technique is the same as the formula for the annual rate of return technique. Is Tom correct? What is the formula for the cash payback technique?
4. Two types of present value tables may be used with the discounted cash flow techniques. Identify the tables and the circumstance(s) when each table should be used.
5. What is the decision rule under the net present value method?
6. Discuss the factors that determine the appropriate discount rate to use when calculating the net present value.
7. What simplifying assumptions were made in the chapter regarding calculation of net present value?
8. What are some examples of potential intangible benefits of investment proposals? Why do these intangible benefits complicate the capital budgeting evaluation

process? What might happen if intangible benefits are ignored in a capital budgeting decision?
9. What steps can be taken to incorporate intangible benefits into the capital budget evaluation process?
10. What advantages does the profitability index provide over direct comparison of net present value when comparing two projects?
11. What is a post-audit? What are the potential benefits of a post-audit?
12. Identify the steps required in using the internal rate of return method when the net annual cash flows are equal.
13. El Cajon Company uses the internal rate of return method. What is the decision rule for this method?
14. What are the strengths of the annual rate of return approach? What are its weaknesses?
15. Your classmate, Mike Dawson, is confused about the factors that are included in the annual rate of return technique. What is the formula for this technique?
16. Sveta Pace is trying to understand the term "cost of capital." Define the term and indicate its relevance to the decision rule under the internal rate of return technique.

BRIEF EXERCISES

BE12-1 Bella Company is considering purchasing new equipment for $450,000. It is expected that the equipment will produce net annual cash flows of $50,000 over its 10-year useful life. Annual depreciation will be $45,000. Compute the cash payback period.

Compute the cash payback period for a capital investment.
(LO 2), AP

BE12-2 Hsung Company accumulates the following data concerning a proposed capital investment: cash cost $215,000, net annual cash flows $40,000, present value factor of cash inflows for 10 years 5.65 (rounded). Determine the net present value, and indicate whether the investment should be made.

Compute net present value of an investment.
(LO 3), AN

BE12-3 Magic Corporation, an amusement park, is considering a capital investment in a new exhibit. The exhibit would cost $136,000 and have an estimated useful life of 5 years. It will be sold for $65,000 at that time. (Amusement parks need to rotate exhibits to keep people interested.) It is expected to increase net annual cash flows by $25,000. The company's borrowing rate is 8%. Its cost of capital is 10%. Calculate the net present value of this project to the company.

Compute net present value of an investment.
(LO 3), AP

BE12-4 Caine Bottling Corporation is considering the purchase of a new bottling machine. The machine would cost $200,000 and has an estimated useful life of 8 years with zero salvage value. Management estimates that the new bottling machine will provide net annual cash flows of $34,000. Management also believes that the new bottling machine will save the company money because it is expected to be more reliable than other machines, and thus will reduce downtime. How much would the reduction in downtime have to be worth in order for the project to be acceptable? Assume a discount rate of 9%. (*Hint:* Calculate the net present value.)

Compute net present value of an investment and consider intangible benefits.
(LO 3, 4), AN

BE12-5 Beacon Company is considering two different, mutually exclusive capital expenditure proposals. Project A will cost $400,000, has an expected useful life of 10 years, a salvage value of zero, and is expected to increase net annual cash flows by $70,000. Project B will cost $280,000, has an expected useful life of 10 years, a salvage value of zero, and is expected to increase net annual cash flows by $50,000. A discount rate of 9% is appropriate for both projects. Compute the net present value and profitability index of each project. Which project should be accepted?

Compute net present value and profitability index.
(LO 3, 5), AN

Perform a post-audit.

(LO 6), AN

BE12-6 Quillen Company is performing a post-audit of a project completed one year ago. The initial estimates were that the project would cost $250,000, would have a useful life of 9 years, zero salvage value, and would result in net annual cash flows of $46,000 per year. Now that the investment has been in operation for 1 year, revised figures indicate that it actually cost $260,000, will have a useful life of 11 years, and will produce net annual cash flows of $39,000 per year. Evaluate the success of the project. Assume a discount rate of 10%.

Calculate internal rate of return.

(LO 7), AP

BE12-7 Horowitz Company is evaluating the purchase of a rebuilt spot-welding machine to be used in the manufacture of a new product. The machine will cost $176,000, has an estimated useful life of 7 years, a salvage value of zero, and will increase net annual cash flows by $33,740. What is its approximate internal rate of return?

Calculate internal rate of return.

(LO 7), AN

BE12-8 Viera Corporation is considering investing in a new facility. The estimated cost of the facility is $2,045,000. It will be used for 12 years, then sold for $716,000. The facility will generate annual cash inflows of $400,000 and will need new annual cash outflows of $150,000. The company has a required rate of return of 7%. Calculate the internal rate of return on this project, and discuss whether the project should be accepted.

Compute annual rate of return.

(LO 8), AP

BE12-9 Mecha Oil Company is considering investing in a new oil well. It is expected that the oil well will increase annual revenues by $130,000 and will increase annual expenses by $70,000 including depreciation. The oil well will cost $470,000 and will have a $10,000 salvage value at the end of its 10-year useful life. Calculate the annual rate of return.

> DO IT! REVIEW

Compute the cash payback period for an investment.

(LO 2), AP

DO IT! **12-1** Wallowa Company is considering a long-term investment project called ZIP. ZIP will require an investment of $120,000. It will have a useful life of 4 years and no salvage value. Annual cash inflows would increase by $80,000, and annual cash outflows would increase by $40,000. Compute the cash payback period.

Calculate net present value of an investment.

(LO 3), AN

DO IT! **12-2** Wallowa Company is considering a long-term investment project called ZIP. ZIP will require an investment of $120,000. It will have a useful life of 4 years and no salvage value. Annual cash inflows would increase by $80,000, and annual cash outflows would increase by $40,000. The company's required rate of return is 12%. Calculate the net present value on this project and discuss whether it should be accepted.

Calculate internal rate of return.

(LO 7), AN

DO IT! **12-3** Wallowa Company is considering a long-term investment project called ZIP. ZIP will require an investment of $120,000. It will have a useful life of 4 years and no salvage value. Annual cash inflows would increase by $80,000, and annual cash outflows would increase by $40,000. The company's required rate of return is 12%. Calculate the internal rate of return on this project and discuss whether it should be accepted.

Calculate annual rate of return.

(LO 8), AP

DO IT! **12-4** Wallowa Company is considering a long-term investment project called ZIP. ZIP will require an investment of $120,000. It will have a useful life of 4 years and no salvage value. Annual revenues would increase by $80,000, and annual expenses (excluding depreciation) would increase by $40,000. Wallowa uses the straight-line method to compute depreciation expense. The company's required rate of return is 12%. Compute the annual rate of return.

✔ **The Navigator**

EXERCISES

Compute cash payback and net present value.

(LO 2, 3), AN

E12-1 Palo Alto Corporation is considering purchasing a new delivery truck. The truck has many advantages over the company's current truck (not the least of which is that it runs). The new truck would cost $56,000. Because of the increased capacity, reduced maintenance costs, and increased fuel economy, the new truck is expected to generate cost savings of $7,500. At the end of 8 years the company will sell the truck for an estimated

$27,000. Traditionally the company has used a rule of thumb that a proposal should not be accepted unless it has a payback period that is less than 50% of the asset's estimated useful life. Larry Newton, a new manager, has suggested that the company should not rely solely on the payback approach, but should also employ the net present value method when evaluating new projects. The company's cost of capital is 8%.

Instructions
(a) Compute the cash payback period and net present value of the proposed investment.
(b) Does the project meet the company's cash payback criteria? Does it meet the net present value criteria for acceptance? Discuss your results.

E12-2 Doug's Custom Construction Company is considering three new projects, each requiring an equipment investment of $22,000. Each project will last for 3 years and produce the following net annual cash flows.

Compute cash payback period and net present value.

(LO 2, 3), AN

Year	AA	BB	CC
1	$ 7,000	$10,000	$13,000
2	9,000	10,000	12,000
3	12,000	10,000	11,000
Total	$28,000	$30,000	$36,000

The equipment's salvage value is zero, and Doug uses straight-line depreciation. Doug will not accept any project with a cash payback period over 2 years. Doug's required rate of return is 12%.

Instructions
(a) Compute each project's payback period, indicating the most desirable project and the least desirable project using this method. (Round to two decimals and assume in your computations that cash flows occur evenly throughout the year.)
(b) Compute the net present value of each project. Does your evaluation change? (Round to nearest dollar.)

E12-3 Hiland Inc. manufactures snowsuits. Hiland is considering purchasing a new sewing machine at a cost of $2.45 million. Its existing machine was purchased five years ago at a price of $1.8 million; six months ago, Hiland spent $55,000 to keep it operational. The existing sewing machine can be sold today for $260,000. The new sewing machine would require a one-time, $85,000 training cost. Operating costs would decrease by the following amounts for years 1 to 7:

Calculate net present value and apply decision rule.

(LO 3), AN

Year	1	$390,000
	2	400,000
	3	411,000
	4	426,000
	5	434,000
	6	435,000
	7	436,000

The new sewing machine would be depreciated according to the declining-balance method at a rate of 20%. The salvage value is expected to be $350,000. This new equipment would require maintenance costs of $100,000 at the end of the fifth year. The cost of capital is 9%.

Instructions
Use the net present value method to determine whether Hiland should purchase the new machine to replace the existing machine, and state the reason for your conclusion.

(CGA adapted)

E12-4 BAK Corp. is considering purchasing one of two new diagnostic machines. Either machine would make it possible for the company to bid on jobs that it currently isn't equipped to do. Estimates regarding each machine are provided below.

Compute net present value and profitability index.

(LO 3, 5), AN

	Machine A	Machine B
Original cost	$75,500	$180,000
Estimated life	8 years	8 years
Salvage value	–0–	–0–
Estimated annual cash inflows	$20,000	$40,000
Estimated annual cash outflows	$5,000	$10,000

Determine internal rate of return.

(LO 7), AN

Instructions
Calculate the net present value and profitability index of each machine. Assume a 9% discount rate. Which machine should be purchased?

E12-5 Eisler Corporation is involved in the business of injection molding of plastics. It is considering the purchase of a new computer-aided design and manufacturing machine for $430,000. The company believes that with this new machine it will improve productivity and increase quality, resulting in an increase in net annual cash flows of $101,000 for the next 6 years. Management requires a 10% rate of return on all new investments.

Instructions
Calculate the internal rate of return on this new machine. Should the investment be accepted?

Calculate cash payback period, internal rate of return, and apply decision rules.

(LO 2, 7), AN

E12-6 BSU Inc. wants to purchase a new machine for $29,300, excluding $1,500 of installation costs. The old machine was bought five years ago and had an expected economic life of 10 years without salvage value. This old machine now has a book value of $2,000, and BSU Inc. expects to sell it for that amount. The new machine would decrease operating costs by $7,000 each year of its economic life. The straight-line depreciation method would be used for the new machine, for a six-year period with no salvage value.

Instructions
(a) Determine the cash payback period.
(b) Determine the approximate internal rate of return.
(c) Assuming the company has a required rate of return of 10%, state your conclusion on whether the new machine should be purchased.

(CGA adapted)

Determine internal rate of return.

(LO 7), AN

E12-7 Ueker Company is considering three capital expenditure projects. Relevant data for the projects are as follows.

Project	Investment	Annual Income	Life of Project
22A	$240,000	$16,700	6 years
23A	270,000	20,600	9 years
24A	280,000	17,500	7 years

Annual income is constant over the life of the project. Each project is expected to have zero salvage value at the end of the project. Ueker Company uses the straight-line method of depreciation.

Instructions
(a) Determine the internal rate of return for each project. Round the internal rate of return factor to three decimals.
(b) If Ueker Company's required rate of return is 11%, which projects are acceptable?

Calculate annual rate of return.

(LO 8), AP

E12-8 Pierre's Hair Salon is considering opening a new location in French Lick, California. The cost of building a new salon is $300,000. A new salon will normally generate annual revenues of $70,000, with annual expenses (including depreciation) of $41,500. At the end of 15 years the salon will have a salvage value of $80,000.

Instructions
Calculate the annual rate of return on the project.

Compute cash payback period and annual rate of return.

(LO 2, 8), AP

E12-9 Brady Service Center just purchased an automobile hoist for $35,000. The hoist has an 8-year life and an estimated salvage value of $3,000. Installation costs and freight charges were $3,300 and $700, respectively. Brady uses straight-line depreciation.
   The new hoist will be used to replace mufflers and tires on automobiles. Brady estimates that the new hoist will enable his mechanics to replace five extra mufflers per week. Each muffler sells for $72 installed. The cost of a muffler is $36, and the labor cost to install a muffler is $12.

Instructions
(a) Compute the cash payback period for the new hoist.
(b) Compute the annual rate of return for the new hoist. (Round to one decimal.)

E12-10 Vilas Company is considering a capital investment of $190,000 in additional productive facilities. The new machinery is expected to have a useful life of 5 years with no salvage value. Depreciation is by the straight-line method. During the life of the investment, annual net income and net annual cash flows are expected to be $12,000 and $50,000, respectively. Vilas has a 12% cost of capital rate, which is the required rate of return on the investment.

Compute annual rate of return, cash payback period, and net present value.

(LO 2, 3, 8), AP

Instructions
(Round to two decimals.)
(a) Compute (1) the cash payback period and (2) the annual rate of return on the proposed capital expenditure.
(b) Using the discounted cash flow technique, compute the net present value.

E12-11 BAP Corporation is reviewing an investment proposal. The initial cost and estimates of the book value of the investment at the end of each year, the net cash flows for each year, and the net income for each year are presented in the schedule below. All cash flows are assumed to take place at the end of the year. The salvage value of the investment at the end of each year is equal to its book value. There would be no salvage value at the end of the investment's life.

Calculate payback, annual rate of return, and net present value.

(LO 2, 3, 8), AP

Investment Proposal

Year	Initial Cost and Book Value	Annual Cash Flows	Annual Net Income
0	$105,000		
1	70,000	$45,000	$10,000
2	42,000	40,000	12,000
3	21,000	35,000	14,000
4	7,000	30,000	16,000
5	0	25,000	18,000

BAP Corporation uses a 12% target rate of return for new investment proposals.

Instructions
(a) What is the cash payback period for this proposal?
(b) What is the annual rate of return for the investment?
(c) What is the net present value of the investment?

(CMA-Canada adapted)

EXERCISES: SET B AND CHALLENGE EXERCISES

Visit the book's companion website, at **www.wiley.com/college/weygandt**, and choose the Student Companion site to access Exercise Set B and Challenge Exercises.

PROBLEMS: SET A

P12-1A Henkel Company is considering three long-term capital investment proposals. Each investment has a useful life of 5 years. Relevant data on each project are as follows.

Compute annual rate of return, cash payback, and net present value.

(LO 2, 3, 8), AN

	Project Kilo	Project Lima	Project Oscar
Capital investment	$150,000	$165,000	$200,000
Annual net income:			
Year 1	14,000	18,000	27,000
2	14,000	17,000	23,000
3	14,000	16,000	21,000
4	14,000	12,000	13,000
5	14,000	9,000	12,000
Total	$ 70,000	$ 72,000	$ 96,000

Depreciation is computed by the straight-line method with no salvage value. The company's cost of capital is 15%. (Assume that cash flows occur evenly throughout the year.)

Instructions

(b) L $(4,016); O $2,163

(a) Compute the cash payback period for each project. (Round to two decimals.)
(b) Compute the net present value for each project. (Round to nearest dollar.)
(c) Compute the annual rate of return for each project. (Round to two decimals.) (*Hint:* Use average annual net income in your computation.)
(d) Rank the projects on each of the foregoing bases. Which project do you recommend?

Compute annual rate of return, cash payback, and net present value.

(LO 2, 3, 8), AN

P12-2A Lon Timur is an accounting major at a midwestern state university located approximately 60 miles from a major city. Many of the students attending the university are from the metropolitan area and visit their homes regularly on the weekends. Lon, an entrepreneur at heart, realizes that few good commuting alternatives are available for students doing weekend travel. He believes that a weekend commuting service could be organized and run profitably from several suburban and downtown shopping mall locations. Lon has gathered the following investment information.

1. Five used vans would cost a total of $75,000 to purchase and would have a 3-year useful life with negligible salvage value. Lon plans to use straight-line depreciation.
2. Ten drivers would have to be employed at a total payroll expense of $48,000.
3. Other annual out-of-pocket expenses associated with running the commuter service would include Gasoline $16,000, Maintenance $3,300, Repairs $4,000, Insurance $4,200, Advertising $2,500.
4. Lon has visited several financial institutions to discuss funding. The best interest rate he has been able to negotiate is 15%. Use this rate for cost of capital.
5. Lon expects each van to make ten round trips weekly and carry an average of six students each trip. The service is expected to operate 30 weeks each year, and each student will be charged $12.00 for a round-trip ticket.

Instructions

(a) (1) $5,000

(b) (1) 2.5 years

(a) Determine the annual (1) net income and (2) net annual cash flows for the commuter service.
(b) Compute (1) the cash payback period and (2) the annual rate of return. (Round to two decimals.)
(c) Compute the net present value of the commuter service. (Round to the nearest dollar.)
(d)  What should Lon conclude from these computations?

Compute net present value, profitability index, and internal rate of return.

(LO 3, 5, 7), AN

P12-3A Goltra Clinic is considering investing in new heart-monitoring equipment. It has two options: Option A would have an initial lower cost but would require a significant expenditure for rebuilding after 4 years. Option B would require no rebuilding expenditure, but its maintenance costs would be higher. Since the Option B machine is of initial higher quality, it is expected to have a salvage value at the end of its useful life. The following estimates were made of the cash flows. The company's cost of capital is 8%.

	Option A	Option B
Initial cost	$160,000	$227,000
Annual cash inflows	$70,000	$80,000
Annual cash outflows	$30,000	$26,000
Cost to rebuild (end of year 4)	$50,000	$0
Salvage value	$0	$8,000
Estimated useful life	7 years	7 years

Instructions

(a) (1) NPV A $11,503
(3) IRR B 15%

(a) Compute the (1) net present value, (2) profitability index, and (3) internal rate of return for each option. (*Hint:* To solve for internal rate of return, experiment with alternative discount rates to arrive at a net present value of zero.)
(b) Which option should be accepted?

Compute net present value considering intangible benefits.

(LO 3, 4), E

P12-4A Jane's Auto Care is considering the purchase of a new tow truck. The garage doesn't currently have a tow truck, and the $60,000 price tag for a new truck would represent a major expenditure. Jane Austen, owner of the garage, has compiled the estimates shown on the next page in trying to determine whether the tow truck should be purchased.

Initial cost	$60,000
Estimated useful life	8 years
Net annual cash flows from towing	$8,000
Overhaul costs (end of year 4)	$6,000
Salvage value	$12,000

Jane's good friend, Rick Ryan, stopped by. He is trying to convince Jane that the tow truck will have other benefits that Jane hasn't even considered. First, he says, cars that need towing need to be fixed. Thus, when Jane tows them to her facility, her repair revenues will increase. Second, he notes that the tow truck could have a plow mounted on it, thus saving Jane the cost of plowing her parking lot. (Rick will give her a used plow blade for free if Jane will plow Rick's driveway.) Third, he notes that the truck will generate goodwill; people who are rescued by Jane's tow truck will feel grateful and might be more inclined to use her service station in the future or buy gas there. Fourth, the tow truck will have "Jane's Auto Care" on its doors, hood, and back tailgate—a form of free advertising wherever the tow truck goes. Rick estimates that, at a minimum, these benefits would be worth the following.

Additional annual net cash flows from repair work	$3,000
Annual savings from plowing	750
Additional annual net cash flows from customer "goodwill"	1,000
Additional annual net cash flows resulting from free advertising	750

The company's cost of capital is 9%.

Instructions
(a) Calculate the net present value, ignoring the additional benefits described by Rick. Should the tow truck be purchased?
(b) Calculate the net present value, incorporating the additional benefits suggested by Rick. Should the tow truck be purchased?
(c) Suppose Rick has been overly optimistic in his assessment of the value of the additional benefits. At a minimum, how much would the additional benefits have to be worth in order for the project to be accepted?

(a) NPV $(13,950)

(b) NPV $16,491

P12-5A Goldbloom Corp. is thinking about opening a soccer camp in southern California. To start the camp, Goldbloom would need to purchase land and build four soccer fields and a sleeping and dining facility to house 150 soccer players. Each year, the camp would be run for 8 sessions of 1 week each. The company would hire college soccer players as coaches. The camp attendees would be male and female soccer players ages 12–18. Property values in southern California have enjoyed a steady increase in value. It is expected that after using the facility for 20 years, Goldbloom can sell the property for more than it was originally purchased for. The following amounts have been estimated.

Compute net present value and internal rate of return with sensitivity analysis.

(LO 3, 7), E

Cost of land	$300,000
Cost to build soccer fields, dorm and dining facility	$600,000
Annual cash inflows assuming 150 players and 8 weeks	$940,000
Annual cash outflows	$840,000
Estimated useful life	20 years
Salvage value	$1,500,000
Discount rate	8%

Instructions
(a) Calculate the net present value of the project.
(b) To gauge the sensitivity of the project to these estimates, assume that if only 125 players attend each week, annual cash inflows will be $800,000 and annual cash outflows will be $750,000. What is the net present value using these alternative estimates? Discuss your findings.
(c) Assuming the original facts, what is the net present value if the project is actually riskier than first assumed and an 11% discount rate is more appropriate?
(d) Assume that during the first 5 years, the annual net cash flows each year were only $40,000. At the end of the fifth year, the company is running low on cash, so management decides to sell the property for $1,332,000. What was the actual internal rate of return on the project? Explain how this return was possible given that the camp did not appear to be successful.

(a) NPV $403,640

(d) IRR 12%

PROBLEMS: SET B

Compute annual rate of return, cash payback, and net present value.

(LO 2, 3, 8), AN

P12-1B The Borders and Noble partnership is considering three long-term capital investment proposals. Each investment has a useful life of 5 years. Relevant data on each project are as follows.

	Project Mary	Project Winnie	Project Sarah
Capital investment	$140,000	$175,000	$190,000
Annual net income:			
Year 1	$10,000	$12,500	$19,000
2	10,000	12,000	16,000
3	10,000	11,000	14,000
4	10,000	8,000	9,000
5	10,000	6,000	8,000
Total	$50,000	$49,500	$66,000

Depreciation is computed by the straight-line method with no salvage value. The company's cost of capital is 12%. (Assume cash flows occur evenly throughout the year.)

Instructions

(b) M $(3,018); S $(3,075)

(a) Compute the cash payback period for each project. (Round to two decimals.)
(b) Compute the net present value for each project. (Round to nearest dollar.)
(c) Compute the annual rate of return for each project. (Round to two decimals.) (*Hint:* Use average annual net income in your computation.)
(d) Rank the projects on each of the foregoing bases. Which project do you recommend?

Compute annual rate of return, cash payback, and net present value.

(LO 2, 3, 8), AN

P12-2B Ben Paul is an accounting major at a western university located approximately 60 miles from a major city. Many of the students attending the university are from the metropolitan area and visit their homes regularly on the weekends. Ben, an entrepreneur at heart, realizes that few good commuting alternatives are available for students doing weekend travel. He believes that a weekend commuting service could be organized and run profitably from several suburban and downtown shopping mall locations. Ben has gathered the following investment information.

1. Five used vans would cost a total of $90,000 to purchase and would have a 3-year useful life with negligible salvage value. Ben plans to use straight-line depreciation.
2. Ten drivers would have to be employed at a total payroll expense of $43,000.
3. Other annual out-of-pocket expenses associated with running the commuter service would include Gasoline $26,000, Maintenance $4,000, Repairs $5,300, Insurance $4,500, Advertising $2,200.
4. Ben desires to earn a return of 15% on his investment.
5. Ben expects each van to make ten round trips weekly and carry an average of six students each trip. The service is expected to operate 32 weeks each year, and each student will be charged $15 for a round-trip ticket.

Instructions

(a) (1) $29,000

(a) Determine the annual (1) net income and (2) net annual cash flows for the commuter service.

(b) (1) 1.53 years

(b) Compute (1) the cash payback period and (2) the annual rate of return. (Round to two decimals.)
(c) Compute the net present value of the commuter service. (Round to the nearest dollar.)
(d) ✏️ What should Ben conclude from these computations?

Compute net present value, profitability index, and internal rate of return.

(LO 3, 5, 7), AN

P12-3B Platteville Eye Clinic is considering investing in new optical-scanning equipment. It has two options: Option A would have an initial lower cost but would require a significant expenditure for rebuilding after 3 years. Option B would require no rebuilding expenditure, but its maintenance costs would be higher. Since the Option B machine is of initial higher quality, it is expected to have a salvage value at the end of its useful life. The following estimates were made of the cash flows. The company's cost of capital is 11%.

	Option A	Option B
Initial cost	$100,000	$160,000
Annual cash inflows	$56,000	$60,000
Annual cash outflows	$24,000	$24,000
Cost to rebuild (end of year 3)	$53,000	$0
Salvage value	$0	$24,000
Estimated useful life	6 years	6 years

Instructions

(a) Compute the (1) net present value, (2) profitability index, and (3) internal rate of return for each option. (*Hint:* To solve for internal rate of return, experiment with alternative discount rates to arrive at a net present value of zero.)

(b) Which option should be accepted?

(a) (1) NPV A $(3,376)
(3) IRR B 12%

P12-4B Isaac's Auto Repair is considering the purchase of a new tow truck. The garage doesn't currently have a tow truck, and the $65,000 price tag for a new truck would represent a major expenditure for the garage. Isaac Mayer, owner of the garage, has compiled the following estimates in trying to determine whether to purchase the truck.

Compute net present value considering intangible benefits.

(LO 3, 4), E

Initial cost	$65,000
Estimated useful life	8 years
Net annual cash inflows from towing	$9,600
Overhaul costs (end of year 4)	$7,000
Salvage value	$16,000

Isaac's good friend, Brad Jolie, stopped by. He is trying to convince Isaac that the tow truck will have other benefits that Isaac hasn't even considered. First, he says, cars that need towing need to be fixed. Thus, when Isaac tows them to his facility his repair revenues will increase. Second, he notes that the tow truck could have a plow mounted on it, thus saving Isaac the cost of plowing his parking lot. (Brad will give him a used plow blade for free if Isaac will plow Brad's driveway.) Third, he notes that the truck will generate goodwill; that is, people who are rescued by Isaac and his tow truck will feel grateful and might be more inclined to use his service station in the future or buy gas there. Fourth, the tow truck will have "Isaac's Auto Repair" on its doors, hood, and back tailgate—a form of free advertising wherever the tow truck goes.

Brad estimates that, at a minimum, these benefits would be worth the following.

Additional annual net cash flows from repair work	$2,600
Annual savings from plowing	600
Additional annual net cash flows from customer "goodwill"	1,200
Additional annual net cash flows resulting from free advertising	500

The company's cost of capital is 10%.

Instructions

(a) Calculate the net present value, ignoring the additional benefits described by Brad. Should the tow truck be purchased?

(b) Calculate the net present value, incorporating the additional benefits suggested by Brad. Should the tow truck be purchased?

(c) Suppose Brad has been overly optimistic in his assessment of the value of the additional benefits. At a minimum, how much would the additional benefits have to be worth in order for the project to be accepted?

(a) NPV $(11,102)

(b) NPV $15,039

P12-5B Lewis Corp. is thinking about opening a basketball camp in Texas. In order to start the camp, the company would need to purchase land and build eight basketball courts and a dormitory-type sleeping and dining facility to house 110 basketball players. Each year, the camp would be run for 8 sessions of 1 week each. The company would hire college basketball players as coaches. The camp attendees would be male and female basketball players ages 12 to 18. Property values in Texas have enjoyed a steady increase in value. It is expected that after using the facility for 20 years, Lewis can sell the property for more than it was originally purchased for. The amounts shown on the next page have been estimated.

Compute net present value and internal rate of return with sensitivity analysis.

(LO 3, 7), E

Cost of land	$200,000
Cost to build dorm and dining facility	$350,000
Annual cash inflows assuming 110 players and 8 weeks	$700,000
Annual cash outflows	$570,000
Estimated useful life	20 years
Salvage value	$700,000
Discount rate	12%

Instructions

(a) NPV $493,596

(a) Calculate the net present value of the project.

(b) To gauge the sensitivity of the project to these estimates, assume that if only 90 campers attend each week, annual cash inflows will be $570,000 and annual cash outflows will be $508,000. What is the net present value using these alternative estimates? Discuss your findings.

(c) Assuming the original facts, what is the net present value if the project is actually riskier than first assumed, and a 15% discount rate is more appropriate?

(d) IRR 15%

(d) Assume that during the first 5 years the annual net cash inflows each year were only $65,000. At the end of the fifth year, the company is running low on cash, so management decides to sell the property for $668,000. What was the actual internal rate of return on the project? Explain how this return was possible given that the camp did not appear to be successful.

PROBLEMS: SET C

Visit the book's companion website, at **www.wiley.com/college/weygandt**, and choose the Student Companion site to access Problem Set C.

WATERWAYS CONTINUING PROBLEM

(This is a continuation of the Waterways Problem from Chapters 1–11.)

WCP12 Waterways Corporation puts much emphasis on cash flow when it plans for capital investments. The company chose its discount rate of 8% based on the rate of return it must pay its owners and creditors. Using that rate, Waterways then uses different methods to determine the best decisions for making capital outlays. Waterways is considering buying five new backhoes to replace the backhoes it now has. This problem asks you to evaluate that decision, using various capital budgeting techniques.

Go to the book's companion website, **www.wiley.com/college/weygandt**, *to find the remainder of this problem.*

Broadening Your PERSPECTIVE

Management Decision-Making

Decision-Making at Current Designs

BYP12-1 A company that manufactures recreational pedal boats has approached Mike Cichanowski to ask if he would be interested in using Current Designs' rotomold expertise and equipment to produce some of the pedal boat components. Mike is intrigued by the idea and thinks it would be an interesting way of complementing the present product line.

One of Mike's hesitations about the proposal is that the pedal boats are a different shape than the kayaks that Current Designs produces. As a result, the company would need to buy an additional rotomold oven in order to produce the pedal boat components. This project clearly involves risks, and Mike wants to make sure that the returns justify the risks. In this case, since this is a new venture, Mike thinks that a 15% discount rate is appropriate to use to evaluate the project.

As an intern at Current Designs, Mike has asked you to prepare an initial evaluation of this proposal. To aid in your analysis, he has provided the following information and assumptions.

1. The new rotomold oven will have a cost of $256,000, a salvage value of $0, and an 8-year useful life. Straight-line depreciation will be used.
2. The projected revenues, costs, and results for each of the 8 years of this project are as follows.

Sales		$220,000
Less:		
Manufacturing costs	$140,000	
Depreciation	32,000	
Shipping and administrative costs	22,000	194,000
Income before income taxes		26,000
Income tax expense		10,800
Net income		$ 15,200

Instructions
(a) Compute the annual rate of return. (Round to two decimal places.)
(b) Compute the payback period. (Round to two decimal places.)
(c) Compute the NPV using a discount rate of 9%. (Round to nearest dollar.) Should the proposal be accepted using this discount rate?
(d) Compute the NPV using a discount rate of 15%. (Round to nearest dollar.) Should the proposal be accepted using this discount rate?

Decision-Making Across the Organization

BYP12-2 Luang Company is considering the purchase of a new machine. Its invoice price is $122,000, freight charges are estimated to be $3,000, and installation costs are expected to be $5,000. Salvage value of the new machine is expected to be zero after a useful life of 4 years. Existing equipment could be retained and used for an additional 4 years if the new machine is not purchased. At that time, the salvage value of the equipment would be zero. If the new machine is purchased now, the existing machine would be scrapped. Luang's accountant, Lisa Hsung, has accumulated the following data regarding annual sales and expenses with and without the new machine.

1. Without the new machine, Luang can sell 10,000 units of product annually at a per unit selling price of $100. If the new unit is purchased, the number of units produced and sold would increase by 25%, and the selling price would remain the same.
2. The new machine is faster than the old machine, and it is more efficient in its usage of materials. With the old machine the gross profit rate will be 28.5% of sales, whereas the rate will be 30% of sales with the new machine.
3. Annual selling expenses are $160,000 with the current equipment. Because the new equipment would produce a greater number of units to be sold, annual selling expenses are expected to increase by 10% if it is purchased.
4. Annual administrative expenses are expected to be $100,000 with the old machine, and $112,000 with the new machine.
5. The current book value of the existing machine is $40,000. Luang uses straight-line depreciation.
6. Luang's management has a required rate of return of 15% on its investment and a cash payback period of no more than 3 years.

Instructions
With the class divided into groups, answer the following. (Ignore income tax effects.)
(a) Calculate the annual rate of return for the new machine. (Round to two decimals.)
(b) Compute the cash payback period for the new machine. (Round to two decimals.)
(c) Compute the net present value of the new machine. (Round to the nearest dollar.)
(d) On the basis of the foregoing data, would you recommend that Luang buy the machine? Why?

Managerial Analysis

BYP12-3 Hawke Skateboards is considering building a new plant. Bob Skerritt, the company's marketing manager, is an enthusiastic supporter of the new plant. Lucy Liu, the company's chief financial officer, is not so sure that the plant is a good idea. Currently, the company purchases its skateboards from foreign manufacturers. The following figures were estimated regarding the construction of a new plant.

Cost of plant	$4,000,000	Estimated useful life	15 years
Annual cash inflows	4,000,000	Salvage value	$2,000,000
Annual cash outflows	3,540,000	Discount rate	11%

Bob Skerritt believes that these figures understate the true potential value of the plant. He suggests that by manufacturing its own skateboards the company will benefit from a "buy American" patriotism that he believes is common among skateboarders. He also notes that the firm has had numerous quality problems with the skateboards manufactured by its suppliers. He suggests that the inconsistent quality has resulted in lost sales, increased warranty claims, and some costly lawsuits. Overall, he believes sales will be $200,000 higher than projected above, and that the savings from lower warranty costs and legal costs will be $60,000 per year. He also believes that the project is not as risky as assumed above, and that a 9% discount rate is more reasonable.

Instructions

Answer each of the following.

(a) Compute the net present value of the project based on the original projections.
(b) Compute the net present value incorporating Bob's estimates of the value of the intangible benefits, but still using the 11% discount rate.
(c) Compute the net present value using the original estimates, but employing the 9% discount rate that Bob suggests is more appropriate.
(d) Comment on your findings.

Real-World Focus

BYP12-4 Tecumseh Products Company has its headquarters in Tecumseh, Michigan. It describes itself as "a global multinational corporation producing mechanical and electrical components essential to industries creating end-products for health, comfort, and convenience." The following was excerpted from the management discussion and analysis section of a recent annual report.

Tecumseh Products Company
Management Discussion and Analysis

The company has invested approximately $50 million in a scroll compressor manufacturing facility in Tecumseh, Michigan. After experiencing setbacks in developing a commercially acceptable scroll compressor, the Company is currently testing a new generation of scroll product. The Company is unable to predict when, or if, it will offer a scroll compressor for commercial sale, but it does anticipate that reaching volume production will require a significant additional investment. Given such additional investment and current market conditions, management is currently reviewing its options with respect to scroll product improvement, cost reductions, joint ventures and alternative new products.

Instructions

Discuss issues the company should consider and techniques the company should employ to determine whether to continue pursuing this project.

BYP12-5 Campbell Soup Company is an international provider of soup products. Management is very interested in continuing to grow the company in its core business, while "spinning off" those businesses that are not part of its core operation.

Address: **www.campbellsoups.com**, or go to **www.wiley.com/college/weygandt**

Steps

1. Go to the home page of Campbell Soup Company at the address shown above.
2. Choose the current annual report.

Instructions

Review the financial statements and management's discussion and analysis, and answer the following questions.

(a) What was the total amount of capital expenditures in the current year, and how does this amount compare with the previous year?

(b) What interest rate did the company pay on new borrowings in the current year?

(c) Assume that this year's capital expenditures are expected to increase cash flows by $42 million. What is the expected internal rate of return (IRR) for these capital expenditures? (Assume a 10-year period for the cash flows.)

Critical Thinking

Communication Activity

BYP12-6 Refer back to E12-9 to address the following.

Instructions

Prepare a memo to Maria Fierro, your supervisor. Show your calculations from E12-9, (a) and (b). In one or two paragraphs, discuss important nonfinancial considerations. Make any assumptions you believe to be necessary. Make a recommendation based on your analysis.

Ethics Case

BYP12-7 NuComp Company operates in a state where corporate taxes and workers' compensation insurance rates have recently doubled. NuComp's president has just assigned you the task of preparing an economic analysis and making a recommendation relative to moving the entire operation to Missouri. The president is slightly in favor of such a move because Missouri is his boyhood home and he also owns a fishing lodge there.

You have just completed building your dream house, moved in, and sodded the lawn. Your children are all doing well in school and sports and, along with your spouse, want no part of a move to Missouri. If the company does move, so will you because the town is a one-industry community and you and your spouse will have to move to have employment. Moving when everyone else does will cause you to take a big loss on the sale of your house. The same hardships will be suffered by your coworkers, and the town will be devastated.

In compiling the costs of moving versus not moving, you have latitude in the assumptions you make, the estimates you compute, and the discount rates and time periods you project. You are in a position to influence the decision singlehandedly.

Instructions

(a) Who are the stakeholders in this situation?

(b) What are the ethical issues in this situation?

(c) What would you do in this situation?

All About You

BYP12-8 Numerous articles have been written that identify early warning signs that you might be getting into trouble with your personal debt load. You can find many good articles on this topic on the Web.

Instructions

Find an article that identifies early warning signs of personal debt trouble. Write up a summary of the article and bring your summary and the article to class to share.

Considering Your Costs and Benefits

BYP12-9 The March 31, 2011, edition of the *Wall Street Journal* includes an article by Russell Gold entitled "Solar Gains Traction—Thanks to Subsidies."

Instructions

Read the article and answer the following questions.

(a) What was the total cost of the solar panels installed? What was the "out-of-pocket" cost to the couple?

(b) Using the total annual electricity bill of $5,000 mentioned in the story, what is the cash payback of the project using the total cost? What is the cash payback based on the "out-of-pocket" cost?

(c) Solar panel manufactures estimate that solar panels can last up to 40 years with only minor maintenance costs. Assuming no maintenance costs, a 6% rate of interest, a more conservative 20-year life, and zero salvage value, what is the net present value of the project based on the total cost? What is the net present value of the project based on the "out-of-pocket" cost?

(d) What was the wholesale price of panels per watt at the time the article was written? At what price per watt does the article say that subsidies no longer be needed? Does this price appear to be achievable?

Answers to Chapter Questions

Answers to Insight and Accounting Across the Organization Questions

p. 554 Can You Hear Me—Better? Q: Based on the potentially slow initial adoption of 4G by customers, how might the conclusions of a cash payback analysis of Verizon's 4G investment differ from a present value analysis? **A:** If the initial adoption of 4G by customers is slow, then the amount of cash received in the early years will be low. This would lengthen the cash payback period, making it unlikely that the investment would get high marks with this test. However, the long-run potential of 4G is probably quite high as more people switch to smart phones and consequently increase their use of services that benefit from a high-speed connection. These later cash flows may well be large enough that they provide a positive net present value amount.

p. 558 It Need Not Cost an Arm and a Leg Q: In addition to the obvious humanitarian benefit of reducing serious injuries, how else might the manufacturer of this product convince potential customers of its worth? **A:** Serious injuries cost employers huge sums, which can sometimes force small companies out of business. In addition to the obvious humanitarian benefit, the manufacturer can demonstrate that this device is a sound financial investment in terms of reduced health-care and workers' compensation costs and fewer hours missed due to injury. Also, as the device gains wider acceptance, employers that do not have the device may ultimately be found negligent with regard to worker safety.

p. 560 Wide-Screen Capacity Q: What implications does the excess capacity have for the cash payback and net present value calculations of these investments? **A:** Because the companies have excess capacity, they are not selling as many units as expected. Also, to increase sales, they are being forced to cut selling prices in order to sell units. Therefore, the revenues that they generate are lower than the amounts that would have been estimated when the plants were planned and built. This means that cash payback periods are longer and net present values are lower than desired levels.

p. 561 Seeing the Big Picture Q: How important is the choice of discount rate in making capital budgeting decisions? **A:** The point of this discussion is that errors in implementation, as well as the accuracy of the estimated future benefits and costs as measured by cash inflows and outflows, are what matter the most when making capital expenditure decisions. While the choice of discount rates will result in incremental differences in present value calculations, "missing the big picture" has the potential to cause much bigger decision errors. Underestimating potential future cash inflows can result in missed opportunities. Underestimating future costs can result in failed investments.

Answers to Self-Test Questions

1. d   2. c   3. d   4. b ($48,000 ÷ $7,000) > ($75,000 ÷ $12,000)   5. a   6. b   7. d   8. d   9. c
10. c ($18,112 + $80,000) ÷ $80,000   11. a   12. c   13. d ($60,000 ÷ $15,400) = IRR factor   14. d
15. a $15,000 ÷ [($120,000 + $20,000) ÷ 2]

Statement of Cash Flows

Got Cash?

In today's environment, companies must be ready to respond to changes quickly in order to survive and thrive. This requires that they manage their cash very carefully. One company that managed cash successfully in its early years was Microsoft. During those years, the company paid much of its payroll with stock options (rights to purchase company stock in the future at a given price) instead of cash. This strategy conserved cash and turned more than a thousand of its employees into millionaires during the company's first 20 years of business.

In recent years, Microsoft has had a different kind of cash problem. Now that it has reached a more "mature" stage in life, it generates so much cash—roughly $1 billion per month—that it cannot always figure out what to do with it. At one time, Microsoft had accumulated $60 billion.

The company said it was accumulating cash to invest in new opportunities, buy other companies, and pay off pending lawsuits. But for many years, the federal government blocked attempts by Microsoft to buy anything other than small firms because it feared that purchase of a large firm would only increase Microsoft's monopolistic position.

Microsoft's stockholders have complained for years that holding all this cash was putting a drag on the company's profitability. Why? Because Microsoft had the cash invested in very low-yielding government securities.

✔ The Navigator

☐ Scan Learning Objectives

☐ Read Feature Story

☐ Read Preview

☐ Read Text and answer **DO IT!** p. 591
   ☐ p. 599 ☐ p. 602 ☐ p. 605

☐ Work Using the Decision Toolkit p. 606

☐ Review Summary of Learning Objectives

☐ Work Comprehensive **DO IT!** **1** p. 607
   ☐ **2** p. 622

☐ Answer Self-Test Questions

☐ Complete Assignments

☐ Go to **WileyPLUS** for practice and tutorials

Learning Objectives

After studying this chapter, you should be able to:

1 Indicate the usefulness of the statement of cash flows.

2 Distinguish among operating, investing, and financing activities.

3 Prepare a statement of cash flows using the indirect method.

4 Analyze the statement of cash flows.

Stockholders felt that the company either should find new investment projects that would bring higher returns, or return some of the cash to stockholders.

Finally, Microsoft announced a plan to return cash to stockholders, by paying a special one-time $32 billion dividend. This special dividend was so large that, according to the U.S. Commerce Department, it caused total personal income in the United States to rise by 3.7% in one month—the largest increase ever recorded by the agency. (It also made the holiday season brighter, especially for retailers in the Seattle area.) Microsoft also doubled its regular annual dividend to $3.50 per share. Further, it announced that it would spend another $30 billion buying treasury stock. In addition, Microsoft more recently offered to buy Yahoo! for

$44.6 billion (Yahoo! declined the offer). Dividends, stock buybacks, and acquisitions will help to deplete some of its massive cash horde. But, as you will see in this chapter, for a cash-generating machine like Microsoft, the company will be anything but cash-starved.

Interestingly, in 2010 Google found itself in a position similar to Microsoft's. Its cash pile of $26.5 billion was nearly 20% of the company's value. That's enough to pay a dividend of $80 per share. Unless it can find large, worthwhile projects to invest in, Google will also need to return a big chunk of its cash to shareholders.

Source: "Business: An End to Growth? Microsoft's Cash Bonanza," *The Economist* (July 23, 2005), p. 61.

✔ **The Navigator**

Preview of **Chapter 13**

The balance sheet, income statement, and retained earnings statement do not always show the whole picture of the financial condition of a company or institution. In fact, looking at the financial statements of some well-known companies, a thoughtful investor might ask questions like these: How did Eastman Kodak finance cash dividends of $649 million in a year in which it earned only $17 million? How could United Airlines purchase new planes that cost $1.9 billion in a year in which it reported a net loss of over $2 billion? How did the companies that spent a combined fantastic $3.4 trillion on mergers and acquisitions in a recent year finance those deals? Answers to these and similar questions can be found in this chapter, which presents the statement of cash flows.

The content and organization of this chapter are as follows.

STATEMENT OF CASH FLOWS		
Statement of Cash Flows: Usefulness and Format	**Preparing the Statement of Cash Flows—Indirect Method**	**Using Cash Flows to Evaluate a Company**
• Usefulness • Classifications • Significant noncash activities • Format • Preparation • Indirect and direct methods	• Step 1: Operating activities • Step 2: Investing and financing activities • Step 3: Net change in cash	• Free cash flow

✔ **The Navigator**

Statement of Cash Flows: Usefulness and Format

The balance sheet, income statement, and retained earnings statement provide only limited information about a company's cash flows (cash receipts and cash payments). For example, comparative balance sheets show the increase in property, plant, and equipment during the year. But, they do not show how the additions were financed or paid for. The income statement shows net income. But, it does not indicate the amount of cash generated by operating activities. The retained earnings statement shows cash dividends declared but not the cash dividends paid during the year. None of these statements presents a detailed summary of where cash came from and how it was used.

Usefulness of the Statement of Cash Flows

> **LEARNING OBJECTIVE 1**
>
> Indicate the usefulness of the statement of cash flows.

The **statement of cash flows** reports the cash receipts, cash payments, and net change in cash resulting from operating, investing, and financing activities during a period. The information in a statement of cash flows should help investors, creditors, and others assess:

1. **The entity's ability to generate future cash flows.** By examining relationships between items in the statement of cash flows, investors can make predictions of the amounts, timing, and uncertainty of future cash flows better than they can from accrual-basis data.

2. **The entity's ability to pay dividends and meet obligations.** If a company does not have adequate cash, it cannot pay employees, settle debts, or pay dividends. Employees, creditors, and stockholders should be particularly interested in this statement because it alone shows the flows of cash in a business.

> ### 🤝 Ethics Note
>
> Though we would discourage reliance on cash flows to the exclusion of accrual accounting, comparing cash from operations to net income can reveal important information about the "quality" of reported net income. Such a comparison can reveal the extent to which net income provides a good measure of actual performance.

3. **The reasons for the difference between net income and net cash provided (used) by operating activities.** Net income provides information on the success or failure of a business. However, some financial statement users are critical of accrual-basis net income because it requires many estimates. As a result, users often challenge the reliability of the number. Such is not the case with cash. Many readers of the statement of cash flows want to know the reasons for the difference between net income and net cash provided by operating activities. Then, they can assess for themselves the reliability of the income number.

4. **The cash investing and financing transactions during the period.** By examining a company's investing and financing transactions, a financial statement reader can better understand why assets and liabilities changed during the period.

Classification of Cash Flows

> **LEARNING OBJECTIVE 2**
>
> Distinguish among operating, investing, and financing activities.

The statement of cash flows classifies cash receipts and cash payments as operating, investing, and financing activities. Transactions and other events characteristic of each kind of activity are as follows.

1. **Operating activities** include the cash effects of transactions that create revenues and expenses. They thus enter into the determination of net income.

2. **Investing activities** include (a) acquiring and disposing of investments and property, plant, and equipment, and (b) lending money and collecting the loans.

3. Financing activities include (a) obtaining cash from issuing debt and repaying the amounts borrowed, and (b) obtaining cash from stockholders, repurchasing shares, and paying dividends.

The operating activities category is the most important. It shows the cash provided by company operations. This source of cash is generally considered to be the best measure of a company's ability to generate sufficient cash to continue as a going concern.

Illustration 13-1 lists typical cash receipts and cash payments within each of the three classifications. **Study the list carefully.** It will prove very useful in solving homework exercises and problems.

TYPES OF CASH INFLOWS AND OUTFLOWS

Illustration 13-1
Typical receipt and payment classifications

Operating activities—Income statement items
   Cash inflows:
      From sale of goods or services.
      From interest received and dividends received.
   Cash outflows:
      To suppliers for inventory.
      To employees for services.
      To government for taxes.
      To lenders for interest.
      To others for expenses.

Operating activities

Investing activities—Changes in investments and long-term assets
   Cash inflows:
      From sale of property, plant, and equipment.
      From sale of investments in debt or equity securities of other entities.
      From collection of principal on loans to other entities.
   Cash outflows:
      To purchase property, plant, and equipment.
      To purchase investments in debt or equity securities of other entities.
      To make loans to other entities.

Investing activities

Financing activities—Changes in long-term liabilities and stockholders' equity
   Cash inflows:
      From sale of common stock.
      From issuance of long-term debt (bonds and notes).
   Cash outflows:
      To stockholders as dividends.
      To redeem long-term debt or reacquire capital stock (treasury stock).

Financing activities

Note the following general guidelines:

1. Operating activities involve income statement items.

2. Investing activities involve cash flows resulting from changes in investments and long-term asset items.

3. Financing activities involve cash flows resulting from changes in long-term liability and stockholders' equity items.

Companies classify as operating activities some cash flows related to investing or financing activities. For example, receipts of investment revenue (interest and dividends) are classified as operating activities. So are payments of interest to lenders. Why are these considered operating activities? **Because companies report these items in the income statement, where results of operations are shown.**

Significant Noncash Activities

Not all of a company's significant activities involve cash. Examples of significant noncash activities are:

1. Direct issuance of common stock to purchase assets.
2. Conversion of bonds into common stock.
3. Direct issuance of debt to purchase assets.
4. Exchanges of plant assets.

    Companies do not report in the body of the statement of cash flows significant financing and investing activities that do not affect cash. Instead, they report these activities in either a **separate schedule** at the bottom of the statement of cash flows or in a **separate note or supplementary schedule** to the financial statements. The reporting of these noncash activities in a separate schedule satisfies the **full disclosure principle**.

    In solving homework assignments, you should present significant noncash investing and financing activities in a separate schedule at the bottom of the statement of cash flows. (See the last entry in Illustration 13-2, on page 591, for an example.)

ACCOUNTING ACROSS THE ORGANIZATION

Net *What?*

Net income is not the same as net cash provided by operating activities. Below are some results from recent annual reports (dollars in millions). Note the wide disparity among these companies, all of which engaged in retail merchandising.

Company	Net Income	Net Cash Provided by Operating Activities
Kohl's Corporation	$ 1,083	$ 1,234
Wal-Mart Stores, Inc.	11,284	20,169
J.C. Penney Company, Inc.	1,153	1,255
Costco Wholesale Corp.	1,082	2,076
Target Corporation	2,849	4,125

? In general, why do differences exist between net income and net cash provided by operating activities? (See page 649.)

Format of the Statement of Cash Flows

The general format of the statement of cash flows presents the results of the three activities discussed previously—operating, investing, and financing—plus the significant noncash investing and financing activities. Illustration 13-2 shows a widely used form of the statement of cash flows.

Company Name Statement of Cash Flows Period Covered			**Illustration 13-2** Format of statement of cash flows
Cash flows from operating activities			
(List of individual items)	XX		
Net cash provided (used) by operating activities		XXX	
Cash flows from investing activities			
(List of individual inflows and outflows)	XX		
Net cash provided (used) by investing activities		XXX	
Cash flows from financing activities			
(List of individual inflows and outflows)	XX		
Net cash provided (used) by financing activities		XXX	
Net increase (decrease) in cash		XXX	
Cash at beginning of period		XXX	
Cash at end of period		XXX	
Noncash investing and financing activities			
(List of individual noncash transactions)		XXX	

The cash flows from operating activities section always appears first, followed by the investing activities section and then the financing activities section. The sum of the operating, investing, and financing sections equals the net increase or decrease in cash for the period. This amount is combined with the beginning cash balance to arrive at the ending cash balance—the same amount reported on the balance sheet.

> DO IT!

Classification of Cash Flows

Action Plan

✔ Identify the three types of activities used to report all cash inflows and outflows.

✔ Report as operating activities the cash effects of transactions that create revenues and expenses and enter into the determination of net income.

✔ Report as investing activities transactions that (a) acquire and dispose of investments

During its first week, Duffy & Stevenson Company had these transactions.

1. Issued 100,000 shares of $5 par value common stock for $800,000 cash.
2. Borrowed $200,000 from Castle Bank, signing a 5-year note bearing 8% interest.
3. Purchased two semi-trailer trucks for $170,000 cash.
4. Paid employees $12,000 for salaries and wages.
5. Collected $20,000 cash for services provided.

Classify each of these transactions by type of cash flow activity.

Action Plan (cont'd.)	Solution
and long-term assets and (b) lend money and collect loans.	
✔ Report as financing activities transactions that (a) obtain cash from issuing debt and repay the amounts borrowed and (b) obtain cash from stockholders and pay them dividends.	

Solution

1. Financing activity	4. Operating activity
2. Financing activity	5. Operating activity
3. Investing activity	

Related exercise material: **BE13-1, BE13-2, BE13-3, E13-1, E13-2, E13-3, and DO IT! 13-1.**

✔ **The Navigator**

Preparing the Statement of Cash Flows

Companies prepare the statement of cash flows differently from the three other basic financial statements. First, it is not prepared from an adjusted trial balance. It requires detailed information concerning the changes in account balances that occurred between two points in time. An adjusted trial balance will not provide the necessary data. Second, the statement of cash flows deals with cash receipts and payments. As a result, the company **must adjust** the effects of the use of accrual accounting **to determine cash flows**.

The information to prepare this statement usually comes from three sources:

- **Comparative balance sheets.** Information in the comparative balance sheets indicates the amount of the changes in assets, liabilities, and stockholders' equities from the beginning to the end of the period.

- **Current income statement.** Information in this statement helps determine the amount of cash provided or used by operations during the period.

- **Additional information.** Such information includes transaction data that are needed to determine how cash was provided or used during the period.

Preparing the statement of cash flows from these data sources involves three major steps, explained in Illustration 13-3 on the next page.

Indirect and Direct Methods

Usage of Methods

99% Indirect Method

1% Direct Method

In order to perform step 1, a company **must convert net income from an accrual basis to a cash basis**. This conversion may be done by either of two methods: (1) the indirect method or (2) the direct method. **Both methods arrive at the same total amount** for "Net cash provided by operating activities." They differ in **how** they arrive at the amount.

The **indirect method** adjusts net income for items that do not affect cash. A great majority of companies (99%) use this method, as shown in the chart on the left.[1] Companies favor the indirect method for two reasons: (1) It is easier and less costly to prepare, and (2) it focuses on the differences between net income and net cash flow from operating activities.

The **direct method** shows operating cash receipts and payments, making it more consistent with the objective of a statement of cash flows. The FASB has expressed a preference for the direct method but allows the use of either method.

The next section illustrates the more popular indirect method. Appendix 13B illustrates the direct method.

---

[1]*Accounting Trends and Techniques—2010* (New York: American Institute of Certified Public Accountants, 2010).

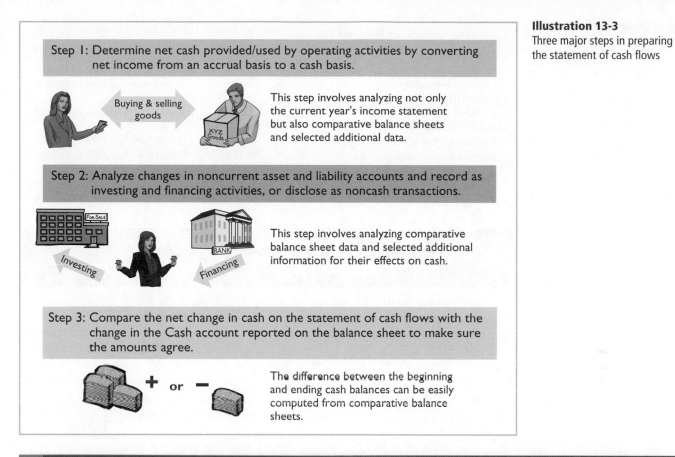

Illustration 13-3
Three major steps in preparing the statement of cash flows

Step 1: Determine net cash provided/used by operating activities by converting net income from an accrual basis to a cash basis.

Buying & selling goods

This step involves analyzing not only the current year's income statement but also comparative balance sheets and selected additional data.

Step 2: Analyze changes in noncurrent asset and liability accounts and record as investing and financing activities, or disclose as noncash transactions.

Investing   Financing

This step involves analyzing comparative balance sheet data and selected additional information for their effects on cash.

Step 3: Compare the net change in cash on the statement of cash flows with the change in the Cash account reported on the balance sheet to make sure the amounts agree.

+ or −

The difference between the beginning and ending cash balances can be easily computed from comparative balance sheets.

Preparing the Statement of Cash Flows—Indirect Method

To explain how to prepare a statement of cash flows using the indirect method, we use financial information from Computer Services Company. Illustration 13-4 presents Computer Services' current- and previous-year balance sheets, its current-year income statement, and related financial information for the current year.

LEARNING OBJECTIVE   3

Prepare a statement of cash flows using the indirect method.

Illustration 13-4
Comparative balance sheets, income statement, and additional information for Computer Services Company

Computer Services Company
Comparative Balance Sheets
December 31

Assets	2014	2013	Change in Account Balance Increase/Decrease
Current assets			
Cash	$ 55,000	$ 33,000	$ 22,000 Increase
Accounts receivable	20,000	30,000	10,000 Decrease
Inventory	15,000	10,000	5,000 Increase
Prepaid expenses	5,000	1,000	4,000 Increase
Property, plant, and equipment			
Land	130,000	20,000	110,000 Increase
Buildings	160,000	40,000	120,000 Increase
Accumulated depreciation—buildings	(11,000)	(5,000)	6,000 Increase
Equipment	27,000	10,000	17,000 Increase
Accumulated depreciation—equipment	(3,000)	(1,000)	2,000 Increase
Total assets	$398,000	$138,000	

Liabilities and Stockholders' Equity

Current liabilities			
Accounts payable	$ 28,000	$ 12,000	$ 16,000 Increase
Income taxes payable	6,000	8,000	2,000 Decrease
Long-term liabilities			
Bonds payable	130,000	20,000	110,000 Increase
Stockholders' equity			
Common stock	70,000	50,000	20,000 Increase
Retained earnings	164,000	48,000	116,000 Increase
Total liabilities and stockholders' equity	$398,000	$138,000	

Computer Services Company
Income Statement
For the Year Ended December 31, 2014

Sales revenue		$507,000
Cost of goods sold	$150,000	
Operating expenses (excluding depreciation)	111,000	
Depreciation expense	9,000	
Loss on disposal of plant assets	3,000	
Interest expense	42,000	315,000
Income before income tax		192,000
Income tax expense		47,000
Net income		$145,000

Additional information for 2014:
1. Depreciation expense was comprised of $6,000 for building and $3,000 for equipment.
2. The company sold equipment with a book value of $7,000 (cost $8,000, less accumulated depreciation $1,000) for $4,000 cash.
3. Issued $110,000 of long-term bonds in direct exchange for land.
4. A building costing $120,000 was purchased for cash. Equipment costing $25,000 was also purchased for cash.
5. Issued common stock for $20,000 cash.
6. The company declared and paid a $29,000 cash dividend.

We will now apply the three steps to the information provided for Computer Services Company. *(Appendix 13C demonstrates an approach that employs T-accounts to prepare the statement of cash flows. Many students find this approach helpful. We encourage you to give it a try as you walk through the Computer Services example.)*

Step 1: Operating Activities

DETERMINE NET CASH PROVIDED/USED BY OPERATING ACTIVITIES BY CONVERTING NET INCOME FROM AN ACCRUAL BASIS TO A CASH BASIS

To determine net cash provided by operating activities under the indirect method, companies **adjust net income in numerous ways**. A useful starting point is to understand **why** net income must be converted to net cash provided by operating activities.

Under generally accepted accounting principles, most companies use the accrual basis of accounting. This basis requires that companies record revenue when earned and record expenses when incurred. Earned revenues may include credit sales for which the company has not yet collected cash. Expenses incurred may include some items that the company has not yet paid in cash. Thus, net income under the accrual basis is not the same as net cash provided by operating activities.

Therefore, under the indirect method, companies must adjust net income to convert certain items to the cash basis. The indirect method (or reconciliation method) starts with net income and converts it to net cash provided by operating activities. Illustration 13-5 lists the three types of adjustments.

Net Income	+/−	Adjustments	=	Net Cash Provided/ Used by Operating Activities
		• **Add back noncash expenses**, such as depreciation expense, amortization, or depletion.		
		• **Deduct gains and add losses** that resulted from investing and financing activities.		
		• **Analyze changes** to noncash current asset and current liability accounts.		

Illustration 13-5
Three types of adjustments to convert net income to net cash provided by operating activities

We explain the three types of adjustments in the next three sections.

DEPRECIATION EXPENSE

Computer Services' income statement reports depreciation expense of $9,000. Although depreciation expense reduces net income, it does not reduce cash. In other words, depreciation expense is a noncash charge. The company must add it back to net income to arrive at net cash provided by operating activities. Computer Services reports depreciation expense in the statement of cash flows as shown below.

Helpful Hint
Depreciation is similar to any other expense in that it reduces net income. It differs in that it does not involve a current cash outflow. That is why it must be *added back* to net income to arrive at cash provided by operating activities.

Illustration 13-6
Adjustment for depreciation

Cash flows from operating activities	
Net income	$145,000
Adjustments to reconcile net income to net cash provided by operating activities:	
Depreciation expense	**9,000**
Net cash provided by operating activities	$154,000

As the first adjustment to net income in the statement of cash flows, companies frequently list depreciation and similar noncash charges such as amortization of intangible assets, depletion expense, and bad debt expense.

LOSS ON DISPOSAL OF PLANT ASSETS

Illustration 13-1 (page 589) states that cash received from the sale (disposal) of plant assets should be reported in the investing activities section. Because of this, **companies must eliminate from net income all gains and losses related to the disposal of plant assets, to arrive at cash provided by operating activities**.

In our example, Computer Services' income statement reports a $3,000 loss on disposal of plant assets (book value $7,000, less $4,000 cash received from disposal of plant assets). The company's loss of $3,000 should not be included in the operating activities section of the statement of cash flows. Illustration 13-7 shows that the $3,000 loss is eliminated by adding $3,000 back to net income to arrive at net cash provided by operating activities.

Illustration 13-7
Adjustment for loss on disposal of plant assets

Cash flows from operating activities		
Net income		$145,000
Adjustments to reconcile net income to net cash provided by operating activities:		
Depreciation expense	$9,000	
Loss on disposal of plant assets	**3,000**	12,000
Net cash provided by operating activities		$157,000

If a gain on disposal occurs, the company deducts the gain from its net income in order to determine net cash provided by operating activities. **In the case of either a gain or a loss, companies report the actual amount of cash received from the sale as a source of cash in the investing activities section of the statement of cash flows.**

CHANGES TO NONCASH CURRENT ASSET AND CURRENT LIABILITY ACCOUNTS

A final adjustment in reconciling net income to net cash provided by operating activities involves examining all changes in current asset and current liability accounts. The accrual accounting process records revenues in the period earned and expenses in the period incurred. For example, companies use Accounts Receivable to record amounts owed to the company for sales that have been made but for which cash collections have not yet been received. They use the Prepaid Insurance account to reflect insurance that has been paid for, but which has not yet expired, and therefore has not been expensed. Similarly, the Salaries and Wages Payable account reflects salaries and wages expense that has been incurred by the company but has not been paid.

As a result, we need to adjust net income for these accruals and prepayments to determine net cash provided by operating activities. Thus, we must analyze the change in each current asset and current liability account to determine its impact on net income and cash.

CHANGES IN NONCASH CURRENT ASSETS. The adjustments required for changes in noncash current asset accounts are as follows. **Deduct from net income increases in current asset accounts, and add to net income decreases in current asset accounts, to arrive at net cash provided by operating activities.** We can observe these relationships by analyzing the accounts of Computer Services Company.

DECREASE IN ACCOUNTS RECEIVABLE Computer Services Company's accounts receivable decreased by $10,000 (from $30,000 to $20,000) during the period. For Computer Services, this means that cash receipts were $10,000 higher than sales revenue. The Accounts Receivable account in Illustration 13-8 shows that Computer Services Company had $507,000 in sales revenue (as reported on the income statement), but it collected $517,000 in cash.

Illustration 13-8
Analysis of accounts receivable

	Accounts Receivable			
1/1/14	Balance	30,000	**Receipts from customers**	**517,000**
	Sales revenue	**507,000**		
12/31/14	Balance	20,000		

To adjust net income to net cash provided by operating activities, the company adds to net income the decrease of $10,000 in accounts receivable (see Illustration 13-9). When the Accounts Receivable balance increases, cash receipts are lower than sales revenue earned under the accrual basis. Therefore, the company deducts from net income the amount of the increase in accounts receivable, to arrive at net cash provided by operating activities.

INCREASE IN INVENTORY Computer Services Company's Inventory balance increased $5,000 (from $10,000 to $15,000) during the period. The change in the Inventory account reflects the difference between the amount of inventory purchased and the amount sold. For Computer Services, this means that the cost of merchandise purchased exceeded the cost of goods sold by $5,000. As a result, cost of goods sold does not reflect $5,000 of cash payments made for merchandise. The company deducts from net income this inventory increase of $5,000 during the period, to arrive at net cash provided by operating activities (see Illustration 13-9). If inventory decreases, the company adds to net income the amount of the change, to arrive at net cash provided by operating activities.

INCREASE IN PREPAID EXPENSES Computer Services' prepaid expenses increased during the period by $4,000. This means that cash paid for expenses is higher than expenses reported on an accrual basis. In other words, the company has made cash payments in the current period, but will not charge expenses to income until future periods (as charges to the income statement). To adjust net income to net cash provided by operating activities, the company deducts from net income the $4,000 increase in prepaid expenses (see Illustration 13-9).

			Illustration 13-9
Cash flows from operating activities			Adjustments for changes in current asset accounts
Net income		$145,000	
Adjustments to reconcile net income to net cash			
provided by operating activities:			
Depreciation expense	$ 9,000		
Loss on disposal of plant assets	3,000		
Decrease in accounts receivable	**10,000**		
Increase in inventory	**(5,000)**		
Increase in prepaid expenses	**(4,000)**	13,000	
Net cash provided by operating activities		$158,000	

If prepaid expenses decrease, reported expenses are higher than the expenses paid. Therefore, the company adds to net income the decrease in prepaid expenses, to arrive at net cash provided by operating activities.

CHANGES IN CURRENT LIABILITIES. The adjustments required for changes in current liability accounts are as follows. **Add to net income increases in current liability accounts, and deduct from net income decreases in current liability accounts, to arrive at net cash provided by operating activities.**

INCREASE IN ACCOUNTS PAYABLE For Computer Services Company, Accounts Payable increased by $16,000 (from $12,000 to $28,000) during the period. That means the company received $16,000 more in goods than it actually paid for. As shown in Illustration 13-10 (page 598), to adjust net income to determine net cash provided by operating activities, the company adds to net income the $16,000 increase in Accounts Payable.

DECREASE IN INCOME TAXES PAYABLE When a company incurs income tax expense but has not yet paid its taxes, it records income taxes payable. A change in the Income Taxes Payable account reflects the difference between income tax expense incurred and income tax actually paid. Computer Services' Income Taxes Payable account decreased by $2,000. That means the $47,000 of income tax expense reported on the income statement was $2,000 less than the amount of taxes paid during the period of $49,000. As shown in Illustration 13-10, to adjust net income to a cash basis, the company must reduce net income by $2,000.

Illustration 13-10
Adjustments for changes in current liability accounts

Cash flows from operating activities		
Net income		$145,000
Adjustments to reconcile net income to net cash provided by operating activities:		
Depreciation expense	$ 9,000	
Loss on disposal of plant assets	3,000	
Decrease in accounts receivable	10,000	
Increase in inventory	(5,000)	
Increase in prepaid expenses	(4,000)	
Increase in accounts payable	**16,000**	
Decrease in income taxes payable	**(2,000)**	27,000
Net cash provided by operating activities		$172,000

Illustration 13-10 shows that, after starting with net income of $145,000, the sum of all of the adjustments to net income was $27,000. This resulted in net cash provided by operating activities of $172,000.

Summary of Conversion to Net Cash Provided by Operating Activities—Indirect Method

As shown in the previous illustrations, the statement of cash flows prepared by the indirect method starts with net income. It then adds or deducts items to arrive at net cash provided by operating activities. The required adjustments are of three types:

1. Noncash charges such as depreciation, amortization, and depletion.

2. Gains and losses on disposal of plant assets.

3. Changes in noncash current asset and current liability accounts.

Illustration 13-11 provides a summary of these changes.

Illustration 13-11
Adjustments required to convert net income to net cash provided by operating activities

		Adjustments Required to Convert Net Income to Net Cash Provided by Operating Activities
Noncash Charges	Depreciation expense	Add
	Patent amortization expense	Add
	Depletion expense	Add
Gains and Losses	Loss on disposal of plant assets	Add
	Gain on disposal of plant assets	Deduct
Changes in Current Assets and Current Liabilities	Increase in current asset account	Deduct
	Decrease in current asset account	Add
	Increase in current liability account	Add
	Decrease in current liability account	Deduct

ETHICS INSIGHT

Cash Flow Isn't Always What It Seems

Some managers have taken actions that artificially increase cash flow from operating activities. They do this by moving negative amounts out of the operating section and into the investing or financing section.

For example, WorldCom, Inc. disclosed that it had improperly capitalized expenses: It had moved $3.8 billion of cash outflows from the "Cash from operating activities" section of the statement of cash flows to the "Investing activities" section, thereby greatly enhancing cash provided by operating activities. Similarly, Dynegy, Inc. restated its statement of cash flows because it had improperly included in operating activities, instead of in financing activities, $300 million from natural gas trading. The restatement resulted in a drop of 37% in cash flow from operating activities.

Source: Henny Sender, "Sadly, These Days Even Cash Flow Isn't Always What It Seems to Be," *Wall Street Journal* (May 8, 2002).

? For what reasons might managers at WorldCom and at Dynegy take the actions noted above? (See page 649.)

> DO IT!

Cash from Operating Activities

Action Plan

✔ Add noncash charges such as depreciation back to net income to compute net cash provided by operating activities.

✔ Deduct from net income gains on disposal of plant assets, or add losses back to net income, to compute net cash provided by operating activities.

✔ Use changes in non-cash current asset and current liability accounts to compute net cash provided by operating activities.

Josh's PhotoPlus reported net income of $73,000 for 2014. Included in the income statement were depreciation expense of $7,000 and a gain on disposal of plant assets of $2,500. Josh's comparative balance sheets show the following balances.

	12/31/13	12/31/14
Accounts receivable	$17,000	$21,000
Accounts payable	6,000	2,200

Calculate net cash provided by operating activities for Josh's PhotoPlus.

Solution

Cash flows from operating activities		
Net income		$73,000
Adjustments to reconcile net income to net cash provided by operating activities:		
Depreciation expense	$ 7,000	
Gain on disposal of plant assets	(2,500)	
Increase in accounts receivable	(4,000)	
Decrease in accounts payable	(3,800)	(3,300)
Net cash provided by operating activities		$69,700

Related exercise material: **BE13-4, BE13-5, BE13-6, BE13-7, E13-4, E13-5, E13-6, E13-7, E13-8, and** DO IT! **13-2.**

✔ **The Navigator**

Step 2: Investing and Financing Activities

ANALYZE CHANGES IN NONCURRENT ASSET AND LIABILITY ACCOUNTS AND RECORD AS INVESTING AND FINANCING ACTIVITIES, OR DISCLOSE AS NONCASH TRANSACTIONS

INCREASE IN LAND As indicated from the change in the Land account and the additional information, the company purchased land of $110,000 through the issuance of long-term bonds. The issuance of bonds payable for land has no effect on cash. But, it is a significant noncash investing and financing activity that merits disclosure in a separate schedule. (See Illustration 13-13 on page 601.)

INCREASE IN BUILDINGS As the additional data indicate, Computer Services Company acquired an office building for $120,000 cash. This is a cash outflow reported in the investing section. (See Illustration 13-13 on page 601.)

INCREASE IN EQUIPMENT The Equipment account increased $17,000. The additional information explains that this was a net increase that resulted from two transactions: (1) a purchase of equipment of $25,000, and (2) the sale for $4,000 of equipment costing $8,000. These transactions are investing activities. The company should report each transaction separately. Thus, it reports the purchase of equipment as an outflow of cash for $25,000. It reports the sale as an inflow of cash for $4,000. The T-account below shows the reasons for the change in this account during the year.

Illustration 13-12
Analysis of equipment

	Equipment			
1/1/14	Balance	10,000	Cost of equipment sold	8,000
	Purchase of equipment	**25,000**		
12/31/14	Balance	27,000		

The following entry shows the details of the equipment sale transaction.

A = L + SE
+4,000
+1,000
    −3,000 Exp
−8,000

Cash Flows
+4,000

Cash	4,000	
Accumulated Depreciation—Equipment	1,000	
Loss on Disposal of Plant Assets	3,000	
Equipment		8,000

INCREASE IN BONDS PAYABLE The Bonds Payable account increased $110,000. As indicated in the additional information, the company acquired land from the issuance of these bonds. It reports this noncash transaction in a separate schedule at the bottom of the statement.

Helpful Hint
When companies issue stocks or bonds for cash, the actual proceeds will appear in the statement of cash flows as a financing inflow (rather than the par value of the stocks or face value of bonds).

INCREASE IN COMMON STOCK The balance sheet reports an increase in Common Stock of $20,000. The additional information section notes that this increase resulted from the issuance of new shares of stock. This is a cash inflow reported in the financing section.

INCREASE IN RETAINED EARNINGS Retained earnings increased $116,000 during the year. This increase can be explained by two factors: (1) Net income of $145,000 increased retained earnings. (2) Dividends of $29,000 decreased retained earnings. The company adjusts net income to net cash provided by operating activities in the operating activities section. Payment of the dividends (not the declaration) is a **cash outflow that the company reports as a financing activity**.

ANATOMY OF A FRAUD

For more than a decade, the top executives at the Italian dairy products company Parmalat engaged in multiple frauds. The company overstated cash and other assets by more than $1 billion while understating liabilities by between $8 and $12 billion. Much of the fraud involved creating fictitious sources and uses of cash. Some of these activities incorporated sophisticated financial transactions with subsidiaries created with the help of large international financial institutions. However, much of the fraud employed very basic, even sloppy, forgery of documents. For example, when outside auditors requested confirmation of bank accounts (such as a fake $4.8 billion account in the Cayman Islands), documents were created on scanners, with signatures that were cut and pasted from other documents. These were then passed through a fax machine numerous times to make them look real (if difficult to read). Similarly, fictitious bills were created in order to divert funds to other businesses owned by the Tanzi family (who controlled Parmalat).

Total take: Billions of dollars

THE MISSING CONTROL

Independent Internal Verification. Internal auditors at the company should have independently verified bank accounts and major transfers of cash to outside companies that were controlled by the Tanzi family.

STATEMENT OF CASH FLOWS—2014

Using the previous information, we can now prepare a statement of cash flows for 2014 for Computer Services Company as shown in Illustration 13-13.

Step 3: Net Change in Cash

COMPARE THE NET CHANGE IN CASH ON THE STATEMENT OF CASH FLOWS WITH THE CHANGE IN THE CASH ACCOUNT REPORTED ON THE BALANCE SHEET TO MAKE SURE THE AMOUNTS AGREE

Illustration 13-13 indicates that the net change in cash during the period was an increase of $22,000. This agrees with the change in Cash account reported on the balance sheet in Illustration 13-4 (page 593).

Illustration 13-13
Statement of cash flows, 2014—indirect method

| Computer Services Company | | |
| Statement of Cash Flows—Indirect Method | | |
For the Year Ended December 31, 2014		
Cash flows from operating activities		
Net income		$ 145,000
Adjustments to reconcile net income to net cash		
provided by operating activities:		
Depreciation expense	$ 9,000	
Loss on disposal of plant assets	3,000	
Decrease in accounts receivable	10,000	
Increase in inventory	(5,000)	
Increase in prepaid expenses	(4,000)	
Increase in accounts payable	16,000	
Decrease in income taxes payable	(2,000)	27,000
Net cash provided by operating activities		172,000
Cash flows from investing activities		
Purchase of building	(120,000)	
Purchase of equipment	(25,000)	
Disposal of plant assets	4,000	
Net cash used by investing activities		(141,000)

Helpful Hint
Note that in the investing and financing activities sections, positive numbers indicate cash inflows (receipts), and negative numbers indicate cash outflows (payments).

Illustration 13-13
(cont'd.)

Cash flows from financing activities		
Issuance of common stock	20,000	
Payment of cash dividends	(29,000)	
Net cash used by financing activities		(9,000)
Net increase in cash		22,000
Cash at beginning of period		33,000
Cash at end of period		$ 55,000
Noncash investing and financing activities		
Issuance of bonds payable to purchase land		$ 110,000

> DO IT!

Indirect Method

Helpful Hint
1. Determine net cash provided/used by operating activities, recognizing that operating activities generally relate to changes in current assets and current liabilities.
2. Determine net cash provided/used by investing activities, recognizing that investing activities generally relate to changes in noncurrent assets.
3. Determine net cash provided/used by financing activities, recognizing that financing activities generally relate to changes in long-term liabilities and stockholders' equity accounts.

Use the information below to prepare a statement of cash flows using the indirect method.

Reynolds Company
Comparative Balance Sheets
December 31

Assets	2014	2013	Change Increase/Decrease
Cash	$ 54,000	$ 37,000	$ 17,000 Increase
Accounts receivable	68,000	26,000	42,000 Increase
Inventory	54,000	–0–	54,000 Increase
Prepaid expenses	4,000	6,000	2,000 Decrease
Land	75,000	70,000	5,000 Increase
Buildings	200,000	200,000	–0–
Accumulated depreciation—buildings	(21,000)	(11,000)	10,000 Increase
Equipment	193,000	68,000	125,000 Increase
Accumulated depreciation—equipment	(28,000)	(10,000)	18,000 Increase
Totals	$599,000	$386,000	

Liabilities and Stockholders' Equity			
Accounts payable	$ 23,000	$ 40,000	$ 17,000 Decrease
Accrued expenses payable	10,000	–0–	10,000 Increase
Bonds payable	140,000	150,000	10,000 Decrease
Common stock ($1 par)	220,000	60,000	160,000 Increase
Retained earnings	206,000	136,000	70,000 Increase
Totals	$599,000	$386,000	

Reynolds Company
Income Statement
For the Year Ended December 31, 2014

Sales revenue		$890,000
Cost of goods sold	$465,000	
Operating expenses	221,000	
Interest expense	12,000	
Loss on disposal of plant assets	2,000	700,000
Income before income taxes		190,000
Income tax expense		65,000
Net income		$125,000

Additional information:

1. Operating expenses include depreciation expense of $33,000.
2. Equipment with a cost of $41,000 and a book value of $36,000 was sold for $34,000 cash.
3. Land was sold at its book value for cash.
4. Interest expense of $12,000 was paid in cash.
5. Equipment with a cost of $166,000 was purchased for cash.
6. Bonds of $10,000 were redeemed at their face value for cash.
7. Common stock ($1 par) of $130,000 was issued for cash.
8. Cash dividends of $55,000 were declared and paid in 2014.
9. Common stock of $30,000 was issued in exchange for land.

Solution

Action Plan

✔ Determine net cash provided/used by operating activities by adjusting net income for items that did not affect cash.

✔ Determine net cash provided/used by investing activities and financing activities.

✔ Determine the net increase/decrease in cash.

Reynolds Company Statement of Cash Flows—Indirect Method For the Year Ended December 31, 2014		
Cash flows from operating activities		
Net income		$ 125,000
Adjustments to reconcile net income to net cash provided by operating activities:		
Depreciation expense	$ 33,000	
Loss on disposal of plant assets	2,000	
Increase in accounts receivable	(12,000)	
Increase in inventory	(54,000)	
Decrease in prepaid expenses	2,000	
Decrease in accounts payable	(17,000)	
Increase in accrued expenses payable	10,000	(66,000)
Net cash provided by operating activities		59,000
Cash flows from investing activities		
Sale of land	25,000	
Disposal of plant assets	34,000	
Purchase of equipment	(166,000)	
Net cash used by investing activities		(107,000)
Cash flows from financing activities		
Redemption of bonds	(10,000)	
Sale of common stock	130,000	
Payment of dividends	(55,000)	
Net cash provided by financing activities		65,000
Net increase in cash		17,000
Cash at beginning of period		37,000
Cash at end of period		$ 54,000
Noncash investing and financing activities		
Issued common stock in exchange for land		$ 30,000

Related exercise material: **BE13-4, BE13-5, BE13-6, BE13-7, E13-4, E13-5, E13-6, E13-7, E13-8, and E13-9.**

✔ **The Navigator**

Using Cash Flows to Evaluate a Company

LEARNING OBJECTIVE   **4**

Analyze the statement of cash flows.

Traditionally, investors and creditors have most commonly used ratios based on numbers derived from accrual accounting. These days, cash-based ratios are gaining increased acceptance among analysts.

Free Cash Flow

In the statement of cash flows, cash provided by operating activities is intended to indicate the cash-generating capability of the company. Analysts have noted, however, that **cash provided by operating activities fails to take into account that a company must invest in new fixed assets** just to maintain its current level of operations. Companies also must at least **maintain dividends at current levels** to satisfy investors. The measurement of free cash flow provides additional insight regarding a company's cash-generating ability. **Free cash flow** describes the cash remaining from operations after adjustment for capital expenditures and dividends.

Consider the following example: Suppose that MPC produced and sold 10,000 personal computers this year. It reported $100,000 cash provided by operating activities. In order to maintain production at 10,000 computers, MPC invested $15,000 in equipment. It chose to pay $5,000 in dividends. Its free cash flow was $80,000 ($100,000 − $15,000 − $5,000). The company could use this $80,000 either to purchase new assets to expand the business or to pay an $80,000 dividend and continue to produce 10,000 computers. In practice, free cash flow is often calculated with the formula in Illustration 13-14. (Alternative definitions also exist.)

Illustration 13-14
Free cash flow

Free Cash Flow	=	Cash Provided by Operating Activities	−	Capital Expenditures	−	Cash Dividends

Illustration 13-15 provides basic information (in billions) excerpted from the 2009 statement of cash flows of Microsoft Corporation.

Illustration 13-15
Microsoft cash flow information
($ in millions)

Microsoft Corporation
Statement of Cash Flows (partial)
2009

Cash provided by operating activities		$ 19,037
Cash flows from investing activities		
Additions to property and equipment	$ (3,119)	
Purchases of investments	(36,850)	
Sales of investments	19,806	
Acquisitions of companies	(868)	
Maturities of investments	6,191	
Other	(930)	
Cash used by investing activities		(15,770)
Cash paid for dividends		(4,468)

Microsoft's free cash flow is calculated as shown in Illustration 13-16.

Cash provided by operating activities	$ 19,037
Less: Expenditures on property, plant, and equipment	3,119
Dividends paid	4,468
Free cash flow	**$11,450**

Illustration 13-16
Calculation of Microsoft's free cash flow ($ in millions)

Microsoft generated approximately $11.4 billion of free cash flow. This is a tremendous amount of cash generated in a single year. It is available for the acquisition of new assets, the retirement of stock or debt, or the payment of dividends.

Also note that Microsoft's cash from operations of $19 billion exceeds its 2009 net income of $14.6 billion. This lends additional credibility to Microsoft's income number as an indicator of potential future performance. If anything, Microsoft's net income might understate its actual performance.

As another example, consider Oracle Corporation, one of the world's largest sellers of database software and information management services. Like Microsoft, its success depends on continuing to improve its existing products while developing new products to keep pace with rapid changes in technology. Oracle's free cash flow for 2009 was $7.5 billion. This is impressive but significantly less than Microsoft's amazing ability to generate cash.

DECISION TOOLKIT

DECISION CHECKPOINTS	INFO NEEDED FOR DECISION	TOOL TO USE FOR DECISION	HOW TO EVALUATE RESULTS
How much cash did the company generate to either expand operations or pay dividends?	Cash provided by operating activities, cash spent on fixed assets, and cash dividends	$\text{Free cash flow} = \text{Cash provided by operations} - \text{Capital expenditures} - \text{Cash dividends}$	Significant free cash flow indicates greater potential to finance new investment and pay additional dividends.

> DO IT!

Free Cash Flow

Chicago Corporation issued the following statement of cash flows for 2014.

Chicago Corporation
Statement of Cash Flows—Indirect Method
For the Year Ended December 31, 2014

Cash flows from operating activities		
Net income		$ 19,000
Adjustments to reconcile net income to net cash provided by operating activities:		
Depreciation expense	$ 8,100	
Loss on disposal of plant assets	1,300	
Decrease in accounts receivable	6,900	
Increase in inventory	(4,000)	
Decrease in accounts payable	(2,000)	10,300
Net cash provided by operating activities		29,300

Cash flows from investing activities		
Sale of investments	1,100	
Purchase of equipment	(19,000)	
Net cash used by investing activities		(17,900)
Cash flows from financing activities		
Issuance of stock	10,000	
Payment on long-term note payable	(5,000)	
Payment for dividends	(9,000)	
Net cash used by financing activities		(4,000)
Net increase in cash		7,400
Cash at beginning of year		10,000
Cash at end of year		$ 17,400

(a) Compute free cash flow for Chicago Corporation. (b) Explain why free cash flow often provides better information than "Net cash provided by operating activities."

Solution

Action Plan

✔ Compute free cash flow as: Cash provided by operating activities – Capital expenditures – Cash dividends.

(a) Free cash flow = $29,300 – $19,000 – $9,000 = $1,300

(b) Cash provided by operating activities fails to take into account that a company must invest in new plant assets just to maintain the current level of operations. Companies must also maintain dividends at current levels to satisfy investors. The measurement of free cash flow provides additional insight regarding a company's cash-generating ability.

Related exercise material: **BE13-8, BE13-9, BE13-10, BE13-11, E13-7, E13-9, and** DO IT! **13-3.**

✔ **The Navigator**

USING THE **DECISION TOOLKIT**

Intel Corporation is the leading producer of computer chips for personal computers. It makes the hugely successful Pentium chip. Its primary competitor is AMD (formerly Advanced Micro Devices). The two are vicious competitors, with frequent lawsuits filed between them. Financial statement data for Intel are provided below.

Instructions

Calculate free cash flow for Intel, and compare it with AMD's free cash flow, which was $7 million.

Intel Corporation
Statements of Cash Flows
For the Years Ended 12/27/09 and 12/29/08
(in millions)

	2009	2008
Net cash provided by operating activities	$11,170	$10,926
Net cash used for investing activities	(7,965)	(5,865)
Net cash used for financing activities	(2,568)	(9,018)
Net increase (decrease) in cash and cash equivalents	$ 637	$ (3,957)

Note. Cash spent on property, plant, and equipment in 2009 was $4,515. Cash paid for dividends was $3,108.

Solution

Intel's free cash flow is $3,547 million ($11,170 – $4,515 – $3,108). Compared to AMD's $7 million, this gives Intel a huge advantage in the ability to move quickly to invest in new projects.

✔ **The Navigator**

SUMMARY OF LEARNING OBJECTIVES

✔ The Navigator

1 Indicate the usefulness of the statement of cash flows. The statement of cash flows provides information about the cash receipts, cash payments, and net change in cash resulting from the operating, investing, and financing activities of a company during the period.

2 Distinguish among operating, investing, and financing activities. Operating activities include the cash effects of transactions that enter into the determination of net income. Investing activities involve cash flows resulting from changes in investments and long-term asset items. Financing activities involve cash flows resulting from changes in long-term liability and stockholders' equity items.

3 Prepare a statement of cash flows using the indirect method. The preparation of a statement of cash flows

involves three major steps: (1) Determine net cash provided/used by operating activities by converting net income from an accrual basis to a cash basis. (2) Analyze changes in noncurrent asset and liability accounts and record as investing and financing activities, or disclose as noncash transactions. (3) Compare the net change in cash on the statement of cash flows with the change in the Cash account reported on the balance sheet to make sure the amounts agree.

4 Analyze the statement of cash flows. Free cash flow indicates the amount of cash a company generated during the current year that is available for the payment of additional dividends or for expansion.

DECISION TOOLKIT A SUMMARY

DECISION CHECKPOINTS	INFO NEEDED FOR DECISION	TOOL TO USE FOR DECISION	HOW TO EVALUATE RESULTS
How much cash did the company generate to either expand operations or pay dividends?	Cash provided by operating activities, cash spent on fixed assets, and cash dividends	$\text{Free cash flow} = \begin{matrix}\text{Cash} \\ \text{provided} \\ \text{by} \\ \text{operating} \\ \text{activities}\end{matrix} - \begin{matrix}\text{Capital} \\ \text{expen-} \\ \text{ditures}\end{matrix} - \begin{matrix}\text{Cash} \\ \text{divi-} \\ \text{dends}\end{matrix}$	Significant free cash flow indicates greater potential to finance new investment and pay additional dividends.

> Comprehensive DO IT! 1

The income statement for the year ended December 31, 2014, for Kosinski Company contains the following condensed information.

Kosinski Company
Income Statement
For the Year Ended December 31, 2014

Sales revenue		$6,583,000
Operating expenses (excluding depreciation)	$4,920,000	
Depreciation expense	880,000	5,800,000
Income before income taxes		783,000
Income tax expense		353,000
Net income		$ 430,000

Included in operating expenses is a $24,000 loss resulting from the sale of machinery for $270,000 cash. Machinery was purchased at a cost of $750,000.

The following balances are reported on Kosinski's comparative balance sheets at December 31.

Kosinski Company
Comparative Balance Sheets (partial)

	2014	2013
Cash	$672,000	$130,000
Accounts receivable	775,000	610,000
Inventory	834,000	867,000
Accounts payable	521,000	501,000

Income tax expense of $353,000 represents the amount paid in 2014. Dividends declared and paid in 2014 totaled $200,000.

Instructions

Prepare the statement of cash flows using the indirect method.

Solution to Comprehensive DO IT! 1

Kosinski Company
Statement of Cash Flows—Indirect Method
For the Year Ended December 31, 2014

Cash flows from operating activities		
Net income		$ 430,000
Adjustments to reconcile net income to net cash provided by operating activities:		
Depreciation expense	$ 880,000	
Loss on disposal of plant assets	24,000	
Increase in accounts receivable	(165,000)	
Decrease in inventory	33,000	
Increase in accounts payable	20,000	792,000
Net cash provided by operating activities		1,222,000
Cash flows from investing activities		
Disposal of plant assets	270,000	
Purchase of machinery	(750,000)	
Net cash used by investing activities		(480,000)
Cash flows from financing activities		
Payment of cash dividends		(200,000)
Net increase in cash		542,000
Cash at beginning of period		130,000
Cash at end of period		$ 672,000

✔ **The Navigator**

APPENDIX 13A USING A WORKSHEET TO PREPARE THE STATEMENT OF CASH FLOWS—INDIRECT METHOD

When preparing a statement of cash flows, companies may need to make numerous adjustments of net income. In such cases, they often use **a worksheet to assemble and classify the data that will appear on the statement**. The worksheet is merely an aid in preparing the statement. Its use is optional. Illustration 13A-1 shows the skeleton format of the worksheet for preparation of the statement of cash flows.

The following guidelines are important in preparing a worksheet.

1. In the balance sheet accounts section, **list accounts with debit balances separately from those with credit balances**. This means, for example, that Accumulated Depreciation appears under credit balances and not as a contra account under debit balances. Enter the beginning and ending balances of each account in the appropriate columns. Enter as reconciling items in the two middle columns the transactions that caused the change in the account balance during the year.

    After all reconciling items have been entered, each line pertaining to a balance sheet account should "foot across." That is, the beginning balance plus or minus the reconciling item(s) must equal the ending balance. When this

Illustration 13A-1
Format of worksheet

		XYZ Company.xls				
Home	Insert	Page Layout Formulas Data Review View				
P18		fx				
	A	B	C	D	E	
1						
2		**XYZ Company**				
3		Worksheet				
4		Statement of Cash Flows For the Year Ended . . .				
5						
6		End of			End of	
7		Last Year	Reconciling Items		Current Year	
8	**Balance Sheet Accounts**	Balances	Debit	Credit	Balances	
9	Debit balance accounts	XX	XX	XX	XX	
10		XX	XX	XX	XX	
11	Totals	XXX			XXX	
12	Credit balance accounts	XX	XX	XX	XX	
13		XX	XX	XX	XX	
14	Totals	XXX			XXX	
15						
16	**Statement of Cash**					
17	**Flows Effects**					
18	Operating activities					
19	Net income		XX			
20	Adjustments to net income		XX	XX		
21	Investing activities					
22	Receipts and payments		XX	XX		
23	Financing activities					
24	Receipts and payments		XX	XX		
25	Totals		XXX	XXX		
26	Increase (decrease) in cash		(XX)	XX		
27	Totals		XXX	XXX		
28						

agreement exists for all balance sheet accounts, all changes in account balances have been reconciled.

2. The bottom portion of the worksheet consists of the operating, investing, and financing activities sections. It provides the information necessary to prepare the formal statement of cash flows. **Enter inflows of cash as debits in the reconciling columns. Enter outflows of cash as credits in the reconciling columns.** Thus, in this section, the sale of equipment for cash at book value appears as a debit under investing activities. Similarly, the purchase of land for cash appears as a credit under investing activities.

3. **The reconciling items shown in the worksheet are not entered in any journal or posted to any account.** They do not represent either adjustments or corrections of the balance sheet accounts. They are used only to facilitate the preparation of the statement of cash flows.

Preparing the Worksheet

As in the case of worksheets illustrated in earlier chapters, preparing a worksheet involves a series of prescribed steps. The steps in this case are:

1. Enter in the balance sheet accounts section the balance sheet accounts and their beginning and ending balances.

2. Enter in the reconciling columns of the worksheet the data that explain the changes in the balance sheet accounts other than cash and their effects on the statement of cash flows.

3. Enter on the cash line and at the bottom of the worksheet the increase or decrease in cash. This entry should enable the totals of the reconciling columns to be in agreement.

To illustrate the preparation of a worksheet, we will use the 2014 data for Computer Services Company. Your familiarity with these data (from the chapter) should help you understand the use of a worksheet. For ease of reference, the comparative balance sheets, income statement, and selected data for 2014 are presented in Illustration 13A-2.

DETERMINING THE RECONCILING ITEMS

Companies can use one of several approaches to determine the reconciling items. For example, they can first complete the changes affecting net cash provided

Illustration 13A-2
Comparative balance sheets, income statement, and additional information for Computer Services Company

	Computer Services Company.xls		
Home Insert Page Layout Formulas Data Review View			
P18 *fx*			
A	**B**	**C**	**D**
1	**Computer Services Company**		
2	**Comparative Balance Sheets**		
3	**December 31**		
4			**Change in**
5			**Account Balance**
6 **Assets**	**2014**	**2013**	**Increase/Decrease**
7 Current assets			
8 Cash	$ 55,000	$ 33,000	$ 22,000 Increase
9 Accounts receivable	20,000	30,000	10,000 Decrease
10 Inventory	15,000	10,000	5,000 Increase
11 Prepaid expenses	5,000	1,000	4,000 Increase
12 Property, plant, and equipment			
13 Land	130,000	20,000	110,000 Increase
14 Buildings	160,000	40,000	120,000 Increase
15 Accumulated depreciation—buildings	(11,000)	(5,000)	6,000 Increase
16 Equipment	27,000	10,000	17,000 Increase
17 Accumulated depreciation—equipment	(3,000)	(1,000)	2,000 Increase
18 Total	$398,000	$138,000	
19			
20 **Liabilities and Stockholders' Equity**			
21 Current liabilities			
22 Accounts payable	$ 28,000	$ 12,000	$ 16,000 Increase
23 Income taxes payable	6,000	8,000	2,000 Decrease
24 Long-term liabilities			
25 Bonds payable	130,000	20,000	110,000 Increase
26 Stockholders' equity			
27 Common stock	70,000	50,000	20,000 Increase
28 Retained earnings	164,000	48,000	116,000 Increase
29 Total liabilities and stockholders' equity	$398,000	$138,000	

Illustration 13A-2
(cont'd.)

	A	B	C	D	
	🖫 ⤺ ⤻ ⤵	Computer Services Company.xls			
	Home Insert Page Layout Formulas Data Review View				
	P18	fx			
1					
2		**Computer Services Company**			
3		**Income Statement**			
4		**For the Year Ended December 31, 2014**			
5	Sales revenue				$507,000
6	Cost of goods sold			$150,000	
7	Operating expenses (excluding depreciation)			111,000	
8	Depreciation expense			9,000	
9	Loss on disposal of plant assets			3,000	
10	Interest expense			42,000	315,000
11	Income before income tax				192,000
12	Income tax expense				47,000
13	Net income				$145,000
14					

Additional information for 2014:

1. Depreciation expense was comprised of $6,000 for building and $3,000 for equipment.
2. The company sold equipment with a book value of $7,000 (cost $8,000, less accumulated depreciation $1,000) for $4,000 cash.
3. Issued $110,000 of long-term bonds in direct exchange for land.
4. A building costing $120,000 was purchased for cash. Equipment costing $25,000 was also purchased for cash.
5. Issued common stock for $20,000 cash.
6. The company declared and paid a $29,000 cash dividend.

by operating activities, and then can determine the effects of financing and investing transactions. Or, they can analyze the balance sheet accounts in the order in which they are listed on the worksheet. We will follow this latter approach for Computer Services, except for cash. As indicated in step 3, **cash is handled last**.

ACCOUNTS RECEIVABLE The decrease of $10,000 in accounts receivable means that cash collections from sales revenue are higher than the sales revenue reported in the income statement. To convert net income to net cash provided by operating activities, we add the decrease of $10,000 to net income. The entry in the reconciling columns of the worksheet is:

| (a) | Operating—Decrease in Accounts Receivable | 10,000 | |
| | Accounts Receivable | | 10,000 |

INVENTORY Computer Services Company's inventory balance increases $5,000 during the period. The Inventory account reflects the difference between the amount of inventory that the company purchased and the amount that it sold. For Computer Services, this means that the cost of merchandise purchased exceeds the cost of goods sold by $5,000. As a result, cost of goods sold does not reflect $5,000 of cash payments made for merchandise. We deduct this inventory increase of $5,000 during the period from net income to arrive at net cash provided by operating activities. The worksheet entry is:

| (b) | Inventory | 5,000 | |
| | Operating—Increase in Inventory | | 5,000 |

PREPAID EXPENSES An increase of $4,000 in prepaid expenses means that expenses deducted in determining net income are less than expenses that were paid in cash. We deduct the increase of $4,000 from net income in determining net cash provided by operating activities. The worksheet entry is:

| (c) | Prepaid Expenses | 4,000 | |
| | Operating—Increase in Prepaid Expenses | | 4,000 |

Helpful Hint
These amounts are asterisked in the worksheet to indicate that they result from a significant noncash transaction.

LAND The increase in land of $110,000 resulted from a purchase through the issuance of long-term bonds. The company should report this transaction as a significant noncash investing and financing activity. The worksheet entry is:

| (d) | Land | 110,000 | |
| | Bonds Payable | | 110,000 |

BUILDINGS The cash purchase of a building for $120,000 is an investing activity cash outflow. The entry in the reconciling columns of the worksheet is:

| (e) | Buildings | 120,000 | |
| | Investing—Purchase of Building | | 120,000 |

EQUIPMENT The increase in equipment of $17,000 resulted from a cash purchase of $25,000 and the sale of equipment costing $8,000. The book value of the equipment was $7,000, the cash proceeds were $4,000, and a loss of $3,000 was recorded. The worksheet entries are:

| (f) | Equipment | 25,000 | |
| | Investing—Purchase of Equipment | | 25,000 |

(g)	Investing—Disposal of Plant Assets	4,000	
	Operating—Loss on Disposal of Plant Assets	3,000	
	Accumulated Depreciation—Equipment	1,000	
	Equipment		8,000

ACCOUNTS PAYABLE We must add the increase of $16,000 in accounts payable to net income to determine net cash provided by operating activities. The worksheet entry is:

| (h) | Operating—Increase in Accounts Payable | 16,000 | |
| | Accounts Payable | | 16,000 |

INCOME TAXES PAYABLE When a company incurs income tax expense but has not yet paid its taxes, it records income taxes payable. A change in the Income Taxes Payable account reflects the difference between income tax expense incurred and income tax actually paid. Computer Services' Income Taxes Payable account decreases by $2,000. That means the $47,000 of income tax expense reported on the income statement was $2,000 less than the amount of taxes paid during the period of $49,000. To adjust net income to a cash basis, we must reduce net income by $2,000. The worksheet entry is:

(i)	Income Taxes Payable	2,000	
	Operating—Decrease in Income Taxes		
	Payable		2,000

BONDS PAYABLE The increase of $110,000 in this account resulted from the issuance of bonds for land. This is a significant noncash investing and financing activity. Worksheet entry (d) above is the only entry necessary.

COMMON STOCK The balance sheet reports an increase in Common Stock of $20,000. The additional information section notes that this increase resulted from the issuance of new shares of stock. This is a cash inflow reported in the financing section. The worksheet entry is:

| (j) | Financing—Issuance of Common Stock | 20,000 | |
| | Common Stock | | 20,000 |

ACCUMULATED DEPRECIATION—BUILDINGS, AND ACCUMULATED DEPRECIATION—EQUIPMENT Increases in these accounts of $6,000 and $3,000, respectively, resulted from depreciation expense. Depreciation expense is a **noncash charge that we must add to net income** to determine net cash provided by operating activities. The worksheet entries are:

| (k) | Operating—Depreciation Expense | 6,000 | |
| | Accumulated Depreciation—Buildings | | 6,000 |

| (l) | Operating—Depreciation Expense | 3,000 | |
| | Accumulated Depreciation—Equipment | | 3,000 |

RETAINED EARNINGS The $116,000 increase in retained earnings resulted from net income of $145,000 and the declaration and payment of a $29,000 cash dividend. Net income is included in net cash provided by operating activities, and the dividends are a financing activity cash outflow. The entries in the reconciling columns of the worksheet are:

| (m) | Operating—Net Income | 145,000 | |
| | Retained Earnings | | 145,000 |

| (n) | Retained Earnings | 29,000 | |
| | Financing—Payment of Dividends | | 29,000 |

DISPOSITION OF CHANGE IN CASH The firm's cash increased $22,000 in 2014. The final entry on the worksheet, therefore, is:

| (o) | Cash | 22,000 | |
| | Increase in Cash | | 22,000 |

As shown in the worksheet, we enter the increase in cash in the reconciling credit column as a **balancing** amount. This entry should complete the reconciliation of the changes in the balance sheet accounts. Also, it should permit the totals of the reconciling columns to be in agreement. When all changes have been explained and the reconciling columns are in agreement, the reconciling columns are ruled to complete the worksheet. The completed worksheet for Computer Services Company is shown in Illustration 13A-3 (page 614).

Illustration 13A-3
Completed worksheet—
indirect method

	Computer Services Company.xls				
P18	*fx*				
	A	B	C	D	E
	Computer Services Company				
	Worksheet				
	Statement of Cash Flows For the Year Ended December 31, 2014				
		Balance	Reconciling Items		Balance
	Balance Sheet Accounts	**12/31/13**	**Debit**	**Credit**	**12/31/14**
7	Debits				
8	Cash	33,000	(o) 22,000		55,000
9	Accounts Receivable	30,000		(a) 10,000	20,000
10	Inventory	10,000	(b) 5,000		15,000
11	Prepaid Expenses	1,000	(c) 4,000		5,000
12	Land	20,000	(d) 110,000*		130,000
13	Buildings	40,000	(e) 120,000		160,000
14	Equipment	10,000	(f) 25,000	(g) 8,000	27,000
15	Total	144,000			412,000
16	Credits				
17	Accounts Payable	12,000		(h) 16,000	28,000
18	Income Taxes Payable	8,000	(i) 2,000		6,000
19	Bonds Payable	20,000		(d) 110,000*	130,000
20	Accumulated Depreciation—Buildings	5,000		(k) 6,000	11,000
21	Accumulated Depreciation—Equipment	1,000	(g) 1,000	(l) 3,000	3,000
22	Common Stock	50,000		(j) 20,000	70,000
23	Retained Earnings	48,000	(n) 29,000	(m) 145,000	164,000
24	Total	144,000			412,000
25					
26	**Statement of Cash Flows Effects**				
27	Operating activities				
28	Net income		(m) 145,000		
29	Decrease in accounts receivable		(a) 10,000		
30	Increase in inventory			(b) 5,000	
31	Increase in prepaid expenses			(c) 4,000	
32	Increase in accounts payable		(h) 16,000		
33	Decrease in income taxes payable			(i) 2,000	
34	Depreciation expense		(k) 6,000		
35			(l) 3,000		
36	Loss on disposal of plant assets		(g) 3,000		
37	Investing activities				
38	Purchase of building			(e) 120,000	
39	Purchase of equipment			(f) 25,000	
40	Disposal of plant assets		(g) 4,000		
41	Financing activities				
42	Issuance of common stock		(j) 20,000		
43	Payment of dividends			(n) 29,000	
44	Totals		525,000	503,000	
45	Increase in cash			(o) 22,000	
46	Totals		525,000	525,000	
47					
	* Significant noncash investing and financing activity.				

SUMMARY OF LEARNING OBJECTIVE FOR APPENDIX 13A

✔ The Navigator

5 Explain how to use a worksheet to prepare the statement of cash flows using the indirect method. When there are numerous adjustments, a worksheet can be a helpful tool in preparing the statement of cash flows. Key guidelines for using a worksheet are: (1) List accounts with debit balances separately from those with credit balances. (2) In the reconciling columns in the bottom portion of the worksheet, show cash inflows as debits and cash outflows as credits. (3) Do not enter reconciling items in any journal or account, but use them only to help prepare the statement of cash flows.

The steps in preparing the worksheet are: (1) Enter beginning and ending balances of balance sheet accounts. (2) Enter debits and credits in reconciling columns. (3) Enter the increase or decrease in cash in two places as a balancing amount.

APPENDIX 13B STATEMENT OF CASH FLOWS—DIRECT METHOD

To explain and illustrate the direct method, we will use the transactions of Computer Services Company for 2014, to prepare a statement of cash flows. Illustration 13B-1 presents information related to 2014 for Computer Services Company.

LEARNING OBJECTIVE   6

Prepare a statement of cash flows using the direct method.

Illustration 13B-1
Comparative balance sheets, income statement, and additional information for Computer Services Company

Computer Services Company
Comparative Balance Sheets
December 31

Assets	2014	2013	Change in Account Balance Increase/Decrease
Current assets			
Cash	$ 55,000	$ 33,000	$ 22,000 Increase
Accounts receivable	20,000	30,000	10,000 Decrease
Inventory	15,000	10,000	5,000 Increase
Prepaid expenses	5,000	1,000	4,000 Increase
Property, plant, and equipment			
Land	130,000	20,000	110,000 Increase
Buildings	160,000	40,000	120,000 Increase
Accumulated depreciation— buildings	(11,000)	(5,000)	6,000 Increase
Equipment	27,000	10,000	17,000 Increase
Accumulated depreciation— equipment	(3,000)	(1,000)	2,000 Increase
Total assets	$398,000	$138,000	

Liabilities and Stockholders' Equity	2014	2013	Change in Account Balance Increase/Decrease
Current liabilities			
Accounts payable	$ 28,000	$ 12,000	$ 16,000 Increase
Income taxes payable	6,000	8,000	2,000 Decrease
Long-term liabilities			
Bonds payable	130,000	20,000	110,000 Increase
Stockholders' equity			
Common stock	70,000	50,000	20,000 Increase
Retained earnings	164,000	48,000	116,000 Increase
Total liabilities and stockholders' equity	$398,000	$138,000	

Computer Services Company Income Statement For the Year Ended December 31, 2014		
Revenues		$507,000
Cost of goods sold	$150,000	
Operating expenses (excluding depreciation)	111,000	
Depreciation expense	9,000	
Loss on disposal of plant assets	3,000	
Interest expense	42,000	315,000
Income before income tax		192,000
Income tax expense		47,000
Net income		$145,000

Additional information for 2014:
1. Depreciation expense was comprised of $6,000 for building and $3,000 for equipment.
2. The company sold equipment with a book value of $7,000 (cost $8,000, less accumulated depreciation $1,000) for $4,000 cash.
3. Issued $110,000 of long-term bonds in direct exchange for land.
4. A building costing $120,000 was purchased for cash. Equipment costing $25,000 was also purchased for cash.
5. Issued common stock for $20,000 cash.
6. The company declared and paid a $29,000 cash dividend.

To prepare a statement of cash flows under the direct approach, we will apply the three steps outlined in Illustration 13-3 (page 593).

Step 1: Operating Activities

DETERMINE NET CASH PROVIDED/USED BY OPERATING ACTIVITIES BY CONVERTING NET INCOME FROM AN ACCRUAL BASIS TO A CASH BASIS
Under the **direct method**, companies compute net cash provided by operating activities by **adjusting each item in the income statement** from the accrual basis to the cash basis. To simplify and condense the operating activities section, companies **report only major classes of operating cash receipts and cash payments**. For these major classes, the difference between cash receipts and cash payments is the net cash provided by operating activities. These relationships are as shown in Illustration 13B-2.

An efficient way to apply the direct method is to analyze the items reported in the income statement in the order in which they are listed. We then determine cash receipts and cash payments related to these revenues and expenses. The following pages present the adjustments required to prepare a statement of cash flows for Computer Services Company using the direct approach.

CASH RECEIPTS FROM CUSTOMERS The income statement for Computer Services Company reported revenues from customers of $507,000. How much of that was cash receipts? To answer that, companies need to consider the change in accounts receivable during the year. When accounts receivable increase during the year, revenues on an accrual basis are higher than cash receipts from customers. Operations led to revenues, but not all of these revenues resulted in cash receipts.

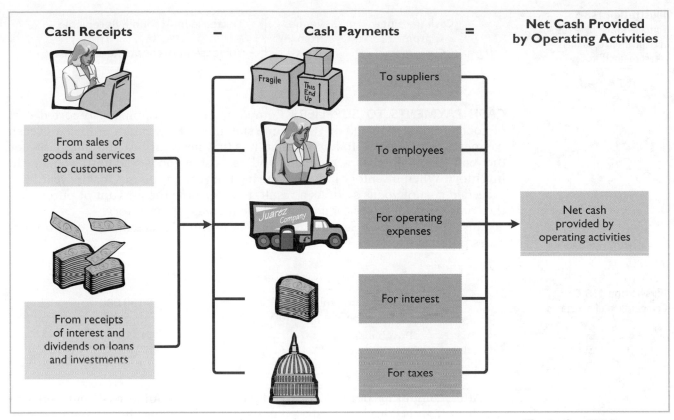

Cash Receipts	−	Cash Payments	=	Net Cash Provided by Operating Activities

Illustration 13B-2
Major classes of cash receipts and payments

To determine the amount of cash receipts, the company deducts from sales revenues the increase in accounts receivable. On the other hand, there may be a decrease in accounts receivable. That would occur if cash receipts from customers exceeded sales revenues. In that case, the company adds to sales revenues the decrease in accounts receivable. For Computer Services Company, accounts receivable decreased $10,000. Thus, cash receipts from customers were $517,000, computed as shown in Illustration 13B-3.

Revenues from sales	$ 507,000
Add: Decrease in accounts receivable	10,000
Cash receipts from customers	**$517,000**

Illustration 13B-3
Computation of cash receipts from customers

Computer Services can also determine cash receipts from customers from an analysis of the Accounts Receivable account, as shown in Illustration 13B-4.

Accounts Receivable

1/1/14	Balance	30,000	**Receipts from customers**	**517,000**
	Revenues from sales	507,000		
12/31/14	Balance	20,000		

Illustration 13B-4
Analysis of accounts receivable

Helpful Hint
The T-account shows that revenue plus decrease in receivables equals cash receipts.

Illustration 13B-5 (page 618) shows the relationships among cash receipts from customers, revenues from sales, and changes in accounts receivable.

Illustration 13B-5
Formula to compute cash receipts from customers—direct method

Cash Receipts from Customers	=	Revenues from Sales	{	+ Decrease in Accounts Receivable
				or
				− Increase in Accounts Receivable

CASH PAYMENTS TO SUPPLIERS Computer Services Company reported cost of goods sold of $150,000 on its income statement. How much of that was cash payments to suppliers? To answer that, it is first necessary to find purchases for the year. To find purchases, companies adjust cost of goods sold for the change in inventory. When inventory increases during the year, purchases for the year have exceeded cost of goods sold. As a result, to determine the amount of purchases, the company adds to cost of goods sold the increase in inventory.

In 2014, Computer Services Company's inventory increased $5,000. It computes purchases as follows.

Illustration 13B-6
Computation of purchases

Cost of goods sold	$ 150,000
Add: Increase in inventory	5,000
Purchases	**$155,000**

After computing purchases, a company can determine cash payments to suppliers. This is done by adjusting purchases for the change in accounts payable. When accounts payable increase during the year, purchases on an accrual basis are higher than they are on a cash basis. As a result, to determine cash payments to suppliers, a company deducts from purchases the increase in accounts payable. On the other hand, if cash payments to suppliers exceed purchases, there may be a decrease in accounts payable. In that case, a company adds to purchases the decrease in accounts payable. For Computer Services Company, cash payments to suppliers were $139,000, computed as follows.

Illustration 13B-7
Computation of cash payments to suppliers

Purchases	$ 155,000
Deduct: Increase in accounts payable	16,000
Cash payments to suppliers	**$139,000**

Computer Services also can determine cash payments to suppliers from an analysis of the Accounts Payable account, as shown in Illustration 13B-8.

Illustration 13B-8
Analysis of accounts payable

Accounts Payable					
Payments to suppliers	**139,000**	1/1/14	Balance		12,000
			Purchases		155,000
		12/31/14	Balance		28,000

Helpful Hint
The T-account shows that purchases less increase in accounts payable equals payments to suppliers.

Illustration 13B-9 shows the relationships among cash payments to suppliers, cost of goods sold, changes in inventory, and changes in accounts payable.

Cash Payments to Suppliers	=	Cost of Goods Sold	{	+ Increase in Inventory or − Decrease in Inventory	{	+ Decrease in Accounts Payable or − Increase in Accounts Payable

Illustration 13B-9
Formula to compute cash payments to suppliers—direct method

CASH PAYMENTS FOR OPERATING EXPENSES Computer Services reported on its income statement operating expenses of $111,000. How much of that amount was cash paid for operating expenses? To answer that, we need to adjust this amount for any changes in prepaid expenses and accrued expenses payable. For example, if prepaid expenses increased during the year, cash paid for operating expenses is higher than operating expenses reported on the income statement. To convert operating expenses to cash payments for operating expenses, a company adds the increase in prepaid expenses to operating expenses. On the other hand, if prepaid expenses decrease during the year, it deducts the decrease from operating expenses.

Companies must also adjust operating expenses for changes in accrued expenses payable. When accrued expenses payable increase during the year, operating expenses on an accrual basis are higher than they are in a cash basis. As a result, to determine cash payments for operating expenses, a company deducts from operating expenses an increase in accrued expenses payable. On the other hand, a company adds to operating expenses a decrease in accrued expenses payable because cash payments exceed operating expenses.

Computer Services Company's cash payments for operating expenses were $115,000, computed as follows.

Operating expenses	$ 111,000
Add: Increase in prepaid expenses	4,000
Cash payments for operating expenses	**$115,000**

Illustration 13B-10
Computation of cash payments for operating expenses

Illustration 13B-11 shows the relationships among cash payments for operating expenses, changes in prepaid expenses, and changes in accrued expenses payable.

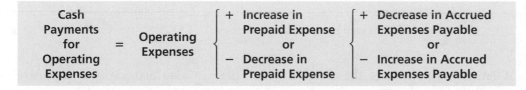

Cash Payments for Operating Expenses	=	Operating Expenses	{	+ Increase in Prepaid Expense or − Decrease in Prepaid Expense	{	+ Decrease in Accrued Expenses Payable or − Increase in Accrued Expenses Payable

Illustration 13B-11
Formula to compute cash payments for operating expenses—direct method

DEPRECIATION EXPENSE AND DISPOSAL OF PLANT ASSETS Computer Services' depreciation expense in 2014 was $9,000. Depreciation expense is not shown on a statement of cash flows under the direct method because it is a noncash charge. If the amount for operating expenses includes depreciation expense, operating expenses must be reduced by the amount of depreciation to determine cash payments for operating expenses.

The loss on disposal of plant assets of $3,000 is also a noncash charge. The loss on disposal of plant assets reduces net income, but it does not reduce cash. Thus, the loss on disposal of plant assets is not shown on the statement of cash flows under the direct method.

Other charges to expense that do not require the use of cash, such as the amortization of intangible assets, depletion expense, and bad debt expense, are treated in the same manner as depreciation.

CASH PAYMENTS FOR INTEREST Computer Services reported on the income statement interest expense of $42,000. Since the balance sheet did not include an accrual for interest payable for 2013 or 2014, the amount reported as expense is the same as the amount of interest paid.

CASH PAYMENTS FOR INCOME TAXES Computer Services reported income tax expense of $47,000 on the income statement. Income taxes payable, however, decreased $2,000. This decrease means that income taxes paid were more than income taxes reported in the income statement. Cash payments for income taxes were, therefore, $49,000 as shown below.

Illustration 13B-12
Computation of cash payments for income taxes

Income tax expense	$ 47,000
Add: Decrease in income taxes payable	2,000
Cash payments for income taxes	**$49,000**

Illustration 13B-13 shows the relationships among cash payments for income taxes, income tax expense, and changes in income taxes payable.

Illustration 13B-13
Formula to compute cash payments for income taxes—direct method

Cash Payments for Income Taxes	=	Income Tax Expense	+ Decrease in Income Taxes Payable
			or
			− Increase in Income Taxes Payable

The operating activities section of the statement of cash flows of Computer Services Company is shown in Illustration 13B-14.

Illustration 13B-14
Operating activities section of the statement of cash flows

Cash flows from operating activities		
Cash receipts from customers		$517,000
Less: Cash payments:		
To suppliers	$139,000	
For operating expenses	115,000	
For interest expense	42,000	
For income taxes	49,000	345,000
Net cash provided by operating activities		$172,000

When a company uses the direct method, it must also provide in a **separate schedule** (not shown here) the net cash flows from operating activities as computed under the indirect method.

Step 2: Investing and Financing Activities

ANALYZE CHANGES IN NONCURRENT ASSET AND LIABILITY ACCOUNTS AND RECORD AS INVESTING AND FINANCING ACTIVITIES, OR DISCLOSE AS NONCASH TRANSACTIONS

Helpful Hint
The investing and financing activities are measured and reported the same under both the direct and indirect methods.

INCREASE IN LAND As indicated from the change in the Land account and the additional information, the company purchased land of $110,000 by directly exchanging bonds for land. The exchange of bonds payable for land has no effect on cash. But, it is a significant noncash investing and financing activity that merits disclosure in a separate schedule. (See Illustration 13B-16 on page 622.)

INCREASE IN BUILDINGS As the additional data indicate, Computer Services Company acquired an office building for $120,000 cash. This is a cash outflow reported in the investing section. (See Illustration 13B-16 on page 622.)

INCREASE IN EQUIPMENT The Equipment account increased $17,000. The additional information explains that this was a net increase that resulted from two transactions: (1) a purchase of equipment of $25,000, and (2) the sale for $4,000 of equipment costing $8,000. These transactions are investing activities. The company should report each transaction separately. The statement in Illustration 13B-16 reports the purchase of equipment as an outflow of cash for $25,000. It reports the sale as an inflow of cash for $4,000. The T-account below shows the reasons for the change in this account during the year.

Illustration 13B-15
Analysis of equipment

Equipment			
1/1/14 Balance	10,000	Cost of equipment sold	8,000
Purchase of equipment	**25,000**		
12/31/14 Balance	27,000		

The following entry shows the details of the equipment sale transaction.

Cash	4,000	
Accumulated Depreciation	1,000	
Loss on Disposal of Plant Assets	3,000	
Equipment		8,000

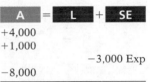

```
+4,000
+1,000
                    -3,000 Exp
-8,000
```

Cash Flows
+4,000

INCREASE IN BONDS PAYABLE The Bonds Payable account increased $110,000. As indicated in the additional information, the company acquired land by directly exchanging bonds for land. Illustration 13B-16 reports this noncash transaction in a separate schedule at the bottom of the statement.

INCREASE IN COMMON STOCK The balance sheet reports an increase in Common Stock of $20,000. The additional information section notes that this increase resulted from the issuance of new shares of stock. This is a cash inflow reported in the financing section in Illustration 13B-16.

INCREASE IN RETAINED EARNINGS Retained earnings increased $116,000 during the year. This increase can be explained by two factors: (1) Net income of $145,000 increased retained earnings and (2) dividends of $29,000 decreased retained earnings. The company adjusts net income to net cash provided by operating activities in the operating activities section. **Payment** of the dividends (not the declaration) is a **cash outflow that the company reports as a financing activity in Illustration 13B-16**.

Helpful Hint
When companies issue stocks or bonds for cash, the actual proceeds will appear in the statement of cash flows as a financing inflow (rather than the par value of the stocks or face value of bonds).

STATEMENT OF CASH FLOWS—2014
Illustration 13B-16 shows the statement of cash flows for Computer Services Company.

Step 3: Net Change in Cash

COMPARE THE NET CHANGE IN CASH ON THE STATEMENT OF CASH FLOWS WITH THE CHANGE IN THE CASH ACCOUNT REPORTED ON THE BALANCE SHEET TO MAKE SURE THE AMOUNTS AGREE
Illustration 13B-16 indicates that the net change in cash during the period was an increase of $22,000. This agrees with the change in balances in the cash account reported on the balance sheets in Illustration 13B-1 (page 615).

Illustration 13B-16
Statement of cash flows,
2014—direct method

Computer Services Company		
Statement of Cash Flows—Direct Method		
For the Year Ended December 31, 2014		
Cash flows from operating activities		
Cash receipts from customers		$ 517,000
Less: Cash payments:		
To suppliers	$ 139,000	
For operating expenses	115,000	
For income taxes	49,000	
For interest expense	42,000	345,000
Net cash provided by operating activities		172,000
Cash flows from investing activities		
Disposal of plant assets	4,000	
Purchase of building	(120,000)	
Purchase of equipment	(25,000)	
Net cash used by investing activities		(141,000)
Cash flows from financing activities		
Issuance of common stock	20,000	
Payment of cash dividends	(29,000)	
Net cash used by financing activities		(9,000)
Net increase in cash		22,000
Cash at beginning of period		33,000
Cash at end of period		$ 55,000
Noncash investing and financing activities		
Issuance of bonds payable to purchase land		$ 110,000

SUMMARY OF LEARNING OBJECTIVE FOR APPENDIX 13B

✔ **The Navigator**

6 Prepare a statement of cash flows using the direct method.
The preparation of the statement of cash flows involves three major steps: (1) Determine net cash provided/ used by operating activities by converting net income from an accrual basis to a cash basis. (2) Analyze changes in noncurrent asset and liability accounts and record as investing and financing activities, or disclose as non-cash transactions. (3) Compare the net change in cash on the statement of cash flows with the change in the cash account reported on the balance sheet to make sure the amounts agree. The direct method reports cash receipts less cash payments to arrive at net cash provided by operating activities.

> Comprehensive **DO IT! 2**

The income statement for Kosinski Company contains the following condensed information.

Kosinski Company
Income Statement
For the Year Ended December 31, 2014

Sales revenue		$6,583,000
Operating expenses, excluding depreciation	$4,920,000	
Depreciation expense	880,000	5,800,000
Income before income taxes		783,000
Income tax expense		353,000
Net income		$ 430,000

Included in operating expenses is a $24,000 loss resulting from the sale of machinery for $270,000 cash. Machinery was purchased at a cost of $750,000. The following balances are reported on Kosinski's comparative balance sheet at December 31.

Kosinski Company
Comparative Balance Sheets (partial)

	2014	2013
Cash	$672,000	$130,000
Accounts receivable	775,000	610,000
Inventory	834,000	867,000
Accounts payable	521,000	501,000

Income tax expense of $353,000 represents the amount paid in 2014. Dividends declared and paid in 2014 totaled $200,000.

Instructions

Prepare the statement of cash flows using the direct method.

Solution to Comprehensive DO IT! 2

Action Plan

✔ Determine net cash from operating activities. Each item in the income statement must be adjusted to the cash basis.

✔ Determine net cash from investing activities. Investing activities generally relate to changes in noncurrent assets.

✔ Determine net cash from financing activities. Financing activities generally relate to changes in long-term liabilities and stockholders' equity accounts.

Kosinski Company
Statement of Cash Flows—Direct Method
For the Year Ended December 31, 2014

Cash flows from operating activities			
Cash collections from customers			$6,418,000*
Cash payments:			
For operating expenses		$4,843,000**	
For income taxes		353,000	5,196,000
Net cash provided by operating activities			1,222,000
Cash flows from investing activities			
Disposal of plant assets		270,000	
Purchase of machinery		(750,000)	
Net cash used by investing activities			(480,000)
Cash flows from financing activities			
Payment of cash dividends		(200,000)	
Net cash used by financing activities			(200,000)
Net increase in cash			542,000
Cash at beginning of period			130,000
Cash at end of period			$ 672,000

Direct-Method Computations:

*Computation of cash collections from customers:	
Sales revenue per the income statement	$6,583,000
Deduct: Increase in accounts receivable	(165,000)
Cash collections from customers	$6,418,000
**Computation of cash payments for operating expenses:	
Operating expenses per the income statement	$4,920,000
Deduct: Loss on disposal of plant assets	(24,000)
Deduct: Decrease in inventories	(33,000)
Deduct: Increase in accounts payable	(20,000)
Cash payments for operating expenses	$4,843,000

✔ **The Navigator**

APPENDIX **13C**   STATEMENT OF CASH FLOWS—T-ACCOUNT APPROACH

Many people like to use T-accounts to provide structure to the preparation of a statement of cash flows. The use of T-accounts is based on the accounting equation. The basic equation is:

> **Assets = Liabilities + Equity**

Now, let's rewrite the left-hand side as:

> **Cash + Noncash Assets = Liabilities + Equity**

Next, rewrite the equation by subtracting Noncash Assets from each side to isolate Cash on the left-hand side:

> **Cash = Liabilities + Equity − Noncash Assets**

Finally, if we insert the Δ symbol (which means "change in"), we have:

> **Δ Cash = Δ Liabilities + Δ Equity − Δ Noncash Assets**

What this means is that the change in cash is equal to the change in all of the other balance sheet accounts. Another way to think about this is that if we analyze the changes in all of the noncash balance sheet accounts, we will explain the change in the Cash account. This, of course, is exactly what we are trying to do with the statement of cash flows.

To implement this approach, first prepare a large Cash T-account, with sections for operating, investing, and financing activities. Then, prepare smaller T-accounts for all of the other noncash balance sheet accounts. Insert the beginning and ending balances for each of these accounts. Once you have done this, then walk through the steps outlined below. As you walk through the steps, enter debit and credit amounts into the affected accounts. When all of the changes in the T-accounts have been explained, you are done. To demonstrate, we will apply this approach to the example of Computer Services Company that is presented in the chapter. Each of the adjustments in Illustration 13C-1 is numbered so you can follow them through the T-accounts.

1. Post net income as a debit to the operating section of the Cash T-account and a credit to Retained Earnings. Make sure to label all adjustments to the Cash T-account. It also helps to number each adjustment so you can trace all of them if you make an error.

2. Post depreciation expense as a debit to the operating section of Cash and a credit to each of the appropriate accumulated depreciation accounts.

3. Post any gains or losses on the sale of property, plant, and equipment. To do this, it is best to first prepare the journal entry that was recorded at the time of the sale and then post each element of the journal entry. For example, for Computer Services the entry was:

Cash	4,000	
Accumulated Depreciation—Equipment	1,000	
Loss on Disposal of Plant Assets	3,000	
Equipment		8,000

The $4,000 cash entry is a source of cash in the investing section of the Cash account. Accumulated Depreciation—Equipment is debited for $1,000. The Loss on Disposal of Plant Assets is a debit to the operating section of the Cash T-account. Finally, Equipment is credited for $8,000.

4–8. Next, post each of the changes to the noncash current asset and current liability accounts. For example, to explain the $10,000 decline in Computer Services' Accounts Receivable, credit Accounts Receivable for $10,000 and debit the operating section of the Cash T-account for $10,000.

9. Analyze the changes in the noncurrent accounts. Land was purchased by issuing Bonds Payable. This requires a debit to Land for $110,000 and a credit to Bonds Payable for $110,000. Note that this is a significant noncash event that requires disclosure at the bottom of the statement of cash flows.

10. Buildings is debited for $120,000, and the investing section of the Cash T-account is credited for $120,000 as a use of cash from investing.

11. Equipment is debited for $25,000 and the investing section of the Cash T-account is credited for $25,000 as a use of cash from investing.

12. Common Stock is credited for $20,000 for the issuance of shares of stock, and the financing section of the Cash T-account is debited for $20,000.

13. Retained Earnings is debited to reflect the payment of the $29,000 dividend, and the financing section of the Cash T-account is credited to reflect the use of Cash.

Illustration 13C-1
T-account approach

Cash

Operating			
(1) Net income	145,000	5,000	Inventory (5)
(2) Depreciation expense	9,000	4,000	Prepaid expenses (6)
(3) Loss on disposal of plant assets	3,000	2,000	Income taxes payable (8)
(4) Accounts receivable	10,000		
(7) Accounts payable	16,000		
Net cash provided by operating activities	172,000		
Investing			
(3) Disposal of plant assets	4,000	120,000	Purchased building (10)
		25,000	Purchased equipment (11)
		141,000	Net cash used by investing activities
Financing			
(12) Issued common stock	20,000	29,000	Dividend paid (13)
		9,000	Net cash used by financing activities
	22,000		

Accounts Receivable		Inventory		Prepaid Expenses		Land	
30,000		10,000		1,000		20,000	
	10,000 (4)	(5) 5,000		(6) 4,000		(9) 110,000	
20,000		15,000		5,000		130,000	

Buildings		Accumulated Depreciation—Buildings		Equipment		Accumulated Depreciation—Equipment	
40,000			5,000	10,000			1,000
(10) 120,000			6,000 (2)	(11) 25,000	8,000 (3)	(3) 1,000	3,000 (2)
160,000			11,000	27,000			3,000

Accounts Payable		Income Taxes Payable		Bonds Payable		Common Stock		Retained Earnings	
	12,000		8,000		20,000		50,000		48,000
	16,000 (7)	(8) 2,000			110,000 (9)		20,000 (12)		145,000 (1)
	28,000		6,000		130,000		70,000	(13) 29,000	
									164,000

At this point, all of the changes in the noncash accounts have been explained. All that remains is to subtotal each section of the Cash T-account and agree the total change in cash with the change shown on the balance sheet. Once this is done, the information in the Cash T-account can be used to prepare a statement of cash flows.

GLOSSARY

Direct method A method of determining net cash provided by operating activities by adjusting each item in the income statement from the accrual basis to the cash basis. (p. 592, 616).

Financing activities Cash flow activities that include (a) obtaining cash from issuing debt and repaying the amounts borrowed and (b) obtaining cash from stockholders, repurchasing shares, and paying dividends. (p. 589).

Free cash flow Cash provided by operating activities adjusted for capital expenditures and dividends paid. (p. 604).

Indirect method A method of preparing a statement of cash flows in which net income is adjusted for items that do not affect cash, to determine net cash provided by operating activities. (p. 592).

Investing activities Cash flow activities that include (a) acquiring and disposing of investments and property, plant, and equipment and (b) lending money and collecting the loans. (p. 588).

Operating activities Cash flow activities that include the cash effects of transactions that create revenues and expenses and thus enter into the determination of net income. (p. 588).

Statement of cash flows A basic financial statement that provides information about the cash receipts, cash payments, and net change in cash during a period, resulting from operating, investing, and financing activities. (p. 588).

Self-Test, Brief Exercises, Exercises, Problem Set A, and many more resources are available for practice in WileyPLUS.

Note: All Questions, Exercises, and Problems marked with an asterisk relate to material in the appendices to the chapter.

SELF-TEST QUESTIONS

Answers are at the end of the chapter.

(LO 1) **1.** Which of the following is *incorrect* about the statement of cash flows?
  (a) It is a fourth basic financial statement.
  (b) It provides information about cash receipts and cash payments of an entity during a period.
  (c) It reconciles the ending cash account balance to the balance per the bank statement.
  (d) It provides information about the operating, investing, and financing activities of the business.

(LO 1) **2.** Which of the following will *not* be reported in the statement of cash flows?
  (a) The net change in plant assets during the year.
  (b) Cash payments for plant assets purchased during the year.
  (c) Cash receipts from sales of plant assets during the year.
  (d) How acquisitions of plant assets during the year were financed.

3. The statement of cash flows classifies cash receipts (LO 2) and cash payments by these activities:
  (a) operating and nonoperating.
  (b) investing, financing, and operating.
  (c) financing, operating, and nonoperating.
  (d) investing, financing, and nonoperating.

4. Which is an example of a cash flow from an operating (LO 2) activity?
  (a) Payment of cash to lenders for interest.
  (b) Receipt of cash from the sale of capital stock.
  (c) Payment of cash dividends to the company's stockholders.
  (d) None of the above.

5. Which is an example of a cash flow from an investing (LO 2) activity?
  (a) Receipt of cash from the issuance of bonds payable.
  (b) Payment of cash to repurchase outstanding capital stock.

(c) Receipt of cash from the sale of equipment.

(d) Payment of cash to suppliers for inventory.

(LO 2) 6. Cash dividends paid to stockholders are classified on the statement of cash flows as:

(a) operating activities.

(b) investing activities.

(c) a combination of (a) and (b).

(d) financing activities.

(LO 2) 7. Which is an example of a cash flow from a financing activity?

(a) Receipt of cash from sale of land.

(b) Issuance of debt for cash.

(c) Purchase of equipment for cash.

(d) None of the above.

(LO 2) 8. Which of the following is *incorrect* about the statement of cash flows?

(a) The direct method may be used to report cash provided by operations.

(b) The statement shows the cash provided (used) for three categories of activity.

(c) The operating section is the last section of the statement.

(d) The indirect method may be used to report cash provided by operations.

Questions 9 through 11 apply only to the indirect method.

(LO 3) 9. Net income is $132,000, accounts payable increased $10,000 during the year, inventory decreased $6,000 during the year, and accounts receivable increased $12,000 during the year. Under the indirect method, what is net cash provided by operating activities?

(a) $102,000.   (c) $124,000.

(b) $112,000.   (d) $136,000.

(LO 3) 10. Items that are added back to net income in determining cash provided by operating activities under the indirect method do *not* include:

(a) depreciation expense.

(b) an increase in inventory.

(c) amortization expense.

(d) loss on sale of equipment.

(LO 3) 11. The following data are available for Allen Clapp Corporation.

Net income	$200,000
Depreciation expense	40,000
Dividends paid	60,000
Gain on sale of land	10,000
Decrease in accounts receivable	20,000
Decrease in accounts payable	30,000

Net cash provided by operating activities is:

(a) $160,000.   (c) $240,000.

(b) $220,000.   (d) $280,000.

(LO 3) 12. The following data are available for Orange Peels Corporation.

Sale of land	$100,000
Sale of equipment	50,000
Issuance of common stock	70,000
Purchase of equipment	30,000
Payment of cash dividends	60,000

Net cash provided by investing activities is:

(a) $120,000.   (c) $150,000.

(b) $130,000.   (d) $190,000.

13. The following data are available for Something (LO 3) Strange!

Increase in accounts payable	$ 40,000
Increase in bonds payable	100,000
Sale of investment	50,000
Issuance of common stock	60,000
Payment of cash dividends	30,000

Net cash provided by financing activities is:

(a) $90,000.   (c) $160,000.

(b) $130,000.   (d) $170,000.

14. The statement of cash flows should *not* be used to (LO 4) evaluate an entity's ability to:

(a) earn net income.

(b) generate future cash flows.

(c) pay dividends.

(d) meet obligations.

15. Free cash flow provides an indication of a company's (LO 4) ability to:

(a) generate net income.

(b) generate cash to pay dividends.

(c) generate cash to invest in new capital expenditures.

(d) Both (b) and (c).

*16. In a worksheet for the statement of cash flows, a de- (LO 5) crease in accounts receivable is entered in the reconciling columns as a credit to Accounts Receivable and a debit in the:

(a) investing activities section.

(b) operating activities section.

(c) financing activities section.

(d) None of the above.

*17. In a worksheet for the statement of cash flows, a (LO 5) worksheet entry that includes a credit to accumulated depreciation will also include a:

(a) credit in the operating section and a debit in another section.

(b) debit in the operating section.

(c) debit in the investing section.

(d) debit in the financing section.

Questions 18 and 19 apply only to the direct method.

*18. The beginning balance in accounts receivable is (LO 6) $44,000, the ending balance is $42,000, and sales during the period are $129,000. What are cash receipts from customers?

(a) $127,000.   (c) $131,000.

(b) $129,000.   (d) $141,000.

*19. Which of the following items is reported on a state- (LO 6) ment of cash flows prepared by the direct method?

(a) Loss on sale of building.

(b) Increase in accounts receivable.

(c) Depreciation expense.

(d) Cash payments to suppliers.

Go to the book's companion website, www.wiley.com/college/weygandt, for additional Self-Test Questions.

✔ The Navigator

QUESTIONS

1. (a) What is a statement of cash flows?
   (b) Nick Johns maintains that the statement of cash flows is an optional financial statement. Do you agree? Explain.
2. What questions about cash are answered by the statement of cash flows?
3. Distinguish among the three types of activities reported in the statement of cash flows.
4. (a) What are the major sources (inflows) of cash in a statement of cash flows?
   (b) What are the major uses (outflows) of cash?
5. Why is it important to disclose certain noncash transactions? How should they be disclosed?
6. Wilma Flintstone and Barny Rublestone were discussing the format of the statement of cash flows of Saltwater Candy Co. At the bottom of Saltwater Candy's statement of cash flows was a separate section entitled "Noncash investing and financing activities." Give three examples of significant noncash transactions that would be reported in this section.
7. Why is it necessary to use comparative balance sheets, a current income statement, and certain transaction data in preparing a statement of cash flows?
8. Contrast the advantages and disadvantages of the direct and indirect methods of preparing the statement of cash flows. Are both methods acceptable? Which method is preferred by the FASB? Which method is more popular?
9. When the total cash inflows exceed the total cash outflows in the statement of cash flows, how and where is this excess identified?
10. Describe the indirect method for determining net cash provided (used) by operating activities.
11. Why is it necessary to convert accrual-based net income to cash-basis income when preparing a statement of cash flows?
12. The president of Ferneti Company is puzzled. During the last year, the company experienced a net loss of $800,000, yet its cash increased $300,000 during the same period of time. Explain to the president how this could occur.
13. Identify five items that are adjustments to convert net income to net cash provided by operating activities under the indirect method.
14. Why and how is depreciation expense reported in a statement prepared using the indirect method?
15. Why is the statement of cash flows useful?
16. During 2014, Singletree Company exchanged $1,700,000 of its common stock for land. Indicate how the transaction would be reported on a statement of cash flows, if at all.
*17. Why is it advantageous to use a worksheet when preparing a statement of cash flows? Is a worksheet required to prepare a statement of cash flows?
*18. Describe the direct method for determining net cash provided by operating activities.
*19. Give the formulas under the direct method for computing (a) cash receipts from customers and (b) cash payments to suppliers.
*20. Aloha Inc. reported sales of $2 million for 2014. Accounts receivable decreased $200,000 and accounts payable increased $300,000. Compute cash receipts from customers, assuming that the receivable and payable transactions related to operations.
*21. In the direct method, why is depreciation expense not reported in the cash flows from operating activities section?
22. **PEPSICO** In its 2010 statement of cash flows (see *www.pepsico.com*), what amount did PepsiCo report for net cash (a) provided by operating activities, (b) used for investing activities, and (c) used for financing activities?

BRIEF EXERCISES

Indicate statement presentation of selected transactions.

(LO 2), AP

BE13-1 Each of the items below must be considered in preparing a statement of cash flows for Alpha-Omega Co. for the year ended December 31, 2014. For each item, state how it should be shown in the statement of cash flows for 2014.
(a) Issued bonds for $150,000 cash.
(b) Purchased equipment for $200,000 cash.
(c) Sold land costing $50,000 for $50,000 cash.
(d) Declared and paid a $20,000 cash dividend.

Classify items by activities.

(LO 2), C

BE13-2 Classify each item as an operating, investing, or financing activity. Assume all items involve cash unless there is information to the contrary.
(a) Purchase of equipment.
(b) Sale of building.
(c) Redemption of bonds.
(d) Depreciation.
(e) Payment of dividends.
(f) Issuance of capital stock.

BE13-3 The following T-account is a summary of the Cash account of Wiegman Company.

Cash (Summary Form)

Balance, Jan. 1	8,000		
Receipts from customers	364,000	Payments for goods	200,000
Dividends on stock investments	6,000	Payments for operating expenses	140,000
Proceeds from sale of equipment	36,000	Interest paid	10,000
Proceeds from issuance of		Taxes paid	8,000
bonds payable	500,000	Dividends paid	60,000
Balance, Dec. 31	496,000		

What amount of net cash provided (used) by financing activities should be reported in the statement of cash flows?

BE13-4 Mokena, Inc. reported net income of $2.0 million in 2014. Depreciation for the year was $160,000, accounts receivable increased $350,000, and accounts payable increased $280,000. Compute net cash provided by operating activities using the indirect method.

BE13-5 The net income for Lodi Co. for 2014 was $250,000. For 2014, depreciation on plant assets was $70,000, and the company incurred a gain on disposal of plant assets of $12,000. Compute net cash provided by operating activities under the indirect method.

BE13-6 The comparative balance sheets for Tobemory Company show these changes in noncash current asset accounts: accounts receivable increase $80,000, prepaid expenses decrease $28,000, and inventories decrease $30,000. Compute net cash provided by operating activities using the indirect method assuming that net income is $250,000.

BE13-7 The T-accounts for Equipment and the related Accumulated Depreciation—Equipment for Ada Company at the end of 2014 are shown here.

Equipment				**Accumulated Depreciation—Equipment**			
Beg. bal.	80,000	Disposals	22,000	Disposals	8,500	Beg. bal.	44,500
Acquisitions	41,600					Depr. exp.	12,000
End. bal.	99,600					End. bal.	48,000

In addition, Ada Company's income statement reported a loss on disposal of plant assets of $6,500. What amount was reported on the statement of cash flows as "cash flow from disposal of plant assets"?

BE13-8 In a recent year, Cypress Semiconductor Corporation reported cash provided by operating activities of $155,397,000, cash used in investing of $207,628,000, and cash used in financing of $33,372,000. In addition, cash spent for fixed assets during the period was $130,820,000. No dividends were paid. Calculate free cash flow.

BE13-9 Wruck Corporation reported cash provided by operating activities of $450,000, cash used by investing activities of $150,000, and cash provided by financing activities of $80,000. In addition, cash spent for capital assets during the period was $250,000. No dividends were paid. Calculate free cash flow.

BE13-10 In a recent quarter, Alliance Atlantis Communications Inc. reported cash provided by operating activities of $45,000,000 and revenues of $265,800,000. Cash spent on plant asset additions during the quarter was $1,400,000. Calculate free cash flow.

BE13-11 The management of Russel Inc. is trying to decide whether it can increase its dividend. During the current year, it reported net income of $875,000. It had cash provided by operating activities of $643,000, paid cash dividends of $80,000, and had capital expenditures of $280,000. Compute the company's free cash flow, and discuss whether an increase in the dividend appears warranted. What other factors should be considered?

*BE13-12 During the year, prepaid expenses decreased $6,500, and accrued expenses increased $2,000. Indicate how the changes in prepaid expenses and accrued expenses payable should be entered in the reconciling columns of a worksheet. Assume that beginning balances were prepaid expenses $18,600 and accrued expenses payable $8,200.

Compute receipts from customers—direct method.

(LO 6), AP

*BE13-13 Columbia Sportswear Company had accounts receivable of $205,025,000 at the beginning of a recent year, and $267,653,000 at year-end. Sales revenues were $1,085,307,000 for the year. What is the amount of cash receipts from customers?

Compute cash payments for income taxes—direct method.

(LO 6), AP

*BE13-14 Kinsey Corporation reported income taxes of $360,000,000 on its 2014 income statement, income taxes payable of $277,000,000 at December 31, 2013, and $525,000,000 at December 31, 2014. What amount of cash payments were made for income taxes during 2014?

Compute cash payments for operating expenses—direct method.

(LO 6), AP

*BE13-15 Yaddof Corporation reports operating expenses of $70,000 excluding depreciation expense of $15,000 for 2014. During the year, prepaid expenses decreased $6,800 and accrued expenses payable increased $4,500. Compute the cash payments for operating expenses in 2014.

> DO IT! REVIEW

Classify transactions by type of cash flow activity.

(LO 2), C

DO IT! 13-1 Piekarski Corporation had the following transactions.

1. Issued $200,000 of bonds payable.
2. Paid utilities expense.
3. Issued 500 shares of preferred stock for $45,000.
4. Sold land and a building for $250,000.
5. Lent $30,000 to Zarembski Corporation, receiving Zarembski's 1-year, 12% note.

Classify each of these transactions by type of cash flow activity (operating, investing, or financing).

Calculate net cash from operating activities.

(LO 3), C, AP

DO IT! 13-2 Jojo Photography reported net income of $100,000 for 2014. Included in the income statement were depreciation expense of $4,000, amortization expense of $3,000, and a gain on disposal of plant assets of $3,900. Jojo's comparative balance sheets show the following balances.

	12/31/13	12/31/14
Accounts receivable	$27,000	$21,000
Accounts payable	6,000	9,200

Calculate net cash provided by operating activities for Jojo Photography.

Compute and discuss free cash flow.

(LO 4), C, AN

DO IT! 13-3 Zielinski Corporation issued the following statement of cash flows for 2014.

Zielinski Corporation
Statement of Cash Flows—Indirect Method
For the Year Ended December 31, 2014

Cash flows from operating activities		
Net income		$ 59,000
Adjustments to reconcile net income to net cash provided by operating activities:		
Depreciation expense	$ 9,100	
Decrease in accounts receivable	8,500	
Loss on disposal of plant assets	3,300	
Increase in inventory	(5,000)	
Decrease in accounts payable	(2,500)	13,400
Net cash provided by operating activities		72,400
Cash flows from investing activities		
Sale of investments	3,100	
Purchase of equipment	(26,000)	
Net cash used by investing activities		(22,900)

Cash flows from financing activities		
Issuance of stock	20,000	
Payment on long-term note payable	(10,000)	
Payment for dividends	(18,000)	
Net cash used by financing activities		(8,000)
Net increase in cash		41,500
Cash at beginning of year		13,000
Cash at end of year		$ 54,500

(a) Compute free cash flow for Zielinski Corporation. (b) Explain why free cash flow often provides better information than "Net cash provided by operating activities."

✔ **The Navigator**

EXERCISES

E13-1 Quarshee Corporation had these transactions during 2014.
(a) Issued $50,000 par value common stock for cash.
(b) Purchased a machine for $30,000, giving a long-term note in exchange.
(c) Issued $200,000 par value common stock upon conversion of bonds having a face value of $200,000.
(d) Declared and paid a cash dividend of $18,000.
(e) Sold a long-term investment with a cost of $15,000 for $15,000 cash.
(f) Collected $16,000 of accounts receivable.
(g) Paid $18,000 on accounts payable.

Classify transactions by type of activity.

(LO 2), C

Instructions
Analyze the transactions and indicate whether each transaction resulted in a cash flow from operating activities, investing activities, financing activities, or noncash investing and financing activities.

E13-2 An analysis of comparative balance sheets, the current year's income statement, and the general ledger accounts of Solomon Corp. uncovered the following items. Assume all items involve cash unless there is information to the contrary.

Classify transactions by type of activity.

(LO 2), C

(a) Payment of interest on notes payable.
(b) Exchange of land for patent.
(c) Sale of building at book value.
(d) Payment of dividends.
(e) Depreciation.
(f) Receipt of dividends on investment in stock.
(g) Receipt of interest on notes receivable.

(h) Issuance of capital stock.
(i) Amortization of patent.
(j) Issuance of bonds for land.
(k) Purchase of land.
(l) Conversion of bonds into common stock.
(m) Loss on sale of land.
(n) Retirement of bonds.

Instructions
Indicate how each item should be classified in the statement of cash flows using these four major classifications: operating activity (indirect method), investing activity, financing activity, and significant noncash investing and financing activity.

E13-3 Tim Latimer Corporation had the following transactions.

1. Sold land (cost $12,000) for $10,000.
2. Issued common stock for $22,000.
3. Recorded depreciation on buildings for $14,000.
4. Paid salaries of $7,000.
5. Issued 1,000 shares of $1 par value common stock for equipment worth $9,000.
6. Sold equipment (cost $10,000, accumulated depreciation $8,000) for $3,200.

Prepare journal entry and determine effect on cash flows.

(LO 2), AP

Instructions
For each transaction above, (a) prepare the journal entry, and (b) indicate how it would affect the statement of cash flows under the indirect method.

*Prepare the operating
activities section—indirect
method.*

(LO 3), AP

E13-4 Bracewell Company reported net income of $195,000 for 2014. Bracewell also reported depreciation expense of $40,000 and a gain of $5,000 on disposal of plant assets. The comparative balance sheet shows an increase in accounts receivable of $15,000 for the year, a $17,000 increase in accounts payable, and a $4,000 decrease in prepaid expenses.

Instructions

Prepare the operating activities section of the statement of cash flows for 2014. Use the indirect method.

*Prepare the operating
activities section—indirect
method.*

(LO 3), AP

E13-5 The current sections of Nasreen Inc.'s balance sheets at December 31, 2013 and 2014, are presented here. Nasreen's net income for 2014 was $153,000. Depreciation expense was $24,000.

	2014	2013
Current assets		
Cash	$105,000	$ 99,000
Accounts receivable	110,000	79,000
Inventory	158,000	172,000
Prepaid expenses	27,000	25,000
Total current assets	$400,000	$375,000
Current liabilities		
Accrued expenses payable	$ 15,000	$ 9,000
Accounts payable	85,000	95,000
Total current liabilities	$100,000	$104,000

Instructions

Prepare the net cash provided by operating activities section of the company's statement of cash flows for the year ended December 31, 2014, using the indirect method.

*Prepare partial statement of
cash flows—indirect method.*

(LO 3), AN

E13-6 The three accounts shown below appear in the general ledger of Chaudry Corp. during 2014.

Equipment

Date		Debit	Credit	Balance
Jan. 1	Balance			160,000
July 31	Purchase of equipment	70,000		230,000
Sept. 2	Cost of equipment constructed	53,000		283,000
Nov. 10	Cost of equipment sold		49,000	234,000

Accumulated Depreciation—Equipment

Date		Debit	Credit	Balance
Jan. 1	Balance			71,000
Nov. 10	Accumulated depreciation on equipment sold	28,000		43,000
Dec. 31	Depreciation for year		23,000	66,000

Retained Earnings

Date		Debit	Credit	Balance
Jan. 1	Balance			105,000
Aug. 23	Dividends (cash)	17,000		88,000
Dec. 31	Net income		67,000	155,000

Instructions

From the postings in the accounts, indicate how the information is reported on a statement of cash flows using the indirect method. The loss on disposal of plant assets was $5,000. (*Hint:* Cost of equipment constructed is reported in the investing activities section as a decrease in cash of $53,000.)

E13-7 Meera Corporation's comparative balance sheets are presented below.

Prepare statement of cash flows and compute free cash flow.

(LO 3, 4), AP

Meera Corporation
Comparative Balance Sheets
December 31

	2014	2013
Cash	$ 14,700	$ 10,700
Accounts receivable	20,800	23,400
Land	20,000	26,000
Buildings	70,000	70,000
Accumulated depreciation—buildings	(15,000)	(10,000)
Total	$110,500	$120,100
Accounts payable	$ 12,370	$ 28,100
Common stock	75,000	72,000
Retained earnings	23,130	20,000
Total	$110,500	$120,100

Additional information:

1. Net income was $22,630. Dividends declared and paid were $19,500.
2. All other changes in noncurrent account balances had a direct effect on cash flows, except the change in accumulated depreciation. The land was sold for $5,000.

Instructions

(a) Prepare a statement of cash flows for 2014 using the indirect method.
(b) Compute free cash flow.

E13-8 Here are comparative balance sheets for Syal Company.

Prepare a statement of cash flows—indirect method.

(LO 3), AP

Syal Company
Comparative Balance Sheets
December 31

Assets	2014	2013
Cash	$ 73,000	$ 33,000
Accounts receivable	85,000	71,000
Inventory	170,000	187,000
Land	73,000	100,000
Equipment	260,000	200,000
Accumulated depreciation—equipment	(66,000)	(34,000)
Total	$595,000	$557,000

Liabilities and Stockholders' Equity	2014	2013
Accounts payable	$ 35,000	$ 47,000
Bonds payable	150,000	200,000
Common stock ($1 par)	216,000	174,000
Retained earnings	194,000	136,000
Total	$595,000	$557,000

Additional information:

1. Net income for 2014 was $103,000.
2. Depreciation expense was $32,000.
3. Cash dividends of $45,000 were declared and paid.
4. Bonds payable amounting to $50,000 were redeemed for cash $50,000.
5. Common stock was issued for $42,000 cash.
6. No equipment was sold during 2014.
7. Land was sold for its book value of $27,000.

Instructions

Prepare a statement of cash flows for 2014 using the indirect method.

Prepare statement of cash flows and compute free cash flow.

(LO 3, 4), AP

E13-9 Cassandra Corporation's comparative balance sheets are presented below.

Cassandra Corporation
Comparative Balance Sheets
December 31

	2014	2013
Cash	$ 17,000	$ 17,700
Accounts receivable	25,200	22,300
Investments	20,000	16,000
Equipment	60,000	70,000
Accumulated depreciation—equipment	(14,000)	(10,000)
Total	$108,200	$116,000
Accounts payable	$ 14,600	$ 11,100
Bonds payable	10,000	30,000
Common stock	50,000	45,000
Retained earnings	33,600	29,900
Total	$108,200	$116,000

Additional information:

1. Net income was $18,300. Dividends declared and paid were $14,600.
2. Equipment which cost $10,000 and had accumulated depreciation of $1,800 was sold for $3,500.
3. All other changes in noncurrent account balances had a direct effect on cash flows, except the change in accumulated depreciation.

Instructions
(a) Prepare a statement of cash flows for 2014 using the indirect method.
(b) Compute free cash flow.

Prepare a worksheet.

(LO 5), AP

*E13-10 Comparative balance sheets for Erisa Magambo Company are presented below.

Erisa Magambo Company
Comparative Balance Sheets
December 31

Assets	2014	2013
Cash	$ 58,000	$ 22,000
Accounts receivable	85,000	76,000
Inventory	180,000	187,000
Land	75,000	100,000
Equipment	250,000	200,000
Accumulated depreciation—equipment	(66,000)	(42,000)
Total	$582,000	$543,000
Liabilities and Stockholders' Equity		
Accounts payable	$ 34,000	$ 45,000
Bonds payable	150,000	200,000
Common stock ($1 par)	214,000	164,000
Retained earnings	184,000	134,000
Total	$582,000	$543,000

Additional information:

1. Net income for 2014 was $120,000.
2. Cash dividends of $70,000 were declared and paid.
3. Bonds payable amounting to $50,000 were redeemed for cash $50,000.
4. Common stock was issued for $50,000 cash.
5. Depreciation expense was $24,000.
6. Sales for the year were $978,000.

Instructions
Prepare a worksheet for a statement of cash flows for 2014 using the indirect method. Enter the reconciling items directly on the worksheet, using letters to cross-reference each entry.

*E13-11 Dumezweni Company completed its first year of operations on December 31, 2014. Its initial income statement showed that Dumezweni had revenues of $195,000 and operating expenses of $78,000. Accounts receivable and accounts payable at year-end were $60,000 and $25,000, respectively. Assume that accounts payable related to operating expenses. (Ignore income taxes.)

Compute cash provided by operating activities—direct method.

(LO 6), AP

Instructions
Compute net cash provided by operating activities using the direct method.

*E13-12 A recent income statement for McDonald's Corporation shows cost of goods sold $4,527.8 million and operating expenses (including depreciation expense of $1,120 million) $10,517.6 million. The comparative balance sheet for the year shows that inventory increased $17.1 million, prepaid expenses increased $65.3 million, accounts payable (merchandise suppliers) increased $139.6 million, and accrued expenses payable increased $190.6 million.

Compute cash payments—direct method.

(LO 6), AP

Instructions
Using the direct method, compute (a) cash payments to suppliers and (b) cash payments for operating expenses.

*E13-13 The 2014 accounting records of Liz Ten Transport reveal these transactions and events.

Compute cash flow from operating activities—direct method.

(LO 6), AP

Payment of interest	$10,000	Collection of accounts receivable	$190,000
Cash sales	50,000	Payment of salaries and wages	57,000
Receipt of dividend		Depreciation expense	16,000
revenue	18,000	Proceeds from disposal of	
Payment of income taxes	16,000	plant assets	12,000
Net income	38,000	Purchase of equipment for cash	22,000
Payment of accounts payable		Loss on disposal of plant assets	3,000
for merchandise	115,000	Payment of dividends	14,000
Payment for land	74,000	Payment of operating expenses	28,000

Instructions
Prepare the cash flows from operating activities section using the direct method. (Not all of the items will be used.)

*E13-14 The following information is taken from the 2014 general ledger of Okonedo Company.

Calculate cash flows—direct method.

(LO 6), AP

Rent	Rent expense	$ 40,000
	Prepaid rent, January 1	5,600
	Prepaid rent, December 31	9,000
Salaries	Salaries and wages expense	$ 65,000
	Salaries and wages payable, January 1	10,000
	Salaries and wages payable, December 31	8,000
Sales	Sales revenue	$170,000
	Accounts receivable, January 1	19,000
	Accounts receivable, December 31	7,000

Instructions
In each case, compute the amount that should be reported in the operating activities section of the statement of cash flows under the direct method.

EXERCISES: SET B AND CHALLENGE EXERCISES

Visit the book's companion website, at **www.wiley.com/college/weygandt**, and choose the Student Companion site to access Exercise Set B and Challenge Exercises.

PROBLEMS: SET A

P13-1A You are provided with the following transactions that took place during a recent fiscal year.

Distinguish among operating, investing, and financing activities.   (LO 2), C

Transaction	Statement of Cash Flow Activity Affected	Cash Inflow, Outflow, or No Effect?
(a) Recorded depreciation expense on the plant assets.		
(b) Recorded and paid interest expense.		
(c) Recorded cash proceeds from a sale of plant assets.		
(d) Acquired land by issuing common stock.		
(e) Paid a cash dividend to preferred stockholders.		
(f) Paid a cash dividend to common stockholders.		
(g) Recorded cash sales.		
(h) Recorded sales on account.		
(i) Purchased inventory for cash.		
(j) Purchased inventory on account.		

Instructions

Complete the table indicating whether each item (1) affects operating (O) activities, investing (I) activities, financing (F) activities, or is a noncash (NC) transaction reported in a separate schedule; and (2) represents a cash inflow or cash outflow or has no cash flow effect. Assume use of the indirect approach.

Determine cash flow effects of changes in equity accounts.

(LO 3), AN

P13-2A The following account balances relate to the stockholders' equity accounts of Chipo Corp. at year-end.

	2014	2013
Common stock, 10,500 and 10,000 shares, respectively, for 2014 and 2013	$155,000	$130,000
Preferred stock, 5,000 shares	125,000	125,000
Retained earnings	300,000	250,000

A small stock dividend was declared and issued in 2014. The market value of the shares was $11,200. Cash dividends were $16,000 in both 2014 and 2013. The common stock has no par or stated value.

Instructions

(a) Net income $77,200

(a) What was the amount of net income reported by Chipo Corp. in 2014?

(b) Determine the amounts of any cash inflows or outflows related to the common stock and dividend accounts in 2014.

(c) Indicate where each of the cash inflows or outflows identified in (b) would be classified on the statement of cash flows.

Prepare the operating activities section—indirect method.

(LO 3), AP

P13-3A The income statement of Toby Zed Company is presented here.

Toby Zed Company
Income Statement
For the Year Ended November 30, 2014

Sales revenue		$7,500,000
Cost of goods sold		
Beginning inventory	$1,900,000	
Purchases	4,400,000	
Goods available for sale	6,300,000	
Ending inventory	1,400,000	
Total cost of goods sold		4,900,000
Gross profit		2,600,000
Operating expenses		1,150,000
Net income		$1,450,000

Additional information:

1. Accounts receivable increased $200,000 during the year, and inventory decreased $500,000.
2. Prepaid expenses increased $175,000 during the year.

3. Accounts payable to suppliers of merchandise decreased $340,000 during the year.
4. Accrued expenses payable decreased $105,000 during the year.
5. Operating expenses include depreciation expense of $85,000.

Instructions

Prepare the operating activities section of the statement of cash flows for the year ended November 30, 2014, for Toby Zed Company, using the indirect method.

Cash from operations $1,215,000

*P13-4A Data for Toby Zed Company are presented in P13-3A.

Prepare the oper. activities section—direct method.

(LO 6), AP

Cash from oper. $1,215,000

Instructions

Prepare the operating activities section of the statement of cash flows using the direct method.

P13-5A Rattigan Company's income statement contained the condensed information below.

Prepare the operating activities section—indirect method.

(LO 3), AP

Rattigan Company
Income Statement
For the Year Ended December 31, 2014

Sales revenue		$970,000
Operating expenses, excluding depreciation	$624,000	
Depreciation expense	55,000	
Loss on disposal of plant assets	25,000	704,000
Income before income taxes		266,000
Income tax expense		40,000
Net income		$226,000

Rattigan's balance sheet contained the comparative data at December 31, shown below.

	2014	2013
Accounts receivable	$75,000	$60,000
Accounts payable	41,000	27,000
Income taxes payable	13,000	7,000

Accounts payable pertain to operating expenses.

Instructions

Prepare the operating activities section of the statement of cash flows using the indirect method.

Cash from operations $311,000

*P13-6A Data for Rattigan Company are presented in P13-5A.

Prepare the oper. activities section—direct method.

(LO 6), AP

Instructions

Prepare the operating activities section of the statement of cash flows using the direct method.

Cash from oper. $311,000

P13-7A Presented below and on the next page are the financial statements of Rajesh Company.

Rajesh Company
Comparative Balance Sheets
December 31

Prepare a statement of cash flows—indirect method, and compute free cash flow.

(LO 3, 4), AP, AN

Assets	2014	2013
Cash	$ 37,000	$ 20,000
Accounts receivable	33,000	14,000
Inventory	30,000	20,000
Equipment	60,000	78,000
Accumulated depreciation—equipment	(29,000)	(24,000)
Total	$131,000	$108,000

Liabilities and Stockholders' Equity	2014	2013
Accounts payable	$ 29,000	$ 15,000
Income taxes payable	7,000	8,000
Bonds payable	27,000	33,000
Common stock	18,000	14,000
Retained earnings	50,000	38,000
Total	$131,000	$108,000

Rajesh Company
Income Statement
For the Year Ended December 31, 2014

Sales revenue	$242,000
Cost of goods sold	175,000
Gross profit	67,000
Operating expenses	24,000
Income from operations	43,000
Interest expense	3,000
Income before income taxes	40,000
Income tax expense	8,000
Net income	$ 32,000

Additional data:

1. Depreciation expense is 13,300.
2. Dividends declared and paid were $20,000.
3. During the year, equipment was sold for $9,700 cash. This equipment cost $18,000 originally and had accumulated depreciation of $8,300 at the time of sale.

Instructions

(a) Prepare a statement of cash flows using the indirect method.
(b) Compute free cash flow.

(a) Cash from operations
$29,300

Prepare a statement of cash flows—direct method, and compute free cash flow.

(LO 4, 6), AP, AN

*P13-8A Data for Rajesh Company are presented in P13-7A. Further analysis reveals the following.

1. Accounts payable pertain to merchandise suppliers.
2. All operating expenses except for depreciation were paid in cash.
3. All depreciation expense is in the operating expenses.
4. All sales and purchases are on account.

Instructions

(a) Prepare a statement of cash flows for Rajesh Company using the direct method.
(b) Compute free cash flow.

(a) Cash from operations
$29,300

Prepare a statement of cash flows—indirect method.

(LO 3), AP

P13-9A Condensed financial data of Sinjh Inc. follow.

Sinjh Inc.
Comparative Balance Sheets
December 31

Assets	2014	2013
Cash	$100,350	$ 48,400
Accounts receivable	92,800	33,000
Inventory	112,500	102,850
Prepaid expenses	29,300	26,000
Long-term investments	140,000	114,000
Plant assets	265,000	242,500
Accumulated depreciation	(47,000)	(52,000)
Total	$692,950	$514,750

Liabilities and Stockholders' Equity		
Accounts payable	$112,000	$ 67,300
Accrued expenses payable	16,500	17,000
Bonds payable	110,000	150,000
Common stock	220,000	175,000
Retained earnings	234,450	105,450
Total	$692,950	$514,750

Sinjh Inc.
Income Statement
For the Year Ended December 31, 2014

Sales	$392,780	
Gain on disposal of plant assets	5,000	$397,780
Less:		
Cost of goods sold	135,460	
Operating expenses, excluding depreciation	12,410	
Depreciation expense	45,000	
Income taxes	27,280	
Interest expense	4,730	224,880
Net income		$172,900

Additional information:

1. New plant assets costing $80,000 were purchased for cash during the year.
2. Old plant assets having an original cost of $57,500 and accumulated depreciation of $50,000 were sold for $12,500 cash.
3. Bonds payable matured and were paid off at face value for cash.
4. A cash dividend of $43,900 was declared and paid during the year.

Instructions
Prepare a statement of cash flows using the indirect method.

Cash from operations $184,350

*P13-10A Data for Sinjh Inc. are presented in P13-9A. Further analysis reveals that accounts payable pertain to merchandise creditors.

Prepare a statement of cash flows—direct method.

(LO 6), AP

Instructions
Prepare a statement of cash flows for Sinjh Inc. using the direct method.

Cash from operations $184,350

P13-11A The comparative balance sheets for Strackman Lux Company as of December 31 are presented below.

Prepare a statement of cash flows—indirect method.

(LO 3), AP

Strackman Lux Company
Comparative Balance Sheets
December 31

Assets	2014	2013
Cash	$ 59,520	$ 45,000
Accounts receivable	44,000	62,000
Inventory	154,550	142,000
Prepaid expenses	15,280	21,000
Land	145,000	130,000
Equipment	228,000	155,000
Accumulated depreciation—equipment	(45,000)	(35,000)
Buildings	200,000	200,000
Accumulated depreciation—buildings	(60,000)	(40,000)
Total	$741,350	$680,000

Liabilities and Stockholders' Equity	2014	2013
Accounts payable	$ 46,350	$ 40,000
Bonds payable	300,000	300,000
Common stock, $1 par	195,000	160,000
Retained earnings	200,000	180,000
Total	$741,350	$680,000

Additional information:

1. Operating expenses include depreciation expense of $40,000.
2. Land was sold for cash at book value of $20,000.

3. Cash dividends of $25,000 were paid.
4. Net income for 2014 was $45,000.

Cash from operations $108,520

5. Equipment was purchased for $95,000 cash. In addition, equipment costing $22,000 with a book value of $12,000 was sold for $6,000 cash.
6. Issued 35,000 shares of $1 par value common stock in exchange for land with a fair value of $35,000.

Instructions

Prepare a statement of cash flows for the year ended December 31, 2014, using the indirect method.

Prepare a worksheet—indirect method.

(LO 5), AP

*P13-12A Condensed financial data of Jhutti Company appear below.

Jhutti Company
Comparative Balance Sheets
December 31

Assets	2014	2013
Cash	$ 90,300	$ 47,250
Accounts receivable	80,900	57,000
Inventory	121,900	102,650
Investments	84,000	87,000
Equipment	250,000	205,000
Accumulated depreciation—equipment	(46,600)	(40,000)
	$580,500	$458,900

Liabilities and Stockholders' Equity		
Accounts payable	$ 53,400	$ 48,280
Accrued expenses payable	12,100	18,830
Bonds payable	100,000	70,000
Common stock	240,000	200,000
Retained earnings	175,000	121,790
	$580,500	$458,900

Jhutti Company
Income Statement
For the Year Ended December 31, 2014

Sales revenue	$297,500	
Gain on disposal of plant assets	8,550	$306,050
Less:		
Cost of goods sold	99,460	
Operating expenses (excluding depreciation expense)	14,670	
Depreciation expense	47,900	
Income taxes	7,270	
Interest expense	2,940	172,240
Net income		$133,810

Additional information:

1. Equipment costing $92,000 was purchased for cash during the year.
2. Investments were sold at cost.
3. Equipment costing $47,000 was sold for $14,250, resulting in gain of $8,550.
4. A cash dividend of $80,600 was declared and paid during the year.

Instructions

Reconciling items total $580,910

Prepare a worksheet for the statement of cash flows using the indirect method. Enter the reconciling items directly in the worksheet columns, using letters to cross-reference each entry.

PROBLEMS: SET B

P13-1B You are provided with the following transactions that took place during a recent fiscal year.

Distinguish among operating, investing, and financing activities.

(LO 2), C

Transaction	Statement of Cash Flow Activity Affected	Cash Inflow, Outflow, or No Effect?
(a) Recorded depreciation expense on the plant assets.		
(b) Incurred a loss on disposal of plant assets.		
(c) Acquired a building by paying cash.		
(d) Made principal repayments on a mortgage.		
(e) Issued common stock.		
(f) Purchased shares of another company to be held as a long-term equity investment.		
(g) Paid cash dividends to common stockholders.		
(h) Sold inventory on credit. The company uses a perpetual inventory system.		
(i) Purchased inventory on credit.		
(j) Paid wages to employees.		

Instructions

Complete the table indicating whether each item (1) affects operating (O) activities, investing (I) activities, financing (F) activities, or is a noncash (NC) transaction reported in a separate schedule; and (2) represents a cash inflow or cash outflow or has no cash flow effect. Assume use of the indirect approach.

P13-2B The following selected account balances relate to the plant asset accounts of Raji Inc. at year-end.

Determine cash flow effects of changes in plant asset accounts.

(LO 3), AN

	2014	2013
Accumulated depreciation—buildings	$337,500	$300,000
Accumulated depreciation—equipment	145,000	93,000
Buildings	750,000	750,000
Depreciation expense	101,500	85,500
Equipment	300,000	250,000
Land	100,000	70,000
Loss on disposal of plant assets	7,000	0

Additional information:

1. Raji purchased $90,000 of equipment and $30,000 of land for cash in 2014.
2. Raji also sold equipment in 2014.
3. Depreciation expense in 2014 was $37,500 on building and $64,000 on equipment.

Instructions

(a) Determine the amounts of any cash inflows or outflows related to the plant asset accounts in 2014.

(b) Indicate where each of the cash inflows or outflows identified in (a) would be classified on the statement of cash flows.

(a) Cash proceeds $21,000

P13-3B The income statement of Asquith Company is presented on the next page.

Prepare the operating activities section—indirect method.

Additional information:

1. Accounts receivable decreased $230,000 during the year, and inventory increased $120,000.

2. Prepaid expenses increased $125,000 during the year.

(LO 3), AP

3. Accounts payable to merchandise suppliers increased $50,000 during the year.
4. Accrued expenses payable increased $155,000 during the year.

Asquith Company
Income Statement
For the Year Ended December 31, 2014

Sales revenue		$5,250,000
Cost of goods sold		
Beginning inventory	$1,780,000	
Purchases	3,430,000	
Goods available for sale	5,210,000	
Ending inventory	1,900,000	
Total cost of goods sold		3,310,000
Gross profit		1,940,000
Operating expenses		
Depreciation expense	95,000	
Amortization expense	20,000	
Other expenses	945,000	1,060,000
Net income		$ 880,000

Instructions

Cash from operations
$1,185,000

Prepare the operating activities section of the statement of cash flows for the year ended December 31, 2014, for Asquith Company, using the indirect method.

Prepare the operating activities section—direct method.

*P13-4B Data for Asquith Company are presented in P13-3B.

(LO 6), AP

Instructions

Cash from operations $1,185,000

Prepare the operating activities section of the statement of cash flows using the direct method.

Prepare the operating activities section—indirect method.

P13-5B The income statement of Anne Droid Inc. reported the following condensed information.

(LO 3), AP

Anne Droid Inc.
Income Statement
For the Year Ended December 31, 2014

Sales revenue	$551,000
Operating expenses	400,000
Income from operations	151,000
Income tax expense	36,000
Net income	$115,000

Anne Droid's balance sheet contained these comparative data at December 31.

	2014	2013
Accounts receivable	$55,000	$70,000
Accounts payable	40,000	51,000
Income taxes payable	12,000	4,000

Anne Droid has no depreciable assets. Accounts payable pertain to operating expenses.

Instructions

Cash from operations $127,000

Prepare the operating activities section of the statement of cash flows using the indirect method.

Prepare the operating activities section—direct method.

*P13-6B Data for Anne Droid Inc. are presented in P13-5B.

(LO 6), AP

Instructions

Cash from operations $127,000

Prepare the operating activities section of the statement of cash flows using the direct method.

P13-7B Presented below are the financial statements of Rocastle Company.

Prepare a statement of cash flows—indirect method, and compute free cash flow.

(LO 3, 4), AP, AN

Rocastle Company
Comparative Balance Sheets
December 31

Assets		2014		2013
Cash		$ 18,000		$ 33,000
Accounts receivable		25,000		14,000
Inventory		45,000		25,000
Equipment	$ 70,000		$ 78,000	
Less: Accumulated depreciation—				
equipment	(27,000)	43,000	(24,000)	54,000
Total		$131,000		$126,000

Liabilities and Stockholders' Equity		2014		2013
Accounts payable		$ 31,000		$ 43,000
Income taxes payable		24,000		20,000
Bonds payable		20,000		10,000
Common stock		25,000		25,000
Retained earnings		31,000		28,000
Total		$131,000		$126,000

Rocastle Company
Income Statement
For the Year Ended December 31, 2014

Sales revenue	$286,000
Cost of goods sold	204,000
Gross profit	82,000
Operating expenses	37,000
Income from operations	45,000
Interest expense	7,000
Income before income taxes	38,000
Income tax expense	10,000
Net income	$ 28,000

Additional data:

1. Depreciation expense was $6,000.
2. Dividends of $25,000 were declared and paid.
3. During the year, equipment was sold for $12,000 cash. This equipment cost $15,000 originally and had accumulated depreciation of $3,000 at the time of sale.
4. Additional equipment was purchased for $7,000 cash.

Instructions
(a) Prepare a statement of cash flows using the indirect method.
(b) Compute free cash flow.

(a) Cash from operations
  $(5,000)

*P13-8B Data for Rocastle Company are presented in P13-7B. Further analysis reveals the following.

Prepare a statement of cash flows—direct method, and compute free cash flow.

(LO 4, 6), AP, AN

1. Accounts payable pertains to merchandise creditors.
2. All operating expenses except for depreciation are paid in cash.
3. All depreciation expense is in the operating expenses.
4. All sales and purchases are on account.

Instructions
(a) Prepare a statement of cash flows using the direct method.
(b) Compute free cash flow.

(a) Cash from operations
  $(5,000)

Prepare a statement of cash flows—indirect method.

(LO 3), AP

P13-9B Condensed financial data of Minnie Hooper Company are shown below.

Minnie Hooper Company
Comparative Balance Sheets
December 31

Assets	2014	2013
Cash	$ 93,600	$ 33,400
Accounts receivable	63,200	37,000
Inventory	124,500	102,650
Investments	79,500	107,000
Plant assets	318,000	205,000
Accumulated depreciation	(44,000)	(40,000)
Total	$634,800	$445,050

Liabilities and Stockholders' Equity		
Accounts payable	$ 56,600	$ 48,280
Accrued expenses payable	15,100	18,830
Bonds payable	140,000	70,000
Common stock	250,000	200,000
Retained earnings	173,100	107,940
Total	$634,800	$445,050

Minnie Hooper Company
Income Statement
For the Year Ended December 31, 2014

Sales revenue		$297,500
Less:		
Cost of goods sold	$99,460	
Operating expenses, excluding depreciation expense	19,670	
Depreciation expense	25,000	
Loss on disposal of plant assets	5,000	
Income taxes	37,270	
Interest expense	2,940	189,340
Net income		$108,160

Additional information:

1. New plant assets costing $149,000 were purchased for cash during the year.
2. Investments were sold at cost.
3. Plant assets costing $36,000 were sold for $10,000, resulting in a loss of $5,000.
4. A cash dividend of $43,000 was declared and paid during the year.

Instructions

Prepare a statement of cash flows using the indirect method.

Cash from operations $94,700

Prepare a statement of cash flows—direct method.

(LO 6), AP

Cash from operations $94,700

*P13-10B Data for Minnie Hooper Company are presented in P13-9B. Further analysis reveals that accounts payable pertain to merchandise creditors.

Instructions

Prepare a statement of cash flows for Minnie Hooper Company using the direct method.

Prepare a statement of cash flows—indirect method.

(LO 3), AP

P13-11B Presented on next page are the comparative balance sheets for Vernet Company at December 31.

Vernet Company
Comparative Balance Sheets
December 31

Assets	2014	2013
Cash	$ 41,460	$ 57,000
Accounts receivable	77,000	64,000
Inventory	170,000	140,000
Prepaid expenses	12,140	16,540
Land	140,000	150,000
Equipment	215,000	175,000
Accumulated depreciation—equipment	(70,000)	(42,000)
Buildings	250,000	250,000
Accumulated depreciation—buildings	(70,000)	(50,000)
Total	$765,600	$760,540

Liabilities and Stockholders' Equity		
Accounts payable	$ 58,000	$ 45,000
Bonds payable	265,000	265,000
Common stock, $1 par	275,000	250,000
Retained earnings	167,600	200,540
Total	$765,600	$760,540

Additional information:

1. Operating expenses include depreciation expense $57,000 and charges from prepaid expenses of $4,400.
2. Land was sold for cash at cost for $35,000
3. Cash dividends of $82,940 were paid.
4. Net income for 2014 was $50,000.
5. Equipment was purchased for $80,000 cash. In addition, equipment costing $40,000 with a book value of $31,000 was sold for $37,000 cash.
6. Issued 25,000 shares of $1 par value common stock in exchange for land with a fair value of $25,000

Instructions
Prepare a statement of cash flows for 2014 using the indirect method.

Cash from operations $75,400

PROBLEMS: SET C

Visit the book's companion website, at **www.wiley.com/college/weygandt**, and choose the Student Companion site to access Problem Set C.

WATERWAYS CONTINUING PROBLEM

(This is a continuation of the Waterways Problem from Chapters 1–12.)

WCP13 Waterways prepared the balance sheet and income statement for the irrigation installation division for 2014. Now the company also needs to prepare a statement of cash flows for the same division. This problem asks you to prepare a statement of cash flows and to calculate cash-basis measures.

Go to the book's companion website, **www.wiley.com/college/weygandt**, *to find the completion of this problem.*

Broadening Your **PERSPECTIVE**

Financial Reporting and Analysis

Financial Reporting Problem: PepsiCo, Inc.

 PEPSICO

BYP13-1 Refer to the financial statements of PepsiCo, presented at **www.pepsico.com**, and answer the following questions.

(a) What was the amount of net cash provided by operating activities for the year ended December 25, 2010? For the year ended December 26, 2009?

(b) What was the amount of increase or decrease in cash and cash equivalents for the year ended December 25, 2010? For the year ended December 26, 2009?

(c) Which method of computing net cash provided by operating activities does PepsiCo use?

(d) From your analysis of the 2010 statement of cash flows, did the change in accounts and notes receivable require or provide cash? Did the change in inventories require or provide cash? Did the change in accounts payable and other current liabilities require or provide cash?

(e) What was the net outflow or inflow of cash from investing activities for the year ended December 25, 2010?

(f) What was the amount of interest paid in the year ended December 25, 2010? What was the amount of income taxes paid in the year ended December 25, 2010? (See Note 14.)

Comparative Analysis Problem:
PepsiCo, Inc. vs. The Coca-Cola Company

PEPSICO

BYP13-2 PepsiCo's financial statements are presented at **www.pepsico.com**. Financial statements of The Coca-Cola Company are presented at **www.coca-cola.com**.

Instructions

(a) Based on the information contained in these financial statements, compute free cash flow for each company.

(b) What conclusions concerning the management of cash can be drawn from these data?

Decision-Making Across the Organization

BYP13-3 Norman Roads and Sara Mesa are examining the following statement of cash flows for Del Carpio Company for the year ended January 31, 2014.

Del Carpio Company
Statement of Cash Flows
For the Year Ended January 31, 2014

Sources of cash	
From sales of merchandise	$350,000
From sale of capital stock	405,000
From sale of investment (purchased below)	85,000
From depreciation	75,000
From issuance of note for truck	25,000
From interest on investments	6,000
Total sources of cash	946,000

Uses of cash	
For purchase of fixtures and equipment	320,000
For merchandise purchased for resale	245,000
For operating expenses (including depreciation)	160,000
For purchase of investment	75,000
For purchase of truck by issuance of note	25,000
For purchase of treasury stock	15,000
For interest on note payable	5,000
Total uses of cash	845,000
Net increase in cash	$101,000

Norman claims that Del Carpio's statement of cash flows is an excellent portrayal of a superb first year with cash increasing $101,000. Sara replies that it was not a superb first year. Rather, she says, the year was an operating failure, the statement is presented incorrectly, and $101,000 is not the actual increase in cash. The cash balance at the beginning of the year was $140,000.

Instructions
With the class divided into groups, answer the following.
(a) Using the data provided, prepare a statement of cash flows in proper form using the indirect method. The only noncash items in the income statement are depreciation and the gain from the sale of the investment.
(b) With whom do you agree, Norman or Sara? Explain your position.

Real-World Focus

BYP13-4 Purpose: Learn about the SEC.

Address: **www.sec.gov/index.html,** or go to **www.wiley.com/college/weygandt**

From the SEC homepage, choose **About the SEC**.

Instructions
Answer the following questions.
(a) How many enforcement actions does the SEC take each year against securities law violators? What are typical infractions?
(b) After the Depression, Congress passed the Securities Acts of 1933 and 1934 to improve investor confidence in the markets. What two "common sense" notions are these laws based on?
(c) Who was the President of the United States at the time of the creation of the SEC? Who was the first SEC Chairperson?

BYP13-5 Purpose: Use the Internet to view SEC filings.

Address: **biz.yahoo.com/i,** or go to **www.wiley.com/college/weygandt**

Steps:
1. Type in a company name.
2. Choose **Profile**.
3. Choose **SEC Filings**. (This will take you to Yahoo-Edgar Online.)

Instructions
Answer the following questions.
(a) What company did you select?
(b) Which filing is the most recent? What is the date?
(c) What other recent SEC filings are available for your viewing?

Critical Thinking

Communication Activity

BYP13-6 Bart Sampson, the owner-president of Computer Services Company, is unfamiliar with the statement of cash flows that you, as his accountant, prepared. He asks for further explanation.

Instructions

Write him a brief memo explaining the form and content of the statement of cash flows as shown in Illustration 13-13 (page 601).

Ethics Case

BYP13-7 Babbit Corp. is a medium-sized wholesaler of automotive parts. It has 10 stockholders who have been paid a total of $1 million in cash dividends for 8 consecutive years. The board's policy requires that, for this dividend to be declared, net cash provided by operating activities as reported in Babbit's current year's statement of cash flows must exceed $1 million. President and CEO Milton Williams's job is secure so long as he produces annual operating cash flows to support the usual dividend.

At the end of the current year, controller Jerry Roberts presents president Milton Williams with some disappointing news: The net cash provided by operating activities is calculated by the indirect method to be only $970,000. The president says to Jerry, "We must get that amount above $1 million. Isn't there some way to increase operating cash flow by another $30,000?" Jerry answers, "These figures were prepared by my assistant. I'll go back to my office and see what I can do." The president replies, "I know you won't let me down, Jerry."

Upon close scrutiny of the statement of cash flows, Jerry concludes that he can get the operating cash flows above $1 million by reclassifying a $60,000, 2-year note payable listed in the financing activities section as "Proceeds from bank loan—$60,000." He will report the note instead as "Increase in payables—$60,000" and treat it as an adjustment of net income in the operating activities section. He returns to the president, saying, "You can tell the board to declare their usual dividend. Our net cash flow provided by operating activities is $1,030,000." "Good man, Jerry! I knew I could count on you," exults the president.

Instructions

(a) Who are the stakeholders in this situation?
(b) Was there anything unethical about the president's actions? Was there anything unethical about the controller's actions?
(c) Are the board members or anyone else likely to discover the misclassification?

All About You

BYP13-8 In this chapter, you learned that companies prepare a statement of cash flows in order to keep track of their sources and uses of cash and to help them plan for their future cash needs. Planning for your own short- and long-term cash needs is every bit as important as it is for a company.

Instructions

Read the article ("Financial Uh-Oh? No Problem") provided at **www.fool.com/personal-finance/ saving/index.aspx**, and answer the following questions.

(a) Describe the three factors that determine how much money you should set aside for short-term needs.
(b) How many months of living expenses does the article suggest to set aside?
(c) Estimate how much you should set aside based upon your current situation. Are you closer to Cliff's scenario or to Prudence's?

Answers to Chapter Questions

Answers to Insight and Accounting Across the Organization Questions

p. 590 Net *What*? Q: In general, why do differences exist between net income and net cash provided by operating activities? **A:** The differences are explained by differences in the timing of the reporting of revenues and expenses under accrual accounting versus cash. Under accrual accounting, companies report revenues when earned, even if cash hasn't been received, and they report expenses when incurred, even if cash hasn't been paid.

p. 599 Cash Flow Isn't Always What It Seems Q: For what reasons might managers at WorldCom and at Dynegy take the actions noted above? **A:** Analysts increasingly use cash flow-based measures of income, such as cash flow provided by operations, in addition to net income. More investors now focus on cash flow from operations, and some compensation contracts now have bonuses tied to cash flow numbers. Thus, some managers have taken actions that artificially increase cash flow from operations.

Answers to Self-Test Questions

1. c **2.** a **3.** b **4.** a **5.** c **6.** d **7.** b **8.** c **9.** d ($132,000 + $10,000 + $6,000 − $12,000)
10. b **11.** b ($200,000 + $40,000 − $10,000 + $20,000 − $30,000) **12.** a ($100,000 + $50,000 − $30,000) **13.** b ($100,000 + $60,000 − $30,000) **14.** a **15.** d *16.* b *17.* b *18.* c [$129,000 + ($44,000 − $42,000)] *19.* d

✔ Remember to go back to The Navigator box on the chapter opening page and check off your completed work.

Chapter 14

Financial Statement Analysis

Feature Story

It Pays to Be Patient

A recent issue of *Forbes* magazine listed Warren Buffett as the richest person in the world. His estimated wealth was $62 billion, give or take a few million. How much is $62 billion? If you invested $62 billion in an investment earning just 4%, you could spend $6.8 million per day—every day—forever. How did Mr. Buffett amass this wealth? Through careful investing.

However, if you think you might want to follow Mr. Buffett's example and transform your humble nest-egg into a mountain of cash, be warned: His techniques have been widely circulated and emulated, but never practiced with the same degree of success.

Mr. Buffett epitomizes a "value investor." To this day, he applies the same basic techniques he learned in the 1950s from the great value investor Benjamin Graham. That means he spends his time looking for companies that have good long-term potential but are currently under-priced. He invests in companies that have low exposure to debt and that reinvest their earnings for future growth. He does not get caught up in fads or the latest trend. Instead, he looks for companies in industries with sound economics and ones that have high returns on stockholders' equity. He looks for steady earnings trends and high margins.

Mr. Buffett sat out on the dot-com mania in the 1990s. When other investors put lots of money into

✔ **The Navigator**

☐ Scan Learning Objectives

☐ Read Feature Story

☐ Read Preview

☐ Read Text and answer **DO IT!** p. 656
    ☐ p. 670 ☐ p. 675 ☐ p. 677

☐ Work Using the Decision Toolkit p. 678

☐ Review Summary of Learning Objectives

☐ Work Comprehensive **DO IT!** p. 682

☐ Answer Self-Test Questions

☐ Complete Assignments

☐ Go to **WileyPLUS** for practice and tutorials

Learning Objectives

After studying this chapter, you should be able to:

1 Discuss the need for comparative analysis.

2 Identify the tools of financial statement analysis.

3 Explain and apply horizontal analysis.

4 Describe and apply vertical analysis.

5 Identify and compute ratios used in analyzing a firm's liquidity, profitability, and solvency.

6 Understand the concept of earning power, and how irregular items are presented.

7 Understand the concept of quality of earnings.

✔ The Navigator

fledgling high-tech firms, Mr. Buffett did not bite. He simply did not find any dot-com companies that met his criteria. Of course, he didn't get to enjoy the stock price boom on the way up. On the other hand, he didn't have to ride the price back down to Earth either. Instead, when the dot-com bubble burst, and nearly everyone else was suffering from investment shock, he swooped in and scooped up deals on companies that he had been following for years.

So, how does Mr. Buffett spend his money? Basically, he doesn't! He still lives in the same house that he purchased in Omaha, Nebraska, in 1958 for $31,500. He still drives his own car (a Cadillac DTS). And in case you were thinking that his kids are riding the road to Easy Street, think again. Mr. Buffett has committed to giving virtually all of his money to charity before he dies.

So, given that neither you nor anyone else will be inheriting Mr. Buffett's riches, you should probably start honing your financial analysis skills. A good way for you to begin your career as a successful investor is to master the fundamentals of financial analysis discussed in this chapter.

✔ **The Navigator**

Preview of **Chapter 14**

We can learn an important lesson from Warren Buffett: Study companies carefully if you wish to invest. Do not get caught up in fads but instead find companies that are financially healthy. Using some of the basic decision tools presented in this book, you can perform a rudimentary analysis on any U.S. company and draw basic conclusions about its financial health. Although it would not be wise for you to bet your life savings on a company's stock relying solely on your current level of knowledge, we strongly encourage you to practice your new skills wherever possible. Only with practice will you improve your ability to interpret financial numbers.

Before unleashing you on the world of high finance, we will present a few more important concepts and techniques, as well as provide you with one more comprehensive review of corporate financial statements. We use all of the decision tools presented in this text to analyze a single company—J.C. Penney Company, one of the country's oldest and largest retail store chains.

The content and organization of Chapter 14 are as follows.

FINANCIAL STATEMENT ANALYSIS				
Basics of Financial Statement Analysis	**Horizontal and Vertical Analysis**	**Ratio Analysis**	**Earning Power and Irregular Items**	**Quality of Earnings**
• Need for comparative analysis • Tools of analysis	• Balance sheet • Income statement • Retained earnings statement	• Liquidity • Profitability • Solvency • Summary	• Discontinued operations • Extraordinary items • Changes in accounting principle • Comprehensive income	• Alternative accounting methods • Pro forma income • Improper recognition

✔ **The Navigator**

Basics of Financial Statement Analysis

Analyzing financial statements involves evaluating three characteristics: a company's liquidity, profitability, and solvency. A **short-term creditor**, such as a bank, is primarily interested in liquidity—the ability of the borrower to pay obligations when they come due. The liquidity of the borrower is extremely important in evaluating the safety of a loan. A **long-term creditor**, such as a bondholder, looks to profitability and solvency measures that indicate the company's ability to survive over a long period of time. Long-term creditors consider such measures as the amount of debt in the company's capital structure and its ability to meet interest payments. Similarly, **stockholders** look at the profitability and solvency of the company. They want to assess the likelihood of dividends and the growth potential of the stock.

Need for Comparative Analysis

LEARNING OBJECTIVE 1

Discuss the need for comparative analysis.

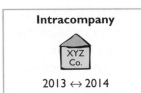

Every item reported in a financial statement has significance. When J.C. Penney Company, Inc. reports cash and cash equivalents of $3 billion on its balance sheet, we know the company had that amount of cash on the balance sheet date. But, we do not know whether the amount represents an increase over prior years, or whether it is adequate in relation to the company's need for cash. To obtain such information, we need to compare the amount of cash with other financial statement data.

Comparisons can be made on a number of different bases. Three are illustrated in this chapter.

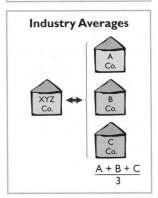

1. **Intracompany basis.** Comparisons within a company are often useful to detect changes in financial relationships and significant trends. For example, a comparison of J.C. Penney's current year's cash amount with the prior year's cash amount shows either an increase or a decrease. Likewise, a comparison of J.C. Penney's year-end cash amount with the amount of its total assets at year-end shows the proportion of total assets in the form of cash.

2. **Industry averages.** Comparisons with industry averages provide information about a company's relative position within the industry. For example, financial statement readers can compare J.C. Penney's financial data with the averages for its industry compiled by financial rating organizations such as Dun & Bradstreet, Moody's, and Standard & Poor's, or with information provided on the Internet by organizations such as Yahoo! on its financial site.

3. **Intercompany basis.** Comparisons with other companies provide insight into a company's competitive position. For example, investors can compare J.C. Penney's total sales for the year with the total sales of its competitors in retail, such as Sears.

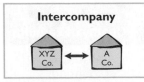

Tools of Analysis

LEARNING OBJECTIVE 2

Identify the tools of financial statement analysis.

We use various tools to evaluate the significance of financial statement data. Three commonly used tools are as follows.

- **Horizontal analysis** evaluates a series of financial statement data over a period of time.
- **Vertical analysis** evaluates financial statement data by expressing each item in a financial statement as a percentage of a base amount.
- **Ratio analysis** expresses the relationship among selected items of financial statement data.

Horizontal analysis is used primarily in intracompany comparisons. Two features in published financial statements facilitate this type of comparison. First, each of the basic financial statements presents comparative financial data for a minimum of two years. Second, a summary of selected financial data is presented for a series of five to 10 years or more. *Vertical analysis* is used in both intra- and intercompany comparisons. *Ratio analysis* is used in all three types of comparisons. In the following sections, we explain and illustrate each of the three types of analysis.

Horizontal Analysis

Horizontal analysis, also called **trend analysis**, is a technique for evaluating a series of financial statement data over a period of time. Its purpose is to determine the increase or decrease that has taken place. This change may be expressed as either an amount or a percentage. For example, Illustration 14-1 shows recent net sales figures of J.C. Penney Company.

LEARNING OBJECTIVE	3
Explain and apply horizontal analysis.	

J.C. Penney Company
Net Sales (In millions)

2009	2008	2007
$17,556	$18,486	$19,860

Illustration 14-1
J.C. Penney Company's net sales

If we assume that 2007 is the base year, we can measure all percentage increases or decreases from this base period amount as follows.

$$\text{Change Since Base Period} = \frac{\text{Current Year Amount} - \text{Base Year Amount}}{\text{Base Year Amount}}$$

Illustration 14-2
Formula for horizontal analysis of changes since base period

For example, we can determine that net sales for J.C. Penney decreased from 2007 to 2008 approximately 6.9% [($18,486 − $19,860) ÷ $19,860]. Similarly, we can determine that net sales decreased from 2007 to 2009 approximately 11.6% [($17,556 − $19,860) ÷ $19,860].

Alternatively, we can express current year sales as a percentage of the base period. We do this by dividing the current year amount by the base year amount, as shown below.

$$\text{Current Results in Relation to Base Period} = \frac{\text{Current Year Amount}}{\text{Base Year Amount}}$$

Illustration 14-3
Formula for horizontal analysis of current year in relation to base year

Illustration 14-4 (page 654) presents this analysis for J.C. Penney for a three-year period using 2007 as the base period.

Illustration 14-4
Horizontal analysis of J.C.
Penney Company's net sales
in relation to base period

J.C. Penney Company		
Net Sales (in millions)		
in relation to base period 2007		
2009	**2008**	**2007**
$17,556	$18,486	$19,860
88.4%	93.1%	100%

Balance Sheet

To further illustrate horizontal analysis, we will use the financial statements of Quality Department Store Inc., a fictional retailer. Illustration 14-5 presents a horizontal analysis of its two-year condensed balance sheets, showing dollar and percentage changes.

Illustration 14-5
Horizontal analysis of
balance sheets

Quality Department Store Inc.				
Condensed Balance Sheets				
December 31				
			Increase or (Decrease) during 2009	
	2009	**2008**	**Amount**	**Percent**
Assets				
Current assets	$1,020,000	$ 945,000	**$ 75,000**	**7.9%**
Plant assets (net)	800,000	632,500	**167,500**	**26.5%**
Intangible assets	15,000	17,500	**(2,500)**	**(14.3%)**
Total assets	$1,835,000	$1,595,000	**$240,000**	**15.0%**
Liabilities				
Current liabilities	$ 344,500	$ 303,000	**$ 41,500**	**13.7%**
Long-term liabilities	487,500	497,000	**(9,500)**	**(1.9%)**
Total liabilities	832,000	800,000	**32,000**	**4.0%**
Stockholders' Equity				
Common stock, $1 par	275,400	270,000	**5,400**	**2.0%**
Retained earnings	727,600	525,000	**202,600**	**38.6%**
Total stockholders' equity	1,003,000	795,000	**208,000**	**26.2%**
Total liabilities and stockholders' equity	$1,835,000	$1,595,000	**$240,000**	**15.0%**

The comparative balance sheets in Illustration 14-5 show that a number of significant changes have occurred in Quality Department Store's financial structure from 2008 to 2009:

- In the assets section, plant assets (net) increased $167,500, or 26.5%.
- In the liabilities section, current liabilities increased $41,500, or 13.7%.
- In the stockholders' equity section, retained earnings increased $202,600, or 38.6%.

These changes suggest that the company expanded its asset base during 2009 and **financed this expansion primarily by retaining income** rather than assuming additional long-term debt.

Income Statement

Illustration 14-6 presents a horizontal analysis of the two-year condensed income statements of Quality Department Store Inc. for the years 2009 and 2008. Horizontal analysis of the income statements shows the following changes:

- Net sales increased $260,000, or 14.2% ($260,000 ÷ $1,837,000).
- Cost of goods sold increased $141,000, or 12.4% ($141,000 ÷ $1,140,000).
- Total operating expenses increased $37,000, or 11.6% ($37,000 ÷ $320,000).

Overall, gross profit and net income were up substantially. Gross profit increased 17.1%, and net income, 26.5%. Quality's profit trend appears favorable.

Illustration 14-6
Horizontal analysis of income statements

Quality Department Store Inc. Condensed Income Statements For the Years Ended December 31				
			Increase or (Decrease) during 2009	
	2009	**2008**	**Amount**	**Percent**
Sales revenue	$2,195,000	$1,960,000	**$235,000**	**12.0%**
Sales returns and allowances	98,000	123,000	**(25,000)**	**(20.3%)**
Net sales	2,097,000	1,837,000	**260,000**	**14.2%**
Cost of goods sold	1,281,000	1,140,000	**141,000**	**12.4%**
Gross profit	816,000	697,000	**119,000**	**17.1%**
Selling expenses	253,000	211,500	**41,500**	**19.6%**
Administrative expenses	104,000	108,500	**(4,500)**	**(4.1%)**
Total operating expenses	357,000	320,000	**37,000**	**11.6%**
Income from operations	459,000	377,000	**82,000**	**21.8%**
Other revenues and gains				
Interest and dividends	9,000	11,000	**(2,000)**	**(18.2%)**
Other expenses and losses				
Interest expense	36,000	40,500	**(4,500)**	**(11.1%)**
Income before income taxes	432,000	347,500	**84,500**	**24.3%**
Income tax expense	168,200	139,000	**29,200**	**21.0%**
Net income	$ 263,800	$ 208,500	**$ 55,300**	**26.5%**

Helpful Hint
Note that though the amount column is additive (the total is $55,300), the percentage column is not additive (26.5% is not the total). A separate percentage has been calculated for each item.

Retained Earnings Statement

Illustration 14-7 (page 656) presents a horizontal analysis of Quality Department Store's comparative retained earnings statements. Analyzed horizontally, net income increased $55,300, or 26.5%, whereas dividends on the common stock increased only $1,200, or 2%. We saw in the horizontal analysis of the balance sheet that ending retained earnings increased 38.6%. As indicated earlier, the company retained a significant portion of net income to finance additional plant facilities.

Horizontal analysis of changes from period to period is relatively straightforward and is quite useful. But, complications can occur in making the computations. If an item has no value in a base year or preceding year but does have a value in the next year, we cannot compute a percentage change. Similarly, if a negative amount appears in the base or preceding period and a positive amount exists the following year (or vice versa), no percentage change can be computed.

Illustration 14-7
Horizontal analysis of retained earnings statements

Quality Department Store Inc. Retained Earnings Statements For the Years Ended December 31				
			Increase or (Decrease) during 2009	
	2009	**2008**	**Amount**	**Percent**
Retained earnings, Jan. 1	$525,000	$376,500	$148,500	39.4%
Add: Net income	263,800	208,500	55,300	26.5%
	788,800	585,000	203,800	
Deduct: Dividends	61,200	60,000	1,200	2.0%
Retained earnings, Dec. 31	$727,600	$525,000	$202,600	38.6%

DECISION TOOLKIT

DECISION CHECKPOINTS	INFO NEEDED FOR DECISION	TOOL TO USE FOR DECISION	HOW TO EVALUATE RESULTS
How do the company's financial position and operating results compare with those of the previous period?	Income statement and balance sheet	Comparative financial statements should be prepared over at least two years, with the first year reported being the base year. Changes in each line item relative to the base year should be presented both by amount and by percentage. This is called *horizontal analysis*.	Significant changes should be investigated to determine the reason for the change.

> DO IT!

Horizontal Analysis

Summary financial information for Rosepatch Company is as follows.

	December 31, 2014	December 31, 2013
Current assets	$234,000	$180,000
Plant assets (net)	756,000	420,000
Total assets	$990,000	$600,000

Compute the amount and percentage changes in 2014 using horizontal analysis, assuming 2013 is the base year.

Solution

Action Plan

✔ Find the percentage change by dividing the amount of the increase by the 2013 amount (base year).

	Increase in 2014	
	Amount	**Percent**
Current assets	$ 54,000	30% [($234,000 − $180,000) ÷ $180,000]
Plant assets (net)	336,000	80% [($756,000 − $420,000) ÷ $420,000]
Total assets	$390,000	65% [($990,000 − $600,000) ÷ $600,000]

Related exercise material: **BE14-2, BE14-3, BE14-5, BE14-6, BE14-7, E14-1, E14-3, E14-4,** and **DO IT! 14-1.**

✔ **The Navigator**

Vertical Analysis

Vertical analysis, also called **common-size analysis**, is a technique that expresses each financial statement item as a percentage of a base amount. On a balance sheet we might say that current assets are 22% of total assets—*total assets* being the base amount. Or on an income statement, we might say that selling expenses are 16% of net sales—net sales being the base amount.

LEARNING OBJECTIVE   4

Describe and apply vertical analysis.

Balance Sheet

Illustration 14-8 presents the vertical analysis of Quality Department Store Inc.'s comparative balance sheets. The base for the asset items is **total assets**. The base for the liability and stockholders' equity items is **total liabilities and stockholders' equity**.

Illustration 14-8
Vertical analysis of balance sheets

Quality Department Store Inc.
Condensed Balance Sheets
December 31

	2009		2008	
	Amount	**Percent**	**Amount**	**Percent**
Assets				
Current assets	$1,020,000	**55.6%**	$ 945,000	**59.2%**
Plant assets (net)	800,000	**43.6%**	632,500	**39.7%**
Intangible assets	15,000	**0.8%**	17,500	**1.1%**
Total assets	$1,835,000	**100.0%**	$1,595,000	**100.0%**
Liabilities				
Current liabilities	$ 344,500	**18.8%**	$ 303,000	**19.0%**
Long-term liabilities	487,500	**26.5%**	497,000	**31.2%**
Total liabilities	832,000	**45.3%**	800,000	**50.2%**
Stockholders' Equity				
Common stock, $1 par	275,400	**15.0%**	270,000	**16.9%**
Retained earnings	727,600	**39.7%**	525,000	**32.9%**
Total stockholders' equity	1,003,000	**54.7%**	795,000	**49.8%**
Total liabilities and stockholders' equity	$1,835,000	**100.0%**	$1,595,000	**100.0%**

Helpful Hint
The formula for calculating these balance sheet percentages is:
$$\frac{\text{Each item on B/S}}{\text{Total assets}} = \%$$

Vertical analysis shows the relative size of each category in the balance sheet. It also can show the **percentage change** in the individual asset, liability, and stockholders' equity items. For example, we can see that current assets decreased from 59.2% of total assets in 2008 to 55.6% in 2009 (even though the absolute dollar amount increased $75,000 in that time). Plant assets (net) have increased from 39.7% to 43.6% of total assets. Retained earnings have increased from 32.9% to 39.7% of total liabilities and stockholders' equity. These results reinforce the earlier observations that **Quality is choosing to finance its growth through retention of earnings rather than through issuing additional debt**.

Income Statement

Illustration 14-9 (page 658) shows vertical analysis of Quality's income statements. Cost of goods sold as a percentage of net sales declined 1% (62.1% vs. 61.1%),

Quality Department Store Inc.
Condensed Income Statements
For the Years Ended December 31

	2009 Amount	2009 Percent	2008 Amount	2008 Percent
Sales revenue	$2,195,000	104.7%	$1,960,000	106.7%
Sales returns and allowances	98,000	4.7%	123,000	6.7%
Net sales	2,097,000	100.0%	1,837,000	100.0%
Cost of goods sold	1,281,000	61.1%	1,140,000	62.1%
Gross profit	816,000	38.9%	697,000	37.9%
Selling expenses	253,000	12.0%	211,500	11.5%
Administrative expenses	104,000	5.0%	108,500	5.9%
Total operating expenses	357,000	17.0%	320,000	17.4%
Income from operations	459,000	21.9%	377,000	20.5%
Other revenues and gains				
Interest and dividends	9,000	0.4%	11,000	0.6%
Other expenses and losses				
Interest expense	36,000	1.7%	40,500	2.2%
Income before income taxes	432,000	20.6%	347,500	18.9%
Income tax expense	168,200	8.0%	139,000	7.5%
Net income	$ 263,800	12.6%	$ 208,500	11.4%

and total operating expenses declined 0.4% (17.4% vs. 17.0%). As a result, it is not surprising to see net income as a percentage of net sales increase from 11.4% to 12.6%. Quality appears to be a profitable business that is becoming even more successful.

An associated benefit of vertical analysis is that it enables you to compare companies of different sizes. For example, Quality's main competitor is a JC Penney store in a nearby town. Using vertical analysis, we can compare the condensed income statements of Quality Department Store Inc. (a small retail company) with J.C. Penney Company, Inc. (a giant international retailer), as shown in Illustration 14-10.[1]

Condensed Income Statements
(in thousands)

	Quality Department Store Inc. Dollars	Quality Department Store Inc. Percent	J.C. Penney Company Dollars	J.C. Penney Company Percent
Net sales	$2,097	100.0%	$17,556,000	100.0%
Cost of goods sold	1,281	61.1%	10,646,000	60.6%
Gross profit	816	38.9%	6,910,000	39.4%
Selling and administrative expenses	357	17.0%	6,247,000	35.6%
Income from operations	459	21.9%	663,000	3.8%
Other expenses and revenues (including income taxes)	195	9.3%	412,000	2.4%
Net income	$ 264	12.6%	$ 251,000	1.4%

---

[1]*2009 Annual Report*, J.C. Penney Company, Inc. (Dallas, Texas).

J.C. Penney's net sales are 8,372 times greater than the net sales of relatively tiny Quality Department Store. But vertical analysis eliminates this difference in size. The percentages show that Quality's and J.C. Penney's gross profit rates were comparable at 38.9% and 39.4%. However, the percentages related to income from operations were significantly different at 21.9% and 3.7%. This disparity can be attributed to Quality's selling and administrative expense percentage (17%) which is much lower than J.C. Penney's (35.7%). Although J.C. Penney earned net income more than 951 times larger than Quality's, J.C. Penney's net income as a **percentage of each sales dollar** (1.4%) is only 11% of Quality's (12.6%).

DECISION TOOLKIT

DECISION CHECKPOINTS	INFO NEEDED FOR DECISION	TOOL TO USE FOR DECISION	HOW TO EVALUATE RESULTS
How do the relationships between items in this year's financial statements compare with those of last year or those of competitors?	Income statement and balance sheet	Each line item on the income statement should be presented as a percentage of net sales, and each line item on the balance sheet should be presented as a percentage of total assets or total liabilities and stockholders' equity. These percentages should be investigated for differences either across years in the same company or in the same year across different companies. This is called *vertical analysis*.	Any significant differences either across years or between companies should be investigated to determine the cause.

Ratio Analysis

Ratio analysis expresses the relationship among selected items of financial statement data. A **ratio** expresses the mathematical relationship between one quantity and another. The relationship is expressed in terms of either a percentage, a rate, or a simple proportion. To illustrate, in 2010 Nike, Inc., had current assets of $10,959.2 million and current liabilities of $3,364.2 million. We can find the relationship between these two measures by dividing current assets by current liabilities. The alternative means of expression are:

> **LEARNING OBJECTIVE 5**
>
> **Identify and compute ratios used in analyzing a firm's liquidity, profitability, and solvency.**

Percentage:	Current assets are 326% of current liabilities.
Rate:	Current assets are 3.26 times current liabilities.
Proportion:	The relationship of current assets to liabilities is 3.26:1.

To analyze the primary financial statements, we can use ratios to evaluate liquidity, profitability, and solvency. Illustration 14-11 (page 660) describes these classifications.

Ratios can provide clues to underlying conditions that may not be apparent from individual financial statement components. However, a single ratio by itself is not very meaningful. Thus, in the discussion of ratios we will use the following types of comparisons.

1. **Intracompany comparisons** for two years for Quality Department Store.

2. **Industry average comparisons** based on median ratios for department stores.

3. **Intercompany comparisons** based on J.C. Penney Company as Quality Department Store's principal competitor.

Illustration 14-11
Financial ratio classifications

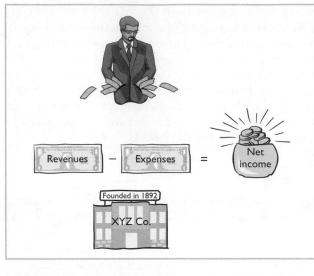

Liquidity Ratios

Measure short-term ability of the company to pay its maturing obligations and to meet unexpected needs for cash

Profitability Ratios

Measure the income or operating success of a company for a given period of time

Solvency Ratios

Measure the ability of the company to survive over a long period of time

ANATOMY OF A FRAUD

Sometimes, relationships between numbers can be used by companies to detect fraud. The numeric relationships that can reveal fraud can be such things as financial ratios that appear abnormal, or statistical abnormalities in the numbers themselves. For example, the fact that WorldCom's line costs, as a percentage of either total expenses or revenues, differed very significantly from its competitors should have alerted people to the possibility of fraud. Or, consider the case of a bank manager, who cooperated with a group of his friends to defraud the bank's credit card department. The manager's friends would apply for credit cards and then run up balances of slightly less than $5,000. The bank had a policy of allowing bank personnel to write off balances of less than $5,000 without seeking supervisor approval. The fraud was detected by applying statistical analysis based on Benford's Law. Benford's Law states that in a random collection of numbers, the frequency of lower digits (e.g., 1, 2, or 3) should be much higher than higher digits (e.g., 7, 8, or 9). In this case, bank auditors analyzed the first two digits of amounts written off. There was a spike at 48 and 49, which was not consistent with what would be expected if the numbers were random.

Total take: Thousands of dollars

THE MISSING CONTROL

Independent Internal Verification. While it might be efficient to allow employees to write off accounts below a certain level, it is important that these write-offs be reviewed and verified periodically. Such a review would likely call attention to an employee with large amounts of write-offs, or in this case, write-offs that were frequently very close to the approval threshold.

Source: Mark J. Nigrini, "I've Got Your Number," *Journal of Accountancy Online* (May 1999).

Liquidity Ratios

Liquidity ratios measure the short-term ability of the company to pay its maturing obligations and to meet unexpected needs for cash. Short-term creditors such as bankers and suppliers are particularly interested in assessing liquidity. The ratios we can use to determine the company's short-term debt-paying ability are the current ratio, the acid-test ratio, receivables turnover, and inventory turnover.

1. CURRENT RATIO

The **current ratio** is a widely used measure for evaluating a company's liquidity and short-term debt-paying ability. The ratio is computed by dividing current assets by current liabilities. Illustration 14-12 shows the 2009 and 2008 current ratios for Quality Department Store and comparative data.

$$\text{Current Ratio} = \frac{\text{Current Assets}}{\text{Current Liabilities}}$$

Quality Department Store	
2009	**2008**
$\dfrac{\$1,020,000}{\$344,500} = 2.96{:}1$	$\dfrac{\$945,000}{\$303,000} = 3.12{:}1$
Industry average	J.C. Penney Company
1.70:1	**2.05:1**

Illustration 14-12
Current ratio

What does the ratio actually mean? The 2009 ratio of 2.96:1 means that for every dollar of current liabilities, Quality has $2.96 of current assets. Quality's current ratio has decreased in the current year. But, compared to the industry average of 1.70:1, Quality appears to be reasonably liquid. J.C. Penney has a current ratio of 2.05:1, which indicates it has adequate current assets relative to its current liabilities.

The current ratio is sometimes referred to as the **working capital ratio**; **working capital** is current assets minus current liabilities. The current ratio is a more dependable indicator of liquidity than working capital. Two companies with the same amount of working capital may have significantly different current ratios.

The current ratio is only one measure of liquidity. It does not take into account the **composition** of the current assets. For example, a satisfactory current ratio does not disclose the fact that a portion of the current assets may be tied up in slow-moving inventory. A dollar of cash would be more readily available to pay the bills than a dollar of slow-moving inventory.

2. ACID-TEST RATIO

The **acid-test (quick) ratio** is a measure of a company's immediate short-term liquidity. We compute this ratio by dividing the sum of cash, short-term investments, and net receivables by current liabilities. Thus, it is an important complement to the current ratio. For example, assume that the current assets of Quality Department Store for 2009 and 2008 consist of the items shown in Illustration 14-13.

Quality Department Store Inc. Balance Sheet (partial)		
	2009	**2008**
Current assets		
Cash	$ 100,000	$155,000
Short-term investments	20,000	70,000
Receivables (net*)	230,000	180,000
Inventory	620,000	500,000
Prepaid expenses	50,000	40,000
Total current assets	$1,020,000	$ 945,000

*Allowance for doubtful accounts is $10,000 at the end of each year.

Illustration 14-13
Current assets of Quality Department Store

Helpful Hint
Can any company operate successfully without working capital? Yes, if it has very predictable cash flows and solid earnings. A number of companies (e.g., Whirlpool, American Standard, and Campbell's Soup) are pursuing this goal. The rationale: Less money tied up in working capital means more money to invest in the business.

Cash, short-term investments, and receivables (net) are highly liquid compared to inventory and prepaid expenses. The inventory may not be readily saleable, and the prepaid expenses may not be transferable to others. Thus, the acid-test ratio measures **immediate** liquidity. The 2009 and 2008 acid-test ratios for Quality Department Store and comparative data are as follows.

Illustration 14-14
Acid-test ratio

$$\text{Acid-Test Ratio} = \frac{\text{Cash + Short-Term Investments + Receivables (Net)}}{\text{Current Liabilities}}$$

Quality Department Store

2009	2008
$\dfrac{\$100,000 + \$20,000 + \$230,000}{\$344,500} = 1.02{:}1$	$\dfrac{\$155,000 + \$70,000 + \$180,000}{\$303,000} = 1.34{:}1$
Industry average	J.C. Penney Company
0.70:1	**1.05:1**

The ratio has declined in 2009. Is an acid-test ratio of 1.02:1 adequate? This depends on the industry and the economy. When compared with the industry average of 0.70:1 and J.C. Penney's of 1.05:1, Quality's acid-test ratio seems adequate.

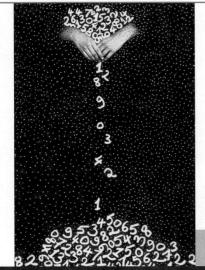

INVESTOR INSIGHT

How to Manage the Current Ratio

The apparent simplicity of the current ratio can have real-world limitations because adding equal amounts to both the numerator and the denominator causes the ratio to decrease.

Assume, for example, that a company has $2,000,000 of current assets and $1,000,000 of current liabilities; its current ratio is 2:1. If it purchases $1,000,000 of inventory on account, it will have $3,000,000 of current assets and $2,000,000 of current liabilities; its current ratio decreases to 1.5:1. If, instead, the company pays off $500,000 of its current liabilities, it will have $1,500,000 of current assets and $500,000 of current liabilities; its current ratio increases to 3:1. Thus, any trend analysis should be done with care because the ratio is susceptible to quick changes and is easily influenced by management.

? How might management influence a company's current ratio? (See page 703.)

3. RECEIVABLES TURNOVER

We can measure liquidity by how quickly a company can convert certain assets to cash. How liquid, for example, are the receivables? The ratio used to assess the liquidity of the receivables is **receivables turnover**. It measures the number of times, on average, the company collects receivables during the period. We compute receivables turnover by dividing net credit sales (net sales less cash sales) by the average net receivables. Unless seasonal factors are significant, average net receivables can be computed from the beginning and ending balances of the net receivables.[2]

Assume that all sales are credit sales. The balance of net receivables at the beginning of 2008 is $200,000. Illustration 14-15 shows the receivables turnover

---

[2]If seasonal factors are significant, the average receivables balance might be determined by using monthly amounts.

for Quality Department Store and comparative data. Quality's receivables turnover improved in 2009. The turnover of 10.2 times is substantially lower than J.C. Penney's 37.2 times, and is also lower than the department store industry's average of 46.4 times.

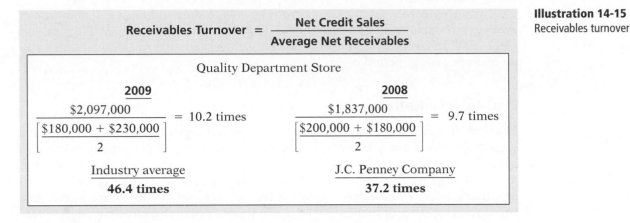

Illustration 14-15
Receivables turnover

AVERAGE COLLECTION PERIOD A popular variant of the receivables turnover ratio is to convert it to an **average collection period** in terms of days. To do so, we divide the receivables turnover ratio into 365 days. For example, the receivables turnover of 10.2 times divided into 365 days gives an average collection period of approximately 36 days. This means that receivables are collected on average every 36 days, or about every 5 weeks. Analysts frequently use the average collection period to assess the effectiveness of a company's credit and collection policies. The general rule is that the collection period should not greatly exceed the credit term period (the time allowed for payment).

4. INVENTORY TURNOVER

Inventory turnover measures the number of times, on average, the inventory is sold during the period. Its purpose is to measure the liquidity of the inventory. We compute the inventory turnover by dividing cost of goods sold by the average inventory. Unless seasonal factors are significant, we can use the beginning and ending inventory balances to compute average inventory.

Assuming that the inventory balance for Quality Department Store at the beginning of 2008 was $450,000, its inventory turnover and comparative data are as shown in Illustration 14-16. Quality's inventory turnover declined slightly in 2009. The turnover of 2.3 times is low compared with the industry average of 4.3 and J.C. Penney's 3.1. Generally, the faster the inventory turnover, the less cash a company has tied up in inventory and the less the chance of inventory obsolescence.

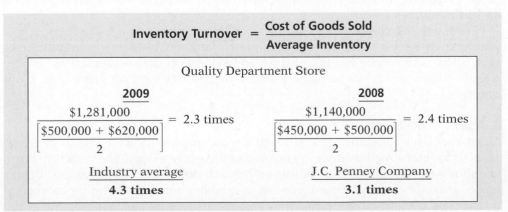

Illustration 14-16
Inventory turnover

DAYS IN INVENTORY A variant of inventory turnover is the **days in inventory**. We calculate it by dividing the inventory turnover into 365. For example, Quality's 2009 inventory turnover of 2.3 times divided into 365 is approximately 159 days. An average selling time of 159 days is also high compared with the industry average of 84.9 days (365 ÷ 4.3) and J.C. Penney's 117.7 days (365 ÷ 3.1).

Inventory turnover ratios vary considerably among industries. For example, grocery store chains have a turnover of 17.1 times and an average selling period of 21 days. In contrast, jewelry stores have an average turnover of 0.80 times and an average selling period of 456 days.

Profitability Ratios

Profitability ratios measure the income or operating success of a company for a given period of time. Income, or the lack of it, affects the company's ability to obtain debt and equity financing. It also affects the company's liquidity position and the company's ability to grow. As a consequence, both creditors and investors are interested in evaluating earning power—profitability. Analysts frequently use profitability as the ultimate test of management's operating effectiveness.

5. PROFIT MARGIN

Alternative Terminology
Profit margin is also called the *rate of return on sales*.

Profit margin is a measure of the percentage of each dollar of sales that results in net income. We can compute it by dividing net income by net sales. Illustration 14-17 shows Quality Department Store's profit margin and comparative data.

Illustration 14-17
Profit margin

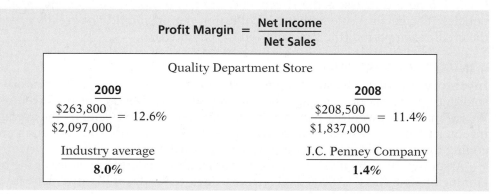

$$\text{Profit Margin} = \frac{\text{Net Income}}{\text{Net Sales}}$$

Quality Department Store

2009	2008
$\dfrac{\$263,800}{\$2,097,000} = 12.6\%$	$\dfrac{\$208,500}{\$1,837,000} = 11.4\%$
Industry average	J.C. Penney Company
8.0%	**1.4%**

Quality experienced an increase in its profit margin from 2008 to 2009. Its profit margin is unusually high in comparison with the industry average of 8% and J.C. Penney's 1.4%.

High-volume (high inventory turnover) businesses, such as grocery stores (Safeway or Kroger) and discount stores (Kmart or Wal-Mart), generally experience low profit margins. In contrast, low-volume businesses, such as jewelry stores (Tiffany & Co.) or airplane manufacturers (Boeing Co.), have high profit margins.

6. ASSET TURNOVER

Asset turnover measures how efficiently a company uses its assets to generate sales. It is determined by dividing net sales by average assets. The resulting number shows the dollars of sales produced by each dollar invested in assets. Unless seasonal factors are significant, we can use the beginning and ending balance of total assets to determine average total assets. Assuming that total assets at the beginning of 2008 were $1,446,000, the 2009 and 2008 asset turnover for Quality Department Store and comparative data are shown in Illustration 14-18.

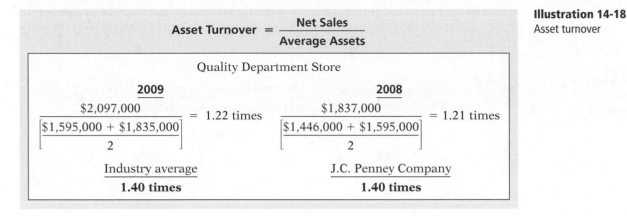

Illustration 14-18
Asset turnover

Asset turnover shows that in 2009 Quality generated sales of $1.22 for each dollar it had invested in assets. The ratio changed very little from 2008 to 2009. Quality's asset turnover is below both the industry average of 1.40 times and J.C. Penney's ratio of 1.40 times.

Asset turnover ratios vary considerably among industries. For example, a large utility company like Consolidated Edison (New York) has a ratio of 0.40 times, and the large grocery chain Kroger Stores has a ratio of 3.4 times.

7. RETURN ON ASSETS

An overall measure of profitability is **return on assets**. We compute this ratio by dividing net income by average assets. The 2009 and 2008 return on assets for Quality Department Store and comparative data are shown below.

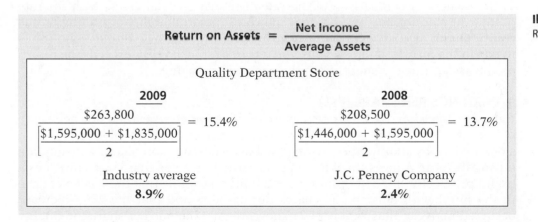

Illustration 14-19
Return on assets

Quality's return on assets improved from 2008 to 2009. Its return of 15.4% is very high compared with the department store industry average of 8.9% and J.C. Penney's 2.4%.

8. RETURN ON COMMON STOCKHOLDERS' EQUITY

Another widely used profitability ratio is **return on common stockholders' equity**. It measures profitability from the common stockholders' viewpoint. This ratio shows how many dollars of net income the company earned for each dollar invested by the owners. We compute it by dividing net income available to common stockholders by average common stockholders' equity. When a company has preferred stock, we must deduct **preferred dividend** requirements from net income to compute income available to common stockholders. Similarly, we deduct the par value of preferred stock (or call price, if applicable) from total stockholders' equity to determine the amount of common stockholders' equity used in this ratio. Assuming that common stockholders' equity at the beginning of 2008 was $667,000, Illustration 14-20 shows the 2009 and 2008 ratios for Quality Department Store and comparative data.

Illustration 14-20
Return on common stockholders' equity

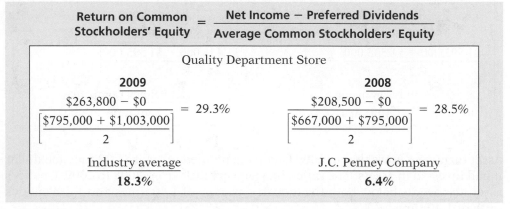

$$\text{Return on Common Stockholders' Equity} = \frac{\text{Net Income} - \text{Preferred Dividends}}{\text{Average Common Stockholders' Equity}}$$

Quality Department Store

2009	2008
$\dfrac{\$263,800 - \$0}{\left[\dfrac{\$795,000 + \$1,003,000}{2}\right]} = 29.3\%$	$\dfrac{\$208,500 - \$0}{\left[\dfrac{\$667,000 + \$795,000}{2}\right]} = 28.5\%$
Industry average **18.3%**	J.C. Penney Company **6.4%**

Quality's rate of return on common stockholders' equity is high at 29.3%, considering an industry average of 18.3% and a rate of 6.4% for J.C. Penney.

Note also that Quality's rate of return on stockholders' equity (29.3%) is substantially higher than its rate of return on assets (15.4%). The reason is that Quality has made effective use of **leverage**. **Leveraging** or **trading on the equity** at a gain means that the company has borrowed money at a lower rate of interest than it is able to earn by using the borrowed money. Leverage enables Quality Department Store to use money supplied by nonowners to increase the return to the owners. A comparison of the rate of return on total assets with the rate of interest paid for borrowed money indicates the profitability of trading on the equity. Quality Department Store earns more on its borrowed funds than it has to pay in the form of interest. Thus, the return to stockholders exceeds the return on the assets, due to benefits from the positive leveraging.

9. EARNINGS PER SHARE (EPS)

Earnings per share (EPS) is a measure of the net income earned on each share of common stock. It is computed by dividing net income available to common stockholders by the number of weighted-average common shares outstanding during the year. A measure of net income earned on a per share basis provides a useful perspective for determining profitability. Assuming that there is no change in the number of outstanding shares during 2008 and that the 2009 increase occurred midyear, Illustration 14-21 shows the net income per share for Quality Department Store for 2009 and 2008.

Illustration 14-21
Earnings per share

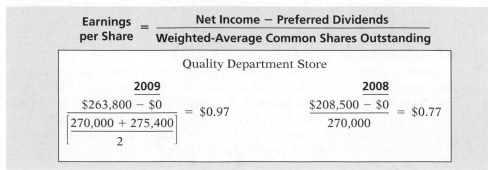

$$\text{Earnings per Share} = \frac{\text{Net Income} - \text{Preferred Dividends}}{\text{Weighted-Average Common Shares Outstanding}}$$

Quality Department Store

2009	2008
$\dfrac{\$263,800 - \$0}{\left[\dfrac{270,000 + 275,400}{2}\right]} = \$0.97$	$\dfrac{\$208,500 - \$0}{270,000} = \$0.77$

Note that no industry or J.C. Penney data are presented. Such comparisons are not meaningful because of the wide variations in the number of shares of outstanding stock among companies. The only meaningful EPS comparison is an intracompany trend comparison: Quality's earnings per share increased 20 cents per share in 2009. This represents a 26% increase over the 2008 earnings per share of 77 cents.

The terms "earnings per share" and "net income per share" refer to the amount of net income applicable to each share of **common stock**. Therefore, in computing EPS, if there are preferred dividends declared for the period, we must deduct them from net income to determine income available to the common stockholders.

10. PRICE-EARNINGS RATIO

The **price-earnings (P-E) ratio** is an oft-quoted measure of the ratio of the market price of each share of common stock to the earnings per share. The price-earnings (P-E) ratio reflects investors' assessments of a company's future earnings. We compute it by dividing the market price per share of the stock by earnings per share. Assuming that the market price of Quality Department Store Inc. stock is $8 in 2008 and $12 in 2009, the price-earnings ratio computation is as follows.

Illustration 14-22
Price-earnings ratio

$$\text{Price-Earnings Ratio} = \frac{\text{Market Price per Share of Stock}}{\text{Earnings per Share}}$$

Quality Department Store

2009	2008
$\dfrac{\$12.00}{\$0.97} = 12.4 \text{ times}$	$\dfrac{\$8.00}{\$0.77} = 10.4 \text{ times}$
Industry average	J.C. Penney Company
21.3 times	**17.2 times**

In 2009, each share of Quality's stock sold for 12.4 times the amount that the company earned on each share. Quality's price-earnings ratio is lower than the industry average of 21.3 times, and also lower than the ratio of 17.2 times for J.C. Penney. The average price-earnings ratio for the stocks that constitute the Standard and Poor's 500 Index (500 largest U.S. firms) in early 2009 was approximately 19.1 times.

11. PAYOUT RATIO

The **payout ratio** measures the percentage of earnings distributed in the form of cash dividends. We compute it by dividing cash dividends by net income. Companies that have high growth rates generally have low payout ratios because they reinvest most of their net income into the business. The 2009 and 2008 payout ratios for Quality Department Store are computed as shown in Illustration 14-23.

Illustration 14-23
Payout ratio

$$\text{Payout Ratio} = \frac{\text{Cash Dividends}}{\text{Net Income}}$$

Quality Department Store

2009	2008
$\dfrac{\$61,200}{\$263,800} = 23.2\%$	$\dfrac{\$60,000}{\$208,500} = 28.8\%$
Industry average	J.C. Penney Company
16.1%	**63.0%**

Quality's payout ratio is higher than the industry average payout ratio of 16.1%. J.C. Penney's ratio is very high because its net income in 2009 was quite low.

Solvency Ratios

Solvency ratios measure the ability of a company to survive over a long period of time. Long-term creditors and stockholders are particularly interested in a company's ability to pay interest as it comes due and to repay the face value of debt at maturity. Debt to total assets and times interest earned are two ratios that provide information about debt-paying ability.

12. DEBT TO TOTAL ASSETS RATIO

The **debt to total assets ratio** measures the percentage of the total assets that creditors provide. We compute it by dividing total debt (both current and long-term liabilities) by total assets. This ratio indicates the company's degree of leverage. It also provides some indication of the company's ability to withstand losses without impairing the interests of creditors. The higher the percentage of debt to total assets, the greater the risk that the company may be unable to meet its maturing obligations. The 2009 and 2008 ratios for Quality Department Store and comparative data are as follows.

Illustration 14-24
Debt to total assets ratio

$$\text{Debt to Total Assets Ratio} = \frac{\text{Total Debt}}{\text{Total Assets}}$$

Quality Department Store

2009	2008
$\dfrac{\$832,000}{\$1,835,000} = 45.3\%$	$\dfrac{\$800,000}{\$1,595,000} = 50.2\%$
Industry average	J.C. Penney Company
34.2%	**62.0%**

A ratio of 45.3% means that creditors have provided 45.3% of Quality Department Store's total assets. Quality's 45.3% is above the industry average of 34.2%. It is considerably below the high 62.0% ratio of J.C. Penney. The lower the ratio, the more equity "buffer" there is available to the creditors. Thus, from the creditors' point of view, a low ratio of debt to total assets is usually desirable.

The adequacy of this ratio is often judged in the light of the company's earnings. Generally, companies with relatively stable earnings (such as public utilities) have higher debt to total assets ratios than cyclical companies with widely fluctuating earnings (such as many high-tech companies).

13. TIMES INTEREST EARNED

Alternative Terminology
Times interest earned is also called *interest coverage*.

Times interest earned provides an indication of the company's ability to meet interest payments as they come due. We compute it by dividing income before interest expense and income taxes by interest expense. Illustration 14-25 shows the 2009 and 2008 ratios for Quality Department Store and comparative data. Note that times interest earned uses income before income taxes and interest expense. This represents the amount available to cover interest. For Quality Department Store, the 2009 amount of $468,000 is computed by taking the income before income taxes of $432,000 and adding back the $36,000 of interest expense.

$$\text{Times Interest Earned} = \frac{\text{Income before Income Taxes and Interest Expense}}{\text{Interest Expense}}$$

Quality Department Store

2009	2008
$\dfrac{\$468,000}{\$36,000} = 13$ times	$\dfrac{\$388,000}{\$40,500} = 9.6$ times
Industry average	J.C. Penney Company
16.1 times	**2.9 times**

Illustration 14-25
Times interest earned

Quality's interest expense is well covered at 13 times, compared with the industry average of 16.1 times and J.C. Penney's 2.9 times.

Summary of Ratios

Illustration 14-26 summarizes the ratios discussed in this chapter. The summary includes the formula and purpose or use of each ratio.

Illustration 14-26
Summary of liquidity, profitability, and solvency ratios

Ratio	Formula	Purpose or Use
Liquidity Ratios		
1. Current ratio	$\dfrac{\text{Current assets}}{\text{Current liabilities}}$	Measures short-term debt-paying ability.
2. Acid-test (quick) ratio	$\dfrac{\text{Cash + Short-term investments + Receivables (net)}}{\text{Current liabilities}}$	Measures immediate short-term liquidity.
3. Receivables turnover	$\dfrac{\text{Net credit sales}}{\text{Average net receivables}}$	Measures liquidity of receivables.
4. Inventory turnover	$\dfrac{\text{Cost of goods sold}}{\text{Average inventory}}$	Measures liquidity of inventory.
Profitability Ratios		
5. Profit margin	$\dfrac{\text{Net income}}{\text{Net sales}}$	Measures net income generated by each dollar of sales.
6. Asset turnover	$\dfrac{\text{Net sales}}{\text{Average assets}}$	Measures how efficiently assets are used to generate sales.
7. Return on assets	$\dfrac{\text{Net income}}{\text{Average assets}}$	Measures overall profitability of assets.
8. Return on common stockholders' equity	$\dfrac{\text{Net income} - \text{Preferred dividends}}{\text{Average common stockholders' equity}}$	Measures profitability of owners' investment.
9. Earnings per share (EPS)	$\dfrac{\text{Net income} - \text{Preferred dividends}}{\text{Weighted-average common shares outstanding}}$	Measures net income earned on each share of common stock.
10. Price-earnings (P-E) ratio	$\dfrac{\text{Market price per share of stock}}{\text{Earnings per share}}$	Measures the ratio of the market price per share to earnings per share.
11. Payout ratio	$\dfrac{\text{Cash dividends}}{\text{Net income}}$	Measures percentage of earnings distributed in the form of cash dividends.

Illustration 14-26
(cont'd.)

Ratio	Formula	Purpose or Use
Solvency Ratios		
12. Debt to total assets ratio	$\dfrac{\text{Total debt}}{\text{Total assets}}$	Measures the percentage of total assets provided by creditors.
13. Times interest earned	$\dfrac{\text{Income before income taxes and interest expense}}{\text{Interest expense}}$	Measures ability to meet interest payments as they come due.

> DO IT!

Ratio Analysis

The condensed financial statements of John Cully Company, for the years ended June 30, 2014 and 2013, are presented below.

John Cully Company
Balance Sheets
June 30

	(in thousands)	
Assets	**2014**	**2013**
Current assets		
Cash and cash equivalents	$ 553.3	$ 611.6
Accounts receivable (net)	776.6	664.9
Inventory	768.3	653.5
Prepaid expenses and other current assets	204.4	269.2
Total current assets	2,302.6	2,199.2
Property, plant, and equipment (net)	694.2	647.0
Investments	12.3	12.6
Intangibles and other assets	876.7	849.3
Total assets	$3,885.8	$3,708.1
Liabilities and Stockholders' Equity		
Current liabilities	$1,497.7	$1,322.0
Long-term liabilities	679.5	637.1
Stockholders' equity—common	1,708.6	1,749.0
Total liabilities and stockholders' equity	$3,885.8	$3,708.1

John Cully Company
Income Statements
For the Year Ended June 30

	(in thousands)	
	2014	**2013**
Sales revenue	$6,336.3	$5,790.4
Costs and expenses		
Cost of goods sold	1,617.4	1,476.3
Selling and administrative expenses	4,007.6	3,679.0
Interest expense	13.9	27.1
Total costs and expenses	5,638.9	5,182.4
Income before income taxes	697.4	608.0
Income tax expense	291.3	232.6
Net income	$ 406.1	$ 375.4

Compute the following ratios for 2014 and 2013.

(a) Current ratio.

(b) Inventory turnover. (Inventory on 6/30/12 was $599.0.)

(c) Profit margin ratio.

(d) Return on assets. (Assets on 6/30/12 were $3,349.9.)

(e) Return on common stockholders' equity. (Stockholders' equity on 6/30/12 was $1,795.9.)

(f) Debt to total assets ratio.

(g) Times interest earned.

Solution

Action Plan

✔ Remember that the current ratio includes all current assets. The acid-test ratio uses only cash, short-term investments, and net receivables.

✔ Use average balances for turnover ratios like inventory, receivables, and assets.

	2014	2013
(a) Current ratio:		
$2,302.6 ÷ $1,497.7 =	1.5:1	
$2,199.2 ÷ $1,322.0 =		1.7:1
(b) Inventory turnover:		
$1,617.4 ÷ [($768.3 + $653.5) ÷ 2] =	2.3 times	
$1,476.3 ÷ [($653.5 + $599.0) ÷ 2] =		2.4 times
(c) Profit margin:		
$406.1 ÷ $6,336.3	6.4%	
$375.4 ÷ $5,790.4		6.5%
(d) Return on assets:		
$406.1 ÷ [($3,885.8 + $3,708.1) ÷ 2] –	10.7%	
$375.4 ÷ [($3,708.1 + $3,349.9) ÷ 2] =		10.6%
(e) Return on common stockholders' equity:		
$406.1 – $0 ÷ [($1,708.6 + $1,749.0) ÷ 2] =	23.5%	
$375.4 – $0 ÷ [($1,749.0 + $1,795.9) ÷ 2] –		21.2%
(f) Debt to total assets ratio:		
($1,497.7 + $679.5) ÷ $3,885.8 =	56.0%	
($1,322.0 + $637.1) ÷ $3,708.1 =		52.8%
(g) Times interest earned:		
($406.1 + $291.3 + $13.9) ÷ $13.9 =	51.2 times	
($375.4 + $232.6 + $27.1) ÷ $27.1 =		23.4 times

Related exercise material: **BE14-9, BE14-10, BE14-12, BE14-13, E14-5, E14-7, E14-8, E14-9, E14-11, and** DO IT! **14-2.**

✔ **The Navigator**

Earning Power and Irregular Items

Users of financial statements are interested in the concept of earning power. **Earning power** means the normal level of income to be obtained in the future. Earning power differs from actual net income by the amount of irregular revenues, expenses, gains, and losses. Users are interested in earning power because it helps them derive an estimate of future earnings without the "noise" of irregular items.

> **LEARNING OBJECTIVE   6**
>
> **Understand the concept of earning power, and how irregular items are presented.**

For users of financial statements to determine earning power or regular income, the "irregular" items are separately identified on the income statement. Companies report two types of "irregular" items.

1. Discontinued operations.

2. Extraordinary items.

These "irregular" items are reported net of income taxes. That is, the income statement first reports income tax on the income before "irregular" items. Then the amount of tax for each of the listed "irregular" items is computed. The general concept is "let the tax follow income or loss."

Discontinued Operations

Discontinued operations refers to the disposal of a **significant component** of a business, such as the elimination of a major class of customers, or an entire activity. For example, to downsize its operations, General Dynamics Corp. sold its missile business to Hughes Aircraft Co. for $450 million. In its income statement, General Dynamics reported the sale in a separate section entitled "Discontinued operations."

Following the disposal of a significant component, the company should report on its income statement both income from continuing operations and income (or loss) from discontinued operations. **The income (loss) from discontinued operations consists of two parts: the income (loss) from operations and the gain (loss) on disposal of the segment.**

To illustrate, assume that during 2014 Acro Energy Inc. has income before income taxes of $800,000. During 2014, Acro discontinued and sold its unprofitable chemical division. The loss in 2014 from chemical operations (net of $60,000 taxes) was $140,000. The loss on disposal of the chemical division (net of $30,000 taxes) was $70,000. Assuming a 30% tax rate on income, Illustration 14-27 shows Acro's income statement presentation.

Illustration 14-27
Statement presentation of discontinued operations

Helpful Hint
Observe the dual disclosures: (1) The results of operations of the discontinued division must be eliminated from the results of continuing operations. (2) The company must also report the disposal of the operation.

Acro Energy Inc. Income Statement (partial) For the Year Ended December 31, 2014		
Income before income taxes		$800,000
Income tax expense		240,000
Income from continuing operations		560,000
Discontinued operations		
Loss from operations of chemical division, net of $60,000 income tax saving	$140,000	
Loss from disposal of chemical division, net of $30,000 income tax saving	70,000	210,000
Net income		$350,000

Note that the statement uses the caption "Income from continuing operations," and adds a new section "Discontinued operations." **The new section reports both the operating loss and the loss on disposal net of applicable income taxes.** This presentation clearly indicates the separate effects of continuing operations and discontinued operations on net income.

DECISION TOOLKIT

DECISION CHECKPOINTS	INFO NEEDED FOR DECISION	TOOL TO USE FOR DECISION	HOW TO EVALUATE RESULTS
Has the company sold any major components of its business?	Discontinued operations section of income statement	Anything reported in this section indicates that the company has discontinued a major component of its business.	If a major component has been discontinued, its results during the current period should not be included in estimates of future net income.

Extraordinary Items

Extraordinary items are events and transactions that meet two conditions: They are (1) **unusual in nature,** and (2) **infrequent in occurrence**. To be *unusual*, the item should be abnormal and only incidentally related to the company's customary activities. To be *infrequent*, the item should not be reasonably expected to recur in the foreseeable future.

A company must evaluate both criteria in terms of its operating environment. Thus, Weyerhaeuser Co. reported the $36 million in damages to its timberland caused by the volcanic eruption of Mount St. Helens as an extraordinary item. The eruption was both unusual and infrequent. In contrast, Florida Citrus Company does not report frost damage to its citrus crop as an extraordinary item, because frost damage is not infrequent. Illustration 14-28 shows the classification of extraordinary and ordinary items.

Illustration 14-28
Examples of extraordinary and ordinary items

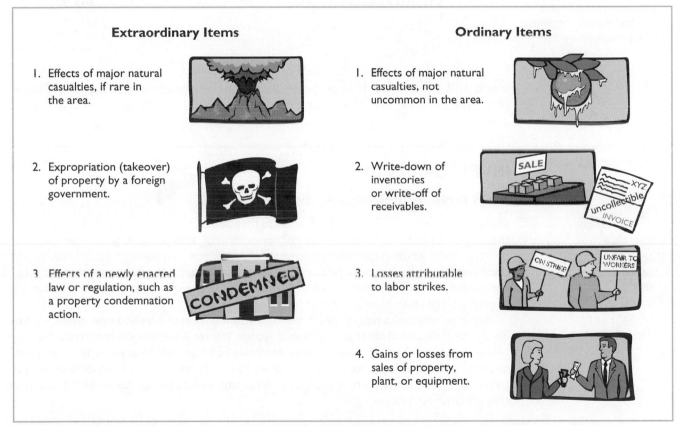

Extraordinary Items

1. Effects of major natural casualties, if rare in the area.

2. Expropriation (takeover) of property by a foreign government.

3. Effects of a newly enacted law or regulation, such as a property condemnation action.

Ordinary Items

1. Effects of major natural casualties, not uncommon in the area.

2. Write-down of inventories or write-off of receivables.

3. Losses attributable to labor strikes.

4. Gains or losses from sales of property, plant, or equipment.

Companies report extraordinary items net of taxes in a separate section of the income statement, immediately below discontinued operations. To illustrate, assume that in 2014 a foreign government expropriated property held as an investment by Acro Energy Inc. If the loss is $70,000 before applicable income taxes of $21,000, the income statement will report a deduction of $49,000, as shown in Illustration 14-29 (page 674). When there is an extraordinary item to report, the company adds the caption "Income before extraordinary item" immediately before the section for the extraordinary item. This presentation clearly indicates the effect of the extraordinary item on net income.

What if a transaction or event meets one (but not both) of the criteria for an extraordinary item? In that case, the company reports it under either "Other revenues and gains" or "Other expenses and losses" at its gross amount (not net of tax). This is true, for example, of gains (losses) resulting from the sale of property,

Illustration 14-29
Statement presentation of extraordinary items

Acro Energy Inc. Income Statement (partial) For the Year Ended December 31, 2014		
Income before income taxes		$800,000
Income tax expense		240,000
Income from continuing operations		560,000
Discontinued operations		
Loss from operations of chemical division, net of $60,000 income tax saving	$140,000	
Loss from disposal of chemical division, net of $30,000 income tax saving	70,000	210,000
Income before extraordinary item		350,000
Extraordinary item		
Expropriation of investment, net of $21,000 income tax saving		**49,000**
Net income		$301,000

Helpful Hint
If there are no discontinued operations, the third line of the income statement would be labeled "Income before extraordinary item."

plant, and equipment. It is quite common for companies to use the label "Non-recurring charges" for losses that do not meet the extraordinary item criteria.

INVESTOR INSIGHT

What Does "Non-Recurring" Really Mean?

Many companies incur restructuring charges as they attempt to reduce costs. They often label these items in the income statement as "non-recurring" charges to suggest that they are isolated events which are unlikely to occur in future periods. The question for analysts is, are these costs really one-time, "non-recurring" events, or do they reflect problems that the company will be facing for many periods in the future? If they are one-time events, they can be largely ignored when trying to predict future earnings.

But some companies report "one-time" restructuring charges over and over again. For example, toothpaste and other consumer-goods giant Procter & Gamble Co. reported a restructuring charge in 12 consecutive quarters. Motorola had "special" charges in 14-consecutive quarters. On the other hand, other companies have a restructuring charge only once in a five- or ten-year period. There appears to be no substitute for careful analysis of the numbers that comprise net income.

? If a company takes a large restructuring charge, what is the effect on the company's current income statement versus future ones? (See page 703.)

DECISION TOOLKIT

DECISION CHECKPOINTS	INFO NEEDED FOR DECISION	TOOL TO USE FOR DECISION	HOW TO EVALUATE RESULTS
Has the company experienced any extraordinary events or transactions?	Extraordinary item section of income statement	Anything reported in this section indicates that the company experienced an event that was both unusual and infrequent.	These items should usually be ignored in estimating future net income.

Changes in Accounting Principle

For ease of comparison, users of financial statements expect companies to prepare such statements on a basis **consistent** with the preceding period. A **change in accounting principle** occurs when the principle used in the current year is different from the one used in the preceding year. Accounting rules permit a change when management can show that the new principle is preferable to the old principle. An example is a change in inventory costing methods (such as FIFO to average-cost).

Companies report most changes in accounting principle retroactively. That is, they report both the current period and previous periods using the new principle. As a result, the same principle applies in all periods. This treatment improves the ability to compare results across years.

DECISION TOOLKIT

DECISION CHECKPOINTS	INFO NEEDED FOR DECISION	TOOL TO USE FOR DECISION	HOW TO EVALUATE RESULTS
Has the company changed any of its accounting principles?	Effect of change in accounting principle on current and prior periods	Management indicates that the new principle is preferable to the old principle.	Examine current and prior years reported, using new-principle basis to assess trends for estimating future income.

Comprehensive Income

The income statement reports most revenues, expenses, gains, and losses recognized during the period. However, over time, specific exceptions to this general practice have developed. Certain items now bypass income and are reported directly in stockholders' equity.

Companies do not include in income any unrealized gains and losses on available-for-sale securities. Instead, they report such gains and losses in the balance sheet as adjustments to stockholders' equity. Why are these gains and losses on available-for-sale securities excluded from net income? Because disclosing them separately (1) reduces the volatility of net income due to fluctuations in fair value, yet (2) informs the financial statement user of the gain or loss that would be incurred if the securities were sold at fair value.

Many analysts have expressed concern over the significant increase in the number of items that bypass the income statement. They feel that such reporting has reduced the usefulness of the income statement. To address this concern, in addition to reporting net income, a company must also report comprehensive income. **Comprehensive income** includes all changes in stockholders' equity during a period except those resulting from investments by stockholders and distributions to stockholders. A number of alternative formats for reporting comprehensive income are allowed. These formats are discussed in advanced accounting courses.

> ### Ethics Note
> Changes in accounting principle should result in financial statements that are more informative for statement users. They should *not* be used to artificially improve the reported performance or financial position of the corporation.

> DO IT!

Irregular Items   In its proposed 2014 income statement, AIR Corporation reports income before income taxes $400,000, extraordinary loss due to earthquake $100,000, income taxes $120,000 (not including irregular items), loss on operation of discontinued flower division $50,000, and loss on disposal of discontinued flower division $90,000. The income tax rate is 30%. Prepare a correct income statement, beginning with "Income before income taxes."

Action Plan

✔ Recall that a loss is extraordinary if it is both unusual and infrequent.

✔ Disclose the income tax effect of each component of income, beginning with income before any irregular items.

✔ Show discontinued operations before extraordinary items.

Solution

Air Corporation Income Statement (partial) For the Year Ended December 31, 2014		
Income before income taxes		$400,000
Income tax expense		120,000
Income from continuing operations		280,000
Discontinued operations		
Loss from operation of flower division, net of $15,000 tax saving	$35,000	
Loss on disposal of flower division, net of $27,000 tax saving	63,000	98,000
Income before extraordinary item		182,000
Extraordinary earthquake loss, net of $30,000 tax saving		70,000
Net income		$112,000

Related exercise material: **BE14-14, BE14-15, E14-12, E14-13, and** DO IT! **14-3.**

✔ The Navigator

Quality of Earnings

LEARNING OBJECTIVE **7**

Understand the concept of quality of earnings.

In evaluating the financial performance of a company, the quality of a company's earnings is of extreme importance to analysts. A company that has a high **quality of earnings** provides full and transparent information that will not confuse or mislead users of the financial statements.

The issue of quality of earnings has taken on increasing importance because recent accounting scandals suggest that some companies are spending too much time managing their income and not enough time managing their business. Here are some of the factors affecting quality of earnings.

Alternative Accounting Methods

Variations among companies in the application of generally accepted accounting principles may hamper comparability and reduce quality of earnings. For example, one company may use the FIFO method of inventory costing, while another company in the same industry may use LIFO. If inventory is a significant asset to both companies, it is unlikely that their current ratios are comparable. For example, if General Motors Corporation had used FIFO instead of LIFO for inventory valuation, its inventories in a recent year would have been 26% higher, which significantly affects the current ratio (and other ratios as well).

In addition to differences in inventory costing methods, differences also exist in reporting such items as depreciation, depletion, and amortization. Although these differences in accounting methods might be detectable from reading the notes to the financial statements, adjusting the financial data to compensate for the different methods is often difficult, if not impossible.

Pro Forma Income

Companies whose stock is publicly traded are required to present their income statement following generally accepted accounting principles (GAAP). In recent years, many companies have also reported a second measure of income, called pro forma income. **Pro forma income** usually excludes items that the company thinks are unusual or non-recurring. For example, at one time, Cisco Systems (a high-tech company) reported a quarterly net loss under GAAP of $2.7 billion. Cisco reported pro forma income for the same quarter as a profit of $230 million. This large difference in profits between GAAP income numbers and pro forma income is not unusual these days. For example, during one 9-month period the 100 largest firms on the Nasdaq stock exchange reported a total pro forma income of $19.1 billion, but a total loss as measured by GAAP of $82.3 billion—a difference of about $100 billion!

To compute pro forma income, companies generally can exclude any items they deem inappropriate for measuring their performance. Many analysts and investors are critical of the practice of using pro forma income because these numbers often make companies look better than they really are. As the financial press noted, pro forma numbers might be called EBS, which stands for "earnings before bad stuff." Companies, on the other hand, argue that pro forma numbers more clearly indicate sustainable income because they exclude unusual and non-recurring expenses. "Cisco's technique gives readers of financial statements a clear picture of Cisco's normal business activities," the company said in a statement issued in response to questions about its pro forma income accounting.

The SEC has provided some guidance on how companies should present pro forma information. Stay tuned: Everyone seems to agree that pro forma numbers can be useful if they provide insights into determining a company's sustainable income. However, many companies have abused the flexibility that pro forma numbers allow and have used the measure as a way to put their companies in a good light.

Improper Recognition

Because some managers have felt pressure from Wall Street to continually increase earnings, they have manipulated the earnings numbers to meet these expectations. The most common abuse is the improper recognition of revenue. One practice that companies are using is *channel stuffing*: Offering deep discounts on their products to customers, companies encourage their customers to buy early (stuff the channel) rather than later. This lets the company report good earnings in the current period, but it often leads to a disaster in subsequent periods because customers have no need for additional goods. To illustrate, Bristol-Myers Squibb at one time indicated that it used sales incentives to encourage wholesalers to buy more drugs than needed to meet patients' demands. As a result, the company had to issue revised financial statements showing corrected revenues and income.

Another practice is the improper capitalization of operating expenses. The classic case is WorldCom. It capitalized over $7 billion dollars of operating expenses so that it would report positive net income. In other situations, companies fail to report all their liabilities. Enron had promised to make payments on certain contracts if financial difficulty developed, but these guarantees were not reported as liabilities. In addition, disclosure was so lacking in transparency that it was impossible to understand what was happening at the company.

> **DO IT!**

Quality of Earnings, Financial Statement Analysis

Match each of the following terms with the phrase that it best matches.

Comprehensive income	Vertical analysis
Quality of earnings	Pro forma income
Solvency ratio	Extraordinary item

1. _____ Measures the ability of the company to survive over a long period of time.
2. _____ Usually excludes items that a company thinks are unusual or non-recurring.
3. _____ Includes all changes in stockholders' equity during a period except those resulting from investments by stockholders and distributions to stockholders.
4. _____ Indicates the level of full and transparent information provided to users of the financial statements.
5. _____ Describes events and transactions that are unusual in nature and infrequent in occurrence.
6. _____ Expresses each item within a financial statement as a percentage of a base amount.

Solution

Action Plan

✔ Develop a sound understanding of basic methods used for financial reporting.

✔ Understand the use of fundamental analysis techniques.

1. Solvency ratio: Measures the ability of the company to survive over a long period of time.
2. Pro forma income: Usually excludes items that a company thinks are unusual or non-recurring.
3. Comprehensive income: Includes all changes in stockholders' equity during a period except those resulting from investments by stockholders and distributions to stockholders.
4. Quality of earnings: Indicates the level of full and transparent information provided to users of the financial statements.
5. Extraordinary item: Describes events and transactions that are unusual in nature and infrequent in occurrence.
6. Vertical analysis: Expresses each item within a financial statement as a percentage of a base amount.

Related exercise material: **DO IT!** **14-4.**

✔ **The Navigator**

USING THE **DECISION TOOLKIT**

In analyzing a company, you should always investigate an extended period of time in order to determine whether the condition and performance of the company are changing. The condensed financial statements of Kellogg Company for 2009 and 2008 are presented here.

Kellogg Company, Inc.
Balance Sheets
December 31 (in millions)

Assets	2009	2008
Current assets		
Cash	$ 334	$ 255
Accounts receivable (net)	1,093	1,100
Inventories	910	897
Other current assets	221	269
Total current assets	2,558	2,521
Property (net)	3,010	2,933
Other assets	5,632	5,492
Total assets	$11,200	$10,946
Liabilities and Stockholders' Equity		
Current liabilities	$ 2,288	$ 3,552
Long-term liabilities	6,637	5,939
Stockholders' equity—common	2,275	1,455
Total liabilities and stockholders' equity	$11,200	$10,946

Kellogg Company, Inc. Condensed Income Statements For the Years Ended December 31 (in millions)		
	2009	**2008**
Net sales	$12,575	$12,822
Cost of goods sold	7,184	7,455
Gross profit	5,391	5,367
Selling and administrative expenses	3,390	3,414
Income from operations	2,001	1,953
Interest expense	295	308
Other (income) expense, net	18	12
Income before income taxes	1,688	1,633
Income tax expense	476	485
Net income	$ 1,212	$ 1,148

Instructions

Compute the following ratios for Kellogg for 2009 and discuss your findings (2008 values are provided for comparison).

1. Liquidity:
   (a) Current ratio (2008: .71:1).
   (b) Inventory turnover ratio (2008: 8.2 times).

2. Solvency:
   (a) Debt to total assets ratio (2008: 87%).
   (b) Times interest earned ratio (2008: 6.3 times).

3. Profitability:
   (a) Return on assets ratio (2008: 10.6%).
   (b) Profit margin ratio (2008: 9.0%).
   (c) Return on common stockholders' equity ratio (2008: 65%).

Solution

1. Liquidity
   (a) Current ratio:

   $$2009: \frac{\$2,558}{\$2,288} = 1.12:1 \qquad 2008: \ .71:1$$

   (b) Inventory turnover ratio:

   $$2009: \frac{\$7,184}{(\$910 + \$897)/2} = 8.0 \text{ times} \qquad 2008: \ 8.2 \text{ times}$$

We see that between 2008 and 2009, the current ratio increased substantially. The inventory turnover ratio decreased slightly. The current ratio indicates that the company was more liquid in 2009.

2. Solvency
   (a) Debt to total assets ratio:

   $$2009: \frac{\$2,288 + \$6,637}{\$11,200} = 80\% \qquad 2008: \ 87\%$$

   (b) Times interest earned ratio:

   $$2009: \frac{\$1,212 + \$476 + \$295}{\$295} = 6.7 \text{ times} \qquad 2008: \ 6.3 \text{ times}$$

Kellogg's solvency as measured by the debt to total assets ratio improved slightly in 2009. We also can see that the times interest earned ratio improved.

3. Profitability
   (a) Return on assets ratio:

   2009: $\dfrac{\$1{,}212}{(\$11{,}200 + \$10{,}946)/2} = 10.9\%$ 2008: 10.6%

   (b) Profit margin ratio:

   2009: $\dfrac{\$1{,}212}{\$12{,}575} = 9.6\%$ 2008: 9.0%

   (c) Return on common stockholders' equity ratio:

   2009: $\dfrac{\$1{,}212}{(\$2{,}275 + \$1{,}455)/2} = 65\%$ 2008: 65%

   Kellogg's return on assets ratio increased. Its profit margin ratio also increased, but its return on stockholders' equity held constant.

   ✔ **The Navigator**

SUMMARY OF LEARNING OBJECTIVES   ✔ The Navigator

1 Discuss the need for comparative analysis. There are three bases of comparison: (1) Intracompany, which compares an item or financial relationship with other data within a company. (2) Industry, which compares company data with industry averages. (3) Intercompany, which compares an item or financial relationship of a company with data of one or more competing companies.

2 Identify the tools of financial statement analysis. Financial statements can be analyzed horizontally, vertically, and with ratios.

3 Explain and apply horizontal analysis. Horizontal analysis is a technique for evaluating a series of data over a period of time to determine the increase or decrease that has taken place, expressed as either an amount or a percentage.

4 Describe and apply vertical analysis. Vertical analysis is a technique that expresses each item within a financial statement in terms of a percentage of a relevant total or a base amount.

5 Identify and compute ratios used in analyzing a firm's liquidity, profitability, and solvency. The formula and purpose of each ratio was presented in Illustration 14-26 (pages 669–670).

6 Understand the concept of earning power, and how irregular items are presented. Earning power refers to a company's ability to sustain its profits from operations. "Irregular items"—discontinued operations and extraordinary items—are presented net of tax below income from continuing operations to highlight their unusual nature.

7 Understand the concept of quality of earnings. A high quality of earnings provides full and transparent information that will not confuse or mislead users of the financial statements. Issues related to quality of earnings are (1) alternative accounting methods, (2) pro forma income, and (3) improper recognition.

DECISION TOOLKIT A SUMMARY 🧰

DECISION CHECKPOINTS	INFO NEEDED FOR DECISION	TOOL TO USE FOR DECISION	HOW TO EVALUATE RESULTS
How do the company's financial position and operating results compare with those of the previous period?	Income statement and balance sheet	Comparative financial statements should be prepared over at least two years, with the first year reported being the base year. Changes in each line item relative to the base year should be presented both by amount and by percentage. This is called *horizontal analysis*.	Significant changes should be investigated to determine the reason for the change.

DECISION CHECKPOINTS	INFO NEEDED FOR DECISION	TOOL TO USE FOR DECISION	HOW TO EVALUATE RESULTS
How do the relationships between items in this year's financial statements compare with those of last year or those of competitors?	Income statement and balance sheet	Each line item on the income statement should be presented as a percentage of net sales, and each line item on the balance sheet should be presented as a percentage of total assets or total liabilities and stockholders' equity. These percentages should be investigated for differences either across years in the same company or in the same year across different companies. This is called *vertical analysis*.	Any significant differences either across years or between companies should be investigated to determine the cause.
Has the company sold any major components of its business?	Discontinued operations section of income statement	Anything reported in this section indicates that the company has discontinued a major component of its business.	If a major component has been discontinued, its results during the current period should not be included in estimates of future net income.
Has the company experienced any extraordinary events or transactions?	Extraordinary item section of income statement	Anything reported in this section indicates that the company experienced an event that was both unusual and infrequent.	These items should usually be ignored in estimating future net income.
Has the company changed any of its accounting principles?	Effect of change in accounting principle on current and prior periods	Management indicates that the new principle is preferable to the old principle.	Examine current and prior years' reported income, using new-principle basis to assess trends for estimating future income.

GLOSSARY

Acid-test (quick) ratio A measure of a company's immediate short-term liquidity; computed by dividing the sum of cash, short-term investments, and net receivables by current liabilities. (p. 661).

Asset turnover A measure of how efficiently a company uses its assets to generate sales; computed by dividing net sales by average assets. (p. 664).

Change in accounting principle The use of a principle in the current year that is different from the one used in the preceding year. (p. 675).

Comprehensive income Includes all changes in stockholders' equity during a period except those resulting from investments by stockholders and distributions to stockholders. (p. 675).

Current ratio A measure used to evaluate a company's liquidity and short-term debt-paying ability; computed by dividing current assets by current liabilities. (p. 661).

Debt to total assets ratio Measures the percentage of total assets provided by creditors; computed by dividing total debt by total assets. (p. 668).

Discontinued operations The disposal of a significant segment of a business. (p. 672).

Earnings per share (EPS) The net income earned on each share of common stock; computed by dividing net income minus preferred dividends (if any) by the number of weighted-average common shares outstanding. (p. 666).

Extraordinary items Events and transactions that are unusual in nature and infrequent in occurrence. (p. 673).

Horizontal analysis A technique for evaluating a series of financial statement data over a period of time, to determine the increase (decrease) that has taken place, expressed as either an amount or a percentage. (p. 653).

Inventory turnover A measure of the liquidity of inventory; computed by dividing cost of goods sold by average inventory. (p. 663).

Leveraging See *Trading on the equity*. (p. 666).

Liquidity ratios Measures of the short-term ability of the company to pay its maturing obligations and to meet unexpected needs for cash. (p. 660).

Payout ratio Measures the percentage of earnings distributed in the form of cash dividends; computed by dividing cash dividends by net income. (p. 667).

Price-earnings (P-E) ratio Measures the ratio of the market price of each share of common stock to the earnings per share; computed by dividing the market price of the stock by earnings per share. (p. 667).

Profitability ratios Measures of the income or operating success of a company for a given period of time. (p. 664).

Profit margin Measures the percentage of each dollar of sales that results in net income; computed by dividing net income by net sales. (p. 664).

Pro forma income A measure of income that usually excludes items that a company thinks are unusual or non-recurring. (p. 677).

Quality of earnings Indicates the level of full and transparent information provided to users of the financial statements. (p. 676).

Ratio An expression of the mathematical relationship between one quantity and another. The relationship may be expressed either as a percentage, a rate, or a simple proportion. (p. 659).

Ratio analysis A technique for evaluating financial statements that expresses the relationship between selected financial statement data. (p. 659).

Receivables turnover A measure of the liquidity of receivables; computed by dividing net credit sales by average net receivables. (p. 662).

Return on assets An overall measure of profitability; computed by dividing net income by average assets. (p. 665).

Return on common stockholders' equity Measures the dollars of net income earned for each dollar invested by the owners; computed by dividing net income minus preferred dividends (if any) by average common stockholders' equity. (p. 665).

Solvency ratios Measures of the ability of the company to survive over a long period of time. (p. 668).

Times interest earned Measures a company's ability to meet interest payments as they come due; computed by dividing income before interest expense and income taxes by interest expense. (p. 668).

Trading on the equity Borrowing money at a lower rate of interest than can be earned by using the borrowed money. (p. 666).

Vertical analysis A technique for evaluating financial statement data that expresses each item within a financial statement as a percent of a base amount. (p. 657).

> Comprehensive **DO IT!**

The events and transactions of Dever Corporation for the year ending December 31, 2014, resulted in the following data.

Cost of goods sold	$2,600,000
Net sales	4,400,000
Other expenses and losses	9,600
Other revenues and gains	5,600
Selling and administrative expenses	1,100,000
Income from operations of plastics division	70,000
Gain from disposal of plastics division	500,000
Loss from tornado disaster (extraordinary loss)	600,000

Analysis reveals that:

1. All items are before the applicable income tax rate of 30%.

2. The plastics division was sold on July 1.

3. All operating data for the plastics division have been segregated.

Instructions
Prepare an income statement for the year.

Solution to Comprehensive DO IT!

Action Plan

✔ Report material items not typical of continuing operations in separate sections, net of taxes.

✔ Associate income taxes with the item that affects the taxes.

✔ Apply the corporate tax rate to income before income taxes to determine tax expense.

✔ Recall that all data presented in determining income before income taxes are the same as for unincorporated companies.

Dever Corporation
Income Statement
For the Year Ended December 31, 2014

Net sales		$4,400,000
Cost of goods sold		2,600,000
Gross profit		1,800,000
Selling and administrative expenses		1,100,000
Income from operations		700,000
Other revenues and gains	$ 5,600	
Other expenses and losses	9,600	4,000
Income before income taxes		696,000
Income tax expense ($696,000 × 30%)		208,800
Income from continuing operations		487,200
Discontinued operations		
Income from operations of plastics division, net of		
$21,000 income taxes ($70,000 × 30%)	49,000	
Gain from disposal of plastics division, net of $150,000		
income taxes ($500,000 × 30%)	350,000	399,000
Income before extraordinary item		886,200
Extraordinary item		
Tornado loss, net of $180,000 income tax saving		
($600,000 × 30%)		420,000
Net income		$ 466,200

✔ **The Navigator**

 Self-Test, Brief Exercises, Exercises, Problem Set A, and many more resources are available for practice in WileyPLUS.

SELF-TEST QUESTIONS

Answers are at the end of the chapter.

(LO 1)   **1.** Comparisons of data within a company are an example of the following comparative basis:
(a) Industry averages.
(b) Intracompany.
(c) Intercompany.
(d) Both (b) and (c).

(LO 3)   **2.** In horizontal analysis, each item is expressed as a percentage of the:
(a) net income amount.
(b) stockholders' equity amount.
(c) total assets amount.
(d) base year amount.

(LO 4)   **3.** In vertical analysis, the base amount for depreciation expense is generally:

(a) net sales.
(b) depreciation expense in a previous year.
(c) gross profit.
(d) fixed assets.

4. The following schedule is a display of what type of (LO 4) analysis?

	Amount	Percent
Current assets	$200,000	25%
Property, plant, and equipment	600,000	75%
Total assets	$800,000	

(a) Horizontal analysis.   (c) Vertical analysis.
(b) Differential analysis. (d) Ratio analysis.

(LO 3)   **5.** Sammy Corporation reported net sales of $300,000, $330,000, and $360,000 in the years, 2012, 2013, and 2014, respectively. If 2012 is the base year, what is the trend percentage for 2014?
(a) 77%.   (c) 120%.
(b) 108%.   (d) 130%.

(LO 5)   **6.** Which of the following measures is an evaluation of a firm's ability to pay current liabilities?
(a) Acid-test ratio.   (c) Both (a) and (b).
(b) Current ratio.   (d) None of the above.

(LO 5)   **7.** A measure useful in evaluating the efficiency in managing inventories is:
(a) inventory turnover.
(b) average days to sell inventory.
(c) Both (a) and (b).
(d) None of the above.

Use the following financial statement information as of the end of each year to answer Self-Test Questions 8–12.

	2014	2013
Inventory	$ 54,000	$ 48,000
Current assets	81,000	106,000
Total assets	382,000	326,000
Current liabilities	27,000	36,000
Total liabilities	102,000	88,000
Preferred stock	40,000	40,000
Common stockholders' equity	240,000	198,000
Net sales	784,000	697,000
Cost of goods sold	306,000	277,000
Net income	134,000	90,000
Tax expense	22,000	18,000
Interest expense	12,000	12,000
Dividends paid to preferred stockholders	4,000	4,000
Dividends paid to common stockholders	15,000	10,000

(LO 5)   **8.** Compute the days in inventory for 2014.
(a) 64.4 days.   (c) 6 days.
(b) 60.8 days.   (d) 24 days.

9. Compute the current ratio for 2014.   (LO 5)
(a) 1.26:1.   (c) .80:1.
(b) 3.0:1.   (d) 3.75:1.

10. Compute the profit margin ratio for 2014.   (LO 5)
(a) 17.1%.   (c) 37.9%.
(b) 18.1%.   (d) 5.9%.

11. Compute the return on common stockholders' equity (LO 5) for 2014.
(a) 47.9%.   (c) 61.2%.
(b) 51.7%.   (d) 59.4%.

12. Compute the times interest earned for 2014.   (LO 5)
(a) 11.2 times.   (c) 14.0 times.
(b) 65.3 times.   (d) 13.0 times.

13. In reporting discontinued operations, the income (LO 6) statement should show in a special section:
(a) gains and losses on the disposal of the discontinued segment.
(b) gains and losses from operations of the discontinued segment.
(c) Both (a) and (b).
(d) Neither (a) nor (b).

14. Scout Corporation has income before taxes of (LO 6) $400,000 and an extraordinary loss of $100,000. If the income tax rate is 25% on all items, the income statement should show income before extraordinary items and extraordinary items, respectively, of:
(a) $325,000 and $100,000.
(b) $325,000 and $75,000.
(c) $300,000 and $100,000
(d) $300,000 and $75,000.

15. Which situation below might indicate a company has (LO 7) a low quality of earnings?
(a) The same accounting principles are used each year.
(b) Revenue is recognized when earned.
(c) Maintenance costs are expensed as incurred.
(d) The company is continually reporting pro forma income numbers.

Go to the book's companion website, **www.wiley.com/college/weygandt**, for additional Self-Test Questions.

✔ **The Navigator**

QUESTIONS

1. (a) Kurt Gibson believes that the analysis of financial statements is directed at two characteristics of a company: liquidity and profitability. Is Kurt correct? Explain.
(b) Are short-term creditors, long-term creditors, and stockholders interested primarily in the same characteristics of a company? Explain.

2. (a) Distinguish among the following bases of comparison: (1) intracompany, (2) industry averages, and (3) intercompany.
(b) Give the principal value of using each of the three bases of comparison.

3. Two popular methods of financial statement analysis are horizontal analysis and vertical analysis. Explain the difference between these two methods.

4. (a) If Nimoy Company had net income of $350,000 in 2013 and it experienced a 22.4% increase in net income for 2014, what is its net income for 2014?
(b) If five cents of every dollar of Nimoy revenue is net income in 2013, what is the dollar amount of 2013 revenue?

5. What is a ratio? What are the different ways of expressing the relationship of two amounts? What information does a ratio provide?

6. Name the major ratios useful in assessing (a) liquidity and (b) solvency.

7. Maribel Ortiz is puzzled. Her company had a profit margin of 10% in 2014. She feels that this is an indication that the company is doing well. Gordon Liddy, her accountant, says that more information is needed to determine the firm's financial well-being. Who is correct? Why?

8. What do the following classes of ratios measure? (a) Liquidity ratios. (b) Profitability ratios. (c) Solvency ratios.

9. What is the difference between the current ratio and the acid-test ratio?

10. Monte Company, a retail store, has a receivables turnover of 4.5 times. The industry average is 12.5 times. Does Monte have a collection problem with its receivables?

11. Which ratios should be used to help answer the following questions?
    (a) How efficient is a company in using its assets to produce sales?
    (b) How near to sale is the inventory on hand?
    (c) How many dollars of net income were earned for each dollar invested by the owners?
    (d) How able is a company to meet interest charges as they fall due?

12. The price-earnings ratio of General Motors (automobile builder) was 8, and the price-earnings ratio of Microsoft (computer software) was 38. Which company did the stock market favor? Explain.

13. What is the formula for computing the payout ratio? Would you expect this ratio to be high or low for a growth company?

14. Holding all other factors constant, indicate whether each of the following changes generally signals good or bad news about a company.
    (a) Increase in profit margin.
    (b) Decrease in inventory turnover.
    (c) Increase in the current ratio.
    (d) Decrease in earnings per share.
    (e) Increase in price-earnings ratio.
    (f) Increase in debt to total assets ratio.
    (g) Decrease in times interest earned.

15. The return on assets for Miller Corporation is 7.6%. During the same year, Miller's return on common stockholders' equity is 12.8%. What is the explanation for the difference in the two rates?

16. Which two ratios do you think should be of greatest interest to:
    (a) A pension fund considering the purchase of 20-year bonds?
    (b) A bank contemplating a short-term loan?
    (c) A common stockholder?

17. Why must preferred stock dividends be subtracted from net income in computing earnings per share?

18. (a) What is meant by trading on the equity?
    (b) How would you determine the profitability of trading on the equity?

19. Tillman Inc. has net income of $160,000, weighted-average shares of common stock outstanding of 50,000, and preferred dividends for the period of $30,000. What is Tillman's earnings per share of common stock? Pat Tillman, the president of Tillman Inc., believes the computed EPS of the company is high. Comment.

20. Why is it important to report discontinued operations separately from income from continuing operations?

21. You are considering investing in Cherokee Transportation. The company reports 2014 earnings per share of $6.50 on income before extraordinary items and $4.75 on net income. Which EPS figure would you consider more relevant to your investment decision? Why?

22. MRT Inc. reported 2013 earnings per share of $3.20 and had no extraordinary items. In 2014, EPS on income before extraordinary items was $2.99, and EPS on net income was $3.49. Is this a favorable trend?

23. Indicate which of the following items would be reported as an extraordinary item in Muerte Corporation's income statement.
    (a) Loss from damages caused by volcano eruption.
    (b) Loss from sale of temporary investments.
    (c) Loss attributable to a labor strike.
    (d) Loss caused when manufacture of a product was prohibited by the Food and Drug Administration.
    (e) Loss from flood damage. (The nearby Black River floods every 2 to 3 years.)
    (f) Write-down of obsolete inventory.
    (g) Expropriation of a factory by a foreign government.

24. Identify and explain factors that affect quality of earnings.

25. **PEPSICO** Identify the specific sections in PepsiCo's 2010 annual report (*www.pepsico.com*) where horizontal and vertical analyses of financial data are presented.

BRIEF EXERCISES

Follow the rounding procedures used in the chapter.

BE14-1 You recently received a letter from your Uncle Liam. A portion of the letter is presented below.

You know that I have a significant amount of money I saved over the years. I am thinking about starting an investment program. I want to do the investing myself, based on my

Discuss need for comparative analysis.

(LO 1), C

own research and analysis of financial statements. I know that you are studying account-ing, so I have a couple of questions for you. I have heard that different users of financial statements are interested in different characteristics of companies. Is this true, and, if so, why? Also, some of my friends, who are already investing, have told me that comparisons involving a company's financial data can be made on a number of different bases. Can you explain these bases to me?

Instructions

▭▭▭▭▷ Write a letter to your Uncle Liam which answers his questions.

Identify and use tools of financial statement analysis.

(LO 2, 3, 4, 5), K, AP

BE14-2 Maria Fierro Corporation reported the following amounts in 2012, 2013, and 2014.

	2012	**2013**	**2014**
Current assets	$220,000	$230,000	$240,000
Current liabilities	$160,000	$170,000	$184,000
Total assets	$500,000	$600,000	$630,000

Instructions

(a) Identify and describe the three tools of financial statement analysis. (b) Perform each of the three types of analysis on Maria Fierro's current assets.

Prepare horizontal analysis.

(LO 3), AP

BE14-3 Using the following data from the comparative balance sheet of Dotte Company, illustrate horizontal analysis.

	December 31, 2014	**December 31, 2013**
Accounts receivable	$ 520,000	$ 350,000
Inventory	$ 840,000	$ 500,000
Total assets	$2,500,000	$3,000,000

Prepare vertical analysis.

(LO 4), AP

BE14-4 Using the same data presented above in BE14-3 for Dotte Company, illustrate vertical analysis.

Calculate percentage of change.

(LO 3), AP

BE14-5 Net income was $550,000 in 2012, $475,000 in 2013, and $525,000 in 2014. What is the percentage of change from (a) 2012 to 2013 and (b) 2013 to 2014? Is the change an increase or a decrease?

Calculate net income.

(LO 3), AP

BE14-6 If Valdamorte Company had net income of $560,000 in 2014 and it experienced a 40% increase in net income over 2013, what was its 2013 net income?

Calculate change in net income.

(LO 3), AP

BE14-7 Horizontal analysis (trend analysis) percentages for Kemplar Company's sales, cost of goods sold, and expenses are shown below.

Horizontal Analysis	**2014**	**2013**	**2012**
Sales	97.8	105.3	100.0
Cost of goods sold	103.0	96.0	100.0
Expenses	108.2	99.3	100.0

Did Kemplar's net income increase, decrease, or remain unchanged over the 3-year period?

Calculate change in net income.

(LO 4), AP

BE14-8 Vertical analysis (common size) percentages for Dagman Company's sales, cost of goods sold, and expenses are shown below.

Vertical Analysis	**2014**	**2013**	**2012**
Sales	100.0	100.0	100.0
Cost of goods sold	59.2	62.4	64.5
Expenses	25.0	25.6	27.5

Did Dagman's net income as a percentage of sales increase, decrease, or remain unchanged over the 3-year period? Provide numerical support for your answer.

BE14-9 Selected condensed data taken from a recent balance sheet of Morino Inc. are as follows.

Calculate liquidity ratios.
(LO 5), AP

Morino Inc.
Balance Sheet (partial)

Cash	$ 8,113,000
Short-term investments	4,947,000
Accounts receivable	12,545,000
Inventory	14,814,000
Other current assets	6,271,000
Total current assets	$46,690,000
Total current liabilities	$40,600,000

What are the (a) working capital, (b) current ratio, and (c) acid-test ratio?

BE14-10 Huntsinger Corporation has net income of $12.76 million and net revenue of $88 million in 2014. Its assets are $14 million at the beginning of the year and $18 million at the end of the year. What are Huntsinger's (a) asset turnover and (b) profit margin?

Calculate profitability ratios.
(LO 5), AP

BE14-11 The following data are taken from the financial statements of Gladow Company.

Evaluate collection of accounts receivable.
(LO 5), AN

	2014	2013
Accounts receivable (net), end of year	$ 550,000	$ 520,000
Net sales on account	3,745,000	3,000,000
Terms for all sales are 1/10, n/60.		

(a) Compute for each year (1) the receivables turnover and (2) the average collection period. At the end of 2012, accounts receivable (net) was $480,000.
(b) ▆▆▆▆▆➤ What conclusions about the management of accounts receivable can be drawn from these data?

BE14-12 The following data are from the income statements of Charles Company.

Evaluate management of inventory.
(LO 5), AN

	2014	2013
Sales	$6,420,000	$6,240,000
Beginning inventory	980,000	860,000
Purchases	4,440,000	4,720,000
Ending inventory	1,020,000	980,000

(a) Compute for each year (1) the inventory turnover and (2) the average days to sell the inventory.
(b) ▆▆▆▆▆➤ What conclusions concerning the management of the inventory can be drawn from these data?

BE14-13 Ming Company has stockholders' equity of $400,000 and net income of $68,000. It has a payout ratio of 20% and a rate of return on assets of 16%. How much did Ming pay in cash dividends, and what were its average assets?

Calculate profitability ratios.
(LO 5), AN

BE14-14 An inexperienced accountant for Reeves Corporation showed the following in the income statement: income before income taxes and extraordinary item $500,000, and extraordinary loss from flood (before taxes) $80,000. The extraordinary loss and taxable income are both subject to a 30% tax rate. Prepare a correct income statement.

Prepare income statement including extraordinary items.
(LO 6), AP

BE14-15 On June 30, Blevins Corporation discontinued its operations in Europe. During the year, the operating loss was $350,000 before taxes. On September 1, Blevins disposed of its European facilities at a pretax loss of $150,000. The applicable tax rate is 30%. Show the discontinued operations section of the income statement.

Prepare discontinued operations section of income statement.
(LO 6), AP

> ## DO IT! REVIEW

Prepare horizontal analysis.
(LO 3), AP

DO IT! **14-1** Summary financial information for Rapture Company is as follows.

	December 31, 2014	December 31, 2013
Current assets	$ 199,000	$225,000
Plant assets	821,000	750,000
Total assets	$1,020,000	$975,000

Compute the amount and percentage changes in 2014 using horizontal analysis, assuming 2013 is the base year.

Compute ratios.
(LO 5), AP

DO IT! **14-2** The condensed financial statements of Soule Company for the years 2013 and 2014 are presented below.

Soule Company
Balance Sheets
December 31

	2014	2013
Current assets		
Cash and cash equivalents	$ 330	$ 360
Accounts receivable (net)	470	433
Inventory	430	390
Prepaid expenses	120	160
Total current assets	1,350	1,343
Property, plant, and equipment	420	380
Investments	10	10
Intangibles and other assets	530	510
Total assets	$2,310	$2,243
Current liabilities	$ 900	$ 810
Long-term liabilities	390	393
Stockholders' equity—common	1,020	1,040
Total liabilities and stockholders' equity	$2,310	$2,243

Soule Company
Income Statements
For the Years Ended December 31

	2014	2013
Sales revenue	$4,000	$3,600
Costs and expenses		
Cost of goods sold	984	895
Selling and administrative expenses	2,400	2,330
Interest expense	10	20
Total costs and expenses	3,394	3,245
Income before income taxes	606	355
Income tax expense	242	142
Net income	$ 364	$ 213

Compute the following ratios for 2014 and 2013.
(a) Current ratio.
(b) Inventory turnover. (Inventory on 12/31/12 was $326.)
(c) Profit margin ratio.
(d) Return on assets. (Assets on 12/31/12 were $2,100.)

(e) Return on common stockholders' equity. (Stockholders' equity on 12/31/12 was $960.)
(f) Debt to total assets ratio.
(g) Times interest earned.

DO IT! **14-3** In its proposed 2014 income statement, Grinders Corporation reports income before income taxes $500,000, extraordinary loss due to earthquake $160,000, income taxes $175,000 (not including irregular items), loss on operation of discontinued music division $60,000, and gain on disposal of discontinued music division $40,000. The income tax rate is 35%. Prepare a correct income statement, beginning with income before income taxes.

Prepare income statement, including irregular items.

(LO 6), AP

DO IT! **14-4** Match each of the following terms with the phrase that it best matches.

Match terms relating to quality of earnings and financial statement analysis.

(LO 3, 4, 5, 6, 7), C

Quality of earnings   Pro forma income
Current ratio   Discontinued operations
Horizontal analysis   Comprehensive income

1. _____ A measure used to evaluate a company's liquidity.
2. _____ Usually excludes items that a company thinks are unusual or non-recurring.
3. _____ Indicates the level of full and transparent information provided to users of the financial statements.
4. _____ The disposal of a significant segment of a business.
5. _____ Determines increases or decreases in a series of financial statement data.
6. _____ Includes all changes in stockholders' equity during a period except those resulting from investments by stockholders and distributions to stockholders.

✔ **The Navigator**

EXERCISES

Follow the rounding procedures used in the chapter.

E14-1 Financial information for Gallup Inc. is presented below.

Prepare horizontal analysis.

(LO 3), AP

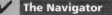

	December 31, 2014	December 31, 2013
Current assets	$128,000	$100,000
Plant assets (net)	396,000	330,000
Current liabilities	91,000	70,000
Long-term liabilities	138,700	95,000
Common stock, $1 par	159,000	115,000
Retained earnings	135,300	150,000

Instructions
Prepare a schedule showing a horizontal analysis for 2014 using 2013 as the base year.

E14-2 Operating data for Conard Corporation are presented below.

Prepare vertical analysis.

(LO 4), AP

	2014	2013
Net sales	$750,000	$600,000
Cost of goods sold	480,000	408,000
Selling expenses	105,000	84,000
Administrative expenses	75,000	54,000
Income tax expense	36,000	18,000
Net income	54,000	36,000

Instructions
Prepare a schedule showing a vertical analysis for 2014 and 2013.

Prepare horizontal and vertical analyses.

(LO 3, 4), AP

E14-3 The comparative condensed balance sheets of Garcia Corporation are presented below.

Garcia Corporation
Comparative Condensed Balance Sheets
December 31

	2014	2013
Assets		
Current assets	$ 76,000	$ 80,000
Property, plant, and equipment (net)	100,000	90,000
Intangibles	24,000	40,000
Total assets	$200,000	$210,000
Liabilities and stockholders' equity		
Current liabilities	$ 40,000	$ 48,000
Long-term liabilities	140,000	150,000
Stockholders' equity	20,000	12,000
Total liabilities and stockholders' equity	$200,000	$210,000

Instructions

(a) Prepare a horizontal analysis of the balance sheet data for Garcia Corporation using 2013 as a base.

(b) Prepare a vertical analysis of the balance sheet data for Garcia Corporation in columnar form for 2014.

Prepare horizontal and vertical analyses.

(LO 3, 4), AP

E14-4 The comparative condensed income statements of Hendi Corporation are shown below.

Hendi Corporation
Comparative Condensed Income Statements
For the Years Ended December 31

	2014	2013
Net sales	$600,000	$500,000
Cost of goods sold	468,000	400,000
Gross profit	132,000	100,000
Operating expenses	60,000	54,000
Net income	$ 72,000	$ 46,000

Instructions

(a) Prepare a horizontal analysis of the income statement data for Hendi Corporation using 2013 as a base. (Show the amounts of increase or decrease.)

(b) Prepare a vertical analysis of the income statement data for Hendi Corporation in columnar form for both years.

Compute liquidity ratios and compare results.

(LO 5), AN

E14-5 Nordstrom, Inc. operates department stores in numerous states. Selected financial statement data for the year ending January 30, 2010, are shown below.

Nordstrom, Inc.
Balance Sheet (partial)

(in millions)	End-of-Year	Beginning-of-Year
Cash and cash equivalents	$ 795	$ 72
Accounts receivable (net)	2,035	1,942
Merchandise inventory	898	900
Prepaid expenses	88	93
Other current assets	238	210
Total current assets	$4,054	$3,217
Total current liabilities	$2,014	$1,601

For the year, net sales were $8,258 and cost of goods sold was $5,328 (in millions).

Instructions
(a) Compute the four liquidity ratios at the end of the year.
(b) Using the data in the chapter, compare Nordstrom's liquidity with (1) that of J.C. Penney Company, and (2) the industry averages for department stores.

E14-6 Bennis Incorporated had the following transactions occur involving current assets and current liabilities during February 2013.

Perform current and acid-test ratio analysis.

(LO 5), AP

Feb.	3	Accounts receivable of $15,000 are collected.
	7	Equipment is purchased for $28,000 cash.
	11	Paid $3,000 for a 3-year insurance policy.
	14	Accounts payable of $12,000 are paid.
	18	Cash dividends of $5,000 are declared.

Additional information:

1. As of February 1, 2013, current assets were $140,000, and current liabilities were $50,000.
2. As of February 1, 2013, current assets included $10,000 of inventory and $5,000 of pre-paid expenses.

Instructions
(a) Compute the current ratio as of the beginning of the month and after each transaction.
(b) Compute the acid-test ratio as of the beginning of the month and after each transaction.

E14-7 Willingham Company has the following comparative balance sheet data.

Compute selected ratios.

(LO 5), AP

Willingham Company
Balance Sheets
December 31

	2014	2013
Cash	$ 10,000	$ 30,000
Receivables (net)	70,000	50,000
Inventory	60,000	50,000
Plant assets (net)	205,000	190,000
	$345,000	$320,000
Accounts payable	$ 50,000	$ 60,000
Mortgage payable (15%)	100,000	100,000
Common stock, $10 par	140,000	120,000
Retained earnings	55,000	40,000
	$345,000	$320,000

Additional information for 2014:

1. Net income was $25,000.
2. Sales on account were $410,000. Sales returns and allowances were $20,000.
3. Cost of goods sold was $187,000.

Instructions
Compute the following ratios at December 31, 2014.

(a) Current. (c) Receivables turnover.
(b) Acid-test. (d) Inventory turnover.

E14-8 Selected comparative statement data for Molini Products Company are presented below. All balance sheet data are as of December 31.

Compute selected ratios.

(LO 5), AP

	2014	2013
Net sales	$700,000	$680,000
Cost of goods sold	480,000	400,000
Interest expense	7,000	5,000
Net income	42,000	34,000
Accounts receivable	120,000	100,000
Inventory	85,000	75,000
Total assets	580,000	540,000
Total common stockholders' equity	425,000	325,000

Instructions

Compute the following ratios for 2014.

(a) Profit margin.
(b) Asset turnover.
(c) Return on assets.
(d) Return on common stockholders' equity.

Compute selected ratios.

(LO 5), AP

E14-9 The income statement for Christiansen, Inc., appears below.

Christiansen, Inc.
Income Statement
For the Year Ended December 31, 2014

Net sales	$400,000
Cost of goods sold	235,000
Gross profit	165,000
Expenses (including $14,000 interest and $17,000 income taxes)	105,000
Net income	$ 60,000

Additional information:

1. The weighted-average common shares outstanding in 2014 were 30,000 shares.
2. The market price of Christiansen, Inc. stock was $10.80 in 2014.
3. Cash dividends of $21,000 were paid, $6,000 of which were to preferred stockholders.

Instructions

Compute the following ratios for 2014.

(a) Earnings per share.
(b) Price-earnings.
(c) Payout.
(d) Times interest earned.

Compute amounts from ratios.

(LO 5), AP

E14-10 Rees Corporation experienced a fire on December 31, 2014, in which its financial records were partially destroyed. It has been able to salvage some of the records and has ascertained the following balances.

	December 31, 2014	December 31, 2013
Cash	$ 30,000	$ 10,000
Receivables (net)	73,000	126,000
Inventory	200,000	180,000
Accounts payable	50,000	90,000
Notes payable	30,000	60,000
Common stock, $100 par	400,000	400,000
Retained earnings	134,000	122,000

Additional information:

1. The inventory turnover is 3.4 times.
2. The return on common stockholders' equity is 25%. The company had no additional paid-in capital.
3. The receivables turnover is 8.8 times.
4. The return on assets is 20%.
5. Total assets at December 31, 2013, were $650,000.

Instructions

Compute the following for Rees Corporation.

(a) Cost of goods sold for 2014.
(b) Net sales (credit) for 2014.
(c) Net income for 2014.
(d) Total assets at December 31, 2014.

E14-11 Yadier Corporation's comparative balance sheets are presented below.

Compute ratios.
(LO 5), AP

Yadier Corporation
Balance Sheets
December 31

	2014	2013
Cash	$ 4,300	$ 3,700
Accounts receivable	22,000	24,000
Inventory	10,000	7,000
Land	20,000	26,000
Buildings	70,000	70,000
Accumulated depreciation—buildings	(15,000)	(10,000)
Total	$111,300	$120,700
Accounts payable	$ 12,000	$ 31,100
Common stock	75,000	69,000
Retained earnings	24,300	20,600
Total	$111,300	$120,700

Yadier's 2014 income statement included net sales of $100,000, cost of goods sold of $60,350, and net income of $14,000.

Instructions
Compute the following ratios for 2014.

(a) Current ratio.
(b) Acid-test ratio.
(c) Receivables turnover.
(d) Inventory turnover.
(e) Profit margin.
(f) Asset turnover.
(g) Return on assets.
(h) Return on common stockholders' equity.
(i) Debt to total assets ratio.

E14-12 For its fiscal year ending October 31, 2014, Douglas Corporation reports the following partial data shown below.

Prepare a correct income statement.
(LO 6), AP

Income before income taxes	$550,000
Income tax expense (30% × $410,000)	123,000
Income before extraordinary items	427,000
Extraordinary loss from flood	140,000
Net income	$287,000

The flood loss is considered an extraordinary item. The income tax rate is 30% on all items.

Instructions
(a) Prepare a correct income statement, beginning with income before income taxes.
(b) ▱▱▱▱▷ Explain in memo form why the income statement data are misleading.

E14-13 Maulder Corporation has income from continuing operations of $290,000 for the year ended December 31, 2014. It also has the following items (before considering income taxes).

Prepare income statement.
(LO 6), AP

1. An extraordinary loss of $70,000.
2. A gain of $35,000 on the discontinuance of a division.
3. A correction of an error in last year's financial statements that resulted in a $25,000 understatement of 2013 net income.

Assume all items are subject to income taxes at a 30% tax rate.

Instructions
(a) Prepare an income statement, beginning with income from continuing operations.
(b) Indicate the statement presentation of any item not included in (a) above.

EXERCISES: SET B AND CHALLENGE EXERCISES

Visit the book's companion website, at **www.wiley.com/college/weygandt**, and choose the Student Companion site to access Exercise Set B and Challenge Exercises.

PROBLEMS

Follow the rounding procedures used in the chapter.

Prepare vertical analysis and comment on profitability.

(LO 4, 5), AN

P14-1 Comparative statement data for Lionel Company and Barrymore Company, two competitors, appear below. All balance sheet data are as of December 31, 2014, and December 31, 2013.

	Lionel Company		Barrymore Company	
	2014	**2013**	**2014**	**2013**
Net sales	$1,549,035		$339,038	
Cost of goods sold	1,053,345		237,325	
Operating expenses	278,825		77,979	
Interest expense	7,745		2,034	
Income tax expense	61,960		8,476	
Current assets	401,584	$388,020	86,450	$ 82,581
Plant assets (net)	596,920	575,610	142,842	128,927
Current liabilities	65,015	75,507	19,618	14,654
Long-term liabilities	102,500	84,000	16,711	11,989
Common stock, $5 par	578,765	578,765	137,435	137,435
Retained earnings	252,224	225,358	55,528	47,430

Instructions

(a) Prepare a vertical analysis of the 2014 income statement data for Lionel Company and Barrymore Company in columnar form.

(b) ▭▭▭▶ Comment on the relative profitability of the companies by computing the return on assets and the return on common stockholders' equity ratios for both companies.

Compute ratios from balance sheet and income statement.

(LO 5), AP, AN

P14-2 The comparative statements of Larker Tool Company are presented below.

Larker Tool Company
Income Statement
For the Years Ended December 31

	2014	2013
Net sales	$1,818,500	$1,750,500
Cost of goods sold	1,011,500	996,000
Gross profit	807,000	754,500
Selling and administrative expense	516,000	479,000
Income from operations	291,000	275,500
Other expenses and losses		
Interest expense	15,000	14,000
Income before income taxes	276,000	261,500
Income tax expense	84,000	77,000
Net income	$ 192,000	$ 184,500

Larker Tool Company
Balance Sheets
December 31

Assets	2014	2013
Current assets		
Cash	$ 60,100	$ 64,200
Short-term investments	69,000	50,000
Accounts receivable (net)	105,750	102,800
Inventory	110,950	115,500
Total current assets	345,800	332,500
Plant assets (net)	600,300	520,300
Total assets	$946,100	$852,800
Liabilities and Stockholders' Equity		
Current liabilities		
Accounts payable	$160,000	$145,400
Income taxes payable	43,500	42,000
Total current liabilities	203,500	187,400
Bonds payable	200,000	200,000
Total liabilities	403,500	387,400
Stockholders' equity		
Common stock ($5 par)	300,000	300,000
Retained earnings	242,600	165,400
Total stockholders' equity	542,600	465,400
Total liabilities and stockholders' equity	$946,100	$852,800

All sales were on account.

Instructions
Compute the following ratios for 2014. (Weighted-average common shares in 2014 were 60,000.)

(a) Earnings per share.
(b) Return on common stockholders' equity.
(c) Return on assets.
(d) Current.
(e) Acid-test.

(f) Receivables turnover.
(g) Inventory turnover.
(h) Times interest earned.
(i) Asset turnover.
(j) Debt to total assets.

P14-3 Condensed balance sheet and income statement data for Clarence Corporation appear below and on page 696.

Perform ratio analysis, and evaluate financial position and operating results.

(LO 5), AP, AN

Clarence Corporation
Balance Sheets
December 31

	2014	2013	2012
Cash	$ 25,000	$ 20,000	$ 18,000
Receivables (net)	50,000	45,000	48,000
Other current assets	90,000	95,000	64,000
Investments	75,000	70,000	45,000
Plant and equipment (net)	400,000	370,000	358,000
	$640,000	$600,000	$533,000
Current liabilities	$ 70,000	$ 75,000	$ 70,000
Long-term debt	80,000	85,000	50,000
Common stock, $10 par	345,000	315,000	300,000
Retained earnings	145,000	125,000	113,000
	$640,000	$600,000	$533,000

Clarence Corporation
Income Statement
For the Years Ended December 31

	2014	2013
Sales revenue	$740,000	$700,000
Less: Sales returns and allowances	40,000	60,000
Net sales	700,000	640,000
Cost of goods sold	420,000	400,000
Gross profit	280,000	240,000
Operating expenses (including income taxes)	238,000	208,000
Net income	$ 42,000	$ 32,000

Additional information:

1. The market price of Clarence's common stock was $4.00, $5.00, and $8.00 for 2012, 2013, and 2014, respectively.
2. All dividends were paid in cash.

Instructions
(a) Compute the following ratios for 2013 and 2014.
  (1) Profit margin.
  (2) Asset turnover.
  (3) Earnings per share. (Weighted-average common shares in 2014 were 32,000 and in 2013 were 31,000.)
  (4) Price-earnings.
  (5) Payout.
  (6) Debt to total assets.
(b) ▭▭▭▭▷ Based on the ratios calculated, discuss briefly the improvement or lack thereof in financial position and operating results from 2013 to 2014 of Clarence Corporation.

Compute ratios, and comment on overall liquidity and profitability.

(LO 5), AN

P14-4 Financial information for Ernie Bishop Company is presented below.

Ernie Bishop Company
Balance Sheets
December 31

Assets	2013	2012
Cash	$ 70,000	$ 65,000
Short-term investments	52,000	40,000
Receivables (net)	98,000	80,000
Inventory	125,000	135,000
Prepaid expenses	29,000	23,000
Land	130,000	130,000
Building and equipment (net)	168,000	175,000
	$672,000	$648,000

Liabilities and Stockholders' Equity		
Notes payable	$100,000	$100,000
Accounts payable	48,000	42,000
Accrued liabilities	44,000	40,000
Bonds payable, due 2014	150,000	150,000
Common stock, $10 par	200,000	200,000
Retained earnings	130,000	116,000
	$672,000	$648,000

Ernie Bishop Company
Income Statement
For the Years Ended December 31

	2013	2012
Net sales	$858,000	$798,000
Cost of goods sold	611,000	575,000
Gross profit	247,000	223,000
Operating expenses	204,500	181,000
Net income	$ 42,500	$ 42,000

Additional information:

1. Inventory at the beginning of 2012 was $118,000.
2. Total assets at the beginning of 2012 were $632,000.
3. No common stock transactions occurred during 2012 or 2013.
4. All sales were on account.
5. Receivables (net) at the beginning of 2012 were $88,000.

Instructions

(a) Indicate, by using ratios, the change in liquidity and profitability of Ernie Bishop Company from 2012 to 2013. (*Note:* Not all profitability ratios can be computed.)

(b) Given below are three independent situations and a ratio that may be affected. For each situation, compute the affected ratio (1) as of December 31, 2013, and (2) as of December 31, 2014, after giving effect to the situation. Net income for 2014 was $50,000. Total assets on December 31, 2014, were $700,000.

Situation	Ratio
(1) 18,000 shares of common stock were sold at par on July 1, 2014.	Return on common stockholders' equity
(2) All of the notes payable were paid in 2014. The only change in liabilities was that the notes payable were paid.	Debt to total assets
(3) Market price of common stock was $9 on December 31, 2013, and $12.50 on December 31, 2014.	Price-earnings ratio

P14-5 Selected financial data of Target and Wal-Mart Stores, Inc. for a recent year are presented here (in millions).

Compute selected ratios, and compare liquidity, profitability, and solvency for two companies.

(LO 5), AP

	Target Corporation	Wal-Mart Stores, Inc.
	Income Statement Data for Year	
Net sales	$67,390	$405,046
Cost of goods sold	45,725	304,657
Selling and administrative expenses	13,469	79,607
Interest expense	757	1,884
Other income (expense)	(2,944)	2,576
Income tax expense	1,575	7,139
Net income	$ 2,920	$ 14,335
	Balance Sheet Data (End of Year)	
Current assets	$17,213	$ 48,331
Noncurrent assets	26,492	122,375
Total assets	$43,705	$170,706
Current liabilities	$10,070	$ 55,561
Long-term debt	18,148	44,396
Total stockholders' equity	15,487	70,749
Total liabilities and stockholders' equity	$43,705	$170,706

	Target Corporation	Wal-Mart Stores, Inc.
	Beginning-of-Year Balances	
Total assets	$44,533	$163,429
Total stockholders' equity	15,347	65,285
Current liabilities	11,327	55,390
Total liabilities	29,186	96,350
	Other Data	
Average net receivables	$ 6,560	$ 4,025
Average inventory	7,388	33,836
Net cash provided by operating activities	5,271	26,249

Instructions

(a) For each company, compute the following ratios.

(1) Current.	(7) Asset turnover.
(2) Receivables turnover.	(8) Return on assets.
(3) Average collection period.	(9) Return on common stockholders' equity.
(4) Inventory turnover.	(10) Debt to total assets.
(5) Days in inventory.	(11) Times interest earned.
(6) Profit margin.	

(b) Compare the liquidity, profitability, and solvency of the two companies.

Compute numerous ratios.

(LO 5), AP

P14-6 The comparative statements of Beulah Company are presented below.

Beulah Company
Income Statement
For the Years Ended December 31

	2014	2013
Net sales (all on account)	$500,000	$420,000
Expenses		
Cost of goods sold	315,000	254,000
Selling and administrative	120,800	114,800
Interest expense	7,500	6,500
Income tax expense	20,000	15,000
Total expenses	463,300	390,300
Net income	$ 36,700	$ 29,700

Beulah Company
Balance Sheets
December 31

Assets	2014	2013
Current assets		
Cash	$ 21,000	$ 18,000
Short-term investments	18,000	15,000
Accounts receivable (net)	85,000	75,000
Inventory	80,000	60,000
Total current assets	204,000	168,000
Plant assets (net)	423,000	383,000
Total assets	$627,000	$551,000

Liabilities and Stockholders' Equity

Current liabilities		
Accounts payable	$122,000	$110,000
Income taxes payable	12,000	11,000
Total current liabilities	134,000	121,000
Long-term liabilities		
Bonds payable	120,000	80,000
Total liabilities	254,000	201,000
Stockholders' equity		
Common stock ($5 par)	150,000	150,000
Retained earnings	223,000	200,000
Total stockholders' equity	373,000	350,000
Total liabilities and stockholders' equity	$627,000	$551,000

Additional data:
The common stock recently sold at $19.50 per share.

Instructions
Compute the following ratios for 2014.
(a) Current.
(b) Acid-test.
(c) Receivables turnover.
(d) Inventory turnover.
(e) Profit margin.
(f) Asset turnover.
(g) Return on assets.

(h) Return on common stockholders' equity.
(i) Earnings per share.
(j) Price-earnings.
(k) Payout.
(l) Debt to total assets.
(m) Times interest earned.

P14-7 Presented below is an incomplete income statement and an incomplete comparative balance sheet of Bondi Corporation.

Compute missing information given a set of ratios.

(LO 5), AN

Bondi Corporation
Income Statement
For the Year Ended December 31, 2014

Net sales	$10,500,000
Cost of goods sold	?
Gross profit	?
Operating expenses	1,500,000
Income from operations	?
Other expenses and losses	
Interest expense	?
Income before income taxes	?
Income tax expense	550,000
Net income	$?

Bondi Corporation
Balance Sheets
December 31

Assets	2014	2013
Current assets		
Cash	$ 480,000	$ 375,000
Accounts receivable (net)	?	950,000
Inventory	?	1,720,000
Total current assets	?	3,045,000
Plant assets (net)	4,620,000	4,455,000
Total assets	$?	$7,500,000

Assets	2014	2013
Liabilities and Stockholders' Equity		
Current liabilities	$?	$ 825,000
Long-term notes payable	?	3,300,000
Total liabilities	?	4,125,000
Common stock, $1 par	3,000,000	3,000,000
Retained earnings	400,000	375,000
Total stockholders' equity	3,400,000	3,375,000
Total liabilities and stockholders' equity	$?	$7,500,000

Additional information:

1. The receivables turnover for 2014 is 10 times.
2. All sales are on account.
3. The profit margin for 2014 is 14.5%.
4. Return on assets is 20% for 2014.
5. The current ratio on December 31, 2014, is 3.0.
6. The inventory turnover for 2014 is 4.2 times.

Instructions

Compute the missing information given the ratios above. Show computations. (*Note:* Start with one ratio and derive as much information as possible from it before trying another ratio. List all missing amounts under the ratio used to find the information.)

Prepare income statement with discontinued operations and extraordinary loss.

(LO 6), AP

P14-8 Violet Bick Corporation owns a number of cruise ships and a chain of hotels. The hotels, which have not been profitable, were discontinued on September 1, 2014. The 2014 operating results for the company were as follows.

Operating revenues	$12,900,000
Operating expenses	8,700,000
Operating income	$ 4,200,000

Analysis discloses that these data include the operating results of the hotel chain, which were operating revenues $2,000,000 and operating expenses $2,500,000. The hotels were sold at a gain of $300,000 before taxes. This gain is not included in the operating results. During the year, Violet Bick suffered an extraordinary loss of $700,000 before taxes, which is not included in the operating results. In 2014, the company had other expenses and losses of $200,000, which are not included in the operating results. The corporation is in the 30% income tax bracket.

Instructions

Prepare a condensed income statement.

Prepare income statement with nontypical items.

(LO 6), AP

P14-9 The ledger of Gower Corporation at December 31, 2014, contains the following summary data.

Net sales	$1,600,000	Cost of goods sold	$1,100,000
Selling expenses	70,000	Administrative expenses	90,000
Other revenues and gains	22,000	Other expenses and losses	28,000

Your analysis reveals the following additional information that is not included in the above data.

1. The entire puzzles division was discontinued on August 31. The income from operations for this division before income taxes was $15,000. The puzzles division was sold at a loss of $80,000 before income taxes.
2. On May 15, company property was expropriated for an interstate highway. The settlement resulted in an extraordinary gain of $100,000 before income taxes.
3. The income tax rate on all items is 30%.

Instructions

Prepare an income statement for the year ended December 31, 2014. Use the format illustrated in the Comprehensive **DO IT!** (page 683).

PROBLEMS: SET B

Visit the book's companion website, at **www.wiley.com/college/weygandt**, and choose the Student Companion site to access Problem Set B.

WATERWAYS CONTINUING PROBLEM

(*Note:* This is a continuation of the Waterways Problem from Chapters 1–13.)

CCC14 Waterways Corporation has proposed comparative balance sheets and income statements for 2013 and 2014. This problem asks you to prepare horizontal and vertical analyses of the income statements and to calculate various ratios.

Go to the book's companion website, **www.wiley.com/college/weygandt**, *to see the completion of this problem.*

Broadening Your **PERSPECTIVE**

Financial Reporting and Analysis

Financial Reporting Problem: PepsiCo, Inc.

BYP14-1 Your parents are considering investing in PepsiCo common stock. They ask you, as an accounting expert, to make an analysis of the company for them. You can access the current annual report of PepsiCo at **www.pepsico.com**. Note that all dollar amounts are in millions.

Instructions
(Follow the approach in the chapter for rounding numbers.)
(a) Make a 5-year trend analysis, using 2006 as the base year, of (1) net sales and (2) net income. Comment on the significance of the trend results.
(b) Compute for 2010 and 2009 the (1) profit margin, (2) asset turnover, (3) return on assets, and (4) return on common stockholders' equity. How would you evaluate PepsiCo's profitability? Total assets at December 31, 2008, were $35,994 and total stockholders' equity at December 31, 2008, was $12,203.
(c) Compute for 2010 and 2009 the (1) debt to total assets and (2) times interest earned ratio. How would you evaluate PepsiCo's long-term solvency?
(d) What information outside the annual report may also be useful to your parents in making a decision about PepsiCo, Inc.?

Comparative Analysis Problem:
PepsiCo, Inc. vs. The Coca-Cola Company

BYP14-2 PepsiCo's financial statements are presented at **www.pepsico.com**. Financial statements of The Coca-Cola Company are presented at **www.coca-cola.com**.

Instructions
(a) Based on the information contained in these financial statements, determine each of the following for each company.
   (1) The percentage increase (decrease) in (i) net sales and (ii) net income from 2009 to 2010.
   (2) The percentage increase in (i) total assets and (ii) total common stockholders' (shareholders') equity from 2009 to 2010.

(3) The basic earnings per share and price-earnings ratio for 2010. (For both PepsiCo and Coca-Cola, use the basic earnings per share.) Coca-Cola's common stock had a market price of $65.77 at the end of fiscal-year 2010, and PepsiCo's common stock had a market price of $65.69.

(b) What conclusions concerning the two companies can be drawn from these data?

Decision-Making Across the Organization

BYP14-3 As the CPA for Bonita Inc., you have been asked to develop some key ratios from the comparative financial statements. This information is to be used to convince creditors that the company is solvent and will continue as a going concern. The data requested and the computations developed from the financial statements follow.

	2014	2013
Current ratio	3.4 times	2.1 times
Acid-test ratio	.8 times	1.3 times
Asset turnover	2.6 times	2.2 times
Net income	Up 32%	Down 9%
Earnings per share	$3.20	$2.50

Instructions
With the class divided into groups, complete the following.

Bonita Inc. asks you to prepare a list of brief comments stating how each of these items supports the solvency and going-concern potential of the business. The company wishes to use these comments to support its presentation of data to its creditors. You are to prepare the comments as requested, giving the implications and the limitations of each item separately. Then prepare a collective inference that may be drawn from the individual items about Bonita's solvency and going-concern potential.

Real-World Focus

BYP14-4 The Management Discussion and Analysis section of an annual report addresses corporate performance for the year, and sometimes uses financial ratios to support its claims.

Address: **www.ibm.com/investor/tools/index.phtml** or go to **www.wiley.com/college/weygandt**

Steps
1. Choose **How to read annual reports** (in the Guides section).
2. Choose **Anatomy**.

Instructions
Using the information from the above site, answer the following questions.
(a) What are the optional elements that are often included in an annual report?
(b) What are the elements of an annual report that are required by the SEC?
(c) Describe the contents of the Management Discussion.
(d) Describe the contents of the Auditors' Report.
(e) Describe the contents of the Selected Financial Data.

Critical Thinking

Communication Activity

BYP14-5 Kyle Benson is the CEO of Macarty's Electronics. Benson is an expert engineer but a novice in accounting. He asks you to explain (1) the bases for comparison in analyzing Macarty's financial statements, and (2) the factors affecting quality of earnings.

Instructions
Write a letter to Kyle Benson that explains the bases for comparison and factors affecting quality of earnings.

Ethics Case

BYP14-6 Robert Turnbull, president of Turnbull Industries, wishes to issue a press release to bolster his company's image and maybe even its stock price, which has been gradually falling. As controller,

you have been asked to provide a list of 20 financial ratios along with some other operating statistics relative to Turnbull Industries' first quarter financials and operations.

Two days after you provide the ratios and data requested, Perry Jarvis, the public relations director of Turnbull, asks you to prove the accuracy of the financial and operating data contained in the press release written by the president and edited by Perry. In the press release, the president highlights the sales increase of 25% over last year's first quarter and the positive change in the current ratio from 1.5:1 last year to 3:1 this year. He also emphasizes that production was up 50% over the prior year's first quarter.

You note that the press release contains only positive or improved ratios and none of the negative or deteriorated ratios. For instance, no mention is made that the debt to total assets ratio has increased from 35% to 55%, that inventories are up 89%, and that while the current ratio improved, the acid-test ratio fell from 1:1 to. 5:1. Nor is there any mention that the reported profit for the quarter would have been a loss had not the estimated lives of Turnbull's plant and machinery been increased by 30%. Perry emphasized, "The prez wants this release by early this afternoon."

Instructions
(a) Who are the stakeholders in this situation?
(b) Is there anything unethical in president Turnbull's actions?
(c) Should you as controller remain silent? Does Perry have any responsibility?

All About You

BYP14-7 In this chapter, you learned how to use many tools for performing a financial analysis of a company. When making personal investments, however, it is most likely that you won't be buying stocks and bonds in individual companies. Instead, when most people want to invest in stock, they buy mutual funds. By investing in a mutual fund, you reduce your risk because the fund diversifies by buying the stock of a variety of different companies, bonds, and other investments, depending on the stated goals of the fund.

Before you invest in a fund, you will need to decide what type of fund you want. For example, do you want a fund that has the potential of high growth (but also high risk), or are you looking for lower risk and a steady stream of income? Do you want a fund that invests only in U.S. companies, or do you want one that invests globally? Many resources are available to help you with these types of decisions.

Instructions
Go to **http://web.archive.org/web/20050210200843/http://www.cnb1.com/invallocmdl.htm** and complete the investment allocation questionnaire. Add up your total points to determine the type of investment fund that would be appropriate for you.

Answers to Chapter Questions

Answers to Insight and Accounting Across the Organization Questions

p. 662 How to Manage the Current Ratio Q: How might management influence a company's current ratio? **A:** Management can affect the current ratio by speeding up or withholding payments on accounts payable just before the balance sheet date. Management can alter the cash balance by increasing or decreasing long-term assets or long-term debt, or by issuing or purchasing common stock.

p. 674 What Does "Non-Recurring" Really Mean? Q: If a company takes a large restructuring charge, what is the effect on the company's current income statement versus future ones? **A:** The current period's net income can be greatly diminished by a large restructuring charge. The net incomes in future periods can be enhanced because they are relieved of costs (e.g., depreciation and labor expenses) that would have been charged to them.

Answers to Self-Test Questions

1. b **2.** d **3.** a **4.** c **5.** c ($360,000 ÷ 300,000) **6.** c **7.** c **8.** b $306,000 ÷ [($54,000 + $48,000) ÷ 2] = 6; 365 ÷ 6 **9.** b ($81,000 ÷ $27,000) **10.** a $134,000 ÷ $784,000 **11.** d ($134,000 − $4,000) ÷ [($240,000 + $198,000) ÷ 2] **12.** c ($134,000 + $22,000 + $12,000) ÷ $12,000 **13.** c **14.** d ($400,000 − (25% × $400,000); $100,000 − (25% × $100,000) **15.** d

✔ **Remember to go back to The Navigator box on the chapter opening page and check off your completed work.**

Learning Objectives

After studying this appendix, you should be able to:

1 Distinguish between simple and compound interest.

2 Solve for future value of a single amount.

3 Solve for future value of an annuity.

4 Identify the variables fundamental to solving present value problems.

5 Solve for present value of a single amount.

6 Solve for present value of an annuity.

7 Compute the present value of notes and bonds.

8 Compute the present values in capital budgeting situations.

9 Use a financial calculator to solve time value of money problems.

Would you rather receive $1,000 today or a year from now? You should prefer to receive the $1,000 today because you can invest the $1,000 and earn interest on it. As a result, you will have more than $1,000 a year from now. What this example illustrates is the concept of the **time value of money**. Everyone prefers to receive money today rather than in the future because of the interest factor.

Nature of Interest

Interest is payment for the use of another person's money. It is the difference between the amount borrowed or invested (called the **principal**) and the amount repaid or collected. The amount of interest to be paid or collected is usually stated as a rate over a specific period of time. The rate of interest is generally stated as an annual rate.

> **LEARNING OBJECTIVE 1**
>
> Distinguish between simple and compound interest.

The amount of interest involved in any financing transaction is based on three elements:

1. **Principal (p):** The original amount borrowed or invested.
2. **Interest Rate (i):** An annual percentage of the principal.
3. **Time (n):** The number of years that the principal is borrowed or invested.

Simple Interest

Simple interest is computed on the principal amount only. It is the return on the principal for one period. Simple interest is usually expressed as shown in Illustration A-1.

$$\text{Interest} = \underset{p}{\text{Principal}} \times \underset{i}{\text{Rate}} \times \underset{n}{\text{Time}}$$

For example, if you borrowed $5,000 for 2 years at a simple interest rate of 12% annually, you would pay $1,200 in total interest, computed as follows:

$$
\begin{aligned}
\text{Interest} &= p \times i \times n \\
&= \$5,000 \times .12 \times 2 \\
&= \$1,200
\end{aligned}
$$

Illustration A-1
Interest computation

Compound Interest

Compound interest is computed on principal **and** on any interest earned that has not been paid or withdrawn. It is the return on (or growth of) the principal for two or more time periods. Compounding computes interest not only on the principal but also on the interest earned to date on that principal, assuming the interest is left on deposit.

To illustrate the difference between simple and compound interest, assume that you deposit $1,000 in Bank Two, where it will earn simple interest of 9% per year, and you deposit another $1,000 in Citizens Bank, where it will earn compound interest of 9% per year compounded annually. Also assume that in both cases you will not withdraw any cash until three years from the date of deposit. Illustration A-2 shows the computation of interest to be received and the accumulated year-end balances.

Illustration A-2
Simple versus compound interest

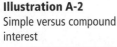

Bank Two				Citizens Bank		
Simple Interest Calculation	Simple Interest	Accumulated Year-End Balance		Compound Interest Calculation	Compound Interest	Accumulated Year-End Balance
Year 1 $1,000.00 × 9%	$ 90.00	$1,090.00		Year 1 $1,000.00 × 9%	$ 90.00	$1,090.00
Year 2 $1,000.00 × 9%	90.00	$1,180.00		Year 2 $1,090.00 × 9%	98.10	$1,188.10
Year 3 $1,000.00 × 9%	90.00	$1,270.00		Year 3 $1,188.10 × 9%	106.93	$1,295.03
	$ 270.00				$ 295.03	

$25.03 Difference

Note in Illustration A-2 that simple interest uses the initial principal of $1,000 to compute the interest in all three years. Compound interest uses the accumulated balance (principal plus interest to date) at each year-end to compute interest in the succeeding year—which explains why your compound interest account is larger.

Obviously, if you had a choice between investing your money at simple interest or at compound interest, you would choose compound interest, all other things—especially risk—being equal. In the example, compounding provides $25.03 of additional interest income. For practical purposes, compounding assumes that unpaid interest earned becomes a part of the principal, and the accumulated balance at the end of each year becomes the new principal on which interest is earned during the next year.

Illustration A-2 indicates that you should invest your money at the bank that compounds interest. Most business situations use compound interest. Simple interest is generally applicable only to short-term situations of one year or less.

Future Value Concepts

Future Value of a Single Amount

The **future value of a single amount** is the value at a future date of a given amount invested, assuming compound interest. For example, in Illustration A-2, $1,295.03 is the future value of the $1,000 investment earning 9% for three years. The $1,295.03 could be determined more easily by using the following formula.

$$FV = p \times (1 + i)^n$$

Illustration A-3
Formula for future value

where:

FV = future value of a single amount
p = principal (or present value; the value today)
i = interest rate for one period
n = number of periods

The $1,295.03 is computed as follows.

$$
\begin{aligned}
FV &= p \times (1 + i)^n \\
&= \$1,000 \times (1 + .09)^3 \\
&= \$1,000 \times 1.29503 \\
&= \$1,295.03
\end{aligned}
$$

The 1.29503 is computed by multiplying (1.09 × 1.09 × 1.09). The amounts in this example can be depicted in the time diagram shown in Illustration A-4.

Illustration A-4
Time diagram

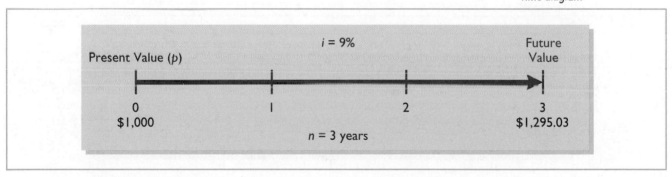

Another method used to compute the future value of a single amount involves a compound interest table. This table shows the future value of 1 for n periods. Table 1 on the next page is such a table.

In Table 1, n is the number of compounding periods, the percentages are the periodic interest rates, and the 5-digit decimal numbers in the respective columns are the future value of 1 factors. In using Table 1, you would multiply the principal amount by the future value factor for the specified number of periods and interest rate. For example, the future value factor for two periods at 9% is 1.18810. Multiplying this factor by $1,000 equals $1,188.10—which is the accumulated balance at the end of year 2 in the Citizens Bank example in Illustration A-2. The $1,295.03 accumulated balance at the end of the third year can be calculated from Table 1 by multiplying the future value factor for three periods (1.29503) by the $1,000.

The demonstration problem in Illustration A-5 (page A-4) shows how to use Table 1.

TABLE 1 Future Value of 1

(*n*) Periods	4%	5%	6%	7%	8%	9%	10%	11%	12%	15%
0	1.00000	1.00000	1.00000	1.00000	1.00000	1.00000	1.00000	1.00000	1.00000	1.00000
1	1.04000	1.05000	1.06000	1.07000	1.08000	1.09000	1.10000	1.11000	1.12000	1.15000
2	1.08160	1.10250	1.12360	1.14490	1.16640	1.18810	1.21000	1.23210	1.25440	1.32250
3	1.12486	1.15763	1.19102	1.22504	1.25971	1.29503	1.33100	1.36763	1.40493	1.52088
4	1.16986	1.21551	1.26248	1.31080	1.36049	1.41158	1.46410	1.51807	1.57352	1.74901
5	1.21665	1.27628	1.33823	1.40255	1.46933	1.53862	1.61051	1.68506	1.76234	2.01136
6	1.26532	1.34010	1.41852	1.50073	1.58687	1.67710	1.77156	1.87041	1.97382	2.31306
7	1.31593	1.40710	1.50363	1.60578	1.71382	1.82804	1.94872	2.07616	2.21068	2.66002
8	1.36857	1.47746	1.59385	1.71819	1.85093	1.99256	2.14359	2.30454	2.47596	3.05902
9	1.42331	1.55133	1.68948	1.83846	1.99900	2.17189	2.35795	2.55803	2.77308	3.51788
10	1.48024	1.62889	1.79085	1.96715	2.15892	2.36736	2.59374	2.83942	3.10585	4.04556
11	1.53945	1.71034	1.89830	2.10485	2.33164	2.58043	2.85312	3.15176	3.47855	4.65239
12	1.60103	1.79586	2.01220	2.25219	2.51817	2.81267	3.13843	3.49845	3.89598	5.35025
13	1.66507	1.88565	2.13293	2.40985	2.71962	3.06581	3.45227	3.88328	4.36349	6.15279
14	1.73168	1.97993	2.26090	2.57853	2.93719	3.34173	3.79750	4.31044	4.88711	7.07571
15	1.80094	2.07893	2.39656	2.75903	3.17217	3.64248	4.17725	4.78459	5.47357	8.13706
16	1.87298	2.18287	2.54035	2.95216	3.42594	3.97031	4.59497	5.31089	6.13039	9.35762
17	1.94790	2.29202	2.69277	3.15882	3.70002	4.32763	5.05447	5.89509	6.86604	10.76126
18	2.02582	2.40662	2.85434	3.37993	3.99602	4.71712	5.55992	6.54355	7.68997	12.37545
19	2.10685	2.52695	3.02560	3.61653	4.31570	5.14166	6.11591	7.26334	8.61276	14.23177
20	2.19112	2.65330	3.20714	3.86968	4.66096	5.60441	6.72750	8.06231	9.64629	16.36654

John and Mary Rich invested $20,000 in a savings account paying 6% interest at the time their son, Mike, was born. The money is to be used by Mike for his college education. On his 18th birthday, Mike withdraws the money from his savings account. How much did Mike withdraw from his account?

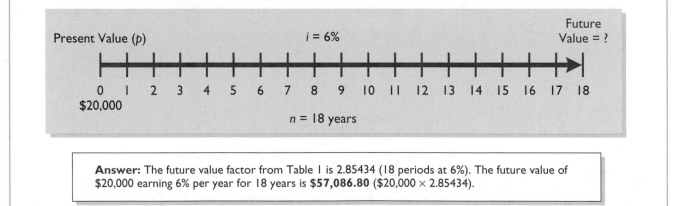

Present Value (*p*)   *i* = 6%   Future Value = ?

0 1 2 3 4 5 6 7 8 9 10 11 12 13 14 15 16 17 18
$20,000

n = 18 years

Answer: The future value factor from Table 1 is 2.85434 (18 periods at 6%). The future value of $20,000 earning 6% per year for 18 years is **$57,086.80** ($20,000 × 2.85434).

Illustration A-5
Demonstration problem—
Using Table 1 for *FV* of 1

Future Value of an Annuity

LEARNING OBJECTIVE   3

Solve for future value of an annuity.

The preceding discussion involved the accumulation of only a single principal sum. Individuals and businesses frequently encounter situations in which a **series** of equal dollar amounts are to be paid or received at evenly spaced time intervals (periodically), such as loans or lease (rental) contracts. A series of payments or receipts of equal dollar amounts is referred to as an **annuity**.

The **future value of an annuity** is the sum of all the payments (receipts) plus the accumulated compound interest on them. In computing the future value of an annuity, it is necessary to know (1) the interest rate, (2) the number of payments (receipts), and (3) the amount of the periodic payments (receipts).

To illustrate the computation of the future value of an annuity, assume that you invest $2,000 at the end of each year for three years at 5% interest compounded annually. This situation is depicted in the time diagram in Illustration A-6.

Illustration A-6
Time diagram for a three-year annuity

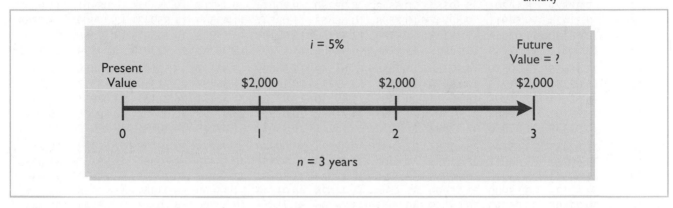

The $2,000 invested at the end of year 1 will earn interest for two years (years 2 and 3), and the $2,000 invested at the end of year 2 will earn interest for one year (year 3). However, the last $2,000 investment (made at the end of year 3) will not earn any interest. The future value of these periodic payments could be computed using the future value factors from Table 1, as shown in Illustration A-7.

Illustration A-7
Future value of periodic payment computation

Invested at End of Year	Number of Compounding Periods	Amount Invested	×	Future Value of 1 Factor at 5%	=	Future Value
1	2	$2,000	×	1.10250		$ 2,205
2	1	$2,000	×	1.05000		2,100
3	0	$2,000	×	1.00000		2,000
				3.15250		**$6,305**

The first $2,000 investment is multiplied by the future value factor for two periods (1.1025) because two years' interest will accumulate on it (in years 2 and 3). The second $2,000 investment will earn only one year's interest (in year 3) and therefore is multiplied by the future value factor for one year (1.0500). The final $2,000 investment is made at the end of the third year and will not earn any interest. Thus $n = 0$ and the future value factor is 1.00000. Consequently, the future value of the last $2,000 invested is only $2,000 since it does not accumulate any interest.

Calculating the future value of each individual cash flow is required when the periodic payments or receipts are not equal in each period. However, when the periodic payments (receipts) are **the same in each period**, the future value can be computed by using a future value of an annuity of 1 table. Table 2 (page A-6) is such a table.

TABLE 2   Future Value of an Annuity of 1

(n) Payments	4%	5%	6%	7%	8%	9%	10%	11%	12%	15%
1	1.00000	1.00000	1.00000	1.0000	1.00000	1.00000	1.00000	1.00000	1.00000	1.00000
2	2.04000	2.05000	2.06000	2.0700	2.08000	2.09000	2.10000	2.11000	2.12000	2.15000
3	3.12160	3.15250	3.18360	3.2149	3.24640	3.27810	3.31000	3.34210	3.37440	3.47250
4	4.24646	4.31013	4.37462	4.4399	4.50611	4.57313	4.64100	4.70973	4.77933	4.99338
5	5.41632	5.52563	5.63709	5.7507	5.86660	5.98471	6.10510	6.22780	6.35285	6.74238
6	6.63298	6.80191	6.97532	7.1533	7.33592	7.52334	7.71561	7.91286	8.11519	8.75374
7	7.89829	8.14201	8.39384	8.6540	8.92280	9.20044	9.48717	9.78327	10.08901	11.06680
8	9.21423	9.54911	9.89747	10.2598	10.63663	11.02847	11.43589	11.85943	12.29969	13.72682
9	10.58280	11.02656	11.49132	11.9780	12.48756	13.02104	13.57948	14.16397	14.77566	16.78584
10	12.00611	12.57789	13.18079	13.8164	14.48656	15.19293	15.93743	16.72201	17.54874	20.30372
11	13.48635	14.20679	14.97164	15.7836	16.64549	17.56029	18.53117	19.56143	20.65458	24.34928
12	15.02581	15.91713	16.86994	17.8885	18.97713	20.14072	21.38428	22.71319	24.13313	29.00167
13	16.62684	17.71298	18.88214	20.1406	21.49530	22.95339	24.52271	26.21164	28.02911	34.35192
14	18.29191	19.59863	21.01507	22.5505	24.21492	26.01919	27.97498	30.09492	32.39260	40.50471
15	20.02359	21.57856	23.27597	25.1290	27.15211	29.36092	31.77248	34.40536	37.27972	47.58041
16	21.82453	23.65749	25.67253	27.8881	30.32428	33.00340	35.94973	39.18995	42.75328	55.71747
17	23.69751	25.84037	28.21288	30.8402	33.75023	36.97351	40.54470	44.50084	48.88367	65.07509
18	25.64541	28.13238	30.90565	33.9990	37.45024	41.30134	45.59917	50.39593	55.74972	75.83636
19	27.67123	30.53900	33.75999	37.3790	41.44626	46.01846	51.15909	56.93949	63.43968	88.21181
20	29.77808	33.06595	36.78559	40.9955	45.76196	51.16012	57.27500	64.20283	72.05244	102.44358

Table 2 shows the future value of 1 to be received periodically for a given number of payments. It assumes that each payment is made at the **end** of each period. We can see from Table 2 that the future value of an annuity of 1 factor for three payments at 5% is 3.15250. The future value factor is the total of the three individual future value factors was shown in Illustration A-7. Multiplying this amount by the annual investment of $2,000 produces a future value of $6,305.

The demonstration problem in Illustration A-8 shows how to use Table 2.

Illustration A-8
Demonstration problem—Using Table 2 for *FV* of an annuity of 1

John and Char Lewis' daughter, Debra, has just started high school. They decide to start a college fund for her and will invest $2,500 in a savings account at the end of each year she is in high school (4 payments total). The account will earn 6% interest compounded annually. How much will be in the college fund at the time Debra graduates from high school?

Answer: The future value factor from Table 2 is 4.37462 (4 payments at 6%). The future value of $2,500 invested each year for 4 years at 6% interest is **$10,936.55** ($2,500 × 4.37462).

Present Value Concepts

Present Value Variables

The **present value** is the value now of a given amount to be paid or received in the future, assuming compound interest. The present value, like the future value, is based on three variables: (1) the dollar amount to be received (future amount), (2) the length of time until the amount is received (number of periods), and (3) the interest rate (the discount rate). The process of determining the present value is referred to as **discounting the future amount**.

Present value computations are used in measuring many items. For example, the present value of principal and interest payments is used to determine the market price of a bond. Determining the amount to be reported for notes payable and lease liabilities also involves present value computations. In addition, capital budgeting and other investment proposals are evaluated using present value computations. Finally, all rate of return and internal rate of return computations involve present value techniques.

LEARNING OBJECTIVE 4

Identify the variables fundamental to solving present value problems.

Present Value of a Single Amount

To illustrate present value, assume that you want to invest a sum of money today that will provide $1,000 at the end of one year. What amount would you need to invest today to have $1,000 one year from now? If you want a 10% rate of return, the investment or present value is $909.09 ($1,000 ÷ 1.10). The formula for calculating present value is shown in Illustration A-9.

LEARNING OBJECTIVE 5

Solve for present value of a single amount.

$$\text{Present Value} = \text{Future Value} \div (1 + i)^n$$

Illustration A-9
Formula for present value

The computation of $1,000 discounted at 10% for one year is as follows.

$$
\begin{aligned}
PV &= FV \div (1 + i)^n \\
&= \$1,000 \div (1 + .10)^1 \\
&= \$1,000 \div 1.10 \\
&= \$909.09
\end{aligned}
$$

The future amount ($1,000), the discount rate (10%), and the number of periods (1) are known. The variables in this situation can be depicted in the time diagram in Illustration A-10.

Illustration A-10
Finding present value if discounted for one period

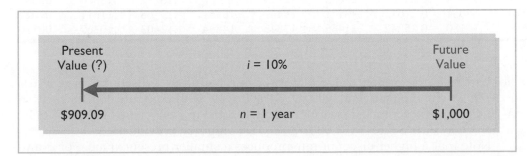

If the single amount of $1,000 is to be received **in two years** and discounted at 10% [$PV = \$1,000 \div (1 + .10)^2$], its present value is $826.45 [($1,000 ÷ 1.21), depicted as shown in Illustration A-11 on the next page.

Illustration A-11
Finding present value if
discounted for two periods

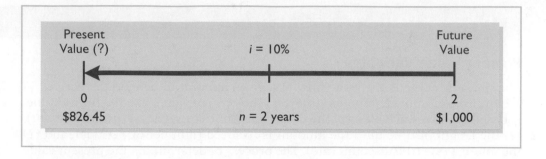

The present value of 1 may also be determined through tables that show the present value of 1 for n periods. In Table 3, below, n is the number of discounting periods involved. The percentages are the periodic interest rates or discount rates, and the 5-digit decimal numbers in the respective columns are the present value of 1 factors.

When using Table 3, the future value is multiplied by the present value factor specified at the intersection of the number of periods and the discount rate.

TABLE 3　Present Value of 1

(n) Periods	4%	5%	6%	7%	8%	9%	10%	11%	12%	15%
1	.96154	.95238	.94340	0.93458	.92593	.91743	.90909	.90090	.89286	.86957
2	.92456	.90703	.89000	0.87344	.85734	.84168	.82645	.81162	.79719	.75614
3	.88900	.86384	.83962	0.81630	.79383	.77218	.75132	.73119	.71178	.65752
4	.85480	.82270	.79209	0.76290	.73503	.70843	.68301	.65873	.63552	.57175
5	.82193	.78353	.74726	0.71299	.68058	.64993	.62092	.59345	.56743	.49718
6	.79031	.74622	.70496	0.66634	.63017	.59627	.56447	.53464	.50663	.43233
7	.75992	.71068	.66506	0.62275	.58349	.54703	.51316	.48166	.45235	.37594
8	.73069	.67684	.62741	0.58201	.54027	.50187	.46651	.43393	.40388	.32690
9	.70259	.64461	.59190	0.54393	.50025	.46043	.42410	.39092	.36061	.28426
10	.67556	.61391	.55839	0.50835	.46319	.42241	.38554	.35218	.32197	.24719
11	.64958	.58468	.52679	0.47509	.42888	.38753	.35049	.31728	.28748	.21494
12	.62460	.55684	.49697	0.44401	.39711	.35554	.31863	.28584	.25668	.18691
13	.60057	.53032	.46884	0.41496	.36770	.32618	.28966	.25751	.22917	.16253
14	.57748	.50507	.44230	0.38782	.34046	.29925	.26333	.23199	.20462	.14133
15	.55526	.48102	.41727	0.36245	.31524	.27454	.23939	.20900	.18270	.12289
16	.53391	.45811	.39365	0.33873	.29189	.25187	.21763	.18829	.16312	.10687
17	.51337	.43630	.37136	0.31657	.27027	.23107	.19785	.16963	.14564	.09293
18	.49363	.41552	.35034	0.29586	.25025	.21199	.17986	.15282	.13004	.08081
19	.47464	.39573	.33051	0.27615	.23171	.19449	.16351	.13768	.11611	.07027
20	.45639	.37689	.31180	0.25842	.21455	.17843	.14864	.12403	.10367	.06110

For example, the present value factor for one period at a discount rate of 10% is .90909, which equals the $909.09 ($1,000 × .90909) computed in Illustration A-10. For two periods at a discount rate of 10%, the present value factor is .82645, which equals the $826.45 ($1,000 × .82645) computed previously.

Note that a higher discount rate produces a smaller present value. For example, using a 15% discount rate, the present value of $1,000 due one year from now is $869.57, versus $909.09 at 10%. Also note that the further removed from the present the future value is, the smaller the present value. For example, using the same discount rate of 10%, the present value of $1,000 due in **five years** is $620.92. The present value of $1,000 due in **one year** is $909.09, a difference of $288.17.

The following two demonstration problems (Illustrations A-12 and A-13) illustrate how to use Table 3.

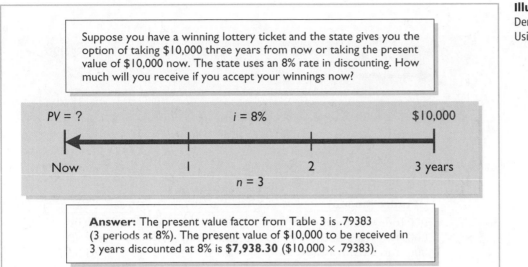

Illustration A-12
Demonstration problem—
Using Table 3 for *PV* of 1

Suppose you have a winning lottery ticket and the state gives you the option of taking $10,000 three years from now or taking the present value of $10,000 now. The state uses an 8% rate in discounting. How much will you receive if you accept your winnings now?

PV = ?   i = 8% $10,000

Now   1   2   3 years

n = 3

Answer: The present value factor from Table 3 is .79383 (3 periods at 8%). The present value of $10,000 to be received in 3 years discounted at 8% is **$7,938.30** ($10,000 × .79383).

Illustration A-13
Demonstration problem—
Using Table 3 for *PV* of 1

Determine the amount you must deposit today in your SUPER savings account, paying 9% interest, in order to accumulate $5,000 for a down payment 4 years from now on a new car.

PV = ?   i = 9% $5,000

Today   1   2   3   4 years

n = 4

Answer: The present value factor from Table 3 is .70843 (4 periods at 9%). The present value of $5,000 to be received in 4 years discounted at 9% is **$3,542.15** ($5,000 × .70843).

Present Value of an Annuity

The preceding discussion involved the discounting of only a single future amount. Businesses and individuals frequently engage in transactions in which a series of equal dollar amounts are to be received or paid at evenly spaced time intervals (periodically). Examples of a series of periodic receipts or payments are loan agreements, installment sales, mortgage notes, lease (rental) contracts, and pension obligations. As discussed earlier, these periodic receipts or payments are **annuities**.

The **present value of an annuity** is the value now of a series of future receipts or payments, discounted assuming compound interest. In computing the present value of an annuity, it is necessary to know (1) the discount rate, (2) the number of payments (receipts), and (3) the amount of the periodic receipts or payments. To illustrate the computation of the present value of an annuity, assume that you

LEARNING OBJECTIVE   6

Solve for present value of an annuity.

will receive $1,000 cash annually for three years at a time when the discount rate is 10%. This situation is depicted in the time diagram in Illustration A-14. Illustration A-15 shows the computation of its present value in this situation.

Illustration A-14
Time diagram for a three-year annuity

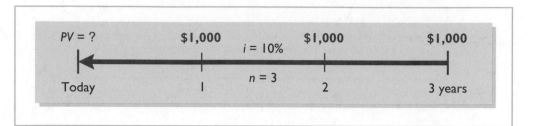

Illustration A-15
Present value of a series of future amounts computation

Future Amount	×	Present Value of 1 Factor at 10%	=	Present Value
$1,000 (one year away)		.90909		$ 909.09
1,000 (two years away)		.82645		826.45
1,000 (three years away)		.75132		751.32
		2.48686		**$2,486.86**

This method of calculation is required when the periodic cash flows are not uniform in each period. However, when the future receipts are the same in each period, an annuity table can be used. As illustrated in Table 4 below, an annuity table shows the present value of 1 to be received periodically for a given number of payments. It assumes that each payment is made at the end of each period.

TABLE 4   Present Value of an Annuity of 1

(n) Payments	4%	5%	6%	7%	8%	9%	10%	11%	12%	15%
1	.96154	.95238	.94340	0.93458	.92593	.91743	.90909	.90090	.89286	.86957
2	1.88609	1.85941	1.83339	1.80802	1.78326	1.75911	1.73554	1.71252	1.69005	1.62571
3	2.77509	2.72325	2.67301	2.62432	2.57710	2.53130	2.48685	2.44371	2.40183	2.28323
4	3.62990	3.54595	3.46511	3.38721	3.31213	3.23972	3.16986	3.10245	3.03735	2.85498
5	4.45182	4.32948	4.21236	4.10020	3.99271	3.88965	3.79079	3.69590	3.60478	3.35216
6	5.24214	5.07569	4.91732	4.76654	4.62288	4.48592	4.35526	4.23054	4.11141	3.78448
7	6.00205	5.78637	5.58238	5.38929	5.20637	5.03295	4.86842	4.71220	4.56376	4.16042
8	6.73274	6.46321	6.20979	5.97130	5.74664	5.53482	5.33493	5.14612	4.96764	4.48732
9	7.43533	7.10782	6.80169	6.51523	6.24689	5.99525	5.75902	5.53705	5.32825	4.77158
10	8.11090	7.72173	7.36009	7.02358	6.71008	6.41766	6.14457	5.88923	5.65022	5.01877
11	8.76048	8.30641	7.88687	7.49867	7.13896	6.80519	6.49506	6.20652	5.93770	5.23371
12	9.38507	8.86325	8.38384	7.94269	7.53608	7.16073	6.81369	6.49236	6.19437	5.42062
13	9.98565	9.39357	8.85268	8.35765	7.90378	7.48690	7.10336	6.74987	6.42355	5.58315
14	10.56312	9.89864	9.29498	8.74547	8.24424	7.78615	7.36669	6.98187	6.62817	5.72448
15	11.11839	10.37966	9.71225	9.10791	8.55948	8.06069	7.60608	7.19087	6.81086	5.84737
16	11.65230	10.83777	10.10590	9.44665	8.85137	8.31256	7.82371	7.37916	6.97399	5.95424
17	12.16567	11.27407	10.47726	9.76322	9.12164	8.54363	8.02155	7.54879	7.11963	6.04716
18	12.65930	11.68959	10.82760	10.05909	9.37189	8.75563	8.20141	7.70162	7.24967	6.12797
19	13.13394	12.08532	11.15812	10.33560	9.60360	8.95012	8.36492	7.83929	7.36578	6.19823
20	13.59033	12.46221	11.46992	10.59401	9.81815	9.12855	8.51356	7.96333	7.46944	6.25933

Table 4 shows that the present value of an annuity of 1 factor for three payments at 10% is 2.48685.[1] This present value factor is the total of the three individual present value factors, as shown in Illustration A-15. Applying this amount to the annual cash flow of $1,000 produces a present value of $2,486.85.

The following demonstration problem (Illustration A-16) illustrates how to use Table 4.

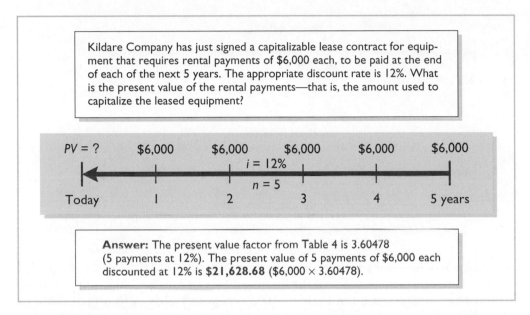

Kildare Company has just signed a capitalizable lease contract for equipment that requires rental payments of $6,000 each, to be paid at the end of each of the next 5 years. The appropriate discount rate is 12%. What is the present value of the rental payments—that is, the amount used to capitalize the leased equipment?

PV = ? $6,000 $6,000 $6,000 $6,000 $6,000
                                   $i = 12\%$
                                    $n = 5$
Today   1   2   3   4   5 years

Answer: The present value factor from Table 4 is 3.60478 (5 payments at 12%). The present value of 5 payments of $6,000 each discounted at 12% is **$21,628.68** ($6,000 × 3.60478).

Illustration A-16
Demonstration problem—Using Table 4 for *PV* of an annuity of 1

Time Periods and Discounting

In the preceding calculations, the discounting was done on an annual basis using an annual interest rate. Discounting may also be done over shorter periods of time such as monthly, quarterly, or semiannually.

When the time frame is less than one year, it is necessary to convert the annual interest rate to the applicable time frame. Assume, for example, that the investor in Illustration A-14 received $500 **semiannually** for three years instead of $1,000 annually. In this case, the number of periods becomes six (3 × 2), the discount rate is 5% (10% ÷ 2), the present value factor from Table 4 is 5.07569 (6 periods at 5%), and the present value of the future cash flows is $2,537.85 (5.07569 × $500). This amount is slightly higher than the $2,486.86 computed in Illustration A-15 because interest is computed twice during the same year. That is, during the second half of the year, interest is earned on the first half-year's interest.

Computing the Present Value of a Long-Term Note or Bond

The present value (or market price) of a long-term note or bond is a function of three variables: (1) the payment amounts, (2) the length of time until the amounts are paid, and (3) the discount rate. Our illustration (on the next page) uses a five-year bond issue.

LEARNING OBJECTIVE   7

Compute the present value of notes and bonds.

---

[1]The difference of .00001 between 2.48686 and 2.48685 is due to rounding.

The first variable (dollars to be paid) is made up of two elements: (1) a series of interest payments (an annuity) and (2) the principal amount (a single sum). To compute the present value of the bond, both the interest payments and the principal amount must be discounted—two different computations. The time diagrams for a bond due in five years are shown in Illustration A-17.

Illustration A-17
Present value of a bond time diagram

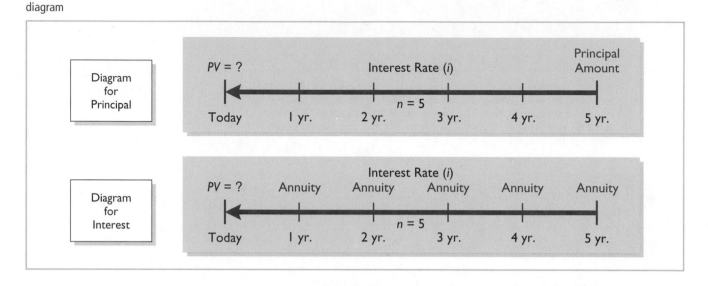

When the investor's market interest rate is equal to the bond's contractual interest rate, the present value of the bonds will equal the face value of the bonds. To illustrate, assume a bond issue of 10%, five-year bonds with a face value of $100,000 with interest payable **semiannually** on January 1 and July 1. If the discount rate is the same as the contractual rate, the bonds will sell at face value. In this case, the investor will receive (1) $100,000 at maturity and (2) a series of ten $5,000 interest payments [($100,000 × 10%) ÷ 2] over the term of the bonds. The length of time is expressed in terms of interest periods—in this case—10, and the discount rate per interest period, 5%. The following time diagram (Illustration A-18) depicts the variables involved in this discounting situation.

Illustration A-18
Time diagram for present value of a 10%, five-year bond paying interest semiannually

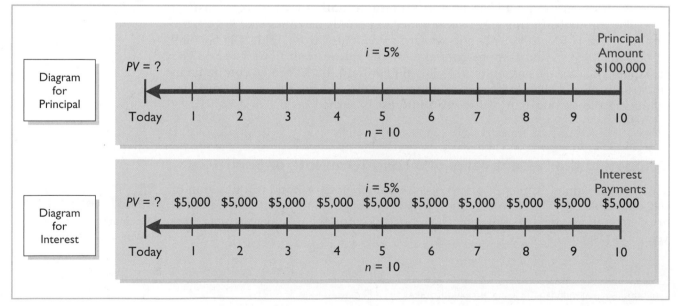

Illustration A-19 shows the computation of the present value of these bonds.

Illustration A-19
Present value of principal and
interest—face value

10% Contractual Rate—10% Discount Rate

Present value of principal to be received at maturity	
$100,000 × *PV* of 1 due in 10 periods at 5%	
$100,000 × .61391 (Table 3)	$ 61,391
Present value of interest to be received periodically	
over the term of the bonds	
$5,000 × *PV* of 1 due periodically for 10 periods at 5%	
$5,000 × 7.72173 (Table 4)	38,609*
Present value of bonds	**$100,000**

*Rounded

Now assume that the investor's required rate of return is 12%, not 10%. The future amounts are again $100,000 and $5,000, respectively, but now a discount rate of 6% (12% ÷ 2) must be used. The present value of the bonds is $92,639, as computed in Illustration A-20.

Illustration A-20
Present value of principal
and interest—discount

10% Contractual Rate—12% Discount Rate

Present value of principal to be received at maturity	
$100,000 × .55839 (Table 3)	$ 55,839
Present value of interest to be received periodically	
over the term of the bonds	
$5,000 × 7.36009 (Table 4)	36,800
Present value of bonds	**$92,639**

Conversely, if the discount rate is 8% and the contractual rate is 10%, the present value of the bonds is $108,111, computed as shown in Illustration A-21.

10% Contractual Rate—8% Discount Rate

Present value of principal to be received at maturity	
$100,000 × .67556 (Table 3)	$ 67,556
Present value of interest to be received periodically	
over the term of the bonds	
$5,000 × 8.11090 (Table 4)	40,555
Present value of bonds	**$108,111**

The above discussion relied on present value tables in solving present value problems. Calculators may also be used to compute present values without the use of these tables. Many calculators, especially financial calculators, have present value (*PV*) functions that allow you to calculate present values by merely inputting the proper amount, discount rate, periods, and pressing the PV key. We discuss the use of financial calculators in the next section.

Computing the Present Values in a Capital Budgeting Decision

The decision to make long-term capital investments is best evaluated using discounting techniques that recognize the time value of money. To do this, many companies calculate the present value of the cash flows involved in a capital investment.

To illustrate, Nagel-Siebert Trucking Company, a cross-country freight carrier in Montgomery, Illinois, is considering adding another truck to its fleet because of a purchasing opportunity. Navistar Inc., Nagel-Siebert's primary supplier of overland rigs, is overstocked and offers to sell its biggest rig for $154,000 cash payable upon delivery. Nagel-Siebert knows that the rig will produce a net cash flow per year of $40,000 for five years (received at the end of each year), at which time it will be sold for an estimated salvage value of $35,000. Nagel-Siebert's discount rate in evaluating capital expenditures is 10%. Should Nagel-Siebert commit to the purchase of this rig?

The cash flows that must be discounted to present value by Nagel-Siebert are as follows.

Cash payable on delivery (today): $154,000.

Net cash flow from operating the rig: $40,000 for 5 years (at the end of each year).

Cash received from sale of rig at the end of 5 years: $35,000.

The time diagrams for the latter two cash flows are shown in Illustration A-22.

Illustration A-22
Time diagrams for Nagel-Siebert Trucking Company

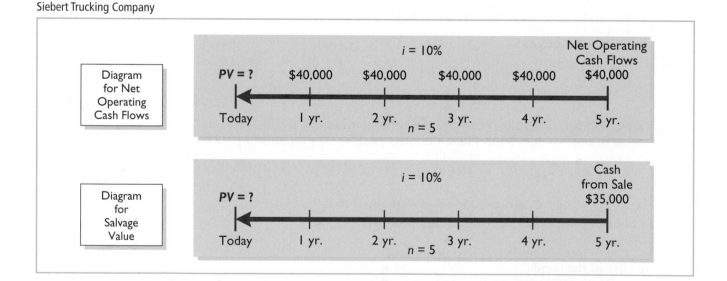

Notice from the diagrams that computing the present value of the net operating cash flows ($40,000 at the end of each year) is **discounting an annuity** (Table 4), while computing the present value of the $35,000 salvage value is **discounting a single sum** (Table 3). The computation of these present values is shown in Illustration A-23.

Illustration A-23
Present value computations
at 10%

Present Values Using a 10% Discount Rate

Present value of net operating cash flows received annually over 5 years:
$40,000 × PV of 1 received annually for 5 years at 10%
$40,000 × 3.79079 $ 151,631.60
Present value of salvage value (cash) to be received in 5 years
$35,000 × PV of 1 received in 5 years at 10%
$35,000 × .62092   21,732.20
Present value of cash **inflows**   173,363.80
Present value cash **outflows** (purchase price due today at 10%):
$154,000 × PV of 1 due today
$154,000 × 1.00000   (154,000.00)
Net present value   **$ 19,363.80**

Because the present value of the cash receipts (inflows) of $173,363.80 ($151,631.60 + $21,732.20) exceeds the present value of the cash payments (outflows) of $154,000.00, the net present value of $19,363.80 is positive, and **the decision to invest should be accepted**.

Now assume that Nagle-Siebert uses a discount rate of 15%, not 10%, because it wants a greater return on it investments in capital assets. The cash receipts and cash payments by Nagel-Siebert are the same. The present values of these receipts and cash payments discounted at 15% are shown in Illustration A-24.

Illustration A-24
Present value computations
at 15%

Present Values Using a 15% Discount Rate

Present value of net operating cash flows received annually
over 5 years at 15%
$40,000 × 3.35216 $ 134,086.40
Present value of salvage value (cash) to be received in 5 years at 15%
$35,000 × .49718   17,401.30
Present value of cash **inflows** $ 151,487.70
Present value of cash **outflows** (purchase price due today at 15%):
$154,000 × 1.00000   (154,000.00)
Net present value   **$ (2,512.30)**

Because the present value of the cash payments (outflows) of $154,000 exceeds the present value of the cash receipts (inflows) of $151,487.70 ($134,086.40 + $17,401.30), the net present value of $2,512.30 is negative, and **the investment should be rejected**.

The above discussion relied on present value tables in solving present value problems. As we show in the next section, calculators may also be used to compute present values without the use of these tables. Some calculators, especially the "business" or financial calculators, have present value (PV) functions that allow you to calculate present values by merely identifying the proper amount, discount rate, periods, and pressing the PV key.

Using Financial Calculators

Business professionals, once they have mastered the underlying concepts in sections 1 and 2, often use a financial calculator to solve time value of money problems. In many cases, they must use calculators if interest rates or time periods do not correspond with the information provided in the compound interest tables.

To use financial calculators, you enter the time value of money variables into the calculator. Illustration A-25 shows the five most common keys used to solve time value of money problems.[2]

Illustration A-25
Financial calculator keys

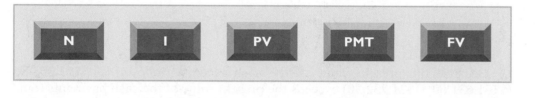

where:

N	=	number of periods
I	=	interest rate per period (some calculators use I/YR or i)
PV	=	present value (occurs at the beginning of the first period)
PMT	=	payment (all payments are equal, and none are skipped)
FV	=	future value (occurs at the end of the last period)

In solving time value of money problems in this appendix, you will generally be given three of four variables and will have to solve for the remaining variable. The fifth key (the key not used) is given a value of zero to ensure that this variable is not used in the computation.

Present value of a Single Sum

To illustrate how to solve a present value problem using a financial calculator, assume that you want to know the present value of $84,253 to be received in five years, discounted at 11% compounded annually. Illustration A-26 depicts this problem.

Illustration A-26
Calculator solution for present value of a single sum

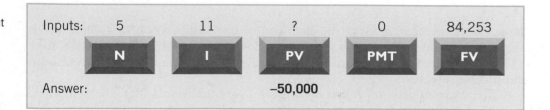

Inputs: 5   11   ?   0   84,253

N   I   PV   PMT   FV

Answer: −50,000

---

[2]On many calculators, these keys are actual buttons on the face of the calculator; on others, they appear on the display after the user accesses a present value menu.

Illustration A-26 shows you the information (inputs) to enter into the calculator: N = 5, I = 11, PMT = 0, and FV = 84,253. You then press PV for the answer: −$50,000. As indicated, the PMT key was given a value of zero because a series of payments did not occur in this problem.

PLUS AND MINUS

The use of plus and minus signs in time value of money problems with a financial calculator can be confusing. Most financial calculators are programmed so that the positive and negative cash flows in any problem offset each other. In the present value problem above, we identified the $84,253 future value initial investment as a positive (inflow); the answer −$50,000 was shown as a negative amount, reflecting a cash outflow. If the 84,253 were entered as a negative, then the final answer would have been reported as a positive 50,000.

Hopefully, the sign convention will not cause confusion. If you understand what is required in a problem, you should be able to interpret a positive or negative amount in determining the solution to a problem.

COMPOUNDING PERIODS

In the problem above, we assumed that compounding occurs once a year. Some financial calculators have a default setting, which assumes that compounding occurs 12 times a year. You must determine what default period has been programmed into your calculator and change it as necessary to arrive at the proper compounding period.

ROUNDING

Most financial calculators store and calculate using 12 decimal places. As a result, because compound interest tables generally have factors only up to five decimal places, a slight difference in the final answer can result. In most time value of money problems, the final answer will not include more than two decimal places.

Present Value of an Annuity

To illustrate how to solve a present value of an annuity problem using a financial calculator, assume that you are asked to determine the present value of rental receipts of $6,000 each to be received at the end of each of the next five years, when discounted at 12%, as pictured in Illustration A-27.

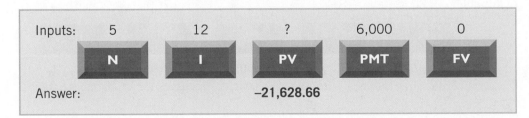

Illustration A-27
Calculator solution for present value of an annuity

In this case, you enter N = 5, I = 12, PMT = 6,000, FV = 0, and then press PV to arrive at the answer of −$21,628.66.

Useful Applications of the Financial Calculator

With a financial calculator, you can solve for any interest rate or for any number of periods in a time value of money problem. Here are some examples of these applications.

AUTO LOAN

Assume you are financing the purchase of a used car with a three-year loan. The loan has a 9.5% stated annual interest rate, compounded monthly. The price of the car is $6,000, and you want to determine the monthly payments, assuming that the payments start one month after the purchase. This problem is pictured in Illustration A-28.

Illustration A-28
Calculator solution for auto loan payments

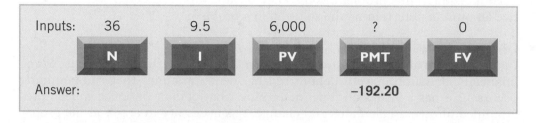

To solve this problem, you enter N = 36 (12 × 3), I = 9.5, PV = 6,000, FV = 0, and than press PMT. You will find that the monthly payments will be $192.20. Note that the payment key is usually programmed for 12 payments per year. Thus, you must change the default (compounding period) if the payments are other than monthly.

MORTGAGE LOAN AMOUNT

Let's say you evaluating financing options for a loan on a house. You decide that the maximum mortgage payment you can afford is $700 per month. The annual interest rate is 8.4%. If you get a mortgage that requires you to make monthly payments over a 15-year period, what is the maximum home loan you can afford? Illustration A-29 depicts this problem.

Illustration A-29
Calculator solution for mortgage amount

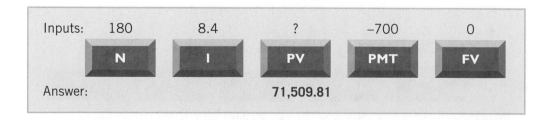

You enter N = 180 (12 × 15 years), I = 8.4, PMT = −700, FV = 0, and press PV. With the payments-per-year key set at 12, you find a present value of $71,509.81— the maximum home loan you can afford, given that you want to keep your mortgage payments at $700. Note that by changing any of the variables, you can quickly conduct "what-if" analyses for different situations.

SUMMARY OF LEARNING OBJECTIVES

✔ **The Navigator**

1 **Distinguish between simple and compound interest.** Simple interest is computed on the principal only, while compound interest is computed on the principal and any interest earned that has not been withdrawn.

2 **Solve for future value of a single amount.** Prepare a time diagram of the problem. Identify the principal amount, the number of compounding periods, and the interest rate. Using the future value of 1 table, multiply the principal amount by the future value factor specified at the intersection of the number of periods and the interest rate.

3 **Solve for future value of an annuity.** Prepare a time diagram of the problem. Identify the amount of the periodic payments (receipts), the number of payments (receipts), and the interest rate. Using the future value of an annuity of 1 table, multiply the amount of the payments by the future value factor specified at the intersection of the number of periods and the interest rate.

4 **Identify the variables fundamental to solving present value problems.** The following three variables are fundamental to solving present value problems: (1) the future amount, (2) the number of periods, and (3) the interest rate (the discount rate).

5 **Solve for present value of a single amount.** Prepare a time diagram of the problem. Identify the future amount, the number of discounting periods, and the discount (interest) rate. Using the present value of a single amount table, multiply the future amount by the present value factor specified at the intersection of the number of periods and the discount rate.

6 **Solve for present value of an annuity.** Prepare a time diagram of the problem. Identify the amount of future periodic receipts or payment (annuities), the number of payments (receipts), and the discount (interest) rate. Using the present value of an annuity of 1 table, multiply the amount of the annuity by the present value factor specified at the intersection of the number of payments and the interest rate.

7 **Compute the present value of notes and bonds.** Determine the present value of the principal amount: Multiply the principal amount (a single future amount) by the present value factor (from the present value of 1 table) intersecting at the number of periods (number of interest payments) and the discount rate. Determine the present value of the series of interest payments: Multiply the amount of the interest payment by the present value factor (from the present value of an annuity of 1 table) intersecting at the number of periods (number of interest payments) and the discount rate. Add the present value of the principal amount to the present value of the interest payments to arrive at the present value of the note or bond.

8 **Compute the present values in capital budgeting situations.** Compute the present values of all cash inflows and all cash outflows related to the capital budgeting proposal (an investment-type decision). If the **net** present value is positive, accept the proposal (make the investment). If the **net** present value is negative, reject the proposal (do not make the investment).

9 **Use a financial calculator to solve time value of money problems.** Financial calculators can be used to solve the same and additional problems as those solved with time value of money tables. Enter into the financial calculator the amounts for all of the known elements of a time value of money problem (periods, interest rate, payments, future or present value), and it solves for the unknown element. Particularly useful situations involve interest rates and compounding periods not presented in the tables.

GLOSSARY

Annuity A series of equal dollar amounts to be paid or received at evenly space time intervals (periodically). (p. A-4).

Compound interest The interest computed on the principal and any interest earned that has not been paid or withdrawn. (p. A-2).

Discounting the future amount(s) The process of determining present value. (p. A-7).

Future value of a single amount The value at a future date of a given amount invested, assuming compound interest. (p. A-2).

Future value of an annuity The sum of all the payments (receipts) plus the accumulated compound interest on them. (p. A-5).

Interest Payment for the use of another person's money. (p. A-1).

Present value The value now of a given amount to be paid or received in the future assuming compound interest. (p. A-7).

Present value of an annuity The value now of a series of future receipts or payments, discounted assuming compound interest. (p. A-9).

Principal The amount borrowed or invested. (p. A-1).

Simple interest The interest computed on the principal only. (p. A-1).

BRIEF EXERCISES

(Use tables to solve exercises BEA-1 to BEA-25.)

Compute the future value of a single amount.

(LO 2), AP

BEA-1 Randy Owen invested $9,000 at 5% annual interest, and left the money invested without withdrawing any of the interest for 12 years. At the end of the 12 years, Randy withdrew the accumulated amount of money. (a) What amount did Randy withdraw, assuming the investment earns simple interest? (b) What amount did Randy withdraw, assuming the investment earns interest compounded annually?

Use future value tables.

(LO 2, 3), C

BEA-2 For each of the following cases, indicate (a) to what interest rate columns and (b) to what number of periods you would refer in looking up the future value factor.

(1) In Table 1 (future value of 1):

	Annual Rate	Number of Years Invested	Compounded
Case A	5%	3	Annually
Case B	12%	4	Semiannually

(2) In Table 2 (future value of an annuity of 1):

	Annual Rate	Number of Years Invested	Compounded
Case A	3%	8	Annually
Case B	8%	6	Semiannually

Compute the future value of a single amount.

(LO 2), AP

BEA-3 Joyce Company signed a lease for an office building for a period of 12 years. Under the lease agreement, a security deposit of $8,400 is made. The deposit will be returned at the expiration of the lease with interest compounded at 4% per year. What amount will Joyce receive at the time the lease expires?

Compute the future value of an annuity.

(LO 3), AP

BEA-4 Bates Company issued $1,000,000, 10-year bonds and agreed to make annual sinking fund deposits of $78,000. The deposits are made at the end of each year into an account paying 6% annual interest. What amount will be in the sinking fund at the end of 12 years?

Compute the future value of a single amount and of an annuity.

(LO 2, 3), AP

BEA-5 Frank and Maureen Fantazzi invested $5,000 in a savings account paying 5% annual interest when their daughter, Angela, was born. They also deposited $1,000 on each of her birthdays until she was 18 (including her 18th birthday). How much was in the savings account on her 18th birthday (after the last deposit)?

Compute the future value of a single amount.

(LO 2), AP

BEA-6 Hugh Curtin borrowed $35,000 on July 1, 2014. This amount plus accrued interest at 8% compounded annually is to be repaid on July 1, 2019. How much will Hugh have to repay on July 1, 2019?

Use present value tables.

(LO 5, 6), C

BEA-7 For each of the following cases, indicate (a) to what interest rate columns and (b) to what number of periods you would refer in looking up the discount rate.

(1) In Table 3 (present value of 1):

	Annual Rate	Number of Years Involved	Discounts per Year
Case A	12%	7	Annually
Case B	8%	11	Annually
Case C	6%	8	Semiannually

(2) In Table 4 (present value of an annuity of 1):

	Annual Rate	Number of Years Involved	Number of Payments Involved	Frequency of Payments
Case A	10%	20	20	Annually
Case B	10%	7	7	Annually
Case C	8%	5	10	Semiannually

BEA-8 (a) What is the present value of $25,000 due 9 periods from now, discounted at 10%?

      (b) What is the present value of $25,000 to be received at the end of each of 6 periods, discounted at 9%?

Determine present values.
(LO 5, 6), AP

BEA-9 Chaffee Company is considering an investment that will return a lump sum of $750,000 six years from now. What amount should Chaffee Company pay for this investment to earn an 8% return?

Compute the present value of a single amount investment.
(LO 5), AP

BEA-10 Lloyd Company earns 6% on an investment that will return $450,000 eight years from now. What is the amount Lloyd should invest now to earn this rate of return?

Compute the present value of a single amount investment.
(LO 5), AP

BEA-11 Arthur Company is considering investing in an annuity contract that will return $46,000 annually at the end of each year for 15 years. What amount should Arthur Company pay for this investment if it earns an 8% return?

Compute the present value of an annuity investment.
(LO 6), AP

BEA-12 Kaehler Enterprises earns 5% on an investment that pays back $80,000 at the end of each of the next 6 years. What is the amount Kaehler Enterprises invested to earn the 5% rate of return?

Compute the present value of an annually investment.
(LO 6), AP

BEA-13 Hanna Railroad Co. is about to issue $300,000 of 10-year bonds paying an 11% interest rate, with interest payable semiannually. The discount rate for such securities is 10%. How much can Hanna expect to receive for the sale of these bonds?

Compute the present value of bonds.
(LO 5, 6, 7), AP

BEA-14 Assume the same information as BEA-13 except that the discount rate is 12% instead of 10%. In this case, how much can Hanna expect to receive from the sale of these bonds?

Compute the present value of bonds.
(LO 5, 6, 7), AP

BEA-15 Tomas Taco Company receives a $65,000, 6-year note bearing interest of 4% (paid annually) from a customer at a time when the discount rate is 6%. What is the present value of the note received by Tomas?

Compute the present value of a note.
(LO 5, 6, 7), AP

BEA-16 Gleason Enterprises issued 6%, 8-year, $2,500,000 par value bonds that pay interest semiannually on October 1 and April 1. The bonds are dated April 1, 2014, and are issued on that date. The discount rate of interest for such bonds on April 1, 2014, is 8%. What cash proceeds did Gleason receive from issuance of the bonds?

Compute the present value of bonds.
(LO 5, 6, 7), AP

BEA-17 Mark Barton owns a garage and is contemplating purchasing a tire retreading machine for $18,000. After estimating costs and revenues, Mark projects a net cash inflow from the retreading machine of $3,200 annually for 8 years. Mark hopes to earn a return of 9% on such investments. What is the present value of the retreading operation? Should Mark purchase the retreading machine?

Compute the present value of a machine for purposes of making a purchase decision.
(LO 6, 7), AP

BEA-18 Frazier Company issues a 10%, 5-year mortgage note on January 1, 2014, to obtain financing for new equipment. Land is used as collateral for the note. The terms provide for semiannual installment payments of $48,850. What were the cash proceeds received from the issuance of the note?

Compute the present value of a note.
(LO 6), AP

BEA-19 Leffler Company is considering purchasing equipment. The equipment will produce the following cash inflows: Year 1, $40,000; Year 2, $45,000; and Year 3, $50,000. Leffler requires a minimum rate of return of 8%. What is the maximum price Leffler should pay for this equipment?

Compute the maximum price to pay for a machine.
(LO 6, 7), AP

BEA-20 If Colleen Mooney invests $4,765.50 now and she will receive $12,000 at the end of 12 years, what annual rate of interest will Colleen earn on her investment? (*Hint:* Use Table 3.)

Compute the interest rate on a single amount.
(LO 5), AN

BEA-21 Wayne Kurt has been offered the opportunity of investing $29,319 now. The investment will earn 11% per year and at the end of that time will return Wayne $75,000. How many years must Wayne wait to receive $75,000? (*Hint:* Use Table 3.)

Compute the number of periods of a single amount.
(LO 5), AN

Compute the interest rate on an annuity.

(LO 6), AN

BEA-22 Joanne Quick made an investment of $10,271.38. From this investment, she will receive $1,200 annually for the next 15 years starting one year from now. What rate of interest will Joanne's investment be earning for her? (*Hint:* Use Table 4.)

Compute the number of periods of an annuity.

(LO 6), AN

BEA-23 Patty Schleis invests $6,542.83 now for a series of $1,300 annual returns beginning one year from now. Patty will earn a return of 9% on the initial investment. How many annual payments of $1,300 will Patty receive? (*Hint:* Use Table 4.)

Compute the present value of a machine for purposes of making a purchase decision.

(LO 8), AP

BEA-24 Barney Googal owns a garage and is contemplating purchasing a tire retreading machine for $12,820. After estimating costs and revenues, Barney projects a net cash inflow from the retreading machine of $2,700 annually for 7 years. Barney hopes to earn a return of 9% on such investments. What is the present value of the retreading operation? Should Barney Googal purchase the retreading machine?

Compute the maximum price to pay for a machine.

(LO 8), AP

BEA-25 Ramos Company is considering purchasing equipment. The equipment will produce the following cash inflows: Year 1, $20,000; Year 2, $30,000; Year 3, $40,000. Ramos requires a minimum rate of return of 11%. What is the maximum price Ramos should pay for this equipment?

Determine interest rate.

(LO 8), AP

BEA-26 Carly Simon wishes to invest $18,000 on July 1, 2014, and have it accumulate to $50,000 by July 1, 2024. Use a financial calculator to determine at what exact annual rate of interest Carly must invest the $18,000.

Determine interest rate.

(LO 9), AP

BEA-27 On July 17, 2014, James Taylor borrowed $60,000 from his grandfather to open a clothing store. Starting July 17, 2015, James has to make 10 equal annual payments of $8,860 each to repay the loan. Use a financial calculator to determine what interest rate James is paying.

Determine interest rate.

(LO 9), AP

BEA-28 As the purchaser of a new house, Carrie Underwood has signed a mortgage note to pay the Nashville National Bank and Trust Co. $8,400 every 6 months for 20 years, at the end of which time she will own the house. At the date the mortgage is signed, the purchase price was $198,000 and Underwood made a down payment of $20,000. The first payment will be made 6 months after the date the mortgage is signed. Using a financial calculator, compute the exact rate of interest earned on the mortgage by the bank.

Various time value of money situations.

(LO 9), AP

BEA-29 Using a financial calculator, solve for the unknowns in each of the following situations.

(a) On June 1, 2013, Holly Golightly purchases lakefront property from her neighbor, George Peppard, and agrees to pay the purchase price in seven payments of $16,000 each, the first payment to be payable June 1, 2014. (Assume that interest compounded at an annual rate of 6.9% is implicit in the payments.) What is the purchase price of the property?

(b) On January 1, 2013, Sammis Corporation purchased 200 of the $1,000 face value, 7% coupon, 10-year bonds of Malone Inc. The bonds mature on January 1, 2021, and pay interest annually beginning January 1, 2014. Sammis purchased the bonds to yield 8.65%. How much did Sammis pay for the bonds?

Various time value of money situations.

(LO 9), AP

BEA-30 Using a financial calculator, provide a solution to each of the following situations.

(a) Lynn Anglin owes a debt of $42,000 from the purchase of her new sport utility vehicle. The debt bears annual interest of 7.8% compounded monthly. Lynn wishes to pay the debt and interest in equal monthly payments over 8 years, beginning one month hence. What equal monthly payments will pay off the debt and interest?

(b) On January 1, 2014, Roger Molony offers to buy Dave Feeney's used snowmobile for $8,000, payable in five equal annual installments, which are to include 7.25% interest on the unpaid balance and a portion of the principal. If the first payment is to be made on December 31, 2014, how much will each payment be?

Management accountants have an obligation to the organizations they serve, their profession, the public, and themselves to maintain the highest standards of ethical conduct. In recognition of this obligation, the **Institute of Management Accountants** has published and promoted the following standards of ethical conduct for management accountants.

IMA Statement of Ethical Professional Practice

Members of IMA shall behave ethically. A commitment to ethical professional practice includes: overarching principles that express our values, and standards that guide our conduct.

Principles

IMA's overarching ethical principles include: Honesty, Fairness, Objectivity, and Responsibility. Members shall act in accordance with these principles and shall encourage others within their organizations to adhere to them.

Standards

A member's failure to comply with the following standards may result in disciplinary action.

I. COMPETENCE

Each member has a responsibility to:

1. Maintain an appropriate level of professional expertise by continually developing knowledge and skills.
2. Perform professional duties in accordance with relevant laws, regulations, and technical standards.
3. Provide decision support information and recommendations that are accurate, clear, concise, and timely.
4. Recognize and communicate professional limitations or other constraints that would preclude responsible judgment or successful performance of an activity.

II. CONFIDENTIALITY

Each member has a responsibility to:

1. Keep information confidential except when disclosure is authorized or legally required.
2. Inform all relevant parties regarding appropriate use of confidential information. Monitor subordinates' activities to ensure compliance.
3. Refrain from using confidential information for unethical or illegal advantage.

III. INTEGRITY

Each member has a responsibility to:

1. Mitigate actual conflicts of interest. Regularly communicate with business associates to avoid apparent conflicts of interest. Advise all parties of any potential conflicts.

2. Refrain from engaging in any conduct that would prejudice carrying out duties ethically.

3. Abstain from engaging in or supporting any activity that might discredit the profession.

IV. CREDIBILITY

Each member has a responsibility to:

1. Communicate information fairly and objectively.

2. Disclose all relevant information that could reasonably be expected to influence an intended user's understanding of the reports, analyses, or recommendations.

3. Disclose delays or deficiencies in information, timeliness, processing, or internal controls in conformance with organization policy and/or applicable law.

Resolution of Ethical Conflict

In applying the Standards of Ethical Professional Practice, you may encounter problems identifying unethical behavior or resolving an ethical conflict. When faced with ethical issues, you should follow your organization's established policies on the resolution of such conflict. If these policies do not resolve the ethical conflict, you should consider the following courses of action:

1. Discuss the issue with your immediate supervisor except when it appears that the supervisor is involved. In that case, present the issue to the next level. If you cannot achieve a satisfactory resolution, submit the issue to the next management level. If your immediate superior is the chief executive officer or equivalent, the acceptable reviewing authority may be a group such as the audit committee, executive committee, board of directors, board of trustees, or owners. Contact with levels above the immediate superior should be initiated only with your superior's knowledge, assuming he or she is not involved. Communication of such problems to authorities or individuals not employed or engaged by the organization is not considered appropriate, unless you believe there is a clear violation of the law.

2. Clarify relevant ethical issues by initiating a confidential discussion with an IMA Ethics Counselor or other impartial advisor to obtain a better understanding of possible courses of action.

3. Consult your own attorney as to legal obligations and rights concerning the ethical conflict.

Source: Institute of Management Accountants, *www.imanet.org/pdf/981.pdf.* Reprinted by permission.

Cases for Management Decision-Making

The complete cases are available for viewing or download at the book's companion website that accompanies this textbook, at *www.wiley.com/college/weygandt*. To solve these cases, it will be necessary to use the tools learned within the chapters.

Suggested Uses of Cases

Case	Overview
CASE 1 *Greetings Inc.:* *Job Order Costing*	This case is the first in a series of four cases that presents a business situation in which a traditional retailer decides to employ Internet technology to expand its sales opportunities. It requires the student to employ traditional job order costing techniques and then requests an evaluation of the resulting product costs. (Related to Chapter 2, Job Order Costing.)
CASE 2 *Greetings Inc.:* *Activity-Based* *Costing*	This case focuses on decision-making benefits of activity-based costing relative to the traditional approach. It also offers an opportunity to discuss the cost/benefit trade-off between simple ABC systems versus refined systems, and the potential benefit of using capacity rather than expected sales when allocating fixed overhead costs. (Related to Chapter 4, Activity-Based Costing.)
CASE 3 *Greetings Inc.:* *Transfer Pricing* *Issues*	This case illustrates the importance of proper transfer pricing for decision-making as well as performance evaluation. The student is required to evaluate profitability using two different transfer pricing approaches and comment on the terms of the proposed transfer pricing agreement. (Related to Chapter 8, Pricing.)
CASE 4 *Greetings Inc.:* *Capital Budgeting*	This case is set in an environment in which the company is searching for new opportunities for growth. It requires evaluation of a proposal based on initial estimates as well as sensitivity analysis. It also requires evaluation of the underlying assumptions used in the analysis. (Related to Chapter 12, Planning for Capital Investments.)
CASE 5 *Auburn Circular* *Club Pro Rodeo* *Roundup*	This comprehensive case is designed to be used as a capstone activity at the end of the course. It deals with a not-for-profit service company. The case involves many managerial accounting issues that would be common for a start-up business. (Related to Chapter 5, Cost-Volume-Profit; Chapter 7, Incremental Analysis; and Chapter 9, Budgetary Planning.)

CASE 6	This case focuses on setting up a new business. In plan-
Sweats Galore	ning for this new business, the preparation of budgets is
	emphasized. In addition, an understanding of cost-volume-
	profit relationships is required. (Related to Chapter 5, Cost-
	Volume-Profit, and Chapter 9, Budgetary Planning.)

CASE 7	This comprehensive case involves finding the cost for a
Armstrong Helmet	given product. In addition, it explores cost-volume-profit
Company	relationships. It requires the preparation of a set of budgets.
	(Related to Chapter 1, Managerial Accounting; Chapter 5,
	Cost-Volume-Profit; Chapter 9, Budgetary Planning; Chap-
	ter 10, Budgetary Control and Responsibility Accounting;
	Chapter 11, Standard Costs and Balanced Scorecard; and
	Chapter 12, Planning for Capital Investments.)

To access the full text of these cases, go to the book's companion website at **www.wiley.com/college/weygandt**.

Photo Credits

Company Index

A

adidas, 21
Allegiant Airlines, 19
Alliance Atlantic Communications, Inc., 629
Amazon.com, 8, 196–197, 300, 331, 389
AMD, 606
American Airlines, 5, 205, 512
American Express, 153, 296, 331
American LaFrance, 49, 50, 60
American Van Lines, 438
Ampex, 561
Anchor Glass Container Corporation, 45–46
Anytime Fitness, 289
Apple, 335, 381
Armani, 334
Armour, 302
AT&T, 5, 153, 199

B

Babcock Ice Cream, 406–407
Balanced Scorecard Institute, 543
Barnes and Noble, 233
Ben & Jerry's Homemade, Inc., 50, 94–96, 100
Beverly Hills Fan Company, 328–329
Boeing Company, 8, 18, 298, 664
Briggs and Stratton, 466
Bristol-Meyers Squibb, 677
Buck Knives, 307
Burlington Northern Railroad, 253, 290
Burton Snowboards, 16

C

Campbell Soup Company, 5, 561, 566–567, 582–583
Carnival Corporation, 546
Caterpillar, 11, 100, 104, 153, 167
Chase, 513
ChevronTexaco, 334
Chrysler, 510
Cisco Systems, 251, 449, 677
Clark Equipment Company, 148

Clark-Hurth, 148
Clarus Technologies, 380
The Coca-Cola Company, 10, 21, 100, 232–233, 466, 646, 701–702
Columbia Sportswear Company, 630
Compumotor, 148
Computer Associates International, Inc., 490
Conservation International, 510
Consolidated Edison, 665
Consumers Packaging Inc., 45
Costco Wholesale Corp., 590
Current Designs, 2–5, 9, 10, 13, 14, 43–44, 88–89, 141, 190–191, 231, 285–286, 326–327, 377, 426–427, 487–488, 540–541, 580–581
Curves, 289
Cypress Semiconductor Corporation, 629

D

Dell Computer, 5, 20, 167, 547
Del Monte Foods Company, 287
Delta Airlines, 304, 512
Dick's Sporting Goods, 12
Disney, see Walt Disney
Dow, 11
Duke Energy Corporation, 199, 439, 454
Dun & Bradstreet, 652
Dynastar, 293
Dynegy, Inc., 599

E

Eastman Kodak, 104, 587
East Valley Hospital, 191
Eli Lilly, 466
Enron, 5, 677
Ethan Allen, 301
E*Trade, 251
ExxonMobil, 50, 96, 302, 334, 547

F

Facebook, 6, 253
FedEx Corporation, 5, 287–288
FlightServe, 211, 234

Florida Citrus Company, 673
Ford Motor Company, 111, 205, 244, 335, 454
Fox Broadcasting, 441

G

Ganong Bros. Ltd., 233
General Dynamics Corp., 672
General Electric (GE), 6, 21, 67, 92, 104
General Mills, 96, 159
General Motors (GM), 5, 20, 51, 292, 293, 298, 335, 676, 685
Gibson Greetings, Inc., 292
Glassmaster Company, 542–543
GM, see General Motors
Goldman Sachs, 66
Gold's Gym, 144
Goodyear, 305
Google, 335, 381, 587
Gulf Craft, 125

H

Hard Candy, 144
Harley-Davidson, 167
Hershey, 99
Hewlett-Packard (HP) Corporation, 5, 18, 21, 153, 168, 244, 292, 298, 309, 512
Hilton Hotels Corporation, 21, 144, 199
Holland America Line, 457, 546, 555
Honda, 451
HP, see Hewlett-Packard Corporation
H&R Block, 97
Hughes Aircraft Co., 153, 672

I

IBM, 8, 50, 153, 498
Ideal Manufacturing Company, 191–192
Intel Corporation, 111, 236–237, 244, 333, 334, 606
iSuppli, 57

J

J. C. Penney Company, Inc., 590, 652–654, 658–659, 661, 663–669, 691
Jiffy Lube, 97
Jif Peanut Butter, 125
John Deere Company, 152
Josten's, Inc., 512

K

Kellogg Company, 50, 96, 103–111, 116–121, 205, 505, 678–680
Kmart, 328, 664
Kohl's Corporation, 590
Komag, 253
Kraft Foods, 505
Kroger Stores, 664, 665

L

Levi Strauss, 336, 381
Louis Vuitton, 6
Lucent, 5

M

McDonald's Corporation, 496, 635
McDonnell Douglas, 8
Madison Square Garden, 389
Mahany Welding Supply, 156
Marriott Hotels, 199, 438
Massachusetts General Hospital, 198
Mayo Clinic, 66
Merck & Co., Inc., 334, 379
Microsoft Corporation, 4, 332, 586–587, 604–605, 685
Moody's, 652
Motorola, 674
Museum of Contemporary Art (Los Angeles, California), 406

N

NASCAR, 159
NBCUniversal, 441, 492
Network Computing Devices Inc., 428–429
Nike, Inc., 8, 199, 251, 292, 659
Nissan, 547
Nordstrom, Inc., 690–691

O

1-800-GOT-JUNK?, 434–435
Oracle Corporation, 605
Oral-B Laboratories, 293

P

Pandora, 253
Parker Hannifin Corporation, 148, 340
Parlex Corporation, 90
Parmalat, 601
Patriarch Partners, 48, 49
Penske Automotive Group, 512–513
PepsiCo, Inc., 628, 646, 685, 701–702
P&G, *see* Procter & Gamble
Philip Morris, 293
Positively-You.com, 382–383, 386
Pratt and Whitney, 67
Precor Company, 144, 145, 164–165
PriceWaterhouseCoopers, 66
Princeton University, 406
Procter & Gamble (P&G), 12, 153, 449, 498, 674

Q

Quad Graphics, 50
Quaker Oats, 125, 293

R

Reebok, 199
Renault, 547

S

Safeway, 664
San Diego Zoo, 446
Sanford Corp., 516–517
SAP, 20
Sara Lee, 10, 292
Schering-Plough, 8
Sears, 652
Sharp, 560
Sherwin Williams, 96
Siebel Systems, 451
Siemens AG, 466
Smart Balance, 288
Snap Fitness, 289
Solectron Corporation, 293, 309
Southwest Airlines, 198
Standard & Poor's, 652
Starbucks, 21, 335, 494–495, 510, 545
Sunbeam, 308
Susan's Chili Factory, 501, 545

T

Target Corporation, 590, 697–698
Tecumseh Products Company, 582
Tektronix, 153

Texas Instruments, 561
3M, 246
Tiffany & Co., 664
Time Warner, 345, 387
Toyota, 19, 21, 335, 352
Trek, 301, 345
Twitter, 253

U

U-Haul, 201
Unilever, 513
United Airlines, 198, 244, 512, 515, 545, 587
U.S. Navy, 498
United States Steel Corp., 205
University of Wisconsin, 406
USX, 96

V

Verizon, 554, 584

W

Wal-Mart Stores, Inc., 21, 336, 381, 513, 590, 664, 697–698
Walt Disney, 50, 345
Warner Bros. Motion Pictures, 125
Wenonah Canoe, 2, 3, 43
Westinghouse, 352, 561
Weyerhaeuser Co., 673
Whirlpool, 11
Willard & Shullman Group Ltd., 385
World Bank, 498
WorldCom, Inc., 599, 649, 660

X

Xerox, 5
XM Satellite Radio Holdings, 397

Y

Yahoo! Inc., 587, 652

Z

Zappos.com, 332–333
Zoom Kitchen, 247
Zoran, 334

A

ABC. *See* Activity-based costing
ABM (activity-based management), 157–159
Absorption costing:
  deciding when to use, 262–264
  defined, 256
  example of, 257, 259–262
  variable costing vs., 256–265
Absorption-cost pricing, 355–357
Accounting. *See also* Managerial accounting; Responsibility accounting
  accrual, 548, 592–595, 610–620
  and budgeting, 384
  cash, 548, 592–595, 616–620
  cost, 50
  financial, 4, 5
Accounting equation, 624
Accounting principle, change in, 675
Accounts payable, 403, 597, 612
Accounts receivable, 403, 596–597, 611
Accrual accounting, 592–595
  cash accounting vs., 548
  and net income, 592–595, 616–620
Accumulated depreciation, 403, 613
Accumulating manufacturing costs, 51–54, 64
  factory labor, 53
  in job order and process cost systems, 97
  overhead, 53–54
  raw materials, 52–53
Acid-test (quick) ratios, 661–662, 669
Activity(-ies), 147
  batch-level, 159–161
  classification of, 159–161
  coordination of, 384
  in cost behavior analysis, 198
  facility-level, 160, 161
  financing, 588–590, 600–601, 620–621
  identification/classification of, 149, 150

investing, 588–590, 600–601, 620–621
noncash, 590, 596–598
non-value-added, 157–158
operating, 588–590, 594–599, 604, 616–620
product-level, 159–161
in statement of cash flows, 588–592
unit-level, 159, 160
value-added, 157
and variable/fixed costs, 198, 199
Activity bases, 59, 60
Activity-based costing (ABC), 20, 144–170
  and activity-based management, 157–159
  activity-based overhead rates, 150–151
  benefits of, 155
  classification of activity levels in, 159–161
  cost drivers in, 150
  and cost pools, 150, 155
  for employee evaluations, 156
  in Greetings, Inc. case study, CA-1
  and incremental analysis, 308
  limitations of, 155
  and overhead costs, 150–152, 500
  in service industries, 153, 161–165
  traditional costing vs., 146–154
  unit costs under, 149–154
  when to use, 156–157
Activity-based management (ABM), 157–159
Activity-based overhead rates, 149–151
Activity cost pools, 147–148, 150
Activity flowcharts, 157–158
Activity index, 198
  for flexible budgets, 438, 442
  relevant range of, 201
  for static budgets, 437
Actual cost (in total variance), 503
Adjusted trial balances, 592

Administrative expenses. *See* Selling and administrative expenses
After-tax total contribution margin, 351, 352
Airline industry, 19, 153, 211, 515
Analysis. *See also* Cost-volume-profit; Financial statement analysis
  break-even, 209–213, 216, 239–240
  comparative, 652
  cost behavior, 198–205
  and effective budgeting, 384–385
  incremental, 292–311, 351
  regression, 204
  risk, 560
  sensitivity, 560
Annual rate of return method, 564–565
Annuities, A-9
  discounting, A-14
  future value of, A-4–A-6
  present value of, A-9–A-11, 17
Applications, pricing of, 335
Assets:
  current, 596–597, 661
  fixed, 604
  long-term, 589
  noncurrent, 600–601, 620–621
  operating, 458, 460
  plant, 595–596, 619
  return on, 665, 669
  total, 657, 668, 670
Asset turnover, 664–665, 669
Assigning manufacturing costs, 54–58, 64, 99–102
  to cost of goods sold, 63, 101
  of factory labor, 57–58, 100
  to finished goods, 62–63, 101
  in job order costing, 54–58, 67, 98
  of manufacturing overhead, 58–61, 101
  to next department, 101
  in process costing, 52, 98–102
  of raw materials, 55–57, 99–100
Audit committees, 8

Auto loans, A-18
Automation:
    and activity base for overhead, 60
    and cost structure, 251
    and CVP analysis, 241–242
    and fixed costs, 199
    and manufacturing in U.S., 11
    and the value chain, 20
Automobile industry, 335, 513
Available-for-sale securities, 675
Available funds, 549
Average collection period, 663
Awareness of operations,
        management's, 384

B
Balanced scorecard, 20–21, 512–515
    defined, 513
    perspectives employed with,
        513–515
Balance sheet(s), 15–16
    budgeted, 402–403
    comparative, 592
    horizontal analysis of, 654
    in job order costing, 68
    and statement of cash flows,
        601–602
    vertical analysis of, 657
Balancing amount, 613
Banks, 513, 652
Base period, horizontal analysis,
        653–654
Batches, 50
Batch-level activities, 159–161
Before-tax total contribution margin,
        351, 352
Beginning work in process
        inventory, 13
Behavior:
    and budgeting, 386–387
    and equipment retention/
        replacement, 305
    and performance evaluations,
        450–451
Benford's Law, 660
Bezos, Jeff, 196, 300
Big-screen televisions, 560
Boards of directors, 6, 8
Bonds, present value of, A-11–A-13
Bondholders, 652
Bonds payable, 600, 613, 621
Book value, 305
Borrowers, liquidity of, 652
Bottlenecks, 20
Bowline, Lyle, 382
Break-even analysis, 209–213, 216
    contribution margin technique for,
        210–211
    and CVP analysis, 209–213, 216,
        239–240

and CVP graph, 211–212
    defined, 209
    equation for, 210
Break-even point, 207
    and conversion rates, 242
    on CVP graph, 212
    defined, 207, 209
    formula for, 240
    identifying, 209
    in sales dollars, 210
    in sales units, 210–211
Brock, Paula, 446
Budget(s), 384. See also Budgeting
    cash, 399–402, 404
    defined, 384
    direct labor, 395
    direct materials, 392–393
    financial, 388, 399–404
    flexible, 438–447, 451, 455
    government, 390, 405–406
    manufacturing overhead, 395–396
    master, 387–388, 392–393, 437–438
    merchandise purchases, 404–405
    operating, 389–399
    production, 390–391
    sales, 389–390
    selling and administrative
        expense, 396
    standards vs., 496
    static, 437–440
Budgetary control, 436–447
    defined, 436–437
    with flexible budgets, 438–447
    with static budget reports, 437–438
Budgetary goals, 450
Budgetary optimism, 390
Budgetary planning, 382–411
    budgeting basics, 384–389
    financial budgets, 399–404
    in nonmanufacturing companies,
        404–407
    operating budgets, 389–399
Budgetary slack, 387
Budget committees, 386
Budgeted balance sheet, 402–403
Budgeted income statement,
        396–399
Budgeting, 384–389. See also Capital
        budgeting
    and accounting, 384
    benefits of, 384
    effective, 384–385
    human behavior affected by,
        386–387
    length of budget period, 385
    long-range planning vs., 387
    and master budget, 387–388
    for merchandisers, 404–405
    for nonmanufacturing companies,
        404–407

for not-for-profit organizations,
        405–406
    process of, 385–386
    responsibility accounting vs., 448
    for service enterprises, 405, 406
Budget period, 385
Budget reforecasting, 446
Budget reports, 436
    flexible, 445–447
    for responsibility accounting,
        451–454
    static, 437–438
Buffett, Warren, 253, 650–651
Buildings:
    on budgeted balance sheet, 403
    on statement of cash flows, 600,
        612, 621
Burden. See Manufacturing overhead
Businesses. See also Service
        companies
    manufacturing, 292–293
    nonmanufacturing, 404–407
    small, 385
    standards for, 496–497
    virtual, 351
Business calculators. See Financial
    calculators
Business environment, CVP analysis
    in, 241–242
Business ethics, 7–8
Buswell, Diane, 44, 190, 231,
        326–327, 426, 541

C
Calculators. See Financial calculators
Capacity, 297, 346–348, 500
Capital:
    cost of, 554
    working, 661
Capital budgeting, 546–569
    annual rate of return method used
        in, 564–566
    authorization process, 548
    and cash flow information,
        548–549
    cash payback technique used in,
        550–551
    computing time and present values
        in, A-14–A-15
    defined, 547
    evaluation process for, 548–549
    and free cash flow, 604
    in Greetings, Inc. case study, CA-1
    intangible benefits in, 557–559
    internal rate of return method
        used in, 562–564
    with mutually exclusive projects,
        559–560
    net present value method used in,
        551–561, 564

and post-audits, 561
and risk analysis, 560
Capitalization of operating
    expenses, 677
Carpenter, Jake Burton, 16
Cash. *See also* Net cash
    in budgeted balance sheet, 403
    disposition of change in, 613
    liquidity of, 661–662
    net change in, 601–602, 621
Cash accounting, 548, 592–595,
    616–620
Cash budget, 399–402, 404
Cash disbursements section
    (cash budget), 400
Cash flow(s). *See also* Statement of
    cash flows
    and capital budgeting, 548–549
    for company evaluation, 604–606
    discounted cash flow techniques,
        551–564
    equal, 552–553, 562
    free, 604–606
    inflows, 548, 549, 609
    net annual, 550
    in net present value method, 555
    of not-for-profit organizations, 405
    outflows, 548, 549, 600, 609, 621
    predicting, 588
    unequal, 553, 563
Cash flow numbers, 548
Cash inflows, 548, 549, 609
Cash outflows, 548, 549, 600, 609, 621
Cash payback technique, 550–551
Cash payments, 617–619
Cash receipts, 616–617
Cash receipts section
    (cash budget), 399
CEO (chief executive officer), 6, 8
CFO (chief financial officer), 7, 8
Change in accounting principle, 675
Channel stuffing, 677
Charges:
    material loading, 341–343
    non-recurring, 674
    restructuring, 674
    in time-and-materials pricing,
        342–343
Chemical industry, 513
Chief executive officer (CEO), 6, 8
Chief financial officer (CFO), 7, 8
Cichanowski, Mike, 2, 3, 43, 44, 326,
    327, 540, 580–581
CM. *See* Contribution margin
COLAs (cost of living adjustments),
    499
Collaboration, 449
Collections:
    average collection period, 663
    schedule of expected, 400

Common-size analysis. *See* Vertical
    analysis
Common stock, 666–667
    on budgeted balance sheet, 403
    issuance of, for cash, 600
    on statement of cash flows,
        613, 621
Common stockholders' equity, return
    on, 665–666, 669
Companies. *See* Businesses
Comparative analysis, 652
Comparative balance sheets, 588, 592
Comparisons, 652, 653, 659
Compensation programs, 449
Competence, B-1
Competitive advantage, 340
Competitive markets, pricing in,
    334–335
Completion percentages, 103
Components, cost of, 57
Composition (current assets), 661
Compounding periods, A-3, 17
Compound interest, A-2–A-4
Comprehensive income, 675
Computer systems industry, 513
Confidentiality, B-1–B-2
Conflict resolution, B-2
Constraints, theory of, 20, 249
Continuous 12-month budgets, 385
Continuous improvement, 158
Contribution margin (CM), 206–207,
    238, 247
    per unit, 207–208, 249
    ratios, 208–209, 211, 240, 252
    and tax rates, 351, 352
    of unprofitable segments/
        products, 306
    weighted-average, 244–247
Control(s). *See also* Budgetary
        control
    and activity-based costing, 155
    with budgets, 384
    cost, 350
    internal, 8, 55
Control accounts, 54, 56, 62
Controllable costs, 448–450, 455–458
Controllable margin, 456–458, 460
Controllable revenues, 449, 456, 457
Controllable variance, 509, 521–522
Controller, 7
Controlling, as management
    function, 5–6
Conversion costs, 103, 108, 117–118
Conversion rates, 242
Corporate social responsibility,
    21, 510
Corporate strategy, pricing in, 335
Corporate turn-arounds, 48–49
Cost(s), 9–12. *See also specific types*
    of ABC implementation, 155

in CVP analysis, 239
and equivalent units
    computations, 120
in financial statements, 12–19
of morale, 308
underestimating, 51
Cost accounting, 50
Cost accounting systems, 50, 111
    absorption costing, 256–265
    activity-based. *See* Activity-based
        costing changes in, 156
    and cost-plus pricing, 337–339
    defined, 50
    job order costing. *See* Job order
        cost systems
    operations costing, 111
    process costing. *See* Process cost
        systems standard, 518–521
    target costing, 335–336
    traditional, 146–154, 162
    variable. *See* Variable costing
Cost-based transfer price, 349–350
Cost behavior analysis, 198–205
    fixed costs in, 199–200
    and identification of variable and
        fixed costs, 205
    mixed costs in, 201–204
    relevant range in, 200–201
    variable costs in, 198–199
Cost centers, 454, 455
Cost control, 350
Cost determination, 4
Cost drivers, 100, 147–150
Cost flows:
    and job order costing, 51–68,
        97–98
    and process costing, 97–99
Costing and costing systems. *See* Cost
    accounting systems
Cost of capital, 554
Cost of goods manufactured, 12–15
Cost of goods manufactured
    schedule, 12, 14–15, 68
Cost of goods purchased, 12
Cost of goods sold, 63, 69, 101, 512
Cost of living adjustments
    (COLAs), 499
Cost of transfer to cost of goods
    sold, 101
Cost of transfer to finished
    goods, 101
Cost of transfer to next
    department, 101
Cost-plus pricing, 66, 337–339
Cost pools:
    and ABC, 150, 155
    activity, 147–148, 150
    allocating overhead to,
        149, 150
    overhead, 147

Cost reconciliation schedule, 108–109, 119–120
Cost structures, 251–252
    and break-even point, 252
    and contribution margin ratio, 252
    and margin of safety ratio, 252
    and operating leverage, 252–255
Cost-volume-profit (CVP) analysis, 206–217, 236–267
    absorption vs. variable costing in, 256–265
    assumptions of, 206
    and break-even analysis, 209–213, 216, 239–240
    and business environment, 241–242
    components of, 206
    computations in, 239–241
    concepts in, 238–239
    cost structure and operating leverage in, 251–255
    margin of safety in, 215–217, 240–241
    and sales mix, 244–251
    and target net income, 213–216, 240
    and variances, 512
Cost-volume-profit (CVP) graph, 211–212, 214–215
Cost-volume-profit (CVP) income statement, 206–209
    and contribution margin per unit, 207–208
    and contribution margin ratio, 208–209
    variances on, 512
Credibility, B-2
Credits:
    from manufacturing costs, 54
    on statement of cash flows worksheet, 608, 609
Credit balance, 69
Creditors, 652, 660
Cruise industry, 546–547
Current assets, 596–597, 661
Current liability, 596–598
Current ratio, 661, 662, 669
Curvilinear relationship (of cost and activity), 200
Customer perspective (balanced scorecard), 513, 514
Customer service, 308
Cutoff rate, 552, 554
CVP analysis. See Cost-volume-profit analysis
CVP graph. See Cost-volume-profit graph
CVP income statement. See Cost-volume-profit income statement

D
Data entry (for job order costing), 67
Days in inventory, 664
Debits:
    from manufacturing costs, 54
    on statement of cash flows worksheet, 608, 609
Debit balance, 69
Debt to total assets ratio, 668, 670
Decentralization, 448
Decision-making process, 294–296
    as capital budgeting consideration, 549
    cases for management decision-making, CA-1–CA-2
    make-or-buy decisions, 292–293, 298–300
    sell-or-process-further decision, 301–304
Defects, 168
Degree of operating leverage, 253
Departmental overhead costs (report), 437
Depreciation, accumulated, 403, 613
Depreciation expense, 595, 619–620
Differential analysis. See Incremental analysis
Direct fixed costs, 455–456
Directing, as management function, 5
Direct labor, 10, 146, 499
Direct labor budget, 395
Direct labor price standard (direct labor rate standard), 499
Direct labor quantity standard (direct labor efficiency standard), 499
Direct labor variances, 506–508
Direct materials, 10, 499
Direct materials budget, 392–393
Direct materials price standard, 498
Direct materials quantity standard, 498–499
Direct materials variances, 503–506
Direct method (statement of cash flows), 592, 615–623
Discontinued operations, 672
Discounts (on selling price), 241
Discounted cash flow techniques:
    comparing, 564
    defined, 551
    internal rate of return method, 562–564
    net present value method, 551–561, 564
Discounting, A-7, 11, 14
Discounting the future amount, A-7
Discount rate, 552, 554
Dividends, 588, 604, 621, 665–666
Documentation, cost system, 98

Dot-com bubble, 650–651
Dunlap, Al "Chainsaw," 308

E
Early warning system, budgeting as, 384
Earned revenues, 594–595
Earnings. See also Retained earnings statements
    quality of, 676–680
    retained, 403, 600, 613, 621
    volatility of, 235–236
Earnings per share (EPS), 666–667, 669
Earning power, 671–676
    and changes in accounting principle, 675
    and comprehensive income, 675
    defined, 671
    and irregular items, 671–676
Economic downturns, 390
Emphasis (of budgeting vs. long-range planning), 387
Employees:
    efficiency of, 508
    evaluations of, 156
    misallocation of, 507, 508
    safety of, 558
    skilled, 204, 508
Ending work in process inventory, 13
Enterprise resource planning (ERP) software systems, 20
EPS (earnings per share), 666–667, 669
Equal Employment Opportunity Act, 496
Equipment:
    on budgeted balance sheet, 403
    disposal of plant assets, 595–596, 619
    incremental analysis for, 304–305
    replacement of, 304–305
    retention of, 304–305
    on statement of cash flows, 600, 612, 621
Equity:
    stockholders', 589, 657, 665–666, 669
    trading on the, 666
Equivalent units of production, 102–105, 115–116
    for conversion costs, 117–118
    FIFO method computation, 115–121
    for materials, 117–118
    for process cost reports, 107
    weighted-average method computation, 102–105
ERP (enterprise resource planning) software systems, 20

Ethics:
  and budgeting, 387
  business, 7–8
  and cash flow from operating
    activities, 599
  and changes in accounting
    principle, 675
  and competence, B-1
  and confidentiality, B-1–B-2
  and conflict resolution, B-2
  and credibility, B-2
  in determining equivalent
    units, 103
  and documentation, 55
  and fees, 18
  and IMA, B-1–B-2
  and incentives, 8
  and integrity, B-2
  and make-or-buy decisions, 299
  principles of, B-1
  and quality of net reported
    income, 588
  and standards, 497, B-1–B-2
  and taxes, 352
  of transferring profits, 352
Eurich, Beecher, 94, 95
Evaluation process (capital
  budgeting), 548–549
Excess capacity, 347–348
Exotic Newcastle Disease, 446
Expected input and output, service
  revenue from, 405
Expenses:
  in accrual accounting, 595
  depreciation, 595, 619–620
  operating, 619, 677
  prepaid, 597, 612
  selling and administrative, 356,
    396, 437, 438
External sales, 334–341
  cost-plus pricing for, 337–339
  and target costing, 335–336
  time-and-material pricing for,
    341–344
  variable-cost pricing for,
    339–340
Extraordinary items, 673–674

F
Facility-level activities, 160, 161
Factory labor costs:
  accumulating, 53
  assigning, 57–58, 100
Factory overhead. *See* Manufacturing
  overhead
Fair Labor Standards Act, 496
FASB (Financial Accounting
  Standards Board), 592
Favorable variances, 502, 512
Feedback, 450

FIFO method. *See* First-in, first-out
  method
Financial accounting, 4, 5
Financial Accounting Standards
  Board (FASB), 592
Financial budgets, 388, 399–404
  and budgeted balance sheet,
    402–403
  cash budget, 399–402, 404
Financial calculators, A-16–A-18
  applications of, A-18
  and compounding period, A-17
  keys on, A-16
  minus signs on, A-17
  plus signs on, A-17
  present value function on,
    A-16–A-17
  rounding on, A-17
Financial information, 294
Financial measures, 514
Financial perspective (balanced
  scorecard), 513, 514
Financial statement(s). *See also*
  specific statements
  cost of goods manufactured, 12–15
  cost of goods manufactured
    schedule, 12, 14–15, 68
  job cost data on, 68–71
  management's responsibility for, 8
  manufacturing costs reflected in,
    12–19
  standard costs and variances
    on, 512
Financial statement analysis,
  650–683
  of earning power, 671–676
  horizontal analysis, 653–656
  irregular items, 671–676
  need for, 652
  quality of earnings, 676–680
  ratio analysis, 659–671
  tools for, 652–653
  vertical analysis, 657–659
Financing activities, 588–590
  in direct method, 620–621
  in indirect method, 600–601
  net cash provided by, 600–601,
    620–621
Financing section (cash budget), 400
Finished goods:
  assigning costs to, 62–63
  transfer to, 101
Finished goods inventory, 62, 403
First-in, first-out (FIFO) method,
  115–121
  and cost reconciliation schedule,
    119–120
  and equivalent units of production,
    115–118
  and physical unit flow, 116–117

  and production cost report,
    120, 121
  and unit production costs, 118–119
  weighted-average method vs., 120
Fixed assets, 604
Fixed costs:
  in break-even analysis, 211
  computing, with high-low method,
    203–204
  and controllable margin, 460
  in cost behavior analysis, 199–200
  on CVP graph, 212
  in flexible budgets, 442–444
  identifying, with cost behavior
    analysis, 205
  in incremental analysis, 296, 297
  overhead, 395–396
  per unit, 339
  in responsibility accounting,
    455–456
  static budget for, 438
Flexible budget(s), 438–447, 451
  budgetary control with, 438–447
  and budget reforecasting, 446
  case study, 442–445
  for cost centers, 455
  development of, 440–441
  performance evaluations with,
    445–446
  reasons to use, 439–440
Flexible budget reports, 445–447
Flexible manufacturing, 451
Flowcharts, activity, 157–158
Forecasts:
  budget reforecasting, 446
  sales, 385–386, 389, 510
Fragrance manufacturers, 250
Franchising, 435
Fraud, 601, 660
Free cash flows, 604–606
Free-shipping subscriptions, 300
Full costing. *See* Absorption costing
Full-cost pricing, 339–340, 355
Full disclosure principle, 590
Future value:
  of annuities, A-4–A-6
  of single amounts, A-2–A-4

G
Gains, unrealized, 675
Generally accepted accounting
  practices (GAAP), 676, 677
  and absorption-cost pricing, 355
  and accrual accounting, 594
  net income measured under, 262
Globalization, 351–352
Global Responsibility Report, 510
Government budgets, 390, 405–406
Graham, Benjamin, 650
Growth, 196–197, 345

H

Herold, Cameron, 434–435
High-inventory turnover, 664
High-low method, 203–204
Horizontal (trend) analysis, 653–656
    of balance sheets, 654
    of income statements, 655
    of retained earnings statements,
        655–656
Hourly fees, 344
"House" (television show), 441
Hsieh, Tony, 332, 333
Human behavior. *See* Behavior
Hurdle rate, 552, 554

I

Ideal standards, 497
IMA. *See* Institute of Management
    Accountants
IMA *Statement of Ethical
    Professional Practice*, 8,
    B-1–B-2
Incentives, 8
Income. *See also* Net income
    comprehensive, 675
    from discontinued operations, 672
    pro forma, 676–677
    residual, 465–467
    target net, 213–216, 240
Income (margin) measure, 458
Income statement(s), 12–13, 437, 592
    budgeted, 396–399
    CVP, 206–209, 512
    horizontal analysis of, 655
    in job order costing, 68
    operating activities on, 589–590,
        616
    statement of cash flows vs., 588
    variances disclosed on, 512
    vertical analysis of, 657–659
Income tax payable, 598,
    612–613, 620
Incremental analysis, 292–311
    and activity-based costing,
        308–309
    approach used in, 294–296
    defined, 294
    for elimination of unprofitable
        segments, 305–307
    for equipment retention/
        replacement, 304–305
    for make-or-buy decision, 298–300
    for outsourcing, 351
    qualitative factors in, 308
    for sell-or-process-further decision,
        301–304
    with special orders, 296–297
    types of, 296–307
    in virtual companies, 351
Incremental overhead costs, 308

Independence (of capital projects),
    549
Independent internal verification,
    601, 660
Indirect fixed costs, 456
Indirect labor, 10
Indirect manufacturing costs. *See*
    Manufacturing overhead
Indirect materials, 10
Indirect method (statement of cash
    flows), 592–603, 608–615
    direct method vs., 592
    investing and financing activities,
        cash from, 600–601
    and net change in cash, 601–602
    operating activities, net cash from,
        594–599
    worksheets for, 608–615
Industry averages, 652, 659
In process inventories, 168
Institute of Management Accountants
    (IMA), 8, 46, B-1–B-2
Intangible benefits (net present value
    method), 557–558
Integrity, B-2
Intercompany comparisons,
    652, 653, 659
Interest, A-1–A-4
    cash payments for, 620
    compound, A-2–A-4
    simple, A-1
Interest coverage (times interest
    earned), 668–670
Interest rates, A-1
Internal audit staff, 7
Internal controls, 8, 55
Internal process perspective
    (balanced scorecard), 513, 514
Internal rate of return (IRR),
    562–564
Internal rate of return method,
    562–565
    advantages of, 565
    decision rule for, 563, 565
    net present value method vs., 564
Internal sales, 345–354. *See also*
    Transfer pricing
Internet, 211, 242
Intracompany comparisons,
    652, 653, 659
Inventoriable costs. *See* Product
    cost(s)
Inventory(-ies):
    beginning work in process, 13
    days in, 664
    in direct materials budgets, 392
    ending work in process, 13
    finished goods, 62, 403
    of merchandising and
        manufacturing companies, 15–16

and net income, 597
    perpetual inventory systems, 50
    in process, 168
    product costs as, 11
    in production budgets, 390–391
    raw materials, 52–53, 403
    on statement of cash flows
        worksheet, 611–612
    work in process, 54–55, 61
Inventory methods:
    just-in-time, 20
    periodic, 12, 13
    perpetual, 50
Inventory turnover, 663–664, 669
    formula for, 669
    high, 664
Investing activities, 588–590
    in direct method, 620–621
    in indirect method, 600–601
    net cash provided by, 600–601,
        620–621
Investment(s):
    and interest, A-2
    short-term, 661–662
Investment centers, 454, 458–462
iPhones, 57
IRR (internal rate of return),
    562–564
Irregular items, 671–676
    discontinued operations, 672
    and earning power, 671–676
    extraordinary items, 673–674

J

Japan, 153
JIT (just-in-time) inventory method,
    20
JIT (just-in-time) processing,
    166–168
Jobs:
    in job order cost systems, 50
    in time-and-materials pricing,
        342–343
Job cost sheets, 54–55
Job order cost systems, 48–74, 111
    accumulating costs in, 51–54, 64
    advantages and disadvantages of,
        67–68
    assigning costs in, 54–58,
        62–64, 67
    and cost accounting systems,
        50–51
    features of, 50
    flow of costs in, 51–68
    in Greetings, Inc. case study, CA-1
    journal entries in, 518–520
    ledger accounts in, 520
    manufacturing costs, 52–62
    manufacturing overhead costs,
        58–62

process costing vs., 50–51, 96–98
recording of costs in, 50
reporting job cost data, 68–71
for service companies, 65–67
standard cost, 518–521
Joint costs, 302–303
Joint products, 302–303
Journal entries, 99–102, 518–520
Just-in-case philosophy, 166
Just-in-time (JIT) inventory
    method, 20
Just-in-time (JIT) processing,
    166–168

L
Labor:
    direct, 10, 146, 395, 499
    indirect, 10
    and variable costs, 199
Labor costs:
    direct, 146, 499
    factory, 53, 57–58, 100
    in time-and-material pricing,
        341–342
Labor price variances (LPVs),
    506–508
Labor quantity variances, 506–508
Labor reports, 437
Labor variances, 503, 506–508
Land, 600, 612, 620
Leadership in Energy and
    Efficient Design (LEED)
    Certification, 144
Lean manufacturing, 19, 204
Learning and growth perspective
    (balanced scorecard),
    513, 514
Ledgers, 54, 520
LEED (Leadership in Energy
    and Efficient Design)
    Certification, 144
Leverage, 666
Leveraging, 666
Liability(-ies):
    current, 596–598
    long-term, 589
    noncurrent, 600–601, 620–621
    total, 657
Limited resources, 248–251, 559
Lin, Alfred, 332, 333
Linear cost assumption, 200, 201
Line positions, 6
Linkages (in balanced scorecard
    approach), 514, 515
Liquidity, 652
    of borrower, 652
    of cash, 661–662
    immediate, 662
    of receivables, 662–663
    short-term, 661–662

Liquidity ratios, 660–664
    acid-test ratio, 661–662
    average collection period, 663
    current ratio, 661, 662
    days in inventory, 664
    inventory turnover, 663–664
    receivables turnover, 662–663
    summary of, 669
Loans, 652, A-18
Long-range planning, 387
Long-term assets, 589
Long-term creditors, 652
Long-term liabilities, 589
Long term notes, A-11–A-13
Losses:
    from discontinued operations, 672
    unrealized, 675
Low-volume enterprises, 664
LPVs (labor price variances),
    506–508
Ludgon, Duane, 49
Luxury goods, 6

M
Machine hours, 60, 100, 146
Machine time used, 100
Make-or-buy decision:
    incremental analysis for, 298–300
    opportunity cost in, 299
    and outsourcing, 292–293
Management (managers):
    awareness of operations, 384
    decision making process of,
        294–296
    decisions of, 155
    and financial statements, 8
    functions of, 4–6
    in participative budgeting, 386–387
    usefulness of ABC for, 164
Management, activity-based, 157–159
Management by exception, 449–450
Managerial accounting, 4–9
    activities of, 4
    current trends in, 19–25
    defined, 4
    financial accounting vs., 4, 5
Manufacturing, 9
    automated factories in, 11
    flexible, 451
    lean, 6, 19
    merchandising vs., 9
Manufacturing companies:
    deciding to move, 307
    financial statements for, 12, 15–16
    outsourcing by, 292–293
Manufacturing costs, 9–18. See also
    Manufacturing overhead
    accumulating, 51–54, 64, 97
    assigning. See Assigning
        manufacturing costs

calculating, for absorption-cost
    pricing, 356
direct labor, 10
direct materials, 10
in financial statements, 12–19
in job order costing, 52–62, 97
in process costing, 97, 99–102
in static budget, 438
total, 13, 108
Manufacturing costs incurred in the
    prior period, 13
Manufacturing overhead, 10
    accumulating costs of, 53–54
    assigning costs of, 58–61, 101
    over-/underapplied, 69–71
    standard rate per unit, 500
    in year-end balance, 69–71
Manufacturing overhead budget,
    395–396
Manufacturing overhead variances,
    508–511
Margin (income) measure, 458
Margin of safety, 215–216, 240–241
Margin of safety ratio, 215, 241
Market-based transfer price, 350–351
Market niche, 335
Market positioning, 561
Markup, 337–338
    for absorption-cost pricing, 356
    and competitive advantage, 340
    for variable-cost pricing, 358
Master budgets, 387–388, 393–394,
    437–438
Material(s). See also Raw materials
    direct, 10, 499
    equivalent units of production,
        117–118
    indirect, 10
    pricing, 341–344
Materiality, 450
Material loading charge, 341–343
Materials price variance (MPV),
    503–505
Materials quantity variance, 503–505
Materials requisition slips, 55–57, 99
Materials variances, 503–506
Matrix, variance analysis,
    504, 505, 508
MBA calculators. See Financial
    calculators
Merchandise purchases budget,
    404–405
Merchandisers, 404–405
Merchandising, 9
Merchandising companies, 12, 15–16
Minimum rate of return, 466
Minimum transfer price, 346–348
Minus signs (in time value of money
    problems), A-17
Misallocation of workers, 507, 508

Mixed costs, 201–204
Money, time value of. *See* Time value
    of money
Morale, cost of, 308
Mortgage loans, calculating, A-18
Motivation, 384, 451
Movie industry, 461
MPV (materials price variance),
    503–505
Mutually exclusive projects, 559–560

N
Negotiated transfer prices, 346–349
    with excess capacity, 347–348
    with no excess capacity, 346–347
    variable costs in, 348
Net annual cash flow, 550
Net cash:
    from financing activities, 600–601,
        620–621
    from investing activities, 600–601,
        620–621
    net income vs., 590
    from operating activities, 588,
        594–601, 604, 616–620
Net change in cash, 601–602, 621
Net income, 590
    and absorption vs. variable
        costing, 259, 261–264
    and contribution margin, 245
    net cash vs., 590
    as percentage of sales dollars, 659
    as performance measure, 588
    per share, 667
    and sell-or-process-further
        decisions, 301
    on statement of cash flows,
        592–595
    target, 213–216, 240
    and unprofitable segments/
        products, 305–306
Net present value (NPV), 552
Net present value method, 551–561
    assumptions of, 555
    for equal annual cash flows,
        552–553
    example, 556
    intangible benefits in, 557–558
    internal rate of return method
        vs., 564
    with mutually exclusive projects,
        559–560
    and post-auditing, 561
    and risk analysis, 560
    for unequal annual cash flows, 553
No excess capacity, 346–347
Noncash activities:
    changes of, 596–598
    on statement of cash flows, 590
Noncontrollable costs, 449, 456

Noncurrent assets, 600–601, 620–621
Noncurrent liabilities, 600–601,
    620–621
Nonfinancial information, 294
Nonfinancial measures, 513–515
Nonmanufacturing companies,
    404–407
    merchandisers, 404–405
    not-for-profit organizations,
        405–406
    service enterprises, 405
Non-recurring charges, 674
Non-value-added activities, 157–158
Normal capacity, 500
Normal range, 200–201
Normal standards, 497
Notes (on statements of cash
    flow), 590
Notes, long-term, A-11–A-13
Not-for-profit organizations, 405–406
NPV (net present value), 552. *See
    also* Net present value method

O
Olympic Games, 402
Onward (Howard Schultz), 495
Open Standards Benchmarking
    Collaborative, 498
Operating activities, 588–590
    in direct method, 616–620
    in indirect method, 594–599
    net cash provided by, 588,
        594–599, 604, 616–620
Operating assets, 458, 460
Operating budgets, 389–399
    and budgeted income statement,
        396–399
    defined, 387–388
    direct labor budget, 395
    direct materials budget, 392–393
    manufacturing overhead budget,
        395–396
    preparation of, 389–399
    production budget, 390–391
    sales budget, 389–390
    selling and administrative expense
        budget, 396
Operating expenses, 619, 677
Operating leverage, 252–255
Operations costing, 111
Opportunity costs, 295
    in make-or-buy decision, 299
    and no excess capacity, 346–347
Optimism, budgetary, 390
Orders:
    accepting, at special prices, 296–297
    incremental analysis for, 296–297
Ordinary items, 673
Organizational structure, 6–7, 384
Organization charts, 6, 7

Outsourcing:
    and cost structure, 251
    by manufacturers, 292–293
    and transfer pricing, 351
Overapplied overhead, 69–71
Overhead. *See also* Manufacturing
    overhead
    assigning, to products, 149,
        151–153
    departmental overhead costs, 437
    and direct labor, 146
    inefficient use of, 509–510
    in job order costing, 67–68
    manufacturing overhead budget,
        395–396
    overapplied and underapplied,
        69–71
Overhead controllable variance, 509,
    521–522
Overhead costs:
    and ABC, 155
    assigning, to products, 151–152
    departmental, 437
    incremental, 308
    in service industries, 161, 163–164
Overhead cost pools, 148, 149
Overhead rates:
    activity-based, 149–151
    computing, 149–151
    predetermined, 59–60, 64, 146,
        499–500
Overhead variance, 508–511,
    521–523
Overhead volume variance,
    509, 522–523
Overspending, 406

P
Participative budgeting, 386–387
Payback period, 550, 551
Payments:
    cash, 617–619
    schedule of expected, 400, 401
Payout ratio, 667–669
P-E (price-earnings ratio), 667, 669
People, planet, profit. *See* Triple
    bottom line
Percentage change (in vertical
    analysis), 657
Percentage of sales dollars, net
    income as, 659
Performance, fees based on, 344
Performance evaluation, 449–451,
    461–462
    with flexible budgets, 445–446
    principles of, 449–451
    and residual income, 465–467
    with static budgets, 438–440
Performance measures, 20–21,
    120, 457

Period costs, 11
Periodic inventory system, 12, 13
Perpetual inventory systems, 50
Pharmaceutical industry, 334
Physical unit(s), 106–107
   and FIFO method, 116–117
   in process costing, 106–107,
    116–117
Planning. *See also* Budgetary
   planning
   and budgeting, 384
   as management function, 5
Plant assets, disposal of, 595–596, 619
Plus signs (in time value of money
   problems), A-17
Post-audits, 561
Practical range, 200–201
Predetermined overhead rates,
   59–60, 64, 146, 499–500
Preferred dividends, 665–666
Preferred stock, 665–666
Prenumbering, 55
Prepaid expenses, 597, 612
Present value, A-7. *See also* Net
   present value method
   of annuities, A-9–A-11, 17
   calculator functions for, A-13, 15
   in capital budgeting decisions,
    A-14–A-15
   of long-term notes/bonds, A-11–A-13
   of single amounts, A-7–A-9
   of single sums, A-16–A-17
   variables affecting, A-7
Present value (PV) key, A-13, 15
Price-earnings (P-E) ratio, 667, 669
Price takers, 334
Pricing, 332–360
   absorption-cost, 355–357
   in competitive markets, 334–335
   in corporate strategy, 335
   cost-plus costing, 66, 337–339
   and equivalent units
    computations, 120
   for external sales, 334–341
   full-cost, 339–340, 355
   for internal sales, 345–351
   for services, 341–344
   target costing, 335–336
   time-and-material, 341–344
   transfer. *See* Transfer pricing
   variable-cost, 339–341, 357–359
Principal, A-1
Process cost systems, 50–51, 94–123
   assigning manufacturing costs in,
    99–102
   cost reconciliation schedule,
    preparation of, 108–109
   equivalent units of production,
    computation of, 102–105, 107,
    115–120

   and flow of costs, 99
   job order costing vs., 50–51, 96–98
   operations costing, 111
   physical unit flow, computation of,
    106–107
   preparing production cost report,
    109–110
   and production cost report,
    105–109
   for service companies, 97
   unit production costs,
    computation of, 107–108
   uses of, 96
Product cost(s), 10
   as inventory, 11
   in manufacturing costs, 17
   overhead as, 151–152
   period costs vs., 11
   for service industries, 18–19
Production budget, 390–391
Production cost reports:
   and FIFO method, 120, 121
   in process costing, 105–110,
    120, 121
Production department, 505,
   508–510
Product-level activities, 159–161
Profitability, 652
   of capital expenditure, 564
   of capital projects, 551
   and growth, 196–197
   and standard costs, 501
Profitability index, 559–560
Profitability ratios, 660, 664–668
   asset turnover, 664–665
   earnings per share, 666–667
   payout ratio, 667–668
   price-earnings ratio, 667
   profit margin, 664
   return on assets, 665
   return on common stockholders'
    equity, 665–666
   summary of, 669
Profit centers, 454–457
Profit margin, 664, 669
Pro forma income, 676–677
Proportions, 659
"Pull approach," 167
Purchasing department, 504, 505
"Push approach," 166
PV (present value) key, A-13, 15

Q

Quality of earnings, 676–680
   alternative accounting methods
    for, 676
   improper recognition of, 677
   and pro forma income,
    676–677
Quick ratios, 661–662, 669

R

Railroads, 259
Rates, 659
Rate of return on sales. *See* Profit
   margin
Ratio(s), 659
   acid-test, 661–662, 669
   asset turnover, 664–665, 669
   average collection period, 663
   current, 661, 662, 669
   days in inventory, 664
   debt to total assets ratio, 668, 670
   earnings per share, 666–667
   inventory turnover, 663–664, 669
   liquidity, 660–664, 669
   margin of safety, 215, 241
   payout, 667–669
   price-earnings, 667, 669
   profitability, 660, 664–669
   profit margin, 664
   quick, 661–662, 669
   receivables turnover, 662–663, 669
   return on assets, 665
   return on common stockholders'
    equity, 665–666
   solvency, 660, 668–670
   summary of, 669–670
   times interest earned, 668–669
   working capital, 661
Ratio analysis, 652, 659–671
   with liquidity ratios, 660–664
   with profitability ratios, 664–668
   with solvency ratios, 668–669
Raw materials, 10
   accumulating costs of, 52–53
   assigning costs of, 55–57, 99–100
   in direct materials standards, 498
   stockpiling, 393
Raw materials inventory, 52–53, 403
Receivables, liquidity of, 662–663
Receivables turnover, 662–663, 669
Recessions, 204, 344
Reconciliation method. *See* Indirect
   method (statement of cash
   flows)
Reconciling items, 608–613
Regional banking industry, 513
Regression analysis, 204
Regulations, 496. *See also* Standards
Relevant costs, 295, 297, 298, 305
Relevant range:
   of activity index, 201
   in cost behavior analysis, 200–201
Remanufactured goods, 104
Reporting:
   determining costs vs., 4
   performance evaluation, 451
Required rate of return, 552, 554
Research (for effective budgeting),
   384–385

Residual income, 465–467
Resources:
    activity level and control/use of,
        160–161
    ERP software systems, 20
    limited, 248–251, 559
Responsibility accounting,
        447–464. *See also*
        Responsibility centers
    budgeting vs., 448
    and collaboration, 449
    conditions for, 447–448
    with controllable vs.
        noncontrollable revenues
        and costs, 449
    performance evaluation in,
        449–451
    reporting system for, 451–454
Responsibility centers, 454–464
    behavior affecting, 450–451
    cost centers, 454, 455
    investment centers, 458–462
    profit centers, 454–457
Responsibility reporting system,
        451–454
    for investment centers, 458
    for profit centers, 456–457
Restructuring charges, 674
Retained earnings:
    on budgeted balance sheet, 403
    on statement of cash flows,
        600, 613, 621
Retained earnings statements:
    horizontal analysis of, 655–656
    statement of cash flows vs., 588
Return on assets, 665, 669
Return on common stockholders'
        equity, 665–666, 669
Return on investment (ROI), 458
    and absorption-cost pricing,
        356–357
    and cost-plus pricing, 338–339
    disadvantage of, 465
    improvement of, 459–460
    judgmental factors in, 458–459
    for movie industry, 461
    with positive or zero net present
        value, 552
    residual income vs., 465–466
    and variable-cost pricing, 359
Revenues:
    controllable, 449, 456, 457
    earned, 594–595
    service, 405
Risk (in capital budgeting), 549
Risk analysis, 560
ROI. *See* Return on investment
Rolling Stones, 215, 234
Rounding, A-17

S
Safety:
    employee, 558
    margin of, 215–216, 240–241
Sales:
    and controllable margin, 460
    on CVP graph, 212
    external, 334–341
    internal, 345–354. *See also*
        Transfer pricing and margin
        of safety, 240
Sales budgets, 389–390
Sales department, 509, 510
Sales dollars:
    break-even point in, 210, 246–247
    for target net income, 214
Sales forecasts, 385–386, 389, 510
Sales mix, 244–251
    and break-even analysis, 244–248
    defined, 244
    with limited resources, 248–251
Sales reports, 437
Sales units:
    break-even point in, 210–211,
        244–245
    for target net income, 213–214
Sarbanes-Oxley Act (SOX), 8
Schedules:
    cost of goods manufactured,
        12, 14–15, 68
    cost reconciliation, 108–109,
        119–120
    of expected payments and
        collections, 400, 401
    for statements of cash flows,
        590, 620
Schultz, Howard, 494–495
Scrap reports, 437
Scudamore, Brian, 434
Securities, available-for-sale, 675
Securities and Exchange
        Commission (SEC), 677
Selling and administrative expenses,
        356, 396, 438
Selling and administrative expense
        budget, 396
Selling expenses report, 437
Selling price. *See also* Target selling
        price
    discounts on, 241
    unit, 210
Sell-or-process-further decision,
        301–304
    for multiple products, 302–303
    for single products, 301
Sensitivity analysis, 560
Service companies:
    activity-based costing in, 156,
        161–165
    airline baggage handling costs, 153

balanced scorecard approach
        in, 513
    break-even and margin of safety
        in, 211, 215
    budgetary optimism in, 390
    budgeting in, 402, 405, 406,
        441, 446
    contribution margin in, 247
    credit card companies, 296
    fees of, 344
    free-shipping subscriptions, 300
    job order costing for, 65–67
    operating leverage of, 253
    pricing, 344
    process costing for, 97
    product costing for, 18–19
    standard costs in, 496
    traditional costing in, 162
Service contracts, 67
Short-term creditors, 652, 660
Short-term liquidity, 661–662
Significant variances, 511
Simple interest, A-1
Single amount:
    future value of, A-2–A-4
    present value of, A-7–A-9
Single sum:
    discounting, A-14
    present value of, A-16–A-17
Skilled workers, 204, 508
Small businesses, 385
Social responsibility, corporate,
        21, 510
Solvency, 652
Solvency ratios, 660, 668–669
    debt to total assets ratio, 668
    summary of, 670
    times interest earned, 668–669
SOX (Sarbanes-Oxley Act), 8
Spending variance, 509
Split-off point, 302
Staff positions, 6, 7
Standards:
    budgets vs., 496
    need for, 496
    normal vs. ideal, 497
Standard costs, 496–512
    advantages of, 496
    controlling costs with, 501
    defined, 496
    direct labor standards, 499
    and direct labor variances, 506–508
    direct materials standards, 498–499
    and direct materials variances,
        503–506
    on financial statements, 512
    ideal vs. normal standards, 497
    manufacturing overhead, 499–500
    and manufacturing overhead
        variances, 508–511

and reporting variances, 511
setting, 496–501
and statement presentation of
    variances, 512
total standard cost per unit, 500
in total variance, 503
variances affecting, 502–505
Standard cost, job order cost
    accounting system, 518–521
    journal entries, 518–520
    ledger accounts, 520
Standard direct labor cost per
    unit, 499
Standard direct materials cost per
    unit, 499
Standard hours allowed, 509, 521
Standard manufacturing overhead
    rate per unit, 500
Standards of Ethical Professional
    Practice, B-1–B-2
Standard predetermined overhead
    rate, 499–500
Statement of cash flows, 586–626
    activity classifications in, 588–592
    balance sheet vs., 588, 601–602
    for company evaluation, 604–606
    direct method, 592, 615–623
    format of, 590–591
    and free cash flows, 604–606
    income statements vs., 588
    indirect method, 592–603, 608–615
    noncash activities on, 590
    preparation of, 592–603
    retained earnings statements
        vs., 588
    T-account method, 624–626
    usefulness of, 588
    worksheets for preparing, 608–615
Static budget(s), 437–440. See also
    Master budgets
Static budget reports, 437–438
Stock(s). See also Common stock
    issuance of, for cash, 600
    preferred, 665–666
    on statement of cash flows,
        613, 621
Stockholders, 6, 652
Stockholders' equity, 589, 657,
    665–666, 669
Stockpiling of raw materials, 393
Subsidiary ledger, 54
Sunk costs, 295, 302, 305
Supplementary schedules, 590
Suppliers:
    cash payments to, 618–619
    CVP analysis and price changes
        from, 242
    dependability of, 168
Sustainable business practices, 21
Swinmum, Nick, 332

T
T-account approach (statement of
    cash flows), 624–626
Target costs, 335–336
Target net income, 213–216, 240
Target selling price, 337–338,
    340–341
    for absorption-cost pricing, 356
    for variable-cost pricing, 358
Taxes:
    global differences in rates, 351–352
    income tax payable, 598,
        612–613, 620
Telecommunications companies, 18
Theory of constraints, 20, 249
Thill, Dave, 44, 89, 540
Thrune, Rick, 44, 141
Tilton, Glenn, 515
Tilton, Lynn, 48, 49
Time (in time value of money), A-1
Time-and-material pricing, 341–344
Time periods:
    average collection, 663
    base, 653–654
    budget, 385
    for budgeting vs. long-range
        planning, 387
    compounding, A-3, 17
    and discounting, A-11
    payback, 550, 551
    in process cost systems, 51
Times interest earned, 668–670
Time tickets, 57–58
Time value of money, A-1–A-19
    and capital budgeting, 551
    future value of an annuity, A-4–A-6
    future value of a single amount,
        A-2–A-4
    and incremental analysis, 296
    and interest, A-1–A-2
    present values, A-7–A-16
    and use of financial calculators,
        A-16–A-18
TLV (total labor variance), 506
TMV (total materials variance), 503
Total assets, 668, 670
Total costs (on CVP graph), 212
Total costs accounted for, 109
Total cost of work in process, 13
Total costs to be accounted for, 109
Total labor variance (TLV), 506
Total liabilities, 657
Total manufacturing costs, 13, 108
Total materials variance (TMV), 503
Total overhead variance, 508–509
Total quality management (TQM)
    systems, 20, 168
Total standard cost per unit, 500
Total units accounted for, 106
Total units to be accounted for, 106

Total variance, 502–503
TQM (total quality management)
    systems, 20, 168
Traceable costs. See Fixed costs
Trading on the equity, 666
Traditional costing:
    activity-based costing vs., 146–154
    in service industries, 162
    unit costs under, 152
Transfer prices, 345
Transfer pricing, 345
    abuse of, 352
    cost-based, 349–350
    in global environment, 351–352
    in Greetings, Inc. case study, CA-1
    market-based, 350–351
    negotiated, 346–349
    and outsourcing, 351
    tax rates affecting, 351–352
Treasurer, 7
Trend analysis. See Horizontal
    analysis
Trend forecasting, 561
Triple bottom line (people, planet,
    profit):
    corporate social responsibility, 21
    remanufactured goods, 104
    at Starbucks, 510
    vertical farming, 200
Turnover:
    asset, 664–665, 669
    high-inventory, 664
    inventory, 663–664, 669
    receivables, 662–663, 669

U
Underapplied overhead, 69–71
Underestimating costs, 51
Unfavorable variances, 502, 512
Unionized workers, 507
Units completed, costing for, 109
Unit conversion cost, 108
Unit costs:
    with activity-based costing,
        152–153
    calculating, for variable-cost
        pricing, 357–358
    in job order and process cost
        systems, 98
    with traditional costing, 152
Units in process, costing for, 109
Unit-level activities, 159, 160
Unit materials cost, 108
Unit production costs:
    defined, 107
    with FIFO method, 118–119
    in process costing, 107–108,
        118–119
Unit selling prices, 210
Units started and completed, 115

Unit variable costs, 210
Unprofitable segments, 305–307
Unrealized gains and losses, 675
Unskilled workers, 508

V
Value(s), 5
    adding, 5, 157
    book, 305
    future, A-2–A-6
    measurement of, 5
    net present, 552
    present, A-7–A-17
    time value of money, A-1–A-19
Value-added activities, 157
Value chain, 19–20
Value investing, 650–651
Variable cost(s):
    computing, with high-low method,
        203–204
    and controllable margin, 460
    in cost behavior analysis,
        198–199, 205
    on CVP graph, 212
    in flexible budgets, 442–444
    in incremental analysis, 296, 297
    in negotiated transfer pricing, 348
    overhead, 395–396
    unit, 210

Variable costing. *See also specific
        topics*, e.g.: Job costing
    absorption costing vs., 256–265
    deciding when to use, 262–264
    defined, 256
    example of, 258–262
    potential advantages of, 264–265
Variable cost per unit, 203
Variable-cost pricing, 339–341,
        357–359
Variances:
    controllable, 509, 521–522
    disclosing, 512
    favorable, 502, 512
    labor, 503, 506–508
    and management by exception, 511
    materials, 503–506
    overhead, 508–511, 521–523
    reporting, 511
    spending, 509
    in standard cost accounting
        systems, 518–520
    total, 502–503
    unfavorable, 502, 512
Vertical (common-size) analysis,
        652, 657–659
    of balance sheets, 657
    of income statements, 657–659
Vertical farming, 200

Vertical growth, 345
Vice president of operations, 7
Virtual companies, 351
Volatility (of earnings), 235–236
Volume-based cost allocation, 160

W
Wages, 507
Weighted-average contribution
        margin, 244–247
Weighted-average method, 102–105,
        120
Welch, Deb, 44, 540
Wireless service providers, 554
Work force (for JIT), 168
Working capital, 661
Working capital ratio, 661
Work in process accounts, 98
Work in process inventory, 54–55, 61
Worksheets (for indirect method),
        608–615
Write-offs, 660

Y
Year-end balance, 69

RAPID REVIEW
Chapter Content

MANAGERIAL ACCOUNTING (Chapter 1)

Characteristics of Managerial Accounting

Primary users	Internal users
Reports	Internal reports issued as needed
Purpose	Special purpose for a particular user
Content	Pertains to subunits, may be detailed, use of relevant data
Verification	No independent audits

Types of Manufacturing Costs

Direct materials	Raw materials directly associated with finished product
Direct labor	Work of employees directly associated with turning raw materials into finished product
Manufacturing overhead	Costs indirectly associated with manufacture of finished product

JOB ORDER AND PROCESS COSTING (Chapters 2 and 3)

Types of Accounting Systems

Job order	Costs are assigned to each unit or each batch of goods
Process cost	Costs are applied to similar products that are mass-produced in a continuous fashion

Job Order and Process Cost Flow

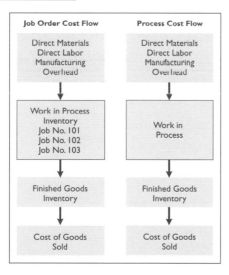

ACTIVITY-BASED COSTING (Chapter 4)

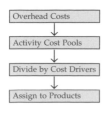

Activity-based costing involves the following four steps:
1. Identify and classify the major activities involved in the manufacture of specific products, and allocate the manufacturing overhead costs to the appropriate cost pools.
2. Identify the cost driver that has a strong correlation to the costs accumulated in the cost pool.
3. Compute the overhead rate for each cost driver.
4. Assign manufacturing overhead costs for each cost pool to products, using the overhead rates (cost per driver).

COST-VOLUME-PROFIT (Chapters 5 and 6)

Types of Costs

Variable costs	Vary in total directly and proportionally with changes in activity level
Fixed costs	Remain the same in total regardless of change in activity level
Mixed costs	Contain both a fixed and a variable element

CVP Income Statement Format

	Total	Per Unit
Sales	\$xx	\$xx
Variable costs	xx	xx
Contribution margin	xx	\$xx
Fixed costs	xx	
Net income	\$xx	

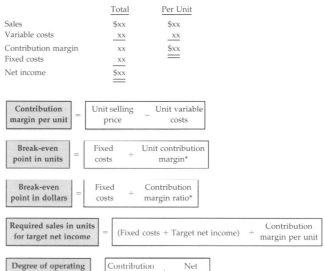

*For multiple products, use weighted-average.

INCREMENTAL ANALYSIS (Chapter 7)

1. Identify the relevant costs associated with each alternative. **Relevant costs** are those costs and revenues that differ across alternatives. Choose the alternative that maximizes net income.
2. **Opportunity costs** are those benefits that are given up when one alternative is chosen instead of another one. Opportunity costs are relevant costs.
3. **Sunk costs** have already been incurred and will not be changed or avoided by any future decision. Sunk costs are not relevant costs.

PRICING (Chapter 8)

External Pricing

Transfer Pricing

Minimum transfer price	=	Variable cost + Opportunity cost

RAPID REVIEW
Chapter Content

BUDGETS (Chapter 9)

Components of the Master Budget

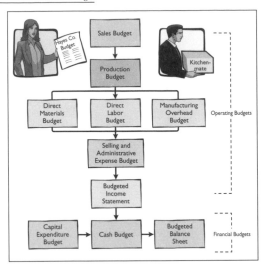

RESPONSIBILITY ACCOUNTING (Chapter 10)

Types of Responsibility Centers

Cost	Profit	Investment
Expenses only	Expenses and Revenues	Expenses and Revenues and ROI

Return on Investment

$$\text{Return on investment (ROI)} = \frac{\text{Investment center controllable margin}}{\text{Average investment center operating assets}}$$

STANDARD COSTS (Chapter 11)

Standard Cost Variances

$$\text{Total materials variance} = \text{Materials price variance} + \text{Materials quantity variance}$$

$$\text{Total labor variance} = \text{Labor price variance} + \text{Labor quantity variance}$$

$$\text{Total overhead variance} = \text{Overhead controllable variance} + \text{Overhead volume variance}$$

Balanced Scorecard

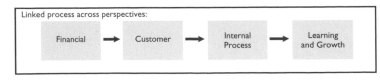

Linked process across perspectives:

Financial → Customer → Internal Process → Learning and Growth

---

Materials price variance $= (AQ \times AP) - (AQ \times SP)$

Materials quantity variance $= (AQ \times SP) - (SQ \times SP)$

Labor price variance $= (AH \times AR) - (AH \times SR)$

Labor quantity variance $= (AH \times SR) - (SH \times SR)$

* Overhead controllable variance $=$ Actual overhead $-$ Overhead budgeted

* Overhead volume variance $=$ Fixed overhead rate $\times$ (Normal capacity $-$ Standard hours allowed)

*Appendix coverage

CAPITAL BUDGETING (Chapter 12)

Annual Rate of Return

$$\text{Annual rate of return} = \text{Expected annual net income} \div \text{Average investment}$$

Cash Payback

$$\text{Cash payback period} = \text{Cost of capital investment} \div \text{Annual cash inflow}$$

Discounted Cash Flow Approaches

Net Present Value	Internal Rate of Return
Compute net present value (a dollar amount). If net present value is zero or positive, accept the proposal. If net present value is negative, reject the proposal.	Compute internal rate of return (a percentage). If internal rate of return is equal to or greater than the minimum required rate of return, accept the proposal. If internal rate of return is less than the minimum rate, reject the proposal.

STATEMENT OF CASH FLOWS (Chapter 13)

Cash flows from operating activities (**indirect method**)

Net income		
Add:	Losses on disposals of assets	$ X
	Amortization and depreciation	X
	Decreases in noncash current assets	X
	Increases in current liabilities	X
Deduct:	Gains on disposals of assets	(X)
	Increases in noncash current assets	(X)
	Decreases in current liabilities	(X)
Net cash provided (used) by operating activities		$ X

Cash flows from operating activities (**direct method**)

Cash receipts
(Examples: from sales of goods and services to customers, from receipts of interest and dividends on loans and investments) $ X

Cash payments
(Examples: to suppliers, for operating expenses, for interest, for taxes)   (X)

Cash provided (used) by operating activities $ X